CW00764754

The Penguin Book of Greek and Latin Lyric Verse

The Penguin Book of Greek and Latin Lyric Verse

Translated and Edited by
CHRISTOPHER CHILDERS

Afterword by
GLENN MOST

PENGUIN BOOKS

PENGUIN CLASSICS

UK | USA | Canada | Ireland | Australia
India | New Zealand | South Africa

Penguin Books is part of the Penguin Random House group of companies
whose addresses can be found at global.penguinrandomhouse.com

Penguin
Random House
UK

First published in Penguin Classics 2023
001

Translation and editorial matter copyright © Christopher Childers, 2023

Afterword copyright © Glenn Most, 2023

The moral right of the translator has been asserted

Set in 10.5/14pt Sabon LT Std
Typeset by Jouve (UK), Milton Keynes
Printed and bound in Great Britain by Clays Ltd, Elcograf S.p.A.

The authorized representative in the EEA is Penguin Random House Ireland,
Morrison Chambers, 32 Nassau Street, Dublin D02 YH68

A CIP catalogue record for this book is available from the British Library

ISBN: 978-0-241-56744-9

For Robert G. Kirkpatrick, Jr., 1940–2004
vagae moderatori summo iuventae

Contents

Note on Lyric   xiii

Translator's Preface   xv

Note on Meters   xxvii

Note on the Text(s)   xlv

Acknowledgments   xlvii

The Archaic Period   1

  Archilochus   5

  Semonides of Amorgos   16

  Callinus   21

  Tyrtaeus   22

  Mimnermus   27

  Alcman   31

  Sappho   38

  Alcaeus   55

  Solon   68

  Theognis and the *Theognidea*   76

  Phocylides   86

  Demodocus   88

  Stesichorus   89

    Geryon   90

    Helen   92

    The *Theban Saga*   93

    The *Sack of Troy*   94

  Ibycus   96

Anacreon   100

Xenophanes   109

Hipponax   114

Simonides   120

    Lyrics   121

    Elegies   128

    Epigrams   129

Pindar   134

    Olympian Odes   135

    Pythian Odes   146

    Fragments from Other Genres   155

Bacchylides   165

The Classical Period   187

Timocreon of Rhodes   193

Ion of Chios   196

Praxilla   198

Corinna   199

Timotheus   204

Ariphron of Sicyon   213

Philoxenus   215

'Plato'   221

Aristotle   223

Aristonous of Corinth   226

Philodamus of Scarphea   229

Hermolochus   233

Anonymous Classical Lyric   234

Folk Songs   242

Scolia   245

Post-Classical Greek Lyric 249

  Callimachus 255

    The *Aetia* 258

    The *Iambi* 261

    The *Hymns* 269

    Epigrams 276

  Theocritus 282

  The *Greek Anthology* 299

    Epigrams from the *Garland of Meleager* 301

      Philetas of Samos 301

      Erinna 302

      Anyte 302

      Asclepiades 303

      Leonidas of Tarentum 306

      Phalaecus 310

      Nossis 310

      Heraclitus of Halicarnassus 312

      Posidippus of Pella 312

      Hedylus 313

      Rhianus 313

      Dioscorides 313

      Mnasalces 315

      Theodoridas 316

      Alcaeus of Messene 317

      Theaetetus 318

      Diotimus 318

      Tymnes 319

      Pancrates 319

      Phanias 320

Antipater of Sidon   320

Anonymous   323

Meleager   326

Epigrams from the *Garland of Philip*   332

Philodemus   333

Crinagoras   339

Erucius   343

Zonas   344

Antipater of Thessalonica   344

Apollonides   346

Marcus Argentarius   347

Bianor   351

Antiphilus of Byzantium   351

Automedon   352

Evenus   354

Maccius   354

Antiphanes of Macedonia   354

Philip of Thessalonica   355

Anacreontea   357

Latin Lyric   365

Catullus   373

Polymetric Poems   376

Longer Poems   388

Elegies and Epigrams   394

Virgil   398

Tibullus   411

Propertius   421

Sulpicia   446

The 'Sulpicia Elegist'   447

Sulpicia   451

Horace   453

  Epodes   456

  Odes   462

Ovid   492

  Amores   494

  Tristia   512

  Letters from Pontus   521

Statius   527

Martial   533

Afterword: What Is Lyric?   557

Abbreviations   567

Notes   571

Index of Genres   895

Index of Poets   903

Index of First Lines   905

Thematic Index   925

Note on Lyric

This book is a hybrid work. Embedded within it is an anthology of Greek and Latin lyric poetry as the ancients would have understood it – and it can be navigated as such, by those readers and students who wish to do so, using the Index of Genres at the back (pp. 895). Surrounding and interleaving that strict core is something wider, more generous and no doubt more idiosyncratic: a survey of the poetry written by Hellenes, Alexandrians and Romans, covering roughly the period from 800 BCE to 100 CE, and selected according to the lens of our own, altogether more inclusive twenty-first-century understanding of the lyric.

The ancient definition is clear enough. It prescribes a mode of performance – a song sung to the accompaniment of a lyre – and a set of meters associated with it. The songs so performed were the work of the canonical Nine Lyric Poets, spanning the Greek world and active between the seventh and fifth centuries BCE: Alcman and Anacreon (pp. 31–7 and 100–108); the Lesbian poets Sappho and Alcaeus (pp. 38–54 and 55–67); Stesichorus pp. 89–95), Ibycus and Simonides (pp. 96–9 and 120–33); and Pindar and Bacchylides (pp. 134–64 and 165–85). To these might be added, from Latin verse, perhaps as few as two poems by Catullus (poems 11 and 51, pp. 380 and 387), and a heaping of Horace's *Odes* (pp. 462–91).

Opposed to such classical clarity is the understanding native to anglophone poetry. For us, 'lyric' has evolved to refer roughly to poems of short to moderate length, either isolated or forming part of a discontinuous sequence of vignettes, which seem to speak personally (in the poet's voice or in that of a mask) and/or to verge toward song. Our lyric poem is often redolent of the everyday. It is what T. S. Eliot called 'the voice of the poet talking to himself', and what Gail McConnell, quoting

Denise Riley, terms 'the form of writing closest to . . . "the voice without a mouth that is inner speech"'. It is not epic, like Homer, nor is it dramatic, like Greek tragedy. It is the mode that in the last two centuries has come to dominate English verse almost completely.

Iambus (invective), elegy, sympotic (drinking-party) poetry, epigram, Latin love elegy – even certain fragments which the historical accident of damage and decay has imbued with an aura of lyric mystery: this volume includes much fascinating and affecting material that falls outside the strict definition of lyric, and yet which, seen through this anglophone lens, looks markedly lyrical. It also includes much that does *not* now strike us as lyrical. Yet to have told only part of the story of these genres would have been to do a disservice to the larger projects – the mental categories, aims and objectives – of the poets who wrote in them.

Included too, finally, are a small handful of poems which represent an exception even to these capacious rules, but without which the picture formed of key moments in the art form's development would have been incomplete. These are the excerpts from Callimachus' didactic poem *Aetia* (*Causes*, pp. 258–61), and the pastoral inclusions from Theocritus' *Idylls* (pp. 283–98) and Virgil's *Eclogues* (pp. 400–410), and they are explained at the relevant places.

In short, then, anyone looking for a picture of what ancient poets were up to when they weren't composing, with grand ambition, national epics, manuals in verse or masterpieces for the tragic or comic stage – when they were singing to the gods, or their friends, or otherwise opening little verbal windows into their life and times – can find it here. Readers interested in gaining a deeper insight into the more technical questions of genre and the lyric, meanwhile, can refer to Glenn Most's generous Afterword to this volume, 'What Is Lyric?' (pp. 557–66).

Translator's Preface

The Penguin Book of Greek and Latin Lyric Verse has been an epic undertaking: in a sort of personal odyssey, it has detained me for ten years now. And, viewed in the light of much-longer-established trends in the translation of the Classics, it might look somewhat unusual. For one thing, while readers are used to omnibus translations of Greek lyric poetry – a practical necessity, given that the material is often too fragmentary, and too scant, to present in isolation – we are less used to volumes of Latin lyric, and even less to the combination of both Greek and Latin verse in a single volume, as here. For another, we are accustomed to translations by many hands: one kind of book will often gather the work of multiple translators, each tackling a different poet, and communicating, by way of the varying styles and attitudes of the translators, the variety of authors anthologized; a second kind applies this hundred-handed approach to a single poet – Horace (pp. 453–91), say – and thus highlights the capacity of its original to 'contain multitudes'. Finally, the prevailing tastes of the last thirty or fifty years have tended noticeably toward unrhymed, free verse translation.

In the present volume, the situation is different. Here, more than eighty poets spanning eight centuries are translated by a single hand, and according to consistent principles. And not just that: the translations that result also use a great number of the English language's traditional resources of meter, stanza and rhyme – I hope to thrilling, or at times soothing, or, generally, enjoyable effect. But why?

The formal choice is the easiest explained. Neither free verse nor prose is particularly well suited to communicating what has always struck me as a fundamental characteristic of classical verse, namely, its lapidary quality, its sense of being intricately and solidly made, as if the poet had chiseled the words into stone. I don't mean that free verse *cannot* seem this way – Basil Bunting's *Briggflatts* is only one of the obvious counterexamples; I only mean that, *as a form*, free verse seems to me more interested in *what* is being said than *how*; the utterance itself must be poetry, not merely dressed as poetry. In this way, the wigs and corsets of so-called 'formal verse' are stripped away to show more of the human body beneath, and appreciation moves from the elegant turn of phrase or the stately fulfillment of syntax and stanza to the individuality of the voice and the (perceived) honesty of the emotion. However crude that précis is, it outlines a way of thinking about poetry which has made aesthetic and historical sense for a while now, but which I believe would have seemed thoroughly alien to the poets compassed in this book. For them, a poet's authority was predicated not so much on interior qualities of sincerity, or authenticity, or visionary derangement, as on the solid, objective evidence of what they could do with words. The language of Greek and Latin verse is *marked* as poetic by any number of usages that diverge on the one hand from everyday speech and on the other from prose: poetic diction, elaborate word order, and, especially, metrical patterns, often quite intricate, repeated like clockwork across lines and stanzas, which, at least in the earliest lyrics, may well have conjured traditional melodies or even steps to a dance. It is this sense of marked and patterned language which my more formal strategies seek to communicate. True, ancient Greek and Latin poetry did not use rhyme, but it had many meters; English is much more metrically limited – attempts to shape it into such mysteries to the anglophone reader as choriambs or dactylo-epitrites tend, to my ear, to sound muddy and inscrutable – but, as if in compensation, the history of English poetry has given it a wealth of kinds and patternings of rhyme.

These strategies, in turn, have allowed me to employ, throughout these hundreds of pages of verse, a consistent formal approach, and thereby, I hope, to show the reader – in a way that is simply not possible when each text has its own translator – both what these various poets and poems have in common, and what divides them: how they stand out from, and rub shoulders with, one another, even when their authors lived hundreds of years apart. I think of these contextual richnesses as a kind of 'thickness', commandingly present in the original language but all too often lost in translation. My highest hope is that this volume might make such thickness freshly available to the anglophone reader.

Of course, a translation – whatever else it may be – is always the result of a translator's personal experience of a text. If this talk of 'thicknesses' sounds very abstract, then an account of my own experiences in first coming to discover the treasure trove that this poetry represents might help to shed more light on the aims and approach of the present anthology.

At the start, when the hard work of studying grammar was over, when, with lots of help and difficulty, I was finally able to read poetry composed in ancient Greek and Latin, you could say I was like one wandering in a forest, enchanted by the beauty of individual trees, but with little sense of where I was or what I was looking at. In the first place, I was drunk on music – a common enough experience for the young poetry enthusiast dabbling in foreign tongues with more enthusiasm than expertise. One of the first Latin poems I ever read was the fourth Eclogue of Virgil (p. 403); long before I could make much of Virgil's Latin, I was convinced that in his dactylic hexameters I had encountered the true cadence of prophecy. Latin sounded solid and sonorous to my ears, a bit orotund, but sturdily constructed on a frame of consonants. Greek, by contrast, seemed light and full of air, an ambrosial distillation of sunlight and simplicity, elemental passions and hard-won wisdom. It also offered a breathtaking variety of rhythms, tones and dialects. Of course, I loved the limpidities of Sappho (pp. 38–54), her mesmerizing vowels, and the light-hearted lilt of Anacreon (pp. 100–108), but I was perhaps most struck by Alcman's *Partheneion* (p. 32), how singable it was, and how strange: his old Peloponnesian Doric felt as if the classical Attic Greek I had learned in school had wandered off to the Galapagos and gone wild.

But, in time, even a natural novice ceases to be one; over many walks in the woods, a sense of the forest begins to condense. By dint of practice, I got better at reading, and my understanding increased. I learned to listen not only with the sensual ear, but with the mind as well; to enjoy not only the delights of mystification, the ensorcellments of strangeness, but the more sober pleasures of comprehension and discernment. And what I mostly began to discern were the interconnections between texts and contexts: the rootedness of early Greek poetry in occasion and ceremony; the rootedness, in turn, of later poetry in what had gone before. It was as if a map was forming in my head, in which poems no longer seemed to be isolated statements, but part of a grand conversation. This phenomenon, far from lessening the fascination of individual poems, intensified it. The very language felt denser, thicker, with relations and implications, and meter seemed not ornamental but essential to that thickness. The different meters, first employed by the Greeks and later adapted by the Romans, began to seem like a sort of musical code – the 'iambus', used for invective and general scurrility; the song forms, ranging from the straightforward melodiousness of Anacreon and the enthralling harmonies of Sappho to the dazzling complexities of Pindar's triads (pp. 134–64); the ubiquitous elegiac couplets, neatly alternating between loping hexameters and pointed pentameters. This poetic DNA, once fathomed, revealed family resemblances among poets, affinities and enmities, carrying conversations and heated arguments down through the centuries. The music I first fell in love with did not disappear, but revealed itself to be part of a larger meaning.

A translator decides what is most important and translates accordingly. The decision is necessarily subjective. If classical poetry is thought of as a kind of forest, whose trees are the individual poems, my translations in this anthology seek to convey both the beauty of the trees themselves and the shape of the forest as a whole. They wish, first, to be musical, but to be so in such a way that their musical shapes reveal something about each poem's genealogy and position in the grand conversation, just as tree species are revealed by the shape of their leaves: the spiky, five-pronged maple; the birch and elm leaves, like toothy eggs; the heart-shaped linden. The translations accomplish this by using the resources of English poetry – regular meter, mostly iambic; stanzas; and rhyme – to generate a musical shape which corresponds to the Greek or Latin originals. This analogy, once established, is maintained throughout.

Let me illustrate as briefly as I can. In what follows, I will present a few excerpts of Archaic Greek poetry, in different meters, alongside excerpts from later Latin verse which employ the same meters, all with their English translations. The original of the first, from the Spartan martial elegist Tyrtaeus (pp. 22–6), is in elegiac couplets:

Tyrtaeus 10 (late seventh century BCE; p. 23):

‿ ‿‿ |‿ ‿ ‿|‿ ‿ ‿ ‿ |‿ ‿|‿ ‿ ‿|‿ ‿
ὦ νέοι, ἀλλὰ μάχεσθε παρ᾽ ἀλλήλοισι μένοντες,

‿ ‿ ‿|‿ ‿ | ‿ ‖‿ ‿ ‿ ‿ ‿ ‿ ‿
μηδὲ φυγῆς αἰσχρῆς ἄρχετε μηδὲ φόβου . . .

‿ ‿ ‿|‿‿ ‿| ‿ ‿| ‿ ‿‿| ‿ ‿ ‿|‿ ‿
τοὺς δὲ παλαιοτέρους, ὧν οὐκέτι γούνατ᾽ ἐλαφρά,

‿ ‿ ‿| ‿ ‿ |‿ ‖ ‿ ‿‿ ‿ ‿ ‿‿ ‿
μὴ καταλείποντες φεύγετε, τοὺς γεραιούς.

> Young men, get up! Stand side by side and fight,
> and don't give in to fear or shameful flight! . . .
> Think of the old, their knees no longer light –
> don't turn your back on them and take to flight!

Whether the English reader simply has an instinct for the rhythms and sounds of English poetry as she reads it aloud – always the best way of 'hearing' any poem – or has the expertise necessary to recognize that this first excerpt is translated into pairs of rhymed iambic pentameter lines (known in English poetics as 'heroic couplets'), she will hopefully perceive the family resemblance, the musical genetic code, when the form reappears over half a millennium later, both in the original language and in my English translations of the Latin poetry of the first century BCE:

Ovid, Amores *1.9 (circa 16 BCE–2 CE; p. 495):*

‿‿‿ |‿ ‿ ‿|‿ ‿ ‿ ‿|‿ ‿‿| ‿ ‿ ‿|‿ ‿
Militat omnis amans, et habet sua castra Cupido;

‿ ‿‿| ‿ ‿ ‿ ‿‖ ‿‿‿ ‿ ‿ ‿ ‿
Attice, crede mihi, militat omnis amans.

‿ ‿| ‿ ‿ ‿‿|‿ ‿ ‿|‿ ‿ ‿ | ‿ ‿‿|‿ ‿
quae bell(o) est habilis, Veneri quoque convenit aetas.

‿ ‿ ‿|‿ ‿|‿ ‖ ‿ ‿ ‿ ‿‿ ‿ ‿
turpe senex miles, turpe senilis amor.

Each lover is a soldier on campaign.
Cupid, too, has tents pitched on the plain.
Believe me, Atticus, when I maintain
each lover is a soldier on campaign.
Both war and Venus want a youth still green;
old soldiers and aged lovers are obscene.

What does this coincidence of meter tell us? Well, Ovid's modus operandi is to ring witty, often shocking variations on conventional wisdom.
Here, the echo of martial elegy can be seen to lie in the background of
the *militia amoris* (warfare of love) motif, a trope inherited by Ovid as
part of his chosen genre of love elegy, which he, with characteristic
insouciance, elaborates to absurdity, in this poem and elsewhere. In
seeking to associate the lover, a figure firmly identified with delinquency
by Romans and Spartans alike, with the industry and dignity of the
soldier, Ovid commits an irreverence for which Tyrtaeus probably
would have wanted him whipped; and whether his conscious target was
Tyrtaeus himself or only the genre of which Tyrtaeus is here the figurehead, it may not be irrelevant that in travestying the subject matter he
also uses the meter.

Undoubtedly relevant, on the other hand, are the metrical concurrences
of the next two examples. In the first, the original is taken from the scabrous iambic poet Hipponax (pp. 114–19), written in a form of his own
invention called 'limping iambics' – here rendered into English as unrhymed
(or irregularly rhymed) iambic hexameters – and it is no coincidence that
Catullus (pp. 373–97) then casts his swaggering Latin polemic in the
humorously clunky meter of that earlier virtuoso of invective.

Hipponax 3+3a (circa 540–530 BCE; p. 115):

⏑ – ⏑ –⊢ – ⏑ – | – – – –
ἔβωσε Μαίης παῖδα, Κυλλήνης πάλμων.
– – ⏑ – | ⏑ – ⏑ – | ⏑ – – ⏑
Ἑρμῆ κυνάγχα, Μηιονιστὶ Κανδαῦλα,
– – ⏑ – | ⏑ – ⏑ – | ⏑ – – – –
φωρῶν ἑταῖρε, δεῦρό μοι σκαπαρδεῦσαι.

He called on Maia's son, grand poobah of Cyllene:
'Dog-Choker, Hermes, whom the Lydians call "Candaules",
buddy of burglars, come and save my ass already!'

Catullus 37 (circa 60s–50s BCE; p. 384):

ᴗ–   ᴗ –|ᴗ –   ᴗ – |ᴗ – – –
Salax taberna vosque contubernales,

– – ᴗ–|– – ᴗ –|ᴗ – – ᴗ
a pilleatis nona fratribus pila,

ᴗ –   ᴗ –|ᴗ – ᴗ – |ᴗ–   – ᴗ
solis putatis esse mentulas vobis . . .

You pubic pub, and you, its pubey regulars,
nine doors down from the bonnet-wearing Dioscuri,
you think, I guess, the only cocks in town are yours . . .

In the third example, the original is from the drinking songs of the
Mytilenean Alcaeus (pp. 55–67), composed in a meter called 'greater
asclepiads'. Alcaeus was one of the favorite poets of the Roman
Horace; and here, Horace's *carpe diem* ode uses the same meter, while
simultaneously elevating the Mytilenean's gruff particularity to universality and transcendence. Both are rendered into English in iambic
tetrameter couplets, set end-to-end to make internally rhyming eight-
beat lines:

Alcaeus 346 (circa 600 BCE; p. 65):

 – – –   ᴗ ᴗ –| – ᴗ ᴗ– | – ᴗ ᴗ – ᴗ –
πώνωμεν· τί τὰ λύχν' ὀμμένομεν; δάκτυλος ἀμέρα·

 – –– ᴗ ᴗ –|– ᴗ ᴗ – |–ᴗ ᴗ – ᴗ –
κὰδ δᾶερρε κυλίχναις μεγάλαις, ἄϊτα, ποικίλαις.

Drink! Is it lamps we're waiting for? A finger of day is left, no
    more.
Come on, my man, break out the great wine goblets, massy
    and ornate.

Horace, Odes *1.11* (*circa 23 BCE; pp. 467–8*):

‾ ‾‾ ∪∪‾ |‾∪∪ ‾ |‾ ‾∪∪ ∪‾
Tyrrhenum! sapias, vina liques, et spatio brevi

‾ ‾ ‾ ∪∪‾|‾ ∪∪ ‾|‾∪∪‾ ∪∪
spem longam reseces. dum loquimur, fugerit invida

‾‾ ‾∪∪‾|‾ ∪∪‾|‾∪∪ ‾∪‾
aetas: carpe diem, quam minimum credula postero.

...Be wise; have taste; let the wine decant, and prune back your
extravagant hopes for forever. Life is brief. While we sit talking, Time,
that thief, escapes. Don't let your life delay until tomorrow: pluck today.

The reader may indulge one further example. The Greek stanza which
bears Sappho's name is a languid, haunting, minor-key sort of quatrain,
consisting of three eleven-syllable lines followed by a truncated five-syllable
close. (Some deny that there should be a line break between the third and
fourth lines, but the matter is, strictly speaking, academic.) Here is the
opening of one of Sappho's most famous poems, fragment 31 (p. 44):

‾ ∪‾ ‾ ‾∪∪‾ ∪‾ ∪
φαίνεταί μοι κῆνος ἴσος θέοισιν

‾ ∪ ‾‾ ‾∪∪‾ ∪‾ ‾
ἔμμεν' ὤνηρ, ὄττις ἐνάντιός τοι

‾ ∪‾ ‾ ‾∪∪ ‾∪ ‾ ‾
ἰσδάνει καὶ πλάσιον ἆδυ φωνεί-

‾ ∪∪ ‾‾
σας ὐπακούει

‾ ∪‾ ∪ ‾∪∪‾
καὶ γελαίσας ἰμέροεν . . .

He seems like the gods' equal, that man, whoever he is, who takes his seat so close
across from you, and listens raptly to
          your lilting voice

and lovely laughter . . .

Five centuries or so later, both Catullus and Horace used Sappho's stanza to hold a conversation with her, and each other:

> *Catullus 51 (p. 387):*
>
> ‒ ᴜ ‒ ‒ ‒ ᴜ ᴜ‒ ᴜ ‒ᴜ
> Ille mi par esse deo videtur,
>
> ‒ ᴜ ‒ ‒ ‒ ᴜ ᴜ‒ᴜ ‒ ‒
> ille, si fas est, superare divos,
>
> ‒ ᴜ ‒ ‒ ‒ ᴜ ᴜ‒ ᴜ ‒ ‒
> qui sedens adversus identidem te
>
> ‒ ᴜ ᴜ ‒ ᴜ
> spectat et audit
>
> ‒ ᴜ ‒ ‒ ‒
> dulce ridentem . . .

> > The equal of a god that man appears,
> > better than gods, if it's not blasphemy,
> > who sits across from you, and stares, and hears
> > > continually
> >
> > your lovely laughter . . .

> *Horace, Odes 1.22 (p. 468):*
>
> ‒ ᴜ ‒ ‒ ‒ ᴜ ᴜ‒ ᴜ ‒ ‒
> pone sub curru nimium propinqui
>
> ‒ᴜ ‒ ‒ ‒ ᴜ ᴜ ‒ ᴜ ‒ ‒
> solis in terra domibus negata:
>
> ‒ ᴜ ‒ ‒ ‒ ᴜ ᴜ ᴜ ‒ ‒
> dulce ridentem Lalagen amabo,
>
> ‒ ᴜ ‒ ‒ ‒
> dulce loquentem.

> > [T]ake me to where the sun swoops lower, faster,
> > so low there are no towns or houses built;
> > I'll still love Lalage for her lovely laughter,
> > > her lovely lilt.

These three poems are among their authors' most celebrated, and I love each one individually, but I am fascinated by their interrelationships. The origin of Sappho's stanza, whether she invented it herself, or merely made more and better use of it than anyone before or after, is lost to history; but when Catullus tackles it, he uses Sappho's poem and legacy to work out something personal, about femininity and masculinity, poetry and political ambition, Greekness and Romanness. By contrast, Horace's chief model was Alcaeus, who also wrote poems in sapphics, which means that Horace often uses the sapphic without any reference to Sappho. Here, however, when he quotes Catullus translating Sappho, and even adds back in the 'lovely lilt' (*dulce loquentem*) which appeared in Sappho's original (ἄδυ φωνείσας) but which Catullus left out, both poets are very much on his mind. Horace's poem, as I hear it, is a bit arch, a bit critical of his predecessors, but fondly so; he wants to show himself a different kind of poet from the other two, but takes the time to say, as it were, 'That Sapphic stuff that Catullus got himself mixed up in – isn't it silly? But, ah, what a lovely lilt!'

One need not notice a stanza form to enjoy a poem, of course, any more than one needs to know that a tree is a poplar, or a willow, to find it beautiful. Notice or not, however, the poems in this volume carry a density of musical meaning that connects them to their context, and raises fascinating questions – just as it gives us rich information, or tantalizing hints – about poetic lineage, cultural influence and evolution, and authorial intent. It is a density I perceive whenever I read these poems in Greek or Latin, though I have seldom seen it rendered into English.

I am indebted to a number of excellent previous translations. I rely on the donnish prose of the Loeb Classical Library, published by Harvard University, to supply the defects of my own scholarship. Of more literary translations, I love the playful exuberance of James Michie, Aaron Poochigian and A. E. Stallings, the rhythmical inventiveness of Richmond Lattimore, Charles Martin and Jim Powell, the plainspoken intimacies of Willis Barnstone and David Ferry, the wit of Daryl Hine, the evocative literalism of Anne Carson (*If Not, Winter* is a brilliant title!). Editions and anthologies edited by J. D. McClatchy, Diane Rayor and William W. Batstone, and the Norton leviathan (Peter Constantine, Rachel Hadas,

Edmund Keeley, Karen Van Dyck, editors), all translated by various hands, contain a lot of first-class work. And that goes for many others as well.

I hope, however, that my translation offers something that the others have not: not only the excitement of individual poems, individual poets, but also the shape of the forest, dark and difficult to interpret though it often is. My ambition has been to transplant both the forest *and* the trees of classical lyric verse into English, without missing one for the other. If a reader gets from these translations some sense of the musical charge and variety that so excited me in my own early encounters with Greco-Roman lyric, along, perhaps, with a slight feeling of strangeness, straddling the gap between antiquity and today, then my translation will be a success. Should a reader spend a little more time with the book, however, I hope that a larger sense of interrelation, of an ecosystem, will also start to emerge: the recognition that certain kinds of lines and stanzas signal certain kinds of poetry; that the very *shapes* of stanzas suggest one poem's affinity to, or difference from, another; that even an obvious instance of debt or derivation points out something important about a poet's craft or expressive choices. I hope, in short, that reading a poem in this volume might feel a little less like encountering a Greek statue or Roman mosaic in a museum, and a little more like seeing it in the atrium of the villa it was made for, along a road of cobblestones precisely rutted by the wheels of untold trundling wagons.

Christopher Childers
Baltimore, MD, January 2022

Note on Meters

Classical Quantity, English Stress

Beginning from a foundation of three basic types of meter, the Greeks elaborated a metrical system of great sophistication and complexity, a few small patches of which the Romans tamed and turned to their own purposes. Many readers of poetry in English will be familiar with certain of the more famous Greco-Roman meters – the dactylic hexameter, the sapphic – and may well know of attempts by writers like Thomas Campion and Alfred Lord Tennyson, among others, to do what the Romans did to the Greeks and adapt classical meters to English. This approach, while it has produced some interesting results and some fine poems, is not followed in the present volume, owing to what I perceive as a fundamental difference between Greco-Roman and English verse. In what follows, I will attempt to explain, in brief, the basic principles of classical, as opposed to English, meters, and shed some light on the various metrical and formal patternings I employ in rendering classical verse into English.

Greek and Latin meters are quantitative, that is, based on syllable quantity or length (the time it takes to pronounce a syllable), while English meter is qualitative, that is, based on syllable quality or stress (the force with which a syllable is pronounced). In Greek and Latin, syllable length is fixed, while stress in English is relative: syllables are pronounced more or less forcefully in relation to each other. Words of two or more syllables have fixed stress (you don't put the empHAsis on the wrong sylLABle, as they say), but monosyllables (like 'let', 'me', 'not', 'the', 'true', etc.) do not have stress in themselves, but only in relation to other words in the line or sentence where they are found. This feature of English (or is it a bug?) has long bedeviled metricians, who squabble heatedly about whether, in Shakespeare's famous line, we should say 'LET me NOT to the MARriage of TRUE MINDS / adMIT imPEDIMENTS' or 'let ME not TO the MARriage OF true MINDS'. The latter may at first sound less natural, but what if the speaker wanted to recuse himself in particular, to wit: 'Let *others* admit impediments, but not *me*'? Stress is, at least in part, a function of tone, and a matter of interpretation.

A related characteristic of stress in English is that it tends to alternate. Whether we know it or not, our anglophone ears, outside of chants at sporting events and protest rallies, do not like strings of three or more stressed or unstressed syllables – utter a bunch of monosyllables in a row, and some will step out, as it were, into the aural spotlight, while others will shrink back demurely. This tendency makes English unsuited to imitating the runs of long and short syllables so frequent in Greco-Roman verse: we have to use monosyllables, and then, once we do, their stresses start slipping and sliding, muddying the rhythm – which, inasmuch as it is already unfamiliar, needs to be precisely rendered to be heard by the nonspecialist reader. Strict imitation of classical measures in English therefore strikes me as both quixotic (especially when it comes to some of the more recondite rhythms of Greek choral lyric) and self-stymieing, since the precision required to make foreign meters intelligible precludes expressive variation of a sort the Greeks and Romans themselves often employed when they made verbal stress clash with syllable length. Such expressive variations are, however, fully possible in traditional (stress-based, mostly iambic) English meters, which centuries of exercise have rendered hardy enough to absorb a bit of rough treatment. This anthology, therefore, has preferred not to imitate the metrical rhythms of the Greek and Latin poems it translates, but instead to seek analogous forms for classical line and stanza shapes from among the resources of traditional English prosody.

I've said already that there are three basic types or categories of classical meter; they are the *dactylic*, the *iambic* and the *aeolic*. Dactylic meters consist of *dactyls* (a long syllable followed by two short, – ∪ ∪, the same in Greek as in English), often interchangeable with *spondees* (two long syllables, – –). A Greek or Latin *iambus* is like its English equivalent (∪ –), except it contains twice as many syllables (x – ∪ –), so *iambic trimeter* in Greek to the anglophone ear sounds like hexameter, and iambic dimeter sounds like tetrameter. The base of *aeolic* meters is the *choriamb* (– ∪ ∪ –). These are the building blocks from which the whole splendid edifice is constructed.

It should further be remarked that meters are either *stichic* or *strophic*. A *stich* consists of a single metrical line – dactylic hexameter, say, or iambic pentameter – which is repeated, line by line, for an entire poem. A *strophe* (or stanza) consists of several different types or lengths of line, arranged into a pattern which then becomes the unit of repetition – readers familiar with anglophone poetry might find it helpful to think of the elaborate stanza forms of George Herbert, Thomas Hardy or Marianne Moore. Sometimes, when strophes are used frequently, they become recognized forms, and are given names, like the *sapphic* and the *alcaic*. Other times, they are one-offs, used only in the particular poem in which they appear; in this case, we can call them *nonce strophes* (or nonce stanzas).

Generally, strophes in classical lyric are distinguished in two other chief ways. The first distinction is between *choral* strophes (that is, those performed by a chorus) and *monodic* strophes (those performed by an individual singer). The second is between *monostrophic* poems, in which the unit of repetition is a single strophe, and *triadic* poems, in which the unit of repetition consists of three strophes, called the *strophe, antistrophe* and *epode* (turn, counter-turn and stand). *Monostrophes*, depending on their length and complexity, can be either monodic or choral; but triads are thought to be exclusively choral. It should be obvious that, by reading a poem on a page, we cannot say for sure whether it was originally performed by a single individual or a chorus. Yet it is generally assumed that larger, more complex monostrophes (such as Alcman's *partheneia*, pp. 32–7), and all triadic poems (such as Pindar's victory odes, pp. 135–55), were performed chorally, while the simpler, shorter monostrophes of Aeolic poetry were intended for monodic performance.

In between the stich and the strophe, finally, is the *distich*, or couplet, in which repetition alternates between two different types of metrical lines; the most common of these is the *elegiac couplet*, famously illustrated by Samuel Taylor Coleridge in the lines

> In the hexameter rises the fountain's silvery column,
> In the pentameter aye falling in melody back.

NB

Many meters are associated with particular genres, moods or tones, while others are 'unmarked', meaning either that they were used in all manner of different poems, or that not enough examples survive to generalize about their associations.

In what follows, as elsewhere in this volume,

- – indicates a long syllable;
- ᴗ indicates a short syllable, about half the length of a long;
- × indicates an *anceps*, a metrical position that can be occupied by either a long or a short syllable; and
- ‖ indicates a *caesura* or pause in the line.

Dactylic and Iambic Meters

DACTYLIC HEXAMETER

stichic

SCANSION: Six feet, the first four being dactyls or spondees, the fifth usually a dactyl and the sixth a spondee or anceps.

ASSOCIATIONS: Widely used in narrative and discursive verse of all sorts. Its primary associations are with High Poetry – epic, didactic, hymns – but it is also employed in pastoral (perhaps Theocritus first used it to give his rustic peasants a literary air) and is the chief meter of Roman satire (Horace, Persius, Juvenal).

TRANSLATED HERE AS:

A Loose blank verse with liberal use of feminine (unstressed) line endings.

B (*when the poem is an epigram, or feels like one*) Stricter iambic pentameter, often rhymed.

C (*when the poem frames an internal story or song*) Blank verse for framing lines; rhymed iambic pentameter for the embedded song.

EXAMPLES: A: *Xenophanes 11–34* (*pp. 112–13*); *Praxilla* (*p. 198*); *Callimachus*, Hymns 2 (*p. 269*); *Catullus 60* (*p. 388*). B: *Alcman 26* (*p. 36*); *Sappho 104–5* (*p. 51*); *Phocylides 3–6* (*pp. 86–7*). C: *Theocritus*, Idylls (*pp. 283–98*); *Catullus 62* (*p. 388*); *Virgil*, Eclogues (*pp. 400–410*); *Statius*, Silvae 2.4 (*p. 528*).

ELEGIAC COUPLETS

distichic

SCANSION: Two lines, the first a dactylic hexameter and the second an *elegiac pentameter*, meaning two and a half feet of dactyls or spondees followed by a *dactylic hemiepes* (– ∪ ∪ – ∪ ∪ –).

ASSOCIATIONS: Inscriptions and epitaphs; the genre of elegy ('sympotic' or drinking-party elegy; martial elegy; public elegy; love elegy); the Greek and Latin epigram.

TRANSLATED HERE AS: Rhymed iambic pentameter ('heroic') couplets, with occasional triplets.

EXAMPLES: *Archilochus 1–13* (*pp. 6–7*) *and the* Achaeans at Mysia (*p. 7*); *Callinus* (*p. 21*); *Tyrtaeus* (*pp. 22–6*); *Mimnermus* (*pp. 28–30*); *Solon 4–27* (*pp. 69–73*); *Theognis and the* Theognidea (*pp. 77–85*); *Phocylides 1* (*p. 86*); *Demodocus* (*p. 88*); *Anacreon, Elegy 2* (*p. 108*); *Xenophanes 1–8* (*pp. 110–12*); *Simonides*, Elegies (*pp. 128–9*) *and*

Epigrams (*pp. 129–33*); *Timocreon of Rhodes, Elegy 10 (p. 195); Ion of Chios, Elegy 26 (p. 197); Timotheus,* Epitaph for Euripides (*p. 212*); 'Plato' (*pp. 221–2*); *Aristotle 673 (p. 225); Callimachus,* Aetia (*pp. 258–61*), Hymns 5 (*p. 272*) *and* Epigrams (*pp. 276–81*); *most of the* Greek Anthology (*pp. 304–56*); *Catullus 65–109 (pp. 390–97); Tibullus (pp. 413–20); Propertius (pp. 423–45); Sulpicia (pp. 447–52); Ovid,* Amores (*pp. 494–511*), Tristia (*pp. 512–20*) *and* Letters from Pontus (*pp. 521–6*); *Martial* 1.23, 1.32, 1.34, 1.68, 1.73, 1.79 (*pp. 535–7*), *etc.*

IAMBIC TRIMETER

stichic

SCANSION: Three iambic feet (× – ∪ –).

ASSOCIATIONS: Relatively unmarked, but especially associated with iambus, a genre known for invective and profanity. Its use as the main conversational meter in Greek drama suggests a deep association with lively first-person speech.

TRANSLATED HERE AS: Stricter iambic pentameter, usually blank, occasionally rhymed (for epigrammatic effect).

EXAMPLES: *Archilochus 19–48 (pp. 8–9) and 201–13 (p. 15); Semonides of Amorgos (pp. 16–20); Solon 36 (p. 75).*

TROCHAIC TETRAMETER

stichic

SCANSION: Four feet, each a trochee (– ∪ – ×).

ASSOCIATIONS: Iambus; colloquial speech; invective and polemic. Found frequently in Archaic poetry, but not afterwards.

TRANSLATED HERE AS: Iambic heptameter (fourteeners), with and without rhyme.

EXAMPLES: *Archilochus 105–31 (pp. 9–12); Sappho 132 (p. 53); Solon 33 and 34 (p. 74); Anacreon 419 (p. 108); Hipponax 120+121 (p. 119).*

'LIMPING IAMBIC' OR SCAZON

stichic

SCANSION: Iambic trimeter, with the final long and short of each line reversed.

ASSOCIATIONS: Intentional and humorous clunkiness; the metrical inversion of the last two syllables creates the limp (Greek *skazein*, 'to limp'; the other Greek term, *choliambic*, derives from *cholos*, 'lame') that gives it its name. Said to have been invented by Hipponax, it was revived by Callimachus and then most notably used by Catullus and Martial.

TRANSLATED HERE AS: Iambic hexameters, with and without rhyme.

EXAMPLES: *Hipponax 3–78 (pp. 115–17); Callimachus,* Iambi *1–4 (pp. 261–4); Catullus 8 (p. 379), 22 (p. 382), 31 (p. 383) and 37 (p. 384); Martial 1.10 (p. 535), 4.81 (p. 542) and 10.92 (p. 551).*

EPODIC METERS

distichic / strophic

SCANSION: Any of a number of combinations of dactylic and/or iambic lines into repeating strophes of two, three or four lines (the latter often a repeated distich). Examples include dactylic hemiepes alternating with iambic dimeter; iambic trimeter with dactylic hemiepes; iambic trimeter with iambic dimeter; etc.

ASSOCIATIONS: Generally associated with iambus and invective, though Horace also uses them for some of his most melancholy and moving exhortations.

TRANSLATED HERE AS:

A Tercets or quatrains with irregular line lengths and variable rhyme schemes, taking their cue from the originals while maintaining differentiation from *glyconic tercets* (see below).
B (*when alternating dactylic hexameter and dactylic hemiepes*) A five-line stanza.

EXAMPLES: A: *Archilochus 168, 184, 188 and 191 (p. 12) and 196a (p. 13); Hipponax 115 and 117 (p. 119); Theodoridas 15 (p. 316); Horace,* Epodes *(pp. 456–61) and Odes 1.4 (p. 464); Martial 1.61 (p. 536).* B: *Horace,* Odes 4.7 *(p. 489).*

Aeolic Meters

The aeolic meters use long feet of many varieties, but they are alike in almost always featuring a *choriamb* (– ∪ ∪ –) at the beginning or middle of the foot. Though the basic aeolic metrical units are numerous, and each has a name, only three – variously tweaked and expanded – form the crucial building blocks of the presentation that follows. They are:

• the *glyconic* (– – – ∪ ∪ – ∪ –), by far the most common;
• the *pherecretean* (– – – ∪ ∪ – –), a catalectic glyconic (that is, with the final syllable omitted); and
• the *hagesichorean* (– – ∪ – ∪ – –).

AEOLIC *OR* SAPPHIC PENTAMETER

stichic / glyconic

SCANSION: $--- \cup\cup - \cup\cup - \cup -$

ASSOCIATIONS: Originally the meter of Sappho's second book (in Alexandrian recension) and Theocritus' second book of *Idylls* (only one poem from which has survived). For Theocritus, the meter pointed to Sappho; for Sappho and perhaps Alcaeus, the meter may have had Homeric associations, owing to the relatively large proportion of epic / Ionic dialect forms.

TRANSLATED HERE AS: Anglo-Saxon-style alliterative tetrameter, with a visual caesura.

EXAMPLES: *Sappho 44–9 (pp. 45–6), 115 (p. 52) and 130–31 (p. 53); Alcaeus 38a (p. 57), 141 (p. 62) and 364 (p. 67).*

FIRST *OR* LESSER ASCLEPIAD

stichic / glyconic

SCANSION: $--- \cup\cup - \| - \cup\cup - \cup -$

ASSOCIATIONS: Named for the Hellenistic poet Asclepiades (pp. 303–6), who apparently used it frequently, though no examples of his survive. Often employed as part of a strophe, more rarely as a stich; see the other 'asclepiad' meters, below.

TRANSLATED HERE AS: Accentual hexameter, with a visual caesura.

EXAMPLES: *Alcaeus 70 (p. 59) and 130b (p. 61); Horace,* Odes *1.1 (p. 462) and 3.30 (p. 487).*

Greater Asclepiad

stichic or *distichic* / *glyconic*

SCANSION: $--- \cup \cup -- \cup \cup -- \cup \cup - \cup -$

ASSOCIATIONS: Sappho's third book (in Alexandrian recension) consisted entirely of poems in this meter; frequent also in Alcaeus, and in anonymous drinking songs (*scolia*); for Horace, at any rate, wine and the symposium seem to be the relevant associations. In Greek, it is generally arranged into distichs; in Latin, it is treated as a stich.

TRANSLATED HERE AS: Iambic octameter lines, with an internal rhyme falling on the fourth and eighth beats instead of a visual caesura.

EXAMPLES: *Sappho 53–6 (p. 47); Alcaeus 345–8 (pp. 65–6); Scolia 902–8 (p. 247); Horace, Odes 1.11 (p. 467).*

Hagesichorean with Double Choriambic Expansion

stichic

SCANSION: $-- \cup \cup -- \cup \cup -- \cup \cup - \cup --$

ASSOCIATIONS: Unknown. The meter is obviously close in effect to the greater asclepiad. The 'hagesichorean' itself is so named because, in its unexpanded form ($-- \cup \cup - \cup --$), it is used in the strophe of Alcman's *Partheneion* (p. 32).

TRANSLATED HERE AS: Eight-beat lines with internal rhyme variously located.

EXAMPLES: *Sappho 58a–b (pp. 47–8) and 81 (p. 48).*

GLYCONIC TERCETS

strophic / glyconic

SCANSION: Three-line strophes consisting of one or two pure glyconics, and one or two glyconics expanded in various ways.

TRANSLATED HERE AS: Tercets of four- and five-beat lines, generally rhymed AAA, where one of the As is a slant or half rhyme (to distinguish them from epodic tercets, which generally have one unrhymed line, or which rhyme AAB CCB).

EXAMPLES: *Sappho 94–8 (pp. 48–50); Anacreon 388 (p. 106).*

PHALAECIAN HENDECASYLLABLE

stichic / glyconic

SCANSION: – – – ∪ ∪ – ∪ – ∪ – ×

ASSOCIATIONS: Named after Phalaecus (p. 310), the only extant example of whose work in this meter is not sufficiently interesting to include here. Catullus and Martial use it flexibly, for satire and invective, for 'slice of life' anecdote and for reflections on love, friendship and happiness.

TRANSLATED HERE AS: Loose tetrameter lines, irregularly rhymed.

EXAMPLES: *Catullus 5 (p. 377), 10 (p. 379), 16 (p. 382), 41–6 (pp. 385–6) and 50 (p. 387); Martial 1.1 (p. 535), 1.117 (p. 537), 2.33 (p. 538), 3.53 (p. 540), 5.20 (p. 543), 5.73 (p. 544), 6.19 (p. 544), 6.82 (p. 545), 7.39 (p. 546), 7.95–8.69 (p. 547), 10.47 (p. 549), 11.63 (p. 551), 12.18 (p. 553), 12.20 (p. 554) and 12.34 (p. 554).*

SAPPHIC

strophic

SCANSION: $- \cup - - - \cup \cup - \cup - \times$

$- \cup - - - \cup \cup - \cup - \times$

$- \cup - - - \cup \cup - \cup - \times$

$- \cup \cup - -$

ASSOCIATIONS: Perhaps Sappho and Alcaeus associated the strophe with hymns and prayers; later generations associated it with Sappho and Aeolic poetry generally. To my ear, it combines a restless forward movement with a musical 'dying fall'. Sappho's entire first book (in Alexandrian recension) was in this meter.

TRANSLATED HERE AS: Quatrains, consisting of three lines in loose iambic pentameter and one line of iambic dimeter. ABAB rhyme scheme.

EXAMPLES: *Sappho 1–41 (pp. 39–45); Alcaeus 34 (p. 57), 42 (p. 58), 45 (p. 58), 69 (p. 59), 283 (p. 63), 308b (p. 64), 362 (p. 66); Catullus 11 (p. 380) and 51 (p. 387); Horace, Odes 1.22 (p. 468), 1.38 (p. 471), 3.18 (p. 485) and 4.11 (p. 490).*

ALCAIC

strophic

SCANSION: (*in Alcaeus and Sappho*)

$\times - \cup - \times - \cup \cup - \cup -$

$\times - \cup - \times - \cup \cup - \cup -$

$\times - \cup - \times - \cup - -$

$- \cup \cup - \cup \cup - \cup - -$

(in Horace)

$--\cup--\|-\cup\cup-\cup-$

$--\cup--\|-\cup\cup-\cup-$

$--\cup---\cup--$

$-\cup\cup-\cup\cup-\cup--$

ASSOCIATION: Predominantly with Alcaeus, and thus with the sort of politically engaged and wine-soused poetry he practiced.

TRANSLATED HERE AS: Quatrains, with 5–5–3–4 or 5–5–4–4 beats to a line, with a bit of roughness, often a choriamb, in each of the first two lines, and a dactyl or two in the fourth. ABAB rhyme scheme.

EXAMPLES: *Sappho 137 (p. 53); Alcaeus 6 (p. 56), 72–129 (pp. 59–60), 208 (p. 62), 298 (p. 63), 332 (p. 64), 335 (p. 65) and 338 (p. 65); Horace, Odes 1.9 (p. 466), 1.37 (p. 470), 2.3 (p. 471), 2.7 (p. 000), 2.13 (p. 474), 2.14 (p. 476), 2.20 (p. 477), 3.1–3.5 (pp. 478–80) and 3.23 (p. 485); Statius,* Silvae 4.5 (p. 529).

Asclepiadean Quatrains

strophic / aeolic

SCANSION: Grouped under this heading is a variety of quatrains, each of which combines two or three lesser asclepiads with another Aeolic metrical element: glyconics, glyconics + iambus, glyconics and pherecreteans, or other obscure metrical fauna (hipponacteans and telesilleans).

ASSOCIATION: Alcaeus has two extant poems in asclepiadean strophes, both of which are polemically political. Horace, by contrast, seems to use asclepiadeans for poems more Hellenistic in inspiration, with situations and motifs evocative of epigrams from the Greek Anthology (pp. 000-00).

TRANSLATED HERE AS: Quatrains, with various approaches to rhyme, but usually (except in version C) containing an accentual hexameter with caesura (see First or Lesser Asclepiad, p. 000, above). Both of Alcaeus' poems in the measure are one-offs, while Horace uses three varieties of asclepiadean quatrain (A, B and C), below.

EXAMPLES: *Alcaeus 70 (p. 000) and 130b (p. 000). Horace,* ASCLEPIA-DEAN A: *Odes 1.6 (p. 000) and 1.24 (p. 000);* ASCLEPIADEAN B: *Odes 1.5 (p. 000), 1.23 (p. 000), and 3.13 (p. 000);* ASCLEPIADEAN C: *Odes 1.3 (p. 000), 3.9 (p. 000), 3.25 (p. 000), and 4.1 (p. 000).*

Minor Ionic

stichic / distichic / strophic

SCANSION: ∪ ∪ – –, arranged in various line lengths and stanza patterns.

ASSOCIATIONS: Inasmuch as ionics are associated with the region of Ionia, they may suggest a certain languid softness, shading into lubricity. Geographically speaking, Ionia is plainly not part of Aeolia; but Ionic meters strike my ear as perhaps more polished, and more frivolous, variations on Aeolic ones, with the ionic foot, both major (– – ∪ ∪) and minor, as an *anaclastic* (reconfigured) choriamb.

TRANSLATED HERE AS: Rhyming dimeter couplets, presented variously in two-, four- or eight-beat lines.

EXAMPLES: *Alcman 46 (p. 36); Alcaeus 10b (p. 56); Anacreon 352 (p. 103); Corinna 654 (p. 000, in a strophe); Horace,* Odes 3.12 *(p. 483).*

ANACREONTIC I

strophic / ionic

SCANSION: Strophes consisting mainly of the *anacreontic* or *anaclastic ionic dimeter*, a slightly scrambled lesser ionic line (◡◡ – ◡ – ◡ – –) with an occasional pure ionic dimeter (◡◡ – – ◡◡ – –) thrown in for variety.

ASSOCIATIONS: Song, wine and the symposium. Along with Anacreontics II and III, this is one of the meters characteristically used by Anacreon and associated with his brand of light-hearted drunkenness and literary polish; all three are among the most purely lilting and frolicsome in Greek poetry.

TRANSLATED HERE AS: Accentual trimeter for the 'anacreontic' lines, and two lines of rhyming dimeter for the pure ionics.

EXAMPLES: *Anacreon 356 (p. 103), 395 (p. 106), 396 (p. 107) and 400 (p. 107); Anacreontea 46 (p. 362) and 53 (p. 365).*

ANACREONTIC II

strophic / glyconic / pherecretean

SCANSION: Three glyconics followed by a pherecretean.

TRANSLATED HERE AS: Accentual tetrameters for the glyconics, and accentual trimeters for the pherecreteans. Irregularly rhymed.

EXAMPLES: *Anacreon 348 (p. 103) and 357–61 (pp. 104–5); Aristonous of Corinth, Paean to Apollo (p. 227); Catullus 34 (p. 383).*

ANACREONTIC III

stichic

SCANSION: Iambic dimeter catalectic: $\times - \cup - \cup - \times$.

TRANSLATED HERE AS: Iambic trimeter, irregularly rhymed.

EXAMPLES: Anacreontea *1–35* (*pp. 358–62*).

Choral Strophes

All of the *monodic* strophes covered so far have been *monostrophic*; yet, as mentioned above, *choral strophes* can be either *monostrophic* or *triadic*. They differ further from the monodic strophes by being 'nonce' forms, one-offs, composed for particular occasions, and particular choruses, perhaps even to fit original melodies and choreographies also composed for the occasion. At any rate, it is hard to imagine audiences following the extraordinary complexity of some of the stanzas of Pindar and Bacchylides without the additional cues of music and dance.

While a monostrophic ode repeats one stanza form for the entire poem, a triadic ode employs a *strophe*, *antistrophe* and *epode*, in which the strophe and antistrophe have the same meter, but the epode follows its own pattern; thus the unit of repetition is the entire three-part structure. The translations in this book imitate the basic concept of the monostrophic or triadic choral ode by inventing a nonce stanza in English, of comparable size and complexity to the Greek (there is nothing like this in Latin), and repeating it as appropriate. In addition, the stanzas of monostrophic poems are marked *Str.* for 'strophe', while those of triadic poems are marked *Str.*, *Ant.*, *Ep.*, for 'strophe', 'antistrophe', 'epode'. To get the idea, a reader might compare the stanzas in Alcman's monostrophic *Partheneion* (p. 32) with one of the triadic victory odes of Pindar (pp. 135–55).

With fragments, it can be difficult to tell whether we are dealing with

a monostrophe or a triad, or even (in the case of two- or three-line fragments) with a much smaller unit of repetition. The following poems are
clearly monostrophic: Alcman 1 (p. 32) and 3 (p. 34); Simonides 542 (p.
123); Pindar, Dithyramb 2 (p. 158), Frr. 122 (p. 161) and 124a+b (p.
163); Bacchylides, fragment 20b (p. 185); Timocreon of Rhodes 727 (p.
194); Corinna 654 and 690 (p. 203); Ariphron 813 (p. 213); Aristonous
of Corinth, *Hymn to Hestia* (p. 226) and *Paean to Apollo* (p. 227);
Philodamus, *Paean to Dionysus* (p. 229); and the Anonymous *Hymn to
Zeus on Mount Dicte, Crete* (p. 234). The following poems are triadic:
Stesichorus, *Geryon* (p. 90) and the *Theban Saga* (p. 93); Ibycus 282 (p.
97); Simonides 543 (p. 124); and most of Pindar (pp. 135–64) and
Bacchylides (pp. 167–85).

Note on the Text

To list all of the editions and editors consulted for these translations would require several pages of interest only, or mainly, to the sort of specialist who doesn't really need a book like this one to begin with. I shall not do so. Instead, I will direct readers interested in tracking down the texts I have translated to the Loeb Classical Library editions (published by Harvard University Press) and their own notes on their texts. There are three broad exceptions to this rule. (1) In cases where the text was disputed or in disrepair (for example, Propertius, pp. 421–45), I felt free to consult the available scholarly editions and make my own determinations. (2) For minor gaps in fragmentary papyri, I consulted the various *apparatus critici* in the scholarly editions and translated the supplements which struck me as (*a*) poetically attractive and (*b*) not philologically implausible. Such instances are indicated in square brackets [ ]. (3) Finally, for poems published subsequent to the most recent Loeb editions (for example, Archilochus' *Achaeans at Mysia*, p. 7, or Simonides' *Plataea Elegy*, p. 128), I used the most authoritative scholarly texts and commentaries I could find.

The following pages contain many fragmentary poems. These often begin or end abruptly, as indeed they do in the papyri where they are often found. In general, line numbering tries to reproduce what we know or can reasonably deduce about the length of such poems. For example, if a poem starts on a line other than line 1, it is because the papyrus contains one or more lines that are too scrappy to translate, though we can see that the lines are there. Lacunas within poems are indicated by ellipses. When we know their length, it is indicated by the line numbering; but when the extent of the gap is unknown, the line numbering proceeds as if there were no gap. Sometimes fragments are combined, whether because they share some thematic resemblance, are presented by our sources in close proximity to each other, or both; sometimes they clearly come from the same poem, but may or may not be consecutive. In all instances, the location of the join is indicated in the margin and (where helpful) explained in the Notes at the end of the book.

The numeration of early Greek poetry – both poems and fragments – follows the Loeb editions of Douglas Gerber and David Campbell, which in turn follow the standard editions of scholars such as Diehl, Lobel, Snell, West and Page. It is perhaps worth noting that the Greek lyric poets, other than Sappho and Alcaeus, were published most authoritatively in the *Poetae Melici Graeci* of Denys Page. Page began with Alcman (pp. 31–7), to whom he assigned numbers 1–177, then followed with Stesichorus (numbers 178–281), Ibycus (282–345), and the rest, concluding with 'Minor Lyric Poets' (696–1045). Thus if Aristotle has a fragment numbered 842 (p. 224), it does not mean that more than 800 fragments of Aristotle's poetry survive, merely that this fragment came 842nd in Page's omnibus edition. (One exception to this is Stesichorus, for whom I used the edition of M. Davies and P. J. Finglass.) Poems of the *Greek Anthology*, because I wished to present them by author rather than preserving the *Anthology*'s original thematic arrangement, follow the numeration in the editions of Gow–Page (*Hellenistic Epigrams* and *The Garland of Philip*) and Page (*Further Greek Epigrams*). Poems published after these scholarly editions (and thus ill-integrated into the standard numeration) are generally given blandly descriptive English titles.

Unless otherwise stated, translations from both modern and ancient languages in the Notes are my own.

Acknowledgments

A book thirteen years in the making has been touched by too many hands to do justice to in an Acknowledgments page such as this – not if I had ten tongues, ten mouths and a heart of bronze within me, as the poet said. Be that as it may, three men who are no longer around to read it claim pride of place – Robert Kirkpatrick, without whose guidance I never would have studied Greek and Latin to begin with, and whose encouragement in the field of verse proved decisive; Peter Carson, late of Penguin, whom I never met but whose original conception this book once was, and who believed, even when I didn't, that I was the man for the job; and my father – my greatest regret being that I failed to finish it in time for him to thumb its pages with pride.

Much gratitude is also due the living. A.E. Stallings and Nathan Costa have believed in, supported and guided me for longer than the book has been in progress. Invaluable advice and encouragement were graciously provided by Ryan Wilson, Dylan Carpenter, Armen Davoudian, David Yezzi, Mary Jo Salter, James Arthur, Andrew Motion and everyone else, students and faculty, of the Writing Seminars at Johns Hopkins University. So much that is good and coherent in the anthology is owed to the editorial acuity, immense erudition and moderating influence of Donald Futers at Penguin, and copy-editor Kit Shepherd. Much thanks also belongs to the Classics Department of the University of North Carolina at Chapel Hill, especially Patrick Lee Miller, Peter Smith, William H. Race, Sharon James, Jim O'Hara and Sara Mack, among others, who nourished me in my love of ancient literature and language; in addition, my beloved teachers Alan Shapiro, Larry Goldberg, and Walid Sakaan also deserve the deepest appreciation. Finally, I have been surrounded and heartened all along by the loving kindness and magnanimous generosity of friends and family, including my mother Jennifer Childers and brother Patrick Childers, and my beloved friends and colleagues Wallace Simpson, Jason Pedicone, Sean Northrup, Swayam Bagaria, Sean Byrnes, Daniel J. McCaffery Esq., Sasha Mahool Potts and Sanaz Nourmohammadi. (I hope she is proud of me.) Needless to say, whatever errors and infelicities the book contains are attributable to none of the above, and probably the result of my failing to heed their good advice. My sincerest apologies go out to everyone I have not mentioned but should have.

I have benefited enormously by the support and generosity, at different times, of Saint Andrew's School, the Johns Hopkins University Writing Seminars, and Gilman School. I was supported by the Columbia University Classics Department as a visiting scholar, by the Paideia Institute with a Brightheart Fellowship, and by the NEA with a Translator's Grant. Finally, grateful acknowledgment is made to the editors of the following journals, in which some of these translations initially appeared: *The Kenyon Review*, *The Hopkins Review*, *Agni*, *Harvard Review Online*, *The Columbia Review Online*, *PN Review*, *Smartish Pace*, *Literary Matters*, *Literary Imagination*, *Arion*, *Parnassus*, *Classical Outlook*, *Eidolon*, *The New Criterion*, *Atavic*, *Kin*, *New Walk*, *Peacock Journal*, *Snakeskin*, *The Raintown Review*, *Able Muse Review*, *New Haven Review* and *Metamorphoses*. Horace *Odes* 2.10 was republished by the Adrian Brinkerhoff Poetry Foundation and Propertius 2.28 in *The Penguin Book of Elegy*, edited by Andrew Motion and Stephen Regan. Simonides 584 will appear in *The Poetry Pharmacy Forever*.

The Archaic Period (circa 800–479 BCE)

SONG CULTURE: *SOPHIA*

Our story begins around 650 BCE, give or take a hundred years, among the islands, archipelagos and peninsulas of what today we call Greece and Turkey. Then, as now, the landscape was scattered with the remnants of Mycenaean palace society, whose collapse at the end of the Bronze Age (around 1200 BCE) had left behind colossal ruins; at this point, the people had lived among those ruins for centuries, without remembering who built them, or how. Of course, there was no internet or television, but neither were there cinemas or theaters, concert halls or opera houses; there were no schools, or even books. There was writing – its appearance around 800 coincided with the end of the period we call 'Dark' and the beginning of the one we call 'Archaic' – but it still had a low profile in the collective consciousness, and was found mostly on dedications and inscriptions, where, since most people could not read, the words would have served more to impress than to enlighten.

Had you been there, you might have lived in a small town (to you quite large) of maybe 7,000–10,000 people – possibly Thebes in central Boeotia, whether by the Cadmeia, the old Mycenaean citadel defended by its famous seven gates, or on the fertile Aonian plain north of the acropolis. You might have hailed from the bustling multicultural port of half-Anatolian Mytilene, islanded from its island (Lesbos) by the narrow Euripus strait, its two major harbors looking toward Sardis and the Lydian mainland. Or, then again, you might have dwelt in Elis, along the Peneus River in the Peloponnese, a once-small settlement now expanding rapidly thanks to its management of the Funeral Games of Pelops. (The latter were otherwise known as the Olympics – a real growth industry.) In each place, you would have spoken a different dialect of the language we today call 'Greek', though you would not have

called yourself 'a Greek': your people would have been Thebans, Mytileneans, Eleans. Even the group identities these communities possessed
as members of a given *polis* (or 'city-state' in English) were of no great
antiquity. It was only within the last few generations that changing weather patterns had allowed agricultural production to pick up, causing a
mini-boom in population and bringing people closer to their neighbors.
The 'cities' they now inhabited represented a novel and uneasy sort of
compromise, marked more by competitive cooperation, or cooperative
competition, than by anything much in the way of centralized organization or institutions.

It was through song that you knew who you were. These identities
were a product, above all, of stories (*mythoi*), and these, made more
memorable by rhythm, melody and dance, were at the heart of religious
festivals, like the Kallisteia or the Adonia, which recurred regularly
throughout the year. The already heady atmosphere of such events was
heightened further by the primal frisson of slaughter, the taste of meat
(a rare and fortifying indulgence), intoxicating drink and the smell of
incense – all good for health and morale. Song invested the mysteries of
the landscape with meaning: that mound across the river was the tomb
of Pelops; the impossibly large stones of this circuit wall, relics of the
Bronze Age, were coaxed into place by the lyre of Amphion; and the
whole island of Lesbos was understood to derive its musical potency
from the singing severed head of Orpheus, which had washed over the
sea to its shores from Thrace. Every visible remnant of the bygone Age
of Heroes, every sacred grove and shrine, had its story and its god.

Song was your school and your training ground. As a boy you sang
and danced the *paean* at the temple of Apollo Ismenius on the Ismenus
River, where you learned orderly and graceful movement through rhythm,
keeping time with the other boys – skills which would later serve you well
in the military formation called the *phalanx*. Elegiac couplets sung after
dinner taught elegance in speech and action, and put words both to the
unbelievable sweetness and shocking violence of sexual desire (*eros*) and
to the god who inflicted it. Praise poetry (*epainos*) articulated shared
values, offering a sort of road map to excellence (*arete*), while iambus
(*psogos*, blame poetry) made you laugh and taught you how not to
become a laughing stock yourself. When it was time to mourn, dirges
(*threnoi*) conjured tears with the visionary beauty of the life to come.

Song revealed the justice within the status quo: the oligarchs of Thebes, it was implied, ruled by right, for they were *Spartoi*, men sown by Cadmus from the dragon's teeth, descendants of Earth and Ares; or so the songs claimed. The world was a *hierarchy* – a 'holy order' or arrangement (*cosmos*) – with gods at the top and monsters at the bottom, encompassed always by chaos and death, but with powerful allies, too, on the side of order and civilization, and with the city as its microcosm. Finally, song, though it inculcated the discipline of the social order, also offered an escape from it, a sort of release valve, in the licentious whirlings of the dithyramb, sung by a chorus in honor of Dionysus. Away from the battle-field, it was in song and dance that you felt most a part of your community; and the musical stories stayed with you as models to emulate or avoid, framed and explained by the aphorisms of the poets in their wisdom.

What was the Wisdom (*Sophia*) of the poets? It was their ability to make poetry. First, *Sophia* was memory – the remembering of old stories, and the invention of new ones, which they could compose so as to make others remember. Memory (*Mnemosyne*) was the Mother of the Muses, and the poets were Masters of Truth (truth, *a-letheia*, literally 'not forget-ting'). Thus poetry conserved what happened in the past, and conveyed what it meant for the present. Second, *Sophia* was inspiration, the gift of the Muses. When poets remembered or invented a story or poem, at first it wasn't in their heads, and then it was. How did it get there? Where did the words come from? It must have been that their friends, the Muses, sent them: everything extraordinary had its god. Finally, *Sophia* was the composer's expertise, the command of complex melodies, rhythms and stanzas, the deft deployment of diction – all that would come in time to be called *techne*. 'Technique' was the outward manifestation of the poet's inward authority. It publicized their friendship with the Muses, who gave the words, and with the Graces (*Charites*), who added sweetness and pleasure. Both authority and truth were built into the song itself; it was True, because it was unforgotten, and unforgettable.

How did songs survive their first performance and become memory, when they might so easily have vanished without a trace, sung once and then forgotten? Writing, of course, was the key, though exactly when it entered the process is hard to say for sure. The poets themselves wrote; or they composed in their heads, and dictated to literate scribes; or their songs were written down by chorus members after the fact, much as parts of Shakespeare's First Folio would be more than 2,000 years later. In the rest of society, meanwhile, songs were widely learned and memorized, sung in the fields and after dinner, on shipboard and in exile, diffusing through the Greek world until in Athens a man named Solon (pp. 68–75), himself a poet and politician, while in attendance at an aristocrats' drinking party called a *symposium*, could hear his nephew sing a song by a Mytilenean named Sappho (pp. 38–54), and say to him, 'Teach me that song, so I can learn it and die.' Throughout the so-called Archaic period, the oral culture of song coexisted with the written word, which nonetheless continued to gain more and more currency – until, in the middle of the fifth century, Herodotus could compete with Homer by writing (yes, writing!) his monumental history of the Persian Wars in prose.

In that same century, the spread of literacy reached a tipping point, which, though it did not put an immediate end to the earlier song culture, was the beginning of the end. The Greeks of that time blamed the development on Cadmus, the mythical 'Easterner' and founder of Thebes who, when he traveled from Phoenicia to search for his sister Europa, kidnapped by Zeus, was said to have brought the first written letters with him. Yet it was not the old Phoenician syllabary that Cadmus brought. That system had been one in which only consonant sounds were represented, leaving vowels to be supplied by the reader's knowledge, but Cadmus' cargo was something else, something quite new in the history of the world: a true alphabet, in which every significant sound of the language, vowels as well as consonants, had been abstracted into symbols.

The new alphabet proved the perfect instrument for writing down Greek poetry, whose rhythms and meters were based above all on vowels. This tool of abstraction would enable the Theban Pindar to send his elaborate odes to Sicily across the sea at the height of the Lyric Age; and yet, in time, it also enabled the Athenian Plato to undermine the traditional authority of the poets and challenge their culturally embedded Archaic wisdom with an intellectual and absolute idea. When Plato asked not 'What does Homer say is good?' but 'What is Goodness, itself by itself?' he was at the vanguard of a new generation of thinkers bidding to supplant the singers as the true 'Lovers of Wisdom' (the original meaning of 'philosophers', from Greek *philo* + *sophia*). And the singers would have to respond.

That, however, is for the next section. For now, it is the Archaic period, and Archilochus is clearing his throat.

Archilochus

Archilochus was born on the Cycladic island of Paros some time near the beginning of the seventh century BCE. His father, Telesicles, was reportedly involved in Paros' colonization of Thasos in the northern Aegean near Thrace, and we are told by a fifth-century source that Archilochus 'went to Thasos from Paros because of poverty'. He is known for his feud with one Lycambes, a denizen of Paros said to have promised Archilochus the hand of Neobule, one of his daughters, and then to have broken his oath. Incensed, Archilochus attacked Lycambes and his family in fierce iambics, driving the girls to hang themselves. (Recent scholars, pointing to the similarity between 'Lycambes' and 'iambus', have suggested that he and his daughters may have been stock figures of the genre, rather than real people.) By the third century, Archilochus had come to be worshiped as a hero on his native Paros, at a shrine called the Archilocheion.

According to the literary scholars of Hellenistic Alexandria, Archilochus was the first of the three canonical iambic poets (the other two being Semonides of Amorgos, pp. 16–20, and Hipponax, pp. 114–19). As the founder of the genre, he was often placed beside Homer and Hesiod, the progenitors of epic and didactic poetry, respectively (and thus not featured in this volume). More recently, he has been credited with the invention of the 'Lyric I' for first-person narrative in verse, and even of the 'confessional' (associated in the mid-twentieth century with such major American poets as Anne Sexton, Robert Lowell and Sylvia Plath). Personal speech may, however, have been as conventional in iambus as objectivity was in epic; and we cannot always tell, from the meager fragments at our disposal, whether the poet is speaking in his own voice or in a character's (see fragment 122, p. 10, and note). However that may be, to modern ways of thinking, Archilochus' tonal and formal range, his liveliness, his vividness and his concision – in short, his voice – more than justify the esteem in which the ancients held him.

Like many of the poets in this book, Archilochus' work survives almost entirely in fragments, either found on tattered papyri or quoted by later authors. The following translations represent a liberal selection.

1

I serve Lord Ares on the battlefield,
and the sweet Muses' gift is mine to wield.

2°

My bread's aboard ship, aboard ship is my wine,
and, as I drink aboard ship, I recline.

3°

You won't see many bent bows, nor a throng
of slings, when Ares drives both sides headlong
over the plain; the groans will come from swords.
This is the fighting style the spear-famed lords
have mastered in Euboea.

4

Come, bring the cup across this man-of-war
to every oarsman; unstop the cask, and pour
the red wine to the dregs, until we're toast.
There's no way we'll stay sober at this post.

5°

Some Thracian now enjoys the faultless shield
I tossed in bushes, fleeing the battlefield
to save my skin. To hell with it! Why curse?
Who cares? I'll get another one no worse.

11°

I can't cure this by weeping, nor can I
make matters worse by giving fun a try.

13

No man or government will fault our grief,
Pericles, turning to feast on wine and beef,°
such brave souls has the sea's confounding din
dashed to the depths, submerging our lungs in
surges of pain. But for such helpless ill,
my friend, the gods have given us this pill:
endurance. All men hurt – now less, now more.
It's our turn now to groan and drain the sore;
soon it will be another's. Make it fast –
endure. Put girlish grieving in the past.   10

The Achaeans at Mysia°

When a god goads us with necessity,
don't rant at 'gutless weaklings' – I say we
did well to cut and run! Flight can be right
at times: the whole Greek host once took to flight,
those mighty spearmen, routed by one man –
by Telephus, displaced Arcadian.°
So urgent is the force of fate. The slain
clogged the sweet-flowing Caicus, and the plain°
of Mysia; the finely greaved Greek bands,
dying in droves at his relentless hands,   10
turned backward to the booming beach in haste;
those men – the gods' own kith and kin – now raced
for shelter to the ships, they who had come
with Agamemnon to raze Ilium.
Off-course, along that coastline, they'd sailed down
and were assailing Teuthras' lovely town,°

both men and horses snorting battle fury
deludedly. But soon they all were sorry –
20   how quick they'd breached Troy's towers, so they thought,
in wheat-rich Mysia, and all for naught.
Heracles came, and roared at his son's mettle,
indomitable in the dust of battle –
Telephus, who made Achaea cut and run
like cowards, fighting like his father's son.

19

I don't want golden Gyges' anything –°
no envy here. A god's perks do not pique
my interest. I don't hanker to be king.
All that's too far away. My sight's too weak.

21+22°

21   This island, arching like an ass's backbone,
stands covered over with a savage forest;
22   it isn't beautiful, desirable
or lovely, as around the stream of Siris.°

30+31°

30   Glowing with pleasure, she held a myrtle sprig
and beautiful rose flower,
31   and her hair
spilled shadows on her shoulders and her back.

41

A kingfisher
perched on a jutting rock and beat its wings.

42

Like a Phrygian or a Thracian sucking
beer through a straw, she knelt down hard at work.

48

their nurse brought them, with scented hair and breasts,
so even an old man would be turned on,
Glaucus°

105°

Look, Glaucus, as the breakers thrash the bottomless ocean there
and over Gyrae's peaks a column of cloud stands straight and sheer;°
it means a storm is coming and – when we least expect it – fear.

108

Be my ally, Lord Hephaestus: hear your supplicant;
be kindly now, and grant the kinds of favor that you grant.

114

I don't like tall generals who strut with a long stride,
and brag about their curls and style their whiskers when they shave.
Give me a little one instead, with stumpy legs bowed wide,
who plants his feet firm on the ground, is full of heart, and brave.

115°

Leophilus is leader now, Leophilus has sway,
it all rests with Leophilus; Leophilus, hooray!

116°

So long, Paros, with those figs and that seafaring life!

118

How I wish that I could touch the hand of Neobule!

119°

[I] fell on that hard-working wineskin and began to thrust
belly against belly, thigh on thigh.

120+121°

120   For I know how to strike up Dionysus' lovely strain,
       the dithyramb, even as wine lightning-bolts my brain,°
121   and I can lead the Lesbian paean as pipers play along.°

122°

No more surprises now, no stunning miracles, no thought
unthinkable, since heaven's father, Zeus, saw fit to blot
the midday with sheer midnight, overshadowing the sun,
and with that shadow fear and trembling fell on everyone.
From now on no occurrences, no worries or wild hopes
are past belief; from now on there's no call for shock or wonder,
not if you see the dolphins crop the mountains and treetops,
while woodland creatures graze each oceanic glen and copse –
the dolphins' home – and frisk with pleasure through the
      breakers' thunder.

124

To Pericles°

One time you came to visit in the true Myconian style,°
draining neat wine by the carafe, freeloading all the while,
no cash in hand, no invitation, like you were our friend,
obedient only to your belly's hunger to transcend
the bounds of shamelessness

125

Like a man parched for water, so I long to skirmish with you.

126

I know how to do one major thing:
repay someone who makes me suffer with brutal suffering.

128

O heart, my heart, turned upside down by cares that have no cures,
get up, thrust out your chest, and take a stand – don't be afraid! –
go face your enemies now hunkering in their ambuscade
with firmness. Don't be overjoyed if victory is yours,
and if you lose don't head home wailing, or collapse dismayed.
No, grieve when things are rotten, and enjoy your days of bliss,
but not too much – know all men's lives are up and down like this.

130

Chalk it all up to the gods; for they have often caught
men fallen down on the black earth and picked them up again,
and often, too, they've pummeled even well-established men,
and piled misfortunes high on them, laid out by the onslaught;
and the man roams – no food, no work – beside himself, distraught.

131

Glaucus, son of Leptines, our hearts are built this way,°
to change their weather as the weather changes every day.

168°

Hey, it's Sunshine, Sweetheart's son,
    My best friend by a mile!
This story is *hilarious*;
    It's bound to make you smile.

184

    Bent on deceit, she carried
water in one hand; in the other, fire.

188

The Cologne Papyrus

Your skin has lost the bloom of spring,
    dryness is withering
your furrow; fetid age now holds you fast.
    The beauty and the tender grace
    of your once-lovely face
have rushed away before the wintry blast
    buffeting you from arctic climes,
    and many, many times

191°

In my desire for sex, blind lust
    coiled deep in my chest
and drenched my vision in a heavy mist,
    stealing the weak wits from my breast.

193

I lie here pierced with longing,
lifeless and wretched; the gods have speared my bones
and the fierce pangs come thronging.

196

Lust, that makes limbs slack,
my friend, has knocked me on my back.

196a°

The Cologne Papyrus

'. . . wholly restraining yourself,
and I'll endure in the same way.

But if your longing's urgent and can't wait,
there is a girl in our house
right now whose need for you is great,

a lovely maiden, soft and delicate.
I think that her beauty is perfect.
With her you can be intimate.'

She finished, and I answered her in haste:
'Dearest Amphímedo's daughter –   10
how noble and refined, how chaste

your mother was, whom the rank earth holds tight! –
the goddess has given the young
so many methods of delight

besides the sacred act, and one will do.
The rest we will mull over later,
calling on heaven, me and you,

when you're more ripe, and we have calm to think.
          I'll do what you tell me to do.
20   You've brought my longing to the brink.

But don't begrudge, my dear, my passing through
          the entryway under the lintel
     to the grass gardens where, I'm telling you,

I'm headed. Neobule? What a laugh!
          Somebody else can have her.
     She's twice your age, too ripe by half,

her girlish bloom has blown, the flower died,
          her charms are a thing of the past.
     Her lust cannot be satisfied;

30   she's shown how drunk with it, how crazed she is.
          To the crows, to the gallows with her!
     Let no one sentence me to this:

to take on such a woman as my wife.
          I'd be a joke to the neighbors!
     I much prefer you in my life,

since you don't lie or try to cheat with others.
          But she is hot-tempered and harsh,
     and welcomes many men as lovers.

I fear if I move too fast or rush in early,
40   like the proverbial bitch°
     I'll bear blind offspring prematurely.'

I said no more, but took her to a bed
          of grasses and blossoming flowers,
     and laid her down. Behind her head

I laced an arm, and spread my tunic over
        her as she fussed like a fawn,
    and held her, moving to uncover

her breasts, which I took hold of gently, sleek
        young flesh she revealed to my eyes
    that showed her springtime near its peak;   50

and stroking her whole lovely body there
        I let out a spurt of the white stuff,
    with one hand in her yellow hair.

201°

The fox knows many tricks, the hedgehog one,
but it's a big one.

212

The ship sat on a knife-edge
between the waves and wind.°

213

They gave their lives into the waves' embrace.

Semonides of Amorgos

Semonides of Amorgos (first half of the seventh century BCE) – to be distinguished from Simonides of Ceos (pp. 120–33) – was, along with Archilochus (pp. 5–15) and Hipponax (pp. 114–19), one of the three canonical iambic poets as established by the scholars of Hellenistic Alexandria; all three are shadowy figures, but Semonides is much the most mysterious to us. We are told he was born on Samos, but like Archilochus he led a colonizing expedition, and was ultimately linked with the colony he founded on the Cycladic island of Amorgos. Just as Archilochus attacked Lycambes (p. 5), and Hipponax set his sights on his own target, the sculptor Bupalus (p. 114), so Semonides' preferred punching bag was one Orodoecides – at least, that's what we are told eight centuries later by the satirist Lucian of Samosata, though Orodoecides is not mentioned in any of the extant fragments. To Semonides is attributed a long elegiac poem of which nothing survives, possibly a *History of Samos*, as well as a collection of iambics. From what remains it is difficult to get a general sense of Semonides' poetry beyond a certain grimly hectoring pessimism and tedious misogyny.

1°

The will of Zeus the Thunderer, my boy,
holds and fixes the end of everything,
but men are dumb, blind creatures of the day,
who live like grazing herds, with no idea
of how the god will bring things to their end.
Meanwhile, hopeful bravado keeps us rushing
in hot pursuit of the impossible;
we wait for the next morning, or next season,
and no one thinks that he won't wake tomorrow
10   in bed with money and the ruling class.
But loathsome old age gets there first and takes

this man before his time, while that one coughs
his life away, and war mows others down
on a forced march to darkness underground.
Some men are buffeted by hurricanes
on the high seas, and drown in churning breakers,
who couldn't make a living on dry land;
while others tie the noose that breaks their necks,
and leave the sunlight by a choice demise.
Thus, nothing is unmixed with evil; thousands   20
of deaths and sorrows and surprise disasters
wait on us. But if we'd take my advice,
we wouldn't lust for misery, or twist
our hearts over the rack of bitter pain.

2+3

If we had sense, we wouldn't think about   2
or mourn the dead more than a single day.
For we'll be dead a long time, but we live   3
a few years only, and we live them badly.

7°

In the beginning, god created women
with different characters. One's from a sow
bristling with hair. Everything in her house
is smeared with muck and scattered on the floor.
And she herself, unwashed, in unwashed clothes,
sits there beside the shit-heap and gets fat.
    He made another from a fiendish fox:
she's an authority on everything.
She misses nothing bad, and nothing good,
and mostly she considers bad things good,   10
and good things bad. Her moods are always changing.
    One's from a snappish bitch – just like her mother,°
she's got to hear it all, and know it all,
and sneaks and seeks, and peers and pries all over,

yapping no matter if there's no one there.
Threats are no good; a man can't shut her up,
not if he takes a rock in rage and breaks
her teeth, or if he murmurs soothingly,
not even if she's sitting there with guests,
but she just yaps and yaps, unflappably.

The gods made one from earth, and made her gimpy,
her husband's damaged goods. Such a wife
has no idea of what's bad or good;
the only thing she knows is how to eat.
And even when the winter makes her shiver,
she's too dumb to scoot closer to the fire.

One's from the ocean; she's a paradox.
One day she smiles and sparkles with delight,
so houseguests will admire her and say,
'There's no one in the world who's got a wife
better than this one, or more beautiful.'
But the next day her husband can't get close
or even look at her, because she's crazy,
defensive as a bitch around her pups,
relentless, and at war with everyone,
treating her friends and enemies the same.
Just as the sea in summer lies becalmed,
all innocence and imperturbable,
gladdening sailors, but before long's crazed,
raging with waves that crash like thunderclaps –
that's what this sort of woman's moods are like.
The ocean's character is always changing.

One's from a gray ass used to being beaten;
only when forced and cussed she grudgingly
gives in and works, and then the work she does
is good enough. Meanwhile, all day and night,
she eats in corners, eats beside the hearth,
and takes on lovers like she takes in food,°
sleeping with anyone who comes along.

One's from a weasel – that one's miserable.°
There's nothing beautiful, desirable,

20

30

40

50

delightful or attractive about her.
She's crazy about sex but sickening,
and makes the man she sleeps with want to puke.
She's always stealing, pissing off the neighbors,
and eats the food reserved for sacrifices.

  A gorgeous mare with an exquisite mane
bore one; she turns her nose at drudgery,
makes others do it. She won't touch a millstone,
handle a sieve, shovel the shit from the house°   60
or sit close to the stove (she can't stand soot).
Her husband's forced to love her – and his debt.
Two or three times a day she takes warm baths,
scrubs off the dirt, anoints herself with scents,
and that luxuriant hair – she always wears it
combed straight and long, and shadows it with flowers.
She's an exquisite sight for other men,
but to her husband she's a royal pain,
unless he's some crowned head or tyrant-type,
the kind of man who likes this kind of woman.   70

  One's from a monkey. This one is the worst,°
the greatest curse that Zeus has thrust on men.
Her face is so disgusting, when she goes
around the city, everybody laughs.
Her neck is stumpy. Her gait lurches weirdly,
no ass, all knees and elbows – god, poor guy,
who has to sleep with that monstrosity!
She's cunning, though, knows lots of twists and turns,
just like a monkey. Mockery doesn't faze her.
She's no help ever, always on the lookout,   80
scanning and planning all day every day
for opportunities to do her worst.

  One's from a bee. Her husband struck it lucky,°
since she's the only one that's not a nightmare.
Under her care, his livelihood improves,
his household flourishes, and she grows old
cherished by a man she cherishes,
and rears a fine, distinguished family.

Her grace outshines all other women; grace
90   touched by the gods surrounds her with its glow.
She doesn't like to gossip with the girls
when they all get together, talking sex.
Such women are the best and most discerning
that Zeus bestows to grace a husband's life.

     Zeus has it fixed so all these other species
of women are here with men, and here to stay.
But the worst curse Zeus has devised is this:
women. A husband who believes his wife
has something to contribute is in trouble.
100   Not once will a man make it a whole day
in a good mood if he lives with a woman,
or easily from his own home kick out
Hunger, a hated houseguest, hostile god.
And when her man is happiest at home,
because of the gods' help or human kindness,
she drums up some complaint and arms for battle.
Where there's a woman, men can't in good conscience
put up a distant guest, much less a neighbor.
And wives who seem most virtuous – it's true –
110   turn out to be most vicious in the end:
the husband gapes there dumbly, while the neighbors
are titillated, chuckling at his blindness.
And everyone still remembers to speak well
of his own wife, but badmouths other people's,
and we don't see we're all in the same boat.
For this is the greatest curse that Zeus devised,
clapping us with these ankle fetters we
can't shake off, ever, since so many men
went down to Hades fighting for a woman.°

Callinus

Callinus (mid-seventh century BCE) came from Ephesus, one of the twelve Ionian cities in Asia Minor. Very little is known about him; besides the one long fragment, only a few scattered lines remain, though the skill and vigor of fragment 1 show that he was a talented poet. It is a shame so little of his work survives.

1°

How long, boys, will you lie there and hang back?°
Where is your heart? The neighbors see how slack
you are – aren't you ashamed? You think we stand
at peace, while war is general in the land! . . .°
and dying, hurl your spear one final time!
A man earns shining honor in the strife,
fighting to save his country, children, wife
from the foe's hands. When the Fates cut your thread –
that's when you'll die. So come, charge straight ahead,
with spear held high and heart behind your shield   10
unwavering, when you first take the field.
No man, not even of immortal blood,
is destined to escape from death for good.
A man who flees the strife and battersome
thudding of spears to die in his own home
will not be loved or missed at all in town;
but great and common mourn a soldier down.
For when a brave man dies, we grieve and pine;
alive, he's honored like one half-divine.
The people see him as a bastion,   20
who does the work of many, all alone.

Tyrtaeus

The Spartan elegiac poet Tyrtaeus (late seventh century BCE) wrote five books, under the headings of the *Spartan Constitution* or *Eunomia* (*Good Order*), *Exhortations* and *Marching Songs* (or *Battle Songs*; some titles will have comprised more than one book). Of these, our most substantial surviving fragments are from the *Exhortations*; we have little of the *Eunomia* and nothing of the *Marching Songs*. Tyrtaeus was said to have played a prominent role in the Second Messenian War (circa 620–600 BCE), in which the Spartans suppressed a revolt of the helots, the enslaved population of neighboring Messenia. We are told that he recited his elegies during the darkest moments of the war to inspire the Spartans not to give up fighting, and even that he declaimed them behind the front lines during battle to inspire the soldiers and discourage the weak ones from deserting. The latter is unlikely; more probably his poems were sung within or in front of the kings' tent on campaigns and at the messes during peacetime.

Later Greeks, incredulous that the Spartans could have produced a poet of any sort, claimed that Tyrtaeus was a limping, dim-witted schoolmaster sent to Sparta from Athens in response to an oracle; the story smacks of Athenian chauvinism. The Spartan king Leonidas reportedly found Tyrtaeus' poems 'good for enflaming the hearts of young warriors', and they remained popular in Sparta long after the subjugation of Messenia had been completed. Though Tyrtaeus is not a poet of the first rank, his imagery is vivid, his phrases are often striking and well turned, and his extant fragments are essential to our understanding of elegy in general and martial elegy in particular.

10

It's beautiful for a brave man to fall
fighting in front when home and country call,°
but the most brutal, harshest thing of all

is leaving one's hometown and fertile soil
to scrape by on a beggar's life and toil,
with his whole family wandering together:
small children, wife, dear mother and old father.
For everyone he meets is hostile to him;
base poverty and neediness undo him;
he soils his family name; his looks desert him;   10
and all dishonor stains, all hardships hurt him.
Therefore, since men don't care for or admire
such homeless exiles, or the line they sire,
let us fight for this land with spirits high;
don't cling to life; it's for our sons we die!
Young men, get up! Stand side by side and fight,
and don't give in to fear or shameful flight!
No, steel your fighting spirit to the strife;
when you face men, don't be in love with life.
Think of the old, their knees no longer light –   20
don't turn your back on them and take to flight!
Appalling, when an old man in the fray
falls in the front while young ones shy away,
his head already white, his gray beard mussed,
exhaling his brave spirit in the dust,
his hands clutching his bloodied private parts –
appalling sight, one to incense your hearts! –
stripped naked. But a youth – all is becoming
for him, while his springtime is bright and blooming;
alive, he's what men praise and women want;   30
he's beautiful, too, fallen at the front.
Now, everyone, stand wide, get a good grip
with both feet, hold your ground, and bite your lip!

11

Come, you sons of unconquered Heracles!°
Zeus isn't yet among your enemies.
Be brave! Don't fear that mob of men, don't fly,
but march straight at them, with your shields held high,

despising life, and loving the black night
of death as much as you love the sun's light.
You know how ruinous the actions are
of tear-stained Ares, you've felt the pulse of war,
you've been with those who chase, and those who flee;
in both you've reached and passed satiety.
Soldiers who dare line up and make a stand,
who gain the front and battle hand to hand –
those men survive, and shield the company;
but flight erases acts of bravery.
No one could list, when someone loses face,
all the misfortunes that attend disgrace.
It's awful when a man's pierced through the back
because he fled an enemy attack,
and shameful when a corpse with spearpoint thrust
between its shoulder blades lies in the dust.
Now, everyone, stand wide, get a good grip
with both feet, hold your ground, and bite your lip.
Make sure thighs, shins, chest, shoulders are concealed
behind the belly of your massive shield,
in your right hand heft your mighty spear,
and nod your plumed crest, flashing awe and fear.
By doing mighty deeds you learn to fight.
With shield in hand, don't steer clear of the flight
of arrows, but get close, close as you can,
and with your sword or long spear strike your man!
Go in, thrust foot to foot and chest to chest,
helmet to helmet, plumed crest to plumed crest,
clash shield on shield and fight your man, so near
you wrest away his sword, or seize his spear.
Crouch down on every side, you light-armed ones,
behind the shields, and let fly with huge stones
at them, or fling your polished javelin,
standing hard by the heavy-armored men.

12°

I'd never praise a man or pay him heed
if he excels in wrestling or in speed,
not if he has a Cyclops' size and might,
or outstrips Thracian Boreas in flight,°
not if Adrastus' tongue drips with less honey,°
or Cinyras and Midas have less money,°
not if Tithonus is less fair to see,°
or Tantalus' son less a king than he,°
not if he's famed for every kind of glory
except for bravery and battle fury.   10
A man who can't watch when the fight gets gory,
or lunge at foes from close range and shed blood –
in war that man will never be called good.
This is true excellence, this is the best
prize youth can garner, and the loveliest.
For the whole city reaps the benefits
when a man stands in front and never quits,
doggedly holding ground, and risks his life,
forgetting flight, his heart steeled to the strife,
urging the man he stands by to endure –   20
this is the man that we call good in war.
Quickly he routs the foes packed side by side
and, bristling, keenly stems the battle's tide.
But if, in the front ranks, death cuts him down,
he glorifies his father, townsmen, town,
with his shield punctured, where he was hard-pressed,
and holes punched through his breastplate and his breast.
Then youths and elders mourn the soldier slain;
the whole town wails for him in grief and pain,
and people point his sons out, and his tomb,   30
and his sons' sons, and all his line to come.
His name, his glory, do not cease to sound;
he is immortal, though beneath the ground,
because he stood and fought and proved his mettle

for land and children, and was killed in battle.
But if he dodges death that brings distress,
and makes his brave boast good by his success,
everyone honors him, old men and boys;
he enters Hades after many joys,
40   and stands out in old age, when no one will
dishonor or defraud or wish him ill,
and young men, those his age, and elders greet
him at the benches, giving up their seat.
Now, men, each give your all to gain this height
of excellence; don't let up in the fight!

Mimnermus

Mimnermus (circa 660–600 BCE), an elegiac poet from Asia Minor, was born in Smyrna (modern İzmir) around the time when it was invaded by the Lydian king Gyges. (At some later point he was mistakenly claimed by the people of Colophon.) The Smyrnaeans defeated Gyges at the Hermus River (now the Gediz) around 660, and it is possible that Mimnermus' name, which means 'Remember the Hermus', was chosen to commemorate the victory. Smyrna was eventually sacked by Alyattes, a successor of Gyges and the father of the famously wealthy Croesus, around 600, and Mimnermus is assumed to have died either at the time of that conflict, or shortly before. Fragment 14 (p. 30) refers back to the first battle at the Hermus and may well exhort the Smyrnaeans on the eve of the second.

We are told Mimnermus produced two books in his lifetime, most likely the *Nanno*, a collection of elegiac poems on various topics, and the *Smyrneis*, a long historical elegy about Smyrna's victory over Gyges and the Lydians, of which fragment 13 (not included herein) is all that remains. The *Nanno* is said to have been named after a girl pipe-player whom Mimnermus loved; most, if not all, of our fragments of his poetry come from this collection. Though there is little evidence in his surviving poems, he was thought of by later generations primarily as a love poet; what our extant verses do show is that, while no early Greek poet has a positive view of old age (with the partial exception of Solon, pp. 68–75), none of them were as depressive or obsessive about it as Mimnermus.

He was revered by such authors as Callimachus (in *Aetia* 1.1, lines 11–12, p. 258) and Propertius (pp. 421–45) for his lovely concision and polished, lapidary style. Besides Archilochus (pp. 5–15), Mimnermus is easily the most skilled of the Archaic elegists.

I

What life, what pleasure, without golden Love?°
Let me drop dead when I have had enough
of secret trysts, love-gifts and the love-bed,
flowers of youth whose joys are harvested
by men and women. But when the pain sets in
of age, deforming even handsome men,
cruel worries always wear us down for spite;
we get no pleasure looking on the light;
women do not respect us; boys are cold.
10   That's how bitter the god made getting old.

2

We are like leaves born in the teeming spring,°
basking in sunlight, swiftly burgeoning;
like them, for an arm's length of time, we live°
happy and young, and what the gods will give
we don't suspect. Presences wrapped in gloom
are always near, one holding out the doom
of age, another, death. And youth won't last;
its fruit, like one day's worth of sun, dies fast.
And when this season dwindles and is gone,
10   it's better being dead than living on.
For troubles swarm the heart: one man will blow
his savings, and lose everything but woe;
another man wants children most of all,
and, wanting them, goes down to Hades' hall;
disease destroys a third. For Zeus the king
gives everyone a share of suffering.

3

When a man's past his prime, though handsome once,
he isn't loved or honored by his sons.

4

Zeus gave Tithonus an everlasting curse:°
old age, at least as bad as death, and worse.

5

[Suddenly speechless sweat rivers my face
and my heart flutters at the charm and grace
of boys my age in bloom. If this could last!]°
But like a pleasant dream that fades too fast
youth withers; suddenly above your head°
old age hangs pain and ugliness and dread;
dishonored, foul, disfiguring, it wounds
the mind and sight of those whom it surrounds.

6°

May my fate take me after sixty years
without the pain of sickness or sad fears.

7

Live for yourself, not reputation. Yes,
you will be criticized, now more, now less.

11+11a°

Jason could not have done it on his own,   11
brought back the great fleece to the brutal throne
of Pelias, prize won through hard exertion,
or even made it to the stream of ocean . . .
Aeëtes' city, where the great halls hold   11a
the sun's swift rays in storerooms made of gold
by ocean's edge, where godlike Jason went.

12°

For all the sun does every day is work.
He never has a chance to rest or shirk,
he and his horses, once rosy-fingered Dawn
leaves ocean for the sky and brings day on.
At night he's carried back across the seas
all the way from the Hesperides
asleep in a hollow, golden, wingèd cup
made by Hephaestus, skimming the water's top
to Aethiopia, where his steeds stand
10   till Dawn awakes and rises overland.
Hyperion's son then mounts his chariot°

14°

That none today could rival that man's might
I've gathered from the old, who saw him fight
with spear in hand and rout the serried ranks
of Lydian horsemen hard by Hermus' banks.
At no time could Athena criticize
his heartfelt fury, when amid the cries
of bloody war he barreled to the front,
into the rain of spears, and bore the brunt.
For not one of his enemies was more
10   suited to the brutal work of war
when he came on, swift as the blazing sun

Alcman

Alcman, one of the canonical Nine Lyric Poets, was active in the mid- to late seventh century BCE. A Spartan, he composed in a local dialect on local themes. As with Tyrtaeus (pp. 22–6), later Greeks, surprised that Sparta should have produced a poet of note, argued that Alcman was really from Sardis in Lydia, probably because they misread the dialect of fragment 16 (p. 35). Alcman is said to have composed six books of poetry – the first two of which the scholars of Hellenistic Alexandria classified as *partheneia* (maiden-songs), the genre for which Alcman was most famous – as well as something called the *Diving Women*, perhaps a long narrative poem, otherwise unknown. Alcman is also credited with wedding hymns and erotic poetry. As with other Archaic poets, the stories told about Alcman – for example, that he was a man of large appetites for food and sex – are clearly derived from his verse. Alcman was also widely reputed to have been the teacher of the legendary minstrel and dolphin-charmer Arion (see Anonymous Classical Lyric, fragment 939, p. 239). Aristotle mentions, unpleasantly, that Alcman died of pubic lice.

The text of Alcman's first fragment, constantly gesturing beyond itself toward sights we cannot see and meanings at which we can only guess, has provoked numerous interpretations. Some see the poem as the script of an initiation ceremony for the female chorus, or as an *epithalamion* (wedding song) in which (in one version of this interpretation) Agido might be the bride, and Hagesichora a cult title of the goddess Helen. Given such difficulties, it is no wonder that Alcman's oeuvre should have provoked serious attention among the Alexandrians; as evidence of their attentions, we have the twelve papyrus fragments and six fragments of commentaries found in an ancient trash heap at Oxyrhynchus in Egypt from the late 1890s onward, as well as mentions of monographs on his poetry written between the third century BCE and the first century CE.

For us today, his work exerts a similar pull, and probably for similar reasons – chief among them, that its parochial rootedness in local tradition provides tantalizing access to a spectacle and a society we cannot quite grasp. Apart from whatever it may have meant in the context of his contemporary Sparta, Alcman's poetry was also known for its sweetness and charm, its lightness of touch and delicacy of rhythm; one of his fragments (26, p. 36) is among the most beautiful of Archaic lyric. Taken together, his surviving poems show us – through a glass, darkly – an ancient Spartan song culture more musical and more in love with life than that oppressively martial people afterwards became.

1°

The Partheneion

Str. 6   There *is* revenge the gods exact.
               He's happy who lives weaving
          the fabric of each daily act
               in goodness, without grieving.°
40   But me, I hymn the luminous
               auroral Agido,°
          who calls the sun to shine for us,
               her glow like sunlight's glow.
     The sparkler, though, who mounts our spectacle°
          won't let me cover her with blame or praise,
               herself as unsurpassable
          as a black horse among dream-flocks that graze
     in meadows of dreams, with the rock of the world
               for roof –
     a powerful thoroughbred victor with thunderous hoof.

Str. 7   Just look at her! This sable steed
51   by the Black Sea was foaled.
          My cousin's of a Lydian breed,
               her mane of unmixed gold:
          Silvery Hagesíchora, Chorus
               Queen, whose countenance –°
          but why use words when she's before us?
               There, at the head of the dance!

Next, rosy Agido will come, soon now,
a Scythian horse behind the Lydian.°
    For as we bring around the plow   60
and its due season, at the cusp of dawn
the Pleiades, hanging aloft in ambrosial night
like fiery Sirius, are battling us, light to light.°

    No purple cloth's enough to make   *Str. 8*
      our choir safe from harm,
    no, nor a glittering, chased-gold snake
      worn as a holy charm,
    no Lydian garland dark-eyed girls
      slip on to general awe,
    nor Nanno with her gorgeous curls,   70
      nor godlike Areta.
Cleësithera? – no; not Thylacis;
in that dark house all mortals praise, don't say,°
    'I wish to stand by Astaphis,
I wish that Philylla would look my way,
and Damáreta, lovely Ianthemis . . .' No – when I near
Hagesíchora's radiant countenance, I disappear.°

    Where Hagesíchora plies her dance   *Str. 9*
      on ankles fine and small,
    look – Agido! Their radiance   80
      applauds our festival.
    Gods who accomplish every goal,
      please hear us as we pray;
    fulfillment is in your control.
      And, Lady, if I may,
who mount our dance, I'm just a girl, whose voice°
pours from the sky in vain, like the mournful owl's;°
    I long to make the heart rejoice
of healing Dawn, the lightener of our toils.
Away from Hagesíchora on pathways of peace   90
we plant our maidenly steps in sublime release.

Str. 10   For in a [chariot every horse]
                   will let the trace-horse lead;
               and a ship's helmsman sets the course
                   which all the sailors heed.
               When Sirens sing, we give way then –
                   they're goddesses of heaven,
               and sing in perfect steps of ten;
                   we stumble at eleven.°
100   The melody is lovely as a swan's
               paddling the Xanthus, and the yellow hair°

3°

The Second Partheneion

Str. 1   Olympian singers, [now descend!
               The longing for a ne]w song [brims
               inside] my heart. I w[ant] to hear
                   the [maide]n voices [send
5   into the lof]ty air their lovely hymns . . .
7   will clear my eyes of sleep and bend
                   my footsteps to the gathering [where
9   I'll join the dance] and toss my yellow hair . . .°

Str. 6   while longing makes their knees go weak.
62   More than in sleep or death they melt
               for her. Her sweetness doesn't go unfelt.°

Str. 7   Astymeloisa makes no reply
               to me as she bears the anadem
               of flowers – like a shooting star°
                   that sparks in the vivid sky,
68   or like soft feathers, or a gold-green stem . . .
70   her elegant feet passed by.
               The dewy Cypriot attars shed
               their fragrant blessings on her [lovely] head.

[So A]stymeloisa [marches] through   *Str. 8*
the crowd, the people's favorite,
and takes [my heart along with her.]
    And I say [this to you:] ...   76
May [the gods] show me favor, too,   79
    and bring her close, lay my soft hand
in hers, and let [me serve at her co]mmand.

14

Come, Muse, whose hymns and high notes ring,
    unquenchable singer, strike
up a new strain for the maidens to sing.

16°

He wasn't any backward yokel
or cretin ignorant what art is,
no shepherd son of Thessaly
or rude Erysichean local –°
no, no, he came from lofty Sardis.

17

Someday I'll give you a tripod pot, where you
    can store your grain. It's a big pot
as yet untouched by fire, but soon to brim
    with fava mash – which Alcman, who°
eats anything and everything, likes hot
    after the solstice. Not for him
the froufrou canapés; no, he seeks out
    the common fare the people eat.

26°

No more, you honey-voiced maidens whose songs have a
    holy power,
can my frame bear my weight. I wish, I wish that I were
a kingfisher aloft with you halcyons over the sea-foam in flower,
an ocean-colored holy bird, light-hearted, sure.

39

    his music and his lyrics
Alcman devised by listening
to the clickering tongue of the partridge sing°

40

    and I know the airs of every
bird

41

On one side, steel; and on the other,
    the lovely lyre-playing.

46

The Muses, dressed   in their saffron best,
to Zeus's son,   whose arrows stun°
from far away, had this to say:

56

High on the mountains, when the gods enjoy
    their torchlight-thronged festivities,
you'd take that golden barrel of a cup,°

the sort that shepherd swains employ,
and with your own hands fill it up
with lion's milk, to clabber for Argus's killer a great firm cheese.°

58

Not Cypris, that
          is her childish brat,
                    Love, at his pranks,
                              maniacal
as he flits and skips
          on the blooming tips –
                    no touching, thanks! –
                              of the galingale.

59a+b°

Again, Love, doing Aphrodite's bidding,   59a
invades my heart and heats it with his sweetness.

This gift of the charming Muses was unveiled   59b
by that happiest of girls –
Megalostrata, with the golden curls.

82

The young ladies scattered, their jobs half done,
like birds when a hawk swoops in front of the sun.

89°

Asleep are all the mountain peaks and the crevasses,
          the headlands and high torrents,
     and all the tribes of earth-fed creeping things,
     the beasts that haunt the hills, and the bee-races,
          and the monsters deep in the sea's dark currents;
     and asleep are the clans of the birds with their long wings.

Sappho

Such details as are known of Sappho's life are distressingly sparse. One of the canonical Nine Lyric Poets, and commonly referred to as the 'Tenth Muse', she was probably born in Mytilene on the island of Lesbos, probably around 630 BCE, and probably knew Alcaeus (pp. 55–67) and the elected tyrant (*aisymnetes*) Pittacus. She had a mother and a daughter both named Cleis, and her brothers were Charaxus (see fragment 5, p. 41), Larichus and Eurygyus (or Erigyus). She seems to have gone into exile in Sicily around 600, though, unlike those of her countryman Alcaeus, her political activities and affiliations are obscure. We know next to nothing about pre-existing traditions of Aeolic song (was Sappho a traditionalist? an innovator?) or about the social framework in which she composed and performed, and which allowed her to become famous: for instance, were there female companies or associations (*hetaireiai*) on Lesbos, in parallel to the male ones? In other words, what we know of both her life and work is made up almost entirely of gaps.

Any reading of Sappho must engage imaginatively with those gaps – especially with the interrelated unknowns of how the poems were composed, performed and passed down. In doing so, all readers, and eras, inevitably invent their own Sappho, rewriting her tattered manuscript like a palimpsest. There is the Sappho depicted on the comic stage of Athens in the fourth century BCE: a voracious heterosexual, wife of 'Dick Allcock from the Isle of Man' (Cercylas of Andros), who, rejected by the beautiful Phaon, commits suicide with a leap into the sea. This Sappho is taken up by Ovid (or an imitator of Ovid) in an epistle which contributed much to the seventeenth-century view of Sappho as a victim of her own desire. In that century, she seemed a primitive voice, an exponent of softness and grace, in contrast to the sophistications of her 'literary husband' Anacreon (pp. 100–108) and the public grandiloquence of Pindar (pp. 134–64). For the Romantics, 'burning Sappho' was lionized for her subjectivity, and her suffering – her emotionalism,

distasteful to the eighteenth century, became in the nineteenth the mark
of genius. Later, the Decadent poet Swinburne followed Charles Baudelaire and the Marquis de Sade in embracing her lesbianism – or
Sapphism – for them indistinguishable from a light sadomasochism (as
in Swinburne's 'Anactoria': 'I feel thy blood against my blood: my pain
/ Pains thee . . .') or, at any rate, a transgressive and passionate sexuality.
In the twentieth century, we had – and still have today – Sappho the
schoolteacher; Sappho the priestess; Sappho the proto-Imagiste,
admired by Ezra Pound and Hilda Doolittle (H.D.); Sappho the liber-
ated woman; Sappho the queer icon; and that Sappho whom we read as
much with yearning for what isn't there as with pleasure in what is – the
Sappho whom the accidents of history have turned into a metaphor for
her chief subject, loss.

1°

O deathless Aphrodite, enthroned in glamor,°
wile-weaver, Zeus's daughter, take my part,
I pray, and do not yoke, with pain and fever,
   Lady, my heart,

but come here now, if you ever heard my voice
with a heedful ear when I called to you on high,
and, going from your father's golden house,
   came down the sky

charioted out of heaven in a hurry
through mid-air by a team of lovely sparrows,°   10
their wingbeats whirring in a crowded flurry
   over the furrows,

and there they were, and you – as a smile played
on your immortal lips, o Blessed One,
you asked what was the matter now, what made
   me call *again,*

what was the main thing that my maniac
heart hoped would happen. 'Sappho, what love or lust
must I persuade this time to take you back?
20   *Now* who's unjust?

For if she's running now, she will soon pursue;°
if she says no to gifts, she'll give them soon;
and if she feels no love, and refuses to,
          she'll change her tune.'

Appear to me now again. Release me from
desire's stranglehold. Fulfill, provide
all that my heart has hoped for. Goddess, come
          fight at my side.

                              2°

Come to this holy place from your Cretan home°
and join me here, where the orchard trees are dense
with the charm of apples, and the altars fume
          with frankincense.

Here, through the apple boughs, the lapse of water
sounds icy-clear, and here, rose-shadow fills
the grass, as through the leaf-light and leaf-flutter
          a trance distills.

And here are meadows where the buds of spring
10   exuberantly bloom, where horses graze,
11   and, honey-sweet, the wind goes whispering . . .

13   Come hither, Cypris; nectar is in the bowl.
Mix it well with feasting and good will;
from your gold cups fill ours, pouring with all
          your grace and skill.°

5°

For my sake, Lady Nereids, please grant
my brother his return with life and limb
intact – and anything his heart may want,
            give it to him.

Let him atone for all the wrong he's done,
and be a joy to friends, a misery
to foes, and may he never be again
            a nobody,

but take a bit more heed of his sister's honor
in his decisions, and [provide relief,]   10
for hearts [his] suffering has [caused to suffer,]
            from all our grief

[at Doricha's in]fluence. Gossip in town
could quickly have become a real blood-letter,
and caused a scandal if ever there was one.
            But he [learned better]

before too long – and what could be [better] than
for him to learn [the value of] reputation?
But you, exalted Cypris

15

And, Cypris, about Doricha: don't let°
her find you so compliant now as then,
or gloat about how longingly he sought
            her arms *again*.

16°

Some say that horsemen, some a host on foot
is loveliest of all that the dark lands boast,
and some say warships; but I say it's what
    you love the most.

How effortless to make this perfectly
clear to you all, since the incomparable
Helen, that beauty more than human – *she*
    forsook her noble,

her royal husband and sailed for Troy, with all
10   concern for her dear parents and dear child
forgotten – [despite her woman's self-control,]
12   misled, beguiled . . .

15   And now I'm thinking of Anactoria,
        who isn't here:

thinking of how I'd rather see her sway,
her dancer's walk and sparkle, her face beaming,
than all of Lydia's chariots and array
20   of soldiers gleaming.

17°

Queen Hera, on this ground [the chorus rings,]
let your grace [waft and fan] our festival
which Atreus' sons founded, mighty kings°
    who did your will

when they, their epic tribulations over –
both those that they endured at Ilium
and when they landed here – could not discover
    the sea-route home

until they turned to you and Thyone's son,°
the thirsted-for, and to the guest god, Zeus.
And now we [too do what] of old was done
    in holiness

and b[eauty, as our g]irls and women [draw
near to your altar in a great pro]cession,
and lift in measure, [gladly and with awe,
    the u]lulation.

22°

    Now take your lyre and sing
of Gongyla, Abanthis, I command you,°
until the same Desire on the wing
    flutters around you,

you lovely girl. For she was flustered when
she saw your flowing dress. It makes me happy.
Her Holiness herself, the Cyprian,
    was angry at me

once when I prayed

23°

Each time I look into your eyes reveals
beauty to match Hermione's, I swear;°
even comparing you to Helen feels
    perfectly fair.

26

What can a woman do, if you don't love [her,]
Cypris, slave driver, but be ill with craving?
[When all] she wants to do is hi[de] her fever,
    [but you] keep driving?

Idly [you churn] the billows; you split me open
[with lo]nging that, [alas], makes my knees [slack;
the sto]rm will swa[mp the stays], but it wouldn't happen
    [if you'd hold back]°

27

But you too, even you, at one time [were]
a girl [who lov]ed to sing. Ponder the whole
affair inside you, and then grant us your
    blessing in full,

since, [as you see,] we're going to a wedding.
So come on, turn the girls loose right away
and let us go, and may the gods see [no]thing
    [ugly] today.

30°

    and all night let
the maidens hymn your love and your lady's, gowned
    in violet.

Go, call your bachelor friends whose age is right.
Don't even dream of dozing off; keep up!
Think of the clear-voiced nightingale – tonight
    we get *less* sleep.

31°

He seems like the gods' equal, that man, whoever he is, who takes his seat so close
across from you, and listens raptly to
    your lilting voice

and lovely laughter, which, as it wafts by,°
sets the heart in my ribcage fluttering;
as soon as I glance at you a moment, I
      can't say a thing,

and my tongue stiffens into silence, thin
flames underneath my skin prickle and spark,   10
a rush of blood booms in my ears, and then
      my eyes go dark,

and sweat pours coldly over me, and all
my body shakes, suddenly sallower
than summer grass, and death, I fear and feel,
      is very near.

But I must feel it all, since even a poor°

34°

The stars that in their glimmering orbits hover
around the gorgeous Moon go dim and hide
whenever she is full and beaming over
      the countryside.

41

and toward you who are lovely my regard
      will never alter

44°

'Hector and company   are heading here now
from sacred Thebe   and Placia's streams,°
on board with playful-eyed   pretty Andromache,
sailing her dowry   across the salt sea:
there's gold in abundance,   bracelets and bangles,
with royal robes,   beautiful baubles,

and countless cups   of silver, and ivories.'
So the herald spoke.   Spryly, Hector's
beloved father   leapt to his feet,
10   and through the wide city   word went to friends.
The Trojans tied   mules to the traces
of carriage-cars   that glide in comfort,
and matrons and maidens   flocked to the feast.
Priam's daughters   paraded apart;
young heroes yoked   horses to chariots . . .°

They entered Ilium   together, like gods.
The sweetness of pipes   and lyre-sounds swirled.
Castanets kept time.   Holy and clear,
the maidens' hymn,   more than human,
20   struck the skies.   In every street,
cups and pitchers   poured, and cassia
mingled its fragrance   with myrrh and frankincense.
Elderly women   whooped and warbled,°
and all the fellows   in fine falsetto
called, *Paean! Paean!*   Lyre-Player,°
awesome Archer!   So godlike Andromache
and Hector were hailed   in their wedding hymn.

47

Love hit my heart
like a gust that shakes   oaks high on the rocks.

48

You came, when I   was wild with wanting;
you cooled my heart   which craving made hot.

49°

Atthis, I loved you   long ago;
you seemed like a little   graceless girl.

53

You with the arms of roses, Zeus's daughters, come here, holy Graces

54

and out of heaven, Love came down and had a purple mantle on

55°

You'll lie low when you're dead, and be forgotten by posterity.
No one will think of you with love, who never plucked the roses of
Pieria; in Hades' hall, you'll be, as here, invisible,°
and flit about, where none can mark, among the shadows in the dark.

56

Of girls who gaze upon the sun, I can't imagine even one
will come in future to possess a comparable artfulness.

58a°

Dear girls, [I'm still possessed] of the lovely gifts [of the Muses,]
    violet-dressed;
[I'm still in love with song] and the lyre's voice that rings as it sings
    along.

But now this flesh and body, [once so supple,] old age has already
[got in its clutches,] and my head [is white] where all the black has
    fled.

My heart, heavy with freight, beats slow; my knees buckle beneath
    my weight –
knees which were as springy once as a small fawn's, and as quick to
    dance.

And so I groan, and groan anew. But what else can a
    body do?
No one made from a mortal mold can go on living and not
    get old.

Even rosy-forearmed Dawn, they say, once spirited away
10   Tithonus to the farthest-flung brink of the world when he
    was young

and lovely, and love [stung her.] Even so, he couldn't help
    but grow
old and gray in the gray years' clutch and blur. But time
    could not touch her.

58b

But *I*'m in love with the soft and sensuous. This [is my fire], and this
passion of mine has given its beauty to the sun, its sheen to heaven.

81

Now, Dica, with soft hands cull some anise strands,
plait the blooms and stalks and wreathe your lovely locks.
The Graces in bliss prefer a garlanded blossomer,
but turn their backs and neither love nor bless the
    blossomless.

94°

I honestly wish that I were dead.
As she was leaving me, she stood and said,

letting a flood of crying fall,
'Oh, Sappho, it's been terrible
for us. I'm leaving you against my will.'

I said to her in answer, 'Go.
    Go and farewell, and as you do,
remember me, how I – we – cared for you.

    But if you can't remember, let me
remind you . . .   10
                and we *have* been happy: 11

    think how, while I stood by your side,
        you'd gather roses for your head,
or crocus, or violets, and go garlanded;

    think of the necklaces you'd hang
        around your neck in a woven string,
trimming the supple skin with blossoming;

    remember, on your limbs and hair –
        nothing could be queenlier –
the spicy lavishness of floral myrrh,   20

    and the soft bed where you would sate
        your craving for the delicate . . .'

                        95

Gongyla . . .°
some sign, surely . . .
and [Hermes] came . . .°

I said, 'My Lord . . .
    By the great goddess, there's no more
happiness left for me in an earthly morning.

The longing's on me now to die, to go
    witness Acheron in its flowing
through dewy banks where lotus flowers grow.'

96

in Sardis,
2   where frequently she still remembers us . . .°

3   you always did impress her
            as like a goddess in the flesh,
      and when you sang it was her greatest pleasure.

      Lydian now, she outshines the ladies there
            as, after the sun has dipped his flaring°
      head, the moon's rose fingers brush the air

      and shutter all the stars, and an equal luster
10   shimmers the ocean's salty surf
      and lights the meadows where the flowers cluster,

      where the dew scatters spangles and the rose
            riots, where melilot uncloses
      blossoms and, delicate, the chervil blows.

      So she goes back and forth, and still recalls her
            dear Atthis with desire, and mulls
      what happened to you and, no doubt, it galls her.

98a+b°

98a   once, my mother said,

      when she was young, far the most sought
            accessory a girl could get
      was a purple headband – that's what people thought

      most flattering, the height of fashion.
            But any blonde whose locks out-flash
      the torch's hair should opt for decoration

more suitable: a simple braid
of flowers blooming on her head.
Just recently, an intricately made   10

headband from Sardis . . .

Cleis, I have no way to get   *98b*
ahold of an elaborate
headband for you

102

I can't do this weaving,   sweet mother, since in truth
Cypris is besieging   me with love of a youth.

104°

O evening star, you bring home everything
the brilliant Dawn disperses as she warms;
you bring back sheep, and bring goats back, and bring
children back home into their mother's arms.

105a°

An apple on a bough hangs redly, sweetly,
high on the highest limb, against the sky.
The pickers leave it be, but don't completely
leave it – they reached for it; it was too high.

105c°

a hyacinth, which shepherds in the mountains
trample, and the petals purple the ground

110a°

The doorman's feet stretch seven fathoms;
five oxen died to make his sandals;
ten cobblers cobbled them together,
and it was hard work, too.

111°

Carpenters, raise the roof up! There is –
　　Sing *Hymen, Hymen!* –°
no room, no room.
The groom is coming, big as Ares –
　　Sing *Hymen, Hymen!* –
he's big, this groom.

112°

O husband, blessed now the request made in your prayers
　　is granted –
the wedding's done; she's yours! You won the hand of the girl you
　　wanted.
O bride, he'll prize your honeyed eyes, your body's pride and grace,
while Love's mystique flushes each cheek and streams from your
　　beaming face,
for Aphrodite has made you mighty

114°

Where, o where, Virginity, where have you gone, deserting me?
I shall not come to you again; I shall not come again.

115°

Bridegroom, how do you seem to me?
Just like a slender sapling tree.

116°

Honored guests, goodnight, and goodnight, bride.

121

If you care for me, take a younger woman
    into your bed, to share it;
but I would never live with someone
I'm older than – I couldn't bear it.

130

Love's got me again, that impossible,
limb-loosening, bittersweet animal

131

Now that the thought of me rubs you raw,
Atthis, you flit to Andromeda.°

132

I have a child as gorgeous as gold flowers, and I love her.
Her name is Cleis, and there's nothing I would take above her,°
not all of Lydia, nor lovely

137°

I need to tell you something, but shame stops me . . .

Well, if you really cared for what's good and right,
and your tongue weren't always dredging up filth to spray,
        contrition wouldn't cloud your sight,
    and you would say what you have to say.

140°

Lady of Cyprus, Adonis is dying – what should we do?
Beat your breasts, maidens, and shred your clothes.

141°

The mixing bowl
stood there, brim-full,
and Hermes poured ambrosia round the room;
then the gods all
let offerings fall
from lifted cups, and drank health to the groom,
with every blessing.

147

Someone, someday, I say, will remember us.

154

The full moon showed,
and the women stood
around the altar

160

Now I'll sing beautifully to my companions
to make them happy.

168b°

The moon drops down the sky.
The Pleiades have gone.
Midnight. Time crawls by.
I lie down alone.

Alcaeus

Alcaeus of Mytilene (flourished circa 600 BCE), one of the canonical Nine Lyric Poets, was an aristocrat and revolutionary of Lesbos, the author of *stasiotika* (factional songs) and a rough contemporary of Sappho (pp. 38–54) – whether older or younger is hard to say. His poems are composed for the upper-class drinking party known as the *symposium*, and specifically for Alcaeus' own *hetaireia*, or company: a club of partisans, led perhaps by his brother Antimenidas, which strove against clubs of other elite families for power in Mytilene – mostly without success. Alcaeus' band did manage to overthrow the tyrant Melanchrus around the time of the Battle of Sigeum (against Athens, in 612 or 608 BCE). When Alcaeus' enemy Myrsilus seized power, however, the company's second attempted coup – which seems to have included a failed assassination of Myrsilus – was betrayed. Alcaeus went into exile for the first time, at the city of Pyrrha, about ten miles from Mytilene. The man who betrayed their faction, Pittacus, had come to fame at Sigeum when he defeated the Athenian general and Olympic champion Phrynon in single combat. Alcaeus himself had dropped his shield and fled from that battle; nonetheless, the poet-deserter never hesitated to attack the victorious war hero for his low birth: Pittacus was of Thracian descent.

With Alcaeus at Pyrrha, Myrsilus and Pittacus shared power in Mytilene. When Myrsilus died, Alcaeus exulted, no doubt feeling that his own hour had come at last; but he and his clan were soundly defeated by Pittacus and forced into a second exile. Around this time, Pittacus became *aisymnetes* (elected tyrant), a position which he held for ten years (597/6–588/7 BCE), then voluntarily relinquished, to live as a private citizen until his death in 577/6. At some point during his rule, Pittacus – later numbered along with Solon of Athens (pp. 68–75) among the Seven Sages of Archaic Greece – pardoned Alcaeus, and declared: 'Pardon is better than vengeance.' But the poet's revolutionary reflex was too strong; he did something – alas, we have no idea what – to provoke the tyrant

once again, and was sent into a third exile. While we do not have Alcaeus'
date of death, he probably lived into old age.

   According to Dionysius of Halicarnassus, 'Without the prosody,
[Alcaeus' poems] would be mere political rhetoric', though he also says
they are 'endowed with genius, compressed and pleasant, possessing
intensity'. The Romantic strain which finds an antithesis between 'rhetoric' and 'poetry' may these days be a bit passé; I hope so. Alcaeus is
perhaps not a great poet, but his eye is keen, his phrasing forceful, his
rhythms virtuosic and he may have invented the 'ship of state' allegory
(see fragment 6 below, and note). That, and his profound impact on the
Roman Horace (pp. 453–91), constitute his enduring legacy, long after
the causes he fought for have been consigned to footnotes.

6°

> This roller, like the roller before it, slaps
> our boat again, and it'll be hell to bail
> 3   once it gets in the ship's …
>
> 7   quick as we can, let's cobble
> some cover together and run to port.
>
> No shrinking violets now! Not a man of you
> 10   can stand to waver: the crisis is here, that's clear.
> Just think what we've been through,
> muster your manhood, and persevere!
>
> Let's none of us besmirch with lily livers
> the honor of fathers sleeping six feet under

10b

> Alas for me in my misery, forced to share in all sorts of care!°
> There's no way to heal the wound I feel.
> So the stag bells, and the sound wells in the doe's faint heart

34

Leave the island where Pelops once was master,°
o Leda's powerful progeny, and Zeus's;
to me – here, now – appear and look kindly, Castor
        and Polydeuces,

you who, astride your horses, galloping, whizzing,
crisscross the whole of the sea and the wide earth,
and easily rescue people from the freezing
        waters of death,

leaping through crow's-nests, high over rowers pulling,
flickering forestays, distantly radiant,   10
to the black ship in its night of trial revealing
        your corposant.°

38a°

Drink and get drunk   with me, Melanippus!°
You think, once you've crossed   the currents of Acheron

swirling, you'll see   the immaculate sunlight
again? Don't aim   above your orbit.

King Sisyphus, Aeolus'   boy, believed°
he could crack death –   and he was our cleverest.

Despite that wiliness,   his doom demanded
he twice traverse   Acheron's torrent,

and Cronus' son sentenced him   to subterranean
toil. Pay attention: don't hope too much.   10

We're young now, and need –   now, if ever –
to weather whatever   god will give.

42°

The story goes that your bad behavior cruelly
cost Priam and his sons, when you made trouble
fall on them, Helen, and Zeus's flame turned holy
    Troy into rubble.

Not a whit like you was the delicate
bride of Aeacus' son, who invited all°
the gods to attend his wedding, and took her out
    of Nereus' hall

to Chiron's house, and undid her maiden garter.°
10   Then the love grew green between Lord Peleus
and Thetis, Nereus's foremost daughter,
    who bore, in less

than a year, the greatest half-god, heaven-cherished
Achilles, charioteer of chestnut horses.°
But thanks to Helen that city in Phrygia perished
    with all its forces.

45

The loveliest of rivers where you race
by Aenus, pouring into the churning sea,°
3   Hebrus, you thunder through the land of Thrace . . . °

5   Your currents many maiden palms have cupped
to wash their gorgeous thighs within your stream,
handling your waves like scented unguents, rapt
    as in a dream.

69

Frustrated by recent setbacks, Father Zeus,°
the Lydians laid two thousand staters down°
with us, that we might enter and reduce
        that holy town,°

though we had never once done them a service:
they didn't know us. Then *he* claimed – sly old fox –°
it would be easy, and thought we wouldn't notice
        his barefaced tricks.

70

      Joining   the party, a playful lyre
plays on. He, feasting   among the rout of blowhards boasting°
to no effect . . .   3

Let him wolf down –   as he and Myrsilus did – our town,°   6
that groom just grafted into   the house of Atreus,°
till the War-Lord   bids us once more take up the sword.
For now, though, let's let go   the hold rage has on us.

Let's take a pause   from turning in the ceaseless jaws   10
of internecine warfare   some god saw fit to start,
who stooped to guide   the people to madness and suicide,
but gave Pittacus glory   to gratify his heart.

72°

vehemently . . .   3
They fill their cups with neat wine, and night and day
        the basin splashes with flung drops . . .   5

None of that's ever far from the Thracian's thought,°   7
from the first cup he topples and sets to sinking;

he dimples the water's top all night,
10   and the base of the basin keeps clanking and clinking.

How is it, born from such a brood as that,
you have the same reputation as freeborn men
        whom a storied line begat?

73

Pounded by thrashing waves, [storm-thumped and sodden,]
she says she wants to battle [the rainy winters]
        no more, but hit some hidden
        sandbank and [shiver her sides to splinters.]°

Let her go [where she's going. As for me,]
I want to forget all that, and enjoy our youth,
        [my friend,] in company
        with you and Bycchis

119°

Already your time is past, and your prime is spent.
What fruit you had is gathered, though there are hopes
        your shoot – once excellent –
        will still produce its share of grapes.

129

            The Lesbians erected,
    for all to share, this grand and conspicuous
            sanctuary, and constructed°
        altars within for the gods in bliss,

    honoring first the Suppliants' Bulwark, Zeus;
    then you, our Mother, Queen of Aeolia,°
            goddess most glorious;
        and thirdly, Him Who Eats Meat Raw,

Lord Dionysus, called Kemelius.°
Come, holy ones, to our aid in toil and trial,   10
      we pray. Give ear to us
    and bring to an end this cruel exile.

May the Spirit of Vengeance shadow Hyrrhas's son°
Pittacus, from that day when we vowed not
      to [forsake] one of our own
    and slit [the sacrifice's throat,]

swearing we'd die and put on a cloak of earth,
killed by the onslaught of the opposition,
      or else we'd deal them death
    and deliver the people from tribulation.   20

But conscience never bothered our friend Paunch,°
who trampled easily upon his oath;
      and now he's eating us for lunch,
    gobbling the city [and citizens both.]°

130b°

                  my life is like some hick's –
o god, it's all so wretched –   stranded out in the sticks.
    I long to hear the herald summon,
Agesilaidas,   the citizens to come in°

from my seat on the council.   All that my people owned –
my father and his father –   all they grew old around,
    among our citizenry riven
by crimes against each other,   I'm dispossessed of, driven

into this hinterland,   exiled and solitary
as Onomacles, dwelling   in thickets the wolves harry . . .°   10

I live, and steer my footsteps   out of the way of trouble,   16

where girls of Lesbos, silken   in skirts that swish the ground,
compete to dazzle the judges   of beauty, and all around
          the otherworldly echoes ring
20   of holy ululation,   their yearly offering.°

You gods upon Olympus,   how long until [you pluck me]
out of this swarm [of sorrows?]

140°

                    The great house scintillates
brazenly, its whole ceiling decked for war,
                    arrayed with the radiance
of helmets under plumes of white horsehair
                    down-nodding – ornaments
for fighting men. Covering the pegs where
                    they hang in a lambent wash
are greaves to wall the smashing arrows out.
                    Corselets – all of fresh
10   linen – and hollow shields lie strewn about.°
          Broadswords from Chalcis shine°
nearby, with many tunics, many belts.
          Since we first toed this line
and took up arms, we've thought of little else.

141

This man in pursuit   of supreme power°
will topple the town;   the balance is tipping.

208°

Which way the winds are blowing, I can't tell.
From here, now from there, breakers are rocking the keel;
          we're swept along in the swell
          right through the riotous heart of the gale,

stumbling and straining under the storm to bail
the bilge – now up past the masthold, swamping it –
    and big holes in the sail
  open out on sky-fragments opposite.

283

setting the heart in Argive Helen's chest°
to fluttering. Then she, gone insane with passion,
followed the Trojan prince, that traitorous guest,
    over the ocean,

convincing herself to leave her daughter lonely,
to leave her husband's luxurious bed behind
and yield to love, while the daughter of Zeus and Dione°
    mastered her mind . . .   8

          So many brothers, fallen   10
onto the plain of Troy, the dark earth holds
    because of Helen;

and many chariots tumbled in the dust,
and many dark-eyed heroes underfoot
were trampled

298°

heaping humiliation on the head   2
    of each wrongdoer. Now
    [clap them in shackles] and stone them dead!

The Greeks would have been better off by far
had they just killed Athena's enemy;
    sailing by Aegae's shore,°
    they would have found a friendlier sea.

For Priam's daughter had sought out [the statue] in
10   the temple of Pallas Abounding in War's Rewards,
            and clasped her by the chin,°
12   while the city sang with enemy swords . . .

13   They killed Deiphobus as well;°
over the city's breastworks, cries of pain
            [rose wailing,] and the wail
of children carried across the plain.°

[Then Ajax] reached, in a blind, bloodthirsty rage,
[that temple] of the Holy Virgin, Pallas,
            who, of the gods, treats sacrilege
20   with the most unforgiving malice.

As the girl quailed by the [holy] statue's side,
with both [his hands] the Locrian seized her there
            [and dragged her out], not terrified
            [of the daughter] of Zeus, the Bringer of War,

[whose eyes flash daggers.] Now those eyes rolled livid
and she flew awful over the wine-dark main
            to make the darkness gravid
            with the sudden blast of a hurricane.°

308b°

All hail, Lord of Cyllene, you're the one°
my heart would hymn, whom on the vertical
mountaintop Maia bore to Cronus' son,
            the king of all.

332°

High time to get drunk now and to drink with all
the strength we've got, since Myrsilus is no more

333

wine shines right through a man

335

Rehearsing our sorrows won't get us anywhere;
it's no use dwelling on woes in which we're sunk.
          The only cure, Bycchis my dear,°
is getting the wine and getting drunk.

338°

Now Zeus is sleeting, and out of heaven a mighty
storm is pouring; the ice-choked streams stand still . . .   2

Forget the blizzard! We'll overcome it yet.   5
Stoke up the fire, dole out a healthy portion
          of mixed wine, honey-sweet,
     and prop up your head on a nice, plump cushion.

345

What are these birds, come from the sea – the world's
     uttermost boundary –
these long-winged widgeon ducks, with necks covered
     in particolored flecks?

346

Drink! Is it lamps we're waiting for? A finger of day is left,
     no more.°
Come on, my man, break out the great wine goblets, massy
     and ornate.

With the grape's gift, Semele's son and Zeus's gave oblivion°
from suffering to mortal men. One part to two, mix water in –°

make sure they're full up to the brim! – and set the goblets
    rim to rim
and elbowing

347°

Wet your whistle – have some wine! Soon Sirius will rise
    and shine;
the weather's bad, and the sweltering is sweating every thirsty
    thing.

Leaf-shadowed, the cicada sings sweetly; from underneath his
    wings
4   he pours a ceaseless, high-pitched shimmer-music, while the
    blaze of summer . . .°

5   Now, while the bloom is on the thistle, women are most
    inclined to tustle
but men are drained by the dog days, their knees and heads
    baked in the blaze

348

                             over that city –°
that spineless city, darkly fated – to tyranny they elevated
Pittacus, debased in birth, whom the crowds praise for all they're
    worth°

362

Let somebody come over and surround
    our necks with woven strands of dill in bloom,
    and cover our chests with unguent, till we're drowned
        in sweet perfume.

364

Poverty's pain,   an impossible evil.
She crushes countries   with her sister, Surrender.°

366

Come on, my boy, it's time for wine and truth.

Solon

Solon (circa 640–560 BCE) was hailed by later Greeks as one of the Seven Sages of Archaic Greece (along with Pittacus of Mytilene: see the introduction to Alcaeus, p. 55). He was a figure of major importance to the Athenian political consciousness, and consequently the Archaic poet most discussed in ancient sources. Nevertheless, questions persist about the accuracy of the information we have about his life, and even the authorship of his poems has been questioned. The tradition depicts him as statesman and lawgiver par excellence, whose compromise between rival factions of rich and poor paved the way, some half a century later, to the mature Athenian democratic constitution. He served as *archon* (Athenian chief executive) in 594/3, and around this time is said to have canceled public and private debts, divided the citizenry into four classes based on wealth and reformed the judicial system to admit all classes as jurors. His reforms provided some relief to the commoners and enlarged their participation in politics, while nonetheless ensuring that the nobility's level of influence and activity remained higher than that of the masses. Still, members of all classes were unhappy – many had wanted him to become tyrant, and mocked him when he refused – and Solon is said to have absented himself from Athens for ten years, traveling to Egypt, Lydia and Cyprus, before returning in time to warn the Athenians – to no avail – of the tyrannical ambitions of his kinsman Pisistratus.

Plutarch tells us that Solon first composed verses for his own amusement, but later used his poetry to defend and justify his political choices. It is notable, however, how vividly Solon's verse – in marked contrast to Sappho's (pp. 38–54) mysterious privacy – illustrates the almost complete absence of any perceived contradiction between poetry and public affairs in the Archaic period. Whether his poems were performed in the *agora* (marketplace) or the more traditional setting of the symposium, they contain much that is generically Panhellenic – that is, timelessly, universally Greek – and overlap in several places with the elegies of Theognis (pp. 76–85). However, there are specific references as well; and

though not as polished in their style as, for example, those of Mimnermus (pp. 27–30), the poems are lively and intelligent, striking a delicate
rhetorical balance between the tastes and interests of the aristocrats and
the commons – just as Solon himself struck that balance in politics.

4°

Our state will never perish by decree
of Zeus, or by the gods' antipathy,
for Power's daughter, valiant Pallas, stands
our guardian and shields us with her hands.
No – but seduced by greed, deprived of sense,
we squander Athens' old magnificence;
our leaders know no justice, but it's sure
their arrogance will earn a brutal cure.
They don't know how – their gluttony has no measure –
to share a civil feast in peace and pleasure   10
and, creatures of injustice, they grow rich . . .°
From sacred and from public property
alike they steal, and do not spare a jot,
while Justice's once-grand foundations rot.
She knows what is and was, but does not say,
yet comes at last to make the guilty pay.
It's coming on, this wound we cannot flee;
the city's on the brink of slavery,
which rouses sleeping war and civil strife,
and costs many a lovely youth his life.   20
She's ground down swiftly by her enemies
and Justice's, in hatched conspiracies –
such evils throng the people, while the poor
in droves are driven to a foreign shore,
and sold as slaves, bound shamefully in chains . . .°
So public ill seeks each man's door, and knocks;
no longer kept out by his gates and locks,
it leaps over the wall, and finds him, though
he hides as deep inside as he can go.
I've taught the Athenians what my heart wills.   30

Disorder brings the city countless ills.
But Lawfulness will lead to harmony,
and clap chains on the unjust as they flee;
she smooths what's rough, stalls outrage, stops the flood
of excess and nips ruin in the bud,
makes crooked verdicts straight and tames with reason
acts of arrogance, stifles acts of treason,
stifles the roar of strife. When she rules us,
man's state is prudent and harmonious.

5

I gave the mass such privilege as was due it,
and did not strip its honor or add to it.
The ruling class, whose riches all men want –
I made sure it would suffer no affront.
I sheltered both sides with my mighty shield,
let neither wrongly win, or wrongly yield.

6

The masses will obey their leaders best
when not too unrestrained, or too oppressed.
Excess breeds outrage, wherever benefit°
accrues to men whose minds aren't tuned to it.

9°

Out of stormclouds, snow falls and hailstones crash,
and thunderclaps burst from a lightning-flash;
from great men ruin comes, and tyranny:
the masses blindly rush to slavery.
Hard to restrain a man, once he is too
exalted. We must think now what to do.

11°

If your mistakes have brought you grief and shame,
the fault is yours; don't give the gods the blame.
You bolstered those men with a bodyguard,°
and earned this slavery as just reward.
In private, each of you is like the fox;
but as a group, your heads are full of rocks.
You hang on every word these con men spew,
but barely even notice what they *do*.

13°

Daughters of Zeus and Memory, you fair
Muses of Pieria, hear my prayer.°
Grant that I prosper with the gods, have good
repute for virtue with the multitude;
be loved by friends, by those who hate me, feared –
bitter to them, but by my friends, revered.
I long for wealth, though not to win my sums
unjustly; vengeful Justice always comes.
But wealth that the gods give is always sure:
from deepest roots to highest crown, secure.   10
The wealth men honor comes disordered, won
outrageously – Injustice drives it on
unwilling, and swift Ruin follows it.
It starts off small, as when a blaze is lit,
meager at first, soon dangerously strong.
Men can't sustain outrageousness for long;
but always Zeus looks to the end, and fast
as when the clouds flee from the sudden blast
of a spring storm, which churns the barren deeps
and raises waves, then through the plowed fields sweeps,   20
flattening wheat, until it gains the sheer
heights of the gods' heaven, and leaves them clear,
so that on fruitful earth the warm sunlight

spills lovely, and there's not a cloud in sight –
so fast comes Zeus's vengeance. Not like men's,
who get worked up at every small offense;
no – Zeus sees everyone who carries crime
deep in his heart: all is revealed in time.
Some pay now, some pay later, and some flee,
30   dodging the gods' pursuing destiny,
but not forever; the guiltless reap the grim
rewards – their sons, or their sons after them.
So mortals, great and mean, and rich and poor,
all think our lives are bearing fruit, before
disaster; then we wail, and try to cope.
Till then, we gawk and coddle empty hope.
One man, whom pangs oppress and fevers drain,
imagines he'll be healthy, free from pain;
one of low station thinks he'll scale the height,
40   and be good-looking, though he looks a fright;
one's bound by poverty, without a cent,
but still believes he'll soon be affluent.
We rush toward different things. One man will roam
the fishy ocean, desperate to bring home
boatloads of profit, blown in the brute winds' strife.
The one thing he won't scrimp and save? His life.
Another labors, cleaving field and wood,
for a whole year – the plow's his livelihood.
Another understands Hephaestus' and
50   Athena's crafts, and lives by his own hand.°
Another has the Muses' gifts at heart,
versed in the measures of their lovely art.
Apollo made another man a seer;
he knows when far disaster's drawing near
with the gods' help; fate comes, at all events,
and rites and augury are no defense.
Paean has taught his skill with drugs and salves°
to others – doctors, who can't cure themselves.
So often from slight pains, great pains begin
60   that can't be healed with soothing medicine;

but someone else, delirious with pain,
is lightly touched, and he feels good again.
For Fate gives mortal men both good and ill;
there's no escaping the immortals' will.
Danger's in everything, and no one knows,
when something has begun, how it will close.
One man would do what's right, but unawares
falls into folly and disaster's snares;
another, doing ill, the gods still bless
with fortune and release from foolishness.   70
Wealth has no limit that stands manifest
for men, and those whose living is the best
work twice as hard. What could sate everyone?
From the gods, profits come to mortal men,
the source of ruin, which now this man is sent,°
now that, when Zeus decrees their punishment.

24

Two men have wealth: one owns estates replete
with gold and silver, farmlands full of wheat,
horses and mules. The other's is as great:
clothing and shoes to wear, food on his plate,
and, when the season comes, a boy and wife,
and youthful joys in harmony with life.
That is true wealth, since multitudinous
possessions can't be brought to Hades' house,
and none's so rich as to bribe death, or grim
disease, or stop old age from chasing him.   10

27°

At seven years, a boy's still infantile;
the first teeth come and go in his young smile.
In the next seven, when god makes it so,
the signs of puberty begin to show.
His body strengthens in the third, his skin

darkens, and peach-fuzz starts to shade his chin.
When, in the fourth, his strength is at its best,
he puts his manly courage to the test.
In the fifth, a man is at the marrying age;
he fathers sons to form his lineage.
In the sixth age, he disciplines his mind;
his youthful foolishness is left behind.
Then in the seventh, mind and tongue drip gold;
the eighth as well. That's fourteen years, all told.
In the ninth age, he still has eloquence,
but speech and wisdom show less excellence.
Then, if he makes it to the tenth at last,
no one will say death came for him too fast.

33°

'This Solon is no wise man – why, he doesn't have a clue!
He wouldn't take the blessings that the god plopped in his lap.
He caught his prey, and stared at it awhile, but didn't draw
the huge net tight, and lost it. Lost his mind and courage both.
If I could rule in Athens, stage a coup, take all those riches,
be tyrant for a day – just one! – the next I'd let them flay
my skin into a wine sack and wipe out my family name.'

34

And others came for plunder, with high hopes to strike it rich;°
these people thought there was an ample windfall on the way,
that I, despite my gentle words, would turn tyrannical.
Their foolish hopes were disappointed; now, they're mad about it,
and shoot black looks at me as if I were their mortal foe.
Enough's enough! With the gods' help, I did just what I promised,
and not those other worthless things. The violence of a tyrant°
holds no appeal, no more than divvying our country's rich
farmland among the lowborn and the nobles equally.

36°

The goals I summoned the assembly for:
did I fail to achieve a single one?
In the just court of Time, I call to witness
the mother of the Powers on Olympus,
the dark and mighty Earth, from whom my hands
lifted the boundary stones that scarred her sides.°
She was enslaved before. Now, she is free.
I've brought so many sons of Athens home,
sold off as slaves – some with, some without justice –
to this god-founded land, and many debtors,   10
fugitives from duress, who had forgotten
our Attic tongue, as wanderers will do.
And those constrained by shameful slavery
right here, and trembling at their masters' whims –
I freed them too. Using both force and justice
in harmony, I exercised my power
and did this, and completed what I promised.
I wrote laws fair to great and mean alike,
and fashioned a straightforward path to justice
for every man. If some rapacious fool   20
had goaded on the people as I did,
he would have lost them. And I, if I'd agreed
to pass the laws desired by the nobles,
or then again, the ones the people wanted,
I would have cost this city many men.
So I set safeguards on all sides, and whirled
like a wolf held at bay by snapping hounds.

Theognis and the *Theognidea*

Theognis of Megara lived probably around the late seventh to the mid-sixth century BCE. Besides the ancient debate about whether he was from Megara near Corinth or Megara Hyblaea in Sicily (the former is more likely), almost no biographical information about Theognis survives. His poetry portrays him as a conservative, old-guard aristocrat threatened by the tumultuous politics of his day. It is possible he lived in the time of Theagenes, who became tyrant of Megara around 630 or 620 and reigned some years before being succeeded by a mild government of oligarchs, followed in turn by a revolutionary democratic one (circa 600). When the democrats took over, they drove the oligarchs into exile, but the oligarchs reclaimed power around 550 and maintained it for the rest of the Archaic period. Theognis would have been a member of the oligarchic class, wary of the demagogic Theagenes as he grew in power, and eventually dispossessed and exiled, either by the tyrant or democratic revolutionaries. It's also possible, however, that Theognis was born in the sixth century, well after the brief reign of Theagenes – in which case his poetry must refer to events we know nothing about.

Theognis is the earliest Archaic Greek poet (aside from Homer and Hesiod) whose work is preserved in a continuous manuscript, instead of fragmentary papyri or quotes from later authors. Unfortunately, we can't know how many of these poems are actually by Theognis. Though headed *Theognis*, the manuscript is an anthology of elegies for performance at symposia, and includes poems belonging to Tyrtaeus (pp. 22–6), Mimnermus (pp. 27–30) and Solon (pp. 68–75), among others; in addition, there are poems from as late as 490–480 BCE, too late for the historical Theognis, whatever his exact date. The manuscript is in two books, the first comprising 1,230 lines on typical sympotic (symposium-esque) themes; the second, 159 lines erotic or pederastic in nature. (The poems in Book 2 are widely believed to have been culled from their places in the original collection at a late date by some prudish Christian bowdlerizer.) In the collection, poem endings are not marked,

so the division into individual poems is guesswork, and a subject of
scholarly dispute; here, a new poem is indicated by a stanza break.

Many of Theognis' poems are addressed to a young man called
'Cyrnus' or 'Polypaedes' (son of Polypais), presumably Theognis' boy
love, or *eromenos*. His mention in a poem is often taken as a sign of
Theognis' authorship. Scholars assign poems containing his name to
'Theognis', while poems without it are called 'Theognidean'. In all likelihood, some of these *Theognidea* actually are by Theognis, just as others
will be the work of unknown poets from Megara, and still others un-
recognizable poems by famous poets, or, indeed, traditional sayings or
aphorisms.

> Now, Cyrnus, let these verses bear my seal°
> of art and wisdom, so no thief can steal   20
> my words uncaught, or make a good line worse,
> and all will say, 'This is Theognis' verse,
> from Megara; the whole world knows his name.'
> Yet I can't please the whole town all the same.
> No wonder, Polypaedes. Not everyone
> is even pleased by Zeus, come rain or sun.
> I'll give you kind advice, the kind I had
> from nobles, Cyrnus, when I was a lad.
> Be prudent. Don't pursue, to your own shame,
> unjust success, or affluence, or fame.   30
> Know that I'm right. Avoid the company
> of base men; stick with the nobility.°
> Nobles have power – please them, take your seat
> with them, and drink with them, and with them eat.
> Good men will teach good things, but you'll erase
> the sense you have, if you befriend the base.
> Stick with the nobles. Someday you'll agree
> I give good counsel to those dear to me.
>
> This city's pregnant, Cyrnus, with, I fear,°
> a tyrant who will fix the outrage here.°   40
> The people still have sense; the leaders, though,
> are sunk in baseness deep as men can go.

Nobles have never been a city's bane,
but when the base give violence free rein,
draining the public, acquitting the unjust,
all for their private gain and power-lust,
don't think the town will long be free from riot,
Cyrnus, though now engrossed in peace and quiet,
since this is still what makes a base heart warm:
50   the private gain accrued at public harm.
From this comes faction, kin by kinfolk slain,
and tyrants. May this city dodge that pain.

This city's still a city; the citizens°
have changed, Cyrnus; they used to wear goatskins°
55   and live like deer outside the city walls,
in equal ignorance of rights and laws.
They're nobles now, and the once-noble, base,
Polypaedes – unbearable disgrace.
1111   The vulgar, not the nobles, hold the honors;°
1112   nobles are marrying their lowborn daughters.
All con and mock each other; neither station
60   has proper attitudes or education.
Polypaedes, befriend no one sincerely,
no matter what you need, however dearly.
Talk like you love them all and know them well,
but if there's something serious, don't tell
a soul. This way, you'll learn how wretches view
the world, though you still can't trust what they'll do,
for they love treachery, deceit and lies,
like hopeless men, assured of their demise.

Cyrnus, don't seek or trust a lowborn man
70   when you have something serious to plan,
but, when you need advice, go to great trouble
and travel many miles for someone noble.

105   Helping the base is fruitless charity –
might as well sow the wide and white-capped sea.°

Sow the wide sea, no crops will come of it;
help out the base, there'll be no benefit.
The base cannot be satisfied. Make one
mistake, your former friendship is undone.   110
But noble men do not forget the good
that they've received; they show their gratitude.

Cyrnus, it's easy for the connoisseur
to spot when gold or silver is impure;
bankruptcy's something people can endure.   120
But if a friend's intent conceals deceit,°
if his breast hides the false heart of a cheat,
that is the greatest con the god has wrought,
and the most painful of them all to spot.
A person's mind remains unknowable
till put to proof like a draft animal.
And you can't judge by waiting one more day;
appearances still lead the mind astray.

Cyrnus, don't wish for sterling qualities
or riches. Luck's the only thing there is.   130

Cyrnus, the gods alone give gain and ruin –
let no one claim that either's all his doing –
and none can tell if effort they expend   135
will turn out well or badly in the end.
One thinks he'll fail, but triumph swells his sails;
one thinks his work will prosper, but he fails.
No one has everything he longs for by him,
since barriers of helplessness deny him.   140
Our thoughts and hopes are vain, our knowledge nil.
The gods bring to fruition what they will.

Don't taunt a man, annoyed at some affront,°   155
with soul-destroying poverty and want.
Now Zeus's scales lean that way, and now this.°
You're wealthy now, and now you're penniless.

*

There are so many miseries, no one

168   is truly blessed who lives beneath the sun.

When someone who is just and innocent°
gains wealth from Zeus, his wealth is permanent.
But when greed and injustice give us reason

200   to break our oaths and profit out of season,
we think we've made a killing, but we're still
ruined at last: the gods will have their will.
Yet people are misled, when they see crime
unpunished; they don't know: gods take their time.
One man pays for his deeds, and then disaster
no longer threatens his whole line thereafter.
Another justice skips, for ruthless death
lights on his eyelids first, and stops his breath.

My heart, adopt a shifting attitude;°
turn to your friends a mirror of their mood.

215   Be like the slippery octopus, whose hue
changes to match the rock it's clinging to.°
Now match this one, now take a different shade.
It's better to be supple than too staid.

I've made you wings, to soar above the sea°
and over all the earth, effortlessly
aloft; at every feast and festival°

240   you're present, flitting on the lips of all,°
and fine boys fittingly, for all to hear,
to clear-toned pipes with voices fine and clear
shall sing of you. And when you've perished, bound
for Hades' wailful halls deep in the ground,
death shall not silence your undying fame;
the generations shall preserve your name,
Cyrnus; you'll roam through Greece, the Cyclades,
and cross the fishes' realm, the barren seas,
but not on horseback; the dazzling charm and virtue

250   of the violet-wreathed Muses shall escort you.

For all who love their gifts, or ever will,
while earth still stands, and while the sun shines still –
you'll give their music its material.
Yet you won't even offer me some mild
respect, but lie to me, like I'm a child.

   I'm mad among the mad, but when I fall°
   in with the just, I'm the most just of all.   314

Olympian Zeus, come, grant my prayer, and hurry!
Give me some good to balance all this worry,
or let me die, if I don't find relief
from these sad cares. May I pay grief with grief.
This is my lot: no vengeance I can see   345
against the men who stripped my property°
by force. I'm like the dog who crossed the rough
torrent in winter, then shook the water off.°
I'd drink their black blood! May some spirit strike
them down and grant the ending I would like.   350

   When a man suffers much, his heart contracts,
   Cyrnus, but after vengeance, it will wax.   362

Zeus, my friend, I don't know what to say.
You rule us all, have honor, endless sway.
To you, our minds and hearts are manifest;   375
o king, your power is the highest, best.
Then, son of Cronus, how can you appraise
just men and sinners with an equal gaze,
whether they practice temperate good sense,
or villainy and wanton violence?   380
Are there no rules from heaven to obey?
No road to take and please the gods, no way?
Some men get wealth and ease, while others, free
from base outrageousness, get poverty,
mother of helplessness, which, though they long
for justice, goads the heart toward doing wrong,

wounding the spirit with necessity.
A man endures the shame unwillingly,
yielding to need, which teaches crime, inciting

390   lies, and deception, and destructive fighting.
There's nothing worse – he couldn't want to less –
but need gives birth to bitter helplessness.
In poverty, who's base and who is nobler
is clearly seen, whenever need takes over.
The noble's thoughts, attuned to justice, bear
the judgment he was born with, straight and square,
but neither bad nor good times suit base minds;
the noble, though, must tolerate both kinds,
respect his friends, shun false oaths, which bring danger,

400   and carefully steer clear of the gods' anger.

425   Not to be born is of all things the best,°
not being, by the sun's fierce rays, oppressed;
once born, it's best to vanish straight away
through Hades' gate and lie beneath the clay.

Wash me, and the water from my crown
pure and unsullied always will rush down.
Apply the touchstone; everywhere my sheen°

450   will be like yellow gold, unalloyed, clean.
No mold can root on it, no verdigris
darken its bloom of lasting purity.

Poor Clearistus! Now you've crossed the sea°

512   and come, impoverished, here to poverty.

515   I'll share the best I've got. And if a guest
comes who's your friend, choose seats as you think best.°
I'll give you what I have, but won't spring for

518   exotic niceties if you want more.

513   I'll fill your ship, beneath the banks of oars,

514   with gods' gifts, Clearistus, and with ours.
If someone asks you how I'm doing, say,

520   'Poor for the rich, but for the poor, okay:

He can put up an old friend on his own;
just don't make him put up with more than one.'

I wouldn't chafe at nobles' gatherings,
Simonides, if I still had my things.°
My wealth is slipping off; want has suppressed
my voice, but I see better than the rest   670
how, with our white sails down, we veer and tack
out beyond Melos, through a night of black,°
and nobody will bail as breakers crest
over the gunwales; everyone's hard-pressed
to save himself. Our noble pilot, who
kept expert watch, they sacked – that's what they do.
Order's destroyed, possessions commandeered;
equable shares for all have disappeared.
Bagmen are captains; nobles serve the base;
I fear a wave will deal the coup de grace.   680
These are my riddles, hidden for the noble.°
The wise man will divine the coming trouble.

May Zeus on high and all the luminous
gods in their bliss stretch right hands over us
to keep this city safe, and may Apollo
straighten our judgments, and make straight words follow.
Now, let's have hymns, from pipes and lyre strings,   761
and, pouring the immortals' offerings,°
let's drink, and banter brightly, and drink more,
with no fear of the Medes or looming war.°
Cheering our hearts like this, or even better,
let's drown our cares and pass the time together
divertingly, and may all fatal, fey
spirits, cruel age, and death stay far away.

Phoebus, you built this towering bastion,
Alcathous, to honor Pelops' son;°
you, therefore, drive the insolently bold   775
Medes from our city, so that we may hold°

hecatombs in your honor come the spring,
and revel in the lyre and banqueting,
dance paeans round your altar, shout and cheer.°
780   For I see the Greeks squabbling and I fear°
their madness may prove deadly. Be our savior,
Phoebus; guard this city; grant us favor.

I went once to the land of Sicily,°
and to vine-rich Euboea on the sea,
785   famed Sparta, and Eurotas lined with rushes,°
and everyone who welcomed me was gracious,
and yet with them I found no joy or mirth.
A homeland is the sweetest place on earth.

Let's give our hearts to feasting and not shirk,°
while we're up to it, pleasure's luscious work.
985   For youth, fast as a feeling, gleams and passes,
more swiftly than a charging courser races
the spearman on its back into the heat
of battle, thundering joyful through the wheat.

Ah happy, lucky, blessed is he who goes°
to Hades' dark domain untouched by woes,
1015   before he's forced to overstep, or shrink
from foes, or learn what his friends really think.

Gracious, a noble's words; his deeds have grace;
1168   but the winds blow the base words of the base.

I heard it, Polypaedes, heard the shrill°
crane trumpeting the time had come to till
the land once more. It pierced my heart with cold,
1200   since others hold the fields I used to hold,
and no mules pull the curving plow for me.
Now I have crossed a wide expanse of sea°

*

Boy, you're like a horse who left my pen;°
now full of barley, you've come back again.   1250
You want your noble charioteer, your meadow,
your cooling spring, your groves of dappled shadow.

   Boy, your body's handsome, but you wear
   a crown of willful daftness on your hair.   1260
   Your moods wheel like a raptor, on a dime,
   for other men persuade you every time.

Love has her season too, when burgeoning°   1275
flowers come blanketing the land in spring.
Then Love leaves gorgeous Cyprus and goes forth
moving among us, seeding all the earth.

Your heart knows boyhood's blooming time goes by   1305
faster than a footrace; therefore untie
me, mighty boy, lest you too meet with scorn,
subdued by the cruel goddess, Cyprus-born,
as you subdue me now. Be on your guard
that no boy ever makes your life so hard.   1310

   Happy the man at home all day, who lies°   1335
   by a fine boy and gets his exercise.

Bitter and sweet, and dear and desperate,
is young love, till the lover quenches it,
Cyrnus; it's sweet when slaked, but if it goes   1355
unslaked, then it's the bitterest of woes.

   Happy is that boy-lover with no notion°   1375
   of the deep sea or nightfall on the ocean.

Phocylides

Phocylides (early sixth century BCE) was most likely a philosopher-poet from Miletus – one of the twelve Ionian cities of Asia Minor – who composed a collection of brief aphorisms intended probably as instruction for the young. Alternatively, he may have been a 'wise man' figure, named by the maxims' true author as the ostensible source of their authority. As poetry, his verse tends to plod, and is rendered here with a kind of homespun lumpiness. His ponderous habit of attaching his name to quite banal utterances may strike us as eccentric, but this is a common feature of wisdom literature in many early traditions. The ancients associated him with Theognis (pp. 76–85) and assumed they were contemporaries.

I

This, too, a saying of Phocylides:
On Leros all the citizens are sleaze.°
It's not, 'One is, one isn't' – every man
save Procles. And he too is Lerian.

3

This, too, a saying of Phocylides:
Who cares that some folks are nobly born, if they
are total buffoons in all they think or say?

5

This, too, a saying of Phocylides:
Friends should stand up for friends, when gossips wheeze
around the town, and spew duplicitese.

6

[*This, too, a saying of Phocylides:*]
Try never to go in hock to some low peasant:
they knock when you're not ready. It's unpleasant.

Demodocus

Nothing is known of Demodocus of Leros except the following barbed response to a poem, attributed to Phocylides of Miletus (pp. 86–7), which had mocked his native island.

I

A saying of Demodocus, this too:
Not all Milesians are moronic, true;
they only do the things that morons do.

Stesichorus

According to the first-century CE Roman rhetorician Quintilian, Stesichorus (circa 632–556 BCE) 'sustained on the lyre the weight of epic song'. One of the canonical Nine Lyric Poets, he is traditionally associated with Himera on the north coast of Sicily, but also with other towns of Sicily and Greek Italy (also known as Magna Graecia, 'Great Greece'). The diligent editors of Alexandria gathered his collected works into a reported twenty-six books – nine more than his closest competitor, Pindar (pp. 134–64). Stesichorus is thus a poet of vast scale and amplitude; detractors would say diffuseness. The ancients considered him the inventor of triadic form – the strophe–antistrophe–epode structure, often rendered as 'turn, counter-turn and stand', which we find in later choral poetry – and considered it a sign of boorishness not to know 'the three of Stesichorus'. He lavished this technical innovation on mythical stories spun out at epic length: his *Geryon* was at least 1,300 lines, perhaps quite a bit longer, while his *Oresteia* and *Helen* filled two books each.

'Stesichorus' means 'Establisher of the Chorus' – a nom de plume he is said to have adopted over his given name, Tisias – and in antiquity his poems were generally assumed to have been performed chorally. Modern scholars have questioned that ancient assumption, mostly on the grounds of the sheer stamina that such a performance would have required; today, many prefer to see Stesichorus as a figure like the bard Demodocus in the *Odyssey*, strumming and singing as dancers danced. Among those books of his not excerpted here are three more starring Heracles (*Cycnus*, *Cerberus*, *Scylla*), as well as the *Boar-Hunters* (featuring Meleager; see Bacchylides 5, lines 69–218, pp. 173–7), *Europa*, *Eriphyle*, the *Funeral Games of Pelias* and the *Returns from Troy*. Stesichorus was an important forerunner of Pindar and Attic drama; and, in fact, it is likely that we know more of his poetry than we are even aware of, due to his (now incalculable) influence on Pindar, the tragedians and Virgil (pp. 398–410).

Geryon°

8a

Str./Ant.   Then did Hyperion's powerful son embark°
      in his golden cup, that he might traverse the ocean
      and arrive at the bottom of evening, holy and dark,
      to his mother and wife and the children of his devotion,
      while into the grove and the shade of the laurels went
         the scion of Zeus, [most excellent.]°

10

Str./Ant.   as the waves rolled
   they crossed the salt deep and came to the gods' gorgeous island°
   where the Hesperides have their dwellings of gold

15°

Ant.   [the offspring of mighty Chrysaor and] undying°
4   [Callirhoë] spoke then, replying:

Ep.   'Don't try to stop m[y heart from being brave
      with talk of the cold of the g]rave,
7   nor [beg me] . . .
8   for if [I could share in] Olympian ways,
      [immortal] and agele[ss all of my days,
     it might be] better [to endure]
11   reproaches . . .

Str.   'and, [skulking from the strength of Heracles,
14   to witness] my stables emptied, [my cattle dr]iven.
     But if, my frie[nd, I am doomed to old] age and [disease,]
     to live for a d[ay far aw]ay from the blisses of heaven,
     it's better I now [should suffer wha]tever may come
      by fate [than let opprobrium]

and shame [dog me and all m]y posterity,   *Ant.*
[when people sing o]f Chrysaor's son hereafter.   20
May *that* not be the blessed gods' decree!
About my cattle . . .'

16+17°

seeing him coming, his mother said . . .°   *16*, l. 3. *Str.*

'Heartbroken woman! I, forlorn   *17*, l. 2. *Ep.*
in the son and the ills I've borne!
Geryon, I'm pleading, hugging your knees:
    if I ever suckled you at my breast . . .   5
    by your dear mother's side, at ease . . .   8
happiness . . .'   9

[She spoke, and threw open her sce]nted robe   *Str.*

18°

[Not one st]ood by Zeus, [the gods' uni]versal [king.   *Ep.*

Then gray-]eyed Athena [eloquent]ly [said   *Str.*
to her uncle,] the mighty-[hearted] stallion-master:
['Come on,] remember [the prom]ise th[at you made;
don't dream of saving Ger]yon from death [and disaster] . . .'

19°

[Heracles decided] the greatest advantage lay   *Str.*
    in fighting covertly [from far away] . . .   8

                for he was strong.   *Ant.*
[On th]at side Heracles plotted bitter slaughter.   10
[And Geryon] shielded his chest, but the [other flung
a rock at his temple; straightway with a mighty clatter]
the helmet [leapt] from his hea[d, and the hor]sehair crest
    [fell to] the ground [and lay at rest,]

Ep.   for malig[nant Spirits of Death] on their rapid wings°
                who determine [the issue of things]
17   [had batted i]t down [swiftly] to the earth . . .

Str.   bringing the bitter end of death,
28   with [doom] affixed to the head of the barb, and all
                dabbled with blood and [virulent] gall,

Ant.   the death-agonies of the Hydra, that murder machine°
31   with the glittering neck. Between his eyebrows it glided,
            the arrow silent and thievish, and slicing clean
            through flesh and bone, as the heavenly ones provided,
            thrust up through the top of the skull. Then the red gore flowed,
                staining his breastplate and limbs with blood,

Ep.   and Geryon's neck lolled to the side, and drooped,
                like a poppy whose petals have dropped°
            suddenly, and all its delicate beauty is spoiled

Helen°

85

                    Because Tyndareus once,
            worshiping all the gods with sacrifice,
        forgot just onc – the Cyprian, whose gifts are a balm to life –
            she, in her anger, made his daughters wife°
                to many men, twice married, more than twice,
            leavers-of-lords-in-the-lurch

88

Many were the quinces cast°
              at the king's chariot as it passed,°
     and many the myrtle leaves
  and the plaited rings of violets and the twined rose-wreaths

91a°

The Palinode

No, no, it isn't true, that tale:
on sturdy ships you did *not* sail,
nor reach the Trojan citadel

The *Theban Saga*

97°

'Don't fan our fears   *Ant.* 10
        and swell our crying,   202
  or sink my future hopes with this
    dark prophesying!

'Not grindingly always, without a respite, do   *Ep.* 10
   the deathless gods commit mankind
across the holy earth to strife and war;
no, not to friendship either, since the mind
of men shifts daily, when they want it to.
I pray Apollo, Lord Who Works from Far,
   not all your prophecies come true!   210

'But if the Fates have spun this destiny,   *Str.* 11
to watch my children each by the other slain,
let me yield now to Death the despicable,
   before I see

             pain heaped on pain,
                      tear-stained, groan-wracked:
             my children dead in the palace hall,
                my city sacked.

Ant. 11   'Listen, my sons, dear sons, obey my words.
             This is what *I* envision: one will hold
220   sway in his native Thebes, and one take all his father's herds
             and all his gold
                    and get him gone –
             whoever pulls the shorter straw
                when lots are drawn.

Ep. 11   'For this alone, I think, may obviate
             the evil destiny revealed
         by the inspired seer's prophecy,
         whether the son of Cronus means to shield
         Lord Cadmus' living lineage and state
230   a good while longer from calamity,
            or we must face some other fate.'

Str. 12   So spoke the lady, and her words allayed°
         the quarrel brewing in the palace halls;
         Tiresias joined his vatic voice to hers,
            and her sons obeyed.°

The *Sack of Troy*

100°

Ant.   Come, goddess, tell me how, by the lovely purling
           Simois, the man°
           whom that goddess' will –
        Athena, awe-surrounded – taught
        wise measures and a measured skill

achieved surpassing glory, not
as warrior hurling
battle cries, but artisan:
as engineer of the day that would destroy
the spacious ways of Troy.   10

For Zeus's daughter   *Ep.*
saw him forever fetching water
for kings and pitied him

103°

'Go, hurry right   *Ep.*
to the temple on the city's height,
you Trojans and confederates, and pay
no mind to arguments that say
we should destroy this horse, high-towering
tithe-offering,
this image sacred to the goddess' name,
covering ourselves with shame;
no, let us respect instead our Lady's wrath . . .'

Ibycus

An important, if shadowy, precursor to Simonides (pp. 120–33), Pindar (pp. 134–64) and Bacchylides (pp. 165–85), Ibycus flourished in the second half of the sixth century. One of the canonical Nine Lyric Poets, he was born in Rhegium, at the southern tip of Italy on the strait of Messina (modern Reggio Calabria), though he seems to have traveled widely throughout the Greek world, to Sicily, Sicyon, Sparta and Samos, where he may have been invited as a court poet by the tyrant Polycrates (who ruled circa 535–522), and where he probably met Anacreon (pp. 100–108). His main subjects were myth, love and praise; quite a few papyrus fragments (mostly too scrappy to include here, alas) give a sense of names he mentioned, either at length or in passing (for example, Heracles, Peleus, Geryon, Oedipus, Ino, Ganymede) and suggest he may also have composed proto-epinicians (victory odes), a generation or two before Simonides is supposed to have invented the genre.

As far as we can tell, in Ibycus' poetry the mythical elements are not generally elaborated for their own sake, but subordinated to the focus of the poem's praise or desire, as in his most substantial fragment, 282 (p. 97). If that poem's attitude can be taken as characteristic of Ibycus' work, his poetry may have recast the harsh heroic values of Homer in a softer, more sensuous vein, with a premium placed on love and beauty, rather than excellence and honor – though for Ibycus *eros* is hardly all sweetness and light, but, rather, a force of nature, irresistible and devastating. (The epithet 'boy-crazy', conferred on Ibycus by ancient readers, is hardly undermined by his extant works.) It is a shame so little survives of his reported seven Alexandrian volumes; fragment 286 (p. 99) in particular is one of the most evocative remnants of Greek erotic verse.

282°

from Argos, by Zeus's will, they sailed°   *Ant.*
to the town – great, famous, prosperous –
  where the son of Dardanus,
Priam, held sway, and laid it waste;

  and, all for the allure   *Ep.*
of Helen and her blond locks, bore
that strife of song, that tearful war;°
and ruin came at last to Troy's long-suffering stronghold
from the Cyprian, whose hair is gold.

But Paris, and the hosts he fooled,   *Str.*
my heart has no design to hymn;   11
  no, nor Cassandra's slim
ankles, or Priam's other boys,

or the day – unspeakable! – when Troy's   *Ant.*
high gates were forced; nor shall I sing
  of the splendid swaggering
valor of heroes whom the well-tooled

  ships hauled to Troy in their hollows   *Ep.*
to be its bane – fine, manly fellows
ruled by the man the army follows,   20
the noble son of Atreus, Pleisthenes' offspring,°
Lord Agamemnon, Greece's king.

Those things the Muses, Helicon's   *Str.*
lore-learned ladies, could repeat;
  but where is the mortal so fleet
of tongue as to tally each detail:°

Ant.   how many ships Aulis saw set sail°
               from Argos on the Aegean main,
                  that at the horse-pasturing plain
30   of Troy unladed their cargo of bronze-

Ep.   spear-wielders, Greece's host –
              with rapid Achilles, the foremost
              in spearcraft that Greek arms could boast,
    and Telamon's son Ajax, huge and resolute, [whose dire
              courage saved the ships from] fire;°

Str.   [and, with them,] prettiest in Greece,
37   Cyanippus went to Ilium . . .°

Ant.   and the son of Hyllis with gold-wrought girdle,
41   Zeuxippus, who both sides declared –°
               Trojans and Greeks – compared
              to Troilus in shapeliness,°

Ep.   like orichalc beside°
              gold that's been triply purified.
              Like theirs, your beauty shall abide
     immortally, Polycrates, in glory ever young,°
              by virtue of my fame and song.

282C.I

             you're on the lips
    [of our whole party], o Comeliness divine,°
who fed the boy [in fields of red rose]-cups
           that bloom by [Aphrodite's] shrine.
         [Your garl]and must have smelled delicious
        [on him, sweet] thing, whom fragrance washes
           and flatters still, whom goddesses
           have bless[ed with beauty's] softnesses.
But Justice [clearly quit] their holy [choir:°
10   all night] my body has felt like lead,

[and all night] an unsleeping fire
[sends thoughts] and pictures racing through my head.

286°

In spring, the Cretan quinces grow°
    flowering by the streams that flow
    irriguous where the virginal
gardens of the Maidens are, and all°
the vines increase and twine their shade above
the blossoms on the grapes. But for me love
    never at any season sleeps –
    like Thracian Boreas, when he sweeps°
crackling with lightning and wild fire
from the Cyprian in fits of mad desire,   10
    and scorching, murky, shameless, shoots
    and shudders my heart at the very roots.

287°

Love once again out from under his eyelids of jet
    is making me melt with smoldering looks,
    and from his deep bag of magical tricks
is tangling me up in his mother's unbreakable net.°
    I shake at his coming, and my pulse races,
    as when, in old age, a prizewinning horse°
is yoked once again to the chariot's traces
    but balks when he walks on the course.

288

Euryalus, bloom of the ocean-eyed Graces,
sweetheart of Seasons with beautiful tresses,°
Cypris and Sweet Talk with eyes soft-lidded
nursed you in meadows where roses are bedded.

Anacreon

Anacreon of Teos lived around 585/70–500/485 BCE. One of the canonical Nine Lyric Poets, he was a lover of the symposium, of wine and of love, and a friend and confidant of tyrants. He was probably already a mature poet when he joined his fellow Teians in their flight from the Persian invasion of Ionia to Abdera in Thrace, circa 545. Sometime afterwards, Anacreon was invited to Samos by the tyrant Polycrates, who ruled circa 535–522; there he will have met the older Ibycus (pp. 96–9).

We're told that Anacreon's poetry was 'full of the name of Polycrates', though no mentions of the tyrant survive. Herodotus even says that Anacreon was with Polycrates when the messenger from Oroetes, the Persian governor or 'satrap' of Lydia who eventually tricked and murdered the tyrant, first arrived. After Polycrates' death, Hipparchus, brother of the Athenian tyrant Hippias, sent a fifty-oared warship – the poet was evidently precious cargo! – to fetch Anacreon to Athens; there, he joined Simonides (pp. 120–33) and made friends with the politician and general Xanthippus, father of the statesman Pericles, who would later erect a statue of his father near one of Anacreon on the Acropolis. Hipparchus was assassinated in 514, and Hippias driven out in 510. At this point Anacreon may have visited Thessaly, or he may have simply settled down in Athens, where he died at the ripe age of eighty-five, choking, as legend has it, on a grape pip.

Such are the vagaries of history that Anacreon's most influential legacy is a body of much later poetry which he did not write – see the *Anacreontea* (pp. 357–64). As a jovial old man he became an archetype of the convivial sophisticate or genteel debauchee, whose wit and polish contrasted with the raw emotion of Sappho (pp. 38–54) and the inspired loftiness of Pindar (pp. 134–64). The *anacreontic* was both a meter – which Anacreon himself used (for example, fragments 356 and 395, pp. 103, 106), and might have invented – and a genre of light-hearted drinking poem practiced by poets of the sixteenth and seventeenth centuries such as Pierre de Ronsard, Ben Jonson, Robert Herrick and Richard Lovelace. The popular image of Anacreon is not so much inaccurate – the stereotype does not fall far from the tree – as incomplete. Anacreon's own poetry is less narrow, and at the same time more trenchant, than the charming squibs written in his name; there is polemic that looks back to Archilochus (pp. 5–15), and a real satirical sting that looks forward to the development of the epigram, especially as practiced by Catullus (pp. 373–97) and Martial (pp. 533–55). Anacreon's poems are easy of access, generalizable but not generic, and suggestively layered in a way that belies their simplicity; his poetry is no less high art for being delivered with a lilt and a wink.

346 fragment 1°

and then, moreover, you're
on edge, you fresh-faced, pretty little thing.

[Your mother] tries to hold you tight,
keeping you out of sight
and safe at home, but you [slip off, to feed]

on hyacinths in pastureland
where Cypris's own hand
ties down the mares she had unyoked and freed.

[And now] you've plunged headfirst into
[the public square,] where you   10
make lots of people's hearts go pitter-pat –

you highway, Herotime, you°
service avenue

346 fragment 4

That boxing left me black and blue,
[but] I can hold my head upright.
All thanks [and credit] go to you,

[Dio]nysus, for my flight
and freedom from Love's chains and screws
which Aphrodite twists to bruise.

Let's have a jar of wine brought in;
let's have some bubbling water brought

347a°

and that hair of yours, which softly
    shadowed your exquisite neck.

Now your noggin's all baldheaded;
hair has miserably fled it;
scabrous hands have smeared the shredded
clumps in dust and in disgrace.

Iron snipped it in a jiffy,
and I'm feeling sick and sniffy –
what's a fellow good for if he
    couldn't manage to save Thrace?°

347b°

I have heard that famous dear – she
keeps repeating, sad and bleary,
these complaints upon the dreary
    vagaries of destiny:

'Think of all the good you'd do me,
Mother, if you took and threw me
in the boiling, dark, unruly
    waves of the uncaring sea.'

348°

Queen of the Wild, with golden hair,
daughter of Zeus, Slayer of Deer,
    Artemis, hear my prayer.
Now, where Lethaeus' current whirls,
you watch and smile down from above
upon that city of the brave,°
for you are not the shepherd of
    some mob of beasts and churls.

352

    Megistes, that
    good pussycat,
    for ten months now
    has bound his brow
    in a willow wreath,
    and wet his teeth
    with the raw wine
    he thinks is fine.

356°

My boy, bring me the bowl;
I'll quaff until I sputter.
Combine five ladles-full
of wine with ten of water,
so once more I can gladly
play the raucous
man of Bacchus
without behaving badly.

Enough of these Thracian bashes,°
with ruckus over wine
and hooting and loud crashes.

10

Let's drink with class – divine
hymns on our lips
and modest sips.

357

O Lord, whom Love, that tames and dazes,
and Aphrodite, fresh as roses,
        and nymphs with wine-dark gazes
surround in play through every clearing
on the high mountains where you stray,
I'm begging, come to me today
with friendly heart; hear what I pray
        and may it please your hearing:
be Cleobulus' counselor,°
Dionysus; make him purr
        Yes to my overture.

10

358

Hitting me again today
with a purple ball, Love urges me
toward this bright-sandaled thing, to see
        whether she wants to play.
But she's a Lesbian born and bred,
and laughs at me, for my white hair,
then opens her mouth wide to stare
        at another sort of head.°

359

I'm in love with Cleobulus.
Cleobulus makes me jealous;
Cleobulus is my solace.
        I ogle Cleobulus.

360

Girlish glancer, whom I pursue,
you never notice when I'm near,
or that the reining charioteer
    yanking my heart is you.

361

Amalthea's horn obsesses°
me not at all, nor do I want
a hundred-fifty-year-long stint
    as ruler of Tartessus.°

373

I had cake (honey-sesame)
    for dinner – just a bite –
but drained a jug of wine entire,
    then took my lovely lyre
and played it sweetly, tenderly,
    for my sweet girl's delight.

376

Look at me climbing, yet again,
tipsy with love, to Leucas' top, all ready for my belly flop°

381b

and threw the shield down nigh where   the lovely stream
    flows by there°

388

He used to wear this cap, striped like a wasp, so tight it hurt,°
and wore the leather wrapper of a cheap shield, caked with dirt,
a swatch of ox he called a shirt;
and from his ears hung wooden dice, and he liked hitting on
fishmongers' wives, and whores-by-choice – the dirtbag
    Artemon,°
whose livelihood was one big con.
And if you checked the wheel or stocks you'd always find him
    there;
his back was crisscrossed with the cracks of whips, and all his
    hair
was gone, his head and beard plucked bare.°
10   An ivory sunshade's in his hand now; his ears boast gold bijoux;
he rides now in a chi-chi landau, Miss Cyce's *petit chou*,°
and does all that the ladies do.

389

You doll to strangers, you're no tease;
I need a nip – I'm thirsty – pretty please?

395°

My temples have turned gray;
my head's a shock of white;
sweet youth has gone away,
my old teeth are a sight,
and there's no doubt
I'm running out
of life and life's delight.

So I often think of death
and sob on the fearful rack.

It's grim, the downward path,
and Hades' rooms are black,
and well I know
that once we go
below, we won't be back.

396

Bring wine and water; bring
a garland with flowery thatch –
quick, boy! I'm challenging
Love to a boxing match.°

398

Hysteria and brouhaha –
those are the dice of Love.°

400

Fleeing from Love again
I went to Pythomander's

408

gingerly,
as to a wee
suckling fawn,°
a newborn who has strayed:
his mother gone,
he's lost, in the woods, afraid.

413

Love like a smith
hit me with
his massive hammer yet again,
then took me to a freezing stream
and dropped me in.

417°

Why so cagey, Thracian filly,
        glancing at me, all side-eyed?
Why do you insist on running?
        You don't think that I can ride?

I could slide the bridle on you
        easy, take you for a spin,
maneuver you around the turnposts,
        make you gallop, rein you in.

As it is, you munch the meadows,
        free and frisky as you please,
lacking anyone to ride you
        with a jockey's expertise.

419

First of my friends, Aristocleides, for your bravery,
you gave your youth to save your fatherland from slavery.

Elegy 2

The guest who stands and drones by the brimming wine
on war and weeping is no friend of mine,
but one who tucks in with an appetite
and mixes love with music is all right.

Xenophanes

Xenophanes of Colophon (circa 570/60–478/68 BCE) was a wandering Ionian poet and philosopher. It is disputed whether he was more poet or philosopher; members of both groups compete in claiming or disowning him depending on how they rank his work. He is often seen as an early ambassador of a new intellectual age, a freethinker whose criticism of prior tradition helped bridge the gap between Homer and Plato. Bertrand Russell describes the Ionian intellectual spirit of which Xenophanes partook and to which he contributed: 'It was not *only* scientific; it was imaginative and vigorous and filled with the delight of adventure. They were interested in everything – meteors and eclipses, fishes and whirlwinds, religion, and morality; with a penetrating intellect they combined the zest of children.' Xenophanes came after Pythagoras (whom he chides; see fragment 7a, p. 111) and before Heraclitus (who chides him as having learning but not understanding).

Along with his elegies, Xenophanes is reported to have composed satires and a poem titled *On Nature*, as well as poetic accounts of the foundation of Colophon and the colonization of Elea. Perhaps for this reason, as well as certain superficial similarities in their thought, he is said to have been the teacher of Parmenides of Elea. Xenophanes' philosophy, however, seems little related to the Eleatic school of Parmenides. That school maintained that sense-perceptions and reason are incompatible, on the basis that perceptions find motion and change everywhere, while reason, starting from the proposition that 'Non-Being cannot be', asserts that they are impossible; consequently, Parmenides and company chose to side with reason, rejecting sense-data as deceptive and fallacious. It is not clear that Xenophanes has much to say on this matter, either for or against; what little he does say may, perhaps, bear on the Eleatic notion of a continuous, indivisible One (see fragment 23–26, p. 112). As far as can be discerned, Xenophanes' philosophy addressed the nature of personal excellence, the unity of the divine, the operations of the natural world, and the relation between truth and opinion. Skeptic philosophers (such as Timon of Phlius) quote him with approval and many of his ideas are taken up, without acknowledgment, by Plato. As a roving gadfly of high moral seriousness intent on questioning traditional pieties and bedeviling sacred cows, Xenophanes comes across as an earlier prototype – more strident, less subtly ironic – of Plato's Socrates.

1°

So now the floor and cups are clean and all
our hands, and each brow wears a coronal.
A servant sets out saucers spiced with scent;
the wine bowl is abrim with merriment.
More wine, with floral scent and mellow flavor,
stands by, and promises to flow forever,
and incense crackles, holy to the nose,
and water, sweet and cold and limpid, flows.°
Nearby is a resplendent table spread
10   with cheese, thick honey and gold-toasted bread.
A central altar bears all sorts of bloom,
and melody and mirth suffuse the room.
Now to Zeus first our buoyant hearts must raise
religious tales, pure words and perfect praise,
once offerings have been poured, and prayers upsent
that hands be ever just and innocent –°
for this is always more convenient
than vicious insolence. Now, it is right
to drink, and gratify the appetite,
20   but not so much you can't walk home alone°
(unless you're old – then use a chaperone).
Praise men whom drink reveals, deep down, as noble,
who make of virtue all their thought and trouble.
But Giants, Titans, Centaurs of old legend –°
ignore those frauds that our forebears imagined;°
scorn bloody schisms, which no one wise applauds,°
and nurture good ideas of the gods.

2

If a man wins the footrace, or prevails
at the pentathlon in Olympia's vales°
by Pisa's stream, where Zeus's temple is,
or makes the wrestling, or the boxing, his,
or wins that horrible 'pancration',°
the people's eyes are full of his renown;
at the next games, he gets an honored seat;
the city council pays for him to eat
with public funds – his is a prize windfall;°
winners on horseback, too, they get it all,   10
though they deserve far less than I, whose force is
Wisdom beyond the force of men and horses.°
But this is neither just nor sensible,
that muscle should outrank the wise man's skill.
Not if the people boast of an elite
boxer, nor wrestler, no, nor pentathlete,
not if one's swiftness makes him a great runner –
the strength in games held in the highest honor –
would it mean better laws or better peace.
How little cities see their joys increase   20
when Pisa's banks prove some athlete the better –
a thing that never makes the coffers fatter.

7a°

Once, when he saw a puppy being whipped,
they say Pythagoras was grieved, and quipped:
'Enough! Stop whipping him. This is the soul
of one I loved. I know him by his yowl.'

8°

Now my ideas for sixty-seven years
have tossed through Greece, striking the country's ears;
and before that, I say I was alive,
if I still know the truth, for twenty-five.

11°

Homer and Hesiod have larded the gods with all kinds
of crimes we mortals hold in contempt, and censure:
filching and fornication and fooling each other.

15°

But if oxen had hands, or horses or lions had them,
or could draw with their hands and make art like the art of humans,
the horses would make their deities look like horses,
the oxen would make them like oxen, and each would picture
their gods with the same sorts of bodies as they have themselves.

16

Aethiopian gods are dark-skinned with flat noses,
while Thrace's gods have red hair and blue eyes.

23–26°

23   One god, who is greatest among both gods and humans,
in no way like human beings, not in form or thought.°
24   Entire he sees, entire conceives; he hears entire;
25   without effort the force of his mind sets all things shaking,
26   while he stays in the same place forever, never departing.
It isn't correct to think of him roaming around.

*o

All space is brimming with god, his ears in all places,
deep in the stones, and over the earth, and in men
ourselves, whatever design a man's heart conceals.

30

The sea is the source of water, the source of wind.
Without the great sea there would be no winds to blow,
no rivers to flow, no shower of waters from heaven;
for the great sea is the parent of clouds and winds,
the begetter of rivers.

34

No man has pierced through to the truth; none will unravel
all the gods' mysteries or all of the subjects I've touched on.
If someone gets lucky – the best that can happen – and utters
the truth of the world as it is, he still wouldn't know it.
But everyone has their opinions – that's all they've got.

Hipponax

Credited with the invention of parody and the 'limping iambic' – a meter also used by Callimachus (pp. 255–81), Catullus (pp. 373–97) and Martial (pp. 533–55) – Hipponax of Ephesus was an Ionian iambic poet who flourished around 540–530 BCE. He is said to have been banished from his hometown of Ephesus in Asia Minor by the otherwise unknown tyrants Athenagoras and Comas, and to have settled at neighboring Clazomenae (modern Urla). The chief event known from his life, possibly derived from later readings of his work, is his quarrel with the sculptors Bupalus and Athenis, who made a statue of him and exhibited it to public ridicule. (He is said to have been repulsively ugly.) Hipponax responded by assailing them in verse until they committed suicide – a story no doubt modeled on Archilochus' feud with Lycambes and his daughters (see p. 5).

Despite Hipponax's status as one of the three canonical iambic poets (along with Archilochus, pp. 5–15, and Semonides of Amorgos, pp. 16–20), only around 180 fragments, totaling 200-odd complete lines, of his verse have survived, out of perhaps two or three books compiled by the editors of Alexandria. They are notable for their Ionian atmosphere, their colorful, sometimes recherché vocabulary (complete with foreign loan words) and their shocking obscenity, which includes sexual farce as lewd as anything left us by antiquity. Generally, moderns have tried to make Hipponax fit into our own cultural categories, seeing him as a trickster-poet, a moralist, a proletarian, a beatnik, a *poète maudit* in the line of nineteenth-century poets-against-society like Charles Baudelaire, Paul Verlaine or Arthur Rimbaud, or even an ironist whose main target is taken to be the poems' own sleazy speaker – the aristocratic versifier donning a lower-class (or nouveau riche) mask for the sake of satire. To me, he seems an ancient predecessor of François Villon, the late medieval French poet best known for his scabrous, intelligent, unreverential verse and his repeated run-ins with the law. At all events, his poetry does provide the main model and precedent for the comedy of Aristophanes, and had an enduring influence on the Alexandrians, especially Callimachus in his *Iambi*, and through him on Callimachus' Roman inheritors.

3+3a°

He called on Maia's son, grand poobah of Cyllene:°   3
'Dog-Choker, Hermes, whom the Lydians call "Candaules",°   3a
buddy of burglars, come and save my ass already!'

12

As if to stiff the Erythraeans, the literal°
motherfucker, Bupalus, now *in flagrante*°
with Arete, tugged his degenerate foreskin back°

14

straight from the bucket
first he, then Arete, were taking pulls of wine,
toasting each other

16°

With a good bird – a heron – on the right, I went
to Arete at nightfall, where I pitched my tent

17

then she bent over lampward, Arete, for me

19

Who midwifed your cord-snipping, you accident,
and scrubbed and sponged the filth off while you wriggled?

26+26a°

26   One of them lived it up on Easy Street, Hog Heaven,°
      stuffing himself on steaks of tuna *au vin aigre*°
      daily, the way the eunuchs do in Lampsacus,°
      until he ate up his whole patrimony. Now
      he breaks rocks with a spade while munching on some measly
      miserable figs and barley bread, slave stuff . . . °
26a   not tucking into pheasant or *lapin rôti au four*,
      not doctoring his pancakes with a spritz of sesame,
      not drizzling honeycomb over his hot waffles.

28

Mimnes, who boast an asshole as big as your whole back:°
stop painting snakes on trireme-sides from stem to stern
beneath the oarlocks – awful omen for the helmsman.
You slave-born slave, invoke Sabazius already,°
to stop it sinking venom in the poor guy's leg!°

32°

Dear Hermes, Hermes, Maia's kid, Cyllene's kingpin,°
I do implore thee. Uff da! I'm shivering all over,
3   my teeth are cla-cla-clacking . . .
4   Give Hipponax a widdle coat, a widdle nightie,
      some widdle sandals, widdle booties and, say, sixty
      gold pieces, and I'll call us all paid up. Capisce?

34

Hey, where's that furry coat, my antidote to freezing?
You didn't give it yet. Where are those furry booties?
Now, give them now! My goddamn chilblains are exploding.

36

Wealth's never found his way to *my* house – too damn blind –
or said, 'Hey, Hipponax, here's thirty silver pieces,
with assets, etc.' I'm telling you, he's chicken.°

38

Zeus, Father Zeus, grand poobah up on Mount Olympus,
grand poobah of payola, I want gold. Let me have it!

39°

I'll give up and give in, all groans, to a bad fate,
if you don't send, *right now*, a barley bushel I
can brew and swig to take the edge off my bad state.°

68

There are two happy days in a woman's life: the day
she marries, and the day her corpse is dragged away.

78°

                          he sacrificed,
at the Cabiri temple, under the Star of Bullsplat,°
a little bait fish, while dung beetles . . .°   12
then went home, where he stuffed his face with mulberries   13
and, dyeing the head of his cock red with the mulberry juice,
he spat on it three times and masturbated

84°

     she came
     with pubes like pennyroyal
     and then she asked me

and we were on the ground
our clothes were off
and we were kissing and biting
and looking through the doors
not wanting anyone
to take us naked
10   now she was really eager
and I was screwing her
                              and I pulled
the tip out like a sausage hanging out to dry
a big *fuck you* to Bupalus
and straight away
following our activities we rested
and I was like a sail gone slack

92°

She spewed some Lydian magic, in the dialect
2   of Uranus, and said, 'Your anus . . .'
3   and my balls and prick
she caned with a fig switch, like I was a scapegoat,°
pinned down by split wood pegs
that was a sticky wicket, double trouble
the fig switch on the one side
falling from above
me spattering shit below
10   my asshole stank, and the bouquet enticed
a swarm of beetles, more than fifty of them, buzzing.
And some of them assailed
and pelted me, and others piqued their pricks
and fell upon the gaping
doors of Buttopia

115°

tossed in the slap of the waves.   4
May the man-bunned goons of Salmydessus give him,°
    washed up on the beach in the raw,
stiff as a plank, bone-chilled, their warmest welcome:
    the crusts of a slave to gnaw,
abundant indignities. And may he cough up
    seaweed, spat from the sea,   10
as his teeth clack and he lies like a dog, face-down,
    emptied of energy,
there where the brine meets beach . . .   13
    All this and more I would send   14
his way, who wronged me, trampling his promises.
    He used to be my friend.

117°

then you scoot close. Hipponax, more than most,
    is onto you, on your case,
and Ariphantus too. Happy the man
    who's never seen your face,
you pickpocket. You smell like a goat. Go to the potter°
    Aeschylides, pick a fight;
he picked your pocket . . . and now
    your thievery's all in the light.

120+121°

Here, hold my cloak, I'm going to bash the eye of Bupalus.   120
You know I'm ambidextrous and my punches never miss.   121

Simonides

Simonides of Ceos (circa 556/2–468/4 BCE) – now Kea, in the Cyclades – is a singular figure in Archaic Greek poetry, who perhaps did more than any other to effect the transition from the Archaic to the Classical age. The only one of the canonical Nine Lyric Poets whose number of total books, in Alexandrian recension, is unknown, he wrote *threnoi* (dirges, laments for the dead), encomia (praise poems), epigrams, paeans (or hymns to Apollo), dithyrambs (or choral odes in honor of Dionysus), assorted other hymns, prayers and curses, and is thought to have invented the epinician (or victory ode – though on this, see Ibycus, p. 96). He composed lyric poems and elegies on the Persian Wars, including a *Reign of Cambyses and Darius*, a *Sea-Battle of Artemisium*, a *Sea-Battle of Salamis*, and the recently discovered *Plataea Elegy*, which evokes Achilles as it praises the Spartans for their leading role in the great victory over Persia (see p. 128). He points forward to Pindar (pp. 134–64) and Bacchylides (pp. 165–85), and, through them, to Attic drama, as well as to the sophists (such as Protagoras and Gorgias) criticized by Plato for casuistry and lack of principle.

The ancients liked to talk about Simonides more than they liked to quote his poems. He is a byword for venality; he is said to have kept two boxes, one marked 'favors', the other 'fees'; the first was always empty and the second always full of cash. To Aristotle, he is a stock miser; Xenophanes (pp. 109–13) calls him a 'skinflint'. He is credited with the invention of the mnemonic technique known as the 'memory palace', and the addition of four letters to the Greek alphabet – ω (*omega*), ε (*epsilon*), ζ (*zeta*) and φ (*phi*). He is called the first literary theorist, for his much-quoted quips that 'a word is a picture of things' and 'painting is silent poetry; poetry is painting that speaks'. In his poems, he is a self-consciously Panhellenic craftsman, the first to work in both elegiac and lyric modes, synthesizing in himself both the Doric and Aeolic traditions.

All this points to why Anne Carson views Simonides as 'the smartest person in the fifth century B.C.': he combines a high capacity for abstract thought with a penchant for reflecting analytically on his own activities and traditions. A cynic before there were Cynics, he was able to (re)formulate conventional wisdom, and to do so in quotable remarks, without ever being constrained by it. While, for Pindar, culture and society are everywhere charged and enchanted by divinity, Simonides sees through such mumbo-jumbo to the bottom line, the quid pro quo, and is content to auction his skills to the highest bidder. His 'chief merit' as a poet, according to the first-century CE Roman rhetorician Quintilian, 'lies in the power to excite pity'; Catullus (pp. 373–97) asks his friend for a consolation 'sadder than the tears of Simonides'. For the elegiac mode that such commentary has in mind, see Simonides' *Lament of Danaë* below (fragment 543, p. 124) – though it is hard, in his case, not to think of an anecdote about the young Beethoven:

> [Beethoven] knew how to produce such an effect upon every hearer that frequently not an eye remained dry, while many would break out into loud sobs ... After ending an improvisation of this kind he would burst into loud laughter and banter his hearers on the emotion he had caused in them. 'You are fools!' he would say.

Simonides is unsentimental and unillusioned; more clear-eyed than compassionate, he keeps the world at a safe distance, does his job – which he regards mostly as a problem of technique – gets paid and goes. He is a consummate craftsman, a burster of bubbles, a man who has things all figured out. He is, as Philip Larkin might say, 'intensely sad'.

Lyrics

520°

The strength of man
is slight; incurable, his case.
In his short span
of life are pangs on pangs.
And over every head in the same way hangs
death, which none can flee,
and is allotted equally
to noble men and base.

521°

You, who are man, do not foretell   what tomorrow will be like,
or, if someone's doing well,   how long he will stay fortunate;
            not even the long-winged bluebottle can zip so quick
                    this way, then that.

522

    All things – great excellences and fortunes – are in one boat
        bound for Charybdis's horrible throat.°

524°

        even to battle-deserters Death catches up

526

        No man, no city, without god
        has ever managed greatness in anything.
        God is all-wise and all-accomplishing.
        We are the downtrodden and overawed.

527

        There comes no pain, no crime
    out of the blue to mortal dread.
                        In a short time
        god turns the world on its head.

531°

        Those who died at Thermopylae
                        died reaping
    transcendent opportunity
                    and an immortal lot;

their tomb an altar, they have praise for pity, fame for weeping,
  and sleep in such a shroud as neither rot
  nor all-subduing Time can stain or crease.°
These heroes earned, to tend their holy plot,
  the reverent esteem of Greece –
and this can Spartan Leonidas, whose estate°
is crowned with manliness and glory that will not abate,
  corroborate.

538

Necessity's behest:
a lark must have its crest.

541°

[His] judgment sifts the noble from the vile.°
The doorless mouths of slanderers eject
  smoke without fire or effect,
  while gold is incorruptible,
  and Truth remains omnipotent.
But only to a few does the god grant
excellence to the end. Yes, being noble
  is no light task: indomitable
  greed, or the gadfly Cypris sends,
  weaving her wiles, or the appetite   10
  to harvest honor's dividends°
beats many down in their despite.
A man who can't, until his death,
tread only on the righteous path°

542°

It's arduous truly to perfect
one's hands, feet, intellect,
and grow foursquare in goodness, without flaw . . .   3

11   Though he was wise, and what he said
                    is widely bruited,
        the apophthegm of Pittacus, to wit,°
            'A good man's a hard thing to be,'
                    doesn't ring true to me.
            Only a god can manage it
        for good; when woes inexorably coerce
            a man, he's cheapened and depressed.
        Good times make all men better, bad times worse.
20   [But those the gods love most are far the best.]

            That's the reason *I* won't pursue
                    hopes that can't come true,
        and throw my life away to do what none
            who eat the fruit of the wide earth can:
                    become a flawless man.
            I'll let you know if I find one.
        Meanwhile, anyone who doesn't cause
                    evil to others willingly
        I shower with affection and applause;
30   but even gods can't fight necessity . . .

33   [I'm not a scold. He's good enough for me
            who isn't base] or void of sense;
                    who knows a town's defense
            is law; who's free of infirmity.
        A man like that is safe from my attacks.
                For the influx of imbeciles
        will never end. I call that good which lacks
40   dilution by the sorriest of ills.

                    543°

            The Lament of Danaë

Ant.   As she was buffeted
                    in the fancy ark by wild
                squalls and choppy seas,

                              when her fears
                      knocked her to her knees,
                      then her cheeks ran with tears,
            and she folded Perseus in her arms, and said,
                      'How I have suffered, child!

            'But you, with your infant character,   *Ep.*
                      sleep on, and do not stir,
                          serene in the gales   10
            that drive the unhappy vessel with its bronze nails
                      through the glossy murk
                                          and the lustrous dark,
                          while the skimmed spray
                      of rollers that slap
                                  and pass
            leaps over your head. But you don't pay
                      them any mind,
                      or hear any sound in the wind,
                      snug in your purple wrap –
                          you cherub face!°
            Oh, if you really believed our fear was fear,   20
            you'd lend your little ear
                                  to what I say.

            'Which is: my babe, enjoy your slumber;   *Str.*
            and may the ocean sleep, and sleep our sorrows without number.
                      O Father Zeus, I wish some new
                      course would occur to you!
            If anything I pray is overbold
                      or out of tune with justice,
                      pardon me.'

                              553

            and they dissolved in tears as the unweaned
            child of Eurydice the violet-crowned°
            exhaled his soul, all sweetness at the end

567°

Over the head of Orpheus a throng
of numberless birds flew,
and fish in a plumb-line flung
themselves from the sea's deep blue
at his beautiful song.

579°

There is an old vignette
that Excellence abides on rocks supremely hard to climb,
and there she tends her holy place [in company sublime.]
Hardly a mortal sees her face, unless
his inmost heart is rent by sweat
and he attains the peak of manliness.

581°

Who in the world whose mind is right
would flatter Cleobulus, Lindus' king? –
who, against ever-flowing rivers and the buds of spring
and the sun's fire and the gold moon's light
and ocean's churning monotone,
opposed a statue's might!
All things that are are less than gods,
and even mortal hands can shatter stone.
His comment was a clod's.

584

What sort of life could satisfy the heart
apart from pleasure?
What tyrant's treasure
be worth the having?
Pleasure apart,
not even a god's life would be worth living.

586

when the nightingale goes warbling,
full-throated, at the start of spring

595°

No windy bluster, filling the leaves with noise,
was kicked up then –
                                        the sort that, rising,
could have stopped the honeyed voice
                                        from hypnotizing
            the ears of men.

597

o herald of spring and its fragrance sweet and clean,
famed swallow, with your blueblack sheen

598

the force of Seeming subjugates even Truth

604°

not even the beauty of wisdom is a blessing,
when or wherever the god of health is missing

651

For mortals, best is a healthy constitution;
next is a fine physique and good complexion;
third, to have riches of honest acquisition;
fourth, to be young among your friends' affection.

Elegies

11°

The Plataea Elegy

            [and you collapsed, as when
a larch] or pine in so[me high, lonely glen

3   fa]lls to the woodmen's blows . . .°

5   [The whole] host [wept then, as with honor due]
in Patroclus's u[rn they planted you.
No mortal creature of an hour ki]lled you;
it was Apollo's hand [that struck and stilled you.
Incen]sed at Priam's sons, [Pallas attacked

10   that fa]mous tow[n with Hera – which they sacked,°
because of do]uble-dealing Pa[ris. Crime]
is caught by Justice' chario[t in time.
So Greece's b]est, Achaea's chieftains, burned
that storied [citad]el, and then re[turned
under] a rain of praise unperi[shing
from o]ne the dark-haired Muses tau[ght to sing°
all t]ruth, who made them themes for y[oung me]n's song –
[these dem]igods whose lifespans were not lon[g.
Grandson of sea-]blue Nereus, goodbye,

20   [whom his imm]ortal daughter bore; but I°
[invoke,] o Muse, your name, so o[ft repeated,]
my ally, [if you answer] when entreated:
[make m]y song fair, w[ell-framed and g]enerous,
[that af]ter-time may sp[eak of] those of us
[who stood their ground and fought] so none s[hould see]
the da[y of Greece and S]parta's [slav]ery;
[their cour]age unforgotten, they earned fame
as high as heaven, and a deathless [name.
From Sparta, and Eu]rotas' banks, their forces°

30   [marched forth] with Zeus's scions skilled in horses,
[the Tyndarid]s, and Menelaus, might[y]°
monarch, shepherds of their [native c]ity,

led [by the offsp]ring of Cleombrotus ...   33

                noblest Pausanias.°   34

[They reached the Isthmu]s soon, Corinth's renowned

towers, and Pelops' is[land's farthest bound,]°

then Nisus' [ancient] city, [Megara] ...°   37

[From heaven's om]ens they took confidence,   39

[and ro]uted, at El[eusis' l]ush expanse,°

[the Medes from the dominio]ns of Pan[dion,°

helped by the pr]ophet, [Iamus's scion.]°

19+20°

This is the best thing said by the Chian bard:°   19

'Like lives of the leaves, even so are the lives of men.'

But few whose ears have taken his words in

have taken them to heart. For each man clings

to Hope, which in a young man wells and springs ...

As long as his youth's lovely bloom is open,   20

in his light heart he dreams what will not happen.

Of age and death to come he does not brood,

or ponder sickness, while his health is good.

Imbeciles think this way, and do not know   10

how quickly primes and lifetimes come and go

for us. But since *you* know, till you depart

be patient, and on good things feast your heart.

Epigrams°

1°

Hipparchus slain! New dawn makes Athens brighten,

thanks to Harmodius and Aristogiton.

2°

Although a glen of Dirphys cradles us,°
our public tomb is by the Euripus –°
and justly, since we gave to the consuming
fog of war our youth when it was blooming.

3°

In iron chains their enemies are pinched,
now Athens' sons with deeds of war have quenched
the flame of Chalcis' and Boeotia's malice.
These mares – tithe of the spoils – they give to Pallas.

6°

This stone marks famed Megistias's slaughter
at the Medes' hands across Spercheus' water –°
a prophet who, though he saw death at hand,
would not abandon Sparta's high command.

7°

Earth holds them in their glory, these who died
here, Spartan Leonidas, by your side,°
who faced in battle the overwhelming forces
of the Medes' myriad bows and myriad horses.

8°

If to die well is of all high acts best,
that chance was given us before the rest,
who sought a crown of freedom for all Greece,
and sleep with praises that will never cease.

9°

With fame imperishable these have endowed
their country, when they entered death's dark cloud.
They died, but are not dead; their valor's story
lifts them from Hades into light and glory.

22a°

Against three million Persians in this spot
four thousands from the Peloponnesus fought.°

22b°

Go tell the men of Sparta, passerby,
that we obeyed them well, and here we lie.

27°

Before this plaque, you won, Simonides,
fifty-six tripods, bulls and victories;
fifty-six choruses of men you taught
have mounted Triumph's glorious chariot.

28°

In Adimantus' days, the tripod went°
to Antíochus' tribe. It was magnificent.°
One Aristides, Xenóphilus's son,
headed the fifty dancers when they won,°
and Simonides, their trainer, was praised greatly:
the son of Leóprepes, when he was eighty.

40a+b+c°

40a   Out of this city to Troy's great battlefield
         with Atreus' sons Menestheus once sailed,°
         among the ranks of Greeks thick-corsleted
         outstanding in command, as Homer said.
         We rightly name the Athenians, therefore,
         Marshals of Manly Courage and of War.

40b   *They* had endurance, who at Eion once
         beside the Strymon's waves on the Medes' sons
         first forced hot hunger and cold war, and found
10   attrition can drive foes into the ground.

40c   So Athens to the leaders of that action
         set up these Herms in thanks for benefaction;
         which men of later days shall not ignore,
         but for the greater good will go to war.°

45°

Not since the day Europe from Asia parted,
and Ares seized our cities, reckless-hearted;
never before has earthborn humanity
seen such a feat take place on land *and* sea:
on Cyprus swarms of Medes were killed ashore,
and at sea a hundred Phoenician men-of-war
were captured full of fighters. Hugely battered
by War's both fists, all Asia groaned and shuddered.

46°

These brave, who fought the bowmen Medes beside
Eurymedon, gave their glorious youth and died –
whether on foot or shipboard, spearmen all,
whose valor earned them this memorial.

84°

The men who murdered me, may Zeus destroy;
may those who buried me live on in joy.

85°

Thanks to this man, Simonides is living;
therefore the live one pays the dead thanksgiving.

Pindar

In antiquity, the Theban Pindar (circa 518–438 BCE) was not only ranked among the canonical Nine Lyric Poets, but also widely considered the greatest of the bunch, and a master – with Aeschylus – of what Dionysius of Halicarnassus called the 'austere style'. The modern consensus, however, is stated by Voltaire when he addresses Pindar as a genius who says

> nothing in poems that never end;
> savant whose panpipe smartly plays
> stuff everyone's supposed to praise
> and nobody can comprehend.

Two more recent critics relate Pindar's poems to an incident from Vasari's *Life of Michelangelo*, when the Renaissance artist's patron commissioned 'surely the best snowman the world has ever seen'. Like the snow, our memory of the rich contexts for which Pindar composed – the athletes he praised, the celebrations at which he praised them, the patrons who commissioned the odes, and so much more – has melted utterly away, leaving only the craggy landscape of the odes behind.

The genre for which Pindar is known, the epinician (victory ode), was not in vogue for very long. Simonides (p. 120–33; or perhaps Ibycus, p. 96–9) invented it one generation before Pindar, and it died more or less with him. Yet Pindar's reputation as an athletic super-fan is an accident of history, since, of the seventeen books in which the editors of Hellenistic Alexandria gathered and published his work, athletic odes made up only four. (Each bears the name of the Panhellenic 'games', or sporting festival, it celebrates, arranged by the Alexandrians in descending order of prestige: the Olympic Games; then the Pythian; then the Nemean; then the Isthmian.) His other thirteen volumes contain hymns, paeans (hymns to Apollo), dithyrambs (choral odes for Dionysus), *prosodia* (processional hymns), *partheneia* (maiden-songs), hyporchemes (dancing hymns), encomia (praise poems) and *threnoi* (funeral dirges).

Almost two-thirds of his poetry addresses the gods; even when speaking to men, his sensibility is deeply religious.

As a Panhellenic poet, Pindar was in high demand throughout the Greek world and traveled widely in it, accepting commissions and training choruses. Indeed, his poetry seems largely, if not entirely, choral. Though he spoke frankly of his 'mercenary Muse', he was no cynic, and not a mere flatterer-for-hire; praise was for him a way of life and sustained the fabric of civilization. The universe he inhabited was a *cosmos* in the root sense of 'order, arrangement', with gods at the top, monsters at the bottom, and humans in a just hierarchy between, fully dependent on the divine. Human events (like athletic games) find their meaning within the system of religious, political and social relations that comprise culture; the odes' goal is to adumbrate this meaning. Meanwhile, their architectural organization recapitulates the cosmic order, thereby affirming it and ensuring the efficacy of Pindar's praise.

If his thought is sometimes hard to follow, it's because his art applies extraordinary pressure to language, with transitions looking backward and forward, aphorisms that fit their particular context but resonate beyond it, and sentences that move between ideas with a fluidity which might, for English readers, recall John Milton or, among nearer contemporaries, Derek Walcott. Pindar tends to think in structural units too large to be comprehended easily, and the effort required to interpret his odes' grammar and argument might be said to parallel the difficulties faced by any observer of world affairs who seeks to fit human events into an order both natural and divine. But the pattern – and the purpose – are there.

Olympian Odes°

Olympian 1°

For Hieron of Syracuse, Winner, Single Horse Race, 476 BCE°

Water is best, while of all riches, gold,°   *Str. 1*
like fire in the dark, shines well apart.
But if it's games, my heart,

you want to hymn, what star could you behold
more warm or more unrivaled in the air
   than the bright sun,
  or what contest compare
to Zeus's at Olympia? Not one.
From that source, poems that all of us repeat
10 are launched in wise men's minds, as they entreat°
and offer praises up to Cronus' son
at the rich and happy hearth of Hieron,

Ant. 1 who, plucking such success as few are able,
wields just sway in flock-rich Sicily,
   and shines in the poetry
  we men recite around his friendly table.°
Now take your lyre, play something Doric, Pindar,°
   if Pisa's grace°
  and Pherenicus' splendor°
20 delight you and inspire you to praise
where praise is due. For that sleek thoroughbred
did not need any goading as he sped
past the Alpheus, and flying ever faster°
won victory and power for his master,

Ep. 1 the king of Syracuse, who loves his horses,
   whose fame beams like a star
in the colony of Pelops, where the course is°
   and where the good men are.
Pelops impressed the powerful Earth-Holder,
30 Poseidon, with a passion that ran hot,
dazzling the deity with his ivory shoulder
when spinster Clotho pulled him from the stainless pot.°
There are so many things hard to believe!
  And yet, when men talk, as they do,
  they don't always hold to what's true,
  but with their colorful fancies weave
elaborate lies intended to deceive.

When Eloquence, which gives men such delight,   *Str. 2*
adds honor to what cannot be conceived,
     it often is believed;   40
yet future days are wise and see what's right.
It's proper for a man to speak no shame
     of gods in glory;
     that way, there's less blame.
Son of Tantalus, here's a different story
than others tell about you: when your father
feasted the gods – a favor for their favor –
in friendly Sipylus, nothing was uncouth;°
but the Lord of the Trident snatched you in your youth

on golden horses, driven by lust and need,   *Ant. 2*
and took you to the honored home of Zeus,   51
     where, for the same use,
the gods' king afterwards brought Ganymede.°
But when you'd vanished, and your mother's men,
     hard though they searched,
     could not find you again,
some envious neighbor secretly besmirched
your story, saying that your folks had you
pared and minced and boiled up in a stew,
then to the gods, when you were quite inert,   60
ladled you out and served you for dessert.

But I could not dishonor in my verse   *Ep.2*
     any immortal god
or say that one's a glutton: slanderers
     rarely come to good.
Yet if Olympus' keepers ever blessed
a man with honor, it was Tantalus,
who, fraught with appetite, could not digest
his happiness, and won this prize in Tartarus
when folly made him ruinously blind: 70
     under a stone of monstrous size°
     hung by the Father, he tries and tries

to free himself, still unresigned,
and despair bears with full weight on his mind.

Str. 3   He's fourth in hell among the famous three,°
suffering pains and helpless for reprieve
        because he sought to give
his friends the cup of immortality –
nectar he stole from deathless benefactors.°
80   No man can trick them;
        his hopes are empty specters,
whoever tries, and he their hapless victim.
And so the gods cast Pelops back in grief
to rejoin men on earth whose lot is brief.
When he'd grown up, and fuzz darkened his chin,
he thought he'd seek a marriage he could win

Ant. 3   with famous Hippodamia, the king
of Pisa's daughter. One night, he went alone°
        to where the gray waves groan
90   and called the Trident Lord, deep-thundering;
who came, and Pelops said, 'If you in heaven
            still honor us
        for gifts of love we've given,
hold back the bronze spear of Oenomaus,
and in a peerless chariot speed me
to Elis; bring me power and victory.
By now he's murdered thirteen men who seek
his daughter's hand, and puts off, week to week,

Ep. 3   her wedding. Danger and achievement never
100   attract the cowardly.
But who could stomach – since no one lives forever –
        a life's obscurity,
attempting nothing fine for honor's sake
and doting on his dotage, to no end?
Not me; this is the test I'll undertake.
But you, fulfill my prayer, and treat me as a friend.'°

He spoke; Poseidon granted his desire,
   and glorified him and his love
   with gifts straight from the gods above:
   a chariot flashing golden fire   110
and wingèd horses that can never tire.

He bested Oenomaus, taking the king's°   *Str. 4*
   daughter to share his bed, and raised six sons –
      commanding, royal ones –
all fired with passion to achieve great things.
Entombed now by the Alpheus he rests,
      and drinks his fill
    of worship, where the guests
from far and wide throng Zeus's festival,°
and fame from the races and displays of force   120
blazes abroad from the Olympic course
of Pelops, and each victor feels the balm
of triumph waft through all his days a calm –

as far as games can give it; for the pleasure   *Ant. 4*
renewed each day brings men most happiness.
    But to crown that man's success
with a horseman's tune in an Aeolic measure°
is now my task; no host alive displays
      more noble skill
    to robe in folds of praise,   130
more deeds of mastery, more lordly will.
The god who guards you makes it his concern
to help you reach the dreams for which you yearn,
Hieron; if he doesn't leave his place,
I hope to praise an even sweeter race

in the swift chariot, as I trace back°   *Ep. 4*
    the road of eloquence
to Cronus' sun-struck hill, and Zeus's track.°
    The Muse in my defense
has strung the strongest arrow on my strings.   140

Though many men are great in many ways,
   the highest pinnacle is crowned by kings.
Cast your gaze no farther. There is no higher praise.
   May you continue drinking that rare air
      for your whole life; and may I come
      with victors to the podium,
      and in the wisdom that I share°
may I outshine all Hellenes everywhere.

Olympian 7°

For Diagoras of Rhodes, Winner, Boxing, 464 BCE

Str. 1   As whose largesse with lavish hand should lift
    a bowl bubbling with vintage, effervescent,
    and toast – 'My home to yours!' – then hand it down,
        ungrudging gift
    of solid gold, most precious he possessed,
    to his young son-in-law to be, to crown
    the drinking party and the gracious present
    and honor their betrothal with his best,
    while all his friends at the symposium
10   envy them both the harmonies to come –

Ant. 1   So I pour nectar out, gift of the Muses,
    sweet fruit of thought, to win the blessing of
    those Pytho and Olympia bestow°
        with crowns and prizes.
    Happy the man always encompassed round
    with good repute. The Grace that makes life glow°
    and blossom as in sunlight looks with love
    now here, now there, and sheds the honeyed sound
    of lyres often, and often too inspires
20   pipes to entwine their voices with the lyre's.

Ep. 1   Now as both musics fill the air,
      I've disembarked with Diagoras

and hymns for Aphrodite's daughter,
the Rose arisen from deep water,°
Rhodes, the bride of Helius.
So shall I praise a puncher who fights fair,
a bruising boxer built with brawn to spare,
    crowned lately at Castalia's spring
    and at the Alpheus, and sing°
    his father Damagetus' praise,   30
    a man whom Justice cherishes;
    whose family dwells by the coastline where
the huge headland of Asia juts its chin,
in the Three Towns of spear-skilled Argive men.°

From its first dawning I shall proclaim their common   *Str. 2*
history, with Tlapolemus at the center,°
the progeny of Heracles, great father
            of superhuman
offspring, through whom the Rhodians are descended
from Zeus, while by Tlapolemus's mother   40
Astydameia, they're children of Amyntor.°
But mortal minds have always hung suspended
among countless confusions, dark with doubt,
and it is past our power to find out

what now and at the end of an event   *Ant. 2*
will prove best for a man. Witness the bastard
brother of Alcmene, Licymnius:°
            he, as he went
away from Midea's perfumed recesses°
to Tiryns, met Rhodes' founder Tlapolemus,   50
who took up his tough staff of olive, mastered
by anger, and struck and killed him. Passion oppresses
even a wise man's wits, and makes him err.
And so he sought the god in Delphi; where°

    out of the depths spices suffuse,   *Ep. 2*
    He of the Golden Hair commanded°

          Tlapolemus straightway to sail
          from Lerna's beaches to the vale°
          which the enormous sea surrounded,
60   and to the city blessed of old with snows
          of gold, sent down by heaven's king, from whose°
              temples once the cunning cracks
              dealt deftly by the bronze-forged axe
              of masterful Hephaestus sped
              Athena; she from her father's head
              leapt fiercely, with a cry that rose
          on high and sent a shudder through the Sky;
          and Earth, all-mother, shuddered at that cry.

Str. 3   Now at that time, the godhead whose face lights
70   the mortal world, the son of Hyperion,°
          had charged his favored children to exalt her°
                 with solemn rites
          in her unending praise, and to allot her
          in all men's view her first (then only) altar,
          to burn their holy offerings thereon
          and warm the hearts of Father and of Daughter,
          whose spear thrums thunder. So should Reverence treasure
          Insight, wellspring of excellence and pleasure

Ant. 3   – for unforeseen, the cloud that makes men blind
80   comes down, and the straight road, which else would carry
          our steps unerring, dark with forgetfulness
                swerves out of mind.
          So up they went, but nobody recalled
          the seeds of fire. On the acropolis
          they had to consecrate the sanctuary
          without flame, but a sudden gold cloud veiled
          the peak, sent from the Father, and sent down
          snows all of gold, at which the Gray-Eyed One°

Ep. 3   upon their hands and labors set
90   an artistry superior

to all that earthborn skill can fashion,
   so that their streets crawled with creation,
   with forms that seemed to breathe and stir,
and their fame flowered. But the best wit,°
though taught by art, is never counterfeit.
   And we've heard also this tale told°
   by our old fathers: when of old
   Zeus and the other gods in glory
   were portioning out their territory,
   Rhodes had not arisen yet   100
to common view on the great face of the sea,
but dwelt below in deep obscurity.

When the gods' lots were drawn, one was not there   *Str. 4*
and so was not accorded a demesne;
though a great god, Helius had been cut
        out of his share.
Zeus, when he was informed of the omission,
was planning a repeat allotment, but
Helius demurred, for he had seen,
borne up from the deep bed of the gray ocean,   110
an island rising rich in nourishment,
where many flocks and men could be content.

And so Zeus asked of golden-chapleted   *Ant. 4*
Lachesis on the instant that she not°
refuse the gods' great oath with both hands high
        over her head,
but join to his their mutual consents
that, once uncovered to the dazzling sky
on the wave's breast, Rhodes would become the lot
and prize of Helius for all time thence.   120
And so his words, rooted in truth, came true
and took root. Out of the stirred sea Rhodes grew

   up like a plant, and is the Sun's   *Ep. 4*
   domain, dear to the sire of

the hot sharp beams, who steers the courses
of fire-radiating horses.
He long ago combined in love
with Rhodes the nymph, and they had seven sons°
whose birthright was supreme intelligence.

130   To one was born the triple band°
of Lindus and Camirus and
Ialysus, the eldest one.
When each boy came into his own,
they divvied their inheritance
of land in three, and husbanded their claims.
Today, the towns of Rhodes still bear their names.

Str. 5   And there he whom the former Tirynthians
hail as their founder, Tlapolemus, receives,
as if a god, the sweet emolument
140   of bitter chance:
a ritual procession smoke sublimes
from flocking altars, and a grand event°
of judgments and fair flowers. With those wreaths
Diagoras is twice laureled, but four times
at the famed Isthmus; twice in a row he won
crowns at Nemea, and among the stone

Ant. 5   of Athens. Argive bronze proclaims his fame's°
extent; bronze prizes know him well
at Thebes's gates, and in Arcadia,
150   and annual games
held in Boeotia and Pellana's lap.
Six times he has been crowned by Aegina,
and still at Megara the stone lists tell
Diagoras's triumphs. O mountaintop
Monarch of Atabyrium, Zeus, Father,°
bless my Olympian music with your favor

Ep. 5   and honor the supremacy
of so much boxing excellence.

May he receive and still return
the high esteem his talents earn   160
from foreigners and citizens
alike, whose path is straight and true and free
from moral violence, whose clarity
of thinking clearly has accrued
the wisdom of his noble brood.
Hide not in dark the seed you share
with Callianax – you, the heir
of Eratus, whose jubilee°
fills all the city. But in a flash of fate
the winds shift, gusting now this way, now that.   170

Olympian 12°

For Ergoteles of Himera, Winner, Long Race, 466 BCE°

To you, daughter of Freeborn Zeus, I pray;°   *Str.*
still dote on the might of Himera, and stay,
   o Fortune, our deliverance!
   At sea you helm the speeding fleet;
   on land you pilot soldiers' feet,
   and steer debates when councils meet.
How windily on the voyage, in suspense,
   now rising up, now sinking low,
delusory and useless, men's hopes blow.

No god has yet conveyed a certain omen   *Ant.*
of what will happen next to any human.   11
   Their minds are shrouded; they keep mum,
   and the day pounces on blind eyes.
   How often confident surmise
   is contradicted by surprise!
Some find their pleasures overthrown, while some
   on whom foul tempests fell all night
in no time turn despair to deep delight.

Ep.   Son of Philanor, think how you might have shed,°
20   like an infighting cock at the local hearth
       where it was bred,°
      your racing laurels – your renown
      an ignominious sacrifice –
      had you not fled from your hometown
      on Crete, the Cnossus of your birth,
    where man-unmanning civil war sees red.°
  Ergoteles, now that the Isthmus, and now that Pytho (twice)°
 and Olympia have watched you go in glory, garlanded,
     you cup the nymphs' warm waters in your hand,°
30   at home again in your adopted land.

Pythian Odes°

Pythian 3°

For Hieron of Syracuse,
Winner, Single Horse Race

Str. 1   I wish that Chiron – sovereign
    offspring of Philyra and Uranus's heir,°
     Cronus – if *my* tongue be allowed to pray
      a prayer heard everywhere –
     I wish that Chiron were alive today;
     not gone away, but ruling Pelion,
     a fearsome creature, but a friend to men;
     I wish that he could be as when
     he brought up that solicitous
10   artisan of the worn-out body's ease,
      the hero Asclepius,°
    who cured all kinds and colors of disease.

Ant. 1   Before his mother, Phlegyas's
    daughter, with help from Eileithyia, Nurse of Birth,°
     could bring her boy to term, she had to go
      to Hades under earth,

by Artemis's golden shafts laid low,
just as Apollo had contrived. (When Zeus's
children aim their anger, the blow hits.)
    But she, poor thing, had lost her wits;   20
    belittling their wrath, she shared
another's bed, in secret from her father,°
    although the flowing-haired
Apollo had already coupled with her

    and she was big with god's immaculate offspring.   *Ep. 1*
She couldn't bide her time until the marriage feast should bring°
the lifted voice of the wedding hymn and of the serenades
    which girls her age are thrilled to sing as daylight fades
and they assemble in a choir.   No, she succumbed to her desire
for the unknown and far away, as many have before.   30
    There is a vain light-mindedness prone to ignore
and disregard good things at hand, with distant ones in view,
    while chasing dreams that won't, and can't, come true.

    That mortal error caused the crisis,   *Str. 2*
and silken-robed, self-willed Coronis was misled
    when first the stranger came from Arcady
        and she slept in his bed.
The Vigilant One was not deceived. Though he
was off in Pytho's seat of sacrifices,
the shrine he rules forever, Phoebus knew,   40
    trusting his right opinion to
    the truest messenger, his mind
that knows all things. He does not suffer lies;°
    no man nor god can find
the words or deeds that will unsight his eyes.

    Then, when he knew her trick and sin   *Ant. 2*
with Ischys the interloper, and their ill-omened tryst,
    he sent his sister, with a rage upwelling
        that nothing can resist,
    to Lakereia, where the girl was dwelling°   50

beside Lake Boebias's edge. And then°
her fortune turned and cold fate came to cast her
down in the general disaster,
as with her many neighbors died.°
Sometimes a conflagration leaps from one
spark up a mountainside,
and a whole forest, great and deep, is gone.

Ep. 2   When the girl's relatives had laid her on the pyre,
and around her Hephaestus' hungry tongues were licking higher
60   over the pyre's wooden walls, 'Enough!' Apollo said,
'My soul can't bear to see my own son dead,
snuffed terribly in his mother's womb   with the hard justice of
her doom.'
He spoke, and in a single step had reached the child, and tore him
out of her body as the fires parted for him,
and took him to Magnesia, to the Centaur's cave, to learn
to heal the ills that make men throb and burn.

Str. 3   All those who came to him, their skin
blooming with sores, or cicatriced with hard steel-slashes,
or bruised by a rock a distant sling unloosed,
70   or feverish with hot flashes
in summer, or, in winter, blue from frost –
soothing the many agonies they were in,
he nursed them back to health; to some, he'd sing
sweet spells that eased their suffering,
and some sipped cures from a proffered cup;
for some, full-body ointments salved their pain;
and sometimes he took up
the knife, and helped them stand upright again.

Ant. 3   But profit even casts its spell
80   on wisdom. He too was enticed by the unmatched
incentive, pressed into his palm, of gold,
to bring a man, once snatched
by death, to life again. Then thunder rolled

and fire flashed from Zeus's hand; both fell
headlong, the breath knocked from their chests in one
    instant as their doom came down.
    We must not beg the gods for more
than what befits our all-too-mortal powers,
      while our poor wits ignore
what's at our feet, what sort of life is ours.   90

Do not, dear heart, pursue a dream of deathlessness,   *Ep. 3*
but drain the store of means and measures which you do possess.°
Yet if sagacious Chiron still were living in his cave,°
   and if my honeyed hymns could conjure up a salve
to charm his heart somehow, I would   persuade him to endow the
                                      good
men of today, whom fevers scorch and burn, with such another
    healer whose father was Apollo or his Father;
and then my ship would cleave the sea to the Sicilian coast,
    to Arethusa, Aetna and my host,°

      the king who rules in Syracuse –   *Str. 4*
kindly to citizens, to good men openhanded,   101
    a father for awed guests to muse upon.
      And I, if I had landed,
would have come bearing double benison:
golden good health and a victorious
    jubilee to adorn the laurels clipped
    when Pherenicus' speed outstripped
    the field at Pytho way back when.
And when I'd crossed the sea to where you are,
      I swear, I would have been   110
a light more luminous than any star.

    But as it is, I want to pray   *Ant. 4*
to the Great Mother, whose holy shrine is near my door –°
    that High One whom, with Pan, the girls most nights
      so musically implore.
If you can rightly plumb the depths and heights

of speech, you've learned from what the old ones say,
　　Hieron: that, for every good we're given,
　　　　two evils are dispensed by heaven.°
120　　　　Such blows the foolish fail to weather,
　　who are not able to endure with grace;
　　　　but better men fare better,
　　and wear their blessings bright upon their face.

Ep. 4　　Think what a share of happiness is yours: if good
　　luck ever smiles, it's on a prince who leads a multitude.
　　Not Aeacus' son Peleus or Cadmus, the gods' double,
　　　　though called the happiest of men, lived free from trouble –
although it's said of both heroes　　　that from beneath gold-
　　　　　　　　　　　　　　　　　　banded brows
　　the Muses sang the hymn when they were wed to their helpmates:
130　　Harmonia to Cadmus, in Thebes's seven gates,
　　and Peleus on Pelion to famous Thetis – she
　　　　who sprung from that shrewd Ancient of the Sea –°

Str. 5　　　　and the gods sat around their table,
　　and they, upon their golden thrones, beheld the presence
　　of Cronus' royal sons and daughters and
　　　　accepted wedding presents.
　　So Zeus's grace sufficed to countermand
　　their former agonies, and they were able
　　once more to make their spirits stand upright.
140　　　　Yet time soon brought to Cadmus' sight
　　three of his daughters' bitter end,°
　　and a good part of his contentment fled –
　　　　although Zeus did descend
　　to white-armed Semele in desire's bed.°

Ant. 5　　　　But Peleus's only boy,
　　whom deathless Thetis bore to him in Phthia, struck°
　　in battle by an arrow, gave up the ghost,

as with the pyre's smoke
the wails came rising from the whole Greek host.
If there are men so wise as to enjoy   150
what gifts they have from heaven, it is they
        whose feet are planted on Truth's Way.
The winds with their high-flying blasts
are always shifting, now this way, now that.
        No mortal gladness lasts
for long, when it comes down with its full weight.

To be small when constrained and great in grandeur's   *Ep. 5*
                                                sway –
so I aspire. I shall embrace the fortune of the day°
with mind and heart and serve it well with my own means and
                                                measures.
    And if a god should grant me wealth with all its pleasures,   160
I hope my future fame will be   a tower to posterity.
We hear Sarpedon's name and Nestor's ring from men's
        rapt lips in lines that echo thanks to the artisans,
the wise ones who made poems. The great songs publish and
                                                declare°
        a fame that lasts. But it is hard, and rare.

Pythian 8°

For Aristomenes of Aegina, Winner, Wrestling (Boys' Division), 446 BCE

O Calm, well-wisher, Justice's daughter,°   *Str. 1*
you who make great cities greater
        and hold the highest keys
        of wars and counsels, take this wreath
of honor won at Pytho by Aristomenes;
for you know when to bless
                            men with a gift of gentleness
and when to welcome gifts that men bequeath.

Ant. 1   When someone drives relentless spite
                        deep in his heart, you meet his might
10   roughly and force your brash
                        and overbearing enemy
                  into the bilge. Porphyrion was just so rash,°
            not knowing you'd prove his bane
                                    when he attacked. The sweetest gain°
                  is garnered when it's given willingly.

Ep. 1   But violence in time trips up all violent blustering.
            Neither hundred-headed Typhus nor the Giants' king°
                        could slip your grasp, for lightning struck them down;
                        Apollo's arrows also, whose good will°
                  welcomed Xenarces' son from Cirrha, with a crown°
20   of Mount Parnassus' laurel and a Doric festival.

Str. 2   Sheltered in the Graces' hands
                        this righteous island city stands°
                        touching the feats of glory
                        the Aeacids performed, her fame°
            unblemished from the first, extolled in song and story
            for heroes she has raised
                                    to pinnacles where they are praised
                  for winning contests, battles and acclaim.

Ant. 2   Her men, too, are preeminent,
                        but I can't raise a monument
30   with lyre and gentle singing
                        to all her virtues; that would bore
            and chafe my audience. Here at my feet comes springing
            the song I owe the last
                                    great honor, child, that you amassed:
                  my art will give it wings and let it soar.

Ep. 2   Following your uncles' steps, you don't disgrace their names,
            for Theognetus took the crown at the Olympic Games,°
                  Clitomachus, too, at the Isthmians.°

Your glory swells your clan's, and illustrates
Amphiaraus' riddle, when he beheld the sons°
at spearpoint hold their ground before Thebes of the seven gates;   40

    watching the Epigones come back   *Str. 3*
    again from Argos to attack,
        he said, as they fought on:
    'How clear a father's spirit shines
forth in his sons, with nature's light! I see my own,
Alcmaeon, as he wields
            the dappled dragon on his shield's°
    bright boss at Cadmus' gates in the front lines.

    'But for Adrastus, the hero who°   *Ant. 3*
    met with defeat his first time through,
        the omens now are better   50
    for his campaign, though not at home.
For he, alone of the Greek force, will have to gather
the bones of his dead son,
            but with the gods will soldier on
    and his whole host unscathed at last will come

'to Abas' spacious avenues.' So spoke, with prophet's sight,°   *Ep. 3*
Amphiaraus. I too hail Alcmaeon with delight,
    crown him with wreaths, splash him with melody,
    for en route to the navel of the earth,
    he – my neighbor, guard of all my property –
he met me with his gift of sight inherited at birth.°   60

    And you, Lord of the Long-Range Bow,°   *Str. 4*
    to whose bright shrine all peoples go
        in Delphi's lofty dell,
    where you bestowed, there at your seat,
    the best of joys; and earlier at home as well,
you gave on your feast day
            the Fivefold Crown to take away:°
    Apollo, everything that I may meet –

Ant. 4   with willing mind I pray to see
                       it all in proper harmony.
70   As Justice takes her place°
                       beside our band in joyful song,
          I ask the gods, Xenarces, not to grudge you grace,
          for many think that men
                                        who win without long discipline
                       are geniuses among the foolish throng

Ep. 4   and helm their lives with clever stratagems which they have
                                                              planned.
          But such things are not in men's power; a god grants them,
                                                         whose hand
                       now lifts one up and pins another down.
                       Compete with measure, Aristomenes.
                    At Megara and Marathon you hold the crown,
80   and home, at Hera's games, your hard work earned three
                                                            victories.

Str. 5   Onto four bodies from above
                       with violent thoughts you pounced, and strove.
                       For them, Pytho bestowed
                       no happy homecoming, no wreath;
                    no mothers' tears of joy, no welcome laughter flowed
          at their return. They slink
                                        down alleyways instead, and shrink
                       clear of their foes, clamped in disaster's teeth.

Ant. 5   But one who gains some new success
                       on wings of soaring manliness
90   and splendid hope takes flight
                       toward future deeds, for he has caught
                    a passion beyond wealth. In no time, man's delight
          bursts into bloom, but just
                                        as fast collapses in the dust,
                       shaken by a breeze, a shift in thought.

One day we live. What is someone? What is no one? A dream   *Ep. 5*
of a shadow, man; no more. But when the heavens shed their gleam,
     our life grows sweet and light shines over us.
     Dear Mother Aegina, safeguard this city's
voyage of freedom, with Zeus and with King Aeacus,
and Peleus, and noble Telamon, and with Achilles.°   100

Fragments from Other Genres

from *Hymn 1*

To Zeus°

29°

   Well: shall we hymn Ismenus River
or golden-spindled Melia, his mother,
or else the sacred Race of the Dragon, or
Cadmus, or Thebe in her deep-blue crown,
or Heracles and his all-daring power,
   or the delectable renown
of Dionysus, or the wedding of
white-armed Harmonia?

30

   Themis, who counsels only right,°
child of the Sky, first traveled on the light-
irradiated road from the deep sources
of ocean when the Fates escorted her
upward on the backs of golden horses
   to Mount Olympus' hallowed stair
at the wellspring of time, to be the wife
of Zeus the Savior, and she bore to him
the Seasons, each with a golden diadem,°
   truth-charged, bright with the fruit of life.   10

33c

Hail to you, heaven's seedling, love°
most intimately dear to the children of
Leto, whose locks are luminous as flame;
you, daughter of the deep, fixed on the breast
of the wide world, a miracle men name
        twice-holy Delos, while the Blest
which are upon Olympus call you star
of their blue firmament, so brightly far°

33d

For Delos in the early days was tossed
over the sea's face, buffeted by the gust
and countergust of every wind that blows,
till Leto, Coeus' daughter, desperate
because she felt the fast-approaching throes
        of birth, no sooner set her foot
on Delian soil than from the deep earth's bed
four column-drums with roots of adamant
rose straight and square, and held the pediment
10   of rock-hewn Delos riveted
upon their capitals, and made it fast.
And soon she was delivered, and at last
beheld the offspring of her blessedness

from *Paean 6*

For the Delphians at Delphi°

Str. 1   By Zeus who rules Olympus, I implore
                you, golden Pytho, famous for
                prophetic sight, and also pray
            the Graces and Aphrodite, that I may
                be welcome in this holy hour°
                as prophet of the Muses' power.

For when I heard Castalia's spate
run gushing from the brazen gate°
unushered by men's song and dance,°
I came to liberate your clan's   10
honor, and mine, from the unmusical°
abyss. As a child heeds his mother's call,
    I listened to my heart and made
    the journey to the holy glade
    and temple of Apollo, rife
    with coronals and festal life,
    where Leto's son loves to receive
    the hymns the Delphic maidens weave
here at the leaf-dark navel of the world,°
    pounding the ground with footsteps whirled   20
    in rhythm . . .

and what cause set the deathless ones at odds,   *Ep. 1*
    the gods are able to apprise   51
    those art and poetry make wise;
but mortals otherwise cannot find out.
    You virgin Muses past all doubt
    know all that is – that is your due,
    your thunder-clouded father's too,
    and Mnemósyne's – therefore
give me your ear. I long for nothing more
than honey's sweet distillate on my tongue,
    here at the gods' guest-feast among   60
    men come from far and wide to hallow
      Loxias Apollo.°

from *Paean 9*

For the Thebans°

Mother of vision, beam of the sun,   *Str. 1*
what have you, distant seer, done,
o highest of stars, who have found a way

to hide in the depths of the day?
Why have you plunged into helpless night
wisdom's road, and all human might,
as you steal swiftly out of sight?
Are you foreshadowing some dark surprise?
   By Zeus, I pray, swift charioteer,

10   that now
                somehow
you quell this universal fear:
o Lady, let it harmlessly allude

14   to Thebes's greater good! . . .

Ant. 1   But what do you mean? Is it some new war,

20   or the crops' collapse, or a blizzard more
brutal than words, or civilian gore
besmirching the city, or the huge outpouring
   of ocean rising to swamp the plain,
                each field
                congealed
with ice, or a summer torrential with rain;
or will you flood the planet, and replace
   mankind with some new race?

Dithyramb 2°

Heracles, or Cerberus

For the Thebans

Str. 1   Before now, dancers in the dithyramb
                slunk forth in single file,
and from their lips the hissing sigmas came

4   in false, discordant style . . .°
7   aware
            what kind of Bacchic rites are there
            among the sons of Uranus

10   beneath the sceptered sway of Zeus
filling his palace halls. Where Cybele,

Great Mother, shadows forth her majesty,
    the ritual onset
  is a whirling circle of tambourines,
  then clatterings of the castanet
and torchlight flickering under yellow pines.
And there the Naiads' cries go echoing,
    and crazy passions
    and ululations
echo as necks are tossed in the seething ring.   20
And there the thunderbolt breathes fire as it shakes
fast in the hand of Omnipotence; there shakes the spear
  of Ares, and Pallas' shield, immune to fear,
  seethes with the sibilance of a thousand snakes.°

Light comes the foot of Artemis, who stalks   *Str. 2*
    alone through wild environs,
now in the grip of Bacchus as she yokes
    her chariot with lions:
  even the savage herd entices
  the heart of holy Dionysus.   30
    And now I lift my voice,
  the Muse's herald and first choice,
  with words of wisdom to address
  the gorgeous dancing floors of Greece,
and to praise Thebes with mighty chariots laden,
where once the hand of the beloved maiden
    Harmonia, it is said,
  was wooed and won by the lofty wit
  of Cadmus, and the two were wed.
Zeus spoke. She heard his voice, and heeded it,   40
and bore a daughter famous the world over°

Dithyramb 4°

For the Athenians

Come join the dance, Oympians!
Come let your grace and glory pour
over our dancing floor,
as you approach the clouds of scent and citizens
thronging the city's navel and famed center,
the finely sculptured marketplace; oh enter
holy Athens, and receive
these garlands plaited violets weave,
these blooms of song spring nurses.

10 From Zeus first with a lambent play of verses
I come next to the god whom ivy tethers,
whom our hymns name Bull-Bellower and Huge Shouter,
the offspring of the loftiest of fathers
and Semele, Cadmus' daughter.°
Like all the great diviners, I
let no bright truth escape my eye.
The Seasons in their purple dresses throw°
open their rooms and usher forth the spring
nectar of blooms that sweetly grow and blow.

20 Now, now the violets are carpeting
the deathless earth with lovelinesses,
and roses brighten mortal tresses,
and echoing chants and dulcet pipe-songs spread
as dance greets Semele full-circleted.

Hyporchemes°

108a+b°

108a When god shows where to set forth from
on any enterprise, the route
runs straight to triumph's podium:
how loftily your labors will turn out!

For god can, from the depths of night,   *108b*
call forth the clean and uncorrupted light;
and can in shrouds of cloudy dark
conceal the day's pure spark.

109

The citizen who would increase
the general joy in sunlight and sweet weather
should seek illuminating Peace,
which makes men better,
and spurn uncivil strife, that bringer of wrath
and poverty, that nurse who ruins youth

110

To those who haven't been, war seems a dear
privilege; but those who know it watch it coming near
with nothing but pounding fear.

Scolia°

122°

Priestesses of Persuasion, dears   *Str. 1*
who with Corinthian opulence
will greet her many guests, and yours, and burn the yellow tears
of wood-fresh frankincense,
while high devotion wings you ever higher
to heavenly Aphrodite, mother of desire:

children, yours is the privilege   *Str. 2*
to pluck, in love's sweet vineyard, free
from all dishonor, the exquisite fruit of your green age.
For when Necessity   10
urges, all work is noble . . .

Str. 3   But I would know what the Isthmus's seigneurs will say of this
16   beginning I have given
                my banquet-song, whose honeyed phrases summon
                harmonies for women the people hold in common.

Str. 4   When gold is pure, the touchstone proves
20   its worth . . .°
21   Lady of Cyprus, here into your sanctuary's groves
                          Xenophon has led
                a flock of girls a hundred strong to grass,
            in glad thanksgiving that you brought his prayers to pass.

123°

For Theoxenus of Tenedos

Str.   Heart, you should pluck love's harvest in good time,
                not when you're past, but in, your prime;
                yet anyone who witnesses
                Theoxenus' sun-sparkle eyes
                        and does not feel
                        desire overspill
            must have a heart annealed of adamant or steel

Ant.   in frigid flame, coal-black; must be a man
                despised by the bright-eyed Cyprian,
10   or slave away, a drudge for cash;
                or with uxorious panache
                        plow nothing but
                        a single frigid rut.
            But I, in Aphrodite's warmth like the sunshot

Ep.   wax of the holy bee,
                        dissolve each time I see
            the fresh young bodies of the fresh young boys.
                And now, in Tenedos, is one
                Persuasion, Graciousness and Poise

delight to wait upon: 20
Hagesilas's charming son.

124a+b°

For Thrasybulus of Acragas°

Dear Thrasybulus, here: I'm sending you this little craft   124a
of lovely song for after you have eaten. May it sweeten
your spirited camaraderie and vivify each draft

of Bacchic grapes and Attic cups, and goad you to keep going.
For when the tedious weight of human pain begins to strain   124b
out of the heart, the seas turn gold and all alike go rowing

easily through abundance to a beach of make-believe,
where the have-nots have what they crave, and those who have

Threnoi (Dirges)

129°

and while night overshadows
the upper world, the sun shines on the lower
with its full power,°
and there, in red-rose-raddled meadows,
souls of the righteous have their residence
among the cool shade-canopies
of trees loaded with golden fruit, and trees
of frankincense;
and there they take their leisure,
some horseback-riding, some in training, some   10
absorbed in games or dice, while others strum
the lyre for their pleasure,
and flourishing takes root and blooms
amidst all this,
spreading an unadulterated bliss,

and sweet perfumes
suffuse the lovely landscape, for they never tire
of sacrifice,
and mingle every kind of spice
20   at the gods' altars while each beaconing fire
kindles still higher.

131b

for over every mortal frame
indomitable Death has staked his claim;
still, there's a likeness of our life which keeps
alive, and is the only thing the gods
have given of themselves. It sleeps
while we're awake, but, when the body nods,
in dream on dream it renders clear
the judgment, harsh or sweet, that's drawing near.

137°

Happy the man who sees, before he goes
below, the Mysteries; he knows life's course°
and end, and knows
its fountainhead is god, the primal source.

140d

What is god?
What isn't?

Bacchylides

Bacchylides (circa 520/10–450 BCE) was born in Iulis on the Cycladic island of Ceos (now Kea); his mother was the sister of the poet Simonides (pp. 120–33). Tradition held him to be Pindar's (pp. 134–64) younger contemporary and rival, though they were probably about the same age; as for the rivalry, that idea was probably derived (none too securely) from Pindar's poetry. They do at least seem to have competed for commissions: both poets wrote odes in praise of the Syracusan tyrant Hieron's victory in the horse race at the Olympic Games of 476 BCE (see Pindar's Olympian 1, p. 135, and Bacchylides' poem 5, p. 171), but only Bacchylides got the nod to eulogize Hieron's more prestigious Olympic chariot victory of 468 (see poem 3, p. 167); perhaps Hieron preferred the Ionian poet's easy fluency to the clotted sublimities of the Boeotian. The librarians of Hellenistic Alexandria edited Bacchylides' works in nine volumes: epinicians (victory odes), hymns, paeans (hymns to Apollo), dithyrambs (choral odes for Dionysus), *prosodia* (processional hymns), *partheneia* (maiden-songs), hyporchemes (dancing hymns), encomia (praise songs) and love songs (all genres also attested for Pindar, except the love songs). Almost nothing else is known of Bacchylides' life, except for a brief note in Plutarch that he did his best work while in exile in the Peloponnese. He probably did not outlive his latest datable ode, composed in 452 BCE, by very long.

Bacchylides may well have been the least influential major poet in this anthology, for the simple reason that he went almost completely unread for much of the twenty-three hundred or so years between his death and the turn of the twentieth century. He had little impact on subsequent generations: the poets of the later fifth and fourth centuries make no reference to him. He was rediscovered at Alexandria by Callimachus (pp. 255–81) in the mid-third century BCE; edited between 260 and 180 BCE, and included by the scholar Aristarchus of Samothrace, head of the great Library, in the canon of Nine Lyric Poets (see Note on Lyric, p. xiii); damned with faint praise in the first (or perhaps third) century

CE by the author of *On the Sublime*; and remained popular, at least in Egypt, until the middle of the fourth century CE – he was also a particular favorite of the emperor Julian the Apostate (330–63 CE). After that, the trail goes silent until his second rediscovery, by the papyrologists Bernard Grenfell and Arthur Hunt in 1896/7, among the many thousands of scraps they unearthed on the site of an ancient rubbish dump near Oxyrhynchus in Egypt. To this papyrus roll, now held at the British Museum, we owe the entire book of Bacchylides' victory odes (sixteen poems or fragments), the first half of his book of dithyrambs (fifteen poems or fragments) and sixty-six further fragments.

Yet, despite the importance of the find, the reception Bacchylides received was, once again, lukewarm. At the time, the great German philologist Wilamowitz wrote that we 'sought in him a great poet, who in the end did not quite materialize'. Again and again he was compared with Pindar, and found wanting. It's true that Bacchylides is easier to read. From Stesichorus (pp. 89–95) he inherited, and passed on to the Alexandrian poets, a Homeric approach to narrative – unlike Pindar, he does not jump excitedly around, but tells his stories chronologically and dramatically, with an un-Pindaric focus on characters' emotions. (The classicist Adam Parry describes his style as occupying 'a beautiful midway point between Homer and Pindar'.) His syntax is simple and straightforward, his language descriptive; he is fond of color, gesture and contrast; he loves epithets, and lays them on thick at important moments. Structurally, he is less elaborate than Pindar, and less inclined to call attention to his own mythical innovations. (It may be that his approach is a reaction to, or against, Pindar's complexities.) And yet we should not allow Bacchylides to fool us with his stylistic modesty: just because he is willing to be under-read does not mean he should be. Bacchylides' poetry may be simple, but it is built to last; that it almost didn't is no fault of his. We might even hope that his period of greatest influence remains ahead of him.

3

For Hieron of Syracuse, Chariot Race,
Olympic Games, 468 BCE°

Hail, Clio, hymn Demeter's name,°   *Str. 1*
Sicily's queen, where fruits abound;°
her Daughter's too, the violet-crowned,°
and, o profuse of sweetnesses, acclaim
    Hieron's each rapid horse
    galloping down Olympia's course

    beside wide-roiling Alpheus,°   *Ant. 1*
    flanked by Splendor as they sped,
    and Victory, which strides ahead,
further to glorify the prosperous   10
    son of Deinomenes, supreme°
    at winning garlands and esteem,

      at whose success a loud   *Ep. 1*
      cheer thundered from the crowd:
      o triply fortunate,°
      whose Zeus-apportioned lot
    and privilege is to command
    the greatest army in the land,
who will not hide, in night's black cerements,
      your towering affluence!   20

The consecrated shrines are brimming   *Str. 2*
with cattle sacrifice and feasts,
and kindliness of hosts and guests
brims in the streets, and a gold light is gleaming
    from intricate tripods that soar°
    on high and coruscate before

    the great precinct and temple doors   *Ant. 2*
    of Phoebus's devotion, where

the Delphians confer their care
30   beside Castalia's fountain and pure source.°
To god, to god, let glory wing.
There is no greater flourishing.

Ep. 2   Consider the high king°
of stallion-mastering
Lydia: when the decree
of Fate had finally,

through Zeus's might, been consummated,°
and Sardis had capitulated
to Persian hordes, the Lord of the Gold Lyre,
40   Apollo, from the fire

Str. 3   saved Croesus. Facing down a grim
day he had never hoped to see,
he would not wait for slavery
with wave on wave of tears to come for him.
And so in front of his bronze-walled
courtyard he ordered to be piled

Ant. 3   a pyre, and climbed it by the side°
of his beloved wife and pigtailed
daughters as they wept and wailed
50   hopelessly, and would not be mollified.
Now on the platform's top he stands
and to steep heaven lifts his hands

Ep. 3   and cries, 'O awful Source
of overweening force,
where is our human share
of heaven's thanks? And where
is Lord Apollo, Leto's son?°
My father's palace is undone;
The myriad [gifts I sent to Pytho once°
60   have garnered no response;]

the city's [sacked, and the marauder   *Str. 4*
Medes are in it, bent on slaughter;]°
the currents of Pactolus' water,
once eddying with gold, are red with murder;°
the women are – outrageousness! –
dragged from the sturdy palaces;

now things I used to hate delight me;   *Ant. 4*
oblivion alone is sweet.'
He ceased, and bade the servant set°
the wooden frame alight, and he moved lightly.   70
A cry leapt from his daughters' lips,
and mother-ward their fingertips°

went reaching, since the ending   *Ep. 4*
mortals can see impending
provokes the most despair.
But when the muscular
knot of flame came leaping on,
sparking with horror, Zeus sent down
a cloud like a black shroud over the light
and doused the fire's might.   80

No miracle exceeds the scope   *Str. 5*
of reason when a god's concern
dreams up and does it. Delos-born°
Apollo swooped and swept the old man up
north to the Hyperboreans°
with his slim-ankled daughters, since

his pious openhandedness   *Ant. 5*
had excelled all who went before
in sending holy Pytho more
and richer gifts. But of all those in Greece   90
alive today, there isn't one,
incomparable Hieron,

Ep. 5   so rash as to pretend
that he has, or could send
more gold to Loxias°
than you. Whoever has
not gorged himself on grudges must
acclaim you, warrior and [robust]
equestrian, who wield the courteous
100   sway [of the guest god,] Zeus,

Str. 6   and who enjoy the friendship of
103   the Muses decked in violet crowns . . .
106   Life is brief,

Ant. 6   and Hope, with ineffectual wings,
baffles our minds that live for one
day long. Admetus, Pheres' son,°
110   heard these words from Apollo, whose bowstrings
are strung for distance: you, since you
are mortal, ought to nourish two

Ep. 6   ideas: that you may
not see another day
beyond tomorrow's sun,
and that you may live on
for fifty years with wealth to spare.
Look for felicity in fair
and righteous action. For of all profit, this
120   provides the highest bliss.

Str. 7   The sense I speak shall find its way
to the mind primed to understand.
The deeps of air may not be stained;
seawater may not fester and decay;
gold is delight; and yet, to slough°
our winter of senescence off

and come again to the green glade   *Ant. 7*
    of youth once manhood has commenced,
    the law is adamant against.
Yes, but the light of greatness does not fade   130
    as bodies do; the Muse's power
    still tends the blaze. The fairest flower

    of blessing, Hieron,   *Ep. 7*
    you've shown to everyone.
    But silence will not shout
    the owed adornment out
for excellence, and as men tell
    your true deeds, they will hymn as well
my gift of honeyed harmony, and hail
    the Cean nightingale.°   140

5°

For Hieron of Syracuse, Winner,
Single Horse Race, Olympic Games, 476 BCE

O lord whom gracious fortune blesses°   *Str. 1*
    with rule of stallion-driving
Syracuse – whose wit assesses,
    as much as any living,
the life-enlivening gifts of art
    of the violet-crowned Muses
exactingly – relax your heart
    which Righteousness suffuses
and cares surround, and bend your mind
    hither, toward this hymn   10
bearing the lissome Graces' hand
    in its fine-woven trim,°
which now from Ceos, your guest-friend,°
    famed servant of the golden-
wreathed Urania, I send°
    the famed town you're extolled in.

The bottom of my heart rejoices
   to pour a flood of choicest

Ant. 1   praise for Hieron. On high°
20   with a rapid roll and glide
of great wings slicing the deep sky,
     the eagle, bird of wide-
reigning Zeus whose thunder roars,
     in the full swell of his power
serenely, confidently soars
     where little songbirds cower
and trill timidity. No height
     of earth is high enough
to stop or interrupt his flight,
30   no sea swollen so rough –
though it is weariless, the sea.
     Through void air without end
he aims his feathers' finery
     and rides the western wind,
conspicuous against the skies,
     and humans lift up eyes.

Ep. 1   Both that, and also this:
there are a thousand paths my hymn might take
     to praise your worthiness
40   for sable-braided Victory's sake°
and for the brazen-chested warlord, Ares,
     o lordly sons of Deinomenes.
For you, I hope that heaven never wearies
     of generosities.
        Gold-armed Dawn°
     lately gazed upon
the chestnut mane of that famous racer
Pherenicus, storm-outpacer,
       victorious
50   beside the widely roiling Alpheus,

and crowned in Pytho's sacred space.° *Str.* 2
 I swear and give my word,
hand on the ground, that in no race°
 yet has a horse out-spurred
his pole position as he shot
 straight to the final post;
no courser's dust yet soiled his coat.
 He gallops like the gust
of the North Wind as he obeys
 the jockey urging him on   60
to triumph, winning cheers and praise
 for welcoming Hieron.
Happy the man to whom god gives°
 a share in noble deeds;
who, envied by all comers, lives
 with all he wants and needs.
No earthbound mortal yet has had
 good only, and no bad.°

The story goes that once from slender-°   *Ant.* 2
 ankled Persephone's house°   70
the undefeatable son of thunder-
 fulminating Zeus,
Heracles, the gate-crusher, dragged
 up out of the lightless hole
a dog, his slavering maw tooth-jagged,°
 the unendurable
Echidna's awful whelp. And there,
 beside Cocytus swirling,
he saw the souls wracked with despair
 and suffering, like whirling   80
leaves in the teeth of the wind that ropes°
 along the sun-stunned height
of Ida's sheep-sustaining slopes.°
 One stood out, shedding light:
the shade of that spear-champion,
 Porthaon's bold grandson

Ep. 2   Meleager, bright
          in flashing arms. He had no sooner caught
              our wondrous hero's sight,
90   than fair Alcmene's son stretched taut
          the string of his great bow from hook to hook°
              until it twangled, and unlidded
          the cover of his quiver, and he took
              an arrow out, bronze-headed.
                  Then, eye to eye,
              that warrior ghost drew nigh
          to Heracles, and there addressed him,
              drawing on a deeper wisdom:
                  'Don't shrink and start,
100   son of great Zeus; be still and calm your heart.

Str. 3   It would be vain to launch a dread
                  arrow with your strong arm
          against these souls of the spent dead;
                  they can do you no harm.'
          He spoke; Amphitryon's lordly breed°
              answered him, astounded:
          'What god or mortal raised a seed
                  like you? Where were you tended?
          Who cut you down? How long until
110   Hera in her fair
          ceinture demands he come to kill
                  me too? But that affair
          we must leave up to Pallas' whim,°
                  She of the Golden Locks.'
          Then Meleager answered him
              with tears streaking his cheeks:
          'To counter the gods' purposes
                  for earthborn mortals is

Ant. 3   a hard, hard thing to do. If this
120   weren't true, bloom-decorated,
          majestic, white-armed Artemis

might have been placated
and dropped her wrath when Oeneus,
   expert in spur and saddle,
my father, offered sacrifice°
   of goats and red-backed cattle
in great abundance. But the grudge
   was lodged deep in her core;
the virgin goddess would not budge.
   And so she sent a boar,°   130
flood-fulsome, a huge, ruthless brute,
   to Calydon's lovely plain,
who tusked the vine rows up by the root.°
   Then many sheep were slain;
and of the many men who crossed
   its path, all, all were lost.

   'For six days, without rest,   *Ep. 3*
we waged a wretched war – we, the amassed
   Aetolians, Greece's best –°
to kill it, on and on. At last,   140
when deity gave the victory to us,°
   we turned our thought to burying
our comrades gutted by the thunderous
   terribly charging thing.
   And among others
   were my two bravest brothers,
dear Agelaus and Ancaeus,
beloved of my heart, Althaea's
   children, raised
in Oeneus's hall which all have praised.   150

   'But murderous fate made plans to slaughter   *Str. 4*
   still more before it stopped.
For Leto's fire-minded daughter,°
   the Huntress, had not dropped
her wrath. We fought the battle-tried
   tough Curetes, on and on,°

over the fire-colored hide.
　　　And I cut many down,
including my mother's brothers, quick
160　　　　　Iphiclus, good Aphares,
strong runners both. But in the thick
　　　of battle, iron Ares,
heartless, does not specify
　　　who is or is not a friend;
blindly the spears and arrows fly,
　　　the enemy is thinned,
and in the melee, death diffuses
　　　however the god chooses.

Ant. 4　　　'One wretched woman, fire-minded,
170　　　　　gave none of that a thought:
Thestius' daughter, my grief-blinded
　　　mother, who did not
blanch to devise my death, or flinch:
　　　from the decorative chest
she took the kindling into which
　　　my swift doom was compressed
and lit a flame, and let it burn.
　　　For so the Fates had spun
that, when it was consumed, my turn
180　　　　　and term of life was done.°
Then, I was killing Clymenus,
　　　a youth at the height of his powers,
exquisite son of Daipylus.°
　　　I'd caught him in front of the towers –
the Curetes were on the run
　　　back to the ancient town

Ep. 4　　　　'of Pleuron, their strong fort.°
I felt life's sweetness ebb from me, and pass;°
　　　my strength and breath grew short.
190　　　And then I, wretched, wept, alas,
and exhaled life, and left my youth behind.'

They say that day was the only one
when, pitying the lot of humankind,
    the son of Amphitryon –
      whom no war-shout
    has ever struck with doubt
or troubled with emotion yet –
felt teardrops make his eyelids wet.
    He answered, torn:
'Best is for mortals never to be born,°   200

    'never to see the sunlight pierce   *Str. 5*
      their darkness. But what way
forward is there in shedding tears?°
      Better instead to say
the next exploit that we intend
      and do it. Tell me, come,
does Oeneus, the war god's friend,
      have in his royal home
a torch-bright, still-unmastered daughter
      of noble build, like yours?   210
For I would gladly wish to wed her.'°
      That spirit tried in wars,
brave Meleager, answered, 'Yes.
      I left Deianira there,°
her neck lit up with loveliness,
      fresh still, still unaware
of the gold touch of the Cyprian
      who so ensorcells men.'

    Now let your well-made chariot,   *Ant. 5*
      white-armed Calliope,°   220
halt here: sing heaven's king, begot°
      of Cronus, his Majesty
Olympian Zeus, and sing the course
      of inexhaustible
Alpheus, and Pelops' force,
      and Pisa, where at the full°

height of his fame and racing powers
   Pherenicus galloped on
and brought to Syracuse's towers
   and conquering Hieron
230
a leaf from gracious fortune's tree.°
   We must, with both our hands,
heave off ill will and jealousy,
   and praise – so Truth demands –
whatever mortal should succeed
   at doing some great deed.

Ep. 5   A man once, a Boeotian,
the honeyed Muses' servant, Hesiod,
   aptly expressed this notion:
240
   'Who earns the good regard of god
will also find that mortals praise his name.'°
   Yes, it was easy to persuade
my tongue to send these words freighted with fame,
   these words which have not strayed
    from the just road,
   to Hieron's abode;
the roots they nourish will produce
a crown of joy. All-Father Zeus,
   perpetuate
250
this house in peace which nothing can negate.

17°

Paean for the Ceans at Delos

Str. 1 The ocean-colored prow was knifing toward
   Crete, and it held on board
twice-seven young ones, splendid Ionians,°
   and Theseus, who fearlessly stands
   wherever spears are thudding,
and the ship, full sails aflash in the sun, was scudding
   before the northerly breezes surging

at aegis-wielding Athena's august urging.°
But Minos's heart was throbbing under the tight
    grip of the appetite-   10
wreathed Cyprian, at whose godhead
the whole world shudders in a kind of dread.
    The girl was there; the king was weak
    to keep his hand back any more;
    he touched the white skin of her cheek,
    and Eriboea shouted for°
    Pandion's heir, in his bronze plate,°
Theseus, who saw and stared, irate,
    eyebrows furrowing icily
    while his heart split in agony.   20
He spoke: 'O son of unexampled Zeus,
        this is abuse!
    Unholy urges overwhelm
    your heart; you are not at the helm.
Don't perpetrate this arrogant attack.
        Hold back.

'Whatever portion almighty Fate has given   *Ant. 1*
    us by the will of heaven,
duly tipping the Scales of Justice, we
    shall welcome it as our destiny   30
    no matter what day it
arrives. But don't indulge this importunate
    gross hankering. For even if
the mother who bore you under Ida's cliff°
was Phoenix's child, wide-famed for love, nonpareil°
    in power to beguile,
    and Zeus himself was your dear father;
still, Poseidon and rich Pittheus's daughter°
    were joined, and I am whom she bore,
    after the Sea King went to lift   40
    the veil of woven gold she wore,
    the violet-braided Nereids' gift.
Therefore, your Majesty, at pain

of groans to come, I urge you to abstain
   from force. I would not gaze upon
   the kindly light of the deathless Dawn
again, if I should let you harm one hair
     on these youths here,
   with overtures that they oppose.
50   Before that, we will come to blows,
and then who wins between us, and who loses,
      god chooses.'

Ep. 1   So spoke the hero, bold with spears,
   and all on board were struck with awe
   at his sheer brazenness and fierce
forthrightness. But the son-in-law
   of Helius seethed with bitter anger,°
   and wove a novel machination.
   He said, 'O Zeus, my father, stronger
60   than strong, give ear. If the Phoenician
   maiden with those arms like snow
   bore me to you, now crack the skies
with lightning's flickering flame-haired glow –
   a sign that all can recognize.
You, Theseus – if Aethra of Troezen bore you to
earth-shattering Poseidon, into these blue
    depths throw yourself, and bring
     this golden ring
   bright on my finger, sumptuous,
70   back to the light. Now, to your father's house
    boldly go under,
   and Cronus' son, the Lord of Thunder,
   Ruler of All, will make it clear
whether this prayer of mine has reached his ear.'

Str. 2   And Zeus at the height of power heard his prayer.
    He found it pure, and fair,
and for Minos his dear son chose to engender
   a brilliant, overwhelming splendor

and let, for all to see,
his lightning fly. The hero who fearlessly   80
    stands in the press of war caught sight
of the omen and was smitten with delight.
He lifted both his hands to the glory of heaven
        and spoke: 'What Zeus has given
    me, Theseus, is past dispute.
Now, take your plunge into the snarling throat
    of sea, and let your father, Lord
    Poseidon, son of Cronus, stoke
    your glory, not to be ignored
    through the deep-forested earth.' He spoke,   90
    and Theseus did not hesitate,
but stood on the sturdy stern deck and leapt straight
    into the sanctum of the sea,
    which opened for him willingly.
The son of Zeus beheld, and was astounded.
        Still, he commanded
    the ship rigged out with expertise
    to hold its course before the breeze,
while Fate charted its own tack, had its own ending
        impending.   100

The timber scuddingly kept on running, fast   *Ant. 2*
        ahead of the northerly gust
urging it onward. And that whole youthful crew
    from Athens was terribly shaken to view
        the ocean wave close over
their hero's head, and their lily eyes were aquiver
    with tears of grievous apprehension,
dreading the worst. But down to his father's mansion,
the Lord of Horses, great Theseus was riding°
        on the backs of the salt-abiding   110
    dolphins, and he rapidly°
arrived at the gods' palaces in the sea.
    And there amazement makes him dumb
    to witness the resplendent girls

of blessed Nereus, as from°
their glistening bodies brilliance purls
like flame, and on their hair, around
their brows, gold-woven coronets are wound;
joy fills their hearts and overbrims

120   as they waltz lightly on fluent limbs.
And there he saw his father's cherished bride,
superb ox-eyed
Amphitrite in those always
charmingly appointed hallways,
who swathed his shoulders in sea-colored royal
apparel

Ep. 2   and set a circlet, dark with roses,
impeccable, on his thick-curled head,
which Aphrodite, whose sly poses

130   beguile, gave her when she was wed.
No mortal of sound wisdom should
think anything the Powers do
incredible – for now he stood
hard by the shapely stern, and oh!
what hopes he dashed, how he upset
Cnossus' king and general,°
emerging from the sea unwet,
provoking wonder in them all
as the gods' gifts on his bright body shone,

140   and the girls of Athens, each with a splendid throne,
in newly minted joy let out
a jubilant shout,
and the sea made a joyful noise,
and all the young men there with lovely voice
lifted their paeans.
Now may these choirs of the Ceans,
o Lord of Delos, warm your heart,
and let the rain of grace from heaven start.

19°

For the Athenians

The paths are numberless which wind   *Str.*
through songs ambrosia interfuses,
when a man holds within his mind
the gifts of the Pierian Muses;
and with their eyes like violets
the Graces bearing coronets°
come shedding honor on his songs like dew.
    Now, lauded ingenuity
    of Ceos, come and weave for me°
and gorgeous, god-loved Athens something new.   10
    You are Calliope's elect,°
    whom she has singled out and decked
    with prizes better than the rest;
therefore the road you travel will be best.
Once, out of Argos' stallion country, sped
the precious cow, the child of Inachus,
rose-fingered Io, led along by Zeus°
    whose sway is wide and deep; she fled

from Argus' eyes that never rest,   *Ant.*
    vigilant from every quarter,°   20
    to whom the high and mightiest
    gold-robed queen Hera gave the order,
    without the balm of sleep or bed,
    to keep watch on that cow whose head
blossomed with horns. And not in broad daylight
    nor in the nighttime's holy shade
    could Hermes, Maia's son, evade
the sentry Argus' ever-watchful sight.
    Now, whether Argus, void of mirth,°
    the son of Giant-birthing Earth,°   30
    had his life snuffed by a stone flung
from Zeus' quicksilver herald's hand (no tongue

can compass all the pain the gods intend),
or if the Pierian Muses' melodies
finally gave his ceaseless labors ease,
    lulling his eyes shut in the end,

Ep.   for me the securest path
        runs straight to the aftermath,
    when Io to the flowery Nile
40   came with a gadfly on her tail,
and there gave birth to Epaphus
the son of Zeus, the glorious
monarch of the linen-dressed
Egyptians, honored past the rest°
for fathering the greatest line of men:°
Agenor, who sired Cadmus; Cadmus then
in Thebes of the seven gates sired Semele,
        and she
    was mother of holy Dionysus,
50   at whose approach each Bacchant rises,
    lord of the radiant reveling,
for whom our choirs decked in garlands sing.

from Fragment 4°

Paean to Apollo at Asine

Str. 3   For mortals it is Peace gives birth°
62   to wealth, which magnifies their worth;
in Peace the honeyed tongues of music bloom,
    and flaxen tongues of flame consume
65   bull-shanks and fleecy sheep-thighs for the taste
of gods, at altars art and skill have graced;
in Peace the young men concentrate their passion
on exercise, reed pipes and celebration,
    while iron shield-grips shield the plain
    brown spider toiling at her skein,

and two-edged sword-blades and the thrust-   *Ant. 3*
   sharp points of spears grow dull with rust . . .   72
Nowhere the trumpet's bronze cacophony   75
is heard, nor do the well-sealed eyelids see
the honeyed hush of sleep despoiled in strife
at dawn, whose light breaks only to assuage.
   Street-feasts and revels never tire,
   and lovely love songs rise like fire.

Fragment 20b

Encomium for Alexander, Prince of Macedon°

Lyre, leap down from your peg! Don't linger,
clear-throated, seven-noted singer.°
Into my hands! I'm spreading the splendor
of the Muses' golden wing over Alexander,

   the toast of every Twentieth dinner,°
   when delicious duress kindles the tender
   hearts of the young as their goblets hover
and Aphrodite's promise makes them quiver,

   mixing with Dionysus' favor,
   who fills their thoughts with soaring fervor: 10
   straightway they're sacking metropolises
and lording it over entire populaces

   while gold and ivory gleam in their houses
   and on the bright ocean a fleet of scows is
   speeding from Egypt with wheat and lucre –
for these are the kinds of dreams that absorb each drinker.°

The Classical Period (479–323 BCE)

THE NEW MUSIC

After Orpheus was torn limb from limb, the myths tell us, his four-stringed lyre and severed head, still singing, went rolling down the River Hebrus (now the Maritsa) and out to sea, finally washing ashore at the city of Antissa on Lesbos. Fishermen found the lyre and gave it to Terpander, a native of Antissa, who added three strings and founded a genre of musical performance called *citharoedia* (singing to cithara accompaniment). Competing before a festival crowd, often for quite exorbitant prizes, the Terpandrean *citharode* would perform one of eight or ten *nomoi*, or 'nomes' (pronounced 'gnomes'). Nomes were somewhat like jazz standards, except that they were less tune than template; they had a fixed harmonic and rhythmic character and associated musical motifs, but no prescribed melody or lyrics. To accompany the music, citharodes would often select (or create) texts: frequently, these would be heroic narratives, especially episodes from Homer or the *Homeric Hymns*, or stories from Stesichorus (pp. 89–95) and elsewhere. As in jazz or classical Indian raga, the requirements of the *nomos* left plenty of room for original expression and improvisation.

In practice, citharodes were the rock stars of the ancient world, but, in origin, they were something even more: bringers not only of musical but also of political harmony, *eunomia*, 'law and order' – 'law' being the root sense of the Greek word *nomos*. Here, too, Terpander was a pioneer. In the seventh century BCE, he traveled from Lesbos to Sparta, and, in 676, he founded and triumphed in the musical competitions of the Carneia, the most ancient and prestigious citharodic contest, held yearly as part of a Spartan festival in honor of Apollo. Sparta had fallen into unrest, and Terpander's gift of good musical order helped restore *eunomia* in the polity as well. Terpander came to be revered at Sparta as a second lawgiver, a musical version of Lycurgus, the semi-legendary figure famous for drawing up the Spartan constitution; thereafter, in Terpander's honor, citharodes from Lesbos always performed first at the Carneia, and they usually won. A line from Sappho (pp. 38–54) proves that the primacy of Lesbos' musicians had become proverbial: 'Superior, as the songster from Lesbos is to all others from elsewhere.'

Enter the Classical era – conventionally dated from the Greeks' defeat of Persia in 479 to the death of Alexander the Great in 323 – and Timotheus of Miletus, the Classical world's most famous, or infamous, citharode (pp. 204–12). This period, which saw the rise and fall of democratic Athens, and has received its name thanks to the efflorescence of specifically Athenian literature – drama, oratory, history and philosophy – was not, however, rich in lyric poetry, for reasons that will become clear. This was an era in which new modes of performance were beginning to take over from the old-fashioned lyric of Simonides (pp. 120–33), say, or Pindar (pp. 134–64). Much of the style and many of the strategies of the Archaic lyricists we met in the last section had been subsumed and incorporated into the new synthesis of Attic drama (of which our earliest extant example, Aeschylus' *Persians*, was produced in 472 BCE), while the construction of civic identity, once the job of poetry, had fallen mainly to public oratory in the courts and assemblies. Instrumental music had gained in popularity, thanks in large part to the famous piper (*aulete*) Pronomus of Thebes. Before Pronomus, one instrument had been required for the Dorian mode, another for the Phrygian or the Lydian; but he now invented a device to allow a single pair of pipes (*auloi*, singular *aulos*) to modulate between modes.

To keep up with the pipers, citharodes introduced innovations of their own, in a movement now known as 'the New Music'. To match the versatility of the *aulos*, they added strings to the cithara; now they, too, could modulate between harmonies and modes, which they did with a verve that appalled traditionalists. The last great Lesbian citharode, Phrynis of Mytilene, developed a form of 'free verse' (*apolelymenon*), doing away with regular, recurring melodies and rhythms (the triadic form of Stesichorus, Pindar, and Bacchylides, pp. 165–85) for the sake of local embellishments and expressive effects. There were now long passages of imitative music – that is, music which attempted to mimic the sound and character of natural and human phenomena, for example by using dissonance to evoke storms or battles. Singing became actorly: now comic, now tragic, each performer was a one-man ensemble cast. In earlier lyric, musical settings were mostly simple enough that they could be reperformed at the aristocratic symposium – even Pindar and Bacchylides must have enjoyed a fair amount of reperformance – but this was professional music; amateurs could not play it. The distance from the old-style lyric of Simonides to the New Music of Timotheus is similar to that from *Eine Kleine Nachtmusik*, which Mozart composed to be pleasantly performable throughout the drawing rooms of Europe, to the histrionics of Liszt, impossible to play except by the virtuoso in concert.

Timotheus' most famous performance was surely the debut of his new nome, the *Persians* (p. 205), heavily influenced by Aeschylus' fifty-plus-year-old play of the same name, though with plenty of modern innovations of its own. The debut likely took place in Athens, perhaps at the Great Panathenaea – the major Athenian civic festival in honor of Athena, held once every four years starting in 566 BCE. The present year, we will imagine, is 410 BCE. The city is at war with Sparta, which will end crushingly six years later – but, in this window of time, there is still room for hope. The audience are crowded into the Odeion of Pericles, a concert hall originally built with timbers from the Persian ships taken by the Athenians in the great naval victory at Salamis in 480 BCE. The citharode (as we know mostly from depictions in vase-paintings) wears a rich purple robe falling straight to his slippered feet, his shoulders draped with a gold-embroidered mantle. In his left arm he holds a splendid concert cithara, made of ivory, broad and heavy, with a resonant sounding-board, while in his right hand he raises aloft the ivory plectrum with which he will strike his music from the strings. From the bottom of the sound box hangs a lush cloth designed to billow hypnotically as his body sways. On his hair (a shock of red, much-mocked) is a gold-wrought olive crown, an advertisement of previous victories.

The crowd, far from bating their breath, may be actively hostile – Timotheus had already run afoul of the authorities at the Carneia, and we are told that he had been hissed during an earlier performance. He has at least one partisan in the crowd, however: no less a personage than the tragedian Euripides, very old by now, who, it is reported, 'recognized how great [Timotheus was] in this branch of art', and may even have helped compose the words to the *Persians*. Perhaps, perhaps not – but

Timotheus is the man on stage. His plectrum falls, the first note sounds, and the song begins to cast its spell. Gradually, whether thanks to the innovative music, the riveting delivery or the power and novelty of the poetry, the posture of the crowd transforms from resistance to enchantment. As the music tightens its grip, they listen more and more with their bodies – clapping and shouting, feeling the action physically and miming it. The music is emotional, the matter patriotic, the diction 'dithyrambic' – aggressively novel, straining Greek to its limits, full of weird kennings and compound epithets. There is no aesthetic detachment in this crowd. They are entranced, physically, mentally and emotionally. In the end, the contest is no contest: Timotheus wins in a landslide.

At least one man, however, may have been in that crowd who was not won over, a writer to whose life and work all of Western philosophy has justly been called a footnote – perhaps the first person to write the word *philosophia*, meaning 'love of wisdom'. As we saw already in the introduction to the Archaic period (p. 4), Plato's was no longer the wisdom of the poets; indeed, he was to be the inaugurator of a new rationalism which, in time, would prove staggeringly consequential. Already isolated from the crowd's enthusiasm by hard-won habits of mind, Plato would have taken in Timotheus' performance from an ironic, contemptuous distance. Of course, much of that contempt was run-of-the-mill elitism, the leisured aristocrat's dismissal of all things lowbrow, demotic and professional. Yet when Plato would later write (at 'white heat', as the scholar Eric Havelock has speculated) the polemical tenth book of his *Republic*, in which poets are evicted once and for all from the just society, there was something bigger and deeper at work than mere class snobbery.

Lurking in the background to Plato's famous quarrel with poetry, Havelock has detected what might be termed 'epistemic warfare': not merely a struggle between rival pedagogies, but a critical stage in the forging of the modern mind. For Plato, poetic song was a technology of mind-control, which could seduce and subject the individual intelligence to the unconsidered sway of collective consciousness. He responded with a mind-altering strategy of his own: dialogues designed not so much to expound a new educational system as to be one. Plato did not wish merely to persuade his fellow Athenians; he wanted, literally, to change their minds.

In post-Enlightenment democracies, it has often been taken for granted that the goal of education is to teach 'critical thinking', which we might describe as the ability to distinguish a proposition's beauty (or ugliness) from its truth (or falsehood). In oral poetry, by contrast, beauty is both the guarantor of truth and the vehicle of its conveyance: it is as if delicious food were understood not only to be appetizing but also, by *virtue* of being delicious, sure to be healthy. That such a concept of veracity strikes us as patently false belongs, I would suggest, to the achievement of Plato. His conception of 'forms' as timeless ideas with greater reality than the physical world, which merely imitates them; his insistence on abstracting concepts such as 'Goodness' or 'Justice' from the web of associations, aphorisms and traditions in which they were enmeshed, and considering them in splendid isolation, as concepts whole in themselves: these constituted a wholesale assault on the contingent and culturally specific mode of knowing which song culture – that culture whose storage of knowledge and experience depended on the mnemonic device of sung poetry – had inculcated. For one raised under the old regime, to read Plato's works carefully was to emerge changed, endowed with a power of abstraction sufficient to dismantle the mental edifice of the existing culture and melt it clean away. Still more importantly, from this anthology's point of view, it was also to find oneself newly endowed with a conception of poetry not as beautiful truth but as potentially delusive enchantment – and newly equipped to recognize and resist the greater part of its deceptions.

It is a paradoxical consequence of Plato's success that few Platonists, from Plotinus through Shelley to our own day, have felt the need to follow him in his crusade against poetry. Indeed, his victory was so complete that, when he won his rationalizing war, it was no longer easy to see what he had been fighting against, because it had, in a sense, ceased to exist. Minds had indeed changed; the beast was defanged, the tiger turned into a house cat. Poetry was now an aesthetic endeavor, rather than an existential one; a high-toned entertainment, not a drug that hijacked the mind and body.

Of course, Plato was not the only thinker in the fifth and fourth centuries BCE moving away from the collectivism of song culture in a more critical and individualistic direction: perhaps he only finished what Simonides had begun. Simonides, unusually for his time, had struck an ironic attitude toward conventional wisdom, and had had no patience for its typical contradictions (see the introduction to Simonides, pp. 120–21).

The sophists, too – those itinerant teachers of rhetoric and manipulation who came in for a drubbing in Plato's dialogues – had been teaching criticism and cynicism as avenues of exploitation for a while now, so the countercultural winds were blowing Plato's way. Perhaps his triumph had been inevitable from the beginning, ever since the Greeks adopted and adapted from Phoenicia the original tool of abstraction, the Greek alphabet (see the introduction to the Archaic period, p. 4). Literacy had become widespread – is it surprising that Plato's epistemic revolution should have followed the written word, as crops follow the plow?

The significance of Plato's views for the history of Greco-Roman poetry was twofold, though it did not begin to emerge until at least fifty years after his death, and in faraway Alexandria: city of scholarship, home to antiquity's most storied library. First, while Plato's critique of poetry mostly did not impact the ongoing reception of Homer, it clung to Timotheus, as well as to other poets of his generation like Phrynis of Mytilene and Cinesias of Athens; they receive precious little praise from our sources, and though the librarians of Alexandria could have chosen to edit and publish them, they did not. In their eyes, the illiterate crowds who followed the citharodes must have seemed little more than mobs – hardly (they may have thought) a contemporary expression of the same phenomenon that had surrounded the exalted Homer and Stesichorus. As such, this era of lyric poetry, the Classical period, is scantily attested in the remains that have come down to us.

Second, and more importantly, the poets who came after Plato – at least the ones whose work has survived and whom we consider the major writers of their age, the scholar-poets of Alexandria – had all read him. Plato's works and the tide of the times had not just done away with the oral poetic mindset; they had rendered it invisible – or, if not invisible, then at least embarrassingly demotic and un-chic. Song culture was as alien to the scholarly elite of Alexandria as it is to us. For them, poetry had become a less totalizing, more intellectual experience, approached mainly through reading and writing. This thoroughgoing adoption of book culture would have profound implications for the kind of verse these influential *philologoi* (lovers of words) scribbled down in their erudite enclave, while the unread citharodes of Alexandria, Timotheus' heirs, still swayed the untutored throngs in the enraptured streets.

Timocreon of Rhodes

Timocreon (early fifth century BCE), from Ialysus on Rhodes, was a poet, pentathlete, and playwright of the Old Comedy, best known for his attacks against the eminent, and eminently attackable, Athenian general Themistocles. Themistocles was an Athenian patriot and popular politician whose low birth and demagogic tactics rankled aristocrats, even as his advocacy of Athenian naval power led directly to the first major victory of the Greeks over the Persian king Xerxes, in the sea-battle at Salamis in 480; later, however, Themistocles' anti-Spartan machinations resulted in his ostracism and exile. At any rate, Timocreon's single-mindedness resembles both Archilochus' fixation on Lycambes (p. 5) and Hipponax's on Bupalus (p. 114) – though, unlike Lycambes and Bupalus, Themistocles is an indubitably historical figure.

In antiquity, Timocreon was branded a 'Medizer' – that is, a partisan of Persian rule, and a traitor to the Greek cause. The tag implies individual choice – as if Timocreon had weighed the alternatives of freedom and slavery and chosen the latter. Such labeling, while effective as slander, obscures the fact that by 480 BCE the Rhodians, whether they liked it or not, had been under Persian control for some time; it is at least plausible that, for an ambitious Rhodian Greek of the period, the path of prestige and advancement ran not through Athens but to the Persian capital, Susa. This may point toward the reality behind one colorful anecdote about Timocreon, which relates that, in a visit to the Persian court, he showed off his prowess before the assembled worthies by beating up a bunch of expendable flunkies and then continuing to punch the air: he may only have been doing the sort of thing ambitious Rhodians often did (albeit in his own inimitable way).

Most of Timocreon's work is lost; all of his poems that have survived did so because Plutarch quoted them in his *Life of Themistocles*. According to classicist Eva Stehle, they belonged to a 'shared liturgy among banqueters of certain persuasions' – those 'persuasions' being anti-Themistoclean or anti-Athenian (which is not to say that Timocreon's

vendetta against Themistocles lacked its own very personal flavor).
Timocreon's, finally, is a voice from one of the forgotten byways of history, speaking for many Greeks who, for whatever reason, threw their
lot in with the Persian king and were shown by later events to have
chosen poorly.

727°

You there might want to praise Pausanias;
Xanthippus, you; you, Leotychidas.
    Me, I like Aristides. He's°
    the best man the Athenian state
has yet exported, since Themistocles,
    reviled by him, gained Leto's hate –°

cold-blooded, double-dealing, two-faced bastard,
whose heart a crooked, silvery payoff mastered
    not to restore Timocreon,
10   his host and friend, to his old haunt,
Ialysus. Three silver talents – done! –
    and he sailed straight to Hades' taint.

Some he restored wrongfully; some his navy
drove off; some he murdered. Stuffed with gravy,°
    ridiculous, he sold his cold
    meat to the whole Corinthian strip;°
    they prayed they never would behold
that prick again, and ate, and filled him up.°

729°

Well, well! Timocreon is not
the only one whose tail was docked,
who 'pledged allegiance to the Medes';
there's lots of other 'good-for-nothings'!
And lots of other foxes, too.

731°

Would that none had caught your scent,
purblind Wealth, on sea or land,
or on the Asian continent!
Would that you had been constrained
in Acheron or Tartarus's pit!
The source of mortal suffering? You're it.

Elegy 10°

That bunk that blew in from Ceos? I thought it stunk.
I thought it stunk like hell, that Cean bunk.

Ion of Chios

Ion of Chios (born circa 490–480 BCE) flourished during the so-called *Pentekontaetia*, the 'fifty-year period' between the Persian and Peloponnesian wars (479–431), and died in the 420s, the first decade of the war with Sparta. He was a vastly prolific writer of poetry and prose, who impressed later authors, such as Callimachus (pp. 255–81), with his *polyeideia* (proficiency in many genres). Known mostly as a tragedian, he also composed satyr plays, comedies, dithyrambs, epigrams, paeans, drinking songs (*scolia*), encomia (praise poems), elegies, epic poems, prose histories and philosophical works (he was a card-carrying Pythagorean). In his prose *Epidemiai* (*Visits*), he may have invented the genre of memoir; there he described various encounters with the leading lights of the day, both at home on Chios, and in Athens, where, having first come as a very young man, he got to know the statesman Cimon, whom he liked, as well as Aeschylus, Sophocles, Socrates and others. He was cool toward Cimon's chief political rival, Pericles, perhaps because both he and Pericles were in love with the same woman, a certain Chrysilla. Their mutual antipathy could also have been political: Ion and Cimon were both admirers of Sparta, whereas Pericles' aggressively 'Athens First' policy eventually led to the Peloponnesian War. The mere handful of fragments surviving from Ion's vast body of work justify one ancient historian's characterization of him as 'bibulous' and given to tippling. Ion of Chios is not to be confused with the eponymous Ion, a rhapsode from Ephesus, met in the dialogue by Plato.

744

impossible
boy, whose face is like a bull,°
young and not young,
best escort of the Loves who trail behind,

uproarious; by whom our thoughts are flung
aloft, o wine, the master of mankind.

745°

We waited for the star of dawn,
                    the air-traverser,
white-winged precursor
                                of the sun.

746°

His body pummeled, pummeled in each eye,
        he does not falter; he is brave.
As his strength ebbs, he lifts his battle cry –
        he'd rather die than be a slave.

Elegy 26

for wise old Dionysus with his thyrsus°
made wine the subject of all kinds of verses
through all of Greece, at every princely spread,
since the first vinestalk raised its clustering head
up from the earth and stretched luxuriant limbs
skyward, and from the thickly budded stems
burst children, silent till they loudly plopped
on top of each other. When the ructions stopped,
we milked the juice with grateful pain – self-grown
elixir bringing joys to everyone.   10
The offspring? Feasting, dancing, jubilee.
King Wine shows noble men's nobility.
Now, Father Bacchus, joy of the garland-crowned,
lord of the lively board which healths go round,
I greet you; beautiful heightener, supply
good drink, fair play and right thoughts, till I die!

Praxilla

Praxilla of Sicyon – a city in the northern Peloponnese – flourished around 450 BCE. Little survives of her work and less is known of her. She was said by the third-century CE grammarian Athenaeus in his encyclopedic *Scholars at Dinner* to have been a famous composer of drinking songs (*scolia* see p. 245); she was also praised, around the time of Augustus, by Antipater of Thessalonica (pp. 344–6) as one of the nine mortal Muses.

The following fragment – spoken by Adonis in the underworld – was quoted by the second-century CE rhetorician Zenobius in his *Proverbs* to illustrate the expression 'Sillier than Praxilla's Adonis'. 'For anyone who lists cucumbers and the rest alongside sun and moon,' Zenobius explains, 'can only be regarded as feeble-minded.'

747

The loveliest thing I left is the light of the sun;
next comes the brightness of stars and the face of the moon,
and after, cucumbers in season, and apples, and pears.

Corinna

Corinna, hailing from Tanagra in Boeotia, near Thebes, is supposed by the ancients to have flourished in the fifth century BCE, though many modern scholars date her as late as the third century BCE. She was much admired in antiquity. Antipater of Thessalonica (pp. 344–6) makes her one of the nine mortal Muses; Propertius (pp. 421–45) and Statius (pp. 527–32) sing her praises; Ovid (pp. 492–526) names his mistress in the *Amores* after her. Plutarch tells how she once famously criticized Pindar's treatment of myth (see Pindar's fragment 29, p. 155). When the geographer Pausanias visited Tanagra in the mid-second century CE, he saw 'a picture of Corinna tying her hair with a ribbon she won for her victory over Pindar at Thebes'. Dubious traditions make her variously Pindar's teacher (in the *Metrical Life of Pindar*, l. 9) or his fellow student (in the tenth-century CE Byzantine encyclopedia called the *Suda*; their teacher was the poetess Myrtis). The *Suda* adds that Corinna won no fewer than five victories over him (Pindar was supposedly so angry about this that he called her a 'sow'). Yet in a fragment quoted by one grammarian of the second century CE, Corinna 'finds fault' with Myrtis for competing with Pindar 'as a woman'.

Most scholars rightly disregard these stories. Instead, many of them consider her a Hellenistic poet, given that her language, vocabulary, meter, style and subject matter seem products of a later age; her manuscripts, for example, are written in a Boeotian dialect of about 200 BCE. Antipater's mention of her circa 20 BCE–20 CE is the earliest we have; M. L. West finds 'an intrinsic implausibility in the hypothesis that Corinna's poetry survived underground for something over two centuries, finally to emerge and become a best-seller'. Even if we can't resolve the question, we can dismiss it in good conscience: in the words of one scholar, G. M. Kirkwood, Corinna 'was so little influenced by and had so little influence on Greek poetry that it does not matter much at which date she wrote'.

Corinna is a local poet par excellence: both her dialect and the myths she chooses to tell are heavily regional. If she were a fifth-century poet, she would certainly cut against the historical grain of gradually increasing Pan-hellenism, traced in the arc that runs from Alcman (pp. 31–7) to Pindar. Then, too, Corinna is a woman. Though the attitudes expressed in these meager fragments fall some way short of feminism, she does still seem to have conceived of her audience as largely, or entirely, female (see, for example, fragment 655 below), and to have chosen myths on such tradi-tionally 'feminine' subjects as marriage, motherhood and child-rearing (see the *Singing Match* and the *Daughters of Asopus*, below). Was she a more Homeric Sappho? The fragments are not quite impressive enough for that. Like many of the scanty fragments collected here as examples of Classical lyric, Corinna speaks to us from the margins of history, and our know-ledge, tantalizing but attenuated, makes it hard to say much more.

654a°

The Singing Match

12   '... the Curetes   hid the goddess's°
        baby away,   and the small god lay
        in the cave's blind;   the crooked mind
        of Cronus all the while was left
    in ignorance of blessed Rhea's theft,

        'for which she won   sublime renown
        among the splendid   gods.' He ended,
        and the Muses pressed   all the Blest
20   straightway to hide   their votes inside
        the urn's gold-glamored scintillance,
    and all the deities rose up at once.

        Cithaeron's score   proved superior.°
        Then blurting out   with a great shout,
        Hermes said   the coveted
        triumph was his,   and the gods in bliss
        decked him in wreaths of victory,
    and his heart overflowed with ecstasy.

But severe throes began to close
and fasten on Mount Helicon;   30
with a great groan he tore a stone,
smooth and sleek, from his high peak,
and from that height with wretched moans
he shattered it into ten thousand stones.°

654b

The Daughters of Asopus°

'. . . And of your daughters, Zeus, the royal head°   12
  and father of all, has married three;
    and three of them have wed
  Poseidon, Sovereign of the Sea;
and two are consorts of Apollo's bed;

'and one of them has wed Maia's divine
  son, Hermes. For the blandishments
    of Love and the Cyprian
  seduced the gods to your residence,   20
to seek in secret, and to take, all nine.

'And soon your girls will mother lineages
  of heroes and half-gods whose worth
    and glory shall be ageless,
  whose seed shall cover the whole earth.
For so to me the tripod's voice presages –

'Acraephen, perfect in veracity,
  of all my father's fifty sons
    alone endowed to see
  intentions of the holy ones   30
and speak them with supreme authority.

'By gift of Phoebus, Euonymus first reckoned°
　　what the prophetic tripods meant
　　　　and uttered what they beckoned,
　　till he was forced into banishment
by Hyrieus, who held the honor second –°

'Poseidon's son. Orion was the third,
　　my family's father, whose enterprise
　　　　saw his homeland restored;°
　　now that he dwells among the skies,
on me this honored role has been conferred.

'Thus have I learned to speak the truths I'm given,
　　unerring and oracular:
　　　　but you – fight everliving
　　gods no more, nor mourn, who are
father-in-law to deities in heaven.'

So spoke the prophet, wholly sanctified.
　　Asopus took hold of his right
　　　　hand, now teary-eyed
　　in the efflux of his delight,
and answered him as follows while he cried

655

　　Terpsichore requires verses!°
　　I am to sing fine narratives
　　to the lovely ladies in white dresses
　　here in Tanagra town, which gives
a joyful shout that echoes out to hear
　　my words' chattering river ringing clear . . .
　　　　Now in the finery of my art
　　　　I'll dress tales that our fathers heard;
　　　　listen, ladies, and I shall start.
　　　　So many times my tuneful word
has bedecked Cephisus, our originator;°

40

50

6
10

Orion's greatness too, begetter
   of fifty high and mighty sons
   with nymphs encountered on his hunts;°
   and lovely Libye I've sung°

690°

Orestes

   Leaving the sea-stream, Dawn
   down from the sky has drawn
   the moon's unworldly glow;
   meanwhile, the Seasons flow
   from Zeus, ambrosial king,
   among the buds of spring;
and the feet of the choruses toil lightly,
delighted through the seven-gated city

Timotheus

Timotheus of Miletus (circa 450–360 BCE) was, as David Campbell writes, either the most distinguished or the most outrageous of the New Musicians, depending on your point of view. A citharode (singer to a cithara accompaniment) from the Ionian cities of Asia Minor, he composed some nineteen cithara-pieces (or nomes), eighteen dithyrambs, and numerous hymns, encomia (praise poems), preludes and other works. Titles known from his oeuvre include the dithyrambs *Madness of Ajax*, *Birthpangs of Semele*, *Elpenor* and *Scylla*, along with other pieces (probably nomes), such as *Nauplius*, *Niobe*, *Cyclops*, *Laertes* and *Sons of Phineus*, and the citharodic nome translated here, the *Persians*.

Timotheus was the most successful and popular lyric poet of his day – perhaps in all of antiquity. Around 415 BCE, he defeated his older contemporary, Phrynis of Mytilene, in a citharodic competition; by 400, he was widely acknowledged as the most famous, or infamous, poet of his generation. Later, he was invited to join the court of King Archelaus of Macedon and the brilliant artistic circle assembled there, which included the tragedians Euripides and Agathon, the epic poet Choerilus and the painter Zeuxis. For 700 years after his death, his work was constantly reperformed, from the fourth century BCE until the third century CE; no other lyric poet – not even Pindar (pp. 134–64) – had ever received such treatment. In his *Metaphysics*, Aristotle claims that, 'If there had been no Timotheus, we should not possess much of our music.'

Yet the popular success of Timotheus and the other New Musicians is the stick their critics have used to beat them. Of Timotheus, the tenth-century Byzantine encyclopedia, the *Suda*, simply says: 'He led ancient music into degeneration.' Plutarch, Aristoxenus (a student of Aristotle's whose treatise on the *Elements of Harmony* survives) and others attacked his 'love of novelty', his mixing of rhythms and musical modes in a single work, his abandonment of metrical repetitions in strophes and antistrophes (*apolelymenon*, a kind of free verse), and his actorly (imitative) delivery. Comic playwrights make fun of the 'twists' or 'bends' in his musical style, and his melodic 'ant tracks' – perhaps the sort of runs of notes we would associate with a guitar solo more difficult than musical, in which the virtuoso shreds just to show he can. Popular enjoyment of these features led to their being politicized as 'democratic', and earned the scorn of writers like Plato, who is withering in his contempt for what he called the 'theatocracy', or rule by the sort of vulgarians who like the theater. Modern scholars – no doubt the same who recoiled in horror on learning that Greek marbles were actually painted – have mostly followed the lead of the ancient snobs; see, for example, H. J. Rose in 1934, for whom Timotheus' 'restless and undignified' meters suggested 'the modern horrors of "jazz"'. It is hard to take such shrill dismissals seriously.

And yet it is also hard to refute them. Timotheus' *Persians* is an unpleasant sort of poem, without much in the way of human sympathy to temper the sensationalism of its violent language and extreme emotions. Two thousand years later, his bold political statements and extravagant novelties have lost their resonance, leaving behind a monument to demotic xenophobia; the outlandish compounds and kennings seem no more than stylistic counterparts to the ugly jingoism which worked the crowds into a lather: anything to get the people going. As a point on the timeline of Greek song culture, Timotheus' work is unquestionably of enormous value and interest; but, as art, its unvarnished populism and pursuit of novelty above all else seem of a piece with the poem's dearth of humanity and insight.

from the Persians°

791

[the Greek ships bashed the enemy boats]
and smashed their firry arms off.°
Now, what side the [irresistible] force
jolted, crunching the oars –
the sailors pitched that way; but if
[a rock-shelf] on the other dealt the crack   10
that snapped the oar-blades while the pine planks groaned,

they all pitched back;
and when ships' guts were [helplessly] exposed
and the flax-wound ribs yawned through the wound,°
some of them, pelted by the [glittering fierce
plunge] of lead weights from the yardarms, went°
under, while others nosed
down headlong with all their ornament°
chewed off by the iron ram, as [spears,]

20   thong-bound and [murder-bent,]°
leapt out of hands, and [air-incumbent,] dropped
down like Ares, down like flame
on limbs that twitched awhile, and stopped.
And hard-compacted [shot] with a killing aim
whistled, and wood-split skewers like pricks for an ox°
flew coiled in fiery cloaks,
and brazenly snouted arrows with huge wings
hurtled from bowstrings
in droves to the hecatomb of slaughter.

30   And so the ocean's emerald hair°
waving in furrowed fields of water
incarnadined with sailor-spatter;
and battle cries and screams were everywhere
wedded. As one the barbarous fleet
dissolved, unkempt, into wild retreat
over the breast of Amphitrite, decked°
in finery fish-stippled and light-flecked.
    But here a man [in the watery] plain,°
once the lord of a domain

40   a daylong journey crossed,
now islanded amid the breakers, beat
the infected main
with hands and [feet;]
battered and tossed
[toward extinction], he [cast about]
for some way out,

47   but equally encompassed [on all sides] . . .°
49   he called the sea-lord, Father . . .

When the winds died in one direction, from   60
another they kicked up, and water no
wine tempered, afroth with foam,°
flooded his gullet, where food should go;
and when salt-froth sputtered
up from his mouth and lungs, in a shrill
strangled voice – he had had more than his fill –
beside himself, gone in the head, he spluttered
threats and gnashed his teeth in a rage at the sea,°
his waterlogged corpse's certain grave:
'Well, aren't you brave!   70
Forgetting how recently
Xerxes collared your insubordinate neck
with shackles of flax? Soon the oarage°
of pinnacle-inseminated pine
at my liege's beck –
ha, ha! yes, mine, he's mine! –
will churn your guts and circumscribe your salt
pastures with sailors scavenging for forage –
you gadflydemented paleoloathsome traitor-
ous pet the breakneck hurricanes love to assault°   80
and batter!'
He hacked the words out, wracked and writhing,
and drooled sea-scum, and coughed up the briny, seething
deeps in the midst of his labored and panicked breathing.
        And so the barbarous Persian fleet°
raced backward in full-blown retreat,
a different hazard splintering each wreck
as they sailed down the channel's bottleneck,
and vessels' montane sea-legs kept
leaping from hands, and brilliantly enameled   90
children of the gumline leapt°
from heads being pummeled,
and everywhere breath was going,
and light had ceased its glowing
for the roiling glut of corpses no longer rowing
the star-strewn sea;°

the beaches, too, were overflowing.
And others sat on a headland fronting the surges
in naked immobility,
100   shrieking, tear-splashing,
wailing, breast-bashing,
wailing their lamentations, wailing dirges.
And up out from despair
they called upon their homeland: 'O my dear
ravines of Mysia, trees in your greeny hair,°
deliver us from here
where we are driven by the gales;
for these bodies of ours will never gain
our native soil again
110   if your help fails . . .°
115   Oh how I wish my lord
had never built that bridge
enabling us to ford
such distances abroad!
Then Mount Tmolus' ridge
120   and Lydian Sardis never would have seen°
us hurry off to fight the Greek war god!
How hard for a refugee
to find asylum from catastrophe!
Where can we flee?
The Queen, the Queen,
oh she alone could free us back to joy! –
the Mountain Mother, gathering us to Troy,
if we could fall before the calyxes
black-petaling her robe, and clasp her knees
130   with our unweathered lovelinesses
and beg her, *Please,*
o goddess Mother of the golden tresses,
save me, oh save me
from this hard lot so hard to flee!
Otherwise we'll be marked out for the slaughter
by the keen cutthroat steel, that deadpan plotter,
or else shipsmashing, billowdashing breezes,

extinguishers of breath,
with northers howling till night freezes
will be our death,   140
or else the currents will soon strip
our woven warmth away in the savage rip,
and I shall lie pathetic here, a fresh
meal for the clans of birds that feast on flesh.'
    Lamenting in this vein, they carried on
weeping. When one of their new Greek masters,
steeled to the hilt, would seize
a native son
of Phrygia rich in pastures°
and drag him off, yanking his hair, all fight   150
gone out of him, he would clasp tight
the soldier's knees
and beg him, mixing broken Greek
with Oriental speak,
as he unstopped his throat with a thin yowl
in hot pursuit of the Ionian tongue:
'Me you speak how?°
What say?
I come back never here, no how, no way.
This time my master me here brung.   160
In future, father, no more, now.
No more come back!
No more attack!
I stay on Ecbatana, Sardis, Susa.°
Never again I bother you, sir.
Big god of me, Artimus,°
will watch me out on Ephesus.'
    And they, as they beat their escape,
backward paced in extreme haste,
flinging their two-faced   170
weapons away, and raked their cheeks with their nails,
and shredded the elegant warp and drape
of their Persian cloaks, tuning
their high-pitched Asiatic wails

to dirges choked with many tongues, all groaning;°
and none in the Great King's company could avert
their frightened cries
or unpeel their eyes
from all the horror coming, and the hurt.

180 And the Great King, when he saw the confused rout°
of his host break backward into a headlong rush,
fell to his knees and mortified his flesh.
Adrift on the breakers of failure he cried out,
'Woe to my house razed to the ground!°
You Greek ships, searing like summer stars, whose rage
contrived to drown and maim
so many ships and soldiers my own age! –
whom those ships shall never carry, bound
back toward home again; instead

190 the smokeblack heart and feral thews of flame
will coil them round,
while all of Persia shudders with despair,
weeps itself sick.
Oh awful weight of fate that led
me here to Greece! You, come, and quick,
harness my four-horse chariot; you there,
load up the mule-carts with our immense
riches past measure,
and burn down all the tents!

200 We cannot let them profit from our treasure!'

    But all the Greeks erected trophies
in Zeus's holiest of holies,
and 'Paean! Paean!' their great shout –°
'Hail, Lord of Remedy!' – rang out,
as the deep thud of their dancing beat
joy's measures with high-stepping feet.

    O Paean, Paean, you who feed the fire
of my newfangled Muse with her gold lyre,
be with me as my helper, god of healing.

210 For now the great and noble
antiquely venerable

rulers of Sparta, I mean the people, swelling
in youthful efflorescence, come
with smoldering odium
at me
and chase me with the torch of obloquy,
since (they say) I do
violence to their old Muse with my new.°
Yet whether a man is young, old, my own peer –
my music bids them all come near and hear;   220
but those who would abuse the ancient Muse,
the enemies of song – them I accuse,
I banish them from earshot, far from me,
keen criers of uncouth cacophony.
Orpheus, son of Calliope,°
with his kaleidoscopic Muse, first plied
the tortoise lyre in Pieria;°
Terpander then,
from Lesbos in Aeolia,
pride of Antissa, vied and multiplied   230
his Muse to the tune of ten
fit strains; and now Timotheus has given
the lyre new life with his eleven
taut strings of rhythm and sweet song,
as he throws wide
the Muse's treasury
and all its many rooms of melody.
Miletus raised him, whose folk belong°
at the forefront of Greece,
linked in a league twelve cities strong.°   240
But you, Far-Shooting Pythian, consent°
to come and bless this city with increase
of fortune for its people, and release
from worry, and good government –
the rule of law that tends the bloom of peace.

796°

Those ancient songs I do not sing.
My new, improved ones are the thing.
Zeus is a young man, and is king;
Cronus's sway was yesterday.
Let passé Muses pass away!

Epitaph for Euripides°

Euripides' memory all Hellas owns,
though Macedon, his deathplace, claims his bones.
Hailing from Athens, Greece's Greece, he's praised
by myriads his Muse pleased and amazed.

Ariphron of Sicyon

Almost nothing is known of Ariphron save the justly famous poem translated below. It comes down to us thanks to the third-century CE grammarian Athenaeus, who quotes it at the end of his encyclopedic *Scholars at Dinner*. A copy was erected at the sanctuary of Asclepius at Epidaurus, probably in the late fifth or early fourth century, though the poem could have been composed as late as the third century BCE. Its continuing popularity into the second century CE is attested by the rhetorician Maximus of Tyre and the satirist Lucian of Samosata, who calls it 'that extremely well-known song on everyone's lips'. Athenaeus refers to the poem as a paean, though it lacks any of the genre's formal hallmarks. In form and content its closest parallel is probably Aristotle's 'Hymn to Excellence' (poem 842, p. 224). Thematically, the poem is anticipated by Simonides 604 (p. 127), and the popular drinking song attributed to him, poem 651 (p. 127).

813

O Health, among the Blest
the best and worthiest
of mortal worship, may
I pass what life remains to me, I pray,
in your good graces, while
you linger by my side, and smile.
For no enjoyments are complete and good –
not wealth or children, not the royal might
that makes a man a god,
not the sexual delight   10
we hunt with Aphrodite's secret coils,
or any other pleasure humans know
from heaven, not the breathing space when toils
dissolve – but, gracious Health, bathed in your glow

they gleam and effloresce,
and the sweet-lilting Graces come to bless.
But without you there is no happiness.

Philoxenus

The excerpt translated below, from the *Feast* (*Deipnon*), is the work of one Philoxenus, but exactly which Philoxenus is a quandary; even the third-century CE grammarian Athenaeus, who quoted the poem extensively in his encyclopedic *Scholars at Dinner*, was not sure. It could be Philoxenus of Cythera (circa 435–380), a dithyrambic poet of the New Music (see the introduction to the Classical Period, pp. 187–92), whose lost poem *Cyclops* (or *Galatea*) probably mocked a nome by Timotheus (pp. 204–12) also called *Cyclops*, while simultaneously inventing the love affair between Polyphemus and Galatea which Theocritus would later make famous (Idyll 11, p. 296; see also Callimachus' *Epigram 3*, p. 276). On the other hand, it could also be the Cytherean's contemporary, Philoxenus of Leucas, a noted glutton and author of a cookbook (the *Opsartysia*) in dactylic hexameters.

The present poem's subject matter – relentlessly gastronomic, with possible parodic intent – recalls the Middle Comedy, the style that dominated the Athenian comic stage between Aristophanes and Menander, one of whose favorite stock characters was a windbag cook always flourishing his culinary science. Its dramatic setting has affinities with earlier symposium-poetry, like that of Xenophanes (pp. 109–13) and Ion of Chios (pp. 196–7). Its metrical form, meanwhile – astrophic, or *apolelymenon* – recalls the so-called 'New Music' (see the *Persians* of Timotheus, p. 205).

The gastronomic content of the *Feast*, unhelpfully, could support its authorship by either of the Philoxenoi, the first having been almost as notable a gourmand as the second. Its metrical form, however, points to the first, Philoxenus of Cythera. If he was the author, then it might have been written to describe or lampoon the lavish banquets held by Dionysius I of Syracuse, in whose court the poet spent time. This Philoxenus eventually ran afoul of Dionysius, either because he panned the tyrant's verses, or seduced his mistress, or both. The poet was sent to the quarries, but he escaped, and spent the rest of his life traveling and performing throughout Greece. He died in Ephesus.

from the Feast

836b+c

836b   And two boys, working double,
              brought us a polished table,

              and one for another group,
              and more for the rest, until
              the room filled up,

              and the lamps' high circle of light
              made their sheen bright,

              and they heaped the tables with dishes
              and side dishes and lots of sauces
10   and the thrill of every delicious

              and subtle and colorful art
              for seasoning life
              and capturing the heart.

              And others brought snow-white bread
              in baskets of woven reed,

              and afterwards, chum, we got
              not a three-legged pot

              but a huge, wide tray
              of eels, conger and moray,

20   gleaming and replete,
              such as the gods would eat°

              with relish. And next, a plate
              came out, no less great,
              with a perfect circle of skate,

and dogfish fillets
were brought in little crocks,
and others held stingrays,°

and there was another dish
with succulent squid, and many-
tentacled cuttlefish,   30

whose flesh is so delicate.
And then, still piping hot

and wreathed in steam,
an empty-bellied bream,

big as the table, was provided,
followed by fried and breaded

calamari, and we were served
shrimps cooked to a golden brown,
their small backs curved,

and savory herb-green cakes   40
with crackly phyllo flakes,

and wheat cakes too were brought,
sweet-sour, fully dressed°
and big as a three-legged pot,

the kind that we both call – I know it well –
'the Navel of the Meal'.°

And then – it's true, I swear! –
an enormous whole-roasted tuna
came from right over there,

nice and hot, with a slit   50
carved all the way under it,

exposing the belly steak,
which if you and I could make

disappear forever
and never have to stop,
we'd do it in a snap,

happily. But to pick up
the thread where I let it drop,

59   the feast . . .

61   No one could enumerate
precisely all we were served
that day, but a giddy heat

precipitates me on.
Then chitlins came from a piglet
raised in the house, with his loin

and his lungs, all piping hot,
and the severed head was brought
of an unweaned baby goat,
70   strangled, boiled, and split

through the eyes, with boiled ribs, and the best
odds and ends of the rest,

gooey with fat: carvings
of head-parts, snouts and trotters,
all of the choicest servings

seasoned with silphium,°
and other roasted and boiled
cutlets of kid and lamb,

and sausages made from the sweet
sweet cuts of shoulder meat 80

of lamb and kid combined,
which is the gods' favorite kind.

You'd have eaten every bit of it,
chum! Then we were brought
baby rooster, and rabbit,

and partridges and pigeon
were piled up hot for us in enormous profusion,

and soft-folded bread
came side by side
with a sweet spread 90
of yellow honey,
with milk-curd everyone said

looked cheese-like, but was runny
and soft, and of course I agreed.
But then our whole company

were full of drink and food
and in a contented mood,

and servants cleared each platter
away, and boys came out
and washed our hands with water, 100

soothing and warmly scented
with iris-infused soap.
However much each person wanted

they poured, and gave us all
a clean white linen towel,

and ambrosial lotion, and set
a garland on every head°

108   of woven violet . . .

836c   But now we've come

110   to the point in the symposium
when our hands are clean, and it's time
for a toast. Here, chum,

to you!
Accept this cup,
brimming with wine and dew.

This gift, so mellow and pleasant,
is Bacchus's way of enhancing
the savor of the present.°

'Plato'

Plato the philosopher lived from around 425 to around 348 BCE. While it is not intrinsically implausible that that enemy of poetry should have composed the stuff – he clearly loved it, and kicks the poets out of his *Republic* with more than a shred of regret – it is universally agreed that these compositions under his name are the work of a later age. Some, anthologized by Meleager (pp. 326–32), were likely composed circa 250 BCE; others probably date somewhere between 100 BCE and 100 CE.

1°

You watch the stars, my star. Were I the wide
heavens, then I would watch you, starry-eyed.

2°

While you were still alive, your brightness shone
above like Phosphorus, the star of dawn;
now, gone below, among the dead you are
as bright as Hesperus, the evening star.

3°

As I was giving Agathon a kiss,
my soul caught at my lips, sap that she is –
she'd hoped to go to him, and to be his.

4

Here, take this apple, and, if you love me°
truly, respond with your virginity.
If (heaven forbid!) you do not, nonetheless
take it, and think how brief is loveliness.

5

I am an apple, fruit of your lover's praying.°
Say yes, Xanthippe. We are both decaying.°

Aristotle

Aristotle of Stagira (384–322 BCE), student of Plato and tutor to Greece's greatest conqueror, Alexander of Macedon, became in time so influential – and, for a number of centuries, so definitive – that he is known to history simply as 'the Philosopher'. Despite his deep connection to Plato, Aristotle went his own way intellectually, and in 334 founded a new philosophical school in Athens, the Lyceum, which became home to the 'Peripatetic' philosophers, so called because they adopted Aristotle's method of walking around the gardens as they philosophized. (*Peripatein* in Greek means 'to walk around'.) It was at the Lyceum that Aristotle wrote the bulk of his prodigious philosophical output – probably more than 200 works, of which around thirty have survived, covering subjects ranging from natural philosophy (science) to practical philosophy (ethics and politics), and from logic and metaphysics to poetics. Aristotle's writings formed the core of the Lyceum's substantial private library, the first of its kind in Greece, after which the Library of Alexandria was later modeled.

Aristotle's extant works are not generally known for their elegance of style, since they were mostly not intended for publication but written as lecture notes for his students. However, his dialogues, which have not survived, are supposed to have been very elegant indeed; and, at any rate, the slender surviving poetic output translated here argues that he was certainly capable of writing well.

On poem 842, known as the 'Hymn to Excellence', there hangs a rather fascinating tale. The poem was written to honor Aristotle's friend Hermias, the tyrant of Atarneus in Asia Minor, who welcomed Aristotle during his wanderings after the death of Plato. Around 345/4 BCE, Hermias had been tortured to death at Susa by the Persian king Artaxerxes III, who wanted information about the plans of Philip II of Macedon; but Hermias' lips were sealed. Before he died, he sent a letter to his friends that 'he had done nothing unworthy of philosophy or shameful'. Deeply moved, Aristotle composed his hymn and made it customary at the Lyceum to sing it every day after meals. Later, following the death of Alexander in 323 BCE, when Aristotle's Macedonian connections made him vulnerable to anti-Macedonian sentiment in Athens, the philosopher was accused of impiety, on the grounds that he had written a paean for a mortal man. Aristotle's defense was that the poem was not a paean at all, but a *scolion*, a drinking song, and therefore no crime. In this way the Philosopher was brought to trial on a matter of poetic genre, and probably convicted, too, since he went into exile around this time and died not long afterwards.

842°

   Greatness, the cause of humanity's sweat and striving,
      the loftiest reason for living,
     who in Greece would not be jealous
   of one fated to die for your beauty's sake,
   Lady, or else to labor without break?
     You feed the mind the food of solace,
      greater than gold, good as divine,
  more soothing than mothers are and soft-eyed sleep.
     In quest of the power you define,
10   Heracles and Leda's sons could keep°
      enduring endless toils and pains.
   For love of you, Achilles and Ajax went
     down to the house where Hades reigns;
   and for your beautiful embodiment
   Atarneus's native son was taken°
   and left the fire of the sun forsaken.
   But now Hermias and his glorious
     deeds shall never die,
   sung by the Muses, daughters of Memory,
20   who also sing the majesty of Zeus,
      the Lord of Welcoming, forever,
   and Lord of Friendship which no fate can sever.

673

For Plato°

Eudemus, coming to famous Attica,°
upreared an altar in the grip of awe
to sanctify the friendship of a man°
lip-service of the wicked dare not stain,
the first or only man to demonstrate
in his own life and writings and debate
that the good man and happy man are one.
Now none can ever do what he has done.

Aristonous of Corinth

Aristonous of Corinth lived in the third quarter of the fourth century BCE. He is the author of two hymns intended for performance in honor of specific gods at religious festivals in Delphi, found on stone inscriptions in the Athenian treasure house there. A public decree inscribed in the 'archonship [chief magistracy] of Damochares' (334/3 BCE) grants to Aristonous a number of privileges at Delphi 'because of the hymns to the gods that he composed'. These privileges included first rights to consult the oracle, front-row seats in the theater, honorary citizenship rights, and the title of 'Benefactor'. Aristonous' elegant compositions are subtly original without seeming to be: unlike Pindar (pp. 134–64), he does not emphasize, but downplays, his divergence from canonical narratives. The poet's Athens-centric perspective is somewhat surprising given his Corinthian origin.

Hymn to Hestia°

O sacred, sacramental queen,
Hestia, we hymn you, focus of
Olympus and the laurel grove
of Pytho and the innermost
interior of Earth's navel, where you're seen°
dancing through Phoebus' precinct, lofty-gated,
joyfully engrossed
as tripods utter oracles, and Apollo
strikes his golden lyre, seven-noted,
joining with you to magnify the mellow
gladness of immortals his hymns hallow.
Greetings and gladness to you, daughter
of Cronus and Rhea, you alone who burn
bright fire on each venerated altar
to deathlessness, o Hestia; in return

10

for piety,
grant us pious prosperity,
to weave forever round your glistening seat
and altar on our dancing feet.

Paean to Apollo°

At Pytho's sacrosanct foundation,
the Rock of Delphi, without fail
full of oracular vibration,
　　　you dwell – *hail, Paean, hail!* –
Coeus' daughter Leto's great
and treasured gift, and Zeus's too,
who's uppermost where gods debate:
　　　o Paean, hail to you!

And there, descanting from between
the god-built tripods, you exhale
prophetic breath upon the green-
　　　haired laurel – *Paean, hail!*
Out of your sanctum, quick with awe,
with plangent lyre you construe
the future and its holy law –
　　　o, Paean, hail to you!

At Zeus's will, supremely strong,
you cleansed yourself in Tempe's vale,
then Pallas ushered you along
　　　to Pytho – *Paean, hail!* –
to cajole Themis, divinely coiffed,
and Gaea, nurse of flowers, to
seat you where incense soars aloft –
　　　o Paean, hail to you!

Athena's temple ever since°
has stood on Delphi's eastern trail
before yours: deathless recompense –

hail, Paean! Paean, hail! –
for gracious deeds of olden days.
30   With memory forever new
and tribute high your grace repays
        Athena's – *hail to you!*

And other gods, with gifts they gave,
thank you: Poseidon's sacred dale,
the nymphs in their Corycian cave –°
        hail, Paean! Paean, hail! –
and Bacchus who, on even years,
is lit with torches all night through,
where august Artemis trains fierce
40   watchdogs – *o hail to you!*

There, from Parnassus' bubbling
crevasses, you lave your graceful, pale
body in Castalia's spring –°
        hail, Paean! Paean, hail!
May piety win prosperity;
may you smile on our hymns, and view
us worthy of your charity.
        O Paean, hail to you!

Philodamus of Scarphea

Philodamus of Scarphea (a town in Locris, near Thermopylae) lived in the third quarter of the fourth century BCE. Like Aristonous of Corinth (pp. 226–8), he was granted numerous special privileges at Delphi in return for a hymn – the *Paean to Dionysus*, below. First published in 1895, the poem was found inscribed on the paving stones of Delphi's Sacred Way, face-down. A prose text beneath it claims that the poem was composed and performed during the 'archonship [chief magistracy] of Etymondas', which the current best guess assigns to 340/39 BCE. This was a turbulent time in Greece: the Athenian orator Demosthenes had convinced his fellow citizens to break their treaty with Philip II of Macedon, who responded by marching into the heart of Phocis in central Greece and pitching camp at Elatea. The next year, at the Battle of Chaeronea (338 BCE), Philip would decisively crush the Greek allies, effectively putting an end to Greek independence. Philodamus' poem is unconcerned with these events, its attention being claimed instead by the destruction of the Delphic temple of Apollo by an earthquake three decades earlier, in 373, and the slowness of the reconstruction works (not finished until about 320). In the poem, the god Apollo urges the 'Delphic Board' of Amphictyons – of which Philip II was a member – to speed things up, and describes some of the statuary he'd like to see put in place; he also has his sights set on liturgical reform. The poem is both compelling in its own right and offers a fascinating glimpse of the interdependence and mutual reinforcement of various kinds of authority – mythical/religious, political and poetic – at the epicenter of Greek spirituality.

Paean to Dionysus°

> Lord Dithyramb, the Bacchants' Lord,°   *Str. 1*
> the Ululated-At, great Bull,
> great Bellower, the Ivy-Haired,
> come grace our springtime festival!

Euoi, Bacchus! Paean, Healer, hail!°
   Whom once, in Thebes, where Bacchants howl,
   Thyone, blessed with a lovely child°
   by Zeus, gave birth to you, and all
   the gods danced; all the mortals smiled,
10   Bacchus, now that you were here.
Hail, Paean, Healer, Deliverer; appear!
Preserve this city, through your charity,
   in blest prosperity.

Str. 2   Then Cadmus's [illustrious]
   plains joined the Bacchic dance, as well
   as Minyan Orchomenus;°
   Euboea too, the bountiful –
Euoi, Bacchus! Paean, Healer, hail!
   When all of Delphi's hallowed land,
20   vineyard of hymns, danced too, you showed
   your body like a starry brand
   in Delphic maidens' hands, and stood
   upon Parnassus, rugged, sheer:
Hail, Paean, Healer, Deliverer; appear!
Preserve this city, through your charity,
   in blest prosperity.

Str. 3   With passion your godhead infuses,
   you brought your midnight ritual,
   awash in torchlight, to Eleusis'
30   ever-blooming inner hall.
Euoi, Bacchus! Paean, Healer, hail!
   There all Greece joins the locals who
   administer the Mysteries,°
   thankful to call, Iacchus, you,°
   and take, from mortal toil, the ease
   you give, the breathing space you clear.
Hail, Paean, Healer, Deliverer; appear!
Preserve this city, through your charity,
39   *in blest prosperity . . .*

In that blest land you did not tarry,°   *Str. 5*
but passed through Thessaly, to scale   54
to Mount Olympus' sanctuary,
and to the famed Pierian vale –°
Euoi, Bacchus! Paean, Healer, hail!
The Muses, crowned in ivy, came
and sang a circular serenade:°
Deathless Paean, of deathless fame!   60
leapt from their lips. Apollo played
the prelude at the hymn's premiere.
Hail, Paean, Healer, Deliverer; appear!
Preserve this city, through your charity,
      in blest prosperity . . .°   65

Phoebus orders the Delphic Board,   *Str. 9*
and ASAP, to fulfill   106
the restoration, lest the Lord°
Who Shoots from Far let his wrath fall –
Euoi, Bacchus! Paean, Healer, hail! –
and to display this hymn to all   110
the holy kindred progeny
of gods at their Guest-Festival,°
while suppliants from all Greece see
the sacrificial fires rear.
Hail, Paean, Healer, Deliverer; appear!
Preserve this city, through your charity,
      in blest prosperity.

Happy the race of men who build°   *Str. 10*
Lord Phoebus' holy house, which shall
not ever age or be defiled;°   120
happy, and prosperous as well –
Euoi, Bacchus! Paean, Healer, hail! –
all golden, upon gold slopes where,
Paean, goddesses in a ring
surround you, waving a branch, your hair
bright white with ivory, glistering

under the local laurel you wear.°
Hail, Paean, Healer, Deliverer; appear!
Preserve this city, through your charity,
130   *in blest prosperity.*

Str. 11   And at the four-year Pythian Games
the god had ministers install
contests of circular dithyrambs°
and a sacrificial ritual –
Euoi, Bacchus! Paean, Healer, hail! –
for Bacchus, and a chariot
with two gold lions, an effigy
like to the sunrise, delicate;°
and consecrate to his sanctity
140   a cave to be his proper sphere.°
Hail, Paean, Healer, Deliverer; appear!
Preserve this city, through your charity,
in blest prosperity.

Str. 12   Come all, receive your Bacchic Lord,
and call Lord Dionysus; call
him as you pour forth, ivy-haired,
and dance in every street through all –
Euoi, Bacchus! Paean, Healer, hail! –
149   of Hellas, hallowed, prosperous . . .
153   O Lord of Health, all hail, and cheer.
Hail, Paean, Healer, Deliverer; appear!
Preserve this city, through your charity,
in blest prosperity.

Hermolochus

Hermolochus is nothing more than a name. His one poem, translated below, comes down to us thanks to the fifth-century CE anthologist Ioannes Stobaeus, who quoted it in his *Extracts*. It is probably not complete.

846

Life has no maps, nor any grounds for confidence;
    we drift, unmoored, among the accidents.
  Hope is a comfort, yes, but no one mortal knows
    the coming fate to which he goes
with any exactitude. God steers us all through the dice-throws
    of danger, and even on our happiest day –
  suddenly, into our faces, the other way –
    an ill wind blows.

Anonymous Classical Lyric

The following poems by many hands have come down to us without attribution. They are of various provenance: a number are cult hymns, many of which were found inscribed on stones at different religious sites, while others were quoted by writers who did not bother to name the authors. Dates range widely, and at any rate are difficult to determine with precision (for discussion, see the endnotes to individual poems). Not all of these poems are strictly from the Classical period; however, if they are late, they are late imitations of earlier literary and religious lyric styles.

Hymn to Zeus on Mount Dicte, Crete°

Hail, Young Man, mightiest of all,
I greet you! Son of Cronus, hail,
invincible font of light, whose stance
is at the head of the immortal ones;
come back to Dicte, as the year's circle runs
its course; smile on our song and dance.
The plectrum shuttles on the lyre;
pipe music mixes with the strings;
around your altar now, our choir
stands at the wall and sings:
Hail, Young Man, mightiest of all,
I greet you! Son of Cronus, hail,
invincible font of light, whose stance
is at the head of the immortal ones;
come back to Dicte, as the year's circle runs
its course; smile on our song and dance.
For, deathless Infant, it was here
[the Curetes] from Rhea's hands°
received and [hid] you, [beating spear]

10

on shield [in a leaping dance.]   20
Hail, Young Man, mightiest of all,
I greet you! Son of Cronus, hail,
invincible font of light, whose stance
is at the head of the immortal ones;
come back to Dicte, as the year's circle runs
    its course; smile on our song and dance . . .   26
    a beautiful new dawn.   30
Hail, Young Man, mightiest of all,
I greet you! Son of Cronus, hail,
invincible font of light, whose stance
is at the head of the immortal ones;
come back to Dicte, as the year's circle runs
    its course; smile on our song and dance.
The Seasons brought forth yearly bounty,
and men took Justice for their king,
and Peace that loves and proffers plenty
    ruled every living thing.°   40
Hail, Young Man, mightiest of all,
I greet you! Son of Cronus, hail,
invincible font of light, whose stance
is at the head of the immortal ones;
come back to Dicte, as the year's circle runs
    its course; smile on our song and dance.
With you, lord, let the vats be filled;
leap into the tall crops, and leap
into our houses, now fulfilled,
    and into the fleece of sheep.   50
Hail, Young Man, mightiest of all,
I greet you! Son of Cronus, hail,
invincible font of light, whose stance
is at the head of the immortal ones;
come back to Dicte, as the year's circle runs
    its course; smile on our song and dance.
Leap into each seagoing ship
and every town within our border;
leap into our young men, and leap

60   into the civic order.
Hail, Young Man, mightiest of all,
I greet you! Son of Cronus, hail,
invincible font of light, whose stance
is at the head of the immortal ones;
come back to Dicte, as the year's circle runs
its course; smile on our song and dance.

934°

Inscription from Erythrae (380–360 BCE)

Sing Paean, boys, the Famed for Art:
Leto's son, with his long-range dart –
         hail, Paean, hail! –
who benefited all mankind
when with Coronis he combined
in love, in the land of Phlegyas –°
hail, Paean! – hail, Asclepius
the god whose name is endless fame –
         hail, Paean, hail!

10   Podalirius was his son,
Machaon too, and Medicine –°
         hail, Paean, hail! –
and Panacea, and the rosy face
of Radiance – Gentleness
bore them, along with Health, the wholly
glorious, and wholly holy –
hail, Paean! – hail, Asclepius,
the god whose name is endless fame –
         hail, Paean, hail!

20   I greet you! With a gracious gaze
smile on our city's spacious ways –°
         hail, Paean, hail! –
Approve our plea, and let us see

the sunlight in felicity,
rejoicing with good Health, the wholly
glorious, and wholly holy –
hail, Paean! – hail, Asclepius,
the god whose name is endless fame –
                    hail, Paean, hail!

935°

Hymn to Cybele

Descend from on high, divine
[Pierians], here, and praise°
the gods' Great Mother; raise
your voice, twine it with mine,
tell how, through mountains and valleys,
she wandered here and there,
unkempt her [immortal] hair,
frantic and far from solace,
till Zeus, whose thunder thrums,
perceived her roving about   10
and took up his lightning bolt
and tried to take her drums,
and split the cliffs, and tried
to take the drums from her hands:
'Quit roaming the hinterlands!°
Come back where the gods abide!
Or else! – there might be violence
from gray-eyed wolves, or lions.'
'I shan't unless I am given
the regions I am worth: 20
one full half of the earth,
and one full half of heaven,
and thirdly, half the sea.
That done, you shall prevail.'
O Mother of Heaven, hail!
Hail to your Majesty!

936°

Hymn to Pan

Pan, I sing you, lord of nymphs,
god whom every Naiad fancies,
adept of allegretto, adding
gilding to the golden dances.

With panache your Panpipes, wispy-
sweet, god-panting, waken echoes,
while, feet bouncing to the beat, you
jitterbug through shady grottos.

Pantomiming all the world,
10   good at dancing, and good-looking,
blond-goateed, you're very striking.

To the gods in their euphoria
on starry-eyed Olympus goes a
panoramic, airy aria,
spritzing musical ambrosia.

Sea and earth for all they're worth
greet you, our pantocosmic pillar,
great pantocrat, the all-controller.
Pan, greetings; greetings, Pan!

937°

Hymn to All the Gods at Epidaurus

Asclepius' high virtuosity.
And also call that duo, Zeus's Twins,°
and the reverence of the Graces,
and the resonance of the Muses,
the Fates with benign designs,

and the tireless Sun and the Moon's full round
and all of the lights with which heaven is crowned,°
bright signs and tokens for us.
Hail to you all, undying and divine,
you gods and goddesses – preserve this shrine   10
of Epidaurus
in excellent working order
and full of Greeks from every quarter –
o you in victory rejoicing,
holy authors of all blessing.

939°

Arion's Song

Sublimest of deities,
Poseidon, Lord of the Sea's
populous womb, whose trident is all gold,
who have the whole planet to hold –
around you creatures of the ocean
ply their circle dance that swims,
gills flashing, with a darting motion,
lightly on their finny limbs;
and slick-necked pups with blunt round noses,
quicksilver dolphins, lovers of the Muses,   10
Amphitrite's oceanic kids,°
nurslings of the goddess Nereids.
Thanks to you I managed to escape
when I was bobbing aimlessly
in the swells off Sicily,
and you took me up on your arching backs
and plowed the ocean's wavy plain
through furrows free from human tracks
and set me down again
in Pelops' country, on Taenarus's cape,°   20
after double-dealing men
from the seaworthy hollow ship hurled me
into the bruise-dark billows of the sea.

988°

Not diamonds or gold in its lustrousness – most rare gleam
in a life always baffling to mortal hopes –
not couches of silver so fire our esteem
      as they dazzle and glow,
nor do acres of farmland far as the eye can see,
entirely self-sufficient, teeming with crops,
      affect us so
as noble hearts in unanimity.

1010

    when he said this, the distantly radiant
    ambrosial face of Day,
    spurring its horses, left him and went
    away

1018a+b°

Hymn to the Fates

1018a   Hear me, o Fates, you who sit,
    of all the gods, nearest to Zeus's throne
      and weave your infinite
    snares which grant escape to none
    with ever-varying intent
    on shuttles made of adamant:
1018b   Apportioners, Spinners and Allotters,°
    exquisitely limbed Midnight's daughters,
      hear my prayer,
10   you dreaded Powers past compare
      on earth and in the air:
    send us the lovely triplets throned at the height
    of light – Justice, good Order with her bright
    rose-tinted countenance, and the fair sight
      of garland-wearing Peace –°

that this heartbroken place may find release
from suffering, and our misfortunes cease.

1019

Hymn to Fortune

O Fortune, start and finish line
for mortals, you who fill the seat
of Wisdom, from which you assign
the honors for which men compete –
you bless more often than you curse,
grace flickers lambent from your golden wings,
     and what your scales disburse
is blessedest and best of mortal things.
In trials you find a way where there is none;
in darkness you unveil a brighter sun: 10
what god is greater than you are? Not one.

Folk Songs

Like the poems of the Anonymous Classical Lyric section (pp. 234–41), the following anonymous songs come down to us in quotations from various authors, among them the grammarian Athenaeus, the Stoic Roman emperor Marcus Aurelius, and the biographer and essayist Plutarch, and no doubt represent traditional songs sung by regular folks in places like Rhodes, Athens, Sparta and Mytilene. For more information, see the endnotes to individual songs.

848°

The swallow, the swallow is here!
And he's bringing the beautiful clear
weather and prime of the year!
His belly is white
and his back is black.
Oh, won't you come out
from your chockablock
pantry and bring us a little fruit cake
and a cupful of wine and a basket of cheese
10   and wheat, pretty please?
(The swallow will also eat lentils and peas.)
  Have we got to go, or will we get it?
Fork it over, or you'll regret it!
We'll take your door or the lintel above it
or the pretty wife hiding behind it.
(She's little enough, we'd think nothing of it.)
But if you're going to give us anything,
make it a fatty and not a skinny thing!
Open, open! The swallow bids.
20   We're not old men here, we're just kids.

852°

Where are my roses, where are my violets,
    where is my beautiful celery?
Here are your roses, here are your violets,
    here is your beautiful celery.

853°

Come on, what's wrong with you? Don't stay
    and give us both away!
Get up before my man comes back
if you don't want him to attack
and do some awful injury
to you and me, poor little me!
Can't you see the sunlight play
    on the windowsill? It's day!

854°

Rain, rain, sweet Zeus, let it rain
down on Athens, field and plain.

856°

You stalwart sons of citizens,
men of Sparta's well-manned land,
grip your shields in your left hand
and bravely raise your javelins.
Don't balk, don't let death frighten you,
for that is not what Spartans do.

859°

Away, away with the dire
owl, the midnight crier!
Away to the wharves with it, far
from where the people are.

869°

Grind, mill, grind the barley down
as King Pittacus once ground down
the folks in Mytilene town.

873°

O graced with grace and the bloom of health,
you boys of noble blood,
don't grudge to spread your beauty's wealth
among the great and good –
for limb-dissolving Love
in step with bravery
sinews the soldiers of
Thracian Chalcidice.

Scolia

All of the following short anonymous pieces are quoted by the third-century CE grammarian Athenaeus in Book 15 of his encyclopedic *Scholars at Dinner* as *scolia*: drinking songs for performance at the symposium after dinner. The genre's most accomplished practitioners included Alcaeus (pp. 55–67), Anacreon (pp. 100–108), Simonides (pp. 120–33) and Pindar (pp. 134–64); no doubt many couplets of the *Theognidea* (pp. 76–85), with which these poems overlap thematically, also fit the bill. We are told that the postprandial singing proceeded according to a three-part program: first, the entire company sang together in unison; second, everyone sang individually, responding to or 'capping' the previous singer's offering (see Timocreon of Rhodes 727 11.1–3, p. 194, and note); third, the most talented would then offer more virtuoso fare, beyond the range of the rest. The songs gathered by Athenaeus appear to be of the second type. Why they were called *scolia* ('twisters' or 'zigzags') was a question that engaged and perplexed ancient scholars; suggestions include: (1) because they were in reality quite straightforward, and someone was being sarcastic; (2) because the singing proceeded in a zigzag manner from person to person; and (3) because the third type of song, which concluded the symposium, was in fact quite tricky to perform. Whatever the truth, these little songs are all simple and relaxed, with a demotic air.

889°

I wish we could see the truth of appearances
by opening a man's chest and looking in,
and then, when we close it again,
befriend the one who is what he says he is!

892°

The crab spoke up
with the snake in its grip:
'A true friend's a straight-shooter, trusty,
never double-tongued and twisty.'

893°

Like Harmodius and Aristogiton's,
a myrtle bouquet will hide *my* sword –°
our two tyrant-killing titans
who saw equality restored.°

895°

I'll hide my sword in a myrtle bouquet
like Aristogiton and Harmodius,
who at the festival managed to slay°
the tyrant Hipparchus, delivering us.

896°

Harmodius and Aristogiton's
immortality is assured,
our two tyrant-killing titans
who saw equality restored.°

900°

I wish, I wish I could be a lyre of ivory,
held by the pretty hands of boys in the Bacchic dance!

901

I wish I could be a grand clay bowl, well thrown by hand,
held in the lovely clench of a lovely and innocent wench!

902

Join me in drink and youth and daring, join me in love and
    garland-wearing,
and when I do – you, act insane; when I hold back, you, too, abstain.°

903

My friend, turn over any stone and you will find a scorpion.
Don't let it sting you! Treachery thrives in the places you can't see.

904°

'Now this here ac'rn may be mine, but I want that 'un!' thinks the
    swine.
And me, I've got this lovely girl, but want to give that one a whirl.

905

The prostitute's and bath attendant's chosen trades share this
    resemblance:
both have one tub, and only one, for men with scruples and
    men with none.

908

True honor, mortal and divine, is due that man who would decline
to screw a friend or play the fink; at any rate, that's what I think.

909°

My riches are in my sword and my spear together,
and the shield that defends my skin with excellent leather;
I stomp sweet wine from the grapevine
with them, with them I farm my fields and pastures,
with them I rule my indentured horde.

Those scared to wield their sword and their spear together
and shield their tender skin with excellent leather
all fall before these knees of mine
and kiss my feet, and call me Master of Masters,
10   and Mighty King, and Overlord.

Post-Classical Greek Lyric (from 323 BCE)

LIBRARY AND MUSEUM

The third century BCE. Alexandria – or Alexandria-by-Egypt, as it was known to both Greece and Rome – was midway through its first century of existence and already the chief city of the Mediterranean: it was more stable than its biggest rivals, such as Macedon's capital, Pella, and Seleucia's capital, Antioch-on-the-Orontes; more mature than Rome and Carthage, which, though on the rise, were still parochial powers and cultural backwaters; more free and fortunate than Athens and Thebes. These last two were mere shadows of their former glory, Thebes having been razed by Alexander the Great in 335, while Athens had been reduced to a blue-chip possession in the high-stakes Monopoly game played between Macedonian dynasts. This is not the place to expound the political and military exploits of the tumultuous preceding century and a half: from Athens' loss of the Peloponnesian War and capitulation to Sparta in 404, to Sparta's own rapid decline, and the meteoric rise of Thebes; to the crushing defeat inflicted by the Macedonian monarch Philip II on the combined Athenian and Theban forces at Chaeronea in 338; to Philip's assassination in 336, and his son Alexander's invasion and conquest of Persia and advance into India, as one spectacular victory followed another, until his sudden death, without an heir, in Babylon in 323; to the ensuing chaos, as Alexander's generals, called the 'Successors', carved up his vast conquests among themselves and proceeded to fight over the pieces. One of those Successors, Ptolemy, son of Lagus, took a precious piece indeed – Alexander's embalmed corpse – and spirited it to the capital of his newly claimed province in North Africa: Alexandria, where the prestige of the Conqueror's physical presence fueled that of the thriving city which bore his name.

Alexandria's heyday was at hand. It boasted a new lighthouse, a wonder of the world, on Pharos Island, and the first temple of the new god Serapis, a Greco-Egyptian fusion strongly associated with the new regime. A soon-to-be-renowned gymnasium, with 600-foot long porticoes, was going up. On the north shore, the Ptolemies' enormous palace complex included the magnificent Museum (not a museum in the modern sense but a temple of the Muses), to which the famous Library of Alexandria was attached. At the intersection of the 100-foot-wide central thoroughfare with the Street of the Soma (the Body) was the golden tomb of the deified Alexander. But the glory of the Macedonian conqueror did not shine in his city's architecture alone: a numerous fleet filled its harbor, exotic animals populated its zoological gardens and the greatest minds of the age toiled in its Library.

Alexandria's was not the first library in the Greek world – that, we are told, was established by the Athenian tyrant Pisistratus (who reigned from around 567 to 528/7 BCE) – but it certainly was the greatest. Founded in 295 BCE, it was modeled after Aristotle's Lyceum in Athens. Its first president, Demetrius of Phalerum, was fresh from his previous gig playing Macedonian puppet-ruler of Athens; before that, he had been a student of Aristotle and of Aristotle's successor, Theophrastus, and knew the Lyceum's library intimately. Ptolemy had given him 'vast sums of money' – according to the *Letter of Aristeas* – 'for the purpose of collecting together, as far as he possibly could, all the books in the world', with the initial target set at 500,000 volumes. To reach that goal, Demetrius ordered that all ships putting into Alexandria should be scoured for books. When found, they would be confiscated and copied, the copies returned to the books' owners and the originals preserved in the Library under the heading 'from the ships'. Ptolemy played a similar trick on the city of Athens; he put fifteen talents down to borrow the official Athenian edition of the tragedians Aeschylus, Sophocles and Euripides for copying, then kept the originals, returned the new copies and cheerfully forfeited the money.

Books were acquired by fair means as well as foul: Demetrius also commissioned translations into Greek from books in (among other languages) Assyrian, Egyptian, Latin and Hebrew, including the epoch-making Septuagint, the Greek translation of the Torah. Invited by the Ptolemies and tempted by their resources, luminaries flocked from all corners of the Greek world to the paradisal Brotherhood of the

Muses. From Thrace on the Greek mainland and the Dodecanesian island of Cos, as well as nearby Samos and Rhodes, from all over Greek Asia Minor – Chalcedon, Byzantium, Lampsacus, Ephesus, Cnidus – and from Cyrene and Pelusium in Egypt itself, came the historians and scholars of Homer, the mathematicians and physicists, the naturalists, astronomers and geographers, the doctors and proto-humanists, all eager to join the greatest community of learning ever assembled. The gathered geniuses included the textual critic Zenodotus of Ephesus, who first edited Homer; the medical researcher Herophilus of Chalcedon, who concluded that the brain, and the not the heart, is the seat of intelligence; the mathematician Aristarchus of Samos, responsible for an early heliocentric model of the solar system, and the Alexandrian native Euclid, often referred to as 'the father of geometry'.

Old Lesbos, as we have seen, laid claim to the lyre and legacy of Orpheus; the Alexandria of the Ptolemies followed suit, although – with the sort of variation-within-repetition that would become a hallmark of its literature – it chose the semi-legendary citharode Arion instead. The following poem, freely translated from the epigrammatist Posidippus of Pella, illustrates the point. Dedicated to Arsinoë II, sister and wife to the Alexandrian monarch Ptolemy II Philadelphus, with whom she reigned from perhaps as early as 280 until her death in the 260s BCE, it was first published in 2001, after being discovered on a papyrus roll used as part of a mummy case:

> This lyre that Arion used to play
> his dolphin brought to you, Arsinoë.
> He found it bobbing on the waves, past hope,
> and (second act of salvage) scooped it up
> to stir, when it made land safe on his tail,
> the antiphon of every nightingale.

The dolphin who had once saved Arion on his back when pirates made him walk the plank now carried his lyre to the Egyptian coast, to Pharos Island and the Nile's Canopic mouth, where he received a grateful and melodious response from all the country's nightingales. Whether those nightingales represent poems – as in Callimachus' elegy (*Ep.* p. 34, 280) for his friend Heraclitus of Halicarnassus (p. 312, not the Presocratic philosopher) – or the poets who wrote them, or both, the work of the Alexandrians is conceived in response to a Panhellenic inheritance of literature and learning; and this is as true of the epigrams of Posidippus (p. 312) and Asclepiades (pp. 303–6) as it is of the 'mimes' (comedic mini-dramas) of Herodas and the inventive, erudite and, ultimately, lost epics and tragedies of the literary group called 'the Pleiad'. Nor is it less true of the verse of Alexandria's three greatest writers, Callimachus (pp. 255–81), Theocritus (pp. 282–98) and Apollonius of Rhodes (an epic poet, excluded from this volume on generic grounds). Symbolized by Arion's lyre, that inheritance was no mere idea: it had physical being in the myriad books salvaged by the flocks of scholars, editors and librarians who thronged the Library and Museum, which one cynical wag famously called the 'Birdcage of the Muses'.

But where did this Alexandrian bibliomania come from? Were the Ptolemies really such avid readers? In a word, no, though they did employ their distinguished scholars as personal tutors and propagandists. Above all else, the Library and Museum that they founded earned them enormous prestige. While the ensemble cast of Successors, seduced by Alexander's pipedream of a unified empire, kept picking each other off like characters in a prestige TV dramedy, the Ptolemies sublimated their universalist ambitions into the cultural sphere: universal dominion gave way to universal knowledge. Ptolemaic munificence drew the scholars and scholar-poets of the Greek world like bees to pollen. Once there, they often found waspish ways to spoil their readerly paradise through bickering and infighting; but then they were, after all, de facto members of the royal court and bound by the same codes of competitive gift exchange (or competitive erudition) as other courtiers. The Successors' geopolitical tempest had its counterpart in the teapot of the Museum.

We should not be surprised that the work of these scholars, mostly the editing and cataloguing of texts, took the form it did. After Alexander, the center of the Greek world had shifted to its periphery; the Greeks of Alexandria, originally from all corners, now lived cheek by jowl with an Egyptian people Herodotus describes as having 'established for themselves manners and customs in a way opposite to other men in almost all matters'. The Hellenic cultural inheritance seemed to be under threat. The odes of Alcman (pp. 31–7) and Pindar (pp. 134–64) were already deeply obscure, in their dialect, occasion and reference, and daily becoming more so. Greeks from smaller communities, now in diaspora, found their familiar local traditions on the brink of disappearing. There was thus more at stake than is easily perceived in the arcane learning and chatty digressiveness which today we associate with 'Alexandrianism'. Behind a work like Callimachus' *Aetia* (*Causes*, pp. 258–61) on the origins of countless unusual customs was an ambition to create a sort of Panhellenic poetic encyclopedia, encompassing all that was humanly fascinating from old Greece in an elegant new synthesis intended to dazzle and delight. Another possible reason, then, besides scholarly disdain of the demotic, that we have so little of the New Music (see the introduction to the Classical Period, pp. 187–92) beloved of Alexandria's *hoi polloi*: the scholars never edited it, because its ubiquity meant they didn't need to.

Something old, something borrowed and something new: this was the formula for creativity in Hellenistic Alexandria. Consider, for example, the city's new deity, Serapis, compounded from gods both Greek and Egyptian: his name combined those of the Egyptian gods Osiris and the bull Apis, worshiped at Memphis, while his iconography derived from the newly yoked Greek trinity of Zeus (the sky-father), Asclepius (god of medicine) and Hades/Pluto (lord of the dead). In a similar way, the poet Callimachus grafted the details gleaned from his wide ranging among the Library shelves onto the age-old genres of hymn, elegy and iambus, and transplanted the results to the hothouse intellectual climate of the Museum.

Callimachus' brand of Alexandrianism has often been dismissed, by those who prefer the plainspoken straight talk of early Greek lyric, as 'bookish'; but in his defense one might observe that it is almost impossible now to imagine what a new thing Alexandrian 'book culture' actually was, or how the very act of reading and writing answered, incidentally or not, Plato's quarrel with poetry. Plato objected to the way oral poets must surrender control to the sway of the song as it forms itself in real time in their minds and mouths, sweeping the audience along with it; but the writer has time to research, think, weigh words and formulate principles, and the reader to reflect and judge. The new literary self-consciousness proved beguiling, and the scholar-poets of Alexandria devoted more time than we might like to articulating and arguing about their literary principles, as well as to cultivating a vast

erudition which, to them, must have seemed a sign not of aesthetic ener-
vation but health and genius itself.

For some readers, therefore, an exercise of historical imagination
may be required; if we are to indulge the Alexandrians in their ludic
learnedness, their aestheticism, their swaggering literary polemic, we
must reach back to a time before the suspicion of texts had become
ingrained, when 'writers' and 'readers' were exciting new categories and
there seemed to be only one Library in the world worthy of the name.
The least we can say is that their poetry sheds light on the differences
between a text-based and an oral poetic culture. The typical virtues of
'Alexandrianism' – its small scale and humble subject matter, its technical polish and flaunted allusiveness, as well as what we might call its
Ars Poetica instinct and its carefulness in the organization of its books –
would all be picked up by the Romans and passed by them into the
mainstream of medieval and modern European poetry. Surrounded by
more books than they could ever read, the denizens of the Library were
kids in a candy store, gluttons in the timeless new world of text where
they were free to feast at leisure. Small wonder, then, that a Callimachus, holed up with his books, shunning Timotheus, reading and
responding to Plato, invented literary poetry.

Callimachus

Scholarly, ingenious, playful, prickly, Callimachus of Cyrene (circa 310–240 BCE) was the greatest poet of his age and an Alexandrian par excellence; indeed, he was progenitor, high priest and avatar of what today we term 'Alexandrianism', a term which conjures (among other things) extravagant erudition, literary self-consciousness, generic experimentation and cross-pollination, and technical polish. Born in Cyrene, a Greek city on the Libyan coast about 700 miles west of Alexandria, Callimachus spent most of his life in the capital, as a courtier to both Ptolemy II Philadelphus and Ptolemy III Euergetes. One source claims that, when young, he was a schoolteacher in the Alexandrian suburb of Eleusis, another that he was a 'youth of the court' – the latter implies higher birth, and is, at first sight, more likely. Callimachus never headed the Library, but he was one of its most productive scholars; his more than 800 books included a thorough bibliography of its vast holdings (he is often said to have 'invented' bibliographical science), alongside many works with titles such as *Foundations of Islands and Cities*, *On the Rivers of Europe* and *On Wonders and Miracles in Italy*. His poetry displays a similarly compendious bookishness. He was constantly picking quarrels with critics, whom he attacks in his extant poems. The most prominent was said to be Apollonius – 'of Rhodes' supposedly having been attached to his name only after he fled there to escape Callimachus' salvos. But, like most good stories about ancient poets, this latter claim seems to have been the invention of a later age.

Amartyron ouden aeido: 'I sing nothing without a witness' (or 'nothing unattested'), Callimachus writes in his fragment 612. It appears to be a classic truth-claim, descended directly from the epiphany granted by the Muses to Hesiod, the didactic poet and Homer's rough contemporary, at the beginning of his *Theogony*. There, appearing as he grazes his sheep on Mount Helicon, the Muses tell Hesiod: 'We know how to fangle falsehoods that sound true / but we also know the truth, when we want to tell it' – the implication being that Hesiod, with their help, will be speaking the truth. For him, the Muses are sources of divine inspiration; in Callimachus, especially in the first two books of his aetiological work, the *Aetia*, they speak from the shelves of scrolls. The poet presents himself as a compiler, sifting and rewriting what has already been written. And yet there are reasons not to take him at his word. By the third century BCE, poets had fully absorbed the heckling of such eminences as Xenophanes (pp. 109–13) and Plato; they treated the traditional truth-claims of oral poetry with healthy irony, if not outright cynicism. As poet, Callimachus may claim to be a Good and Truthful Scholar, but his tongue is often firmly in his cheek. Elsewhere he says: 'I'd like my lies, when I tell them, to be convincing.'

The question of originality is tricky here. Though there is no reason to assume that Callimachus' nerdy enthusiasms (for aetiology, say) are not authentic, and he does write personally at times (see, for instance, Iambus 12, p. 266); and though, in fact, his writing is full of personality, of voice – still, regardless of all this, if we want creation *ex nihilo* (out of nothing), or *ex vivo* (from the life), Callimachus is not our poet. Despite (and because of) his indebtedness to other authors, however, Callimachus was a great innovator. He may well have been the first poet to make extensive use of prose as a source for verse – a thing Shakespeare also did, when, for example, he made a rather ordinary passage from North's Plutarch, describing Cleopatra's appearance on a barge, into one of the most transcendent passages of poetry in *Antony and Cleopatra*. Callimachus opened up poetry to new subjects and attitudes. He introduced technical refinements to the dactylic hexameter. He was among the first to arrange his own poems into books. His Hymns 2 (p. 269) and 5 (p. 272) deploy a new kind of *mimesis*, or imitation of life, intended to evoke cult ceremonies for readers who were not actually present. And, in passages we have come to call 'programmatic', he formulated aesthetic principles, which he proclaimed in verse: for example, his preference for poetry that was 'slender' and polished; for pure streams (of diction) and untrodden paths (of subject matter). These had an immense influence on Roman poets in particular; and, even when their 'project' diverged from his, they borrowed his way of asserting it. In particular, the Prologue to his *Aetia* (1.1, p. 258) became the single most influential piece of Greek literature in Rome, leaving its mark on compositions by Virgil (pp. 398–410), Propertius (pp. 421–45), Horace (pp. 453–91) and Ovid (pp. 492–526).

A further word on the *Aetia*. The inclusion of selections from that work in the present volume is, on generic grounds, difficult to justify. Though the poem is elegiac in meter and, to some extent, in subject matter (for example, the symposium scene in the *Banquet of Pollis*, p. 259), its operative mode is best described as 'didactic'. The works which are closest to it in spirit and style – Propertius' fourth book of *Elegies* and Ovid's learned long elegy about the Roman calendar, the *Fasti* – are for the most part excluded for reasons of genre and space (though two unrepresentative poems from Propertius' Book 4 are given: see pp. 440 and 442). I would argue, however, that Callimachus is such a central figure, such an important hinge between the oral poetics of the Archaic lyricists – composers for the literal or figurative stage – and the literary poetry of the Romans – writers for the page – that he deserves a more well-rounded selection than would appear if, on generic grounds, I included samples taken from only the *Iambi* and the *Epigrams*. As such, an exception has, in this case, been made: an idiosyncratic one, admittedly, but one that I believe is justified.

Callimachus was an aesthete, an intellectual entertainer and a polemicist; he was smarter and better than other Alexandrian writers, and he was pleased to say so. For me, his playful bookishness recalls a triumvirate of modern writers – Constantine Cavafy, Jorge Luis Borges and Umberto Eco – who share with Callimachus, and each other, a fascination with the arcana of history and an unabashed obsession with libraries and reading. In the end, Callimachus' scholarly attainments may have been surpassed by the librarians who came after him, but his influence – and his exquisite Greek – never were.

The *Aetia*°

1.1°

Prologue: To the Critics

You're [always] croaking at my music's strains,
Telchines, cretins whom the Muse disdains,°
since I've made no uninterrupted song
of kings or heroes, thousands of lines long,
but speak in little spurts, as children do,°
despite the many decades I've lived through.
[Hear] this, Telchines: 'Tribe [both dull and vile,]
trained just to simmer in your vicious bile:
[I] write slight poems – [so what?] The tender stalk
10   *Demeter* bears outweighs the mighty [*Oak*,]°
and of Mimnermus' volumes, it's the Fine,
not the Fat Woman, proves his verse divine.°
Let cranes fly far, from Egypt up to Thrace,
to wage their war against the Pygmy race;°
from far away let Scythian arrows fall
upon the Mede; but poems are sweeter small.°
Damned cross-eyed yokels! Measure my success°
not by the Persian chain, but artfulness.°
I can't bear thunder in my poetry –
20   don't seek it there! It's Zeus who booms, not me.'
For, when I first had taken pen in hand,
Lycian Apollo uttered this command.°
[He said, 'My friend,] a bard's tending should render
his sacrifices fat, but his Muse slender.
I say this too: don't stumble through a rut
that wagons leave, or drive your chariot
through others' tracks or down wide roads, but tread
an unworn path, though tightly limited.'
[Agreed:] my readers love the high, clear voice
30   [of the cicada,] not the ass's noise.°
Let others honk the donkey's flop-eared cry;

let me be delicate, be winged, ah, fly
forever, singing as I sip the dew –
[bountiful] manna of the holy blue –
and shed old age, for me as ponderous
as Sicily atop Enceladus.°
[No matter;] Muses, once they've glorified
a man in youth, in age stand by his side.

Fragment 178+2.43°

The Banquet of Pollis

[For Pollis didn't skimp on or] ignore   *Fr. 178*
the Festival of the Cask-Opening or
Orestes' Pitcher-Feast, which slaves adore;
but now it was your yearly feast he kept,
Erigone, whom Attic women wept,°
with some like-minded friends, and, in addition,
one new to Alexandria, an Ician
by birth, here on some personal affair,
fresh off the boat. We grabbed a couch to share,
not by design, but Homer's aphorism –   10
'the god leads like to like' – must have some wisdom,°
since we both hated chugging unmixed drafts
like Thracians, but preferred petite carafes.°
In the third round of drinks, when I had learned
his name and family, I told him as I turned,
'It's really true, the rule, "Wine should be cut
with water, yes, but also scuttlebutt."°
It's on us – since these Ganymedes won't pour it
with ladles, and your pointed looks won't score it
from gazes of unbending condescension,   20
now free men must compete for slaves' attention –
to drop it like a drug into the cup
ourselves, Theogenes, and drink it up.
Come on, and tell me everything I yearn
to hear from you. Here's what I'd like to learn:

what's Thessaly to Icus? Why latch on
to Peleus, the royal Myrmidon?°
And why do girls, at his descent to hell,
bring [bread] and onions, as [I've heard] them tell
30   who know, [because they've sailed on distant seas]
and on your own. [Not me, Theogenes,
on yours] or any other. If you will,
explain; my ears are primed to drink their fill.'
I ceased, [and thus replied that mariner:]°
'O three times blessed – and few are happier –
if you've lived free of ships and sea; my home,
far more than a shearwater's, is the foam . . .'°

2.43   And all that graced my head on that occasion –
the fragrant wreaths, the silky golden lotion –
40   soon staled and faded; and of all I ate
that settled in my stomach – that ingrate! –
nothing endures; but our discussion's strains
are with me still. Only the word remains.°

3.64°

The Tomb of Simonides

Lake Camarina drained could not bring doom°
like wiping out a pious person's tomb.
My own here, built by Acragas for me,
heeding the laws of hospitality,°
the shocking tyrant Phoenix's caprices –°
maybe you've heard of him? – tore all to pieces.
He built my stone into the balustrade
and didn't heed or read the part that said,
I lie here, offspring of Leoprepes,
10   *the sage of Ceos, who knew subtleties*
unnumbered, and who first revealed the key°
to unlock palaces of memory.°
Nor, Dioscuri, did he care about

how you, with the hall crumbling, lured me out,
and the roof fell on Scopas' head, and I –
I was the only guest who didn't die.°

4.112

Epilogue

[Light of the spangled sash,] the Graces' [star]°
and [mother of our] queen, you truly are°
all goodness, all fulfillment, in the words
[of the great bard] to whom, among his herds,°
the Muses spoke beside the hoof-struck spring:°
farewell, and go, increased in everything.
Zeus, save our royal house, and now, adieu;
I'm off on foot to prose's pastures new.°

The *Iambi*

1°

Listen to Hipponax! And can the disbelief.
Blown in from boonies where a dime buys you an ox,°
I bring *Iambics*, yes, but not about my beef
with Bupalus . . .°   4

      You 'moderns', birdbrained flocks,°   6
[ode-loaded] and pipe-plastered, dazed Dionysiacs
or Muse-[enthused, confused,] Apollo's [woozy hacks:]
come cram Serapis' shrine, the one outside of town,°
where the old fraud who dreamt up 'Panachaean Zeus',   10
Euhemerus, rants and jots his blasphemous drivel down . . .°

Phoebus! – like wasps from earth, or flies around a goat-   26
herd, or Delphians as they mob a bull whose throat
they've cut, these worthies swarm. Hecate, what a crew!°
The bald one there will blow hot air until he's blue,
so no one takes his coat.   30

                     Enough! Shut up. Take notes.
A certain Bathycles once, an Arcadian –°
it won't take long, wise guy, don't screw your nose at me!
I don't have time to waste; soon, soon I will be gone,
alas, back down the churning heart of Acheron –
in olden days this Bathycles was thriving, blessed
with every gift and godsend which conduces to
days of felicity, as men (and gods!) attest.
When he was on the brink of sinking into his long, last
repose – since he'd had a good life – he had his sons,
40   now old enough to marry, stand around the bed
on both sides (since he was bedridden with the gout),
and propping himself, like a guest at a symposium,
up on a feeble elbow, eyes uplifted, said:
'My sons, my anchors to the world I'm passing from . . .'°

52   His son sailed to Miletus, having judged the prize
should go to Thales, in most things supremely wise,
who'd also charted the sidereal career
of the two Bears, by which Phoenician sailors steer.°
What luck! The scion of the Moon's Forerunner found°
the old man, staff in hand and scratching on the ground
of Phoebus' shrine at Didyma a figure which°
Trojan Euphorbus, reincarnate, had first written:°
60   a right triangle in a circle. (He'd made the pitch,°
Pythagoras, that mooing meat should be verboten,
persuading the Italians – some of them at least –
whom hard times and bad gods denied a proper feast.)°
Amphalces reached into his bag as he went up
to Thales and took out the solid golden cup
and said, 'My pops told me to judge you and your peers –
all seven of you – and to choose the best and brightest
to give this goblet to. Here, you're the winner. Cheers.'
But Thales, holding his stick, while letting one hand sift
70   thoughtfully through his beard, still scribbling in the dirt,
replied, 'I'm sorry, but I can't accept this gift.

Yet if you do not want to disobey your father,
then Bias of Priene . . .'°

It came to Solon. Solon sent the cup to Chilon . . .

And the gift circled back to Thales once again . . .

Thales devotes me to Miletus' guardian,   76
Phoebus – a prize which Thales has twice won.°

3°

Apollo, how I wish I lived in bygone days,
[when, with the Muses,] you enjoyed esteem, and praise . . .°   2

Now Euthydemus' mother's [bargained the boy away   24
to a rich lover,] they won't give the time of day
to me – [but when] I told [the pretty thing] hello,
he gave me his right hand, and set my heart [aglow,]
and said this was a lucky day, and promised me
that we'd be close from then on – almost family!
But I, [at least,] was brought up not to lie or cheat,   30
[and, when I looked at him,] I thought I saw the Good.
And now I see the gods don't care [when a boy's faith
goes bad,] and I'm a wreck. More lucrative by far
to worship Cybele in a gown down to my feet,°
shrieking to Phrygian pipes, and tossing my wild hair,
crying, *Alas for the goddess' lover! Alas, the death
of poor Adonis!* No, this imbecile pursued°
the Muse. It's bread I baked myself; now time to eat.°

4°

The Quarrel of the Olive and the Laurel

1   Simus, you're one of us then? You? That's what you think? . . .°

6   It's an old Lydian story. Listen. There was a quarrel
     on Tmolus once between an olive and a laurel . . .°

21   '[Picture a slave whose tunic covers just one shoulder:]
     the naked right is sunburnt; the left, which the tunic sleeves,
     is white as a snake's belly – hey, just like your leaves!°
     But me – is there a door I don't adorn? A house?
     What priestly or prophetic rites don't use my boughs?
     The Pythia pronounces from a laurel throne;°
     her song is all of laurel, her bed with laurel strewn.
     But, imbecilic olive, didn't Branchus stanch°
     the pique Apollo felt toward the Ionians
30   by chanting, twice or thrice, what no one understands°
     and striking all the people with a laurel branch?
     And then, Athenians – I join their feast and dance
     at Pytho, where the victors wear a crown of me,
     and from the hills of Tempe I'm brought by Dorians
     to Delphi in lustration of Phoebus' victory.°
     For I am sacrosanct, unschooled in mortal care or
     sorrow or the winding path of the pallbearer –
     for I am pure, and not to trample underfoot.
     But, imbecilic olive, whenever people have
40   a body to cremate, or bury in a grave,
     they put on wreaths of you, and scatter you beneath –
     [what an indignity!] – those ribs deprived of breath.'
     She spoke so far, no farther. Then oil's progenitor
     with quiet strength dismissed her arguments and her:
     'My pretty, pretty friend, there, at your speech's end,
     just like Apollo's swan, you sang my greatest beauty –
     and may I never weary of that signal duty.
     Yes, I see off men slain in war, who proved most brave,

lying beneath the corpse, or honoring the grave.
And I, when the grandkids of Tethys great and gray,   50
or venerable Tithonus, carry the coffin out,°
pursue the path they tread myself, and straw their way.
That gives me deeper joy than what you brag about,
parading out of Tempe. Since you also brought
this up – how am I not a far more precious prize
than you, when the great games held at Olympia
outdistance Delphi's? But discretion here is wise,
and I don't want to compliment or criticize.
I've listened now for a bit to these two twittering birds
chitchatting in my branches. I'll repeat their words: 60
Where did the laurel come from?

                    – Oh, just from dampened earth,
like pine and oak, and like holm oak and galingale.°
And what about the olive?

                    – Pallas caused her birth
in old days when the arbiter with serpent tail
gave Attica to her, and not the Seaweed Lord.°
That's round one to the olive! But which Death-Defeater°
gives honor to which tree?

                    – The laurel is adored
by Phoebus, and the olive by Athena, her creator.
I won't decide between the gods. That's a dead heat.
But what's the laurel's fruit like? What is it used for?   70
– You can't make oil from it. It's not to drink or eat.
You *can* cook olive cakes, a favorite of the poor,
and you can press an oil which nourishes the skin,
or make those pickled olives Theseus once ate.°
That's round two to the olive. A decisive win!
Whose branches do men tender when they supplicate?
– The olive's!

        A third point – the laurel's down again!
(Oh boy, these cheeky chatterboxes sure aren't terse!
Crows, don't your beaks ever wear out, or get hoarse?)
Whose is that sacred trunk the Delians protect?   80
– Well, that's the olive where the pregnant Leto rested . . .°

[*In all of these respects*] *the olive is the winner!*'°

90   The olive ended. Wounded by her words, the laurel
fumed; more than at first now spoiling for the quarrel,
she was about to wade back in, when a dowdy old
frump of a thornbush in a hedge before the wall
spoke up – since she was close by and had heard it all –
'Ladies, let's let it rest! How nasty! A bystander
who hates us would be thrilled. Let's cease to bandy cruel
invective back and forth. Since all this is, is slander.'
And now the laurel, glaring blackly as a bull
at her, said, 'Eyesore among vegetables, you blight,
100   you think you – you – are one of us? May Zeus's might°
fend off such ridicule. Nearness to you is slow
unsavory strangulation. No! By Phoebus, no!
By Cybele, no! By the waters of Pactolus°

12°

Artemis, [you haunt] the Cretan pastures°
washed by Amnisus, and Dic[te's ridges,]°
honored *in Ephesus and highest heaven –*°
from those haunts a week ago we summoned
you *to ease the birth of Leo's daughter;*°
now, we beg you, grace the hearth [of Leo]°
once again to celebrate her birthday.
For, when called, [you enter] *righteous* cities,
though you love to gaze upon your mountains.°
10   And you, gorgeous spinners, *whose fine fabrics*
spread spell-binding nets across the hilltops,
[come and sing] – this time, not for a wedding;
[praise her fath]er's justice and [right action,]
lord of all this [loveliness] *we look on.*
He deserves our finest, you can trust me,
me, your humble servant, who speaks only
truth, who knows the tomb on Crete is empty,
who couldn't claim that Zeus, your father, perished:°
therefore, goddesses, receive with favor

these sincerest prayers for Leo's daughter.   20
I shall sing a new song for the newborn.
        Once, while Hera [bustled round preparing]
her own Hebe's one-week birthday banquet,
all the other gods sat on Olympus
arguing: who'd bring the finest present?
Zeus allotted her no middling [honor,
making her cupbearer to all heaven.
Mai]den Pallas brought a raft of playthings,
gorgeously engraved with shifting pi[ctures.]
He who guards [King Apis'] realm, Poseidon,°   30
came with toys of orichalc and amber
[from Etru]ria, whole *armloads of them,°*
lovelier than gold, and more expensive.
Envoys from the mother *of earth's bounty°*
[brou]ght *sublime bouquets of fruits and flowers,*
[with heartfelt ex]cuses *for her absence:*
she was shedding lonely tea[rs,] *lamenting*
her girl [snatched] *by that grim* robber baron's°
horses clattering down pathless shadows.
But [the blacksmith came, club-footed, shuffling,]°   40
fairest worker of t[he famous makers;
wobbling on bow l]egs, he brought all ma[nner]
of superb and golden masterpieces.
[So the gods, in fr]iendly competition,
jockeyed *vainly* to eclipse their e[quals.]
You *arrived then*, Delian Apollo,
[unencumb]ered by the ancient treasures
[sanctuaried in your ho]use at Pytho;°
[on the verge of grab]bing a gold tripod,
with prophetic ears you heard it shouting: 50
['No! Leave me] at home; *take her a poem!*'°
Now you strode inside, and started singing:
'*Gods, those gifts are gorgeous that you've offered,*
gorgeous; but the one I [bear] is different.
Phoebus, all your art and skill are needed
to surpass Hephaestus' gold creations –

gold, which Indian canines unbury°
easily – I mean the ants, dog-bodied,
lugging it on wings from the earth's innards.

60 Often gold devolves onto the vulgar
house, but disregards time-honored [greatness;]
Righteousness, and Zeus, and *love of Justice* –
people trample on their backs, and kick them,
but not gold! It's their favorite affliction.°
From your presents – even from Athena's –
though designed and chiseled with precision,
future days will leach away the luster;
only my exquisite gift will linger:
while my smooth cheek blooms with youth eternal,

70 while the wolf still hunts the kid, and hungers,
while desire leads the feet *of lovers*
after the fleeting scent of satisfaction,
so long, nymph, my song shall sing your praises
and preserve you, ever green and golden.'
At that, all the gods rose in ovation
and declared Apollo the clear victor.
Now I have to imitate *the master*
if my gift will praise her to the ages.
Let me, Lord! T[he girl is no]t a stranger:

80 we're rela[ted through my mot]her's family.
Moved by [this and more, o hea]lth of maidens,
leave the cliffs of Crete behind, and hurry:
[blessings of the beau]tiful are needed
to adorn a beau[tiful occasion.]
Make a beeline here, and grace our speeches,
goddess, with the glow of good *intentions.*
And you, Leo, brother of my boyhood,
find in my affection more than money:
the poor poet with no gold to offer

90 *offers what he can of golden verses.*

The *Hymns*

Hymn 2°

To Apollo

Look, look how the crown of Apollo's laurel is shivering!°
The whole shrine shudders. Off with you, temple-profaners!°
I hear his beautiful feet move. Phoebus is knocking.
Don't you see the delicious nod of the Delian palm tree°
suddenly stirring – the swan on the updraft, descanting?
Doorbars, leap, leap from your latches! Doorways,
turn on your hinges! Deity is not distant.
Prepare, youths, for the paean and the dance.
  Apollo appears to merit, not to the many.
Those who behold him are great; who don't, are nothing.   10
We here shall witness you, Far-Shooter, and prosper.
No boy should silence his lyre, or let his footsteps'
fervor be muffled, when such godhead comes home,
if he wants to be married, or offer gray locks in the future,°
or maintain his town walls firm on their ancient foundations.
Boys, I'm impressed – that's the use for the tortoise shell!°
  Keep a holy hush for the paean, all you who hear it.°
The sea falls silent, whenever bards start hymning
the equipment of Pythian Phoebus, the bow and the lyre.°
Thetis stifles her wails for her son, Achilles,   20
whenever she hears the *All hail, Paean, Paean!*
The tear-stained cliff face puts aside affliction,°
that live wet rock which Phrygia holds immobile,
marble that once was a woman, mouth wide, lamenting.
Cry *Hail! All hail!* Nobody should fight with immortals.
Who battles the blessed gods, would battle my king;°
whoever would battle my king, would battle Apollo.
Apollo will honor the chorus that for him will hymn
their hearts out; he's sovereign, and sits at Zeus's right.
Our chorus won't sing to Phoebus for one day only;   30
to hymn him, a bottomless wellspring of music, is easy!

For Apollo's cloak is gold, and a gold pin clasps it;°
his lyre is gold, and golden his bow and his quiver;
his sandals are golden. Apollo has gold in profusion,
and property also – just look at his precinct at Pytho.
He is handsome and youthful forever; never has Phoebus
felt, on his girlish cheeks, the least touch of peach-fuzz.
Onto the ground his tresses drip essence of incense,
yet the locks of Apollo exude not a sweat of oil-beads
40 but Universal Healing, and every city
whose earth those droplets dampen is whole forever.

    Apollo, expansive in artistry – whose range is wider?
He's patron to masters of bows and melodious bards,
for airs and archery both have his special attention.
He's god of diviners and oracles, and is the teacher
of doctors who know, through him, how to stave off death.

    And we've called him Lord of the Herdsmen since the interlude°
when, by Amphrysus' banks, he pastured the yoke-mares,°
his passionate heart beating hot for unmarried Admetus.°
50 Easily cattle increase their numbers, and she-goats
are never without young ones in a flock whose grazing
Apollo's gaze is over; the ewes are never
milkless or lambless, but they are all always nursing,
and the mother of one calf soon is a mother of twins.

    And when they map and measure some new town,°
men follow Phoebus, the lover of many a city
foundation; Phoebus himself weaves plans for cities.
The god was four years old at his first foundation,
beside the oval lake on beautiful Delos.
60 Artemis, ceaselessly hunting on Cynthus, brought back°
a bounty of goats' heads, and Phoebus braided the altar:
he built up its base out of horns, and fashioned its sides
from horns, and wove horns into its circling wall.
So Phoebus learned how to frame his first foundations.

    My deep-loamed city Phoebus revealed to Battus°
as his clan made for Libya; in the shape of a raven,
propitious, he led the way, and swore to our sovereigns
their walls would be there. Apollo's word is truthful.

Many, Apollo, appeal to you as Boedromius,
many as Clarian; everywhere, everyone calls you.   70
But me, I call you Carneius – my people's custom.°
Carneius, Sparta was your first great foundation;
Thera came second, and third was my city, Cyrene.
The sixth generation after Oedipus
brought you from Sparta to Thera; from Thera, laconic
Aristoteles settled you where the Asbystians dwelt,°
and built an exquisite abode for you, and in the city
ordained yearly festival rites, in which, at their life's end,°
o Lord, in your honor numberless bull-knees buckle.

    Carneian Lord, hail, hail! In spring, your altars   80
are dressed with all the flowers, in all their colors,
the Seasons open to dewdrops Zephyrus exhales;°
in winter, they wear sweet saffron. The flame burns always;
no ashes ever batten on last night's coals.
How Phoebus relished the dance which our warriors in war-belts
danced with the blond-haired Libyan women the first time°
the time of Carneia approached its appointed season,
when the Dorians still could not draw near to the waters
of Cyre, but dwelt in the dense-wooded vales of Azilis.°
The Lord himself saw them, and showed them the way to his bride   90
on the high-horned Myrtle Hill where Hypseus' daughter°
had slain the lion that ravaged Eurypylus' cattle.°
Apollo had never beheld a dance more godlike,
nor blessed a city with as many good things as Cyrene,
recalling the nymph he had taken. And there is no god
whom Battus' descendants have honored over Apollo.

    We hear *O Paean, Paean* – a refrain the people
of Delphi hit on for you first, on the occasion
when you aired your expertise with the golden bow.
Making for Pytho, you met an appalling, demonic,   100
god-haunting serpent. Using up all of your arrows,°
you speedily slew him, and all your people applauded:
'*O Paean*, speed an arrow!' You were born to be°
a source of succor – praise you've deserved ever after.

    Envy covertly buzzed in Apollo's ear:°

'I don't care for poets whose song is less large than the sea is.'
Apollo kicked Envy away with his foot, and answered:
'Assyria's river is vast indeed, but its churning
lymph rolls sewage and sediment down in abundance.
110   Demeter's Bees don't carry her water from any
source – the holy springs they sip at flow slightly
but purely, and theirs is the most exquisite of waters.'
    Hail, Lord! Let Criticism slink where Envy slunk to.

Hymn 5°

To Athena

All you who wait on Pallas' bath, come forth,°
come forth! The holy mares paw at the earth –°
I hear them whicker. The goddess will appear.
Come quick, you fair-haired Argive girls, come here!
Athena never washed her limbs before
she'd rinsed her horses of the dust of war,
not when she brought back from the lawless brood
of Giants weapons spattered with their blood;°
no, first by far she loosed her chargers' necks
10   from the car's yoke and scoured the sweaty flecks
of grime in ocean's streams, and cleansed the spit
and crusted froth from mouths that champed the bit.
Achaean girls, no scents, and no scent-bottle
(I hear the axles of her wagon rattle);
no scents, you bath attendants, nor scent-chalice
(such mingled attars don't appeal to Pallas),
no mirror either: *her* looks are always fair.
On Ida, too, with Paris judging there,°
her godhead neither gazed on gleaming brass
20   nor in the Simois's swirling glass;°
and nor did Hera; but Cypris took the limpid
mirror and primped each lock, and then reprimped it,
while Pallas ran twice sixty double stades,°
like Helen's brothers through Eurotas' glades,°

so that, when she had deftly kneaded in
her extra virgin oil to coat her skin,
a flush rushed to her cheeks, as ruddy-fresh
as a spring rose, or pomegranate flesh.
So bring a manly oil – just olive, please –
like Castor uses, and like Heracles,°   30
and bring a golden comb, to unentwine
her tangled locks, once they've been washed and shine.
    Come forth, Athena! Your beloved band
of Argos' maiden daughters is at hand!
And now they're bearing Diomedes' Shield,
a custom Eumedes, your priest, revealed°
to elder Argives, a man in your esteem,
who, when he learned about the people's scheme
to kill him, fled with your Palladium°
out to the Crean Mount, and made his home –   40
the Crean Mount, I say, on rocks now called
the Pallatids – and there had you installed.°
Come out, Athena, gold-helmed, you who shatter
cities, who love the shields' and horses' clatter.
Today, avoid the river, water-fetchers!
Argos, today let fountains fill your pitchers;
today, slaves, Physadeia brings your water,
or Amymone, Danaus's daughter.°
The hills will pour Inachus' wholesome torrent,°
with gold and flowers swirling in the current,   50
for Pallas' lovely bath. You men, beware
to gaze upon the goddess bathing there!
Argos is in her hand, and any man
who sees her naked won't see home again.
Come out, Athena! Meanwhile, I'll regale
these girls with – not mine, but another's tale.°
    There was a nymph in Thebes once, idolized
by Pallas, of her whole train the most prized,
Tiresias's mother; the two spent
no time apart, for when Athena went   60
to Thespiae, or drove through the corn-crowned

farms of Boeotia, Haliartus-bound,
or made for Coronea's fragrant woods,
with altars where the Coralius floods,°
she rode beside the goddess on the way;
and never did the others dance or play
but Chariclo was always at the fore.°
Yet she, too, had her share of tears in store,
though Pallas loved her like a second self.
One time, they'd shed their dresses on a shelf
of Helicon, and in the horse's spring°
were bathing. A noon hush held everything.
The two were bathing. The hour was noontide.°
A mighty hush held all the mountainside.
Tiresias approached the holy place
alone, a beard just shadowing his face,
with dogs at heel, thirsting unspeakably°
for the cool water – not, poor fool, to see
what he ought not, the naked deity.
Athena spoke to him, despite her wrath:
'What fate has driven you on this hard path,
Eueres' son, now bound to lose your sight?'
She ceased, and the boy's eyes were full of night.
He stood, knees locked in anguish, robbed of words,
for blank desertion seized his vocal chords.
Chariclo cried, 'Mistress, what did you do
to my poor son? Are all gods friends like you?
Unhappy boy, she took away your eyes!
Because you saw Athena's chest and thighs,
now you won't see the sun again. O woe,
o hills, o Helicon where I shall go
no more, what a great price for loss so slight:
he took a few deer, and you took his sight.'
She threw her arms around her cherished son
and cried as nightingales do, on and on,°
frenzied with grieving, and the goddess heard her.
Athena made this speech, for pity stirred her:
'Good lady, all those words so fierce and wild –

70

80

90

rethink them, please. *I* didn't blind your child.
It's not Athena's joy to quench the spark   100
in children's eyes. But Cronus' law is stark:
Whoso beholds, without the god's consent,
a god at large, shall come to punishment.
Good lady, this can never be undone
henceforth: such is the thread that the Fates spun
the day your boy was born. Now take the blow,
son of Eueres; pay the debt you owe.
What prayers Autonoë will make one day,°
what offerings Aristaeus, when they pray
their son Actaeon had escaped so lightly.   110
Although he joins the chase alongside mighty
Artemis, neither hunts nor arrows shot
beside her in the hills shall ease his lot
when he by accident shall glimpse the stream
laving the goddess. Then his former team
will taste their master's flesh, and, as she mourns,
his mother seek his bones in brush and thorns.
Oh you, most heaven-blessed of womankind,
she'll say, *whose son came home again, though blind!*
My dear, please cease to keen. Because of you,   120
I'll see your son has many blessings too:
he'll always be renowned, a paragon
of prophecy, surpassing everyone.
He'll know which birds are favorable, which fly
on an ill wind, which fail to signify.
For Cadmus he shall speak the will divine,
Boeotia too, and Labdacus's line.°
I'll give him a great staff to steer his feet,
and years on years before his life's complete.
Alone among the shades he'll still be wise   130
and honored by great Hades when he dies.'°
She spoke, and gave her nod. When Pallas nods
her will is done – to her alone of gods
her father Zeus gave his full range of powers.
It was no womb she sprang from, o bath-drawers,

but Zeus's head, that head that will not nod –
[nor will his] daughter's – in deceit or fraud.°
    Now, now: Athena comes in truth! Prepare
her welcome, girls – the task is yours to share –
140   with greetings and with prayers and chanted hymns.
Hail, shield of Argos, where Inachus brims!
Hail, driving horses forth and home in glory:
o goddess, save our Argive territory!

Epigrams°

1

Hunters, dear Epicydes, stalk the hare
and track the roe deer through the mountain air
in frost and snow; but when they cry, 'Bullseye!
And there's the animal', they let it lie.
So with my heart, which chases fleeing prey,
but when a catch lies waiting, turns away.

2°

I hate the Epic Cycle, and refuse°
to fight through crowds on busy avenues;
I don't like boys who get around, or springs
in public squares: I loathe all common things.
Lysanias, you're fair, fair, no mistaking.
(An echo, as it fades, says, 'No, he's taken.')

3°

What a love-charm the Cyclops hit upon –
that Polyphemus was no simpleton.
The Muses, Philip, soothe the wounded heart;°
there's no more potent medicine than art.
Starvation too, though evil, has one good

effect: it drives boy-fever from the blood.
Against you, callous Love, I have two cures –
so listen, kiddo: clip those wings of yours.
You don't scare me one bit. My pantry stocks
both remedies against your bitter shocks.

5

Toast Diocles. Again! Let glasses clink,
and keep the river god far from our drink.°
He's fair, o Achelous, fair – but fine,°
deny it: let his beauty be all mine!

8°

Archinus, if my own free choice convinced me
to serenade your door, hold it against me;
but please forget, if my deeds were not free,
your outrage, and my importunity.
Love and the grape compelled me – wouldn't let
me not go, or not be importunate.
I didn't call your name, but kissed the jamb.
If that was criminal, well, then I am.

10

'Menecrates, I'll catch you! Better fly!'
That was June 20th. Then on July
the 10th, the ox came to the yoke. All praise
to Hermes! (I won't sweat the twenty days.)

11

Ionis thrilled when Callignotus swore
he'd never love a man or woman more.
Swore, but the tale is true: the gods above
ignore all oaths sworn in the grip of love.°

He burns now for a man, and of last week's
Ionis he no longer thinks or speaks.

13

Our guest was wounded, and we didn't see,
though didn't we hear him sighing painfully
at the third round of toasts, when from his crown
of roses all the petals drifted down?
He's badly burnt, you gods, and that belief
is no wild guess: a thief can track a thief.

14°

I was a shellfish, Cypris by the Sea;
now I'm your shell: Selene gifted me,
a nautilus who steered my way through gales
with halyard-tentacles to hoist my sails,
but in the goddess Calm, I rowed with all
my feet (my name's from being *nautical*)
until the strand of Ceos sheltered me
and I became your toy, Arsinoë,
where the kingfishers won't, now I'm ashore,
lay eggs inside my chambers any more.
Bless Clinias's daughter, who can turn a
good deed, a native of Aeolian Smyrna.

15

There are four Graces – the three have just made room
for a fourth one, still dripping with perfume:
Berenice, bright among those brilliant faces.°
Without her light, the Graces are not Graces.

29°

All you who pass this tombstone, know that I
was both the father of and fathered by
Cyrene's son Callimachus. You ought°
to know them both. One was a patriot
who girded on his country's arms, and fought;
the other sang what Envy cannot blot.

30

Here lies the blood of Battus, who could write°
in Homer's key, and drink and joke all night.

31

– Does Charidas lie here? *You mean, I guess,*
Arimmas of Cyrene's son? Then yes.
– Say, Charidas, what is it like below?
No light. – Is there an upward passage? *No.*
– And Pluto? *Just a fable.* – Then we're through – !
I've told the truth. But if the truth appalls,
an ox goes for a dime in Hades' halls.°

32

We buried Melanippus in the morning;
that evening, Basilo died, without warning,
by her own hand, for she preferred to end it
than live unbrothered. So twin grief descended
on Aristippus, and Cyrene swooned
to see that thriving house, that gaping wound.

34

When I heard, Heraclitus, you were dead,°
I thought of all the suns we'd talked to bed
those nights, and the tears came. Dear guest, I know
that you were ashes long and long ago,
and yet your nightingales are singing still:
Death kills all things, but them he cannot kill.

37

The daughters of all Samos still ask after
the chatty Crathis, clever, quick to laughter,
their sweetest friend, whose tongue was never still;
but here she sleeps the sleep all daughters will.

41

Here Saon of Acanthus shuts each eye
in holy sleep. Don't say that good men die.

45

If only sailing ships had never been!°
Sopolis, son of Diocleides, then
would not rot on the waves, while we go by
his empty tomb, and read his name, and cry.

46

After twelve years, here Philip had to lay
Nicoteles, his son, his hope, away.

50

Who are you, stranger? A corpse wrecked on the foam;
Leontichus found me, and made this tomb,
mourning his own life hard by death. For full
restless he roams the oceans, like a gull.

51

Timon, is Dark or Light worse? You can tell,°
you're dead. *The Dark – there's more of you in hell.*

53

Ambracian Cleómbrotus said, 'Sun, farewell!'
and leapt right off a rampart into hell.
No awful sight ordained his dying; he'd o-
nly skimmed some metaphysics: Plato's *Phaedo*.°

58

A poet has the planet's briefest boast
when he triumphs: 'Winning,' he says, at most.
But if things turn out badly, and you say,
'Hey, how'd it go?', he says, 'The other way.'
Let that last speech belong to those who cheat;
but for me, Lord, let's keep it short and sweet!

63°

May you too sleep through nights like those you force
on me, Conopion, by your cold doors.
May you too sleep the sleep you bring on me,
too pitiless to dream of sympathy.
The neighbors pity; you wouldn't dream of it;
but when you're gray – soon, soon! – you won't forget.

Theocritus

Theocritus (mid-third century BCE) was famous in antiquity as the inventor of pastoral, also known as 'bucolic' or 'oxherd songs' (from Greek *boukolos*, 'oxherd' or 'herdsman'). It's a likely enough inference from his poems – and biographies agree – that he was a native of Syracuse and spent much of his life on the island of Cos in the Dodecanese. It's also plausible that he visited Alexandria, where he obtained the patronage of Ptolemy II Philadelphus and could have met Callimachus (pp. 255–81), as well as the epic poet and librarian Apollonius of Rhodes; there's certainly evidence of reciprocal influence and allusion throughout the work of all three men. Most scholars believe Theocritus to have been the youngest of the lot, but the precise chronology is in doubt and ultimately impossible to prove.

In being commonly referred to as 'idylls' (from *eidyllia*, 'little types'; *eclogae* is the Latin translation, meaning 'short pieces' or 'selections'), Theocritus' poems are unique in all of Greek verse. Indeed, the literary meaning of 'idyll', at least at first, seems merely to be 'a poem written by Theocritus'. Why this should be so is far from clear. What is clear, though, is that his importance, for us as for the ancients, lies in his invention of bucolic. Not all Theocritus' idylls are bucolic, or pastoral; in this selection, neither Idyll 2, the monologue of a broken-hearted mistress (p. 286), nor Idyll 10, a dialogue between two reapers (p. 294), has anything to do with herdsmen. Many, but not all, are 'mimes' (*mimoi*, mini-plays), a genre invented by Theocritus' Sicilian countryman Herodas, while the occasional use of rhetorical or narrative frames (as in Idyll 11, p. 296) recalls the Platonic dialogue. Many of his idylls are set on Sicily, with the exception, in this volume, of Idylls 2 and 7 (pp. 286 and 291), which are on Cos, and Idyll 10, which could be anywhere; the action, such as it is, mostly takes place in a timeless and idealized landscape free from labor and piracy, though Idyll 11 belongs to the mythical past. Theocritus' poetry simultaneously invites and resists generalization: if Theocritus thought of himself as inventing something, it would be hard to define what it was based on his own pleasingly varied output. Pastoral crystallized as a genre only in his wake; and the familiarity of certain tropes and motifs should not disguise the fact that, when Theocritus was writing, nothing comparable yet existed in Greek. He may not have known exactly what he was doing, but he must have known it was new.

Bucolic is not, strictly speaking, a lyric form. It is, rather, a sophisticated literary hybrid, with an epic meter and a dramatic structure wrapped around a core of song that, in its highly stylized way, does represent or recapitulate one of the closest things ancient poetry offers to pure lyric: namely, the simple tunes sung by country folk to while away the long hours spent pasturing sheep or harvesting grain, in a rustic song culture which may have had its roots in the real third-century BCE Sicilian countryside and which Theocritus may have experienced directly. It's those lyric cores that are primarily extracted here from Idylls 1 and 7.

What Theocritus made of bucolic has enjoyed enormous influence. Starting in the Renaissance, pastoral was for centuries a sort of rite of passage for major poets, from Edmund Spenser in *The Shepheardes Calender* (1579) to Robert Frost in *North of Boston* (1914) – though this is due less to the direct influence of the *Idylls* than to the *Eclogues* of Theocritus' greatest imitator, Virgil (pp. 398–410). Nonetheless, Theocritus deserves attention not only for his historical importance and portrayals of country life but as an artist of profound originality and skill, with a keen eye for character and a deep sense of mystery and wildness.

from Idyll 1°

The Death of Daphnis

Muses, strike up, strike up the country song.
I, Thyrsis of Aetna, sweet-voiced Thyrsis, speak:°
Where, where were you, nymphs, during Daphnis' fever?°
In Tempe and Peneus? Pindus' peak?
For you weren't near Anapus' mighty river,   70
on Aetna, or by Acis' sacred creek.°

Muses, strike up, strike up the country song.
For him the wolves, for him the jackals howled;
grief-stricken lions in the thickets growled.
Muses, strike up, strike up the country song.
There by his feet the bovine herd converges;
the steers, calves, bulls and heifers low their dirges.
Muses, strike up, strike up the country song.
First from the hill came Hermes. He said, 'Oh,°

80   Daphnis, who did this? Whom did you love so?'
Muses, strike up, strike up the country song.
The oxherds, shepherds, goatherds all came over°
wondering what was wrong. Priapus then
came and cried out, 'Poor Daphnis, why this fever?
A girl goes round each spring and woody glen –
Muses, strike up, strike up the country song –
searching for you. Wrong-headed, powerless!°
An oxherd once, you're like goatherds who shed
tears as they see the nannies' friskiness

90   in heat, and wish they'd been born goats instead –
Muses, strike up, strike up the country song –
just so, you watch the maidens laugh, heartsore
that you can't dance with them, and tears descend.'
The oxherd, though, made no reply, but bore
his bitter love right to the bitter end.
Keep singing, Muses, sing the country song.
Now Cypris came, sweet-smiling, in a set
mask for the heaviness beneath the sweet.
She said, 'You boasted you could throw Love, yet

100   here you are, Daphnis, pinned by him, and beat.'°
Keep singing, Muses, sing the country song.
Then Daphnis answered, 'Vengeful martinet,
unbearable, man's enemy-in-chief,
you think I'm done for? All my suns are set?
Even in hell, Daphnis will give Love grief.
Keep singing, Muses, sing the country song.
You and an oxherd once – Go on, turn tail!°
Ida, Anchises, oaks and galingale

are waiting. Go, beslut the bee-loud vale.°
   Keep singing, Muses, sing the country song.   110
Adonis is ripe and ready, herding sheep
and hunting hares, and things that charge and leap.°
   Keep singing, Muses, sing the country song.
Tell Diomedes at close quarters, "See,
I've crushed the oxherd Daphnis; fight with me!"°
   Keep singing, Muses, sing the country song.
O wolves, o jackals, bears that live in dens,
farewell. No more shall oxherd Daphnis dwell
among your woods, your thickets, and your glens.
Farewell, o Arethusa, and you, swell°   120
of floods down Thybris, lovely streams, farewell.°
   Keep singing, Muses, sing the country song.
I am that Daphnis led his cows to pasture
and to the water – the bulls', the heifers' master.
   Keep singing, Muses, sing the country song.
Pan, Pan, if it's Lycaeus' heights you roam,
or Maenalus, come down to Sicily,°
leaving Callisto's crag and the sheer tomb
of Lycaon's seed, where the gods love to be –°
   Muses, leave off, leave off the country song –   130
come, Lord, and take this pipe of honeyed breath,
sweet with compacted wax, whose lovely lip
good binding winds around – for now to Death,
King Death, Love drags me down with iron grip.
   Muses, leave off, leave off the country song.
Brambles, bear violets; and bear violets, furze!
Let all be changed: let pears make pine-boughs sag,
let bright narcissus bloom on junipers,
since Daphnis dies; let the hound flee the stag,
and let the screech owl in the mountains shout   140
down at the nightingale, and drown him out.'°
   Muses, leave off, leave off the country song.
He spoke, and ceased. And Aphrodite bent,
wanting to raise him up, but all his thread
the Fates had measured out. So Daphnis went

down to the stream; the whirlpool laved that head°
the Muses loved, and nymphs did not resent.
    Muses, leave off, leave off the country song.

Well! Give me the goat and cup, so I can milk her
150   and offer a libation to the Muses.
A thousand greetings, Muses, and goodbye!
Someday I'll sing you something even sweeter.

Idyll 2°

The Spell

Where are my bay leaves? Thestylis, bring them!
Where are my cordials? Crown the cup with wool,
fine crimson wool, so that my magic art
may bind my love, now grown intractable.
It's twelve days since the villain visited;
he doesn't know if I'm alive or dead,
and hasn't knocked, not once! Oh, faithless heart! –
the Loves have handed it to someone else,
it's clear. I'll go to Timagetus' gym°
10   tomorrow and berate him to his face;
now, though, I'll bind him with my fire spells.
Daemonic Moon, shine fair, while quietly°
to you and subterranean Hecate,°
whose dark epiphany makes dog-hearts race
beside the corpse-mounds where the black blood flows,
I'll murmur incantations. Hail, o dire
goddess! Secure the end of my desire
and make my spells good as the sorceresses',
Circe's and Medea's, and good as those
20   of Perimede with the golden tresses.°
    Catch, magic wheel, my man, and bring him home.°
First, char the barley, Thestylis. What's the matter?°
There, on the fire, scatter the barley grains!
You think I'm joking? Do you have any brains?

Scatter, and say, 'It's Delphis' bones I scatter.'
    Catch, magic wheel, my man, and bring him home.
Delphis hurt me. For him I burn the bay.
Just as it pops and sparks and in a flash
is swallowed by the blaze, and leaves no ash,
so may the flames melt Delphis' flesh away.   30
    Catch, magic wheel, my man, and bring him home.
I'll burn the bran now. You, who break hell's bonds
and gates of adamant, o Artemis –
the dogs howl in the alleys, Thestylis!
The goddess is at the crossroads. Clash the bronze!°
    Catch, magic wheel, my man, and bring him home.
The winds are silent; silent stands the sea,
but far from silent churns my hidden strife,
for I, no more a virgin, not a wife,
am burning for the man who ruined me.   40
    Catch, magic wheel, my man, and bring him home.
As this wax melts by Cypris, may that man,
Delphis of Myndus, melt with love and burn.
As Cypris makes this bronze bullroarer turn,°
may he be whirled out to my door again.
    Catch, magic wheel, my man, and bring him home.
I tip my cup three times, three times implore:
whether a woman holds him, or a man,
may Delphis never think of them again,
forgotten like Ariadne on the shore.°   50
    Catch, magic wheel, my man, and bring him home.
A weed in Arcady, hippomanes,°
drives colts and mares mad in the hills they roam;
bring Delphis, likewise maddened, to my home,
straight from the wrestling floor, all bright with grease.
    Catch, magic wheel, my man, and bring him home.
This bit of cloak-fringe Delphis lost – now I
shred it and feed it to the ramping fire.
Why cling to me like a swamp leech, Desire –
you curse, you killer! – draining my black blood dry?   60
    Catch, magic wheel, my man, and bring him home.

Tomorrow I'll grind and brew some lizard mush.
Now, while it's night, Thestylis, take this powder
to crush before his door, and say, no louder
than a whisper, 'It's Delphis' bones I crush.'
 Catch, magic wheel, my man, and bring him home.
Alone now, I can mourn the mess I've made –
where should I start? Who caused this pain of mine?
My friend Anaxo joined in the parade°

70 as basket-bearer at Artemis's shrine;°
great beasts, a lioness even, were displayed.
 Behold my love, Queen Moon; behold the start.°
Theumaridas's nurse, who lived next door
(gods rest her soul!), a Thracian, pled with me
to go; I yielded, to my woe, and wore
a shawl of Clearista's, shimmery,
over my linen dress that brushed the floor.
 Behold my love, Queen Moon; behold the start.
Halfway along, by Lycon's, I caught sight

80 of Delphis and Eudamippus in the road;
their beards were like sunflowers, but more bright;
and brighter, Moon, than yours, their torsos glowed,
oiled from the toil of wrestling, slick with light.
 Behold my love, Queen Moon; behold the start.
I saw him, I went mad, a foolish blaze
caught in my heart, my beauty drained away;
I couldn't see the show, and it's a haze
how I got home, where, feverish, I lay
bedridden, shaking, for ten nights, ten days.

90 *Behold my love, Queen Moon; behold the start.*
My skin was jaundiced, as with yellow dye;
my hair fell out in clumps, and I was weak,
just bones and skin. Whose help did I not try?
What hag adept in charms did I not seek?
Nothing was any use, and time flew by.
 Behold my love, Queen Moon; behold the start.
I told my slave the truth: 'It's killing me,
Thestylis; I'm sick, and all for him,

the Myndian boy. Quick, find a remedy,
and go keep watch at Timagetus' gym –   100
that's where he goes, and where he loves to be.
  Behold my love, Queen Moon; behold the start.
When he's alone – be subtle! – beckon. Say,
"Simaetha wants to talk" – and lead him here.'
That's what I said. She went, and shortly they
were at my door. When I saw him appear,
athletic and glistening in the entryway –
  behold my love, Queen Moon; behold the start –
my body froze, colder than snow, dewfall
of sweat beaded my forehead, not a peep   110
of sound I made, more speechless than a small
child whimpering for its mother in its sleep,
and I tensed, rigid as a waxwork doll.°
  Behold my love, Queen Moon; behold the start.
Heartless, he glanced at me, then to the floor,
and sat down on the couch, and sitting, said,
'You beat me here, Simaetha, by no more,
as soon as your message came, than I outsped
Philinus that time when we raced before.°
  Behold my love, Queen Moon; behold the start.   120
I would have come, though – by sweet Love, it's true –°
right around nightfall, with four friends, or three,
with apples of Dionysus all for you,°
wreathed in white poplar, Heracles' holy tree,°
with bands of crimson cloth all woven through.
  Behold my love, Queen Moon; behold the start.
Then, if you'd let me in, what pure delight
(since the boys say I'm fast, and no mean catch);
and, if you'd kissed me once, I'd have slept tight.
But if you'd met me with a fastened latch,   130
I'd have brought axe and torch on the next night.
  Behold my love, Queen Moon; behold the start.
To Cypris first my utmost thanks are due,
but after Cypris, lady, for your gracious
hand from the oven, I, half-cooked, thank you.°

It's true: Love's furnace really is more vicious
than Lipara's, where Hephaestus lights the flue.°
   Behold my love, Queen Moon; behold the start.
Love, too, with a kind of fear, bewildering Love

140 makes virgins venture from their rooms and hallways
and brides desert the still-warm bed sheets of
husbands.'
              He ceased. I took his hand and lay
beside him on the couch, too trusting always.
Then skin warmed skin, our faces flushed with heat,
we whispered low, and what we said was sweet.
No need, dear Moon, to draw my story out:
the deed was done; we came to our desire.
Till yesterday, I had no cause for doubt –
he was in love with me; I felt the same.

150 But then Philista's and Melixo's mother came –
Philista was our flute-girl – just today,°
when, out of ocean, sweeping ever higher,
the steeds brought Dawn in veils of rosy flame;°
she told me many things, and said as well
that Delphis was in love, though couldn't say
if it was with a woman or a man,
but knew that toasts to Love and unmixed wine°
were always on his lips. She said he ran
off in the end, announcing he was bound

160 to wreathe that house. That's what she had to tell°
and she's no liar – he used to come around
three or four times a day, and leave with me
his flask of oil. But I last saw the boy
twelve days ago. Yes, he has some new toy
and I am clean forgot. So now I'll bind
him with my spells: he'll knock on Hades' door –
by Fate, I swear! – if he won't knock on mine.
For my case holds concoctions black with danger,
recipes gleaned from an Assyrian stranger.°

170 Farewell, Moon, turn your horses toward the sea,
and I'll endure my longing as before.

Farewell, Queen Moon, poised on your throne of light,
and farewell all you stars that trail behind
the frictionless and flying car of Night.

from Idyll 7°

The Harvest Festival

LYCIDAS

Ageanax will smoothly sail the brine,°
making for Mytilene, when waves flee
the South Wind's blast, the Kids at evening shine°   60
and Orion wets his ankles in the sea –
if Lycidas, in Love's volcano caught,
he deigns to save. My love of him runs hot.
And halcyons shall lay the waves to rest°
and the winds' clash that churns the deep seaweed –
halcyons, by the Nereids loved best
of birds; loved, too, by all the waters feed.
May all things bless Ageanax's way;
may he end safe in Mytilene bay.
And on that day around my brow I'll twine   70
roses, or dill, or snowdrops, and I'll sit
beside the fire with my Ptelean wine,°
and drink, and eat beans cooked in the firepit.
Fleabane, asphodel and celery,
deep as my arm, will strew my bed of grass;
I'll toast Ageanax in luxury
and lip my lifted cup, and drain the glass.
From Lycope and from Acharnia°
shepherds will pipe, and Tityrus will sing
how oxherd Daphnis fell for Xenea,°   80
how the hills grieved and oaks stood sorrowing
for Daphnis by the Himera while he°
melted with fever like the snows that wend
down from Mount Haemus, Athos, Rhodope,
or mighty Caucasus at the world's end.°

And I'll hear how that wicked, reckless master
 in a chest locked his goatherd, still alive;
how to that cedar box, out of the pasture,
the blunt bees brought the soft food of the hive,
90   because those lips were sweetened by the Muses.°
Blessed Comátas, you too were fed with roses;
you too were locked in a box while the kind hive
fed you with honeycomb through a brutal spring.
Ah, how I wish that you were still alive!°
I'd graze your goats to listen to you sing,
divine Comatas; meanwhile, you'd recline
97   and spread your honey under oak or pine.

SIMICHIDAS
104   The Loves sneezed for Simichidas. The poor°
guy feels for Myrto as spring makes he-goats feel.
But his best friend, Aratus, hungers for°
a boy, and suffers. Gentle, nay, genteel
Aristis knows, whom Phoebus would not bar°
from lyric singing where his tripods are:°
110   Aratus loves a boy, and his bones burn.
O Pan, for Homole plain is yours by lot,°
to my friend's arms, unbidden, make him turn,
if it's Philinus that he wants, or not;°
and if you do, I hope you get off scot-
free from the boys with their sea-onion flails
who whip your statue when the hunting fails.°
But if you won't, may bites and scratches score
your body; may you sleep in nettles; may
you tramp the hills of Thrace while snowstorms pour
120   near Hebrus, facing north, and far away
in Aethiopian summers, take your flock
south of the Nile, beneath the Blemyes' rock.°
From Byblis', Hyetis' and Oecus' creeks,°
and blond Dione's peak that shears the air,°
leave now, o Loves with apples in your cheeks,
and let fly at Philinus, now so fair;

let fly! He hurts my friend, and doesn't care.
He's pear-like, overripe; the women say,°
'Philinus, how your petals drop away!'
Aratus, no more vigils at the sill;   130
we'll scuff the porch no more. Let the shrill cock
benumb another in the morning chill,
and Molon go alone for the headlock.°
Now let's have peace of mind, and have a gray°
crone spit on us to keep bad luck at bay.°

I ceased. He, chuckling coolly as before,
in token of our friendship in the Muses
gave me the staff, then curved off to the left
toward Pyxa. Eucritus and fair Amyntas°
and I turned north, to Phrasidamus's,   140
and, in a deep bed of sweet-smelling rushes
and fresh-cut vine-leaves, lay luxuriating.
Over our heads, the elm and poplar boughs
swished in the breeze; nearby, a sacred spring
from the nymphs' cave purled cool and crystalline,
while dusky in the shadows the cicadas
chattered away, and distant nightingales
made a low murmur from the bramble thickets.
The lark sang, and the linnet; turtledoves
moaned, and the bees buzzed droning by the water.   150
The smells were of rich harvest and fruit hanging.
Pears at our feet and apples from bent boughs
were rolling everywhere, and blackthorn branches
were bowing, dense with berries, to the ground.
We cracked the seals from off the four-year vintage.
O nymphs of Castalia, lofty Parnassians,°
was it from such a bowl old Chiron served
Heracles under Pholus's rock roof?°
Was this the sort of nectar that the shepherd
who lobbed whole hills at troopships near Anapus –°   160
the massive Polyphemus – quaffed that time°
when his light feet went twinkling through the sheepfolds?

Yes, nymphs, and your waters tempered it, beside°
the altar of Demeter of the Threshing.
Here in her heap of winnowed grain may I
return to plant my shovel, while she smiles°
and holds the sheaves and poppies in each hand.

Idyll 10°

The Reapers

MILON

Bucaeus, what's wrong, buddy? Why this moping?
You can't cut your swath straight, like you used to,°
or keep up with the next guy. Look, you're straggling
like an old sheep whose toes have caught a thorn.
What will you do this afternoon or evening
if you can't even mow your row this morning?

BUCAEUS

Milon, chip off a tough block, you late-reaper,
haven't you ever longed for someone absent?

MILON

Never. What good is longing when you're working?

BUCAEUS

10   Haven't you spent one sleepless night for love?

MILON

No, and I hope not to. Hard to retrain
a dog once he's picked up a taste for guts.

BUCAEUS

Well, *I'm* in love. Have been for ten days now.

MILON

It's jars of sweet wine for you! I drink sour thimbles.

BUCAEUS

Sure, *that's* why no one's hoed my yard in months.°

MILON

So who's the kid who's got you in this muddle?

BUCAEUS

It's Polybotas' girl, the one who piped
for reapers lately at Hippocion's.

MILON

The gods *are* just! You asked for it; you got it.
Now you can spoon all night with a praying mantis!°   20

BUCAEUS

You're mocking me. Wealth's not the only blind god –
remember reckless Love. Don't put on airs.

MILON

I'm not. But you, just drop those sheaves, and sing
some sweet love-ditty for the girl, to make
the work go lighter. You always were a singer.

BUCAEUS

My slender girl, Pierian Muses, sing,°
for all you touch soon sets to blossoming.
Lovely Bombyca, they call you Syrian,
skinny and sunburnt; but I say 'honey-skin'.
Dark are the hyacinth and violet,   30
but theirs are the first blooms wreath-makers get.
Clover has goats, and goats have wolves, beguiled;
cranes chase the plow; it's you who drive me wild.
If I were rich as Croesus was of old,
we two would stand for Cypris, cast in gold,
you with your pipes, an apple or a rose,
I wearing brand-new shoes, and brand-new clothes.
Lovely Bombyca, your voice is a bouquet,
your feet white dice, your moods – well, I can't say.

MILON

Our boy's a poet – we had no idea!   40
Look how he tuned the manner to the matter,
and me with this big beard, and all for nothing!
Well, try this song, by the divine Lityerses:°

Fruitful Demeter, lavish of your bounty,
make our toil easy and our harvest plenty.

Bind up those piles, boys, so no one can say,
'These men are weak as fig-wood; dock their pay!'
The stalks you cut should face the north or west,
since that's the way the cornstalks plump the best,
50   *and nobody should stop at noon to sleep –*
it's then the corn is easiest to reap.
Start up the reaping when the lark awakes,
stop when he sleeps; high heat is time for breaks.
Frogs have it good, boys! They don't need to call
for 'Drinks! More drinks!' Their swamp has got it all.
More lentils, cook, you skinflint! Or it's fitting
for you to cut your thumb off cumin-splitting.

Now *that's* the sort of thing that men should sing
who labor in the sun. That starveling love
60   of yours, Bucaeus – save it for your mommy,
to croon some morning when she's sleeping in.

Idyll 11°

The Cyclops

Seems to me, Nicias, that there's no cure°
for love, no preparation, balm or powder,
except the Muses. Their medicine is sweet;
it goes down easy, but it's hard to find.
I know you know it well, since you're a doctor
and poet popular with all the Nine.
It's how the Cyclops made the best of things
in the old days – our Polyphemus – when
he fell in love with famous Galatea
10   as the first peach-fuzz touched his cheeks and chin.
He wooed her not with apples, roses, rings,
but with pure wildness – all the rest seemed silly.
His sheep flocked from the pastures and went home
all by themselves, while, feverish on the shore,
laved by seaweed, he sang to Galatea
as the dawn broke, and nursed the bitter wound

which Aphrodite's shaft fixed in his gut.
But he did find that cure. High on a rock
he gazed out on the waves and sang this song:

> *My Galatea, fair and shearling-soft,*   20
> *firm as an unripe grape, as white as cream,*
> *and shyer than a calf, why blow me off?*
> *For you won't come ashore but while I dream,*
> *and when the dream lets go, you run away,*
> *like a sheep fleeing a wolf that's after it.°*
> *You came to pluck a hyacinth bouquet*
> *with Mama on the day my flame was lit.°*
> *I led you up the hillside the whole way.*
> *From that day on, I loved. I couldn't quit.*
> *But lordy, you – no, you don't care a bit.*   30
> *I know, I know what's got you spooked, my dear:*
> *it's this one bushy eyebrow way up high*
> *in an unbroken line from ear to ear,*
> *and these flared nostrils, and this single eye.*
> *Set that aside, my herd's a thousand strong;*
> *I milk them and the milk I drink's the best.*
> *And cheese for me's in season all year long;*
> *there's so much cheese my cheese trays are oppressed.*
> *I can outpipe all the Cyclopses here,*
> *and all night long I sing these purdy airs*   40
> *about us, my sweet apple, while I rear*
> *eleven collared fawns and four cub bears.*
> *Oh, just come here, and you'll make out all right;*
> *leave the blue ocean sloshing on the sands.*
> *Inside my cave you'll have a pleasant night:*
> *there's laurels there, and slender cypress-stands,*
> *dark ivy, and the grapevine, sweet and low;*
> *and melting freshets Aetna with its trees*
> *pours like ambrosia from its fields of snow.*
> *Who'd rather live beneath the crashing seas?*   50
> *If I'm too shaggy, I've got lots of oak*
> *and, under ash, a flame that will not die:*

come singe my hair and heart until they smoke;
and singe my favorite thing, my single eye.°
If Mama gave me gills, I'd dive below
and kiss, if not your mouth, your hand instead;
and I'd bring you narcissus, white as snow,
or poppies with their petals soft and red.
Not both at once, though – nature don't allow:
60   one buds in summer, one's a winter bud.
I'll learn to swim, at least; I'll learn right now,
and find out why you like it in the flood –
if I could meet some seadog to teach me how!
Oh, Galatea, come out and forget
to go back home, as I have on this spot;
come watch and milk my sheep with me and set
the cheese with rennet drops to make it clot.
It's all my Mama's fault, and I blame her:
she never put a good word in with you,
70   and sees me every day get skinnier.
I'll tell her my head's throbbing, my feet too,
so I can make her suffer like I do.
Cyclops, Cyclops, what's happened to your head?
You'd be far wiser weaving crates for cheese
or getting fodder for your lambs instead.
Milk what you have; why chase the one that flees?
You'll find another, purdier, maybe:
all the girls call at night, 'Come have some fun!'
and when I hear, they titter, Tee-hee-hee.
80   On land I, even I, could be someone.

So Polyphemus shepherded his love
with music that did more than money could.°

The *Greek Anthology*

The *Greek Anthology* is a collection of around 4,100 epigrams written over more than a millennium, from the Archaic to the Byzantine periods. It is largely derived from a manuscript known as the *Palatine Anthology* (*Anthologia Palatina*), founded on a text compiled by the Byzantine schoolmaster Constantine Cephalas between 930 and 980 CE. Cephalas based his work on three earlier anthologies, the stand-alone versions of which are now lost: the *Garland of Meleager* (circa 100–90 BCE) and the *Garland of Philip* (40s or 50s CE) – so called because *anthologia* is Greek for 'gathering of flowers' – and the *Byzantine Cycle* of Agathias, which dates from the sixth century CE. Only the first two *Garlands* fall within the scope of this volume.

The epigram is so named due to its origin in inscriptions – *epi* (upon) + *gramma* (letter, writing) is an exact equivalent of the Latin *in* + *scriptum* – and the brevity of the form (generally two to eight lines in length) arises in the first place from the fact that, when chiseling text onto stone, space is limited and costs are high. The poems of the *Greek Anthology*, however, with a few exceptions, tend to be literary rather than inscriptional: they are written to be read in books, not scratched onto stone. Where they pretend to physical presence, whether in a temple or on a tomb, we should generally be skeptical.

The genre has often been thought quintessentially Hellenistic, for reasons both negative and positive: negative criticisms emphasize the artificiality of the exercise and the very circumscribed nature of its ambitions; more positive ones, the scope for polish that brevity affords, the interest in quotidian subjects not previously thought fit for poetry, the considerable charm of many of the poems, etc. It was during the Hellenistic period, too, that epigram and elegy began to merge, due first of all to an overlap in meter – the same couplets which Theognis (pp. 76–85) sang to his disgruntled fellow Megarians were also uniquely suited to the brief and pointed statements inscriptions required – and, secondly, because the brevity of epigram made it easy to trade one's favorites at a party, or even to compose one on the fly. It is thus a function of the new, literary emphasis of the age that erotic and sympotic epigrams take up a major chunk of the *Greek Anthology*, along with dedications and epitaphs.

The *Greek Anthology* is arranged thematically, according to the following scheme: Book 1, Christian epigrams; Book 2, epigrams by Christodorus of Egyptian Thebes (flourished late fifth–early sixth century CE); Book 3, epigrams purportedly about a second-century BCE Pergamene temple, but likely as late as the second to sixth century CE; Book 4, verse proems (introductions) to the various source anthologies; Book 5, love poems for women; Book 6, temple dedications; Book 7, sepulchral poems; Book 8, epigrams by the fourth-century CE theologian St. Gregory of Nazianzus; Book 9, descriptive poems; Book 10, ethical pieces; Book 11, convivial poems; and Book 12, love poems for boys, probably from the first to the second century CE (Cephalas' separation of love poems for boys from those for women was the work of a later, more censorious age). Book 13 contains poems in unusual meters; Book 14, riddles and math problems; Book 15, miscellanies; and Book 16, poems lost from the *Palatine Anthology* but included in an inferior anthology compiled in 1301 by Maximus Planudes and based on Cephalas' anthology. The selection here concentrates on poems from Books 5–7 and 9–11 taken from the *Garlands* of Meleager of Gadara (pp. 301–32) and Philip of Thessalonica (pp. 332–56) and tries to avoid later intrusions. Presentation is roughly chronological.

Many of the poets included in the *Greek Anthology* are shadowy figures about whom little is known. Most have disputed or indeterminate chronology; many are no more than names, some of which (like 'Diodorus' or 'Evenus') may belong to two or more different poets. The same goes for the poems' myriad speakers and addressees – some may well have indicated real people, even acquaintances of the poets; others no doubt were stock names, intended to conjure a type or veil a personal criticism. In either case, the litany of names, mostly unknown to history, carries a specificity more poignant for its elusiveness. Where something can be said about a name, I have tried to say it in a note; otherwise, I have passed over them in silence. In the same way, I have provided brief introductions below for each *Garland* and for those *Garland*-authors for whom such an introduction is possible.

EPIGRAMS FROM THE
GARLAND OF MELEAGER

The *Garland of Meleager* dates to the decade of 100–90 BCE. It is named for its anthologist and one of its most prominent poets, Meleager of Gadara (p. 326–32). Meleager's original collection probably comprised around 6,000 lines in four books, of which about 4,500 are preserved in the *Greek Anthology*. Like Constantine Cephalas' *Palatine Anthology* (p. 299), Meleager's anthology was organized thematically, under the headings of erotic poems, temple dedications, sepulchral poems and descriptive poems – but we do not know in what order. Though Meleager anthologized epigrams from Archilochus (pp. 5–15) onward, only post-Classical poets who survive exclusively as epigrammatists are given below; the epigrams of poets whose work in other genres also survives, such as Simonides (pp. 120–33) or Callimachus (pp. 255–81), may be found with their respective authors.

Philetas of Samos

Philetas of Samos (mid-fourth century BCE) may or may not be the same as the more famous Philitas of Cos, whose elegies were so important to Propertius (pp. 421–45). These are the only two epigrams ascribed to the name.

I

Nicias, now past her fiftieth year,
Love's darling, hangs in Cypris' shrine her gear:
sandals, curled wig, prized girdle and bronze mirror,
whose gleaming face is not subject to error,
and all those things men can't make mention of.
You see here the whole panoply of Love.

2

The crushing gravestone says, 'Hades took hold
of small Theodota, who was not old.'
But the small one speaks up: 'Father, do not
lament. Disaster is our mortal lot.'

Erinna

Erinna flourished circa 350 BCE, and supposedly died at the tender age
of nineteen, soon after lamenting the death of her comrade Baucis in a
poem called the *Distaff*; its 300 hexameters were widely said to rival
Homer. The *Greek Anthology* preserves three poems attributed to her,
all of which may be by later imitators. A tribute to Erinna can be found
in Antipater of Sidon's poem 58 (p. 322).

I

O column, o Sirens, o urn with anguished air
who hold what scanty ashes Death could spare,
bid them 'Farewell' who pass before my stone,
whether from other towns, or from my own,
and say I died a young bride, that the name
my father gave was Baucis, that I came
from Tenos, so they know, and make it clear
my friend Erinna left these verses here.

Anyte

Anyte, who flourished circa 300 BCE in Tegea in Arcadia, was known
among the first generation of Hellenistic poets as the 'female Homer' for
her thoroughgoing and learned saturation in Homeric language. A skilled
composer of quatrains, she distinguishes herself chiefly by the contents of
her verses, which include epitaphs for women and pets, and pastoral

descriptive epigrams. She is a pioneering poet of the commonplace, one of the first to write epigrams on such humble subject matter. Her most dedicated imitator in the *Greek Anthology* is Mnasalces (pp. 315–16).

5

Cleina has often wailed beside this tomb,
lamenting her dear daughter's early doom,
calling Philaenis, who, before she married,
across tear-colored Acheron was carried.

9°

This Damis built for his brave horse, who died°
when Ares drove his spear through the thick hide
in front, and from the tawny breast the blood
frothed black, and soaked into the thirsty mud.

13°

The kids have muzzled you, poor billy goat,
and fastened purple reins upon your throat,
and riding you like jockeys on a course, they
circle the shrine, whose god enjoys their horseplay.

16

Sit in the shade where the laurel riots green,
sip from the spring that bubbles sweet and clean,
and give your body, breathless from the heat
of harvesting, to the West Wind to beat.

Asclepiades

Asclepiades of Samos (circa 340–260 BCE) was the first poet we know of to adapt the sympotic love poetry of elegy to the pseudo-inscriptional compression of epigram. Born on Samos in the eastern Aegean while the island was under Athenian control, he is likely to have spent some time in Sicily (whence the nickname 'Sicelidas', 'the Sicilian'), and, more speculatively, in Alexandria, where he may have befriended the younger poets Posidippus of Pella (p. 312) and Hedylus (p. 313), whose verse he influenced and with whom he is often associated. At some point Asclepiades' name attached itself to a lyric meter quite unrelated to epigram, already used long before his time by Sappho (pp. 38–54) and Alcaeus (pp. 55–67), and later much employed by Horace (pp. 453–91); it is therefore likely that Asclepiades wrote in other meters and genres (particularly the lyric) and with a wider range than Meleager's anthologizing has happened to preserve. Admired and imitated by Callimachus in his epigrams (pp. 276–81), Asclepiades stands at the head of a long line of erotic epigrammatists which includes Meleager (pp. 326–32), Philodemus (pp. 333–9) and Argentarius (pp. 347–50).

1°

Sweet in the summer heat to gulp down snow,
and sweet for sailors to make out the glow
of the Spring Wreath when zephyrs start to blow,°
but sweeter still when one sheet covers two
lovers, and both give Cypris' rites their due.

2

Saving yourself?! What for? When you've crossed over
to Hades' house, you'll never find a lover.
Love's joys are for the living. Once we're gone,
my girl, our ashes mix in Acheron.°

4

Siren Hermione and I once played;
Cypris, she wore a rainbow belt that said
in golden letters, 'Love me forever, and
soon, when another holds me, understand.'

5

Didyme's eyes have ravished me; I stare
and melt like candlewax to see her there.
What if she's darker? Coal is dark, but it
glows like a rose's calyx when it's lit.

6

Here, Lady Cypris, by your temple door
the golden spur Lysidice once wore
beside her lovely ankle she hangs up
to you – she always rode her steed on top,
so lithe her thighs weren't reddened as she rode,
and always finished, and didn't need a goad.

12°

Hang here above this door, garlands my pain
has watered (lovers' eyes are full of rain),
and do not shed your leaves too soon, my wreath;
but when the door swings and he stands beneath,
shake out your cloud upon his head, that so
his shining locks may drink deep of my woe.

15

Not twenty-two, and life is too much for me.
Why burn me, Loves? Why do you prick and gore me?
And if I die, what happens? Clearly you
punks will keep dicing, as you always do.°

16°

Asclepiades, drink! Why all these tears?
Cypris has taken many prisoners;

many have suffered from the barbs of Lust.
You're not dead yet; why grovel in the dust?
Drink the wine straight. Dawn's fingernail shows thin:
will a lamp lead us off to bed again?
Another round, my loveless, luckless friend!
Soon we'll sleep through a night that does not end.

17

Whatever life is left me, for god's sake,
lay off, o Loves! Just give my heart a break.
Or change your darts to lightning and let fly,
blasting the pile of ash that once was I.
Let fly, o Loves, let fly! You've wasted me,
and all I ask is this small courtesy.

42°

Long winter night. The Pleiades have set.°
I pace her porch in rain, shivering and wet,
desperate for her, the liar. The goddess' arrow,
flame-cured, burns worse than love; it boils my marrow.

Leonidas of Tarentum

Leonidas of Tarentum (which the Greeks called Taras, and which is
now Taranto) flourished around 290 BCE. He is among the most
popular and imitated epigrammatists in the *Greek Anthology*. A poet
of the common people, and thus heir to Anyte (pp. 302–3), he deploys
an ornate Greek style, replete with recherché vocabulary and striking
neologisms, to elevate hunters, farmers, fishermen, weavers, etc., to
the dignity of verse. His commitment to the simple life, self-sufficiency
and contentment with little has its philosophical roots in the Cynicism
of Diogenes of Sinope. Among the many authors influenced by Leonidas' combination of style and subject matter, this volume includes
Theodoridas (pp. 316–17), Phanias (p. 320), Antipater of Sidon

(pp. 320–23), Erucius (p. 343), Zonas (p. 344), Antiphilus of Byzantium (pp. 351–2), Evenus (p. 354), Maccius (p. 354) and the anthologist Philip of Thessalonica (pp. 355–6).

5

Cool waters rushing where the rock is cleft,
greetings; and greetings, nymphs, whittled and left
by country hands! You rocks that ring the rim,
and you, you thousand dolls splashed at the brim,
greetings! Aristocles leaves you this cup
which quenched his thirst when he was burning up.

17

Dust is enough for me. Let a too-great
tower of wealth crush others with its weight.
What do I care, once dead, who knows where I,
Calliteles' son Alexander, lie?

19

Shepherds who walk these hills in the wind's teeth
feeding your goats and shaggy sheep, bequeath
Cleitagoras this kindness, sweet though small,
owed to Persephone, who's under all.
May your sheep greet me, while your shepherd's reed
flutes softly from a near rock as they feed.
In the new spring, may locals deck my tomb
with a wreath woven from many a gathered bloom,
and may a ewe, her udder full of cream,
mother of pretty lambs, send forth a stream   10
of milk onto my stone. We dead *can* see
the living blessed for acts of charity.

21°

Traveler, though the stone at my grave-mound
looks small and hardly sits above the ground,
don't blame Philaenis. From the bramble thicket
she cared two years for me, her songster cricket,
her piping hopper, and she cherished me
because my reedy voice made melody.
And when I died, she left this little shrine
in tribute to those varied tunes of mine.

33

Don't let the drifter's lifestyle grind you down,
ranging from land to land, and town to town.
Don't be ground down. Get you a hut, though bare,
that has a little hearth to warm the air,
some meager barley bread – no gourmet stuff –
kneaded by your own hands in the stone trough,
and mint, a sprig of thyme, or just a bit
of coarse salt, slightly sweet, to season it.

45

Here Philocles has hung on Hermes' wall
his clattering boxwood rattle and his ball,
the jacks that drove him mad, his top, all dear
toys of the childhood that he hangs up here.

57

Sober Eubulus lies here. Let's recall°
him and drink up: Hades dry-docks us all.

71

Ah, Anticles! and ah me, who upon
the pyre laid, in his prime, my only son!
You perished at eighteen, my child, and left
my old age racked and weeping and bereft.
Would I could join you in the dark! No sight
of dawn or the keen sun brings me delight.
Ah poor, doomed Anticles, assuage my pain;
take me from here to be with you again!

77

Infinite, man, the days before your birth,
and infinite will be your time in earth.
What is the span of life left till you sink
but an eye-blink, or less than an eye-blink?
Your life is short, hemmed in, and what there is
is bitter, worse than death's indignities.
Would you, who are but scaffolds built of bone,
take to the sky as if it were your own?
Your toil is vain. Look, see the maggot sit
on the thread at the end of the warp and ruin it . . .°   10
Each morning ask how well you feel, how strong,   13
and live within your means your whole life long,
always remembering, while you walk above,
what wisps of straw your frame is fashioned of.

85°

It's sailing season! Swallows are on the wing
chitchatting, and the zephyr's freshening;
the fields bloom, and the sea, furrowed by violent
windlash and whitecaps, finally is silent.
Now weigh the anchors, sailor, and untie
the hawsers, fill your sheets with wind, and fly!

It's I, Priapus of the Port, who order°
you off on every trade, to every quarter.

91°

Not only do I sing sweet melodies,
warmed by the summer heat high in the trees,
feasting on dainty dewdrops, all unpaid
by passersby for any serenade,
but you can see me on Athena's spear,
next to her helmet, singing in her ear.
As I receive the Muses' fond attention,
so she has mine: the pipe was her invention.°

Phalaecus

5

Cease from seafaring, if you would survive
to ripe old age; get you a plow to drive.
Landlubbers' lives are long, but it is rare
to find a mariner who has gray hair.

Nossis

Nossis (flourished circa 275 BCE) was an aristocrat from Epizephyrian
Locri (now simply Locri) in Calabria, on the toe of Italy. A literary
descendant of Sappho (pp. 38–54), in most of her extant epigrams
Nossis celebrates mature female beauty. Other influences include Erinna
(p. 302), Anyte (pp. 302–3) and Asclepiades (pp. 303–6).

1

'Nothing is sweeter than love; no goods compete.
I'd even spit out honey – it's not sweet.'
So Nossis says. You girls Love hasn't kissed
don't know the sorts of roses that exist.

3

Hera most high, who often stoop to view
the smoking altars Croton keeps for you,°
accept these linens we two wove together,
Theophilis and Nossis, her famed daughter.

4

Let's go to Cypris' temple and behold°
her statue, highly wrought and made of gold,
which Polyarchis gave, whose living came
from her own body, and her beauty's flame.

5

Samytha's gift, I'm sure, will satisfy
Cypris: this net her locks were governed by,
for it is intricate and fragrant now
as nectar she daubs on Adonis' brow.°

11

You're off to Mytilene, land of dances,
to drink in Sappho's petaled elegances?
Say I'm the Muses' friend, a Locrian,
and that my name is Nossis, and pass on.

Heraclitus of Halicarnassus

This is that same Heraclitus who is mourned famously by Callimachus in his epigram 34 (p. 280). Little is known of him, and none other of his 'nightingales' survives – though the quality of this one makes us wish there were more.

I

The earth is freshly dug, and the leaves wave
and drop from garlands draped about the grave.
Traveler, come, let's read the stone and find
whose scoured bones it says are here enshrined.
'I'm Aretemias, kind Euphro's wife,
from Cnidus. Birthpangs brought me twins in life:°
one helps my husband in infirmity;
one, to remind me of him, came with me.'

Posidippus of Pella

(Early–mid-third century BCE)

I

Come, Attic jug, let Bacchus' raindrops spill;
drench our cocktail potluck. Refresh, refill!°
Silence Cleanthes; let learned Zeno bleat°
no more. We'll talk of Love the bittersweet.°

2

No tears, no wheedling; I won't swallow it,
Philaenis. I know, *I'm* your favorite –
when we're together. And when you're undressed
with someone else, you say you love him best.

Hedylus

2

That wine, those toasts, Nicagoras' love, all crept
up on Aglaonice, and she slept.
Now she in Cypris' temple leaves these spoils
of maiden love, still sweet with dripping oils:
her sheer slip, and the shawl ripped from her breast,
witnesses to his wildness and her rest.

Rhianus

(Mid-third century BCE)

10

Under a plane tree Dexionicus trapped
a holy blackbird, and held it while it flapped
its wings, wretchedly screeching the whole time.
But I, dear Love, and Graces in your prime,
wish I were thrush or blackbird, so the boy
would hold me while I shrilled and sobbed with joy.

Dioscorides

1

They drive me wild, those chatty lips flushed rose,
heart-melters, portals where ambrosia flows;
those eyes, that with soul-snaring lightning-flashes
lasso my longing under batting lashes,
and then that shapely, matching, milky bosom,
seat of desire, better than any blossom.°
But why lead dogs to bones? Secrets, once spouted,
escape. Midas's reeds know all about it.°

2°

Athenium sang the *Horse*, and did me wrong,
since I caught flame with Ilium at the song.
What took the Greeks ten years took her a minute.
So Troy was conquered, and I too within it.

3

Adonis, by your bier she wounded me°
beating her own breast – Aristonoe.
If she would do as much beside *my* tomb,
I'd join you on the ferry now – make room!

6

Arsinoë gave Sosipater her oath
of loving loyalty and common troth.
She lied; her oaths were empty; his wounds linger;
and still the gods have yet to lift a finger.
Hard by her doorbar, Hymen, when she's wed,°
may you hear dirges from the perjured bed.

16

Chaste Atys, chambermaid of Cybele,°
inspired with a bitter ecstasy,
from Pessinus for Sardis once set out°
in frenzy, while the wind-blasts whipped about
his raving hair. He ventured on until
the fervor of his passion had grown still
and twilight fell, and then he ducked inside
a cave just off the road where he could hide.
A lion jumped his path, a hulking brute
10   brave men would tremble at. He stood there mute,
speechless with fear, till some god made him take

his kettledrum and give it a good shake.
At once, the boldest of the beasts, in fear
of that deep thunder, sped off like a deer,
spooked by the noise. 'This chamber in the rocks,'
he cried, 'Great Mother, and this chatterbox°
that scared him off, I consecrate in thanks
to you by the Sangarias's banks.'°

30°

To Pitana Thrasybulus was borne°
flat on his shield, with seven punctures torn°
straight through his chest in front. Tynnichus laid
his bloodied boy upon the pyre, and said,
'Tears are for cowards. I will not shed one
for you, dear boy, both my and Sparta's son.'

32°

Demaeneta sent eight to the war zone°
and buried all of them beneath one stone.
Said, 'Sparta, hail!' – letting no teardrop fall –
'I bore these boys for you.' And that was all.

Mnasalces

(Mid- to late third century BCE)

8

Now heaven's birds can rest their wings and sit
on this sweet plane tree, since he's under it –
the Melian Poemander, who no more
coats fowlers' canes with birdlime, as before.

11°

Say 'Seagull', for she's buried here, my friend,
the lightest thing on land, mare like the wind,
who made such voyages as ships can make,
and flew the full twelve stades like her namesake.°

Theodoridas

(Late third century BCE)

2

To all the nymphs on Amarynthus' sheer°
slopes Charisthenius now hallows here
this gold hairpin, and these shorn youthful locks,°
along with a holy-water-sprinkled ox.
The boy shines like a star, or like a colt
who has cast off his downy newborn coat.

12

Staffless, Cinesias, you walked the road,
and paid the debt to Hades that you owed,
still hearty in old age. Thus, you'll be better
received by Acheron, an honest debtor.

15

Here lies Mnasalces, writer of elegies,
      Plataea's son.°
His Muse is a copy of Simonides –°
      a knock-off one;
his dithyrambics, loud and tedious
      as bottles droning.

He's dead. Let's not throw stones. Were he with us,
  we would start stoning.

19

A shipwrecked man lies here. Stranger, no slowing,
for when we sank, the other ships kept going.

Alcaeus of Messene

(Late third–early second century BCE)

2

More fiercely, Bacchus, than the Cyclops when°
he'd gorged his belly on the flesh of men,
I'm drinking, yes, I'm drinking, and wish I
had shattered Philip's skull and drunk it dry –°
Philip, who mixes guests a poisoned cup
and serves the blood of friends, and laps it up.

6

I hate Love. Why, why won't the god pursue°
wild beasts, instead of running my heart through?
Why should a god hunt men? Or what august°
prize does he gain for grinding me to dust?

7

On Protarchus

He hates his beauty now, but give him time.
Meanwhile, it sprints on with the torch, his prime.°

14

All Hellas, Pylades, wails for you gone,°
and shears her unkempt hair close to the bone,
and Phoebus doffed the laurel, as is due,
from hair no shears can cut, to honor you;
the Muses wept, Asopus stopped his flow°
and listened to their lifted voice of woe,
and dancing ceased in Bacchus's abode,
when you descended by that iron road.

Theaetetus

3

Phileas' brilliance seemed to have no peers;
let those who envy him choke on their tears.
Fame is an empty gift. By Styx's stream
Thersites and Minos share the same esteem.°

Diotimus

1

O Artemis, torch-wielder, Savioress,
rest here, on Pollis' land, Bright One, and bless
him and his offspring with light freely given –
he knows the Scales of Right that are in heaven.
And, goddess, may the Graces deign to pass
with their light sandals through his flowering grass.

10

Back to the barn through snow, of their own will,
the cows came home at evening from the hill.
But, ah, Therimachus beneath the oak
sleeps the long sleep, laid down by heaven's stroke.

Tymnes

(Third or second century BCE)

2

My dear Philaenis, don't be too distressed
that the Nile doesn't water where you rest
in Eleutherna. There's one thoroughfare°
below – for everyone, from everywhere.

5

This tomb holds the white hound from Melite,°
who guarded Eumelus most faithfully.
Alive he was called Bull, but now his bark
is muted in the pathways of the dark.

Pancrates

1

Polycrates gives hammer, tongs and pliers
to you, Hephaestus, from his forge's fires:
pounding the anvil, he earned his family
a livelihood, and drove off poverty.

Phanias

2

His pointing stick, his strap, its nearby mate,
the fennel rod to rap boys on the pate,
the supple switch which he kept so well oiled,
his skullcap (he was bald), his shoe (one-soled):
Callon, weighed down by age, gives all these tools
to Hermes, relics of his life in schools.

7

Thessalian Eugethes once rejected
his mirror, and the towel where hair collected,
his reed comb, the felt strip where he set razors,
his sharp nail-cleaners and his blunted scissors,
nail-clippers, blades and chair, and property,
and ran from stroppery to sophistry
in Epicurus' garden-party school.°
He listened to the lyre like a fool,
and would have starved to death, but that he ran
10   back home, and started barbering again.

Antipater of Sidon

Antipater of Sidon, from Phoenicia in the Greek East, lived between
around 170 and 100 BCE. He was an older contemporary of Meleager
(pp. 326–32), adept at imitating and varying the epigrams of others,
chiefly Leonidas of Tarentum (pp. 306–10). The Roman orator and
statesman Cicero tells us in *De Oratore*, his treatise on the ideal orator,
that 'Antipater made a habit of improvising hexameters and other verses
in various meters and forms, and, being a man of genius, with a good
memory, was able to train himself so that, whenever he decided to take
to verse, the words would follow on their own.' He was admired by

Meleager and his work proved influential in the subsequent development of the epigram. There is always the danger of confusing the
Sidonian's work with that of the later poet, Antipater of Thessalonica
(pp. 344–6), not only because of the coincidence of their names, but also
because of their strong literary resemblance.

22

I, who once chased off starlings and the crane –
that sky-high Thracian pirate! – from the grain,
Alcimenes, was whirling my leather sling
to keep the feathered cloud from settling,
when a thirst-snake at my ankles broke the skin°
and, pumping from his cheeks the venom in,
put out my light. Thus, gazing in the air,
I overlooked my feet and the death there.

23

She who was lapped in purple, love and gold,
more melting than soft Cypris – her I hold,
Lais of Corinth which the oceans ring,°
more whitely shining than Pirene's spring,°
a mortal Cytherea, with more who sought her°
than flocked to wed Tyndareus's daughter,°
plucking her favors and her purchased love;
whose tomb the scent of saffron floats above,
whose skull, still wet with sweet emollients,
and gleaming locks still exhale frankincense;   10
whose death was mourned by Aphrodite raking
her lovely cheeks, and Love bent double, shaking.
Had she not made her bed one all could lease,
a second Trojan War had riven Greece.

26

When Cleodemus, still a suckling, was
blasted by truly Thracian Boreas°
and slipped from shipboard into the roiling sea
and the waves quenched his tiny infancy –
pitiless Ino, you turned him a cold shoulder,
though your son, Melicertes, was no older.°

41°

High time for ships to surge their ocean path,
unfurrowed by dumb swells or fits of froth,
now while the martin builds his rounded home
under the eaves, and laughing meadows bloom.
Now, coil your dripping cables, sailors; weigh
the anchor rooting in the harbor clay
and hoist your sails. It's I who urge you on,
Priapus of the Harbor, Bacchus' son.°

51

Hippe has put up her luxuriant
entangled curls and touched her brow with scent,
for she must wed; and I, her hairband, pray
that Artemis shcd graces on her way.
At once with groom and offspring – double joys –
now bless this maiden, who still loves her toys.

58

Erinna's themes are few, her poem not long,°
and yet the Muse co-authored her brief song.
Thus she is not forgotten, not embayed
in midnight's shrouding wings of dusk and shade.
But we, unnumbered swarms who follow, all

lie moldering in the dark beyond recall.
More sweet the swan lifts her small voice to sing
than jackdaws cackling in the clouds of spring.

59°

Where is that charm the world flocked to behold,
Corinth? Your crown of towers? Your wealth of old?
Where are your temples now? Your houses? Wives?
Your myriad citizens with busy lives?
No trace of you is left, o desolate,
since war seized all you had, and swallowed it.
We Nereids, alone inviolate,
are left, like halcyons, to mourn your fate.°

61

Antiodemus, nursed with Cypris' milk,
lulled from her babyhood on purple silk,
heartthrob of Hooch, louche-crooning halcyon,°
whose glances melt like slumber in the sun,
whose limbs move like the water in a stream,
who has no bones in her, who is pure cream,
has crossed to Italy, where her soft charms
will drive Rome to lay down its wars and arms.

Anonymous

4°

My love stays here; don't let it go elsewhere,
Cypris. I hate a love that others share.

6

Plastered on words – I drink my madness neat –
armed with delirium, I'll hit the street
and sing my way to her, though Zeus above
hurl down his worst. Who cares? My shield is Love.

8

Lovers of boys, rest from your fruitless toil;
stop slaving; empty hopes make our blood boil.°
Might as well bail the sea onto dry land,
or count each granule of Saharan sand,
as dote on boys' affections, though they vaunt
a beauty mortals and immortals want.
Friends, look! See how I tender empty hands,
my toil poured out like water on the sands.

10°

Damn raucous birds, be silent! Leave me be,
with my boy's dainty body warming me.
Nightingales in the branches, I'm beseeching –
how you girls chatter on! – please, stop screeching.

35

This magic wheel of Nico's, on a string°
of purple wool, carved out of shimmering
amethyst crystal, filigreed with gold,
Lady of Cyprus, now is yours to hold,
a present from the witch of Thessaly°
in gratitude for hospitality;
it draws girls from their rooms, men home from sea.

47

Hades, implacable, unswerving, why
did tiniest Callaischron have to die?
Persephone plays 'Peek-a-boo! Guess who?'
in her house; his is full of gall and rue.

49

Awful to mourn the death of groom or bride,
but worst of all is when the pair have died,
as when the roof, in their first night of bliss,
caved on Lycaenion and Eupolis
and hushed the wedding hymn. No grief like this
with which you, Nicis, mourned your perished son,
and you, Theodicus, your daughter gone.

50

You Naiads, and you drafty stalls, in spring
inform the bees as they start foraging
that old Leucippus, chasing a scampering hare,
died when the winter night tightened its snare.
He'll tend his swarms no more; and vales and rills,
where sheep graze, miss their neighbor from the hills.

52

I sing steep Rhegium in Italy,
that coastline drinking the Sicilian sea,
where, underneath an elm tree's leafy shade,
Ibycus the *bon vivant* was laid,°
lover of boys and lyres; all around
thick ivy climbs and white reeds fence his mound.°

53°

So long untaken, uninvaded, Sparta,
Greek smoke now billows on Eurotas' water.°
Your shade is gone. Your birds nest on the ground.
Your wolves' ears strain for sheep, but hear no sound.

Meleager

Meleager of Gadara flourished around 95 BCE. As he tells us in a flotilla
of autobiographical epitaphs, he was born in Syria, raised in Tyre and
spent his later life on the island of Cos, where he compiled his *Garland*,
an anthology of epigrams by his own hand and others', dedicated to
one Diocles (see poem 129, p. 332). Meleager also wrote prose satires
about which little is known, save that they were modeled after the
Graces of his Gadarene countryman Menippus, a Cynic whose prosi-
metrical works, now lost, also influenced such later writers as Marcus
Terentius Varro and Lucian of Samosata. Meleager was an amatory
poet, once memorably (and, in my view, unfairly) dismissed for his
'*iostephanous* [violet-garlanded] and tawdry muse'; his poems ring original variations on familiar themes, in language that is lively, lucid and
picturesque. In the narrow limits within which he operates, Meleager is
one of the *Greek Anthology*'s most enjoyable poets.

4

Shh, stranger, softly! With the dead devout
the old man sleeps the sleep that none may doubt –
Meleager, Eucrates' boy, the one
who dressed Love and the Muse with grace and fun.
Tyre and Gadara sustained his prime,
and Cos nursed him in his declining time.
Naidius! Phoenicians, and *Salaam!*
you Syrians; Greeks, *Chaire!* Say the same.°

6

Love's awful, awful! But what's the value of
always groaning and sighing 'Awful Love'?
The boy just laughs and savors the refrain,
as I berate him, feasting on my pain!
How is it possible, Queen of Desire,
that, born from blue-green sea, you mothered fire?°

23

By Timo's curls that love to be caressed,
by Demo's scented skin that baffles rest,
by trysts with Ilias, and all the rites
and revels my sleepless lamp has witnessed nights,
my lips still boast a shred of breath, at most:
Love, ask for it, and I'll give up the ghost.

25°

Asclepias, with her oceanic eyes,°
cajoles us all onto her ship of sighs.

29

Sweetly you pluck the lyre, Zenophila;
how sweet, by Pan, the music that you play!
Where can I run? The Loves are everywhere,
and leave no room even to breathe the air.
Beauty, the Muse or Graces fuel this yearning,
or – no, all three at once! I'm burning, burning.

31

Now snowdrops are in bloom, as daffodils
make eyes at rain, and lilies light the hills;
now, too, Zenophila, sweet bud of spring,
Love's love, Persuasion's rose, is blossoming.
Meadows, why laugh, and flaunt your scented hair?
She's sweeter than the sweetest bloom you bear.

36

Zenophila the rosebud is asleep.
Like Sleep, I wish I (winglessly) could creep
under her lids. Though even Zeus is prone
to yield to Sleep, I want her all my own!

41

My soul says: 'Heliodora's trouble; go!
Think of the jealous tears . . .' I know, I know.
I just don't have the strength. She warns me, too –
whispers, through kisses, 'You know I'm bad for you.'

42

To the Cupbearer

Top off the wine, and toast, and toast again,
'To Heliodora!' Swirl the sweet name in.
That garland – yes, from last night – hand it over,
dripping with perfume, to remind me of her.
The rose, the lover's friend – look! – sheds a tear
since she is gone, and not in my arms here.

46

I'll weave snowdrops with dainty daffodillies
and myrtle berries; I'll weave laughing lilies
and fragrant crocus and the crimson clothes
of hyacinths, and weave Love's love, the rose,
until the finely plaited wreath unfurls
petals through Heliodora's perfumed curls.

49

Heliodora's nail is Love's own dart:
scratching the skin, it goes straight to the heart.

52

O need for Heliodora, nights awake,
o tears and joys of Dawn's hooked nails that rake –
has our love been forgotten? Does no shred
of kisses shared still warm her frigid bed?
Are her bedfellows tears? Does she embrace
my ghost in dreams and kiss the cloudy face?
Or does she take new loves? Lamp, guard her lonely!
I bought you for our love, and our love only.

56°

Tears are my gift, tears terrible to shed,
Heliodora, for you among the dead:
the last drops of our love. I stand before
your grave, remembering, and let them pour.
So Meleager mourns you he adores,
and sends his empty gifts to Styx's shores.
Where is she, tender, longed-for? Oh, the tomb
has her, has her! Dust blots the perfect bloom.
All-nursing Earth, this girl – wept like no other –
embrace her in your arms and rock her, Mother.   10

65°

I was a speedy, big-eared bunny, torn
clear of my mother right when I was born,
and rescued by the love and nurturing
of Phanion, who fed me buds of spring.
I didn't miss my mother then, but died
from too much eating, fat and satisfied.
She put my grave beside her bed, so near
that in her dreams she'll always see it there.

69

Only you two were privy to the oath,
o Lamp and holy Night, sworn by us both:
I promised not to leave; he promised love,
and we called you as witnesses thereof.
But, Lamp, he wrote in water what he said,°
and now you shine for others in his bed.

71°

Take her this message, Dorcas. Say it one,
two, three times over, the whole thing. Well? Run!
Don't loiter, fly! One second! Dorcas, stay!
You haven't got it all. Why run away?
There's more to add! Instead – oh, I'm a twit!
Say nothing. Just that – no, say all of it.
Don't hold back, speak! But oh, what do I need
you for? I'm coming too; look, here, I'll lead!

72°

I know. No – shh! No tricks. I've found you out.
I know it all. No swearing; there's no doubt.
The whole time! – oh, you sleep alone, do you?

What shameless lies! 'No, no,' she says, 'it's true!'
What about that fop Cleon? Or, instead –
but why rail on? Go now, bitch. Out of bed!
No, wait – you want to visit him, it's clear.
I'll make your day, and make you stay right here.

79

At noon I saw the boy Alexis where
summer was combing fruit from her long hair.
I stopped mid-road, burned by two lasers, one
of love from the boy's eyes, one from the sun.
Night quenched the last, but a fair phantom burst
into my dreams, and burned more than the first.
So sleep, that eases labor, made me sweat
with sight of beauty, flame that burns me yet.

90

To the Son of Polyxenus

Fair Heraclitus' beauty has declined:
a curtain blocks all comers from behind.°
Now, child, don't be too proud with *your* physique,
for Nemesis can grow on either cheek.°

94°

Theron is dead to me, and the once-hot
flame of Apollodotus has winked out.
I love the love of women. Let goatherds grind
some goat's or gigolo's unkempt behind.

102

I'd fight off Zeus himself, if he should try
to make Myiscus carry cups on high.°
But Zeus says, 'I'm not jealous – why so ashen?
I shall not strike. My pain has taught compassion.'°
That's what he says, but if I see a fly,°
I blanch and tremble, knowing he might lie.

103

Myiscus' eyes first pierced my haughty heart,
as yet unwounded by Desire's dart.°
He cried, 'I've got him! Look, I'm trampling down
the scholar's arrogance that was his crown!'
I sucked in breath, then said, 'Why be impressed?
Love brought down even Zeus from heaven's crest!'°

129

I – glyph that signifies the finish line,°
sentinel where the column meets the spine –
proclaim that Meleager's task is done
of rolling all the poets into one
great garland; that for Diocles he made
this crown of flowers which shall never fade.
Coiled like a serpent's back, I sit apart,
enthroned and final to his work of art.

EPIGRAMS FROM THE GARLAND OF PHILIP

The *Garland of Philip*, intended as an extension of Meleager's (pp. 301–32), takes up where the earlier leaves off; it begins with Meleager's younger contemporary Philodemus (below), also from Gadara. Dedicated to one Camillus, it was presented to the Roman emperor in the 40s or 50s CE. The original anthology was organized alphabetically by the first letter of each poem's first word and may have contained 4,500 lines in three books, of which about 3,500 are preserved in the *Greek Anthology*. Philip of Thessalonica is not among the better poets in his own collection, and as such his presence here has been kept to a minimum (pp. 355–6).

Philodemus

Philodemus of Gadara (circa 110–40 BCE) was born in Syria but spent much of his life first in Athens, where he studied Epicurean philosophy with Zeno of Sidon, then in Italy, under the patronage of Lucius Calpurnius Piso Caesoninus, Julius Caesar's father-in-law and a political enemy of Cicero. In Italy from the 60s on, Philodemus lived at the so-called 'Villa of the Papyri' (likely the villa of Piso) in Herculaneum – famously, with Pompeii, one of the two cities buried by the eruption of Vesuvius in 79 CE. Philodemus' extensive library of Epicurean philosophical texts in Greek was discovered there by Bourbon excavators, beginning between 1750 and 1755. Evidently, during the eruption, the denizens of the villa had been trying to rescue and remove the books when they succumbed to the volcano; some of the scrolls were found still in their pigeonholes on the shelves, others in carrying boxes to which they had been moved. Unfortunately, the scrolls, carbonized by the eruption, proved extremely difficult to unroll and read, and much of their content was jumbled or destroyed in the attempt. Recent advances in papyrology, especially involving microscopes and multispectral imaging techniques, are aiding in the editing and publication of the volumes, which is nonetheless still extremely difficult and painstaking work. At any rate, whether the library belonged to Philodemus or his patron Piso, it included many of the poet's prose works – among them his treatise *On Poetry*, in which he claims that neither truth nor utility is necessary in poetry, that what counts is instead the melding of various elements, namely thought, diction, composition, euphony and so on. In and around Naples, Philodemus was a prominent member of an Epicurean circle, headed by the philosopher Siro, which also included Virgil (pp. 398–410) and Virgil's friends the epic poet Lucius Varius Rufus (addressed in Horace, *Odes* 1.6, p. 466), the literary critic Quintilius Varus (see Horace, *Odes* 1.24, p. 469), the poet Plotius Tucca and possibly Horace himself. Philodemus, then, besides being probably the most talented poet in Philip's *Garland*, is a fascinating minor presence at the margins of a major period of Roman and indeed world literary history.

1°

The tacit lamp, trustworthy bystander
that will not speak what no one ought to hear –
now make it drunk with oil, and disappear:
alone of gods, Love does not hanker for
spectators. And, Philaenis, shut the door.
Now, Xantho, let's – and you, love-loving bed,
learn everything that's better left unsaid.

2

For sixty years of seasons Grace has made it,
and yet her hair's still black and thickly braided;
each breast still stands, a brilliant marble cone,
without a girdle's help, firm on its own;
ambrosia bathes her skin, unwrinkled still,
still graceful, still with love's come-hither skill.
Lovers who love a passion ripe to burst,
forget her age, go to her, quench your thirst.

3°

Each time Cydilla holds me, if I call
by day, or venture boldly at nightfall,°

I know I cut a clifftop path, I know
I stake my life each time on a dice-throw.
What good is knowing? Each time you drag me here,
wild Love, I know I have no thought of fear.

5

'My dear, I pay with love the love I find,
but when I'm bitten, I bite back in kind.
Try not to hurt a lover crazy for you,
or rouse the Muses' rancor to abhor you.'
Though I kept up my warnings, you ignored them,
as deaf as the Ionian Sea toward them.°
And now, while you cry bitterly and whine,
I sit in Naias' lap, or she in mine.°

6

I loved Demo of Paphos. Fair enough.
Then, Demo the Samian. Still, normal stuff.
The third was from Nysa. It wasn't funny, this.°
Then the fourth Demo came from Argolis.
I guess the Fates were feeling polysemous
to name this Demo-lover Philodemus.°

8°

Philainion is short, and somewhat brown,
but, ah, her skin is softer than fresh down,°
her hair is curlier than celery,
Queen Cypris murmurs less enchantingly,
and then, she'll do it all – often, for free!
I'll love this girl, o golden Love, until
I find another one more perfect still.

9°

Night's Moon, horned Moon of the dance that lasts all night,
shine, Moon, shine through the shutters; spread your light
on golden Callistion, for gods above
are free to gaze on mortal beds of love.
You'll bless us both, Moon, for you've felt the same:
Endymion once set *your* heart aflame.°

12°

O feet, o calves, o thighs I'd die to taste,
o perfect bum, o honeypot, o waist,
o shoulders, breasts, o slim neck that I crave,
o hands, o eyes that make me melt and rave,
o rolling hips, o pure technique, delicious
use of the tongue, o cries that grant my wishes!
What if she's Flora, from Campania,°
and can't sing any Sappho? Andromeda,
Perseus' lover, came from India!°

14

Xantho, my fragrant Muse-faced waxwork toy,
sweet lilter, the winged Passions' pride and joy,
strum me a scent with your dewy touch; alone
I must sleep in a single bed of stone
a deathless length of days. Come, love, repeat
that song again – yes, that one. Yes. So sweet.

15

Cypris, sea-calmer, Cypris, who adore°
grooms and just men, and for them go to war;
who mothered Love, borne on the stormwinds' roar;

me, Cypris, riven, kicked from my saffron bed,
soul battered by Celtic winds and blizzarded,
me the trustworthy, me the pacifist,
whom your blue breakers, Cypris, toss and twist,
o lover of harbors and the rites of love,
now moor me, Cypris, safe in Naias' cove.°

16°

Demo and Thermion are killing me!
One streetwalks; one has her virginity.
I fondle one, the other not. By your
sway, Cypris, I don't know which I prefer!
I'll say the virgin Demo. I don't chafe
over loose change, but long to pick the safe.

17°

Now seven years have joined with thirty, ripped
pages out of my life's manuscript;
Xanthippe, now the white hairs sprinkling me
herald an era of maturity.
Yet I still love carousing, love the lyre;
my heart, unquenchable, still stokes the fire.
Muses, my mistresses, hurry and come
conclude this poem, and this delirium.°

18°

I've loved; who hasn't? I've reveled in her name;
who's skipped those rites, or hasn't fanned that flame?
I've raved. But why? Isn't a god to blame?
But all that's done. I'm old, I should be wise –
so the gray hair supplanting black implies.
I played when it was time, but now I find
playtime is past. I'll elevate my mind.

19°

O Melicertes, and you too, sea-green
Leucothea, guardian spirit, ocean's queen,°
o Nereid choruses, Poseidon king,
breakers, and Thracian Zephyrs freshening –°
be gracious; waft me, through the broad wave bound,
safe to Piraeus, gratefully aground.°

20

The chickpea's rife, the rose is at its prime
right now, and cabbage cut for the first time;
the sprats are sizzling, we have fresh salt-cheese,
and tender curly heads of lettuces.
But, Sosylus, we can't climb for the view
or stroll the beach the way we often do;
Antigenes and Bacchius, so merry
yesterday, today we have to bury.

21°

Again the lyre, again the snowdrop bloom,
the Chian wine, the Syrian perfume;
the orgy again, again the drunken whore:
I hate them all. They'll drive me mad no more.
No, give me narcissus garlands for my head,
essence of saffron, and flute-song instead;
also, some wine from Lesbos, just a touch,
and a young wife, who won't leave home too much.

23°

Piso, tomorrow your poet-friend will tow°
you to eat at his beggar's bungalow –

a feast for the Twentieth! Though your house boasts°
udders and Chian wine for fancy toasts,°
at mine you'll see your faithful friends, and hear
words sweeter than ever struck Phaeacian ear;°
And if you think of me in future, too,
I'll host a richer Twentieth for you.

25

John Doe gives Jane (who isn't that good-looking!)
five talents for one night of nervous fucking.°
Lysianassa (cuter, all can see)
accepts five drachmas for twelve nights with me.
Either I've lost my mind, or that guy should
have an axe part him from his nuts for good.

27°

Once I was good for five or nine. Now – one,
struggling from nightfall till the rising sun.
The thing, already at half-mast so often,
is slowly dying. The nail is in the coffin!
Old age, old age, I have so little steel
right now – what happens when you come for real?

Crinagoras

Crinagoras of Mytilene (circa 70 BCE–20 CE) was a person of standing on his native Lesbos and, along with Philodemus (pp. 333–9), one of the best poets in the *Garland of Philip*. Inscriptions from the wall of the old fortress at Mytilene attest to Crinagoras' presence on three embassies, the first and second to Julius Caesar in 48/7 and 45 BCE respectively, and the third to Augustus in Spain in 26/5 BCE. He was thus, as the philologist Denys Page comments, 'the accredited representative of an illustrious city overseas, acceptable in the highest society at Rome', and

in his poems he speaks with familiarity of members of the imperial
family: the first two Roman emperors, Augustus and his stepson Tiberius, as well as Tiberius' nephew and adopted son Germanicus, and
others. For the most part, Crinagoras' epigrams seem to arise directly
from his experience, and bear the stamp of a distinct personality. His
metrical technique, rougher than is usual in the authors collected in
Philip's and Meleager's *Garlands*, contributes to the impression of an
authentic speaking voice.

3

Proclus, this spearlike silver pen, with fine
divided double nib, buffed to a shine,
rushing the page with flow both smooth and swift,
Crinagoras sends you as a birthday gift,
small emblem of great tenderness, which will
join you in practicing your newest skill.

4

This feather from a hook-beaked eagle's wing,
steel-sharpened, glazed with dark enameling,
deft to dislodge the bits of food that stick
between the teeth with its sympathetic pick,
Lucius, though small, is sign of no small favor
felt by Crinagoras, who's

                Yours, as ever –

9

To Zeus Accomplisher and Artemis
who eases labor pangs we offer this
sacrament on a longed-for day of bliss:
my brother vowed, when his chin still was bare,
his cheeks' first youthful bloom of downy hair.°
Accept, gods; guide Eucleides all the way
from this new beard until his hair is gray.

10

Marcellus, spoil-rich from the western war,°
when he set foot on Italy's craggy shore,
shaved his first beard. It was his country's plan°
to send a boy and welcome home a man.

15

My mother was named Earth, and earth's dark mat°
hides me in death. This earth's no worse than that:
in this earth I'll lie long; as for the other,
withering sunstroke stole me from my mother.
Now far from home I lie, true Inachus,
the wept-for servant of Crinagoras.

17°

Islands before have yielded their unknown
titles and taken men's names for their own.
So you too, Spines, should be Love's Islands; none°
will grudge your name changed to a better one.
The boy, whose father heaped your dirt above
his grave, had both the bloom and name of Love.
O boneyard island, o beach-pounding sea –
lie lightly on him, you; you, quietly.

18

For Selene°

The Moon herself, climbing on evening's skirt,
went dark, to veil with night her grief and hurt:
she saw her lovely namesake, void of breath,
had sunk down darkling to the King of Death.
To you, Moon gave the beauty of her light
in life; in death, she shared your utter night.

19

Small, home-born Hymnis the sweet-talker, shine
of Evander's eye, his darling, at age nine
you stole, implacable King Death; why send
so soon for one bound to you in the end?

20

Philostratus, hapless in your happiness,°
where are your scepters now, that kings' largesse
which propped up your prestige and made you grand
both on the Nile and in Judaean land?
All that you toiled for foreigners have got,
and Ostracina's sands will see you rot.

27

Not if the whole sea up the coast comes pouring,
not if the whole Rhine seethes with Germans warring,
will Rome be harmed at all, as long as Romans
trust Caesar's right-hand rule and right-hand omens.°
So Zeus's holy oaks stand rooted fast
and deep, but dead leaves flee the tempest's blast.

33

Earthquake, most shuddersome of cataclysms,
whether the sea or wind shake up your schisms,
don't hurt my house, just built. No fear resembles
the terror that I've known when the earth trembles.

34

Holy heart of the great Earthshaker, be°
good to all those who cross the Aegean Sea;
gracious, you gave me, fleeing a Thracian squall,°
safe harbor – sweetest thing I ever saw.

35

Although your life is sedentary, and
you've never sailed, or hiked on the dry land,
still, go to Attica, to see those nights
at the great temples, and Demeter's rites;°
alive, you'll be less troubled, and you'll go
lightlier to the majority below.

37

What immigrants, o abject, have replaced°
what citizens! Alas for Greece disgraced!
Corinth, I'd have you lower than the low,
more deserted than desert sands, than know
you in the grubby hands of shopworn slaves
chafing the ancient Bacchiads in their graves.°

48

How long will you shiver in the clouds, poor dope,
flapping your wings of unsubstantial hope,
dreaming of riches, sketching countless schemes?
Nothing just comes. Mortals need more than dreams.
Look to the Muses' gifts; leave all the hollow
vague pipedreams for the idiots to follow.

Erucius

(Flourished circa 50 BCE)

13

Although he's underground, pour out a splash
of pitch on Parthenius, who talked such trash°
and slimed the Muses, hocking gobs of snot,

spewing his loathsome elegiac rot,
and even dared to claim, with unhinged tongue,
the *Odyssey* is dirt, the *Iliad* dung.
Now with the Furies' choker cinched around
his neck, he drinks Cocytus, gagged and bound.°

Zonas

5

I'll pile this cold shore-shingle in a heap
above your head, above your frigid sleep.
Your mother never wailed before your tomb,
or saw your sea-lashed corpse, your watery doom.
You're tenant now of a hostile, barren reach
of flatland next to an Aegean beach.
So take your tears, your little lot of sand,
stranger, whose trade meant death in a strange land.

9

Pass me the cup, shaped of the selfsame clay
I was made from, and shall become someday.

Antipater of Thessalonica

Antipater of Thessalonica (flourished circa 20 BCE–20 CE) lived about
100 years later than his Sidonian namesake (pp. 320–23). The Piso his
poems name as patron was Lucius Calpurnius Piso Frugi (48 BCE–32
CE), a prominent figure of the early Empire and son of the Calpurnius
Piso associated with Philodemus (pp. 333–9). It is often difficult to tell
this Antipater's poems from those of Antipater of Sidon.

3

Boeotian Helicon, once from your course
Hesiod sipped at eloquence's source.°
But here's a boy who bears your name and brings
Italian wine poured out from gayer springs.
I'd rather drink one cup of what he pours
than thousands from that horsey hole of yours!°

7°

Day breaks, Chrysilla; the cock is urging on –
and has been a good while – the jealous Dawn.
Go to hell, jealous bird, who drive me, sighing,
home to my pupils' ceaseless speechifying.
You're getting old, Tithonus, or why chase
Aurora so early from your own embrace?°

20°

Pipe down, get out, dull tribe, thorn-gatherers,
with 'kirtles', 'cressets', 'piscicles' in your verse,
who sip from sacred springs most soberly,
then pretzel poems into obscurity.
Today, it's toasts – Archilochus is up,
and manly Homer. No water in this cup.

37

Neither the setting of the Pleiades°
nor rough-hewn boulders dashed by roaring seas
nor heaven's lightning scares me like the stinking
rat who can quote my words since he's not drinking.°

38

I shall die young – so says astrology.
It's true, Seleucus. Doesn't bother me!
All take one path to Hades; I'll make out
Minos the sooner, the shorter is my route.°
Let's drink, since wine is both a horse and highway
downward; let walkers waddle their slow byway.°

80

Two traps: one plucked a fat thrush from the air,
one caught a blackbird in its horsehair snare.
The first one's plaited collar never let
the fat thrush fly off into the sunset;
the other set the sacred songbird free.
Even deaf snares are moved by melody.

82°

Don't touch the millstone, grinding girls; sleep on,
although the cock proclaims the crack of dawn.
Demeter has engaged nymphs to take up°
your hands' hard work; they leap on the wheeltop
and set the axle whirling – which rotates,
with its ring of teeth, the millstone's hollow weights.
If we can profit from Demeter's wage
sans sweat, *sans* toil, this is the Golden Age!°

96

Summer is over, Epicles, and bright
in the Plowman's belt, we see Arcturus' light.°
Already the hook is haunting the grape-cluster,
and huts are roofed against the wintry bluster,
but there's no warm wool clothing in your closet.
You'll shrivel up, and say Arcturus caused it.

Apollonides

8

Menoetes, offspring of Diaphanes
the Samian, was scuttled in the seas
between Syros and Delos with his freight.
His was a sacred task that couldn't wait –
ah, but an ailing father's no defense
against the ocean's vast indifference.

27°

You're sleeping, though your cup is shouting, friend,
'Wake up! Don't savor training for your end.'
Don't hold back, Diodorus, drain the cup
with draft on draft until you can't stand up.
Days without drink are long, long. Get up, now!
Already wisdom's white is on our brow.

Marcus Argentarius

Marcus Argentarius (born around 30–20 BCE) is probably the same Argentarius mentioned frequently in the *Controversies* of the Elder Seneca. If so, Argentarius' teacher was Cicero's enemy, the rhetorician Lucius Cestius Pius, whom Cicero's son once had whipped at a banquet for his calumnies against Cicero. Argentarius was Cestius' pupil, but not his friend: he used to swear 'by the ghost of Cestius' while the latter was still alive; Cestius in turn called Argentarius his monkey. According to the philologist Denys Page, Argentarius was a 'fluent, witty, and often malicious speaker'. In the art of epigram he is a student of Meleager (pp. 326–32), deeply imbued with the style and spirit of his master, and one of the most enjoyable contributors to the *Garland of Philip*, surpassed only by Philodemus (pp. 333–9) and Crinagoras (pp. 339–43).

1

You gold-horned Moon, do you see – and you, swarms
of fiery stars that sleep in Ocean's arms –
how scented Ariste cut me loose and went,
and six days later I've lost the witch's scent?
Still, I know how to find her. Look, I'll send
Love's silver bloodhounds, noses to the wind.°

2

Melissa, you're the same as your namesake,
the bee; take this to heart, and no mistake:°
when you kiss me, your lips are sweet as honey,
but you sting cruelly when you ask for money.

6

Take off those nets, coy, cruel Lysidice;
don't slink and roll your ass to torture me.
That's a sheer, gauzy thing you're wrapped up in –
I see, and I don't see, your naked skin.
You think you're cute? Well, I too have a thing,
rock-hard, that needs a gauzy covering.

7

Menophila's tasted everything. Her stars
are different – *very* different – from ours,
or that's the gossip of her kept-girl friends.
Chaldeans, take her for one, or several spins –°
her heavens harbor *both* the Dog and Twins.°

10°

A female love is best for us, if we
approach our love with moral gravity.

But if it's boys you yearn for, be assured
your perverse fever can be quickly cured.
Just turn Menophila around, and thus
pretend you're buggering Menophilus.

11°

Sweet-scented Isias, though your limbs breathe
scent ten times over, come, accept this wreath
which now is in full bloom, which one day's time
will witness blown – a symbol of your prime.

12

I fell for young Alcippe hard, when she
yielded and let me bed her, secretly.
Our two hearts, frightened somebody might come
and see our hidden love, beat like one drum.
Her mother found us – heard the squeaking bed –°
looked, and 'By Hermes, I get halves!' she said.°

13°

Breastbone glued to breastbone, breast to breast,
my lips upon Antigone's lips pressed,
skin against skin – but of the rest I'll sing
no more; the lamplight witnessed everything.

15°

Reading the *Works and Days* of Hesiod,
I noticed Pyrrha coming up the road.
I flung the book and shouted, 'You old jerk,
Hesiod, why give me all this *work*?'

16°

Why rip me, rooster, from sweet dreams? The charms
of Pyrrha's form have flitted from my arms.
I gave you flocks of hens, and made you king –
you punk, is this your 'Thanks for everything'?
By Serapis' altar, I swear, I can't ignore it!°
And you, you'll get the altar where I swore it.

23

Lie here for Cypris, loaded flask of mine,
slim-necked sister to the cup of wine,
friend to the feast of peers, who glug and splash,
you daughter of our potluck bottle-bash,°
my self-taught refill-pourer, bosom-buddy
of lovers' toasts, *garçon* who's always ready;
wino, lie here, the gift of Marcus, who
praised you, old pilgrim, when he offered you.

26

Watching the stars pulse in their golden trances
I dance; I've given up on human dances.
A crown blooms in my hair as I inspire,
with Muse-inspired touch, my singing lyre.
So I've designed it well, this life of mine:
both Lyre and Crown belong in the Design.°

30

Dead, you'll possess five feet, and not see one
of life's delights, no sliver of the sun.
So drain your wine cup straight, joy on your face,
Cincius, gorgeous wife in your embrace.
You think that Wisdom's deathless? You should dwell
on Zeno and Cleanthes deep in hell.°

Bianor

(Alive in 17 CE)

2

I was lamenting my Theonoë,
but, since our child still lived, less bitterly.
Now jealous Doom has snatched the baby too,
and robbed me, child, of all I had left – you.
Persephone, heed a father, grief-oppressed:
lay the babe on its buried mother's breast.

Antiphilus of Byzantium

1

Lady, I don't have much, and yet I boast
the man whose heart is yours has more than most.
But take this fleecy robe, as soft as moss,
flower-bright, with a purple flower's gloss,
this rose wool, and this spikenard in a green
glass flagon to anoint your hair's dark sheen:
the wool will show your skill while the robe dresses
your skin and clouds of scent float on your tresses.

2

I am a quince from the last year, kept fresh°
in my young skin, with smooth, unblemished flesh,
as downy as a newborn, wrinkle-free,
with branch and leafage still attached to me,
winter's unlooked-for gift. But for you, queen,
even the snow and ice will bring forth green.

9

Just let me sleep in the stern on a strawy bed
while raindrops drum the awning overhead
and fire licks up through the hearthstones where
the kettle pops and crackles noise and air,
while I observe the deckhand slice the meat,
then sit at a plank above the bridge and eat.
And so it happened: sea-wind soughing, give
and take – the common folk know how to live.

16

Queen of the Wayside, Antiphilus offers you°
this hat in token of his passing through,
for you have heard his prayers, and blessed his route.
The gift is tiny, goddess, but devout.
Protect it from the clutches of some thief,
I pray: even slight crimes can come to grief.

33

Lofty oak-branches, helping men evade
the scorching heatwave in your spreading shade,
more densely leafed than roof-tiles, noontide boughs,
house to the pigeons, the cicadas' house,
protect me, too, sprawled out beneath your hair,
refugee from the sun that burns the air.

Automedon

1°

I love that Asian dancing girl who drips
sex from her shaking hips to her fingertips,
not for the way we drool through every dance,

or how she softly flutters her soft hands;
no, but she stomachs wrinkles, and she will
gyrate at sagging poles with equal skill;
she tongues, kneads, tickles and – just let her flex
her leg on yours, the dead wood resurrects.

2°

Call her; you're ready. But what will you do
when she arrives, Automedon? Think it through.
You're limper than a parsnip. What used to rise
upright, alive, flops dead between your thighs.
People will mock you, venturing from shore
dismasted – rowing, but without an oar.

7

I dined last on goat's foot and a ten-day-old
stalk of yellow cabbage, tough and cold.
I will not name my host. He isn't nice –
so tetchy – and he might invite me twice.

11

The other day for dinner I dropped by
Coach Demetrius – what a lucky guy!
One boy sat on his lap, one boy was glued
against his arm, one poured wine, one brought food –
exquisite squad. I joked, with some delight,
'Coach, do you also work them out at night?'

Evenus

7°

If hate is pain and love is pain, I would
opt for the pain that does me the most good.

Maccius

1°

Philistion, always difficult, who never,
without the clink of silver, took a lover,
has seemed more mellow lately. It's not strange,
the seeming; but I think there's no real change.
A cobra can be tamed, every so often;
but when it bites, you end up in a coffin.

10°

Lord, come yourself, and join us at a bound;
vat-trampler, lead our labor's nightly round.
Whiten your foot, bare to the nimble knee,
the dance's servant; give it energy!
Fill up the casks with fluent wine, and take
this goat in thanks, Blest One, and this meal-cake.

Antiphanes of Macedonia

1

Cypris loosed from her breast her sensual,
beguiling sash for you and let it fall,°
so you could force all hearts to be your throne,
Ino – but you've ensorcelled mine alone.

6

Whoever shuns the flute or the divine
twangling of strings, or aged, ambrosial wine,
pine-torches, boys, wreaths, perfumes, while he crunches
soundlessly creeping interest and skips lunches,
stingy against himself – he's dead to me,
a cheese-rind-scraping corpse. I leave him be.

7°

Our time is brief, however much we've got,
poor things, even if old age should be our lot;
our prime's still briefer. While we're fresh and strong,
let it all overflow: drink, passion, song,
for soon it's wintry age, when no one fucks
or gets it up – not for a thousand bucks.

9°

You busybody grammar-mongers, brutes
who tear up others' verses by the roots,
bookworms that nest in thorns, sad, shriveled pricks,
soilures of greatness, rancid ordure slicks,
plague of poets, Erinna's flunky claque,°
dogs who leap when Callimachus says, 'Attack!'
bedbugs who bite your betters' backs, black goo
blocking beginners' eyes – fuck off. Fuck you.

Philip of Thessalonica

The anthologist (flourished circa 40s or 50s CE), about whom little is
known. See the introduction to the epigrams from the *Garland of Philip*,
above (pp. 333).

55

What hill – deserted, sunless – brought you forth,
you feral vine from Scythia in the North,°
or what snow-beaten Alp, with icy crust,
or iron-mothering Iberian dust,
could make a vine so sour; could produce
such unripe clusters of such caustic juice?
I need your hands, Lycurgus, to uproot°
this misbegetting vine – stem, branch and shoot.

ANACREONTEA

The *Anacreontea* are a collection of sixty or so anonymous poems composed for the symposium between the second century BCE and the sixth
century CE. Included as an appendix to the tenth-century manuscript of
the *Greek Anthology*, they were incorrectly identified as the work of
Anacreon (pp. 100–108) and published under that name in 1554 by the
French printer Henri Estienne (aka Stephanus). Instantly influential, this
ersatz Anacreon was widely imitated both in French (by poets such as
Pierre de Ronsard and Rémy Belleau), and in English (by Ben Jonson,
Robert Herrick, Richard Lovelace, Abraham Cowley and Joseph Addi-
son, among many others). 'Anacreonticks' – which in Greek refers to a
particular meter used by Anacreon, for example, in fragments 356 (p.
103) and 395 (p. 106), and which became the most frequently occurring
meter of the *Anacreontea* – was used to refer to any light, convivial
poem in the style of the Pseudo-Anacreon. At least one such composition's legacy is still with us in the present day: in eighteenth-century
London, a drinking club called the Anacreontic Society selected as its
'constitutional song' a tune called 'To Anacreon in Heaven', which, when
combined with lyrics taken from a poem about the defense of Fort
McHenry in Maryland against a British naval bombardment during the
War of 1812, eventually turned into the 'Star-Spangled Banner'.

After more than two centuries of careful philology and new archaeological discoveries, we have access to quite a bit more Greek lyric poetry
today than the readers of the early modern era were ever able to enjoy.
For them, the 'Anacreon' of these poems provided an appealing alternative to the public-minded sublimity of Pindar (pp. 134–64) and the
erotic intensities of Sappho (pp. 38–54) – the latter of whom was said,
erroneously, to have been Anacreon's wife, on the basis of an ancient
misreading of Anacreon's fragment 358 (p. 104) and encouraged by
Stephanus' printing of the *Anacreontea* together with all of the then-
known fragments of Sappho. The Anacreon imagined by the early
moderns is a private poet, frivolous and sophisticated, a day-seizing

lover of banquets, wine and boys. The Archaic Anacreon was all of
those things in part, but he was also much more; what the poets of the
Anacreontea did, in effect, was to isolate their master's most obvious
characteristics and make them the delimiters of a genre. The poetry thus
produced over centuries of playful banter is highly stylized, dripping
with wine and sex, and narrow in subject matter, situation and effect.
But it is no less graceful and charming for all that.

1

I dreamt the Troubadour
from Teos stood before
my eyes – Anacreon!
I ran, hearing him speak,
hugged him, and kissed his cheek –
not young, but handsome still;
handsome, and sensual.
He smelled of wine, and shook.
To steady him, Love took
10   him by the hand, and led.
The garland from his head
he gave me for my own:
it smelled like Anacreon.
Then I, bumptious buffoon,
I raised it, I put it on,
and since that day, for me,
no day's been passion-free.

4

Put silver to the hammer
for me, Hephaestus; solder –
no, not a suit of armor°
(do I look like a fighter?) –
make me an empty flagon,°
as deep as you can fashion,
and make the decoration –

no, not the stars or Wagon
or dull Orion – please!
What have the Pleiades   10
or Plowman done for me?°
Apply your artistry
to vines laughing with glaucous
grapes beside handsome Bacchus.

7°

The girls are all appalled:
'You're old, Anacreon.
Look in the mirror, there.
All of your hair is gone.
You are completely bald.'
When it comes to my hair,
if I have some, or none,
I'm not sure. But I know this:
the older a man is,
the sooner his life will be done,   10
the more he should have his fun.

8

The wealth of Gyges, Lord
of Sardis, makes me bored.°
There are no grudges in me,
no tyrants whom I envy.
I like when perfume's smeared
and dripping from my beard;
I like it when I wear
a rose crown in my hair.
I care about today –
tomorrow, who can say?   10

9°

By god, don't make a stink
if I want to drink, and drink
the whole cup at a draught.
I want to be daft, daft, daught!
Daft as Alcmaeon was,
and Orestes, who lost his shoes.
(Each of them murdered his mother.)°
Me, I don't want to murder,
just guzzle wine, and be
10   absurd, and yet absurder –
deranged as Heracles
when he took Iphitus' bow
after he laid him low;°
deranged as Ajax, shielded,
but not from the blade he wielded.°
I, with this wreath I've made,
this cup that makes me glad –
not with a bow, or blade –
I want to be mad, mad, mad!

10

Swallow, you windbag, you,
what do you think I should do?
Should I go get my scissors
and clip your flipping wings?
Or should I take a razor,
like Tereus did once,
and cut out your tongue as it sings?°
Why did you let your jealous
early morning tra-la-las
10   ruin my dreams of Bathyllus?°

21

The earth imbibes the rain,
and so do all the trees;
seas drink the streams that run;
the sun imbibes the seas;
the moon imbibes the sun.
Friend, spare the diatribe
if I also imbibe.

22

Tantalus' daughter grew
into a Phrygian rock;°
Pandion's daughter flew
away in a swallow-flock.°
If you'd give me a look,
I'd grow into your mirror;
I'd turn into your cloak
if you would be my wearer.
I'd be a crystal stream
for you to bathe within.　　　　　　　10
I'd be a scented cream –
just rub me on your skin.
I'd be a necklace pearl;
a band for your breast I'd be;
your sandal, too, if, girl,
you'd walk all over me.

26°

Your theme is Thebes' attack;
his, Troy's battle cries;
but I sing my own sack.
No ships wrought my demise,
no soldiery, no horse,
but another, stranger force
arrowing out of her eyes.

35

Love once overlooked
a bee asleep in the cup
of a rose, and he was pricked.
It got his fingertip.
His wailing wasn't pretty.
Half-running and half-flying
to ravishing Aphrodite,
he cried, 'Mother, I'm dying!
I'm killed! I'm going to croak!
10   A snake with wings bit me,
quite small – what country folk
call by the name of *bee*.'
She said, 'If bee stings prove
to cause such suffering,
what do you think, my Love,
happens to those you sting?'

46

See how the springtime uncloses,
at the Graces' behest, the roses,
        and the sea's wild
        billows grow mild
in a calm the calm sky composes.

See the duck slip
   under, tail up;
see the crane at his journey's beginning,
and the sun more brilliantly shining,
and the shadows of clouds as they scatter,   10
and the manors of mortals grow brighter,
and the olive, that tentative sprouter.
The nectars in Bacchus's bower
   begin to brim
   from leaf to limb
and the fruits of the earth are in flower.

53°

When I gaze at handsome young men,
then my youth comes back again,
and, as old as I am, I take flight,
and the dance is my only delight.
I'll go mad, I'll toss my head!
I want to be garlanded –
give me one! And see that gray
old age stays far away!
With the young men, young as I am,
let me dance, and bring me a dram   10
of Bacchus' autumnal liquor,
and you'll witness an old man's vigor
who has learned how phrases are turned,
who has learned how to drink, and has learned
   to go insane
   and stay urbane.

60b

O my heart, why has the best
delirium got you possessed?
Now pick up your spear and heave
it into the bullseye and leave.

The deity-conquering bow
of the Cyprian – let it go.
Let the songs of Anacreon
be your glorious paragon.
To the beautiful boys lift up
the beautiful words in your cup,
and let the ambrosia we drain
provide some cessation of pain,
as we tipple and keep far
from the heat of the summer star.

Latin Lyric (mid-first century BCE–104 CE)

CONQUEST AND RIVALRY

Spring, 207 BCE. In the eleventh year of the second war with Carthage, Rome was in a state of dread, thanks to a series of terrifying portents: stones raining from the sky, temples lightning-struck, rivers of blood. At Capua in the south, a night-sentry was mauled by a wolf. In Frusino (modern Frosinone, in the central Italian region of Latium, near Rome), a baby was born, the size of a four-year-old; no one could tell if the child was male or female. Soothsayers were consulted, expiations performed and the hermaphrodite, sealed in a chest, was flung into the sea.

The threat was very real: the Carthaginian general Hasdrubal Barca, on the march with an army of 30,000, had crossed the Italian Alps, and hoped to join forces with his brother Hannibal in the south. For ten years now, Hannibal's military genius had ranged over Italy, dealing Rome one defeat after another; the people feared that, once allied with his brother's formidable army, he would be invincible. Of course, the Romans could not have known that the reversal of their enemies' fortunes was only months away. The situation was urgent: the gods had to be propitiated, and the favor of Juno, Rome's patron goddess, regained. A great rite was held in the Greek style: two white cows were marched through the Carmental Gate into the city, followed by two cypress-wood statues of Juno the Queen; behind them, twenty-seven maidens in long robes processed solemnly, singing a hymn to Juno – 'a song which', writes the historian Titus Livius, over 200 years later, 'to the untrained minds of that time may have deserved praise, but now, if repeated, would be repellent and uncouth'. The hymn was a *partheneion*, a 'maiden-song' of the sort previously composed by Alcman (pp. 31–7), Pindar (pp. 134–64) and Bacchylides (pp. 165–85); and its author was a man called Livius Andronicus.

Livius was at least half Greek, perhaps a slave or a freedman, possibly from Tarentum (Greek Taras, modern Taranto) in Magna Graecia, on the instep of the Italian boot. Some thirty years earlier – in 240 BCE, when Callimachus (pp. 255–81) was either recently dead or about to be – he had also been commissioned to translate a Greek tragedy into Latin, in celebration of Rome's recent victory in the previous major war against Carthage. That translation had been the first of its kind, and Livius had followed it soon after with another, still more consequential: that of Homer's *Odyssey* into the native Italian verse form, the saturnian. These translations were literary achievements, but they were also more than that. They represented, in fact, nothing less than the inauguration of Latin literature.

Literature in Latin thus has its origins in translation from Greek, and it is never without the double consciousness of the translator. Always there is that negotiation between a source and a target: between a foreign, sometimes ancient, set of conventions and contexts, and the needs and expectations of the present. To modern habits of thinking, this fact may call the originality of Latin literature into question, and with it its value: the Romans were so *derivative*, some will say. The truth is that translating a foreign literature was, in the third century BCE, perhaps the most original thing the Romans could have done.

As the classicist Denis Feeney has said, 'literature in the ancient world turns out to be "that which does not get translated"'. Medicine, divination, astronomy, astrology, science, mathematics – texts concerning such useful subjects as these had indeed passed from language to language long before the emergence of Rome; but what we call 'literature' must have been deemed too culturally specific, too impractical. The Greeks certainly never translated it; like today's Americans, they were stubborn monoglots, fascinated by the cultures of peoples they ruled, but with no interest in their languages. The last of the Ptolemies, Cleopatra, was also the first who had even bothered to learn Egyptian. Meanwhile, the Etruscans and other Italian peoples (Sabellians, Umbrians, Messapians) seem simply not to have possessed anything we would call 'literature', either oral or written. Nor, for that matter, did the Romans, before 240.

Roman literature belonged to the wider pattern of cultural interchange with Greece – a dynamic that included rivalry and conquest, assimilation and backlash. Early poet-translators like Livius and his exact contemporary Gnaeus Naevius (circa 270–201 BCE) were the most Romanizing of writers. They avoided Greek expressions and used the highly alliterative and rhythmical saturnian verse form, which, however, lacked a clear metrical structure. Livius' 'versions' (the Latin word for 'translate' is *vertere*, 'to turn' or 'to transform') catered to the differing requirements of the Roman stage and sensibility, which – less restrained and more emphatic than the Greeks' own – tended toward pathos, intensity and color. In doing so, they took many liberties: indeed, in 'turning' his models into Latin, Livius always rewrote them as he saw fit, changing anything from words and phrases to settings and plots. He strove, in fact, to outdo his originals. For Roman writers in general, from Livius to St. Jerome, the fourth-century CE theologian who translated the Bible into Latin, translation was a form of conquest; they plundered what they needed and discarded what they didn't.

Meanwhile, in the hundred years after Livius' first translation, Rome was busy conquering Greece – a process completed by the statesman and general Lucius Mummius when he sacked Corinth in 146 BCE. In a surprising reversal of the normal prerogative of conquest, rather than imposing their own culture on the vanquished, Roman elites almost universally learned the Greek language and Greek letters; Roman literature, like Roman culture, drew ever closer to the Greek, leading the poet Horace (pp. 453–91) to remark a century or more later, 'Greece, taken, took its feral captor captive'. Rome's first great epic poet, Quintus Ennius (circa 239–169 BCE), even claimed to be the reincarnation of Homer; in his epic on Roman history, the *Annals*, he became the first to adapt the Greek hexameter to Latin. It quickly set the poetic standard, driving the saturnian into extinction. For the hundred or so years following his death, Ennius was the major figure of Latin literature, which, through his mediation, came to be informed by Homeric epic, Attic tragedy and the New Comedy.

Lyric poetry was not, at this time, a prominent genre. Epic and drama, the form into which lyric had evolved, were the real crowd-pleasers, while lyric itself would have had an old-fashioned air and seemed removed from the daily life of Latins. That began to change, however, in the first century BCE.

Parthenius of Nicaea, often called 'the prophet of the Callimachean school' at Rome, was brought to Italy as a prisoner of war in 72 BCE, in all likelihood by the poet Gaius Helvius Cinna. At first a slave, he may then have been freed on account of his education. True to the gospel of Callimachus and of Callimachus' fellow Alexandrian Euphorion of Chalcis (then much read, but now almost entirely lost), Parthenius helped to spread the Alexandrian taste for small-scale verse of intricate erudition in a refined style. By that time, Ennius' hexameter works of the previous century had already come to seem old-fashioned. They had been composed in bulk, admitting into the flood of their eloquence the occasional infelicity or solecism, which must have set Parthenius' teeth on edge. No doubt, too, there was a gauche earnestness to Ennius – a sense of buy-in to traditional values – at which Parthenius' chic protégés would have rolled their eyes.

It was those protégés who now came to the fore. These trendy young things, known to history as the 'New Poets' (or 'Neoterics'), included Catullus (pp. 373–97) and such friends of his as Cinna and Gaius Licinius Calvus (see Catullus 50, p. 387). They embraced the personal and the flippant, obsessively polishing their verses and eschewing unfashionable patriotism and boring grandeur. To Catullus – for our purposes the first Latin lyric poet – love, not politics, was the central experience of life, even if he also had very Roman reservations about this view (see poem 51, p. 387). His ambivalent example inaugurated a subversive strain in Latin poetry, a sense of unease with Roman mores, which would never thereafter be wholly absent. Dignity (*dignitas*), influence (*auctoritas*), strictness (*severitas*), and the particular seriousness (*gravitas*) of the lawmaker, the statesman and the accomplished soldier: these were the traditional values of Rome, and they were inherently hostile to the poetry – as, no doubt, also to the adulterous lifestyles – of Catullus and the love elegists.

There were, moreover, many grounds for disaffection in the Italy of the first century BCE. From the 90s to the 30s, the peninsula was riven with internecine conflict: there was the Social War between Rome and her Italian allies (*socii*), who wanted Roman citizenship, followed by three civil wars between the most powerful men of the time, in the course of which the centuries-old Republican system of Roman government was forever transformed. The first, fought between the popular politician-general Gaius Marius, and his former lieutenant, the hardened aristocrat Lucius Cornelius Sulla, laid the ruinous groundwork; Sulla became the first Roman to march on the city of Rome and to

make lists of his enemies, and both men at different times established
tyrannical rule over the capital. The second and third are known to
almost everyone. In the second, Marius' nephew Julius Caesar, a ruth-
lessly brilliant general and politician, triumphed over his chief associate
and rival, Pompey the Great, to deliver the death blow to the old Republic; and finally, after the assassination of Caesar, there came the third,
between his nephew and adopted son, Octavian, and Mark Antony,
Caesar's quondam general and friend, consort to Caesar's consort, the
last of the Ptolemies, Cleopatra. Octavian won, and with himself as
First Citizen (*princeps*) would refashion the government as an Empire.

In the wake of his decisive victory at Actium in 31 BCE, Octavian (soon
to be Augustus: the name was voted him by the Senate in 27) recognized
the exhaustion of the country and its people; both cities and confidence
needed rebuilding. Promoting peace and his own regime went hand in
hand; he had to persuade the citizenry that his supremacy – which it
would have been perfectly natural for Romans to construe as a backward
slide into a tyranny not unlike that of the monarchs under which the city
had labored for its first 250-odd years – was not the mere triumph of a
faction, to be resented and resisted, but the endpoint toward which the
Republic had always been tending; not a traumatic break, but a continuity of Roman character and a culmination of Roman greatness. To
accomplish this goal, he used every means of propaganda at his disposal,
including poetry. Under the judicious eye of Gaius Cilnius Maecenas, a
sort of Augustan 'Minister of Culture' and patron of patrons, the place of
poetry was moved from the periphery of Roman society to the center.

This shift, along, perhaps, with a certain psychic need persisting in
the post-traumatic landscape, helps explain the increased pursuit of
gravity and grandeur, the willingness to assume the role of public poet,
in writers like Virgil (pp. 398–410), Horace (in his 'Roman Odes', pp.
478–82, and *Centennial Hymn*) and, occasionally, Propertius (in his
fourth book of *Elegies*, pp. 440–45) and Ovid (in parts of the *Metamorphoses* and the *Fasti*). If the previous generation, with Catullus at their
head, had set aside Ennian grandiosity in order to experiment with
Alexandrian polish and erudition, now this new generation of Augus-
tans could take the Latin style they had achieved for granted, and
expand its scope. They effected a reintegration and recuperation: a new,
broader synthesis of Greek form with Roman content, of the New

Poets' stylistic innovations with a more public-facing stance – sometimes in clear alignment with Augustus' political program, and sometimes less so. The result was less a translation than a transfusion of the prestigious Greek past into the language and life of Rome. Its two greatest monuments are Virgil's *Aeneid* and Horace's *Odes*.

This is not to say that Catullan subversion died out. Even Horace and Virgil, the poets most closely allied with the Augustan regime, are not without a strain of it; one senses in them the scarred consciousness of a devil's bargain between Republican freedom and Augustan peace. But it is preeminently the love elegists (Propertius in most of his work, Tibullus, pp. 411–20, and the young Ovid, pp. 494–511) who pick up where Catullus left off.

Where did love elegy come from? No one has been able to explain exactly how the new genre sprang up, with its conventional situations, tropes and motifs seemingly intact from the start, like a louche Athena from the bawdy brain of Zeus. Naturally, there were precedents. Like Catullus with Lesbia, the elegists are generally obsessed with (if never entirely faithful to) one particular beloved. Unlike Catullus, however, they write exclusively in one meter: elegiac couplets. The meter and typical length – say, twenty to sixty lines; although some are longer – recall Greek public elegies such as Simonides' *Plataea Elegy* (p. 128); but the subject matter, love for love's sake, is ostentatiously frivolous and private, and especially so by Roman lights. The amatory focus of love elegy in turn evokes the Hellenistic epigrams of poets like Asclepiades (pp. 303–6), Meleager (pp. 326–32) and Philodemus (pp. 333–9), which share the elegists' obsession with the strain of seduction, the bliss of success and the frustrations of failure; but the Greeks frequently address such poems to young boys, while the Romans are almost exclusively heterosexual. The Greek epigrams evoke the urgent but fleeting lusts of a night's debaucheries, while the Romans conjure a whole life and identity constructed around erotic obsession. Finally, the situation of the elegist, that of a free young man trying to persuade a sophisticated courtesan through arguments and, occasionally, gifts, resembles the typical protagonist of the Greek New Comedy of Menander, and his third- and second-century BCE Roman adaptors, Plautus and Terence – though, unlike in comedy, the elegist neither desires marriage, nor even considers it.

The various elements, then, of Roman love elegy are to be found scattered throughout prior literature, but the particular synthesis the genre represents is limited to the brief period of its flourishing in Rome, lasting less than half a century, from the 40s BCE to around the turn of the millennium. The missing link is Gaius Cornelius Gallus (*c.*70–26 BCE), love elegy's inventor, who, along with Virgil, studied under Parthenius, and provides a sort of bridge between the cynicism of Catullus and his circle and the Augustan project of Roman propriety and national myth-making. Unfortunately, Gallus' poetry does not survive. Instead, we have, more or less complete, the corpus of three poets whose work, un-Augustan if not outright anti-Augustan, substitutes for the *virtus* (manliness, courage, virtue) of the idealized Roman citizen the proudly decadent *nequitia* (lewdness, levity, wastefulness, sloth) of the dedicated lover.

The beginning of love elegy's demise should perhaps be dated to 1 CE, when Ovid published the second edition of his *Amores*. A 'smiling destroyer' (as Italian classicist Gian Biagio Conte puts it), Ovid further subverted an already subversive genre, dissolving it in its own contradictions, by showing up its characteristic postures as exactly that: postures. His infatuation with one woman (Corinna), for example, soon becomes an infatuation with all women, or, at least, most of them (2.4, p. 499); his protestations of fidelity, a key motif of the genre, are humorously revealed as rhetorical lies (2.8, p. 502); perhaps most strikingly, the conceit of *militia amoris* (the warfare of love), whereby earlier elegists sought to set their decadent vocation on an equal footing with the soldier's, is pushed past the breaking point and rendered ridiculous (1.9, p. 495; 2.12, p. 505), and he even shows how the 'bloodless triumph' of sexual conquest nearly leads to his mistress's death by abortion (2.13, p. 506). (Ovid never hesitated to sacrifice good taste in pursuit of an effect.) One might go so far as to say that Ovid, by showing more interest in genre and convention than the woman he is supposedly in love with, points up the same tendency – more muted, perhaps, but no less present – in the other, less campy elegists, and hence exposes the genre's inherent self-regard: in love elegy, love itself is just a trope. In the end, Latin love elegy died with Ovid, in exile beside the Black Sea, three years after the death of Augustus, who had exiled him.

So far, the story of Roman poetry has almost exclusively been that of a literature fixated on a foreign inheritance: that of colonized Greece. With Ovid that begins to change. First Andronicus and Naevius Romanized

Greek poetry, then Ennius, with Homeric ambition, Grecized their Roman poetry. Catullus played Callimachus to Ennius' Homer, introducing a level of polish which Virgil, Horace and Ovid would take for granted, and even improve on, while they in turn, each in their own way, widened their ambitions and their sense of themselves as public poets. Yet for Ovid, the only poet so far who was young enough to have missed the worst of the civil wars of the 40s and 30s, the older generation were already classics; he already felt himself belated. He therefore looks as much or more to his Roman predecessors, especially Virgil, as to the Greeks, and in this he is followed by the poets of the early Empire: Statius (pp. 527–32), in his epic poetry, explicitly acknowledges his debt to Virgil, while the epigrammatist Martial (pp. 533–55) pays fervent homage to Catullus – though it is not so much Catullus' passionate subjectivity that Martial borrows as his wittily pointed malice.

In 17 BCE, Augustus, to celebrate the restoration and renewal which he wished his regime to represent, staged the Centennial or 'Secular' Games. A *saeculum* was a period of 110 years, at which interval an oracle had declared the games should be held. (They had last been staged in the 140s BCE.) In the 40s, Virgil had heralded the birth of the new *saeculum* with his fourth Eclogue (p. 403), but now, two years after his death, it was Horace whom the *princeps* would tap to compose the official hymn. On the third day of celebrations, following sacrifices by Augustus and his right-hand man, Marcus Vipsanius Agrippa, a chorus of twenty-seven freeborn youths and as many maidens sang, first on the Palatine, then on the Capitoline, the two most preeminent of Rome's fabled seven hills, words that Horace had taught them in the measure of Sappho:

> Kind Sun, ever the same yet other still,
> who carry and bury the day in the sky's dome,
> your beams touch nothing – no, and never will –
>   greater than Rome!

If that portion of Livy's *History of Rome* which covered this signal event survived, we might expect the historian to admire the poet's metrical mastery, verbal polish and sufficiency of statement, and thus to note how far, since the *partheneion* of Livius Andronicus, both the Roman state, and the state of Roman poetry, had come.

Catullus

Gaius Valerius Catullus (circa 84–54 BCE) was the most talented poet of the late Republic. He hailed from Verona, in what today is northern Italy but by the Romans was called Cisalpine or Transpadane Gaul (that is, Gaul on *this* side of the Alps but on *that* side of the Po). Little is known of his life; the one datable event is his stint on the staff of Gaius Memmius, governor of Bithynia, on the southern Black Sea coast of Asia Minor, between 57 and 56 BCE. Catullus did not care for Bithynia, and complained about his time there in his poetry after he returned; it wasn't so much the corruption of Rome's governance that he deplored as his own failure to be enriched by it (see poem 10, p. 379). Catullus' father was a friend of Julius Caesar, whom he often hosted at his villa on Lake Benacus (modern Garda, near Verona) in the winters between Caesar's campaigns in Transalpine Gaul (Gaul-across-the-Alps) in the 50s BCE. In his poems, Catullus launches several attacks on Caesar and his associates, which they must have found very annoying; still, Suetonius tells us that, the minute Catullus apologized, 'Caesar invited the poet to dinner that very same day, and continued his usual friendly relations with Catullus' father'.

Catullus also had a brother whom he loved, whose death in Asia Minor, near Troy, he mourns in several poems; he visited the grave while he was in Bithynia (see poem 101, p. 397). The other major event in Catullus' life was his adulterous affair with the woman he calls 'Lesbia', probably Clodia Metelli, wife of Quintus Metellus Celer (consul 60, died 59 BCE), and sister of the notorious demagogue Publius Clodius Pulcher, who happened to be on a short list of Cicero's Least Favorite People. In the collection of Catullus' verse that has survived to us, known simply as the *Carmina*, or *Poems*, the affair is not presented in chronological order; it has proved impossible to rearrange the poems into anything resembling a timeline, though that has not stopped scholars from trying. We are told that he died at the tender age of thirty.

Catullus is often thought of as the chief surviving representative of a 'new school' of poets who first introduced Alexandrian-style poetry to Rome – that is, the sort of poetry practiced by Callimachus (pp. 255–81), Theocritus (pp. 282–98) and other denizens of the Library of Alexandria, from the third to the first centuries BCE. For Catullus and his circle, this poetry must have been a sexily youthful alternative to the old-fashioned shagginess of poets like Ennius, Lucretius and Cicero, who at one time was widely considered not only Rome's best orator, but also her best poet (see the introduction to Latin Lyric, p. 368). The idea that they formed a school is derived from three passages in Cicero, all dripping with contempt. In one, he mocks what he takes to be their florid style in a verse he tells his friend Atticus he can sell to one of those 'newer' poets (*neoteroi* in Greek, from which comes another name for their grouping, the 'Neoterics'); in the others, he inveighs against the tendency of these 'New Poets' (*poetae novi*, now, in Latin) and 'songbirds of Euphorion' (of Chalcis, a poet associated with Callimachus) to tout their own exquisitely hip new style at the expense of the old literary lions. No doubt much of his annoyance derived from his own demotion, as the tides of taste carried him out to sea, from the best poet in Rome to a crotchety afterthought. Besides Catullus, the main New Poets were his friends or acquaintances, like Marcus Furius Bibaculus, Gaius Licinius Calvus, Gaius Helvius Cinna and Publius Terentius Varro Atacinus. Whether or not we are ultimately justified in calling these poets a 'school', there is no doubt that Catullus and his friends introduced something genuinely new into Latin literature.

We have already seen how much of the newness of Alexandrian poetry was rooted in its textuality, and in the space opened by text for theorizing and polemicizing (see the introduction to Post-Classical Greek Lyric, pp. 253–4). Catullus now imported Callimachus' opposition to grandeur and gaucheness, as well as his taste for the polemical, to first-century Italy. Where the old stuff was rough, verbose, moralizing and sententiously Roman, the new stuff was polished, concise, amoral, clever, learned and coded as culturally 'Greek'. Of course, Catullus was hardly a paint-by-numbers sort of poet; in channeling what Callimachus might have written if he were a fiery young fop from Verona with a chip on his shoulder and a hole in his heart, Catullus wrote not Callimachus' poetry but his own. His example was followed; in their own ways, Horace (pp. 453–91), the elegists (Tibullus, pp. 411–20,

Propertius, pp. 421–45, Ovid, pp. 492–526) and Martial (pp. 533–55) all looked to Catullus as to a pioneer, and even Virgil's (pp. 398–410) achievement, though far grander, would have been inconceivable without him.

We have no idea what, if anything, Catullus had to do with organizing the collection we possess. The *Carmina* manuscript is based on a single codex which turned up in Verona in the late thirteenth or early fourteenth century; it is fabled by one romantic but unfortunately improbable myth to have been discovered either under a wine barrel or, still more fancifully, *in* it, used as a bung. This codex was copied three times and then promptly went missing, never to be found again. (Catullus' poetry was unknown between late antiquity and the early Renaissance.) It is divided into three parts: polymetric poems (poems 1–60), longer poems (61–8) and elegies and epigrams (69–116). The 'polymetrics' are written in various meters, mostly lyric or iambic. The longer poems, mostly written in dactylic hexameter and elegiac couplets, consist of *epithalamia* (wedding poems), mini-epics and two lengthy elegies, one of which (poem 68b, p. 391) is a clear precursor to Latin love elegy. The last section, entirely in elegiac couplets, consists of Hellenistic-style epigrams, one of which (poem 76, p. 395) is extended to the cusp of elegy.

Catullus was clearly inspired by Callimachus' generic diversity: his range is astonishing, and runs the gamut from the most vulgar obscenity to the loftiest poeticism, from proto-confessionalism to epic-style objectivity, from light-hearted banter to bitter invective, with every shade of intensity in between. All this variety is held together on the one hand by the poet's depth of feeling (vehemence in affection and reproach, obsession with fidelity and betrayal), and on the other by his psychological conflictedness (between sincerity and irony, politics and aesthetics, Rome and Greece). Catullus is among the most fascinating poets of antiquity, and one of the best.

Polymetric Poems

1°

Who gets this smart new chapbook, freshly
buffed by hand, still smoking hot?
You do, Cornelius, since you°
were always kind to these squibs of mine:
the one Italian brave enough
to fit all history in three volumes –
what learning, gods! And what hard work!°
Well, here: good, bad or mediocre,
it's yours – and, maiden Patroness,
may it at least outlast its maker.°

2

Sparrow, my sweetheart's favorite baby –°
she loves to keep you in her lap,
to poke your beak with her fingertip,
beckoning you to nip and peck it;
so, when the lovely one I long for
wants to release some pent-up tension,
the cuteness of your capers, maybe,
can comfort her anxiety –
I wish, when I was in that mood,
that you could do the same for me! . . .°
I'd like it as Atalanta liked,°
they say, that little golden apple
that loosened up her tight-wound girdle.°

3°

Weep, you Venuses and Cupids;°
dishes and dreamboats, start weeping!
My sweetheart's sparrow has dropped dead,

her sparrow, her most favorite baby,
that she loved more than anything.
This pet, so smoothly tuneful, knew her
better than she knew her mother.
Never hopping off her lap,
it flitted this way, flitted that,
cheep-cheep-cheeping to her alone; but now   10
it skips and pecks the Path of Shadows
to a dark cage no bird has flown.
But you be damned, dread maw of hell,
devourer of the beautiful;
you stole a pretty pet, my sparrow.
O dreadful crime! Poor baby sparrow!
It's your fault now that there's no keeping
my sweetheart's puffy eyes from weeping.

5

My Lesbia, let's live and love!
And what the crabbed old crows are mouthing
we'll hold as worth – oh, less than nothing!°
Suns in succession set and rise,
but we, when our brief daylight dies,
must sleep one everlasting sleep.
Give me a thousand kisses, then
a hundred, then another thousand,
another hundred then, and then
a thousand, then a hundred more;°   10
then after many, many thousands,
we'll jumble the numbers up, lose count,
and foil the jealous fogeys' jinxes
by muddling the true amount.°

6

Flavius, your new girlfriend – spill!°
No holding back! Or maybe she's
a hayseed, or an imbecile?
That's clearly it: you've fallen for
a scrawny, syphilitic whore.
I know – it *is* embarrassing.
I know your nights have not been lonely –
your bedposts, without speaking, shout,
slathered in wreaths and flavored oils,

10   with sheets and pillows, left *and* right,
bedraggled, and the bedframe reeling
all around the bedroom, squealing.°
Sealed lips do nothing; truth gets out.
How's that? You're pale; your hygiene's sliding
from late nights in the saddle, riding.
So dish, whether she's bad, or worse;
and I'll praise you two lovebirds high
as heaven in my sparkling verse.

7°

How many kisses must come before
Catullus has had enough and more?°
asks Lesbia, and I reply:
count up the desert sands that lie
in Libyan Cyrene, home°
to the world's stash of silphium,°
between Jove-Ammon's sweaty shrine°
and old King Battus' holy tomb;°
or count the stars in the tacit sky

10   that spy on furtive mortal loves,
and *that*'s how many will satisfy
and glut Catullus – a sum too high
for stale voyeurs to count or curse
with evil spells or an evil eye.°

8

Catullus, lovesick, heartsick, quit this stupid mooning.°
You see that it's all over. Give up now. You're dumped.
It's true that, once, for you, the brightest suns were shining:
when love would lead you on, and you would follow after –
you loved her then, as no girl ever will be loved.
You wanted her, and she, she never disapproved,
and all your days were banter, teasing, tickling, laughter.
It's true that, once, for you, the brightest suns were shining.
She doesn't want you now. Stop wanting her. (You can't.)
She's turned her back on you. Stop chasing her. Don't live   10
a sniveling invalid. Don't wobble. Be like flint.
Adios, darling. Now Catullus' heart is flint.°
He will not visit you or ask what you won't give.
But you'll repent when nobody visits any more.
Look out for that, she-devil! Then what will your life be?
Who'll praise your beauty then? And who'll knock at your door?
Whose spoil will your affection be? Whose property?
Whose lips will you bite now? Whose kisses will you savor?
But you, Catullus, be like flint. Do not waver.

10

I was just loafing in the Forum
when Varus took me to meet his lover.°
Now that one was a firecracker –
no dummy either, and a looker.
Well, I showed up, and we got talking
on this and that, and someone brought
the business up, in Bithynia –°
I must have made a killing there.
My answer was plain truth: no one,
not magistrates or office workers,   10
could grease our palms to slick our hair,
because the governor, that fucker,

is fucking everybody over –
to him, his staff's not worth a pube.
'Surely,' they said, 'you earned enough
to buy yourself some litter-bearers –
Bithynia's where the vogue began.'°
I, wanting to impress her, said,
'Well, yes, I was exaggerating.
20 Things weren't so bad I couldn't manage
eight sturdy backs for a sedan.'
(Of course, I didn't have one man
with a neck strong enough to hoist
the broken-down old cot I sleep on.)
Then that sly slut said, 'Oh, you *must*
lend them to me, Catullus, just
one day, to take me to Serapis.'°
So I replied, 'Tomorrow morning,
those men that I just said were mine –
30 what *was* I thinking? What I meant was,
they're my buddy's, Gaius Cinna's.°
But mine, or his, who cares? I don't.
I use them any time I want.
But go on splitting hairs, ball-buster,
who won't ignore some harmless bluster!'

11

To Furius and Aurelius°

You'd stick beside Catullus, your old friend,
if he takes off for India's farthest reaches,°
where the eastern ocean at the world's end
  batters the beaches;

or even for the Caspian, or Iran,
or the soft Arabs, Parthia's archer host,°
or where the Nile's sevenfold waters span
  and darken the coast;

or if he crosses the Alps to see firsthand
great Caesar's monuments, the Gaulish Rhine, 10
the violent Channel, and British hinterland
    beyond the brine.°

Friends braced to do with me what I have to do,
where or whatever the gods' will leads me towards,
go and address my girl; pass on these few
    ungentle words:

Let her live and enjoy her crowd of pricks,
letting three hundred at once into her skirt,
not true to any, but using all her tricks
    to make them spurt. 20

Don't let her call me a lover or a friend;
it's *her* fault that my love is fallen now
like a shy flower touched at the meadow's end°
    by a passing plow.

13°

Come to my place, you'll dine in style,
gods willing, in a few days' while,
Fabullus – if you bring the dinner,°
the cute girl and the wine, the wit
and belly laughs to season it;
bring all that, *bello*, and, I promise,
you'll dine in style; but I can't pull it
off with cobwebs in my wallet.
Though I *can* pour you friendship, neat,
and what's more sumptuous and sweet: 10
a scent Love's choicest powers chose
to lavish on my dearest dear –
a smell that when, my friend, you smell it,
your prayer will be to be all nose.

16°

I'll fuck you in the ass and throat,
Aurelius and Furius:°
both of you tend to play the bitch.
You read my poems and labeled *me* –
since they're a little titillating –
a shameless pervert, and indecent.
A poet ought to keep his life
decent, not his poetry;°
it gives the poems charm and wit
10   if they're a little titillating,
a little shameless, and can get
a fellow going, make him itch –
not boys, I mean, but hairy geezers
who can't get up below the belt.
You read about those thousand kisses°
and thought I wasn't man enough?
I'll fuck you in the ass and throat.

22

Varus, you said *Suffenus*. I know you know him well:°
a prince of urbanity, always impeccable.
And yet the poems he writes are really, really long;°
I think he must be guilty of ten thousand lines
or more – and not repurposing old paper either,°
but writing on fresh reams of overpriced octavo,
with brand-new dowels, red leather bindings, parchment
    wrappers,
ruled straight with pencil marks, buffed evenly with pumice.
And when you read these things, this polished gentleman,
10   this dapper wag, doesn't he seem to metamorphose
before your eyes into a gravedigger and goatfucker?
Well. What is going on? This scintillating wit –
if that does justice to his brilliant conversation! –

suddenly turns duller than the dullest inbred yokel
as soon as he picks up a pen, and this same guy
is never happier than when he's writing poems,
he's so thrilled and enthralled by his own company.
Are all of us fooling ourselves? Who hasn't got,
somewhere, in some respect, a serving of Suffenus?
Everybody has a blind spot. We can track   20
the baggage that we see, but not what's on our back.

31

Sweet Sirmio, dearest of waterfronts – lake isles,°
sea isles, peninsulas, where Neptune, salt or fresh,
plashes in glassy pools, or makes the big waves crash –
with what a leap of the heart I look on you at last,
awash with disbelief I've left Bithynia,
that I'm alive, intact, and I've made it home today.
What could be sweeter than when worries drain away,
when, in the bone-fatigue of an interminable journey
ended, the mind unclenches by the family fire
and we slip melting in the bed of our desire?   10
This, this is the one thing that pays for so much pain.
Hello, exquisite Sirmio, beam for your beaming
master; and you, Lydian lake-water, gleaming°
with giddiness, wind-tickled, laugh: I'm home again!

34°

Under Diana's faithful wing
unmarried girls and boys are carried;
to Diana we unmarried
    boys and girls now sing.

Your mother Leto gave you birth,
o greatest Jove's great progeny;
at Delos, by an olive tree,
    she placed you on the earth.°

Now you are mistress of the mountains,
and of the forests growing green.
The hidden coverts call you queen,
       and sweetly sounding fountains.

As Midwife Juno, you're the boon°
the pregnant pray to in their plight;
and Triple One, by your false light°
       you're also called the Moon.°

O goddess, on a monthly route
you chart your annual career,
and fill farmhouses every year
       with stores of grain and fruit.

Whatever name, o holy one,
would please you most, by your good grace
watch over Romulus's race,
       as you have always done.

37

You pubic pub, and you, its pubey regulars,
nine doors down from the bonnet-wearing Dioscuri,°
you think, I guess, the only cocks in town are yours,
that you're the only ones to score a bit of tail
and fuck her brains out, that we're all repulsive goats?
You sit, lined up a hundred strong (or is it two?)
and think I lack the balls, you worthless sacks of shit,
to skull-fuck all two hundred of you where you sit?
That's what you think, but I am coming with graffiti,
to stuff your tavern's face with a shit-ton of dicks.
Since she who has abandoned me, my former sweetie,
whom I once loved as no girl ever will be loved,°
the one I fought my biggest wars for, likes to mix
now with the likes of you, and all you classy gents
make love to her, and you – this part is most obscene –

you demimonde sex fiends, horndogs of the latrine;
you too, worst of the worst, bigwig of flocculence,
born in the Land of Shaggy Rabbits, Iberia's son,°
Egnatius, whose thick beard gives you your *bon ton* –
that, and the Spanish piss that keeps your teeth so clean.   20

41

Ameana, you've been fucked silly –
you want ten thousand from me? Really?
You? With that revolting schnoz?
The sidepiece of bankrupt Mamurra?°
Family members, benefactors –
the girl's sick! Call her friends and doctors:
she's never asked a looking glass
the market value of her ass.

45°

Holding his Acme in his lap,
Septimius exclaimed, 'My dove,
if I'm not desperately in love,
if I don't mean to be your lover
with no letup till my life's over,
if I am not more deathly smitten
than anyone Love's ever bitten,
through Indian or Saharan drouth
I'll leap alone in a lion's mouth.'
As on the left, so on the right,   10
Love sneezed approval and delight.°
Then Acme lightly raised her head,
and with those lips, rose-madder red,
she kissed his sweet, besotted eyes.
'Septimius, my life,' she sighs,
'let us be servants to one love
our whole lives through, so I can prove
my molten marrow with more heat

more fiercely melts for you, my sweet.'
20   *As on the left, so on the right,*
Love sneezed approval and delight.
And now, from this auspicious start,
they love and are loved with one heart.
Septimius loves Acme, smitten,
beyond all Syria and Britain;
for Acme, Septimius alone
can give her joy or make her moan.
Who's seen felicity like this?
Have lovers ever known such bliss?

46°

Spring is here, and the cold is melting;
the sky's wild equinoctial pelting
gives way before the playful zephyrs.
Now say goodbye to Troy, Catullus,
and the hot farmland of Nicaea:°
you're off to see the best of Asia!
Excitement has you flutter-hearted;
your fidgety feet can't wait to roam.
You treasured colleagues, *sayonara!*
10   A long way off our journeys started,
and many roads will take us home.

48°

If I could kiss-kiss-kiss, nonstop,
your honeyed eyes, Juventius,
three hundred thousand times, the yield
would not sate me, not unless our crop
of kisses were more numerous
than grains of wheat in a golden field.

50

Yesterday, Calvus, we were free°
to play and reply in poetry,
now cute and classy, now off-color.
We would each scribble a verse in turn,
fooling with meters, drinking, kidding,
giving as good as we were getting.
And when I left, I was on fire,
abuzz with your smart style and wit;
food couldn't slacken my desire,
sleep wouldn't ease my eyes a bit,   10
but I tossed wildly all night through,
restless for the sun to rise
so I could talk and be with you.
Exhausted from so much exertion,
limbs sprawling on the bed, half-dead,
I wrote this poem for you, sweet cheeks,
to lay bare my acute condition.
Beware to hurt me now, I pray,
my darling, and don't spurn my prayer,
so Nemesis won't make you pay:°   20
she's easily provoked – beware.

51°

The equal of a god that man appears,
better than gods, if it's not blasphemy,
who sits across from you, and stares, and hears
          continually

your lovely laughter, which, in my despair,°
siphons my senses; soon as I look upon
you, Lesbia, I'm dumb, and don't know where
          my voice has gone;

my tongue grows heavy, underneath my skin
10   a thin flame drips, my ears ring with a bright
and tinny sound, and my eyes are veiled within
    a twofold night.

Free time, Catullus, that's what's killing you!
Free time fuels your fidgeting and your flings.
Free time has leveled prosperous cities, too,
    and mighty kings.

58

Lesbia, Caelius, Lesbia,°
that very Lesbia Catullus
loved more than life and all his dears,
on corners now and in back-alleys
shucks lordly Remus' sons and heirs.

60°

So: a lioness bore you on African bluffs,
or Scylla, crotch surrounded by canine mewls and woofs,°
since you can be so cruel, so flinty, as to pause
over a suppliant, and hear his dying call
unmoved, and spit on him, you heartless animal – !

Longer Poems

62°

It's Venus! On your feet, boys! Venus, long
awaited, crowns Olympus with her light.°
The bride will come; we'll sing the wedding song.
Stop feasting and get up! The time is right.
Hymen o Hymenaeus, Hymen, come!°

Girls, did you see the boys? Then on your feet!
It seems Mount Oeta sports the star of night.°
You saw how fast they leapt, each from his seat?
They leapt to sing; they're spoiling for a fight.
Hymen o Hymenaeus, Hymen, come!   10

To win the laurel, fellows, won't be easy:
look at them practicing what they've rehearsed!
They've got it down by heart. Yes, they've been busy –
no wonder, since they're utterly immersed.
Victory loves hard work, so they should smoke us.
We've listened, but we've been woolgathering.
Let's pull ourselves together now, and focus;
We'll answer them, and they're about to sing.
Hymen o Hymenaeus, Hymen, come!

Could heaven, evening star, burn crueler light?°   20
You tear the daughter from her mother's arms
while the girl clings and holds her mother tight,
to serve her fervid husband with her charms.
What city's sack could be more cruel than this?
Hymen o Hymenaeus, Hymen, come!

Could heaven, evening star, show sweeter fire?
You seal betrothals when you shine your light,
betrothals both sides settled and desire;
our loves are joined when your flame climbs in sight.
What gods could give a more transcendent bliss?   30
Hymen o Hymenaeus, Hymen, come!

Ladies, the evening star stole one of us . . .°

you rouse the guards you shine your light upon;
thieves hide at night, whom you come back and seize,
the evening star become the star of dawn.
But let them fabricate their gripes and taunt you;
so what? They chide, but silently, they want you.
Hymen o Hymenaeus, Hymen, come!

A garden wall surrounds a secret flower°
40   which no herd tramples down, no plow destroys;
the breezes soothe it, sunshine feeds, rains shower,
and many girls desire it, many boys.
But when a nail deflowers it and shears it,
no boys or girls desire it any more.
Thus with virginity, while she reveres it;
but when it's plucked, and she's no longer pure,
no boys will speak to her, and girls are numb.
Hymen o Hymenaeus, Hymen, come!

A barren field bears an unmarried vine
50   that never climbs aloft or brings forth fruit,
but bends low with its brittle weight to twine
its stem-tip on the ground back to its root:
the farmers all, and all the steers, ignore it.
But if the same vine to an elm is wed,
the farmers all, and all the steers, care for it.
A virgin thus grows old, unhusbanded;
But when it's time to take the marriage oath,
she's loved by husband and by father both.

Now   maiden, don't resist, and don't delay.
60   Don't fight the man your father gave you to –
your father and your mother – but obey.
Not all your maidenhead belongs to you:
one say's your father's; your mother has a say,
the third say's yours – don't fight the other two,
who dowered you and gave you to the groom.
Hymen o Hymenaeus, Hymen, come!

65

Though constant grief confounds me and its fetters,
Hortalus, keep me from the Maids of Letters,°
and though my mind and heart are weak to press
the Muses' fruit, still drowning in distress –

for recently my brother wet his toe,
death-pale, in turbid Lethe's sluggish flow,
and took Rhoeteum's Trojan dirt for pall,°
ripped from my eyes by scanty burial . . .   8
dear brother, dearer to me than life, will I   10
never see you again? I'll always love you,
I'll always make sad music because of you,
as Procne in the shade trees sings her pain,
mourning for Itylus, so early slain.°
Yet, Hortalus, despite my grief, I send
lines of Battiades to you, my friend,°
so you won't think your plea, cast to the wind
in vain, has tumbled headlong from my mind
the way an apple, the hushed gift of a lover –
when the girl jumps at the entrance of her mother,   20
forgetful, poor thing, it was in her clothes –
spills from her virgin lap, and, as it goes
rolling away now in a headlong streak,
a guilty blush suffuses her sad cheek.°

68b°

Sing Allius! I can't hush, goddesses,°
how much he helped me, or what that help was;
so that the ages, in forgetful flight,
won't wrap his gift invisibly in night,
I'll tell you, and you'll publish it to many,°
and make my page a gossipy old granny . . .   46
and, when he's dead, his fame will only grow: 48
no spider's subtle lacework will subsume
the name on Allius' forgotten tomb.°   50
    You know the fever the two-natured Dame
of Cyprus sicked on me, that crazy flame°
which broiled me like Sicilian magma, or
the scalding springs Thermopylae's named for,
when my sad eyes were swamps of ceaseless crying,
and the wet weather kept my cheeks from drying.

As when a mossed stone on a mountain summit
exhales a lucid freshet sluicing from it
which roping headlong downhill soon gets sent
60   slaloming through a populous settlement
to a sweat-drenched wayfarer – largesse sweet
when the ground cracks and gapes in withering heat;
or as when sailors squalls have slapped and sprayed,
begging now Pollux's, now Castor's aid,°
are brushed and buoyed by a gentler wind –
that's how it felt, that favor from my friend.
Where all was locked and barred, he cleared a space:
with me, and my sweetheart, he shared his place,
so we could cultivate the love between us.
70   That's where, with soft footfall, a gleaming Venus,
she came; her radiant feet caressed the sleeked
flags of the foyer, when her sandal squeaked –°
as Laodamia, who loved her spouse
Protesilaus, first stepped in the house°
he'd just begun – in vain, because his new
bride overlooked the sacrifices due.°
O Nemesis, I pray, do not dispose°
me to some reckless act the gods oppose!
For Laodamia – her husband lost –
80   soon learned what that unbloodied altar cost,
forced to release her new love's neck before
a second winter swelled the first one's store
of hungry kisses shared from dusk to dawn
to keep her going when her love was gone:
he whom the Fates knew doom would soon destroy
if he should sail against the walls of Troy.
For Troy had just begun, with Helen's seizure,
summoning Greece's greatest to besiege her:
Troy – cursed name! – that butcher of the brave,
90   all Europe's and all Asia's common grave,
which even, in a cruel blow, stole from me°
my brother. Brother lost, o agony!
No more you'll see the day's each light-drenched hue;

now all my house is in the grave with you;
with you all of my joys and pleasures perished,
which you sustained in life with love I cherished.
Now, far from those you loved, not resting in
known plots, beside the ashes of your kin,
you're held in hostile Troy, in Troy that brings
no joy, off at the savage edge of things.   100
That's where the young, the pick of Greece, it's said,
abandoning their hearths, from all sides sped,
so Paris and the slut he stole would cease
to frolic in their bridal bed at peace.
And, gorgeous Laodamia, that's where
your husband, more beloved than life, than air,
was lost, and love's implacable undertow
engulfed you into an abyss as low –
as deep – as the pit the Greeks say drained and dried
Pheneus' swamps by Mount Cyllene's side:°   110
that pit the son who wasn't Amphitryon's°
tunneled out of the mountain's marrow once –
after he drove bronze birds from Stymphalus°
with his enchanted bow that couldn't miss,
the minion of a lesser man – before°
he swelled the ranks of deities that wore
the flagstones smooth at Mount Olympus' door
and Hebe was not a virgin any more.°
But deeper than that pit was the deep love
your untamed heart bowed to the bridle of –   120
more than the love felt by an old granddad
for his daughter's son, the son he never had,
the late-born heir to his ancestral loot,
whose naming in his will at last would mute
the sleazy glee surrounding his deathbed,
driving the vultures from his hoary head;°
more than the love a snowy dove has ever
felt for her mate, who show (it's said) a fever
more cheeky, as they peck and pluck their kisses,
than the most lascivious and flighty missus.°   130

Your love alone was more consuming than
all those, bound always to one golden man.
   No whit less lovingly, or slightly less,
my sweetheart brought herself to my caress,
while Cupid, saffron-robed and gleaming white,
kept fluttering round her to the left and right.
If I alone am not enough for her
I won't deter the odd discreet affair,
so I don't seem dull and conventional.
140   For even Juno, queen of heaven's hall,
has choked back bile at rank abuse above,
knowing the vices of all-randy Jove.
But it's all wrong to liken men and gods . . .°

Elegies and Epigrams

70°

My girl tells me there's no one she'd prefer
to marry her – not even Jupiter.
Her words: but what a woman tells her lover
she ought to write in wind or running water.°

72

You used to say I was your only love,
Lesbia, and that you'd take me over Jove.
I cared for more than sex – I loved you all,
as a father loves his sons and sons-in-law.°
I know you now. My flame grows more severe,
the cheaper and more faithless you appear.
How can this be, you ask? Your callousness
drives me to love you more, and like you less.

76°

If memories of good deeds do any good
for one who knows he's acted as he should,
who never broke faith once, or swore in vain
a holy pact he knew he would profane,°
what happiness your long old age has earned,
Catullus, from this passion unreturned!
Yes, all the good deeds men can say or do
for anyone were said and done by you,
and all have vanished from her thankless life.
So why torment yourself? Why twist the knife?   10
Why not come back, stand strong against your woes,
give up this misery the gods oppose?
It's hard, so soon, to let such long love drop;
it's hard, but as you're able, make it stop!
You have one hope, one chance at life, one plan:
let go, no matter if you can't or can.
If you feel pity, gods, or ever think°
to help a soul shuddering at death's brink,
think of me now – my pain, my innocence –
and save me from this poison pestilence   20
slithering through me, numbing every part,
sucking all sense of pleasure from my heart.
I won't ask any more what you won't grant,
that she still love me, or be chaste (she can't!);
I want to move on, and be rid of this
lovesickness. Gods, reward my faithfulness!

83

Lesbia bashes me when hubby's near;°
that's what the imbecile loves most to hear.
You donkey, don't you see? There'd be no danger
in silence, but she spits and seethes with anger,
so she both thinks about me, and – this matters! –
she's livid. QED: she burns, and chatters.

84

Not 'commodities', 'commoditae',
says Arrius; 'satyrs' are 'satori'.°
He beams; our sidelong glances verify
the erudition of his 'satori'.
Clearly these are words he grew up with –
his mother's, freedman uncle's and their kith.
He sailed for Syria; our ears were easy,
without that dialect to drive them crazy,
until we heard what we'd thought gone for good –
a notice from abroad that chilled our blood:
it seems we've got new atlases to buy,
since Syrians now go by 'Syriae'.

10

85°

I hate and I love. How can that be? you scoff.
Don't know – I feel it. It's breaking me in half.

92

Lesbia never stops complaining of
me this, me that: damned if she's not in love.
The proof? I'm the same way. I'm always mad
at her, but damned if I don't love her bad!

99°

Horsing around, I stole a kiss from you,
whose sweetness sweet ambrosia can't outdo.
You made me pay, sweetheart Juventius;
more than an hour, I hung upon that cross,
while I wept for forgiveness and could not
assuage your wrath's severity one jot.
And that whole time, you washed your little lips

with tears, and scrubbed them with your fingertips,
so no trace of my own lips would persist,
as if it was a filthy whore you'd kissed.   10
And now, with hateful love, you still defy me,
and, every way you can, you crucify me,
making your sweet ambrosial kiss taste more
bitter to me than bitter hellebore.°
Your punishment has my heart in so much pain,
I'll never steal another kiss again.

101°

Conveyed through many nations, many seas,°
brother, I've come to these sad obsequies,
to bear you proper rites of burial
and call your ashes, mute beyond recall,°
since Fortune sundered us from one another –
how far, alas, from your deserts, dear brother!
These sorry gifts, of old inherited,°
gifts which our fathers' fathers gave their dead:
take them, soaked where your brother's teardrops fell,
and, brother, for all time, hail and farewell.   10

109

'Light-hearted love', my life, you offer me,
and offer it in perpetuity.
Great gods, make her speak true, make her sincere,
draw from her heart of hearts the words I hear,
so we may live the life she's speaking of,
in steadfast bonds of loyalty and love.°

Virgil

Publius Vergilius Maro (70–19 BCE) was Rome's greatest poet but not, strictly, a lyricist. He is responsible for three major works: the pastoral *Eclogues* (published around 38 BCE), minor-key verse dramas featuring shepherds and goatherds, modeled on Theocritus' *Idylls* (pp. 283–98); the didactic *Georgics* (29 BCE), a verse treatise on farming in four books; and the epic *Aeneid* (published after Virgil's death in 19 BCE), which tells of Aeneas' heroic quest, after the fall of Troy, to reach Italy and establish the Roman people.

For most of his life, Virgil's love of the countryside conspired with his melancholy constitution to keep him away from Rome. Born in the small village of Andes, near Mantua in northern Italy, to a humble father, he was educated first in Cremona, then in Milan and finally in Rome. Unlike his near-contemporary Catullus (pp. 373–97, likewise a native of the region the Romans called Transpadane Gaul, 'Gaul-across-the-Po'), he had no affinity for city life. Tall and dark, with a slow, 'almost uneducated' way of speaking (but a 'sweet and wonderfully effective' delivery of his own poetry), Virgil avoided Rome; on the rare occasions that he did go there, he spent much of his time hiding from the public eye. (Ovid, pp. 492–526, boasts that, as a young man, he 'saw Virgil once'.) Instead, Virgil preferred Campania, in and around Naples, where he studied with the famous Epicurean philosopher Siro and his protégé, the epigrammatist Philodemus (pp. 333–9); also present were the literary critic Quintilius Varus (see Horace, *Odes* 1.24, p. 469) and the epic poets Lucius Varius Rufus (see *Odes* 1.6, p. 466), and Plotius Tucca; even Horace himself probably joined them. It was Varius and Plotius whom the emperor Augustus entrusted with the posthumous editing of the *Aeneid*, in contravention of Virgil's deathbed wish that the unfinished work be burned.

Both Virgil and Horace were dedicated Epicureans of Philodemus' and Siro's school – albeit, in their poetry anyway, eclectic ones; but where a native jolliness made Horace a natural 'porker from the sty of

Epicurus', Virgil's quest for unperturbedness came from a darker place, a soulful melancholy marked by the tumultuous century into which he had been born. It is hard to say what impact the vicious decade of inter-necine violence from 91 to 80 BCE – first between Rome and the Italians, then between the populist general Marius and Sulla, his aristocratic antagonist – may have had on the physical and psychic landscape he encountered as a child; but there is no doubt that the nearly twenty years of civil war that stretched from Julius Caesar's crossing of the Rubicon in 49 to Octavian's decisive victory at Actium in 31 had left deep scars. Virgil was an Italian first and a Roman second, and always more temperamentally inclined toward lament than celebration. When Octavian was evicting the poet's Mantuan neighbors to settle veterans of Philippi, the battle of 42 BCE in which the pro-Caesarian party defeated the band of Caesar's assassins, led by Marcus Junius Brutus and Gaius Cassius Longinus, Virgil managed to keep his family farm thanks to the intervention of his early patron, Gaius Asinius Pollio (see Eclogue 4, p. 403); but his poems on the subject (Eclogues 1 not incl-luded here, and 9, p. 405) weigh his personal gratitude against the general grief. The *Georgics* and the *Aeneid* are similarly unillusioned about the price of peace and progress, even (or especially) when, in the *Aeneid*, all Virgil's considerable gifts are bent toward celebrating the Augustan regime as the climax of history.

Of the four Eclogues included here, Eclogues 2 and 9 are the most typical, while 4 and 10 are not particularly characteristic either of the gorgeous little volume in which they appear, or of Virgil's work in general; but their literary-historical significance is beyond dispute. In the *Eclogues* (the title means *Selections*, and is itself a Latinization of the Greek *Eidyl-lia*, or *Idylls*), Virgil imitates Theocritus, and nowhere more closely than in the second Eclogue's (p. 400) play on Idyll 11 (p. 296). He also varies him; in his tenth Eclogue (p. 408), for example, Virgil shifts the scene from Sicily, the setting of Theocritus' bucolics, to Arcadia, a mountain-ous region of the central Peloponnese destined to be the home of pastoral poetry for all time to come. (He plainly did not intend to position Arca-dia as the mythical utopia which, for the writers of the Renaissance, it became.) The *Georgics* in turn imitate Hesiod, while the *Aeneid* Roman-izes Homer. This particular progression in the writer's work from one genre to the next, from pastoral to georgic to epic, became known as the

'Wheel of Virgil' (*rota Vergiliana*) and served as a model, with variations, for centuries of ambitious poets – Ovid and Statius (pp. 527–32),
Dante and Petrarch, Spenser and Milton – as they planned and navigated their careers. Of all the incalculable contributions to subsequent
poetry made by Virgil, whom T. S. Eliot rightly called (for better or
worse) 'the classic of all Europe', this is not the least.

Virgil died in 19 BCE at the age of fifty-one. He had traveled to Greece
intending to spend the next three years finishing the *Aeneid*, and then
to devote the rest of his life to philosophy; but, meeting Augustus in
Athens, he was invited – or perhaps ordered – to return to Rome. On
the way, he fell sick. He passed away on 21 September in the harbor
of Brundisium (modern Brindisi), in a region then known as Calabria,
and was buried in Naples. He supposedly left behind this epitaph,
which, to judge by its modesty, may well be genuine:

Whom Mantua bore and Calabria claimed, death lands
in Naples. I sang of meadows, farms, commands.

Eclogue 2°

Corydon

Poor Corydon was yearning for Alexis,
their owner's handsome sweetheart; the shepherd had
no hope. And still among the shadowy
tall beechtops he would come, and go, and come,
and there, alone with his unkempt complaints,
he buffeted the wild woods, all for nothing:

> So: songs *can't touch your heart, or make you mourn?*
> *You'd like me dead, Alexis? Oh, you're cruel!*
> *While livestock make for shady spots, to cool,*
10   *and lizards lie low in the greeny thorn,*
> *and Thestylis scoops the fresh herbs up, to pound*
> *for reapers drooping from the boiling swelter,*
> *I trace your steps – alone, and far from shelter,*
> *where harsh cicadas rasp the only sound.*

Wouldn't it have been preferable to put
up with Amaryllis' snobbery
and tantrums? Or Menalcas, although he°
is dark, and you are fair? You're handsome, but
don't prize your fair complexion; we pluck all
the blackberries, but let white privets fall.   20
    You hate me, though, and don't ask who I am, or
what store of flocks and milk I have in hand.
A thousand lambs graze my Sicilian land;
I have fresh milk in winter and in summer.
I sing the songs Amphion, Dirce's bane,°
uttered on Attic Aracynthus' height°
to call his sheep. I'm not such a bad sight,
either: the other day, the sea's smooth plane
lay glass and windless, and, to where I stood
on shore, gave back my looks. I wouldn't grudge   30
to take on Daphnis, and let you be judge,°
Alexis – if reflections don't delude.
    Oh, stoop to share my life here, if you can
stomach it: dirt fields, small shacks, deer hunts,
reed pipes to lead your goatish audience.
Soon, soon I'll have you warbling like Pan!°
To marry reeds with wax was Pan's idea;
Pan loves and cares for sheep and shepherds both.
The pipes may chafe your lips, but don't be loth –
what would Amyntas not have done, to be a   40
master like me? My panpipe is an honor,
with seven hemlock stalks of different length,
the gift of old Damoetas' failing strength;
dying, he told me, "You're its second owner."
He spoke; that dolt Amyntas' envy grew.
And these two kids I risked my life to win –
still suckling twice a day, and still with skin
white-flecked – I've saved them, as a gift for you.
A while now, Thestylis has begged me for them.
So be it; you, because they're mine, abhor them.   50

    Come, handsome boy! For you – look! – our nymphs fill
their lily baskets; our cream-white Naiad sets
the tops of poppies with pale violets,
and mixes in narcissus, and fresh dill,
weaves daphne sprigs with fragrant herbs, enfolds
blackberries in a ground of marigolds.
And I'll pick lots of fuzzy, whitish quince,
and chestnuts, apple of Amaryllis' eyes,
and waxy plums – that fruit, too, is a prize –
60   and you, o laurels; you, too, myrtle fence,
planted nearby to mingle your sweet scents.

    Of course, Alexis hates your offerings,
Corydon; how could the gifts you give outdo
Iollas's – a weepy hick like you?
What, what have I let loose? The South Wind flings
my flowers; boars befoul my crystal springs.

    Madman, why are you running? Even gods
have loved the woods, and Paris, Trojan prince.°
Let towns she built be Pallas' residence;°
70   before all other homes, I choose the woods.
The lion hunts the wolf, the wolf the goat;
the randy goat hunts trefoil blooms, to taste;
Alexis, Corydon hunts you; two-faced
desire lands us all in the same boat.°

    Well, look – the oxen, plows upturned, drag home;
the sun sinks, and the doubled shades extend.
But love still burns me. Love – where is the end?
Corydon, Corydon, what delirium
has twisted you? The vine is half pruned on
80   the leafy elm. Do something someone needs,
like plait an osier basket with soft reeds.
If this Alexis will not cease to shun
your love, well, you can find another one.

Eclogue 4°

The Messianic Eclogue

Sicilian Muses, let's make a grander poem.°
Our lowly tamarisks and orchard stands
don't suit all tastes. If we sing pasturelands,
we'll clothe them in the majesty of Rome.

The last age of the Sibyl's song departs;
the years' great cyclic roll can recommence.°
The Virgin comes, and Saturn's rule restarts;°
down from the towering sky a child descends.
To this boy, who will make the age of vicious
iron give way, that gold may rise again,   10
Diana, Queen of Childbirth, be propitious;
your twin, Apollo, now is sovereign.°

With you in office, Pollio, this sublime°
epoch inaugurates; majestic time
renews its march. During your consulship,
what remnants linger of our ancient crime,°
absolved, shall free the earth from terror's grip.
The child shall live a god, with hero-bands
and bands of gods before him; at their side
he'll shine, conspicuous as he commands   20
the earth his hero-fathers pacified.

To you, child, Earth will give her gifts of green
unplanted: ivy twined with cyclamen;
laughing acanthus and Egyptian bean.
The lion will not menace fold or pen;
unforced, she-goats will seek the milking pail.
Your very cradle will burst into bloom.
The snake and treacherous poison weed will fail,
and the world teem with Syrian perfume.°

30   Then, when you are of age to read the bold
exploits of heroes, and your father's worth;
when you have learned what greatness is, the earth
will slowly spin the wheatfields into gold,
wild briars will bunch with grapes their juice makes dark,
and beads of honey sweat from the oak's bark.

It's true that traces of the ancient fault
will still persist, and drive us to surround
cities with walls, and with our ships insult
the Nereids, and cut ruts in the ground.
40   Another Tiphys then will come to life,°
another *Argo* freighted with choice men
will hoist its sails; new wars will sow new strife,
and great Achilles go to Troy again.°

And yet, when time, that ripens all, has made
a man of you, no one will sail the sea;
no ocean-going pine will ply its trade;
and all the earth will bear all things for free.
No hoe will hack the soil, nor hook the vine;
the hardy farmer will unyoke his team;
50   no lying dyes will teach false threads to gleam;
the ram will stand in his own fields, and shine
with Punic purple now, now saffron fleece,°
and nature clothe the lambs in bold red wool.

In tune with heaven's fixed decree, *O Peace,*
unroll, the spinning Fates have sung, *unspool!*

That time is now. Offspring of gods, assume
the grandeur and inheritance of Jove!
See the world trembling bodily, base to dome,
the earth, the seaways, the deep sky above:
60   see all things overjoyed at what shall come.

Oh then may I have breath, at my life's end,
and strength to sing your every victory:
not if their voices and their parents' blend
could Orpheus or Linus conquer me
in singing: no, not if Apollo twinned
with Linus; with Orpheus, Calliope.°
Should Arcady judge as Pan and I competed,
then Arcady would judge great Pan defeated.°

Come, start to smile upon your mother, boy,
whom you, for near ten months now, have oppressed.   70
Come, smile! Who does not greet his folks with joy
no feast of gods, nor goddess' bed, has blessed.

Eclogue 9°

Lycidas, Moeris

LYCIDAS

Where are you headed, Moeris? The same way
the road leads, to the city?

MOERIS

         Lycidas,
it's come to this – I've lived to witness what
I never thought to fear – some out-of-towner
coming to claim my little patch of country
with 'Shove off, squatters! This here's *my* land now.'
Now crushed, crestfallen, since everything is upside down and out of joint, I'm taking him
these baby goats. I hope they turn out worthless.

LYCIDAS

Didn't I hear that all the leveler land   10
from the hill's foot down to the river's edge
and that old beech clump full of broken crowns,
was rescued by your friend Menalcas' singing?°

MOERIS

Well, yes, that was the rumor. But our songs
can do as much, when armies move in, as
Dodona's doves can when an eagle comes.°
And if I'd not been warned to drop the fight,
just give up, by a crow's screech on my left
out of a hollow holm oak, your friend Moeris

20   would not have lived this long, nor would Menalcas.

LYCIDAS

Who's heard of such an outrage!? Oh, Menalcas,
to have at once your solace, and yourself,
stolen from us! Who else could sing of nymphs,
or scatter flowers through the grass, or plunge
the brooklets in green shade? Or sing that song
I overheard the other day, lips zipped,
as you skipped off to fondle Amaryllis?
Hey, Tityrus, these nannies need a sitter –
I won't be long – just heading round the corner.

30   *Feed them and lead them, when they're fed, to water.*
Only make sure that you don't catch a horn or
something – that billy, he's a real headbutter.°

MOERIS

I prefer this, to Varus, still unfinished:
O Varus, if I do not lose my home°
in Mantua – Mantua, too near the scars
of sad Cremona's wreck – through heaven's dome°
swan-song will strew your name among the stars.

LYCIDAS

If you've got songs to sing, please do, and may
your bees steer clear of Corsica's bitter yews,

40   your cows' milk grow sweet in fields of clover.
Though I'm a poet too, thanks to the Muses,
though I have songs, although the shepherds also
have hailed my efforts that way, I don't trust them.
Nothing I've done yet touches Varius°
or Cinna; I'm a goose that honks at swans.°

MOERIS

I'm working on it. I've been quietly
turning one over in my head – it's not
some humdrum number – if I can remember:
Come here, o Galatea – why should waves°
delight you? Spring shoots color here; here flowers   50
of every hue around the rivers pour;
here the white poplar overhangs the cave's
cool mouth, and thick-necked vines weave shady bowers.
Come here! Let the harsh ocean lash the shore.
And what about that one I heard you singing
alone one cloudless night? I still recall
the rhythms, but the words have slipped my grasp.

LYCIDAS

Why watch the heavens do it all again,
Daphnis, when – look there! – a new star shines°
for Caesar, Venus-born? It makes the grain°   60
grow rich on the joyful tilth, and the grapevines
turn dark on sunny hills. Now, Daphnis, graft your°
pear trees; their fruits will feed your line hereafter.

MOERIS

Time takes it all, our minds too. I remember
how, as a boy, I'd sing the summer days
to bed; but now I have forgotten such
a store of songs, it's like my voice has vanished –
the wolves saw Moeris first. At least you've got°
Menalcas, who can still sing yours for you.

LYCIDAS

Your stalling puts my passion off, not out.   70
Now, all for you, the sea is silent glass,
and look, the winds have hushed their murmuration.
We've made it halfway, since Bianor's tomb°
is coming into sight. Here, where the farmhands
are slashing the lush leaves, let's sit and sing,
Moeris. Set down your kids; we'll reach the town.
But if we're scared the night will marshal rain,

we should keep going, singing while we go –
the road hurts less that way. So we can go
80   on singing, let me help you with your burden.

>   MOERIS
That's enough, boy. Let's just do what we're doing.
We'll sing much better when Menalcas comes.

Eclogue 10°

Gallus

One last time, Arethusa, bless my efforts.°
I owe a song to Gallus, which Lycoris°
might want to hear: how could I cheat my Gallus?
Begin, and may your waters slide beneath
Messina's channel unembittered by°
the spikes of salt. I'll tell the turbulent
passion of Gallus, while my snub-nosed goats
nibble the tender grass. The song will not
fall on deaf ears: the whole wild wood will answer.
10   Which forests hemmed you in, Naiads, while Gallus,°
mistreated, wasted with a lovesick fever?
It wasn't Mount Parnassus or the Pindus°
or Theban Aganippe's springs that stopped you.°
The laurels even, even the tamarisks
mourned, and the piny height of Maenalus
mourned him prostrate beneath that lonely cliff,
and Mount Lycaeus' snow-capped summit mourned.°
The sheep stood round; they're not ashamed of us,
nor, holy poet, should you be of them:
20   even adored Adonis herded sheep.°
The shepherds came, the swineherds came, slow-plodding,
and, wet from winter acorn-gathering,
Menalcas came. Then everybody asked,°
'How, where did such passion start?' Apollo came
and said, 'What's all this lunacy? Your love,
Lycoris, through the bristling camps and snowdrifts

chases another man.' Silvanus came,°
wreathed in a country garland of big lilies
and fennel flowers. Pan, god of Arcady,
came too – we saw him – red-faced with the blood   30
of the dwarf elder, and with cinnabar.°
'When will this end?' he said. 'Love doesn't care
for you; Love's never had his fill of tears,
no more than fields can have their fill of water,
or bees of thyme, or she-goats of green shoots.'
    Then Gallus, groaning, spoke:

                              All that may be.°
Yet still you'll sing my words through Arcady:
only Arcadians can sing with skill.
Oh, my bones then will rest in luxury,
when your pipes tell my love from every hill.°   40
I wish, I wish that I'd been one of you!
I'd have kept sheep, or nursed grapes on the vine.
Then Phyllis or Amyntas would be mine –°
what if Amyntas' skin is dark in hue?
Blueberries have dark skin, and violets too –
or I'd be mad for someone, in vine-shade,
embracing among willows. Phyllis could
plait wreaths for me; Amyntas, serenade.

    Here are cool rills, lush meadows and the wood,
Lycoris; here with you I'd waste my life.   50
Now feverish Love distracts me with the strife
of war and arms and soldiers hot for blood.
You, far from home – don't let me guess too much! –
alone, without me, unrelenting, greet
snow on the Alps and winter on the Rhine.
Don't let those winters wound you with their touch,
or ice-blades lacerate your lovely feet!
I shall retune those Chalcis-songs of mine°
to play on pipes, as you Sicilians do.
Yes, best to suffer with the beasts, in grove   60
and cave, and cut the name that makes me pine

in saplings, which will grow: my love will, too.
Meanwhile, across Mount Maenalus I'll rove
with bands of nymphs, or hunt the toothy boar.°
And all of Mount Parthenius's snows°
won't keep my hounds from clearings they'll enclose.
I see myself now, wandering through the roar
of mountain glades, nocking, on every cliff,
my Parthian bow with Cretan shafts: as if°

70   *those things could cure the wound that makes me wild,*
or human pain could make the harsh god mild.
Now neither woodland nymphs can bring me joy
nor poetry. Be gone, you sylvan grove.
No strain of mine can move the callous boy,
not if I drank the Hebrus' icy flow,°
or ranged the northern plains through sleet and snow,
not if, where elm bark dries and dies, I drove
African sheep while Cancer burned above.
     Love conquers all, and now I yield to Love.°

80   Goddesses, that will do. Your bard has sung
enough, o Muses, while he sat and wove
a homely basket out of slender mallow.
You'll make these musings great enough for Gallus,
for whom my love grows greater by the hour,
as alder saplings shoot up in the spring.
We must rise now. The evening shade hangs heavy
on singers, heavy shade of junipers,
cool shade that wounds the fruit. My she-goats, go:
you're full. Home waits. The evening star is come.

Tibullus

The Roman love elegist and equestrian officer Albius Tibullus (circa 55–18 BCE) hailed from Pedum, perhaps fifteen miles from Rome; as such, he was the only major Latin-language poet who was actually of Latin extraction – the others came from southern Italy (Horace, pp. 453–91, Statius, pp. 527–32), Umbria (Propertius, pp. 421–45), Abruzzo (Ovid, pp. 492–526), Cisalpine Gaul (Catullus, pp. 373–97, Virgil, pp. 398–410) or farther afield (Martial, pp. 533–55, from Spain). Tibullus is second in the traditional and putatively chronological canon of Latin elegists, younger than Gaius Cornelius Gallus (see the introduction to Latin Lyric, p. 371) and older than Propertius, though perhaps not by much. His patron was Marcus Valerius Messalla Corvinus, an orator whose elegance of diction Cicero and the Elder Seneca remarked upon, and whose style Tacitus, in his *Dialogue on Orators*, compares favorably to Cicero's. Messalla's political sympathies were initially Republican, but, seeing the writing on the wall, he sided with Octavian against Mark Antony at the Battle of Actium in 31 BCE, and continued to side with him – albeit somewhat coolly – from then on. A dilettante in philosophy and grammar, and a composer of poetry in Greek, Messalla also included in his circle his niece Sulpicia (pp. 446–52) and the young Ovid; his circle was the second most illustrious of its day, after that of Maecenas (see the introduction to Latin Lyric, p. 369). Tibullus served on Messalla's proconsular staff in Aquitania, where Messalla quashed a rebellion, for which he was voted a triumph in Rome in September 27 BCE; shortly thereafter, possibly a little later than Propertius' Book 1, Tibullus' first book was published. His second cannot have appeared long before his death around 18 BCE, and may well have been issued posthumously.

Tibullus' individuality may best emerge in comparison with his fellow elegists. Unlike Propertius, who has eyes in his poetry for one woman only, Tibullus' two slender books address three different beloveds. Book 1 is dedicated to the poet's romance with Delia, but also contains some poems addressed to a boy called Marathus; Book 2 focuses on an ever more desperate relationship with a woman called, unpromisingly, Nemesis, after the Greek goddess of retribution. According to Apuleius, a prose author of the second century CE, 'Delia' is a pseudonym for 'Plania', but 'Plania' is only a translation of the Greek *Delia* (bright, clear), and we know of no one by that name. Likewise there is no guessing who Marathus or Nemesis may really have been. The poems to Marathus recall Catullus' Hellenistic-style pederastic poems to Juventius (see Catullus' poems 48, p. 386, and 99, p. 396) – the example of which Tibullus is the only elegist to have followed. Tibullus is also the only major Roman poet who never makes explicit mention of his models, and, while he seems plainly influenced by both Callimachus (pp. 255–81) and Theocritus (pp. 282–98), he does not name them. Finally, while both Propertius and Ovid play on the love and warfare dyad (in the *militia amoris* motif; see, for example, Propertius 2.15, p. 429, and Ovid, *Amores* 1.9, p. 495), Tibullus adds a third element, the countryside, which he depicts sometimes in a pastoral, sometimes in a georgic (didactic and conversational) mode, and often as a scene of imaginative escape or amatory servitude.

Until the twentieth century, Tibullus was the most popular of the four love elegists. He was the favorite of the first-century CE rhetorician and educator Quintilian, who called him 'precise and elegant'; Horace addresses him twice in admiring poems (*Odes* 1.33 and *Epistles* 1.4); and Ovid's deep affection is evident in his funeral elegy for Tibullus (*Amores* 3.9, p. 510). More recently, what some critics consider the 'Modernism' of Propertius has drawn more admiration, whereas Tibullus' formal haziness has proved confounding – one German scholar wondered if he suffered from a brain injury. Today, however, the vague, dreamlike way his poems slide from subject to subject will probably seem Tibullus' most modern feature. He does not leap but glides, almost imperceptibly, via a logic of association that lands us, by the poem's end, very far from where we began.

A comparison with Propertius again suggests itself, in fact. It is notable that where the latter's more foursquare and classical construction coincides with a likewise much greater emotional and linguistic violence, Tibullus' gliding is the counterpart of an altogether more pacific, and often outright pacifist, sensibility, extending not only to the military sphere (none of the elegists is what we would call a hawk) but also to the sexual: both Propertius and Ovid are far more 'pro-kink'. Alone among his compatriots, Tibullus appears never to have been turned on by violence; he seems, in fact, genuinely to have abhorred it – even if, in his dreamy country idylls and nightmare cityscapes, the threat of it is never far away.

1.3°

You'll sail without me the Aegean blue,
Messalla – but think of me, you and your crew!
I'm in Phaeacia, sick in a strange land –°
o Death, don't touch me with your grasping hand!
Please, Death, don't touch me – here no mother's cloak
will scoop my bones up, blackened from the smoke,
no sister wash with Syrian perfume°
my ash or weep, hair flowing, at my tomb.
And here's no Delia, who, when I left home,°
I'm told consulted all the gods of Rome.						10
Three times she drew from the boy's urn, and he
replied three times with certain prophecy.°
All signs said I'd be back, and yet those answers
did not prevent her tears, or lingering glances.
I soothed her tears, said all I had to say,
yet still, choked up and anxious, sought delay.
I blamed the birds, or claimed the heavens frowned;
on Saturn's Day, none should be outward bound!°
How often, as I set out, I'd allege
bad omens when I stumbled on the ledge!							20
Let no one dare depart without love's nod,
or go and knowingly defy the god!
Delia, did Isis ever once assist?°
Did those bronze rattles clattering in your fist?
Did it help you to keep pure, to atone,
to bathe and – I remember! – sleep alone?°
Help, goddess, help me now! (For that you are
a healer, paintings in your shrines declare.)
Give Delia what her piety implores,

30   sitting in linen at your temple doors,°
          twice daily, hair unbound, in praiseful trance,
          outstanding among the Alexandrians.
          May I adore the gods of my father's hall
          once more in the monthly incense ritual.°
          How well they lived when Saturn was still king,°
          when none had gone abroad adventuring.
          No ship had mocked the ocean's indigo,
          puffing its sails with all the winds that blow;
          no merchant cruising parts unknown had made
40   great profits in pursuit of foreign trade.
          No yoke had yet subdued a mighty bull,
          no horse had champed the bit, grown tractable;
          no house had doors, nor were there boundary stones
          to mark the property a person owns.
          Oak-honey freely flowed for easy-living
          people who drank what sheep were freely giving.
          There were no feuds, no armies; no one warred;
          no coldly artful smith had shaped a sword.
          Now that Jove reigns, death thrives; now through the vast
50   ocean and earth, death's ways throng thick and fast.
          Peace, Jove, and cease your threats! No lies of mine
          have yet profaned your sanctity divine.
          But if my fated years are over, raise
          a stone above my bones whose legend says:
          Here lies Tibullus, cruelly snuffed while he
          followed Messalla over land and sea.
          But I, so long Love's champion, shall come,
          with Venus leading, to Elysium.°
          Here songs and dances flourish; here sweet notes
60   flute from the flitting birds' exquisite throats,
          the unworked fields waft marjoram, and blooms
          of roses fill kind meadows with perfumes.
          Boys linked with tender maidens in a ring
          play on; Love never ceases skirmishing.
          There, lovers greedy Death has taken wear
          distinguished myrtle garlands in their hair.

But criminals lie dead, in deep night drowned,
surrounded by the midnight river's sound.°
Tisiphone, who never combs her snakes,
storms where the impious mob rushes and quakes.°   70
Black Cerberus, a-seethe with serpents, waits
and hisses as he sits at the brazen gates.°
Juno's assailant there, the all-too-bold
Ixion, on his wheel of pain is rolled,°
and Tityus stretched nine acres on his back
feels ceaseless vultures peck his liver black;°
there is the pool which Tantalus, immersed,
sees slip – again, again! – his bitter thirst.°
Hated of Venus, Danaus's daughters
fill leaky vessels with Lethean waters.°   80
And there may those who ravish Delia stay,
who wished me on this slow tour, far away.°
But you, be true, your purity unmarred,°
while an old crone sits watch, a constant guard.°
She'll tell you stories while the late lamp burns,
your distaff lightens and your spindle turns,
and you, upon your weight of wool intent,
fight sleep until, at long last, you relent.
Then, without warning, sudden, like a clear
harbinger sent from heaven, I'll appear.   90
Whatever state you're in, with hair undone,
or naked feet – come to me, Delia. Run.
I pray, oh may the rosy mares of Dawn°
bring that white daystar in its brilliance on!

1.10°

Who was the first swordsmith, parent of peril?
He must have had a ferrous heart, and feral!°
He brought us the pitched battle, the bloodbath,
and cleared cruel Death a quick and easy path.
Was he to blame? Or have we gored ourselves
with an invention aimed at bears and wolves?

Gold was the goad! Warfare did not exist
when beechwood goblets at the feast sufficed.
There were no forts, no trenches; carefree sleep
10   sought shepherds out among their motley sheep.
Oh for the simple life, not to have known
weapons, or heart-in-throat at warhorns blown!
War calls me now; perhaps some foe already
carries an arrow destined for my body.
Gods of my fathers, help me! – as you did°
when I frisked at your feet, a stripling kid.
Don't blush to be of seasoned wood, not bronze:
thus you were worshiped by the ancient ones.
Then faith was stronger, when, undecked by much,
20   the wooden god adorned his humble hutch.
A splash of vintage, or a corn crown twined
on holy hair sufficed to make him kind.
Then thanks were paid in cakes for prayers come true,
and little daughters offered honey, too.
O Lares, save me from the brazen spears! . . .°
I'll pay you a plump piglet from my sty.
I'll follow in pure robes, my baskets bound
with myrtle wreaths, my head with myrtle crowned,
and please you so. Let someone bold in wars
30   outduel opposing leaders, blessed by Mars,
and then, at table, tell me of his fine
feats as we drink, and map his camps with wine.
How mad to summon Death with war's dark drumming!
He steals in secret, too, and keeps on coming.
No corn or vines below, just the cold barks
of Cerberus and the boatman of the Styx.°
There the gray masses, with burnt hair and cheeks
shredded, meander past sepulchral lakes.
No, praise instead that man old age has slowed,
40   with heirs around him in his small abode.
He tends the sheep himself, his son the lambs;
his wife heats water for their weary limbs.
That's what I pray for, that my old head grays

while I sit recollecting olden days.
Meanwhile, Peace tills the fields – Peace, first to press°
bulls to the curving yoke in priestly dress.
Peace nursed the vines and stored the grape juice up
till fatherly carafe filled filial cup.
Peace shines the hoe and plow, while the sad thrust
of soldiers' steel is seized by dark and rust.   50
Driving his wagon from the grove, the farmer
takes wife and children home, a tipsy charmer;
but when the wars of Venus warm, she whinges°
at her hair torn and doors wrenched from their hinges.
She cries with bruises on her cheeks, while he
cries at his own crazed brawn in victory.
For shameless Love eggs on their verbal violence,
then as they seethe sits in their midst in silence.
Ah, stone and iron is that man who beats
his love! He tears the gods down from their seats.   60
Let it suffice to tear her gauzy dress,
and tear her hair loose from its flourishes;
oh, let her tears suffice! Four times in luck,
that man who makes her weep with just a look!
But one who uses fists – force him afield
far from soft Venus, taxed with stake and shield.
And come, o wholesome Peace, with your corn-spear,
and from your white dress let the fruits fall clear.

2.1°

Come kindly, you who happen on these grounds:
we bless the fields and fruits, and walk the bounds,
as the old rite our fathers used propounds.
Come, Bacchus, sweet grapes looped around each horn°
and dangling free; come, Ceres, crowned with corn.
Let earth take holiday; let farmers bask
in ease; let plows put off their hefty task.
Unloose the yokes, and let the oxen tread
full stables with their bodies garlanded.

10 Let all tasks be for god, all women shirk
  the looming quotas of their wool-wrapped work.
  But you, depart our altars and our sight,
  whom Venus' pleasures gratified last night.
  The gods embrace the chaste. Come with clean dress°
  and hands to cup the fountain's holiness.
  See the bright altars where the lamb is going,
  the white-robed crowds with olive crowns following.
  Gods of our fathers, our fields and our field-hands°
  we cleanse; cast all misfortune from our lands!
20 *Don't taint the harvest with the specious weed;*
  may slow lambs never fear the wolf pack's speed.
  Then bright-faced rustics trusting in the earth
  will heap up firewood on the ardent hearth,
  and gaggles of slaves will laugh before it, weaving
  twigs into houses – proof the farm is thriving.°
  All this I pray. Did you not see the sign
  the entrails smiled? The gods' minds are benign.°
  Now bring the aged Falernian, full of smoke,
  and loose the Chian from its cask of oak.°
30 Wines cheer a holiday: no one should blush
  to stumble drunkenly and play the lush.
  'Health to Messalla!' let each drinker cheer,
  his name on every tongue, though he's not here –
  hero of Aquitania, the lauded°
  pride of his fathers, everywhere applauded:
  come and inspire me, that we may please
  the agricultural divinities.°
  I sing the country and its gods, those teachers
  who offered acorns first to starving creatures.
40 They taught how leaves and branches could be put
  to use, and woven in a little hut;
  it's even said they taught mankind the arts
  of breaking bulls, and fixing wheels to carts.°
  Wild ways were tamed then, planted seeds bore fruits,
  gardens grew lush with irrigated roots;
  then footsteps trod the gold drops of the vine,

and sober water tempered carefree wine.°
Each year under the summer star fields bear
their bounty and we shear their golden hair.
In fields bees pack their springtime hive with blooms,   50
industrious to load the honeycombs.
First farmers, tired out with plowing, beat
rhythms for rustic words with their crude feet,
and with full bellies on parched reeds first played
songs for the gods their garlands had arrayed.
Bacchus, at first some clumsy farmer led
your choral dances, painting his face red.
That's when a he-goat first enriched your thrift –
the sheep's skipper, a memorable gift.°
A country boy first wove a crown from buds   60
in spring and set it on the ancient gods,°
and the white sheep first brought its fleecy curls,
not yet a weight of care, to country girls.
From here came women's work, wool's weighted measure,
the spindles spinning under the thumb's pressure.
The weaver, devotee of Pallas, sings°
without fatigue, as weights thump on warp-strings.
Cupid himself was born among the pastures,°
the flocks and mares whose lust no stallion masters.
He shot his first bow there, not knowing how;   70
alas, he is a practiced expert now!
Now livestock bores him, but he loves to hunt°
maidens and men, and break the arrogant.
He wastes the young man's cash and makes the old
offend his lover's door, shamelessly bold.
At his command, at night, a girl will go
alone past sleeping guards to her young beau;
her foot feels forward, tensing up in stark
suspense, and her blind fingers touch the dark.
Woe comes to all whom cruel Love oppresses;   80
but blessed are those whose brows his breeze caresses!
Come join our feast, but put your bow away,
great god, and snuff your ardent torch, I pray!

Hymn the god's fame, and make a prayer – yes, cry it°
aloud! – for livestock, but keep your own prayers quiet.
Actually, holler even those aloud,
as Phrygian pipes uplift the laughing crowd!
Play on! Night's car is yoked; behind her team°
star-choruses, her children, frisk and gleam;
and soon the hush of Sleep, with dark wingbeat,
will lead the black Dreams in on their strange feet.

Propertius

Most of what we know or believe about the life of the love elegist Sextus Propertius (circa 55–15 BCE) is derived from his poems. He was born into an important provincial family in the hill town of Asisium (Assisi) in Umbria, near Etruscan Perusia (modern Perugia). His father died when he was young, perhaps during Octavian's siege of Perusia in 41–40 BCE. The family's fortune had dwindled when their land was confiscated during the proscriptions of 43–42, when Rome's new masters, the triumvirate of Octavian, Mark Antony and Marcus Aemilius Lepidus, outlawed certain opponents in order to expropriate their wealth; yet they remained affluent enough to remain part of the equestrian order, and to provide Propertius with a first-rate education at Rome.

Propertius aspired to be known as the Roman Callimachus (see pp. 255–281). His first book, variously referred to as the *Monobiblos* (the *Single Volume*, or the *Chapbook*) or just *Cynthia*, probably appeared early in 28 BCE; it is addressed to Gaius Volcacius Tullus, Propertius' patron and possible kinsman (Tullus' family was from Perusia). The book produced a sensation, and Propertius was recruited into the circle of Gaius Cilnius Maecenas (see the introduction to Latin Lyric, p. 369) and given an abode on the Esquiline Hill, the fashionable district where Maecenas lived lavishly on grounds and gardens acquired with money raised during the proscriptions; however, he seems not to have fully 'bought in' to the Augustan program, and may not have gotten along with Maecenas' other poets, especially Horace (pp. 453–91). Propertius' second book appeared in or after 26 BCE; his third sometime after 23; and the fourth, which may have been published posthumously, around 16. Propertius' date of death is unknown, but cannot have been later than 2 or 1 BCE.

Many of the poems in Propertius' first three books depict his tumultuous affair with Cynthia, whose actual name we are told by Apuleius, a prose author of the second century CE, was Hostia. She was probably a real person, though we can't tell from the poems where reality ends and genre begins. Propertius focuses on her with a Catullan single-mindedness that far exceeds the concern of Tibullus (pp. 411–20) for Delia or Nemesis, or of Ovid (pp. 492–526) for his Corinna. Cynthia dominates Propertius' first two books and remains a frequent presence (if now less over-whelmingly so) in the third, which ends with a bitter renunciation of their love. Propertius' fourth book is mostly concerned with Roman aetiologi-cal topics – that is, with stories that purport to explain the origins of Roman customs or traditions, be they mythical, legendary or otherwise – and written in a Callimachean mode; but Cynthia appears again, for the last time, in its two central poems (4.7 and 4.8, pp. 440–45). Propertius' passion is savage, often morbid, and not without a tinge of sadomaso-chism; his flame of love, in Steele Commager's phrase, 'is as much charnel as carnal'. His work has struck many as shockingly anti-military and anti-political, and much criticism of the Augustan regime, both covert and overt, has been perceived in it; nevertheless, unlike Ovid, Propertius managed not to antagonize either Maecenas or Augustus during his lifetime.

Time has mostly not been kind to Propertius. Though admired and imitated by Ovid, and mentioned here and there by others, Propertius disappeared from literature around 95 CE, when the oratorical writer Quintilian damned him with faint praise – lauding Tibullus, he said only, 'Some people prefer Propertius.' It was not until the twelfth century that his poems resurfaced, in the Loire valley of France. The manuscript trad-ition through which his work has survived is suspect: it is not always clear where one poem ends and another begins, and the text is corrupt, garbled by careless copying, interpolations and nonsense. Though he influenced John Donne and Thomas Campion in seventeenth-century England, and excited Petrarch in fourteenth-century Italy and Goethe in eighteenth-century Germany, the desperate state of the text, along with the frequent difficulty and obscurity of Propertius' Latin – often as jagged and violent as his passion – accounts for his neglect by almost all but text-ual scholars until the 1900s. In the first half of that century, Propertius' rough edges made him seem more modern than his Augustan counter-parts, and proved attractive to poets like Ezra Pound and Robert Lowell, whose work was comparably invested in rebelling against smoothness and formality. Still, it's hard to say how much of this jagged quality is due to textual corruption; ancient writers, wherever they mention Propertius, consider him a model of clarity and elegance.

1.1°

Cynthia – it was those eyes – captured me first,°
poor kid, as yet untouched by lust, uncursed.°
Then Love toppled my pride, my stubborn ways;
his feet drove my head down and dropped my gaze,
until the hellion taught me to reject
good girls, and live in excess and neglect.
A year now, and this madness still subdues me;
I'm forced to supplicate gods who refuse me.

Tullus, Milanion spared no drudgery°
to wear down Atalanta's savagery:°   10
he roamed the Virgin Mountain, low and high,°
unhinged, and looked the wild beasts in the eye,
and, when the Centaur's club knocked him a wound,°
sprawled supine on Arcadian rocks and groaned.
That's how he tamed his love, though lightning fast:
so faith and suffering should win at last.°

My limping Love won't use his former art
and can't recall his old map to the heart.
But you who con the moon down, so you claim,
and tend the dark gods by your magic flame,   20
now change my mistress' mind and heart, go on,
and make her face turn paler than my own!
Then I'd grant your Thessalian witchcraft might°
reverse rivers, and siphon the stars' light.

And you who call me back too late, my friends,
find some cure for this heart that sickness rends.
Surgeons could carve me up and I'd be brave,
if free to shout what pain and fury crave.
Take me through far-flung tribes, to the edge of Dawn,
somewhere no girl will know where I have gone.°   30

But you, whom the god blesses, stay behind;
enjoy your safe love, always of one mind.
On me, Venus drives bitter nights and black;
Love's never gone, and never gives me slack.

I warn you, flee this suffering! Cling to
long love; don't trade a known bed for a new.
Whoever hears too late these words of warning,
what pain he'll suffer yet, and ah, what mourning!

I.2°

Why step out, love, with labyrinthine hair,
swishing your Coan silks, light as the air,°
or oil yourself with Syrian spice and lotion,
and flaunt your wares, tricked out in foreign fashion,
spoiling your gorgeousness with style from stores,
dulling the luster naturally yours?
No doctoring can do your beauty good;
Love has no love for gimmicks – he goes nude.
   Look at the colors Nature's hand has sown,
how ivy spreads more lushly on its own,
how in the wild the finest shade trees grow,
and rivers, though untaught, know where to flow.
Mosaics fleck the beach by no design,
and no art can make birdsong more divine.
   Phoebe did not win Castor's love like this,
no frills won Hilaïra Pollux's;°
Phoebus and Idas, by Evenus' shore,
did not fight for his daughter's haute couture,°
and Hippodamia's powdered cheeks aren't what
earned her a place in Pelops' chariot.°
By gems and jewels their looks were never tainted,
pure as the colors that Apelles painted.°
They didn't look for love just anywhere;
virtue, for them, was loveliness to spare.
   I know you love me better than the rest;
with one man's love, a woman's richly dressed;
the more, since Phoebus taught you music, too,
and the Muse gladly gave her lyre to you,
and you have special grace in all your speech,
and all that Venus and Minerva teach.°

10

20

30

You'll always be a love and joy to me,
if you give up this gaudy luxury.

1.3

As languidly as Ariadne lay°
on the bare sand while Theseus sailed away;
or like Andromeda, her first sleep free
from the sheer cliff, the shackles and the sea;°
or tired as a Thracian maenad falls
by Apidanus, after bacchanals;°
so Cynthia slumbered, hands enlaced beneath
her pillowed head, and puffed her quiet breath,
when I lurched in, woozy from drinking too much,
led home in the small hours by the slave's torch.   10
    I inched toward her – not all my wits had fled –
and gingerly pressed my body on the bed;
though two insistent gods, Wine and Desire,
were urging me, lit with a double fire,
to snake my arm beneath her body there
and steal late kisses, brushing back her hair,
while she slept on, I didn't dare encroach
and rouse that tongue so fluent in reproach,
yet couldn't look away, as riveted
as Argus by the horns on Io's head.°   20
    I loosed the flowers from my temples now
and placed them, Cynthia, upon your brow,
smiling to lift your tresses' fallen strands,
and, hushed, gave apples from my beggared hands,°
all gifts I lavished on that thankless sleep,
gifts that her canted lap refused to keep;
every least sigh or movement that she made,
I froze as if it were a sign, afraid
that nightmare terrors pulsed behind her eyes,
or some dream rape was forcing her clenched thighs,   30
    until the flighty moonlight filtered in –
it would have loved to linger on her skin –

unshuttering her eyelids, and she woke.
Elbow propped on a pillow, now she spoke:°
'So. Crawling back to my embrace°
now someone else's door's slammed in your face?
Where did you spend this night, now all but gone,
you'd promised me? You're looking limp and wan.
I wish *your* nights would drag as wretchedly,
40   you deadbeat, as the ones you force on me!
      'At first I cheated sleep by spinning thread,
then, drifting off, tried Orphic song instead,°
and softly mourned the jilted lover's state,
how long, and how alone, we're forced to wait,
till, sheltering in the easeful wings of sleep,
I wept my last complaint, and ceased to weep.'

                              I.II

      While you're in Baiae, Cynthia, at ease°
on the beach near the Road of Hercules,°
or gazing on Avernus, in surprise
that at Misenum Thesprotia's waters rise,°
do you still sometimes dream or think of me?
Do I still haunt your love's periphery?
Or has some rival, offering you his heart,
stolen you from my arms and from my art,°
15   as a false girl, when the guard's gone, will fly,
16   forgetting oaths, and gods she sealed them by?°
      I wish some tiny paddleboat would take
10   you innocently on the Lucrine Lake,°
or Teuthras' easy waves and shallow brim°
would shelter and surround you as you swim,
so no sweet whisperer could take your hand
14   where you lounge softly on the tacit sand!
17   It's not that I don't trust your virtue, just
that Baiae makes all virtue hard to trust.
So if my letter's caused you some distress,
20   forgive me: blame a lover's fearfulness.

How could I care so tenderly for my own
mother, or dream of living with you gone?
You are my parents now, my home and hearth,°
and you are all my joy, and all my mirth.
When I meet friends downcast, or happily,
I tell them, 'Cynthia did this to me.'
Just hurry home from Baiae's wanton heart,
those shores where lovers go to grow apart
and chaste girls trade their virtue in for shame:
Baiae be damned, you stain on love's good name!   30

2.1°

You ask why love, love, love, is all I sing,
with melodies so softly murmuring?
It's no thanks to the Muses, or Apollo;
no, my love leads and makes my genius follow.
Let's say her Coan silks gleam as she goes;°
I'll make a whole book from those silken clothes.
Or say a few locks tumble down untied;
I'll praise her hair until she glows with pride.
If her white fingers pluck a lyre string,
I'm awestruck at the easy fingering;   10
or if her fluttering lids succumb to dreams,
I hatch a thousand new poetic themes;
then, if she fights and wrestles me unclad,
I reel off *Iliad* on *Iliad*.
Whatever she does or mumbles, an immense
epic is born out of her non-events.
If only fate had dealt me out the genius
to trumpet heroes, arms and war, Maecenas,°
I'd skip the Titans piling Ossa on
Olympus, and on Ossa, Pelion,°   20
and ancient Thebes, and Troy, which Homer vaunted,
and the canal through Athos Xerxes wanted,
the reign of Remus, Carthage furious,
the Cimbrian threat, the feats of Marius:°

instead I'd sing your Caesar's deeds and wars,
and after Caesar's greatness, I'd sing yours.
     Yet if I praised him for Mutina, or°
men killed at Philippi in civil war,
or the fleet that fled off the Sicilian shore,
30   Perusia sacked, her households overthrown,
the harbor seized where Ptolemy's lighthouse shone,
or Egypt and the River Nile, brought home
with seven bloodied mouths, a slave to Rome,
or kings that down the Sacred Way have come
in gilded chains, with prows from Actium –
in each campaign, Maecenas, I'd add you,
steadfast in peace and war, heart always true –
true as Patroclus and Pirithöus
(so Theseus and Achilles testify,°
40   one underground, the other in the sky).
     Callimachus, with his voice fine and small,°
couldn't go thundering the Giants' fall;
neither can I, in strident martial verse,
place Caesar with his Trojan ancestors.°
Farmers talk bulls, and sailors, winds and seas;
shepherds count sheep, and soldiers, injuries;
my narrow bed's the field where I wage war:
let's all just ply the trade we're fitted for.
     It's fine to die in love; it's fine, moreover,
50   to love just one; may I be *her* one lover.
Doesn't she say loose women make her mad,
that Helen's conduct mars the *Iliad*?
If I drained Theseus' stepmother's venom,
which her stepson was saved from pouring in him;°
if Circe's herbs unman me, or Medea
cooks me in cauldrons as a panacea:°
because there's just one woman stole my heart,
it's from her house that my cortège will start.
     Doctors have healed most ailments that have wracked us;
60   but love alone eludes the doctors' practice.
Machaon cured limping Philoctetes' pain,°

and Chiron made blind Phoenix see again;°
Asclepius brought back King Minos' son
from death with Cretan herbs – Androgeon;°
and Telephus restored his wounded limb
with rust from the same spear that wounded him.°
But anybody who could cure me could°
manage to smuggle Tantalus some food;
or he could seal and fill that leaky cask,
save the Danaids from their endless task;   70
or he could climb the Caucasus, uncuff
Prometheus and drive the vulture off.

    When fate reclaims this life I have on loan
and I'm a brief name etched on a little stone,
Maecenas, friend my boyhood longed for most,
rightly in life and death my only boast,
if someday chance should lead you near my plot,
there briefly halt your fancy chariot,
address the answerless ash, and shed a tear,°
saying, 'A woman's coldness drove him here.'   80

2.15°

O great good luck! O gorgeous night! O you,
bed, blessed for everything you let us do!
We talked and talked, while the lamp still was lit,
then brawled and brawled, once we'd extinguished it.
Sometimes, with her shirt off, she'd wrestle me,
and then she'd cover up, frustratingly.
When I dozed off, she mocked me: 'Look how lazy!'
then kissed my eyes back open: 'Upsy-daisy!'
How many ways we found to intertwine
our limbs; how long your lips stayed locked on mine!   10

    Don't spoil your moves by veiling them in dark;
eyes take the lead in lighting the love-spark.
On seeing Helen, Paris nearly died,
when she climbed naked from her husband's side;
naked Endymion made Phoebe swoon,°

and he lay naked with the naked moon.
Come naked, then, or I'll go wild and shred
your gown, if you keep wearing it to bed.
Don't get me any hotter; if you do,
20   you'll show your mother arms bruised black and blue.
Your breasts don't sag – that shame can't stop the fun.
It might for mothers, true, but you aren't one.
Let's feast our eyes on love, while we still can:
a night will come when day won't come again.°
      I wish a chain would bind us here forever
in this embrace, a chain no day could sever!
Think of two doves in love, perched wing to wing,
female and male, a perfect coupling.°
Love may be mad, but one who'd limit it
30   is madder still: true love is infinite.
The Sun will sooner darken his bright steeds,°
the wrong crops will be gleaned from the wrong seeds,
rivers will swim upstream back to their source,
and dried-up fish will flop on dry sea-floors,
before another girl will make me sigh.
Alive, I'm hers; I'll be hers when I die.
      But if she'll grant me nights of ecstasy
like this, one year will make a century!
I'll live forever if many more are given:
40   for one night any man can summit heaven.
If everyone desired a life like mine,°
and bedded down beneath the weight of wine,
there'd be no warships, and no swords stained red;
Actium's waves would not roil with our dead,°
and Rome, beset by Romans everywhere,
wouldn't be worn out tearing at her hair.
One thing the future ought to praise me for:
no gods were outraged by my sort of war.
      Drink deep from life, while light still shines for you;
50   all the world's kisses, love, are all too few.
And – as, when garlands wither, petals drop
and drift this way and that in every cup –

we lovers, panting, hoping, far from sorrow,
we too shall meet our fate: perhaps tomorrow.

2.28°

My sweetheart's sick: Jupiter, show some pity!
Keep her death off your hands – she's far too pretty!
Now summer's here, the Dog hangs high and dry,°
boiling the earth, and sweltering in the sky.
But weather's not to blame, nor the sky baking:
it's her slights to the gods, and her oath-breaking.
It leads girls – always has – into despair
when wind and water scatter what they swear.
Was Venus mad you were compared with her?°
She's jealous of any girl thought lovelier.   10
Did you make light of Argive Juno's shrine,°
or say Minerva's eyes are sub-divine?°
You lookers don't know how to stop your nagging:
your beauty's guilty, and your sharp tongue wagging.
But at the last, after so many trials,
a day will come when sweeter weather smiles.
Io spent *her* youth mooing like a cow;°
that cow who drank the Nile's a goddess now.
Ino, who wandered, young, through earth and sea,
wrecked sailors pray to as Leucothoë.   20
Andromeda, vowed to Leviathan,
was saved by Perseus, and wed the man.
Callisto, in bear form, roamed Greece's vales;
at night her stars conduct benighted sails.
But if you're destined for untimely rest,
even your destined burial will be blessed:
you'll speak of beauty's risks with Semele;°
she'll understand, taught by catastrophe.
And Homer's heroines will all defer°
to you and own you their superior.   30
Now, if you can, endure, although you burn:
the god and the god's destiny may turn.   32

35   The spells have failed, the whirligig's not working;
        on the cold hearth, the laurel lies unsmoking;
        the moon will not descend, unfazed, inhuman;
        the horned owl blackly hoots its dire omen.°
        The same ghost ship will take us both as one,
40   hoisting its midnight sails on Acheron.
        Let two lives move you, Jove, if one won't do:
        I live if she lives; if she dies, I die too.

          Help her, I'll write a hymn in gratitude:
        'This girl was saved by Jove the great and good.'
        She'll sit before your feet, and worship you,
        and tell the long tale of her torments through.
33   Juno will pardon your benevolence;
34   when a girl's dying, even she relents.°
47   I pray, Persephone, stay merciful,
        and you, her husband – don't become more cruel!°

          Beauties unnumbered dwell in endless night;
50   let one, just one, still drink the earthly light!
        Fair Tyro's there, and there, Antiope,°
        Europa and perverse Pasiphaë;°
        and all whom ancient Crete and Hellas bore,
        and Thebes, and Priam's kingdom, now no more,
        and Roman beauties immemorial
        are there; the gluttonous pyre has them all.
        No wealth or beauty is immortal here;
        late or soon, our day of death draws near.

          But you, my darling, rescued from death's door,
60   offer Diana the dances that you swore;
        thank Isis, now divine, bovine back then,°
        and pay the nights you owe me – that makes ten!

3.3°

    A dream: I lay on Helicon, in shade,
      beside the spring that Pegasus once made,°
      mouth open, fingers on my lyre strings,
      to hymn your kings' deeds, Alba, and your kings:°

an epic task. I'd bent for a small draft
from the great source which Ennius once quaffed,°
who sang the trophies of Aemilius,°°
the brothers Curii, the Horaces,°
and Fabius triumphing by delaying,°
our rout at Cannae, gods who heard us praying,°   10
then turned and far from Rome drove Hannibal,
and cackling geese that saved the Capitol;°
when Phoebus, watching from his laurel tree,°
propped on his golden lyre, said to me:

    'What's this cascade to you? Are you insane?°
Who made you launch such a heroic strain?
Propertius, here you'll be a poetaster;
your smaller wheels demand a softer pasture.
Your book should be at hand for girls to thumb
on lonely couches till their lovers come.   20
I set your course for you – why deviate?
Your talent's boat won't bear such heavy freight.
With one wet oar, and one oar scraping sand,
you'll stay afloat; it's rough too far from land.'
He spoke, and with his ivory pick he showed,°
banked in the mossy earth, a novel road.

    There was a green cave, with mosaic scenes;°
down from the pumice vault hung tambourines.
That's where the Muses' holy objects lay,°
Pan's reed pipes, a Silenus made of clay;°   30
there Venus' doves, my flock, flutter and preen,°
and dip their dark beaks in the Hippocrene.
There the nine Muses, all with different parts,
busy their tender hands at their own arts:
one plucks the Bacchic ivy; one composes
and sings her songs; one plaits wreaths of roses.°
One of those goddesses laid hold of me
(I guessed, from her fair face, Calliope):°

    'You'll be content to ride your snow-white swans,°
far from the horses' hooves and clashing bronze.   40
Don't blast the battle horn and call your corps

to arms, or circle Helicon with war;
don't worry where Rome breaks the German lines
as legions swarm to Marius's signs,°
or the barbaric Rhine rolls Swabian dead,°
mourning the bodies choking the waves red.
You'll sing wreathed lovers married girls lock out,
the signs of drunken siege, and nightly rout,
so men can outwit husbands with your skill,
50   and sing their cloistered women out at will.'°
She spoke. And now she cups her hands and drips
water Philitas drank upon my lips.°

3.5°

The god of peace is Love. Lovers are wed
to peace: enough to wage our wars in bed!
No base gold plucks at my heartstrings with lust;
I don't drain goblets precious gems encrust;
no thousand bulls plow my Campanian field;
I don't own bronzes Corinth's flames annealed.°
Prometheus made a mess of things that day°
he shaped our senses from his primal clay!
He made our bodies sound, but our thoughts blind;
10   the part he got right should have been the mind.
So now we seek out enemies, brave the weather
through the whole ocean, and string wars together.
    There is no wealth that hell will let you carry;
you bonehead, you'll be naked on the ferry.
Victor and victim take the selfsame ride:
Jugurtha sails by Marius's side.°
Irus and Croesus, beggar and king, are peers;
the best death follows on the fullest years.°
    I'm glad I worshiped Helicon when young,
20   and, arms linked with the Muses, danced and sung;°
I'm also glad to have wine wreathe my mind,
and roses at my temples always twined.
    But when old age prohibits Love's delight,

and slows me, salting my black hairs with white,
then let me study Nature's secret heart,
what Power rules the world's house, with what art,
how the sun rises, how it sets, from where
the moon restores her horns and fills the air,
the source of ocean winds, what Eurus whooshes°
after, why clouds swell and water gushes,   30

    if the world's ramparts will be ground to ash,
why rain wrings out bright rainbows in the wash,
why Pindus' peaks are prone to quake and crack,°
why the sun mourns, and drapes its horses black,
why the Herdsman's plow and cattle set so late,°
why the bright flock of Pleiads congregate,°
or why the ocean stays within its bounds
and the full year in four parts makes its rounds,

    if gods hold court below, and sinners toil,
if Tisiphone's tresses hiss and coil,°   40
if Furies chase Alcmaeon, Phineus wastes,°
if there are wheels, rocks, pools that no one tastes,°
if hell's watchdog is three-jawed Cerberus,°
and if nine acres shortchange Tityus,°
or those are fables human fears have spawned,
and death is death, and nothing lies beyond.

    May my life end so; you who fight for Rome
and love the lists, bring Crassus' standards home!°

3.8°

    Our fight was sweet beneath the lamps last night,
when you spat curses at me, wild with spite,
and, wild with wine, toppled the table and
hurled sloshing goblets with a maddened hand.
Come on, I dare you, strike, and pull my hair;
dig your sweet nails deep in my cheeks, and tear!
Threaten to burn my eyes out, be my guest,
and shred the tunic off my naked chest!
This heat is just a sign of what you feel;

10   women don't rave unless their love is real.
      When a girl rants and skewers your deceit,
she's groveling in the dust at Venus' feet:
if she's the type with handlers always there,
or maenad-like goes solo everywhere,°
if she has nightmares she finds terrifying,
or if some schoolgirl's picture sets her crying,
I've learned to be a true interpreter:
if she torments, she loves you – that is sure.°
If she won't scream at you, there's no desire;
20   may my foes love a girl who feels no fire!
      Let her teeth gouge my neck so rivals see;
let bruises show I've had her there with me.
My pain or yours, I want a love that sears;
I want your cheeks or mine to course with tears,
whether your darkened brow shoots wordless looks,
or your hands write unutterable books.
I hate a dream which no sighs punctuate;
may I be always pale, and she irate.
      Paris enjoyed love more when through the strife
30   of battle he could steal time with his wife;
as Greeks advanced, and Hector beat them back,
in Helen's arms he launched the real attack.°
With you or with my rivals, I won't cease
from fighting: in your case, I don't want peace.
A girl as fine as you would make you sad,
but none exist. Your pride is just – be glad!
      But you, who threw a snare around my bed,°
may moms and in-laws buzz about your head!
Know, if you steal a night of ecstasy,
40   it's not that she likes you: she's mad at me!

3.10°

Why were the Muses smiling by my bed
this morning, with the sunrise flushing red?
Cynthia's birthday! So they signaled me,

and clapped their hands three times, propitiously.
     Oh, may today be cloudless, the winds silent,
and the waves kiss the shore, no longer violent!
May this day's sun reveal no misery.
May the stone stop the tears of Niobe.°
May halcyons rest their plaints, and be at peace,°
and Itys' mother let her sad songs cease.°   10
     Now, love, whose birth rejoicing omens blessed,
get up, and make the prayers the gods request.°
Wash the sleep out with water fresh and pure,
and lightly style your radiant coiffure;
then that first dress that caught me, made me stare –
wear it, and twine some flowers in your hair,
and pray your beauty's power does not wane,
that, throned within my heart, you'll always reign.
     When you have blessed the altar, crowned by boughs,
with sweet smoke, and a bright flame fills the house,°   20
let's spread a feast, till night falls in our cups,
and spritz ourselves with saffron-scented drops.
Tired by dancing, let the hoarse pipes flag,
and let your puckish tongue be free to wag,
and our sweet squabbling drive all dreams away,
and the alley air vibrate with games we play;
we'll toss the dice for answers to our ardor:°
which of us do the boy's wings whiplash harder?°
     When many hours and cups have passed between us,
and the night's sacraments been blessed by Venus,   30
we'll lay us down, and wile the night away,
and come to the conclusion of your day.

3.16°

     The dead of night. A letter comes to me:
she orders me to Tibur, instantly.°
That's Tibur, where the cliffsides whitely flash°
and down into pools the Anio's falls crash.°
What should I do? Ignore the dark, depart,

hope criminals can't hear my pounding heart?°
But say I don't heed her, but heed my fears:
no criminal could be scarier than her tears.
I strayed once, and all that year she exiled me;
10   her hands have never yet dealt with me mildly.
     A lover is holy, though, and can't be harmed,°
not if he strides by Sciron's den unarmed;°
no savages will threaten him with blows,
not if through Scythia's wilderness he goes.°
Moons show the way; stars light each jagged shelf;
Love lifts his torch and leads him on himself.
A mad dog with its slavering jaws steers clear:
the path a lover treads is free of fear.
What fiend would stain his fingers with the thinned
20   blood of a lover who calls Venus friend?°
     What if I knew that if I went I'd die –
but that's a death that I would gladly buy!
She'll wreathe my bier with roses, cast perfume
into the flames, keep vigil at my tomb.
Gods, just don't let her bury me along
the highway where those herds of peasants throng
and scribble insults over lovers' stones.
Far from the road, let a tree shade my bones;
or shroud me in sands which hold no memory;
30   but no roadside memorial for me!°

3.24°

    You're too proud of your beauty, girl: you're wrong.
Your eyes have made you arrogant too long.
Look at the heights to which my love has raised you!
Now I'm embarrassed how my verses praised you.
With mingled charms my poems were all so fraught
that my love thought you were what you were not.
I said your blush was rosy as the dawn,
when all the time that glow was painted on.
    No family friends could rid me of the notion,°

no witches cleanse me in great Neptune's ocean;° 10
I saved myself, *sans* fire or surgery,
though wrecked, I swear, on the Aegean Sea.
My meat was cooked in Venus's bronze pot;°
my hands were bound behind me, chains cinched taut.
But look, my ship – all wreathed – makes port at last;°
I've passed the shoals; my anchor has been cast!
　　Though tempest-tossed, I'm finally feeling fit:
my senses are restored; my wounds have knit.
If you're a goddess, I'll worship at your shrine,
Good Sense! (Jove never heard a prayer of mine.) 20

3.25°

　　I was a joke at parties, feasts, events;
anyone could get laughs at my expense.
Five years I served you with fidelity;
now, gnaw your nails and mourn my constancy.
　　No, tears won't work; I've fallen for that trick –
you always cry to make your falsehoods stick.
Leaving, I'll weep, but tears weigh less than treason;
our well-matched team stumbled, and you're the reason.°
Goodbye, doorways my crying drove to cry,
and, door – which my fist never smashed! – goodbye. 10
　　But you – may years you've painted catch and gall you;°
may wrinkles crack your beauty and appall you;
soon, soon now, mirror-mocked, no longer cute,
you'll tear your hair out by the hoary root.
Shut out in turn, you'll suffer your own scorn;
a hag, you'll mourn as you made others mourn.
This is the crushing future my page sings:
tremble to learn what favor beauty brings.

4.7°

Ghosts do exist. Not all things end with dying.
From the defeated pyre the shade comes flying.
Over my pillow, Cynthia's form leaned,
though buried at a jostling highway's end,°
while my sleep snagged upon love's funeral,
and my bed's empty empire smacked of gall.
She had that hair I saw spread on the pyre,
those eyes; her dress's side was black from fire;
her beryl ring had warped in the flames' flicker;
10   her lips were gone, dissolved in Lethe's liquor.
Her voice was breathing, though, and loud; she cracked
her bony fingers, and then she attacked:
      'Traitor! – no girl can hope that you'll be true –
can sleep already have a hold on you?
Have you forgotten all those trysts we'd keep,°
rubbing my window smooth without a peep,
in the Subura's streets that never sleep?°
The ropes I climbed down, dangling in mid-air,
hand over hand – all to embrace you there?
20   Love at the crossroads, where, my breast on yours,
we heated up the alleys with our wars?
Alas for broken oaths and verbal art
the South Wind, without listening, tore apart!
      'I might – but no one mourned my day of dying! –°
have lived one more, if you had been there crying.
No watcher shook his rattle by my bed,°
and a rough tile gouged my unpillowed head.
Who saw you at my funeral with bowed back?
Who saw your warm tears splash your mourning black?
30   If you were ashamed to follow it past town,°
you could've begged my cortège to slow down.
Why didn't you throw incense on my fire,
ingrate, or call the breeze to fan it higher?
You were too cheap to deck that bier of mine

with wayside flowers, or wash my bones with wine!°
   'Burn Lygdamus! Redden the irons – the slave!
I could taste it, that wine spiked with the grave!
Or Nomas – let her hide her subtle stock
of toxins: burning bricks will make her talk!°
The whore who worked in alleyways, for cheap –°   40
her gold-hemmed skirts now scratch the ground they sweep!
A prattling maid who calls me beautiful
finds herself tasked with extra spinning-wool;°
because she brought my grave a nice bouquet,
a wood block hobbles poor old Petale,
and Lalage is flogged, hung by the hair,
since she invoked my name – how *could* she dare?
You let her melt my gold bust in the fire,
and steal her dowry from my very pyre!
   'You don't deserve it, but I'll check my curses,   50
Propertius: a long while I ruled your verses.
I swear, by the Fates' song none can undo –
may Cerberus purr for me, if I speak true –°
I kept faith. If I lie, may my gravestones
hiss with a viper nesting on my bones!
   'Twin dwellings flank the riverine abyss:
some shades are rowed to that, and some to this.
One boat holds convicts of adultery,
like Clytemnestra and Pasiphaë°
(whose wooden cow masked her debauchery);   60
but others – look! – with garlanded prow come
to the fresh rose fields of Elysium,°
full of bronze cymbals, airs and rhythmic chants,°
where Lydian lyres lead the turbaned dance.
Andromeda and Hypermestra, wives°
unsullied, tell the stories of their lives:
one, how her mother bought her wrongful pains
against the cold rock, clapped in chafing chains;
the other, of the crime her sisters wrought –
appalling! – which her decency would not.   70
Our tears in death confirm the loves we lived –

I hide the way you cheated and deceived.
      'But if you're moved, here's what I'd have you do,
if Chloris' witchcraft hasn't dazzled you:
Parthenie, my old nurse – give her food
and goods; she never fleeced you, though she could.
My Latris, named for service – I revere her! –°
don't let her hold another mistress' mirror.
And all those verses written in my name?
80   Burn them. Don't feed my ashes to your fame.
Keep ivy off my grave, so it won't twine°
my softening bones with its lubricious vine.
Where Anio irrigates the orchard trees
in Tibur's laden fields, and ivories
don't jaundice by the grace of Hercules,°
inscribe a column with a fitting verse
where Roman travelers pass (make sure it's terse!):°
In Tibur golden Cynthia takes repose
and adds her glory to the Anio's.
90   'Don't scoff at dreams that pass the Righteous Gate;°
when dreams have righteousness, then they have weight.
At night we range, loosed nightly from our cell:
nights, Cerberus wanders from the gate of hell.
Come dawn, though, Lethe broadcasts an embargo:
we're borne backward, and Charon weighs his cargo.°
Now others hold you; soon, I will alone;
you'll be mine, and I'll grind you, bone on bone.'
      That was the bitter note she rested on –
then ghosted through my fingers, and was gone.

4.8°

Now hear what shocked the Esquiline last night,°
when the New Gardens saw a crowd take flight!°
      There's an old serpent at Lanuvium,°
protecting and protected. If you come,
your visit, trust me, won't be tiresome.
A sacred cavern's mouth gapes blindly there:

the virgin enters (the path is hard – beware!)
with the snake's offering, when his hunger craves
its yearly due and hissing fills the caves.
The maidens blench to feel their fingertips,   10
when they descend, brushed by the serpent's lips.
The virgin offers morsels, which he takes,
while in her hands the virgin's basket shakes.
If she's been chaste, she gains her parents' arms,
and farmers cheer, 'A good year for the farms!'

    There Cynthia went, drawn in a Gallic chaise,
'for Juno's rites' – really, for Venus's.°
O Appian Way, I pray, describe the tones°
of her triumphal wheels upon your stones!°
What a sight! – Cynthia, her frame above the pole's,   20
driving the team through puddles and potholes.
(I won't describe her carriage's silk top,
those necklaced puppies, or that smooth-chinned fop
who'll sell his life for gladiators' gruel,
once cheeks which he now plucks have furred with wool.)°

    Since she had mocked me with the way she cheats
so often, I thought I'd try some other sheets.
There's a girl, Phyllis, lives near the divine
haunt of Diana on the Aventine.°
She's awful, dry; but when you're drunk, she's fine.   30
And then, fair Teia, by Tarpeia's bluff:°
when she imbibes, one man is not enough.
I thought I'd ask them over for the night:
new spice does wonders for the appetite.

    Our couch was in a garden, screened from view.
Where was my spot? I lay between the two!
Summer's for glassware. Lygdamus ladles in
a classy vintage, top-notch Lesbian.°
Miletus pipes; fresh, artless Byblis lets°
our roses pelt her and her castanets,   40
and the pinched dwarf himself, our Mr. Big,
claps to the boxwood flute and cuts a jig.

    The lamps, though full, were flickering as they burned;°

between courses, a table overturned;
dicing, I tried for Venus with my tosses,
but the damned Dogs kept leaping up with losses.°
Deaf to the girls' song, to their bared breasts, blind,
I balked – Lanuvium was my whole mind –°
when suddenly the gates were fiercely screaking,
50   and the whole foyer thronged with muffled shrieking.
        Now Cynthia bursts the doors – and they go booming –
her hair disheveled, radiantly fuming.
My wine cup drops from slackened fingertips;°
despite the wine stains, pallor takes my lips.
Her eyeballs fulminate a woman's wrath;
the scene is like Troy's sack and aftermath.
She plunges raging nails in Phyllis' cheeks;
'Fire! Neighbors, fire!' Teia shrieks.
The clamor wakes the Romans all around,
60   and the whole alley buzzes, wild with sound.
Hair shredded, dresses slashed, the girls retreat
to the first tavern on the darkened street.
        Exulting in her spoils, she strides apace
toward me, triumphant, and backhands my face;
she bites hard at my neck, so red marks rise,
but rains the most blows on my guilty eyes.
Then, when her arms grew tired of all that flailing,
she dragged out Lygdamus where he was quailing
behind the couch. His eyes beg my assistance –
70   Lygdamus, I can't. We're both resistless.
        Then, grudgingly, she let me seek detente
at last, and touch her feet, a suppliant,
and said, 'If you want pardon for these acts,
here are the terms of peace my law exacts:
you'll skip the flirty Forum's swordplay shows;
you won't stroll Pompey's walks in fancy clothes,
or crane your neck to the theater's top tier,
or look for litters open to your leer.°
And Lygdamus first, cause of all my pains –
80   sell him, with both his ankles clapped in chains.'

These were her terms. I answered, 'I assent.'
She laughed, imperious, omnipotent.
Then everywhere those outside girls had been
she touched with smoke, and washed the threshold clean,
and bade me change the lamps out, oil and taper,
and three times touched my brow with sulfur vapor.
Then when we'd changed the linens and bedspread,
we made peace on our old familiar bed.

Sulpicia

Sulpicia (born around 40 BCE) is the only Roman woman poet whose work has survived in any quantity; there is another, also called Sulpicia, from the time of Domitian (emperor from 81 to 96 CE), but only two of her lines survive. Our Sulpicia was the granddaughter of Servius Sulpicius Rufus – who was elected as one of two consuls, the highest executive office of the Republic, in 51 BCE – and the niece of Tibullus' (pp. 411–20) patron Marcus Valerius Messalla Corvinus. In the literary salons of her uncle, who seems to have been her guardian, she heard the poetry of Tibullus and the young Ovid (pp. 492–526). Her beloved, whom she addresses with surprising frankness, she calls 'Cerinthus' – Greek for 'bee bread', a food for bees made of honey and pollen and similar to wax (*keros* means 'wax' in Greek). The name is thus suggestive both of wax writing tablets and the sweetness of poetry and love.

The poems below are conventionally held to be the work of at least two different authors: the so-called 'Sulpicia elegist' (or 'friend of Sulpicia') as well as Sulpicia herself. Both sequences are found in a third book attached to Tibullus' first two but not written by him. Since the nineteenth century, most scholars have assumed that poems 13–18 are by Sulpicia herself, while poems 8–12 belong to an unknown poet from Messalla's circle. Perhaps this author has worked up Sulpicia's epigrams into real elegy, as prose commentaries (by the dictator Sulla, Cicero and, most famously, Julius Caesar, in his memoirs of the Gallic Wars) were ostensibly written to be worked up later into real history. The elegies add interesting context to the epigrams, but it's hard not to feel that their author suffers in the comparison. The epigrams are in a Catullan vein (see pp. 373–97), with something of his live-wire vulnerability and an imperiousness all Sulpicia's own, while the elegies have an Ovidian wit and smoothness, and a coherent progress-of-love organization; they also frequently echo Ovid and have even been identified as his juvenilia. Yet there is more individuality and interest in the epigrams' idiosyncrasies than in the elegies' invention. Then again, perhaps the stylistic differences between the two groups should be ascribed to genre rather to than the varying talents of their notionally separate poets.

The 'Sulpicia Elegist'

3.8

It's your month, Mars. Sulpicia's dressed the part°
for you. You'll come and see her, if you're smart.
Venus won't mind. But, brawling boy, take care°
that you don't drop your weapons while you stare.
When Love, that little imp, acts up and scorches
Olympus, it's her eyes that light his torches.
No matter what she does or where she goes,
her servant, Beauty, primps her and follows.
Her tresses flatter her when they're unkempt,
and flatter her when they are neatly primped.   10
The heart leaps when she's in her purple gown,
and when her pure white vestments cascade down.
Like her, Vertumnus, on the Deathless Mount,
can wear a thousand looks, all elegant.°
She is the only girl who's worth the price
of softest wools which Tyre has dyed twice,°
and she alone deserves the perfume yields
rich Arabs harvest from their incense fields,
and all the gems the swarthy Indians boast
where the dawn's waters lap the rubied coast.   20
This festive First of March, o Muses, swell
her praise, and, Phoebus, strum your tortoise shell.°
She'll keep this rite up as the years advance.
No girl is worthier of your song and dance.

3.9°

Boar, spare that boy, whether a gentle glade°
shelters you, or the mountain's trackless shade;
don't whet your toothy weapons for the clash!
Love, guard him; bring him home without a gash!
Diana leads him, hunt-obsessed, astray –
I wish all woods and dogs would go away!
What madness drives a man, surrounding valleys
with woven nets, to make his smooth hands callous?
What pleasure sneaks him into beastly caves
10   to scratch, with spines and thorns, his perfect calves?
But if he'd let me join his roving band,
I'd spread nets on the hills with my own hand;
I'd study fleeting deer-tracks, print by print,
and then unleash the dog at a flying sprint.
I'd swear the country's cultured good as it gets,
if we could lie together by the nets!
Then, boar, you could approach and leave at leisure,
if you don't come between us and our pleasure.
With me not there though, love, be celibate,°
20   now you're Diana's thrall, not Venus' pet;
with a hand past reproach pick up your net.
And, girls, just try to cozy up to him –
I hope wild creatures tear you limb from limb!
Oh, leave your father to his hunting fun,
and back into my arms, dear, don't walk – run!

3.10°

Come here! The girl is sick; come bring the cure.
Come, Phoebus, in your unshorn hair's hauteur.
Hear me and hurry, Phoebus; don't be snooty
to lay your healing hands on such a beauty!
Don't let malnourishment increase her pallor,
or her frail body turn some awful color.

May all we fear, each grim infirmity,
be washed by rushing rivers out to sea.
Come, holy one, and bring us any spell
or cordial which can make sick bodies well.   10
Don't kill the boy the thought of her death scares
to death – who's made, for her, uncounted prayers.
Sometimes he prays; sometimes, for her condition,
he blasts the gods with every malediction.
Relax, Cerinthus: god won't harm a lover.°
The girl's protected, if you'll always love her.
No need for weeping. Weeping will be due
that day when – gods forbid! – she's mad at you.
She's yours, you know. She's got you on the brain
and only you. All others' hopes are vain.   20
Be gentle, Phoebus. Your kudos will be splendid
to have saved two lives with one body mended;
yes, you'll be praised and pleased when they, renewed,
vie at your shrine to pay their debts accrued.
The good gods then will bless your newfound wealth,
and secretly wish that they were gods of health.

3.11°

The day, Cerinthus, you were born, I rate°
as holy, and will always celebrate.
That day the Fates established new restraints
on women's hearts, and you, their cocky prince.
I'm burnt worse than the rest, but love the flame,
provided that you also feel the same.
That love – oh, by your eyes, I pray we share it,
and by our secret trysts, and your birth-spirit.°
Spirit, enjoy this incense; bless his plea,°
if his pulse quickens when he thinks of me.   10
But if another has his heart engrossed,
vacate his faithless hearth, o holy ghost.
Venus, be equal: bind us both together
in shared solicitude, or snap my tether.

But no, just bind us both in one strong chain
which no day ever can dissolve in twain.
It's what the boy wants, too, but circumspectly,
since he's embarrassed to say so directly.
But who cares if he hides it, or is open?
20   You know his heart, birth-spirit; make it happen!

3.12°

Dear Juno, birthday goddess, take this mass°
of incense offered by the lettered lass°
who, dressed in her best and ritually clean,
stands beaming at your altars, to be seen.
For all this, goddess, you're her alibi;
but, secretly, she wants to catch an eye.
Let no one come between these lovers' joy!
Smile, goddess. With the same chain, cinch the boy.
You've matched them well, when he won't care to know
10   another belle, nor she another beau.
And may no vigilant doorman blockade them,°
as Love supplies the tricks to help evade him.
Come robed in purple, goddess; nod and shine.
Accept three gifts of cakes, and three of wine.
Her mother tells her, wish for this and that,
but she's in charge, and heeds no autocrat;
there's something else she wants now – she knows what.
She's burning, like an altar when they've lit it;
she wouldn't wish for health if she could get it.
20   Be gracious, Juno, that next year this same
love, older now, may once more bless your name.

Sulpicia

3.13°

Love's come at last – and such a love that I
would think my honor worser injured by
shamefaced dissembling than by frank displaying;
the Queen of Cyprus heard my Muses praying
and dropped him in my lap, and I am his.
Now Venus has fulfilled her promises;
let all my blisses be rehearsed at leisure
by anyone who hasn't known this pleasure.
To write it in a letter, which my man
might never read, or be the last to scan,   10
is not my choice. Yet the transgression thrills,
while making up a face for rumor mills
bores me to tears. I would be spoken of
as worthy lover to a worthy love.

3.14°

My birthday's nearing – miserable day!
With city and Cerinthus far away,
I'll have to spend it on a wretched farm.
What's sweeter than big city life? What charm
could draw a girl to some backwoods chateau,
to Tuscan fields where frigid waters flow?
Uncle Messalla, surely your interest°
in me is too officious – let it rest!
There are itineraries nothing warrants.
Kidnapped like that, I'd have my vital currents   10
of intellect and feeling left behind,
since you won't let me make up my own mind.

3.15°

You've heard!? The trip and weight are off! I'm free!
Now Rome will host my birthday jubilee!
Cheers to my birthday! Let no one neglect it,
which came when you, I think, did not expect it.

3.16°

How nice, Cerinthus, that you feel so free
in everything you do concerning me,
not worrying I'll make a grave mistake!
Yes, chase that bit of skirt, you dashing rake,
that whore in hand-me-downs, that quaint go-getter,
before Sulpicia, Servius's daughter.°
Yet some have got the worry in their head –
they care for us, and are discomfited –
that I will yield my place to a base bed.°

3.17°

Cerinthus, are you worried for me now,
thanks to my achy limbs and feverish brow?
I'd only wish to see this illness through
alive if I believed you wished me to.
What good can good health do if you can learn
that I'm near death with utter unconcern?

3.18°

Never again may I so feed your blaze
of worry, love, as in the last few days,
for never in my wayward youth did I
do anything I'm so embarrassed by
as when, last night, pretending to ignore you,
I left – as if I wasn't burning for you!

Horace

Quintus Horatius Flaccus (8 December 65–27 November 8 BCE) was Rome's greatest lyric poet; he is also the poet in this volume who tells us most about his life. He was born in Venusia (now Venosa), in Apulia in the heart of southern Italy. His freedman father was an auctioneer who provided credit to his buyers and then reaped the interest; his job paid for his son's education in Rome and Athens. There, in 44 BCE, Horace met Marcus Junius Brutus – then fresh from assassinating Julius Caesar – and joined the Republican cause. After Brutus and his fellow tyrannicide Gaius Cassius Longinus were defeated at the Battle of Philippi in Macedonia in 42, Horace, who had fought on the losing side, returned to Rome. He was pardoned, but whatever inheritance he had from his father was confiscated; poverty, he claims, then drove him to poetry. Soon enough he caught the notice of Tibullus' (pp. 411–20) patron Marcus Valerius Messalla Corvinus, as well as of the poet Virgil (pp. 398–410), who introduced him to Augustus' friend and confidant Gaius Cilnius Maecenas (see the introduction to Latin Lyric, p. 369). In 37, Maecenas officially became Horace's patron and gifted him his beloved villa and estate in the Sabine Hills northeast of Rome, sometime after the first book of his *Satires* was published in 35/4.

Horace may have been present at the Battle of Actium in 31 BCE, when the fleets of Antony and Cleopatra were finally defeated by Octavian, who thus united the Roman east and west under his rule as *princeps* (First Citizen). Thereafter, perhaps around 30, Horace published his second book of *Satires* and his *Epodes* (satirical poems written in mostly iambic lines of varying length, which, like Callimachus (pp. 255–81), Horace called *iambi*. The first three books of *Odes* were published as a unit in 23. Thereupon Horace turned to his *Epistles*, of which Book 1 may have come out around 19 and Book 2 around 11/10, about the same time as the fourth book of *Odes*. The highlight of Horace's career was being commissioned by Augustus to write the hymn for the Centennial or 'Secular' Games in 17 BCE (see the introduction to Latin Lyric, p. 372); this may have gotten him back into writing lyric, if he had not been doing so all along. In any event, during the last decade of his life he seems to have distanced himself somewhat from Maecenas and inched closer to Augustus – though Maecenas, on his deathbed, asked Augustus to 'remember Horace as if he were me'. When he died in 8 BCE, Horace was buried near Maecenas on the Esquiline Hill in Rome. In his will, he left all his possessions to the *princeps*.

Horace's relationship to contemporary or 'modern' poetry was complex. Unlike Callimachus and Propertius (pp. 421–45), Horace pointedly refrains from advertising his Alexandrianism. And yet Alexandria was essential to Horace's modernity: anyone who ignored Callimachus would have seemed somewhat like a Georgian sonneteer in the time of T. S. Eliot. Horace was too ambitious for that; besides, Callimachus – by way of the New Poets (see the introduction to Latin Lyric, pp. 367–8) – had taught everyone that the best poetry was highly polished, that slight and elegant was preferable to grand and clumsy. And Horace agreed: hence his Callimachean criticism of his forebear, the satirist Gaius Lucilius, whose writing was 'rough' and whose eloquence was a 'muddy' stream which abundantly coughed up all manner of verses ('two hundred lines an hour'!), including plenty which would have been better left out. The Callimachean reflex is perceptible in the *Odes* as well, where again and again Horace protests the essential modesty of his art – for example, in Ode 1.6 (p. 466), where he refuses to write a grand epic in praise of the *princeps*' right-hand man, Marcus Vipsanius Agrippa, instead preferring to hymn epic battles of flirtation between men and women at dinner parties.

Yet, for all that Horace shared Callimachus' basic project (at least in its broad outlines), still he had no desire to be yet another Callimachus reborn – that was Propertius' schtick. To carve his own niche, Horace looked farther back – as Alexandria itself had done – to Paros and Lesbos, the wellsprings of iambus and lyric. Horace availed himself of the Callimachean (we might call it the 'Poundian') paradox that the most modern poetry could be made by imitating the most ancient. Catullus (pp. 373–97) had shown that the meters of Lesbos were possible in Latin; it fell to Horace to solve the double problem, technical and tonal, of how to produce them consistently and elegantly in a manner consonant with the Augustan age.

Horace wished to maintain both a poetic and an individual identity, separate from the regime; yet he also valued his creature comforts, and lacked any interest in the kind of integrity that led to a Cato's or a Brutus' demise. His poetic solution was thus a personal one as well. The slightness of lyric as a genre, along with frequent protestations of his own slender powers, allowed him to compliment Augustus without constantly writing hymns of adulation. Lyric gave license to his overarching focus on themes of wine, love, philosophy (mostly Epicurean) and the inevitability of death, while his deferential, slightly clownish persona was able to draw laughs, often at his own expense, and soften hard words with the emollient of wit. Could any other poet have refused Augustus' invitation to be the *princeps'* personal secretary without giving offense? Horace did; while, at the same time, his choice of Alcaeus (pp. 55–67) as model allowed him to rise to the grandeur of Augustan political themes when he chose.

Yet Horace was no double agent. After fifty years of civil war, no one in Italy wanted more bloodshed, and Horace – self-serving, but principled, too – was a true friend of the regime. Augustus' absolutism was the price Rome paid for peace, and Horace was Augustus' good-natured, easy-living, self-deprecating, subtly savvy and razor-sharp court poet. He was also, it seems, quite personally close to his patrons, first to Maecenas, and then later to Augustus himself. No doubt many of the personal nuances of Horatian tact – his feel for how a line or image would land with a particular person, the care with which he calibrated his messages, his sense of when to approach the seat of power and when to keep his distance – will have vanished with his addressees. And yet when, for example, Horace celebrates his reunion with a friend from Brutus' army without offending his pro-Caesarian patrons (Ode 2.7, p. 472), or when he addresses a high-minded, philosophical ode to the disfavored Licinius Murena (Ode 2.10, p. 473), whom he manages to warn without incurring any disfavor himself – in all such cases, the odes themselves preserve a fossil record, as it were, of his delicate negotiation between past and present, artistry and authority. If, today, the poems feel so lapidary and inevitable that it's hard to imagine a time when they did not exist, it is testimony both to the superb skill and precision with which Horace weighed his words, and to his enduring influence, impossible to overstate, on English and European poetry.

For, through the ages, Horace, more than any other poet, classical or modern, has taught the speakers of European languages what a lyric poem is; how the lyric mind moves from feeling to form, from particular occasion to universalizing message; how to balance individual personality with technical artistry, and blend humor with wisdom. There is hardly an author, hardly a period, of English literature (to speak narrowly) which a thorough knowledge of Horace does not illuminate; prior to the twentieth century, virtually every significant Western author read him in school (before, say, the First World War, classical education was education, *tout court*), and, for the most part, continued to read him their whole lives. This was as true of his biggest fans, from Quintilian to Nietzsche, as of his relative detractors, like Lord Byron and Matthew Arnold, who find him wanting in one way or another. One might even say that, just as medieval and modern Europe were built on the foundations of a Roman Empire which had been given its most enduring political form, and its most powerful institutional impetus, by Augustus – just, indeed, as the historians and monarchs of Europe have looked to Augustus time and again as a model ruler and exemplar, whether of enlightened despotism or *Realpolitik* – so, too, European (and Europe-derived) lyricists have constructed their own work along the lines laid down by Horace, and have returned to him time and again for new ideas and fresh inspiration.

Epodes

2°

Happy the man who, far from the rat race,°
    lives free of debt and unbeholden,
tilling his father's fields with his own oxen
    as men did when the Age was Golden,
whose slumber no war-trumpets interrupt,
    who doesn't blanch when oceans glower,
who steers clear of the forum and the proud
    vestibules of wealth and power.°
Either he to the poplar trellises°

marries the vines once they're mature,   10
 or watches over mooing herds that amble
  unbothered on the valley floor,
or with his knife prunes off infertile branches
  to intergraft more fruitful stock,
or in clean vessels stores the squeezed-out honey,
  or shears the easygoing flock;
or when, from the tilled fields, Autumn uplifts
  his head, ripe fruits around his brow,°
he thrills to pluck grapes purpler than kings' coats,
  and pears grafted on each bent bough,   20
Priapus, for a gift to you, and you,
  Silvanus, border-guardian.°
He'll sprawl out now under an old holm oak,
  now on a grassy patch of lawn,
as meanwhile in the woods doves make their moan,
  the high banks flank the slipping streams,
and fountain waters bubble up and patter,
  inviting him to easy dreams.
And when Jove adds his wintry thunder to
  the rains and snows the cold begets,   30
with packs of dogs on every side he drives
  toothy boars into waiting nets,°
or stretches the wider mesh on polished poles
  to trick the thrush – which loves to eat –°
and sets snares for the panicky rabbits, and cranes
  just passing through – both tasty meat.
So occupied, who'd not forget the city
  love affairs that hurt the heart?
Yes, with a faithful wife around the house
  to raise the kids and do her part –   40
a Sabine sort, or like the suntanned brides°
  of hardy southern laborers,
to heap the holy hearth with crackly branches°
  before her tired man appears,
and close the wicker pen to milk the flocks
  until their swollen teats are dry,

and pour the sweet young wine, and set the table
    with simple food they didn't buy.
Ah, Lucrine oysters, parrotfish and turbot°
50   could not hold more appeal for me,
not if, swept on by stormy eastern currents,
    a school popped up in our home sea;
then no Moroccan guinea fowl would pass
    my lips, no fancy Asian grouse°
could please me better than the plumpest olives
    plucked from the most productive boughs,
or sorrel, which loves meadowlands, or mallow,
    indigestion's antidote,
or a lamb killed on the Feast of Boundaries,
60   or a wolf-slaughtered baby goat.°
I'll eat all this and with deep joy observe
    my well-fed sheep, now homeward bound,
while oxen, worn out, with slumped necks, plod slowly
    dragging the plows turned back around,
and all the homegrown servants, the farm's wealth,°
    sit by the beaming hearth they've crowned.
So Alfius, the predatory lender,
    planned out his country life with zest,
and dunned his debtors for return of tender
70   *to lend again, at interest.*

13°

The weather has brought the sky low; a scowl on its face,
    it comes down hard, with sleet and snow.
        The Boreal wind out of Thrace°
howls through the wood and the sea – friends, let us seize
    the present opportunity:
        while there's still spring in our knees°
and we look fine, let the clouds of the future clear
    from our smooth brows. You, fetch the wine
        bottled in my birth year,°
10   and speak no more. This turbulence may abate;

god may have kinder days in store.
      Let us luxuriate
with Persian scents in our hair, and Arcadian lyre°
    to lift accumulated care,
        disquiets of late so dire,°
as the good Centaur to his great charge passed on:°
    'O Thetis' dauntless seed, who are°
        a deity's mortal son,
Achilles, Troy lies ahead – those plains that sluice
    with cold Scamander's watershed   20
        and sinuous Simois –°
and no escape for you, since the Fates' loom°
    severs your thread, and your ocean-blue
        mother won't carry you home.
Drink then, and sing, and your destiny will gall less;
    for faced with ugly suffering
        this is our sweetest solace.'

14°

What is this limp lethargy of limb
    that blunts my every whim,
heedless, as if with parched lips I'd drunk deep
    goblets of Lethe's sleep?°
Maecenas, you're killing me with all this nagging.
    God, god is why I'm lagging!
A god keeps these (long-promised, long-impending)
    epodes from their ending.
Bathyllus burned Anacreon, they say,°
    with love – in this same way –   10
who often, on the lyre he carried with him,
    complained in a singsong rhythm.
You're burning, too; but if your gorgeous toy
    shines like the torch of Troy,°
congratulations. Freed Phryne makes me suffer,
    whom one man's not enough for.

16°

Civil war is wasting a second generation°
    and Rome is perishing by her own hand,
though neighboring Marsians failed of her devastation,°
    and Lars Porsena's fell Etruscan band;°
nor could our Capuan rivals, nor the Allobroges, traitors°
    in league with traitors, nor Spartacus's sword°
destroy her, nor Germany's blue-eyed invaders,°
    nor Hannibal, whom our forebears abhorred;°
but we, guilty, blood-cursed, shall be her destroyers,°
10   reduce her to a wild beasts' habitat,
till over the ash a barbarous horseman towers
    triumphant, and his horse-hooves pound it flat,
and Romulus' bones, once sheltered from the weather,°
    he kicks, insulting – pure obscenity.
You wonder, perhaps, how we from these woes together,
    or the best ones of us, at least, might flee.
Be it resolved – nothing is more necessary:
    as the Phocaeans swore an oath and fled°
their fields and hearths, and left each sanctuary
20   to be a den for boars and wolves instead,
we must go wherever our feet will take us, wherever
    sou'westers and siroccos blow our course.
So be it! Or who has a better plan? The favor
    of heaven bids us hurry. To the oars!
But let us swear: 'Return won't be off limits°
    when deep-sunk rocks float up on the sea-foam;
when the Po's floodplain covers Matinus' summits,°
    then we can in good conscience sail back home:
when into the ocean the Apennine goes sprinting;°
30   when prodigies, uncanny, unheard-of,
breed lewdly: the tiger submits to the stag's mounting,
    and hawk commits adultery with dove;°
when trusting herds don't fear the lion's ranting,°
    and sleeked goats in the breakers leap for love.'°

We'll swear, and forswear all reveries of returning,
    and all embark as one, or at least those
more rational than the masses – let limp, unlearning
    despair ignore the signs of doom, and doze.
Now show your spine, men, and shed all female remorse for°
    the Tuscan coast you'll leave behind. Long miles   40
await of encircling ocean. We'll chart a course for
    the fields, the happy fields, and the rich isles°
where the yearly harvest springs without any tilling,
    the vines are never pruned, the grapes are big,
and the olives weigh down the branches without failing,
    ungrafted trees grow dark with each ripe fig,
and all the oaks drip honey, and from high ridges
    fresh water lightly leaps with a cold plash;
the heifer comes happily in when her udder bulges,
    and she-goats willingly make milk-pails splash;   50
no bears at evening surround the sheepfolds, growling;
    no adders in their burrows puff and coil.
And still more delights will amaze us: how the howling
    East Wind won't storm and wash away the soil,
nor will the heat of the sun make good seeds wither:
    by heaven's king they're neither parched nor drowned.
The Argonauts never arrogantly rowed hither;°
    bloodstained Medea never trod this ground;°
no yardarms were ever aimed here by Phoenicians;°
    Ulysses' toilsome crew never appeared.°   60
Here no plagues cull the flock, no constellations'
    furious heat in summer thins the herd.°
These islands Jupiter marked out for the pure in
    spirit when he polluted gold with bronze;
the bronze he toughened with iron, and out of iron°
    my vatic sight proclaims our flight from bonds.°

Odes

1.1°

Maecenas, lordly scion   sprung from Etruscan kings,
o patron and protection,   my glory and delight,
some people love the dust-clouds   kicked up at Olympia°
that settle on the churning   wheels of chariots
grazing the turning posts,   and palm leaves elevating
winners to the exalted   masters of earth and heaven.
One man loves when the random   herdlings of Romulus
rally around him, climbing   the triple rungs of office;°
another, if he imports   and hoards in his own storerooms
10 the whole of the corn harvest   threshed out of Africa.
A third, at his happiest   hoeing the family farm,
you couldn't get to give up   the fields that were his father's
for all the wealth of Asia,   to board a ship from Cyprus
and sail on pins and needles   the stormy Cyclades.
A merchant, in a tizzy   at wild siroccos wrestling°
the Sea of Icarus,   praises the lazy days°
and fields of his hometown;   soon he rebuilds his shattered
freighter fleet, untutored   to live on slender means.
There's some who won't refuse   a swig of the old Massic,°
20 who aren't too proud to take off   a bit of their busy day,
and sprawl, now in the shadow   under the green madrone,
now by the softly bubbling   source of a sacred spring.
Still others love encampments,   the horn and trumpet blaring
their mingled calls to battle,   and warfare, source of mothers'
bitterest grief. The hunter   forgets his sweet young wife,
hunkering down in the blind   under the sky of winter,
no matter if it's deer   his trusty pups are after,
or if a Marsian boar   has burst his woven nets.°
Me, though, a wreath of ivy   adorning my poet's brow
30 will introduce to heaven,   me in the sacred wood
the agile choruses   of nymphs and dancing satyrs°
sequester from the commons,   as long as I'm allowed

the twin pipes of Euterpe,   and Polyhymnia°
remains not loth to tender   her lyre tuned in Lesbos.
Just slip this Roman songster   among the lyric Greeks –°
my elevated noggin   will knock against the stars!

1.3°

    May Venus guide you as you go,°
with help and light from Helen's starry brothers;°
    may Aeolus send one wind to blow°
up from Calabria, and still the others,°

    so that, good ship, you can repay
the debt you owe us all. Release him whole
    and hale in Attica, I pray,
and safeguard Virgil, who is half my soul.°

    He had a heart encased in oak°
and triple bronze, whoever first set sail°   10
    on the fierce sea in a frail bark
with no fear of the hurtling southern gale°

    locked with the northern, wrestling,
or rainy stars, or how the South Wind raves,°
    the Adriatic's fitful king,
mighty to calm, mighty to whip the waves.

    What death could a man fear who looks
unfazed upon the monsters swimming under
    the churned sea, or on your shipwreck rocks,
Acroceraunia, o Cliff of Thunder?°   20

    To no avail the wise god split
the continents with the estranging sea,
    since our keels still race over it,
unholy, sailing where they shouldn't be.

Reckless to flout the ban of gods,
humankind plunges farther, deeper, higher.
Reckless Prometheus's frauds
won for the world of men ill-gotten fire.

When fire out of heaven's hearth
30   was stolen, famine and a new cabal
of fevers infiltrated earth;°
once slow and distant, inescapable

Death suddenly sped up the pace.
Daedalus soared the void empyrean°
on wings denied the human race,
and toiling Hercules sacked Acheron.°

For mortals, nothing is too great;
though our bravado would assail the sky,°
our constant crime will never let
40   Jove lay his anger, or his lightning, by.

1.4°

Spring, and the bitter winter thaws as west winds warm
      the earth,°
      and boats are dragged from storage to the shore.
The cows aren't cooped up in their stalls, or farmer by his
      hearth;
      the white fields shine with ice and frost no more.

Venus leads out her chorus line, a low moon overhead;
      the nymphs and lovely Graces, joining hands,
skip lightly, foot to foot, in time, while Vulcan's fires are fed
      by huge Cyclopes at his stern commands.°

Now that the fields are free of ice, fresh flowers from the
      meadow
10   or sprigs of myrtle grace our shining brows,

and Faunus calls for sacrifice in his groves wreathed in
    shadow,°
        either a goat or lamb to seal our vows.°

Pale Death pounds at the pauper's door and castles of the
    kings,°
        the same for both. Sestius, you're blessed,°
but life's brief compass can't endure our long imaginings.°
        Soon night will hold you, and the Ghosts, half-guessed,°

and Pluto in his paltry house – where, when you've entered in,
        you won't be Lord of Wine when dice decree,°
nor will you lust for Lycidas, for whom all the young men°
        are melting now, and soon the girls will be.   20

1.5°

The Pyrrha Ode

Pyrrha, now who's the skinny   young thing on top of you,°
drizzled in perfume, rolling   on beds of roses laid
      deep in some grotto's shade?
     Who is it for, that blond hair-do

so careful to seem careless?   Poor kid! How many tears
he'll shed at the shifting weather,   surprised by the deities'
      mood swings, and the rough seas
    and black winds, wet behind the ears,

who's so in love now, thinking   you're golden through and through,°
that you'll be free forever,   you'll be forever kind,   10
      and doesn't know the wind
     deceives. Poor bastards, for whom you

glitter before they sail.   Not me – a seaside shrine
shows on a votive plaque that   I've hung this dedication
      to the great Power of Ocean:°
     my sailor's clothes, still wet with brine.

1.6°

Your bard will be Varius, a swan, like Homer, grand,°
who'll limn you brave, victorious against all who defied you
on shipboard or on horseback with Varius beside you,
   soldiering under your command.

But I can't do you justice, Agrippa, no more than rouse
the acid of Achilles, so unschooled in surrender,
or devious Ulysses, cast on the seas to wander,
   or the cruelties of Pelops' house.°

No, I'm too small for grandeur – modesty vetoes it,
10 and my general, my Muse, with lyre averse to wars,
won't let me soar to Caesar's sublime desserts, or yours,
   to slight them with a want of wit.°

But who is the writer worthy of Mars decked out for rage
in adamant, or Trojan dust in a black smear
begriming Meriones, or Diomedes, peer
   of gods, by Pallas' patronage?°

I sing the drunken soirée, I sing of maidens' might,
facing the young men hotly, their nails filed for the war,
whether I'm free, or have someone I'm burning for,
20   in keeping with my custom, light.°

1.9°

The Soracte Ode

See how Soracte, buried in snowdrifts, gleams°
so white, its treetops straining to bear the load
  of winter, as the icy streams
   stand choked in the beds where they once flowed.

Heap the hearth up with firewood to thaw the freeze,
good Thaliarchus, and liberally let me quaff°
      the house Sabine we've aged – more, please –°
   for four years now, from its Greek carafe.

Leave the rest to the gods, who can in a flash
becalm the storm-blasts fighting the churning seas,°   10
      so no breeze stirs the ancient ash,
   and the winds are still in the cypress trees.

Don't ask about tomorrow – run from the news!
Whatever time you get from the hand of chance
      is profit. You're young; don't refuse
   the sweetness of love, don't refuse to dance

now, while your green springtime has no hint of white
old age or death. Now make for the public squares,°
      and for soft whispers in the night
   at the hour appointed for hushed affairs;   20

make for the laughter, traitor of hidden charm,
caught from the corner where she plays hide-and-seek,
      or the love-pledge wrenched from her arm,
   or from her finger, willfully weak.

1.11°

Carpe Diem

Don't ask – it's not for us to know – what end the heavens
   will bestow
on you and me, Leuconoë; ignore all that astrology°
from Babylon. It's better just to bow to what will be,
   and must,
no matter if Jupiter will send more winters, or this one's
   the end
that wears out the Etruscan sea against the rocks, relentlessly.°

Be wise; have taste; let the wine decant, and prune back your
    extravagant°
hopes for forever. Life is brief. While we sit talking, Time,
    that thief,
escapes. Don't let your life delay until tomorrow: pluck today.°

1.22°

A man whose life is whole, whose heart is clean,
Fuscus, does not need Moorish spears to seize on,°
or bows, or quivers of arrows that have been
    tipped with poison,

not if he makes for Libya's sweltering sands,°
or for the Caucasus, where wind whiplashes
the hostile peaks, or for the fabled lands
    the Indus washes.

The proof? A wolf, as I wandered wholly charmed
10   by Lalage, singing of her and lost in thought°
out through my Sabine woods, though I was unarmed,
    took off like a shot;°

a prodigy like Apulia never spied
among its oaks and bellicose environs;
nor has Numidia, that baked and dried
    nursemaid of lions.

Take me to fields that sluggish ice sheets cover,
which no trees break, no summer weather warms,
some region Jupiter's knitted brow scowls over
20   with constant storms;

take me to where the sun swoops lower, faster,
so low there are no towns or houses built;
I'll still love Lalage for her lovely laughter,°
    her lovely lilt.

1.23°

You're running from me, Chloe,   just like a baby deer°
in search of her scared mother   through trackless mountains, lost
      and spooked by every gust
     and tree, wound up with empty fear.

Whether it's new spring breezes   making her shiver and start
at clashing leaves, or whether   a lizard rustles the bush
      it quits in a green rush,
     her small knees judder with her heart.

I'm not some vicious tiger   or ravenous African
lion hot to shatter   and crunch your bones. Don't hide°   10
      there by your mother's side;
     come out! You're ready for a man.

1.24°

What shame is there in weeping?   What limit to desire
for one we loved so dearly?   Strike up the mourning strain,
Melpomene; your father   gave you a voice like rain;°
      set, in your empty hands, the lyre.

So: Quintilius, then,   has gone to his long slumber?°
How could the goddess Honor,   and holy Justice' twin,
immaculate Devotion,   and naked Truth begin
      to seek his like among our number?

Many good men have greeted   his passing with their weeping,
none more than you, dear Virgil.   Alas, your piety°   10
is waste; the gods won't give up   one all too fleetingly
      trusted to our – but not their – keeping.

What if you played more sweetly   than Orpheus could play°
his lyre the trees heard   and followed everywhere –
could fresh blood ever color   an eidolon of air,
        once Mercury has led the way

with his grim wand to pastures   where flocks of shadows graze –
harsh god, and deaf to open   those gates the Fates have sealed?
It hurts; but we must bear it: whatever can't be healed
20   grows lighter with the dream of days.

1.37°

The Cleopatra Ode

High time to drink now, time with unfettered feet°
to pound the ground now; it was high time before
        now, friends, to fix a seat
        for the gods at the feast of our Priests of War.°

To raid the family cellars for noble vintage
was wrong till now, while for the Capitol
        the queen sought waste and wreckage;°
        insane, sought the Empire's funeral,

wielding a flock of 'men' sick from the stink°
10   of their own squalor, possessed by an enervated
        and grasping hope, and drunk
        on luck's sweet liquor. Her fit abated°

when scarcely a ship slipped burning and her blear°
brain, spongy with the Mareotic grape,°
        back to the truth of fear
        flew, far from Italy, flew to escape

Caesar, straining his oars, hawk keen to close
on delicate doves, a hunter stalking a hare
        through Thessaly's vast snows
20   with terrible speed, intent to ensnare

the fate-bedeviled creature – who, steeled to meet°
a nobler end, did not, like a woman, quiver
      at swords, or urge her fleet
    to a secret harbor and trust to cover,

but dared behold, with brow serenely blank,
her realm in rubble; dared with her hands constrain
      sinister asps, and drank
    venom and darkness through every vein;

more terrible now her last choice had been made
not to be reduced to a crownless, common   30
      subject on parade
    for Rome to jeer at, who was no low woman.

1.38°

Please, boy, no crowns of linden for my hair –°
that's just the sort of Persian frill I hate.°
Give up the search for some far country where
      the rose blows late.

You can't improve on a simple myrtle wreath;°
don't even try! These myrtle wreaths look fine
on you as you serve and me as I drink, beneath
      the shade of the vine.

2.3

Remember in uphill climbing to keep a level
temper, and likewise when you're riding high
      do not let too much joy unsettle
    you, Dellius, for you too will die,°

whether you live in ascetic misery,
or take your holidays in a quiet grove
      sprawled on the grass, contentedly
    tippling Falernian Grand Reserve.°

Why should the white poplar and towering pine
10   make friendly shade, entwined so their branches kiss,
            or winding rivers strive to shine
        fleetingly by, if not for this?

Come, bid the boy bring wine and bring perfume°
and roses, all too briefly in flower now –°
            now, while your days and means and doom,
        spun dark by the triple Fates, allow.

You'll leave your expensive tracts, and your place in Rome,°
and, lapped by the Tiber, your rustic pied-à-terre;
            you'll leave, and leave your beachfront home,
20   piled on the whitecaps, to your heir.°

No matter if you're poor, of plebeian birth,
or rich, of Inachus' ancient stock, you'll go;°
            all those who linger on the earth
        fall prey to the pitiless dark below.

One terminus awaits us all, one fate;
all lots are shaken in a single urn,
            and we will draw ours, soon or late,
        to board the ferry, and not return.°

                    2.7°

My friend, who at my side again and again
faced death, campaigning with Brutus' Republican band –
            who brought you back, a citizen,
        to the gods and sky of your fatherland?°

Pompey, my first, most intimate confrère,°
we two so often defeated the dull slow day
            with wine, and crowned our glistening hair
        with the cinnamon scent of the Indian bay!°

At Philippi we both retreated, humbled –°
I dropped my shield and ran (that's not a boast) –°   10
        as we unthreateningly crumbled,
      and our valorous chins bit the ugly dust.

But me, I was saved by Mercury, who plucked°
me through the foe in a mist, as I quailed in fright,
        while you by waves of war were sucked
      back into the heat and the surge of the fight.°

Therefore, feast Jove with the sacrifice you owe,
and rest right here each war-exhausted limb
        under my laurel, and don't be slow
      to plunder the casks with your name on them!   20

Fill the bright goblets with the oblivion°
of Massic wine, and let the conch-jars drown°
        us in perfume. Who will run
      for dewy celery to make a crown,

or myrtle? Venus, whom will the next dice-roll
make king of drinking? No one will know me from°
        a raving Bacchant! It's beautiful
      to go a bit wild when a friend comes home.

                           2.10°

You'll live a better life, Licinius,°
not always braving the open ocean, or –
too scared of storms – always hugging close
        to the rough shore.

Whoever loves and respects the golden mean
lives safe – his roof won't leak and let the rains in;
lives modest, unbegrudged for his obscene
        and gaudy mansion.

Often the tallest pines writhe in the wind's teeth;°
10   the loftiest towers fall with the loudest crash;
the tops of mountains are stricken most beneath
    the lightning's lash.

The man with a heart prepared by philosophy
in bad times hopes for, and in good times fears,
a change of fortune. Jupiter blots the sky;
    the same god clears

the clouds away. If life's hard now, it's not°
forever: sometimes Apollo stirs the silent
Muse with music; his bow's not always taut
20   or his mind violent.

In tight times, spread your canvas, be full of bluff
and bluster; but if you're wise, in good luck's gales
you'll reef it in, so too much wind won't puff
    your swollen sails.

2.13

On a black day that fellow planted you,°
whoever he was, whose temple-pillaging hand
    first nursed you, Tree, and reared you to°
assault his descendants and insult his land.

He's the sort that I can imagine could
have broken a parent's neck; at night he locks in
    his visitors and with their blood
paints bedroom walls. No Black Sea toxin°

exists, no wrong yet dreamt by a criminal,
10   that he's not tried, who in *my* land, you dull
    timber, set you up to fall
on your innocent landlord's innocent skull.

Of all our hours of danger, what man of us°
is fully heedful? The Punic sailor shudders°
      before the stormy Bosporus,°
    blind to disaster from other quarters;

the soldier fears the shots of the Parthian;°
the Parthian, bonds, oak walls, and the fastened latch
      of the Tullianum – but unforeseen°
    Death has caught throngs, and has more to catch.   20

How close I came to facing crepuscular°
Proserpine's realm, Aeacus' judgments, glades°
      where souls of all the righteous are,
    and the plaintive Aeolian serenades

of Sappho among the poplars, her girls around her,
and you, Alcaeus, who more resoundingly°
      apply your golden pick, propounder°
    of warfare and exile and trials at sea!

The shadows, awed at the songs – both yours and hers –
keep holy silence, although the closely packed   30
      populace's ear prefers
    to drink in the battles and tyrants sacked.°

What wonder if the jaws and the ears of the barking
black beast of a hundred heads flop down at this,°
      or if the Furies' twisted, snaking
    curls coil asleep, and do not hiss?°

What if Prometheus and Pelops' father°
beguile their toil with listening, or Orion°
      forgets himself, and hunts no farther
    the skittery lynxes and brave lion?   40

2.14°

The Postumus Ode

Postumus, Postumus, ah, how the fleeting°
years stream onward, nor can your prayerful breath
    make wrinkled old age start retreating
      or stall the unyielding advance of death;

not even triple hecatombs, daily done,°
my friend, can placate Pluto, who never weeps,
    who pins three-bodied Geryon
      and Tityus down where the sad wave sweeps°

holding them fast – a wave that we all, be sure,
10   all who enjoy a share in the earth's good things,
    must sail, no matter if we're poor
      farmers on other men's land, or kings!

To no avail we shy from the wounds of war
and Adriatic breakers that crash and flail;
    each fall, we cower from the roar
      of stinging siroccos, to no avail.°

We shall embark for Cocytus' sludge-black coil,°
languorous eddies where Danaus' daughters fill°
    their pails forever, and the toil
20   of Sisyphus, endlessly on his hill.°

You'll leave your house, your wife who desires to please,
your world behind; and nothing from groves you sow
    except those baneful cypress trees
      will follow its transient lord below.°

Some heir who deserves it more will drink the fine°
Caecuban which your hundred keys preserve,°
    and paint your pavé floor with wine°
    more sumptuous than the pontiffs serve.°

2.20°

Lifted on wings not weak or of common worth°
through liquid air, part bird, part bard, I fly°
    and shall not linger on the earth
    or in cities below me, too great, too high

for Envy's grasp. Not I, though a child of mere°
subsistence, not I, your constant company,°
    my dear Maecenas, shall disappear;
    the waves of the Styx will not touch me.

Already my legs are shriveling and the skin
wrinkles; above, I'm becoming a snow-white   10
    swan, and the airy plumes begin°
    on my fingers and shoulders to prick toward flight.

Already, Daedal Icarus is less notorious.°
To Libya's sandbanks I'll fly, a melodious°
    winged creature soaring north of Boreas,°
    and over the bellowing Bosporus.°

To Colchis and to Dacia, dissembling its dread
of Roman might, I shall not remain unknown,
    or the Geloni, or the well-read
    Ebro, or Gauls who imbibe the Rhône.°   20

My grave will be empty; send lament away –
paid mourners, and beaten breasts, and threnodies.°
    Repress your cries and do not pay
    respects out of place where no death is.

3.1°

Out of the temple, profaners whom I hate.°
Be hushed and holy! High priest of the Muses' word,
     to boys and girls I dedicate
      songs such as no one has ever heard.°

At the power of monarchs subjects shudder in fear,
but over those monarchs the final word is Jove's,
     the Giants' lucent vanquisher,°
      who rattles the world when his eyebrow moves.°

Compare two vineyards: one farmer plants more earth°
10   in larger rows. Or, in the consular
     campaigns, one runs on noble birth,
      another is famed for his character

and judgment, while a third has a large supply
of clients: necessity treats them all the same,°
     indifferently sorts low and high,
      and from one great urn shakes everyone's name.°

See how, at the tyrant's unholy neck, the bright
blade hangs and aims – no flavors of Sicily°
     can please or ease his appetite;
20   no lyre's or songbird's melody

sweetens his sleep. But humble Sleep won't quail
to visit the farmhand's hovel, deep and pure,
     or shady streambanks, or the vale
      of Tempe, where fresh zephyrs stir.°

One whose desires never outstrip his needs
won't blench at the mighty ocean's swell and churn,
     or gale-winds reaching savage speeds
      when Arcturus sets and the Kids return,°

or fret at hopes undone by his farm's deceit,
as hail rips through his vines, and his trees complain°   30
     now that they're bothered by the heat,
    now by a cold snap, now by rain.

Fish feel the ocean shrinking as more and more°
homes heap the deep. At the architect's command,
     the slaves haul landfill to the shore
    while the property owner watches and

disdains firm earth. But Danger and tremulous Doubt
climb every ladder with him, and the tiered sides
     of bronze-beaked triremes can't keep out
    Worry, which hies where the horseman rides.   40

What if no purple robes with a starry shine°
or Phrygian marbles cheer me when I'm down,°
     no fruit of the Falernian vine,°
    no unguents to please an Achaemenid crown,°

no stylish pile of a house, whose columns soar
in Envy's stratosphere? What's that to me?
     Why trade my Sabine valley for°
    the heavier toll of luxury?

3.2°

Now must the lad hard fighting has rendered stout
embrace privation's pinch with a friendly cheer;
     now must our Roman horseman rout
    fierce Parthians scampering under his spear –°

his be the pounding pulse, the life in sight
of heaven, while the tyrant's wife looks on
     his valor from above the fight,
    and the princess, from the bastion,

ah, sighs and prays that her royal fiancé,
10   green in the lists, won't catch that lion's claws
          where he goes ramping through the fray
          with rage in his heart and gore on his jaws.

A fine thing and sweet, to die for the fatherland –°
though Death still catches deserters who cut and run;°
          the young unwarlike are unmanned,
          their fugitive backs and knees undone.

True Manhood knows no scandalous setbacks;°
gleams, in election's light, immaculate;
          nor takes nor yields the sovereign axe°
20   as the popular whim wafts this way or that.

True Manhood treads untrodden paths, and makes
merit immortal – the sky is opening!
          It spurns the massed mob and forsakes
          the muck of the world as it flees on the wing.°

The tact of the faithful also has stored up°
rewards: let none who reveals the mystical
          sacraments of Ceres sup°
          under my roof or unloose my small

boat from its chain. Often the Father of Day,°
30   unheeded, lumps goodness with guilt in the general wrack;
          villainy rarely sprints away
          from Justice that limpingly dogs its back.

3.5°

The Regulus Ode

This we believe: our king in the heavenly spheres
is thunderous Jove; but we'll have a god at hand,
          Augustus, when he yokes the fierce°
          Britons and Parthians to his command.

Is it true – Crassus' troops lie in barbarous beds,
debasing themselves? Grow old at the beck and call
         (oh Senate and customs on their heads!)
     of our enemies, their fathers-in-law?°

Our best men serving a Parthian king; Rome's name
and toga and Twelve Shields all beyond recall,   10
         and Vesta's everliving flame –
     while Jove and the city of Rome don't fall?°

Regulus' foresight sought to put a stop°
to such disgrace when, spurning the outrages
         of a foul peace, he offered up
     himself as a homily to the ages

not to give Romans captured by enemies any
compassion: 'I've seen many a Roman standard°
         embellishing Punic temples, many
     a Roman weapon,' he said, 'surrendered   20

without a fight; I've seen our citizens' hands
yielding to bonds behind their freeborn backs,
         Carthage's doors flung wide, and lands
     replanted we ravaged in our attacks.°

You think a Roman soldier bought back with gold
will still be fierce? No, ransoms just increase
         the damages! Sure as the old
     white never comes back to a dye-soaked fleece,

true Manhood, once discarded, will refuse°
ever again to visit the decadent.   30
         What snared stag fights when he's let loose
     from the net? What man will be valiant

who has trusted a treacherous foe in exchange for breath?
Or crush, who has tamely let his arms be bound
　　　　with biting thongs and quailed at death,
　　　his captors in battle the next time round?

Not knowing whom to accept life from, he scrambles
the laws of peace and warfare. Oh dishonor!
　　　　Oh Italy in shame and shambles,
40　　　and Carthage more lofty by standing on her!'

It's said that he, uncitizened, debarred°
his chaste wife and small sons from kissing him,
　　　　and made them go, fixing his hard
　　　gaze on the ground, a man's gaze, grim,

until, with advice such as none had hazarded,
he'd buttressed the Senate's purpose, weak and cowed,
　　　　and through his grieving comrades sped
　　　to exile, head high above the crowd.

He knew what martyrdom the barbarian
50　　had planned for him, yet parted those who stood
　　　　blocking his path, his countrymen
　　　and family, the way he would

if he set off to the south after lengthy toil,
having settled the cases his clients sent him,
　　　　bound for Venafrum's sunny soil,
　　　or Lacedaemonia's jewel, Tarentum.°

3.9°

HORACE

While I was worthy of your love,
and there was no one you would rather have
　　　embrace your pale white neck, and cling,°
I lived more richly than a Persian king.°

LYDIA

While no one else made your eyes light
and Lydia trumped Chloe in your sight,
    Lydia's was a mighty name
and Romulus's mother had less fame.°

HORACE

Thracian Chloe now rules my heart,°
skillful in verse and music's supple art;   10
    for her, I'd give my final breath
if only fate would rescue her from death.

LYDIA

One passion now burns both of us –
me, and Calaïs, son of Ornytus;°
    for him, I'd die a double death
if fate would only furnish him with breath.

HORACE

What if Love renews old bonds
and we, long parted, bow to the yoke of bronze?
    If Chloe gets kicked out again
and the open door lets Lydia back in?   20

LYDIA

Though he's more gorgeous than a star,
and you're as light as cork, and stormier
    than Adria's insane abyss,°
I'd live with you, I'd die with you, in bliss!

3.12°

NEOBULE

It's a woman's lot that we may not
give our love free rein, or rinse our pain
with a wine-washing, and the tongue-lashing
    of an uncle's wrath
    scares us to death.

Now your basket vanishes, stolen by Venus's
fluttering boy, and the loom and the joy°
of Minerva's duty pales at the beauty°
          of Hebrus – truly°
10   sublime, Neobule,

when he strips and laves, in the Tiber's waves,°
those limbs he's oiled, rider more skilled
than Bellerophon, and not outdone°
          as he speeds to compete
          with fists or feet;

skilled, too, with spear to chase the deer
in a frightened mass through the open grass,
and quick to flush from the underbrush
          the bristling boar
20   he's ready for.°

3.13°

O spring of Bandusia,   brighter than glass, which should
drink many sweet libations,   where flowers ought to float,
          tomorrow you'll have a goat
          to stain your coldness with his blood:°

the lewd herd's little darling,   whose horns mark him a male,
two baby bumps, all raw   and huddled on his head,
          showing that he's been bred
          for sex and fights – to no avail.

The brutal heat of summer   while the fierce Dog Star burns°
10   is powerless to touch you;   your bracing freshets cool
          the ambling sheep, the bull
          exhausted by the plow he turns.

You too will become one day   one of the famous springs,
with me to praise the shady   holly above the niche

of hollow rock, from which
your chattering water leaps and sings.

3.18°

Faunus, who love nymphs on the run, to my°
farm's sunny pastures come with a gentle heart,
and on these nurslings cast a friendly eye
        when you depart –

as long as I offer a kid when the year is full,
and, full in the mixing bowl, Venus's friend,
wine sloshes, and my old altar's agreeable
        odors ascend.

When December's Nones bring round your festival,°
flocks frolic in the fields and take it easy,   10
neighborly villagers laze in grass, and all
        the cows are lazy;

the lambs don't quake at the wolf as it prowls around;
the forest spreads you a carpet of leaf and twig,
and ditch-diggers joyfully cut, on the hated ground,
        a three-step jig.°

3.23°

If, country Phidyle, as soon as the moon is born
you lift your palms to heaven and appease
        the Lares with fresh gifts of corn,°
    a rumbustious pig, and fragrances,

the sirocco won't lay waste to your pregnant grape,°
nor will the rust-blight devastate your crop,
        and your sweet nurslings will escape
    the sickening time when the apples drop.

The sacred sheep that graze by the snowy rills
10   of Algidus, among holm oaks and oaks,°
                or those that roam the Alban Hills
             fattened by pontiffs, will give their necks°

to the priestly axe – that's them, but don't you worry;
such hecatombs do not pertain to you.
                Some fresh-snapped myrtle or rosemary
             crowning your little gods will do.

If the hand touching your altar is undefiled,
though offering no rich sacrificial props,
                your grieving Lares will grow mild
20   when the salted grain gets hot and pops.

3.25°

Bacchus, where to, now that I'm filled and flown
with you? Which groves will know my ecstasy
             as I'm whirled through? Which caves intone
the deathless glory and sublimity

of Caesar, to be sown among
the stars and court of gods where Jove presides?
             My song is a new star, unsung°
by other mouths. As, on the mountainsides,

a sleep-starved Bacchant stares, slack-jawed,
10   at Hebrus and the snow-bright fields of Thrace,
                or at the barbarously foot-trod
Rhodope, so shall I, in a trackless place,°

gaze on the empty groves and rivers
and thrill with awe. King of the Naiad bands,°
                and of the Bacchants, whose strength shivers
             and topples towering ash trees with bare hands,°

mine is no ditty in humble mode,
    no mortal air. This danger is delight,
       Bacchus: to pursue a god,
    with a green vine around my brow, snugged tight.   20

3.30°

I've raised a monument   more permanent than bronze,
loftier than the kingly   decay of pyramids,°
which not the needling raindrops   nor North Wind on the rampage
can ever gnaw to nothing,   no, nor the numberless
centuries in succession,   nor yet the flight of time.°
I shall not wholly perish,   but most of me will go
untouched by the death goddess   to wax forever fresh°
with praise of generations.   As long as the High Priest
and Vestals keeping silence   still scale the Capitol,°
I shall find voice, where vocal   Aufidus pours his floods,°   10
and where the reign of Daunus   shepherds the country people
on fields bereft of water,   I, mighty from slender means,°
the first to lead in triumph   Aeolia's exquisite
music to Roman rhythms.   Now raise the wreath of glory°
won by your power and mine,   Melpomene, and gladly°
consent to lay Apollo's   laurel upon my head.°

4.1°

    Venus, must I rejoin your fray°
after so long on leave? Please, please, don't make me!
    That man I was in the gracious sway
of Cinara is no more. Won't you forsake me,°

    heartless Mother of sweet desire –
me, nearly fifty, too stiff, too long inactive,
    to bow to your soft yoke? Retire
to where the young men's prayers are more attractive!

The time is ripe to seek the house –
as your svelte swans wing you through party-goers –
   the house of Paullus Maximus,°
whose liver will be perfect for your skewers.°

His birth and looks can conquer hearts;
he's forceful in defense before the bar;
   a young man of a hundred arts,
he'll bear your battle standards near and far.

Whenever a richly second-rate
rival amuses Paullus' altitude,
   by the Alban Lake he'll dedicate
your marble likeness roofed with citronwood.°

From there, sweet incense wafting higher
will reach your nostrils, and the mingled measures
   of Phrygian oboe and strummed lyre°
and piccolo will be your constant pleasures;

there, twice a day, the boys and girls
with their white legs will praise your deity,
   footing the triple dance that whirls
and makes the ground shake, like the Salii.°

For me, they've lost their savor now:
women and boys, thrilled hopes that my affections
   will be reciprocated, brow
fresh-wreathed with flowers, drinking competitions.°

So why oh why do the tears start°
at random, Ligurinus, down each cheek?°
   Why, as I'm speaking, does my articulate tongue fail, suddenly stale and weak?°

At night I hold you in my dreams:
    embracing now, now chasing your swift strides
        through Mars's Field; and now it seems°
I chase cruel you through overwhelming tides.°   40

4.7°

The snows have fled; meadows put on their blooms
    and trees their leafy clothes.
      The newborn Earth resumes
her ancient changes; the river, sinking, flows
      in its old repose.

The nymphs and sister Graces dare to dance
    bare in the playful wind.°
      The hour's flashing glance
warns not to hope for more than life will lend:
      This too shall end.   10

Mild zephyrs melt the cold; bold Summer chases
    quickening Spring, to fall
      into the chill embraces
of apple-bearing Autumn, till Winter's pall
      stifles all.

True, swiftly cycling moons can still repair
    the light heaven has lost;
      but we, when we cross where
Tullus, Ancus and Aeneas crossed,°
      are darkness, dust.   20

Who knows if the lofty gods will add tomorrow
    to the sum of days you're here?
      Love the time you borrow;
what you spend yourself, you need not share
      with a grasping heir.°

Yes, we'll go down, and strict Minos allot us°
    our judgment and our place.
      No speeches then, Torquatus,°
no godliness, no aristocratic race°
30   will buy us grace.

Diana does not save inviolate
    Hippolytus who fell;°
      nor can Theseus split
the chains which bind Pirithöus to dwell°
        forgetful in hell.°

4.11°

Phyllis, I have a caskful of Alban wine°
aged over nine years; I have a garden flush°
with celery to crown your head and mine;
    I have a lush

riot of ivy, to tie your hair up nice;
silver smiles in my cupboard; bound with vervain,
my altar's raring for the lamb-sacrifice
    to shed its rain.

My house is abuzz with movement. Back and forth,
10   the maids and serving-boys bustle and scoot,
and flame-tips, twisting, palpitant on the hearth,
    exhale black soot.

You're asking when you're invited to my home?
The party's on the Ides – the holiday°
which splits the month of Venus Born from Foam –°
    April – halfway:

a birthday just as special to me as mine,
a day I celebrate with all thanksgiving:
the day Maecenas, now mellowed like fine wine,
      first graced the living.   20

The boy you're after, Telephus, is trapped°
by a high-class hussy, one of those rich sirens
out of your league; he's happy to be clapped
      in her leg irons.

Your grasping hopes should shrink before Phaethon's°
combustion, while high-flown Pegasus scorning
the earthy burden of Bellerophon's
      a heavy warning

to look to your own limits and not dream past
your level, holding it beyond the pale   30
to dally with unequals. You are my last
      love of them all –

I'll never melt for another girl again.
I want to teach you poems to sing to me
with your sweet voice, since there's no balm for pain
      like poetry.

Ovid

Publius Ovidius Naso (43 BCE–17 CE) was the youngest of the great Augustan poets, and the most prolific. The works selected here as 'lyric' are the *Amores* (*Experiences of Love*: love elegies, published, in two editions, between around 16 BCE and 2 CE) and two collections of epistles from exile: the *Tristia* (*Lamentations*, written around 9–12 CE) and the *Epistulae ex Ponto* (*Letters from Pontus*, circa 13–15 CE). Worth noting among Ovid's voluminous other works are the *Heroides* (*Epistles from Famous Heroines*, circa 13 BCE); the faux-didactic *Ars Amatoria* (*Art of Love*, 2 CE) – in which Ovid's narrator purports to give amatory instruction while constantly undermining himself; the mythological epic the *Metamorphoses* (8 CE); and the *Fasti* (8 CE), a teleological account of the Roman calendar, heavily inspired (like Propertius' fourth book of *Elegies*) by Callimachus' *Aetia* (pp. 258–61).

Ovid was born in Sulmo (modern Sulmona, in Abruzzo in central Italy) to an old equestrian family, wealthy, but without patrician blood or senatorial prestige. As a young man, he frequented the circle of Tibullus' patron, Marcus Valerius Messalla Corvinus (see the introduction to Tibullus, p. 411), where he made an impression at public poetry recitals. Wed three times, with a daughter and a stepdaughter who each married a senator, he owned a townhouse in the neighborhood of the Capitoline Hill in Rome, a villa on the edges of the city and a family estate in Sulmo.

To all eyes, he seemed a successful and affluent habitué of Rome's best circles. So it came as a shock when, in 8 CE, Augustus banished him to a Black Sea port called Tomis (modern Constanța, in Romania) at the outer reaches of the Empire. Augustus issued no statements about the reasons for his decision, though Ovid, in his lengthy, somewhat rambling second book of the *Tristia*, issued many: a 'poem and a mistake', he said – *carmen et error* – were to blame. The poem in question was the *Art of Love*; it seems that Augustus, in the six years since its publication, had grown more censorious, and now finally decided it was beyond the pale. The 'mistake' is unknown: Ovid, deferentially, refuses to say what it was. He had seen, or heard, something he shouldn't have. He had been stupid – but (he insists) it was just a mistake, certainly not premeditated, not a crime. Centuries of speculation have fixed, as the proximate cause, on Augustus' adulterous daughter Julia, whom the *princeps* (First Citizen) had banished in 2 CE, but we will never know. Ovid died in Tomis in 17 CE, three years after the death of Augustus, while revising the *Fasti*. He seems to have been in the process of editing Augustus out, and replacing him instead with praise of his successor, Tiberius, and of the latter's nephew and adopted son Germanicus.

Ovid is unlike the other major Augustan poets in that he had little personal experience of the death throes of the Republic (see the introduction to Latin Lyric, pp. 368–9). The decisive Battle of Actium in 31 BCE was an event of his boyhood, and Augustus' primacy an unavoidable fact of his maturity. The astonishing cultural and propagandistic success of Maecenas' literary patronage (see the introduction to Latin Lyric, p. 369) meant that, by the time Ovid came of age, channels had been established for aspiring poets; perhaps consequently, he lacks the pessimism of Virgil (pp. 398–410), the despair of Tibullus (pp. 411–20), the neurosis of Propertius (421–45) and the guardedness of Horace (pp. 453–91). Instead, he seems well adjusted, comfortable, cocky. His struggles, at least until exile, are mostly literary: acutely conscious of his belatedness, he worked hard to carve himself a niche among monumental elders, and to leave his own work as a model for the ever-more derivative generations of Roman poets to come. He is thus a transitional figure, the first of those who look as much or more to the Golden Age of their Augustan predecessors as to Greek models. His focus is always on other literature, with and against which he constantly plays; he knew how to toy with his audience's expectations, and the wittily flouted convention, and the amusing (occasionally tasteless) shock, are his stock-in-trade. To natural irreverence and insouciance he adds immense fluency and a finicky style. Callimachus – whose influence Ovid also acknowledges (see *Amores* 2.4, lines 19–20, p. 500) – might have raised an eyebrow at Ovid's verbosity, but not at the polish of his verses; each line, each couplet, is as wittily turned as the conceit of the whole.

The sustained hexameters of the *Metamorphoses* apart, Ovid's oeuvre is composed entirely in elegiac couplets, distichs of alternating Latin hexameters and pentameters, all of them neatly closed, all full of repetitions, balances and antitheses which thematize their 'two-ness' more thoroughly than in any other poet except the commonly accepted master of the English couplet, Alexander Pope, who clearly learned a lot from Ovid. Ovid's love for symmetry runs from pairings of words and phrases within individual lines (he delights in such antithetical doublings) to pairs of poems (for example, the diptych about double tablets, *Amores* 1.11 and 1.12, pp. 496–7). It even extends to paired collections: the *Tristia* can be seen as the sad twin of the *Amores*; the *Letters from Pontus*, of the *Heroides*.

Amores°

1.5°

Noon sizzled, and the sun stood overhead.°
I let my limbs relax upon the bed.
The shutters were half open, and half drawn;
the light was like a newly broken dawn,°
before day comes, but after night is gone;
or like the dusk that spreads as sunlight flees,
or light that streams through forest canopies –
a light that even good girls should embrace.
(Propriety can find a hiding place.)
10   But look! – Corinna, in a flowing gown;
on her white neck the parted hair spills down,
as they say famed Semiramis went clothed
for bed, or Lais, whom so many loved.°
I tore the gown – and she looked good in shreds –°
but still she fought to be clothed by the threads;
and while she fought, indifferent to success,
she let me triumph and take off her dress.
She stood there naked; I looked on in awe;
in all her body there was not a flaw.
20   What arms, what shoulders I saw and caressed!
How touchable I found each perfect breast!
Her chest was taut, her belly smooth and long;
how sleek her silhouette! Her thighs, how young!°

Why list it all, when it was all divine?
I pressed her naked body into mine.
Who doesn't know the rest? We had our bliss°
and then we slept. May more noons come like this!

1.9°

Each lover is a soldier on campaign.
Cupid, too, has tents pitched on the plain.°
Believe me, Atticus, when I maintain°
each lover is a soldier on campaign.
Both war and Venus want a youth still green;
old soldiers and aged lovers are obscene.
Generals seek that courage and compliance
which ladies long for in a male alliance.
Both sleep on the hard ground, both do guard duty –
one for his captain, one at the door of beauty.   10
All soldiers travel; a lover is as ready
to march to the world's end behind his lady.
He'll scale the mountains, cross the doubled flow
of storm-fed streams, he'll stride the drifted snow;
he won't gripe, setting sail, at the East Wind's roar,
or wait for the right stars to dip the oar.
Who else puts up with sleet or the night's colder
humors if not the lover and the soldier?
One scouts the enemy army with keen eye;
one tracks his rival's doings like a spy.   20
One to a porch, one to great city-states
lays siege. One knocks at doors; one knocks down gates.
Do soldiers ambush snorers? Sure, it happens –
weaponless enemies are slain with weapons.
So Thracian Rhesus' armies met disaster,°
and you, o captured horses, lost your master.
But lovers, too, are helped by husbands' sleep,
and use their weapons while their foes count sheep.
To slip by guards and sentries is the never-
ending task of soldier and of lover.   30

Both Mars and Venus baffle all conceit:
some get back up, whom you had thought were beat;
some limply fall, whom nothing could defeat.
    So, all who dub love lazy and supine
lay off – it calls for energy, and spine.
Briseis, taken, set Achilles burning –°
attack now, Trojans, while the tide is turning!
Straight from Andromache's arms great Hector sped;
she set the battle helmet on his head.°
40   They say that Agamemnon stopped to stare
at Priam's daughter, stunned by her maenad hair.°
Mars once was fettered by the crafty smith –
that one is Mount Olympus' favorite myth!°
I too was idle, born to forget my belt;°
pillows and shade trees made my mettle melt.
Now love of a lovely girl sinews my nervous
spirit commandingly; I'm at her service!
I fight at night now, always on the move;
who doesn't like to loaf should fall in love!

I.11°

Napé, expert at primping disarrayed
coiffure into good order, no mere maid,
famed for discretion, go-between of genius,
stealthy ambassador to late-night Venus,
who eascd Corinna's doubts, brought her to me,
at times of greatest need, all loyalty –
here, these wax tablets, take to her first thing°
tomorrow. Go straight there – no lingering!
Your veins aren't flint; there's no steel in your heart;
10   you're not some wide-eyed simpleton – you're smart.
Has Cupid shot you, too? It's plausible.
Advancing mine will serve your cause as well!
Say only this, if she's inquisitive,
that it's by hope of seeing her I live;
whatever else she wants, my lines will give.

Look at the time! Approach her when she's free,
and make her read it all, immediately.
Then scrutinize her forehead, how she squints,
and read my future in her countenance.
Make her write back at length, right when she's done –   20
I hate a tablet nothing's written on!
Tell her to pack her lines in and to use all
the margins, to prolong my eyes' perusal.
    Why make her fingers cramp? The tedium!
Let one word take up her whole tablet: *Come!*
Those glorious tablets then, bedecked in bay,
would hang in Venus' shrine without delay,
with this inscription: *Naso offers these*
to Venus, his beloved accessories,
which were, not long ago, mere maple trees.°   30

1.12°

Weep for the news these tablets bring to me!
They say, *I can't today.* A tragedy!
Omens are real, you know. Just now, Napé
tripped on the threshold as she went away.
Napé, next time be careful when you go.
Look sharp; pick up your feet; don't stub your toe!
    Out of my sight, death-notes, you peevish planks,°
and you, wax causing neither joy nor thanks –
wax made from Corsican honey, like enough,
which bees there cull from hemlock – awful stuff.°   10
You blushed, as if by reddish lead made ruddy;°
that wasn't paint, though: you were really bloody.
Lie in the road there, inanimate offenders –
I hope a wagon crushes you to flinders!
The hands were far from clean which felled the tree
and turned you into a commodity.
That tree, too, saw its share of necks in nooses
and gave the public butchers wood for crosses;
it gave hoot-owls foul shade to waul and scowl,

20   and bore the eggs of vulture and scritch-owl.°
        Was it to *these* I gave the crazy mission
        to woo my woman in the key of passion?
        They would do better with a wordy oath
        some dour judge intones with his dry mouth,
        or figuring expenses and amounts
        a miser can weep over as he counts.
              You 'double tablets'! – a fitting sobriquet,
        since double-dealing is your métier.
        Yes, twos are awful omens; they don't pay.
30   Well, here's my curse: may old age gnaw and rot you
        as your wax grays somewhere we've all forgot you.

                        2.1°

        The Son of Sulmo also wrote these pieces –°
        I, Naso, poet of my own caprices.
        Love made me write them – stand back, genteel readers!
        Chaste ears aren't fit to hear my mushy meters.
        I want those girls who meltingly rejoice
        at their love's simper; I want country boys
        love hasn't touched to lend my words their voice;
        and may each young man wounded by the same
        sharpshooting Cupid recognize his flame
10   in mine and know I've felt the same as he,
        reading in intimate conspiracy;
        gobsmacked, he'll ask, 'Who snitched? How did my curse,
        my struggle, end up in this poet's verse?'
              I'd dared embark on that supernal scuff°
        with handsy Gyges – my mouth was big enough –°
        when Earth felt vengeful, and Giants got the jump as
        Pelion piled on Ossa on Olympus.°
        We'd grasped the clouds and lightning, Jove and I,
        which he was going to heave to save the sky –
20   when her door slammed, and Jove and I forgot
        our lightning bolts; Jove exited my thought.
        Forgive me, Jove – your thunder's light on force!

Her door slammed shut with thunder worse than yours.
    Wheedling elegies are my proper arms,
which often soften hard doors with their charms.°
Song brings the blood-horned moon down from the sky,
calls back the Sun's white steeds when they've passed by;
song rips out fangs as serpent jaws explode,
turns rivers back where they've already flowed,
and song has opened doors; and bolts, though oaken,   30
song has cajoled out of their slots, or broken.°
What good would songs of swift Achilles gain me?°
Can either son of Atreus sustain me?
Or he who roamed as many years as fought?
Or Hector, sadly dragged by the chariot?°
But when a lady's looks are called exquisite,
she pays her bard by paying him a visit –
a handsome wage! Goodbye, you famous heroes!
To me, your brilliant deeds and you are zeroes.
But girls, turn all your pretty looks my way,   40
as I transcribe what young Love has to say.

2.4°

I wouldn't dare excuse my grievous faults
with arguments rhetorical and false.
Yes! I confess! My failings are extensive!
But I'll say more – I'll launch a mad offensive!
I hate them – long to give them up – but can't!
It's rough to live with what you can't recant.
I have no willpower, no self-discipline;
I'm like a ship huge currents toss and spin.°
    No single style of beauty has me glamored;
there are so many ways to be enamored.   10
One's modest eyes glance downward, and I'm stung.
Her purity burns me: the trap is sprung.
One's no hayseed, but worldly, forward, fresh;
I dream of bedding her quicksilver flesh.
One's like the Sabines, prudish and forbidding;°

I know she wants to, but she keeps it hidden.
Sophisticates with a refined display
attract me; rustics, with naïveté.
One says Callimachus seems like a peasant
20   next to me; I find her fondness pleasant.
One pans my verses, criticizes, negs;
while she critiques, I want to spread her legs.°
I love a soft footfall; but a loud stomper,
touched by a man, emits a softer whimper.
One sweetly sings, voice effortlessly ringing –
I want to kiss her mouth while she keeps singing.
One's nimble fingers make the lyre trill;
who could resist such deft and handsome skill?
One sways her supple form, a rhythmic mover,
30   and gyrates with soft art, and wins me over –
forget me, since I'm always amorous –
she'd coax Priapus from Hippolytus!°
You, tall as the couch is lengthy – *je t'adore*;°
you're lofty as the heroines of yore.
But *la petite-là* I like too; each sort
defeats my (weak) defenses – tall and short.
One's blowsy – but if she'd revamp her looks . . . !
One wears her dowry, like a million bucks.
40   I like an unsunned and a well-bronzed skin,
but dark complexions also reel me in.°
One's snow-white neck sets off each raven tress:
yes, black-haired Leda also could impress!°
One's locks are golden, like the saffron Dawn –
there's no myth I can't base a passion on.
The young girl thrills me, the mature enchants,
this one by beauty; that, by experience.
      In short, all girls in Rome one might admire
prick my ambition and arouse my fire.

2.6°

Our parrot, parodist from lands of Dawn,
winged scion of distant India, has passed on.
Come, pious flock, and mourn; your brother's gone!
With wingbeats on your breasts, come, feathered races,
and scratch hard claws across your fluffy faces.
Dishevel, not hair, but plumage at the hymn
you sing to top the trumpet's requiem.
Philomela, that Thracian tyrant's crime –
haven't you've mourned it a sufficient time?
For this rare bird retune your grieving plainchant;   10
your Itys *was* a worthy cause, but ancient.°
Mourn, mourn all who on liquid updrafts soar,
but, gentle turtledove, you mourn the more –
you were the parrot's lifelong, loyal friend,°
your heartfelt harmony fast to the end.
Like Pylades and the Argive Orestes,°
just so, while life allowed, you two were besties.
Yes, you were a good pet, of most rare hue,
a canny vocalist: what did that do?
What use you charmed her straightway with your words?   20
In death you're still and sad, crown jewel of birds.
Your wings made emeralds look dull and weak;
you wore rich purple-gold upon your beak.
You echoed speech – no bird was ever better –
with your ungainly and unerring stutter.
Spite silenced you, who balked at beastly wars;
patter and peace were the two loves of yours.
Look how quails always fight, and yet stay strong;
maybe that's why they often live so long.°
You never overate, content with little;   30
your empty beak still fed your love of prattle.
Plain water quenched your thirst; nuts kept you happy,
and poppyseeds sufficed to make you sleepy.
The hungering vulture lives; the kite still circles

in soaring loops; stormclouds still follow grackles;
the crow, loathed by Minerva, Dame of Spears,°
still lives, sometimes as long as ninety years;
while that glib gift, in far-flung climates bred,
the parrot, human dittoist, is dead!

40   Time's greed steals nearly all the finest first,
vouchsafing a full lifespan to the worst:
Thersites saw Protesilaus' death;°
with Hector ash, his brothers still drew breath.

    Why mention all those prayers *she* nervously
prayed for your sake, which the ferocity
of the South Wind whisked off into the sea?
The critical day came, your final one,
when Fate stood over you, your thread all spun;
your failing tongue still found the voice to cry

50   'Corinna' – as the light went out – 'byebye!'

    Adjoining an Elysian hill, a glade°
of grass grows ever green in ilex shade;
There, if we buy the rumor, the devout
birdies all flock; ill-omened ones are out.
There feeds the innocent swan when it deceases;
the phoenix, ever young, sole of its species;
there Juno's peacock spreads her fan, and doves°
in amorous couples peck their dovey loves.°
And there our parrot, ringed by a pious flock,

60   wins welcome and regard through his sweet talk.

    His mound is parrot-sized; he's under it,
beneath a marker where these words just fit:
My mistress' love for me this headstone hints,
who passed the average bird in eloquence.

2.7°

Am I stuck, then, on the defendant's dais?
This is exhausting! Let me rest my case.
If I glance up at Pompey's theater,°
you pluck one from the crowd and harp on her.

Or if some beauty sees me passing by,
you find hushed meanings in her blinking eye.
If I'm nice to some girl, my hair is pulled;
but if I'm mean, you think you're being gulled.
If I look good, my flame for you is dying;
if I look sick, some other has me sighing.   10
If guilty, you should tell me my offense!
The guilty can endure their punishments.
But you accuse me wildly; each 'I swear it, he
is cheating!' cheats your anger of severity.
How slow the low-down flop-eared donkey goes,
limping, demoralized by constant blows!

    And now this howler: the whiz who coiffs your head,
Cypassis, has enjoyed me in your bed!°
I hope the gods send someone more congenial,
should I go looking, than a lowly menial!   20
What freeborn man would so engage a maid,°
or lie with one whose back the whip has flayed?
One who, mark you, is so good with your tresses,
so pleasing and expert with her caresses?
And loyal, too! Sure, I'd try to grab her –
so she could first reject me, and then blabber!
I swear by Venus and by Cupid's bow,°
I swear that I'm not guilty – no, no, no!

2.8°

You, who teach all styles of hair what class is,
suited for coiffing goddesses, Cypassis,
you whom our pleasures proved no philistine,
good in your mistress' service, great in mine –
who blabbed about our physical proclivities?
How did Corinna learn of our activities?
Could I have blushed, or let some signal slip
betraying our hush-hush relationship?

    Yes, I did tell her someone who can covet
a maid's embrace has lost his mind. What of it?   10

Briseis had Achilles on a string;
enslaved Cassandra snared Mycenae's king.°
Both far surpassed my state in dignity;
is a king's pleasure too lowborn for me?
    Yet when she fixed you with her savage pique,
I saw your blushes spread from cheek to cheek.
But when *I* swore, you must have noticed how
much more convincingly I made my vow?
In Venus' name, no less! You, goddess, please°
20   scatter those honest lies in the moist breeze
of the South Wind over Carpathian seas!°
    Repay my kindnesses, sable Cypassis,°
with the sweet tender, now, of your caresses.
Why shake your head, and fangle new distresses?
You've got to please one of your two bosses!
Keep saying no, ingrate, and – fine! – I'll spout
our indiscretions, rat my own self out –°
then what we did, and when, and where, I'll leak,
with each position, encore and technique!

2.10°

You once claimed – I remember! – you, Graecinus! –°
no single man can double up on Venus.
Believing you made me a sitting duck.
Now two girls have me gaga. I'm a schmuck!
Both beauties, both are clothed with elegance;
both are of ravishing accomplishments.
Now this one, and now that, seems lovelier;
I dote on her now; now I dote on *her*.
A pleasure boat caught in the crosswinds' welter,
10   I pitch toward this, now toward the other shelter.°
Your ceaseless sickness has me seeing double,
Venus – isn't one girl enough trouble?
Why add stars to the sky, leaves to the trees?
Why dump more waters in the swollen seas?
Yet this sure beats abstaining from love's charity;

let those I hate live in strait-laced austerity!
Let those I hate in barren beds sleep simply,
flopping their bodies on the mattress limply,
while fierce love interrupts my dreams' dull droning,
and more than my own weight sets the bed groaning.   20
Let love exhaust me – to all killjoys, adieu!
One girl, if she can sate me; if not, two.°
I'm good for it – I'm slender, but with muscle.°
I make up what I lack in bulk with hustle.
Enthusiasm fortifies my thews;
my efforts never yet earned bad reviews.
I've spent whole nights in gusto unabated,
and felt, when morning came, invigorated.
Happy the man shared love is draining, killing;°
oh, let that be the way I die, gods willing!   30
Let soldiers face spear-salvos and a gory
demise to purchase their undying glory;
let money-grubbing merchants, when their ships
have snapped the sea's last nerve, inhale big sips
of salt through shipwrecked, double-crossing lips;
but let me die in Venus' labile throes,
melting with pleasure as my spirit goes;
and let some eulogist be moved to claim,
'This fellow's death and lifestyle were the same.'

2.12°

Laurel of triumph, come, surround my brow!°
I've won! Corinna – look! – is in my arms now.
Her husband, doorman, door, strove to immure her –
my foes, who feared my cleverness would lure her!
A special march of triumph's merited
by this, a victory with no bloodshed.
Forget moats skirting towns, and lowly walls –
a girl's resistance, by my tactics, falls!
      When Troy fell in ten years to many men,°
how little fame did Atreus' sons win?   10

No soldiers fought for mine; it is my own;
the thrust of my achievement's mine alone.
On me, both general and soldiery,
my prayer's fulfillment fell. It fell on me,
my own flagbearer, horse and infantry.
Chance did not succor me. There was no luck:
come, Triumph, won by my own plans and pluck!
  This fight's not new. Had Helen stayed home, Greece
and Asia would have carried on in peace.°
20 The Centaurs and the woodsy Lapiths got
drunk, and mad about a girl, and fought.°
A girl spurred Trojans on to war and glory
once more, Latinus, in your territory.°
And women, in Rome's infancy, gave cause
for Roman sons to battle their in-laws.°
  I've seen bulls fighting for a snowy heifer
while she, observing, made them braver, tougher.
Me, too, like all the rest, Cupid has led
to enter battle – but with no bloodshed.

2.13°

Corinna's reckless bid to bid goodbye
to the new weight she bears has gone awry,
and now she is bedridden, and might die.
She hid from me the danger that she dared;
I should be angry, but instead I'm scared.
Either the child was mine, or – that will do.
I often treat what might be true as true.
  O Queen of Memphis and Paraetonium,
Isis, who cherish Pharos, where the palm
10 flourishes, and Canopus' fertile loam,
who love the wide Nile racing glidingly
to spill, through seven mouths, into the sea,°
I pray you, by the rattles in your hands,°
and by Anubis' worshiped countenance –°

and may Osiris always join your dance,
may slow snakes coil around your laden altar,
may Apis' bullish friendship never falter –°
give ear, and two reprieves at once confer!
For she will save my life, if you'll save her.
On your days, in your name, she's often stood   20
where your priests splash the laurels with their blood.°

 Or you, with laboring women in your charge,
when what they hide has made their bellies large,
come kindly, Ilithyia; hear my cry!°
She's worthy of your help; don't let her die!
With scented smoke I'll make your altars sweet,
and lay, white-robed, my offerings at your feet;
From Naso, for Corinna's preservation
I'll write, if you will offer the occasion.

 You, girl, if times like this permit advice –   30
give up this fight; let this last time suffice!

3.7°

Was she not beautiful? Was she not kempt?
Wasn't it just like I'd so often dreamt?
In vain I held her, sinewless, sedate,
embarrassing the bed with my dead weight.
I wanted to, and so did she, but nothing
could get a rise out of that sluggish, slow thing.
Her arms like ivory, like the snows of Thrace
but whiter, wrapped my neck in an embrace;
she kissed me with her tongue, let our tongues tussle,
with lustful thigh to thigh, muscle to muscle;   10
she coaxed me, called me Daddy, called me Master,
said everything that makes the heart beat faster.
But, as if drugged with hemlock, my entire
body drooped, deserting my desire.
Was I alive or ghost? That flaccid member
was a sad sight, a dumb stump, a felled timber.

What won't old age – should I get there – unbalance,
if youth itself so undersells its talents?
Why be young, and a man? The shameful truth:
she didn't feel my manhood or my youth.
She left my bed as chastely uncaressed as
a priestess tends that deathless flame of Vesta's,°
as sister leaves her brother's side, correct,
with filial affection and respect –
though I had just indulged blond Chlide twice
with no break; Libas, and fair Pitho, thrice.
Corinna once would not be satisfied
with fewer than nine tilts, and I complied.°
    Did drugs from Thessaly inflict this trance?°
Was I spellbound by magic herbs or chants?
Did a witch's red wax effigy transfix
my name and liver with her needle pricks?°
Corn withers on the stalk, stricken by spells,
and spells make waters drain and dry in wells.
Spells strip acorns from oaks, cause grapes to pop
off of the vine, make apples, untouched, drop –
why shouldn't spells be authors of my lapse?
Yes, magic's what enfeebled me, perhaps.
Embarrassment, too, didn't help. First came
failure, compounded soon enough by shame.
    But what a girl to gaze at, and caress
as intimately as her own nightdress!
Her fondling would have made a youth of Nestor,
a human of Tithonus, if he caressed her.°
Yet when she touched me, there was no man there.
What should I pray for now in my next prayer?
No doubt, my bad use of their latest gift
will make the gods regret their lack of thrift.
I wanted to come in, and was admitted.
I wanted her to kiss me, and she did it.
I said, 'Let's go to bed,' and she submitted.
But did I profit by my royal luck, or

fondle, miser-like, my useless lucre?
Tantalus' thirst amid the waves is such,
proprietor of apples he can't touch.°
Who, leaving such a beauty bright and early,
could make a beeline to the temples, purely?
    Maybe she wasn't sexy? Couldn't kiss?
In her inducements, somehow was remiss?
Why, with 'inducements' like that she could coax   60
unyielding adamant, deaf rocks, dumb oaks!
All who were live and man she could have led on;
but I was man no more, or else, a dead one.
When Phemius sings, are deaf crowds the richer?°
Why would blind Homer want a painted picture?
    All pleasures had compelled my private visions;
I'd tried, and tried again, all known positions.
Still, slain before the war, my soldier lay,
worse than a rose that withered yesterday.
Now, look – he's back up, and wants work, though tardy;   70
he's begging for the front now, hale and hardy.
Down, barefaced dog, my own worst part, you owed me!
Your lies, not for the first time, buffaloed me.
You lure me into ambush with no weapon;
I'm humbled by the mess you make me step in.
    The girl was not too good to use her hand
and try, with her soft touch, to bid you stand.
But when her know-how failed to make you stir,
and you were lying there ignoring her,
she said, 'Are you insane? Why would you taunt me?   80
Who made you come to bed if you don't want me?
Either some sorceress has drained your wells
by poking holes in dolls and casting spells,
or you've been having sex with someone else.'
In her loose gown she rose without delay –
how beautifully her bare feet stalked away! –
and, so no one would know we'd had to stop,
she drew a bath to cover up my flop.

3.9°

If Memnon's mother, mistress of the Dawn,
or if Achilles' mother mourned her son,°
if grief leaves even goddesses undone,
then, Elegy, tear your hair, and weep with me!
Alas, how true – too true! – your name will be.°
Your bard, Tibullus, glory of your lyre,
now leaves his empty body on the pyre;
look, Cupid breaks his bow and comes in mourning,
his quiver upside down, his torch not burning;
10 see how his wings are slumped, how sad he goes,
dealing the breast he's bared resounding blows.
The tears are sopping in his unbound hair,
and hoarse sobs choke his chest and shake the air.
Just so, Iulus, they say he left your hall°
after Aeneas', his brother's, funeral.°
Never did Venus groan or suffer more
when her young love was savaged by a boar.°
We holy bards the gods look kindly on –
some think we have a godhead of our own;
20 yet all things holy Death soon steals away,
profaning them with hands that blot the day.
What use was Orpheus' mother, or Apollo;°
what use those songs that charmed the beasts to follow?
That sire wept Linus too through wood and brier,
sang *Aelinon!* to his reluctant lyre.°
And Homer, from whose everlasting fountain
bards sip the spring of the Pierian mountain –°
him too Avernus swallowed in its mire:
poems alone escape the hungry pyre.
30 Yes, poems endure: Troy's glory and her doom;
the web unwoven nightly at the loom.°
Thus Nemesis, thus Delia have a name;°
the first his last, the second his first flame.
What good are Egypt's rattles? What good to moan

and sacrifice? What good you sleep alone?°
Forgive me: when bad fates leave good men stricken,
I doubt the gods are real, and I am shaken.
Live just, die just. Be holy; keep your vows;
still Death will drag you to the charnel house.
Trust in good poems. This tiny urn contains –   40
so little's left! – Tibullus' scant remains.
O holy bard, and did the fires take you?
Did they not shrink to graze on and unmake you?°
They could have burned the golden monuments
and shrines of gods, so rank was their offense!
The Maid of Eryx turns her face away;°
not even she could hold back tears, some say.
Yet this is better than if Phaeacia kept°
your body in its soil, unknown, unwept;
for here your mother seals your eyelids, washes   50
them with her tears, gives last gifts to your ashes;
here, too, your sister joins in her despair
and grieves and tears at her disheveled hair;
beside them Nemesis and Delia moan
and kiss you and won't leave your pyre alone.
'Our love was best,' says Delia, by the pyre.
'You lived so long as I still stoked your fire.'
'Why claim my sorrow?' Nemesis replied.
'His failing grip held *my* hand as he died.'°
If more remains of us than name and shadow,°   60
Tibullus is in the Elysian meadow.
You, young Catullus, ivy on your hair
and Calvus at your side, will meet him there;°
and Gallus, you great heart, if it's untrue
that you betrayed your friend, you'll meet him too.°
They'll join your shade, if shade is more than dust;
Tibullus, you belong among the just.
This urn protect you; may your sleep be sound;
and may your bones lie lightly in the ground.

Tristia°

1.4°

The guardian of Erymanthus' Bear,°
Boötes, sinks to ocean from the air°
and makes the waters stormy that were fair,°
and here I'm scudding the Ionian Sea
unwilling, forced by fear to bravery.
How horrible! The waves chop and winds sweep,
churning the sands up seething from the deep!
Mountain-high on the prow and the curved stern
painted with gods, the breakers lash and churn.
The rigging creaks in the wind, the timbers judder
with the waves' blows; my woes make the boat shudder.
The captain shows his fear; his face has paled;
he's less the sailor now than the assailed.
As a weak jockey's reins, yanked without force,
drop on the neck of his unyielding horse,
our charioteer has given up on steering;
he does not drive, but veers where the waves are veering.
And if the winds won't alter where they're blowing,
the land where I can't go is where we're going.°
For on the left Illyria's disappearing,
and Italy, forbidden me, is nearing.°
Please, winds, don't drive us on where I'm outlawed;
breezes, obey, like me, a mighty god!°
As I cry where I wish and fear to go,
the waves clobber our boat with a huge blow.
Mercy, sea gods, in all your moods of blue!
Jove hates me; I don't need your hatred too.
Enfeebled as I am, keep me alive –
if one who's dead already *can* survive.

3.2°

So. Fate wanted me to visit even far
Scythia, prone beneath the polar star;°
nor Phoebus, nor the Muses in the least –
that well-read clique – have succored their poor priest.
No matter that I've bantered without crime,
more decorous in my life than in my rhyme;°
now, after many trials on land and sea,°
the Pontus's pure colds have welcomed me.°
I'd shunned the great world, born to loaf and shirk,
too soft and too unsuited for real work;   10
but now I bear extremes, and must be brave in
unending treks and sea-routes without haven.
And I've been up to it, my body sharing
my spirit's strength, to bear what's past all bearing.

   Yet in the crossing's perilous immersion,
my griefs were quiet, worn out by exertion;
But when my labor rested, the road finished,
and I had reached the place where I'd be punished,
I cared only for tears, which I let flow
as fulsomely as floods from melting snow.   20
I think of Rome and home, pith of my heart,
that piece of me still there, my missing part.
On the tomb door I've knocked and pounded, but –
alas! – I've always found it tightly shut.
How have I dodged so many swords? Oh, how
has no gale swamped my luckless head by now?
O gods, too constant in your hate for me,
who share the wrath of Rome's great deity,°
I'm begging you, goad on my balky doom;
unlatch the deadbolt; open up the tomb!   30

3.7°

Go to Perilla, hastily scrawled letter,
trusty caretaker of my words, and greet her.
You'll find her with her lovely mother, sitting,
or with her books, among the verse she's writing.
She'll set down every task when you drop in,
and ask you why you've come, and how I've been.
Say I'm alive, but do not wish to be;
time's passage hasn't soothed my misery.
I'm back to couplets, making the words fit,
though verse has never brought me benefit.
Address her: 'Are you working in our line,
still singing in your key, and not in mine?
Besides good looks and manners, native talents,
you have a rarer dowery – your brilliance.
To keep that fecund freshet sluicing clean,
I first led you to drink from Hippocrene.°
I saw it first, when you were young, and tried,
father to daughter, to be friend and guide.
So, if you still burn with the same desire,
Sappho alone will show a brighter fire.
I fear, though, that our fates may prove aligned,
and my downfall will dull your lively mind.
Time was, I'd read your work, and mine to you,
and weigh your lines, and teach you what I knew.
I'd listen to your drafts in their first flush,
and, when I caught you loafing, make you blush.
Perhaps the harm my writing's done to me
has made you fear the selfsame penalty?
Courage, Perilla! Only don't attempt
to teach the art of love; you'll be exempt.°
    'So, put off indolence, sweet prodigy!
Keep practicing your sacred artistry.
Long years will spoil the freshness of your cheeks
and wrinkled age will crease your brow with streaks –

old age, that meets all loveliness with violence,
and steals upon us in a pall of silence.
You'll hear, "But she was pretty once!" and grieve,
and what your mirror shows, you won't believe.
Your fortune's middling (though you merit better),
but let it be immeasurably greater –   40
Luck, at a whim, will still increase or fleece us,
and we'll be Irus, who were lately Croesus.°
No, we have nothing death will not inherit,
except the blessings of the mind and spirit.
Look, I – I've lost you, lost my land, my home;
I'm one whom no more can be taken from;
but my mind's left, my sole delight and friend,
where Caesar's sovereignty does not extend.
And should death, by a sword's cruel stroke, arrive,
my fame, though I have perished, will survive.   50
While Mars's Rome from seven hills shall spread
her rule the whole world over, I'll be read.
On you, though, may our art more kindly smile,
and may the pyre spare you for a while!'

3.13°

Look, it's the barren day that marks my birth,°
and that day's god – a day devoid of worth.°
Cruel god, why add sad years to the sad sum
of an exile? You never should have come.
If you had shame, or cared, if you were kind,
when I left home, you'd not have stalked behind;
that first day – when you learned I was outcast,
my birth a botch – you would have made my last.
Or else, the day I left, in parallel
with my sad friends you would have said, 'Farewell.'   10
     What do you want in Pontus? Did Caesar's wrath°
send you, too, on this far-flung, frozen path?
You clearly want your customary rite,
when I put on my solemn robes of white,

the altar smokes, which floral trimming decks,
its sacred fires crackling with incense flecks,
while I give cakes to mark the genial day,
and with pure lips and cordial heart, I pray.
My life, my minutes, when you reappear,
20   are not the sort that you can ever cheer.
What I need is a funeral altar, hung
with cypress, and a pyre's licking tongue.°
I'm sick of scented prayers that have no power;
I cannot pray in such an evil hour.
Yet if I must pray something, then I pray
you never make another trip this way,
while I must call this hostile outback mine,
the 'Welcoming' (the name is bad) Euxine.°

4.1°

If my books are flawed (they are), please don't abuse them;
reader, think how I wrote them, and excuse them.
Exiled, I seek not laurels but relief,
to dwell on something other than my grief.
They sing, whom chains in mines and ditches fetter –
their untaught measures make the bad task better;
they sing, stooped on the mudbanks, in the team
that slowly tows the loaded barge upstream;
they sing, who synchronize their oars in rhythm,
10   and push and pull, and beat the water with them.
The weary shepherd, propped on staff or rock,
sings through his reeds, and mollifies his flock.
The servant girl sings as she spins her wool
and makes the drudgery endurable.
Achilles, with Briseis taken from him,
turned to his lyre to appease and calm him.°
When Orpheus' music moved the trees and stones,
he sang his love, twice lost, in mournful tones.°
    The Muse consoled me, too, the long road here,
20   the only friend that didn't disappear.

She only has no fear of traps, or swords,
or seas, or stormwinds, or barbarian hordes.
She also knows what error wrought my fall –
that I'm to blame, but I'm no criminal.
Therefore she helps, who harmed me at one time,
when we both stood accused of the same crime.°
I could wish, doomed to be undone by them,
that I had never touched the Muses' hem.°
Now, though? I'm charmed within their sacred grove;
wounded by song, insane, it's song I love.   30
It's like the lotus Ulysses' men embraced:
though it was killing them, they loved the taste.°
The lover knows and clings to his undoing,
and chases the retailer of his ruin.
So I delight in books that have marooned me,
and love the javelin once used to wound me.°

    This zeal of mine may be what madness is,
but madness here has its advantages:
it shakes the mind from its despairing trance,
forgetting, briefly, present circumstance.   40
As a gored Bacchant feels no pain mid-shriek,°
wide-eyed, ecstatic, under Ida's peak,°
so my heart kindles at the thyrsus' blow,
and soars above, beyond, its human woe,
no more aware of exile's aftermath,
the shores of Scythia or heaven's wrath.°
As if I'd quaffed Lethe's oblivion,
all sense of Time, my enemy, is gone.

    I'm right, then, to bestow my praise and care
on goddesses who left Helicon to share   50
in my exile, and lighten my despair,
who did not prove averse, on land or sea,
on shipboard or on foot, to follow me.
I pray that their support may still abide!
The other gods have taken Caesar's side,
submerging me beneath as many pains
as fish have eggs, seas fish and shores sand-grains.

You'll count all flowers in spring, all wheat that grows
in summer, fruits in autumn, winter snows,
60   before the woes which I, unmoored, bereft,
tossed through the world, meet on the Euxine's left.°
        Nor has my luck improved since my arrival;
fate followed me this far, and still is evil.
Here too the ravel of my birth and doom
I recognize – black threads from a black loom.
To skip the ambuscades, the threats of death –
all true, but too extreme to take for truth –
here with the Gets and Bessi life is bleak,°
for one of whom the whole world used to speak!
70   To hide behind a gate and wall is bleak,
still worried your defenses are too weak.
When I was young, I kept far from the front,
and only touched a weapon as a stunt;
old now, I hold a sword and shield to right
and left; the hair my helmet hides is white.°
Now, when the lookout towers raise alarms,
my hands shake as I dress and rush to arms.
With bows and poisoned arrows, savage forces
gallop around the walls on foaming horses.
80   As the wolf snaps up the sheep that's gone astray,
and through the fields and woods drags it away,
so when, outside the gates, they catch a man,
he's property of the barbarian:
they take him prisoner, with chains attached,
or with a poisoned barb have him dispatched.
This is the harrowing place where, cruelly fated –
alas, it's been so long! – I've immigrated.
        And still my Muse her ancient rites and rhymes
warmly revisits in these wretched climes.
90   There's no one to recite to, though – no word
of Latin here is understood when heard.
What choice is there? My judgment is secure.
I read and write for me, my one reviewer;
yet ask, 'Whom are they for, these pains of mine?

Gets or Sarmatians? Will they read one line?"°
How often, as I've written, tears have poured
abundantly, and watermarked each word!
My heart feels its old gashes fresh again,
and my chest streams and sops with the sad rain.
    When I think what I was, what I've become,   100
where chance and change have brought me, and where from;
my wild hand hates itself, its every phrase,
and madly flings poems into the fire's blaze.
Since of so many lines so few still live,
whoever you are, please, as you read, forgive;
and you, forbidden Rome, don't look askance
at poems no better than my circumstance.

4.6°

Time breaks the farmer's bull and makes him bow
his neck, accept the yoke and bear the plow;
time gentles fiery steeds to the rein's restraint,
who learn to bite the bit without complaint;
time, for the African lion, can assuage
his viciousness, subdue his prior rage;
time even conquers the huge elephant,
which to her master grows obedient.
In time, vine-clusters gather and produce
ripe grapes that barely hold their captive juice;   10
in time, the barley stands above its roots,
and the astringent smack is coaxed from fruits.
Time wears the harrow's teeth that turn the clay,
and flint and adamant are worn away;
and time makes angers gradually depart,
and lessens grief, lightens a heavy heart.
Time, then, as it slides by in silence, makes
all things grow less – except my own heartaches.
Since I left home, the threshing floor's been brushed
twice for the harvest; grapes have twice been crushed.   20
Yet I've not learned to live with or live through

this grief; despite the years, it still feels new.
     Sometimes the yoke's refused by the old ox;
faced with the bit, sometimes the tame horse balks.
For me, time's only sharpened my ordeal;
it hasn't changed, but honed, the pain I feel.
The woes that I know now were then unknown;
the more I understand, the worse they've grown.
It's something, too, to bring fresh strength to bear,
30   not dulled by the long slow pressures of despair.
The wrestler just stepped out is charged and wired,
compared to one long lingering has tired.
The glittering gladiator, still unscathed,
defeats the one whose weapons blood has bathed.
The fresh-built ship endures the hurricane,
while an old one is swamped by a little rain.
Now I scarce bear what I once took in stride:
pains that compound as days are multiplied.
As my strength fails and my distress grows stronger,
40   I can't see either lasting too much longer.
My former health and color are quite gone;
a little skin scarce covers so much bone!
My body's sick, but my mind sicker; it
only beholds the bad, and does not quit.
My city's far, and friends who've blessed my life;
and far – far dearer than the rest – my wife.
Nearby: Scythians, Gets in pants (not gowned);°
the things I see, and cannot see, redound.
I have one hope here, and one source of peace:
50   that when I die – ah, soon! – my pain will cease.

Letters from Pontus°

2.4°

To Atticus

Accept this note from Hister's icy crust,°
Atticus, whom I trusted I could trust.
Does your unhappy friend still cross your mind,
or has your love grown weary and declined?
The gods are not so cruel I could allege
you had forgot me without sacrilege.
In my heart, no one ever took your place,
and now, in my mind's eye, I see your face.
We often spoke for hours seriously,
and spent still more in playful repartee.   10
While we conversed, time seemed to flit away;
day was too short for all I had to say.
I'd read my poems – always the latest one –
and you'd determine how my Muse had done.
Your praise surpassed the public's in my eyes,
my efforts richly paid by that rich prize.
To make my book as sharp as I could make it,
when you made a suggestion, I would take it.
You wandered through the forums, arcades, streets
with me; we had adjacent theater seats.°   20
So great a friendship, dear one, bonded us,
we were Achilles and Antilochus.°
Should Lethe's drafts dissolve your cares in bliss,
I'd not believe you could forget all this.°
The long, slow winter days will grow and grow,°
and summer solstice nights be long and slow;
Pontus will sweat, and Babylon see snows,°
lilies smell sweeter than the Paestum rose,°
before our friendship will slip from your heart:
my fate is not that black in any part.   30
But that my confidence not die in doubt,

my trust in you seem gullible, watch out;
preserve, with loyalty, our old affection –
provided you aren't taxed by the connection.

3.3°

To Maximus

If you have a little time for an exiled friend,
Maximus, star of the Fabians, attend°
to what I witnessed, whether we should deem
that it was something dark, or had the gleam
of revelation, or was just a dream.
   Midnight: sifting through shutters, soft moonlight,°
the moon, as always at the mid-month, bright.
I slept the human sleep when cares are shed,
my weary body sprawling on the bed,
when, with a sudden whoosh of air, wing-stirred,
the window moved, and a faint creak was heard.
I jerked onto my left elbow with a start,
all drowsing driven from my pounding heart.
There Love stood, looking different than he had,
hand resting on the maple bedpost, sad,
without the chain or hairband he once wore,
without the neat coiffure he had before.
His curls hung, soft and messy, on his face;
his wings looked mussed, the feathers out of place,
like a dove's back, plucked from the airy blast,
which many hands have dirtied as they passed.
When I knew him (whom do I know more closely?),
my tongue was freed; I started in morosely:
   'You tricked me, boy, to exile in these parts –
better off if I'd never taught your arts!
What? Have you come here, where there's no peace ever,
where the barbaric Hister freezes over?°
If not to see my straits, why come at all?
You know, don't you, that you're responsible?

10

20

You gave me marching orders first when young;°   30
my couplets tripped dictated from your tongue.
You wouldn't grant me a Homeric strain.
I couldn't sing of generals on campaign.
I had gifts – not big ones – as a beginner;
your bow and torches shrunk them, made them thinner.
For while I sang your and your mother's reign,
a major work was too much for my brain.
That wasn't all. I sang on, like a fool,
and with my *Art of Love* took you to school.°
And paid the price: I was forever banned   40
here, to this distant and chaotic land.°
Eumolpus's preceptor, Orpheus,°
was never exiled by his student thus;
Olympus never banished Marsyas;°
Achilles didn't send Chiron to grass,°
and Numa didn't wound Pythagoras.°
My list is long; I could go on, but shouldn't;
I only was uprooted by a student.
I gave you arms; I taught you, shameless creature,
and this was the reward you gave your teacher!   50
You know, though – and could swear – that lawful marriage
was not a rite I wanted to disparage.°
I never wrote for girls with hair not bound
by modest ribbons, whose skirts don't sweep the ground.
Please, tell me when I campaigned to confuse
brides with deceit, and blur whose child was whose.
Those women whose affairs law does not brook
are strictly cautioned not to read my book.
But what's the use, if everyone's convinced
that what I urge there are strict laws against?   60
Oh, may your arrows never miss their mark,
your torches never leave you in the dark,
and Caesar still hold sway the whole world over
(whose ancestor, Aeneas, was your brother),°
if you can somehow get him to relent
and punish me somewhere less inclement.'

Thus much, to the winged boy, I thought I said,
and this is the reply I thought he made:
'By torch and arrows, the weapons that I bear,
70   on Mother's life and Caesar's head, I swear:
you only ever taught me what's permitted;
of any crime your *Art* should be acquitted.
Alas, I wish I could deny it all!
You know the thing that *really* caused your fall.
It would be wrong to give that grief a name –
though you could not pretend you weren't to blame!
"Not crime, mistake!" is what you've always said;
and yet the wrath it roused was merited.
To see and comfort your depressed existence,
80   I flew here over a prodigious distance.
The first time I came here was when my dart,
at Mother's orders, pierced Medea's heart.°
After so long, I've come back to this swamp
for you, my soldier, stalwart of my camp.°
Put off your worries. Caesar's anger eases;
your prayers will conjure up more clement breezes.
Don't fear delay – the time we seek has come.
Tiberius triumphs; joy has taken Rome.°
Your house and sons, and Livia their mother,°
90   are happy, and congratulate each other,
and you, our leader's, and our country's, father.°
Now, while the people cheer, and everywhere
the altars' fragrances perfume the air,
while the gods' temples stand with open doors,
now, we must hope these pleas of ours have force.'°
Either he fled and melted once he spoke,
or I came to myself again, and woke.
    If I believed you'd not support these words,
Maximus, I'd say swans are Memnon's birds.°
100   But no one can get terebinth from rich°
ivory; milk can't curdle into pitch.
Your spirit matches your high birth; your noble
guilelessness is Hercules's double.°

Envy, the laziest vice, creeps into no
high character, but slithers, snake-like, low,
while your mind soars above your lofty birth,
your name and character of equal worth.
Let others harm the weak, their spear-tips smeared
with poison bile, longing to be feared;
but your house helps the weak who count on you.   110
I pray, count me among their number too.

3.7

Words fail me, always saying the same thing –
these useless, endless pleas. Embarrassing.°
My poems are all alike – an awful bore;
you know by heart what they'll be asking for.
You know this one's predictable appeal,
although you haven't broken its wax seal.
This time, I'll change the tenor of my theme,
so I'm not always struggling upstream.
        Forgive the hopes I placed in you, my friends;
here the rehearsal of that error ends.   10
Don't say I weigh on my poor wife, who is
as true as timid and un-worldly-wise.
I'll bear this too – I've borne far worse before.
I barely feel the millstone any more.
The bull bucks at the plow, plucked from the herd;
the yoke chafes at his neck, not yet inured.
But fate's habitual cruelties have become
old news for me; with use, I've gotten numb.
I'm in Get-country now; let me die here,°
driven to fate's implacable frontier.   20
Hope helps us, even unsubstantiated –
some longed-for future we've anticipated;
next comes despair that nothing will restore us,
the certain knowledge all is over for us.
Sometimes, to treat a wound will make it much
larger, which it was better not to touch.

The gentler death is drowning in a blink,
not swimming, swimming, till we tire, and sink.
Why did I ever think I'd move from Thrace
30   and be remanded to some kinder place?
Why did I ever hope for clemency?
Has fortune ever been benign to me?
My torture deepens, each time I rehearse
the woes of exile: they're new again, and worse.
Better for friends to give up their campaign
on my behalf, than that their prayers be vain.
The step which you all fear's a big one, yes;
but there's one who, if asked, would acquiesce.
If Caesar grants just one thing that I crave,
40   I'll die here, by the Black Sea, and be brave.

Statius

Publius Papinius Statius (circa 50–96 CE) is the author of three major works that have survived – the *Thebaid*, the *Silvae* and the *Achilleid* – as well as several more that have not.

Most of what we know about Statius' life and career comes from his elegy for his father, a successful Greek poet and the tutor to the imperial family of the Flavians, who rose from their plebeian beginnings to the heights of power in the civil upheavals that followed the death of the emperor Nero in 68 CE. Born and raised in Naples, Statius then moved to Rome, probably with his father, and perhaps during the reign of Vespasian (69–79 CE). For twelve years – roughly, from 81 to 93 CE – he labored at the *Thebaid*, a Latin epic attempting to imbue the mythical war between the sons of Oedipus for the throne of the Greek city of Thebes with a Virgilian grandeur. Shortly thereafter, he seems to have published the first three books of *Silvae*, gathering occasional poems, that is, those written on request, or in response to particular situations. The *Silvae*'s distinguishing features are its poems' metrical variety and, according to Statius' own prefaces, their speed of composition – he claims not to have spent more than two days on any of them! A fourth book of *Silvae* followed, perhaps in 95 CE, while the fifth seems likely to have been published posthumously, along with his unfinished epic, the *Achilleid*.

Before Statius, Lucan (39–65 CE) had also named a book *Silvae*, meaning 'Woods', or perhaps 'Undergrowth'. The title is somewhat mysterious, but may hint at the miscellaneous nature of the poems, and/or their raw and spontaneous character. Influential in late antiquity, the Statius' *Silvae* disappeared sometime after the fourth century; in the Middle Ages, even Dante, who on the strength of the *Thebaid* gives Statius a major role in the second book of his *Divine Comedy*, hadn't heard of them. In the early fifteenth century, however, they were rediscovered, and enjoyed a brief period of influence. Angelo Poliziano in Italy and John Dryden in England both wrote *Sylvae* of their own, while Ben

Jonson used the title in his books *The Forrest* and *Underwoods*, both miscellanies. (*Underwoods*, in turn, was later borrowed in the nineteenth century for a verse collection by Robert Louis Stevenson, better known for his novels *Treasure Island* and *The Strange Case of Dr. Jekyll and Mr. Hyde*.) Dryden, however, considered that Statius' verse 'wanted the Poyze of Judgement', and his polemics certainly contributed to the decline of Statius' reputation.

In an age whose best writers (the historian Tacitus, the verse-satirist Juvenal and the epigrammatist Martial, pp. 533–55) were disillusioned cynics, Statius' lyric project had a quixotic sincerity, as if striving to affirm ideals his culture no longer believed in. Compared with, say, Martial (who was born even farther from the center of the Empire), Statius seems very much the outsider, desperate to be taken seriously by VIPs whom he perhaps respected more than they deserved. Though his Augustan ambitions can seem anachronistic in the court of the increasingly autocratic Domitian (emperor from 81 to 96 CE), Statius was nonetheless a man of his age. The *Silvae* testifies to what has been called the Flavian culture of 'the impromptu', which sought memorialization of its elaborate showpieces – its lavish dinners and imperial spectacles – in the extemporaneous responses of its poets, orators and wits. In the following poems, all of which come from the *Silvae*, Statius thus mixes an elite literariness with a contemporary taste for warmth, immediacy and display, as, with his ambitious verse, he joins the emperors in their quest for an imperial grandeur.

2.4°

> Parrot, o prince of birds, your owner's favorite,°
> eloquent, quick to impersonate human banter,
> who deadbolted all too soon your cage of silence?
> Just yesterday, we watched you, near death, saunter
> to join us at dinner, and peck up tasty morsels
> spilled from the table, stalking among the couches
> past midnight, chatting and answering with chatter
> long practiced. Forever now your musical speech is
> silenced by Lethe. Away with Cycnus' tale!°
> 10   Not only swans sing their own funeral.

Your spacious house, its reddish dome all gilded,
its silver bars with ivory caps at the edges,
that racketing door your beak would always rattle,
alas, must make its own noise now! Your opulent
prison, now vacant, is party to no prattle.
    Call the bird-poets whom their teacher, Nature,°
imbued with speech's power. Let the raven batter
its breast with wingbeats, and the starling, skilled repeater
of what it hears; those daughters, whose defeaters,
the Muses, made them magpies, and the praters   20
of linked encores, the partridges, the somber
nightingale mourning in her Thracian chamber:
let them all keen, and to the pyre carry
their cousin, chorusing this threnody:
    The glorious parrot, our fluttering race's pride,
the greeny monarch from Eastern realms, has died.
Not peacocks with their tails of many jewels,
not pheasants from cold Colchis, not guinea fowls
Numidia hunts among the humid currents
of the sirocco, are lovelier in appearance.°   30
He said 'Hello' to kings, knew the name of Caesar;
he could play different roles – the people-pleaser,
the chiding friend – and he always had more
to say. You weren't alone, dear Melior,
when he flew free. But he won't be interred
without the honor due to such a bird:
Arabian spice and Sicilian saffron wash his
plumage; Assyrian balsam oils his ashes;°
more fortunate than the phoenix, through clouds of scent°
he'll climb the pyre, still in his prime, unspent.   40

4.5°

Made rich by the goods of my little farm, where old
Alba still tends and stokes her Trojan fire,°
     I greet you, silver-tongued and bold°
Severus, with notes from a novel lyre.

Cruel winter has slunk off now to the Arctic Bear;°
the suns keep climbing higher, the colds are thinned,
      and sea and land are smiling where
    the zephyrs have vanquished the North Wind.°

Now trees are bald no more with the green of spring;
10   now the birds tune their unskilled throats and flute
      the novel songs they're practicing,
    which winter's torpor had rendered mute.

A little land, a crackling hearth, a ceiling
made dark by firelight keep me contented;
      the wine with which my glass is filling
    pours from the cask where it fermented.°

I have no thousands of wooly sheep that bleat,
no bulls lewdly seduced by mooing cows;
      my fields, except when they repeat
20   their verse-intoning owner, drowse –°

these fields which, after my birthplace, my heart prefers
to all the rest, for here the Queen of War, all-
      pure Minerva, crowned my verse
    with Caesar's wreath of golden laurel,°

that time you, with your every fiber, backed
me in delicious risk, my staunch supporter –°
      as Castor quailed at each impact
    when Amycus boxed against his brother.°

Could Leptis Magna have given birth to you
30   way off in Libya? Soon she will field
      Indian harvests, and outdo
    scented Sabaea for cinnamon yield.°

In your sweet infancy, who wouldn't think
you'd toddled on Romulus's every mountain?°
    Or that, since being weaned, you'd drink
    exclusively from Juturna's fountain?°

Your quality's no surprise: you never knew
those African shoals, but came to Italy
    straightway, adopted here, where you
    swam in the waters off Tuscany.   40

You grew up among senators' sons, content
with the narrow equestrian stripe, although your soul°
    is pure patrician, sternly bent
    on many a great and exacting goal.

Phoenician neither in looks nor accent, not
foreign in thought – you're pure Italian-bred!°
    (Plenty of native Romans ought
    to have been Libya-born instead.)

When the Forum bellows, your voice remains upbeat
and yet your eloquence is not for sale;   50
    you never draw your sword in heat,
    but when friends call, you never fail.

But you prefer the peace of rustic sites –
your farm in Veii, once your father's tillage,
    or Monti Ernici's leafy heights,
    or Cures, the ancient Sabine village.°

Here is where you'll polish your footloose prose;
but sometimes lift the lyre you're harboring
    up from your grotto's hushed repose
    and think of me, and make it sing.   60

5.4°

What have I done? What was my fault or fraud,
that I alone of men must live unblessed
by you, sweet youthful Sleep, most gentle god?°
The flocks and herds, the birds, the beasts – all rest;
the treetops nod, and seem to drowse; the roar
of rapids sometimes stills, and the sea's bellow
subsides as tides lie silent on the shore.
But this is the seventh moon to see my hollow
eyes fixed on nothing. Seven times, the flash
10   of Vesper and Lucifer. Each passing Dawn,°
these seven mornings, with her dewy lash
has spritzed my face in pity. Can I go on?
No, not if I had the thousand eyes which kept
Juno's Argus awake through alternation,°
with half wide-open, while the others slept.
But now, if someone in a long night of passion
twined with a girl rebuffs you, from his bed,
come, Sleep, to mine. For all I ask of you
is not your dark wings wrapped around my head
20   (let fortune's favorites pray to be so gifted);
just tap me with your wand's tip – that will do –°
or flit above me lightly, knees uplifted.°

Martial

Marcus Valerius Martialis (circa 40–104 CE) came from a Spanish town called Bilbilis in Aragon, near modern Calatayud; he was born in March, Mars's month – hence his name, *Martialis*. His parents, who probably belonged to the local aristocracy, were clearly wealthy enough to provide him with a first-rate Roman education. Martial moved to Rome in 64, following the example of other Spanish literary talents, including the father-and-son team of the two Senecas (see poem 1.61, p. 536), Lucan, Columella and Quintilian (see 2.90, p. 539). One year later, in 65, the Younger Seneca was forced to commit suicide, as a result of his participation in a failed conspiracy against Nero (emperor from 54 to 68 CE). Martial is often thought to have been a client of Seneca's, since both men had country estates in Nomentum (modern Mentana, fifteen miles northeast of Rome), and it is even imagined that Martial received his estate from Seneca as a gift, either before or after the older man's death. Martial spent thirty-four years in Rome, scraping out a modest, stressful living, if he is to be believed, from various wealthier patrons and the proceeds of his own poetry. By 98 CE, he had had enough. He returned to Bilbilis, where he lived on a country estate gifted to him by a wealthy Spanish widow called Marcella (see 12.31, p. 554). He died there in 104, contemplating a return to Rome.

It may be no coincidence that Martial's departure from Rome in 98 followed the death of the emperor Domitian in 96. Most of Martial's literary career was spent under the patronage of the Flavian dynasty, which spanned the reigns of Vespasian (69–79), Titus (79–81) and Domitian, and Martial makes sure to flatter the last in most of his books: see, for example, poem 4.8 (p. 541). His first publication, the *Book of Spectacles*, had been a collection of epigrams celebrating the inauguration of the Colosseum, or the 'Flavian Amphitheater' as it should more correctly be called, under Titus in 80; but when Domitian ascended to the throne in September 81, Martial became one of his poets, whether he liked it or not. His next two collections – numbered not Books 2 and 3 but 13 and

14 in the manuscripts, presumably because of their obvious differences from the others and their lesser interest – were collections of two-line mottoes describing friendly gifts to be given at dinner parties or at the Saturnalia, the Roman festival of Saturn held annually in December. Martial's first book of epigrams as such (Book 1) was published in 86; these consist of mostly short, often satirical poems, of varying lengths and meters, though elegiac couplets are by far the most common. After 86, Martial produced about a book a year. His Book 11 came out in the year of Domitian's downfall, 96, and his last volume of epigrams, Book 12, contains many poems which address his return to Spain.

It is unclear what drove Martial to dedicate himself so completely to this diminutive genre, though the upshot of his generic single-mindedness was that he invented the epigram as we know it today. Indeed, he set the gold standard for epigrammatists from Ben Jonson in the seventeenth century, through Byron in the nineteenth, to the Americans J. V. Cunningham and Dorothy Parker in the twentieth. Naturally, Martial had his own models, in both Greek and Latin. In Greek, there was the long tradition of Hellenistic epigram, represented in this anthology in the efforts of Callimachus (pp. 255–81) and the selections from the *Greek Anthology* (pp. 299–356); it was, in fact, still active – and still in Greek – under Nero: the *Garland of Philip* (pp. 333–56) may well have been presented at his court in the mid-50s CE, while two epigrammatists there, Lucillius and Nicarchus, certainly influenced Martial. But Martial is something else, the first great master of the kind of pointedness, the 'sting in the tail', we have come to expect from epigram; there is a satirical edge and a sharpness to his lines that the Greek ones rarely possess.

Of all Martial's literary forebears, it is Catullus (pp. 373–97) who comes closest, and he is clearly Martial's primary influence. Yet, as is usual in Roman poetry, Martial is no slavish copyist. His poems are characteristically both less rhetorical and schematic, and less personal, than Catullus'; and while wit is sometimes a byproduct of Catullus' swaggering invective, for Martial it is his *raison d'être*. Humor is not Martial's only mode; his poems also contain generous helpings of easygoing self-deprecation and earthy Epicureanism, both philosophical and gastronomical, to complement the mordancy.

Even outside his literary importance, which is beyond dispute, Martial is fascinating for the light he sheds on daily goings-on in imperial Rome.

His poems are full of the life of the city. In his books, epigrams jostle each other like characters on a crowded Roman street. His two guiding principles are variation and juxtaposition. Beholden to no consistent philosophy, he buys in, or not, to Roman values with an apparently whimsical randomness. Now he is buttering up the rich and powerful; now bursting some cherished bubble. His shamelessness in flattery has earned him a great deal of criticism, but he was, in the end, just trying to get by – and his industrious hustle should win the sympathy of many a latter-day scribbler. Equal parts caustic and ingratiating, Martial sought only to entertain – well, that, and a certain degree of well-fed comfort. That his poems can still produce the kinds of reaction he describes in 6.60 (p. 545) is the measure of his success.

1.1

Here is the man you read and want:
Martial, famous everywhere
for polished little poems with point –
a poet you've lavished more praise on,
kind public, while he lives and breathes
than most enjoy when they're dead and gone.

1.10

Gemellus really wants to marry Maronilla.°
He wheedles, woos, gives gifts, insists; he won't lay off her.
How pretty is she? Ha! Nobody's more disgusting.
What does he like, then? What's his endgame? She's a cougher.°

1.23

You only dine with your bath buddies, Cotta;
there's no invite if you've not shared bathwater.
I know now why I've never been your guest:
you saw me naked and were not impressed.

1.32°

Sabidius, I do not like you – who
knows why? Not I. I know I don't like you.

1.34

You set no guards and do not close the door,
Lesbia, when you cheat and play the whore.°
Voyeurs, not lovers, sate your appetite;
pleasures aren't pleasures when they're out of sight.
Yet drapes are drawn, doors locked, by common hookers;
Memmius' flophouse won't indulge onlookers.
From Chione and Ias learn discretion:°
graveyards lend privacy to their profession.
Is it so hard to do as I instruct?
10   I'm saying 'Don't get caught', not 'Don't get fucked'.

1.61°

Verona loves the works of her best bard;°
    Mantua basks in Virgil's fame;°
Livy sheds honor upon Padua;°
    Stella and Flaccus do the same;°
the swollen Nile applauds Apollodorus;
    Sulmo echoes Ovid's name;°
Córdoba flaunts both Senecas°
    and Lucan's singular acclaim;°
Canius fills Cadiz, Decianus
10   Mérida, with merry glee;
and Bilbilis loves you, Licinianus,°
    and sometimes even mentions me.

1.68

Naevia is Rufus' *idée fixe*:
sad, glad or silent, it's of her he speaks.
He dines, asks questions, nods, or toasts a chum –
all Naevia. It's her, or he keeps mum.
He wrote his father yesterday at morn: 'O
light of my life, o Naevia, *buon giorno*!'

1.73

Nobody cared to take the liberty,
Maecilianus, when your wife was free,
but, now you're guarding her, why, every penis
in Rome is knocking! You're some sort of genius.

1.79

Attalus, you push lawsuits, products, deals;
you're always pushing, spinning your damn wheels.
Agendas pushed? You push a broom, or mop.
Next time, just push yourself from a rooftop.

1.117°

Each time we've met, here's what you've said,
Lupercus: 'I'll rouse my boy, and bid
him borrow your book, then send him speeding
back as soon as I'm done reading.'
Okay, but why disturb the kid?
The Quirinal Pear Tree's quite a haul,°
and the stairs to my flat are very tall;
but what you want's not far at all.
Surely you shop in the Argiletum?°
There's a bookstore facing Caesar's Forum°   10
with posters papering the door there

naming the poets you can score there;
I'm one of them. Ask for Atrectus –
that's the fellow who runs the place.
He'll hand you, from one or another case,
a Martial for five denarii –°
pumice-buffed, with purple dye.
Not worth that much, you say? Smart guy.

2.12

Postumus, you always wear cologne;
your cloud of musk is never just your own.
To smell good, always – something's up, I think.
Postumus, men who always smell good stink.

2.26

Naevia's panting, and her cough won't quit;
she's spattering your lap with snot and spit.
Slow down, Bithynicus! You're not a winner°
just yet. It's not death's door – she wants you in her.

2.33

Philaenis, why, why won't I kiss you?
You're bald, you have one eye, you're red.
It's not a kiss; it's giving head.

2.38

What's in Nomentum, Linus, that I go there?°
I look around, and notice Linus nowhere.

2.53

You want your freedom, Maximus? I doubt it.
But if you do, here's how to go about it:

you'll be free if you don't go out to dine,
if you can stomach Veii's bargain wine,°
if Cinna's golden dishes make you snort,
if basic clothes will do – you know, my sort –
if you can get by with a two-buck whore,
and don't mind stooping, going in your door –
if all this sounds like something you can do,
Parthia's king won't be as free as you.°   10

2.58

Zoilus, my cloak is fraying, yours is fine.
Laugh all you want – mine's fraying, but it's mine.

2.62

You pluck your arms, legs, chest, and keep them slick;
your pubes as well, and shave around your dick.
Your lady likes it – we know, Labienus.°
But tell us for whose sake you pluck your anus.

2.88

Mamercus, though you don't recite or write,
you want to be a poet. That's all right.
Be what you want – just don't write or recite.

2.90

Quintilian, our Roman exemplar,°
for wandering youth both compass and lodestar,
if I, though hardly rich or elderly,
am urgent about life, don't chastise me –
no one can live with too much urgency.
Who would surpass his father's wealth, or stuff
his halls with portraiture, may put life off;
I'm happy with a roof, a smoky hearth

to stain it black, fresh water and green earth.
10   Give me a fat and happy slave, a wife
who doesn't know too much, days free of strife,
nights full of easy sleep – I call that life.°

3.26

You and you only have a large estate;
nobody else has money, or gold plate;
only your pantry has fine china, fine
Massic, and the finest Caecuban wine;°
intelligence and wit are yours alone;
all of these things and more you only own,
Candidus – don't dream I'd disagree! –
although your wife is public property.

3.53

I don't need your face or lips,
your neck, your hands, your legs, your hips,
that ass of yours, or either tit –
but why describe you bit by bit?°
Chloe, I'd happily be free
of you in your entirety.

3.65°

An apple a young beauty bites; fresh puffs
of wind off Corycus's saffron bluffs;°
white-blooming vines, with buds just now revealed;
the cut-grass smell when sheep have cropped a field;
the green earth after a light spritz in summer;
fresh myrtle, the spice harvest, well-thumbed amber,°
which scents the flame when incense makes it flare,°
a wreath recalling nard-anointed hair –°
cruel Diadumenos, your mouth's all this°
10   and more. What if you gave me a real kiss?

3.89

Lettuce and mallow, Phoebus, *might* loosen it –
that look as if you're working hard to shit.°

4.8°

The first two hours bring the morning greeting
to wear us out; the third sets lawyers bleating.
Up through the fifth, Rome's workers, all, are busy;
from hour six to seven, we take it easy.
The eighth sees us oil up for wrestling matches;
the ninth deposits us on dinner couches.
The tenth, Euphemus, likes my little books,
as you direct the genius of your cooks,
when Caesar quaffs ambrosia and is calm,
a modest tipple in his mighty palm.   10
Uncork the wisecracks now! My Muse won't schlep
to Jove's *Good mornings* with her mincing step.

4.24

To Fabianus

Each friend Lycoris courted in her life
she's buried. Introduce her to my wife.

4.48

You adore being buggered, yet you cry
when you've been buggered, Papylus – but why?
You love the deed; why sniffle when it's done?
Do you regret the itch that drove you on?
Or is it rather that you cry a river
because the beloved buggery is over?

4.71

To Safronius Rufus

I've searched through the whole city, head to toe,
for girls who will, but no girl will say no.
Is it a sin, a crime, not comme il faut,
a faux pas? Well, who knows? Girls won't say no.
Is no girl chaste? A thousand are. How so?
The chaste ones won't put out, but won't say no.

4.81

Fabulla read the epigram in which I crow
and carp because no girl in town will tell me no;
now two and three times I've begged her please to throw
a boy a bone. Girl, don't be so *simpatico* –
I only asked that you say no, not *only* no.

4.87

Your Bassa's baby always is nearby
so she can coo at him, 'You sweetie pie!'
And yet – get this, Fabullus – Bassa's heart's
not in it. He's just cover for her farts.

5.9°

Symmachus, I felt a little sick;
you brought your hundred students, double quick.
A hundred cold hands poked and chilled me through.
I didn't have a fever; now I do.

5.16

Instead of writing Major Verse, I make
poems to enjoy – dear reader, for your sake

who read, and fill Rome with my poetry.
But you don't know, my friend, the cost to me –
q.v. as a Treasury lawyer, I could sell°
words to distraught defendants, who'd pay well;
sailors would send me Spanish wine in buckets,
and lots of greasy coins would grime my pockets.
But my books come to supper, or to tea,
and you enjoy them – only if they're free.°   10
Poets of old did not subsist on praise;
Alexis was a knickknack in those days.°
'Bravo! Well said! We think your poems are aces!'
That's your response? You want me pleading cases.

5.20

Sweet Julius, if we were free°
to live without anxiety,
that is, to *truly* live, and measure
our days by the demands of leisure:
palatial homes of the powerful,°
gloomy lawsuits, the boring forum,
ancestral portraits – we'd ignore 'em,
and constitutionals, long chats,
and books, and exercise, and shade,
the Virgo's baths, the colonnade°   10
would be our tasks, our habitats.
But now our lives are not our own,
and our best days are quickly gone –
we spend them now, and pay later.
But no one who knows how to live
would live as a procrastinator.

5.34°

Fronto, my father, mother Flaccilla, here
beside you I inter my dearest dear,
Erotion. Please shield her from the dark,

small as she is, and Cerberus' huge bark.°
It would have been six winters since her birth,
if she had lingered six more days on earth.
With her old patrons, let her now, carefree,
chatter and play, and sometimes mention me.
Lie soft upon her, soil, and you, Earth, do
10   not burden her – she didn't burden you.

5.58

Tomorrow, tomorrow, Postumus, you swear°
you'll live tomorrow – but when will it get here?
Where is it? How far off? And are there maps?
Search Parthia, or Armenia, perhaps.
How old is it? – at least as old as Nestor
or Priam. What's the cost for an investor?°
Tomorrow you'll live? Today is late, I say.
The wise man started living yesterday.

5.73

You're begging me to send my books
and cannot fathom my demurs?
There's a good reason, Theodorus –
I don't want you to send me yours.

5.83

Hunt me, I'll flee you. Flee from me, I'll hunt.
Dindymus, it's my nature. To be blunt:
I don't want wanting. Not wanting's what I want.

6.19°

I'm litigating, not a matter
of mugging, poison or manslaughter –
no, my three goats are gone; I claim

my thievish neighbor is to blame.
The judge says prove it. You take the floor
with Carrhae, the Mithridatic War,°
what devious Hannibal once dared,°
the Sullas and the Mariuses°
and Muciuses, with your throat's°
full power, and no gesture spared.   10
Postumus, what about my goats?

6.60

Rome praises, loves and quotes my little verses.
I'm in all hands, all pockets and all purses.
Faces turn red, or white; jaws yawn, drop, curse –
well, that's more like it! Now *I* like my verse.

6.82

Yesterday, Rufus, a strange guy
was eyeing me with an appraising eye,
keen as a shopper or talent scout.
He stared hard, then he wagged his finger –
'You there,' he said, 'aren't you that Martial
whose wicked wisecracks everyone
who's anyone knows all about?'
I cracked a smile and jerked my head
to say that I was who he said.
'Then why's your coat so bad?' says he.   10
'Because I write bad poetry.'
Let's not repeat this anecdote:
Rufus, please send me a better coat.

7.10

Eros bends over, Linus gives head – who cares,
Olus, how they use those holes of theirs?
Matho's spent millions on the whores he's tupped –

so what? You're not the one that he'll bankrupt.
Sertorius dines till dawn – Olus, so what?
The whole night you saw logs with eyelids shut.
Lupus is deep in hock to Titus – so?
Don't lend the guy a cent, and let him owe.
What *is* your business, though? When *should* you care
10   for something? Olus, you seem unaware.
You're in debt for your toga – that's all you.
No one will lend you a red cent – that too.
Your wife is cheating on you – that's all you.
Your daughter wants her dowry now – that too.
You've got fifteen concerns I could outline,
but if it's your concern, it isn't mine.

7.39°

The endless scurrying about,
the matutinal huff and puff
to say *Buon giorno!* bright and early
to patrons arrogantly surly –
Caelius had had enough!
From now on he would fake the gout.
His methods, though, were too complete:
he daubed and bandaged his poor feet,
and limped and lumbered, stiff and sore.
10   Now – see what diligence and true
precision in deceit can do! –
he isn't faking anymore.

7.65°

Three forums, twenty winters, and your one°
lawsuit, Gargilianus, isn't done?
Poor maniac! For twenty years, you choose
to let this case drag out? Why not just lose?

7.95°

December's bristling with cold,
and yet you, Linus – you don't miss
a chance, no matter where, to hold
up all of Rome with a freezing kiss.
If you'd been slapped or flogged, what worse
revenge could you exact than this?
I wouldn't let my wife or daughter,
dear and adorable as she is,
ply me with kisses in this weather.
But you're more delicate and dainty,   10
with icy snot depending rigid
from your dog-nose, and your beard frigid –
as long and thick as the mohair coats
sheared from Cilicia's and Libya's goats.°
I'd shiver less if I had to greet
a hundred cunt-lickers in a row
or a eunuch fresh from fellatio.°
If you have any human feeling,
Linus, put off these winter smooches
till April openly approaches.   20

8.54

Cruelest of girls that were or are,
but best endowed, and fairest faced,
Catulla, I would rather far
you were less lovely, or less chaste!

8.69

Dead poets from a bygone era
are all you read, applaud, adore.
Forgive me: your applause, Vacerra,°
I'm rather far from dying for.

8.74°

From ophthalmologist to gladiator
you've done the same job, earlier and later.

9.14

This man your food and table have won over –
you think you've found a loyal friend forever?
It's sow paps, mullet, oyster, boar, not you
he likes. If I served those, he'd like me too.

9.15

On seven husbands' tombs, Chloe composed
these words: *Put here by Chloe's hand.* Case closed.

9.21

On Artemidorus and Calliodorus

Artie sold his land for a boy toy,
and Cal bought up the land but sold his boy.
Which one came out on top from the affair?
Cal's plowing here, and Artie's plowing there.

9.81

My audience thinks my lines are first-rate stuff,
but this one poet says that they're too rough.
Aulus, I don't much care. A good host looks
to please the dinner guests, and not the cooks.

10.8°

Paula wanted to marry me. I told her
no – she's too old. (But if she were older . . .)

10.14°

In plush sedans your rouged-up stooges travel;
your riders sweat abroad and kick up gravel;
your purple Baiae villas, pillowed thick,°
turn the seas yellow with their perfume slick;
with Setine wine your crystal goblets drown;°
Venus has never slept in softer down;
yet you, locked out by some conceited whore,
spend all night spraying tears on her deaf door,
racked by the ceaseless sighs in which you're stewed.
Cotta, you're bad off – why? You've got it good.   10

10.47°

Sweet Julius, let me express
my formula for happiness:
money not made but handed down;
a garden plot, a year-round flame;
no time in court, not much in town;
an easy mind, a healthy frame;
the vigor fine pursuits confer;
a frankness fair, but never rude;
a few friends of your caliber;
effortless banter, simple food;   10
evenings not drunk or sunk in worry;
committed sex, but not subdued;
sweet dreams that make the long nights hurry;
to be yourself, not wish for more,
with death not dreaded nor hoped for.

10.48°

It's the eighth hour. Isis' doors are barred;°
the shifts change for the soldiers standing guard.
This is the hour when the baths grow cold –

one hour before, the vapors seethed and boiled;
the sixth shot sparks from Nero's glut of gold.°
Now, Stella, Nepos, Flaccus, Canius
and Cerialis, join me at my house!°
My dinner couch, with its C-shape, has room
for seven, but we're six – would Lupus come?°
From the groundskeeper's wife there's mallow (which is
good for the gut) and other fresh-picked riches:
lettuce, clipped leeks, mint (for indigestion),
arugula as well, which stirs up passion.
We have rue-topped anchovies with egg slices,
and sow-teats in a tuna sauce, with spices.
That's appetizers. For the mains, we'll eat
a kid a wild wolf killed (improves the meat),°
plus the soft bits – set down your knives: no need! –
with cabbage sprouts and fava, accompanied
by ham that's three meals old now, and a whole
chicken; and after, ripe fruits when we're full,
and wine, Nomentum's best – no residue! –
which when Frontinus ran things wasn't new.°
Plus, we'll have candid speech, and friendly laughter,
and nothing to regret the morning after.
We'll talk about our favorite circus sport,
and nobody will land himself in court.°

10.63°

Although this stone is small, do not prefer
the pyramids of Egypt, traveler,
nor Mausolus's stony sepulcher.°
In Caesar's jubilees I twice passed muster;°
until the end my honor kept its luster.
Five girls, five boys to me Juno supplied;
all lived to close my eyelids when I died.
My special glory was my chaste wedlock –
I only ever touched my husband's cock.

10.80

Eros weeps, gazing on the glitz of good°
china, or boys, or costly citronwood;
he sighs and sniffs since he can't buy it all
and mosey home with the entire mall.
How many do the same, but with dry eye?
We mock his tears, but, inwardly, we cry.

10.92°

Marrius, the simple life's devoted friend,
ancient Atina's pride and glory, I commend°
to your safekeeping these twin pines that beautify
my rough Nomentan farm, and the Fauns' sacred grove°
of ilex, and the altars which my foreman's half-
skilled hand upreared for rude Silvanus and loud Jove,°
those altars lambs and kids have often stained with blood;
also Diana's temple, built on sacred earth
which, as you see, the virgin goddess shares with Mars,
her brother, in whose holy month I had my birth;°   10
the laurel stand as well, in which exquisite Flora
escaped Priapus. You, with sacrifice or scent,°
in this small plot will worship every kindly god
and say, 'No matter where it is your Martial went,
through my right hand, an absent priest, he offers you
these rites. Imagine that he's here, and don't be loth,
whatever either asks, to grant it to us both.'

11.63

You watch me bathing, Philomusus,
and want to know what my excuse is:
why the smooth boys I bathe among
are so ridiculously hung.
The *raison d'être* of this squad is:
they bugger nosy busybodies.

11.71

'Hysterical' is Leda's diagnosis.°
She needs a fuck. Her aged husband knows this.
She wrings her hands. Recovery's not worth
the cost! She weeps: just cover her with earth!
But she's so young; he isn't hearing it.
What he no longer does, he will permit.
The nurses all file out; the doctors, in.
Her legs are in the air. Strong medicine!

11.76

I owe ten thousand. Paetus wants it now,
since Bucco squandered his two hundred thou.°
Don't make me pay for someone else's sin.
You lost two hundred thousand; now lose ten.

12.10°

On Africanus

Millionaire seeks billionaire to die and leave him stuff.
Fortune gives many much, but nobody enough.

12.17

You've had this fever now for many days,
Laetinus, and you wonder why it stays.
It bathes with you and travels in your litter.
It tastes your mushrooms, oysters, boar and udder.
It tipples your Falernian and Setine,
and clinks the ice cubes in your Caecuban wine.°
Fragrant with balsam, in a red rose crown,
it lies on purple pillows, stuffed with down.
Lapped in a luxury so fine and famous,
10   why would your fever leave your life for Dama's?°

12.18°

Juvenal, while you no doubt°
are losing sleep to schlep throughout
Diana's hill, or Subura's din,°
haunting the foyers of great men
as your sticky toga flaps to fan you°
and the Caelian Hills compete to drain you,°
I, after many years in Rome,
am back again in my native home,
whose gold and iron are points of pride –
Bilbilis has me countrified.   10
Here work is nice and undemanding.
The turf I tread is savage-sounding –
Platea, Boterdus (Celtic Spain°
has names like that) but there's no strain.
I sleep so much that it's a shock,
sometimes straight through to nine o'clock;°
now I'm recouping my arrears
from thirty sleepless Roman years.
No togas here; here I can wear
whatever's draped on that broken chair.   20
I wake up to the welcome of°
a glowing hearth – an ilex grove
nearby supplies the wood – and pans
cook over it, near where the head maid stands.
Then comes the hunter, a kid that you'd
like to enjoy in a secret wood.
The foreman, with his cheeks still bare,
is almost ripe to cut his hair;°
he gives the help their food, and I
hope this is where I'll live and die!   30

12.20

Why doesn't Themison have a wife?°
Fabullus asks, discomfited.
Well, there's a sister he has instead.

12.31°

These springs, this trellis-woven vine, this shade,
this irrigation channel, this whole glade,
meadows and beds that outdo Paestum's roses,°
green herbs that January never freezes,
the fishpond where the pet eel swims and floats,
the white doves busy in the white dovecotes:
I, after thirty-five years home again,
owe all of this – my house, my small domain –
to my patroness's generosity,
10 Marcella's. If Nausicaä offered me°
the gardens governed by her father's throne,
I'd tell her, 'Thanks, but I prefer my own.'

12.34

Thirty-four years, if I recall,°
we spent together, Julius –°
some days of sweetness, some of gall,
but the good ones were more numerous;
if all the pebbles of either color
were sorted, each in its own stack,
the white heap would outweigh the black.°
Yet, if you'd numb your sorrow's strength,
and flee remorse, or find relief,
10 then keep your loved ones at arm's length –
you'll have less pleasure, and less grief.

12.42

Callistratus and Afer, Rough and Hairy,
married each other as men and maidens marry.
The bride was veiled, the wedding torches shone;
there was a proper epithalamion,
a dowry too. Say, Rome, what's up your sleeve
for this pair next? You want one to conceive?

12.60°

Sweet day, nursling of Mars's month, when I
first saw the sun god's face light up the sky,
if you, long worshiped in a Roman temple,
blush at this country altar, green and simple,
forgive me: on this day my life began,
I want to *live*, not serve as a yes-man.
Should I go pale with fear on my birthday
Sabellus might drink tepid *vin brulé*,
or strain the cloudy Caecuban, intent°
Alauda's tongue should touch no sediment, 10
or stand, and sit, and fuss, and get the door,
the whole meal through, and tend each visitor,
padding with bare feet on the ice-cold floor?
Why stomach all this willingly, and choose
such grovelings as, if ordered, I'd refuse?

12.68°

Parasite – reason I left Rome – awake
already? Go rouse someone on the make!
I'm no attorney skilled at argument;
I'm just a poet, old and indolent,
fond of a thing Rome wouldn't cut me: slack.
If I can't have it here, then I'll go back.

Afterword: What Is Lyric?

By Glenn W. Most

There is no one answer to the question 'What is lyric?', no single definition that could possibly be valid in all places and times. Different cultures
and periods have constructed very different ideas of the genre. To some
extent, these statements might be made about any cultural term. But lyric
is a particularly fascinating concept, since it has always represented a
focal point for larger cultural issues, such as emotion and language, privacy and communication, fantasy and the self. Understanding the various
ways in which it has been understood helps us to understand some of the
most complex and significant aspects of human self-understanding, in
their constancy but also in their variations over time and space. Indeed,
studying the different conceptions of the lyric throughout all the litera-
tures of the world would teach us much about the many kinds of poetry
and of the humans who engage in them. But this brief afterword for a
book of translations from ancient Greek and Latin poetry into English
must obviously limit itself instead to considering only some of the similarities and differences between two understandings of lyric, themselves
internally varied and complex: the ancient Western, and the modern one.

To start at the beginning: in ancient Greece and Rome, all lyric was
sung melodically to the accompaniment of the lyre (and sometimes of
other instruments as well), and the lyre, eventually, gave the genre its
name; in the ancient Greek language, the adjective *lyrikos*, from the
noun *lyra*, signifies anything that has to do with that instrument. This
was not what the first lyric poets would have called their work. In the
earlier stages of the Greek language, during the Archaic and Classical
periods (pp. 1–185 and 187–248), *melikos* – 'melodic', derived from the

noun *melos*, meaning the 'melody' of a bird, a musical instrument or the human voice – was the preferred term for this kind of poetry. The replacement of *melikos* by *lyrikos* coincides with the editorial work of the Alexandrian scholar-poets of the Hellenistic age, who first codified a canon of Nine Lyric Poets (see the Note on Lyric, p. xiii) and helped to turn a living sung tradition into erudite books that preserved a memory of an already distant past.

Whether lyric poetry was called *melikos* or *lyrikos*, however, it was being defined essentially by its musicality. In this regard, lyric poetry differed significantly from the verses of epic and elegiac poetry, which were performed to the accompaniment respectively of a *phorminx* or *cithara* (string instruments related to the *lyra*), or of an *aulos* (a wind instrument similar to our oboe), but which otherwise were recited in much the same way as modern poetry is. The original author of a Greek lyric poem sang it aloud for its original audience, and later performers sang it for later ones. In general, Latin poetry (pp. 365–555) is more bookish than earlier Greek poetry was – perhaps the only lyric composition of the great Roman poets that was actually performed by a singing chorus during its author's lifetime was Horace's *Centennial Hymn* (on which see the introduction to Latin Lyric, p. 372). But even in the Roman world orality continued to play an important role: poets published their works by declaiming them in public readings (people who wanted to own a copy could ask them to allow one to be made from their own text, or could purchase the potentially dodgy products of largely unregulated book factories), and readers usually read the poems aloud.

The meters of all ancient Greek and most ancient Latin verse are not based qualitatively on the opposition between stressed and unstressed syllables, as is the case in most modern European verse, nor, with rare exceptions, are they based on the number of syllables, as for example in some French and Italian verse forms. Instead, they are arranged quantitatively, on the basis of the temporal duration of syllables: the opposition between long and short vowels. All ancient verse, moreover, respects the rules of meter with a precision and strictness that go far beyond what we are accustomed to in modern verse. Within this metrical world of ancient poetry, however, ancient lyric occupies a unique place. In epic and in the spoken parts of drama, for example, every single line has an identical metrical structure, which is repeated, line after line, hundreds or even thousands of times; a few syllables in each line can be indifferently long or short, and some substitutions are permitted, but in general it is astounding how little the metrical scheme varies from one line to the next. The same applies, too, with slight differences, to elegiac couplets and to the trochaic and iambic verse of Archilochus (pp. 5–15) and his Greek and Latin followers. In ancient lyric, by contrast, groups of lines, usually varying in meter – and shorter in length and fewer in number than in epic and the spoken parts of drama – are most often articulated into stanzas or strophes which can be repeated many times. Within lyric verse, there is then a further fundamental distinction, between monodic lyric (sung by a single person) and choral lyric (sung and danced by a chorus): monody usually repeats the same strophic form without variation, however many times, while choral lyric often follows what is called a 'triadic' structure, repeating the first strophe unchanged before adding a third stanza, metrically related but quite different from the first two. This triad of strophe–antistrophe–epode then becomes that choral lyric's large-scale unit of repetition. (For more on the metrical intricacies of classical lyric verse, see the *Note on Meters*, pp. xxvii–xliii.)

The musical accompaniment for ancient poetry was lost in the course of antiquity and is only reflected faintly by such metrical features. That music, however, was merely one especially noticeable aspect of the larger performative context in which ancient lyric had its place. Particularly in the earlier phases of antiquity, most ancients encountered lyric poetry not by reading it on their own in the pages of a book but by hearing it together with other people in oral performance; even when they did read lyric poems, as became more common after the Classical period, the traditional dominance of orality in ancient culture and the cultural privilege accorded to situations of performance meant that the experience of reading was generally felt to be secondary and inferior to that of listening. The civic, religious and social calendars of the ancient world were full of established occasions where the singing of lyric poems formed an essential component. Choral lyrics were performed at religious rituals by choruses that not only sang together but also danced together while they were singing – dithyrambs in honor of Dionysus, paeans for Apollo, hymns for other gods, *partheneia* by choruses of young maidens, tragic and comic choral odes as an essential part of the dramas offered to Dionysus at the Great Dionysia in Athens and at other festivals, and so forth. But choral lyric also belonged to numerous formal civic and social occasions, which might well have had religious overtones but were basically secular in nature: for example, encomia to praise benefactors, epinician odes to celebrate their athletic victories, *epithalamia* to accompany their weddings and threnodies for their funerals. In all these cases, lyric was a public phenomenon, shared by listeners and performers, financed by institutions or patrons.

This public dimension was, in fact, true even in the case of those forms of lyric that strike us modern readers as being more private in nature, especially such monodies as those of Anacreon (pp. 100–108), Sappho (pp. 38–54) and other poets. The typical situation for the performance of ancient monodic lyric, as well as of many kinds of elegies, was the symposium, a drinking party in which upper-class men (or, on the island of Lesbos, upper-class women) got together to celebrate their status, attainments and capacities. Often the capacities in question involved alcoholic tolerance and sexual prowess. But often, too, they involved the ability to perform songs, either new ones that had been composed for the occasion or old ones that were well known and were appropriate to the circumstances. If Alcaeus (pp. 55–67) sings frequently about getting drunk or Anacreon about falling in love, this is not necessarily because Alcaeus happened to be particularly bibulous or Anacreon uncontrollably oversexed, but because experiencing and discussing intoxication and sex were two of the standard activities at ancient symposia. Even if the symposium was private in the sense that it took place at a private house where not everyone was admitted, the privacy involved was not that of a single individual on his or her own, withdrawn from society at large and from groups of other people, but that of a small circle of friends which was set in opposition to other such groups within the city – that is, it was not so much private in our sense as rather a restricted form of public. And the emotions and experiences that this lyric conveyed were shared social phenomena, not private or individual ones.

Christopher Childers's selection of ancient Greek and Latin lyric is generously capacious – though it nonetheless omits many poetic texts that in antiquity would have been considered lyric. There is nothing remarkable in such omissions: for example, evident reasons of space dictate that Childers presents very few of the many extant complete lyric poems of Pindar and Bacchylides (pp. 134–64 and 165–85), as well as only a representative selection of the works of the Hellenistic and later Greek epigrammatists (pp. 299–356) and of the shorter poems of the Latin poets; and considerations of intelligibility require that he leave out a large number of obscure fragments, especially of Greek poetry, which only survive, often in hopelessly corrupted texts, in the form of tiny citations or papyrus scraps.

More noteworthy is Childers's decision to include under the title *The Penguin Book of Greek and Latin Lyric Verse* a large number of poems which, for ancient readers, belonged not to lyric poetry but to other poetic genres. The surviving poems of such Greek poets as Archilochus and Semonides of Amorgos (pp. 16–20), like the *Epodes* of Horace (pp. 456–61), are mostly not lyrics but iambics or trochaics; those of Callinus (p. 21), Tyrtaeus (pp. 22–6), Mimnermus (pp. 27–30), Solon (pp. 68–75) and Theognis (pp. 76–85), like the elegies of Propertius (pp. 421–45), Tibullus (pp. 411–20), Sulpicia (pp. 446–52) and Ovid (pp. 492–526), as well as the Greek and Roman epigrams, are written not in what ancient readers would have identified as lyric meters but in elegiac couplets; the *Idylls* of Theocritus (pp. 283–98) and the *Eclogues* of Virgil (pp. 400–410) belong not to lyric but to pastoral poetry, which is written in the same dactylic hexameters as epic and its subgenre didactic poetry used. Taken strictly, the only poems included in this anthology that would have been recognized in antiquity as belonging to the genre of lyric poetry are those by Alcman (pp. 31–7), Sappho, Alcaeus, Stesichorus (pp. 89–95), Ibycus (pp. 96–9), Anacreon, Simonides (121–7), Pindar, Bacchylides, Corinna (pp. 199–203), Timotheus (pp. 204–12) and a few others (as well as, among the Latin poets, Horace's *Odes*, pp. 462–91, and Catullus' poems in lyric meters, pp. 376–87).

But does this really matter, or is it merely a trivial academic question of obsolete terminology? Should anyone care besides professors? The answer is: yes, and no.

Childers's selection, which transports into the modern anglophone world a broad range of Greek and Latin poetic productions in consistently brilliant and accurate translations, corresponds to a few criteria that are in line, not with the ancient, but with an expansive twenty-first-century understanding of the lyric. The first is that, without any exceptions, the poetic texts translated here are all quite short: aside from the fragmentary texts, which of course are shorter (sometimes much shorter) than the whole compositions of which they once formed part, very few of these poems are much longer than about forty lines, many of them are less than half that length, and even the longest of them can easily be read in a single sitting. More than extended ruminations, they are for the most part flashes of brilliance, gleaming shards shining to us singly from out of the night of antiquity. Second, these verses tend very strongly not only to be spoken by an explicit first person 'I' or 'we' but also to take as their subject matter the experiences and views of that speaker. In this sense, they are mostly autobiographical – whether authentically or, most often, fictitiously so. And third, there is an equally strong tendency for them to focus not so much on the speakers' rational reflections or ethical pronouncements (though these are certainly often present) as on their emotions and passions – above all, love, desire, hatred, contempt, admiration, scorn. We have the impression of encountering here the vicissitudes of a human soul laid bare, which have been transposed into striking language so that they can be shared and become memorable for a wider community – and ultimately, though of course unforeseeably, even for us moderns.

If we moderns can easily understand these criteria, that is because they correspond so exactly to our own general experience of poetry. In English, too, 'lyric' is ultimately derived etymologically from the lyre; but in English, with the exception of the recent use of the plural form 'lyrics' to refer to the words of a popular song, that musical aspect lives on, if at all, only as a kind of etiolated semantic ghost, an ancient poetic aspiration that has by now become, at best, rather quaint. The mode of performance is a fundamental difference between ancient and modern lyric poetry. Almost always, modern poetry is declaimed or recited in a heightened form of ordinary speech, but it is not performed musically: modern poets may claim that they sing, but in fact they mostly do so only in the shower.

Even in an age of poetry slams and of video clips on social media and streaming platforms, it is a safe bet that most of the people who are now reading this book hear verse being recited aloud far less frequently than the ancients did. Our specific mode of experiencing poems thus forms part of our larger experience of reading in general: almost always we read as individuals, silently, in moments of relaxation and with-drawal. We read sitting by a lamp in a comfortable armchair near the radiator, or stretched out on a blanket at the beach, or huddled on a seat in a subway, all alone – or if we're in the company of others, then they are people whose presence does not interfere intolerably with our pleas-ure. We engage in reading poems or other literary texts primarily as a private exercise in enjoyment and self-cultivation, and only secondarily, if at all, in order to acquire membership in the real or imagined commu-nity of other readers of the same kind of literature. The size and shape of the book we read, its external and internal accompanying texts, its pagination and typography and even its paper quality – these all func-tion as guides to help prepare us to understand what kind of text it is that we are dealing with.

Printed as the poems in this volume are, between the covers of a single book, then, it is easy for us to see that all these short, subjective texts have a lot in common with one another. Yet, for ancient readers, they belonged to very different genres – as I have said, well beyond what the ancients understood by 'lyric'; each had its own history, form(s) and social context, and it was this whole larger context, not the manner of the poems' being set down on papyrus, that both shaped their purpose and guided the listener toward a proper understanding. Iambus used the spoken meter, close to the rhythms of ordinary speech, that later became the most common choice for the recited parts of Attic comedies and tragedies and retained a lively, colloquial tone: it could be polemical, and was often abusive toward people who did not share the speaker's values. Elegy, which alternated the dactylic hexameters of epic poetry with a shorter line that was always divided in the middle and was often end-stopped, was used to encourage feelings of solidarity within the closed male groups of the symposium or the battle contin-gent; it was often moralizing and almost never profane. It was most often performed in symposia – as was lyric poetry. Epigrams employed the same meter as elegy but tended to be much shorter. They began as inscriptions on monuments, usually funerary or memorial, and grad-ually developed into a written form that had no relation any longer to stones but could be gathered into anthologies of single poets or groups of poets. These epigrams, in Greek and Latin, could treat of the most diverse subjects – erotic, satirical, sepulchral – and could range from the sublime to the pornographic. Where Latin love elegy comes from, meanwhile, is a question that scholars have never succeeded in answering definitively. It shares the meter of Greek elegy but is far more subjective and passionate than almost anything that has been found in Greek.

Of the three modern criteria for lyric cited earlier, the exclusion of long poetic texts distinguishes lyric above all from epic and its subgenre, didactic poetry, while the restriction to the poet's putative first-person voice opposes lyric not only to epic and didactic (which tell stories about gods, heroes and cosmogony, but only marginally, if ever, about the poet himself), but also to drama (in which the author retires explicitly behind the play's speaking characters). That is why such well-known works as the *Georgics* of Virgil, the *Metamorphoses* of Ovid and the *Satires* of Horace are not translated here, while other, shorter poems of these same authors are.

This generic triad of lyric–epic–drama is a familiar foundational element, within the Western poetic tradition, of much post-Renaissance literary theorization. Ultimately, its appearance of self-evidence may be due to the fact that it can be interpreted as an expression of the three grammatical persons: a first-person 'I' speaks in lyric; a second-person 'you' and a first-person 'I' discourse with one another in drama; and a third-person 'he, she, it' is the subject of the actions and events that epic recounts. This idea seems so simple that it is not surprising that various forms of this generic tripartition have become as widespread in modern times as they have; and yet surprisingly little, if anything, corresponds to it among ancient Greek and Latin poetic theories. A few phrases in Plato and Aristotle might be thought to point vaguely in this general direction; but it was not until the Romantic period, when Goethe (partially anticipated by George Puttenham's *The Arte of English Poesie* of 1589 and by a few other early modern theoreticians) famously defined these three genres as the three 'natural forms of poetry', that this triad became canonical for modern Western poetic theory.

It is, in fact, quite easy to see why this happened then, and not much earlier. Goethe's dictum establishes these three modes as being equivalent, virtually fungible forms of poetic production and reception: poets are now free to choose in which of them to engage their creative energies, depending on their own inclinations and capacities (Goethe chose all three); readers are free to purchase from the bookseller whichever mode or modes they prefer to make the object of their leisure hours, depending on their own tastes and whims. The reader becomes the author's counterpart, equal in power and authority, in a textual relationship mediated by the institutions of the literary marketplace, directed essentially to the economic processes of production and consumption, and concretized above all in the act of individual reading.

But between the eighteenth and nineteenth centuries, in the time of Goethe, these new institutions were only just starting to come into full force and it is only since then that they have come to dominate our world in the ways we know so well. In the centuries that intervened between the fall of the Roman Empire and Goethe's day, a great deal of poetry had been the remunerated work of professional craftsmen who were sponsored by courts to compose verse in order to celebrate suitably the nobility's achievements or to entertain them and their guests, and hence authors were paid not by publishers, literary agents and readers, but by their patrons. The institutions of pre-modern European courtly culture often intervened between poet and reader so that there was a much less immediate relationship between them – both in terms of the primarily transactional one of producer and (paying) consumer, and also in the degree to which the 'I' of the poet merely expressed conventional archetypes and attitudes rather than truly subjective emotions and experiences that chimed with the reader's own most intimate and individual feelings. As a result, it was hard to conceive of lyric poetry as being quite on the same level as drama or epic; and even the notion of lyric poetry itself was fragmented into all the many conceptually distinct ceremonial occasions at which such poems were performed – weddings and funerals, birthdays and commemorations, arrivals and departures, banquets and victories, and so forth. It was only with the decline of pre-modern courtly culture and the rise of the modern bourgeois world in the West that the ceremonial occasions vanished together with the noble courts on which they had been dependent, and the poets had to create their own occasions, ones henceforth, for better and for worse, both untrammeled by and deprived of the formal institutions that had previously served as their mediators, in order to compose poems that would now have to be able to find and reach readers more directly.

To be sure, it is obvious that there were many important differences between the culture and society of ancient Greece and Rome and those of pre-modern Europe. Greece and Rome were slave societies in which only a minority of the inhabitants had civil and political rights; pagan polytheism was far less doctrinaire and far more tolerant of local heterogeneities than Christianity usually was; and the ancient reading public, compared to the dramatic dissemination of reading that resulted from the fifteenth-century invention of the printing press, was minuscule. But nonetheless the experience and the conceptualization of lyric poetry in both periods were far more similar to each other than either of them was to those in the modern West. All this has been transformed by the processes that have helped give rise to the contemporary Western world: the growth of secularization, democratization and the opportunities for privacy and private life; the discoveries and advances in knowledge that have so enhanced our understanding of the ancient past. Now, the surviving examples of this older form of lyric have come to be reinterpreted in ways quite different from those of the times in which they were conceived and composed and from the intervening centuries in which much was preserved but so much was allowed to perish. It is one of the quirks of history that these remnants have been able so to capture the imagination, and so to flourish anew, only because of that thoroughgoing reinterpretation.

Abbreviations

Aen.	*Aeneid*
Aet.	*Aetia* (pp. 258–61)
Alc.	Alcaeus (pp. 55–67)
Alc. Mess.	Alcaeus of Messene (pp. 317–18)
Alcm.	Alcman (pp. 31–7)
Am.	*Amores* (pp. 494–511)
Anac.	Anacreon (pp. 100–108)
Anon.	Anonymous Classical Lyric (pp. 234–41)
Anon. Mel.	Anonymous Poets from the *Garland of Meleager* (323–6)
Ant. Si.	Antipater of Sidon (pp. 320–23)
Ant. Thess.	Antipater of Thessalonica (pp. 344–6)
AP	*Anthologia Palatina, Palatine Anthology*
Ar.	Archilochus (pp. 5–15)
Argent.	Marcus Argentarius (pp. 347–50)
Arist.	Aristonous of Corinth (pp. 226–8)
Ascl.	Asclepiades (pp. 303–6)
Ath.	Athenaeus
Bacch.	Bacchylides (pp. 165–85)
Call.	Callimachus (pp. 255–81)
Cat.	Catullus (pp. 373–97)
Cor.	Corinna (pp. 199–203)
Crin.	Crinagoras (pp. 339–43)
Deip.	*Deipnosophistae, Scholars at Dinner*
Dios.	Dioscorides (pp. 313–15)
Dith.	*Dithyrambs* (pp. 158–60)
Ecl.	*Eclogues* (pp. 400–410)

El.	*Elegies* (pp. 128–9)
Ep.	*Epigrams* (pp. 129–33, 276–81)
Epist.	*Epistulae, Epistles*
Epod.	*Epodes* (pp. 456–61)
Ex Pont.	*Epistulae ex Ponto, Letters from Pontus* (pp. 521–6)
Geo.	*Georgics*
Hdt.	Herodotus
Hes.	Hesiod
HHes.	*Hymn to Hestia* (pp. 226–7)
Hipp.	Hipponax (pp. 114–19)
Hist.	*Histories*
Hom.	Homer
Hor.	Horace (pp. 453–91)
Hy.	*Hymns* (pp. 269–76)
Ia.	*Iambi* (pp. 261–8)
Iby.	Ibycus (pp. 96–9)
Id.	*Idylls* (pp. 283–98)
Il.	*Iliad*
Leo. Tar.	Leonidas of Tarentum (pp. 306–10)
Mart.	Martial (pp. 533–55)
Mel.	Meleager (pp. 326–32)
Met.	*Metamorphoses*
Mimn.	Mimnermus (pp. 27–30)
Nos.	Nossis (pp. 310–11)
Od.	*Odyssey*
Ol.	*Olympian Odes* (pp. 135–46)
Ov.	Ovid (pp. 492–526)
P. Oxy.	Oxyrhynchus Papyrus
Pae.	*Paeans* (pp. 156–8)
PaeAp.	*Paean to Apollo* (pp. 227–8)
PaeDi.	*Paean to Dionysus* (pp. 229–32)
Phil.	Philodemus (pp. 333–9)
Phil. Scar.	Philodamus of Scarphea (pp. 229–32)
Philox.	Philoxenus (pp. 215–20)
Pi.	Pindar (pp. 134–64)
Pos.	Posidippus of Pella (p. 312)

Prop.	Propertius (pp. 421–45)
Py.	*Pythian Odes* (pp. 146–54)
Sap.	Sappho (pp. 38–54)
Silv.	*Silvae* (pp. 528–32)
Sim.	Simonides (pp. 120–33)
Sol.	Solon (pp. 68–75)
Stat.	Statius (pp. 527–32)
Stes.	Stesichorus (pp. 89–95)
Sulp.	Sulpicia (pp. 446–52)
Th.	*Theogony*
Theoc.	Theocritus (pp. 282–98)
Theog.	Theognis (pp. 76–85)
Tib.	Tibullus (pp. 411–20)
Tim.	Timotheus (pp. 204–12)
Tri.	*Tristia* (pp. 512–20)
Tyr.	Tyrtaeus (pp. 22–6)
Vi.	Virgil (pp. 398–410)
W&D	*Works and Days*
Xen.	Xenophanes (pp. 109–13)

Notes

Note on Lyric

xiii. *'the voice of the poet talking to himself'*: T. S. Eliot, 'The Three Voices of Poetry', p. 4.

xiv. *'the form of writing closest to . . .'*: Gail McConnell, 'On Lyric', *The Stinging Fly* 46 (2022), p. 18, referring to Denise Riley, ' "A Voice without a Mouth": Inner Speech', *Qui Parle* 14:2 (2004), pp. 57–104, who in turn follows Beckett (*Texts for Nothing* 13).

THE ARCHAIC PERIOD

4. *Introduction. a man named Solon . . . 'so I can learn it and die'*: Aelian, fr. 187, quoted in Stobaeus, *Extracts* 3.29.58.

Archilochus

5. *Poet Introduction. we are told by a fifth-century source . . .* : Critias, quoted in Aelian's *Various Histories* 10.13.

6. 2. *Doru* in this poem could mean 'ship' or 'spear'; the latter interpretation would give us instead:

> My spear wins me bread, my spear wins me wine,
> and, drinking it, on my spear I recline.

Those who prefer 'ship' often connect this poem with Ar. 4 (p. 6); on the other hand, the author of Scolia 909 (p. 248) seems clearly to have understood it as 'spear'.

3. This poem may refer either to the long-haired Abantes of Hom. *Il.* 2, ll. 536 and 542–4, or to the Lelantine War (*c.*710–650 BCE), fought on the large island of Euboea between the cities of Chalcis and Eretria, in which projectile weapons were reportedly banned. See also Folk Songs 873 (p. 244) and n.

5. While on Thasos, Archilochus joined in the wars with Thrace, from which this poem presumably derives. Ever the iconoclast, here he thumbs his nose at the Greek military imperative, taken most seriously at Sparta, to come back 'with your shield or on it' (Plutarch, *Sayings of Spartan Women* 241f; cf. Dios. 30 and 32, p. 315); the more typical attitude is shown by Plutarch's story (*Customs of the Spartans* 34) that the Spartans drove Archilochus out of their city because he chose flight over fight. This poem either spawned or participated in a mini-genre of poets losing shields; Anacreon (Anac. 381b, p. 105) and Alcaeus (pp. 55–67) composed examples, mostly lost, as did Horace (*Odes* 2.7, p. 472).

7.   11. Plutarch (*How to Study Poetry* 33a–b) connects this couplet to Archilochus' grief over the death of his brother-in-law at sea.

13. l. 2. *Pericles*: A friend of Archilochus, rather than the fifth-century Athenian politician.

The Achaeans at Mysia. Found at *P. Oxy.* 4708 fr. 1, this poem was first published in 2005 and is the earliest mid-length mythological narrative in elegiac couplets (see *Note on Meters*, p. xxxi) that we have. The story comes from one of the poems of the Epic Cycle (see Call. *Ep.* 2, l. 1, p. 276, and n.), the *Cypria*, most commonly attributed to 'Stasinus': the Achaeans get lost on their way to Troy and mistakenly attack Mysia to the north, where they are beaten back by the hero Telephus. Archilochus may intend pointed reference to contemporary events on Paros – perhaps some setback in the (eventually successful) colonization of Thasos. That may be why he leaves out the rest: in the *Cypria*, Telephus is tripped by Dionysus and wounded by Achilles; to cure his wound, he needs rust from Achilles' spear, in exchange for which he leads the Greeks to Troy. Archilochus wants to mock Paros' present ignominy, not hint at future success.

l. 7. *displaced Arcadian*: Telephus was the son of Heracles and Auge, daughter of Aleus, the king of Tegea in Arcadia. An oracle had predicted that Auge's child would kill Aleus' sons, so the king cast them out. She and Telephus ended up in Mysia, Auge marrying the Mysian king Teuthras, who adopted Telephus and made him king of Mysia. Archilochus may emphasize Telephus' Arcadian origins to connect to those of Paros, whose eponymous colonizer was supposed to be the son of the Arcadian Parrhasius.

l. 9. *sweet-flowing Caicus*: A river in northern Turkey (the modern Bakırçay). In the *Iliad* (Bk. 21), Achilles chokes the Scamander with Trojan corpses.

l. 17. *Teuthras' lovely town*: Teuthrantia.

8.   *19. l. 1. Gyges*: The fabulously wealthy king of Lydia in western Turkey, roughly contemporary with Archilochus. This poem is imitated at *Anacreontea* 8 (p. 359).

21+22. The two fragments are quoted in different places but seem to go together. The island is probably Thasos; Archilochus' attitude is not unlike Hesiod's, a second-generation immigrant to Boeotia. Hesiod says of his father (*W&D*, ll. 638–41, trans. Stallings):

> He settled down
> Near Helicon, in Askra, wretched town,
> Bad in winter, harsh in summer, not
> Ever pleasant.

l. 4. *Siris*: Either in southern Italy on the Gulf of Tarentum (modern Taranto), or flowing into the Propontis (the Sea of Marmara) at Cius (modern Gemlik).

30+31. As with the previous fragment(s), these three lines were quoted by two different authors but are joined together by many editors. (The break in the middle of the second line signals the place of the join.)

9.   *48. l. 3. Glaucus*: A friend of Archilochus, whose cenotaph, found on Thasos, dates to the seventh century: 'I am the stone of Leptines' son, Glaucus; Brentes' sons erected me.' He is also addressed in Ar. 105 and 131 (pp. 9 and 12).

105. Our source for these lines tells us that Archilochus, 'embroiled in Thracian troubles, likens the war to a storm at sea'. If so, it is the earliest use of the 'ship of state' metaphor popular in later Greek literature, typically associated with Alcaeus (cf. Alc. 6, p. 56, and 208, p. 62).

l. 2. *Gyrae's peaks*: Either Mount Kyknias on Tenos (north of Paros), or the mythical rocks where the Lesser Ajax met his doom (Hom. *Od.* 4, ll. 500–511).

115. The couplet's end is corrupt in Greek. Leophilus is unknown.

10.   *116*. Some consider the figs an obscene reference to the island's prostitutes, though it may suggest its poverty instead.

119. In the Greek, this fragment's subject could be either 'he' or 'I'.

120+121. These two fragments, mentioned separately by Athenaeus, are combined for ease of presentation.

l. 2. *the dithyramb*: A choral lyric genre in honor of Dionysus, probably characterized more by musical form and performance style than content, though in Alexandria long mythical narrative was thought to be a distinguishing characteristic. Early on, dithyrambs may have been performed in procession, but by the end of the Archaic period if not before choral performance took on a circular form, such that later authors sometimes call it the 'circle dance'. It is believed to have been a precursor to the tragic chorus. Likely examples (some likelier than others) may be found at Sim. 543 (p. 124), Pi. *Dith*. 2 and 4 (pp. 158 and 160), Bacch. 19 (p. 183), Ion 745 (p. 197) and Anon. 939 (p. 239). See also n. on Pi. *Dith*. 2 (p. 158).

l. 3. *Lesbian paean*: The paean, both a cry of thanksgiving (*iē, iē Paian!*) and a poetic genre in honor of Apollo (and related deities, like Asclepius), may have originated on Lesbos; it is also associated with warfare and prayers to be spared from harm. It was typically performed by boys. As a cult title of Apollo in his role of Healer, the name *Paean* goes back to the Mycenaean deity Paiawon. In this collection, *Paean* appears as an epithet at Sap. 44, 1.25 (p. 45), Sol. 13, l. 57 (p. 72), Tim. 791, ll. 203–7 (p. 210), Arist. *PaeAp*. (p. 227) and Anon. 934 (p. 236, where it refers to Asclepius); as a poetic/musical genre at Theog. l. 779 (p. 84), Pi. *Pae*. 6 and 9 (pp. 156 and 157), Bacch. 17 and fr. 4 (pp. 178 and 184), Ariphron 813 (p. 213) and Aristotle 842 (p. 224); and as both at Call. *Hy*. 2 (p. 269). For further discussion of the genre, including its differentiation from the dithyramb (the two could be confused: cf. Bacch. 17), see nn. on the paeans of Pindar (pp. 134–64), Bacchylides (pp. 165–85) and Aristotle (pp. 223–5).

122. Aristotle tells us (*Rhetoric* 1418b28) that Archilochus here represents a father speaking about his daughter – perhaps Lycambes about Neobule (see *Poet Intro*, p. 5). The eclipse referred to is probably that of 648 BCE, though there are also likely candidates in 660, 689 and 711. For the subgenre of eclipse poetry, see Pi. *Pae*. 9 (p. 157) and n.; for the motif of the *adynaton* (catalogue of impossibilities) employed in ll. 5–9, see Prop. 2.1, ll. 67–72 (p. 429) and n.

11.   124. *To Pericles*: See Ar. 13, l. 2 (p. 7) and n.

l. 1. *in the true Myconian style*: Athenaeus tells us (*Deip*. 1.7f–8b) that the inhabitants of Myconus (now Mykonos) 'had a bad name for stinginess and greed because of their poverty and because they lived on a wretched island'; the ancients lacked our enthusiasm for white sand beaches.

12.   *131.* l. *1. Glaucus*: Friend of Archilochus. See Ar. 48, l. 3 (p. 9) and n.

168. According to Athenaeus (*Deip.* 10.415d), somewhere in his poetry Archilochus mocks one Charilaus, son of Erasmon ('Joy of the People, son of Darling', here 'Sunshine, Sweetheart's son'), for his gluttony. Athenaeus' notice is not connected with this fragment, however, which is quoted separately by an author on meters.

191. Like Mimn. 5 (p. 29), a precursor to the influential 'symptomography' in Sap. 31 (p. 44).

13.   *196a, The Cologne Papyrus.* First published in 1974, this papyrus (which also gave us Ar. 188, p. 12, above) is now generally accepted as containing the work of Archilochus. It substantially increased our knowledge of Archaic iambus, suggesting that Archilochus' approach to character assassination may be subtler and more insidious than previously thought. The papyrus picks up somewhere in the middle of the story: Archilochus has approached a girl, perhaps the sister of Neobule (see *Poet Intro*, p. 5), and propositioned her. She responds negatively, recommending abstinence, most likely until marriage (ll. 1–2), or offering another girl (ll. 3–8), probably Neobule. Archilochus assures her that they need not perform 'the sacred act' (l. 15), probably sex, though sometimes thought to refer to marriage. The poem's unusual climax has given rise to an amusing scholarly literature: does the poet keep his word and refrain from penetration, either pleasuring himself or indulging in intercrural intercourse, or has he lied to the girl, and performed 'the sacred act' despite his promise? (A literal rendering of the Greek gives us only 'I expended my white force'.) In any case, if the girl is indeed the sister of Neobule, the narrative, though hardly vituperative in tone, and almost tender, may slander Lycambes anyway, by impugning the virtue of his younger daughter.

14.   l. 40. *like the proverbial bitch*: This tercet alludes to the proverb, 'A hasty bitch bears blind pups.'

15.   *201.* The philosopher Isaiah Berlin wrote a famous essay based on this fragment, in which he divides writers and thinkers into either 'hedgehogs' or 'foxes'. He doesn't say which he considers Archilochus to be.

212. l. *2. between the waves and wind*: Winter gales in the Mediterranean blew up and shifted quickly, creating impossible cross-currents; the impact this fact of life had on the consciousness of classical antiquity can be charted according to its prominence as a poetic topos: cf., e.g., Alc.

208 (p. 62); Sol. 13, l. 45 (p. 72); Pi. *Ol.* 7, l. 170 (p. 145), *Ol.* 12, ll. 7–9 (p. 145), *Py.* 3, ll. 153–4 (p. 151), and fr. 33d, ll. 2–3 (p. 156); Tim. 791, ll. 60–61 (p. 207); Hermolochus 846 (p. 233); Leo. Tar. 85, ll. 3–4 (p. 309); Hor. *Odes* 1.1, l. 15 (p. 462), 1.3, ll. 12–16 (p. 463), 1.5, ll. 10–11 (p. 465) and 1.9, l. 10 (p. 467); Ov. *Am.* 1.9, l. 15 (p. 495), *Am.* 2.10, ll. 9–10 (p. 504) and *Tri.* 1.4 (p. 512); Stat. *Silv.* 4.5, l. 8 (p. 530).

Semonides of Amorgos

16.   *Poet Introduction. that's what we are told eight centuries later*: Lucian of Samosata, *Pseudologistes* 2.

      1. This poem shows that iambics could be used in the same ways and on the same themes as elegiacs; compare Sol. 13 (p. 71), for similar reflections on the vicissitudes of human life.

17.   7. Our longest surviving fragment of Archaic iambus, perhaps composed for a wedding banquet. The poem expresses attitudes recognizable from Hesiod (compare *Th.*, ll. 570–612, and *W&D*, ll. 53–105), and is in debt to the genre of the beast fable, which also influenced Archilochus (see Ar. 201, p. 15; also Ar. 172–81 and 185, not included here). There is disagreement over whether this poem is complete.

      l. 12. *a snappish bitch*: Greeks were less enamored than we are of dogs, which they considered paragons of shamelessness.

18.   l. 48. *and takes on lovers like she takes in food*: 'The ass seems to have owed the great reputation for lubricity which it enjoyed in ancient times to the large penis of the male.' Hugh Lloyd-Jones, *Females of the Species: Semonides on Women*, p. 76.

      l. 50. *One's from a weasel*: Weasels were common domestic mouse-killers up to the fifth century CE. They were 'proverbial for darting about, for lasciviousness, for stealing and for stinking' (Lloyd-Jones, *Females of the Species*, p. 76).

19.   ll. 59–60. *She won't touch a millstone . . .* : The millstone and sieve were for grinding and for sifting and draining corn. A dung-fork was used to clean out the privy.

      l. 71. *One's from a monkey*: The monkey was proverbial for ugliness.

      l. 83. *One's from a bee*: As among us, bees were proverbial for busyness and prudence (*sophrosyne*). Some believe the poem's coda belies the existence of the bee-woman: that, in Semonides' view, she is only a mirage.

20.   l. 119. *a woman*: Helen.

Callinus

21.   *1*. The historical occasion for this exhortation is unknown, but it was clearly part of the general upheaval that also affected Mimnermus' Smyrna (cf. Mimn. 14, p. 30, and n.). In the seventh century BCE, the Cimmerians came down from around the eastern Black Sea and menaced the west coast of Asia Minor. In 652, they sacked Sardis, capital of Lydia, and killed Gyges, its king; a few years later, *c.*645, we are told that a Cimmerian tribe, the Trerians, attacked again, accompanied by Lycians, and took all of Sardis but the citadel; they also destroyed the Ionian city of Magnesia. It is probably in response to one of these Cimmerian threats that Callinus' poem was composed.

l. 1. *lie there*: It is likely that Callinus' poem was performed not on the battlefield but rather in the symposium, as usual for Archaic elegy.

ll. 4–5. Probably at least three lines are missing in this gap.

Tyrtaeus

22.   *Poet Introduction. 'good for enflaming the hearts of young warriors'*: Plutarch, *On the Sagacity of Animals* 1.

10. ll. 1–2. *It's beautiful* . . . : These lines are clearly in the background of Horace's famous *dulce et decorum est*. See Hor. *Odes* 3.2, l. 13 (p. 480).

23.   *11*. l. 1. *sons of unconquered Heracles*: One of the three Dorian tribes (the Spartans were Dorians) claimed descent from Heracles' son Hyllus, as did both of the Spartan royal lines, the Agiads and Eurypontids.

25.   *12*. In this poem, Tyrtaeus redefines the Homeric notion of *arete* (excellence), which for Homer could exist in any activity (e.g., wrestling, running, oratory, etc.). For Tyrtaeus it means one thing and one thing only: steadfastness in battle.

l. 4. *Thracian Boreas*: See n. on Ant. Si. 26, l. 2 (p. 322).

l. 5. *Adrastus' tongue drips with less honey*: Adrastus was a king of Argos, and the only member of the Seven Against Thebes who survived the first attack; perhaps his reputation for eloquence derives from his success in persuading the Epigones to attack Thebes after the failure of the original mission. See Pi. *Py*. 8, ll. 48–55 (p. 153), and n. on l. 39 *ad loc*.

l. 6. *Cinyras and Midas*: Kings respectively of Cyprus and Phrygia. Cinyras is mentioned also by Pindar as being fabulously wealthy (*Nemean* 8,

l. 18), while Midas famously wished for and received the ability to turn everything he touched into gold (Ov. *Met.* 11, ll. 100–145).

l. 7. *Tithonus*: A prince of Troy, loved by the goddess Eos (Dawn). His sad story, in which his goddess lover manages to obtain immortality for him but not eternal youth, so that he withers away (in some versions) into a grasshopper or cicada, is first told in the *Homeric Hymn to Aphrodite*. See also Mimn. 4 (p. 29), Sap. 58a (p. 47), Call. *Ia.* 4, l. 51 (p. 265), Ant. Thess. 7 (p. 345) and Ov. *Am.* 3.7, ll. 43–4 (p. 508) – not to mention Alice Oswald's long poem 'Tithonus' (in *Falling Awake*), and Tennyson's dramatic monologue of the same name.

l. 8. *Tantalus' son*: Pelops. See Pi. *Ol.* 1 (p. 135).

Mimnermus

28.   1. l. 1. *What life, what pleasure* . . . : The question boldly adapts the conventional language of bereavement ('What life is left to me now?') to refer to erotic pleasure.

2. l. 1. *We are like leaves*: Mimnermus may be thinking of Homer (*Il.* 6, l. 146): 'Like leaves that sprout in succession, the men of each new generation.' For further Archaic references to these famous lines of Homer, which influenced Virgil (*Aen.* 6, ll. 309–10) and, through Virgil, Dante (*Inferno* 3, ll. 112–17), see also Sim. *Ep.* 19+20, ll. 1–2 (p. 129) and n., and Bacch. 5, ll. 80–81 (p. 173).

l. 3. *arm's length*: One cubit, which stretched from the elbow to the tip of the middle finger, about 1½ feet; the metaphor here is unprecedented in Greek literature, though cf. Psalm 39:5, 'Behold, thou hast made my days as an handbreadth.'

29.   4. l. 1. *Zeus gave Tithonus an everlasting curse*: See n. on Tyr. 12, l. 7 (p. 25).

5. ll. 1–3. Many scholars combine these lines, found in Theog. ll. 1017–19, with ll. 4–8, which securely belong to Mimnermus. To ll. 1–3, compare Ar. 191 (p. 12) and Sap. 31 (p. 44).

l. 5. *above your head*: Like the rock of Tantalus in Pi. *Ol.* 1, ll. 71–4 (pp. 137–8).

6. Solon (pp. 68–75) takes issue with this sentiment in his fr. 20 (not included here).

11+11a. These two fragments (ll. 1–4, 5–7) come from the same poem, but are not consecutive. The story of Jason and the Argonauts was of great antiquity.

30.   12. Athenaeus (*Deip.* 11.469–70) cites a number of accounts of the sun's voyage in his cup, including those of Stesichorus (*Geryon* 8a, p. 90), Aeschylus and Antimachus (for whom, see further n. on Call. *Hy.* 2, ll. 105–12, pp. 271–2). Cf. Yeats, 'Those Dancing Days Are Gone' (ll. 7–8 *et passim*):

> I carry the sun in a golden cup,
> The moon in a silver bag.

l. 11. *Hyperion's son*: In Homer, the Titan Hyperion is the Sun, but in Hesiod and elsewhere (and once in the *Odyssey*), Hyperion is the Sun's father.

14. In this poem, Mimnermus recalls the first battle at the Hermus to exhort his countrymen – in the manner of Tyrtaeus (pp. 22–6) – on the eve of the second war with the Lydians, *c.*600 BCE (which ended with Smyrna being razed to the ground: see *Poet Intro*, p. 27). The hero he praises is unknown.

Alcman

31.   *Poet Introduction. Alcman died of pubic lice*: Aristotle, *History of Animals* 557a.

32.   *1, The Partheneion*. What we have of Alcm. 1 derives from a papyrus discovered at Saqqara in Egypt in 1855 and preserved today in the Louvre. Despite its incompleteness, it is the most substantial surviving fragment of early choral poetry. Though it may have been longer, Alcman's poem appears to have been composed in ten fourteen-line stanzas, eight of which remain at least partly legible; the mangled first part tells the story of the destruction of the sons of Hippocoön, at the hands of the Dioscuri (the 'Sons of Zeus', Castor and Polydeuces) and (perhaps) Heracles, as part of a feud over Spartan royal succession – at least one source (Scholiast on Euripides, *Orestes* l. 457) tells us that Hippocoön was a bastard, and thus his claim to the throne questionable. The second part, beginning with Str. 6 (where this excerpt picks up), turns to the choral performance. Homoeroticism has often been perceived among the chorus-girls (mentioned by name in Str. 8). My own translation relies on the interpretation of Gloria Ferrari (*Alcman and the Cosmos of Sparta, passim*), according to which the chorus represents the star-cluster of the Hyades (sisters to the Pleiades) at the time of their cosmical setting – that is, the last day on which they are visible before sunrise in the morning sky – singing at the

end of an all-night festival (*pannukhis*), just before sunrise, when Sirius is brightest, to mark the beginning of winter and the rainy season.

ll. 37–9. *He's happy . . .* : A rhetorical trope known as *makarismos* ('proclamation of blessedness', from Greek *makar*, 'blessed'), the most famous example of which is no doubt the opening to Hor. *Epod.* 2 (*Beatus ille*, 'Happy the man . . . ', p. 456). Its opposite is the *schetliasmos* (malediction), for which see Hor. *Odes* 2.13, ll. 1–4 (p. 463) and n. Other examples of *makarismos* in this volume include Theog. ll. 1013–16 (p. 84), 1335–6 (p. 85) and 1375–6 (p. 85); Hipponax 117, ll. 3–5 (p. 119); Pi. *Ol.* 7, ll. 15–16 (p. 140), and fr. 137 (p. 164); Bacch. 3, ll. 15–20 (p. 167), and 5, ll. 63–6 (p. 173); Phil. Scar. *PaeDi.*, ll. 118–27 (pp. 231–2); Ov. *Am.* 2.10, l. 29 (p. 505). Some famous modern examples include Du Bellay's 'Heureux, qui comme Ulysse' and Pope's 'Ode on Solitude' (written when he was eleven!).

l. 41. *Agido*: 'Leader'; here, the Dawn, leader of the sun. Other interpretations emphasize the proximity of Agido to 'Agiad', one of the royal families of Sparta. Of course, if the cosmic interpretation is correct, we should still probably imagine Dawn, Moon and Night as roles played by individual chorus members.

l. 44. *The sparkler . . . who mounts our spectacle*: Aenesimbrota ('She Whom Mortals Praise', i.e., Night), analogized as the *choregus*, the wealthy producer of choral spectacle, mentioned also at ll. 73 and 85–6.

ll. 52–5. *My cousin . . . Chorus Queen*: Hagesichora (Chorus-Leader) is the Moon, daughter of the Titan Hyperion, whose brother, Iapetus, is grandfather to the Pleiades and Hyades. The chorus speaks in the voice of the latter – making the Moon and the chorus first cousins once removed.

33.   l. 59. *a Scythian horse behind the Lydian*: The Black Sea (*Enetic*) horse is black, as the Eneti of Paphlagonia were famous for wearing black robes, while the Lydian (*Ibenian*) horse is golden (a buckskin or champagne?), Lydia being known for wealth, and the Scythian (*Colaxian*) reddish chestnut, as in Homer's 'rosy-fingered Dawn'. The moon is conceived as having a silvery face with a nimbus of golden hair. For other equine comparisons (usually amatory), see Theog. ll. 1249–52 (p. 85), Iby. 287, ll. 6–8 (p. 99), and Anac. 360 (p. 105) and 417 (p. 108).

ll. 62–3. *the Pleiades . . . are battling us*: Both Pleiades and Hyades are faint (unlike Sirius) but important. According to Hesiod (*W&D*, ll. 615–18, trans. Stallings):

> When the stars
> Of the Pleiades, Hyades, and Orion sink,
> That's when it is again high time to think
> Of ploughs.

In Alcman, the language of warfare must relate somehow to the more epic tale, in the poem's first part, about the demise of the sons of Hippocoön.

l. 73. *that dark house all mortals praise*: Aenesimbrota (Night). See n. on l. 44, above.

l. 77. *I disappear*: Like the stars in Sap. 34 (p. 45).

ll. 85-6. *Lady ... who mount our dance*: Aenesimbrota. See n. on l. 44, above.

l. 87. *pours from the sky in vain*: When their brother, Hyas, was killed in a lion hunt, the five sister Hyades died of grief. Transformed into stars, they continue to weep, their tears falling to earth as rain. (Indeed, the ancients commonly derived the name *Hyades* from the Greek verb *hyein*, 'to rain'.)

34.   ll. 96-9. *When Sirens sing ... stumble at eleven*: These fragmentary and difficult lines are construed differently by different scholars. Here, I'll note (with Ferrari, *Alcman and the Cosmos of Sparta*, p. 100) that ten was a mystical number in Pythagorean cosmology, the tetractys of the decad, 'which is the harmony in which the Sirens are' (Iamblichus, *On the Pythagorean Way of Life* 18.82). The myth of Er in Plato's *Republic* (10. 614-21) envisions the cosmos as a whorl of eight concentric circles, each of which carries a Siren emitting a single sound at a single pitch, generating together the music of the spheres. 'Eleven' may refer to the number of chorus members – Str. 8 lists eight names, plus three identifiable by clothing items (purple cloth, gold snake, Lydian garland); alternatively, some think there are ten chorus members (eight names plus Agido and Hagesichora) and eleven Sirens (as depicted on a fourth-century sarcophagus from Ephesus). However that may be, in yielding to the Sirens at the time of their cosmical setting, the chorus of the Hyades obeys a larger cosmic harmony, in contrast to the sons of Hippocoön, who seek to maintain an illegitimate dynasty.

l. 101. *Xanthus*: The swans on the River Xanthus (the modern Eşen) may suggest Apollo's oracle at Patara (also on the Xanthus, in Lycia), where the god was reputed to spend the winter months. The 'yellow hair' is probably Hagesichora's.

582 NOTES TO PAGES 34–6

3, The Second Partheneion. Unfortunately far more mangled than the previous *partheneion*, this maiden-song probably consisted of 126 lines in fourteen nine-line strophes, only three of which (Strr. 1, 7 and 8) are preserved in near-completeness, though at least one line is still missing from each. The 'I' who speaks at the start could belong to the chorus, the poet or Astymeloisa, apparently the lead dancer of this poem. Her name means 'City's Sweetheart' or 'People's Favorite' (as in l. 74). If the poem included a myth, there is no trace of it.

l. 9. Approximately fifty lines are lost before the text picks back up.

l. 63. *for her*: i.e., for Astymeloisa.

ll. 65–6. *the anadem of flowers*: Perhaps either a ritual garland to be offered to Hera, or a decoration marking Astymeloisa out from the rest of the choir.

35.   *16.* According to an anonymous papyrus commentary (*P. Oxy.* 2389), Aristotle cited this poem as proof of Alcman's Lydian origin, probably mistaking 'he' for 'I' due to a quirk of the Doric dialect.

l. 4. *Erysichean*: Erysiche was a town in Acarnania, in Thessaly. Thessalians had a reputation as bumpkins. Accented differently, the Greek word could mean 'carrying a shepherd's crook'.

17. l. 4. *fava mash*: Or lentil, or peas. A basic dietary staple, perhaps associated with a common meal on a ritual occasion. Alcman's widespread reputation in antiquity as a glutton was clearly derived from poems like this one.

36.   *26.* This famous fragment is quoted by Antigonus of Carystus, who tells us: 'When *keryloi* [male halcyons, here "kingfishers"] become weak from old age and are no longer able to fly, the females carry them, taking them on their wings.' There is little evidence for this story, however, and the poem expresses a wish to fly *with* the halcyons, not be carried by them. (For other associations of kingfishers/halcyons, see Theoc. *Id.* 7, l. 64, p. 291, and n.) Many scholars think it may have been sung by Alcman to the choir as a maiden-song prelude, excusing himself from dancing; some go farther and picture the chorus dressed as birds, while one imagines them leaping into the sea, perhaps thinking of Sappho's deadly (and apocryphal) leap from the White Rock of Leucas (see n. on Anac. 376, l. 2, p. 105). Such picturesque speculations are hardly needed to appreciate one of Alcman's most exquisite fragments.

39. l. 3. *the clickering tongue of the partridge*: The Greek for 'partridge' is *kakkabides*, onomatopoeic for the partridge's call (*kakkabi*).

46. l. 2. *Zeus's son*: Apollo.

56. l. 3. *you'd take* . . . : Perhaps Artemis or Dionysus. The rite described does seem clearly Dionysiac in nature.

37.   l. 6. *Argus's killer*: Hermes. Argus was a hundred-eyed Giant, the servant of Hera. She set him to watch over Io, one of Zeus's many extramarital amours, whom the god had transformed into a cow in hopes of escaping notice. According to Ovid (*Met.* 1, ll. 668–721), Hermes/Mercury kills him by boring him to death. Cf. Bacch. 19, ll. 25–33 (pp. 183–4).

59a+b. Athenaeus (*Deip.* 13.600f–601a) quotes these two fragments to prove that the wildly libidinous Alcman fell head over heels for the poetess Megalostrata – but he may have been misreading a *partheneion*.

89. These lines, probably incomplete (Greek literature did not traffic in standalone descriptions of nature), inspired one of Goethe's most beloved poems, the second 'Wanderer's Nightsong' ('Über allen Gipfeln'):

> The high peaks stand
> in silence now.
> No puff of wind
> rustling a bough
> carries to you.
> In all the wood, no song.
> Just wait – not long –
> you will rest too.

Sappho

38.   *Poet Introduction*. *'Dick Allcock from the Isle of Man'*: Holt Parker's felicitous rendering ('Sappho's Schoolmistress', *Transactions of the American Philological Society* 123, 1993, p. 309).

taken up . . . in an epistle: Ovid, *Sappho to Phaon* (*Heroides* 15) – see, further, n. on Anac. 376, l. 2 (p. 105).

39.   *1*. Still our only definitively complete work of Sappho's, this poem is quoted in its entirety by Dionysius of Halicarnassus in his treatise *On Composition* (23) as an example of the 'polished and exuberant' style, owing to the euphony of its vowels and consonants. In form the poem resembles the prayers in Homer (a 'kletic' or invocatory hymn; Homeric examples may be found at *Il.* 1, ll. 37–42; 5, ll. 115–20; 16, ll. 233–48; and especially 10, ll. 284–94), though it avoids the convention of listing

the god's powers, roles and cults, and the worshiper's prior devotions, in order to concentrate on one past narrative of divine aid.

l. 1. *enthroned in glamor*: The first word of Sappho's first poem is a textual crux. I translate the standard reading, *poikilothron*, literally, 'with spangled [i.e., ornate] throne', but *poikilophron*, 'with spangled [i.e., cunning] mind', is equally plausible and almost as well attested.

l. 10. *a team of lovely sparrows*: Sparrows were notoriously lascivious and would have been common then, as now, at temples and sacred precincts; cf. Cat. 2 and 3 (p. 376). Aphrodite's sparrow-chariot is original, but whether the image is humorous or visionary will depend on the beholder.

40. l. 21. *she will soon pursue*: Aphrodite is usually understood to promise that Sappho's beloved will 'change her tune' in respect to Sappho, viz., 'she will soon pursue *you*'; but, as Anne Carson points out (in 'The Justice of Aphrodite in Sappho Fr. 1', *Transactions of the American Philological Association* 110, (1980, pp. 135–42)), the meaning could as well be 'she will soon pursue [someone else]', in which case Aphrodite alludes to the common theme in Greek and Latin literature that sooner or later everyone falls in love. Cf. Call. *Ep.* 63 (p. 281), Mel. 90 (p. 331), Prop. 1.1 (p. 423) and Hor. *Odes* 1.25, 4.1 (p. 487).

2. Copied on a third-century BCE potsherd in an uncomprehending hand (perhaps a student's), this 'kletic' hymn (see n. on Sap. 1, above) seems complete but for the missing l. 12 and, perhaps, a first stanza.

l. 1. *Cretan home*: Perhaps the sanctuary of Aphrodite and Hermes at Kato Symi in southern Crete, active from Minoan (Bronze Age) to Roman times. A semi-mystical Cretan orchard reminiscent of this one is evoked at Iby. 286 (p. 99).

ll. 15–16. *pouring with all your grace and skill*: A less mystical interpretation of this stanza's textual difficulties would have Sappho, not Aphrodite, as the pourer. In that case, the surprising mix of divine 'nectar' with 'feasting and good will' (rather than the expected wine with water) would be more of a playful elegance than sublime transfiguration.

41. 5. A *propempticon*, or 'bon voyage' poem, for Sappho's brother Charaxus, set at the temple of the Nereids, Poseidon and Aphrodite at Pyrrha on Lesbos. Herodotus (*Hist.* 2.135) says Charaxus traded Lesbian wine at Naucratis in north Egypt. While there, he fell in love with a slave girl, whom Herodotus calls Rhodopis but other sources (e.g., Ath. *Deip.* 13.596c–d, and, probably, this poem) name Doricha. After

Charaxus purchased her freedom, Doricha went on to become a famous courtesan – at which Sappho, displeased, vituperated her brother in a poem. It's unlikely we have that poem, though this one may justify this couplet from Ovid's (or his imitator's) *Sappho to Phaon* (*Heroides* 15, ll. 117–18):

Thanks to my loyalty, Charaxus hates me;
for love and frankness, thus he compensates me.

15. l. *1*. *Doricha*: Charaxus' lover; understand Charaxus as the referent of 'he' in l. 3. For these two, see n. on Sap. 5, above.

42. *16*. Sappho's active and approving picture of Helen is often contrasted with those in Alc. 42 and 283, pp. 58 and 63. This poem, among Sappho's most beloved, provides an early and memorable example of the rhetorical structure known as a *priamel* (German for 'preamble'), discussed in the n. on Hor. *Odes* 1.1, ll. 3–34 (pp. 462–3). Sappho's approach continues to inspire contemporary poets, including in the poem that gives Maureen N. McLane's 2017 collection *Some Say* its title:

Some say calamity
and some catastrophe
is beautiful   Some say
porn   Some jolie laide . . .

17. This poem is a cult hymn composed for the Kallisteia, a yearly festival and beauty pageant held in Hera's honor at the temple to her, Zeus and Dionysus at Mesa, in central Lesbos. Cf. Alc. 129 (p. 60), which addresses the same divine trio and may be set at the same temple (as also may Alc. 130b, p. 61).

l. 3. *which Atreus' sons founded*: Agamemnon and Menelaus. According to Homer (*Od.* 3, ll. 130–72), Agamemnon did not accompany Menelaus when he stopped on Lesbos; this poem may therefore represent either a local tradition or an innovation of Sappho's.

43. l. 9. *Thyone's son*: Dionysus. (Thyone is to be identified with Semele; cf. Phil. Scar. *PaeDi.*, l. 7, p. 230, and n.)

22. The fragmentary earlier lines of this poem gave Anne Carson the evocative title of her Sappho translation, *If Not, Winter*.

l. 2. *Gongyla* (also mentioned in Sap. 95, p. 49) appears in the tenth-century CE Byzantine encyclopedia called the *Suda* as one of Sappho's students; a papyrus commentary calls her the 'yoke-mate' (*suzux*) of Gorgo, often thought to be a poetic counterpart and rival of Sappho's.

23. This fragment may be from an *epithalamion* (wedding poem), a genre in which comparisons and similes were common (cf. Sap. 104–16, pp. 51–3, and Cat. 62, p. 388).

l. 2. *Hermione*: The daughter of Helen and Menelaus.

44.   26. ll. 5–8. If this reconstruction is correct, there is an extended 'ocean of passion' conceit (cf. Theog. ll. 1375–6, p. 85, and n.), not unlike Alcaeus' various metaphorical uses of ships, whether in the 'ship of state' – see Alc. 6 (p. 56) and Alc. 208 (p. 62) – or, even more to the point, the probable comparison of ship and courtesan in Alc. 73 (p. 60).

30. Another of Sappho's poems set at a wedding party; cf. Sap. 27 (p. 44), above, and Sap. 104–16 (pp. 51–3), below.

31. This famous poem is quoted in the first- or third-century CE treatise *On the Sublime* attributed to Longinus, with the following comment (10.3, trans. Roberts):

> Are you not amazed how at one instant she summons, as though they were all alien from herself and dispersed, soul, body, ears, tongue, eyes, colour? Uniting contradictions, she is, at one and the same time, hot and cold, in her senses and out of her mind, for she is either terrified or at the point of death. The effect desired is that not one passion only should be seen in her, but a concourse of the passions. All such things occur in the case of lovers, but it is, as I said, the selection of the most striking of them and their combination into a single whole that has produced the singular excellence of the passage.

Sappho's poem was enormously influential on Hellenistic poets and, through them, on the Romans. For similar 'symptomatographies', cf. Ar. 191 (p. 12), Mimn. 5 (p. 29), Theoc. *Id.* 2, ll. 109–13 (p. 289), and Cat. 51 (p. 387).

45.   l. 5. *lovely laughter*: Cf. Cat. 51, l. 5 (p. 387), and Hor. *Odes* 1.22, l. 23 (p. 468) and n.

l. 17. In his quotation, 'Longinus' leaves off after the first line of the fifth stanza. Sappho may claim, as at Theog. ll. 662–3, that 'even the poor' man can become suddenly rich, and that she hopes the same for herself. The fifth stanza was probably the last. Cat. 51 (p. 387) offers a famous free translation of Sappho's first three stanzas, but goes its own way at the end.

34. Quoted in a commentary on Hom. *Il.* 8, ll. 555–61, the famous simile comparing the encamped Trojans to the stars of heaven, beginning (in Pope's version, ll. 687–8):

> As when the moon, refulgent lamp of night,
> O'er heaven's pure azure spreads her sacred light ...

Sappho's stanza may also be a simile, perhaps part of a wedding poem.

44. This poem, though more 'epic' in diction than Sappho's other poetry, also contains non-Homeric details (castanets, frankincense, myrrh and cassia) and is thought to draw its imagery from Sappho's contemporary Lesbos. Many have imagined it performed at weddings, perhaps as a 'mythical proem' before the ceremony proper; but there is no evidence to support or undermine this guess.

l. 2. *Thebe*: Andromache's hometown in northwest Asia Minor at the foot of Mount Placus, nearby the River Placia.

46. l. 15. The gap is of indeterminate length, and may have described the ships' arrival.

l. 23. *whooped and warbled*: This ritual ululation is reminiscent of similar cries at the Kallisteia. Cf. Sap. 17 (p. 42) and n., and Alc. 130b (p. 61) and n.

l. 25. *Paean*: A cry of thanksgiving and a poetic genre in honor of Apollo. See n. on Ar. 120+121, l. 3 (p. 10).

49. These two lines, cited by different sources, may not have been contiguous, but probably derived from the same poem. Atthis also appears in Sap. 96 (p. 50) and Sap. 131 (p. 53).

47. 55. Our sources for this well-known and oft-quoted poem variously gloss the addressee as an uneducated, rich, uncultured and/or ignorant woman. The omission of her name is part of the point.

l. 3. *Pieria*: A region in northeastern Greece where Mount Olympus is located, at the foot of which the Muses were born; nearby Mount Pierus was sacred to them. Pieria contained one of the two main cult centers for worship of the Muses, along with Helicon in Boeotia.

58a. The original 'New Sappho' of the twenty-first century, this poem made international headlines on its discovery in 2004. The papyrus indicates that 58a is a complete poem; 58b must then belong to another. Yet some scholars believe that 58b is the poem's true conclusion, with one couplet missing between it and the end of 58a. If 58a *is* a complete state-ment, as has been argued, any consolation it offers must rely on the subtext of the myth, in which Tithonus (for whom, see Tyr. 12, l. 7, p. 25, and n.), famously withered to a cricket or cicada, will continue singing forever to Eos, the immortal dawn, just as Sappho's poems continue to sing to her girls, despite the poet's bodily decrepitude. The question, how-ever, of whether Sappho would have written such an 'open' ending is itself an open one.

48. 94. It's impossible to tell how many lines are missing from the beginning or who says, 'I honestly wish that I were dead' – Sappho in the present? Sappho in the past? The departing girl? In the first case, we would have to imagine a contradiction between Sappho's current emotions and those she expressed on parting. The end is also ambiguous – the 'craving' sounds sexual, but could easily be for, e.g., sleep.

49. 95. l. 1. *Gongyla*: See Sap. 22, 1.2 (p. 43) and n.

l. 3. *Hermes*: Not a certain supplement, but likely, given Hermes' role as *psychopomp* – conductor of dead souls to the underworld. Cf. Hor. *Odes* 1.24, ll. 16–18 (p. 470).

50. 96. ll. 1–2. *Sardis* was the capital of Lydia, whose Anatolian headland lay directly across from Sappho's Mytilene, easily visible to the naked eye. Lydia's political and cultural influence on Lesbos is affirmed by Sappho (cf. Sap. 16, 98a+b and 132, pp. 42, 50 and 53) and Alcaeus (Alc. 69, p. 59). In this poem, Sappho consoles a former member of her circle, and a favorite of Atthis (also in Sap. 49, p. 46, and 131, p. 53), who has moved there, perhaps to marry.

ll. 7–14. *as, after the sun has dipped* ... : This simile, elaborate in the manner of Homer, is obscure in the extent of its relevance beyond the ini-tial point of comparison. The moon's 'rose fingers' clearly recall Homer's 'rosy-fingered Dawn', though with what referent or effect is also obscure.

98a+b. These two fragments, from the top and bottom of the same papy-rus column, may or may not belong to the same poem. Our sources give Cleis as the name of Sappho's daughter and mother; here, the daughter would be meant (cf. Sap. 132, p. 53). Luxurious Lydian imports may have been limited by the sumptuary laws that the tyrant Pittacus imposed during his ten-year rule of Mytilene; the fragmentary lines following 98b mention the 'Cleanactidae', the family of the earlier tyrant Myrsilus.

51–3. *104–16*. These fragments belong to wedding songs (*epithalamia*); Catul-lus will have borrowed heavily from Sappho's work in the genre in his poem 62 (p. 388), an *epithalamion* where boys and girls sing in competition with each other.

52. *110a*. Like Sap. 111, below, this fragment belongs to a tradition of (often scurrilous) joking practiced at weddings, known to Romans as 'Fescennine verses'. Reference to the groom's shoe size and height probably hinted then, as now, at other notable parts of his anatomy.

111. See n. on Sap. 110a, above.

l. 2. *Hymen*: A god of marriage and weddings, also invoked in Dios. 6, l. 5 (p. 314), and in the refrain of Cat. 62 (p. 388).

53. *131*. l. 2. *Andromeda*: Perhaps Sappho's rival, criticized by Sappho in a textually corrupt fragment for flaunting her ankles in a rustic and unseemly way. (For Atthis, see also Sap. 49, p. 46, and 96, p. 50.)

132. l. 2. *Cleis*: See also Sap. 98a+b (p. 50) and n.

137. Sappho's only extant poem in the alcaic stanza. Aristotle tells us (*Rhetoric* 1367a) that the first line belongs to Alcaeus and the rest is Sappho's response.

54. *140*. Our earliest evidence for the Greek Adonis cult and the festival of the Adonia (see n. on Call. *Ia.* 3, ll. 36–7, p. 263). The first line is probably spoken by a chorus, the second by Aphrodite.

141. Perhaps about the marriage of Peleus and Thetis (cf. Alc. 42, ll. 6–7, p. 58, and n., and Pi. *Py.* 3, ll. 126–36, p. 150). Hermes as the gods' cup-bearer is an oddity unique (Athenaeus tells us, at *Deip.* 10.425c) to Sappho and Alcaeus.

168b. A famous fragment, though problems of dialect render Sappho's authorship doubtful. A. E. Housman has two adaptations in *More Poems*, beginning (in one version) 'The weeping Pleiads wester ...' and (in the other) 'The rainy ...' See also Ascl. 42 (p. 306).

Alcaeus

55. *Poet Introduction. Olympic champion*: According to Diogenes Laertius in his *Life of Pittacus* (1.9.74), Phrynon was a victor in the *pancration*, which was like MMA; see n. on Xen. 2, l. 5 (p. 111).

'*Pardon is better than vengeance*': Diodorus Siculus, *Library of History* 9.12.3.

56. *According to Dionysius of Halicarnassus ...*: Dionysius of Halicarnassus, *On Imitation* 421s.

6. The first three lines are quoted by the grammarian Heraclitus (*Homeric Allegories* 5) as an example of Alcaeus' use of the 'ship of state' metaphor in the time of Myrsilus (see *Poet Intro*, p. 55) – whether before or after he took over the tyranny of Mytilene is impossible to say. (The same commentator also quotes, for the same reason, the entirety of Alc. 208, p. 62.) Subsequent lines are preserved via several scrappy papyri. Other poems with similar (not always clearly political) allegories include Ar. 105 (p. 9), Sap. 26 (p. 43), Alc. 73 (p. 60) and Theog. ll. 667–82 (p. 83).

10b. l. 1. *Alas for me*: The speaker is female. Horace imitates this poem's theme and meter at *Odes* 3.12 (p. 483).

57.   34. l. 1. *Leave the island where Pelops once was master*: In this invocatory hymn, Alcaeus summons Castor and Polydeuces (the Dioscuri, or the 'Sons of Zeus') from Sparta, with which they were associated. The Peloponnese (literally, the 'Island of Pelops') forms the large southern peninsula of Greece, running roughly from Corinth in the north to the southern projections of Cape Malea and the Mani south of Laconia.

l. 12. *your corposant*: Also known as St. Elmo's fire, the corposant is an electrical discharge which plays about the rigging of ships, for which the Dioscuri were thought responsible. The poem probably had three more stanzas and may also have used the 'ship of state' allegory (see n. on Alc. 6, above). Though we have only half the poem, this is the most complete of Alcaeus' hymns.

38a. Of all Alcaeus' drinking poems, this is the one that most anticipates the Horatian style of combining exhortations to drink with premonitions of death and unsettling visions of the afterlife – compare, for example, Hor. *Epod.* 13 (p. 458), *Odes* 2.3 (p. 471) or 2.13 (p. 474), or any number of others.

l. 1. *Drink … with me, Melanippus*: According to Hdt. *Hist.* (5.95.2), Melanippus is also the addressee of the poem in which Alcaeus describes losing his shield in the Battle of Sigeum (see *Poet Intro* p. 55) – apparently a common experience among ancient poets, as shown by Ar. 5 (p. 6), Anac. 381b (p. 105) and Hor. *Odes* 2.7 (p. 472).

l. 5. *King Sisyphus*: See n. on Propertius 3.5, l. 42 (p. 435).

58.   42. Alcaeus' moralistic disapproval of Helen in this poem and in Alc. 283 (p. 63) is often contrasted with Sappho's subtle non-judgment in Sap. 16 (p. 42). One wonders whether Alcaeus knew the uncomplimentary portrayal in Stesichorus' *Helen* (p. 92), which later led to a *palinode*, or

recantation (see Stes. 91a, p. 000). Alcaeus' poem, which certainly ends with l. 16, may be complete.

ll. 5–6. *the delicate bride of Aeacus' son*: The Nereid Thetis. It was at the wedding feast for Thetis' marriage to Aeacus' son Peleus that the uninvited Eris, goddess of discord, dropped her apple, so giving the Trojan War its beginning. As a model of marital fidelity and foil for Helen, Thetis is an odd choice; she did not want to marry Peleus and did not live with him very long after she did.

l. 9. *Chiron*: The wisest and most civilized of the Centaurs, and Peleus' maternal grandfather, whose home on Mount Pelion in Thessaly must have been near Peleus' palace in Phthia. Chiron is commonly depicted as having raised and educated many important Greek heroes, including Achilles, Peleus' son, and there are many myths connecting Peleus and Chiron; but only Alcaeus claims that Peleus and Thetis consummated their marriage in Chiron's cave.

l. 14. *chestnut*: The Greek word, *xanthan*, reminds us of Xanthus, one of Achilles' two immortal horses who prophesied his death at Hom. *Il.* 19, ll. 404–17. The horses were Poseidon's gifts to Peleus at his wedding.

45. l. 2. *Aenus*: Modern Enez (Edirne province, Turkey). This was a Mytilenean colony at the mouth of the River Hebrus, on an important trade route between the Black Sea and the Aegean.

l. 3. *Hebrus*: The Hebrus (modern Maritsa) was the river down which Orpheus' singing, severed head was carried – all the way to Antissa on Lesbos, where it was preserved with his lyre in a temple of Apollo. The possession of the head reputedly gave Lesbos its poetic panache, which became proverbial, as shown by a fragment of Sappho: 'Superior, as the Lesbian singer to those of other lands' (Sap. 106, trans. Campbell).

59.   69. l. 1. *recent setbacks*: It isn't clear which side's; the events related by this poem are otherwise unknown. For some of the broader historical context relevant to this poem concerning the feud between Alcaeus and Pittacus, see *Poet Intro* p. 55.

l. 2. *Lydians*: Lydia at this time (in the reign of Alyattes, father of Croesus) was keenly interested in the politics of Lesbos, and would have been sympathetic to Alcaeus' party.

two thousand staters: According to Denys Page, 'enough to keep 500 men in the field for several months' (*Sappho and Alcaeus: An Introduction to the Study of Ancient Lesbian Poetry*, p. 232).

l. 4. *that holy town*: Perhaps Mytilene or Ira, another city of Lesbos.

l. 6. *sly old fox*: The tyrant Pittacus is the easy guess, to be contrasted with the generous and fair-dealing Lydians.

70. l. 2. *He, feasting*: The tyrant Pittacus, whom Alcaeus calls 'Paunch', or 'Potbelly', at Alc. 129, l. 21 (p. 61). This and the next fragment work to brand Pittacus as power-hungry by way of his gluttony and lowborn manners at the aristocratic symposium.

l. 6. *as he and Myrsilus did*: At one time Pittacus was some sort of co-partner in Myrsilus' tyranny (see *Poet Intro*, p. 55). According to Plutarch, he once told Myrsilus that 'the worst of wild beasts is the tyrant; the worst of tame ones, the flatterer' (*Symposium of the Seven Sages* 147b).

l. 7. *that groom just grafted into the house of Atreus*: Pittacus took a wife from Lesbos' original ruling family, the Penthilids, who traced their ancestry back to Penthilus, Orestes' son and Atreus' descendant.

72. The first two strophes describe the drinking game known as *cottabus* (or *kottabos*). Cups are set to float in a basin at which the drinker flings his wine dregs, trying to sink the cups.

l. 7. *the Thracian's thought*: Referring to Hyrrhas, the Thracian father of Pittacus. Alcaeus frequently mocks the tyrant's low birth (cf. 348, p. 66).

60. 73. ll. 1–4. Denys Page (*Sappho and Alcaeus*, pp. 193–6) sees in this stanza a comparison between a ship and an aging courtesan, but whether courtesan is being likened to ship, or ship to courtesan, is hard to say. Sap. 26, ll. 5–8 (p. 43), may use a similar metaphor.

119. This poem has been read as political allegory, directed as usual at Pittacus, though an erotic meaning seems more likely. The fragmentary next stanza goes on to warn that the grapes will be sour.

129. ll. 2–3. *this grand and conspicuous sanctuary*: This temple to the Lesbian triad of Zeus, Hera and Dionysus may have been the same one, at Mesa in central Lesbos, where the Kallisteia was likely performed – see Sap. 17 (p. 42); or it may have been the one at Cape Phocas on the island's southern coast.

l. 6. *our Mother, Queen of Aeolia*: Hera, probably addressed by name at the beginning of the poem.

61. l. 9. *Kemelius*: The epithet is obscure, but perhaps 'God of Fawns', from *kemas*, 'young deer'.

l. 13. *the Spirit of Vengeance*: One of the Furies – see n. on. Tib. 1.3, ll. 69–70 (p. 415).

l. 21. *our friend Paunch*: i.e., Pittacus (see Alc. 70, l. 2, p. 59, and n.). According to Diogenes Laertius (*Lives of the Philosophers*, 1.4.81), other descriptors applied to the tyrant by Alcaeus include 'chapped feet', 'splay-footed', 'windbag' and 'filthy'.

l. 24. The poem will have ended with the stanza after this one; little of it can be made out, though the tyrant Myrsilus' name is legible.

130b. Another poem of exile, found on the same papyrus as the preceding, and possibly set in the same temple.

l. 4. *Agesilaidas*: Unfortunately unknown.

l. 10. *Onomacles*: An Athenian, otherwise unknown to us, but perhaps one of those whom Alcaeus fought against at the Battle of Sigeum.

62.   ll. 17–20. These lines describe the Kallisteia. See Sap. 17 (p. 42) and n.

140. Discussion of this fragment has centered on whether Alcaeus decorates his 'great house' with weapons that he might actually have used, or whether he deliberately archaizes to evoke a romantic, Homeric atmosphere. A consensus seems to have emerged that he does both at once – viz., describes contemporary arms in terms compatible with a Homeric arsenal – and thus gestures at a continuity between his own *hetaireia* and the Age of Heroes.

ll. 9–10. *Corselets – all of fresh linen*: Alcaeus' mention here is the first clear reference in an ancient language to the linen corselet, which was common as barbarian armor and temple dedications, but rarely worn by Greeks, at least according to the literary evidence, in which corselets are of bronze plate. (One possible exception in Homer is the Lesser Ajax, whose epithet 'linen-breasted', *Il.* 2, l. 529, seems to set him apart from the other soldiers.) However, starting around the sixth century BCE, many red-figure vase-paintings seem to depict corselets of linen (or perhaps leather), and we are told that Alexander the Great wore a double linen breastplate at the Battle of Gaugamela in 331 BCE (Plutarch, *Life of Alexander* 32.8). Writing in the second century CE (a time when cheap iron armor had become widely available), Pausanias (*Description of Greece* 1.21.7) says the linen ones are bad in battle but good for hunting. If Alcaeus and his comrades did indeed wear linen corselets, the reference here will have a contemporary, cutting-edge and distinctly un-epic feel.

l. 11. *Broadswords from Chalcis*: The chief city of the island of Euboea was renowned for its metalworking.

141. l. 1. *This man*: Pittacus, according to a marginal note on the papyrus.

208. Quoted, along with three lines from Alc. 6 (p. 56), by the grammarian Heraclitus in his *Homeric Allegories* 5, who cites it as a clear example of Alcaeus' 'ship of state' allegory. Heraclitus claims that 'the subject is Myrsilus, and the stirring of a tyrannical conspiracy among the Mytileneans'.

63.   283. l. 1. *Argive Helen*: 'Argive' is Helen's usual epithet in Homer. In general, this poem (along with Sap. 44, p. 45) is one of Lesbian lyric's most 'epic' productions. Of course, Alcaeus' apparently 'moralizing' treatment of Helen is often contrasted with Sappho's subtler, more psychological portrayal. Cf. Alc. 42 (p. 58) and Sap. 16 (p. 42).

l. 7. *the daughter of Zeus and Dione*: Aphrodite. This is the parentage favored by Homer (*Il.* 5, ll. 370–71), who makes no mention of the well-known story in Hesiod (*Th.*, ll. 154–206), in which Aphrodite is born from the foam (*aphros*) that boils up when Uranus' testicles, severed by his son Cronus, plop into the ocean near Cythera and Cyprus.

298. This poem (at least fifty-two lines in length and possibly longer) told the story of the Lesser (Locrian) Ajax from the *Sack of Troy* (*Ilioupersis*, one of the poems of the Epic Cycle: see Call. *Ep.* 2, l. 1, p. 276, and n.) and related it to contemporary events (Pittacus' name is discernible in the otherwise illegible l. 47). No doubt Ajax's crime, of dragging the suppliant Cassandra from Athena's temple and raping her, is adduced as a parallel to Pittacus' treachery; Athena's consequent punishment of the whole Greek fleet, shipwrecked in the storm, and Ajax, who is among the many drowned, sounds the note of warning.

l. 7. *Aegae's shore*: Identification uncertain. It could be a town on Euboea, or perhaps a promontory on Lesbos, which, according to Strabo (*Geography* 13.1.68), Sappho called 'Aiga'.

64.   ll. 9–11. *Priam's daughter*, i.e., Cassandra, clasps the statue of Pallas Athena *by the chin*, a normal gesture of supplication among humans but unusual with statues or deities.

l. 13. *Deiphobus*: A son of Priam, who took the lead in the Trojan defense after Hector's death, and married Helen after Paris was killed. He died in the sack of Troy, and his body was mutilated. Aeneas meets his disfigured shade in the underworld in *Aen.* 6, ll. 495–547.

ll. 15–16. *the wail of children*: No doubt we are to think of Hector's infant son Astyanax thrown off the battlements.

l. 28. Following this line, at least two more stanzas describe the storm before Alcaeus returns to contemporary events and his denunciation of Pittacus, but only a few letters at the beginning of each line are preserved.

308b. The first strophe of a hymn to Hermes, on which Horace based his own ode to Mercury/Hermes (*Odes* 1.10).

l. 1. *Cyllene*: A mountain in northeastern Arcadia, site of a particularly ancient cult center of Hermes, and generally held to be the god's birthplace. However, as Hermes is typically said to have been born in a cave, not on top of the mountain (cf. ll. 2–3), there is some reason to suppose Alcaeus may have placed his birth on Olympus instead.

332. These lines, quoted by Athenaeus (*Deip.* 10.430a–c) alongside Alc. 335, 338 and 347 (pp. 65–6) to support his claim that Alcaeus 'is found drinking in all seasons and circumstances', provide the model for the opening of Horace's ode on the death of Cleopatra (1.37, p. 470). For Myrsilus, see *Poet Intro* (p. 55).

65. *335*. l. 3. *Bycchis my dear*: Bycchis is also mentioned in Alc. 73 (p. 60). Contrast Ar. 13, ll. 6–7 (p. 7), where the only cure (or 'pill') is 'endurance'.

338. The model for the opening of Horace's famous *Soracte Ode* (1.9, p. 466); it also influenced Hor. *Epod.* 13 (p. 458).

346. l. 1. *A finger of day*: The image, which Alcaeus may or may not have invented, was proverbial. See the imitation at Ascl. 16 (p. 305).

66. l. 3. *Semele's son and Zeus's*: Dionysus. Semele is a princess of Thebes, daughter of Cadmus and Harmonia, and one of Zeus's many amours. See Phil. Scar. *PaeDi.*, ll. 1–7 (pp. 229–30) and nn.

l. 4. *One part to two, mix water in*: Greeks considered it barbarous to drink unmixed wine. Alcaeus' mixture described here is particularly strong. Hesiod (*W&D*, l. 596) recommends three parts water to one of wine; Anac. 356 (p. 103), two to one (though, elsewhere, Anacreon recommends three to five). In toasts, however, wine was drunk neat: Call. *Ep.* 5 (p. 227); Theoc. *Id.* 2, l. 157 (p. 286) and cf. Ant. Thess. 20 (p. 345).

347. A remarkably close imitation of Hes. *W&D*, ll. 582–9, though translated into Lesbian dialect and meter. Here are Hesiod's lines (trans. Stallings):

> When thistle blooms, and loud Cicada rings
> In a tree, and shrills from underneath his wings
> Clear, ceaseless song, in toilsome summertime,

> That's when she-goats are fattest, wine is prime,
> Women are lustiest, and men instead
> Are at their weakest, parched in knees and head
> By Sirius, and the heat's made their skin dry.

ll. 4–5. Half of a line is missing.

348. l. 1. *that city*: Mytilene.

l. 3. *debased in birth*: Probably because his father was Thracian; cf. the attack on the tyrant Pittacus' parentage at Alc. 72 (p. 59). Anne Pippin Burnett (in *Three Archaic Poets: Archilochus, Alcaeus, Sappho*, p. 117) points out that this epithet (*kakopatrid*) could also mean 'bane of his father (or fatherland)'.

67. 364. l. 2. *Surrender* is sister of Poverty because weapons – especially the *hoplon* shield – cost money; citizens were expected to arm themselves and defend their own property.

Solon

68. *Poet Introduction. Plutarch tells us . . .* : Plutarch, *Life of Solon* 3.3.

69. 4. Famous chiefly for the hymn to Eunomia (Good Order) with which it concludes, this poem recalls Zeus's speech at the beginning of the *Odyssey* (Hom. *Od.* 1, ll. 32–43) as well as the hymn to Zeus at the beginning of Hesiod's *W&D* (ll. 1–10) and his description of the just city (*W&D*, ll. 225–38). Some scholars see here a new conception of Justice, in contrast to Hesiod's, as a natural law or process, rather than as an instrument of the gods' whims. The poem is a fine example of what 'pre-rhetorical' Archaic oratory (that is, before the techniques introduced by the fifth-century sophists) could achieve. It can be read as a response to Theog. ll. 39–52 (pp. 77–8).

ll. 11–12, 25–6. The text is corrupt in these two places; at least three lines are missing.

70. 6. l. 3. *Excess breeds outrage*: This saying later became proverbial. *Koros* (glut, excess), accompanied by complacency, gives birth to *hybris* (insolence, violence, outrage) and finally yields *atē* (foolishness, ruin). Cf. Sol. 4, ll. 9 and 34 (pp. 69, 70), and 13, ll. 11–25 (pp. 71–2).

9. This poem warns of Pisistratus' tyranny (cf. *Poet Intro*, p. 68).

71. 11. Like Sol. 9, this poem reacts to the tyranny of Pisistratus, this time as an 'I told you so!'

l. *3. those men*: Presumably Pisistratus and his circle.

13. Though not explicitly political, this elegy is still concerned with polit-ical themes, especially the acquisition of wealth by just and unjust means. The reflections on the vicissitudes of human fortune (especially ll. 63–70) are right at home with Herodotus' Solon (*Hist.* 1.29–33), who refuses to call any man happy before he has met a happy end. Because of its diffuse-ness, some scholars have sought to divide the elegy into two or more smaller poems; however, for the most part it follows a coherent train of thought while continually circling back to its larger themes. Compare Theog. ll. 197–208 (p. 80) for a similar take on similar themes.

l. 2. *Muses of Pieria*: See n. on Sap. 55, l. 3 (p. 47).

72.   ll. 49–50. Athena and Hephaestus were often worshiped jointly in Athens, where they were patron deities of craftsmen, especially potters, along with their usual associations with weaving and metalworking.

l. 57. *Paean*: See n. on Ar. 120+121, l. 3 (p. 10).

73.   l. 75. It is ambiguous in the Greek whether 'gods' or 'profits' are the source of ruin.

27. Solon's treatment of this common theme gives unusual prominence to the wisdom and eloquence of old age, reminding us of Nestor in the *Iliad* (see n. on Pi. *Py.* 3, ll. 162–4, p. 151). Cf. Shakespeare, *As You Like It* 2.7, ll. 139–65, and Yeats, 'The Four Ages of Man'.

74.   *33*. Solon here ventriloquizes one of his critics among the people who mocked him for refusing the tyranny.

34. l. 1. *others*: Most likely lowborn but reasonably affluent partisans of Solon's who hoped that, by elevating him to the tyranny, they could get some remuneration.

l. 7. *those other worthless things*: Confiscating land to give to his supporters.

75.   *36*. Here Solon offers a political justification for the *seisachtheia*, his can-cellation of debts.

l. 6. *boundary stones*: Stone pillars set up to mark mortgaged land.

Theognis and the *Theognidea*

77.   *19–38*. l. 19. *let these verses bear my seal*: The seal (*sphregis* in Greek) has been variously interpreted as: (1) Cyrnus' name; (2) Theognis' name in l. 22; (3) Theognis' 'art and wisdom' in l. 20; (4) a literal seal placed on

the manuscript; and (5) a metaphorical reference to Theognis writing down what is essentially oral poetry. This translation opts for interpretation no. 3; Douglas E. Gerber's more literal rendering runs, 'For me, a skilled and wise poet, let a seal be placed on these verses' (*Greek Elegiac Poetry*, p. 177). It is unclear how any of these senses would prevent the plagiarism or revision Theognis fears. Whatever is meant, these verses are generally viewed as inaugurating the collection-within-a-collection which concludes at ll. 237–55. For other examples of the *sphregis* in Greek poetry, see Tim. 791, l. 238 (p. 211), Call. *Hy.* 2, ll. 105–12 (pp. 271–2), and Theoc. *Id.* 1, l. 67 (p. 283).

l. 32. *base men*: Theognis' verse is steeped in class-related anxiety. In Greek, words for class tend to convey both social distinctions and judgments of character, not unlike in English ('noble', 'vulgar', etc.). In Theognis, the nobles are so both by birth and by proper upbringing and behavior, while the 'base' lack birth or upbringing or both. One who was nobly born but ill brought up is still 'base' in Theognis' eyes; cf. ll. 57–8 (p. 78).

39–52. Tyrants in Archaic Greece tended to use popular support to vault themselves to power over the oligarchic ruling classes; cf. Sol. 9 (p. 70) and 11 (p. 71), commenting on Pisistratus' rise to tyranny, and Sol. 33–4 (p. 74), defending himself for not claiming the tyranny when he had the chance.

l. 40. *a tyrant*: Perhaps Theagenes (see *Poet Intro*, p. 76).

the outrage: Theognis seems to refer to abuses on the part of his own oligarchical class, which the dreaded tyrant is likely to 'fix'.

78.   53–68. These lines are probably a withering diatribe against the nouveau riche, and not a reaction to the success of the sort of peasant revolution feared by Theognis in the previous poem.

l. 54. *goatskins*: Clothing proper to bumpkins and slaves, not a ruling elite.

ll. 1111–12. Repetitions and illogicalities in the manuscript sometimes cause modern editors to insert verses from one poem into another or to make transpositions within the same poem. Here I have followed one such suggestion.

105–12. ll. 105–6. *Helping the base* ...: Cf. Miguel de Cervantes, *Don Quixote*, Pt. 1, Ch. 23: 'I have always heard, Sancho, that to do good to low-born rabble is to cast water into the sea' (trans. Rutherford).

79.   118–28. ll. 121–8. *if a friend's intent conceals deceit* ...: See Scolia 889 (p. 245) for a similar sentiment.

155–8. Cf. Hes. *W&D*, ll. 717–18 (trans. Stallings):

> Don't ever dare to blame
> A man for soul-destroying Need – it came
> From the everlasting gods.

l. 157. *Zeus's scales*: Zeus's golden scales of justice appear most famously in the *Iliad* (e.g. *Il.* 22, ll. 209–13). In this volume, cf. Bacch. 17, ll. 27–32 (p. 179), Diotimus 1, l. 4 (p. 318), and n. on. Ov. *Am.* 3.9, ll. 1–2 (p. 510).

80.   *197–208.* Some scholars have seen in this poem an imitation of Solon's more famous Elegy 13 (p. 71).

213–18. The popularity of this poem in later antiquity is illustrated by a parody about the sophist Philostratus the Egyptian (cf. Crin. 20, l. 1, p. 342, and n.):

> Be like Philostratus, that genius who
> screwed Cleopatra and took on her hue.
> (Philostratus of Athens, *Lives of the Philosophers* 486)

ll. 215–16. *the slippery octopus, whose hue changes*: Cf. Aristotle, *History of Animals* 622a (trans. Balme):

> The octopus, although stupid (for it even comes towards a man's hand if he puts it under water), is a good house-keeper. For it collects everything into the lair where it happens to live, and after consuming the most useful parts it expels the shells and cases of the crabs and shellfishes and the bones of the small fishes; and it hunts the fishes by changing its colour and making it like whatever stones it is next to. It does the same thing also when frightened.

237–55. This poem is often viewed as an epilogue to the collection-within-a-collection that begins at ll. 19–38 (p. 77). For the theme of literary immortality, compare (e.g.) Hor. *Odes* 2.20 (p. 477) and 3.30 (p. 487).

ll. 237–9. *I've made you wings . . .* : Compare Pi. *Py.* 8, l. 34 (p. 152).

ll. 240–43. *flitting on the lips of all*: Cf. Ov. *Met.* 15, ll. 878–9:

> The people's lips shall read me; in my fame
> through all the centuries, if intimations
> of poets may prove true, I shall live on.

Both Ovid and Horace, *Odes* 2.20 (p. 477), were riffing on the early
Roman epic poet Ennius – *volito vivus per ora virum*, 'I'm still alive on
the lips of men: I fly' – who may in turn have been thinking of Theognis.

81.   *313–14.* A similar sentiment can be found in Scolia 902 (p. 247).

       341–50. l. 346. *the men who stripped my property*: A reference to
       Theognis' dispossession by democratic revolutionaries; see *Poet Intro* (p.
       76), and cf. ll. 667–82 and 1197–1202 (pp. 83 and 84), below.

       ll. 347–8. *I'm like the dog who crossed . . .* : This may be an allusion to an
       otherwise unknown animal fable.

82.   *425–8.* A famous proverb, no doubt earlier than Theognis, reportedly the
       wisdom of Silenus (see n. on Prop. 3.3, l. 30, p. 433) as told to the Phrygian
       king Midas, made much of by Nietzsche at the beginning of *The Birth of
       Tragedy*. Bacchylides voices the same sentiment at Ode 5, l. 200 (p. 177).
       The original anecdote is told by Plutarch, quoting Aristotle, in his *Letter of
       Condolence to Apollonius* 27. See also Yeats, 'A Man Young and Old', XI,
       translating Sophocles' *Oedipus at Colonus*: 'Never to have lived is best,
       ancient writers say . . .'

       447–52. l. 449. *Apply the touchstone*: Gold's quality can be determined
       by the color of the mark it leaves on a dark, fine-grained stone, called a
       'touchstone'.

       511–22. l. 511. We have no independent information about Clearistus.

       l. 516. *choose seats as you think best*: The position of highest honor was
       to the right of the host; this is where Clearistus would recline. However,
       if a friend comes whom Clearistus wants to honor, he could choose to
       give up his seat and take a lesser one.

83.   *667–82.* l. 668. *Simonides*: An otherwise unknown friend of the speaker,
       not the famous poet.

       l. 672. *Melos*: An island in the southwest Cyclades; south of Melos is
       open sea.

       l. 681. *riddles*: Presumably the poem's controlling metaphor. For similar
       allegories, cf. Ar. 105 (p. 9), Sap. 26 (p. 43) and Alc. 6 (p. 56), 73 (p. 60)
       and 208 (p. 62).

       757–68. ll. 761–2. *Now, let's have hymns . . .* : All symposia began with
       hymns and drink offerings to presiding gods or heroes.

       l. 764. *Medes*: i.e., Persians. The Greeks used the names interchangeably after
       Cyrus the Great conquered Media around 550 BCE and incorporated it into

the Persian Empire. Because 'this city' in l. 759 is unidentifiable, the war referred to could be as early as Cyrus' threat to Ionia *c.*546, or the Persian Wars of 490–479, the main subject of Herodotus' *Histories*. In the latter case, we would have a poem, like ll. 773–82, below, manifestly too late to have been composed by the historical Theognis; see *Poet Intro* p. 76.

773–82. l. 774. *Alcathous*: The name of both one of Pelops' sons and the acropolis to the west of Megara. After killing his brother Chrysippus, Alcathous fled from Elis to Megara, where he slew an enormous lion that was ravaging the countryside, then married the king's daughter and won the Megarian crown.

l. 776. *Medes*: See n. on l. 764, above. Since the city in this case is clearly Megara, the invasion must now be that of Xerxes in 480–479 BCE – which means this poem is much too late to be the work of Theognis.

84.   l. 779. *paeans*: See n. on Ar. 120+121, l. 3 (p. 10).

l. 780. *the Greeks squabbling*: Greek unity in the face of the Persian threat was achieved only with great difficulty and at the last minute; cf. Hdt. *Hist.* 7.138–9, 145; 8.49, 56–63, 74–5.

783–8. This poem is often used to prove that Theognis was from mainland Greece, not Sicily; but it need not be Theognis' work at all. It is also a touching example of a priamel; see n. on Hor. *Odes* 1.1, ll. 3–34 (pp. 462–3).

l. 785. *Eurotas lined with rushes*: Laconia's main river, on whose banks Sparta was located.

983–8. *Let's give our hearts to feasting* ... : The sentiment, in itself timeless, is nonetheless reminiscent enough of Theog. ll. 757–68 and 773–82 (p. 83, above) that the context (or likely context) there, of looming war with Persia, may also apply here. Cf. Hor. *Epod.* 13 (p. 458), which bears some resemblance to this poem, especially in ll. 4–8.

1013–16. An example of *makarismos*: see n. on Alcm. 1, ll. 37–9 (p. 32), and cf. Theog. ll. 1335–6 and 1375–6 (p. 85), below. Compare, also, Pi. *ol.* 7, ll. 15–16 (p. 140) and Bacch. 5, ll. 63–6 (p. 173).

1197–202. This moving fragment speaks to Theognis' presumed exile at the hands of democratic revolutionaries; cf. ll. 341–50 and 667–82 (pp. 81 and 83).

l. 1202. The final line is corrupt; little can be made out beyond a reference to 'seafaring' – whether as cause or consequence of the loss of Theognis' land it is impossible to tell.

85.   *1249–52.* With these lines begin the selections from the almost entirely pederastic Bk. 2. These poems were originally scattered throughout the manuscript, but at a late date were excised and collected into their own amoral appendix – which, as Byron remarks, 'saves, in fact, the trouble of an index' (*Don Juan* 1, l. 352).

l. 1. *Boy, you're like a horse*: For other equine comparisons (usually amatory), see Alcm. 1, ll. 47–59 (p. 32), Iby. 287, ll. 6–8 (p. 99), and Anac. 360 (p. 105) and 417 (p. 108).

1275–8. Compare Hor. *Odes* 1.4, ll. 5–8 (p. 464).

1335–6. One of several examples of *makarismos* trope in Theognis. Cf. Theog. ll. 1013–16 (p. 84), above, and ll. 1375–6 (p. 85), below.

1375–6. The same 'ocean of love' metaphor is used perhaps at Sap. 26 (p. 43); clearly at Mel. 6 (p. 327) and 25 (p. 327), Anon. Mel. 8 (p. 324) and Phil. 15 (p. 336); and most notably by Horace in his famous *Pyrrha Ode* (1.5, p. 465). Ovid also plays with it at *Am.* 2.4, ll. 7–8 (p. 499), and 2.10, ll. 9–10 (p. 504).

l. 1. *Happy is that boy-lover ... :* Another example of *makarismos* in Theognis. Cf. Theog. ll. 1013–16 and 1335–6 (pp. 84 and 85), above.

Phocylides

86.   *1. l. 2. Leros*: An island of the Dodecanese in the southeastern Aegean, and a colony of Phocylides' home town of Miletus, lying about thirty-five miles from its parent city on the Ionian coast.

Stesichorus

89.   *Poet Introduction. 'sustained on the lyre ...':* Quintilian, *Institutes of Oratory* 10.1.62.

90.   *Geryon.* The *Geryoneis* is among the best-preserved poems in Stesichorus' meager surviving corpus, though probably no more than 5 percent of it has reached us. At least 1,300 lines, the original was probably the most copious ancient account of Heracles' tenth and, at least among the cup- and vase-painters of the sixth century, most popular labor, to steal Geryon's cattle and bring them back to Argos from the edge of the world; we can't know whether Stesichorus' poem was a cause or effect of their interest. The image of Geryon as a three-headed, three-bodied monster familiar from vase-paintings and writers such as Horace (see Hor. *Odes*

2.14, l. 7, p. 476) seems not to have been contradicted by Stesichorus, who – according to an anonymous ancient commentator on Hesiod's *Theogony* – says Geryon 'has six hands, six feet and is winged'. Most of the poem comes from papyrus fragments found at Oxyrhynchus and first published in 1967; at the time, scholars were surprised by the amount of sympathy Stesichorus seems to show for the doomed monster, who appears to be patterned in important ways on the Homeric hero Sarpedon (see nn. on frr. 15 and 18, below). That sympathy, along with the exiguity of the recovered scraps, fired Anne Carson's imagination in her idiosyncratic and brilliant *Autobiography of Red*.

8a. l. 1. *Hyperion's powerful son*: The Sun. See Mimn. 12, l. 11 (p. 30) and n.

l. 6. *the scion of Zeus*: Heracles, who has come to borrow the sun's cup for his own trip across the sea.

10. l. 2. *they crossed*: Possibly Heracles and his nephew and helper, Iolaus. Others believe the subject may be Eurytion, Geryon's herdsman, and his mother Erytheia, one of the Hesperides.

15. Geryon addresses an unknown friend (possibly Menoetes, herdsman of Hades) who has come to tell him that Geryon's herdsman, Eurytion, is dead and to warn him about Heracles. The speech, often compared to Sarpedon's at Hom. *Il.* 12, ll. 322–8, is clear in its general drift – Geryon resolves to fight, despite misgivings – though some of the details are obscure.

l. 1. *the offspring of mighty Chrysaor*: i.e., Geryon. Chrysaor was the son of Poseidon and Medusa, and the brother of Pegasus.

91.   *16+17*. In these two fragments, Geryon's mother, the sea nymph Callirhoë (Fair-Flowing), tries to convince him not to fight Heracles.

l. 3. At least fifteen lines too fragmentary to translate follow to the end of fr. 16.

18. This fragment represents the council of the gods, who desert Geryon at the crucial moment. The moment recalls the death of Sarpedon, a mortal son of Zeus, in Hom. *Il.* 16, ll. 431–61, when Zeus considers saving Sarpedon's life and Hera upbraids him. The 'stallion-master' in l. 3 is Poseidon.

19. Heracles' tactics of long-range ambush seem calculated to rouse pity for Geryon. First he knocks off Geryon's helmet, then, after the gap in the text, kills one of the heads with a poison arrow; the second, we are told, is sheered off in hand-to-hand combat. There is no way to tell how Stesichorus disposed of the third head; later mythographers, such as Hyginus and Apollodorus, mention only that Heracles killed Geryon 'with a single weapon' (Hyginus, *Fabulae* 30), or that Geryon 'joined battle with [Heracles] and was shot dead' (Apollodorus, *Library* 2.5.10, trans. Frazer).

92. l. 15. *Spirits of Death*: i.e. the Keres, the malevolent equivalents of the Norse Valkyries. They flocked to battlefields to tear free the souls of the fatally wounded and gorge on the blood of their mortal remains.

l. 30. *the Hydra*: This is the first mention in literature of Heracles' famous arrows tipped with the Hydra's poisonous blood.

l. 37. *like a poppy*: To the simile compare Hom. *Il.* 8, ll. 306–8:

> And his head lolled to one side like a garden poppy
> heavy with blooming in the humid spring;
> just so, weighed down by his helmet, his head drooped.

Helen. Plato's *Phaedrus* (243a) tells a story famous in antiquity – that Stesichorus, on writing a poem criticizing Helen, was stricken with blindness. Unlike Homer (whose fabled blindness one legend derives from Helen's anger at the slander of her in his poetry), Stesichorus realized his mistake, and wrote a 'take-back poem' (*palinode*), at which his eyesight was immediately restored. Unfortunately, these three fragments (85, 88 and 91a) are all that remain of both works.

85. l. 4. *his daughters*: Helen and Clytemnestra. This, Stesichorus' first Helen poem, blames her promiscuity and her sister's on their mortal father, the Spartan king Tyndareus. Helen is properly the daughter of Zeus, and a deity herself. As such, like Heracles and Asclepius, she is an example of mythical 'double parentage' (see n. on Pi. *Py.* 3, l. 26, p. 147), while her twin sister, Clytemnestra, was the mortal daughter of Tyndareus. Both, however, could be referred to as 'descendants of Tyndareus'. The same held true of their twin brothers, the Dioscuri, Castor being Tyndareus' mortal, and Polydeuces Zeus's immortal, son.

93. *88*. l. 1. *Many were the quinces cast*: A fertility ritual performed at weddings; on the Saronic island of Aegina, in the nineteenth century, pomegranate seeds and peas were thrown at a bride for the same reason (Frederick J. Simoons, *Plants of Life, Plants of Death*, p. 283). See also Iby. 286, l. 1 (p. 99) and n.

l. 2. *at the king's chariot*: Probably Menelaus', during his wedding with Helen.

91a, The Palinode. Quoted by Socrates in Plato's *Phaedrus*. Evidently, in his *Palinode*, Stesichorus claimed that Paris took a phantom of Helen to Troy while the real Helen preserved her chastity by dwelling with the wise king Proteus in Egypt; the story is also told by Herodotus (*Hist.* 2.112–17) and is the basis for Euripides' *Helen*. Questions of blindness aside, the motivation for the retelling – to affirm the honor of a god or goddess, as Helen was sometimes held to be (see n. on Stes. 85, l. 4, p. 92, above) – is akin to Pindar's revision of the Tantalus myth in *Ol.* 1 (p. 135), and Plato's censure of Homer in the *Republic*; the ancients jibbed at the Homeric 'slander' of deities, under the principle *de superis nil nisi bonum* (speak no ill of the gods).

The Theban Saga. 97. Hesiod tells us (*W&D*, ll. 161–5) that the race of heroes perished in two great conflicts, at Troy and at Thebes. Besides the poems of the Epic or Trojan Cycle, which framed the events of the *Iliad* and the *Odyssey* (see n. on Call. *Ep.* 2, l. 1, p. 276), there was also an epic Theban Cycle, now almost completely lost, which consisted of four separate poems: *Oedipodea, Thebais, Epigonoi* and *Alcmaeonis*. They focus respectively on Oedipus – his arrival in Thebes, his vanquishing of the Sphinx, etc.; the Seven Against Thebes, a conflict provoked by the dispute between Oedipus' sons, Eteocles and Polynices; the Epigones, or children of the Seven, who return to capture Thebes after their fathers' original attack failed; and Alcmaeon, who takes vengeance on his mother, Eriphyle, for her role in the death of his father, Amphiaraus. (See Pi. *Py.* 8, ll. 39–60, p. 153, and nn., for more on these figures.) How much of this sprawling story Stesichorus' account may have covered is unknowable – it is not listed among those of his works whose titles have come down to us. Presumably it was quite long, though, given the level of detail and leisurely pace of the current fragment. In it, the queen of Thebes addresses the seer Tiresias, who has uttered a dire prophecy about the fate of her sons, Eteocles and Polynices; she goes on to unfold her plan for avoiding the bad outcome he predicted.

94.   l. 232. *So spoke the lady*: The name Stesichorus gave the queen is unknown. In the story familiar from Sophocles and Euripides, the queen is Oedipus' mother, Jocasta, whom he marries and by whom he fathers Eteocles, Polynices, Antigone and Ismene. But there were other versions, in the *Odyssey* and elsewhere, and the mother of Oedipus' children is often named Euryganea (or Eurygane; other names are also attested) and may or may not be Oedipus' own mother. Stesichorus' most recent commentators believe that Euryganea is the most likely name here and that Stesichorus' version probably did not involve Oedipal incest.

l. 235. In the gap that follows the end of this excerpt, the queen elaborates on her plan and the lots are drawn; Eteocles wins the kingship and Polynices must depart. The text picks back up with a prophecy of Tiresias to Polynices and Eteocles about the looming disaster their dispute will bring.

The Sack of Troy. 100. This fragment focuses on Epeius, who constructed the Trojan Horse; no doubt Virgil (pp. 398–410) borrowed heavily from it in the second book of his *Aeneid*. It is an antistrophe; in the preceding strophe, we can make out an invocation to the Muse ('goddess . . . maiden, golden- . . .'), which concludes with a 'desire to sing'.

l. 2. *Simois*: One of the two major rivers near Troy (the other was the Scamander).

the man: Epeius. There is a clear echo of the *Odyssey*'s opening ('Goddess, tell me of the man').

103. This epode comes from the Trojan debate about what to do with the horse. The fragmentary lines that follow mention a 'long-winged hawk' and a 'cry', and probably describe a portent which ushers the Trojans toward their destruction.

Ibycus

97.   282. This long papyrus fragment is, according to Denys Page, 'the oldest surviving instance of a purely secular encomium' ('Ibycus' Poem in Honour of Polycrates', *Aegyptus* 31:2 (1951), p. 165). We have the end of the poem but not the beginning; there is no way of knowing how much is missing. The poem has been thought dull because of its extensive borrowing from epic, but Ibycus seems to be asserting an alternative (and characteristic) hierarchy of values, with his emphasis on the obscure Zeuxippus and on Troilus (whose story is told in the *Cypria* of 'Stasinus', the lost Epic Cycle poem about the beginnings of the Trojan War: see Call. *Ep.* 2, l. 1, p. 276, and n.) for their beauty rather than heroic prowess. Sap. 16 (p. 42) offers a similar revaluation of epic values.

l. 1. *they sailed*: i.e., the Greeks. The fragment opens in the middle of an extended riff on the Trojan War.

l. 7. *that strife of song*: In the *apophasis* or *praeteritio* which follows ('But Paris . . . my heart has no design to hymn . . .'), Ibycus 'refuses' his epic subject at length, in part no doubt because it has already been done by Homer and the Epic Cycle.

l. 21. *the noble son of Atreus, Pleisthenes' offspring*: The double patro-
nymic evokes an ancient debate about whether Agamemnon and
Menelaus were sons of Atreus (as in Homer), or of Pleisthenes (as in
Hesiod's *Catalogue of Women*). Ibycus is subtly calling attention to issues
of authority in the epic tradition.

ll. 23–6. *Those things the Muses . . . each detail*: This strophe constitutes
another mixed reference to Hesiod and Homer. The most obvious echo is
of the proem to the 'Catalogue of Ships' in the *Iliad* (*Il.* 2, ll. 484–93),
where Homer attributes his ability to list the ships to the Muses 'who
have their homes on Olympus'. Helicon, however, is where Hesiod's
Muses live, at least at the famous beginning of the *Theogony* (ll. 1–8),
though elsewhere Hesiod employs the Homeric formula (e.g. *Th.*, l. 75).
Other subtle references to Hesiod may recruit him as a kind of ally in
Ibycus' un- or anti-Homeric poetics.

98. l. 27. *Aulis*: The port town in Boeotia, across the strait from Euboea, out
of which the Greeks set sail for Troy. With the fleet becalmed there in the
harbor by the anger of Artemis, Agamemnon was forced to sacrifice his
daughter Iphigenia – a solution which proved expedient for the war
effort, but had a bad effect on his marriage.

ll. 34–5. [*whose dire courage saved the ships from*] *fire*: The only legible
word is *puros*, 'fire'. The reference to Ajax's defense of the ships in *Iliad*
15, ll. 414–746, is just a guess, supplied *exempli gratia*. Ibycus may also
have mentioned Ajax's comrade in that episode, the archer Teucer.

l. 37. *Cyanippus*: An obscure figure mentioned by later authors as a
descendant of the Argive kings Bias and/or Adrastus, but not found in
Homer. Pausanias (*Description of Greece* 2.30.10) says that because
Cyanippus was still a boy, Diomedes commanded the Argives at Troy as
his guardian.

l. 41. *Zeuxippus*: A king of Sicyon, son of Apollo and a Naiad named
Hyllis, whose father was Heracles' son Hyllus.

l. 43. *Troilus*: A Trojan prince and Priam's son, mentioned once in Homer
(*Il.* 24, l. 257). He was renowned for his beauty; his death at the hands of
Achilles (who is sometimes said to have been in love with him) was a
popular subject in sixth- and fifth-century Athenian vase-painting.

l. 44. *orichalc*: An unknown metal, perhaps an alloy of gold, and
evidently very similar to it. It is likely (though not certain) that 'triply
purified' gold is more valuable than orichalc, and thus that Troilus is said
to be even more beautiful than the very beautiful Zeuxippus.

l. 47. *Polycrates*: See *Poet Intro* (p. 96). The praise Ibycus directs at Polycrates' beauty seems an odd thing to say to a tyrant, leading some to wonder if this poem was written for the Samian despot while he was still a boy, before he gained the tyranny.

282c.1.l. 2. *o Comeliness divine*: Charis, goddess of beauty, grace, charm, gratitude, etc.

l. 9. *But Justice clearly quit their holy choir*: Because the boy does not reciprocate Ibycus' intentions.

99.   286. Quoted by Athenaeus (*Deip.* 13.601b) and probably incomplete. The poem's first half reminds us of the sacred grove in Sap. 2 (p. 40), while metaphors for the violence of *eros*/Eros are common in Archaic lyric: e.g., Alcm. 59a+b (p. 37), Sap. 47 (p. 46) and 130 (p. 53), Anac. 413 (p. 108), etc.

l. 1. *quinces*: Or apples – the Greeks considered quinces a variety of apple – from Cydonia in northwest Crete, site of modern-day Chania, where the best Greek variety was found, according to Athenaeus (*Deip.* 3.81a). Apples or quinces were also an erotic symbol (as in 'Plato' 4 and 5, p. 222; Theoc. *Id.* 2, l. 123, p. 289; or Cat. 65, ll. 19–24, p. 391). According to Plutarch, a law of Solon required new brides to eat a quince before sleeping with their husbands, probably to ensure that their offspring would be as plentiful as the fruit's seeds; though Plutarch thought the quince was used as a breath freshener (*Life of Solon* 20.3). See also Stes. 88, l. 1 (p. 93) and n.

l. 4. *the Maidens*: Unidentified; perhaps nymphs, Graces, Muses, or young unmarried human maidens.

l. 8. *Thracian Boreas*: See n. on Ant. Si. 26, l. 2 (p. 322).

287. The anthropomorphizing of Eros here is not Homeric but Hesiodic (*Th.*, ll. 120–22, 201–2), as in poem 282 above (see nn.), and has parallels at Alcm. 58 (p. 37) , Sap. 54 (p. 47), Anac. 358 (p. 104), Anac. 398 (p. 107) and Hor. *Odes* 4.1 (p. 487). The bow and arrows with which Cupid is later endowed may derive from Ibycus' image of Eros as hunter.

l. 4. *his mother's unbreakable net*: Aphrodite is being cast as a huntress, and Cupid as either a dog or a beater. For more on nets in ancient hunting, see n. on Sulp. 3.9, l. 1 (p. 448).

l. 6. *a prizewinning horse*: For other equine imagery in amatory verse, compare Alcm. 1, ll. 47–59 (p. 32), Theog. ll. 1249–52 (p. 85), and Anac. 360 (p. 105) and 417 (p. 108).

288. l. 2. *Seasons with beautiful tresses*: See n. on the anonymous *Hymn to Zeus on Mount Dicte, Crete*, ll. 37–40 (p. 235).

Anacreon

100. *Poet Introduction. his fellow Teians in their flight*: Herodotus describes the Teians' flight to Thrace at 1.168–9 of his *Histories*.

'full of the name of Polycrates': Strabo, *Geography* 14.1.16.

Anacreon was with Polycrates: Hdt. *Hist*. 3.121.

Hipparchus was assassinated: On this event, see Sim. *Ep.* 1 (p. 129) and Scolia 893, 895 and 896 (p. 246) and nn.

101. *346 fragment 1*. This address to a prostitute seems to adumbrate the stages of her slide into decadence. Both this and the next fragment (346 fr. 4) are different poems which come from the same papyrus.

l. 12. *Herotime*: 'Honored of Hera'. The name may indicate high birth.

102. *347a*. This papyrus fragment offers the end of a poem addressed to Smerdies, a boy in Polycrates' court. Apparently Smerdies liked Anacreon better than the tyrant, so Polycrates had his hair cut off in a fit of jealousy.

l. 10. *save Thrace*: A comic exaggeration pointing to Smerdies, who was Thracian.

347b. From the same papyrus as the previous fragment; probably the beginning of a new poem, though not clearly marked as such. Whether or not it refers to Helen, as has been suggested, the lament of the second strophe clearly echoes Helen's words to Hector at Hom. *Il*. 6, ll. 342–8.

103. *348*. To this poem, compare Cat. 34 (p. 383), a hymn to the same deity in the same meter.

l. 6. *that city of the brave*: Magnesia in Anatolia, on the banks of the River Lethaeus (l. 4), a tributary of the Maeander (now the Büyük Menderes). The city boasted a shrine to Artemis of the White Brows (*Leukophryene*). The poem's diplomatic tone may have been literally so: in 522 BCE Polycrates visited Magnesia in hopes of forging an alliance between Samos and the Persian satrap Oroetes, but was tricked and crucified. The poem, which stood first in Anacreon's Alexandrian edition, is at most half-complete.

356. For discussion of Greek habits of wine dilution, see Alc. 346, l. 4 (p. 66) and n. Horace imitates this fragment at *Odes* 1.27; and, together with Anac. 395 (p. 106), it clearly inspired *Anacreontea* 53 (p. 363).

l. 9. *Thracian bashes*: The Thracians were proverbial for boorish drunkenness, unbefitting a civilized Greek. Compare Alcaeus' slander of Pittacus' Thracian descent in Alc. 72 (p. 59) and 348 (p. 66), as well as Call. *Aet.* 178+2.43, ll. 12–13 (p. 259) and n.

104. *357.* l. 9. *Cleobulus' counselor*: Anacreon is punning on Cleobulus' name, which means 'Famed for Counsel' in Greek.

358. ll. 5–8. *a Lesbian born and bred . . . another sort of head*: It's hotly debated whether Anacreon and his audience associated Lesbos, as we do, with female homosexuality, or perhaps with sexual voraciousness, especially fellatio, as did the Greek comedians. Thus, the 'another sort of head' at the poem's end could be (A) a younger person's dark hair, whether male or female; (B) the pubic area of Anacreon; or (C) a woman. The translation tries to preserve the ambiguity. Whatever Anacreon meant, this poem was misread even in antiquity as implying a sexual relationship between Anacreon and the Lesbian poet Sappho (pp. 38–54), giving rise to the tradition that they were man and wife. See *Intro* to the *Anacreontea* (p. 357); see also the imitation at *Anacreontea* 7 (p. 359).

105. *361.* l. 1. *Amalthea's horn*: The horn of plenty, or *cornucopia*. Both Amalthea and the horn are the subject of varying traditions. According to Callimachus' *Hymn to Zeus* (Call. *Hy.* 1, l. 49), Amalthea was the goat who suckled the infant Zeus; ambrosia flowed from one of her horns, nectar from the other. According to others (e.g., Ovid, *Fasti* 5, ll. 115–28), Amalthea was merely the owner of the goat; Ovid adds that, when the goat broke one of its horns against a tree, she carried it, overflowing with fruits, to the infant Zeus. But others tell other stories about the horn (e.g., Apollodorus, *Library* 2.7.5).

l. 4. *Tartessus*: Modern Guadalquivir valley, a fabulously wealthy settlement in southwestern Spain, known for its export of metals like copper and silver, and ruled (according to Hdt. *Hist.* 1.163) by Arganthonius – 'The Silver One': sort of like an ancient El Dorado – for eighty of his 120 years.

376. l. 2. *Leucas' top*: A leap from the White Rock of Leucas was fabled to cure the sufferer of love; in a poem attributed to Ovid (*Sappho to Phaon*, *Heroides* 15, ll. 164–73), a naiad appears in a dream to Sappho, who is smitten with love for the ferryman Phaon, and orders her as follows:

> 'Your love is unreturned,' she said. 'Therefore,
> set sail for Greece and the Ambracian shore.
> From that height, Phoebus sees the seas unfold –

Leucas and Actium, the place is called.
Burning for Pyrrha's love, Deucalion threw
himself unharmed from there into the blue.
When he went under, his stubborn heart grew tame;
love turned and fled; he exited the flame.
Such is the power of Leucas. Go straight there,
and plummet from the summit without fear.'

The poem ends in premonitions of Sappho's own death, attributed by legend to her leap from Leucas.

381b. l. 1. *and threw the shield down*: Cf. Ar. 5 (p. 6) and n.

106. *388*. l. 1. *striped like a wasp*: Perhaps; or perhaps the cap is tied so tight that it bulges above and below the strap that ties it, like a wasp's abdomen.

l. 5. *fishmongers' wives*: Literally, 'breadsellers'. The reputation for lewdness was much the same.

ll. 7–9. The *wheel* was used for punishing the incitement of crimes or riots, the *stocks* fraud, the *whips* any number of crimes, and hair-plucking adultery or other sexual misdemeanors.

l. 11. *Miss Cyce's* petit chou: The Greek is ambiguous whether Cyce (probably a prostitute's name) is Artemon's mother or wife. (*Petit chou*, a French term of endearment meaning, literally, 'little cabbage', here translates *pais Kukes*, 'Cyce's boy'.)

395. Together with Anac. 356 (p. 103), clearly the inspiration for *Anacreontea* 53 (p. 363).

107. *396*. ll. 3–4. *I'm challenging Love to a boxing match*: Or 'I'm *not* challenging' – the two authors who preserve the stanza (Athenaeus, *Deip.* 11.782a, and a fifth-century CE lexicographer called Orion) disagree on this crucial point. For boxing and Love, cf. Anac. 346 fr. 4 (p. 101), above.

398. l. 2. *the dice of Love*: A long-lived trope. See Ascl. 15, l. 4 (p. 305) and n.

408. ll. 2–3. *a wee suckling fawn*: Cf. Hor. *Odes* 1.23 (p. 469).

108. *417*. Our sources quote this well-known and playful poem, quite reasonably, as an example of allegory. Thracian horses were famous, starting with Homer, and the comparison of women to horses was a common erotic trope. For other examples, see Alcm. 1, ll. 47–59 (p. 32), Theog. ll. 1249–52 (p. 85), Iby. 287, ll. 6–8 (p. 99), and Anac. 360 (p. 105).

Xenophanes

109. *Poet Introduction.* '*It was not only scientific . . .*': Bertrand Russell, *History of Western Philosophy*, 'The Atomists', p. 92.

110. 1. This poem (probably incomplete) describing Xenophanes' ideal symposium opens after the end of the meal, with the floors swept and the guests' hands washed. With Xenophanes' vision contrast the orgy of gustatory excess in the *Feast* of Philoxenus (p. 216).

ll. 7–8. *incense . . . water*: Incense was used to purify the room after the meal. The water was for mixing with the wine – cf. Alc. 346, l. 4 (p. 66) and n.

l. 16. *that hands be ever just and innocent*: The prayer, not for the gods' aid or intervention, but for success at just action, is novel, and characteristic of Xenophanes' thought.

l. 20. *not so much you can't walk home alone*: Athenaeus (who quotes this fragment at *Deip.* 10.413c) tells us that Xenophanes' fellow Colophonians were 'so enfeebled by constant drunkenness that some of them never saw the sun rise or set' (*Deip.* 12.526b).

l. 24. *Giants, Titans, Centaurs of old legend*: Xenophanes refers to three important mythical episodes: the *Titanomachy, Gigantomachy* and *Centauromachy*. The first, dealing with the defeat of the primordial gods, the Titans, by the Olympians, is narrated by Hesiod in his *Theogony* (ll. 617–735) and was also the subject of a lost epic poem, often attributed to 'Eumelus of Corinth', the *Titanomachia*. Xenophanes' lines constitute a key piece of evidence that there may also have been an epic poem called the *Gigantomachia*, about the battle of the gods and Giants, though little reference to it survives. The Giants (who may or may not have been 'giants' in our sense) were children of Gaea (Earth), conceived by her in anger over the defeat of the Titans. (The word 'Giant' is derived from Gaea; cf. Bacch. 19, l. 30, p. 83.) Heracles as bowman played a major role in this battle, probably while he was still a mortal. At any rate, these two wars were continually confused and conflated, both with each other and with other assaults on Olympus by such figures as Briareus and Typhus, and Otus and Ephialtes. For more on these two conflicts, see Pi. *Py.* 8, ll. 12–18 (p. 152) and nn.; Call. *Aet.* 1.1, l. 36 (p. 259) and n.; Prop. 2.1, ll. 19–20 (p. 427) and n.; and Ov. *Am.* 2.1, ll. 14–23 (pp. 498–9) and nn. The main accounts of the Centauromachy are found in Diodorus Siculus (*Library of History*, 4.69–70), Plutarch (*Life of Theseus* 30) and Ovid (*Met.* 12, ll. 210–535), though there are plenty of scattered references elsewhere (in this volume, see Ov. *Am.* 2.12, ll. 20–21, p. 506, and n.).

The story goes that, at the wedding feast when Pirithöus, king of the Lapiths (a people of Thessaly), was to marry Hippodamia, the Centaurs got drunk and rowdy and attempted to carry off the bride; a war ensued between the Lapiths and the Centaurs, in which Theseus participated, and the Centaurs were eventually defeated and driven out. Neither the Titans, Giants nor Centaurs were particularly well behaved, though the Centaurs were no doubt the worst of the bunch; at any rate, these legends all share a common theme of order triumphing over chaos, or civilization over savagery – a theme Xenophanes clearly prefers to address through rational exhortation, rather than mythical exempla.

l. 25. *ignore those frauds that our forebears imagined*: No doubt Xenophanes is implicitly criticizing, along with the authors of lost *Titanomachies* and *Gigantomachies* (see previous note), Homer and Hesiod, whom elsewhere he criticizes explicitly (Xen. 11, p. 112). The critique is close to Plato's, who allows no poetry into his *Republic* except 'hymns to the gods and praises of good men' (607a).

l. 26. *scorn bloody schisms*: The reference is possibly to the 'factional songs' (*stasiotika*) of Alcaeus, pp. 55–67.

III. 2. l. 2. *pentathlon*: Long jump, footrace, discus throw, javelin throw and wrestling.

l. 5. *pancration*: A brutal MMA-style bout, fought close to the ground as in Judo, in which 'all manner of force' (the meaning of *pancration*) was permitted except biting and eye-gouging. Xenophanes mentions the Olympic events in the same order as a list of victors found at Oxyrhynchus (*P. Oxy.* 222).

ll. 8–9. *the city council pays for him to eat with public funds*: In the ancient equivalent of a visit to the White House, victorious athletes were fêted and fed at public expense in their town's seat of executive government (*prytaneion*), where they rubbed shoulders with illustrious citizens, foreign ambassadors and other guests of state.

ll. 11–12. *though they deserve far less than I ...*: Similarly Plato in the *Apology* has Socrates, after being convicted of corrupting the youth, propose as his punishment that he be honored at public expense in the *prytaneion*, which he claims he deserves far more than victors in the race of single horses or two- and four-horse chariots (36d).

Wisdom: In the case of Xenophanes, this no doubt refers to 'wisdom' in our sense as well as the more common Greek sense of *sophia* as 'poetic skill'. Cf. Pi. *Ol.* 1, l. 147 (p. 140), as well as *Intro* to the Archaic Period, pp. 1–4.

7a. This humorous squib appears to mock Pythagoras for his doctrine of the transmigration of souls (metempsychosis); Callimachus similarly mocks Pythagoras at *Ia.* 1, l. 59 (p. 262).

112.   *8*. This fragment seems to suggest that Xenophanes left his native Colophon at the age of twenty-five, perhaps in 546/5 BCE, when it was conquered by the Mede Harpagus on behalf of the Persian Empire of Cyrus the Great. Diogenes Laertius (*Lives of the Philosophers* 9.2.18) tells us that Xenophanes lived for a time in Sicily, both at Zancle (modern Messina) and Catana (now Catania); no doubt he traveled widely.

11. Euripides (in the *Heracles*, ll. 1345–6) and Plato (*Republic* 379b) also criticize the poets for impious representations of the gods.

15. Aristotle makes a similar point to this poem in the *Politics* (1252b23–6): 'Wherefore men say that the Gods have a king, because they themselves either are or were in ancient times under the rule of a king. For they imagine, not only the forms of the Gods, but their ways of life to be like their own' (trans. Jowett).

23–26. This statement about the nature of the divine is pieced together from quotes in several different sources: ll. 1–2, Clement, *Miscellanies* 5.109; l. 3, Sextus Empiricus, *Against the Mathematicians* 9.144; l. 4, Simplicius, *Commentary on Aristotle's Physics* 23.19; ll. 5–6, *ibid.* 23.10.

l. 2. *not in form or thought*: Gilbert Murray comments that 'not in thought' is reminiscent 'of the medieval Arab mystic who said that to call God "just" was as foolishly anthropomorphic as to say that he had a beard' (*Greek Studies*, 69).

113.   *. This anonymous fragment is sometimes attributed to Xenophanes but does not have a fragment number.

Hipponax

115.   *3+3a*. Both fragments are quoted by the twelfth-century Byzantine polymath John Tzetzes (*On Lycophron* 219, and *Chiliads* 1, l. 147) and combined here for cleanness of presentation.

l. 1. *He*: Probably the despised sculptor Bupalus; see *Poet Intro* (p. 14). *Cyllene*: See n. on Alc. 308b, l. 1 (p. 64).

l. 2. *Dog-Choker, Hermes*: 'Dog-Choker' appears to be Hipponax's translation of the Lydian word *Candaules*, with reference, perhaps, to Lydian cult, or merely to a skill helpful in burglary.

12. l. 1. *Erythraeans*: Erythrae was a city in Asia Minor, on a sort of midpoint between the Ionian island of Chios and Hipponax's adopted city of Clazomenae. There may be a sexual pun – *erythros*, 'red', was often used to describe the glans of an erect penis. cf. Pi. *Ol.* 1, 1.147 (p. 135)

l. 2. *Bupalus*: A Greek pun on the name (*Bou-phallus* = 'Bullcock') might be intended.

l. 3. *Arete*: Apparently Bupalus' mother.

16. A parody of the Dolon episode from Hom. *Il.* 10, ll. 274–531. Odysseus and Diomedes, having been sent a heron on the right as a good omen by Athena, sneak into the Trojan camp at night and wreak havoc – just as Hipponax appears to be storming enemy territory by cuckolding Bupalus.

116. 26+26a. Both fragments are quoted by Athenaeus (7.304b and 14.645c) and commonly joined by scholars, with or without a lacuna.

l. 1. *One of them*: We seem to be talking about two brothers, one of whom is a glutton and spendthrift.

l. 2. *tuna* au vin aigre: *Myssotos*, a sauce of garlic, cheese and vinegar.

l. 3. *the way the eunuchs do in Lampsacus*: Eunuchs were proverbially gluttonous, and associated with Lampsacus, a city in the northwest of Asia Minor under Persian influence.

l. 6. *miserable figs*: Figs were the cheap food par excellence, these examples being both small and tasteless. Archilocus also expressed distaste for figs at 116 (p. 10; see n. ad loc.). It seems unlikely that the iambicists ever tried them with honey, amaretto and mascarpone.

28. l. 1. *Mimnes* the painter is otherwise unknown.

who boast an asshole as big as your whole back: This epithet for a catamite (*katomochane*) is a parody of the Homeric *kakomechane* (plotter of mischief).

l. 4. *invoke Sabazius*: The Greek text is corrupt; I follow an interpretation that Hipponax wishes Mimnes to call on Sabazius, a Thracian/Phrygian version of Zeus, whom Theophrastus says the superstitious invoke when they find a snake in the house (*Characters* 16.4).

l. 5. *the poor guy*: the helmsman.

32. In this poem Hipponax combines cutesy diminutives with exotic vocabulary to bathetic effect. Many of the items listed are associated with Hermes, e.g., a warm coat was given as a prize at his games in Pellana; he

was known for his winged sandals; and surely the god of thieves would have had no trouble procuring the gold.

l. 1. *Cyllene's kingpin*: See n. on Alc. 308b, l. 1 (p. 64), and cf. Hipp. 3+3a, l. 1 (p. 115), above.

117.   36. l. 3. *he's chicken*: The timidity of wealth/Wealth (Plutus) is a frequent theme of Aristophanes as well, who wrote a whole play (*Plutus*) on the subject – the god has a lot to lose. But Plutus may be particularly scared of crossing paths with the sharp-tongued, cantankerous Hipponax.

39. Here Hipponax asks someone (Hermes?) to provide ingredients for the *kykeon*, a ritual and/or medicinal drink consisting of barley flour mixed with wine, grated cheese and other ingredients, such as the herb penny-royal. It plays a role in the ur-myth of iambus (see the *Homeric Hymn to Demeter*, ll. 198–211, where Iambe's dirty jokes make Demeter laugh and she drinks the *kykeon*, ending her fast), and was consumed as part of the Eleusinian Mysteries (see Phil. Scar. *PaeDi.*, ll 27–36, p. 230, and nn.)

l. 3. *my bad state*: Poverty and hunger, as well as general meanness.

78. This fragment seems to describe an attempt to cure impotence via practical magic.

l. 11. *at the Cabiri temple*: The Cabiri are mysterious, probably non-Hellenic, deities associated with Hephaestus and the islands of Lemnos and Samothrace.

under the Star of Bullsplat: In the original, *Laureon*. Hipponax seems to be punning on *Taureon*, a month in some Greek calendars, and *laure*, 'toilet'. Perhaps if we imagine the constellation Taurus unburdening itself from on high we will approach Hipponax's conception.

l. 12. *a little bait fish*: No doubt with phallic symbolism intended. The line is incomplete.

84. This fragment, like 92 after it, retains Hipponax's characteristic meter, but the mutilated papyrus rarely lets us read more than a half-line at a time.

118.   92. Apparently imitated by Petronius at *Satyricon* 138.1–3, this fragment may depict another magical cure for impotence gone badly wrong.

l. 4. *like I was a scapegoat*: Elsewhere Hipponax has much to say about scapegoats. Apparently they were often caned with fig-branches, e.g., fr. 6:

> Taking him for a scapegoat they cane him during winter,
> whaling away with fig-tree branches and sea-onions.

119. *115.* This anonymous fragment is attributed by many to Archilochus (pp. 5–15). It's a kind of anti-*propempticon* (see n. on Sap. 5, p. 41), imitated by Horace in *Epod.* 10.

l. 5. *Salmydessus*: On the Black Sea, in Thrace. In Homer, the Thracians are frequently referred to as 'top-knotted', in contrast to the Greeks. According to Xenophon (*Anabasis* 7.5.12–13, trans. Brownson):

> [At Salmydessus] many vessels sailing to the Pontus run aground and are wrecked; for there are shoals that extend far and wide. And the Thracians who dwell on this coast have boundary stones set up and each group of them plunder the ships that are wrecked within their own limits; but in earlier days, before they fixed the boundaries, it was said that in the course of their plundering many of them used to be killed by one another.

117. Another anonymous fragment from the same papyrus as the previous poem. It seems as though the addressee may have stolen someone's cloak, then gotten robbed himself by a potter called Aeschylides; Hipponax and Ariphantus know all about it.

ll. 3–5. *Happy the man* . . . : A parodic example of *makarismos* (see n. on Alcm. 1, ll. 37–9, p. 32).

120+121. The two lines are quoted by different sources but commonly combined to express the quintessential Hipponactean moment. Compare Aristophanes' *Lysistrata* (ll. 360–61):

> If somebody would deal their jaws the sort of knock
> Hipponax gave Bupalus, they'd be too sore to talk!

Simonides

120. *Poet Introduction.* 'the smartest person in the fifth century B.C.': Anne Carson, *Economy of the Unlost (Reading Simonides of Keos with Paul Celan)*, p. 10.

121. Simonides' 'chief merit . . .': Quintilian, *Institutes of Oratory*, 10.1.64.

'sadder than the tears of Simonides': Cat. 38, l. 8.

'Beethoven knew how . . .': Carl Czerny, quoted by Lewis Lockwood, 'Beethoven, Florestan, and the Varieties of Heroism', in *Beethoven and His World*, ed. Scott Burnham and Michael P. Steinberg, p. 40.

Lyrics. *520*. Quoted by Plutarch (*Letter of Consolation to Apollonius* 11.107b), these lines probably belong to a dirge.

122. *521*. Our sources tell us that these lines on the impermanence of good fortune derive from a dirge on the Scopadae, Thessaly's ruling family, who were killed when the roof of their banquet-hall collapsed on their heads. The story goes that Simonides was at Crannon in Thessaly visiting the court of the tyrant Scopas. Scopas had commissioned a hymn from him, but only paid for half of it, and told him to ask the Dioscuri for the rest, because the hymn was more about them than him. Just then, two men (Castor and Polydeuces) showed up asking for Simonides; he followed them outside, and the hall promptly collapsed, killing all the other guests. Simonides was later able to identify the bodies of everyone by remembering where they were sitting. From this incident he invented the mnemonic system known as the 'memory palace', which is still used by 'memory athletes' today. Cf. Call., *Tomb of Simonides* (*Aet.* 3.64, p. 260).

522. l. 2. *Charybdis's horrible throat*: The whirlpool-causing sea monster Charybdis first appears in epic (Hom. *Od.* 12, ll. 73–110 and 234–60; Apollonius of Rhodes, *Argonautica* 4, ll. 825–32; Vi. *Aen.* 3, ll. 553–64), where she is paired with Scylla (see Cat. 60, p. 388) as a menace to navigation.

524. Horace echoes this line just after his famous *dulce et decorum est* at *Odes* 3.2, ll. 13–14 (p. 480).

531. The only thing uncontroversial about this fragment is its fame. Everything else – including genre (encomium or dirge), occasion (official funeral, Spartan cult festival or song at the mess-halls), and meter – is in dispute. The poem is probably not complete.

123. ll. 3–5. *their tomb an altar . . .* : These lines are echoed by Horace when he imagines his own tomb as too empty to mourn at *Odes* 2.20, ll. 21–2 (p. 477).

l. 8. *Leonidas*: The Spartan king who led the doomed resistance at Thermopylae. See Sim. *Ep.* 7, 22a and 22b (pp. 130–31), below.

541. This papyrus fragment was discovered among others thought to belong to Simonides, and is generally assigned to him – though style and language make it at least possible that Bacchylides (pp. 165–85) could have written it instead.

l. 1. *His judgment*: Perhaps that of the good man, or Time.

ll. 8–11. *indomitable greed . . . honor's dividends*: The three forces listed here, greed, lust and ambition, often in Greek philosophy represent three different types of lives.

l. 14. Three lines seem to be missing. Perhaps Simonides completed the thought as follows:

> A man who can't, until his death,
> tread only on the righteous path
> *should still be counted virtuous*
> *if he steers clear of crookedness*
> *as best he can.*

542. This fragment is quoted and discussed at length in Plato's dialogue *Protagoras* (339a–347a). Quoting ll. 1–3 and 11–15, the sophist Protagoras accuses Simonides of contradicting himself; Socrates rescues him with a distinction he thinks Simonides is making between *becoming* and *being* good, while quoting selectively from the rest of the poem and offering a few clearly fallacious and sophistic interpretations. *Pace* both interlocutors, Simonides' poem seems to endorse a rather modest and negative view of goodness, as less the presence of virtue than the absence of vice. Complete, the poem probably consisted of four ten-line stanzas, of which ll. 4–10 and 31–2 are passed over by Plato, while ll. 20 and 33–4 are loosely paraphrased in the dialogue.)

124. l. 13. *Pittacus*: Elected tyrant of Mytilene in the early sixth century BCE (see *Intro* to Alcaeus, p. 55) – quoted here in his role of Panhellenic wise man, as one of the Seven Sages of Archaic Greece. (Alcaeus' hatred of him is not relevant.)

543, The Lament of Danaë. This fragment narrates an event from the life of Perseus. He and his mother, Danaë, have been launched out to sea in a carved wooden chest by her father, Acrisius, because of a prophecy that Acrisius would be killed by his grandson (Perseus). The fragment is quoted by Dionysius of Halicarnassus (*On Composition* 26), to support his claim that, when choral poetry is written as prose, it can be difficult to hear its rhythms and distinguish between strophe, antistrophe and epode. Dionysius helps his case by avoiding much metrical overlap in the selections he quotes: he starts with the last seven lines of an (eleven-line) antistrophe, proceeds with the epode and then breaks off seven lines into the next strophe. The selection contains mostly the lament of Danaë, and probably ends with the end of her speech. It may have belonged to a dithyramb or a dirge, but, as we can't tell how the myth was used, we can't be certain.

125. l. 19. *you cherub face*: One might recall *The Tempest*: 'O, a cherubin / Thou wast that did preserve me!' (1.2, ll. 52–3).

553. l. 2. *child of Eurydice*: Wife of Lycurgus, king of Nemea, not Orpheus' beloved. Her child was Archemorus or Opheltes, in whose honor his parents established the Nemean Games (see *Intro* to Pindar, p. 134) after his nurse's neglect resulted in his death by snakebite.

126. *567.* This fragment is the earliest literary reference to the power of Orpheus' song; see n. on Ov. *Tri.* 4.1, ll. 17–18 (p. 516).

579. Based on Hes. *W&D*, ll. 289–92 (trans. Stallings):

> The strait and narrow path the gods have set
> To Virtue is steep and long, and paved with sweat.
> It's hard going at first, but by the time
> You reach the peak, it seems an easy climb
> Uphill as it is.

581. Diogenes Laertius quotes this poem (*Lives of the Philosophers* 1.6. 89–90), probably complete, as a response to Cleobulus, tyrant of Lindus on Rhodes *c.*600 BCE, and sometimes considered one of the Seven Sages of Archaic Greece. According to Diogenes, Cleobulus wrote the following epigram on the Phrygian king Midas:

> I am a girl of bronze on Midas' tomb.
> As long as water flows, and trees grow tall,
> the suns shine when they rise, the moons are bright,
> the rivers ripple, and the ocean froths,
> in this place, on this much-wept tomb, I'll stand,
> informing all who pass me, 'Here lies Midas.'

127. *595.* Quoted by Plutarch (*Table-Talk* 8.3.4) as evidence that sound carries better in windless conditions.

604. Compare Ariphron of Sicyon 813, p. 213.

128. *Elegies. 11, The Plataea Elegy.* A papyrus first published in 1992 (*P. Oxy.* 3965) expanded the number of fragments in M. L. West's first scholarly edition of Simonides' elegiacs from seventeen to ninety-two (many very scrappy). This poem (heavily supplemented by West) provided our first substantial glimpse into a genre we had long known existed: the public elegy on contemporary subjects. Precedents for Simonides' elegy include the *History of Samos* of Semonides of Amorgos (pp. 16–20), the *Eunomia* of Tyrtaeus (pp. 22–6) and the *Smyrneis* of Mimnermus (pp. 27–30),

almost nothing of which survive. The present poem opens with a hymn to Achilles (ll. 1–20), then proceeds to describe the muster of Spartans who defeated Persia at the Battle of Plataea in 479 BCE. Compared with the account in Herodotus (*Histories* Bk. 9), Simonides seems to emphasize Sparta's role at the expense of Athens and the other Greek allies – whether because the poem was commissioned by Sparta, or because the poet rejects some aspect of Herodotus' account, is unclear. (He also may have mentioned the allied Greeks in some part of the poem which is now lost.) The elegy may have been performed at the festival of Zeus the Deliverer, or 'Festival of Freedom' (see also n. on Pi. *Ol.* 12, l. 1, p. 145), instituted at Plataea to celebrate the victory. Other plausible venues include Sparta (perhaps at the temple of Achilles) and/or Delphi.

ll. 1–3. *and you collapsed, as when . . . woodmen's blows*: i.e., Achilles did. The Homeric simile fits the epic tone of the poem, and indeed closely echoes the simile Homer used to describe the death of Sarpedon at the hands of Patroclus at *Il.* 16, ll. 482–3.

l. 10. *that famous town*: Troy. According to Herodotus (*Hist.* 1.5), the Persians regarded the taking of Troy as the beginning of their feud with Greeks.

l. 16. *one the dark-haired Muses taught to sing*: Homer.

l. 20. *his immortal daughter*: Thetis, daughter of the sea god Nereus, mother of Achilles.

l. 29. *Eurotas' banks*: Laconia's main river, on whose banks Sparta was located.

l. 31. *the Tyndarids*: Castor and Polydeuces. It is unclear whether Simonides refers to images of these deities, which were frequently taken along with the Spartans on campaign, or if a divine epiphany is intended.

129. l. 34. *noblest Pausanias*: Pausanias was a member of the Agiad royal family in Sparta and served as regent, after the death of his uncle Leonidas at Thermopylae, for his young cousin Pleistarchus. At Plataea in Boeotia, in 479 BCE, he led Spartan and Tegean forces to what Herodotus called 'the most glorious victory of any known to us' (*Hist.* 9.64, trans. Waterfield). However, he was widely disliked for his arrogance, especially by the Athenians, and suspected of designs on the Spartan throne. Twice accused of 'Medism' (conspiring with Persia) by the senior Spartan magistrates, the ephors, he was released both times for lack of evidence. In 470, however, while fleeing from the ephors, he was bricked up in a temple of Athena, where he starved to death. According to Diodorus Siculus (*Library of History* 11.45), his mother laid the first brick.

l. 36. *Pelops' island's farthest bound*: Cf. Alc. 34, l. 1 (p. 57) and n.

l. 37. *Nisus' ancient city*: Nisus was a mythical king of Megara, some-times said to be the son of the Athenian king Pandion II (see n. on l. 41, below), sometimes of Ares.

l. 40. *at Eleusis' lush expanse*: According to Herodotus (*Hist.* 9.19), the Persians had already vacated Attica for Boeotia by the time the Spartans reached Eleusis; but Simonides misses no opportunity to amplify the Spartans' achievements at the other Greeks' expense.

l. 41. *the Medes*: See Theog. l. 764 (p. 83) and n.

the dominions of Pandion: Probably Attica. Pandion is the name of two legendary Athenian kings, the second of whom (according to some tradi-tions) was driven out and became king of Megara.

l. 42. *the prophet, Iamus's scion*: Tisamenus, made an honorary Spartan due to an oracle which claimed he would win five great victories. See Hdt. *Hist.* 9.33.1–35.2.

19+20. These lines are quoted as a single poem by the anthologist Stobaeus in his *Extracts*. However, the 1992 papyrus (see n. on Sim. *El.* 11, above) makes us doubt that ll. 6–13 really follow ll. 1–5, and wonder whether they might even be from different poems.

ll. 1-2. *the Chian bard . . .*: Homer. The line in question comes from Glau-cus' famous speech at Hom. *Il.* 6, l. 146; Mimn. 2 (p. 28) alludes to it, as does Horace in his *Ars Poetica* (ll. 60–62), where the simile is applied to the coinage and obsolescence of words. Cf. also Bacch. 5, ll. 79–83 (p. 173).

Epigrams. It is impossible to know how many of the epigrams which the *Greek Anthology* attributes to Simonides he actually wrote (see *Intro* to the *Greek Anthology*, pp. 299–300). No doubt some will be anonymous inscriptions from Simonides' era to which his name was attached later; some will be Hellenistic imitations, and/or deliberate forgeries; and some will be genuine. The selections here are no more or less likely to be authentic than any others, but they are representative of the (probably fourth-century BCE) collection of *Simonidea* from which Meleager drew in making his *Garland* (see *Intro*, p. 301).

1. The tyrant Hippias and his brother Hipparchus ruled Athens from their father Pisistratus' death in 528/7 BCE until Hippias was expelled in 510. Thucydides tells us (*Peloponnesian War* 6.56–9) that when Hipparchus' erotic overture was rebuffed by Harmodius, he publicly shamed the latter's sister. Harmodius and his lover, Aristogiton, sought revenge at the festival of the Panathenaea; they planned to assassinate both brothers but only

killed Hipparchus. Harmodius was struck down on the spot, but Aristogiton died under torture. Later, after the expulsion of Hippias, Harmodius and Aristogiton were hailed as liberators; by 477/6 (if not earlier) they were honored with a statue in the *agora* (marketplace), with this epigram inscribed on its base. See also Scolia 893, 895 and 896 (p. 246) for more popular songs on the same subject.

130. 2. This epigram, like *Ep.* 3 after it, relates to a battle between Athens and the Euboean city of Chalcis, along with Chalcis' Boeotian allies, fought in 507/6 and described at Hdt. *Hist.* 5.74–7. It is unclear whether Simonides' poem eulogizes the Athenian or Chalcidian dead.

l. 1. *Dirphys*: A mountain in central Euboea.

l. 2. *Euripus*: The strait separating Euboea from mainland Boeotia.

3. This epigram, famous in antiquity, was inscribed on the base of a bronze statue of a four-horse chariot which the Athenians paid for with money earned from ransoming their Euboean and Boeotian prisoners of war. See also n. on *Ep.* 2, above.

6. The only epigram of Simonides we can be reasonably sure is his. Herodotus tells us (*Hist.* 7.228) that the poet paid for this inscription to honor his friend the prophet Megistias, who, having predicted his own death at Thermopylae, refused to return home to safety even when ordered to do so by the Spartan king Leonidas.

l. 2. *Spercheus' water*: The Spercheios River debouches into the sea just north of Thermopylae.

7. See also Sim. 531 (p. 122), and *Ep.* 22a and 22b (p. 131).

l. 2. *here*: Thermopylae.

130–31. 8, 9. According to Pausanias (*Description of Greece* 9.2.5), on the site of the Battle of Plataea 'the rest of the Hellenes have a common memorial, but there are separate tombs for the Lacedaemonians and for the Athenians who fell, and these have epitaphs by Simonides inscribed on them'. It is a guess, though a pretty good one, that *Ep.* 8 and *Ep.* 9 are those epitaphs; *Ep.* 8 is perhaps more likely to be for the Athenians, *Ep.* 9 for the Spartans.

131. 22*a*. Neither this nor the following epitaph for the dead at Thermopylae is attributed to Simonides by Herodotus, who preserves them (*Hist.* 7.228); cf. n. on Sim. *Ep.* 6, above.

l. 2. *four thousands*: Herodotus estimates the Persian land army at more than 2 million men (with a further half million in the accompanying fleet), and the total Greeks at no more than 7,000 (Hdt. *Hist.* 7.184–5 and 202–3). Of these, a good number fought and died with the Spartan 300 at Thermopylae, but others were sent home by Leonidas before his last stand.

22b. See n. on *Ep.* 22a, above.

27, 28. These two epigrams purport to record Simonides' victories in dithyrambic contests (cf. n. on Ar. 120+121, l. 2, p. 10), though there is a good chance that either or both may be spurious.

28. l. 1. Adimantus' days: That is, 477/6 BCE, when Adimantus was archon in Athens. Simonides' life is traditionally dated 556–468.

l. 2. Antiochus' tribe: In 508/7 BCE, the Athenian politician Cleisthenes had reorganized the citizen body into ten tribes (*phylai*), each named after a local hero; Antiochus, to whose tribe both Simonides and Socrates belonged, was a son of Heracles.

l. 3–4. Aristides . . . headed: Not Aristides the Just, the famous Persian War general and rival of Themistocles (as shown by Plutarch, quoting this poem, in his *Life of Aristides* 1), but another, less consequential man of that name. That he 'headed' the chorus of dancers means he was the *choregus*, i.e., the wealthy producer of the spectacle (cf. Alcm. 1, l. 44, p. 32, and n.).

132. *40a+b+c.* After the Persians withdrew from Greece in 479 BCE following their defeat at Plataea, a few towns in Thrace remained loyal to them, including Eion, on the River Strymon. The Athenian general Cimon besieged and captured Eion in 476. To commemorate the victory, the Athenians erected three Herms (small blocky statues associated with Hermes, sporting a head and male genitalia) in the *agora* inscribed with these three epigrams, one on each base.

l. 2. Menestheus: A legendary king of Athens and leader of their contingent at Troy, included in the 'Catalogue of Ships' at Hom. *Il.* 2, ll. 546–56.

ll. 11–14. So Athens . . . will go to war: Inscription 40c is notably democratic. Aeschines, who preserves the epigrams (*Against Ctesiphon* 183–5), says that the Herms (see poem note) were granted to Cimon's army by the assembly on the condition that none of the generals should be mentioned by name. Aeschines also gives the order of inscriptions as *b, c, a,* but modern editors have found the current arrangement more logical.

45. This epigram commemorates the victory of the Athenians and their allies at the Battle of Cyprus in 449 BCE (see Thucydides, *Peloponnesian War* 1.112) and is probably too late to be by Simonides.

46. Another victory of Cimon's (see n. on Sim. *Ep.* 40a+b+c, above), this one occurred *c.*468 BCE in Pamphylia, in southern Asia Minor, at the River Eurymedon (see Thucydides, *Peloponnesian War* 1.100). If genuine, it would seem to be an inscription erected in Athens over the bones of the dead. Unlike other Greeks, the Athenians made a habit of burying their war dead at home, in the Ceramicus cemetery, rather than on the battlefield. Pausanias tells us that the first such public burial was in 465/4 BCE (*Description of Greece* 1.29.4); it is just possible that Cimon's action after Eurymedon may have set the precedent for the Athenian practice later enshrined in law.

133. *84, 85*. These epigrams were probably composed to shore up the following anecdote about Simonides' life. The story goes that the poet found a corpse on the beach and buried it, adding *Ep.* 84 as an epitaph. That night, the buried man's ghost appeared to him in a dream, and warned him not to board ship the next day. He obeyed; the ship was wrecked; and he added *Ep.* 85.

Pindar

134. *Poet Introduction. circa 518–438* BCE: It will be noted that, for both Pindar and Bacchylides (*c.*520/10–450 BCE) – and even, to a smaller extent, Simonides (*c.*556/2–468/4 BCE) – a substantial part of their careers took place after 479 BCE, the official end of the Archaic and the beginning of the Classical period. These poets seem to me the culmination and apotheosis of the old music (and the process of increasing Panhellenization that characterizes the Archaic period) rather than avatars of the new.

the 'austere style': Dionysius of Halicarnassus, *On Composition* 22.

'nothing in poems that never end ...': Voltaire, *Œuvres complètes*, Ode 17, ll. 6–9.

his 'mercenary muse': Pi. *Isthmian* 2, l. 6.

Two more recent critics: Simon Hornblower and Catherine Morgan (eds.), *Pindar's Poetry, Patrons, and Festivals*, 'Introduction', p. 1.

135. *Olympian Odes*. Associated with Zeus, the Olympic Games, held at Olympia, took place every four years, alternating with the Pythian Games (held at Delphi in honor of Apollo) in much the same way as our own summer and winter Olympics.

Olympian 1. Within Pindar's corpus, the odes were arranged by the Alexandrian editors in descending order, first of the games and second of the events whose victors they celebrate. *Ol.* 1, then, should really be *Ol.* 3, following the two odes honoring the tyrant Theron of Acragas (modern Agrigento) for his victory in the more prestigious four-horse chariot race. Yet *Ol.* 1, we are told, was given pride of place by the early Alexandrian editor Aristophanes of Byzantium because of its praise of the Olympic Games and Pelops, the mythological first competitor at Elis, where the games were held. The precise application of the Pelops story to the ode's main subject is a vexed question, but the myth is clearly appropriate as a narrative of risk, achievement and reward parallel to Hieron's own. *Ol.* 1 is one of Pindar's most beautiful and accessible odes, and gains further coherence from the poet's emphasis throughout on the pursuit and achievement of excellence. Bacch. 5 (p. 171) celebrates the same victory of Hieron's.

For Hieron of Syracuse: Hieron I was tyrant of Syracuse from 478 BCE, when he succeeded his brother Gelon, until his death in 467. He was a formidable power in the politics of Sicily and Calabria, and, like other tyrants before and after him (viz., Polycrates – cf. *Intros* to Ibycus, p. 96, and Anacreon, p. 100; Hipparchus – see *Intro* to Anacreon, p. 100; Archelaus – see *Intro* to Timotheus, p. 204; etc.), played host to an illustrious court of writers and intellectuals, including Aeschylus, Xenophanes (pp. 109–13), Simonides (pp. 120–33), Pindar (pp. 134–64) and Bacchylides (pp. 165–85). His greatest achievement was the defeat of the Etruscans in a naval battle at Cumae in 474 BCE, where he may have commanded the fleet in person. More despotic in style than his brother Gelon, Hieron engaged in various machinations to circumvent the popularity of his other brother, Polyzelus, and, ultimately, to antagonize and then avoid war with his chief Sicilian rival, Theron of Acragas. In this book, Hieron appears chiefly as a competitor (in the role of owner, not jockey) during the Panhellenic games of 476–468, in which his victories in both the single horse and the chariot race were memorialized at different times by Pindar and Bacchylides; of course, Pindar also wrote odes for Hieron's rivals, when he hymned the triumph of Theron in the chariot race of 476 BCE (*Ol.* 2 and 3). Late in life, Hieron suffered from kidney stones, which eventually killed him (Pi. *Py.* 3, p. 146, consoles him in his final illness).

ll. 1–8. *Water is best . . .* : One of Pindar's most famous priamels; see n. on Hor. *Odes* 1.1, ll. 3–34 (pp. 462–3), and also Pi. fr. 29 (p. 155).

136. l. 10. *are launched in wise men's minds*: The metaphor, common in Pindar, of poetry-as-projectile, returns in l. 140. For 'wise men', cf. l. 147, and see *Intro* to the Archaic period, pp. 1–4.

ll. 15–16. *the poetry . . . around his friendly table*: Though the first performances of odes were probably entrusted to a chorus, these lines imagine reperformance by partygoers around the table at symposia as one of the crowning rewards of victory. The sympotic table is a recurring motif of the ode and serves as a unifying element.

l. 17. *Doric*: The precise meaning here is unknown. It could refer to the Doric dialect in which the ode is composed, the Dorian character of Syracuse (a former colony of Corinth), or the Dorian mode, called by an anonymous commentator the 'most dignified'.

l. 18. *Pisa*: The district around Olympia, in the state of Elis.

l. 19. *Pherenicus*: Hieron's horse, 'Prizewinner', also praised at *Py.* 3, l. 107 (p. 149) and extensively in Bacch. 5 (especially at ll. 45–62, pp. 172–3). A sort of ancient Secretariat, Pherenicus was also victorious at the Pythian Games in 478 BCE and perhaps even in 482.

l. 23. *the Alpheus*: The largest river of the Peloponnese, in whose valley lies the sanctuary of Olympia.

l. 27. *the colony of Pelops*: The Peloponnese; cf. n. on Alc. 34, l. 1 (p. 57).

ll. 29–32. *Pelops impressed . . . stainless pot*: Pindar is going to tell two versions of the Pelops story: (A) the traditional version, and (B) his own. (A) claims that Pelops' father, Tantalus, either to impress or test the gods, had his son dismembered in a pot or cauldron and served to feed his immortal guests. Before they realized what had been done, Demeter consumed Pelops' shoulder. Pelops was subsequently reconstituted, and his missing shoulder replaced with one of ivory. Pindar's version (B) denies this (ll. 45–61), claiming instead that Poseidon fell in love with Pelops and snatched him off to Olympus, whereupon some 'envious neighbor' made up (A). The passage at hand (ll. 29–32) appears to be a loose conflation of both versions, preserving the ivory shoulder and cauldron from (A) and Poseidon's love from (B). As often in Pindar, it is a vague teaser, piquing the audience's interest with familiar details, later to be rejected, and unfamiliar details, later to be confirmed.

l. 32. *Clotho*: One of the three Fates; her name means 'Spinster'. See Anon. 1018a+b (p. 240) and n.

137. l. 48. *Sipylus*: A city in Lydia, where Tantalus was king.

ll. 52–3. *where, for the same use . . . Ganymede*: See n. on Mel. 102, l. 2 (p. 332).

l. 71. *under a stone of monstrous size*: Though not as famous as Tantalus' punishment in the *Odyssey* (Hom. *Od.* 11, ll. 582–92), where he finds himself standing in water he can never drink, under boughs of fruit he can never eat, the Rock of Tantalus is mentioned by Archilochus (pp. 5–15), Alcman (pp. 31–7) and Alcaeus (pp. 55–67).

138. l. 75. *the famous three*: Tityus, Sisyphus and Ixion. See, respectively, Tib. 1.3, ll. 75–6 (p. 415) and n.; Propertius 3.5, l. 42 (p. 435) and n.; and Tib. 1.3, ll. 73–4 (p. 415) and n.

l. 79. *nectar he stole*: Unlike the rock, the theft of divine nectar does appear unique to Pindar; because he has denied the dismemberment of Pelops, Pindar must find another reason for Tantalus to end up in hell, where he belongs. Other sources (e.g., Euripides, *Orestes*, ll. 4–10) record Tantalus as guilty of some crime(s) of the tongue, such as sharing secrets of the gods with men.

ll. 87–8. *the king of Pisa*: Oenomaus.

ll. 91–106. '*If you in heaven … treat me as a friend*': Pelops' prayer recalls Achilles' famous choice in Hom. *Il.* 9, ll. 410–16 and also Sarpedon's speech to Glaucus at *Il.* 12, ll. 310–28.

139. l. 112. *He bested Oenomaus*: In the well-known later tradition, Pelops cheats in his race with Oenomaus to win the hand of his daughter Hippodamia by sabotaging the king's chariot so that it crashes and kills him. The race was depicted on the east pediment of the temple of Zeus at Olympia.

ll. 117–19. *and drinks his fill of worship … Zeus's festival*: Triumphant in death, Pelops is portrayed as a symposiast partaking in his rightful share of the blood sacrifices offered to Olympian Zeus, or even to Pelops himself.

l. 127. *Aeolic measure*: Perhaps a reference to meter, dialect or musical mode. It is curious that this ode should be referred to as both 'Aeolic' and 'Doric' (l. 17).

ll. 135–6. *I hope to praise … in the swift chariot*: As the four-horse chariot race was the more prestigious event, Pindar is wishing future success for Hieron and another high-profile commission for himself. Though Hieron would eventually win the Olympic chariot race in 468 BCE, it was Bacchylides, not Pindar, who was hired to celebrate the victory (see Bacch. 3, p. 167).

l. 138. *Cronus' sun-struck hill* was adjacent to Zeus's precinct at Olympia.

140. l. 147. For Pindar's *wisdom* (*sophia*), see *Intro* to the Archaic Period, pp. 1–4, and cf. Xen. 2, ll. 11–12 (p. 111) and n.

Olympian 7. Often called Pindar's most perfect ode, this poem offers ringing praise of its dedicatee, one of antiquity's greatest athletes, as well as of the island of Rhodes. Its three myths, nestled one inside the next like Russian dolls, move progressively backward in time, from Rhodes' founding in the Age of Heroes to the beginnings of the world; in each myth, a mistake or oversight of some sort leads unexpectedly to great good fortune. The dedicatee, Diagoras of Rhodes, won at all four major games (see *Poet Intro*, p. 134), and his sons and grandsons were similarly belaureled. A famous story concerns the Olympics of 448, when one of Diagoras' sons won the boxing and the other the pancration (see n. on Xen. 2, l. 5, p. 111). As they carried their father around the racetrack on their shoulders, a spectator from the crowd shouted, 'Die now, Diagoras, for you cannot ascend to heaven!' – that is, he could not become a god, the only way his state could possibly have improved by that point. He is said to have died on the spot and was considered the happiest of mortals.

l. 13. *Pytho*: See n. on Pi. *Py.* (p. 146).

ll. 15–16. *Happy the man . . .* : An example of *makarismos*: see n. on Alcm. 1, ll. 37–9 (p. 32); and cf. Pi. fr. 137 (p. 164).

141. l. 24. *the Rose arisen from deep water*: Rhodes is both island and nymph. Pindar puns throughout on *Rhodos* (Rhodes) and *rhodon* (rose).

ll. 28–9. *at Castalia's spring . . . at the Alpheus*: i.e., at Delphi (see Pi. *Pae.* 6, ll. 7–8, p. 157, and n.) and Olympia (see n. on Pi. *Ol.* 1, l. 23, p. 136), respectively.

l. 34. *the Three Towns*: Lindus, Camirus and Ialysus; cf. ll. 130–36, below.

spear-skilled Argive men: The Tirynthians who colonized Rhodes with Tlapolemus.

l. 36. *Tlapolemus*: The story Pindar tells, with small alterations, is based on Homer's 'Catalogue of Ships' (*Il.* 2, ll. 653–70). Tlapolemus is later killed by Sarpedon (*Il.* 5, ll. 627–59).

ll. 40–41. . . . *Amyntor*: In Homer, the father of Achilles' tutor, Phoenix. (Homer names Tlapolemus' mother Astyocheia.)

l. 47. *Licymnius*: Tlapolemus' granduncle (Alcmene being the mother of Tlapolemus' father, Heracles).

l. 49. *Midea's perfumed recesses*: Either the Mycenaean fortress of this name, where Licymnius' father, Electryon, was king, or the bedroom of Licymnius' mother, Midea (Electryon's concubine).

l. 54. *he sought the god in Delphi*: Homer does not say so, but Pindar adds this detail, perhaps to emphasize Tlapolemus' wisdom.

l. 56. *He of the Golden Hair*: Apollo.

142. l. 58. *Lerna*, where Heracles slew the Hydra, was an ancient port south of Argos.

ll. 60–61. *snows of gold*: We have transitioned to the second myth. A metaphorical line from Homer ('And Cronus' son poured marvelous wealth down upon them', *Il.* 2, l. 670) has been taken literally, to refer to a Rhodian rain of gold at the time of Athena's birth from Zeus's head.

l. 70. *the son of Hyperion*: Helius, the Sun. See n. on Mimn. 12, l. 11 (p. 30).

l. 71. *his favored children*: The Heliadae (sons of Helius), the first inhabitants of Rhodes. The story is an aetiology (as in Callimachus' *Aetia*, pp. 258–61), an origin myth for the Rhodian custom of fireless sacrifice at Athena's altar.

l. 88. *the Gray-Eyed One*: Athena.

142–3. ll. 90–94. *an artistry superior … their fame flowered*: Pindar alludes to the Telchines, mythical craftsmen of Rhodes, who evidently commanded automata similar to those that serve Hephaestus in Homer (*Il.* 18, ll. 416–20). Cf. Call. *Aet.* 1.1, p. 258, and n. on its l. 2.

143. l. 96. *And we've heard also …* : The transition to the third myth, about how Helius became the god of Rhodes, is more abrupt. In later times, Helius' face was on the island's coinage, and the famous Colossus of Rhodes was an image of him.

l. 114. *Lachesis*: One of the three Fates, whose name means 'She Who Allots'. Cf. Anon. 1018a+b (p. 240).

144. l. 128. *seven sons*: These are the Heliadae of the second myth. See l. 71 and n., above.

l. 130. *To one*: i.e., to Cercaphus.

l. 142. *a grand event*: The Tlapolemeia, pan-Rhodian games in honor of Tlapolemus.

l. 147. *Argive bronze*: A reference to the famous bronze shield awarded as prize in the Games of Hera at Argos; see n. on Call. *Hy.* 5, ll. 35–6 (p. 273).

l. 155. *Atabyrium*: The highest mountaintop of Rhodes.

145. ll. 167–8. *Callianax … Eratus*: Pindar addresses Diagoras; presumably Callianax and Eratus were ancestors of his.

Olympian 12. According to Pausanias (*Description of Greece* 6.4.11), Ergoteles won the long race twice at all four major games (see *Poet Intro*,

p. 134). Originally from Cnossus on Crete, he was driven to Himera on Sicily by political enemies (as Pindar also conveys in his epode, ll. 19–30). This ode was likely composed in honor of a Pythian victory of 466 and was placed among the Olympians by mistake.

Long Race: The *dolichos* was twelve laps of the stadium; as stadia varied in length (the stadium at Olympia was 210 yards, but that at Delphi only 195), so the length of the *dolichos* varied from place to place, but on average it was about twenty stades long, or a little less than 2½ miles.

l. 1. *daughter of Freeborn Zeus*: Tyche (Fortune, Chance) – an appropriate deity to whom to address this ode-as-prayer, given the vicissitudes of Ergoteles' life. 'Freeborn', as an epithet of Zeus (or 'Zeus the Deliverer'), was probably coined after the defeat of Persia (cf. the 'Festival of Freedom' at which Sim. *El.* 11 (p. 128) may have been performed). Here it may be used with reference to Himera's recent liberation from Syracuse.

l. 19. *Philanor*: Ergoteles' father.

146. ll. 20–21. *like an infighting cock at the local hearth where it was bred*: Roosters were associated with Himera and featured on the city's coinage. The cockfight is further emblematic of the civil upheavals of Cnossus; with 'local hearth', Pindar suggests that, had Ergoteles remained on Crete, his fame too would have remained provincial.

l. 26. *man-unmanning*: *Antianeira*, an epithet of Amazons at Hom. *Il.* 3, l. 189, and 6, l. 186.

l. 27. *Pytho*: See n. on *Pythian Odes* (p. 146), below.

l. 29. *the nymphs' warm waters*: The hot springs of Himera were famous, and, as the Termini Imerese, still are.

Pythian Odes. The Pythian Games, associated with Apollo, were held every four years at Delphi, alternating with the Olympic Games. The name 'Pytho' as a synonym for Delphi (frequent in Pindar) is connected with a myth first told in the *Homeric Hymn to Apollo*: shortly after Apollo's birth on Delos (described by Pindar in fr. 33d, p. 156), he went searching for a site at which to found his oracle. When he came to the future site of Delphi on Mount Parnassus (for the Greeks, the center of the earth), he found it defended by an enormous Python, which he slew with his arrows. Sometimes it is specified that Apollo was three days old when he performed this feat, or that he shot his arrows while cradled in his mother Leto's arms. Thereafter the place of the Python's defeat became known as 'Pytho' and Apollo's priestess as the 'Pythia' (or the 'Pythoness', as she used to be known in English). Sometimes, the ancients connected the name 'Python' to the Greek verb *pythesthai*, 'to rot', which is what the Python had done on the spot; at others, they connected it to *pynthanesthai*, 'to seek a response by inquiring', which is certainly what pilgrims at Pytho did; but the etymology is uncertain.

Pythian 3. Not on its face a victory ode, this 'Consolation to Hieron' (for whom, see n. on Pi. *Ol. 1, For Hieron of Syracuse*, p. 135) was included by the Alexandrian editors among the Pythians because it mentions (at ll. 106–8) a past victory of the Syracusan tyrant's horse Pherenicus (Prize-winner) at Delphi, probably in 478 BCE (cf. *Ol. 1*, l. 19, p. 136, and n.). A *felix culpa*, since *Py. 3* is among Pindar's greatest poems. Hieron is sick, and Pindar consoles him *in absentia* with an elaborate promise of poetic immortality, of which the ode is both defense and cause. It is a homily, albeit an indirect one; perhaps Hieron, like Louis XIV, was pleased 'to choose [his] part in a sermon', but not 'to be forced to take it' (see Alfred and Maurice Croiset, *An Abridged History of Greek Literature*, 'Melic Poetry', trans. George F. Heffelbower, p. 142). The advice Pindar offers is both exemplified in the extensive mythical narration – of Asclepius and Coronis at the start, and of Peleus and Cadmus at the end – and woven into the very nature of the consolation. We can only guess at the poem's date, but the late 470s seems plausible – perhaps 474, as Hieron did *not* triumph at Delphi in that year. Later, in 468, when Bacch. 3 (p. 167) congratulates Hieron on finally winning the chariot race at Olympia, his illness – which killed him the following year – is much worse.

ll. 1–2. *Chiron – sovereign offspring of Philyra*: For the Centaur and healer Chiron, see n. on Alc. 42, l. 9 (p. 58). His mother, Philyra, was a sea nymph, one of the many daughters of the Titans Oceanus and Tethys.

ll. 11–14. *Asclepius ... Phlegyas's daughter*: God of medicine, son of Apollo and Coronis (not named until l. 35); cf. Anon. 934 (p. 236) and nn. Phlegyas was king of the Lapiths, a Thessalian people; her brother was Ixion (see Tib. 1.3, ll. 73–4, p. 415, and n.).

l. 14. *Eileithyia*: Goddess of childbirth, sometimes identified with Artemis.

147. ll. 21–2. *she shared another's bed*: Ischys the Arcadian, named at l. 47, though her father had already had her conventionally betrothed to someone else.

l. 26. *She couldn't bide her time ...* : It may seem odd, since Coronis has already lost her virginity outside wedlock to Apollo, that Apollo should not be jealous of her marrying, but should be when she has a premarital affair. Yet perhaps 'double parentage', in this and other cases (cf. Heracles, son of Amphitryon and Zeus at Bacch. 5, 1.105, p. 117, Cat. 686, 1.111, p, 393, or the children of Leda in Stes. 85, l. 4, p. 92, and n.), offers a supernatural explanation for an extraordinary child, which today we would make with reference to 'nature and nurture', 'good genes', etc. In any event, Coronis' affair is culpable because it obscures the issue of the lawful husband; but the miraculous birth assures Asclepius' elevated place in the pantheon as a god of healing, a kind of Apolline Dionysus.

ll. 42–3. *the truest messenger, his mind . . . all things*: Pindar contradicts, by alluding to, the story Hesiod tells in his *Catalogue of Women* (fr. 60), where a raven, rather than his own omniscience, informs Apollo of Coronis' sin; in punishment, the bird is changed from white to black.

l. 50. *Lakereia* was in southeastern Thessaly, near Chiron's home in Magnesia (l. 66).

148. l. 51. *Lake Boebias*: Modern Lake Karla, drained in 1962 for farmland but perhaps one day to be refilled.

ll. 52–4. *cold fate came to cast her down . . .* : i.e., in the form of a plague: Artemis' 'golden shafts' here (l. 17) are disease-bearing, like those of her brother, Apollo. As often happens in myth, an individual's sexual misconduct brings misfortune on the entire community (cf. Oedipus at Thebes).

149. ll. 91–2. *Do not, dear heart . . .* : These lines, among Pindar's most famous, are quoted (in Greek) as the epigraph to Paul Valéry's 'Le Cimetière marin'.

ll. 93–111. *Yet if . . .* : The unreal condition beginning at l. 93 has troubled scholars who believe this poem is, in fact, a victory ode (epinician). Has Pindar come to Sicily (ll. 98–9) and brought a 'jubilee' (*komos*, ll. 103–6) as well as health? Or is he sending a *komos*, without either coming himself or bringing health? It seems easiest to understand him as saying that he has neither come nor brought health, and that this poem is not a *komos*, and it has therefore been classed among the epinicians by mistake. At any rate, what it means for a poet like Pindar (who normally would be expected personally to train the choruses that perform his poems) to send an ode from afar without coming himself is a whole other question, the answer to which presumably involves a written text.

l. 99. *Arethusa*: A spring in Syracuse (for the associated myth, see Vi. *Ecl.* 10, l. 1, p. 408, and n.).

Aetna: A town in Sicily, at the foot of Mount Aetna, founded by Hieron ('my host', named at l. 118) for his son Deinomenes, as recounted by Pindar in *Py*. 1. At one point, it was briefly equivalent to Catana (modern Catania).

l. 113. *the Great Mother, whose holy shrine is near my door*: Cybele (see Anon. 935, p. 237, and n.). Pausanias (*Description of Greece* 9.25.3) and the ancient commentators tell us there was indeed a temple to Cybele in Thebes near Pindar's house (which Alexander the Great famously spared when he destroyed the city in 335 BCE; cf. poem note on Bacch. fr. 20b, p. 185). Pindar's point here seems to be less the content of his prayer (presumably Hieron's recovery) than the fact that Pindar, following his own advice, is pursuing such measures as are readily available.

150. ll. 117–19. *what the old ones say ... dispensed by heaven*: The reference is to Hom. *Il.* 24, ll. 527–8, which most experts, following Plato (*Republic* 379d), take to mean that Zeus has two urns, one of evils, one of blessings; but Pindar understands Homer as speaking of three urns, two of which dispense evils, and only one blessings. Both readings fit the Greek, and it's hard to say whether these lines criticize the other interpretation. It's interesting to note, with Emmet Robbins ('The Gifts of the Gods', in *Thalia Delighting in Song*, p. 186), that most of the exemplary figures of Pindar's ode experience evil and good in a ratio near 2:1. Compare, also, Theog. ll. 1013–14 (p. 84) and Bacch. 5, ll. 167–8 (p. 173).

l. 132. *that shrewd Ancient of the Sea*: The sea god Nereus, possessed of prophetic powers.

l. 141. *three of his daughters*: Ino, Agave and Autonoë; all met with misfortunes. Both Agave and Autonoë saw their sons, Pentheus and Actaeon, dismembered – Actaeon by his own hounds (see n. on Call. *Hy.* 5, ll. 108–19, p. 275) and Pentheus by his own mother and aunts in a Dionysiac frenzy (see Phil. Scar. *PaeDi.*, ll. 14–16, p. 230, and n., not to mention the *Bacchae* of Euripides). Ino, pursued by her Hera-maddened husband, leapt into the sea with her infant son, Melicertes (see Ant. Si. 26, ll. 5–6 (p. 322), and n.). One story has it that the Isthmian Games (for which Pindar also wrote victory odes) were first held for the funeral of Melicertes.

ll. 143–4. *although Zeus did descend ...*: The fact that Semele, Cadmus' fourth daughter, eventually died because of the affair complicates the concession, though she was mother to the god Dionysus; for the story, see n. on Phil. Scar. *PaeDi.*, l. 1 (p. 229). The births of Dionysus and Asclepius are strikingly similar.

ll. 145–6. *Peleus's only boy, whom deathless Thetis bore ...*: Achilles.

151. l. 158. *so I aspire*: Pindar speaks in the first person and leaves Hieron (and us) to apply the poem's lessons on his own.

ll. 162–4. *We hear ... the wise ones who made poems*: Homer again. Sarpedon and Nestor are important supporting characters in the *Iliad*. Sarpedon was a son of Zeus and ally of Troy, who makes several memorable speeches (e.g., *Il.* 12, ll. 310–28: cf. n. on Pi. *Ol.* 1, ll. 91–106, p. 138) before he is killed by Patroclus; see especially Stesichorus' *Geryon* (frr. 15 and 18, pp. 90, 91, and nn.), where Geryon appears to be modeled in important ways on Sarpedon. Nestor, king of Pylos, is portrayed by Homer as a wise old man, Agamemnon's most trusted advisor; see also Ov. *Am.* 3.7, l. 43 (p. 508), Ov. *Ex Pont.* 2.4, l. 22 (p. 521) and n., and Mart. 5.58, l. 5 (p. 544).

Pythian 8. Metaphors of touch and grappling abound in this 'Letter to a Young Athlete', the latest of Pindar's victory odes. The aged poet unfolds for the boy victor Aristomenes a cosmic vision of dark and light, failure and success, violence and peace, mortality and transcendence, locked in a wrestling match. Against this precarious backdrop Pindar sets the brief brightness of youth and victory.

l. 1. *Calm*: Hesychia, peace and quiet, here both political (absence of civil conflict) and personal (repose after toil).

152.   l. 12. *Porphyrion*: The king of the Giants (also mentioned at l. 16). The Gigantomachy (battle with the Giants) is one of Greek myth's foundational wars between Chaos and Order that makes civilization possible; see also Xen. 1, l. 24 (p. 110) and n., Call. *Hy.* 5, ll. 7–8 (p. 272) and n., Prop. 2.1, ll. 19–20 (p. 427), and Ov. *Am.* 2.1, ll. 14–23 (pp. 498–9) and nn.

l. 13. *you'd prove his bane*: That Calm (or Peace) should defeat Chaos in battle is the first of the poem's paradoxical twinnings.

l. 16. *hundred-headed Typhus*: Also known as 'Typhoeus' and sometimes 'Typhaon'. According to Hesiod (*Th.*, ll. 820–68), he is the monstrous offspring of Gaea and Tartarus, who challenges Zeus for the rule of Olympus and is defeated by the thunderbolt; his challenge to heaven seems to have been issued sometime between the Titanomachy and the Gigantomachy (see n. on Xen. 1, l. 24, p. 110). Elsewhere (in the *Homeric Hymn to Apollo*), he is the son of Hera, born in retaliation for Zeus begetting Athena. According to Pindar (in *Py.* 1, ll. 15–28), he is imprisoned underground; stretching from Cumae to Aetna, he belches streams of fire that account for the region's volcanic activity.

l. 18. *Apollo's arrows also*: Here Apollo, by pelting the Giants with arrows, is playing a role elsewhere (for example, in Pi. *Nemean* 1, ll. 67–71) ascribed to Heracles.

l. 19. *Xenarces' son from Cirrha*: i.e., Aristomenes. Cirrha was a port city on the Gulf of Corinth which controlled access to Delphi.

l. 22. *this righteous island city*: Aegina, in the Saronic Gulf.

l. 24. *the Aeacids*: The descendants of Aeacus – Peleus, Telamon, Ajax and Achilles – are patron deities of Aegina often invoked by Pindar in poems for Aeginetan victors. Cf. ll. 99–100, below.

l. 36. *Theognetus*: An epigram from the *Greek Anthology* (16.2) attributed to 'Simonides' celebrates Theognetus' victory:

> Here's Theognetus, child Olympian
> and wrestling champ, who reined opponents in.
> Handsome and full of fight as he is pretty,
> he garlanded his noble fathers' city.

l. 37. *Clitomachus*: Otherwise unknown, though his name in Greek means 'Famed for Fighting'.

153. l. 39. *Amphiaraus' riddle*: Pindar's presentation here of the legendary defeat of the Seven Against Thebes and the aftermath (the eventual triumph of their children, the *Epigonoi* or Epigones) is compressed and elliptical. In the lost epic Theban Cycle (see Stes. 97, p. 93, and nn.), Oedipus' son Polynices and Tydeus (father of the Homeric hero Diomedes) arrive in Argos at the same time, having been exiled from Thebes and Calydon respectively, and marry the daughters of Adrastus, the king of Argos, who promises that he will help them regain their lost kingdoms. They set out for Thebes with an army raised from the Argolid. It is commanded by seven princes, whose names differ in different accounts, but which always include Tydeus and Amphiaraus, along with Adrastus and Polynices. (Amphiaraus, being a prophet, does not want to go, since he knows he will die, but is persuaded by his wife, Eriphyle, Adrastus' sister.) Ten years after the first war failed, the Epigones, again starting from Argos, manage to conquer Thebes, achieving what their fathers could not. In Pindar's poem, the prophet Amphiaraus, fighting in the first war (in which he is destined to die), foretells the success of the second and of his own son, Alcmaeon (who will also take revenge on his mother, Eriphyle, for sending his father Amphiaraus off to die; cf. *Anacreontea* 9, ll. 5–7, p. 360, and n.).

l. 46. *the dappled dragon*: A symbol of Alcmaeon's own gift of prophecy.

l. 48. *Adrastus*: The king of Argos, the leader of the initial campaign and the only one of the Seven to survive, Adrastus succeeds in conquering Thebes the second time around, but at the cost of his son's life.

l. 55. *Abas*: The twelfth king of Argos. Amphiaraus foresees the eventual victorious return of the Epigones to their home base of Argos.

ll. 55–60. . . . *he met me with his gift of sight* . . . : Mysterious lines – what does Pindar mean when he says he met the mythical Alcmaeon on his way to Delphi ('the navel of the earth': cf. Pi. *Pae.* 6, l. 19, p. 157; Philox. 836b+c, l. 46, p. 217, and n.; and Arist. *HHes.*, l. 5, p. 226, and n.)? Whether Pindar actually had such a vision is hard to guess, but poetically, there is a contrast between the violent encounter of Calm and Porphyrion (ll. 8–17) and the poet's joyful meeting with Alcmaeon (an enemy of his native Thebes), along with an emphasis on the kinship of poetry and prophecy.

l. 61. *Lord of the Long-Range Bow*: Apollo.

l. 66. *the Fivefold Crown*: Aristomenes won the pentathlon (cf. Xen. 2, l. 2, p. 111, and n.) at the Delphinia on Aegina, a festival dedicated to Apollo and Artemis.

154. l. 70. *As Justice takes her place*: The mother of Giant-vanquishing Calm, as we're told in l. 1. The ode shifts focus from fathers (Xenarces, Amphiaraus) to mothers, culminating with Mother Aegina (l. 98, below).

155. ll. 98–100. *Dear Mother Aegina* . . . : The ode concludes with a prayer to Aegina as both city and nymph, and her descendants, who become the island's patron heroes: Aeacus, who is her son by Zeus (see nn. on Cor. 654b, p. 201), his sons Peleus and Telamon, and his grandson Achilles (see n. on l. 24, above).

Hymn 1, To Zeus. As the statue of Zeus at Olympia was one of the wonders of the ancient world, this poem, if complete, would be one of the great treasures of Greek literature. We know from an anonymous ancient commentator that it stood at the head of the Alexandrian edition of Pindar and may have employed the wedding of Cadmus and Harmonia (cf. Pi. *Py.* 3, ll. 126–44, p. 150 and *Dith.* 2, ll. 36–41, p. 159) as a frame for the hymn, sung by Apollo and/or the Muses, listing all of Zeus's wives in turn, as in Hes. *Th.*, ll. 886–923.

29. This hymn's first lines – which no doubt originally represented a priamel (see n. on Hor. *Odes* 1.1, ll. 3–34, pp. 462–3) focusing our attention on the hymn's divine subject, Zeus – resonate with the start of

Pindar's Olympian 2. There is a famous (probably apocryphal) story that
Corinna, said (dubiously) to have been Pindar's teacher (see *Intro* to
Corinna, p. 199), once criticized her pupil for not using enough myths in
his poetry. The young Pindar came back with these lines, to which
Corinna responded: 'Sow with the hand, not with the full sack' (Plutarch,
On the Fame of the Athenians, 347f–348a). At any rate, the wedding of
Harmonia to Cadmus (ll. 7–8), which may have been the hymn's mythical
subject, would have been appropriate to a Theban festival setting. Other
references also focus on Thebes: Ismenus (l. 1) was a river near Thebes;
the sea nymph Melia (l. 2) was his mother; the 'Race of the Dragon' (l. 3)
were the *Spartoi*, the 'sown men' of Cadmus (l. 4: see *Intro* to the Archaic
Period, p. 3), the grandfather of Dionysus (l. 7; see n. on Phil. Scar. *PaeDi.*,
l. 1, p. 229); and Thebe (l. 4) was the eponymous nymph of Thebes (see
also Corinna 654b, ll. 12–18, p. 201, and n.). Also important at Thebes
was the cult of Heracles (l. 5), who was born there, and who led the
Thebans in the defeat of their Boeotian arch-rivals Orchomenus on the
way to marrying his first wife.

30. l. 1. *Themis*: 'Divine Order' or 'Law', Zeus's first wife according to
Pindar; but according to Hesiod (*Th.*, l. 901), his second, after Metis
(Wisdom), whom Zeus swallowed when she was already pregnant with
Athena. (For Athena's birth from Zeus's head, see *Ol.* 7, ll. 61–8, p. 142.)

l. 9. *the Seasons*: See n. on the anonymous *Hymn to Zeus on Mount
Dicte, Crete*, ll. 37–40 (p. 235); and cf. Pi. *Dith.* 4, ll. 17–19 (p. 160).

156. 33c. l. 1. *you, heaven's seedling*: The Cycladic island of Delos, where Leto
(Zeus's sixth wife and last before Hera, according to Hesiod) gave birth
to Apollo and Artemis. The famous story, told first in the *Homeric Hymn
to Apollo*, is sketched by Pindar in the next fragment.

ll. 7–8. *star of their blue firmament*: Pindar imaginatively sees our ocean
as a heaven above the gods' heads, with Delos as its North Star.

Paean 6, For the Delphians at Delphi. We possess about two-thirds of this
180-line poem, though only the introductory triad is excerpted here. The
poem goes on, in the second triad, to limn the career of Achilles' son
Neoptolemus at Troy and afterwards, while the third describes the origin
of the island of Aegina.

l. 5. *this holy hour*: The poem was composed for the Theoxenia, 'the
gods' guest-feast' (l. 60), an annual festival held in the ninth Delphian
month (March/April), which entertained various other gods as Apollo's
guests (*xenoi*).

157. ll. 7–8. *Castalia's spate . . . the brazen gate*: The Castalian spring on Mount Parnassus, at Delphi, was associated with Apollo and poetic inspiration. Its waters (still flowing today, and potable!) were used by temple officials to clean the god's cult statue and oracle. The scholia – anonymous ancient commentators – say that the spring flowed out through a bronze spout in the shape of a lion's head.

l. 9. *men's song and dance*: The paean was traditionally a men's genre, orderly, sober, martial. See also n. on Ar. 120+121, l. 3 (p. 10).

ll. 10–11. *your clan's honor, and mine*: Pindar may refer to his specific privileges at Delphi; for example, according to Plutarch, his descendants were entitled to a prime cut of the sacrificial meat at the Theoxenia (*On the Delays in Divine Vengeance*, 557f–558a), an honor which the poet may also have been entitled to while alive (*Metrical Life of Pindar*, ll. 16–18).

l. 19. *leaf-dark navel of the world*: For the epithet, see Pi. *Py*. 8, l. 58 (p. 153), Philox. 836b+c, l. 46 (p. 217) and n., and Arist. *HHes*., l. 5, (p. 226) and n.

l. 62. *Loxias*: A common epithet for Apollo, perhaps 'Riddler', from the riddling (*loxos*, 'slanting', 'oblique') answers given by his oracle at Delphi.

Paean 9, For the Thebans. This fragment forms part of the Archaic sub-genre of eclipse poetry: Archilochus (cf. Ar. 122, p. 10), Mimnermus (pp. 27–30) and Stesichorus (pp. 89–95) also wrote eclipse poems. It reacts to the solar eclipse of either 30 April 463 BCE or 17 February 478 BCE. The poem was performed at the temple of Apollo Ismenius on the Ismenus River at Thebes, and went on to relate some incident from the life of Tenerus, brother of Ismenus, both sons of Apollo and the sea nymph Melia. As god of light and the sun, Apollo is an appropriate addressee for this poem. Pindar employs the paean here in its apotropaic aspect, praying to transmute any bad portents into some local benefit for Thebes.

158. *Dithyramb 2, Heracles, or Cerberus*. Where the paean honors Apollo, the dithyramb honors Dionysus. Where the paean celebrates male solidarity and social order, the dithyramb is wild, unrestrained and transgressive; possibly it also makes more use of extended narrative. This one, according to its title, should have told of Heracles' Twelfth Labor – his descent to the underworld, to capture Cerberus (retold in part at Bacch. 5, ll. 69–218, pp. 173–7); but the two surviving strophes barely get us past the gods at their 'Bacchic rites' (l. 8). The poem may have been quite long. For Heracles' worship at Thebes, see n. on fr. 29 (p. 155), above; for Cybele's (l. 11), see n. on *Py*. 3, l. 113 (p. 149).

ll. 1–4. *Before now ... in false, discordant style*: The present translation, in rendering this vexed passage, follows the interpretation of Armand D'Angour ('How the Dithyramb Got Its Shape', *Classical Quarterly* 47:2, 1997, pp. 331–51), who believes Pindar is glossing the recent transformation of the dithyramb from a single-file procession to a circular chorus (cf. n. on Ar. 120+121, l. 2, p. 10), both more suited to theaters built into hillsides, in which the spectators look down on the performance from above, and more conducive to unison among the singers, allowing them to avoid the unpleasant hissing effect caused by an even slightly staggered pronunciation of words containing *sigma* (the letter *s*). This last problem had famously been addressed by Lasus of Hermione, who, a generation before Pindar, had composed dithyrambs which simply eschewed the letter, like an ancient Georges Perec; but the recent restructuring of the chorus has solved the problem in a simpler, less technically demanding way.

159. ll. 23–4. *Pallas' shield ... a thousand snakes*: This is the aegis, often depicted as a shield carried by Athena, though sometimes it is apparently a breastplate or monster skin. (The truth is that the ancients did not really know what it was, and even Homer himself may not have known.) Often, as apparently here, it is adorned with Medusa's severed snaky head; at *Il.* 2, ll. 448–9, it has a hundred golden tassels, which here seem to have multiplied and become the hissing serpents of Medusa's hair.

l. 41. *a daughter famous the world over*: Semele, Dionysus' mother (see Phil. Scar. *PaeDi.*, ll. 1–7, pp. 229–30, and nn.).

160. *Dithyramb 4, For the Athenians.* Quoted by Dionysius of Halicarnassus (*On Composition* 22), as a representative example of the 'austere style' in poetry (cf. *Poet Intro*, p. 134). The poem was composed for a spring festival of Dionysus – probably the Great Dionysia at Athens; the focus on Semele (l. 14) suggests that Dionysus' birth may have been its theme. Bacch. 19 (p. 183) may also have been composed, in the same genre, for the same event.

l. 14. Pi., Fr. *Cadmus*: 'l. 14. *Semele*. See Phil. Scar. *PaeDi.*, ll. 1–7 (p. 229–30) and nn. For *Cadmus*, see n. on *Hymn* 1, fr. 29 (p. 155), above.

l. 17. *The Seasons*: See n. on the anonymous *Hymn to Zeus on Mount Dicte, Crete*, ll. 37–40 (p. 235); and cf. Pi. fr. 30, ll. 9–10 (p. 155).

Hyporchemes. The Alexandrian edition of Pindar contained two books of hyporchemes, of which only a few fragments survive. Mimetic dance, in which performers acted out the scenes or events described, was the genre's defining feature. The excerpts here suggest the genre's civic concerns. Viewing of, and participation in, such dances was essential training for citizens of a Greek city-state.

108a+b. The two fragments are quoted in different places, but combined by editors.

161. *Scolia.* The Alexandrian book in which these poems were collected was titled *Encomia* – that is, 'praise songs', usually choral, addressed to important men and occasions unrelated to athletic or musical victory – but it included *scolia*, more informal songs, usually solo, to be sung as a toast after a banquet. The former may have been more ambitious but the extant fragments of the latter, all quoted by the charmingly pedantic Athenaeus in his *Scholars at Dinner*, are more substantial and interesting. In them, we find a lightness of touch and an approachability not elsewhere prominent in Pindar.

122. In 464 BCE, the rich Corinthian Xenophon won a double Olympic victory in the stade race and the pentathlon (cf. Xen. 2, l. 2, p. 111, and n.). As was customary in Corinth, a city famed for its *hetairai* and its veneration of Aphrodite, he dedicated a hundred 'hierodules' (temple prostitutes) to the goddess in gratitude. Pindar composed an epinician for the victory (*Ol.* 13) and this *scolion* for the dedication.

162. ll. 19–20. *the touchstone proves its worth*: Cf. Theog. l. 449 (p. 82) and n.

123. We are told, though there is no reason to trust the anecdote, that Pindar died in Argos in the embrace of Theoxenus of Tenedos, the love of his late years and the dedicatee of this poem, his one extant foray into Anacreon's amorous territory (pp. 100–108).

163. *124a+b.* Both fragments are quoted by Athenaeus in *Deip*, Book 11 (at 480c and 782d) and commonly joined.

Threnoi. For Thrasybulus of Acragas: The nephew of the tyrant Theron of Acragas (see n. on Pi. *Ol.* 1, p. 135), whose chariot victories Pindar celebrated in Olympians 2 and 3, and son of the Xenocrates whose chariot victories Pindar celebrated in Pythian 6, and Isthmian 2. Compare Bacch. fr. 20b (p. 185) for genre and theme.

129. Both this and the next fragment (131b) from Pindar's dirges (choral poems of lament for the dead, accompanied by pipe) are quoted by Plutarch in his *Letter of Consolation to Apollonius* (35.120c–e). The mystical vision of the underworld offered by Pindar (here, and in *Ol.* 2) had a great influence on Plato.

ll. 1–3. . . . *the sun shines on the lower* . . . : Callimachus makes a similar claim in his *Victory of Berenice* (*Aet.* 3.54–9, ll. 11–14).

164. *137.* An example of *makarismos*: see n. on Alcm. 1, ll. 37–9 (p. 32); and cf. Pi. *Ol.* 7, ll. 15–16 (p. 140).

l. 2. *the Mysteries*: At Eleusis – cf. Phil. Scar. *PaeDi.*, ll. 27–36 (p. 230) and nn.; Crin. 35 (p. 343); and Hor. *Odes* 3.2, ll. 26–7 (p. 480) and n.

Bacchylides

165. *Poet Introduction. he did his best work while in exile*: Plutarch, *On Exile* 14.

damned with faint praise: Pseudo-Longinus, *On the Sublime* 33.4 (trans. Russell):

> Take lyric poetry: would you rather be Bacchylides or Pindar? Take tragedy: would you rather be Ion of Chios [pp. 196–7] or Sophocles? Ion and Bacchylides are impeccable, uniformly beautiful writers in the polished manner; but it is Pindar and Sophocles who sometimes set the world on fire with their vehemence, for all that their flame often goes out without reason and they collapse dismally.

166. *Wilamowitz wrote*: In D. L. Cairns, *Bacchylides: Five Epinician Odes*, 'General Introduction', p. 16n.

Adam Parry describes: In Bacchylides, *Complete Poems*, trans. Robert Fagles, 'Notes', p. 109, referring to Bacch. 5 (p. 171).

167. *3, For Hieron ... 468* BCE: See n. on Pi. *Ol.* 1, For Hieron of Syracuse (p. 135). Written one year before Hieron's death in 467, this poem celebrates the tyrant's greatest athletic achievement (prayed for by Pindar at *Ol.* 1, ll. 135–6, p. 139) while also consoling him in what must have plainly been his final illness. It is thus a sort of companion to Pindar's own 'Consolation to Hieron', *Py.* 3 (p. 146).

l. 1. *Hail, Clio*: Later the Muse of history, but also associated with lyric, Clio (whose name means 'Proclaimer') is an appropriate addressee. In general, Bacchylides uses the different Muses interchangeably (cf. the references to Urania and Calliope in Bacch. 5, ll. 15 and 220, pp. 171 and 177, below).

l. 2. *Sicily ... where fruits abound*: For the proverbial richness of Sicily, cf. Pi. *Ol.* 1, l. 14 (p. 136).

l. 3. *her Daughter*: After the victory over the Carthaginians at Himera in 480 BCE (see n. on Bacch. 5, l. 40, p. 172), Hieron had dedicated a temple to Demeter and Kore ('Daughter', i.e., Persephone), a cult in which he held a hereditary priesthood. Persephone was particularly associated with Sicily, the usual site of her abduction by Hades (the location of Milton's 'fair field / Of Enna, where Proserpin gathering flowers / Herself a fairer flower by gloomy Dis / Was gathered': *Paradise Lost* 4, ll. 268–71), as well as with the Eleusinian Mysteries and the hope of a beatific life to come; she was thus doubly germane to the ailing Hieron.

l. 7. *wide-roiling Alpheus*: See n. on Pi. *Ol.* 1, l. 23 (p. 136).

l. 11. *son of Deinomenes*: i.e., Hieron, whose father and son shared the name Deinomenes.

l. 15. *o triply fortunate*: To a listening audience without the benefit of punctuation, this *makarismos* (see n. on Alcm. 1, ll. 37–9, p. 32) may seem at first a direct quote of the crowd – though as it goes on, the poet's voice takes over.

ll. 24–5. The scene shifts from the brimming *streets* of Syracuse to the *intricate tripods* at Delphi. These were solid gold dedications made by Hieron and his brother Gelon – in Gelon's case, to commemorate the victory at Himera (cf. n. on l. 3, above); in Hieron's, possibly with reference to the victory at Cumae (see n. on Pi. *Ol.* 1, *For Hieron of Syracuse*, p. 135).

168. l. 30. *Castalia's fountain*: See n. on Pi. *Pae.* 6, ll. 7–8 (p. 157).

l. 33. *Consider the high king*: Croesus. The canonical version of this story, which differs somewhat from Bacchylides', is found at Hdt. *Hist.* 1. 86–7. Both Croesus' rich dedications to Delphi, and his dire circumstances, present an apt analogy to Hieron's own ailing condition.

l. 37. *through Zeus's might*: Herodotus does not involve Zeus, but Bacchylides includes him to strengthen the parallel with Hieron – the Olympics were Zeus's games.

ll. 41–7. *Facing down a grim day ... and climbed it*: In Herodotus' version, the Persian victor Cyrus the Great has the pyre built and orders Croesus placed on it, but Bacchylides grants the defeated king the dignity of agency.

ll. 56–7. *where is Lord Apollo ... ?*: Croesus' indignation is paralleled at Hdt. *Hist.* 1.90. Eventually, instead of executing Croesus, Cyrus enslaves him; Croesus sends his fetters to Delphi and asks 'whether the Greek gods were in the habit of being ungrateful'. The answer: it is 'impossible, even for a god, to escape the apportioned fate' (1.91).

l. 59. *Pytho*: See n. on Pindar, *Pythian Odes* (p. 146).

169. l. 62. *Medes*: See Theog. l. 764 (p. 83) and n.

l. 64. *once eddying with gold*: The River Pactolus, now the Sart Çayı, was famous for its gold dust.

l. 69. *the servant*: Named Euthymus (Of Good Cheer) on a particularly beautiful red-figure amphora at the Louvre, roughly contemporary with Bacchylides' poem and painted by one Myson, which depicts this scene. Besides its beauty, the painting is unusual as well, in that it depicts a historical rather than a mythical subject.

ll. 71–2. *A cry leapt . . . their fingertips*: The mother and daughters do not appear either on Myson's amphora or in Herodotus; Bacchylides may have added them to intensify the emotions of the moment.

ll. 81–3. *No miracle exceeds . . . a god's concern . . .* : For the sentiment, cf. also Bacch. 17, ll. 131–3 (p. 182).

l. 85. *the Hyperboreans*: The inhabitants of a mythical paradise 'Beyond the North Wind' connected with Apollo, who spends the winters there.

170. l. 95. *Loxias*: Apollo. See Pi. *Pae.* 6, l. 62 (p. 157) and n.

l. 109. *Admetus, Pheres' son*: A Thessalian king beloved of Apollo (see Call. *Hy.* 2, ll. 47–54, p. 270, and n. on l. 49), and thus a second mythical parallel for Hieron. Like Croesus, he was also saved from death by Apollo, who, at the hour appointed for his death, convinced the Fates to let another take his place; his wife Alcestis volunteered, and was eventually rescued by Heracles. In this epode, which balances the first, Bacchylides again lets his voice blend in with another speaker's.

l. 125. *gold is delight*: And, used well, purchases delights, such as Hieron's Olympic chariot victory (horses, chariots, charioteers, etc., were naturally quite expensive), and Croesus' miraculous reprieve.

171. l. 140. *the Cean nightingale*: Bacchylides. The contrast of Bacchylides' melodious bird with the majesty and dash of Pindar's preferred eagle (see n. on Bacch. 5, ll. 19–36, p. 172) may well be deliberate.

5. Composed to celebrate the same victory as Pi. *Ol.* 1 (p. 135); Hieron (see n. *ad loc.*, *For Hieron of Syracuse*) did win a second single-horse victory at the Olympics, probably in 472, but probably not with the same horse, Pherenicus (Prizewinner).

l. 1. *O lord*: In this unprecedented beginning, the poem opens with a hymn-style invocation of a mortal, the victorious Hieron.

l. 12. *its fine-woven trim*: An etymology current in the time of Bacchylides and Pindar derived 'hymn' (*hymnos*) from *hyphainein*, 'to weave'.

l. 13. *Ceos*: Modern Kea, an island in the Cyclades, home both to Bacchylides and his uncle Simonides (pp. 120–33).

l. 15. *Urania*: Later the Muse of astronomy, but here just a general representative of the Muses (cf. the invocation of Calliope in l. 220, below, and Clio in Bacch. 3, l. 1, p. 167, and n., above).

172. ll. 19–36. *On high* . . . : To this eagle simile, compare Dante, *Inferno* 4, ll. 95–6, where Virgil is 'that lord of loftiest song, / who flies above the others like an eagle'. Eagle imagery is frequent in Pindar as well, and is likely at the root of the tradition about his antagonistic relationship with Bacchylides. For example, in a poem composed for the same games as this one – to honor the more prestigious four-horse chariot victory of Hieron's rival Sicilian monarch, Theron of Acragas – Pindar writes (*Ol.* 2, ll. 86–8):

> Nature supplies
> true wisdom; learners are like crows who chatter,
> cacophonous and vain, their empty matter
> where Zeus's eagle owns the air.

Is one passage responding to the other? Does Pindar mean that he has the 'true wisdom' of Nature, while Bacchylides is a mere 'learner'? Is Bacchylides the 'Cean nightingale' (see Bacch. 3, l. 140, p. 171, above) one of the 'jackdaws' Pindar derides at Nemean 3, ll. 80–83?

> The eagle's precipitate flight
> outdistances birds, and swoops from a towering height,
> sudden, gaffing its prey,
> while far below the jabbering jackdaws preen.

Pindar also compares himself to an eagle in Nemean 5, ll. 20–21. However, modern scholars tend to regard this tradition of hostility as the fabrication of the poets' commentators and biographers, whose only or chief source of information was the poems themselves, and whose entire method consisted in applying inappropriately personal readings to texts with far more literary concerns. Whatever the case, in the present poem the figure of the eagle surely suggests both the transcendent lordliness of Hieron and the easy flight of Bacchylides' praise. It also anticipates Pherenicus' victorious race in Str. 2, below.

l. 40. *sable-braided Victory*: Bacchylides is also thinking of the victories won by Hieron and his brothers Gelon and Polyzelus – hence '*sons of Deinomenes*' in l. 42 – over the Carthaginians at Himera in 480 BCE (cf. nn. on Bacch. 3, ll. 3 and 24–5, p. 167), as well as Gelon's Olympic chariot victory in 488, and perhaps also Polyzelus' Pythian victory in 478 (or 474) BCE, in honor of which the famous bronze charioteer of Delphi was erected.

l. 45. *Gold-armed Dawn*: The horse races began early in the morning on the second day of the festival, which was the first of events.

173. l. 51. *and crowned in Pytho's sacred space*: Pherenicus had previously won the same event at Delphi (perhaps twice). For Pytho, see n. on Pindar, *Pythian Odes* (p. 146).

l. 53. *hand on the ground*: The gesture marks the solemnity of the oath.

ll. 63–6. *Happy the man* ... : For this *makarismos* motif, see n. on Alcm. 1, ll. 37–9 (p. 32).

ll. 67–8. *No earthbound ... no bad*: Compare Theog. ll. 1013–14 (p. 84) and Pi. *Py.* 3, ll. 116–56 (pp. 149–51), especially ll. 117–19 and n., and ll. 155–6.

173–7. l. 69–218. *The story goes* ... : The mythical section of this ode combines two stories, as far as we can tell for the first time: Heracles' Twelfth Labor – the capture of Cerberus, the many-headed hound of Hades – and Meleager's death as a result of the hunt for the Calydonian Boar and the subsequent war between the Calydonians and the neighboring Curetes. Both Cerberus and the boar are peripheral to the heroes' dramatic encounter, which provides a kind of minor-key contrast to the major key of praise with which the ode opens and closes.

Bacchylides' poem is not the only account of Heracles' meeting with Meleager's ghost, though the story is rare in art and literature. Pindar (pp. 134–64) told it in a poem which survives in an anonymous ancient summary. His main interest in the episode seems to have been Meleager's ghost urging Heracles to marry his sister Deianira (as in ll. 212–18 of the present poem). Pindar then follows Heracles from the underworld to Meleager's homeland of Aetolia, where Heracles out-wrestles the river god Achelous, to whom Deianira has been betrothed, thus winning the maiden's hand. Bacchylides, by contrast, focuses only on the conversation between Heracles and Meleager, in effect ending where Pindar began – with the conversation about marriage. Interestingly, Bacchylides (ll. 206–11) makes Heracles' admiration of Meleager the motive for the desire to marry; in Pindar, it seems rather to have been Meleager's admiration for Heracles which prompted the suggestion. One further difference between Bacchylides' and Pindar's versions involves the story of Meleager's death (ll. 117–91). Pindar apparently did not mention the Boar-Hunt or the war which followed, but that tale is recounted at length in Homer's *Iliad* (*Il.* 9, ll. 529–99; and see n. on l. 130, below). As usual, the question of 'originality' in such matters is impossible to determine. We cannot know which poem – Pindar's or Bacchylides' – came first, or to what extent either or both may be following some lost prior version – as told by Stesichorus in his *Boar-Hunters*, say (see *Intro* to Stesichorus, p. 89), or by a minor epic poet.

l. 70. *Persephone's house*: This *katabasis* (descent into hell) of Heracles is alluded to at Hom. *Il.* 8, ll. 364–9, and *Od.* 11, ll. 621–66.

l. 75. *a dog*: Cerberus, monstrous canine offspring of the snake-woman Echidna (l. 77) and the hundred-headed Typhus (see Pi.*Py.* 8, l.16 p.152 and n.). The hellhound is traditionally depicted with three heads, but see n. on Hor. *Odes* 2.13, ll. 33–4 (p. 475).

ll. 80–81. *like whirling leaves*: These lines show an obvious debt to the famous simile of Homer quoted in Sim. *Ep.* 19+20, l. 2 (p. 129), and also alluded to in Mimn. 2 (p. 28). Virgil may follow Bacchylides directly at *Aen.* 6, ll. 309–10.

l. 83. *Ida's sheep-sustaining slopes*: The Homeric context points toward the Mount Ida about twenty miles southeast of Troy, rather than the Mount Ida on Crete, where the infant Zeus is sometimes said to have been nursed.

174. l. 91. *from hook to hook*: Modeled after Hom. *Od.* 11, ll. 605–8, where Odysseus describes his encounter with the ghost of Heracles in the underworld.

l. 105. *Amphitryon's lordly breed*: Heracles, a famous example of so-called 'double parentage' (see Pi. *Py.* 3, l. 26, p. 147, and n.). Amphitryon was the husband of Alcmene (l. 90, above) and the mortal father of Heracles, whose divine father was Zeus. See also Cat. 68b, l. 111 (p. 393).

l. 113. *Pallas' whim*: As she did with Odysseus, Athena protected Heracles and aided in his labors.

175. ll. 123–5. *dropped her wrath when Oeneus ... great abundance*: Meleager omits the reason for Artemis' wrath – that the king of the Calydonians, Oeneus, had previously forgotten to sacrifice to her (Hom. *Il.* 9, ll. 534–7).

l. 130. *she sent a boar*: The story of the Calydonian Boar, and the war that subsequently broke out over the boar's hide between the

Calydonians and the Curetes, is here much elaborated and embellished
from Phoenix's telling at Hom. *Il.* 9, ll. 538–49. Though Homer's version
is earlier in time, we cannot for that reason consider it more canonical or
less innovative than Bacchylides', as if it were some archetypal original
Bacchylides is varying, for the simple reason that Homer has obviously
tailored the details of his narrative to suit the *Iliad*'s larger dramatic situation. In the *Iliad*, the story is told by Achilles' tutor, Phoenix, who is
trying to persuade his former pupil to return to the fighting at Troy. Phoenix adduces Meleager's story as a negative example of what will happen
if Achilles persists in his current path. In the war over the boar's hide,
Meleager found himself on the opposite side from his mother's brothers,
whom he slew in battle. (His mother, Althaea, was daughter of the
Curetes' king, Thestius.) According to Phoenix, Meleager withdrew from
the battle after Althaea cursed him for killing his uncles, and did not
return to the fray until the enemy was practically beating down the doors;
consequently, he received none of the glory, rewards or gratitude he
would have earned if he had been less intransigent. Phoenix's moral is
clear: Achilles should return to the fighting *now* if he does not want to
suffer Meleager's disgrace. Bacchylides, by contrast, says nothing of sulk-
ing or last-minute heroics; instead, his version makes use of the sort of
folktale elements which the *Iliad* tends to eschew. We therefore have
reason to suspect that Bacchylides' version, though temporally later than
Homer's, may draw on earlier, more 'original' material.

l. 133. *the vine rows*: Perhaps a nod to the name of Oeneus (Wine-King).

l. 139. *Aetolians*: Meleager's homeland of Aetolia, with its capital of
Calydon, was located on the northwest coast of the Gulf of Corinth. The
Iliad (ll. 9.544–5) mentions that Meleager 'gathered from many cities
hunters and hounds', among whom Stesichorus, in his *Boar-Hunters*,
numbers Locrians, Achaeans, Boeotians and Dryopians. But heroes came
from farther afield as well. The famous François Vase, an early sixth-
century BCE black-figure *krater* or wine bowl, specifically names Melanion
(often confused or conflated with Meleager), Atalanta, Peleus, Admetus,
Castor and Polydeuces; Ancaeus, the first to be killed by the boar in this
poem (l. 147), is also depicted as a casualty on the vase. Later authors,
including Ovid and the mythographers Hyginus and Apollodorus, indulge
in increasingly elaborate lists, adding such names as Amphiaraus, Cae-
neus, Jason, Laertes, Pirithöus, Telamon and Theseus.

l. 141. *when deity gave the victory to us*: Atalanta wounded, and Meleager killed, the boar. Meleager's humility here is striking.

l. 153. *Leto's fire-minded daughter*: Artemis. Bacchylides uses the same adjective, *daiphron* – from *dais* (torch), and so, literally, 'fiery-minded', or 'ruinously angry' – to describe both Artemis and Althaea (l. 169, below). The repetition of the *dai-* sound connects to others in the poem, including the name *Deianira*; see n. on l. 214, below.

l. 156. *Curetes*: A people of ancient Aetolia, rival to Meleager's Calydonians. Oeneus was king of the Calydonians, and Thestius (Althaea's father) of the Curetes. They are to be distinguished from the Curetes who protected the infant Zeus (see Cor. 654a, ll. 12–18, p. 200, and n., and the anonymous *Hymn to Zeus on Mount Dicte, Crete*, ll. 17–20, pp. 234–5, and n.).

176. ll. 174–80. ... *the kindling into which my swift doom was compressed* ...: According to Hyginus (*Fabulae* 171), at Meleager's birth one of the Fates, glancing at a log burning on the hearth, prophesied that 'Meleager would live only so long as that log remained unconsumed by flame.' Althaea then extinguished the flame to save her son; but now she takes advantage of the prophecy to wreak her vengeance. The whole story has the air of popular legend; as mentioned above (n. on l. 130) the Log of Doom is the kind of magical element which Homer, in the *Iliad* at least, avoids. We may therefore suspect that Bacchylides, rather than inventing this part of the story, is actually reaching back to an earlier version of the tale which Homer's telling alters for reasons of his own.

l. 183. *Daipylus*: 'The key sound [*dai-*] is also reiterated ... in the perfectly gratuitous name given to Meleager's victim's father' (Anne Pippin Burnett, *The Art of Bacchylides*, p. 144).

l. 187. *Pleuron*: Capital city of the Curetes.

l. 188. *life's sweetness*: 'A rarer notion in early Greek than one might think' (D. L. Cairns, *Bacchylides: Five Epinician Odes*, 'Commentary on Ode 5', p. 240). Cf. Anac. 395, l. 7 (p. 106), Pi. *Py*. 8, ll. 92–7 (pp. 154–5). The Greek phrasing evokes the death of Hector at Hom. *Il*. 22, ll. 361–3.

177. l. 200. *'Best is for mortals never to be born'*: A much more common Greek sentiment. Cf. Theog. l. 425 (p. 82) and n.

ll. 202–3. *But what way forward* ... ?: Bacchylides probably had in mind Achilles' consolatory advice to Priam at Hom. *Il*. 24, l. 549. The ode manages to allude to and condense a remarkable number of Homer's most memorable moments – all likely recognizable to its audience, and to Hieron, whose poetic acumen Bacchylides praises at ll. 3–7 (p. 171).

l. 211. *For I would gladly wish to wed her*: Note that Pindar, as summarized in the n. to ll. 69–218, above, made Meleager suggest the marriage. Bacchylides' difference is of a piece with the poem's thematic emphasis on the gap between human and divine knowledge and the influence of fortune or fate on human life.

l. 214. *Deianira*: In this name (Man-Destroyer), spelled *Daianeira* by Bacchylides, we hear an echo of *daiphron* (fire-minded), used twice above, at ll. 153 and 169. Deianira will eventually be responsible for Heracles' fiery death:

> Love is the unfamiliar Name
> Behind the hands that wove
> The intolerable shirt of flame
> Which human power cannot remove.
>   (T. S. Eliot, 'Little Gidding', IV, ll. 208–11)

Yet the union with Deianira may also look forward to the birth of Heracles' son Hyllus, in accordance with whose rule Pindar says Hieron founded the new city of Aetna (*Py.* 1).

l. 220. *Calliope*: Later the Muse of epic poetry, but here just one of the Muses. Cf. the invocation of Urania in l. 15, above, as well as Clio in Bacch. 3, l. 1 (p. 167) and n.

l. 221. *halt here*: This so-called 'break-off formula' is a common technique in epinician poetry (cf., e.g., Pi. *Ol.* 1, ll. 126–8, p. 139, and *Py.* 3, ll. 112–15, p. 149); here it reinforces the poem's (very Virgilian) subtheme of the limits of human knowledge.

l. 226. *Pisa*: The district around Olympia, in the state of Elis.

178. l. 231. *a leaf from gracious fortune's tree*: An olive crown was the prize of victory at Olympia.

ll. 240–41. Perhaps a summary (not a direct quote!) of Hes. *Th.*, ll. 81–97. This is the only place where Bacchylides refers to a previous poet by name.

17. The story told in this poem, about a showdown between Theseus and Minos over their divine parentage as the Athenians are on their way to Crete, is nowhere mentioned before Bacchylides, which leads us to assume that he invented it himself. It's also probably one of the first poems he ever composed, as a vase by the potter Euphronius of the 490s BCE, when Bacchylides may still have been in his early twenties, clearly illustrates ll. 121–8 of Bacchylides' narrative. The background is the

popular story in which Athens was required to send a periodic tribute of seven youths and seven maidens to the Minotaur as recompense for the death of Minos' son Androgeus. The poem was performed by Bacchylides' countrymen in honor of Apollo at the god's birthplace of Delos (cf. Pi. fr. 33c, p. 156, and n., and fr. 33d, p. 156).

An ancient scholar tells us that this ode's genre was disputed in Alexandria: Callimachus (pp. 255–81) considered it a paean, no doubt influenced by the Delian performance context and the concluding address to Apollo (ll. 146–8, p. 182), but Aristarchus of Samothrace (see *Poet Intro*, p. 165) grouped it among the dithyrambs, on the grounds that only a dithyramb could contain such a long mythical narrative. Aristarchus' opinion carried the day; yet he seems to have been mistaken, with the true generic difference based more in function and performance than narrative content. According to our papyrus, the poem is Dithyramb 3, but I am happy to side with Callimachus and call it a paean. For more on the vexed distinction between paeans and dithyrambs, see nn. on Ar. 120+121, ll. 2–3 (p. 10).

l. 3. *splendid Ionians*: As the poem is to be performed by natives of one Ionian island on another, Bacchylides assimilates Athens as well to the wider pan-Ionian context.

179. l. 8. *aegis-wielding Athena's august urging*: Athena helps Athenians, as usual. For her aegis, see Pi. *Dith.* 2, ll. 23–4 (p. 159) and n.

l. 16. *Eriboea shouted*: Bacchylides plays on the etymology of *Eriboea* (Far-Shouting).

l. 17. *Pandion's heir*: Pandion II (see Sim. *El.* 11, ll. 37 and 41, p. 129, and nn.) was the father of Aegeus, Theseus' mortal father; his acknowledgment here is no obstacle to Theseus also being the son of Poseidon. On mythical 'double parentage', see n. on Pi. *Py.* 3, l. 26 (p. 147) and n.

l. 34. *under Ida's cliff*: This will be the Cretan Mount Ida, rather than the one near Troy.

l. 35. *Phoenix's child*: Europa (see Prop. 2.28, l. 52, p. 432, and n.). This Phoenix, to be distinguished from Achilles' tutor in the *Iliad* (see n. on Bacch. 5, l. 130, p. 175, above), was the eponymous king of Phoenicia, a son of Agenor of Tyre, and either the father of Europa and Cadmus (as here) or their brother (as, presumably, at Bacch. 19, l. 46, p. 184, where Cadmus is the son of Agenor).

l. 38. *Pittheus's daughter*: Aethra. Pittheus was king of Troezen, and a son of Pelops.

180. ll. 56–7. *the son-in-law of Helius*: Minos' wife, Pasiphaë, was a daughter of Helius, sister of Circe and Aeëtes, and aunt of Medea. See also nn. on Prop. 2.1, ll. 53–6 (p. 428), and 2.28, l. 52 (p. 432).

181. l. 109. *the Lord of Horses*: Poseidon is associated with horses, either as their tamer or father.

ll. 109–11. *Theseus was riding . . . dolphins*: Bacchylides may have been influenced by the story of Arion, which we know from Herodotus' account of it at *Hist.* 1.23–4. See also Anon. 939 (p. 239).

181–2. ll. 114–15. *girls of blessed Nereus*: The Nereids (sea nymphs), depicted here as a kind of undersea version of the Muses, in honor of Poseidon and his queen, Amphitrite, dance but (unlike the Muses) do not sing.

182. l. 136. *Cnossus' king and general*: Minos.

183. 19. This dithyramb was probably composed sometime before 460 BCE for the Great Dionysia at Athens. It is the only extant dithyramb of Bacchylides that tells a story related to Dionysus – in this case, his genealogy, via a focus on Io, the great-great-grandmother of his grandfather Cadmus. Compare Pindar's *Dith.* 4 (p. 160), also probably composed for the Great Dionysia.

ll. 4–6. *the Pierian Muses . . . the Graces*: As usual, the Muses inspire the story and subject matter, while the Graces confer the musico-poetic charm that pleases listeners and brings victory in competition (cf. *Intro* to the Archaic Period, p. 3; for other examples, see Pi. *Ol.* 7, ll. 11–20, p. 140, and *Pae.* 6, ll. 4–6, p. 156; Bacch. 5, ll. 11–15, p. 171; and Anon. 937, ll. 3–4, p. 238). For 'Pierian', see n. on. Sap. 55, l. 3 (p. 47).

ll. 8–9. *lauded ingenuity of Ceos*: Bacchylides. These lines would have been performed as a compliment from chorus to poet, though of course the poet is actually complimenting himself.

l. 11. *Calliope's elect*: Calliope is one of the Muses. See Bacch. 5, l. 220 (p. 177) and n.

ll. 16–17. *the child of Inachus, rose-fingered Io*: Inachus was an ancient king of Argos and a river god; his daughter Io caught the eye of Zeus and the wrath of Hera. Zeus, so as not to be taken *in flagrante* with her, transformed her into a cow, which Hera then demanded as a present and summoned the many-eyed watchman Argus to keep guard over. After Hermes set her free by killing Argus, Hera sent a gadfly to torment her, chasing her over the Bosporus ('Cow-Ford', so called because of her crossing) into Asia and down to Egypt, where she became the goddess Isis (see Tib. 1.3, l. 23, p. 413).

l. 20. *vigilant from every quarter*: Bacchylides' depiction of the Giant Argus' entire body as dotted with eyes is consistent with Attic red-figure vases of the fifth century; most versions of the myth allow Argus to keep half his eyes open while the other half sleep, so that he is always on guard. After his death, Juno used his eyes to spangle the tail feathers of the peacock, a bird which became sacred to her thereafter; see Ov. *Am.* 2.6, l. 57 (p. 502) and n.

183–4. ll. 29–36. *Now, whether ... lulling his eyes shut in the end*: The first option, in which Hermes kills Argus with a stone, is depicted on a black-figure amphora from *c.*530 BCE; the other, related by Ovid at *Met.* 1, ll. 682–721, has Hermes tell a long, boring tale and pipe a song that puts the monster to sleep for good. This second version may have been told in Sophocles' (fragmentary) *Inachus* and/or hinted at by Aeschylus (*Prometheus Bound*, ll. 574–5).

183. l. 30. *Giant-birthing Earth*: A *figura etymologica*, as, like the creatures themselves, the word 'Giant' is derived from *Gaea* (Earth); see Xen. 1, l. 24 (p. 110) and n.

184. ll. 43–4. *linen-dressed Egyptians*: Greeks and Romans considered linen the typical Egyptian garment. According to Herodotus (*Hist.* 2.81), the Egyptians 'wear linen tunics with fringes hanging about the legs, called "calasiris", and loose white woolen mantles over these. But nothing woolen is brought into temples, or buried with them: that is impious' (trans. Godley). A Hellenistic hymn to Isis tells us that Egyptian priests deemed hair an impure excrescence; therefore they shaved their entire bodies and refused to wear wool. Herodotus also notes (*Hist.* 2.36) that Egyptians, unlike other peoples, shaved their hair and beard at other times, but let them grow after a death, in mourning.

ll. 45–9. *the greatest line of men ...* : Bacchylides' genealogy leaves out Libye, daughter of Epaphus and mother of Agenor, but is otherwise thorough.

Fragment 4. For performance at the temple of Apollo Pythiaeus in Asine, about five miles southeast of Nauplion. The full poem described how Heracles relocated the people of Asine to their present location from Dryopia in the Parnassus region, when the hero defeated them in war and resettled them by order of Apollo.

l. 61. Peace, in prior Greek thought, is almost exclusively regarded as peace *within* cities, not between or among them. Plato states the typical Greek view: 'in reality every city-state is forever waging an undeclared war against every other city-state' (*Laws* 626a). How this so-called hymn to Peace related to Heracles' war with the Dryopians, or to conditions on the ground at Asine, is impossible to say; what can be said is that Bacchylides' vision here of universal peace is unprecedented before this poem and rare after it (there are echoes in Euripides and Aristophanes), at least until the Roman *Pax Augusta*. Tib. 1.10 (p. 415) may have been inspired by this poem.

185. *Fragment 20b. . . . Alexander, Prince of Macedon*: Son of King Amyntas I and ancestor of Alexander the Great; ruler of Macedon from *c.*495 to 452 BCE. He was later called 'the Philhellene' for his mediation between Greeks and Persians during the Persian Wars (Macedon was a vassal state of Persia). Pindar also wrote poems in praise of this Alexander, in gratitude for which Alexander the Great spared his house when he burned the rest of Thebes to the ground (cf. Pi. *Py.* 3, l. 113, p. 149, and n.). Bacchylides probably wrote this poem before Alexander became king, making it quite possibly the earliest of his surviving works.

l. 2. *seven-noted*: Only a couple of generations later, Ion of Chios (pp. 196–7) used an eleven-stringed lyre and spoke of the seven-string model as old-fashioned; for more on this, see *Intro* to the Classical Period (pp. 187–8) and n. on Tim. 791, ll. 210–18 (pp. 210–11).

l. 5. *every Twentieth dinner*: The 20th of the month seems to have been an occasion for private dinner parties throughout the Greek world; cf. Phil. 23, l. 3 (p. 339).

l. 16. The preceding four stanzas make up the first half of the poem, on the same theme as Pi. fr. 124a+b (p. 163); little from the second half is legible.

THE CLASSICAL PERIOD

188. *Introduction. 'Superior, as the songster from Lesbos . . .'*: Sap. 106.

190. *Plato . . . an ironic, contemptuous distance*: It should be noted that Plato does not mention Timotheus in his extant works; however, he does criticize Cinesias of Athens, who is often associated with Timotheus' brand of musical decadence, and at any rate Plato's dislike of *mimesis* (actorly performance), as well as his *a fortiori* attacks on Homer and the tragedians, make it hard to believe he would not have felt equally or even more strongly about the citharode from Miletus.

at 'white heat': Eric A. Havelock, *Preface to Plato*, p. 239.

Timocreon of Rhodes

193. *Poet Introduction. 'Medizer':* The Medes were a people of Iran, one of the first to be conquered by Cyrus the Great, *c.*550 BCE, and incorporated into the growing Persian Empire. Greco-Roman authors tend to refer to 'Persians' and 'Medes' interchangeably.

one colorful anecdote: Ath. *Deip.* 10.416a–b.

a 'shared liturgy among banqueters . . .': Eva M. Stehle, 'Cold Meats: Timokreon on Themistokles', *American Journal of Philology* 115:4 (1994), p. 509.

194. **727.** The lyric form and deceptively positive opening of this poem may have led Timocreon's audience to expect an encomium; the shift to bitter invective will have been the more memorable because surprising. Timocreon takes aim at his favorite whipping boy, Themistocles (*c.*524–459 BCE), the most ambivalent figure of the Persian Wars: both an undisputed genius, the one man more than any other to whose counsel and leadership the Greeks owed their salvation from Persia – he was the one who persuaded the Athenians to build the fleet which eventually defeated the Persians and allowed Athens to become an imperial power – and an arrogant swaggerer interested exclusively in his own preeminence, and unscrupulous in the pursuit of wealth to achieve political ends, for whom corruption was a legitimate form of *Realpolitik*. His Machiavellian tactics backfired on him, though: like Timocreon, he was accused of Medizing (see *Poet Intro*, p. 193, and fr. 729, p. 194), an accusation which did not need to be proven to ruin him. In Themistocles' case (and others'), the slander eventually fulfilled itself. The Athenian general made his way to the Persian court of Artaxerxes I (ruled 465–424 BCE), and eventually died in exile.

ll. 1–3. *You there might want to praise . . .* : Timocreon opens with a nod to the 'capping' game traditional in symposia, in which each symposiast would try to outdo the other by naming someone more praiseworthy than the last (see *Intro* to Scolia, p. 245). *Pausanias* was the Spartan regent who commanded the allied Greek forces at Plataea in 479 (cf. Sim. *El.* 11, ll. 29–34, pp. 128–9). *Xanthippus* was a friend of the poet Anacreon (see *Intro* to Anacreon, p. 100) and the father of Pericles; he was in charge of the Athenian forces at the Battle of Mycale in 479, while King *Leotychidas* led the Spartan contingent in this victory over the Persians. *Aristides*, known as 'the Just', a rival and foil for the unscrupulous Themistocles, commanded the Athenians at Plataea. Both Xanthippus and Aristides were political opponents of Themistocles, aristocratic where he was a populist. Themistocles campaigned successfully for their ostracism in the mid-480s (cf. ll. 4–5), but they were recalled to Athens in the face of the Persian crisis. Like Themistocles, after the defeat of Persia both Pausanias and Leotychidas fell into disgrace, assailed by accusations of 'Medism', while Xanthippus and Aristides died with their virtuous reputations intact.

l. 6. *Leto's hate*: An allusion to the mostly Ionian defensive alliance formed in 478 under the leadership of Aristides and Athens and known today as the 'Delian League'; its central treasury was located on the Cycladic island of Delos, where Leto gave birth to Apollo and Artemis (cf. Pi. frr. 33c and 33d, p. 156). Thus Timocreon's praise of Aristides 'caps' that of the other leaders because he was the one who masterminded Athenian and Ionian antipathy to Themistocles.

ll. 11–14. *Three silver talents … some he murdered*: Plutarch tells us that, after Salamis, Themistocles sailed around extorting money from the islands (*Life of Themistocles* 21.1). It will have been at this time (if Timocreon's accusation is true) that someone bribed Themistocles not to provide Timocreon with passage back to his hometown of Ialysus on Rhodes – though in Timocreon's invective this was only one instance of the corrupt Themistocles' typical modus operandi: the poet's is not a merely personal grudge.

ll. 14–18. *Stuffed with gravy … filled him up*: I follow Eva Stehle in considering these lines, perplexing in Greek, as obscene double entendre, accusing Themistocles of prostituting himself (Stehle, 'Cold Meats', pp. 516–20).

l. 16. *Corinthian strip*: i.e., the Isthmus of Corinth. Themistocles may have been prominent in the 470s BCE at the Panhellenic Isthmian Games as a representative of Athenian democracy. Corinth, too, was famous for the kind of prostitution insinuated here (cf. Pi. fr. 122, p. 161, and n.). It must be relevant that the Isthmus appeared frequently in obscene jokes as a stand-in for the perineum.

729. In this poem, according to Plutarch, Timocreon reacts to accusations of 'Medism' against Themistocles (*Life of Themistocles* 21.5). Perhaps the phrases in quotes were originally used by Themistocles or his circle against Timocreon.

195. 731. It may be that we should read this poem in the context of Themistocles' famous *philokerdeia* (love of profit) and *pleonexia* (money-grubbing, grasping for more).

Elegy 10. The poet Simonides of Ceos (pp. 120–33) is represented by Plutarch as Themistocles' friend and colleague in venality (*Life of*

Themistocles 5.4–5); little surprise, then, that Timocreon should have feuded with him also. No doubt Simonides responded in kind. The following fake epitaph is attributed to Simonides by Athenaeus (*Deip.* 10.415f) and the *Greek Anthology* (see *Intro* to the *Greek Anthology*, pp. 299–300) and may suggest the kind of thing which made Timocreon hold his nose:

> The tomb of Timocreon of Rhodes? Why, this is it:
> He ate a lot, and drank a lot, and talked a lot of shit.

Ion of Chios

196. *Poet Introduction. Cimon*: Cf. Sim. *Ep.* 40a+b+c (p. 132) and n., and 46 (p. 132) and n.

'bibulous': According to Athenaeus (*Deip.* 10.436f), the historian Baton of Sinope called Ion a 'lover of his cups' and 'extremely amorous'.

744. l. 2. *boy, whose face is like a bull*: Bacchus, often represented by Greek sculptors with bull horns, symbolic of strength and fertility.

197. 745. From a dithyramb; see n. on Ar. 120+121, l. 2 (p. 10).

746. In these lines (probably from a tragedy), Ion recalls cockfights staged by Cimon's father, Miltiades, to exhort his fellow Athenians to courage in the face of the Persian invasion.

Elegy 26. l. 1. *thyrsus*: A gnarled fennel wand wound with leaves and vines of ivy or grape and topped either with a pine cone, a grape-cluster, or ivy leaves and berries. It belonged to Dionysus and his throng of satyrs and maenads, and was brandished by devotees in his worship.

Praxilla

198. *Poet Introduction. a famous composer of drinking songs*: Ath. *Deip.* 15.694a.

spoken by Adonis: For Adonis, see Call. *Ia.* 3, ll. 36–7 (p. 263) and n.

'Sillier than Praxilla's Adonis': Zenobius, *Proverbs* 4.21 (trans. Campbell).

Corinna

199. *Poet Introduction. 'a picture of Corinna …'*: Pausanias, *Description of Greece* 9.22.3.

in a fragment quoted by one grammarian: Apollonius Dyscolus, *Pronouns* 64b–65a.

'*an intrinsic implausibility in the hypothesis . . .*': M. L. West, 'Corinna', *Classical Quarterly* 20:2 (December 1970), p. 286.

'*. . . it does not matter much at which date she wrote*': G. M. Kirkwood, *Early Greek Monody: The History of a Poetic Type*, p. 186.

200. *654a*. This fragment is found in the first column of a second-century CE papyrus from Hermopolis (modern El Ashmunein, Egypt); eleven lines can be counted before the present fragment begins, but only isolated words can be read. The poem is curious, and tells of a singing match/argument (not unlike Call. *Ia*. 4, p. 264) between two mountains: Cithaeron, sacred to Dionysus, on Boeotia's southern border with Attica; and, to the west, the Muses' sacred mountain, Helicon, on the border with Phocis. Cithaeron is the mountain where Oedipus as a baby was left to die and Pentheus was dismembered by Bacchants (cf. n. on Phil. Scar., *PaeDi*, ll. 14–16, p. 230); on Helicon, Tiresias was blinded by Athena (at least according to Callimachus; see *Hy*. 5, ll. 57–134, pp. 273–5) and the Muses appeared to Hesiod (*Th*., ll. 22–34).

ll. 12–18. '*. . . the Curetes . . . the splendid gods*': The quoted song, sung probably by Cithaeron (victors usually speak last), retells a story found in Hes. *Th*., ll. 453–91: the Titan Cronus, having been told by his parents, Earth and Heaven (Gaea and Uranus), that he would one day be overthrown by one of his children, prudently decided to eat them as soon as they were born. Naturally, this upset his wife, Rhea. When it came time to give birth to her sixth and last child (Zeus), Rhea went to her parents, Uranus and Gaea – she and Cronus were siblings as well as spouses – for advice. Gaea told her to satisfy Cronus' appetite with a stone wrapped in swaddling clothes (cf. n. on Arist. *HHes*., l. 5, p. 226), but give the baby Zeus to Gaea to raise. The need to cover up and drown out little Zeus's crying (so as not to arouse Daddy's suspicions) explains the Curetes (l. 12), the young men at arms who beat their weapons, danced and shouted outside the cave (usually located in Mount Ida on Crete) where Zeus was raised; see also the anonymous *Hymn to Zeus on Mount Dicte, Crete*, ll. 17–20 (pp. 234–5) and n. Note that these Curetes are unrelated to those in Bacch. 5, l. 156 (p. 175) and n.

l. 23. *Cithaeron's score proved superior*: Surprising – one would expect the Muses to favor Helicon, their sacred mountain. The outcome may reflect Corinna's regional pride (as a Boeotian) and/or a local commission, e.g., for Thebes, which controlled Plataea in Cithaeron's shadow and had long been associated with the mountain.

201.   l. 34. *ten thousand stones*: On the papyrus, fourteen more fragmentary lines follow this one, before the symbol indicating the end of the poem.

654b. The Daughters of Asopus. This fragment is from a different poem than the previous, found in the second column of the same papyrus, likewise preceded by eleven mostly illegible lines. Asopus is a river in Boeotia. In this poem, the river god learns the fate of his missing daughters (they have all been rustled away by gods) from a prophet called Acraephen, a son of Orion, and hero-founder of a town called Acraephia near the sanctuary of Apollo on Mount Ptoeus. According to Pausanias (*Description of Greece*, 9.20.3), Orion's tomb was also located in Tanagra, Corinna's hometown. In a different version of the story than this poem's, Asopus finds that his daughter Aegina has been kidnapped by Zeus, whom he attacks, only to be driven back to his riverbed by a thunderbolt – a story which explains why the river is so rich in charcoal.

ll. 12–18. *And of your daughters ... Hermes*: According to Maurice Bowra (*Problems in Greek Poetry*, p. 57), the partnering of daughters and gods is as follows: Aegina, Thebe and Plataea were claimed by Zeus; Corcyra, Salamis and Chalcis by Poseidon; Sinope and Thespia by Apollo; and Tanagra by Hermes. For more on those sons of Aegina who feature elsewhere in the present volume, see Pi. *Py.* 8, ll. 99–100 (p. 155) and n.

202.   l. 32. *Euonymus*: According to Stephanus of Byzantium, Euonymus was a son of Cephisus, a river in Boeotia (cf. Cor. 655, l. 14, p. 202); he was the father of the eponymous nymph of the Boeotian town of Aulis. Corinna may have written a poem on the *Daughters of Euonymus*, though interpretation of the title is uncertain; one line survives, quoted in a work called *Pronouns* by the grammarian Apollonius Dyscolus: 'wishing to take her son in her loving arms' (trans. Campbell).

l. 36. *Hyrieus*: Eponymous hero of the Boeotian town of Hyriae and father of Orion.

ll. 38–9. *whose enterprise saw his homeland restored*: Perhaps a reference to the tale told in the fragmentary *Astronomia* (or *Astrologia*), attributed to Hesiod, of Orion's blinding and exile, after drunkenly raping Merope, daughter of Oenopion, king of Chios. Orion was sent by an oracle to the eastern end of the world, where he exposed his eyeballs to the rising sun and was healed, and then was able to return home.

655. l. 1. *Terpsichore*: The Muse of choral song and dance.

l. 14. *Cephisus, our originator*: A Boeotian river and river god.

203. l. 17. *with nymphs encountered on his hunts*: i.e., the daughters of Cephisus (cf. nn. on Cor. 654b, p. 202, above).

l. 18. *lovely Libye*: The grandmother of Cadmus. Cf. his genealogy in Bacch. 19, ll. 41–49 (p. 184), and nn.

690. *Orestes*. The title of this poem is given on the papyrus that preserves the fragment. David Campbell speculates that the piece may have been composed for performance by a girls' choir at the Daphnephoria, the festival of Apollo at Thebes (the 'seven-gated city' in l. 8).

Timotheus

204. *Poet Introduction. as David Campbell writes*: David A. Campbell (ed. and trans.), *Greek Lyric V: The New School of Poetry and Anonymous Songs and Hymns*, 'Introduction', p. 6. See also *Intro* to the Classical Period (pp. 187–92) for more on Timotheus and the New Music.

'*If there had been no Timotheus . . .*': see Aristotle, *Metaphysics* 993b12–19.

205. '*theatocracy*': Plato, *Laws* 701a.

H. J. Rose in 1934: In H. J. Rose, *A Handbook of Greek Literature: From Homer to the Age of Lucian*, 'Hellenistic Poetry', p. 316.

the Persians. Timotheus' *Persians* recounts the Athenian-led Greek victory over the Persians at the naval battle of Salamis in 480 BCE. Pindar and Theognis apart, it is the longest Archaic or Classical lyric text preserved in a single source. The papyrus that gives it to us was found in 1902 in a tomb in Abusir, in Lower Egypt. Dating from the fourth century BCE, it is our oldest papyrus and the one nearest in date to its author's life. The poem was probably performed for the first time in Athens at the Great Panathenaea of 410 BCE. The famous line 'Ares is king. Gold cannot frighten Greece' (quoted elsewhere, but not in the preserved portion) may have alluded to a Spartan treaty with Persia against Athens of 412/11 BCE – gold being Persia's main contribution to the Spartan effort during the Peloponnesian War. In Athens, spirits would have been dampened by the massive failure of the Sicilian expedition in 415–413, but buoyed again by the Athenian victory over Peloponnesians and Persians at Cyzicus in the spring of 410. No doubt Timotheus sought to harness popular enthusiasm and strengthen resolve by bringing new life to the proudest moment of Athens' recent past.

It has been argued, however, that the poem was not performed in Athens at all, since, in the extant text, the city is not mentioned. The fact is striking, but proves little. It is likely that Timotheus hoped to gratify his Athenian audience with implicit praise for their feat at Salamis while also making the poem universal (Panhellenic) enough to allow for performance elsewhere – after all, an itinerant citharode needed repertoire that would work throughout the Greek world. If the *Persians* was premiered in Athens, the performance probably took place in the Odeion of Pericles, a renovation of a trophy (*tropaion*) originally built in 479 BCE from the spoils of Persia: masts and spars from barbarian ships wrecked at Salamis, and even the tent of Xerxes, captured at Plataea. The venue would have given particular resonance to Xerxes' command, at ll. 199–200, to burn the tents, so that his 'riches past measure' do not fall into Greek hands.

Timotheus' *Persians* draws heavily on Aeschylus' play of the same name, our oldest extant tragedy, first performed in 472 BCE. Myriad linguistic similarities perhaps serve to emphasize the poets' vast difference of vision. In the play, the nationalistic pride which both Aeschylus (who fought at Marathon and perhaps also at Salamis) and his audience took in victory is tempered by the adoption of a Persian perspective; in his hands, the Persian disaster becomes a parable for the fickleness of fortune and, perhaps, a warning to the Athenians about the dangers of overreach (*hybris*). It is a deeply humane work and a genuine attempt to grapple with the patterns and themes of history. By contrast, Timotheus' *Persians* speaks far less to its audience's better nature, seeking rather to strengthen social bonds at the expense of the defeated 'other'.

791. ll. 5–6. . . . *smashed their firry arms off.* The papyrus picks up with the Greek ships executing a tactical maneuver (the *diekplous*) designed to break the enemy lines and oars, exposing them to ramming. The 'firry arms' of the ships are fir-wood oars (the first of the poem's many kennings; cf. l. 89).

206. l. 14. *flax-wound ribs*: The ribs of Greek warships were typically reinforced with flax or linen ropes called *hypozomata* 'which ran from stem to stern, under the line of the gunwale' (J. H. Hordern, *The Fragments of Timotheus of Miletus*, 'Commentary on Fragment 791', p. 142).

l. 16. *lead weights*: These weights, called 'dolphins' due to their shape, were a development of naval warfare in the fifth century; they were swung from the yardarms and dropped to punch holes in enemy ships.

l. 18. *ornament*: Greek ships had uncarved prows, while Phoenician triremes (which, along with Syrian, made up the largest part of the Persian fleet) often decorated their bows with a figurehead or tutelary deity.

l. 20. *thong-bound*: The thong (*ankyle*, or *amentum*) attached to the middle of the javelin. 'As the javelin leaves the hand the pull on the amentum gives the javelin a half-turn, and like the rifling of a gun imparts to it a rotatory motion which not only helps it to maintain its direction but increases its carry and penetrating power' (E. Norman Gardiner, *Athletics of the Ancient World*, p. 173).

l. 25. *pricks for an ox*: Timotheus compares these flaming arrows (another development of fifth-century naval warfare) to the ox-goads they visually resembled.

l. 30. *the ocean's emerald hair*: The image is as odd in Greek as in English.

l. 36. *the breast of Amphitrite*: A typical enough metonymy for the surface of the sea. Amphitrite is the daughter of the sea god Nereus and the sea nymph Doris, and consort of Poseidon (cf. Bacch. 17, ll. 121–30, p. 182). She owns the waves at Hom. *Od.* 3, l. 91.

206–7. ll. 38–84. *But here a man in the watery plain . . .*: Among Greeks of the fifth century it was widely known that barbarians were bad or non-swimmers; for Herodotus (*Hist.* 8.89), this is an important explanation for the huge number of Persian deaths at Salamis.

ll. 47–60. For about ten lines the papyrus is too scrappy to make out more than the odd word.

207. ll. 61–2. *water no wine tempered*: If it was barbarous to drink wine unmixed with water, it was primitive and benighted to drink water without wine. Of course, seawater is undrinkable in any case; Timotheus rather cruelly taunts the drowning man with allusion to the refinements of the symposium. See n. at Alc. 346, l. 4 (p. 66).

l. 68. *in a rage at the sea*: Some mockery of 'Oriental emotionalism', which the Greeks stereotyped and considered culpably unmasculine, is no doubt intended.

ll. 71–3. *recently Xerxes collared . . . flax*: Herodotus (*Hist.* 7.35–6) tells how, in 480 BCE, the Persian king Xerxes built two bridges over the Hellespont, each consisting of over 300 boats yoked together by cables of flax and papyrus; it took his invading armies seven days and nights to cross. A previous bridge had been destroyed by a storm; in anger, Xerxes had fetters dropped into the water and 300 lashes administered, while the sea was chastised in words Herodotus calls 'arrogant and barbarous', and which bear significant resemblance to the present speech. For Aeschylus (*Persians*, ll. 70–71, 747–8), bridging the Hellespont was a major act of *hybris* directly connected with the Persian defeat; but Timotheus' version seems deliberately to avoid either divine or moralizing explanations. The cables used to 'yoke' the Hellespont were brought as trophies to Athens in 478, where Timotheus may have seen them.

ll. 79–80. *gadflydemented paleoloathsome* . . . : It is hard to disagree with Maurice Bowra, who calls such locutions 'neologisms of an almost brutal ingenuity' ('Arion and the Dolphin', *Museum Helveticum* 20:3 (1963), p. 125).

207–8. ll. 85–104. *And so the barbarous Persian fleet* . . . : This passage, describing the flight of the Persian ships, is clearly influenced by the messenger speech of Aeschylus' *Persians* (ll. 408–27).

ll. 89–91. *vessels' montane sea-legs . . . children of the gumline*: Kennings for 'oars' and 'teeth' respectively.

l. 96. *star-strewn sea*: Perhaps 'starry with bodies', as in Aeschylus' *Agamemnon* (l. 659): 'We saw the Aegean flowering with corpses.'

208. l. 105. *Mysia*: In northwest Asia Minor, bordering the Troad (cf. Ar., *Achaeans at Mysia*, p. 7). 'Mysian mourning' was proverbial. Also common was the association of foliage with hair.

ll. 111–14. The lines are too scrappy to make out continuous sense.

ll. 119–20. *Mount Tmolus' ridge*: Tmolus in Lydia (modern Mount Bozdağ), with *Sardis* at its foot, was the center of the cult of Cybele ('the Mountain Mother' invoked at ll. 125–34). For Cybele, cf. Anon. 935 (p. 237) and n.

209. l. 149. *Phrygia rich in pastures*: This suppliant is from Celaenae, the capital of Phrygia, at the intersection of the Maeander and the Marsyas rivers. Xerxes built a palace and citadel there upon his return from Greece.

ll. 157–67. '*Me you speak how?* . . .': The broken Greek of this section will have allowed Timotheus to show off his actorly chops; the audience will have been reminded of the comic stage by the style and (perhaps) music.

l. 164. *Ecbatana, Sardis, Susa*: Capitals of Media, Lydia and Persia respectively.

l. 166. *Artimus*: The Phrygian pronunciation of Artemis. The Ephesian cult of Artemis, a mother goddess similar to Cybele, was already famous by the fifth century.

209–10. ll. 171–5. *raked their cheeks ... all groaning*: As at l. 68, Timotheus plays on the Greek stereotype of the overly emotional Oriental; there is also derisive emphasis on Persian luxury in Xerxes' entourage and their elegant clothing.

210. l. 180. *when he saw*: Herodotus tells us (*Hist.* 8.90) that Xerxes watched the battle while sitting on his throne on the headland of Mount Aegaleos, overlooking the bay of Salamis.

ll. 184–95. '*Woe to my house ...*': In contrast to the preceding comic section, the lament of Xerxes is composed, and was no doubt performed, in the style of high tragedy. There are many borrowings from Aeschylus.

ll. 203–9. '*Paean! Paean!*' ... : Apollo; see n. on Ar. 120+121, l. 3 (p. 10). This is the paean as a triumphal song of joy and thanksgiving.

210–11. ll. 210–18. *For now ... (they say) I do violence to their old Muse with my new*: A number of anecdotes inform us that, when Timotheus was performing in a competition in Sparta (probably at the festival of the Carneia: see *Intro* to the Classical Period, p. 189), the conservative ephors – Sparta's senior magistrates – declared him ineligible on the grounds that his lyre had eleven strings, four more than the traditional seven. In one version of this incident, Timotheus points to a nearby statue of Apollo, also holding an eleven-stringed lyre, and is exonerated. In another, he is convicted, and, in the second century CE, the geographer Pausanias saw what was supposed to be his lyre exhibited near the Spartan *agora* (marketplace). That Plutarch tells similar tales not only of Timotheus, but also of Phrynis and Terpander (see *Intro* to the Classical Period, pp. 187–88), suggests that it was a stock literary anecdote, which may well have had its origin as an explanation of the passage at hand.

211. ll. 225–37. *Orpheus ... first plied the tortoise lyre ...* : As recounted in the *Homeric Hymn to Hermes*, early lyres used tortoise shells for sound boxes. Timotheus here further defends himself by claiming his own place in a tradition of innovation, beginning with Orpheus, the mythical inventor of the lyre (see n. on Ov. *Tri.* 4.1, ll. 17–18, p. 516), and moving on to Terpander (see *Intro* to the Classical Period, pp. 187–8). Timotheus seems to claim that Terpander also invented the ten-stringed lyre, though otherwise there is pretty much universal agreement that he used (or invented) the traditional seven-stringed version.

l. 227. *Pieria:* For this musical region, see n. on Sap. 55, l. 3 (p. 47).

l. 238. *him*: Timotheus. The performance concludes with what scholars conventionally term a 'seal' (*sphregis*), in which the poet refers explicitly to himself. There is much speculation about the reasons and purpose behind the *sphregis*, but no sure understanding or agreement. See also Theog. l. 19 (p. 77) and n.

l. 240. *linked in a league twelve cities strong*: Timotheus refers to the Ionian League, formed in the mid-seventh century BCE, and comprising the Greek cities of Miletus, Myus, Priene, Ephesus, Colophon, Lebedus, Teos, Clazomenae, Phocaea, Erythrae, and the islands of Chios and Samos.

l. 241. *Far-Shooting Pythian*: Apollo. Cf. n. on *Pythian Odes* (p. 146).

212. 796. We do not know what poem these lines, quoted in Ath. *Deip.* 3. 122c–d, may have come from. Their stridency makes them seem somewhat earlier than the *Persians*, in which Timotheus appears rather to emphasize continuity with tradition (ll. 225–37).

Epitaph for Euripides. Attributed to Timotheus in a third-century BCE *Life of Euripides*, though Athenaeus and the *Greek Anthology* name the historian Thucydides as the author. Euripides' biographer goes on to say that Timotheus, at a low point in his career, was talked out of suicide by Euripides, who then, as a favor, composed a prelude to the *Persians*, pacifying the poet's detractors and catapulting him to fame and fortune. The anecdote, though hardly trustworthy, nevertheless reflects a real musical and stylistic affinity between the two poets.

Ariphron of Sicyon

213. *Poet Introduction. 'that extremely well-known song . . .':* Lucian of Samosata, *A Slip of the Tongue in Salutation* 6.

Philoxenus

215. *Poet Introduction. Athenaeus, who quoted the poem extensively*: Ath. *Deip.* 15.685d, 4.146f–147e, 11.487b, 11.476e, 14.642f–643d.

216. *836b+c. l. 21. such as the gods would eat*: Would they? The gods enjoyed the smell of burning meat (cf. *Tsiknopempti*, 'Aroma-of-Grilled-Meat Thursday', still part of Greek Carnival celebrations), but seafood was rarely offered – at least outside the work of Hipponax, who makes an offering of a bait fish as a charm against impotence (Hipp. 78, p. 117).

216–17. ll. 24–7. *skate . . . stingrays*: According to Archestratus of Gela, author of a fourth-century BCE poetic guide to Mediterranean gastronomy, stingray is good with olive oil, wine, herbs and grated cheese; skate is served with cheese and silphium (see n. on l. 76, below).

217. l. 43. *sweet-sour*: An agrodolce, with honey and vinegar.

l. 46. *'the Navel of the Meal'*: Presumably these giant cakes resembled in appearance the stone at Delphi, swallowed by Cronus instead of the infant Zeus, and thanks to which Delphi was known as 'the navel (*omphalos*) of the earth'. Cf. Pi. *Py.* 8, ll. 55–60 (p. 153); Pi. *Pae.* 6, l. 19 (p. 157); and Arist. *HHes.*, l. 5 (p. 226), and n.

218. l. 76. *silphium*: An unidentified fennel-like plant, imported from North Africa, where it was over-cultivated so aggressively that it went extinct. Cf. Cat. 7, l. 6 (p. 378), and n.

220. l. 107. *a garland on every head*: Cf. Xen. 1, ll. 1–4 (p. 110), on the beginning of the symposium.

l. 118. Also extant, but not given here, is another long 'parade of foods' quoted at Ath. *Deip.* 14.642f–643d, this time listing desserts ('second tables').

'Plato'

221. 1. This poem and the next are two of the most beautiful epigrams in the *Greek Anthology* (pp. 299–356). Both are clearly Hellenistic in theme and style. They are fancifully said by a writer calling himself 'Aristippus' (the name of a pupil of Socrates) to have been written for a boy called Star (*Aster*).

2. That the morning and evening star were one and the same was widespread knowledge, and presumed by the poet. This epigram was rendered by Percy Bysshe Shelley under the title 'To Stella':

> Thou wert the morning star among the living,
>   Ere thy fair light had fled; –
> Now, having died, thou art as Hesperus, giving
>   New splendour to the dead.

3. The Attic tragedian Agathon (*c.*448–400 BCE) appears as a character in Aristophanes' *Women at the Thesmophoria* and in Plato's *Symposium*, where he gives a frivolously virtuosic speech. Someone, whether the author of the present epigram or the person who attributed it to Plato,

seems to imagine him as the philosopher's beloved (*eromenos*) – absurdly, since he was about twenty years older. This poem was also 'translated' by Shelley, but Agathon has become 'Helena'.

222. 4. l. 1. *take this apple*: Apples are common love tokens in Hellenistic and Roman poetry; see Theoc. *Id.* 2, l. 123 (p. 289) and n., and Cat. 65, ll. 19–24 (p. 391).

5. l. 1. *I am an apple*: See previous note.

l. 2. *Xanthippe*: Socrates' wife, typically portrayed by the ancient sources as an unbearable shrew. To imagine Plato, a man of seemingly homosexual tendencies, courting the much older and generally disliked wife of his beloved teacher seems a rather far-fetched Hellenistic fantasy.

Aristotle

223. *Poet Introduction. 'he had done nothing unworthy ... '*: Didymus, *On Demosthenes* 6.15–16.

224. 842. This poem may owe something to Sim. 579 (p. 126) and, especially, the passage from Hesiod's *Works and Days* that inspired Simonides in turn (see n. *ad loc.*).

l. 10. *Leda's sons*: Castor and Polydeuces, the Dioscuri (Sons of Zeus). Cf. Alc. 34 (p. 57).

l. 15. *Atarneus's native son*: Hermias. See *Poet Intro* (p. 223).

225. 673, *For Plato*. An epigram rather than a lyric fragment, this poem comes from a different edition than Page's *Poetae Melici Graeci* (see *Note on Text(s)*, p. xlvi), with its own numeration system.

l. 1. *Eudemus*: A friend of Aristotle's, from Cyprus. Aristotle composed for him a dialogue, now lost, called *Eudemus, or, On the Soul*.

l. 3. *the friendship of a man*: Plato.

Aristonous of Corinth

226. *Hymn to Hestia*. Hestia was the goddess of the hearth, not of fire – that was Hephaestus – though with the references in this poem to the goddess's 'dancing' (l. 6) we are clearly also to imagine the play of fire on the altar. Yet we should think as much of the dancing chorus, as the poet assimilates the activity of the worshiped deity to that of her mortal worshipers. The occasion for the poem's composition is not known – perhaps the Pythais, an Athenian ritual procession following the route of Apollo's journey

from the island of Delos to Delphi by way of Athens (see n. on Arist. *PaeAp.*, p. 227) and involving the transfer of sacred fire between the two cities.

l. 5. *Earth's navel*: Delphi ('Pytho', l. 4), considered the central hearth of the world by the Greeks, as well as the home of the *omphalos* (navel) stone, thought to have been the stone given by Rhea to Cronus to swallow instead of the infant Zeus (see Cor. 654a, ll. 12–18, p. 200, and n.). After Zeus came of age, he somehow forced Cronus to vomit up his brothers and sisters. According to Hesiod, 'he vomited up first the stone which he had swallowed last. And Zeus set it fast in the wide-pathed earth at goodly Pytho under the glens of Parnassus, to be a sign thenceforth and a marvel to mortal men' (*Th.*, ll. 497–500, trans. Evelyn-White). This stone was washed daily with fresh oil and, for every festival of the gods, dressed with woolen fillets; it is perhaps what Aristonous had in mind with the reference to Hestia's 'glistening seat' (l. 18). Incidentally, the stone, or a later classical reproduction of it, can still be seen at Delphi today. For other references to the *omphalos*, see Pi. *Py.* 8, l. 58 (p. 153), Pi. *Pae.* 6, l. 19 (p. 157), and Philox. 836b+c, l. 46 (p. 217) and n.

227. *Paean to Apollo*. This elegant hymn, which makes its quite original theology seem unexceptional and inevitable, was probably composed for the Delphic Theoxenia, the same 'guest-feast of the gods' at which Pi. *Pae.* 6 (p. 156) and Phil. Scar. *PaeDi.* (p. 229) were performed. Aristonous' poem glosses over or rewrites more violent traditional narratives, and gives Athena a conspicuous position quite possibly designed to gratify an Athenian audience. In the hymn, Apollo slays the Python (cf. n. on Pi. *Py.*, p. 146) off-stage; we are shown only the aftermath of the killing, when Apollo goes to Tempe in Thessaly for ritual purification (ll. 17–18), an act commemorated every eight or nine years by the Delphic festival of the Stepterion. Aristonous combines this tradition with the Athenian story that, after Apollo was born on the Cycladic island of Delos, he first set foot on the mainland in Attica. The odd result is that Apollo goes from Delos to Delphi to Tempe to Athens, and back to Delphi at ll. 17–20; later (ll. 25–32), this episode is adduced to explain the prominence of Athena's temple at Delphi. The intervening lines (ll. 21–4) adapt another tradition, in which previous inhabitants of the oracle are said (with some variation) to have been, first, Gaea (Earth), then Themis (Divine Order, Law), then Apollo. In Euripides (*Iphigenia in Tauris*, ll. 1234–82), the baby Apollo evicts Themis from the oracle, angering Gaea, who takes revenge by sending dream-visions to mortals, usurping Apollo's prophetic prerogative and causing him to seek intervention from Zeus. Characteristically, in Aristonous' version (as also in that of Aeschylus' *Eumenides*, ll. 1–11),

the transfer of power proceeds peacefully, via persuasion. This fits in with the hymn's overarching emphasis on the network of mutual reciprocity (*charis*) and gift exchange among the gods, not inappropriate for the Theoxenia.

l. 25. *Athena's temple*: The temple of Athena Pronaea (Athena 'Before-the-Temple'), which stood about half a mile to the east of the main site of Delphi, in a complex called the Marmaria – also the location of the famous round temple (*tholos*), built in the fourth century BCE, which, with its three standing columns (restored in 1938), is among the most picturesque sights at Delphi today.

228. ll. 34–5. Aristonous here describes aspects of the cultic landscape of Delphi that would no doubt have been more familiar to pilgrims then than now. *Poseidon's sacred dale* may have been associated with the earlier oracle of Gaea on the spot (Poseidon's name is sometimes etymologized as *Posis Gas*, 'Husband of Earth'). The *Corycian cave*, sacred to Pan and the nymphs, is about a four-hour walk from the main site, and is very much worth visiting. For more on the worship of Dionysus at Delphi (ll. 37–8), see Phil. Scar. *PaeDi.* (p. 229) and nn.

ll. 41–3.... *Castalia's spring*: See n. on Pi. *Pae.* 6, ll. 7–8 (p. 157).

Philodamus of Scarphea

229. *Paean to Dionysus*. Composed, like Pindar's *Paean 6* (p. 156) and Aristonous' *Paean to Apollo* (p. 227), for the Delphic Theoxenia in March/April, this hymn self-consciously challenges the usual generic distinction which associates paeans with Apollo and dithyrambs with Dionysus (cf. nn. on Ar. 120+121, ll. 2–3, p. 10). With a boldness that was surely as shocking in the fourth century BCE as upon the poem's rediscovery at the end of the nineteenth century CE, Philodamus appropriates the Apollinian title of *Paean*, 'Healer', for Dionysus, and even has Apollo and the Muses address Dionysus as *Paean* in the fifth strophe. Traditionally, dithyrambs were only performed at Delphi during the winter months, from December to February, when Apollo was away visiting the Hyperboreans, mythical dwellers 'Beyond the North Wind'. Dionysus then departed when Apollo returned, and paeans – and paeans only – were performed from March through November. Philodamus, however, writes a paean to authorize the year-round performance of dithyrambs at Delphi; in the process, he has Apollo install a distinctly Apollinian Dionysus at Delphi as Apollo's double and peer.

Philodamus achieves his effect with recourse to a distinguished Apollinian model – the *Homeric Hymn to Apollo*, which narrates the god's life story in two sections: the first, focused on Apollo's birth on the island of Delos and reception on Mount Olympus; the second, describing his installation at Delphi. Similarly, the first part of Philodamus' poem describes the birth and itinerary of Dionysus, received everywhere with uncomplicated Apolline joy, and culminating in the dithyrambic paean sung to him by the Muses and Apollo (Str. 5); while the second, longer part focuses on Dionysus' installation at Delphi, by decree of Apollo himself, who also urges the 'Delphic Board' of Amphictyons to hurry up and finish restoring his temple already (Str. 9).

l. 1. *Lord Dithyramb*: Besides being the name of a musico-poetic genre, *di-thyramb* is a slightly recherché epithet of Dionysus, which means something like 'Twice Born' – from his mother's womb and his father's thigh. In the familiar story, the jealous Hera tricks Semele into asking Zeus to reveal to her his full glory; she is incinerated, but Zeus rescues the baby from her womb and sews him into his thigh. Compare with the birth of Asclepius as narrated by Pi. *Py.* 3, ll. 13–66 (pp. 146–8).

230. l. 5. The combination of the traditional Bacchic cry *Euoi!* with the Apolline refrain of *Paean, hail!* would have been particularly disorienting to the audience at its first appearance.

l. 7. *Thyone*: The name given to Semele after her divine son rescues her from Hades and brings her to Mount Olympus. The Dionysian minor key of her story is here converted into Apollinian majors.

ll. 14–16. *Then Cadmus's . . . Minyan Orchomenus*: Here, too, Philodamus downplays the violence associated with various Greek cities' reception of Dionysus, usually figured as an unsettling and androgynous Stranger from the East. As told in Euripides' *Bacchae*, Pentheus, the king of Thebes ('Cadmus's . . . plains'), wants to banish Dionysus and his cult; in response, he is driven mad by the god and torn limb from limb by his mother and sisters. Similarly, in the nearby Boeotian city of Orchomenus, the daughters of King Minyas were driven mad when they refused to join the new cult and together they devoured one of their sons (Ov. *Met.* 4, ll. 1–140, 390–415).

ll. 32–3. *the locals who administer the Mysteries* at Eleusis are the Athenians.

l. 34. *Iacchus*: A shadowy minor deity, a son or perhaps husband of Demeter, important to the Eleusinian Mysteries; his name derived from the ritual cry, *Iacche*, sung in the midnight procession from Athens to Eleusis that was held each 20th of Boedromion (September/October). No doubt at least partly owing to the rhyme, Iacchus and Bacchus were identified with each other as early as the fifth century BCE.

231. l. 53. *that blest land*: Perhaps Eleusis, though Dionysus could have traveled anywhere in the missing fourth strophe.

l. 56. *the famed Pierian vale*: See n. on Sap. 55, l. 3 (p. 47).

ll. 58–9. *The Muses . . . circular serenade*: The Muses perform their best imitation of Dionysian maenads – the 'circle dance' here, as usual, conjures a dithyramb (see n. on Ar. 120+121, l. 2, p. 10). Even as the hymn has gone to great lengths to make Dionysus more Apollinian, Apollo and his Muses in turn become more Dionysian.

ll. 65–105. Unfortunately, almost nothing can be read of Strr. 6–8.

l. 107. *the restoration*: In 340/39 BCE, when this paean was performed at Delphi (see *Poet Intro*, p. 229), the temple of Apollo had been rebuilt and re-roofed, but it still wanted the finishing touches: marble slabs for the floor, fluting of columns, and pedimental sculptures. It seems likely that the chief Delphian magistrate of this year, Etymondas, commissioned Philodamus to include these imperatives (voiced by Apollo) in an attempt to mobilize public funds for restoration works which he himself was to oversee for a number of years thereafter.

l. 112. *Guest-Festival*: The Theoxenia (see Pi. *Pae.* 6, l. 5, p. 156, and n.; Arist. *PaeAp.*, p. 227, and n.), whose Panhellenic character (with 'suppliants from all Greece', l. 113) Philodamus is at pains to emphasize.

231–2. ll. 118–27. *Happy the race of men . . .* : An example of the trope of *makarismos*: see n. on Alcm. 1, ll. 37–9 (p. 32).

ll. 119–20. *which shall not ever . . . be defiled*: There is a glancing allusion to the Third Sacred War, when Phocians invaded Delphi in 356 and melted the god's treasures down into coins to pay mercenaries.

ll. 123–7. *all golden . . . under the local laurel you wear*: Philodamus here describes the sculpture of Dionysus on the west pediment of Apollo's temple, or, since it presumably had not yet been built, the plans for it; archaeological remains are exiguous, but substantial enough to confirm the general description, with the exception that the actual statue was not chryselephantine (made of gold and ivory), but marble. Pausanias, too, describes the pediment in similar terms (*Description of Greece*, 10.19.4), but takes the goddesses surrounding Dionysus for maenads; based on this hymn and the un-Dionysian serenity of the figures, however, archaeologists wonder if they are not Muses, albeit Muses in fawn-skins and ivy crowns.

232. ll. 131–3. *Pythian Games . . . circular dithyrambs*: The Pythian Games in honor of Apollo, which took place at Delphi in midsummer, are now to become a venue for dithyrambs, previously performed only in winter.

ll. 136–8. *a chariot . . . effigy like to the sunrise*: Presumably a different statue from the pedimental one described above (ll. 123–7).

l. 140. *a cave*: Probably the Corycian Cave, also sacred to Pan and the nymphs. See Arist. *PaeAp.*, ll. 33–40 (p. 228).

Anonymous Classical Lyric

234. *Hymn to Zeus on Mount Dicte, Crete.* This hymn was discovered inscribed on a stone at a place today called Roussolakkos near both to the Minoan (Bronze-Age) settlement at Palaikastro in eastern Crete, and to Mount Petsophas – ancient Mount Dicte, the mythological birthplace of Zeus. It belonged to a temple of Zeus associated with Dicte and the nearby towns of Praesus, Itanus and Hierapytna, strongholds of the 'Eteocretans', indigenes whose habitation of Crete went back before the Late Bronze Age Mycenaean takeover. The inscription itself dates from the third century CE, but language and style indicate that the poem was composed in the late Classical period. The first temple of Dictaean Zeus was built in the seventh century BCE, on the site of a far more ancient Minoan sanctuary – where, in the late 1980s, excavators from the British School at Athens discovered a chryselephantine (gold and ivory) statuette of a beardless young man from *c.*1500 BCE, thought perhaps to represent the constellation of Orion, whose pre-dawn (heliacal) rising with Sirius indicates the time for winnowing, in July (Hes. *W&D*, ll. 597–8), and whose presence in mid-sky, in September, marks the time to gather the grapes (Hes. *W&D*, ll. 609–11). The hymn and the cult for which it was composed, therefore, seem to reflect the worship of a local Cretan divinity older than, though later assimilated with, the Zeus of the Hellenes, who is nowhere else referred to by the cult title of *Kouros* ('Young Man', l. 1; the reference to Zeus as 'a young man' at Tim. 796, l. 3, p. 212, translates the Greek *neos* instead).

l. 18. *the Curetes from Rhea's hands*: See Cor. 654a, ll. 12–18 (p. 200), and n. We should probably imagine something similar to the loud, leaping dance in armor of these minor deities (ll. 19–20) – which protected Zeus in his infancy – being performed by the young men of eastern Crete when, at the new year, they exhorted Zeus (perhaps conflated here with the pre-Hellenic Orion-figure) in his role as vegetation deity to 'leap' into their fields, houses and ritual with his vivifying and virile power. In this hymn, these 'young men' (l. 59) are closely connected with the unusual epithet given to Zeus (see poem note, above), said to be 'mightiest of all' of them (l. 1).

235. ll. 37–40. *The Seasons ... every living thing*: That is, the Horae, variously identified, but according to Hesiod (*Th.*, ll. 901–3) they were the three daughters of Zeus and Themis ('Divine Law', l. 60) and sisters of the Fates; their names, which sound more political than seasonal, are Dike (Justice), Eirene (Peace) and Eunomia (Good Order). Cf. Iby. 288, l. 2 (p. 99), Pi. fr. 30, ll. 9–10 (p. 155), Pi. *Dith.* 4, ll. 17–19 (p. 160), and Anon. 1018a+b, ll. 12–15 (p. 240).

236. 934. This paean to Asclepius – a god of healing closely associated with Apollo – comes from Erythrae, a city in Asia Minor, facing Chios (cf. Hipp. 12, p. 115). It was found on a marble stele which prescribed a ritual for visitors to the temple: they were to sing a paean to Apollo three times (*O Lord Apollo, protect the young men, protect ...*) while standing or dancing around his altar. On the reverse of the marble is another fragmentary paean to Apollo, along with the present poem. Later inscriptions of this particular composition have also been found at similar complexes in Egypt, Macedonia and Athens, attesting to its widespread popularity. For the paean, see n. on Ar. 120+121, l. 3 (p. 10). Pindar's *Py.* 3, ll. 1–86 (pp. 146–9), gives a more elaborate and literary account of Asclepius' birth and career.

l. 6. *the land of Phlegyas*: Thessaly. Phlegyas was king of the Lapith people of Thessaly, and Coronis was his daughter.

ll. 10–11. *Podalirius ... Machaon*: The healer sons of Asclepius, who accompanied the Greek army to Troy (Hom. *Il.* 2, ll. 730–33); for Machaon see also Prop. 2.1, l. 61 (p. 428) and n. The rest of Asclepius' family members merely personify aspects of health.

l. 21. *our city*: The hymn is intentionally vague, so as to be adaptable to many locations.

237. 935. This poem, probably composed in the fourth or third century BCE, was found (along with the *Hymn to Pan*, Anon. 936, below) in a third- or fourth-century CE inscription at Epidaurus, site of the Greek world's most important sanctuary and cult center of Asclepius. Even there, there was clearly room for other gods. The cult of Cybele was imported into Greece, likely by immigrants from Greek Asia Minor, *c.*600 BCE, and

became increasingly popular from the late fifth century. As sometimes happens, Cybele is here conflated with Rhea, the mother of the gods (l. 3); she is also identified at times with Aphrodite and Demeter. There was a statue of her in Athens, attributed to a pupil of Phidias, which depicted her as a matron seated on a throne with a kettledrum in her hand and a lion at her feet. The kettledrums, or *tympana* (which Zeus twice tries to take in this hymn), were a common feature of her cult, used in her worship – as was her familiarity with lions and wolves, making Zeus's implied threat at ll. 17–18 somewhat farcical. For further mentions of Cybele, see Pi. *Py.* 3, l. 113 (p. 149), and *Dith.* 2, ll. 11–12 (pp. 158–9); Tim. 791, ll. 125–34 (p. 208); Call. *Ia.* 3, l. 34 (p. 263); *Ia.* 5, l. 103 not included herein and Dios. 16 (p. 314).

l. 2. *Pierians*: The Muses. See n. on Sap. 55, l. 3 (p. 47).

ll. 15–24. '*Quit roaming . . .*': Perhaps, here, we should imagine a chorus splitting into two halves, or semichoruses, to play the two roles of this little drama. That would at any rate make the plot, somewhat disjunctive in Greek, easier for an audience to follow. It has been suggested that the tone is comic, whether in the vein of ritual raillery or Hellenistic bathos.

238. 936. This *Hymn to Pan*, preserved like the *Hymn to Cybele* (Anon. 935) in an inscription from Epidaurus (see n. above), was probably composed sometime between the start of the Hellenistic period (323 BCE) and the reign of the Roman emperor Hadrian (117–38 CE). The punning attribution to Pan of a kind of cosmic universality (based on the Greek word *pan*, *panta*, 'all, everything', which is not, however, etymologically related) seems to begin in the Hellenistic period; such punning runs throughout this poem, including on 'pantocrat' (all-ruler) at l. 18. Victor Hugo's 'Le Satyre' seems to owe something to this hymn.

937. Similarly to the previous two hymns, this one to All the Gods comes from an inscription in the shrine of Asclepius at Epidaurus. The carving dates to the second or third century CE, but the hymn itself was likely composed earlier, though how much earlier it is impossible to say (it is surely post-Classical). A cult of All the Gods is attested at Epidaurus as early as the fourth century BCE; throughout the Greek world, such cults grew from the tendency at the end of hymns to add a generalized bow to all gods and goddesses, lest any feel left out and start some mischief.

l. 2. *Zeus's Twins*: Castor and Polydeuces, the Dioscuri (Sons of Zeus).

239. ll. 6–7. *and the tireless Sun . . . with which heaven is crowned*: These two lines are from Hom. *Il.* 18, ll. 484–5. Homeric quotations were common in magical incantations.

939. This charming monologue, which Maurice Bowra thinks was sung by a solo actor while a chorus, representing dolphins, danced around him ('Arion and the Dolphin', *Museum Helveticum* 20:3 (1963), p. 128), is attributed by Aelian to Arion, who (Aelian says) wrote it to thank Poseidon for his delivery from the sea after his ship was seized by pirates (*On the Nature of Animals* 12.45). The story is told in Hdt. *Hist.* 1.23–4; see also Bacch. 17, ll. 109–11 (p. 181) and n. The poem is perhaps a dithyramb, the 'circle dance' (l. 6) being a common genre-defining feature (cf. Phil. Scar. *PaeDi.*, ll. 58–9, p. 231; and see n. on Ar. 120+121, l. 2, p. 10); the style is not unlike that of Timotheus (pp. 204–12), but less outlandishly bold. See *Intro* to Post-Classical Greek Lyric (pp. 251–2) for the symbolic significance of Arion for the Hellenistic poets of Alexandria.

l. 11. *Amphitrite's oceanic kids*: For Amphitrite, see Bacch. 17, ll. 121–30 (p. 182), and Tim. 791, l. 36 (p. 206) and n.

l. 20. *in Pelops' country, on Taenarus's cape*: i.e. the Peloponnese (cf. n. on Alc. 34, l. 1, p. 57). At least by the time of Herodotus there seems to have been a bronze statue at Cape Taenarum (now Cape Matapan, the southernmost tip of the Peloponnese) depicting Arion on the dolphin's back; Pausanias also saw it more than 500 years later (*Description of Greece* 3.25.7).

240. 988. These lines are quoted approvingly (without attribution) in the first *Letter to Dionysius II of Syracuse*, ascribed by tradition to Plato, and sometimes thought to be genuine.

1018a+b. Quoted without attribution by the anthologist Stobaeus in his *Extracts*, this hymn is often assigned to Bacchylides or Simonides. The two fragments (ll. 1–6 and 7–17) may belong to different poems.

l. 7. *Apportioners, Spinners and Allotters*: Aisa (Dispenser of Destiny), Clotho (Spinster) and Lachesis (Disposer of Lots) are the Fates addressed here, varying a little from Hesiod's more canonical trio of Clotho, Lachesis and Atropos (Unpersuadable) at *Th.*, ll. 904–6.

ll. 12–15. *the lovely triplets . . . Peace*: i.e., the Fates' sisters, the Seasons (see the anonymous *Hymn to Zeus on Mount Dicte, Crete*, ll. 37–40, p. 235, and n.).

Folk Songs

242. 848. This delightful song represents a form of trick-or-treat-style begging practiced by children on Rhodes during the month of Boedromion – that

is, at the beginning of spring, in the local calendar (in Athens, Boedromion was an autumn month). The song survived in Greece for a long time and is still taught in schools, though the tradition of 'swallow-caroling' has faded away.

243. 852. These words went along with a popular dance called *Flowers*, in which they were acted out in some way.

853. A semi-bawdy song, addressed by an adulterous wife to her lover. Athenaeus quoted it as an example of a 'Locrian' song (*Deip.* 15.697b–c). There were three non-contiguous regions in central Greece called Locris, which bordered Phocis to the north and south; the implication is that one or other of these was known for a certain kind of raunchy song, which was then called 'Locrian', whether or not the genre came from there.

854. An Athenian prayer, according to the Roman emperor Marcus Aurelius (r. 161–80 CE), who comments that 'one should either pray simply and freely like this or not pray at all' (*Meditations*, 5.7, trans. Campbell).

856. A Spartan marching song, occasionally attributed to Tyrtaeus (pp. 22–6).

244. 859. The screech owl, a familiar of 'malevolent women', according to the ancient grammarian who preserves this apotropaic (evil-averting) squib: Sextus Pompeius Festus, *On the Meaning of Words* Bk. 18 (W. M. Lindsay, ed., *De Verborum Significatu*, p. 414). See also the ill-omened owls at Prop. 2.28, l. 38 (p. 432), and Ov. *Am.* 1.12, ll. 19–20 (pp. 497–8).

869. An anecdote represents Thales of Miletus (one of the Seven Sages of Archaic Greece; cf. Call *Ia* 1, ll. 52–77, (p. 262–63)) claiming that, when he visited Lesbos, his hostess would sing this song as she milled grain by hand. Did these lines come from a poem of Alcaeus (pp. 55–67), or do they represent a wider popular antipathy to the local tyrant, Pittacus? See *Intro* to Alcaeus (p. 55) and, e.g., Alc. 70 (p. 59), 129, ll. 13–24 (p. 61), and 348 (p. 66) for more on his feelings about Pittacus.

873. In the Lelantine War (*c.*710–650 BCE; see also Ar. 3, p. 6, and n.) between the cities of Chalcis and Eretria on the large island of Euboea, armies from Chalcis' Thracian colony of Chalcidice fought on Chalcis' side; one of their soldiers, kissed by his favorite boy before the battle, helped Chalcis earn a decisive victory. Homosexuality was an institution of both the Spartan military and the Theban Sacred Band.

Scolia

245. *Introduction. The genre's most accomplished practitioners ...* : Examples of their *scolia* excerpted in this volume include, but are surely not limited to: Alc. 38a (p. 57), 70 and 72 (p. 59), 332, 333, 335, 338 (pp. 64–5), 346–7 (pp. 65–6), 366 (p. 67); Theog. ll. 757–68 (p. 83) and 983–8 (p. 84); Anac. 346 fr. 4 (p. 101), 356 (p. 103), 396 (p. 107), Elegy 2 (p. 108); Sim. 651 (p. 127); Pi. frr. 122–124a+b (pp. 161–3); and Bacch. fr. 20b (p. 185).

889. See Theog. ll. 121–8 (pp. 79), for a similar sentiment.

246. 892. In a fable of Aesop, the crab kills the snake and proclaims, 'The only straight snake is a dead snake.' The poem seems, in tension with its message, ambiguous: crabs, with their sidewise shuffle, were hardly emblems of straightforwardness. It may also comment somehow on the 'twisty' genre of the *scolion*.

893, 895, 896. For the tyrant-killers Harmodius and Aristogiton, see Sim. *Ep.* 1 (p. 129) and n. One source attributes these songs to an otherwise unknown Callistratus.

893. l. 2. *myrtle bouquet*: No doubt the myrtle branches where the tyrannicides hid their swords were a standard part of the Panathenaic procession during which they made their assassination attempt.

l. 4. *equality*: Isonomia (equality under the law), a key concept in Athenian as in modern democracy.

895. ll. 1–3. *a myrtle bouquet ... at the festival*: See n. on 893, l. 2, above.

896. l. 4. *equality*: See n. on 893, l. 4, above.

900. Performing musicians, both amateur and professional, were focal points for the audience's erotic projections, then as now.

247. 902. l. 2. The same sentiment is given by *Theog.* ll. 313–14 (p. 81). See also Pi. *Py.* 3, l. 157 (p. 151).

904. For the sentiment, cf. Phil. 16 (p. 337).

248. 909. Quoted by Athenaeus as a *scolion* (*Deip.* 15.695f), and attributed to a Cretan called Hibrias (or Hybrias), whom Denys Page suggests may have started out as a public slave before becoming a professional soldier ('The Song of Hybrias the Cretan', *Proceedings of the Cambridge Philological Society* 191 (1965), pp. 62–5). Page muses: 'As a rule, ancient drinking-songs soon became anonymous: there must have been some special reason why the world could not forget that this one was composed

by Hybrias the Cretan' (p. 65) – perhaps they found him funny, and connected his name with the 'overweening arrogance' (*hybris*) of his boast. At any rate, as a piece for general reperformance this poem seems in line with the kind of postprandial fantasizing described by Bacch. fr. 20b (p. 185) and Pi. fr. 124a+b (p. 163). The first line of each stanza echoes Ar. 2 (p. 6), if we take *doru* as 'spear' rather than 'ship' (see n. *ad loc.*).

POST-CLASSICAL GREEK LYRIC

250. *Introduction. 'vast sums of money . . .': Letter of Aristeas* 9 (trans. R. H. Charles).

251. *The dolphin who had once saved Arion*: See Anon. 939 (p. 239) and n.

252. *one cynical wag*: Timon of Phlius, quoted in Ath. *Deip.* 1.22d.

'. . . *opposite to other men in almost all matters'*: Hdt. *Hist.* 2.35.

Callimachus

255. *Poet Introduction. One source claims . . . he was a schoolteacher*: The tenth-century CE Byzantine encyclopedia known as the *Suda* (s.v. 'Callimachus').

another that he was a 'youth of the court': The twelfth-century Byzantine polymath John Tzetzes, quoted in Susan Stephens' 'Introduction', in *Brill's Companion to Callimachus*, p. 11.

critics, whom he attacks in his extant poems: See, for example, *Aet.* 1.1 (p. 258), *Ia.* 1, ll. 6–30 (pp. 61–2), and *Hy.* 2., ll. 105–13 (pp. 271–2).

'*We know how to fangle falsehoods . . .'*: Hes. *Th.*, ll. 26–8.

256. '*I'd like my lies, when I tell them . . .'* : Call. *Hy.* 1 (*To Zeus*), l. 65.

a thing Shakespeare also did: In *Antony and Cleopatra*, 2.2. Cf. Plutarch, *Life of Antony* 26.

257. *the poem is elegiac in meter*: See *Note on Meters* (p. xxxi).

an exception . . . that I believe is justified: The components of the argument for Callimachus' importance are, to some degree, scattered throughout this book. I am persuaded by Eric Havelock's argument in his *Preface to Plato* (*passim*) that much of Plato's criticism of Homeric poetry (see *Intro* to the Classical Period, pp. 190–92) is a criticism of the cultural furniture and mental technology of oral poetry; and it seems to me that Callimachus' efforts showed the way to write poetry after Plato (see *Intro* to Post-Classical Greek Lyric, p. 253), particularly for the

Romans who came after him. On the latter, see especially the *Intros* to Latin Lyric (pp. 365–72), Catullus (pp. 373–5) and Propertius (pp. 421–2). For more on Callimachus in the Alexandrian transition from stage to page, see n. on Call. *Hy.* 2 (p. 269).

258. *Aetia.* The *Aetia* (*Causes*) is a long poem in four books which focuses on 'aetiological' narratives – that is, stories about the origins or causes of various phenomena, mostly cults and rituals. The poem is episodic in structure – there is no consistent attempt to weave the various stories together, as in Ovid's *Metamorphoses.* However, there is a narrative frame in the first two books – the poet dreams that he travels to Mount Helicon in Boeotia, where he meets the Muses and asks them questions about the causes of various things. (This Hesiodic encounter, psychologized by Callimachus into the realm of dreams, became a frequently imitated motif among the Romans; see, for example, Prop. 3.3, p. 432, and n.) The *Aetia*'s third and fourth books, however, abandon the narrative frame to present their aetiologies as discrete stories.

Unlike Callimachus' *Hymns* (pp. 269–76) and *Epigrams* (pp. 276–81), the *Aetia* (and the *Iambi*, pp. 261–8) does not survive in a direct manuscript tradition. For the most part, we rely on papyrus finds – comprising Callimachus' own text, as well as (mostly anonymous) ancient summaries and commentaries – from the trash heaps of Oxyrhynchus for our knowledge of the poem. Major fragments of the *Aetia* were published throughout the twentieth century, between 1910 and 1976; scholars have then done their best to put the fragments in order. (My versions rely on Annette Harder's 2012 text and commentary.) One of the results of this piecemeal publication history is that single episodes, stitched together from multiple papyri, may have several seemingly unrelated fragment numbers attached to them.

1.1, Prologue: To the Critics. This poem, the prologue to Callimachus' *Aetia*, was hugely influential, and contains many tropes we associate with 'Callimacheanism' in the Roman elegists: for echoes of this poem see, e.g., Prop. 2.1, 3.3 (pp. 427 and 432); Hor. *Epod.* 14 (p. 459) and *Odes* 1.6 (p. 466); Ov. *Am.* 2.1 (p. 498); and Mart. 4.8 (p. 541). (Vi. *Ecl.* 6 is also heavily in its debt.) Here Callimachus defends his own style and attacks his critics.

l. 2. *Telchines*: Callimachus calls his critics by the name of the malevolent, pre-Olympian magicians eventually destroyed by Zeus. Associated with islands like Rhodes, Ceos and Crete, they were famed as metalworkers, and the first to cast statues in bronze, but their crude efforts were soon replaced. Cf. Pi. *Ol.* 7, ll. 89–94 (pp. 142–3) and n., which takes a more positive view of their art.

l. 5. *little spurts*: Callimachus probably refers to the discontinuous, episodic nature of the *Aetia*, as contrasted with a more unitary epic. Ovid's *Metamorphoses*, incidentally, manages both types of poem at once: a 'Callimachean' epic which is both episodic and continuous.

ll. 9–10. *The tender stalk* Demeter *bears . . . the mighty* [Oak]: Allusive lines, made more difficult by the fragmentary text and our ignorance of the works alluded to. I assume that *Demeter* is an elegiac poem by Callimachus' predecessor at Alexandria, the scholar-poet Philitas of Cos (cf. n. on Call. *Hy.* 2, l. 110, p. 272), while the *Oak* may have been a different, worse poem. The lines assert a typically Callimachean preference for the small and sophisticated (Demeter's 'tender stalk', i.e., wheat) over the big and unrefined – not only oaks, but also acorns, the crude forage of a time before agriculture (for which, see Tib. 2.1, ll. 38–9, p. 418). The 'tender stalk' may also carry a reference to Philitas' famously emaciated figure; he is described by his younger contemporary Hermesianax as 'gaunt with glosses and lean with lemmata' (fr. 7.77–8), a portrayal echoed by Aelian (*Various Histories* 9.14) and Athenaeus (*Deip.* 9.401d–e).

ll. 11–12. *the Fine, not the Fat Woman*: Perhaps the 'Fine' woman is the *Nanno*, and the 'Fat' the *Smyrneis*, or it could be the other way around (see *Intro* to Mimnermus, p. 27). For another suggestion, see n. on Call. *Hy.* 2, ll. 105–12 (pp. 271–2).

ll. 13–14. *Let cranes fly . . . against the Pygmy race*: The Pygmies, 'that small infantry / Warred on by cranes' (Milton, *Paradise Lost* 1, ll. 575–6; cf. Hom. *Il.* 3, ll. 3–7), were a fabled race of dwarfs, eventually defeated by their avian enemies. Homer has the cranes fly from north to south to fight the Pygmies, but Callimachus reverses the direction of their flight. The Elder Pliny (*Natural History* 4.44) also places the Pygmies in Thrace.

l. 16. *the Mede*: See n. on the *Intro* to Timocreon of Rhodes (p. 193).

l. 17. *Damned cross-eyed yokels*: The envious Telchines (see n. on l. 2, above) spend so much time making the Evil Eye that they have gone cross-eyed.

l. 18. *the Persian chain*: The *schoenus*, a Persian land-measure, was from thirty to sixty stades (approximately 3½–7 miles) in length.

l. 22. *Lycian Apollo*: A standard epithet for Apollo, of unknown significance. While Apollo was worshiped in Lycia, on Mounts Cragus and Ida, and had an important oracle there in Patara, many associate the epithet either with *lykos*, 'wolf', or *lykē*, 'light'.

ll. 29–30. *my readers love the high, clear voice of the cicada*: The tuneless drone of cicadas and similar insects seems to have struck Greeks as particularly musical. In Plato's *Phaedrus* (259b–c), Socrates claims that they are the descendants of early humans who were 'so overwhelmed with the pleasure of singing that they forgot to eat or drink; so they died without even realizing it'. Cf. Sap. 58a (p. 47), and Leo. Tar. 21 (p. 308) and 91 (p. 310).

259. l. 36. *Enceladus*: One of the Giants vanquished in the Gigantomachy; see n. on Xen. 1, l. 24 (p. 110). According to the *Library* of Apollodorus, 'Enceladus fled, but Athena threw on him in his flight the island of Sicily' (1.6.2, trans. Frazer); his battle with Athena was reportedly depicted on the sixth-century temple of Apollo at Delphi (Euripides, *Ion*, ll. 209–11). Pindar, by contrast, has Typhus (or Typhoeus) account for the volcanism of Mount Aetna; see n. on Pi. *Py.* 8, l. 16 (p. 152).

Fragment 178+2.43, The Banquet of Pollis. This fragmentary poem probably stood as the first in Bk. 2 of the *Aetia*. In it, Callimachus attends a dinner party thrown by his Athenian friend Pollis (of whom nothing more is known) and meets a stranger, Theogenes of Icus (modern Alonissos, in the Sporades), whom he plies with questions about an obscure Ician ritual in honor of Achilles' father, Peleus.

ll. 2–5. The three festivals mentioned are all Athenian festivals connected to Dionysus. The first two, the *Cask-Opening* (*Pithoigia*) and the *Pitcher-Feast* (*Choes*), were part of the Anthesteria, held in January or February. The story goes that Orestes, after killing his mother Clytemnestra, came to Athens, whose king, Demophon, was afraid either to turn him away, or to pollute himself and his people through contact with a matricide. Therefore Orestes was allowed to enter, but speak to no one; he sat alone at table and drank his pitcher of wine. The Athenian ritual accordingly involved a form of collective, solitary drunkenness: everyone – laborers, slaves, even children – received their own table and pitcher and drank competitively, in silence. The slaves' participation in this event probably explains both their fondness of it ('which slaves adore', l. 3) and their refusal to pour the wine in l. 18 – they're busy drinking. The third festival Callimachus mentions, held for *Erigone*, was called the *Aiora*, or the 'Swing', and probably took place at a different time. Erigone was the daughter of Icarius, whom Dionysus had taught to make wine. When a group of shepherds became intoxicated for the first time with Icarius' new product, they thought they had been poisoned, and killed him, causing Erigone to hang herself. During the Aiora, dolls were hung by the neck from trees, and fruit was offered to the god.

l. 11. *'the god leads like to like'*: From Hom. *Od.* 17, ll. 217–18. Eumaeus has just brought in the beggar Odysseus, and the goatherd Melantheus says, 'Now indeed the vile leads the vile; as always, the god is bringing like and like together.'

ll. 12–13. *unmixed drafts like Thracians*: The Thracians were barbarians and known for heavy drinking; civilized Greeks drank their wine diluted with water. See Alc. 72 (p. 59) and nn., Alc. 346 l. 4 (p. 65) and n. on its l. 4, and Anac. 356 (p. 103) and nn.

l. 17. *scuttlebutt*: Gossip, the nautical version of water-cooler chitchat, since a scuttlebutt is an open cask of water or drinking fountain on board a vessel.

260. ll. 26–7. *Thessaly ... Icus ... Peleus*: On Icus, there was a hero-cult of Peleus (king of Phthia in Thessaly), involved with his supposedly having died a wretched death there in a cave after a shipwreck.

ll. 29–34. *bring [bread] ... replied that mariner*: The text is badly mutilated. Nothing else is known about the ritual with bread (or perhaps leeks?) and onions.

ll. 37–8. The gap, if these two fragments are correctly joined (see below), is of indeterminate length.

ll. 38–43. *And all that graced ... the word remains*: These lines are found early (ll. 12–17) in the papyrus which gives us the next episode, the *Foundation of Zancle*. The eleven lines which precede this passage, and the twenty-three which follow it, are too scrappy to translate; but the latter, at any rate, joining this section to the next, seem to have involved a long catalogue of Sicilian cities. Annette Harder considers the placement given in this anthology 'tempting'; but, she writes, 'the evidence is not strong enough to regard it as a fact' (*Callimachus, Aetia: Introduction, Text, Translation, and Commentary*, Vol. 2, p. 303).

3.64, *The Tomb of Simonides*: The speaker is the poet Simonides of Ceos (pp. 120–33).

l. 1. *Lake Camarina drained*: The people of the Sicilian town of Camarina wanted to drain their lake, so they consulted an oracle, which said, 'Do not drain Camarina!' They drained the lake anyway, and the town was promptly sacked by enemies who could now approach over land.

l. 4. *laws of hospitality*: Simonides died visiting Acragas (modern Agrigento) as a stranger and was buried there.

l. 5. *the shocking tyrant Phoenix* and his caprices are otherwise unknown.

ll. 10–11. *subtleties unnumbered* may include the four Greek letters ω (*omega*), ε (*epsilon*), ζ (*zeta*) and φ (*phi*), which Simonides is said to have invented (Hyginus, *Fabulae* 277).

l. 12. *palaces of memory*: The memory palace is a spatial mnemonic system, pervasive in the ancient world and still in use today among, e.g., contestants in the Memory Olympics; it involves associating the things one wants to remember with imagined objects or images, 'placed' (so to speak) in specific spots in rooms, buildings or other physical spaces of which one's memories are vivid.

260–61. ll. 13–16. *Nor, Dioscuri . . . who didn't die*: These lines allude to the story of the memory palace's invention, for which see n. on Sim. 521 (p. 122).

261. 4.112, *Epilogue*. l. 1. *Light of the spangled sash*: The conjecture 'spangled' evokes Sap. 1 (p. 39): see n. on its l. 1. For Aphrodite's sash, see also Antiphanes 1 (p. 354) and n.

l. 2. *mother of our queen, you*: Arsinoë II (sister-wife to Ptolemy II Philadelphus; see *Intro* to Post-Classical Greek Lyric, p. 251), who, after her death, became fully deified as a sort of emanation of Aphrodite (cf. Call. *Ep.* 14, p. 278, and n.).

l. 4. *the great bard*: Hesiod. For the allusion here to his poetic epiphany, see *Poet Intro* (pp. 255–6), and the general note on the *Aetia*, above.

l. 5. *the hoof-struck spring*: The Hippocrene (Horse Spring), on Mount Helicon, said to have been formed from the rock by Pegasus' hooves. Cf. also Call. *Hy.* 5, l. 71 (p. 274) and n., Ant. Thess. 3 (p. 345) and nn., Prop. 3.3, l. 2 (p. 432) and n., and Ov. *Tri.* 3.7, l. 16 (p. 514).

l. 8. *prose's pastures new*: Callimachus must mean his *Iambi* (pp. 261–8) here; perhaps he calls them 'prose' because of the awkward gait of the 'limping iambic' (*choliambic*) meter.

Iambi. 1. Callimachus' programmatic first *Iambus* summons to Alexandria the ghost of the mordant Archaic iambicist Hipponax (pp. 114–19), who upbraids Callimachus' fellow Alexandrians and tells the kind of moralizing fable commonly associated with the iambic genre. One of the main ways Callimachus invokes the spirit of Hipponax is by using the 'limping iambic' meter the Ionian invented, rendered here in irregularly rhymed iambic hexameters (see *Note on Meters*, p. xxxiii), though we should also remark that Callimachus' tone, while still satirical, is less scurrilous, more urbane, than his bawdy forebear. Hipponax's poetry, which had been largely forgotten during the fifth and fourth centuries BCE, apparently experienced a major revival during the third, and not only by Callimachus – the 'limping iambic' meter was used by such writers as Herodas and Apollonius of Rhodes, as well as the lesser known iambicists Aeschrion and Charinus. How far Callimachus' use of his model differed from or improved upon his contemporaries' is hard to say; but it proved highly influential, both in setting a precedent in the use of models for later writers (like Horace, pp. 453–91), and in the characteristic way Callimachus pitched his tent (along with Ion of Chios, pp. 196–7) in the camp of *polyeideia* – the notion that a single poet can, perhaps even should, compose in multiple genres.

l. 2. *a dime buys you an ox*: Proverbial of Hades; cf. Call. *Ep.* 31, l. 7 (p. 279).

l. 4. *Bupalus*: For this and other details related to the iambicist, see *Intro* to Hipponax (p. 114).

l. 6. *birdbrained flocks*: Callimachus' Hipponax, with typical brio, addresses various Alexandrian scholars, poets and critics, whom the mutilated ll. 12–25 seem once to have catalogued; among them was certainly an iambic poet – perhaps Callimachus himself.

l. 9. *Serapis' shrine*: Hipponax summons the scholars to the 'Serapeum of Parmenion' (according to the poem's anonymous ancient summary, the *Diegesis*), one of many unidentified temples outside the walls of Alexandria. For Serapis, see *Intro* to Post-Classical Greek Lyric (p. 253).

ll. 10–11. *the old fraud … Euhemerus*: Euhemerus of Messene (early third century BCE), a rationalist writer often attacked as an atheist but later hailed by some Christians as a serious historian who exposed the absurdities of polytheism. (The early Roman epic poet Ennius was famously a translator of Euhemerus.) In his *Sacred History*, Euhemerus described an island called Panachaea where Zeus, represented as a deified former king, had inscribed a copy of his *Personal Accomplishments* on a stele in front of his temple. The present lines may allude to a statue of Euhemerus outside the Serapeum. Cf. also *Ia.* 12, ll. 17–18 (p. 266) and n., where Callimachus takes another dig at 'the old fraud'.

ll. 11–26. The intervening lines (12–25) are in a bad way in the papyrus. For their content, see n. on l. 6, above.

l. 28. *Hecate*: A goddess whose archaic pedigree and sphere of influence are somewhat obscure, but who comes increasingly (in the fifth century BCE and later) to have chthonic and mystical associations, with magic, poison, the night, the moon, etc. She is often invoked as a 'triple' goddess and sometimes represented as having three bodies (cf. Pausanias, *Description of Greece* 2.30.2, and the second-century BCE Altar of Zeus at Pergamum). Her tripartite division encompasses the underworld, where she is a double of Persephone; the crossroads (*trivia* in Latin, a place where three roads meet); and the moon, where she is a double of Artemis/Selene. Broadly speaking, she is portrayed as a kind of dark double to Artemis/Diana, who is similarly regarded as having a triple aspect. Cf. Theoc. *Id.* 2, ll. 13 and 35 (pp. 286, 287), Antiphilus 16, l. 1 (p. 352), and Cat. 34, ll. 15–16 (p. 384).

262–3. ll. 31–77. *A certain Bathycles once ... :* The use of fable was, to all appearances, a major feature of the iambic genre, though only a few Archaic examples survive (for example, Archilochus' exiguous *Fable of the Eagle and the Fox*). Accordingly, Callimachus now has the rebarbative Hipponax address this fable, about the Cup of Bathycles, to the equally rebarbative Alexandrians, in an effort to convince them to be less so. It tells the story of an old man called Bathycles, who on his deathbed instructs one of his sons, Amphalces, to give a golden cup to the wisest of the Seven Sages of Archaic Greece, a group which here includes the Presocratic philosopher Thales of Miletus, the politicians Pittacus of Mytilene (whom Alcaeus, pp. 55–67, hated), Solon of Athens (pp. 68–75), Bias of Priene and Chilon of Sparta, along with the tyrants Periander of Corinth and Cleobulus of Lindus. Unlike the Alexandrians (and this is apparently the point), the sages do not wrangle over the cup or envy each other winning it, but instead pass it around among themselves until it makes a full circle back to its first recipient, Thales, who dedicates it to Apollo. Unfortunately, the state of the papyrus gives us only a few good runs of connected text.

262. ll. 44–52. The gap comprises seven barely legible lines (which are accounted for in the line numbering), followed by a break in the papyrus of around fifteen lines (which aren't counted). In the intervening space, Bathycles has given his golden cup to his middle son, Amphalces, with instructions to pass it on to the 'best of the Seven Sages'. When the text picks up again, Amphalces is bound for Miletus, to give the cup to Thales.

l. 55. *the two Bears, by which Phoenician sailors steer*: Ursa Major and Minor, aka the Big and Little Dippers, the Wagon, the Plow, etc. For the Phoenicians' expertise as sailors, see Hor. *Epod.* 16, l. 59 (p. 461) and n.

l. 56. *The scion of the Moon's Forerunner*: i.e., Amphalces, son (and thus scion) of Bathycles, whose homeland of Arcadia was said to be older than the moon.

l. 58. *Phoebus' shrine at Didyma*: There was a famous temple and oracle of Apollo at Didyma in the territory of Miletus on the Ionian coast.

l. 59. *Trojan Euphorbus*: As part of Pythagoras' famous doctrine of metempsychosis, or the transmigration of souls (also mocked at Xen. 7a, p. 111), the philosopher claimed himself to be a reincarnation of the Trojan hero Euphorbus, who was slain by Menelaus in Hom. *Il.* 17, ll. 43–60. Such digressions were a characteristic element of iambic poetry generally, as well as of Hipponax's performance here.

l. 60. *a right triangle in a circle*: Thales is here introduced in the act of proving the theorem – attributed sometimes to him, sometimes to Pythagoras – that 'the angle in a semicircle is a right angle'.

ll. 60–63. . . . *mooing meat should be verboten* . . .: Pythagoras' doctrine of metempsychosis (see n. on l. 59, above) led him to forbid the eating of meat among his followers at Croton (modern Crotone) in southern Italy; also verboten were beans, which he considered too full of spirit, their flatulent properties being associated with the souls of the transmigrated dead. Callimachus has Hipponax take a cynical view of the former proscription, that the Pythagoreans are really just making a virtue of necessity.

263. ll. 73–6. Around twenty lines are missing from this stretch of the papyrus; we do not know exactly how many. We do, however, know from other sources what they originally contained: the cup makes its rounds from Bias, to Periander, to Solon, to Chilon, to Pittacus, to Cleobulus, and then back to Thales, who dedicates it with the epigram given here as ll. 76–7. The lines that are given at 74–7 are quoted in other sources.

l. 77. The poem does not end at this point; but, while a few more lines are legible, the missing context makes them sadly incomprehensible. (Perhaps Hipponax hectoringly drives his point to the Alexandrians home.)

3. The ancient summary (*Diegesis*) of this poem claims: 'The poet criticizes the present age for valuing money more than excellence, and prefers the previous age, when the opposite opinion prevailed. He also inveighs against a certain Euthydemus for taking venal advantage of his youth and beauty, after he was introduced by his mother to a rich man.' The first part, largely missing, seems to have included a curse on the 'first discoverer' (*protos heuretes*) of metal/gold – a recognizable motif from later

poetry, e.g., Tib. 1.10 (p. 415). Other motifs from this poem – in particular, the impoverished poet and the high-priced beloved – will be familiar to readers of Hellenistic epigram (including Callimachus' own, e.g., *Ep.* 3, p. 276), as well as of Latin love elegy. The poem may be engaged in some kind of conversation or dispute with Plato – 'Euthydemus' (l. 24) is also the name of one of Plato's dialogues, and l. 31's 'I thought I saw the Good' certainly has a Platonic ring to it – but the poem's scrappy state makes it difficult to be more precise.

ll. 2–24. Not much can be made of the first twenty-something lines; at l. 24 the text improves a bit, though the reconstruction here is speculative.

ll. 33–4. *More lucrative ... to worship Cybele*: The Anatolian mother goddess; see Anon. 935 (p. 237) and n. Were priests of Cybele proverbially wealthy? I'm not sure, but they were usually eunuchs (cf. Dios. 16, p. 314, and n.), which would have solved Callimachus' problems in another way.

ll. 36–7. *Alas, the death of poor Adonis*: The cry belongs to the Adonia, a festival held annually in Egypt and a few other locations in honor of the death and rebirth of Aphrodite's lover Adonis, after his genitalia were gored by a boar. (In typical Greek fashion, Callimachus equates Cybele with Aphrodite, and Cybele's divine consort Attis with Adonis.) See Sap. 140 (p. 54); Nos. 5 (p. 311); Dios. 3 (p. 314); Vi. *Ecl.* 10, l. 20 (p. 408); Sulp. 3.9 (p. 448); Ov. *Am.* 3.9, ll. 16–17 (p. 510); and Milton, *Paradise Lost* 1, ll. 446–52: '... While smooth Adonis from his native rock / Ran purple to the sea ...' Adonis' story is told by Ovid at *Met.* 10, ll. 503–59 and 705–39, not to mention Shakespeare's *Venus and Adonis*.

ll. 37–8. *No ... It's bread I baked myself*: The sentiment in these final two lines is reversed at Prop. 3.5, ll. 19–20 (p. 434).

264. 4. In Callimachus' book of *Iambi*, this is the fourth and last poem to be written in the meter invented by Hipponax (see n. on *Ia.* 1, above) before it is reprised in *Ia.* 13 (probably the final poem in the collection; not included here). When *Ia.* 4 opens, Callimachus, according to the ancient summary (*Diegesis*), is apparently quarreling with 'one of his rivals' (whether in poetry, love or something else is unclear) when 'a certain Simus' butts in, attempting to make peace. The poet rounds on him, recounting the fable which occupies the bulk of the poem. It tells of a debate (*agon*) held on Mount Tmolus in Lydia between an olive and a laurel over which tree is superior; after the olive has demolished her opponent, an ugly little thornbush – comparable to Simus – interposes, provoking the laurel's wrath.

It is a strange poem, reminiscent in its way of another curious debate poem, Cor. 654a (p. 200); in this case, the gaps in our text, particularly the opening and the conclusion, do not help. Is Callimachus to be identified with the laurel or the olive? His typical Apolline leanings (as in *Aet.* 1.1, p. 258, *Ia.* 12, p. 266, and *Hy.* 2, p. 269), as well as the parallel role played by his character and the laurel in assailing the interloper, might suggest that the laurel is the poet's surrogate; yet her haphazard and associative arguments are thoroughly dismantled by the olive, who, like the poet, introduces a fable-like device to make her point. (She coyly claims to be quoting a conversation between two birds in her branches: 'nothing without a witness', in Callimachus' own phrase – cf. *Poet Intro*, p. 255 – even if the witness is a made-up one.) Then, too, it is hard to take at face value the poet's assertion that the whole long fable is aimed at the thornbush/Simus; the amount of space given to the debate suggests that the real target might be Callimachus himself and/or his original interlocutor. Sadly, other than the first line (preserved in the ancient summary), we have nothing else of the 'ground situation', either in the lead-up to the fable or in its aftermath. Even so, we can enjoy the *agon*, which is substantially preserved, and get a hint of the Chinese box-like (or Platonic) complexity with which Callimachus couches his tales inside their narrative frame.

ll. 1–21. The majority of the first twenty lines, where they are not completely lost, are so fragmentary that they evade reconstruction.

l. 7. *Tmolus*: A mountain in Lydia (modern Mount Bozdağ).

ll. 21–3. *Picture a slave ... just like your leaves*: The text we can read picks up again with the laurel mocking the olive's leaves for being pale and silvery on the bottom but a more intense green on the top.

l. 26. *The Pythia pronounces from a laurel throne*: See Call. *Hy.* 2, l. 1 (p. 269) and n.

l. 28. *Branchus*: A lover and prophet of Apollo who founded the temple of Apollo at Didyma (where Thales is found at Call. *Ia.* 1, l. 58, p. 262); Callimachus also has a fragmentary poem called *Branchus*, of which a little more than ten lines survive.

l. 30. *what no one understands* refers to a magical nonsense phrase that uses every letter of the Greek alphabet (*knaxzbi chthyptēs phlegmo drōps*).

ll. 32–5. *And then, Athenians ... Phoebus' victory*: The Athenian festival described was a yearly procession from Athens to Delphi called the

Pythais (see n. on Arist. *HHes.*, p. 226). The Dorian one, the Stepterion, commemorated Apollo's ritual purification at Tempe after killing the Python (see n. on Arist. *PaeAp.*, p. 227). For 'Pytho' (l. 34), see n. on Pindar, *Pythian Odes* (p. 146).

265. ll. 50–51. *Tethys* is the wife of Oceanus, *Tithonus* the husband of the Dawn (Eos/Aurora), both here used as types of extreme old age. For Tithonus, see n. on Tyr. 12, l. 7 (p. 25).

l. 62. *holm oak and galingale*: i.e., like pine and oak, ordinary trees.

ll. 63–5. *Pallas caused her birth ... not the Seaweed Lord*: The birds claim that the olive was created by Athena (Pallas) in her famous contest with Poseidon ('the Seaweed Lord'), depicted on the west pediment of the Parthenon. She had given the Athenians an olive tree; he, a saltwater spring. (Both were preserved on the Acropolis.) The 'arbiter with serpent tail' is the Earthborn Cecrops, the mythical first king of Athens, here said to have judged in Athena's favor, upon which she was granted patronage of Athens in preference to the sea god. It is unclear whether the birds omit the laurel's origin story – told most famously by Ovid at *Met.* 1, ll. 452–567 – with a tendentious wink, to help the olive's case, or whether that story was a later invention. In Ovid's version, Apollo falls in love with a nymph named Laurel (*Daphne*), who flees from him, and is eventually turned by her father, the Thessalian river god Peneus, into the tree that bears her name.

l. 66. *round one*: The metaphor the birds are using comes from wrestling. Each point for the olive is a 'takedown' or a 'pin'.

l. 74. *those pickled olives Theseus once ate*: This is a reference to Callimachus' own mini-epic, the *Hecale*, in which the old lady Hecale serves Theseus pickled olives as he takes shelter in her hut, en route to achieving his heroic victory over the bull of Marathon.

sacred trunk ... Leto rested: ll. 80–81. There was a sacred olive tree on the island of Delos, where Leto supposedly rested while giving birth to Apollo and Artemis (cf. Pi. fr. 33c, p. 156, and n., and fr. 33d, p. 156); Callimachus also mentions it in his *Hy.* 4 (*To Delos*, l. 262). Thus the olive demonstrates her superiority to the laurel even in Apollo's territory.

265–6. ll. 81–9. No doubt the missing lines (too mangled to translate) took up and dismantled the rest of the laurel's points.

266. l. 100. *you think you – you – are one of us?*: The laurel's words intentionally recall the first line, reminding us of Simus' interruption of Callimachus' quarrel which triggered the fable in the first place.

l. 104. *the waters of Pactolus*: The River Pactolus (now the Sart Çayı) rises on Mount Tmolus (l. 7, above). After this line, the rest of the poem is beyond recovery.

12. This poem's unusual meter (trochaic trimeter catalectic: i.e., three trochaic feet, the last missing one short syllable) is here rendered as trochaic pentameter. It may have had a precedent in Ar. 197, only one line of which survives: 'Father Zeus, no banquet graced my wedding.'

Ia. 12 frustrates and tantalizes, since almost all of it survives, but in a mangled state; this version is based on suggestions mined from the work of scholar Arnd Kerkhecker, while also inventing some connective material of its own for smoothness of reading. I have sought to use [brackets] as usual to indicate where I am translating a scholar's suggested Greek, and, unusually, *italics* to show where the translation floats free of the Greek into connective material of its own.

The poem is written in honor of one of Callimachus' friends, who is celebrating an infant daughter's 'birthday' or *hebdoma*, a ceremony held one week after her birth. Into this domestic scene Callimachus inserts a narrative describing the *hebdoma* of the goddess Hebe (Youth), to which the gods bring various gifts; Apollo (in clear parallel to Callimachus) surpasses them all with a gift of poetry. Conveniently for Callimachus – who consistently presents himself, with a touch of self-mockery, as deeply impoverished (cf. *Ia.* 3, p. 263) – Apollo (though fabulously wealthy) inveighs against the vulgarity of gold, ending in ll. 69–72 with an *adynaton* (catalogue of impossibilities: see n. on Prop. 2.1, ll. 67–72, p. 429) that emphasizes the immortality, and therefore superiority, of song. Much of the poem adapts Pindar, but where Pindar is grand and visionary, Callimachus is domestic, personal and charming.

So much is clear from the text as it stands. Numerous details, however, are unclear, especially at the beginning, in the catalogue of the gods' gifts and at the end: how does Callimachus move from his invocation of Artemis to Leo's daughter (ll. 4–7)? Who are the 'spinners' invoked at l. 10 – the Muses (as here) or the Fates? Who is it who 'speaks only truth' (ll. 16–17) – the poet, Leo, Apollo, someone else? The poet certainly returns to Artemis at l. 81 ('o health of maidens'), but the conclusions given here both to Apollo's speech and to the poem are my own inventions. I hope the performance is a plausible one, containing more of him than of me, and that it renders more accessible and satisfying one of the most unusually modern and personal poems in the corpus.

l. 1. *Artemis*: Invoked in her identity with Eileithyia as a goddess of childbirth.

l. 2. *Amnisus, and Dic[te's ridges]*: The River Amnisus on Crete starts on Mount Ida and empties into the Aegean near Cnossus; Callimachus associates it with Artemis also in *Hy.* 3 (*To Artemis*, l. 162), as does Apollonius of Rhodes (*Argonautica* 3, ll. 879–84). Artemis' connection with Mount Dicte derives from her association with a Cretan goddess of mountains and the hunt, Britomartis, also known as Dictynna, 'Lady of the Nets', under which name she was depicted as goddess of Dicte.

l. 3. *honored in Ephesus*: See Tim. 791, ll. 166 (p. 209) and n.

ll. 5, 6. *Leo*: A friend of Callimachus, otherwise unknown; first named in the extant text at l. 20.

ll. 8–9. *cities . . . mountains*: Artemis is also associated with both wilderness and civilization at (e.g.) Anac. 348 (p. 103).

ll. 17–18. *the tomb on Crete is empty . . .* : Callimachus takes another swipe at Euhemerus (see *Ia.* 1, ll. 10–11, p. 261, and n.), in whose rationalizing account of the origin of the gods Zeus was evidently a mortal king buried on Crete. The choice of Crete may have something to do with the cult of Zeus the Young Man on Mount Dicte – see the anonymous *Hymn to Zeus on Mount Dicte, Crete* (p. 234) and nn., where Zeus has been thought to stand in for an earlier (pre-Hellenic) vegetation deity, of the sort that dies each year to be reborn with the harvest.

267. l. 30. *[King Apis']* realm: The Isthmus of Corinth, whose patron was Poseidon. (Apis was a mythical king of nearby Argos.)

ll. 31–2. *orichalc . . . [from Etru]ria*: An unknown metal, perhaps an alloy of gold, and evidently very similar to it. Why Callimachus would mention Etruria (or the Etruscans) in connection with Poseidon's gifts is unclear.

l. 34. *the mother of earth's bounty*: Demeter, mother of Persephone.

l. 38. *robber baron*: Hades, who snatched Persephone, as recounted in the *Homeric Hymn to Demeter*.

l. 40. *the blacksmith*: Hephaestus. Callimachus typically refers to the gods not by their names, but by a descriptive periphrasis.

l. 48. *Pytho*: See n. on Pindar, *Pythian Odes* (p. 146).

l. 51. *[. . . Leave me] at home; take her a poem*: Callimachus may be thinking of Pi. *Py.* 9, where, like the tripod, the Centaur Chiron is put in the awkward position of having to prophesy to the god of prophecy. (Callimachus' version is jokier, of course.)

268. l. 57. *Indian canines*: As explained in the next line, this is a kenning for a particular (legendary) species of ant. According to Herodotus, speaking of Afghanistan rather than India (*Hist.* 3.102, trans. Godley):

> In this sandy desert are ants, not as big as dogs but bigger than foxes; the Persian king has some of these, which have been caught there. These ants live underground, digging out the sand in the same way as the ants in Greece, to which they are very similar in shape, and the sand which they carry from the holes is full of gold.

The Elder Pliny conveys similar information in his *Natural History* (11.36). Callimachus' giant ants have wings, perhaps because he conflates them with the gold-guarding griffins beyond the Arimaspians (see Hdt. *Hist.* 4.13 and Pliny, *Natural History* 33.21).

l. 64. *favorite affliction*: The oxymoron looks back to Pindar (*kalon pema* – 'gorgeous curse' – in *Py.* 2, l. 40), and forward to Virgil's 'cursed hunger for gold' (*auri sacra fames, Aen.* 3, l. 57).

269. *Hymns. Hymn 2, To Apollo.* Both this hymn and the *Hymn to Athena* (Call. *Hy.* 5, p. 272) are interesting documents in the Alexandrian slide from stage to page – or from ritual to written – poetry. They are examples of Callimachus' so-called 'mimetic' (imitative) hymns, because they not only provide us with the hymn itself, but describe (or, in Greek terms, 'imitate') its ritual setting, as if to evoke it for audience members (read: readers) who are not physically present. We might think of the difference between a true cult hymn and a 'mimetic' one as like that between seeing and reading a play: when we are actually in the audience, we do not need stage directions, or the playwright's description of the set.

Yet there is also something a bit underdeveloped – certainly, sub-novelistic – about Callimachus' approach to literary imitation. For example, in neither hymn is it quite clear who exactly is speaking. In this one, it seems likeliest that we should understand ll. 1–16 ('Look, look . . . tortoise shell!') as being uttered by the poet, while most of the following lines (ll. 17–104), the hymn or paean proper, are sung by the chorus of boys the poet addresses in l. 16. It is also less than crystal clear, in this hymn at least, where in the Greek world we are: the opening line, with its reference to 'Apollo's laurel', has led many to picture the great temple to Apollo at Delphi, though ll. 71–96 point instead to the festival of the Carneia held in Callimachus' native Cyrene.

It should also be mentioned that, in a general way, Callimachus in his *Hymns* is updating the Archaic model of the Muse-inspired *aoidos* (bard, songster) of the *Homeric Hymns*, just as he updates Hipponax (pp. 114–19) in his *Iambi* (pp. 261–8) and Archaic public elegy in his *Aetia* (pp. 258–61). In recasting Homer (or 'Homer') in the mimetic hymns, Callimachus takes on the role of poet-priest presiding over a ritual, creating what has come to seem a particularly Callimachean affinity between the priest, who excludes the unwashed and impure from the rite, and the poet, who excludes coarse words and unsophisticated readers. This image of the poet-priest would prove an influential one for Roman poets, especially Horace, who sometimes moonlights as a *vates* (the Italian equivalent of the *aoidos*) in much the way Callimachus moonlights as an Alexandrian Homeric bard. See Hor. *Odes* 1.1, l. 35 (p. 463) and n., and 3.1, ll. 1–4 (p. 478) and n.; and cf. also Tib. 2.1, ll. 18–27 (p. 418) and n., and Hor. *Epod.* 16, l. 66 (p. 461) and n.

l. 1. *Apollo's laurel*: The laurel was sacred to Apollo, and associated specifically with his shrine at Delphi, where the priestess (the Pythia: see n. on Pindar, *Pythian Odes*, p. 146) delivered oracles not thus in the lines cited (as she does at Call. *Ia.* 4, ll. 26–7, p. 264), and is even said to have chewed laurel leaves in her oracular trance. Yet, though Delphi is the most obvious reference, Apollo could also have had a laurel tree in Cyrene, since it was common practice to transplant shoots from the Delphic laurel to cult sites at other locations; and, at any rate, a laurel anywhere might be safely referred to as belonging to Apollo.

l. 2. *Off with you, temple-profaners*: Imitated by Horace at *Odes* 3.1, l. 1 (p. 478): *Odi profanum vulgus et arceo* – literally, 'I hate the unclean mob and I cast them out.' 'Profane' means 'outside the temple': see n. *ad loc.*

l. 4. *Delian palm tree*: The tree on the Cycladic island of Delos under which Apollo and Artemis were said to have been born (for the story of the birth, see Pi. Frr. 33c and 33d, p. 156, and nn.). They were also sometimes said to have been born under an olive tree, including by Callimachus himself (see *Ia.* 4, ll. 80–81, p. 265, above). Has the poem's cult setting now moved from Delphi to Delos? Probably we are still in Cyrene, where we know that a bronze replica of this palm stood before the temple of Apollo and the nearby shrine to his mother Leto. The shaking laurel (l. 1) and stirring palm tree (ll. 4–5) may owe something to Arist. *PaeAp.*, ll. 9–12 (p. 227).

l. 14. *offer gray locks*: Hair dedications were frequent in Greek ritual and poetry, most commonly in mourning, as when Achilles and company shear their hair to honor Patroclus in Hom. *Il.* 23, ll. 135–53. A second type of hair dedication involved young men shearing the first locks of their adolescent beards as a thanks-offering for having reached maturity; see Theodoridas 2, l. 3 (p. 316), and Crin. 9 and 10 (pp. 340–41). This passage implies a parallel ceremony, in which old men offer gray hairs in thanks for having made it so far.

l. 16. *tortoise shell*: The lyre. The *Homeric Hymn to Hermes* recounts how the infant Hermes 'first made the tortoise a singer' (l. 25) by using the shell as a sound box. For more on lyres, see Tim. 791, ll. 225–37 (p. 211) and n.

l. 17. *Keep a holy hush . . .* : The speaker likely shifts at this point; see poem note, above.

l. 19. *Pythian Phoebus*: See n. on Pindar, *Pythian Odes* (p. 146).

l. 22. *The tear-stained cliff face*: Niobe, who bragged that she should be esteemed over Leto because she had seven sons and seven daughters while Leto had only one of each. In punishment, Niobe's children were slain by Apollo and Artemis, and she hardened into a weeping rock; see Ov. *Met.* 6, ll. 146–312. She thus makes an apt doublet with Thetis (l. 20), whose son Achilles, according to some sources, was slain by Apollo in disguise as Paris.

l. 26. *my king*: Depending on when this hymn was written, Callimachus must mean either Ptolemy II Philadelphus (r. 282–246 BCE), Magas of Cyrene or Ptolemy III Euergetes (r. 246–221 BCE). Magas, the son of Berenice I and so maternal half-brother of Ptolemy II, wrested control of Cyrene and its surrounding territory away from the Ptolemies between 276 and 250 BCE, during which time he made a marriage alliance with the Seleucids and went to war against Alexandria. If the poem was written for Magas, who also held Apollo's chief priesthood in Cyrene, its mythical marriages may have alluded glancingly to the betrothal of Magas' daughter, Berenice II, to Ptolemy III, sometime in the 250s.

270.   ll. 32–7. *For Apollo's cloak . . . the least touch of peach-fuzz*: Callimachus' description here makes us think of the Apollo of Cyrene, a colossal Roman copy in marble of a second-century BCE Hellenistic bronze statue now housed at the British Museum. Though the Hellenistic original was too late for Callimachus to have known it, it could itself have updated an earlier cult statue which Callimachus would, in fact, have known.

l. 47. *Lord of the Herdsmen*: Nomius, a title also conferred upon Aristaeus, the son of Apollo and Cyrene, the eponymous nymph of Callimachus' hometown, in Pi. *Py.* 9, l. 65; like the lines to come, that poem places much emphasis on Cyrenaean animal husbandry.

l. 48. *Amphrysus*: A river in Thessaly.

l. 49. *Admetus*: A king of Thessaly. In the earlier tradition, Apollo was at one point required to serve him as punishment for killing either the Python or the Cyclopes. (On Zeus's orders, the latter had slain Apollo's own son Asclepius after he brought a dead man back to life; cf. Pi. *Py.* 3, ll. 80–86, pp. 148–9.) Callimachus has reimagined the servitude as erotic, casting Apollo in the role of lover and Admetus as beloved; Tibullus follows suit at 2.3, ll. 11–31:

> Thrall to Admetus, Phoebus did herdsman's duty,
> unaided by his lyre, locks, or beauty;
> nor could his medications cure his heart,
> for love had overcome the doctor's art . . .
> Where's Delos and where's Delphi now, Apollo?
> Love sends you to a tiny hut to wallow.

Admetus receives advice from Apollo at Bacch. 3, ll. 109ff. (p. 170), and figures in an Attic drinking song (*scolion*) preserved in Ath. *Deip.* 15.695c:

> Think of Admetus' story, mate, and learn to love the good and great;
> avoid the wretched and the rude, who only show ingratitude.

In one story regarding Apollo and Admetus (Apollodorus, *Library* 1.9.15), Admetus forgot to sacrifice to Artemis on his wedding day, so she filled his bed with snakes; but Apollo gave him the inside scoop and he was able to clear the premises. Friends in high places do come in handy.

270-71. ll. 55–79. *when they map and measure some new town . . .* : Foundations, whether of temples or cities, were of perennial interest to the Greeks, and a recurring theme in Hellenistic poetry especially. Callimachus varies the narrative from the *Homeric Hymn to Apollo*, ll. 254–5 and 294–5, in which Apollo lays out the foundations for his temple at Delphi; Callimachus replaces that episode with Apollo's building the goat-horn altar at Delos, which was sometimes included among the seven wonders of the ancient world and mentioned at Hom. *Od.* 6, ll. 162–5.

l. 60. *Cynthus*: A mountain on Delos. Artemis slew the goats there whose right-hand horns, held together without mortar or glue, were said to have been used to construct Apollo's famous altar (see previous note).

l. 65. *Battus*: The legendary founder of Cyrene. His descendants were called *Battiadae* or Battiads; Callimachus is often referred to as *Battiades* (Descendant of Battus) in later poetry (see, e.g., Cat. 65, l. 16, p. 391, and n.).

271.   ll. 69–71. Callimachus mentions several cult epithets of Apollo. *Boedro-mius*, common in many parts of the Greek world as both an epithet of Apollo and the name of a month, means something like 'Who Runs to Our Cry for Help' (of which epithet 'source of succor', l. 104, below, is a gloss); it also referred to the victory shout of an army running home to their city. *Clarian*: Claros, a city near Ephesus and the site of an import-ant shrine to Apollo dating from the Archaic period but particularly prominent in the Hellenistic age. *Carneius* means 'Lord of Flocks and Herds' (cf. *Nomius*, l. 47, above) and derives from Sparta, where it has sometimes been thought to preserve an echo of a pre-Dorian deity assimi-lated early to Apollo (not unlike *Paean*, likely derived from the Mycenaean deity Paiawon; see n. on Ar. 120+121, l. 3, p. 10).

l. 76. *Aristoteles*: The formal name of Battus (see n. on l. 65, above). The adjective 'laconic' (l. 75) here plays on both the Dorian origins of Thera (the proverbially tight-lipped Dorians hailed from Laconia) and the speech impediment implied by the nickname 'Battus' (Stutterer).

Asbystians: An indigenous tribe of the North Libyan region, known as the Cyrenaica and dominated by Cyrene.

l. 78. *yearly festival rites*: The major Spartan festival of the Carneia, held in honor of Apollo Carneius; it made the journey to Thera with Spartan colonists, who duly brought it along when they colonized Cyrene (ll. 74–6), a story related in both Pi. *Py.* 4 and Hdt. *Hist.* 4.155.

l. 82. *Zephyrus*: The west wind.

ll. 85–6. The *warriors in war-belts* are Dorian colonists from Thera perform-ing in the first Carneia on Cyrenaean soil; their dancing with the *blond-haired Libyan women* suggests the intermarriage of colonizers and colonized.

l. 89. *Cyre*: A local spring. *Azilis*: The region surrounding the eventual site of Cyrene.

ll. 90–91. *his bride ... Hypseus' daughter*: The nymph Cyrene, whom Apollo abducts while serving Admetus in Thessaly (see n. on l. 49, above); in Pi. *Py.* 9 she is a type of invincible Amazon, an Artemis not unwilling to mate. Hypseus himself was the son of the Thessalian river god Peneus, and king of the Lapiths.

Myrtle Hill translates *Myrtoussa*, probably to be identified with the acropolis of the future city.

l. 91. *Eurypylus*: A legendary Libyan king who offered his realm to anyone who could slay a lion which was laying waste to his fields; Cyrene killed the lion and claimed the kingdom.

l. 101. *god-haunting serpent*: i.e. the Python – see n. on Pi. *Py.* (p. 146).

Using up all of your arrows: Throughout the hymn, Callimachus puns suggestively on the name Apollo and *polus, polu* (much, many). Here, he dials up the sound-play with *allon ep' allo ballon*, 'firing one [arrow] after another' (*ep' allo* in particular sounds like *Apollo*; 'up all of' attempts a similar play).

l. 103. O Paean, *speed an arrow*: Another etymological pun, which serves as an aetiological explanation for the ritual cry *hiē, Paeëon*, which this book tends to translate (with some variation) as 'Hail, Paean, hail!' – a cry said to have derived from Leto's words to her son before attacking the Python: *hiei, pai, ion*, 'Shoot, child, your arrow.'

271-2. ll. 105-12. *Envy covertly buzzed in Apollo's ear . . .* : The *sphregis* (or concluding 'seal'; see Theog. l. 19, p. 77, and n.) of the hymn seems to participate in the same literary-critical debate as a number of Callimachus' other poems (e.g., *Aet.* 1.1, p. 258; *Ep.* 2, p. 276). The particulars are a little obscure, though it has been suggested that 'the sea' (l. 106) in Envy's formulation refers to Homer. This would suggest why Apollo does not reject 'the sea' outright, but creates a new opposition between 'Assyria's river' (l. 108, the Euphrates) and the pure waters of a sacred spring.

In this case, it has been suggested on the basis of the acrostic ('A', 'ly', 'De') found at the beginnings of ll. 108-10, and reproduced here, that the large, dirty river in question may stand in part for the *Lyde* of Antimachus of Colophon (*fl. c.*400 BCE), a work of learned and digressive elegy dedicated to the poet's deceased mistress of that name. Antimachus was a proto-Hellenistic elegist, influenced, like Callimachus, by Mimnermus (pp. 27-30); but, for all their apparent affinities, Callimachus seems to have detested Antimachus' work, finding it overly ornamented and metrically unpolished. (It is possible that the 'Fat Woman' of *Aet.* 1.1, l. 12, p. 258, refers not to any work by Mimnermus but to Antimachus' *Lyde*.)

Demeter's Bees (l. 110) may have both local and poetic reference – there was a spring near the Cyrenaean temple of Demeter and Kore (Persephone), whose priestesses were known as 'Bees' (*Melissae*). *Demeter* was also a poem by Philitas of Cos – a more congenial model than Antimachus – to which Callimachus refers admiringly at *Aet.* 1.1, ll. 9-10 (p. 258). The present passage was particularly influential among Roman poets seeking to flag themselves as Callimachean; it may also be the *fons et origo* of the association between Callimacheanism and water-drinking, whether troped in terms of purity and priestliness, or arid teetotaling (see n. on Ant. Thess. 20, p. 345). It surely influenced Horace's depiction of himself as a 'bee of Matinus' at *Odes* 4.2, ll. 25–32, where he contrasts the modesty of his own art to the rushing river of Pindaric eloquence. For more on Callimacheanism at Rome, see the *Intros* to Latin Lyric (pp. 365–72), Catullus (pp. 373–5) and Propertius (pp. 421–2).

The identity of the critics (*Phthonos* and *Momos*, here 'Envy', l. 105, and 'Criticism', l. 113) is unknown but seems to line up with the philistines Callimachus calls *Telchines* at *Aet.* 1.1, l. 2 (p. 258).

272. *Hymn 5, To Athena.* This hymn – like the previous one, called 'mimetic' because it purports to narrate a ritual in progress (see poem note on *Hy.* 2, above) – is the only one of Callimachus' six hymns written in elegiac couplets. In the ritual it describes, Argive maidens take the Palladium and the Shield of Diomedes (see respectively the nn. on l. 39 and ll. 35–6, below) in a horse-drawn wagon down to the River Inachus to be washed and anointed with olive oil. Such ritual washings of cult images were common; cf. Arist. *PaeAp.*, ll. 41–3 (p. 228). The people of Argos would have kept the Palladium in one of two temples to Athena within the city: either Athena Patroness of Cities (*Polias*) or Athena the Glancing-Eyed (*Oxyderkes*). The latter may be more likely, since, according to the Argives, Diomedes dedicated it to the goddess in thanks for her clearing the mist from his eyes in Hom. *Il.* 5 (see n. on ll. 35–6, below). Certainly the present poem is full of motifs involving blindness, sight and insight. The ritual washing of the statue was apparently an all-female ceremony, appropriate for a virgin goddess, and Callimachus tells the story (ll. 57–107) of how – to dissuade any masculine and, indeed, any un-consented-to mortal voyeurs – the Theban prophet Tiresias was blinded by Athena when he inadvertently caught sight of her bathing.

As so often, Callimachus seems to have sought out a little-known alternative version of a familiar story; in this case, the tale more often encountered is that Tiresias was blinded by Hera for giving his opinion (having himself been both a woman and a man, and tried it both ways) that women get more pleasure from sex than men: cf. Ov. *Met.* 3, ll. 316–38. Callimachus' version probably originated with a fifth-century myth-collector called Pherecydes of Athens. The version of the Actaeon myth also told in this hymn (ll. 108–17) – recounted by Athena as consolation to Tiresias' mother, Chariclo – could be Callimachus' innovation, though some scrappy evidence suggests he may have modeled his version after a (mostly) lost passage of Hesiod. At any rate, unlike the poem's central tale, this secondary one was destined to become mythical canon, when picked up by Ovid (who extends a catalogue of Actaeon's hounds to absurd length) at *Met.* 3, ll. 138–252.

Finally, though Callimachus set the hymn in Argos, he may have done so with a view to his native Cyrene. Athena was an important deity there, anciently associated with Lake Tritonis, where she was said to have bathed after emerging from Zeus's head – no doubt as a post hoc explanation for the mysterious epithet she bears in Homer, *Tritogeneia*, 'Born of Trito'.

l. 1. *All you who wait on Pallas' bath*: The ceremonial bath attendants are all female, though the gender of the speaking voice is never specified.

l. 2. *holy mares*: This refers both to the animals drawing the wagon containing the cult objects in the ritual represented (see poem note, above) and to Athena's mythical horses (ll. 6–12).

ll. 7–8. The role played by Athena in the Olympians' defeat of the Giants was a subject of the ritual garment (*peplos*) woven for her by Athenian girls at the festival of the Great Panathenaea. For the Gigantomachy generally, see n. on Xen. 1, l. 24 (p. 110); and, more specifically, for Athena's defeat of the Giant Enceladus, see Call. *Aet.* 1.1, l. 36 (p. 259) and n.

272–3. ll. 18–28. *On Ida, too, with Paris judging there . . .* : The contrast between Athena's preparations for the Judgment of Paris on Mount Ida, which kicked off the Trojan War, and the doggedly dainty primping of Aphrodite ('Cypris', l. 21) is modeled on a fragmentary satyr play of Sophocles, the *Judgment* (*Krisis*). After exercising, Athena, like a male athlete, anoints herself with simple (unscented) olive oil, olives being sacred to her. The joke, of course, is that she loses the contest; health is no match for makeup. (A proto-Ovidian attitude; compare Ov. *Met.* 1, ll. 497–8, when Apollo sees the uncoiffed hair of Daphne – see n. on Call. *Ia.* 4, ll. 63–5, p. 265 – and thinks, 'What if she styled it a bit?'; also Ov. *Am.* 2.4, ll. 37–8, p. 500.)

l. 20. *the Simois's swirling glass*: The Simois is one of Troy's two major rivers (the other being the Scamander).

l. 23. *twice sixty double stades*: The 'double stade race', or *diaulos*, of which Athena runs 120, took two lengths of the racetrack, 200 yards each way. Athena's morning workout will thus have covered around 48,000 yards or a little over twenty-seven miles.

l. 24. *Helen's brothers*: The Dioscuri (Sons of Zeus), Castor and Polydeuces, associated, like their sister, with Sparta, whose main river was the Eurotas.

273. l. 30. According to Pindar (*Ol.* 3), Heracles introduced the olive tree to the sanctuary at Olympia. During the course of his Third Labor, to capture the Ceryneian Hind, he chased the impossible deer all the way to the mythical paradise of the Hyperboreans (they who dwell 'Beyond the

North Wind'), where he saw olive trees for the first time, and was so astounded by their beauty that he asked and received permission to bring one back to the Peloponnese.

ll. 35–6. *Diomedes' Shield . . . Eumedes*: Diomedes is a major character in the *Iliad*, a favorite of Athena; at *Il.* 5, l. 4, she makes his helmet and shield 'blaze with unwearying fire'; and at l. 127, she removes the mist from his eyes, giving him the visionary power to see gods as well as men on the battlefield, and instructs him to wound Aphrodite when he sees her, which he eventually does – a bit of revenge for her beauty contest defeat. As for his shield, beyond incidental mentions in the *Iliad* (cf. *Il.* 5, l. 4, mentioned above), Diomedes belonged to the royal family of Argos, a town particularly associated with shields: Apollodorus (*Library* 2.2.1) says shields were invented there; a bronze shield was famously the prize given in the games dedicated to Hera (see Pi. *Ol.* 7, l. 147, p. 144, and n.); and the acropolis of the Mycenaean town was on a hill known as *Aspis*, 'the Shield' (later it was moved to another hill, called *Larisa*). The significance of shields at Argos could imply that one, which some may well have associated with Diomedes, was a cult object there, involved perhaps in the worship of Hera or Athena; but nothing else is known either of the afterlife of Diomedes' Shield in particular or of Eumedes beyond what Callimachus tells us.

l. 39. *your Palladium*: A wooden statue of Pallas Athena first mentioned in the lost Epic Cycle poem, the *Little Iliad* (see Call. *Ep.* 2, l. 1, p. 276, and n.). As long as this statue remained within the citadel of Troy, the town could not fall. Its heist was accomplished by Odysseus and Diomedes. Where it ended up next is disputed: Argos, Athens and Rome (via Aeneas) all claimed their Palladium was the real one.

ll. 40–42. *Crean Mount . . . Pallatids*: Their location is unknown, though an ancient commentator claims, rather obviously, that the latter rocks take their name from Pallas Athena.

ll. 47–8. *Physadeia . . . Amymone*: Two of the fifty daughters of the Argive king Danaus (cf. Tib. 1.3, ll. 79–80, p. 415, and n.) and names of important springs providing water to the city of Argos. Physadeia's location is unknown, but Amymone was near Lerna.

l. 49. *Inachus' wholesome torrent*: The central river of the Argive plain. As river god, Inachus was father of Io (cf. Bacch. 19, ll. 16–17, p. 183, and n.), from whom (eventually) both the Argive line of Danaus and the Theban line of Cadmus derive; as the legendary first king of Argos, he supposedly reigned eighteen generations before Heracles.

l. 56. *not mine, but another's tale*: Callimachus' famous claim that 'I sing nothing without a witness' (fr. 612; cf. *Poet Intro*, p. 255) highlights both his reliance on other writers and his interest in naming them as sources in his poetry. (For example, in the narrative of *Acontius and Cydippe* (*Aet.* 3.67–75, ll. 53–77), he summarizes at length the work of historian Xenomedes of Ceos, his source for the tale.) Here he is clearly aware that the myth to come is not widely known, and wants – perhaps with a wink – to defuse our suspicion that he is making it all up. (Contrast Callimachus' approach with Pindar's, who claims vatic insight and religious authority for his own innovations/deviations from canon; see, e.g., his revision of Tantalus' story at *Ol.* 1, ll. 33–79, pp. 136–8, or his tacit unsaying of Hesiod at *Py.* 3, ll. 39–45, p. 147, with the implication that Hesiod is lying, or his authoritative claim at *Dith.* 4, ll. 15–16, p. 160.) In this particular case, Callimachus' sources might be the Argive historians Agias and Dercylus, or the mythographer Pherecydes of Athens.

273–4. ll. 61–4. *Thespiae … Haliartus … Coronea*: Boeotian towns on the northern and eastern slopes of Mount Helicon, where the River Coralius (l. 64) is also located. All three towns had cults of Athena, though the shrine to Athena Itonia at Coronea was the best known and most important, the site of a pan-Boeotian festival in her honor.

274. l. 67. Callimachus withholds the name of *Chariclo* for quite a while after first referring to her ('a nymph in Thebes', l. 57), perhaps as a surprise. In Pindar (*Py.* 4, l. 103), Chariclo is the wife of Chiron, who raises Actaeon, the unfortunate soul who will be brutally punished in ll. 108–19.

l. 71. *the horse's spring*: The Hippocrene, where the Muses appeared to Hesiod. See nn. on Call. *Aet.* 4.112, ll. 4–5 (p. 261); cf. also Ant. Thess. 3 (p. 345) and nn., Prop. 3.3, l. 2 (p. 432) and n., and Ov. *Tri.* 3.7, l. 16 (p. 514).

ll. 72–3. *noon … noontide*: An hour of danger in the country. In Theocritus there is a prohibition against piping at noon for fear of disturbing Pan at his siesta (*Id.* 1, ll. 15–19) – Pan is cranky, and will punish anyone who wakes him. That Tiresias is alone (l. 76) suggests his foolishness – he should be napping too, like the rest of his hunting companions.

l. 77. *thirsting unspeakably*: Properly it is Tiresias' mistake that is unspeakable, not his thirst. (He also has no speaking lines in this hymn.)

l. 95. *and cried as nightingales do*: The nightingale, implicitly identified with Procne grieving over her son Itys (cf. Cat. 65, ll. 13–14, p. 391, and n.), is common in contexts of maternal lament.

275. ll. 108–19. *What prayers* ... : Now familiar to us thanks to Ovid (see poem note, above), this version of the Actaeon myth may well have been Callimachus' original invention; earlier accounts have Actaeon either boasting that he is a better hunter than Artemis or attempting to rape his aunt Semele (later the mother of Dionysus). His mother, *Autonoë*, was a daughter of Cadmus; his father, *Aristaeus*, was the son of Apollo and the nymph Cyrene (cf. n. on Call. *Hy.* 2, l. 47, p. 270). Actaeon is thus a grandson of Cadmus, in whose service Tiresias would begin a prophetic career which was to span seven generations of Thebans (ll. 126–7).

l. 127. *Labdacus*: Cadmus' grandson and Oedipus' grandfather. Given the fraught history of the Theban royal family, Tiresias might have preferred to exercise his gift in less interesting times.

ll. 130–31. *Alone among the shades ... when he dies*: In Hom. *Od.* 11, ll. 100–137, the shade of Tiresias is still able to prophesy helpfully to Odysseus in the underworld, a gift which 'Persephone granted to him alone' (*Od.* 10, ll. 494–5).

276. ll. 132–7. *When Pallas nods* ... : Callimachus has in mind Hom. *Il.* 1, ll. 524–6, when Zeus says to Thetis, 'Come, and I shall nod my head to you, that you may be certain. For this sign from me is the greatest among the immortals, and it is not-to-be-undone' – in Greek, *palinagreton*, the same word Athena uses of Tiresias' punishment, l. 104. For Athena's birth from Zeus's head, see also Pi. *Ol.* 7, ll. 61–8 (p. 142).

Epigrams. Callimachus' epigrams come to us via the *Greek Anthology* (pp. 299–356), where, with sixty-four transmitted, he is among the *Anthology*'s more prolific poets, as well as one of its very best.

2. The epigram expresses an erotic opinion in terms of a literary one, or vice versa. The literary-critical element – Callimachus' disdain for popular poetry like the Epic Cycle, or anything on the beaten path – connects with similar statements at *Aet.* 1.1 (p. 258) and *Hy.* 2, ll. 105–13 (pp. 271–2).

l. 1. *the Epic Cycle*: A collection of epic poems in dactylic hexameter composed on themes related to the Trojan War, which survives today only in summary; the poems were the *Cypria* – commonly attributed to 'Stasinus' – describing the Judgment of Paris (cf. Callimachus' version at *Hy.* 5, ll. 18–28, pp. 272–3, and n.); the *Aethiopis*, about Memnon, a Trojan ally slain by Achilles; the *Little Iliad*, which narrates from the death of Achilles to the building of the Trojan Horse; the *Sack of Troy*, focusing on Achilles' son, Neoptolemus; the *Homecomings*, describing the misadventures of Greek heroes on their return from the war; and the *Telegony*, about Telegonus, Odysseus' son by Circe.

3. This little poem, based on the well-known Hellenistic story of the love of the Cyclops Polyphemus for the sea nymph Galatea, seems to be based on Theoc. *Id.* 11 (p. 296); though the resemblance might be due to reliance on a common source, Philoxenus' late fifth- to early fourth-century dithyramb *Galatea* (see *Intro* to Philoxenus, p. 215).

l. 3. *Philip*: Possibly to be identified with an Alexandrian doctor of this name, mentioned in a papyrus of 240 BCE. (Nicias, the addressee of Theoc. *Id.* 11, p. 296, was also a doctor.)

277. *5.* l. 2. *keep the river god far from our drink*: i.e., do not dilute the neat wine with water. See n. on Alc. 346, l. 4 (p. 66), and cf. Ant. Thess. 20, ll. 5–6, p. 345.

l. 3. *Achelous*: A major river in western Greece.

8. One of many epigrams in the *Greek Anthology* of the 'comastic' type, from *komos*, 'revel' (see also Ascl. 12, p. 305; Anon. Mel. 6, p. 324; Argent. 26, p. 350; and *Anacreontea* 53, p. 363). The *komos* was a festive procession and the source of the word 'comedy'. Such processions could be more or less orderly, but they always involved movement from one place to another; the 'jubilees' for which Pindar (see Pi. *Ol.* 7, l. 168, p. 145, and *Py.* 3, ll. 105–6, p. 149, and n. on ll. 93–111) and Bacchylides (pp. 165–85) composed were *komoi*. By the time of Callimachus, the *komos* is mostly confined to the private sphere of the symposium; drunken revelers leave the party to belabor the door of some beloved, often a courtesan or a boy. This comastic genre was a particular favorite of Asclepiades (pp. 303–6); it is closely allied with the *paraclausithyron*, the 'locked-door song', since that was indeed the usual condition of the beloved's door when the *komos* called. For examples, see Call. *Ep.* 63 (p. 281); Theoc. *Id.* 2, ll. 121–31 (p. 289); Ascl. 12 (p. 305) and 42 (p. 306); Sulp. 3.12, l. 11 (p. 450), Ov. *Am.* 2.1, l. 25 (p. 499); and Mart. 10.14, ll. 7–8 (p. 549).

11. ll. 3–4. *the gods above ignore all oaths sworn in the grip of love*: We first encounter this idea in a fragment of Hesiod (quoted in Apollodorus, *Library* 2.1.3):

> Zeus ruled all oaths sworn in the secret acts
> of Love would be unbinding and unpunished.

A survey merely of the poems in this book shows it was exceedingly common: cf. Ascl. 4 (p. 304); Pos. 2 (p. 312); Dios. 6 (p. 314); Mel. 69 (p. 330); Cat. 65, ll. 17–18 (p. 391), and 70 (p. 394); Prop. 1.11, ll. 15–16 (p. 426), 2.28, ll. 5–8 (p. 431), and 4.7, ll. 22–3 (p. 440); and Ov. *Am.* 2.7, l. 27 (p. 503), and 2.8, ll. 19–21 (p. 504).

278. 14. The epigram records the dedication, by a girl called Selene, daughter of Clinias, of a nautilus shell to Arsinoë II (l. 8), sister-wife of Ptolemy II Philadelphus (see *Intro* to Post-Classical Greek Lyric, p. 251). By her death in the 260s BCE she had been deified and assimilated to Aphrodite-Arsinoë, whose temple ('Cypris by the Sea', l. 1) stood on Cape Zephyrium, near Alexandria.

15. l. 3. *Berenice*: Probably the wife of Ptolemy III Euergetes, but possibly either the wife of Ptolemy I Soter or the daughter of Ptolemy II Philadelphus.

279. 29. An epitaph ostensibly for Callimachus' father, but which conveys information only about Callimachus himself, and his grandfather ('a patriot', l. 4), also named Callimachus.

l. 3. *Cyrene* here refers to the Libyan city and not its eponymous nymph.

30. l. 1. *blood of Battus*: i.e., Callimachus. See Call. *Hy.* 2, l. 65 (p. 270) and n.

31. l. 7. *an ox goes for a dime in Hades' halls*: The cheapness of things in Hades was proverbial. Cf. Cal. *Ia.* 1, l. 2 (p. 261) and n.

280. 34. l. 1. *Heraclitus*: i.e., Heraclitus of Halicarnassus, not to be confused with the Presocratic philosopher Heraclitus of Ephesus. This Heraclitus has one surviving 'nightingale' (l. 5), translated below (p. 312). The present epigram is famously and brilliantly translated by William Johnson Cory: 'They told me, Heraclitus, they told me you were dead . . .'

45. l. 1. *If only sailing ships had never been*: A common sentiment, starting with the first line of Euripides' *Medea*. Cf. also Hor. *Odes* 1.3, ll. 9–16 (p. 463).

281. *51.* l. 1. *Timon*: A legendary Athenian misanthrope, who gives a characteristically salty response. Timon was a popular subject of epigrams.

53. l. 4. The *Phaedo* is the Platonic dialogue in which Socrates famously proclaims the immortality of the soul. This epigram is explicit evidence of Callimachus' ironic, yet profound, engagement with the prose of Plato.

63. A *paraclausithyron* – see n. on Call. *Ep.* 8 (p. 277), above. Many scholars doubt the attribution of this poem to Callimachus; if it is his, it is his only heterosexual love epigram.

Theocritus

283. *Idyll 1, The Death of Daphnis.* In this poem, a shepherd named Thyrsis meets an unnamed goatherd. Thyrsis asks the goatherd to play his pipe, but he declines, and instead asks Thyrsis to sing his famous song about Daphnis; in exchange, he offers Thyrsis an elaborate cup, which is described at length, as well as 'three milkings of a mama goat / who nurses twins and still can fill two pails' (ll. 25–6). This excerpt gives Thyrsis' song, to which Vi. *Ecl.* 5 and 10 (p. 408) are deeply indebted, not to mention the entire subgenre of pastoral elegy ('Lycidas', *Adonais*, etc.), which Theocritus here invents.

l. 67. *I, Thyrsis of Aetna* . . . : For a similar self-referential 'seal' (*sphregis*), see Theog. l. 19 (p. 77) and n. 'Aetna' probably means the town rather than the mountain; see Pi. *Py.* 3, l. 99 (p. 149) and n.

l. 68. *Daphnis*: According to A. S. F. Gow (*Theocritus*, Vol. 2, pp. 1–2), the best-attested account of Daphnis' story, as cobbled together from a number of ancient authors, holds that he was a Sicilian herdsman, and the inventor of bucolic song. His mother, a nymph, abandoned him under a laurel bush (*daphne*), from which he received his name. Daphnis vowed eternal fidelity to a nymph who loved him, but was inebriated and seduced by a princess, which resulted in his blinding. Neither this story nor two others seem reconcilable with the narrative implied by Theocritus here, such that we are left to wonder whether Theocritus has invented the account sketched so allusively in this song, or is drawing on some other source, now unknown. Theocritus' line is famously echoed by Milton's 'Lycidas', l. 50: 'Where were ye, Nymphs . . .'

ll. 69–71. *Tempe*, a valley near Delphi, *Peneus*, the river which flows through it, and *Pindus*, a nearby mountain range, are beauty spots of Thessaly sacred to Apollo and/or the Muses, far from the *Anapus* and *Acis* rivers (modern Anapo and Fiume di Jaci, respectively), which flow by the city of *Aetna* at the foot of its eponymous mountain. The point is that the nymphs would have helped Daphnis had they been at hand, in Sicily, when he was dying; but since they didn't, they must have been somewhere else, perhaps in Thessaly. Compare these lines with Virgil's modeled on them at *Ecl.* 10, ll. 10–13 (p. 408).

284. l. 79. *Hermes*, often named as the father of Pan (l. 126; cf. Anon. 936, p. 238, and n.) and Priapus (l. 83; see n. on Hor. *Epod.* 2, ll. 21–2, p. 457) – and sometimes of Daphnis himself – appears here in his role as a god of shepherds.

l. 82. *oxherds, shepherds, goatherds*: Later scholars constructed a 'bucolic hierarchy' with oxherds at the top and goatherds at the bottom. While oxherds do seem to have somewhat more prestige, the *Idylls* give little evidence that goatherds are socially inferior to shepherds.

l. 87. *powerless*: Priapus seems to blame Daphnis for his 'powerlessness'. Coming from the ithyphallic Priapus, this must imply a failure to consummate his love, which Priapus considers culpable. But why? Is the love unrequited, or somehow off-limits? Has Daphnis vowed himself to chastity, like Hippolytus (see n. on Hor. *Odes* 4.7, l. 32, p. 490)? Or could he perhaps be impotent, possibly injured, like Adonis, whose deadly wound is alluded to at ll. 111–12 (see n. *ad loc.*)? We don't know, nor do we even learn the name of his beloved, though at *Id.* 7, l. 80 (p. 291), Theocritus names a nymph called Xenea, not otherwise known.

ll. 98–100. *the heaviness . . . beat*: This could be grief or anger. If Aphrodite is grieving because she loves Daphnis, she may be the 'girl' at l. 85. Aphrodite's tone here, whether triumphant, chiding or rueful, is hard to pin down. Daphnis' response, however, is plainly indignant.

284–5. ll. 107–9. *You and an oxherd once . . .* : In the passage that follows, Daphnis taunts Aphrodite with three disgraceful or painful interactions with mortals in her life. The first, named here, is her love of the oxherd Anchises on Mount Ida near Troy, which resulted in the birth of Aeneas; the story is told in the *Homeric Hymn to Aphrodite*.

285. l. 109. *bee-loud vale*: There is evidence of an ancient belief that bees were more likely to sting adulterers.

ll. 111–12. *Adonis is ripe and ready . . .* : In the second of Aphrodite's disgraces (see n. on ll. 107–9, above), the goddess fell in love with the beautiful mortal youth Adonis, and mourned for him when he died painfully in a hunting accident, his genitals gored by a boar; Daphnis jeeringly reminds Aphrodite of her lover's death. For Adonis and the Adonia, see n. on Call. *Ia.* 3, ll. 36–7, p. 263.

ll. 114–15. *Tell Diomedes at close quarters . . .* : In the third of Aphrodite's disgraces (see n. on ll. 107–9, above), the hero Diomedes wounds the goddess at Hom. *Il.* 5, ll. 330–51; see also the n. on Call. *Hy.* 5, ll. 35–6 (p. 273).

l. 120. *Arethusa*: A spring in Syracuse; see Vi. *Ecl.* 10, l. 1 (p. 408) and n. Cf. Milton, 'Lycidas', l. 85: 'O fountain Arethuse . . .'

l. 121. *Thybris*: Virgil in the *Aeneid* uses 'Thybris' as a mysterious name for the Tiber (see *Aen.* 8, ll. 330–31), but here it would appear to refer to a mountain or valley, otherwise unknown.

ll. 126–7. *Lycaeus' heights . . . Maenalus*: Two mountains sacred to Pan, in western and eastern Arcadia; the god was born on Lycaeus. Maenalus also appears in Vi. *Ecl.* 10, ll. 15 and 63 (pp. 408 and 409).

ll. 128–9. *Callisto's crag* was a high, wooded mound on the southwest slope of Mount Maenalus. *Lycaon* was a king of Arcadia, and the father of Callisto; his 'seed' refers to Callisto's son Arcas, from whom Arcadia gets its name, and whose tomb was located on Mount Maenalus until it was moved to the Arcadian city of Mantinea at the instigation of an oracle. For Callisto, see Prop. 2.28, ll. 23–4 (p. 431) and n., and n. on Ov. *Tri.* 1.4, l. 1 (p. 512).

ll. 136–41. *Brambles, bear violets . . . drown him out*: A use of the trope of *adynaton* (catalogue of impossibilities); see n. on Prop. 2.1, ll. 67–72 (p. 429).

285–6. ll. 145–6. *So Daphnis went down to the stream*: If 'the stream' refers to Acheron, Theocritus would simply mean that Daphnis died. Alternatively, water could be involved somehow in his death, as when Heracles' beloved Hylas gets dragged into a pool by amorous nymphs in *Id.* 13. Other versions of Daphnis' death have him falling off a cliff, being translated to heaven or turning into a stone.

286. *Idyll 2, The Spell*. This fascinating idyll presents a monologue of the humble Simaetha, who has unfortunately fallen hard for a young man called Delphis, who seems out of her league, and something of a Lothario to boot. After initiating the entanglement via her lone house-slave, Thestylis, Simaetha has not seen Delphis for twelve days. This morning, an acquaintance claims that he is now pursuing someone else; desperate, Simaetha resorts to magic, with Thestylis' help. After Thestylis is sent away, Simaetha tells the story of her affair to what Virgil calls 'the friendly silence of the tacit moon' (*Aen.* 2, l. 255). The poem has often been compared to Theoc. *Id.* 11 (p. 296): though neither monologue accomplishes its objective, both nevertheless succeed in making their speakers feel a little better.

l. 9. *Timagetus' gym*: That Delphis spends most of his time at a wrestling school (*palaistra*) seems, like his self-conscious speech at ll. 117–42, an indicator of class and/or status.

l. 12. *Daemonic Moon*: Simaetha calls the moon a *daimon*, a sort of divine spirit that acts as an intermediary between gods and humans. While the Greek word is the source of our word 'demon', it does not necessarily have any negative connotations, though it does carry the awe and fear of the gods. (Incidentally, W. B. Yeats was fond of the adjective 'daemonic' as pointing to an uncanny power neither wholly devilish nor divine.)

l. 13. *Hecate*: See Call. *Ia.* 1, l. 28 (p. 261) and n.

ll. 19–20. Simaetha names three witches, two very famous and one obscure. *Circe* is best known from Hom. *Od.* 10, where she brews a potion that turns Odysseus' men into swine, but falls in love with Odysseus when her magic fails to work on him. *Medea*, daughter of the Colchian king Aeëtes, falls in love with Jason when he comes to Colchis with the Argonauts, and uses her magic both to help him secure the Golden Fleece and, later, to punish him horribly when he proves unfaithful. (Circe also happens to be Medea's aunt; cf. Prop. 2.1, ll. 53–6, p. 428, and nn.) *Perimede* (Very Cunning) is otherwise unknown, but might be a mistake for *Agamede*, who is mentioned as a sorceress at Hom. *Il.* 11, l. 740.

l. 21. *magic wheel*: We should think of a disk, threaded with string through the center and spun to make a whirring noise while the spell is chanted. The word for this implement in Greek, *iunx*, refers, first, to a nymph called Iunx, who in punishment for an adulterous liaison with Zeus was turned by Hera into a bird also called *iunx*, the wryneck. This bird was affixed spread-eagled to a wheel spun as part of an attraction spell. *Iunx* became the name for the wheel as well, which was used, as probably here, without the bird. We also see it in action in Anon. Mel. 35 (p. 324).

286–8. ll. 22–65. *First, char the barley* . . . : Simaetha's magic is of the 'sympathetic' kind, where the objects used (barley, bay, bran, etc.) stand as symbols of those parts they are intended to affect (bones, flesh, etc.). The fascination with magic in Hellenistic and Roman poetry, especially love elegy, no doubt owes much to this poem; cf. Prop. 2.28, ll. 35–40 (p. 432).

287. l. 35. *The goddess is at the crossroads*: i.e., Hecate (see at l. 13, above).

Clash the bronze: Perhaps cymbals or a bell, and in any case apotropaic (for driving evil away).

l. 44. *bronze bullroarer*: A different implement to the 'magic wheel' of the refrain (see n. on l. 21, above), this was a diamond-shaped piece of wood or metal with a cord attached to the point, which, when swung in a circle, would make a roar that rose in pitch as the speed increased. Cf. the 'whirligig' at Prop. 2.28, l. 35 (p. 432).

l. 50. *forgotten like Ariadne on the shore*: The daughter of the Cretan king Minos fell in love with Theseus and helped him escape from the Labyrinth after he killed the Minotaur; later, he abandoned her on the island of Naxos in the Aegean, because he preferred her sister, Phaedra. There she was ravished by Dionysus, in company with his boisterous band of satyrs and maenads, including Silenus (see n. on Prop. 3.3, ll. 29–30, p. 433). The whole scene of Ariadne's rapture is famously described by Catullus in poem 64 and depicted by Titian in a painting in the National Gallery in London.

l. 52. *hippomanes*: It is impossible to tell what plant is meant here, even if Theocritus has a real one in mind; normally, *hippomanes* would refer to either a growth on the forehead of newborn foals, or the discharge from a mare, both of which were considered aphrodisiacs.

288. ll. 68–9. *where should I start? ... Anaxo joined in the parade*: Festivals were the chief occasions for women to be seen in public, and thus common venues for encounters and seductions.

l. 70. *basket-bearer*: One of the girls who carry baskets containing the things needed for the sacrifice; cf. the ritual at the beginning of Prop. 4.8 (p. 442).

l. 72. *Behold my love, Queen Moon*: According to an ancient commentator, 'It is common for women who are mastered by passion to invoke Selene [the Moon] in prayer'; jilted men apparently pray to Helius, the Sun.

289. ll. 109–13. *my body froze ... rigid as a waxwork doll*: The most famous precedent for such symptomatographies is Sap. 31 (p. 44), but see also Ar. 191 (p. 12), Mimn. 5 (p. 29) and Cat. 51 (p. 387).

l. 119. *Philinus*: This is the name of a celebrated runner of Cos, who was active between 280 and 260 BCE. The island of Cos in the Dodecanese lies just across from Delphis' hometown, Myndus (l. 43), on the mainland, and is the likely setting for this idyll.

ll. 121–31. *I would have come ...*: An example of the *paraclausithyron* (locked-door song) motif: see n. on Call. *Ep.* 8 (p. 277).

l. 123. *apples of Dionysus*: Apples are common love gifts; cf. Callimachus' *Acontius and Cydippe* (*Aet.* 3.67–75), whose story begins when Acontius of Ceos sees the Naxian maiden Cydippe while both are on Delos at a festival of Apollo, and they fall in love at first sight. While Cydippe is sitting near the temple of Artemis, Acontius rolls an especially beautiful apple to her feet, bearing the words 'I swear by Artemis that I shall marry Acontius'; she reads it aloud before realizing what she is saying (compare the apple-based wooing of Atalanta hinted at by Cat. 2, ll. 11–13, p. 376). The newly betrothed lovers return to their islands, and the narrative unfolds from there. In this volume, see Iby. 286, l. 1 (p. 99) and n., 'Plato' 4 and 5 (p. 222), Theoc. *Id.* 11, l. 11 (p. 296), Cat. 65, ll. 19–24 (p. 391), and Prop. 1.3, l. 24 (p. 425).

l. 124. *Heracles' holy tree*: According to Pausanias (*Description of Greece* 5.14.2), Heracles brought the white poplar to Greece from the kingdom of Thesprotis to the northwest. Delphis probably wears it because Heracles is patron of athletes.

l. 135. *you*: Simaetha.

290. l. 137. *Lipara*: Modern Lipari, a volcanic island (the largest in a chain of them) off the north coast of Sicily.

l. 151. *Philista was our flute-girl*: Philista's mother has probably got her gossip from a symposium at which her daughter played the flute.

l. 153. *the steeds brought Dawn*: As often in ancient poetry, the daylight is visualized as riding in a chariot drawn by fiery steeds; cf., for example, the 'rosy mares of Dawn' at Tib. 1.3, l. 93 (p. 415).

l. 157. *unmixed wine*: See Alc. 346, l. 4 (p. 66) and n.

l. 160. *to wreathe that house*: The reference is to hanging wreathes on the door, as part of or following a *komos*; see Call. *Ep.* 8 (p. 277) and n.

l. 169. *Assyrian*: Perhaps here refers to a people on the Black Sea or from Syria. The Greeks credited Easterners with all sorts of potent magic.

Idyll 7, The Harvest Festival. In this poem the narrator, called Simichidas, and two of his friends are journeying to a harvest festival in honor of Demeter, which is being held on the farm of two brothers, Phrasidamus and Antigenes, on the island of Cos. En route, Simichidas meets a goatherd called Lycidas – the latter name is reused by Virgil in his *Ecl.* 9 (p. 405), which borrows heavily from this poem, not to mention in Milton's famous elegy. Simichidas and Lycidas exchange songs and gifts, then Simichidas and company continue on their way, and the festival is described. This translation excerpts the songs of the two protagonists, then closes with the quietly idyllic description of the festival.

Since antiquity, Simichidas has been consistently equated with Theocritus; Lycidas, too, has been thought a mask for various other contemporary poets – Aratus (see n. at l. 106, below), Callimachus (pp. 255–81) or Leonidas of Tarentum (pp. 306–10) – whether rightly or wrongly, no one can say. The form of the poem, an extended first-person narrative *not* cast as a dramatic monologue, is unusual in Greek poetry, Ar. 196a (p. 13) notwithstanding; its most immediate precedents are Platonic dialogues, such as the *Phaedrus* and the *Lysis*. Within that first-person frame, however, the *amoebaean* (alternating) exchange of songs here is typical of pastoral poetry; cf., in this volume, Cat. 62 (p. 388), Vi. *Ecl.* 9, ll. 28–63 (p. 405), and Hor. *Odes* 3.9 (p. 482) and n.

291.   l. 58. *Ageanax*: The name of Lycidas' boy love (*eromenos*), for whom he sings this send-off song (*propempticon*) – 'this ditty I just worked out in the mountains', as he calls it in the preceding line. Evidently Ageanax is due to sail for Lesbos in the stormy autumn. For other *propemptica*, see Sap. 5 (p. 41), Hor. *Odes* 1.3 (p. 463) and Hipponax's (or perhaps Archilochus') anti-*propempticon*, fr. 115 (p. 119).

l. 60. *the Kids*: The *Haedi* are a pair of stars near the constellation Auriga (the Charioteer). Their evening rising, like Orion's morning setting ('wets his ankles', l. 61), was associated with bad weather; cf. Hor. *Odes* 3.1, l. 28 (p. 478) and n. The reference points to a time in late October or early November.

l. 64. *halcyons shall lay the waves to rest*: Halcyons are mythical seabirds, early identified with kingfishers, and most famous as 'birds of calm' ('While birds of calm sit brooding on the charmed wave': Milton, 'On the Morning of Christ's Nativity', l. 68). During the so-called 'halcyon days' – a week-long stretch of calm in the stormy winter – they make their nests and lay their eggs in peace. (Of course, there is a story behind the story: see the account of Ceyx and Alcyone at Ov. *Met.* 11, ll. 410–748.) In this volume, see also Alcm. 26 (p. 36) and n., Ant. Si. 59 and 61 (p. 323), and Prop. 3.10, l. 9 (p. 437).

l. 72. *Ptelean*: The reference is obscure, but there may have been a town called Ptelea on Cos.

l. 78. *From Lycope and from Acharnia*: The place references are obscure. Acharnia (or Acharnae) is a deme in Attica, but could be connected with the Coan deme of Halisarna. Lycope is not otherwise known, but could as easily refer to a place on Cos as elsewhere. Apart from any now-irrecoverable associations, such references may have been employed by Theocritus for color and verisimilitude.

l. 80. *Xenea*: This name for Daphnis' beloved occurs only here. Cf. n. on Theoc. *Id.* 1, l. 87 (p. 284).

l. 82. *Himera*: A river in Sicily.

ll. 84–5. *Haemus, Athos, Rhodope . . . Caucasus*: Snowy northerly mountains, in Thrace and Russia.

292. ll. 86–90. *And I'll hear how . . . were sweetened by the Muses*: There is a story of a Calabrian shepherd who used to sacrifice his master's animals to the Muses. In retaliation, the master shut him up in a box to see if the Muses would save him. When the master opened the box two months later, he found the shepherd alive and the box full of honeycomb.

ll. 91–4. *Comatas . . . still alive*: Comatas, named here only as a mythical poet (a different Comatas is a character in Theoc. *Id.* 5), seems to be different from the goatherd of l. 87, though he apparently endured a similar tribulation. At any rate, his death, lamented in l. 94, is due to his antiquity, not because the bees deserted him.

292–3. ll. 104–35. In fine Hellenistic fashion, Simichidas' song is full of arcane references demonstrating its author's wit and erudition and out of all proportion to the significance of the object discussed, namely, Aratus' love affair.

l. 104. *The Loves sneezed*: Sneezes were good omens; cf. Cat. 45, ll. 10–11 (p. 385) and n.

l. 106. *Aratus*: Like Theoc. *Id.* 6, Simichidas' song is dedicated to one Aratus, who may be the contemporary author of the *Phaenomena* (a didactic poem about astronomy), but more probably is an otherwise unknown Coan friend of Theocritus.

ll. 107–8. *Gentle, nay, genteel Aristis*: Nothing is known of Aristis, nor can we determine what point is made by 'gentle, nay, genteel'.

ll. 108–9. *Phoebus . . . where his tripods are*: i.e., Delphi.

l. 111. *Homole plain*: Perhaps refers to the town Homolion, in the valley of Mount Homole near Tempe in Thessaly. Pan is not otherwise associated with this part of Thessaly.

l. 113. *Philinus*: This *might* be the runner mentioned at Theoc. *Id.* 2, l. 119 (p. 289), but the name was a common one on Cos.

ll. 115–16. *the boys with their sea-onion flails* . . .: This ritual is placed by Theocritus, in the original Greek, in Pan's birthplace, Arcadia. It apparently involved whipping the god's statue with sea-onions or squills when the hunting was bad (like a scapegoat; see Hipp. 92, l. 4, p. 118, and n.), and is not otherwise known.

ll. 119–22. *you tramp the hills of Thrace . . . Blemyes' rock*: These lines are imitated by Virgil at *Ecl.* 10, ll. 75–8 (p. 410). For the Hebrus, see Alc. 45, l. 3 (p. 58), and n. The Blemyes were a tribe of Lower Nubia who lived between Meroë and the Red Sea, but are here envisioned inhabiting a desert south of the source of the Nile.

l. 123. *From Byblis', Hyetis' and Oecus' creeks*: i.e., from Miletus and its environs, where there was a cult of Aphrodite and the Loves on the sacred hill of Oecus.

l. 124. *Dione*: Aphrodite's mother according to Homer (see n. on Alc. 283, l. 7, p. 63), though possibly here used as a name for Aphrodite herself.

293. l. 128. *pear-like, overripe*: Compare Ar. 196a, l. 26 (p. 14).

l. 133. *Molon*: A rival lover and glutton for punishment. Love is here a wrestling school, in which Philinus' suitors get soundly drubbed.

ll. 134–5. *have a gray crone spit on us*: To this day in the Mediterranean, spitting is credited with an apotropaic function, to 'keep bad luck at bay' and ward off the Evil Eye. For a different superstition relating to the latter, see Cat. 5, ll. 11–14 (p. 377) and n., and Cat. 7, ll. 12–14 (p. 378) and n.

l. 139. *Eucritus and fair Amyntas*: Friends of Simichidas, with whom he is traveling. It has been thought that if Theocritus is not to be identified with Simichidas, he might instead be present in the name of Eucritus, which is only one *theta* away from what would have been the Coan spelling of 'Theocritus' (*Theucritus*).

l. 156. *nymphs of Castalia, lofty Parnassians*: See n. on Pi. *Pae.* 6, ll. 7–8 (p. 157).

ll. 157–8. *such a bowl* . . . : The Centaurs Chiron and Pholus entertained Heracles in Arcadia with a wine so marvelous that its aroma brought other Centaurs, who fought a crazed battle with the hero and, despite their numerical advantages, were worsted; the story was told in the mostly lost *Geryon* of Stesichorus (p. 90).

l. 160. *Anapus*: See Theoc. *Id.* 1, l. 70 (p. 283) and n.

l. 161. *quaffed that time*: i.e., when Odysseus got Polyphemus drunk in Hom. *Od.* 9, ll. 345–74. The Cyclops, who was not used to such fine and heady drink, referred to the wine as a 'streamlet of nectar and ambrosia' (l. 360).

294. l. 163. *your waters tempered it*: For the tempering of wine with water, see Alc. 346, l. 4 (p. 66) and n.

ll. 165–6. *may I return to plant my shovel*: The idyll's ending conjures the destination of Odysseus' final voyage as foretold or instructed by Tiresias at Hom. *Od.* 11, ll. 127–32 (trans. Fagles):

> When another traveler falls in with you and calls
> that weight across your shoulder a fan to winnow grain,
> then plant your ... oar in the earth ...
> then journey home.

Idyll 10, The Reapers. This is the only agricultural (as opposed to pastoral) idyll of Theocritus, focused on farmers rather than herdsmen. Its theme, that love is out of place and destructive for the laboring rustic, is Hesiodic.

l. 2. *swath*: The line the reaper cuts in the standing crop.

ll. 14–15. ... *Sure,* that's *why no one's hoed my yard*: Milon implies that Bucaeus must be rich (he drinks sweet wine by the jar), since only the rich can afford to let love distract them from their work. Bucaeus' sarcastic response means that, if he were indeed rich, he could have paid someone to tend the yard which he has neglected, either from lovesickness or because he is always working.

295. l. 20. *praying mantis*: Milon probably means that the girl, called Bombyca (l. 28), is too skinny. It's doubtful whether Greeks knew of the tendency of the female praying mantis to devour the male.

l. 26. *Pierian Muses*: See n. on Sap. 55, l. 3 (p. 47).

l. 43. *the divine Lityerses*: A son of King Midas and the Phrygian inventor of agriculture; a famous reaping song was named for him.

296. *Idyll 11, The Cyclops.* A popular theme in the Hellenistic and Roman periods, the 'Cyclops in love' owes its currency to a satirical dithyramb by Philoxenus of Cythera in the late fifth or early fourth century; he may or may not have been the same Philoxenus whose *Feast* is excerpted above (see *Intro* to Philoxenus, p. 215). According to one tradition, Philoxenus

of Cythera had an affair with Galatea, the mistress of Dionysius I, tyrant of Syracuse; found out, he was imprisoned in the stone-quarries, where he wrote his poem, portraying Dionysius as Polyphemus and himself as Odysseus. In *Id.* 11, the most famous surviving treatment of the theme, Odysseus is only a background presence, putting the focus squarely on the pathos and absurdity of the Cyclops' position. Metrically, the poem is rougher than Theocritus' other idylls and contains a number of rare dialect forms that perhaps depict Polyphemus as a kind of Caliban. Vi. *Ecl.* 2 (p. 400) is an extensive translation or adaptation of this poem. Call. *Ep.* 3 (p. 276) likewise seems to be based on it.

l. 1. *Nicias*: Also the addressee of Theoc. *Id.* 13 and 28 and epigram 8; he is most likely the Nicias to whom are attributed eight undistinguished epigrams in the *Garland of Meleager* (none translated here). We are told that he responded to Theocritus' advice in this poem with a poem of his own, beginning:

> It's true, Theocritus, for love has made
> poets of many who never knew the Muses.

297. l. 25. *like a sheep fleeing a wolf*: Polyphemus here introduces into pastoral a motif in which the desperate lover compares himself to a predator; in denying the similitude, he reinforces it in the mind of the reluctant beloved. Virgil picks up on and expands this hint at *Ecl.* 2 (ll. 71–74), p. 402, and Horace imitates it at *Odes* 1.23, ll. 9–10 (p. 469).

l. 27. *Mama*: Polyphemus' mother was a monstrous sea nymph called Thoösa, the sister of Scylla and Echidna (see, respectively, Cat. 60, l. 2, p. 388, and n., and n. on Bacch. 5, l. 75, p. 173); his father was Poseidon.

298. ll. 53–4. *come singe my hair . . .*: Polyphemus invites Galatea to singe off the excess hair of his chest and unibrow, to make him less repulsive, but with a naive anticipation of his blinding at Odysseus' hands; a similar anticipation is found in l. 63, 'if I could meet some seadog to teach me how'.

l. 82. In Ovid's version of the tale (*Met.* 13, ll. 738–897), Polyphemus' passion remained unrequited after he caught Galatea *in flagrante* with the pretty youth Acis and squashed his successful rival beneath an enormous boulder. Galatea transformed the blood of her former paramour into a river, which still flows near Mount Etna (cf. Theoc. *Id.* 1, l. 71, p. 283).

The *Greek Anthology*

My numbering of epigrams follows the author-based numeration of A. S. F. Gow and Denys Page rather than the thematic arrangement of the *Greek Anthology*. See *Note on the Text* (p. xlvi) and the *Intro* to this section (p. 300).

Epigrams from the *Garland of Meleager*

Anyte

303. 9. The popularity of pet or animal epitaphs in Hellenistic epigram reflects the era's increasing preference for the humble and domestic. The topos makes its way into Latin poetry via Catullus; for examples, cf. Leo. Tar. 21 (p. 308), Mnasalces 11 (p. 316), Tymnes 5 (p. 319), Mel. 65 (p. 330), Cat. 3 (p. 376), Ov. *Am.* 2.6 (p. 501) and Stat. *Silv.* 2.4 (p. 528).

l. 1. *This Damis built*: We should imagine a stone or monument erected by the soldier Damis.

13. This tender scene of children riding a billy goat may derive from a votive painting or relief dedicated at a shrine.

Asclepiades

304. *Poet Introduction. Asclepiades' name attached itself to a lyric meter*: See *Note on Meters* (p. xxxv).

1. This epigram is a priamel, for which see n. on Hor. *Odes* 1.1, ll. 3–34 (pp. 462–3).

l. 3. *the Spring Wreath*: The Corona Borealis, a small constellation representing the ivy crown given to Ariadne by Dionysus after finding her abandoned on Naxos (see n. on Theoc. *Id.* 2, l. 50, p. 287); here its rising at dusk is taken as a sign of the end of winter.

2. l. 4. *our ashes mix*: 'Mixing' in Greek has sexual connotations. Cf. Marvell, 'To His Coy Mistress', ll. 27–8: 'then worms shall try / That long-preserved virginity . . .'

305. 12. This epigram, like 42, is a sort of *paraclausithyron*, or 'locked-door song' (see n. on Call. *Ep.* 8, p. 277).

15. ll. 3–4. *you punks will keep dicing*: The image of Loves (Cupids, *putti*) playing at dice or knucklebones (a primitive game of jacks) goes back to Anac. 398 (p. 107).

16. Cf. Alc. 38a (p. 57) and 346 (p. 65). This poem may have concluded a book of Asclepiades' epigrams.

306. 42. Asclepiades' authorship of this poem (like epigram 12, a 'locked-door song') is disputed.

l. 1. *Pleiades*: Cf. Sap. 168b (p. 54).

Leonidas of Tarentum

308. 21. For the Hellenistic genre of pet epitaphs, see Anyte 9 (p. 303) and n. See also Call. *Aet.* 1.1, ll. 29–30 (p. 258) and n. for the association of crickets and cicadas with poetry (and cf. Leo. Tar. 91, p. 310, below).

57. l. 1. *Eubulus*: The name suggests 'good' or 'wise counsel'.

309. 77. ll. 10–13. I have omitted a corrupt and confusing couplet between these verses. The exhortation to temperance with which the poem concludes, while unexpected (usually such poems take a more *carpe diem* direction), is in accord with Cynic philosophy.

85. A much-imitated poem, whose epigones we find concentrated at the beginning of Bk. 10 of the *Greek Anthology* (epigrams 2, 4, 5, 6, 14, 15, 16); in this volume, see also Ant. Si. 41 (p. 322). The subgenre of 'spring sailing epigram' invented here by Leonidas certainly influenced Cat. 46 (p. 386) and Hor. *Odes* 1.4 (p. 464).

310. l. 7. *Priapus of the Port*: This is the earliest mention of Priapus as a harbor god; cf. Ant. Si. 41 (p. 322), and nn. on Hor. *Odes* 1.4 (p. 464).

91. For the association of cicadas with poetry, cf. Leo. Tar. 21 (p. 308), above, and Call. *Aet.* 1.1, ll. 29–30 (p. 258) and n.

l. 8. *the pipe was her invention*: For Athena's invention of the double-reed pipe, or *aulos*, see, e.g., Pi. *Py.* 12, ll. 17–27.

Nossis

Poet Introduction. Epizephryian Locri: The so-called town of the 'Westerly Locrians', situated in that part of southern Italy known as Magna Graecia, was a colony of Opus in Locris, a region of central Greece.

311. 3. l. 2. *Croton*: Modern Crotone, a Greek city in Calabria, up the coast from Nossis' hometown of Locri. In ancient times, on the southeastern promontory now known as Capo Colonna, Croton boasted a temple to

Hera. The most famous temple of southern Italy, it was described by Livy (*History of Rome* 24.3.3) as 'sacred to all the surrounding peoples' and 'renowned for wealth as well as holiness'.

4. l. 1. *Cypris' temple*: Seaside temples to Aphrodite, where sacred prostitutes plied their trade, mostly for the benefit of sailors, were common; we don't know of such a temple in Nossis' native Locri, but presumably there was one.

5. l. 4. *Adonis' brow*: See Call. *Ia.* 3, ll. 36–7 (p. 263) and n.

Heraclitus of Halicarnassus

312. 1. l. 6. *Cnidus*: A city in southwestern Asia Minor, probably at the site of modern Tekir, across the Gulf of Cos from Heraclitus' Halicarnassus (modern Bodrum).

Posidippus of Pella

1. l. 2. *potluck*: The party is BYOB, as in Argent. 23 (p. 350).

l. 3. *Cleanthes . . . Zeno*: Stoic philosophers, contemporary with Posidippus. Zeno was the founder of Stoicism and Cleanthes was his successor in Athens. Posidippus seems to have had Stoic leanings himself. Cf. Argent. 30, ll. 5–6 (p. 350).

l. 4. *Love the bittersweet*: A famous coinage of Sap. 130 (p. 53).

Dioscorides

313. 1. ll. 1–6. *those chatty lips . . . those eyes . . . milky bosom*: For similar 'catalogues of charms', cf. Phil. 12 (p. 336) and Ov. *Am.* 1.5, ll. 18–23 (p. 494) and n.

l. 8. *Midas's reeds*: As told by Ovid (*Met.* 11, ll. 180–93), when the Phrygian king Midas was given donkey ears for preferring Pan's piping to Apollo's, the only person who knew about them was his barber. The barber whispered the secret into a hole in the ground, but the reeds that grew on the spot found out and told the wind.

314. 2. For a similar theme, cf. *Anacreontea* 26 (p. 362), and the *militia amoris* (warfare of love) trope of Latin love elegy (see Ov. *Am.* 1.9, p. 495, and n.).

3. l. 1. *Adonis*: See Call. *Ia.* 3, ll. 36–7 (p. 263) and n.

6. l. 5. *Hymen*: A god of marriage and weddings, also invoked in Sap. 111 (p. 52) and in the refrain of Cat. 62 (p. 388).

16. l. 1. *Chaste Atys, chambermaid of Cybele*: Atys, or Attis, was both Cybele's divine consort (who castrated himself, died and was reborn) and a name bestowed on Cybele's eunuch priests, as here – hence 'chambermaid'. (Cf. Cat. 63, a lengthy account of a priest called Attis who castrates himself in a fit of religious zeal and then regrets it.) For the goddess Cybele, cf. Anon. 935 (p. 237) and n.

l. 3. *Pessinus*: Modern Ballıhisar, site of Cybele's chief sanctuary in ancient Phrygia; it was located on the Royal Road from Susa to Sardis, once the capital of the ancient kingdom of Lydia, and also a major cult center for the goddess Cybele.

315. l. 16. *chatterbox*: The Greek word (*lalagema*) is related to *Lalage* (Chatterer, Babbler), the name of Horace's mistress in *Odes* 1.22 (p. 468; see n. *ad loc.*), which describe a wolf fleeing the enamored poet just as the lion flees the raving priest in this poem. For Horace, love fulfills the role of protective charm occupied here by Atys' kettledrum, though the effect is less impressive.

l. 18. *Sangarias*: The modern Sakarya, the third longest river of Turkey.

30, 32. The famously stoic patriotism of the Spartans (see, for example, Sim. *Ep.* 6, 7, 9, 22a and 22b, pp. 130–31, and Folk Songs 856, p. 243) was a favorite subject for later ages.

30. l. 1. *Pitana*: One of four pre-Dorian settlements which combined into the town of Sparta. Pitana became the aristocratic district, perhaps in the west of the city.

l. 2. *flat on his shield*: 'With it or on it' was famously how Spartans were told to return from battle; see Ar. 5 (p. 6) and n.

32. l. 1. *Demaeneta*: Her name, which means 'Praise of the People', seems suspiciously relevant.

Mnasalces

316. *11*. For the Hellenistic genre of pet epitaphs, see Anyte 9 (p. 303) and n.

l. 4. *stade*: One length of the track, about 200 yards. A twelve-stade race was a bit less than a mile and a half.

Theodoridas

2. l. 1. *Amarynthus*: A mountain on the west coast of the island of Euboea, facing Attica. There was a temple to Artemis Amarynthia and a cult that spread to Athens.

l. 3. *these shorn youthful locks*: For hair-offerings, see Call. *Hy.* 2, l. 14 (p. 269) and n., and Crin. 9 and 10 (pp. 340–41).

15. ll. 1–2. *Mnasalces ... Plataea's son*: The poet and epigrammatist; see above, p. 315. The 'Plataea' he is from is not the famous Boeotian one, but a village in the territory of Sicyon, in the northern Peloponnese.

l. 3. *Simonides*: See pp. 120–33.

Alcaeus of Messene

317. 2. l. 1. *the Cyclops*: The Polyphemus of the *Odyssey*, not the lovesick one of Theoc. *Id.* 11 (p. 296).

l. 4. *Philip's skull*: Philip V of Macedon, who reigned from 221 to 179 BCE. It is not known what inspired the Messenian Alcaeus' hatred of Philip, though many poisonings and other outrages have been laid to the monarch's discredit. The poet's vehemence certainly reminds us of his Mytilenean namesake's hatred of the tyrant Pittacus (cf., e.g., Alc. 70, p. 59, 129, ll. 13–24, p. 61, and 348, p. 66).

6. l. 1. *I hate Love*: This poem may lie somewhere behind Catullus' famous poem 85 ('I hate and I love', p. 396). Cf. also Anon. Mel. 4 (p. 323) and Evenus 7 (p. 354).

ll. 1–3: *why won't the god pursue wild beasts ...*: Compare Tib. 2.1, ll. 72–81 (p. 419).

7. l. 2. *it sprints on with the torch*: The poem borrows its metaphor from the torch relay – a feature of many Greek festivals – in which runners pass a lit torch, each to the next, instead of a baton.

318. 14. l. 1. *Pylades* of Megalopolis in Arcadia was a well-known citharode who competed at the Panhellenic Nemean Games in 205 BCE with a performance of Timotheus' *Persians* (p. 205).

l. 5. *Asopus*: An ancient note relates this to the Boeotian river (see Cor. 654b, p. 201, and n.), but there were a number of rivers of this name, including one that flows near Nemea before debouching into the Gulf of Corinth at Sicyon.

Theaetetus

3. l. 4. *Thersites and Minos*: Thersites is an ugly, ill-spoken hunchback, and the most despicable of the Greek soldiers at Troy. He has a prominent role in fomenting chaos in Hom. *Il.* 2; cf. Ov. *Am.* 2.6, l. 42 (p. 502). Minos is the legendary king of Crete; cf. n. on Bacch. 17 (p. 178). According to Homer (*Od.* 11, l. 568) and Plato (*Gorgias* 524a), he is one of the judges of the underworld (cf. Ant. Thess. 38, l. 4, p. 346, and Hor. *Odes* 4.7, ll. 26–7, p. 490; also Dante, *Inferno* 5, ll. 4–15). Consequently Minos would, *contra* Theaetetus, have more esteem there than Thersites. Propertius Romanizes Theaetetus' sentiment at 3.5, ll. 15–16 (p. 434).

Tymnes

319. 2. l. 3. *Eleutherna*: A city on Crete. Philaenis has been buried far from her homeland of Egypt.

5. l. 1. *Melite*: The ancient name of Malta, and/or a city there, well known in ancient times for a breed of diminutive dog, perhaps ancestor to the modern Maltese. For the Hellenistic genre of pet epitaphs, see Anyte 9 (p. 303) and n.

Phanias

320. 7. l. 7. *Epicurus' garden-party school*: The philosopher Epicurus, known for advocating the pursuit of pleasure as the main object of life, bought a house with a garden near Athens, where he met with his students and philosophized; after his death, the garden remained in his followers' possession and became a symbol of Epicureanism – pleasurable, private, detached from the cares of the world. Here, Phanias has probably chosen Epicurus for the Greek pun on *koureion*, 'barbershop'.

Antipater of Sidon

Poet Introduction. 'Antipater made a habit . . .': Cicero, *De Oratore* 3.194.

321. 22. l. 5. *thirst-snake*: The Dipsas (from *dipsa*, thirst) was a legendary snake whose bite was supposed to cause intense thirst.

23. l. 3. *Lais of Corinth*: A legendary prostitute in a city legendary for its prostitutes; cf. Pi. fr. 122 (p. 161).

l. 4. *Pirene*: A famous Corinthian spring, said to have been a woman turned to water while mourning her son, whom Artemis had killed. It was transformed by the Romans into an extravagant bath complex, full of white marble, and is well worth visiting.

l. 5. *Cytherea*: An epithet of Aphrodite, 'Lady of Cythera' – Cythera being the island which, along with Cyprus, claimed to have been the site of the goddess's birth.

l. 6. *Tyndareus's daughter*: Helen; for her 'double parentage', see n. on Stes. 85, l. 4 (p. 92). A fragmentary poem of Hesiod's, the *Catalogue of Women*, tells of the suitors who assembled from all over the Greek world to vie for her hand in marriage. Once they had sworn to defend the rights of whichever man Tyndareus chose, he selected Menelaus.

322. 26. l. 2. *Boreas*: The north wind, called 'truly Thracian' both because it blows out of Thrace in the north, and because the Thracians were considered barbarians par excellence.

ll. 5–6. *pitiless Ino ... Melicertes, was no older*: Ino, a daughter of Cadmus, fleeing from her mad husband, the Minyan king Athamas, with her son Melicertes in her arms, jumped into the sea with him; whereupon they were both transformed into sea deities, Ino to Leucothea (White Goddess), and Melicertes to Palaemon. Thereafter Ino/Leucothea made a point of helping seafarers in distress – though not this time. See also Phil. 19 (p. 338) and Prop. 2.28, ll. 19–20 (p. 431).

41. An imitation of Leo. Tar. 85 (p. 309).

l. 8. *Priapus of the Harbor*: See Leo. Tar. 85, l. 7 (p. 310) and n.

58. l. 1. *Erinna*: See p. 302.

323. 59. Lamenting the sack of Corinth by the Roman general Lucius Mummius in 146 BCE (see *Intro* to Latin Lyric, p. 000), this epigram belongs to a tradition of Greek laments for cities which includes Aeschylus' *Persians* and Euripides' *Trojan Women*. Cf. Anon. Mel. 54 (p. 000), and Crin. 37 (p. 343), which laments Corinth's repeopling with Italian freedmen.

l. 8. *like halcyons*: Mythical seabirds early identified with kingfishers, most famous as 'birds of calm'; Antipater's interest in them seems largely to relate to their song (cf. Ant. Si. 61, l. 3). See also n. on Theoc. *Id.* 7, l. 64 (p. 291).

61. l. 3. *Hooch*: This is Methe, goddess of drunkenness.
louche-crooning halcyon: See previous note.

Anonymous

4. Another poem, like Alc. Mess. 6 (p. 317) and Evenus 7 (p. 354), which may lie somewhere in the background of Catullus' poem 85 (p. 396), his most famous couplet. The sentiment here is also interestingly reminiscent of Call. *Ep.* 2 (p. 276).

324. 8. l. 2. *stop slaving*: The language, which no doubt strikes us as hyperbolic, either reflects or anticipates the 'slavery of love' (*servitium amoris*) trope so common in Latin love elegy.

10. Cf. Ant. Thess. 7 (p. 345), Argent. 16 (p. 350) and *Anacreontea* 10 (p. 360) for the same theme.

35. l. 1. *magic wheel*: See Theoc. *Id.* 2, l. 21 (p. 286) and n.

l. 5. *witch of Thessaly*: See Prop. 1.1, l. 23 (p. 423) and n.

325. 52. l. 4. *Ibycus the* bon vivant: The poet (pp. 96–9), from Rhegium (modern Reggio Calabria). Literary epitaphs for famous people, writers or otherwise, were a common subgenre of Hellenistic epigram (of which this is the only example included in this book).

l. 6. *ivy*: Associated with poetry and Dionysus.

326. 53. Perhaps in reference to the invasion of Sparta by the Achaean League under the Arcadian general Philopoemen in 188 BCE, or to Philip V of Macedon's Spartan invasion in 218 BCE, or even to one of those of the Theban general Epaminondas in the 360s BCE. Cf. Ant. Si. 59 (p. 000) and n.

l. 2. *Eurotas*: Laconia's main river, on whose banks Sparta was located.

Meleager

Poet Introduction. 'iostephanous . . . *and tawdry Muse*': The quote is often misattributed to Swinburne, but seems more correctly the sentiment of one George Murray of Magdalen College, Oxford: see Gideon Nisbet, *Greek Epigram in Reception: J. A. Symonds, Oscar Wilde, and the Invention of Desire, 1805–1929*, pp. 195–6.

4. ll. 7–8. *Naidius! . . . Salaam! . . . Chaire!*: 'Greetings!' in Phoenician, Syrian and Greek respectively.

327. 6. l. 6. *born from blue-green sea*: An instance of the 'ocean of love' metaphor; for which, cf. Theog. ll. 1375–6 (p. 85) and n.

25. See previous note.

l. 1. *Asclepias*. A woman's name, unrelated to Asclepius (god of medicine).

329. 56. One of Meleager's most admired poems, and a clear model for Catullus' elegy for his brother, Cat. 101 (p. 397).

330. 65. For the Hellenistic genre of pet epitaphs, see Anyte 9 (p. 303) and n.

69. l. 5. *he wrote in water what he said*: Cf. Cat. 70, ll. 3–4 (p. 394); and, for the untrustworthiness of lovers' vows more generally, see n. on Call. *Ep.* 11, ll. 3–4 (p. 277).

71, 72. Both of these poems exemplify a type of mini-verse drama compressed into epigram which seems to have originated with Asclepiades (pp. 303–6) – a form that A. S. F. Gow has dubbed 'thumb-nail mime' (A. S. F. Gow and D. L. Page, eds., *The Greek Anthology: Hellenistic Epigrams*, Vol. 2, p. 132). Mel. 71 in particular may have inspired Ovid in *Am.* 1.11 (p. 496).

331. 90. l. 2. *a curtain*: i.e., of buttock hair. The above-the-neck variety was not the only sort of beard Greeks found unattractive.

l. 4. *Nemesis*: Goddess of retribution, also invoked at Cat. 50, l. 20 (p. 387), and 68b, l. 77 (p. 392), and by Tibullus, who names a (particularly vengeful) mistress after her (see *Intro to Tibullus*, pp. 411–12); her chief temple was at Rhamnous in northeastern Attica. It is no doubt a trivialization of this goddess's dread power to reduce her to punishing recalcitrant boys with hair, as Meleager says, 'on either cheek'.

94. There was a debate in antiquity about whether to prefer the love of women or of boys. In the *Erotes* (*Affairs of the Heart*) of Lucian (or Pseudo-Lucian), the Athenian Callicratidas favors boys, while the Corinthian Charicles favors women; the former is judged the winner. The dialogue is discussed at length by Foucault in *The History of Sexuality*, Vol. 3, Part 6, Ch. 2. On this theme, cf. also Argent. 10 (p. 348).

332. 102. l. 2. *to make . . . carry cups on high*: The implied reference is to Ganymede, whom Zeus, taking the form of an eagle, ravished and made celestial cupbearer.

l. 4. *My pain has taught compassion*: Zeus, of course, is a noted philanderer. Virgil may be thinking of this line when he has Dido say, 'Schooled in calamity, I've learned to aid the anguished' (*Aen.* 1, l. 630).

l. 5. *if I see a fly*: Zeus could turn into anything, and might well choose a fly to seduce a boy whose name is derived from *myios*, 'fly'.

103. ll. *1–2*. *Myiscus' eyes first pierced* ... : The opening of Prop. 1.1 (p. 423) is famously modeled on this poem.

l. *6*. *Love brought down even Zeus from heaven*: i.e., in pursuit of Ganymede, as hinted at in Mel. 102, l. 2, above.

129. l. *1*. *glyph*: The *coronis* is a symbol used in many extant papyri to indicate the conclusion of a poem, section or work; a coiled, snake-like symbol (cf. l. 7) was a common variation. Phil. 17 (p. 337) and Cat. 1 (p. 376) also engage with physical book-making.

Epigrams from the *Garland of Philip*

333. *Introduction*. *Dedicated to one Camillus*: Perhaps Marcus Furius Camillus, who was elected to the Arval Brethren (a priestly brotherhood drawn from senatorial families) in 38 CE, and stepbrother to Lucius Arruntius Camillus Scribonianus, a quondam consul who was murdered when he rebelled against the emperor Claudius in 42 CE.

presented to the Roman emperor in the 40s or 50s CE: Probably to Nero in the mid-50s, though some have dated it to the reign of Caligula in 40 CE. On the likely dedicatee, see *Intro* to Martial, p. 534.

Philodemus

334. *1*. This poem is a model for Argent. 13 (p. 349) and Ov. *Am.* 1.5, ll. 24–7 (p. 495), which fuses the two.

3. Philodemus provides a humorous counter to the Epicurean teaching that the pleasures of adultery are not worth the fear of punishment – *ataraxia* (lack of perturbation, equanimity) being a key concept and goal for both Epicurus and the Stoics.

l. *2*. *venture boldly at nightfall*: Presumably Cydilla is married and her husband more likely to be home at night (hence the boldness), though Philodemus could also be thinking of the dangers of roaming a city after dark, as in Prop. 3.16 (p. 437).

335. *5*. l. *6*. *Ionian Sea*: Between Italy and Epirus; according to Aeschylus (*Prometheus Bound*, ll. 839–41), named after Io (cf. Bacch. 19, ll. 15–45, pp. 183–4, and nn.).

l. *8*. *Naias* appears again as a refuge from domestic strife in Phil. 15, l. 9 (p. 337).

6. l. 3. *Nysa*: The manuscript reading is uncertain. Other possibilities include Mysia and Hysiae.

l. 6. *Demo-lover Philodemus*: Philodemus puns on his name as 'Demo-Lover', instead of the likelier etymology, 'Lover of the People' (*demos*). That Demo was a common enough name for a woman is shown, in this volume, by Mel. 23 (p. 327) and Phil. 16 (p. 337).

8. For another variation on this theme, see Ov. *Am.* 2.4 ll. 40–1 (p. 499), not to mention Shakespeare, Sonnet 130: 'My mistress' eyes are nothing like the sun . . .'

ll. 1–2. *brown, but* . . . : Probably for reasons of class, fairer skin was conventionally considered more beautiful. Many poets (like Philodemus) were happy to make exceptions. For one exception, see Ov. *Am.* 2.4, l. 41 (p. 500).

336. 9. Denys Page writes of this poem: 'The sensuous tone and exquisite phrasing of this epigram combine to form a style which is hardly to be found in any Greek author earlier than Meleager and Philodemus' (A. S. F. Gow and D. L. Page, eds., *The Greek Anthology: The Garland of Philip and Some Contemporary Epigrams*, Vol. 2, p. 379). Propertius is inspired by it in 1.3, especially ll. 31–2 (p. 425); see also Ov. *Ex Pont.* 3.3, ll. 6–7 (p. 522).

l. 6. *Endymion*: A beautiful young man, variously said to be a shepherd, hunter or king, whose sleep (generally placed on Mount Latmus, now Beşparmak Dağı, in southwestern Anatolia) kindled the passions of Selene, the Moon.

12. Ovid echoes this poem at *Am.* 1.5, ll. 18–23 (p. 494) and n.; cf. also Dios. 1 (p. 313).

l. 7. *Flora, from Campania*: The name 'Flora' is Italian and rustic; Campania is the south Italian region which included Herculaneum, Philodemus' home (see *Poet Intro*, p. 333). Philodemus is implicitly rejecting the fashionable predilection for a *docta puella* ('learned girl', in this case thought of as a Greek courtesan like Lais of Corinth: see Ant. Si. 23, p. 321, and n.) able to charm everyone at the symposium with sophisticated entertainments.

ll. 8–9. *Andromeda* . . . *came from India*: Andromeda was a princess, usually vaguely said to have been Ethiopian, who was rescued from a sea monster and married by the hero Perseus (cf. Prop. 1.3, ll. 3–4, p. 425, 2.28, ll. 21–2, p. 431, and 4.7, ll. 65–8, p. 441). The fact that Philodemus says she is from India merely shows the haziness with which literary Greeks and Romans treated such distant geographical regions; the point here is that 'India' was even more of a far-off backwater than Campania.

15. l. 1. *Cypris, sea-calmer*: Aphrodite, born from the ocean (as noted at Mel. 6, p. 327), has long been considered a sea goddess: see n. at Hor. *Odes* 1.3, l. 1 (p. 463). For other poems and epigrams which combine nautical and erotic themes, see Theog. ll. 1375–6 (p. 85) and n.

337. l. 9. *safe in Naias' cove*: Cf. Phil. 5, l. 8 (p. 335) and n.

16. For the sentiment, cf. Scolia 904 (p. 247).

17, 18. Those bothered by the coincidence of Epicurean philosopher and frivolous poet in one person read this epigram and the next one biographically, and assume that at the age of thirty-seven (17, l. 1) Philodemus, like St. Paul in 1 Corinthians 13:11, put away childish things and turned to serious study. The two poems also provide the basis for Prop. 3.5, ll. 19–30 (pp. 434–5).

17. l. 8. *conclude this poem*: Literally, the Greek says 'write the *coronis*', the 'glyph that signifies the finish line' in Mel. 129, l. 1 (p. 332) and n.

338. *19*. This poem may have been written on Philodemus' voyage from Gadara to Athens to study philosophy (see *Poet Intro*, p. 333).

ll. 1–2. *Melicertes . . . Leucothea*: See n. on Ant. Si. 26, ll. 5–6 (p. 322).

l. 4. *Thracian* just means 'northern' here. Cf. Ant. Si. 26, l. 2 (p. 322) and n.

l. 6. *Piraeus*: The port of Athens.

21. Writes Denys Page: 'Philodemus is saying in effect "I will give up champagne, cigars, and chorus-girls and content myself with claret, Turkish cigarettes, and a young wife"' (*The Greek Anthology: The Garland of Philip*, Vol. 2, p. 391).

23. This poem inaugurated a mini-genre of invitation poems in Roman literature; cf. Cat. 13 (p. 381), Hor. *Odes* 4.11 (p. 490) and Mart. 10.48 (p. 549).

l. 1. *Piso*: See *Intro* to Philodemus (p. 333).

339. l. 3. *the Twentieth*: Epicurus' will stipulated that his followers meet on the 20th of every month for an appropriately Epicurean dinner and discussion; see also n. on Bacch. fr. 20b, l. 5 (p. 185). This epigram presumably represents an early period in Philodemus' and Piso's relationship, when the latter was not yet a committed Epicurean and a regular attendee at such events.

l. 4. *Chian wine for fancy toasts*: Cf. Phil. 21 l. 2 above and n.; and see n. on Tib. 2.1, l. 29 (p. 418).

l. 6. *Phaeacian ear*: The Phaeacians are a mythical people who live on the island of Scheria in the *Odyssey* (equated with Corfu at Tib. 1.3, p. 413); they receive Odysseus when he escapes Calypso's island in Bk. 5, and listen to the tales of his journey in Bks. 9–12 before depositing him back on Ithaca. Philodemus means that the conversation between Piso and himself will be more enthralling than Odysseus' recounting of his fabulous adventures at the Phaeacian court.

25. l. 2. *five talents*: One talent was equivalent to 6,000 drachmas; one drachma would have been about a day's wage for a skilled worker.

27. For other similarly high-minded poems on impotence, cf. Automedon 1 and 2 (pp. 352–3), and Ov. *Am.* 3.7 (p. 507) and n., as well as, naturally, Hipponax's ingenious attempts at a remedy in Hipp. 78 and 92 (pp. 117 and 118).

Crinagoras

Poet Introduction. 'the accredited representative ...': Gow and Page (eds.), *The Greek Anthology: The Garland of Philip*, Vol. 2, p. 212.

340. 9. ll. 4–5. For hair-offerings, cf. Crin. 10, below, and see Call. *Hy.* 2, l. 14 (p. 269) and n., and Theodoridas 2 (p. 316).

341. 10. l. 1. *Marcellus*: M. Claudius Marcellus (42–23 BCE), son of Gaius Claudius Marcellus and Augustus' sister Octavia, whose tragic early death is commemorated most movingly by Virgil at *Aen.* 6, ll. 860–84. The *western war*, waged against the Cantabrians in Spain, was temporarily halted in 25 BCE, the likely date of this epigram.

l. 3. *shaved his first beard*: Cf. Crin. 9 and n., above.

15. l. 1. *Earth*: Ge in Greek was not a common name, but is attested for a freedman.

17. It is likely that the boy named Love (Eros – a common enough name for slaves; cf. Mart. 10.80, p. 551) died during Crinagoras' embassy of 45 BCE (see *Poet Intro*, p. 339) en route either to or from Italy. For another epitaph on a beloved slave, compare Mart. 5.34 (p. 543).

l. 3. *Spines*: The Echinades, an archipelago of rocky islets where the River Achelous empties into the Gulf of Corinth.

18, *For Selene*. Selene ('Moon') here is probably Cleopatra Selene, daughter of Antony and Cleopatra, who may have still been on the throne of Numidia in the second decade CE. This epigram must therefore have been written in Crinagoras' very old age, i.e., in his nineties or upward.

342. 20. l. 1. *Philostratus*: A famed orator, much in favor at the court of Antony and Cleopatra (cf. n. on Theog. ll. 213–18, p. 80). He was eventually pardoned by Octavian and banished to Ostracina (l. 6) on the northern frontier of Egypt. Crinagoras may have met him during his second embassy to Rome in 45 BCE (Cleopatra was in town at the time, along with a large retinue), and learned of his fate during his third embassy in 26/5 BCE (see *Poet Intro*, p. 339).

27. l. 4. *Caesar's right-hand rule*: In all likelihood, Augustus, though it is just possible that the epigram could refer to the campaigns in Germany of Tiberius' adopted son Germanicus in 14–16 CE at the beginning of Tiberius' reign). If so, Crinagoras will have written it in his mid-eighties. 'Right-handed rule' is the opposite of *sinister* (left-handed); it suggests a godlike power to command and strength to guide.

34. l. 1. *the great Earthshaker*: Poseidon.

l. 3. *a Thracian squall*: One out of the north, as at Phil. 19, l. 4 (p. 338).

343. 35. l. 4. *Demeter's rites*: i.e., the Mysteries of Demeter at Eleusis; cf. Pi. fr. 137, l. 2 (p. 164), Phil. Scar. *PaeDi.*, ll. 27–36 (p. 230) and nn., and Hor. *Odes* 3.2, ll. 26–7 (p. 480) and n.

37. l. 1. *What immigrants*: i.e., the Italian freedmen with which Corinth, destroyed by the Roman general Lucius Mummius in 146 BCE (cf. Ant. Si. 59, p. 323, and *Intro* to Latin Lyric, p. 367), was repopulated by Julius Caesar in 44 BCE. These new citizens of Corinth were universally hated by Greeks for being lowborn, for trafficking in relics of Corinth's destruction (cf. Prop. 3.5, l. 6, p. 434) and for building a gladiatorial arena for the first time on Greek soil.

l. 6. *Bacchiads*: An early ruling family of Corinth, overthrown by the tyrant Cypselus in the mid-seventh century BCE; cf. Hdt. *Hist.* 5.92.

Erucius

13. l. 2. *Parthenius*: Probably Parthenius of Nicaea, Alexandrian-style poet and friend and teacher of Virgil (pp. 398–410) and Gaius Cornelius Gallus (see n. on Vi. *Ecl.* 10, l. 2, p. 408). The criticism of the *Iliad* and *Odyssey* attributed to him in this poem may reflect an exaggerated Callimachean preference for the small-scale and refined, though we know of no reason he should stand accused of obscenity. For Parthenius' significance to Roman poetry see *Intro* to Latin Lyric, pp. 367–8.

344. l. 8. *Cocytus*: The River of Lamentation in the underworld.

Antipater of Thessalonica

345. 3. ll. 1-2. *Boeotian Helicon . . . Hesiod sipped*: The mountain in Boeotia, sacred to the Muses, where the Hippocrene spring, formed by the winged horse Pegasus (and therefore called a 'horsey hole' in l. 6), was located. Cf. also Call. *Aet.* 4.112, l. 5 (p. 261) and n., Call. *Hy.* 5, l. 71 (p. 274) and n., Prop. 3.3, l. 2 (p. 432) and n., and Ov. *Tri.* 3.7, l. 16 (p. 514). For the Muses' epiphany to Hesiod on Helicon, see *Intro* to Callimachus (pp. 255-6), and n. on the *Aetia* (p. 258).

ll. 5-6. *I'd rather drink one cup of what he pours . . .*: See n. on Ant. Thess. 20, below.

7. For the theme, cf. Anon. Mel. 10 (p. 324), Argent. 16 (p. 350) and *Anacreontea* 10 (p. 360).

ll. 5-6. For *Tithonus* and his affair with *Aurora* (Eos, the Dawn), see Tyr. 12, l. 7 (p. 25) and n.

20. As sources of poetic inspiration and quarreling, water and wine acquire metapoetic associations in this period, respectively with a 'Callimachean' school – learned, allusive, stylistically 'pure', like a sacred spring (cf. the pure springs sipped by 'Demeter's Bees' in Call. *Hy.* 2, ll. 110-12, p. 272, and see n. *ad. loc.*) – and an 'anti-Callimachean' school, comastic (see n. on Call. *Ep.* 8, p. 277) and sympotic, which looks back to Archilochus (pp. 5-15), Alcaeus (pp. 55-67) and Anacreon (pp. 100-108). (The accusation of teetotaling was not completely fair; Callimachus seems to have enjoyed the occasional tipple, albeit diluted – see the *Banquet of Pollis* (*Aet.* fr. 178+2.43, p. 259).) This opposition is carried forward in altered form among Roman poets, especially by the Callimachean Propertius (pp. 421-45) and the lyric Horace (pp. 453-91), though it is relevant to others as well. Antipater at any rate declares his allegiance not only here but also in epigrams 3, 37 and 38; his fellow anti-Callimacheans in the *Anthology* include Antiphanes of Macedonia (pp. 354-5) and the anthologist Philip of Thessalonica (pp. 355-6).

37. l. 1. *the setting of the Pleiades*: According to Hesiod (*W&D*, ll. 619-22), a harbinger of winter, and the end of the sailing season. Cf. Sap. 168b (p. 54) and Ascl. 42 (p. 306).

l. 4. *since he's not drinking*: See n. on Ant. Thess. 20, above.

346. 38. l. 4. *Minos*: Here a judge of the dead; see n. on Theaetetus 3, l. 4 (p. 318).

ll. 5-6. *Let's drink . . .*: See n. on Ant. Thess. 20, above.

82. This unique epigram celebrates the replacement of a hand-mill with a watermill. It is unclear whether the technology was absolutely new, new to Antipater or newly installed in a particular location. Antipater's slightly older contemporary, Vitruvius, explains the working of the watermill as follows: 'The teeth of the upright drum (which is attached to the axle) compel the teeth of the flat drum and thus drive the rotation of the millstones' (*On Architecture* 10.5.2).

l. 3. Both *Demeter* and *nymphs* here are examples of metonymy: Demeter figuratively oversees the work of grinding the grain she is goddess of; the water nymphs she has hired stand for the river or stream that powers the mill.

ll. 7–8. *Demeter's wage*: i.e., bread. For the *Golden Age*, cf. Tib. 1.3, ll. 35–48 (p. 414) and n.

96. ll. 1–2. The *Plowman* is the constellation of Boötes, whose plow was the Big Dipper; *Arcturus* (the 'Bear Guardian') formed part of Boötes' belt, and its heliacal (pre-dawn) rising occurred around 20 September – the signal for the vintage, according to Hes. *W&D*, ll. 609–11.

Apollonides

347. 27. Cf. Antiphanes 7 (p. 355).

Marcus Argentarius

Poet Introduction. 'by the ghost of Cestius' . . . his monkey: Seneca, *Controversies* 9.3.12.

'fluent, witty, and often malicious . . .': Gow and Page (eds.), *The Greek Anthology: The Garland of Philip*, Vol. 2, p. 166.

348. 1. l. 6. *Love's silver bloodhounds*: Coins, specie. The theme – the unpleasantness of having to pay for sex – is common in epigram (cf. Argent. 2, below, and Maccius 1, p. 354) and the Latin love elegists.

2. ll. 1–2. *Melissa* means 'bee' in Greek.

7. l. 4. *Chaldeans*: Babylonians, known for their expertise in astronomy/astrology. Cf. Hor. *Odes* 1.11, ll. 2–3 (p. 467) and n.

l. 5. *heavens*: This lewd epigram relies on a Greek pun: that *ouranos* means both 'heaven' and 'palate'. The *Dog* and *Twins* harbored by Menophila's *ouranos* refer astronomically to Sirius and Gemini; their sexual implication I will leave to the reader. Her 'heavens' differ from the physical sky because, in the latter, either Sirius or Gemini is always visible, but never both at once.

10. For the hetero- vs. homosexual debate, see Mel. 94 (p. 331) and n.

349. *11*. This little epigram is reminiscent of Edmund Waller's (far superior) 'Go, lovely rose'.

12. l. 5. *the squeaking bed*: Cf. Cat. 6, ll. 11–12 (p. 378).

l. 6. *'By Hermes, I get halves!'*: Denys Page comments: 'The finder of things lost was expected to go shares with any witness of his luck, and Hermes was the god who brought good luck' (*The Greek Anthology: The Garland of Philip*, Vol. 2, p. 172).

13. An imitation of Phil. 1 (p. 334); cf. also Ov. *Am.* 1.5, ll. 24–7 (p. 495), which fuses the two. Argentarius' Antigone has nothing to do with the protagonist of Sophocles' great play.

15. Cf. Austin Dobson, 'Urceus Exit':

> I intended an Ode,
> > And it turned to a Sonnet . . .
> I intended an Ode;
> But Rose crossed the road
> > In her latest new bonnet . . .

350. *16*. Cf. Anon. Mel. 10 (p. 324), Ant. Thess. 7 (p. 345) and *Anacreontea* 10 (p. 360) for the same theme.

l. 5. *Serapis' altar*: For the Hellenistic deity Serapis, see *Intro* to Post-Classical Greek Lyric, p. 253. Whether Argentarius here refers to the Alexandrian temple of Serapis (as at Call. *Ia.* 1, l. 9, p. 261), or the Roman temple to Isis and Serapis (cf. Cat. 10, l. 27, p. 380, and the n. on Tib. 1.3, l. 23, p. 413), or indeed some other public or private shrine, it is impossible to say.

23. l. 4. *potluck bottle-bash*: The feast of peers (a Homeric phrase for a board where everyone shared equally) was evidently BYOB, as in Pos. 1 (p. 312).

26. ll. 5–6. *I've designed it well . . . the Design*: The poem relies on the Greek *kosmos*, which means 'order, arrangement, design' on both a universal and personal scale: hence the derivations of both 'cosmic' and 'cosmetic'.

l. 6. *Lyre and Crown* refers both to the constellations Lyra and Corona Borealis (see n. on Ascl. 1, l. 3, p. 304), and to typical accoutrements of the symposium. Thus, for Argentarius, the presence of these constellations together is evidence that his somewhat decadent lifestyle is in harmony with the heavens and the Order of Things.

30. l. 6. *Zeno and Cleanthes*: See Pos. 1, l. 3 (p. 312) and n.

Antiphilus of Byzantium

351. *2*. l. 1. *a quince*: On the erotic significance of quinces, and their similarity to apples, see Iby. 286, l. 1 (p. 99) and n.

352. *16*. l. 1. *Queen of the Wayside*: Perhaps Artemis or Hecate; see n. on Call. *Ia.* 1, l. 28 (p. 261).

Automedon

352–3. *1, 2*. For more on impotence, cf. Phil. 27 (p. 339), and Ov. *Am.* 3.7 (p. 507) and n.

Evenus

354. *7*. This poem is an example of the raw rhetorical material from which Catullus made his famous couplet, poem 85 (p. 396). In a similar vein, see also Alc. Mess. 6 (p. 317) and Anon. Mel. 4 (p. 323).

Maccius

1. For the theme, compare Argent. 1 and 2 (pp. 247–8).

10. This epigram is unique in the *Greek Anthology* for its rustic realism. Its closest resemblance is to Vi. *Geo.* 2, ll. 7–8:

> O Bacchus, father, come, kick off your boots,
> and stain your bare feet in the unpressed grapes.

Antiphanes of Macedonia

1. l. 2. *sash*: For Aphrodite's *sash* and its aphrodisiac qualities, see Hom. *Il.* 14, ll. 214–23, where she lends it to Hera for the seduction of Zeus; cf. also Call. *Aet.* 4.112, l. 1 (p. 261) and n.

355. *7*. Cf. Apollonides 27 (p. 347).

9. Antiphanes here demonstrates himself to be a member of the anti-Callimachean party: see Ant. Thess. 20 (p. 345) and n.

l. 5. *Erinna's flunky claque*: i.e., pedantic commentators on the work of Erinna (p. 302) – perhaps including authors like Antipater of Sidon, who praises her in his epigram 58 (p. 322) – rather than the work itself.

Philip of Thessalonica

356. *55*. l. 2. *Scythia*: Cf. Ov. *Tri.* 3.2, l. 2 (p. 513) and n.

l. 7. *Lycurgus*: A mythical king of Thrace and an enemy of wine. He got drunk, then tried to rape his mother and afterwards attempted to cut down all the country's grapevines.

Anacreontea

357. *Introduction. a particular meter used by Anacreon*: See *Note on Meters* (p. xli).

358. *4.* l. 3. *a suit of armor*: The poet is thinking of the armor forged by Hephaestus for Achilles, famously described by Homer in *Il.* 18, ll. 478–608. Compare the (admittedly much more serious and far greater) 'Shield of Achilles' of W. H. Auden.

l. 5. *empty flagon*: This vessel may be intended to invoke another famous poetic description (*ekphrasis*), of the rustic drinking cup offered by one herdsman to another in Theoc. *Id.* 1, ll. 27–56, though the decorations mentioned here – the constellations rejected (ll. 8–11) and the vine desired (ll. 13–14) – remind us rather of a cup described in Vi. *Ecl.* 3, ll. 35–43, involving two constellations, riddlingly unspecified, and surrounded by 'a supple vine that clothes its scattered clusters in pale ivy' (l. 39).

359. ll. 8–11. *Wagon ... Orion ... Pleiades ... Plowman*: As the 'suit of armor' (l. 3) invokes the *Iliad*, this list of constellations may well conjure up the *Phaenomena* of Aratus, a didactic Alexandrian poem on the subject of astronomy; thus, the Anacreontic poet rejects the two main poetic genres (epic and didactic) in favor of his own preferred genre of sympotic poetry. The glancing overlap, described above, with Theocritus and his imitator Virgil would seem also to place pastoral somewhere within the spectrum of generic allusions in play here, but whether as a sort of rusticated ally of or adjunct to Anacreontic verse, or as a third poetic rival to be rejected, is unclear.

7. The poem plays on Anac. 358 (p. 104), but is much less ambiguous than the original.

8. ll. 1–2. Gyges, Lord of Sardis: The same proverbially wealthy Lydian king mentioned at Ar. 19 (p. 8), on which this poem is a sympotic variation.

360. *9.* In a manner not far off from that of, e.g., Propertius (pp. 421–45), this poet, justifying his desire to be 'mad, mad, mad' (l. 19), dips into what Philip Larkin called the 'myth-kitty', to bathetic effect.

ll. 5–7. *Alcmaeon* and *Orestes* both killed their treacherous mothers (Eriphyle and Clytemnestra, respectively) and subsequently went insane, pursued by Furies, until they expiated their offenses. For Alcmaeon and Eriphyle, cf. n. on Pi. *Py.* 8, l. 39 (p. 153). Incidentally, they also form the dramatis personae of A. E. Housman's hilarious 'Fragment of a Greek Tragedy', which parodies Aeschylus' *Agamemnon* and Robert Browning's translation of it.

ll. 11–13. *deranged as Heracles* ... : Heracles' first bout of madness, in which he killed his children and wife, saw him saddled with his famous labors; these completed, he went to Oechalia, got in a spat with the local king, Eurytus, and, in a second bout of madness, killed Eurytus' son, Iphitus, who was actually on his side. Our author plainly follows a different version than Homer, who has Iphitus give his bow to Odysseus at *Od.* 21, ll. 13–38.

ll. 14–15. *Ajax ... the blade he wielded*: After losing out to Odysseus in the contest for the dead Achilles' armor, Ajax goes insane and slaughters a herd of sheep; when he eventually comes to his senses, he kills himself for shame. The story is told in Sophocles' surviving play *Ajax*.

10. ll. 6–7. *like Tereus did once* ... : The despotic Thracian king Tereus raped his wife's sister, Philomela, and cut out her tongue. In some versions, she turns into a swallow rather than a nightingale. Cf. n. on Cat. 65, ll. 13–14 (p. 391).

l. 10. *Bathyllus*: One of Anacreon's *eromenoi* (boy loves): see Hor. *Epod.* 14, l. 9 (p. 459) and n. For the aubade theme, cf. Anon. Mel. 10 (p. 324), Ant. Thess. 7 (p. 345) and Argent. 16 (p. 350).

361. *22.* ll. 1–2. *Tantalus' daughter* ... : Niobe. See Call. *Hy.* 2, l. 22 (p. 269) and n.

ll. 3–4. *Pandion's daughter* ... : Either Procne or Philomela (see n. on *Anacreontea* 10, ll. 6–7, above), either or both of whom have variously been said to have transformed into swallows. Pandion here is the first of two legendary kings of Athens bearing that name.

362. 26. As in Dios. 2 (p. 314), the poet has been seduced by a performance of epic poetry, whether of the Theban or the Epic Cycle – for which see, respectively, Stes. 97 (p. 93), and n. on Call. *Ep.* 2, l. 1 (p. 276). Compare also the *militia amoris* (warfare of love) trope of Latin love elegy (see Ov. *Am.* 1.9, p. 495, and n.).

363. 53. The inspiration for this poem clearly combines two surviving fragments of Anac. 356 (p. 103) and 395 (p. 106).

LATIN LYRIC

365. *Introduction. 'a song ... repellent and uncouth'*: Livy, *History of Rome* 27.37.12 (trans. Moore).

366. *'literature ... "that which does not get translated"'*: Denis Feeney, *Beyond Greek: The Beginnings of Latin Literature*, p. 40.

The Greeks certainly never translated it: The Septuagint, the Greek translation of the Hebrew Old Testament, seems an exception; but, *pace* the ancient sources, it was not translated to increase the cultural universality of the Ptolemies' Library; rather, it was produced for Greek-Alexandrian Jews who no longer knew how to read Hebrew, and may actually have helped inspire the (Alexandrian-style) editorial project to stabilize and canonize the Hebrew scriptures which took place between 50 BCE and 73 CE.

367. *Lucius Mummius when he sacked Corinth*: For poetic responses to the event, see Ant. Si. 59 (p. 323) and Crin. 37 (p. 343).

'Greece, taken ... captive': Hor. *Epist.* 2.1, l. 156. See also n. on Hor. *Odes* 3.30, ll. 13–14, p. 487.

'the prophet of the Callimachean school': See Gian Biagio Conte, 'Neoteric Poetry and Catullus', in his *Latin Literature: A History* (trans. Solodow), p. 136.

371. *a 'smiling destroyer' ... Ovid*: Conte, '43 B.C.–A.D. 17: Characteristics of a Period', in *op. cit.*, p. 257.

Catullus

373. *Poet Introduction. 'Caesar invited the poet ... '*: Suetonius, *Life of Julius Caesar* 73 (trans. Rolfe).

374. *Rome's ... best poet*: See Plutarch, *Life of Cicero*, 2.4–5.

three passages in Cicero, all dripping with contempt: Cicero, *Letters to Atticus* 7.2.1; *Orator* 161; *Tusculan Disputations* 3.45.

376. *Polymetric Poems. 1.* In this programmatic poem, Catullus exploits an analogy between the smart appearance of his slender book-roll, freshly buffed with pumice stone, and the pointed, polished little poems it contains. (For other poems touching on physical books and the book trade, see Mel. 129, p. 332, Phil. 17, p. 337, Cat. 22, p. 382, and Mart. 1.117, p. 537.)

l. 3. *Cornelius*: The historian, biographer and poet Cornelius Nepos (*c.* 99–24 BCE), like Catullus a provincial from northern Italy. There is no way to tell which poems exactly are compassed by this dedication – no more than the polymetric poems at a maximum, but probably not all of them.

ll. 5–7. *the one Italian brave enough* ... : Catullus praises Nepos in ambiguous terms for his three-volume universal history (*Chronica*), which does not survive; some of his biographies, however, do, and make for pleasant reading.

ll. 8–10. ... *may it at least outlast its maker*: The concluding prayer recalls a similar prayer addressed by Callimachus to the Graces at the head of his *Aetia* (pp. 258–61):

> That these my elegies may last a while,
> caress them with your gleaming hands, and smile.

Catullus gives the prayer a distinctly Roman twist, by invoking the Muse as his 'maiden Patroness' (being independently wealthy, Catullus needed no other patron, unlike later Augustan poets).

2. l. 1. *Sparrow*: Since the Renaissance, it has been vehemently argued, and vehemently denied, that Lesbia's pet sparrow in poems 2 and 3 should be read as an allegory for the poet's penis. Among the arguments in favor: the Greek word for 'sparrow', *strouthion*, is slang for 'penis', and an epigram of Martial's (11.6) seems to interpret the poem this way. Among those opposed: the Latin for sparrow, *passer*, can also refer to the blue rock thrush, which, unlike the sparrow, makes a good pet. Samuel Butler eulogizes the blue rock thrush in terms that remind us of this poem (*Alps and Sanctuaries of Piedmont and the Canton Ticino*, Ch. 20, pp. 299–300):

> Nobody knows what a bird can do in the way of song until he has heard a *passero solitario* ... All other bird singing is loud, vulgar and

unsympathetic in comparison ... The one I saw flew instantly at my finger when I put it near its cage, but I was not sure whether it did so in anger or play. I thought it liked being listened to, and as long as it chose to sing I was delighted to stay.

ll. 10–11. There are no missing lines in the manuscript; however, the incompleteness of both thought and grammar leads us to suppose that at least one, possibly more, lines have fallen out at this point.

l. 11. *Atalanta*: A mythical huntress and runner, who would challenge potential suitors to a footrace in which the prize for victory was marriage, and the cost of defeat, death. Eventually she was defeated by Milanion (aka Hippomenes), to whom Venus gave three golden apples, and instructions to distract her with them as they ran. The story is told by Ovid at *Met.* 10, ll. 560–681. Cf. Prop. 1.1, ll. 9–16 (p. 423).

ll. 11–13. *I'd like it ... tight-wound girdle*: These lines continuously follow ll. 1–10 in the manuscript, but the sense is broken – what is the 'it' that Catullus would like as Atalanta liked her apple? No answer has met with general approval. It is notable that here and in Cat. 65 (p. 390) Catullus seems to be comparing himself to a woman.

3. The elegy on a dead pet is a common motif in Hellenistic epigram – for other examples, see Anyte 9 (p. 303), Leo. Tar. 21 (p. 308), Mnasalces 11 (p. 316), Tymnes 5 (p. 319), Mel. 65 (p. 330), Ov. *Am.* 2.6 (p. 501) and Stat. *Silv.* 2.4 (p. 528). But Catullus' example is unique in the way it plays against and surprises our generic expectations by transforming at the end from an elegy into a charming and tender little love poem. For the sparrow, see n. on Cat. 2, l. 1, above.

l. 1. *Venuses and Cupids*: The Loves and Graces of the *Anacreontea*, Romanized (cf. *Anacreontea* 1, 35 and 46, pp. 358 and 362).

377.   5. ll. 1–3. *My Lesbia, let's live and love* ... : Catullus' most famous lines have inspired many imitations, including by Thomas Campion – 'My sweetest Lesbia, let us live and love ...' (*A Booke of Ayres* 1, l. 1) – who also imitates Cat. 7 and 8 in this selection. In Yeats's 'The Scholars', the puritanical gossips of Catullus' poem ('the crabbed old crows', l. 2) become philologists:

> Lord, what would they say
> Did their Catullus walk that way?

ll. 7–10. *a thousand, then a hundred* ... : The repetition of the numerals evokes an abacus, with each word like a bead; eventually (l. 12), Catullus shakes the abacus and starts over.

ll. 11–14. ... *muddling the true amount*: The Latin *conturbare* ('jumble the numbers up') is a technical term for concealing assets from creditors in bankruptcy, but Catullus is cheating the Evil Eye, for which an accurate kiss-count would provide ammunition. Cf. nn. on Cat. 7, ll. 12–14, below, and on Theoc. *Id.* 7, ll. 134–5 (p. 293).

378. 6. l. 1. Catullus' friend *Flavius* is otherwise unknown.

ll. 11–12. *the bedframe* ... *squealing*: Cf. Argent. 12, l. 5 (p. 349).

7. This atmospheric poem, like Cat. 5 and 8, is also imitated by Campion (*The Second Booke of Ayres* 18, ll. 11–12):

> Sooner may you count the starres,
> And number hayle downe pouring ...

It showcases not only the 'Alexandrianism' Catullus introduced into Latin poetry (see *Intro* to Latin Lyric, p. 368), but the increased poetic charge with which he invested his learned references. The poem is echoed by Cat. 99 (p. 396), below.

ll. 1–2. *How many kisses* ... : I imagine these lines either in Lesbia's voice or as Catullus' repetition of her (incredulous? impatient?) question.

l. 5. *Cyrene*: A Dorian Greek colony in northwest Africa and the birthplace of Callimachus (see Call. *Hy.* 2, p. 269, and nn.).

l. 6. *silphium*: A fennel-like plant, unidentifiable today, with medicinal and, especially, contraceptive properties; it was the main export of Cyrene until over-cultivation caused its extinction. See also Philox. 836b+c, l. 76 (p. 218).

l. 7. *Jove-Ammon's sweaty shrine*: An oracle, famous throughout the Greco-Roman world, in the Siwa Oasis on the southernmost border of Cyrene's territory.

l. 8. *old King Battus*: Cyrene's legendary founder, whose tomb was in his city's *agora* (marketplace); cf. Call. *Hy.* 2, l. 65 (p. 270) and n.

ll. 12–14. *a sum too high* ... : As in Cat. 5, Catullus hopes to foil the Evil Eye by the uncountability of his kisses – the Latin word he uses, *fascinare*, implies 'binding' with spells (cf. *fasces*, 'bundles'), and is related to Greek *baskania*, 'evil eye', a good old word still current today. Fascinating. Cf.

also Theoc. *Id.* 7, ll. 134–5 (p. 293) and n. for a slightly different tradition relating to the Evil Eye.

379. 8. Cat. 5, 7 and 8 may compass one of the briefest and most intense relationships in literature: from the pure joy of poem 5, to the slight hint of boredom (hers, not his) in poem 7 (ll. 1–2), to the crushing denouement in poem 8; other key moments include what seems to be their first meeting, in Cat. 51 (p. 387), and Catullus' last statement, in Cat. 11 (p. 380). In this poem, Hipponax's meter (by way of Callimachus' *Iambi*, pp. 261–8; see also *Note on Meters*, p. xxxiii) may make the poet even more ridiculous, a bumpkin on a comic stage, an object of cruel fun.

l. 1. *Catullus, lovesick*: In Latin, *Miser Catulle*, famously 'translated' by Celia and Louis Zukofsky as 'Miss her, Catullus?'

ll. 11–12. *Be like flint* . . .: Thomas Campion imitates this poem as he has Cat. 5 and 7, above: 'Harden now thy tyred hart with more then flinty rage . . .' (*The Second Booke of Ayres* 3, l. 1).

10. l. 2. *Varus*: Also the addressee of Cat. 22 (p. 382), he could be one of two people, both from Cremona in northern Italy: Publius Alfenus Varus, a distinguished jurist under Octavian, or Quintilius Varus, friend of Horace (pp. 453–91) and Virgil (pp. 398–410), whose death is mourned in Hor. *Odes* 1.24 (p. 469). Another Catullus poem (Cat. 30), bitterly addressed to one 'Alfenus', perhaps makes the former more likely here (and cf. n. on Vi. *Ecl.* 9, p. 405).

l. 7. *Bithynia*: A Roman province in northern Turkey, on the southern Black Sea coast, which had been bequeathed to Rome by its last puppet ruler in 74 BCE, and was usually joined (for administrative purposes) with the neighboring province of Pontus, finally wrested by Pompey the Great in 63 BCE from one of Rome's bitterest enemies, King Mithridates VI. Catullus worked on the staff of the governor of Bithynia, Gaius Memmius, from 57 to 56 BCE. Young men often went abroad to serve on provincial administrations; it was a way to see the world while making money and connections. This anecdote will have taken place shortly after Catullus' return to Rome, in 56.

380. l. 17. *Bithynia's where the vogue began*: Litters were particularly associated with Bithynia in Republican Rome, since they were in common use there; in Rome, men generally only used them outside the city or for travel, though women loved them, to the point that Caesar sought to restrict their use (Suetonius, *Life of Julius Caesar* 43.1).

l. 27. *Serapis*: See *Intro* to Post-Classical Greek Lyric, p. 253. There was a double temple dedicated to Isis and Serapis in Rome's Campus Martius: cf. Tib. 1.3, l. 23 (p. 413) and n.

l. 31. *Gaius Cinna*: Gaius Helvius Cinna, a noted poet of Catullus' circle, author of an Alexandrian-style epic called *Zmyrna* praised in Cat. 95 (cf. also Vi. *Ecl.* 9, l. 45, p. 406). Cinna was the one who, in all likelihood, brought Parthenius of Nicaea to Rome (see *Intro* to Latin Lyric, p. 367). As depicted in Shakespeare's *Julius Caesar*, he was lynched at the dictator's funeral, mistaken for another Cinna who was actually one of the conspirators. Alexandrianizing poets were everywhere – Governor Memmius was also one, perhaps the dedicatee of Lucretius' *De Rerum Natura* – which would help explain his patronage of Catullus and Cinna.

11, To Furius and Aurelius: This duo is also addressed, separately or together, in six more poems, usually in insulting terms (see, here, Cat. 16, p. 382). The first may be Marcus Furius Bibaculus, a poet from Cremona in northern Italy associated with Catullus' 'neoteric' circle (see *Intro* to Catullus, p. 374); but Aurelius is unknown. Are they genuine antagonists of Catullus, a clueless, hapless pair on whom the poet here lavishes his high style ironically? Or are they actual friends of his, and the abuse-poems light-hearted banter? Modern commentators have often opted for the first interpretation; but there is no evidence that ancient readers heard any irony in Catullus' first three stanzas.

l. 2. *if he takes off*: The temptation is to connect this poem with Catullus' departure for Bithynia (see n. on Cat. 10, l. 7, above), and thus to date it slightly before 57 BCE; but this is impossible, since the reference to 'Caesar' (l. 10) implies a date no earlier than 55, the year Julius Caesar bridged the Rhine and invaded Britain for the first time, as described in Bk. 4 of his *Commentaries*. Therefore the journey, whether real or imagined, which Catullus anticipates making in this poem cannot be attached to any known facts about his life.

l. 6. *Parthia's archer host*: See Hor. *Odes* 2.13, l. 17 (p. 475) and n.

381. ll. 11–12. . . . *beyond the brine*: The poem's journey, from India (l. 2) to Britain (l. 11), has moved east to west, as if following the arc of the setting sun and, implicitly, the sunset of Catullus' love.

ll. 23–4. *like a shy flower* . . . : It is likely that this image, one of Catullus' most pitiful, is related to the 'secret flower' of Cat. 62, ll. 39–44 (p. 390), which represents the fragile virginity of the Roman maiden, and that both images may go back to the trampled hyacinth of Sap. 105c (p. 51).

13. The invitation poem was a conventional genre, represented here by Catullus' contemporary Phil. 23 (p. 338), as well as Hor. *Odes* 4.11 (p. 490) and Mart. 10.48 (p. 549). As in poem 3 (p. 376, above), Catullus

uses a poetic convention as an opportunity for a witty (and, here, slightly surreal) compliment to Lesbia.

l. 3. *Fabullus*: A friend of Catullus', to whom he addresses three poems, all warmly affectionate.

382. 16. Catullus serves warning to all critics who insist on reading him biographically. Unfortunately, the sexual violence threatened by the poem is no outlier: though relations with both sexes were common in Roman high society circles, the passive partner was stigmatized for feminine submissiveness. (Of course, if one takes the point about literal reading to heart, one might doubt the seriousness of the threat.) While Catullus elsewhere seems to associate himself with feminine qualities (see Cat. 2, p. 376, and Cat. 65, p. 390) his posture here is hypermasculine and aggressive.

l. 2. *Aurelius and Furius*: See n. on Cat. 11 (p. 380), above.

ll. 7–8. *A poet ought to keep his life decent, not his poetry*: This persuasively phrased sentiment is often echoed by later poets; cf., e.g., Ov. *Tri.* 3.2, l. 6 (p. 513).

l. 15. *those thousand kisses*: See Cat. 5, l. 7 (p. 377), above.

22. l. 1. *Varus*: See n. on Cat. 10, l. 2 (p. 379), above.

Suffenus: Otherwise unknown. He seems to represent an older, 'Roman' style of poetry, like that of Ennius or Cicero (see *Intro* to Latin Lyric, pp. 367–8), which Catullus finds impossibly dull.

l. 3. *really, really long*: Suffenus hasn't gotten the Callimachean message about short, polished poetry (cf. Call. *Aet.* 1.1, p. 258), but persists in his old-fashioned Roman verbosity.

ll. 5–8. *not repurposing old paper either . . .* : For other poems touching on physical books and the book trade, see Mcl. 129 (p. 332), Phil. 17 (p. 337), Cat. 1, (p. 376) and Mart. 1.117 (p. 537).

383. 31. l. 1. *Sirmio*: Modern Sirmione, about twenty miles northwest of Verona on Lake Garda (ancient Benacus), was the site of Catullus' family villa, to which the poet returned in 56 BCE after his stint on the staff of Governor Memmius in Bithynia (see n. on Cat. 10, l. 7, p. 379); the remains of a Villa di Catullo (dramatically renovated and expanded in the Augustan age, perhaps by the poet's own ancestors) still stand today, and are well worth visiting.

l. 13. The water of Garda is called *Lydian* due to an earlier association of the region with Etruscans, who were thought to be of Lydian origin.

34. Most editors assume that this traditional hymn to Diana was written by Catullus to be read, rather than for any particular cult performance. It may owe something to Anac. 348 (p. 103), a hymn to the same deity in the same meter; see also *Note on Meters* (p. xli).

ll. 5–8. For the birth of Artemis/Diana (and also of Apollo) on the Cycladic island of Delos, see Pi. fr. 33c (p. 156) and n., and fr. 33d (p. 156); for their infant exploits, see Call. *Hy.* 2, ll. 58–64 (p. 270).

384. l. 13. *Midwife Juno*: Ilithyia (Greek Eileithyia; cf. Pi. *Py.* 3, l. 14, p. 146), goddess of childbirth, whose identification with Artemis/Diana is also hinted at by Call. *Ia.* 12 (p. 266). Ovid invokes her at *Am.* 2.13, ll. 22–8 (p. 507).

l. 15. *Triple One*: Hecate, an underworld goddess, also often identified with Artemis/Diana (see Call. *Ia.* 1, l. 28, p. 261, and n.).

l. 16. *the Moon*: As *Phoebe* (the feminine counterpart of her brother Phoebus Apollo) Diana was equated with the moon, as Apollo was with the sun.

37. l. 2. *the bonnet-wearing Dioscuri*: A statue or image of the 'Sons of Zeus', Castor and Pollux, wearing felt bonnets (the *pilleus* cap) stood in front of the temple in Rome dedicated to them. The temple was in the Forum's southeastern corner, apparently 'nine doors down' from Lesbia's favorite pub. See also Alc. 34, l. 1 (p. 57) and n.

l. 12. *whom I once loved as no girl ever will be loved*: Catullus quotes himself from Cat. 8, l. 5 (p. 379).

385. l. 18. *born in the Land of Shaggy Rabbits, Iberia's son*: Egnatius hails from Celtiberia, south of the Ebro River in northeastern Spain, known for its long-haired rabbits. Both Diodorus Siculus and Strabo confirm that Celtiberians did indeed brush their teeth in the manner alleged by Catullus in l. 20; Cat. 39 offers an extended lampoon of Egnatius' toilette.

41. l. 4. *bankrupt Mamurra*: An ostentatiously rich (hence 'bankrupt' – he spends so lavishly he ought to be) crony of Julius Caesar, whose high-priced lady friend apparently did not impress Catullus. This same Mamurra is attacked in Cat. 94, where he is called *Mentula* (Prick).

45. This idyll depicts two lovers, otherwise unidentifiable – a Roman man (Septimius) and a Greek woman (Acme, 'peak, prime, zenith'), probably a freedwoman. The contrast between the way the two think and speak about love may illustrate differences of personality, gender construction or Greek and Roman culture; we might even think of Catullus' own love

affair with Greek poetry (see also, here, Cat. 51, p. 387, and 62, p. 388, and nn., and compare Hor. *Odes* 3.9, p. 482).

ll. 10–11. . . . *Love sneezed* . . . : Sneezes were good omens generally; since the right was lucky for Greeks, and the left for Romans, the double sneeze bodes well for both parties. Catullus may have had a model in mind from Alexandrian pastoral: there are several lucky sneezes in Theocritus. See Theoc. *Id.* 7, l. 104 (p. 292).

386.   46. This poem may owe something to the subgenre of descriptive epigrams about spring (cf. Leo. Tar. 85, p. 309; Ant. Si. 41, p. 322; Hor. *Odes* 1.4, p. 464), but once again Catullus turns the convention to personal use, as he expresses excitement at leaving his post in Bithynia in the spring of 56 BCE and heading home again; see nn. on Cat. 10, l. 7 (p. 379), and Cat. 31, l. 1 (p. 383).

ll. 4–5. *Troy* here refers to the region of Phrygia, which included *Nicaea* (l. 5, modern İznik), the capital of Bithynia, as well as Nicomedia (modern İzmit), a bit farther north, where Catullus was stationed. He clearly intends to do some sightseeing before going back home.

48. The first of two poems (the other is Cat. 99, p. 396) addressed to a boy called Juventius, of whom Catullus is enamored. This poem clearly echoes Cat. 7 (p. 378). For pederasty in Roman poetry, see Hor. *Odes* 1.4, l. 19 (p. 465) and n.

387.   50. l. 1. *Calvus*: Gaius Licinius Calvus (82–47 BCE), poet and orator, was Catullus' closest friend. Three poems are addressed to him; this one, depicting the '*novi poetae* at play' (C. J. Fordyce, *Catullus: A Commentary*, p. 215), is by far the most intimate. Indeed, the intimacy is such that the language seems plainly sexual. Should it be taken literally, as some sort of inside joke, or as a metaphor for Catullus' passionate feelings about poetry? The reciprocity ('giving as good as we were getting', l. 6) may recall the mutual affection of Acme and Septimius in Cat. 45 (p. 385), above.

l. 20. *Nemesis*: Cf. Mel. 90, l. 4 (p. 331) and n., and Cat. 68b, l. 77 (p. 392).

51. If this poem seems familiar, that might be because it is a free translation of Sap. 31 (p. 44). Catullus seems to be applying Sappho's famous description of the physical effects of passion/jealousy to an incident early in his relationship with Lesbia, perhaps even their first meeting. Catullus' Latin may not surpass Sappho's Greek, but it certainly ups the intensity, at least in the first three stanzas. In the fourth, however, which is original to Catullus, he ventriloquizes a voice of conventional Roman morality,

perhaps his own internalized one, or perhaps the sort of thing the 'crabbed old crows' of Cat. 5 (p. 377) were saying. If the speaker's illicit passion for the married woman he calls 'Lesbia' provokes their disapproval, so might the poet's for Sappho's poetry. This poem's roots, then, would reach deep down to the wellspring of Catullan song, encompassing both the young man's love of the forbidden woman and the poet's for the foreign language and literature with and against which he writes his own (for which, see also, here, Cat. 45, p. 385, and 62, p. 388, and nn.).

l. 5. *lovely laughter*: See Hor. *Odes* 1.22, l. 23 (p. 468) and n.

388.   *58*. l. 1. *Caelius*: Probably Marcus Caelius Rufus (also ridiculed in Cat. 69), a political ally of Julius Caesar and the next lover, after Catullus, of the Clodia Metelli generally identified as 'Lesbia'. Cicero defended him in the *Pro Caelio* by attacking, and doing permanent damage to, Clodia's reputation.

60. This wounded *cri de cœur*, the last of the polymetric poems, has models in the *Iliad*, Aeschylus and Euripides, and was reworked by Virgil in Dido's curse on Aeneas in *Aen.* 4, ll. 365–70. Catullus' Latin has an acrostic – NATU CEU AES, 'like bronze by birth' – running down the left and up the right side of the poem, which I have tried to imitate as best I could.

l. 2. *Scylla*: A sea monster, typically represented as a human woman from the waist up, with a fishy tail below, and a pack of ravenous, sailor-eating dogs around her mid-section. She appears first in epic, where she is paired with Charybdis (see Sim. 522, p. 122) as a maritime danger (Hom. *Od.* 12, ll. 73–110 and 234–60; Apollonius of Rhodes, *Argonautica* 4, ll. 825–32; Vi. *Aen.* 3, ll. 420–32 and 553–68). There are also tales of her metamorphosis from a beautiful maiden into a monster due to the jealousy of a goddess, for example, Circe (Ov. *Met.* 14, ll. 8–68) or Amphitrite (Servius at *Aen.* 3, l. 420).

Longer Poems. *62*. This poem transcribes (or purports to) a singing contest between young men and women at a wedding feast, each sitting at separate tables at the bride's father's house, according to the Greek custom. The contest is of the sort, also found in pastoral (cf. Theoc. *Id.* 7, p. 291, and Vi. *Ecl.* 9, p. 405; and see also Hor. *Odes* 3.9, p. 482, and n.), called *amoebaean* or 'alternating' song: the girls sing first, and the boys echo and try to top them; no doubt the respondents have the competitive advantage. It is also rife with the kind of imagery we have come to expect from Greek wedding songs (*epithalamia*); compare, in particular, Sap. 104 and 105c (p. 51). The Hellenism, however, is not thoroughgoing, since the bride is not yet present at this stage in the evening (l. 3), reflecting the custom at Roman weddings but unlike Greek ones. Catullus thus presents a kind of fusion of Greek and Roman traditions; and indeed it is tempting to find in this poem, as elsewhere (e.g., Cat. 45, p. 385, and 51, p. 387, and nn.), a kind of allegory of Catullus' own vision of the marriage, whether cultural or poetic, between Hellenism and *Romanitas* more widely. Literary in conception, the poem was probably not intended for performance at any particular wedding.

ll. 1–2. *It's Venus ... with her light*: Like both Greek and Roman weddings, this one takes place at dusk. Venus here is Vesper/Hesperus, though of course the Romans knew that the evening and morning star were the same planet – cf. l. 35. Olympus stands here for the heavens.

l. 5. *Hymen o Hymenaeus*: This refrain, invoking Hymen, Greek god of marriage ceremonies, is of a traditional sort in wedding hymns (*epithalamia*). See also Sap. 111 (p. 52) and Dios. 6, l. 5 (p. 314).

389. l. 7. *Mount Oeta*: A mountain in the Pindus range of central and northern Greece, about ninety miles south of Olympus.

l. 20. Here the *amoebaean* contest proper begins. The girls sing first, giving the boys the last word. For the address to Venus/Aphrodite ('evening star') in a hymeneal context, cf. Sap. 104 (p. 51).

ll. 32–3. Most of the girls' stanza, and the first line of the boys', is missing. Probably the two stanzas were about the same length.

390. l. 39. *a secret flower*: Cf. Sap. 105c (p. 51) and Cat. 11, ll. 23–4 (p. 381) and n.

65. l. 2. *Hortalus*: Quintus Hortensius Hortalus (114–50 BCE) was a famous oratorical rival of Cicero, as well as consul in 69, and an enthusiast of Catullus' 'new school' of poetry. To judge from this verse epistle, written sometime before Catullus left for Bithynia in 57 (see n. on Cat. 10, l. 7, p. 379), Hortalus had asked him to send some specimen of verse; meanwhile, Catullus was assailed by grief when his brother died in Asia Minor (cf. Cat. 68b, ll. 91–100, pp. 392–3, and Cat. 101, p. 397). Eventually Catullus sent Hortalus a translation of Callimachus, prefaced with this verse epistle.

391. l. 7. *Rhoeteum's Trojan dirt for pall*: The promontory of Rhoeteum, near Troy, was also the burial place of the Greater (Telamonian) Ajax, according to a fragment of Euphorion of Chalcis (for whom, see n. on Vi. *Ecl.* 10, l. 58, p. 409). Catullus visits his brother's grave in poem 101 (p. 397), below.

ll. 13–14. *as Procne ... mourning for Itylus*: Procne was the sister of Philomela, married to the Thracian king Tereus. When Tereus raped Philomela,

Procne killed their son Itylus (or Itys) in revenge; all three were turned into birds – nightingale, swallow and hoopoe. Ovid tells the story at *Met.* 6, ll. 440–674. Cf. *Anacreontea* 10, ll. 6–7 (p. 360) and n., and 22, ll. 3–4 (p. 361) and n.; Prop. 3.10, l. 10 (p. 437); Ov. *Am.* 2.6, ll. 8–11 (p. 501); and Stat. *Silv.* 2.4, l. 22 (p. 529). See also Hor. *Epod.* 14, ll. 1–4 (p. 459) and n. for the possible influence of this passage on Keats's 'Ode to a Nightingale'.

l. 16. *Battiades*: 'Descendant of Battus', i.e., Callimachus: cf. Call. *Hy.* 2, l. 65 (p. 270) and n., and Call. *Ep.* 30 (p. 279). The poem Catullus sends is a translation of Callimachus' *Lock of Berenice* (*Aet.* 4.110), which survives in fragmentary form in Greek, but complete in Catullus' version (Cat. 66).

ll. 19–24. *the way an apple* ... : Another striking simile (cf. Cat. 2, ll. 11–13, p. 376) in which the author of the hypermasculine poem 16 (p. 382) appears to compare himself to a vulnerable young girl. For apples as love gifts, see Theoc. *Id.* 2, l. 123 (p. 289) and n. But the epic style of this simile may remind us more of the touching moment in Hom. *Od.* 23, ll. 233–9, when Penelope, reunited with Odysseus, is compared at length to a shipwrecked (male) sailor who has finally made it to land. Gender reversals apart, the psychological intimacy of the present simile, with its potent mixture of infatuation, secrecy and shame, is all Catullus' own.

68b. This bizarre and wonderful poem, called 'probably the most extraordinary poem in Latin' by R. O. A. M. Lyne (*The Latin Love Poets: From Catullus to Horace*, p. 52), combines four of Catullus' main themes (or obsessions) in close and not always comfortable proximity: the affair with Lesbia, the death of his brother, his affection for his friends, and his erudite Alexandrianism. It is also bedeviled with interpretative difficulties, the first of which involves its relation to Cat. 68a, a verse epistle which is combined with this one in the surviving manuscripts.

   Poem 68a is apparently addressed to a different person: Manius or Manlius, rather than Allius. It also protests (as in Cat. 65, ll. 1–8 p. 390) Catullus' inability to write a poem suitable to the occasion (ll. 31–40):

> And you'll forgive me if, through grief, I scant
> the gift you'd have me give you: I just can't ...
> which, if I could, I would have sent unbidden.

That poem, however, Cat. 68b appears to be. The puzzles and possibilities run still deeper: could, for example, the two suspiciously similar names, Manlius and Allius, conceal the same person, dissociated by textual corruption? Such questions, however, we will leave to one side, as the present excerpt on its own is quite enough to wrestle with.

In Cat. 68b, Catullus empties his cabinet of poetic devices to produce a grand (or grandiose) poetic thanks-offering to his friend Allius. What did Allius do to deserve such an encomium? He let Catullus borrow his house so that he and his mistress – not named but almost certainly Lesbia – could take their flirtation to the next level. Within this frame, the poem itself records almost no action apart from Lesbia's arrival at the entry-way, instead treating us to an intricate and erudite pattern of nesting likenesses. The central comparison likens Catullus and Lesbia to the doomed mythical couple of Protesilaus and Laodamia (see nn. on ll. 72, 74 and 75–6, below), with the further likeness implied of Catullus' affair to a marriage – and wedding poems (*epithalamia*), as a genre, are noted for being rich in similes (see n. on l. 72, below). Yet into and around the central simile a number of others are inset and entwined, like an illuminated manuscript taken over by an almost sentient border. Indeed, the simili-tudinizing is so self-conscious, extravagant and strange that it, rather than the poet's gratitude to Allius or intoxication with Lesbia, has been taken as the poem's chief subject: we have here a meditation on the relationship between life and art or, more to the point, the gap between life and art; about how a poem might describe a person or event and the adequacy of such description, or utter lack thereof.

Nowhere else is Catullus simultaneously so personal and so Alexandrian – usually he is one or the other. It is that combination of confession and erudition which makes it possible to claim Catullus in this poem (and, to a lesser extent, in Cat. 76, p. 395) as the inventor of Latin love elegy. The affinities of Cat. 68b with its elegiac heirs – Prop. 1.3 (p. 425), say, and Ov. *Am.* 1.5 (p. 494) – are obvious: it is an extended poem in elegiac couplets about an urban love affair in the first person which makes frequent, learned use of mythological examples. And yet no poem in subsequent elegy feels much like this one. Catullus has composed no dreamily soft-focused meditation, no fiery tragicomedy of passion and deceit, no set of witty variations on conventional tropes; rather, the psychic material here seems closer to the bone, more galvanic and less controlled, than anything in the elegists, while the poem's austere classicism, more unforgiving in its symmetries than the elegists' chatty digressions, seems correspondingly constructed to hold that material in check. Though the elegists made no secret of their admiration for Catullus, imitating him often and enthusias-tically, it is unclear how influenced they were by this poem; certainly they never wrote anything like it.

l. 41. *Sing Allius*: Catullus invokes the Muses ('goddesses') in hopes that they will help him repay his friend's gift.

l. 45. *I'll tell you, and you'll publish it*: An obvious reversal of the usual formula, in which the Muses are requested to sing to (or through) the poet.

ll. 48–50. *and, when he's dead . . .*: Catullus here seems much more confident of his poem's longevity than elsewhere in his poems; cf. Cat. 1, ll. 8–10 (p. 376) and n.

ll. 51–2. *the two-natured Dame of Cyprus*: Venus/Aphrodite, the bittersweet. A famous coinage of Sap. 130 (p. 53); see also Pos. 1, l. 4 (p. 312).

392. l. 64. *now Pollux's, now Castor's*: The Dioscuri (Sons of Zeus) were patron deities of mariners, thanks to their association with St. Elmo's fire; see n. on Alc. 34, (p. 57).

l. 72. *her sandal squeaked*: A bad omen, of a sort frequent in elegiac poetry; see Tib. 1.3, ll. 19–20 (p. 413). Ovid, in *Laodamia to Protesilaus* (*Heroides* 13, ll. 87–90), depicts Protesilaus stumbling in a similar way when he set forth for Troy. The crossing of the groom's threshold was a key moment in the Roman wedding ceremony; cf. Cat. 61, ll. 159–61:

> The omens smile; now take your little
> golden feet across the threshold
> and through the polished entryway.

Of course, Catullus and Lesbia (unlike Protesilaus and Laodamia; see nn. on ll. 74 and 75–6, below) are not getting married; but Allius' great gift consisted in his allowing Catullus a chance to see, however briefly, what it might be like to be married to her. It is worth noting that similes, so frequent in this poem, happen also to be a constitutive feature of wedding poems (*epithalamia* – cf. Sap. 104–16, pp. 51–3; Cat. 62, p. 388; Hor. *Odes* 1.23, p. 469). Cat. 68b's central move is to compare a doomed mythical marriage to a liaison which isn't a marriage at all – but which Catullus wishes were.

l. 74. *Protesilaus*: The first Greek man killed at Troy (Hom., *Il.* 2, ll. 695–702); see also Ov. *Am.* 2.6, l. 42 (p. 502). Homer does not name Laodamia, but merely says: 'His wife, her two cheeks torn in wailing, was left in Phylace and his house but half established' (*Il.* 2, ll. 700–701, trans. A. T. Murray). Later sources add that they were married for only a day.

ll. 75–6. *his new bride overlooked the sacrifices due*: No other extant source mentions such an oversight by Laodamia, though a fragment of Euripides, from his mostly lost *Protesilaus* (fr. 648), suggests that someone is 'unpurified'.

l. 77. *Nemesis*: Cf. Mel. 90, l. 4 (p. 331) and n., and Cat. 50, l. 20 (p. 387).

392–3. ll. 91–100. *which ... stole from me my brother ...* : Though Laodamia is ostensibly being likened to Lesbia, it turns out, as the simile unfolds, that Protesilaus' heartbroken bride has far more in common with Catullus. The digression about Catullus' brother points out the first way in which this is true: both Laodamia and Catullus lost loved ones at Troy (cf. Cat. 65, p. 390, and 101, p. 397).

393. ll. 109–10. *Pheneus* was a city in Arcadia, southwest of *Mount Cyllene*. Pausanias (*Description of Greece*, 8.14.3) describes a canal ('the pit', l. 109) in the area of Pheneus, said to have been the work of Hercules, over six miles long and about thirty feet wide, which had been dug to carry water from the River Ladon to underground limestone channels. The strange, pedantic simile points out the second major way in which Laodamia is more like Catullus than like Lesbia: if we can judge of the Lesbia poems as a unit, the deep emotions were mostly his, not hers.

l. 111. *the son who wasn't Amphitryon's*: Hercules, interchangeably the son of Amphitryon (his mother Alcmene's husband) and Jupiter. For such 'double parentage', cf. Pi. *Py.* 3, l. 26 (p. 147) and n.

l. 113. *Stymphalus*: An Arcadian town, site of Hercules' Sixth Labor, where he slew the giant, bronze-beaked, man-eating Stymphalian birds with his envenomed arrows, after scaring them up into the air with a rattle.

l. 115. *a lesser man*: Eurystheus, king of Tiryns, Hercules' taskmaster.

l. 118. *Hebe*: The goddess of youth, eventually married to Hercules after he became a god, thus crowning his labors with a reward Catullus could envy.

ll. 121–6. *more than the love ... his hoary head*: This simile, about a grandfather whose late-born grandson allows him to keep his wealth in the family, seems oddly judged as a comparison for the erotic love of either Laodamia or Catullus; but cf. also Cat. 72, ll. 3–4 (p. 394, below). The scene Catullus describes resonates with other instances of legacy hunting or captation in Latin poetry; see n. on Mart. 1.10, l. 4 (p. 535) .

ll. 127–30. *more than the love a snowy dove ...* : Doves were known for mating for life; cf. Prop. 2.15, ll. 27–8 (p. 430), and Ov. *Am.* 2.6, ll. 57–8

(p. 502). Here, however, they remind one more of Lesbia's sparrow (Cat. 2, p. 376), or of Catullus himself in his poems 5 and 7 (pp. 377 and 378). The comparison of Laodamia to a kiss-crazed dove is yet another way in which she reminds us more of Catullus than of Lesbia.

394. l. 143. This line is followed immediately by a lacuna of at least two lines, then another nineteen of verse, not the poem's best, in which Catullus wraps up his account of having received from Lesbia 'furtive thrills in the stunned night', and reiterates his thanks to Allius.

Elegies and Epigrams. 70. This poignant epigram owes something to Call. *Ep.* 11 (p. 277) and probably Mel. 69 (p. 330).

ll. 3–4. *Her words . . . water*: The idea that ineffectual speech is scattered by wind and water is common in Latin poetry, especially love elegy (see, for example, Prop. 2.28, ll. 6–8, p. 431, and Hor. *Odes* 1.5, ll. 5–12, p. 465), while the ephemerality of lovers' vows in general was an ancient commonplace (see n. on Call. *Ep.* 11, ll. 3–4, p. 277). Only here, however, are the false, fleeting words said to be written rather than spoken. One can't help but think of Keats's epitaph: 'Here lies one whose name was writ in water'.

72. ll. 3–4. *I loved you all . . .* : Cf. Cat. 686, ll. 121–6 (p. 393) It has struck more than one commentator that Catullus seems here to be struggling toward a concept, and language, of love more totalizing and transcendent than any commonly employed by, or available to, the Romans of his day. See also n. on Cat. 76, ll. 1–4, below.

395. 76. This poem reaches beyond epigram toward a new genre which would take hold in the next generation: love elegy (see *Intro* to Latin Lyric, pp. 70–71). It is as if the stringent logic of the couplets has pushed Catullus from the buffoonish moping of Cat. 8 (p. 379, this poem's closest analogue) to a more rhetorical and self-righteous brand of soliloquizing.

ll. 1–4. *If memories of good deeds . . . he would profane*: One curious feature of this and several of the epigrams (Cat. 72, p. 394, and Cat. 109, p. 397) is Catullus' use of normally political terms – the so-called 'language of aristocratic obligation'. Late Republican politics in Rome was deeply personal, and founded on an ever-shifting network of individual alliances, backroom agreements and quid pro quos. The kinds of 'good deeds' (l. 1) and 'faithfulness' (l. 26) – and the 'loyalty and love' of Cat. 109, l. 6 (p. 397) – Catullus protests he has rendered Lesbia make him sound, in Latin, as much like a double-crossed senator as a jilted lover. Of course, for many, the 'holy pact' (l. 4), like the *epithalamion* manqué of

68b (see above), conjures marriage – whether ironically, delusionally, wistfully, or ruefully, it is hard to say.

ll. 17–22. *If you feel pity, gods* ... : In this desperate prayer many have found a tormented Christian *avant la lettre*.

83. l. 1. *when hubby's near*: This would be Quintus Caecilius Metellus Celer, at least if Lesbia really is Clodia Metelli; Celer died in 59 BCE, so the poem would presumably need to have been written before then. For the poem's sentiment, cf. Prop. 3.8 (p. 435), especially ll. 16–20.

396. 84. l. 2. *Arrius* may be the Quintus Arrius whom Cicero mentions in his *Brutus* as a talentless but enterprising parvenu orator. Catullus' poem mocks Arrius' pronunciation of the aspirate (i.e., the letter *h*). The use of *h*s (aitches) had been confused in the first century BCE in Rome by the literate classes' increasing fluency in Greek, which employed aspirated stops as part of certain consonants (*theta, chi* and *phi* – θ, χ, φ, respectively). Pronouncing Greek loan words correctly thus displayed a certain kind of education; but those, like Arrius, who lacked this education may have inserted *h*s willy-nilly, not understanding the reasons for their presence or absence, in a gauchely off-target stab at good breeding. For this socially embedded phenomenon, which has no equivalent in American English (British English is apparently a different story), the translation posits another: that of using phony Latin plurals even where utterly inappropriate.

85. See Alc. Mess. 6 (p. 317), Anon. Mel. 4 (p. 323) and Evenus 7 (p. 354) for the background to Catullus' couplet, surely the most analyzed two lines in Latin poetry. Here, as elsewhere, Catullus borrows a conventional motif and turns it to (devastatingly) personal ends.

99. See n. on Cat. 48 (p. 386), above.

397. ll. 13–14. *ambrosial kiss ... bitter hellebore*: Whereas ambrosia, both mythologically and etymologically brings eternal life (*am + brotos* = 'immortal'), hellebore is poisonous and brings death, though in non-lethal amounts it was used as a purgative and a cure for insanity, paralysis, gout and other diseases.

101. Catullus visits his brother's grave in the region around Troy, presumably sometime in 57 BCE, the year he spent in Bithynia (see n. on Cat. 10, l. 7, p. 379). The poem is in the tradition of literary epitaphs in the *Greek Anthology* (pp. 299–356), yet it is not an epitaph; Mel. 56 (p. 329) is closest to it in spirit. For other of Catullus' poems which mourn his brother, see Cat. 65, ll. 1–14 (pp. 390–91), and Cat. 68b, ll. 91–100 (pp. 392–3).

l. 1. *many nations, many seas*: Catullus echoes the famous opening of the *Odyssey* (Hom. *Od.* 1, ll. 3–4):

> He saw the cities of many men and he learned their minds,
> and in his heart suffered many pains on the high sea . . .

l. 4. *call your ashes, mute beyond recall*: Cf. Prop. 2.1, l. 79 (p. 429).

l. 7. *These sorry gifts*: Wine, milk, honey and flowers were the traditional offerings to the shades of ancestors and kin.

109. l. *6. loyalty and love*: For these words as an example of the 'language of aristocratic obligation', see n. on Cat. 76, ll. 1–4 (p. 395), above.

Virgil

398. *Poet Introduction. 'almost uneducated . . . wonderfully effective' delivery*: Donatus, *Life of Virgil* 16 and 28.

Ovid . . . 'saw Virgil once': Ov. *Tri.* 4.10, l. 51.

398–9. *'porker from the sty of Epicurus'*: Hor. *Epist.* 1.4, l. 16.

400. *'the classic of all Europe'*: T. S. Eliot, 'What Is a Classic?', p. 31.

Eclogue 2, Corydon. There is a tradition, given in Donatus' *Life of Virgil* (28–31) and Servius' commentary on this poem (in his n. on l. 15) that Virgil, being partial to boys, fell in love with one Alexander, a slave boy belonging to his patron Gaius Asinius Pollio (see n. on *Ecl.* 4, p. 403, below). When Pollio gave Alexander to Virgil as a gift, Virgil wrote this poem to thank him. According to this tradition, Alexis in the poem stands for Alexander, and Corydon for the poet, though it is not recorded whether Alexander rejected Virgil in the way Alexis rejects Corydon. The Eclogue is a thoroughgoing imitation of Theoc. *Id.* 11 (p. 296), but Virgil has turned Theocritus' Cyclops into a mortal shepherd, not to mention a Roman love elegist, countrified.

401. l. 17. *Menalcas*: See n. on Vi. *Ecl.* 10, l. 23 (p. 408).

l. 25. *Amphion*, brother of Zethus, son of Zeus and the Theban princess Antiope, was an Orpheus-like figure, credited with building the walls of Thebes by his song. *Dirce* was a queen of Thebes, wife of Antiope's uncle Lycus, who tortured Antiope because of the shame resulting from her out-of-wedlock pregnancy (thanks, Zeus!); eventually, in revenge, Amphion and Zethus tied Dirce to the horns of a bull, who trampled her to death. (This brutal execution is vividly depicted by the Farnese Bull, a first-century CE Roman sculpture located in the Archaeological Museum in Naples.) For Antiope, see also Prop. 2.28, l. 51 (p. 432) and n.

l. 26. *Attic Aracynthus' height*: Presumably a mountain in the same range as Mount Cithaeron, on the border of Boeotia and Attica.

l. 31. *Daphnis*: See n. on Theoc. *Id.* 1, l. 68 (p. 283).

l. 36. *Pan*: An Arcadian god, a special patron of pastoral song and (as Corydon tells us in l. 37) the eponymous inventor of the panpipe, which consisted of seven to twenty-one hollow reeds of unequal length, typically glued together with beeswax. See Anon. 936, *Hymn to Pan* (p. 238), and Vi. *Ecl.* 4, ll. 67–8 (p. 405), and *Ecl.* 10, ll. 29–31 (pp. 408–9), and Prop. 3.3, l. 30 (p. 433).

402.   l. 68. *Paris, Trojan prince*: The reference is to Paris' time as a shepherd on Mount Ida, near Troy, when Zeus chose him to decide the quarrel between Hera, Aphrodite and Athena; in the Judgment of Paris, he chose love and beauty, and the Trojan War was set in motion (cf. Callimachus' version at *Hy.* 5, ll. 18–28, pp. 272–3, and n.).

l. 69. *Pallas*: Athena, one of the goddesses Paris did not choose (see n. on l. 68, above), and therefore one of Troy's great enemies and destroyers. The most famous town she built is, of course, Athens.

ll. 71–4. *The lion hunts the wolf . . .* : An imitation and expansion of Theoc. *Id.* 11, l. 25 (p. 297); cf. also Hor. *Odes* 1.23, ll. 9–10 (p. 469).

403.   *Eclogue 4, The Messianic Eclogue.* The year 40 BCE was one in which even the gloomy Virgil found cause for optimism. His friend and patron, Gaius Asinius Pollio (ll. 13–15), a soldier and writer of note, held the consulship. Pollio had just helped broker a deal between the two masters of the Roman world, Octavian Caesar and Mark Antony. Following the defeat of the anti-Caesarians Marcus Junius Brutus and Gaius Cassius Longinus at the Battle of Philippi in 42, relations between the two had been rocky; but in 40, with Pollio negotiating on Antony's behalf and Gaius Cilnius Maecenas (later patron of Propertius, pp. 421–45, and Horace, pp. 453–91) on Octavian's, they temporarily patched things up in the Pact of Brundisium, and Octavian sealed the renewed alliance by giving his sister, Octavia, to Antony in marriage.

Back in Rome, the upheavals and uncertainty of recent years had created a climate of millenarian hysteria: signs and omens were sought and found, the most important having occurred at Julius Caesar's funeral celebration, put on by Octavian in July 44 BCE, when for seven days a comet appeared, hovering in the northern part of the sky, bright and clearly visible from all lands on the earth. (The star's appearance has been independently verified from Chinese astronomical records.) The interpretation which eventually became official was Octavian's: the new star had been spontaneously understood by the funeral crowd to be the soul of Caesar, making his way back to his home among the immortals (cf. Vi. *Ecl.* 9, ll. 59–60, p. 407, and Hor. *Odes* 3.25, ll. 5–6, p. 486). Yet Octavian secretly believed it to portend his own precipitous ascent to the highest echelons of power. In contrast with this upbeat and self-serving interpretation, comets were generally perceived as ominous of catastrophe: flood, famine and civil war. The Sibylline Books were consulted, and prophesied darkly. One Etruscan soothsayer, Vulcanius (or Volcatius), claimed that the comet was a harbinger of the end of the Ninth Age and the beginning of the Tenth – the last in the cycle of ages, according to Etruscan lore.

In the midst of this apocalyptic ferment, Virgil seems to have received the news of Pollio's diplomatic success at Brundisium with visionary ecstasy, and responded with a strange and beautiful poem which has gripped imaginations ever since. Virgil prophesies the birth of a Child, mysterious to us but perhaps not to contemporaries (a future son of the union between Antony and Octavia seems the likeliest option), whose growth and development will coincide with a reversal of the Hesiodic progress of the Races of Man (*W&D*, ll. 109–201) – from decadent Iron, to violent Heroic and back to Gold. Hesiod, of course, speaks of a 'Golden Race'; but Virgil conflates this with the Golden Age, when Saturn (an old Italic deity early identified with Greek Cronus) ruled in Italy, after being overthrown by Jupiter/Zeus – cf. Tib. 1.3, ll. 35–48 (p. 414) and n., Hor. *Epod.* 2, 1.4 (p. 456) and n., Hor. *Epod.* 16 (p. 460) and n., and Hor. *Odes* 1.3 (p. 463) and n. For these other Roman poets, the Golden Age was a blissful period irretrievably lost; Virgil alone prophesies its return.

It is hardly surprising that a poem at once so vatic and so moored to a tenuous political rapprochement, which unfolding circumstances would quickly render moot, should have drifted free of its already transient moorings. In the centuries to come, Christians would consider the poem an inspired prediction of the birth of Christ, and Virgil himself a Christian *avant la lettre*. This was helped by Virgil's own use of Eastern apocalyptica, derived no doubt from the Sibylline Books, and perhaps even from the Septuagint (viz., the Book of Isaiah), to which Virgil could possibly have had access (cf. n. on the *Intro* to Latin Lyric). The Christian understanding of the Eclogue, significant as it has been, may fairly be left to the believer, the theologian and the mystic; it need not concern the literary interpreter, except as a historical curiosity.

Virgil's poem was not originally written as an Eclogue (i.e., a pastoral poem); rather, its few pastoral accoutrements (ll. 1–4, 67–8) were added later, when it was published as part of the book of *Eclogues*. The poem is plainly connected, whether as the influencer or the influenced, to Hor. *Epod.* 16 (p. 460), though we can't tell which poem was written first.

l. 1. *Sicilian Muses*: That is, the Muses of Theocritus' *Idylls* (pp. 283–98), which for the most part were set in Sicily. Virgil announces that in this poem he will leave behind the humble genre of pastoral for more elevated utterance.

l. 6. *the years' great cyclic roll*: Virgil's Latin, *magnus ordo saeclorum*, provides the base for the phrase *novus ordo seclorum*, 'new order of ages', which appears on the Great Seal of the United States of America. In this line and the following, which predict the return of the Virgin Astraea (see next note), Virgil's poem was seen to augur the birth of a new age (*saeculum*) of peace and justice, eventually sacralized by Augustus in 17 BCE (see *Intro* to Latin Lyric, p. 372).

l. 7. *The Virgin*: In the *Phaenomena* of Aratus (ll. 96–136) – a didactic astronomical poem of the third century BCE – the following story is told: when the Golden Race of men populated the earth, the virgin Astraea lived among them and exhorted them to justice; but, when the Silver Race took over, she withdrew to the hills, and visited less frequently, in the late afternoon, to chastise them for their unjust behavior. But the Bronze Race, which succeeded, she loathed so much that she vacated the earth entirely, and fled to the heavens, where she became the constellation Virgo. Virgil is the only ancient author to predict her return to earth. Christians reading this line naturally think of Isaiah 7:14: 'Behold, a virgin shall conceive, and bear a son.'

l. 12. *Apollo, now is sovereign*: Each epoch in the Etruscan scheme of ages (see poem note, above) was presided over by a god. Virgil seems to conceive of Apollo as lord of the penultimate age, preceding the return of Saturn.

l. 13. *Pollio*: Virgil's patron; see poem note, above.

l. 16. *our ancient crime*: The criminality of the present Iron Age – above all, of the recent civil war – will seem ancient from the perspective of the coming one. (Cf. 'the ancient fault' in l. 36). There may be a reference to the Roman ur-crime, Romulus' murder of his twin brother, Remus (cf. Hor. *Epod.* 16, l. 9, p. 460, and n.).

ll. 25–9. *The lion will not menace . . . with Syrian perfume*: These lines were full of significance for Christian interpretations. Besides the obvious passage in Isaiah (11:6: 'The wolf also shall dwell with the lamb, and the leopard shall lie down with the kid; and the calf and the young lion and the fatling together; and a little child shall lead them'), Virgil's lions were understood as Roman emperors persecuting Christian worshipers; the failing snake (l. 28) was the old serpent, the devil; the 'treacherous poison weed' (l. 28), the plausible falsehoods of the pagans; and the dissemination of the Syrian perfume-plant (l. 29) represented the spread of Christian doctrine.

404. l. 40. *Tiphys*: The helmsman of the *Argo* in Apollonius of Rhodes' *Argonautica* 1, ll. 105–8. The *Argo* was the mythical first ship – see Hor. *Epod.* 16, l. 57 (p. 461), and *Odes* 1.3, l. 10 (p. 463) – and, according to Herodotus (*Hist.* 1.2–3), it was believed by the Persians to have helped spark the age-old conflict between East and West which began with the Trojan War: Paris stole Helen from Sparta in the west in retribution for Jason's theft of Medea from Colchis in the east.

ll. 40–43. Similar passages in the *Aeneid* (e.g., 6, ll. 86–94, 10, ll. 26–30) refer with horror to the second Trojan War Aeneas wages in Italy against Turnus, a 'second Achilles'. Here the reincarnation of the Heroic Race seems an ambivalent, intermediary stage as the Ages reverse course back toward the Gold (ll. 44–55).

ll. 51–2. *the ram . . . with Punic purple now, now saffron fleece*: 'The portentous Sibylline tone seems very faint and faraway as we contemplate Virgil's polychromatic ram' (Wendell Clausen, 'Virgil's Messianic Eclogue', in *Poetry and Prophecy: The Beginnings of a Literary Tradition*, ed. James L. Kugel, p. 71). For 'Punic purple', see n. on Sulp. 3.8, l. 16 (p. 447).

405. ll. 64–6. *could Orpheus or Linus . . .*: Both great singers and sons of Apollo, Orpheus by the Muse Calliope. See also Ov. *Am.* 3.9, ll. 22–5 (p. 510) and nn., and Ov. *Tri.* 4.1, ll. 17–18 (p. 516) and n.

ll. 67–8. *Should Arcady judge as Pan and I competed . . .* : Pan was an Arcadian god and a special patron of pastoral song (cf. Vi. *Ecl.* 2, l. 36, p. 401, and n., and *Ecl.* 10, ll. 29–31, pp. 408–9). This grandiose couplet seems to have been added by Virgil as part of the minor adjustments to fit this poem to the pastoral *Eclogues*.

Eclogue 9, Lycidas, Moeris. After the defeat of the anti-Caesarians at the Battle of Philippi in 42 BCE, Mark Antony assumed control of affairs in the eastern Empire while Octavian stayed in Italy to settle veterans from

service on lands confiscated for the purpose. In northern Italy, the process
seems to have begun in 41, when the jurist Publius Alfenus Varus (cf. n.
on Cat. 10, l. 2, p. 379), a native of Cremona, was put in charge. Cremona, the site of Virgil's early education, was one of the chief towns of
northern Italy and only about forty miles from the poet's hometown of
Mantua. It was also marked out, whether by Varus or his henchman
Octavius Musa, as a center for confiscations, which, due to a grudge of
Musa's, were extended into Mantuan territory. According to the biographical tradition recorded by the commentator Servius and in Donatus'
Life, Virgil initially had his land confiscated by Varus; he appealed,
apparently to the other two members of the Land Redistribution Board,
who fortunately for him happened to be his patron, Gaius Asinius Pollio,
and his friend Gaius Cornelius Gallus, and got it restored; but he was
again forcibly driven off, by a centurion called Arrius, only to have his
land returned to him at last by the intervention of Octavian. The story
seems suspiciously likely to have been derived from the two Eclogues (1
and 9) which deal with this traumatic episode. At any rate, in this poem,
the evicted poet Menalcas, generally assumed to be a stand-in for Virgil,
is off petitioning the commissioners for redress of his situation, while his
dependent, the elderly Moeris, is forlornly abandoning his former home.
He is joined by Lycidas, whose station is left vague, but who seems not to
have been directly affected. Lycidas' name – along with many particular
details in the poem – recalls Theoc. *Id.* 7 (p. 291); but, whereas that poem
expresses literary exuberance in an atmosphere of celebration, this one
offers mainly melancholy resignation, and a sense of poetry as a small
and inadequate comfort in a world out of joint.

l. 13. *your friend Menalcas' singing*: See n. on Vi. *Ecl.* 10, l. 23 (p. 408).

406. l. 16. *Dodona's doves*: Dodona was an oracle sacred to Zeus and Dione
      in Epirus, northwestern Greece. Doves were associated with the origins
      of the oracle, as they were with Dione's daughter, Aphrodite; cf. Hdt.
      Hist. 2.55–7.

      ll. 28–32. *Hey, Tityrus . . . headbutter*: At this point, the poem breaks into
      the sort of *amoebaean* (alternating) exchange of songs typical of pastoral
      poetry; cf. Theoc. *Id.* 7 (p. 291), Cat. 62 (p. 388) and Hor. *Odes* 3.9
      (p. 482) for other examples. Each interlocutor in Virgil's poem sings one
      Theocritean song and one more-Roman one. This is Lycidas' Theocritean
      example; his Roman one (ll. 58–63) bookends Moeris' two offerings.

      l. 34. *O Varus*: The land commissioner (see poem note, above). Menalcas
      hopes to flatter Varus into restoring his confiscated plot.

ll. 35–6. *Mantua, too near . . . Cremona's wreck*: See poem note, above.

l. 44. *Varius*: Lucius Varius Rufus, epic poet, praised by Horace at *Odes* 1.6 (p. 466); one of the editors of the *Aeneid* after Virgil's death.

l. 45. *Cinna*: Gaius Helvius Cinna, the neoteric poet (see *Intro* to Catullus, p. 374) and friend of Catullus, murdered in 44 BCE well before the publication of this poem; see n. on Cat. 10, l. 31 (p. 380).

407. l. 49. *Galatea*: The sea nymph beloved of Polyphemus in Theoc. *Id.* 11 (p. 296); this song is based on ll. 43–50 of that poem.

ll. 59–60. *a new star shines for Caesar*: See n. on Hor. *Odes* 3.25, l. 7 (p. 486).

l. 60. *Venus-born*: The Julii traced the origins of their line back to Venus via Aeneas' son Ascanius/Iulus. Cf. Ov. *Am.* 3.9, ll. 14–15 (p. 510), and *Ex Pont.* 3.3, l. 64 (p. 523).

l. 62. *Daphnis*: See n. on Theoc. *Id.* 1, l. 68 (p. 283).

ll. 67–8. *my voice has vanished . . .* : A superstition held that a man would lose his voice when a wolf caught sight of him before he caught sight of the wolf. See Theoc. *Id.* 14, ll. 22–6, and the Elder Pliny, *Natural History* 8.80.

l. 73. *Bianor's tomb*: According to Virgil's ancient commentator, Servius, Bianor was the hero-founder of Mantua, which he named for his mother.

408. *Eclogue 10, Gallus.* Virgil's tenth and final Eclogue is an elaborate tribute to Gaius Cornelius Gallus (see n. on l. 2, below), the father of Latin love elegy and Virgil's friend and fellow student. Virgil's poem transmutes, or translates, Gallus' chosen genre of elegy into pastoral form.

l. 1. *Arethusa*: Arethusa was an Arcadian nymph, a favorite of Artemis/ Diana, committed to chastity. When the river god Alpheus fell for her, she fled, and was transformed by Diana into liquid form and channeled under the ocean to Sicily, where she issued on the island of Ortygia in Syracuse as a freshwater spring, her waters mixed with those of the river god, who had followed her in order to do so. She is thus one of the 'Sicilian Muses' of *Ecl.* 4, l. 1 (p. 403).

l. 2. *I owe a song to Gallus*: Gaius Cornelius Gallus (*c.*70–26 BCE) is Latin love elegy's most elusive ghost. He was a major figure of the late Republic: an important soldier, a friend of Gaius Asinius Pollio (see n. on *Ecl.* 4, p. 403, above) and Octavian, and generally considered (by Ovid, pp. 492–526, and Quintilian) as the father of Latin love elegy. He and Virgil both studied together under Parthenius of Nicaea (see Erucius 13, l. 2, p. 343,

and n., and *Intro* to Latin Lyric, pp. 367–8); the one surviving work of
Parthenius, a collection of summaries of legendary love stories, is dedicated
to Gallus. He chose sides well in the civil wars, and was rewarded by Octavian with an appointment – the first ever – to govern Roman Egypt; there
he somehow disgraced himself, lost Octavian's favor, was recalled by the
Senate, and committed suicide in 27/6 BCE. Afterwards, he was probably
subjected to *damnatio memoriae* – the obliteration of his memory – which
may be why his poems do not survive. Even so, two monuments still carry
his name: one is an obelisk now in St. Peter's Square in the Vatican, another
(in three languages) at Philae, downstream of Aswan on the River Nile. The
fulsome self-promotion of the latter may hint at the nature of his offense.
Other writers suggest that Gallus helped an enemy of the *princeps*, or that
he spoke his mind too freely when drunk.

Despite the wide influence of Gallus' poems, their author's obliteration
was so complete that, until 1979, only one line survived, a geographical
gloss about the River Hypanis separating Asia from Europe. In 1979,
however, a papyrus fragment was published with nine more lines, of
which the four most intelligible run as follows (it is unclear which Caesar,
Julius or Octavian, is being addressed):

> Caesar, how sweet my destiny will seem
> when you are Roman history's greatest theme;
> when, after your return, my eye applauds
> your opulent plunder on the shrines of gods!

Lycoris: The name Gallus gave his beloved in his four books of elegies,
which he probably called *Amores* (*Experiences of Love*, the same title
Ovid used). She was an actress whose real name, we are told, was Volumnia, but whose stage name was Cytheris; at different times, she was the
mistress of the anti-Caesarian Marcus Junius Brutus and of Mark Antony.
'Cytheris', pointing as it does to the lyre (*cithara*), may have suggested
the moniker 'Lycoris', which invokes Apollo via his epithet *Lycoreus*,
employed by Euphorion of Chalcis (see n. on l. 58, below) and also by
Callimachus (*Hymn to Apollo*, l. 19); 'Lycoreus' in turn will have something to do with Apollo's somewhat mysterious association with Lycia
(see n. on Call. *Aet.* 1.1, l. 22, p. 258).

l. 5. *Messina's channel*: The saltwater strait which separates Sicily from
the Italian mainland.

408–9. ll. 10–35. *Which forests ... of green shoots*: Virgil bases his poetic
frame on Theoc. *Id.* 1, ll. 68–100 (pp. 283–4), in which the landscape

grieves for the dying Daphnis while he is visited by a procession of mourners, which includes both herdsmen and deities; but Virgil has transplanted the scene from Sicily to Arcadia (see *Poet Intro*, p. 399).

408. l. 12. *Pindus*: See Theoc. *Id.* 1, l. 69–71 (p. 283) and n.

l. 13. *Aganippe*: A spring on Mount Helicon, said to bestow poetic inspiration on its drinkers (cf. n. on Ant. Thess. 3, ll. 1–2, p. 000).

ll. 15–17. *Maenalus ... Mount Lycaeus*: Two mountains sacred to Pan, in eastern and western Arcadia; the god was born on Lycaeus. Cf. Theoc. *Id.* 1, ll. 126–7, p. 285 and n.

l. 20. *Adonis*: Cf. Theoc. *Id.* 1, l. 111 (p. 285), and see Call. *Ia.* 3, ll. 36–7 (p. 263) and n.

l. 23. *Menalcas*: An important character throughout Virgil's *Eclogues*, with a major speaking role in *Ecl.* 3 and 5; often considered an alter ego of the poet (cf., here, *Ecl.* 2, ll. 17–18, p. 401, and *Ecl.* 9, ll. 13–27, 68–9, 82, pp. 405–8).

l. 27. *Silvanus*: See Hor. *Epod.* 2, ll. 21–2 (p. 457) and n.

408–9. ll. 29–31. *Pan, god of Arcady ...*: Cf. Vi. *Ecl.* 2, l. 36 (p. 401) and n., and *Ecl.* 4, ll. 67–8 (p. 405); see also the *Hymn to Pan* (Anon. 936, p. 238). His face is painted red, like the face of a general in a triumph, or statues of Jupiter during festivals; there may also be a connection to the early days of tragedy, when rustic chorus members painted their faces red (see Tib. 2.1, ll. 56–9, p. 000). The dwarf elder (l. 31), also known as elderwort, is a flowering plant whose berries produce a dark-purple juice.

409. ll. 36–79. *Then Gallus, groaning, spoke ...*: Despite Virgil's use of Theocritus in the previous section, Gallus' monologue here bears no resemblance to Daphnis' in Theoc. *Id.* 1 (ll. 102–41, pp. 284–5), and is probably adapted from Gallus' own poetry. If so, the saturnine dreaminess and fantasias on their own deaths which we find in Tibullus and Propertius (cf., e.g., Tib. 1.3, ll. 4–8, p. 413, and Prop. 2.1, ll. 73–80, p. 429) may well have had a precedent in the father of Latin love elegy. Of course, Virgil himself (*Ecl.* 4 apart) was no joy-monger, and surely infuses Gallus' lament with his own exquisitely gorgeous grief.

ll. 39–40. *Oh, my bones then will rest in luxury ...* : Virgil's couplet seems clearly based on the first two of Gallus' lines to Caesar (see n. on l. 1, above), and may give some sense of how Virgil is surely adapting Gallus' lost work throughout this poem and elsewhere.

l. 43. *Phyllis or Amyntas*: Standard pastoral names, also mentioned in Vi. *Ecl.* 3 (Amyntas also appears in this volume in Theoc. *Id.* 7, l. 139, p. 293, and *Ecl.* 2, ll. 40 and 45, p. 401). Phyllis is typically an object of hetero-sexual passion, Amyntas of homosexual.

l. 58. *Chalcis-songs*: Often taken to be a reference to Euphorion of Chalcis – Hellenistic poet, and court librarian to the Seleucid king Antio-chus the Great (r. 223–187 BCE) – whom Gallus is said to have translated into Latin. A dismissive remark of Cicero's (see *Intro* to Catullus, p. 374) gives us to understand that the heady erudition and obscurity of his verse was influential for Catullus and his 'neoteric' school, of which Gallus may well have been a part. However, skeptics of this tradition point to another, in which one Theocles of Chalcis is said to have been the inventor of the elegiac couplet; in that case, 'Chalcis-songs' would simply refer to Gallus' chosen genre.

l. 64. *hunt the toothy boar*: For another poetic boar-hunt, see Sulp. 3.9 (p. 448).

l. 65. *Mount Parthenius*: The passage bears a clear resemblance to Prop. 1.1, ll. 9–16 (p. 423), where Milanion woos Atalanta on the same Arca-dian mountain.

410.   l. 69. *my Parthian bow with Cretan shafts*: Both Cretans and Parthians (see Hor. *Odes* 2.13, l. 17, p. 475, and n.) were famous archers. In his commentary, Robert Coleman remarks that 'nothing but the best gear will satisfy Gallus even in Arcady' (*Vergil: Eclogues*, p. 291).

ll. 75–8. *not if I drank ... burned above*: Modeled on Theoc. *Id.* 7, ll. 119–22 (p. 292). For the Hebrus, see Alc. 45, l. 3 (p. 58) and n.

l. 79. *Love conquers all*: This famous phrase (*omnia vincit amor*) tends to be quoted with a cheerier affect than the poem warrants.

Tibullus

411.   *Poet Introduction. whose style ... compares favorably to Cicero's*: Tacitus, *Dialogue on Orators* 12 and 17.

412.   *'Delia' is a pseudonym for 'Plania'*: Apuleius, *Apologia* 10.3. 'Delia' (like Propertius' 'Cynthia') is also an epithet of Diana/Artemis, who was born on Delos with her twin, Apollo; see Pi. frr. 33c and 33d (p. 156) and n., and Cat. 34, ll. 5–8 (p. 383); for their infant exploits, see Call. *Hy.* 2, ll. 58–64 (p. 270).

'precise and elegant': Quintilian, *Institutes of Oratory* 10.1.93.

the 'Modernism' of Propertius: See *Intro* to Propertius (p. 422).

one German scholar: J. van Wageningen, 'Tibulls sogenannte Träumereien', *Neue Jahrbücher für das klassische Altertum* 31 (1913), pp. 350–55.

413. *1.3.* Tibullus has set out on an official mission to the east with his patron Marcus Valerius Messalla Corvinus (see *Poet Intro*, p. 411), but fallen ill along the way. Ovid's elegy for Tibullus (*Am.* 3.9, p. 510) makes frequent use of this poem in particular.

l. 3. *Phaeacia*: Corcyra (modern Corfu), which, following Thucydides, Callimachus and Apollonius of Rhodes, Tibullus identifies with the magical land of Phaeacia which hosts Odysseus in Hom. *Od.* 6 and 7 (cf. Phil. 23, l. 6, p. 339, and n.), before his return to Ithaca. Apparently too sick to continue traveling with Messalla, Tibullus has been abandoned here, not unlike Philoctetes on Lemnos.

l. 7. *Syrian perfume*: Roman poets tend to refer vaguely to Eastern perfumes, often confounding Syria and Assyria. The funeral ritual involved extinguishing the pyre, then washing the ashes with milk, wine and perfume, before transferring them to an urn and interring in a *columbarium* (literally, 'dovecote').

l. 9. *Delia*: See *Poet Intro* (pp. 411–12).

ll. 11–12. *Three times she drew from the boy's urn . . .* : In divination by lot, a boy assistant would draw lots from an urn, to be interpreted by a diviner; here, Delia is drawing the lots and the assistant is interpreting them. Cf. Hor. *Odes* 2.3, ll. 26–8 (p. 472), and Hor. *Odes* 3.1, ll. 14–16 (p. 478).

l. 18. *Saturn's Day*: This is the earliest Latin literary reference to Saturday, the Jewish Sabbath. Romans apparently considered it unlucky, and had prohibitions against traveling on that day. For Saturn himself, see. n. on ll. 35–48, below.

l. 23. The Egyptian goddess *Isis* (like Cybele – see Anon. 935, p. 237, and n.) presided over an exotically 'Eastern' mystery religion which took root and flourished in the capital as a result of Roman imperial expansion. In Egypt, Isis was the sister-wife of Osiris (replaced under the Ptolemies by the Hellenistic Serapis; see *Intro* to Post-Classical Greek Lyric, p. 253), and the mother of the falcon-headed Horus. When Osiris was murdered by his brother Seth, god of war, she wandered about lamenting and gathering the pieces of his body to resurrect him; the tale seems to have led Herodotus to associate Isis with Demeter (*Hist.* 2.59). In Greece, Isis was the divinized alter ego of Io, an amour of Zeus, whom Zeus turned into a cow to protect her from Hera's jealousy and whom Hera later chased with a gadfly to Egypt after Hermes set her free by killing the many-eyed watchman Argus (cf. Bacch. 19, ll. 15–45, pp. 183–4, and nn.). In Rome, Isis was a healing deity, mostly worshiped by women, especially lower-class courtesan-types – whence her frequent appearance in the Latin elegists.

Isis worship caught fire in Rome after Augustus annexed Egypt in 30 BCE, following the Battle of Actium (see n. on Hor. *Odes* 1.37, l. 13, p. 470), though the cult had been around for at least half a century already. As with Roman attitudes toward Hellenism, the foreignness of Isis was alternately stigmatized and embraced – a process intensified by her association with the corrupting exoticism of Cleopatra, which made for effective Augustan propaganda. Augustus banned public worship of Isis within the *pomerium* (the sacred boundary of Rome proper), but was ecumenical about her private worship at the temple of Isis and Serapis in the Campus Martius (cf. Cat. 10, l. 27, p. 380, and n.). No doubt the louche, semi-magical glamor of Isis worship was of a piece with the Greek-named beloveds of the elegists; certainly Tibullus emphasizes his own traditional Roman simplicity at ll. 33–4 as a contrast and foil for Delia's religious preferences. See also Prop. 2.28, l. 61 (p. 432), Ov. *Am.* 2.13, ll. 8–21 (pp. 506–7), and Mart. 10.48 1.1 (p. 549).

ll. 24–6. *Did those bronze rattles . . . sleep alone*: The bronze rattle called the *sistrum* was an important element of Isis worship, which also involved periods of purification and religiously prescribed chastity, particularly galling to the elegists. Cf. Tib. 2.1, ll. 12–14 (p. 418).

414. l. 30. *sitting in linen*: For associations of Egyptians and linen, see n. on Bacch. 19, ll. 43–4 (p. 184).

l. 34. *the monthly incense ritual*: i.e., the traditional monthly burning of incense to the Roman gods of the hearth, the *Lares*; see Tib. 1.10, ll. 15–29 (p. 416) and n., below.

ll. 35–48. *Saturn* was an old Italic deity associated with myths of the Golden Age; as the father of Jupiter, he was easily assimilated with the Greek Cronus (see Cor. 654a, ll. 12–18, p. 200, and n.). The usual Roman story goes that, after Saturn/Cronus was overthrown by Zeus/Jupiter, he came to Italy, where he presided over the Golden Age, a time characterized positively by peace and effortless abundance, or, more often, negatively by the absence of all the things that make life hard and painful – seafaring and trade (ll. 37–40), agriculture (ll. 41–2), property (ll. 43–4) and warfare (ll. 47–8). See also Vi. *Ecl.* 4 (p. 403) and n., Hor. *Epod.* 2 (p. 456) and n., Hor. *Epod.* 16 (p. 460) and n., and Hor. *Odes* 1.3 (p. 463) and n.

l. 58. *Elysium*: The 'heavenly' part of the underworld, where the virtuous dead live a life of beatitude, here exclusively populated by Tibullus with virtuous lovers (ll. 59–66). It has long been noted that Tibullus' account of the underworld – one of the earliest that survives in Latin – betrays a specifically elegiac vision. Only here does Venus play the role of *psychopomp* – conductor of dead souls to the underworld – usually assigned to Mercury (cf. Hor. *Odes* 1.24, ll. 16–18, p. 470). Other visions of Elysium in this book are worth comparing with this one – see Prop. 2.28, ll. 25–30 (p. 431), and 4.7, ll. 61–72 (pp. 441–2); and Ov. *Am.* 3.9, ll. 60–67 (p. 511).

415.   l. 68. *midnight river*: The Styx. We are now in Tartarus (ll. 67–82), where the souls of the wicked are punished, and which Tibullus has mostly filled with offenders against love.

ll. 69–70. *Tisiphone . . .* : 'Avenger of Bloodshed'; one of the three Furies, snaky-haired sisters who drive criminals mad on earth and punish them after death.

ll. 71–2. *Cerberus . . . the brazen gates*: See Bacch. 5, ll. 75–7 (p. 173) and n., and cf. Prop. 3.5, l. 43 (p. 435), and 4.7, l. 53 (p. 441), and Hor. *Odes* 2.13, ll. 33–4 (p. 475).

ll. 73–4. . . . *Ixion*: One of the underworld's arch-sinners, often said to have been the son of Phlegyas and brother of Coronis (see Pi. *Py.* 3, ll. 11–14, p. 146, and n., and Anon. 934, ll. 5–6, p. 236). He was tied to an ever-rolling wheel as punishment for the crime of attempting to rape Hera/Juno. (In the event, he failed, copulated with a cloud instead and fathered the race of Centaurs.)

ll. 75–6. *Tityus . . .* : A giant, and son of Zeus, who attempted to rape Leto and was killed by Apollo and Artemis. First placed in the underworld by Homer in *Od.* 11, ll. 576–81, he is chained to the earth, spread out over nine acres, and tormented by two vultures who devour his liver.

ll. 77–8. *Tantalus*, son of Zeus, stands in a pool of water under boughs loaded with figs, pears, pomegranates, apples and olives; but the pool shrinks from his lips as he tries to drink, and the boughs sway out of reach when he tries to eat (see Hom. *Od.* 11, ll. 582–93). The punishment is iconic, but there is confusion about the crime: for two of the most influential versions, that he either served his son Pelops to the gods or stole their immortal nectar, see Pi. *Ol.* 1, ll. 45–79 (pp. 137–8) and nn. However, every other criminal mentioned here by Tibullus sinned against Love; either Tantalus is the odd man out, or Tibullus may have been thinking of a lost Hellenistic elegy according to which Tantalus was punished for abducting Zeus's handsome cupbearer Ganymede; or perhaps he is included simply because (as spelled out by Lucretius at *De Rerum Natura* 4, ll. 1097–102) Tantalus' famous punishment is evocative of the elegiac lover's characteristic frustrations.

ll. 79–80. *Danaus's daughters . . .* : The fifty daughters of Danaus, king of Argos, were engaged to marry the fifty sons of Aegyptus; whether out of abhorrence of marriage, or to save their father from a foretold fate, they killed their husbands on their wedding nights – all except Hypermestra (placed in Elysium by Prop. 4.7, l. 65, p. 441), whose husband, Lynceus, went on to avenge the deaths of his brothers by killing Danaus. Their punishment in Tartarus – not attested until the first century BCE – is to carry water forever in leaky pails.

ll. 81–2. *those who ravish Delia . . . me on this slow tour, far away*: Tibullus transitions back to Rome and Delia by implicitly comparing any rivals he may or may not have to Ixion.

l. 83. *But you*: i.e., Delia.

l. 84. *an old crone . . . constant guard*: Such old ladies in elegy normally serve as madams, shutting out the poor poet, who cannot pay (Prop. 4.5 and Ov. *Am.* 1.8 are well-known portrayals of the type). But in Tibullus' imagination this one, surprisingly, helps Delia – who has become a sort of chaste Penelope – preserve her virtue as the two of them wait for Tibullus' return. The hopeful vision with which the poem concludes is less expectation than hallucination.

l. 93. *the rosy mares of Dawn*: See n. on Theoc. *Id.* 2, l. 153 (p. 290).

1.10. In this poem, which concludes Tibullus' first book, the poet evokes the traditional opposition between the soldier's pursuit of praise and glory and the humble lot of the rustic farmer; the poem's closest parallel is probably Hor. *Epod.* 2 (p. 456). Both Tibullus and Horace associate country living with positively troped motifs of poverty and simplicity, as opposed to greed and moneymaking; yet, in Tibullus, avarice is not given its conventional association (as in Horace) with merchants and moneylenders, but is instead linked to warfare, a civic duty of the Roman man. Thus Tibullus justifies his own pacifism (which he shares with the other elegists) in conventionally moral terms, avoiding the intentional provocations of the un-Roman 'Make love, not war!' creed espoused by Propertius (pp. 421–45) and Ovid (pp. 492–526). Of course, it *was* the case that Roman aristocrats could and did become fabulously wealthy from war – cf. Catullus' attacks on Mamurra (Cat. 41, p. 385, and n.), a lieutenant of Julius Caesar. The usual love themes of elegy are only tangentially touched on by Tibullus here, in the amatory combat of the farmer and his wife at the end of the poem (ll. 51–68). Compare the similarly oblique approach in Tib. 2.1 (p. 417), below.

l. 2. *a ferrous heart, and feral*: The pun (*ferus et ferreus*, 'savage, fierce' and 'of iron') is common in Latin. In these opening lines, Tibullus, being dragged to war – it is impossible to say which one – opens with a traditional curse on the 'first inventor' of the sword. Such curses often lead into nostalgic evocations of simpler, golden times, and so it is here as well (ll. 9–12). Cf. Tib. 1.3, ll. 35–48 (p. 414), and n.

416.   ll. 15–29. *Gods of my fathers ... O Lares ...* : The *Lares* were native Roman deities who protected hearths and farms; they were typically represented as identical twin brothers in short tunics, holding drinking horns and dancing. Painted on walls in little shrines before the hearth, they flanked the painted *genius* of the house (tutelary spirit of the *paterfamilias*); in the form of small statues, they were also displayed on the hearth with the *Penates*, an eclectic group of figurines belonging to a particular family – including both card-carrying members of the pantheon, such as Hercules, Mercury and Apollo, and more idiosyncratic selections, as in the Pompeiian house whose Penates included an amber hippopotamus. The Lares had no Greek equivalent and no mythology, but watched over the places where they were worshiped (hearths, city intersections, farm boundaries, and roads), rewarding with good fortune regular offerings of incense, wine and, on feast days, garlands of flowers (ll. 21–2) and sacrifices of pigs (l. 26). Cf. Tib. 1.3, ll. 33–4 (p. 414), Hor. *Epod.* 2, l. 43 (p. 457) and n., and Hor. *Odes* 3.23 (p. 485) and n.

ll. 25–6. At least two lines are missing.

l. 36. *Cerberus*: See Bacch. 5, ll. 75 (p. 173) and n.
   The *boatman of the Styx* is Charon.

417.   ll. 45–50. *Meanwhile, Peace tills the fields ...* : The hymn to Peace, picked up here and then resumed in the final couplet, may owe something to a similar hymn in Bacch. fr. 4 (p. 184). Tibullus may also have been affected by Augustus' pro-peace propaganda – though he did not live to see the Altar of Peace (completed 9 BCE), he certainly could have seen Augustus close the gates to the temple of Janus, symbolizing an end to war, in 29 and then again in 25 BCE.

ll. 53–66. *the wars of Venus ...* : The idea that it was sexy to fight with one's lover is conventional in Latin love elegy; cf. Prop. 2.15 (p. 429) and

3.8 (p. 435), and Ov. *Am.* 1.5 (p. 494). Tibullus, in criticizing this idea, sounds much more like a traditional Roman moralist than when he inveighs against the evils of war.

2.1. Tibullus' second book opens, unusually, not with mention of his new mistress, the greedily despotic Nemesis (see *Poet Intro*, pp. 411–12), but instead by evoking a country harvest festival – perhaps the Ambarvalia, held in late May, in which members of each household walked the boundaries of their property and sacrificed to 'the agricultural divinities' (l. 37). This interest in ritual is a Callimachean feature (cf. especially Call. *Hy.* 5, p. 272, which Tibullus draws on here), as is Tibullus' assumption of the role of poet-priest (*vates*, Greek *aoidos*: see n. on Call. *Hy.* 2, p. 269), also adopted by Horace in *Epod.* 16, l. 66 (p. 461), and *Odes* 1.1, l. 35 (p. 463), 2.20, l. 2 (p. 477), and 3.1, ll. 1–4 (p. 478). The expected elegiac love themes are again (as in Tib. 1.10, above) introduced obliquely, with the description and invocation of Cupid (ll. 68–71) as a fertility god overseeing the reproduction of livestock; soon, the associative chain takes over and we are back in the city (ll. 74–9), with typical elegiac characters and situations.

l. 4. *each horn*: See n. on Ion of Chios 744, l. 2 (p. 196).

418. ll. 12–14. *But you, depart* … : A period of chastity was commonly required before religious ceremonies (cf. Call. *Hy.* 2, l. 2, p. 269, and Hor. *Odes* 3.1, ll. 1–4, p. 478, and n.) – as Tibullus complains: see Tib. 1.3, ll. 25–6 (p. 413) and n.

ll. 18–25. *Gods of our fathers* … : Tibullus, as poet-priest, offers the ritual prayer; see poem note, above.

ll. 24–5. *gaggles of slaves … weaving twigs*: The slave children building huts of twigs on the green are playing, not working.

ll. 26–7. *the sign the entrails smiled*: Haruspication, a form of divination that involved reading the entrails, and especially livers, of sacrificial victims, had been a specialty of the Etruscans, and early adopted into Roman religion as well.

ll. 28–9. *Falernian … Chian*: Notably fine wines. Falernian (cf. Hor. *Odes* 2.3, l. 8, p. 471, and 3.1, l. 43, p. 479, and Mart. 12.17, l. 5, p. 552) was generally regarded as the second noblest wine of Italy, after the Caecuban (see Hor. *Odes* 2.14, l. 26, p. 477, and n.). Farmed from the slopes of Mount Falernus on the border of Latium and Campania, it is called 'full of smoke' by Tibullus because such wines were often aged in 'smoking rooms' (*fumaria*) powered by bath furnaces. It was best drunk between ten and twenty years old. Greek wines were generally considered even better than Italian; and the Chian, from the island of Chios, near Turkey, was Greece's best – see Phil. 21, l. 2 (p. 338) and n., and 23, l. 4 (p. 339), and n. on Hor. *Odes* 2.14, l. 25 (p. 477).

ll. 32–4. *Messalla ... hero of Aquitania*: After the Battle of Actium (31 BCE; see n. on Hor. *Odes* 1.37, l. 13, p. 470), Tibullus' patron Marcus Valerius Messalla Corvinus was appointed governor of the province of Aquitania, where he quashed a rebellion and received a triumph in September 27 BCE. He is a fitting recipient of toasts as a noted oenophile – Horace in *Odes* 3.21 uncorks a particularly mellow bottle of Massic for him; and in a dialogue of Maecenas' called the *Symposium*, Messalla claims that wine 'makes everything more beautiful' (Servius at *Aen.* 8, l. 310). No doubt he is absent from the present rustic festivities because he is in Rome or somewhere else on important imperial business.

ll. 36–7. *come and inspire me ...* : There is probably an echo here of Call. *Hy.* 5, ll. 55–6 (p. 273).

ll. 42–3. *they taught mankind the arts of breaking bulls*: In Tib. 1.3, ll. 41–2 (p. 414), the art of subduing bulls was presented negatively (alongside the invention of sailing ships and swords, etc.), as signaling the end of the Golden Age; here, with various other farmerly innovations, it is a gift of the 'agricultural divinities' (l. 37), for which they deserve praise and thanks. The ambivalence, which finds in the countryside both healthy, carefree simplicity and unremitting toil, is a keynote of pastoral and georgic not only in Tibullus' eyes, but in urbane literature generally, from Theocritus (pp. 282–98) on.

419. l. 47. *sober water tempered carefree wine*: Virgil, in his *Georgics* (1, l. 9), also describes the dilution of newly discovered wine with water. For Greek attitudes about wine and water, see n. on Alc. 346, l. 4 (p. 66).

ll. 56–9. *Bacchus, at first ... a memorable gift*: These lines allude to the origins of tragedy, always performed in honor of Dionysus/Bacchus, and recall a time when, before the wearing of masks, chorus members painted their faces red with cinnabar. The 'he-goat' (l. 58, *tragos* in Greek) alludes to the etymology of 'tragedy' as 'goat-song', based on the belief that a goat had been the prize for winning performances.

l. 61. *the ancient gods*: That is, the Lares. See Tib. 1.10, ll. 15–29 (p. 416) and n.

l. 66. *The weaver, devotee of Pallas*: Minerva (Pallas) was the goddess of weaving, the traditional occupation of virtuous Roman womanhood. Cf. Hor. *Odes* 3.12, ll. 6–9 (pp. 483–4).

l. 68. *Cupid himself*: Now, with the birth of Cupid, Tibullus maneuvers us back into more familiar elegiac territory. A similar idea is found in the *Pervigilium Veneris* (*Vigil of Venus*), an anonymous poem of the second–fifth centuries CE (ll. 76–9):

> Passion fertilizes fields, the fields know Venus well;
> Love himself, Dione's son, was born there, so men tell.
> While the earth was giving birth, she took him in her lap,
> and among the flowers' whispering kisses brought him up.

ll. 72–81. *Now livestock bores him* . . . : In lines reminiscent of Alc. Mess. 6 (p. 317), Cupid acts like a plague, attacking the animals first, and then the people. Soon Tibullus' imagination is back in the city, lamenting the embarrassing lengths to which the elegiac lover will go for his domineering mistress.

420. ll. 84–7. *Hymn the god's fame* . . . : There may be a further reminiscence here of Call. *Hy.* 5, ll. 138–40 (p. 276).

ll. 88–91. *Night's car is yoked* . . . : The poem's conclusion recalls the end of Theoc. *Id.* 2 (p. 286).

Propertius

421. *Poet Introduction. Cynthia, whose actual name . . . was Hostia*: Apuleius, *Apologia* 10.3.

422. '*is as much charnel as carnal*': Steele Commager, *A Prolegomenon to Propertius*, p. 14.

'*Some people prefer Propertius*': Quintilian, *Institutes of Oratory* 10.1.93.

423. *1.1.* As the programmatic first poem of Propertius' first book, this elegy introduces, in no uncertain terms, the book's subject (Cynthia) and its tone (tortured). For so-called poetic 'programs' in Augustan literature, see n. on Prop. 2.1 (p. 427), below.

l. 1. *Cynthia*: As with Tibullus' Delia, the sobriquet given by Propertius to his beloved is an epithet of Artemis/Diana (after Mount Cynthus on Delos, where she and Apollo were born; cf. Call. *Hy.* 2, l. 60, p. 270).

ll. 1–2. *it was those eyes . . . uncursed*: These lines clearly echo Mel. 103 (p. 332), about the boy Myiscus, illustrating the intimate link between Latin love elegy and Hellenistic epigram (see *Intro* to Latin Lyric, p. 370).

l. 9. *Tullus*: Gaius Volcacius Tullus was Propertius' first patron (see *Poet Intro*, p. 421).

ll. 9–10. *Milanion* ... : As the poem relates, the legendary suitor of the huntress Atalanta (l. 10); the usual story of his courtship (via golden apples) is told in the n. on Cat. 2, l. 11 (p. 376). Propertius, ignoring the golden apples, seizes on more recondite details (see below) as he turns Milanion into a sort of pastoral elegiac lover, not unlike Gallus in Vi. *Ecl.* 10 (see especially ll. 63–71, pp. 409–10, which bear a resemblance to these verses); for another example of hunting in elegy, see Sulp. 3.9 (p. 448).

l. 11. *the Virgin Mountain*: Mount Parthenius in Arcadia, on which Atalanta was exposed as an infant. After being suckled by a she-bear (a familiar of Diana/Artemis), she grew into a wild huntress and fierce custodian of her own virginity, devoting herself to the goddess who had saved her. The implied comparison with Cynthia points at the latter's feral inaccessibility, though she is no virgin.

l. 13. *the Centaur's club*: Hylaeus, with another Centaur, called Rhoecus (Apollodorus, *Library* 3.9.2, Call. *Hy.* 3, l. 221), attempted to rape Atalanta in the Arcadian wilds. She successfully fought them off, apparently with some help from Milanion, who was injured in the process.

ll. 15–16. *That's how he tamed* ... : The point is a revision, or at least a refocusing, of the more familiar story. Not by trickery with golden apples, but by constancy, servitude and suffering – the usual modus operandi of the elegiac lover – Milanion won his bride's hand and heart.

l. 23. *Thessalian witchcraft*: Witches, frequent among the seedy characters encountered by elegists, were often associated with Thessaly (cf. Anon. Mel. 35, p. 324). The enumeration of witches' magical powers (among which the ability to cause eclipses, as at l. 19, was traditionally included) is a common motif of elegy; cf. Prop. 2.28, ll. 35–8 (p. 432), and Ov. *Am.* 2.1, ll. 26–31 (p. 499), and 3.7, ll. 29–38 (p. 508). Tib. 1.2, ll. 43–8, speaks of a 'truthful witch',

> whose magic I've seen make the starlight go
> out of the sky, and torrents halt their flow,
> whose song can split earth open and evoke
> corpses from tombs, bones from the pyre's smoke.

No doubt the vogue for these 'witch passages' in Roman elegy was inspired largely by Theoc. *Id.* 2 (p. 286).

ll. 25–30. *And you who call me … where I have gone*: These lines are recalled at Prop. 3.24, ll. 9–16 (pp. 438–9), where their future-facing imperatives and conditionals are replaced by the past tense of a fait accompli.

424. 1.2. An artful praise of artlessness: Propertius argues for the superiority of natural beauty to cultivation, abundantly supporting his argument with examples from nature and myth.

l. 2. *Coan*: i.e., from Cos, a Greek island in the Dodecanese near Bodrum, Turkey, famed for its gauzy fabric – and also, perhaps not coincidentally, the home of the painter Apelles (l. 22), as well as one of Propertius' favorite elegiac poets, Philitas (cf. Prop. 3.3, l. 52, p. 434, and n.).

ll. 15–16. *Phoebe* and *Hilaïra*, daughters of Leucippus, legendary king of Messenia, were abducted by the Dioscuri (Sons of Zeus), Castor and Pollux/Polydeuces.

ll. 17–18. *Evenus' … daughter*: Marpessa 'of the lovely ankles' (Hom. *Il.* 9, l. 557) – and not, be it noted, 'Marpessa of the Jimmy Choos' – was abducted by Idas from her home in Aetolian Chalcis. Her father Evenus gave chase, only to drown in a river which thereafter took his name. Apollo (Phoebus) later snatched Marpessa from Idas, but Zeus intervened, and she chose Idas over Apollo, because he would grow old with her.

ll. 19–20. For *Pelops'* chariot race with Oenomaus for the hand of his daughter *Hippodamia*, cf. Pi. *Ol.* 1, ll. 85–115 (p. 138–9).

l. 22. *Apelles*: A fourth-century BCE painter from Cos, famous for his naturalistic color. Perhaps the mention of Apelles hints at Propertius' own aesthetic allegiances: he cannot really prefer the untaught artlessness of birdsong (l. 14) to the learned polish he praises so extravagantly below.

ll. 27–30. *Phoebus taught … Venus and Minerva teach*: Propertius articulates the elegiac ideal of the *docta puella*, the 'learned girl' or skilled courtesan who, after a banquet, can gratify male guests with the arts of Apollo (lyre-playing), the Muses (singing) and Venus (sex). Minerva's art – i.e., weaving – however, belongs in the more traditional province of the virtuous Roman maiden. It is worth adding that *doctus* (learned) as used in Latin poetry often implies specifically 'learned in Callimachean poetics': in one of Horace's *Satires*, a character says, 'You know me, I'm *learned*' (1.19, l. 7), by which he means, 'I'm a poet.' Thus the learned skills of the *puella docta* and the *poeta doctus* easily overlap and intermingle (see Ov. *Am.* 2.4, ll. 19–22, p. 500, and n.); neither very much resembles l. 14's untaught simplicity of birdsong.

425. *1.3. ll. 1–6. As languidly as Ariadne* ... : In true elegiac fashion, Propertius likes to pile up his mythical references; cf., in particular, Cat. 68b (p. 391) and Ov. *Am.* 1.5 (p. 494). The poem opens with a comparison of Cynthia's sleeping form, first, to Ariadne abandoned by Theseus on Naxos (cf. Theoc. *Id.* 2, l. 50, p. 287, and n.), and then, by the third comparison, to a maenad ravished by a (rather Propertian) Bacchus.

ll. *3–4. like Andromeda, her first sleep free* ... : The Ethiopian princess, who had been chained to a cliff face as sacrifice to a sea monster, but was saved and married by Perseus. Cf. Prop. 2.28, ll. 21–2 (p. 431).

ll. *5–6. a Thracian maenad* ... : A Bacchant, or ecstatic worshiper of Dionysus, who seems to have wandered from her place of origin in east Thrace (the Thracian Edoni were a people synonymous among the Romans with the rites of Bacchus) to sleep beside the River Apidanus (modern Pharsalitis) in Thessaly.

ll. *19–20. as riveted as Argus* ... *Io's head*: See Bacch. 19, ll. 15–45 (pp. 183–4), and nn.

l. *24. gave apples*: As love tokens. Cf. Cat. 65, ll. 19–24 (p. 391), and see n. on Theoc. *Id.* 2, l. 123 (p. 289).

425–6. ll. *31–4. until the flighty moonlight filtered in* ... : The scene is based on Phil. 9 (p. 336); Ovid also makes use of the motif at *Am.* 1.5 (p. 494) and, with elbow-prop, *Ex Pont.* 3.3, ll. 6–13 (p. 522).

426. ll. *35–46. 'So* ...': It is noteworthy that, so early in the collection, Propertius gives Cynthia a speech of such (apparently unmediated) reproach, since much more typically it is the perspective of the locked-out elegist we are treated to; Cynthia's complaint here seems to foreshadow that of her ghost in Prop. 4.7 (p. 440), the penultimate Cynthia poem in Propertius' oeuvre.

l. *42. Orphic song*: Cynthia, trying to keep awake, may have resorted to singing some of the mystical songs said to have been brought back by Orpheus after his failed attempt to rescue his beloved Eurydice from the underworld; cf. Ov. *Tri.* 4.1, ll. 17–18 (p. 516) and n.

1.11. l. 1. Baiae was a fashionable resort town on the northwest of the Gulf of Naples in southern Italy; it had an air of luxury and decadence, like an ancient Miami Beach. (Ovid says of it, in *Art of Love* 1, ll. 257–8, trans. Michie: 'One man came back with the report: / "That's no health resort!"') Cynthia has gone there; the perpetually jealous Propertius fears the worst.

l. 2. *the Road of Hercules*: A narrow tongue of land, then thought to have been the work of Hercules but probably natural, which separated the Lucrine Lake (l. 10; modern Lago di Lucrino), just north of Baiae, from the sea.

ll. 3–4. *Avernus ... at Misenum Thesprotia's waters rise*: Lake Avernus (modern Lago d'Averno), located near Baiae and the Lucrine Lake, but slightly to the north, was associated with the underworld; it shared its name with another Lake Avernus in Thesprotia, a region of Epirus in what is now northwestern Greece (Hyginus, *Fabulae* 88; Pausanias, *Description of Greece* 1.17.4–5). Misenum (now Miseno), named for Aeneas' ill-fated trumpeter (Vi. *Aen.* 6, ll. 162–76, 212–35), refers to the northwestern cape on the Bay of Naples, about three and a half miles from Baiae. Cape Misenum was home to numerous Republican luxury villas and, later, became the harbor for the imperial fleet. In 37 BCE, Agrippa (see n. on Hor. *Odes* 1.6, l. 1, p. 466) had built a canal connecting the Italian Avernus to the Lucrine Lake and the sea. As at Vi. *Ecl.* 10, ll. 4–6 (p. 408), where the spring Arethusa travels underwater from Greece to Sicily, Propertius now imagines that the Thesprotian Avernus descends from Epirus through the underworld to emerge in Campania, whence, by way of Agrippa's channels, it flows into the sea near Misenum.

ll. 5–8. These lines are clearly reminiscent of Mel. 52 (p. 329), suggesting that in this poem Propertius is adapting a topic from epigram to a specifically Roman setting.

ll. 15–16. *as a false girl ... sealed them by*: I have occasionally followed certain modern editors of Propertius in transposing couplets from one location to another, an expedient often resorted to due to the desperate state of the text (see *Poet Intro*, p. 422).

l. 10. For the *Lucrine Lake*, see notes on ll. 2–4, above.

l. 11. *Teuthras*: Another lake or pool near Baiae.

427. l. 23. *You are my parents now*: Propertius echoes the famous words of Andromache to Hector at Hom. *Il.* 6, l. 429.

2.1. The *recusatio* (refusal poem), common in Augustan 'small genre' poetry (elegy, lyric, pastoral), is an elegant way of complimenting a patron while maintaining a degree of poetic independence: cf. Hor. *Epod.* 14 (p. 459) and *Odes* 1.6 (p. 466); Ov. *Am.* 2.1 (p. 498). Typically the poet 'refuses' some lofty poetic task – an epic in praise of the martial accomplishments of the distinguished addressee – in favor of his preferred, albeit less ambitious, genre and style. Such refusals often stand at or near the head of a book and help to sketch the poet's 'program'. In this, the Augustan poets looked consistently back to the proem of Call. *Aet.* (1.1, p. 258). Such is plainly the case in this programmatic poem for Propertius' second book, in which he sets out his subject matter, love (ll. 1–16); refuses (in courtly style) to write Roman epic in praise of Augustus and his new patron, Gaius Cilnius Maecenas (ll. 17–40); justifies his refusal by the precedent of Callimachus (ll. 41–8); then returns to his preferred matter and manner, protesting his focus on one mistress (ll. 49–58), his incurability (ll. 59–72) and his imminent death (ll. 73–80), all with lavish mythological erudition.

l. 5. *Coan silks*: See n. on Prop. 1.2, l. 2 (p. 424), above.

l. 18. *Maecenas*: The fact that this and Prop. 3.9 are the only poems Propertius addresses to Maecenas (who took over as the poet's patron after the success of Bk. 1) has led scholars to suspect some coolness between Propertius and the Augustan regime; see *Poet Intro* (p. 421).

ll. 19–20. *Ossa ... Olympus ... Pelion*: Mountains in Thessaly. Propertius, not unusually, confuses or conflates the Titanomachy (the battle between the Olympian gods and the Titans: Cronus, Atlas, etc.) with the later Gigantomachy (the battle between the gods and the Giants); see n. on Xen. 1, l. 24 (p. 110). As told at Hom. *Od.* 11, ll. 313–16, the Giants Otus and Ephialtes piled these mountains up to attack the gods; cf. Pi. *Py.* 8, ll. 12–18 (p. 152) and nn. Ovid parodies Propertius' lines (and perhaps corrects them, changing 'Titans' to 'Giants') at *Am.* 2.1, ll. 16–17 (p. 498).

ll. 21–4. *ancient Thebes ... the feats of Marius*: Propertius works, at speed, from distant mythical history toward more recent and more Roman topics. *Thebes* refers to the Theban Cycle (see nn. on Stes. 97, p. 93, and Pi. *Py.* 8, l. 39, p. 153). *Troy*, of course, invokes the *Iliad*. The *canal through Athos* conjures the Persian Wars and a specific episode from Hdt. *Hist.*, 7.22–4. The *reign of Remus* (here substituted for the metrically impossible 'Romulus') evokes the early history of Rome and the first books of Ennius' *Annals* (cf. Prop. 3.3, ll. 6–12, p. 433, and nn.). *Carthage furious* summons the epic treatment of the Punic Wars by Ennius and Naevius (see *Intro* to Latin Lyrics, pp. 365–7). And *Marius* and *the Cimbrian threat* bring us to more recent history, namely, the soldier-statesman Gaius Marius' defeat of the invading German tribes, the Cimbri and Teutones, in 102–101 BCE. Of course, Propertius only mentions all of these topics to dismiss them as inferior to the even more recent victories of Octavian, catalogued immediately below.

428. ll. 27–35. *Mutina . . . Actium*: A catalogue of Octavian's victories in the civil wars. First, those against the anti-Caesarians: Decimus Brutus was defeated at Mutina (Modena) by Mark Antony and the young Octavian in 43 BCE; Marcus Junius Brutus and Gaius Cassius Longinus at *Philippi* in 42; Sextus Pompeius off Naulochus (*the Sicilian shore*) in 36. Then, the wars against Antony and his partisans, chiefly the Perusine War in 41–40 (*Perusia sacked*), when Octavian defeated Mark Antony's brother in an action famous for its cruelty (and inflicted a personal loss on Propertius himself: see *Poet Intro*, p. 421), and the Battle of Actium (31 BCE; see n. on Hor. *Odes* 1.37, l. 13, p. 470), following which *Egypt* was finally annexed (*Ptolemy's lighthouse*, the Pharos of Alexandria, was a wonder of the world). In the resulting triumph of 29 BCE, images of the defeated *Nile* and the famous seven mouths of its delta, along with enemy *kings* in person (including the young son and daughter of Antony and Cleopatra), were paraded through the heart of Rome (*down the Sacred Way*).

ll. 38–9. *Patroclus and Pirithöus*: Beloved friends and sidekicks of Achilles and Theseus, respectively; here their closeness stands for that of Maecenas to Octavian/Augustus.

l. 41. *fine and small*: Propertius may be thinking of Callimachus' comparison of his voice to the cicada's at *Aet.* 1.1, ll. 29–30 (p. 258).

l. 44. *Caesar with his Trojan ancestors*: Augustus' adoption by Julius Caesar made him a member of the Julii, who traced the origins of their line back to Venus via Aeneas' son Ascanius/Iulus.

ll. 53–4. *Theseus' stepmother's venom . . .*: The story of Medea alluded to here is told in Callimachus' *Hecale* and in Ov. *Met.* 7, ll. 419–23. Theseus, as yet unrecognized by his father, King Aegeus, had come to Athens. Aegeus' then-wife, Medea – who had married him after fleeing from Corinth and the deadly revenge she had inflicted on Jason (in Euripides' *Medea*) – identified Theseus as a rival to Medus, her own son by Aegeus. She convinced her husband the newcomer was an enemy, and brewed a poison potion for Aegeus to give his guest; but Aegeus realized Theseus was his son at the last instant and dashed the cup away. Medea was driven out of Athens.

l. 55–6. For *Circe's herbs*, cf. Theoc. *Id.* 2, ll. 19–20 (p. 286) and n. The reference to *Medea's cauldrons* alludes to the story (told in Ov. *Met.* 7, ll. 297–349) of how she brought about the death of her then-husband Jason's enemy, King Pelias of Iolcus – she tricked Pelias' daughters, who wanted to rejuvenate their elderly father, into cutting him up and boiling him in a cauldron: they had seen her do the same with an old ram, which emerged from the boiling water fresh and young; but when they tried the treatment on their father, Medea withheld the magic and the old king met a gruesome end.

ll. 61. *Machaon* was one of the two sons of Asclepius who served as the Greeks' doctors in the *Iliad* (cf. Anon. 934, ll. 10–11, p. 236). In the later *Little Iliad*, one of the poems of the Epic Cycle (see n. on Call. *Ep.* 2, l. 1, p. 276), he cured the snakebitten foot of the great bowman *Philoctetes*, whose archery was needed to conquer Troy.

429. ll. 62. *Chiron* the Centaur (who raised Asclepius in Pi. *Py.* 3, ll. 65–6, p. 148) supposedly cured the blindness of Achilles' teacher *Phoenix*, sometime after he (Phoenix) was banished by his father, Amyntor, but before he made it to the court of Achilles' father, Peleus (cf. Hom. *Il.* 9, ll. 434–605).

ll. 63–4. *Asclepius brought back ... Androgeon*: Asclepius' healing of the Cretan king Minos' son Androgeon (or Androgeus) isn't mentioned elsewhere but might well be the crime for which Asclepius is blasted by Zeus in Pi. *Py.* 3, ll. 80–86 (pp. 148–9); at any rate, Androgeon's death in Athens is the crime the Athenians sought to expiate with regular offerings of youths and maidens to the Minotaur.

ll. 65–6. *Telephus restored ... with rust*: See n. on Ar., *Achaeans at Mysia* (p. 7).

ll. 67–72. *anybody who could cure me could ...* : This list of *adynata* (impossibilities) focuses on famous sinners and their punishments. For *Tantalus* and the Daughters of Danaus (*Danaids*), see nn. on Tib. 1.3, ll. 77–8 and 79–80 (p. 415). *Prometheus* defied Zeus and provided men with fire, for which he was chained to a cliff in the *Caucasus*, where an vulture would drop by every day to eat his liver. For *adynata* generally, cf. Ar. 122, ll. 5–9 (p. 10); Call. *Ia.* 12, ll. 69–70 (p. 268); Theoc. *Id.* 1, ll. 136–41 (p. 285); Prop. 2.15, ll. 31–6 (p. 430); Hor. *Epod.* 16, ll. 25–34 (p. 460); Ov. *Ex Pont.* 2.4, ll. 25–8 (p. 521), and 3.3, ll. 99–101 (p. 524).

l. 79. *answerless ash*: Cf. Cat. 101, l. 4 (p. 397).

2.15. This is one of two genuine 'sex' poems in Latin literature; the other, Ov. *Am.* 1.5 (p. 494), is based on it, especially on its first ten lines or so. This was clearly an important poem for Ovid, who also echoes it in *Am.* 2.12 (p. 505). Compare, too, Prop. 3.8 (p. 435), for its similar commitment to the 'wars of Venus'. Opinion on the present elegy has ranged widely; some scholars, such as A. E. Housman, find it chaotically incoherent, while others have found the combination of ecstatic exclamation with *carpe diem* tinged reflections on mortality among the most compelling passages in Propertius. In general, I hold with the latter group, though the poem does lurch a little bit before it gets going, especially in the abrupt transition at ll. 10–11, where Propertius suddenly shifts from recollected ecstasy to admonition, as if lecturing Cynthia prior to their tryst.

l. 15. *Endymion*: See Phil. 9, l. 6 (p. 336) and n. – one of Propertius' favorite epigrams, already alluded to in Prop. 1.3, ll. 31–4 (p. 000), above. *Phoebe* is the Latin name of Selene, goddess of the moon, often identified with Diana/Artemis.

430. ll. 23–4. *Let's feast . . .* : Here and below (at ll. 49–50), Propertius seems to be thinking of some of Catullus' most famous lines, Cat. 5, ll. 4–6 (p. 377).

ll. 27–8. *Think of two doves . . . a perfect coupling*: Cf. Cat. 68b, ll. 127–30 (p. 393) and n.

ll. 31–6. *The Sun will sooner darken his bright steeds . . .* : This *adynaton* (catalogue of impossibilities: see n. on Prop. 2.1, ll. 67–72, p. 429) clearly inspired Donne's Elegy 15, ll. 27–8:

> Sooner I'll thinke the Sunne will cease to cheare
> The teeming earth, and *that* forget to beare . . .

ll. 41–6. *If everyone desired a life like mine . . .* : An example of the *militia amoris* (warfare of love) trope so common in Latin elegy; see nn. on Ov. Am. 1.9 (p. 000) and Am. 2.12 (p. 000). These lines are echoed by Thomas Campion (*A Booke of Ayres* 1, ll. 7–8):

> If all would lead their lives in love like mee,
> Then bloudie swords and armour should not be . . .

l. 44. *Actium*: See n. on Hor. *Odes* 1.37, l. 13 (p. 470).

431. 2.28. This poem is Propertius' rendition of a standard elegiac theme, the illness of the beloved (cf. Sulp. 3.10, p. 448, and Ov. Am. 2.13, p. 506), which he tackles with a Hellenistic-style combination of myth and magic.

l. 3. *the Dog*: Sirius, Orion's dog, which marked the hottest summer months. Cf. Alc. 347 (p. 66), and W. H. Auden's 'Under Sirius':

> Yes, these are the dog days, Fortunatus:
> The heather lies limp and dead

> On the mountain, the baltering torrent
> Shrunk to a soodling thread ...

ll. 9–12. The trio of *Venus, Juno* and *Minerva* reminds us of the Judgment of Paris, which started the Trojan War (cf. Call. *Hy.* 5, ll. 18–28, pp. 273–3, and n.).

l. 11. *Did you make light of Argive Juno's shrine*: This may refer to an incident involving the daughters of Proetus, king of Argos, who disparaged the temple of Hera/Juno and were driven mad.

l. 12. *Minerva's eyes*: Her gray-green (glaucous) eyes were mocked by other goddesses.

ll. 17–24. Propertius lists four women who endured hardship to be rewarded with apotheosis and/or constellations in their honor: *Io*, who became an Egyptian goddess (cf. Bacch. 19, ll. 15–45, pp. 183–4, and nn.); *Ino*, a sister of Semele (l. 27, below), who, pursued by her maddened husband, threw herself into the sea with her son, Melicertes, and became the goddess *Leucothoë* (or *Leucothea*; cf. Ant. Si. 26, ll. 5–6, p. 322, and n., and Phil. 19, p. 339); *Andromeda*, for whom see n. on Prop. 1.3, ll. 3–4 (p. 425), above; and *Callisto*, an Arcadian princess loved by Jupiter, who was transformed first into a bear, then into the constellation Ursa Major (cf. Ov. *Tri.* 1.4, l. 1, p. 512, and n.).

ll. 26–30. *your destined burial will be blest* ... : The afterlife Propertius envisions for Cynthia here closely resembles the existence which, in Prop. 4.7 (ll. 61–70, p. 441), her ghost claims to have achieved in Elysium.

l. 27. *Semele*: Dionysus' mother. See n. on Phil. Scar. *PaeDi.*, l. 1 (p. 229).

l. 29. *Homer's heroines*: Helen; Odysseus' wife, Penelope; and Hector's wife, Andromache.

432. ll. 35–8. *The spells have failed* ... *its dire omen*: Propertius shows his love of Hellenistic magic with this deeply atmospheric catalogue of failed remedies. The 'whirligig' is the 'bullroarer' of Theoc. *Id.* 2, l. 44 (p. 286) and n., and Anon. Mel. 35 (p. 324). Laurel was commonly burned in magic ceremonies; cf. Theoc. *Id.* 2, ll. 1 and 27–30 (pp. 286 and 287). For the eclipse (or not) of the moon, see Prop. 1.1, ll. 19–20 and 23–4 (p. 423) and n., above; for the 'horned owl', see Folk Songs. 859 (p. 244) and n.

ll. 33–4. *Juno* ... *even she relents*: This couplet, put in different places by different editors, alludes to Juno's inveterate jealousy of her husband Jupiter's amours.

l. 48. *you, her husband*: i.e., Hades.

l. 51. *Tyro* and *Antiope* were princesses of Elis and Thebes, loved by Poseidon and Zeus, respectively. They were persecuted by wicked stepmothers (Sidero and Dirce) and ultimately avenged by their demigod children (Pelias and Amphion; for the latter see n. on Vi. *Ecl.* 2, l. 25, p. 401).

l. 52. *Europa* was a Phoenician princess, abducted to Crete by Zeus in the form of a bull, and the mother of King Minos; *Pasiphaë* was Minos' wife, who – ensconced within a lifesize wooden cow devised by Daedalus – mated with a snow-white bull, the gift of Poseidon, and gave birth to the Minotaur. For Europa, see Bacch. 17, l. 35 (p. 000) and n.; for Pasiphaë, see Bacch. 17, ll. 56-7 (p. 000) and n., and Prop. 4.7, l. 59 (p. 000).

l. 61. *Isis*: The divinized alter ego of Io (ll. 17–18, above); see n. on Tib. 1.3, l. 23 (p. 413).

3.3. The similarity between the first five elegies of Propertius' third book – all rather vatic, ambitious pieces proclaiming his allegiance to Alexandrian poetics and Augustan politics – and the first six odes of Horace's third book (the so-called 'Roman Odes', pp. 478–82) has long been noted. Priority is impossible to determine with any precision, though it does seem likely that Propertius' Bk. 3 came out after 23 BCE (when Horace's first three books of *Odes* were published), thus raising the prospect of *aemulatio* (rivalry) between the two poets. At any rate, like Prop. 2.1 (p. 427) and Roman poetry generally, the present poem owes a great deal to Callimachus' *Aetia* (pp. 258–61). In that poem, the young Callimachus is transported to Mount Helicon in a dream, where the Muses, answering his questions, provide the material for its first two books. In Ennius' later *Annals* (see *Intro* to Latin Lyric, p. 367), the poet's dream is likewise set on Helicon, and he is informed by the ghost of Homer that Homer's soul has transmigrated into his body. Propertius nods to both precedents, but Callimachus is the stronger (cf. n. on ll. 15–24, below).

l. 2. *the spring that Pegasus once made*: The Hippocrene (Horse Spring); see n. on Call. *Aet.* 4.112, l. 5 (p. 261). Cf. also Call. *Hy.* 5, ll. 70–72 (p. 274), Ant. Thess. 3 (p. 345), and Ov. *Tri.* 3.7, l. 16 (p. 514).

l. 4. *Alba*: Not the Gaelic name for Scotland, but Alba Longa, a town of Latium founded by Aeneas' son Ascanius/Iulus and incorporated early into Rome. Propertius is contemplating an epic on early Latium, set between the end of the *Aeneid* and Rome's founding by Romulus.

433. l. 6. *Ennius*: See poem note.

ll. 7–12. *who sang . . . the Capitol*: Propertius lists various great men and famed events in Roman history, mostly from Ennius' *Annals*, but jumbled chronologically, as if to illustrate his unfitness for the task. Cf. the similar lists in Hor. *Epod.* 16, ll. 3–8 (p. 460), and Mart. 6.19, ll. 6–9 (p. 545).

l. 7. *the trophies of Aemilius*: Lucius Aemilius Paullus defeated Perseus, king of Macedon, in 168 BCE and sailed up the Tiber in splendor; the event is described in detail by both Livy (*History of Rome* 45.35.3) and Plutarch (*Life of Aemilius Paullus* 30.1–3). As Ennius died in 169 BCE, he could not have included this episode in his *Annals*.

l. 8. *the brothers Curii* (usually, *Curiatii*) fought the three *Horaces* (*Horatii*) as champions of their respective sides during the early war of Rome and Alba Longa (traditionally, in the mid-seventh century BCE); their battle is described by Livy in his *History of Rome* (1.24–5).

l. 9. *Fabius*: Quintus Fabius Maximus 'Cunctator' (the 'Delayer') helmed the Roman resistance to Hannibal in Italy during the Second Punic War (narrated by Ennius), and was awarded a triumph for his reconquest of Tarentum in 209 BCE; his delaying tactics were at first much maligned by the Romans, but he is now often thought of as a pioneer of guerrilla warfare. For Hannibal, see also *Intro* to Latin Lyric (p. 365), Hor. *Epod.* 16, l. 8 (p. 460) and n., Mart. 6.19, l. 7 (p. 545) and n.

l. 10. *Cannae*: A village in Apulia where Hannibal dealt the Roman army one if its most crushing defeats in 216 BCE. The 'gods who heard us praying' are the Lares – see n. on Tib. 1.10, ll. 15–29 (p. 416) – who are, however, nowhere else credited with saving Rome from Hannibal.

l. 12. *cackling geese*: From Cannae we have gone back in time 170 years, to the Gauls' invasion of Rome probably in 387 BCE, when geese foiled a nighttime assault on the Capitoline Hill by waking the garrison with their squawking (Livy, *History of Rome* 5.47; Plutarch, *Life of Camillus* 26–7).

l. 13. *Phoebus . . . his laurel tree*: Cf. n. on Call. *Hy.* 2, l. 1 (p. 269).

ll. 15–24. *'What's this cascade to you? . . .'*: Compare Apollo's speech to Propertius here with that in Call. *Aet.* 1.1, ll. 23–8 (p. 258); the 'novel road' (l. 26) evokes the 'unworn path' at l. 28 of Callimachus' poem. '[T]alent's boat' (l. 22) shares a metaphor with Dante, *Purgatorio* 1, l. 2: *la navicella del mio ingegno* ('the little bark of my genius').

l. 25. *ivory pick*: The plectrum, used by citharodes to pick the strings of the lyre (cf. *Intro* to the Classical Period, p. 189).

l. 27. *a green cave*: A rusticated grotto, of a type popular for decorating fountains, garden pavilions and so forth.

ll. 29–31. *the Muses' holy objects* ... : Implements and accoutrements appropriate to a mystery religion; since these belong to the Muses, they evoke different poetic genres.

l. 30. *Pan's reed pipes* (see n. on Vi. *Ecl.* 2, l. 36, p. 401) and the *Silenus made of clay* both suggest pastoral poetry. Silenus, a drunk old man on a donkey, is a habitual member of Dionysus' entourage. Sometimes he is a minor deity who, like Proteus (the shapeshifting Old Man of the Sea), will prophesy to anyone able to capture him, as in Vi. *Ecl.* 6; at others, he is a type, like the satyrs and maenads, and there are said to be multiple Sileni.

l. 31. *Venus' doves*: The birds were sacred to the goddess. Propertius calls them 'my flock' because they evoke love poetry.

ll. 33–6. *the nine Muses* may not yet be as thoroughly differentiated by genre as in later ages, but they still suggest different types of poetic activity: 'the Bacchic ivy' (l. 35) evokes tragedy; the one who 'composes and sings her songs' (ll. 35–6) is probably making hymns; the one plaiting rose-wreaths (l. 36) is likely to be associated with lyric/sympotic poetry.

l. 38. *Calliope* means 'beautiful-voiced' but was often said to mean 'beautiful-faced', an easy confusion in Greek.

433–4. ll. 39–50. *'You'll be content* ...': Calliope now explicitly redirects Propertius from Ennian epic back to love elegy.

434. ll. 43–4. *German lines* ... *Marius's signs*: Gaius Marius was a major figure in Roman politics from his first consulship in 107 BCE until his death in 86. One of his greatest victories involved the defeat of the German tribes the Cimbri and Teutones in 102–101 BCE (cf. Prop. 2.1, l. 24, p. 427, and n.). As part of his military reforms, Marius is credited with having fixed the eagle as the legionary ensign, eliminating the other standards of wolf, man-headed ox, horse and boar, which, in addition to it, were previously in use (Elder Pliny, *Natural History* 10.16).

l. 45. *Swabian dead*: The Swabians (Suebi) were a German tribe defeated by Julius Caesar in 58 BCE, and then again by the proconsul Gaius Carrinas in 29.

ll. 47–50. *You'll sing wreathed lovers* ... : This description of the proper subject matter and uses of love elegy strongly echoes Horace's account of lyric in *Odes* 1.6, ll. 17–20 (p. 466).

l. 52. *Philitas*: Philitas of Cos, an Alexandrian elegist, older than Callimachus and often mentioned along with him; little of his work survives (cf. nn. on Call. *Aet.* 1.1, ll. 9–10, p. 258, and *Hy.* 2, l. 110, p. 272). He may or may not be the Philetas of Samos whose two epigrams are given on pp. 301–2.

3.5. Like Cher, this unusual poem looks forward to 'life after love'. It seems to be an expansion of Phil. 17 and 18 (p. 337), though it also bears a strong resemblance to the end of Vi. *Geo.* 2: 'Happy the man,' says Virgil, 'who can fathom the causes of things'(l. 490). The poetry of this period being what it is, we suspect generic implications, i.e., that when Propertius is done with love elegy, he will turn to a more intellectual or didactic kind of poetry; such a suspicion may be borne out by Propertius' aetiologically focused fourth book of elegies.

l. 6. *bronzes Corinth's flames annealed*: When the Roman general Lucius Mummius torched Corinth in 146 BCE (cf. Ant. Si. 59, p. 323, Crin. 37, p. 343, and *Intro* to Latin Lyric, p. 367), the bronzes melted in the flames, making an alloy later much collected.

ll. 7–10. *Prometheus . . .* : One story holds that, after Prometheus created man, his work was criticized by Momus, the god of blame, on the grounds that he should have made the heart visible so good men could be distinguished from bad. Prometheus' name means 'Forethought', and that of his brother, 'Epimetheus', 'Afterthought'. Here both Prometheus and his creation are faulted for their likeness to Epimetheus.

l. 16. *Jugurtha sails by Marius' side*: Gaius Marius (see Prop. 3.3, ll. 43–4, p. 434, and n.) first came to prominence in the war against the Numidian king Jugurtha, which he brought to a successful end in 106 BCE. Propertius' sentiment, drawing an equivalence between a Roman hero and his defeated enemy, is shockingly unpatriotic. For a Greek equivalent, see Theaetetus 3 (p. 318) and n.

ll. 17–18. *Irus*: The beggar of Hom. *Od.* 18. *Croesus*: The Lydian king, proverbial for wealth. Line 18 echoes Solon's injunction to Croesus, in Hdt. *Hist.* 1.32, to call no man happy until he is dead; see also Sol. 13 (p. 71) and n. Ovid also pairs Irus and Croesus, at *Tri.* 3.7, l. 42 (p. 515).

ll. 19–20. *I'm glad I worshiped Helicon . . .* : Propertius expresses the opposite sentiment to Callimachus at *Ia.* 3, ll. 37–8 (p. 263).

435. l. 29. *Eurus*: The east wind.

l. 33. *Pindus*: A mountain range in central and northern Greece; like the rest of the country, earthquake-prone.

l. 35. *the Herdsman* (or *Plowman*) is Boötes (cf. Ant. Thess. 96, p. 346, and Ov. *Tri.* 1.4, l. 2, p. 512), also paired with the Pleiades at *Anacreontea* 4 (p. 358); his *plow and cattle* are the Big Dipper.

l. 36. *Pleiads*: For more on the Pleiades' astronomical behavior, see Alcm. 1, ll. 60–63 (p. 33) and n.

l. 40. *if Tisiphone's tresses hiss . . .* : See Tib. 1.3, l. 69 (p. 415) and n.

l. 41. *Alcmaeon* killed his mother and was chased by the Furies (cf. *Anacreontea* 9, ll. 5–7, p. 360, and n.). The blind *Phineus*, who played host to the Argonauts, was prevented by a plague of Harpies from eating his lavish banquets. Propertius, unusually, imagines both men continuing to suffer in death what they had endured in life.

l. 42. *wheels, rocks, pools*: References to the punishments of Ixion, Sisyphus and Tantalus respectively. For Ixion and Tantalus, see Tib. 1.3, ll. 73–4 and 77–8 (p. 415) and nn. Sisyphus, a son of the wind god Aeolus, is condemned to roll a rock up a hill forever; when it gets near the top, it rolls back down again and he must start over. We do not learn of Sisyphus' crime until the sixth-century BCE writer Pherecydes of Syros. Apparently Sisyphus informed the river god Asopus that Zeus was the one who had abducted Asopus' daughter Aegina; Zeus tried to have Sisyphus killed, but he managed to outwit death not once but twice. When he finally did die for good, Hades assigned him to the rock so he wouldn't be able to escape again. For more on Asopus and the abduction, see Cor. 654b (p. 201) and n. – though the version of the myth involving Sisyphus may have referred to the Peloponnesian Asopus, rather than the Boeotian one Corinna writes about (see n. on Alc. Mess. 14, l. 5, p. 318).

l. 43. *three-jawed Cerberus*: See n. on Bacch. 5, l. 75 (p. 173); and cf. Tib. 1.3, ll. 71–2 (p. 415), Prop. 4.7, l. 53 (p. 441), and Hor. *Odes* 2.13, ll. 33–4 (p. 475) and n.

l. 44. *Tityus*: See Tib. 1.3, ll. 75–6 (p. 415) and n.

l. 48. *Crassus' standards*: See Hor. *Odes* 3.5, ll. 5–8 (p. 481), and n. on 2.13, l. 17 (p. 475); the return of the standards was arranged in 20 BCE, presumably after Propertius' book was published.

3.8. Propertius, much as he also does in Prop. 2.15 (p. 429), states his unequivocal enthusiasm for the 'wars of Venus' abjured by Tibullus at 1.10, ll. 53–66 (p. 417), but waged by Ovid with similar commitment: see *Am.* 1.5 (p. 494).

436. l. 14. *maenad*: A Bacchant, or ecstatic worshiper of Dionysus. Cf. Prop. 1.3, ll. 5-6 (p. 425).

l. 18. *if she torments, she loves you – that is sure*: Cf. Cat. 83 (p. 395).

ll. 29-32. *Paris ... launched the real attack*: Propertius is thinking of the scene in Hom. *Il.* 3 (ll. 380-450) in which Paris, after losing his duel with Menelaus, is whisked by Aphrodite back to his bedroom and Helen.

l. 37. *snare around my bed*: Alludes to the story in Hom. *Od.* 8 (ll. 266-366), where Hephaestus/Vulcan uses a magic net of his own fabrication to catch his wife Aphrodite/Venus in bed with Ares/Mars. Cf. Ov. *Am.* 1.9, l. 42 (p. 496).

3.10. A *genethliacon*, or birthday poem; see n. on Sulp. 3.11 (p. 449). Propertius' example is unique in that he is far more concerned with his own day than with Cynthia's.

437. l. 8. *Niobe*: See Call. *Hy.* 2, ll. 22-4 (p. 269) and n.

l. 9. *halcyons*: See n. on Theoc. *Id.* 7, l. 64 (p. 291).

l. 10. *Itys' mother*: Procne, the nightingale; see Cat. 65, ll. 13-14 (p. 391) and n.

ll. 11-12. *Now, love ... get up*: Compare Robert Herrick, 'Corinna's Going a Maying', ll. 15-16:

> Rise; and put on your Foliage, and be seene
> To come forth, like the Spring-time, fresh and greene ...

ll. 19-20. *When you have blessed the altar ...*: It was customary for a woman to make offerings to a guardian deity (her *Juno*) on her birthday; see n. on Sulp. 3.11 (p. 449), and cf. Sulp. 3.12 (p. 450). Altars were 'crowned' with sacred greenery.

l. 27. *we'll toss the dice ...*: The scene is no doubt similar to that at 4.8, ll. 45-6 (p. 444), and presumably Propertius and Cynthia are competing, like Propertius and his two sidepieces there, for the Venus throw (see n. *ad loc.*). For dice at drinking parties, cf. also Hor. *Odes* 1.4, l. 18 (p. 465), and 2.7, ll. 25-6 (p. 473).

l. 28. *the boy's wings*: i.e., those of Cupid.

3.16. This charming poem illustrates as well as any the subjectivity of Propertius' method. He has received a late-night summons from Cynthia, but we never learn the reason for it, nor whether he ultimately decides to go; instead, we get a Hamlet-like internal monologue as he weighs his options and soon finds his mind wandering.

l. 2. *Tibur*: Modern Tivoli, about twenty miles northeast of Rome.

l. 3. *where the cliff sides whitely flash*: The limestone mountains around Tibur appear white when compared with the volcanic Alban Hills.

l. 4. *the Anio's falls*: The Anio (modern Aniene) has its origin in the Apennines and meets the Tiber in the north of Rome.

437–8.   ll. 5–6. *What should I do? . . . criminals*: Twenty miles was a substantial trip, and night travel was dangerous, since there was no police force to keep the roads clear of bandits.

438.   ll. 11–20. *A lover is holy . . .* : The sentiment is a commonplace of love poetry; see Sulp. 3.10, ll. 15–16 (p. 448), and Hor. *Odes* 1.22 (p. 468) and n.

l. 12. *Sciron's den*: Sciron was one of the monstrous highwaymen killed by Theseus; he terrorized the road between Athens and Megara, on the Isthmus of Corinth, where he would force travelers to wash his feet, then kick them into the sea.

l. 14. *Scythia's wilderness*: Cf. Ov. *Tri.* 3.2, l. 2 (p. 513) and n.

ll. 19–20. *thinned blood*: This relates to the elegiac stereotype of the lover as skinny, pale, feeble and borderline anemic; see also Ov. *Am.* 2.10, l. 23 (p. 505) and n.

l. 30. *no roadside memorial for me*: Burials were not allowed inside city limits, and so massive cemeteries grew up along the roads leading out of them. But Propertius' preference for an out-of-the-way tomb probably has something to do with Callimachus' desire to 'tread / an unworn path' at *Aet.* 1.1, ll. 27–8 (p. 258). Cynthia, at Prop. 4.7, l. 4 (p. 440), ends up with just the kind of burial the poet hopes to avoid.

3.24. This poem and the next, in which Propertius bids Cynthia (and the genre of love elegy) an angry farewell, conclude Bk. 3; in some manuscripts, they are presented as a single poem, but the most reliable one presents them as two.

438–9.   ll. 9–16. *No family friends could rid me of the notion . . .* : These eight lines seem to report the realization of the hopes set forth in ll. 25–30 of Propertius' first poem (1.1, p. 423), which they strongly echo.

439.   l. 10. *no witches cleanse me*: For witches in elegy, see n. on Prop. 1.1, l. 23 (p. 423).

l. 13. *My meat was cooked in Venus's bronze pot*: There is probably a reference here to Phalaris, the semi-legendary tyrant of Acragas (modern Agrigrento) on Sicily, who is said to have roasted victims alive in the belly of a hollow bronze bull sculpted for the purpose.

l. 15. *my ship – all wreathed*: It was customary to garland a ship upon safe arrival in port; cf. the 'garlanded prow' of Prop. 4.7, l. 61 (p. 441).

3.25. See n. on 3.24, above.

l. 8. *our well-matched team stumbled*: The metaphor is of two beasts in harness.

ll. 11–16. *may years you've painted catch and gall you . . .* : Hor. *Odes* 1.25 offers a similar (and similarly unpleasant) curse on an aging woman.

440. 4.7. In his fourth book, Propertius mostly holds to his intention (strongly implied in Prop. 3.24–5, above, as well as, perhaps, 3.5, p. 434) to abandon love elegy and Cynthia for a more intellectual poetry closer to Callimachus' *Aetia* (pp. 258–61). In this and the next poem, however, he returns to his old flame, in the key first of tragedy, then of farce. Here, Cynthia's ghost, fresh from the pyre, comes back to haunt Propertius' dreams. It seems she has been recently buried, and that Propertius is grieving and alone. Whatever the case, it is striking and affecting that, in a genre ostensibly devoted to the beloved, but usually, in reality, entirely focused on the poet's experience and filtered through his subjectivity, Cynthia should be given such a lengthy and indignant swan-song, so full of incidents and details not otherwise compassed in the elegies. (Striking, but not the only example in Propertius: see n. on Prop. 1.3, ll. 35–46, p. 426.) The poem, though itself influenced by the dream of Callimachus (see n. on Prop. 3.3, p. 432), and clearly borrowing from Achilles' dream of Patroclus in Hom. *Il.* 23 (ll. 65–107), has proven deeply influential, not only for ancient poets (cf. Ov. *Ex Pont.* 3.3, p. 522), but also latterly (cf. Goethe, 'Euphrosyne' and Robert Lowell, 'The Ghost').

l. 4. *a jostling highway's end*: Cynthia has apparently found burial in the kind of down-market, high-traffic spot Propertius abjured for his own tomb; cf. Prop. 3.16, l. 30 (p. 438).

l. 15. *Have you forgotten all those trysts*: Similarly Patroclus' ghost, when it appears to Achilles at Hom. *Il.* 23 (ll. 69–71), accuses him of forgetfulness, and demands immediate burial.

l. 17. *the Subura's streets*: The Subura was a low-rent area and a sort of red-light district near where Propertius lived on the fashionable Esquiline

Hill (cf. Prop. 4.8, ll. 1–2, p. 442). Perhaps Cynthia is to be imagined escaping from a brothel, or a lover's house.

440–41. ll. 24–35. *no one mourned my day of dying* ... : At the start of the poem, Propertius seems fresh from the funeral, and rather broken up, throwing some suspicion on Cynthia's claims in these lines.

l. 26. No *watcher shook his rattle by my bed*: It may have been ritual practice to set a guard with a split-reed rattle over the dying, to ward off evil – witches were notorious corpse-snatchers.

l. 30. *past town*: See n. on Prop. 3.16, l. 30 (p. 438).

441. l. 35. *wash my bones with wine*: See n. on Tib. 1.3, l. 7 (p. 413).

ll. 36–9. *Burn Lygdamus!* ... *Or Nomas!* ... : Cynthia accuses Propertius' slaves Lygdamus and Nomas of poisoning her and insists that they be interrogated under torture, with heated metal plates and bricks. (Slaves were not allowed to testify in court *except* under torture.) Lygdamus returns to serve the drinks again in Prop. 4.8, ll. 37–8 (p. 443), below.

ll. 40–47. *The whore who worked in alleyways* ... : Chloris – who, according to Cynthia, is Propertius' new love – goes unnamed until l. 74. Apparently, in Cynthia's absence, she tyrannizes her former faithful servants Petale (Greek for 'leaf') and Lalage (Greek for 'chatterbox', 'babbler'; cf. Hor. *Odes* 1.22, l. 10, p. 468, and n.).

l. 43. *extra spinning-wool*: Tufts of wool to be spun into yarn on a spindle. Slaves received a certain weight (*pensum*) of wool to spin daily.

l. 53. *Cerberus*: See Bacch. 5, ll. 75 (p. 173) and n., and cf. Tib. 1.3, ll. 71–2 (p. 415); Prop. 3.5, l. 43 (p. 435), and Hor. *Odes* 2.13, ll. 33–4 (p. 475). Martial may have been thinking of this line at 5.34, l. 4 (p. 544).

l. 59. *like Clytemnestra and Pasiphaë*: For Clytemnestra, scc Stes. 85, l. 4 (p. 92) and n. While her husband Agamemnon was fighting at Troy, Clytemnestra took up with his cousin Aegisthus, who helped her plan and carry out his murder upon his return. For Pasiphaë, see n. on Prop. 2.28, l. 52 (p. 432).

ll. 61–2. *garlanded prow*: See Prop. 3.24, l. 15 (p. 439) and n. *Elysium*: See Tib. 1.3, l. 58 (p. 414) and n.

l. 63. *bronze cymbals*: Used in the worship of the goddess Cybele, for whom see Anon. 935 (p. 237) and n.

l. 65. *Andromeda*: See n. on Prop. 1.3, ll. 3–4 (p. 425). *Hypermestra*: The one righteous daughter of Danaus; see n. on Tib. 1.3, ll. 79–80 (p. 415).

442. l. 77. *Latris, named for service*: 'Latris' means 'handmaid' in Greek.

l. 81. *ivy*: Associated with poetry and Bacchus.

ll. 84–5. *Tibur's . . . grace of Hercules*: Hercules founded Tibur (modern Tivoli) and had a large shrine there; that ivory kept its color better in Tibur (perhaps due to the sulfur springs) was attributed to his influence. For more on Tibur and its environs, see Prop. 3.16, ll. 1–4 (p. 437) and nn.

ll. 86–7. *inscribe a column . . .* : We should probably imagine Cynthia's epitaph either carved on a small funeral stele, or as a graffito on the public road.

l. 90. *Righteous Gate*: A moralizing variation on Virgil's gates of true and false dreams (horn and ivory, respectively) in *Aen.* 6 (ll. 893–6).

l. 95. *Charon*: The ferryman of the Styx.

4.8. From pathos to bathos, the two Cynthia poems in Bk. 4 give us a less idealized, and perhaps more realistic (or at least more Alexandrian), picture of Propertius' life with Cynthia. Here the account of cult practice at Lanuvium (modern Lanuvio, about twenty miles southeast of Rome; the remains of a temple to Juno Sospita – 'Juno Our Salvation' – are still visible there today) stands as a figure for the showdown with Cynthia: just as the virgin in the ritual is tested (l. 7), so, too, Propertius is tested by Cynthia, and passes, barely; the scene ends with ritual purification and – a sign that the ritual is over – sex. It is a touchingly wistful way to end Propertius' account of his tempestuous affair.

l. 1. *Esquiline*: Propertius lived on Rome's Esquiline Hill (as he tells us in Prop. 3.23, l. 24), near to the rather less salubrious Subura (cf. Prop. 4.7, l. 17, p. 440, and n.).

l. 2. The *New Gardens* were a burial ground recently incorporated into the city by Augustus and converted by Maecenas into a park. The 'crowd' is an exaggeration; it refers merely to the girls Phyllis and Teia at ll. 61–62, below.

442–3. ll. 3–15. *There's an old serpent . . .* : The interest shown in cult practices here is extremely Alexandrian, and of a piece with the rest of Bk. 4 of the *Elegies* (cf. also Ov. *Am.* 2.13, ll. 8–21, p. 506, and nn.), while the farcical realism to come recalls the 'mimes' of Herodas and Theocritus (see *Intro* to Theocritus, p. 282).

443. l. 17. *'for Juno's rites' – really, for Venus's*: Suspicion that women like Cynthia would use religious ceremonies as an excuse for assignations was

common enough, though we should hardly take Propertius' suspicions for fact.

l. 18. *Appian Way*: An ancient and important road running southeast from Rome to Brundisium (modern Brindisi).

ll. 19–20. In the manuscript, an irrelevant couplet is inserted between these two lines, which I have omitted.

ll. 23–5. *that smooth-chinned fop* . . . : Propertius refers to a stereotypical dandy type familiar to his audience, hinting that he will squander his patrimony and then be forced to become a gladiator.

l. 29: *Diana on the Aventine*: The oldest temple to the virgin goddess in Rome was on the Aventine Hill, a somewhat rackety neighborhood. Cf. Mart. 12.18, l. 3 (p. 553).

l. 31. *Tarpeia's bluff*: The Tarpeian Rock was an eighty-foot cliff on the south side of the Capitoline Hill, from the top of which traitors, murderers and criminal slaves were shoved to their deaths. It was named for Tarpeia, a Vestal Virgin who let the enemy Sabines into the citadel in exchange for gold – at least, this is Livy's version (*History of Rome*, 1.11); but Propertius, who treats her story at length in his poem 4.4, has her fall in love with the Sabine commander, Titus Tatius. Tarpeia did not prosper in either account – to punish her treachery, the Sabines, who had benefited from it, crushed her to death with their shields.

ll. 37–8. It's hard to square the present anecdote with the accusation, made by Cynthia's ghost at 4.7, ll. 36–7 (p. 441), that Propertius' servant Lygdamus had poisoned her.

l. 39. *Miletus . . . Byblis*: These performers are named for a father–daughter pair whose story is told by Ovid (*Met.* 9, ll. 446–665). Byblis, the daughter, falls in love with her brother Caunus, who flees from her and her illicit desires; she is driven to madness, and eventually turns into a spring (for which see Theoc. *Id.* 7, l. 123, p. 292, and n.).

443–4. ll. 43–4. *The lamps . . . were flickering . . . a table overturned*: Bad omens.

444.   ll. 45–6. *I tried for Venus . . . but the damned Dogs kept leaping up*: Four four-sided dice were rolled; a 'Venus' (the highest throw) meant all four sides came up different; 'the Dog', a roll of four ones, was the worst throw. 'Originally the die was a four-legged piece of metal: landing on its legs (the commoner result) it was imagined to be a quadruped, on its back a supine woman' (Propertius, *Elegies*, ed. Goold, p. 367). Propertius and Cynthia play a similar game at Prop. 3.10, l. 27 (p. 437), and Horace alludes to the Venus throw at *Odes* 2.7, l. 25 (p. 473).

l. 48. *Lanuvium*: See poem note.

l. 53. *My wine cup drops*: Propertius evokes Odysseus' attack on the suitors at Hom. *Od.* 22, ll. 15–18: 'But Odysseus took aim, and smote him with an arrow in the throat, and clean out through the tender neck passed the point; he sank to one side, and the cup fell from his hand as he was smitten . . .' (trans. A. T. Murray).

ll. 75–8. *the flirty Forum's . . . open to your leer*: Cynthia lists popular places to pick up women, also catalogued by Ovid in *Art of Love* 1, ll. 67–100. The Forum at this time was still used for gladiatorial games on holidays. *Pompey's walks* (or 'colonnade': mentioned, perhaps, in Mart. 5.20, l. 10, p. 543) consisted of a large rectangular portico with a garden in the center containing four rows of plane trees and decorated with statuary; Pompey built it in 55 BCE behind his theater, as a place where spectators could shelter from the rain, and it quickly became a beloved and highly trafficked park. Next door, in the theater, Propertius in cruising mode would be craning his *neck to the . . . top tier* since, by decree of Augustus, women were only allowed to sit in the upper rows, while equestrians (like Propertius) had their designated seating in the first fourteen rows (behind only the senators, who claimed the first row); cf. Ov. *Am.* 2.7, ll. 3–4 (p. 502).

Sulpicia

447. *The 'Sulpicia Elegist'. 3.8. l. 1. It's your month, Mars*: That is, the first day (Kalends) of March, the date of the festival of the Matronalia, when Roman women would sacrifice to Juno, Goddess of Childbirth (Juno Lucina) at her temple on the Esquiline Hill, and then prepare a feast for their female slaves, who were let off work. Roman husbands also prayed for their wives' welfare and gave them gifts; lovers did the same for their beloveds.

l. 3. *Venus won't mind*: i.e., despite her being Mars's wife.

ll. 13–14. *Vertumnus . . .* : An Etruscan deity, adopted in Rome as a god of the seasons, mentioned here for his well-known shapeshifting abilities ('a thousand looks'). Ovid relates his romancing of the Latin goddess of fruitfulness, Pomona, at *Met.* 14, ll. 623–771. Here the author installs Vertumnus on Olympus ('the Deathless Mount') with the assimilated Greek deities.

l. 16. *softest wools which Tyre has dyed twice*: Tyrian or Phoenician ('Punic') purple was an immensely expensive dye made from the murex sea snail, plentiful in the waters along the Phoenician coast (now south-ern Syria and Lebanon); the cost is down to the enormous quantities of snails required – about 30,000 for an ounce of dye. Such purples were a byword for luxury.

l. 22. *tortoise shell*: As recounted in the *Homeric Hymn to Hermes*, early lyres used tortoise shells for sound boxes.

448. 3.9. It is worth considering the possibility that the first person of this poem (as well as of 3.11, below) should be taken at face value, and the authorship attributed to Sulpicia herself; of course, it is even possible that she wrote the third-person elegies, too (see *Poet Intro*, p. 446).

l. 1. *Boar, spare that boy*: In pleading directly with the boar which the 'boy', i.e., Cerinthus (see *Poet Intro*, p. 446), has presumably set out to hunt, the speaker implicitly likens Cerinthus to Adonis, Venus' famously beautiful beloved, who was killed by a boar, and herself to Venus; cf. Call. *Ia.* 3, ll. 36-7 (p. 263) and n. Boar-hunting was a popular aristocratic pastime; nets were used to close off the edges of clearings, and boars were dislodged from their lairs by packs of hounds and driven into them. For other mentions of hunting in elegy, cf., e.g., Prop. 1.1, ll. 9-16 (p. 423), and Gallus' lament at Vi. *Ecl.* 10, ll. 63-71 (pp. 409-10).

l. 19. *love, be celibate*: The poet's fears here echo those of Propertius at 1.11 (p. 426) and 4.8 (p. 442), where he imagines that Cynthia is leaving town to cheat on him.

3.10. The motif of a beloved's illness is common in Latin elegy; cf. Prop. 2.28 (p. 431) and Ov. *Am.* 2.13 (p. 506). If the author of this poem is not Sulpicia herself (see *Poet Intro*, p. 446), he may have learned of her illness from Sulp. 3.17 (p. 452), below; this poem certainly feels more conven-tional than that one.

449. l. 15. *god won't harm a lover*: The invulnerability of the lover is a con-ventional motif, given its most memorable expression at Hor. *Odes* 1.22, ll. 1-8 (p. 468), but also taken up at Prop. 3.16, ll. 11-20 (p. 438), and in Tib. 1.2, ll. 29-35 (quoted in the n. on Hor. 1.22). That it contradicts the equally conventional worry for the ailing beloved plainly did not bother the poet, and need not bother us.

3.11. Like Sulp. 3.12, 3.14 and 3.15, below, this poem belongs to the genre of the birthday poem (*genethliacon*), a specifically Roman genre (or sub-genre) arising from native Italic ritual practice. (Of the non-Latin birthday poems in this anthology, Call. *Ia.* 12, p. 266, celebrates a newborn's *hebdoma*, the one-week anniversary of its birth, and Crin. 3, p. 340, is a Greek poem written under Roman hegemony.)

Pious Romans paid ritual observances annually on the anniversary of their own births and, often, those of family members, friends, patrons and lovers. These rituals involved dressing in white robes and making offerings at the family hearth to the *genius* or *Juno* of the one being celebrated. Every male had a *genius* and every woman a *Juno*. These spirits entered the world at a person's birth and left it at their death; sometimes they were depicted as guardian angels, sometimes as an indwelling essence, and sometimes they were simply treated as synonymous with the individual. When people celebrated their own birthday, they would offer gifts of wine, flowers, incense and barley cakes at the hearth to the *genius* or *Juno*, as well as prayers for continued well-being and promises of a repeat performance next year; the offerings were bloodless, because, in the words of the third-century CE writer Censorinus, 'When on their birthdays our ancestors made yearly offerings to the *genius*, they restrained their hands from slaughter and blood, so as not to deprive others of life on the day when they themselves received it' (*Birthday Book* 2). Relatives and friends would often attend birthday celebrations, sometimes making offerings and prayers themselves, and giving birthday presents; of course, there would also be a celebratory feast.

Much of our knowledge of the details of these ceremonies derives from poems like those included here; see also Prop. 3.10 (p. 436), Ov. *Tri.* 3.13 (p. 515) and Mart. 12.60 (p. 555).

l. 1. *I rate*: On the identity of 'I', see. n. on Sulp. 3.9 (p. 448).

l. 8. *birth-spirit*: i.e., Cerinthus' *genius* (see poem note, above).

l. 9. *bless his plea*: Or 'bless my plea'. The Latin is unclear whether Sulpicia or Cerinthus is making the offering in question; either is possible.

450. *3.12.* See n. on Sulp. 3.11, above.

l. 1. *Dear Juno*: Sulpicia is shown praying to her personal *Juno* or birth-spirit, like Cynthia at Prop. 3.10, ll. 19–20 (p. 437).

l. 2. *the lettered lass*: *Docta puella*, here with specific reference to Sulpicia's poetic skills; cf. Prop. 1.2, ll. 27–30 (p. 424) and n.

l. 11. *may no vigilant doorman blockade them*: This prayer belongs in miniature to the typical elegiac motif of the 'excluded lover' and/or the *paraclausithyron*, the 'locked-door song': see n. on Call. *Ep.* 8 (p. 277).

451-2. *Sulpicia.* 3.13–18. In these epigrams, generally assumed to have been written by Sulpicia herself (see *Poet Intro*, p. 446), the poet speaks with immediacy, from within the events described; the 'Sulpicia elegist' of Sulp. 3.8–12, by contrast, is more performative and less personal. In many ways, the epigrams, in good Catullan fashion, reverse the gendered conventions of elegy: so 3.13 is an unabashed proclamation of female desire; 3.14 and 3.15 reject Tibullan pastoral nostalgia in favor of the city (an attitude Sulpicia shares with Ovid), and also grouse a bit against the powerful Messalla (Sulpicia's uncle and guardian); 3.16 introduces a rift with Cerinthus, offering a scathingly sarcastic rejoinder to the typical elegiac lover, who expects, but does not reciprocate, his beloved's fidelity; 3.17, from within the topos of the ailing female beloved, doubts the sincerity of her lover's concern; and, finally, 3.18, apologizing for a show of feigned frigidity, resolves the rift. In all of this one feels a bracing contrast between the youthful passion and petulance of the speaker and the sophistication and complexity of her phrasing. This, one can't help thinking, is how a true *docta puella* ('learned girl'; see n. on 3.12, l. 2, above) would sound.

451. *3.14.* See nn. on Sulp. 3.11 and 3.13–18, above.

l. 7. *Uncle Messalla*: See *Poet Intro* (p. 446).

452. *3.15.* See nn. on Sulp. 3.11 and 3.13–18, above.

3.16. l. 6. *Servius's daughter*: Sulpicia's father shared his name and his career as a jurist with his own father, Servius Sulpicius Rufus (see *Poet Intro*, p. 446) – although not the older man's senatorial rank.

l. 9. *a base bed*: A haughty reference to the low class of Cerinthus' new 'friend', but also perhaps a pointed reminder to Cerinthus himself that he is of lower status than Sulpicia the equestrian's daughter is.

3.17. See n. on Sulp. 3.13–18, above, and cf. Sulp. 3.10 (p. 448) and n.

Horace

454. *Poet Introduction.* '*remember Horace as if he were me*': Suetonius, *Life of Horace.*

'*rough*' . . . '*muddy*' . . . '*two hundred lines an hour!*': Hor. *Satires* 1.4, ll. 6–13. The terms of Horace's criticism clearly echo Callimachus' description of the Euphrates in *Hy.* 2, ll. 108–9 (p. 272), and see n. *ad loc.*

456. *Epodes.* 2. The reader encountering this poem for the first time ought to read it through before consulting any notes – the last four lines administer

a jolt. Yet the poem's exaggerated idealization of the rustic landscape may have tipped off contemporary readers that something was up: while Virgil, in his *Eclogues* and *Georgics* (to both of which Horace extensively alludes), does not ignore the havoc wrought in the countryside in the 40s and 30s BCE by general brigandage and land confiscations (here, see especially *Ecl.* 9, p. 405, and n.), Horace's speaker seems blissfully unaware. Yet Horace himself is such a committed lover of country living, and the praise of it in this poem so fulsome and apparently sincere, it's hard to know what he was after with his rhapsodically hypocritical loan-shark Alfius (whose name derives from a Greek verb meaning 'to bring in' or 'to fetch'). Perhaps the poem satirizes the facile urban escapism revisited in *Epod.* 16 (ll. 41–62, p. 461) – which, however, the poet offers not as satire, but in despair. In this poem, the unresolved tension between irony and sincerity, mockery and self-mockery, speaker and poet, satire and lyric, helps explain, at least in part, its lasting impact and appeal. For similar themes, see much of Tibullus (especially 1.10, p. 415, and n.), Martial's provincial epigrams (especially 10.92, p. 551) and Horace's *Odes*, throughout (pp. 462–91).

l. 1. *Happy the man* . . . : Probably the most famous *makarismos* (proclamation of blessedness, from Greek *makar*, 'blessed') in classical poetry. For further examples, see n. on Alcm. 1, ll. 37–9 (p. 32).

ll. 7–8. *proud vestibules of wealth and power*: Country dwellers do not make the rounds of the *salutatio* (morning call), at which clients attended on their patrons. Martial particularly hated this custom; cf. especially Mart. 12.18, ll. 1–6 (p. 553), but also 4.8, ll. 1–2 (p. 541) and poem note, 5.20, ll. 5–7 (p. 543), and 7.39 (p. 546).

456–7. ll. 9–36. *Either he to the poplar trellises* . . . : This passage proceeds seasonally, with activities generally performed in spring (ll. 9–16: viticulture, cattle-rearing, grafting, beekeeping and sheep-shearing) giving way to the autumn grape-harvest (ll. 17–22). If, as seems likely, the idyllic relaxations of ll. 23–8 belong to summer rather than autumn, perhaps the jumble reflects Alfius' confused ideas about the country. He is not wrong, though, that hunting (ll. 29–36) is a winter activity, though its purpose is less to procure 'tasty meat' (l. 36) than to protect the herds from predators.

457. ll. 17–18. *Autumn uplifts his head* . . . : The image belongs to a long lineage of personifications of autumn. Cf. Keats, 'To Autumn', where the season is depicted with a 'laden head' (l. 20) and 'hair soft-lifted by the winnowing wind' (l. 15).

ll. 21–2. *Priapus . . . and you, Silvanus*: Deities of the garden and of forests and villas, respectively, here receiving first fruits from the grape harvest – the sort of unpretentious sacrifices characteristic of country religion. Priapus is an ithyphallic country deity of Eastern provenance (his cult originated in Lampsacus, in northwestern Asia Minor), often associated with Pan. Under Roman influence he took over functions previously assigned to Pan. Wooden statues of Priapus were placed in orchards and gardens to deter thieves (the enormous erect phallus was the threat). The role of 'border-guardian' assigned to Silvanus more usually belongs to Terminus (see n. on ll. 59–60, below).

ll. 31–2. *with packs of dogs . . . waiting nets*: For more on boar-hunting, see Sulp. 3.9 (p. 448) and nn.

ll. 33–4. *stretches the wider mesh . . . to trick the thrush*: Fowlers used two canes or poles with a net stretched between them; the birds were coaxed into the net by means of bait, and then the poles were collapsed, trapping the bird. That Alfius envisions a 'wider mesh' for catching thrush than boars may further suggest his ignorance of the country. Mnasalces 8 (p. 315) is an epitaph for a fowler, who however used birdlime instead of nets.

l. 41. *Sabine sort*: Sabine women were known, at least traditionally, as hard workers of old-fashioned virtue. Cf. Ov. *Am.* 2.4, l. 15 (p. 499). Sabinum (modern Sabina) was a region northeast of Rome in the central Apennines. There is a ruined villa often identified with Horace's own Sabine farm (cf. Hor. *Odes* 1.22, p. 468, and 3.13, p. 484) near Licenza.

l. 43. *holy hearth*: The hearth is called holy because the household gods, the Lares and Penates, were kept and worshiped there: see n. on Tib. 1.10, ll. 15–29 (p. 416). Cf. also Hor. *Odes* 3.23 (p. 485), below.

458. l. 49. *Lucrine oysters, parrotfish and turbot*: All luxurious delicacies. The oysters come from the Lucrine Lake (modern Lago di Lucrino), near the resort town of Baiae (cf. Prop. 1.11, p. 426). Parrotfish were native to the eastern Mediterranean, while the best turbot came from the Adriatic coast near Ravenna.

ll. 53–4. *guinea fowl . . . grouse*: Expensive and exotic delicacies from North Africa and Asia Minor, respectively; cf. Stat. *Silv.* 2.4, ll. 27–30 (p. 529).

ll. 59–60. *the Feast of Boundaries . . .* : The Terminalia, held on 23 February in honor of Terminus, the god of boundaries, identified with the boundary stones that marked one piece of property from another. Livestock was too valuable to kill and eat, so country folk ate meat only on special occasions – or when a wolf got hold of a poor lamb or kid. Plutarch claims that the meat of animals killed by wolves is especially tender (*Table-Talk* 2.9); he is echoed by Mart. 10.48, l. 17 (p. 550).

l. 65. *homegrown servants*: Servants born within a household were considered more reliable than those brought in from outside, and a better index of wealth. The picture resembles Tibullus' rustic festival at 2.1, ll. 22–5 (p. 418).

13. This poem, among the most admired and ode-like of Horace's epodes, has its closest parallel in *Odes* 1.9 (p. 466); both go back to a common ancestor in Alc. 338 (p. 65), but this one also owes something to Alc. 38a (p. 57). For Horace, the poem's stormy backdrop is clearly as much political as meteorological, though it is difficult to pinpoint where exactly we are in the period between the battles of Philippi (42 BCE) and Actium (31 BCE) – see n. on l. 15, below.

l. 3. *The Boreal wind out of Thrace*: See n. on Ant. Si. 26, l. 2 (p. 322).

l. 6. *while there's still spring in our knees*: Horace may have been thinking of Theog. ll. 983–8 (p. 84); if so, the possible context there, of looming war with Persia, surely contributes to the present atmosphere of dread. My pun on 'spring' tries to catch the flavor of Horace's synesthetic 'while our knees are still green' (*dum virent genua*).

l. 9. *bottled in my birth year*: 65 BCE. Roman wine jars were labeled with the year of the vintage, by way of the name of the consul(s) of that year; Lucius Manlius Torquatus was consul in 65.

459. l. 13. *Persian scents . . . Arcadian lyre*: 'Persian' signals both the perfume's origin in Syria, once part of the Persian Empire, and the association of Persian kings with extravagant luxury (cf. Hor. *Odes* 1.38, l. 2, p. 471, 3.1, l. 44, p. 479, and 3.9, l. 4, p. 482). The lyre is called 'Arcadian' because it was invented by the infant Mercury on Mount Cyllene in Arcadia (as recounted in the *Homeric Hymn to Hermes*). Horace had a special attachment to Mercury, under whose star he was born and who, he claims in *Odes* 2.7, l. 13 (p. 473), saved his life at Philippi.

l. 15. *disquiets of late so dire*: It is most satisfying to imagine that this scene takes place in the run-up to the Battle of Philippi in 42 BCE, when Horace fought on Marcus Junius Brutus' losing side against Octavian and Mark Antony. If so, this poem would be a dispatch from the time remembered with retrospective fondness in *Odes* 2.7, ll. 5–8 (p. 472), when Horace and his friend 'so often defeated the dull slow day / with wine'. However, there is nothing to stop the poem from being set as late as the climactic Battle of Actium in 31 BCE (see n. on Hor. *Odes* 1.37, l. 13, p. 470).

l. 16. *the good Centaur*: Chiron, who helped deliver Achilles and brought him up (cf. Alc. 42, ll. 9–14, p. 58, Ov. *Ex Pont.* 3.3, l. 45, p. 523). Pindar refers several times to Chiron's tutelage of Achilles, for example, in *Nemean* 3 and *Py.* 6.

l. 17. *Thetis' dauntless seed*: The Nereid Thetis was Achilles' mother, later called 'ocean-blue' (l. 23) because of her association with the sea (cf. also Sim. *El.* 11, ll. 19–20, p. 128). If the poem is connected with the Battle of Philippi (in Macedonia), then the emphasis on sea-crossing is particularly appropriate.

ll. 20–21. *Scamander's watershed ... Simois*: The two rivers of Troy; their mention here may look forward to Hom. *Il.* 21, when Achilles fills both rivers with corpses, and is saved in his battle against the river god Scamander by Hephaestus/Vulcan, who boils his waters.

l. 22. *and no escape for you*: One common thread of Achilles' legend involves his decision to go to Troy, when he chose a short, glorious life over a long, inglorious one (cf. Hom. *Il.* 9, ll. 410–16). Chiron (whom Pindar also endows with prophetic powers – see n. on Call. *Ia.* 12, l. 51, p. 267) here underlines the fatalism of Achilles' choice, in a way many readers of this poem have found ill-suited to the context: if Horace is trying to cheer his comrades up on the eve of a great battle (see n. on l. 15, above), shouldn't he have chosen a more inspiring story? However, on the other side one might note that the *carpe diem* theme is always balanced by the inevitability of death (see Hor. *Odes* 1.11, p. 467, and nn.); and, at any rate, the real point may be the contrast between Achilles' lot and the present situation: 'If Achilles, who knew he was going to die, could drink his cares away,' Horace seems to be saying, 'then we, too, *a fortiori*, should be able to do so; after all, unlike him, we may survive.'

14. Horace offers a jokey excuse to his patron Maecenas, who has been pestering him to finish his *Epodes*.

ll. 1–4. *limp lethargy of limb ... goblets of Lethe's sleep*: An English novice doctor called John Keats found these lines oddly compelling:

> My heart aches, and a drowsy numbness pains
> My sense, as though of hemlock I had drunk,
> Or emptied some dull opiate to the drains
> One minute past, and Lethe-wards had sunk ...

In 1929, Edmund Blunden thought it likely enough 'that Keats had his Horace in his hand that day when he sat under the plum tree at Lawn Bank, and presently began to write' his 'Ode to a Nightingale' ('Keats and His Predecessors', *London Mercury* 20, 1929, p. 292). In Horace's epode, there is a conspiracy of lethargy and Lethe, torpor and forgetfulness, which both impedes and provokes poetry – one thinks of Keats's celebration, in his letters and his verse, of 'delicious diligent Indolence'. Horace's poem is a variation on the *recusatio* (refusal poem; see n. on Prop. 2.1, p. 427). Cat. 65 (p. 390) plays on similar themes, offering the orator Hortalus an apology for his belatedness, though Catullus' excuse is more substantial than Horace's: his brother's death prevents him from writing. In that poem, Catullus compares his own music to the nightingale's (see ll. 12–13, and n.). Keats also lost a brother at an early age; he, too, was obsessed with the great poem he should have been writing (he thought of his odes as minor works). At any rate, in transmuting these two little Latin poems (Horace's is just a squib) into one of the great lyrics of English literature, Keats used the Romans exactly as they used each other and the Greeks before them – including, of course, Callimachus, whose reference to the poems of his dead friend Heraclitus as 'nightingales' (*Ep.* 34, l. 5, p. 280) may also have been fluttering somewhere in Keats's brain that April of 1819.

l. 9. *Bathyllus*: The name given by tradition to Anacreon's *eromenos* (boy love) at Polycrates' court, on Samos; cf. *Anacreontea* 10, l. 10 (p. 360) – Horace would have considered Anacreon the author of the *Anacreontea* (see *Intro* to the *Anacreontea*, pp. 357–8). Tacitus also tells us that Maecenas was in love at one point in his life with a freedman actor called Bathyllus (*Annals* 1.54).

l. 14. *the torch of Troy*: Helen; some ancient authors record an etymology that connects her name to the Greek *helene*, 'torch'.

460. 16. This epode, a harangue to fellow citizens to flee to the Blessed Isles, escaping a Rome decimated by civil war (see *Intro* to Latin Lyric, pp. 368–9), seems clearly modeled, in its public stance, on Archaic elegy and iambus; we may think in particular of Archilochus' *Achaeans at Mysia* (p. 7), in which the poet argues that 'Flight can be right / at times' (ll. 3–4), and which, like Horace's poem, has its own ironies and ambiguities. This one is an early epode, perhaps the earliest, and certainly composed before 38 BCE, the year Horace was introduced to his patron and Octavian's confidant, Maecenas: the poet takes a dimmer view of *both* sides in the conflict than he could have done under Maecenas' wing. The penultimate

poem of Horace's book, *Epod.* 16 makes a fascinating pair with *Epod.* 2, both extended fantasies of escape into an idealized rustic world. The two poems also contrast: *Epod.* 16 has immediate political motivation, and – though the message is hardly straightforward – the speaker is clearly Horace himself. It demands to be read not only against the broad back-drop of Golden Age utopias (cf. Tib. 1.3, ll. 35–48, p. 415, and n.; Hor. *Epod.* 2, p. 456, and n.; Hor. *Odes* 1.3, p. 463, and n.), but with and against one especially famous example in particular: Vi. *Ecl.* 4 (p. 403). While Virgil predicts the dawn of a new Golden Age of peace and pros-perity, Horace advises wholesale flight to an imaginary place where Golden Age-like conditions obtain. Though we can't say for sure which poem was written first, it seems more likely that Horace's bleaker vision answers the visionary optimism of the Eclogue, rather than the other way around. Interpretation of the epode is a vexed question, but Horace cannot have intended his 'modest proposal' to be taken at face value. Instead, its very implausibility surely reflects the despair and *aporia* of the civil-war years in Rome, perhaps even Horace's own helplessness after fighting on the losing side at the Battle of Philippi in 42, when he was routed and put to flight (cf. *Odes* 2.7, ll. 9–12, p. 473 and nn.); it may also reflect the need, in those years, for a poetry which could itself be a place to flee to.

l. 1. *Civil war is wasting a second generation*: This is commonly read in two ways: either the two generations are (A) that of Sulla and Marius (83–81 BCE), followed by (B) that of Caesar and Pompey, Antony and Octavian (49–30); or (A) that of Caesar and Pompey, followed by (B) that of their children Octavian and Sextus Pompeius (44–35). (Cf. *Intro* to Latin Lyric, pp. 368–9; Prop. 2.1, ll. 27–35, p. 428, and n.; and Hor. *Odes* 2.7, ll. 1–16, pp. 472–3, and nn.) The second option seems preferable, as Horace himself was involved in the Battle of Philippi, which concluded the previous generation's war.

ll. 3–8. Horace catalogues Rome's bitterest enemies. Cf. the lists in Prop. 3.3, ll. 7–12 (p. 433), and Mart. 6.19, ll. 6–9 (p. 545).

l. 3. *Marsians*: An Italic people, known for their ferocity, who joined with other Roman allies against Rome in the so-called 'Social War' of 91–88 BCE, a sort of proto-civil war in which Sulla rose to prominence (see *Intro* to Latin Lyric, p. 368). Their chief city was Marruvium (modern San Benedetto dei Marsi), on the shores of the Fucine Lake (Lago Fucino, drained 1878) in western Abruzzo, sixty miles or so east of Rome.

l. 4. *Lars Porsena's fell Etruscan band*: The legendary Etruscan king of Clusium (modern Chiusi, in Tuscany), who tried to reinstate Tarquin the Proud (Tarquinius Superbus) as king of Rome after the latter was deposed by Lucius Junius Brutus and the Republic founded, supposedly at the end of the sixth century BCE (cf. Livy, *History of Rome* 2.9–13).

l. 5. *our Capuan rivals*: Capua, the richest city of Campania, defected to Hannibal's side (see l. 8) during the Second Punic War; it had hoped to replace Rome as the preeminent city of Italy after the war.

Allobroges: A Gallic tribe dwelling just across the Alps, in the area between Vienna and Geneva. In general, Gauls were considered shifty and untrust-worthy, and their sack of Rome *c*.387 BCE (cf. Prop. 3.3, l. 12, p. 433, and n.) left a lasting impression on Roman consciousness. However, the Allo-broges in particular may be mentioned both for their role in the Catilinarian conspiracy of 63 BCE, when they informed on the Roman rebels who were seeking their allegiance, and for their own rebellions before and after, in 66 and 61 (not to mention a third uprising in 38), hence 'traitors in league with traitors'.

l. 6. *Spartacus*: A gladiator who led a slave revolt in Campania in 73–71 BCE, defeating Roman armies several times before he was finally stopped by the future triumvir Marcus Licinius Crassus (see n. on Hor. *Odes* 2.13, l. 17, p. 475).

l. 7. *Germany's blue-eyed invaders*: The Cimbri and Teutones, nomadic tribes from Jutland, who defeated two Roman armies before they were driven off by Gaius Marius in 102–101 BCE. Cf. Prop. 2.1, l. 24 (p. 427), and 3.3, ll. 43–4 (p. 434) and n.

l. 8. *Hannibal*: The Carthaginian general (247–183/2 BCE) was Rome's greatest enemy who, in the Second Punic War (218–201 BCE), came clos-est to defeating them. See also *Intro* to Latin Lyric (p. 365), Prop. 3.3, ll. 9–11 (p. 433) and nn., and Mart. 6.19, l. 7 (p. 545) and n.

l. 9. *blood-cursed*: The curse accrued as a result of Rome's original sin, Romulus' murder of his brother Remus at the founding of the city, was adduced as an explanation for all manner of crises (cf. Vi. *Ecl.* 4, l. 16, p. 403, and n.).

l. 13. *Romulus' bones*: Entombed in the Forum behind the speaker's plat-form (*Rostra*), these were believed to have talismanic power to protect the city.

l. 18. *the Phocaeans*: Phocaea was an Ionian Greek city on the western coast of Turkey (modern Foça). Its inhabitants abandoned their city in

540 BCE, when Persia was poised to conquer it, and sailed first to Chios and then to Corsica; Herodotus tells the story at *Hist.* 1.163–6. Setting out, 'they pronounced a mighty curse on any of their own people who should linger behind the expedition to Corsica; besides this, they sank in the sea a bar of iron and swore never to come back to Phocaea until the bar should surface again' (*Hist.* 1.165, trans. Grene).

ll. 25–34. *But let us swear* . . . : The oath operates via the literary trope of *adynaton* (catalogue of impossibilities); see n. on Prop. 2.1, ll. 67–72 (p. 429).

l. 26. *when deep-sunk rocks* . . . : This first item in the list recalls the Phocaeans' oath (see n. on l. 18, above).

l. 27. The *Po* washing Mount *Matinus* involves two impossibilities: water flowing uphill, and a river of northern Italy transplanting itself to the south. Matinus' precise location is disputed, but it may have been near the modern hamlet of Matino on the heel of the Italian boot. W. H. Auden fans will think of 'As I Walked Out One Evening': 'I'll love you, dear, I'll love you / Till . . . the river jumps over the mountain . . .' (ll. 9–11).

l. 29. *the Apennine goes sprinting*: The Apennines are a landlocked mountain range in central Italy, and thus doubly unable to sprint into the ocean.

l. 32. *hawk commits adultery with dove*: A prodigy both because doves are mating outside their species, with their predators, and because they mated for life (cf. Cat. 68b, ll. 127–30, p. 398, and n.).

l. 33. *when trusting herds don't fear the lion's ranting*: A likely nod to Vi. *Ecl.* 4, l. 25 (p. 403): 'The lion will not menace fold or pen'. What for Virgil represents visionary ecstasy, prophetic of a new Golden Age, is for Horace a contrafactual impossibility.

l. 34. *sleeked goats in the breakers leap*: An echo of Archilochus' 'woodland creatures' that 'frisk with pleasure through the breakers' thunder' (Ar. 122, ll. 8–9, p. 10).

461. l. 39. *female remorse*: Horace's misogynistic phrasing echoes Ar. 13, l. 10 (p. 7): 'Put girlish grieving in the past.'

l. 42. *happy fields* . . . *rich isles*: In the Hellenistic period, the increasing tendency to rationalize old myths identified the Blessed Isles – in Homer, vaguely positioned at the world's edge (*Od.* 4, ll. 563–8) – with the Canary Islands off the Atlantic coast of Morocco. Plutarch describes these islands as the destination where the anti-Sullan guerrilla leader in Spain, Quintus Sertorius (*c.*120–72 BCE), hoped to retire from war and politics (*Life of Sertorius* 8–9.1); unfortunately, he was killed by his own army before he got the chance. Horace's largely negative conception of the Blessed Isles has much in common with Virgil's more positive vision of the new Golden Age in *Ecl.* 4 (p. 403). It is interesting to note, in conjunction with the poem's emphasis on oaths (ll. 35–8), that Pindar places 'all those who kept their oaths' in his own Blessed Isles (*Ol.* 2, ll. 65–8), while more than half of Herodotus' Phocaeans 'were seized with such homesickness and pity for their city and the places they knew that they proved false to their oath and sailed back to Phocaea' (*Hist.* 1.165, trans. Grene).

l. 57. *Argonauts*: The first sailors in the first ship, hence their 'arrogance'. The Blessed Isles are unsullied by contact with the outside world. (There is irony in the fact that in this particular iteration they may only be reached by ship: shipbuilding was typically listed among the innovations that mark the end of the Golden Age; cf. Tib. 1.3, ll. 35–40, p. 414, and n.) Again Horace nods to *Ecl.* 4 (ll. 40–42, p. 404), which foresees the second coming of the *Argo*, before all seafaring is to cease for good (ll. 44–6).

l. 58. *bloodstained Medea*: The *Argo*'s most infamous passenger, whose veil was soaked with the blood of her murdered brother Apsyrtus (Apollonius of Rhodes, *Argonautica* 4, ll. 471–4).

l. 59. *Phoenicians*: Proverbially enterprising sailors, especially in the southern and westerly directions. According to Herodotus (*Hist.* 4.42), the Egyptian Pharaoh Necho II (r. 610–595 BCE) sent a group of Phoenicians to circumnavigate Africa, which they did. They set sail from the Red Sea, then voyaged south and west around the Cape of Good Hope, when they had the 'the sun on their right hand' – a verisimilar detail Herodotus reports while claiming not to believe it – before they turned north and, after more than two years, entered the Mediterranean through the Pillars of Hercules. Another famous Carthaginian sailor, Hanno the Navigator, attempted a similar voyage *c.*480 BCE; he may have ventured as far south as Gabon on the West African coast. His journey is described in the *Periplus of Hanno*, translated from Punic into Greek in the fifth century BCE. Of course, if negative connotations are needed (to match the Argonauts, Medea and Ulysses' crew), Horace may also be making use of the Phoenicians' reputation for piracy and/or their kidnapping of Greek women, as in Hdt. *Hist.* 1.1.

l. 60. *Ulysses' toilsome crew*: In Latin literature, Ulysses was an archetype of bad leadership, cruelty and double-dealing, rather than the
multifaceted and 'complicated man' (trans. Wilson) that is Homer's
Odysseus. No doubt Horace is obliquely entering Hellenistic disputes
about the geography of Odysseus' wanderings ('never appeared').

ll. 61–2. *Here no plagues* ... : Many believe this couplet to have been
misplaced by a copyist, as it would fit better above, among the list of the
island's natural advantages. From Homer on, Orion's dog, Sirius, has heralded the most dangerously hot part of summer; see n. on Prop. 2.28, l. 3
(p. 431), and cf. Hor. *Odes* 3.13, ll. 9–10.

ll. 63–5. ... *polluted gold with bronze* ... *toughened with iron*: Horace
compresses the usual four metallic 'races' of man to three, eliminating the
silver. At ll. 9–10, above, Horace accounted himself and his audience
among the 'guilty, blood-cursed' generation, but by ll. 63–4 they must be
pure in spirit to enter the Blessed Isles – another irony which obviously
undermines Horace's 'plan'.

l. 66. *my vatic sight*: A reference to the *vates*, the ancient Italic poet-
priest, and an example of the tendency to Romanize Greek models – in
this case, that role of which Callimachus is the most prominent Greek
exemplar, the *aoidos*. On the latter see n. on Call. *Hy.* 2 (p. 269); for its
Romanized form, cf. also Tib. 2.1, ll. 18–25 (p. 418) and n., and Hor.
Odes 1.1, l. 35 (p. 463) and n., 2.20, l. 2 (p. 477) and n., and 3.1, ll. 1–4
(p. 478) and n.

462–7. *Odes. 1.1–1.9.* The first nine odes of Horace's first book are conventionally referred to as the 'Parade Odes' because they parade in succession
most of the meters and themes of the next three books; Horace does not
repeat a stanzaic form until 1.10.

462. *1.1.* The initial poem in a book of ancient poetry accomplished several
functions. It sets out a program for the book (cf. n. on Prop. 2.1, p. 427),
which is something like characterizing the poet's brand: positioning him,
explicitly or implicitly, among available genres and styles, selecting key
models or predecessors, establishing a tone or attitude, etc. It often also
dedicated the book to a friend or patron – as, e.g., in Cat. 1 (p. 376), Prop.
1.1 (p. 423) and 2.1 (p. 427), and Mart. 1.1 (p. 535; though Martial also
prefixed a dedication to his book in prose). In this case, Horace dedicates
not only this first book or poem but the whole of *Odes* Bks. 1–3, which he
published as a unit in 23 BCE, to his patron Maecenas, whose wealth and
generosity toward poets have made his name a byword for literary patronage. This poem's meter (stichic lesser asclepiads: see *Note on Meters*,

p. xxxv) will be reprised in the last poem of Bk. 3 (3.30, p. 487) – which, together with *Odes* 2.20 (p. 477) and this poem, are the only three odes in which Horace speaks directly about his own achievement.

462–3. ll. 3–34. *some people ... Me, though ...* : This is classical poetry's most famous example of what scholars have labeled a *priamel* (German for 'preamble'): a particular kind of list, which ticks off various options as 'foils' ('some people ...', l. 3; 'One man ...', l. 7; 'another ...', l. 9; etc.) to focus our attention on the final element or 'cap' ('Me, though ...', ll. 29–34). Pindar is particularly known for this device (cf. *Ol.* 1, ll. 1–8, pp. 135–6; but also *Ol.* 2, ll. 1–8, imitated by Horace at *Odes* 1.12; and probably also the opening of Pi. fr. 29, p. 155); but other examples may be found at Sap. 16, ll. 1–4 (p. 42), Theog. ll. 783–8 (p. 84), Ascl. 1 (p. 304), and Shakespeare's Sonnet 91 ('Some glory in their birth, some in their skill ...').

Given the Pindaric associations of the priamel, it is interesting that the first 'type' of person Horace lists (ll. 3–6) conjures the epinician poet as much as the athletes he celebrates – issuing, no doubt, a coded challenge to Pindar himself, as the consensus chief of the canonical Nine Lyric Poets (see *Note on Lyric*, p. xiii). There are, indeed, nine figures glossed in the poem – the athlete (ll. 3–6), the politician (ll. 7–8), the trader (ll. 9–10), the farmer and the sailor (ll. 11–14), the merchant (ll. 15–18), the loafer (ll. 19–22), the soldier (ll. 23–5), the hunter (ll. 25–8) – and it is tempting to read them in terms of literary genre: besides epinician, we have rhetoric (the politician), georgic (the farmer), pastoral (the loafer), epic (the soldier) and cynegetic (the hunter), though it is difficult to see how some of the figures (viz., the trader, the sailor and the merchant) fit into this scheme. Be that as it may, with the politician the types become markedly Roman, suggesting that, though Horace may be starting from Greek prototypes, he is impressing on them his own definitively Italian stamp.

ll. 7–8. *One man ...* : Despite their Romanness, these lines, following as they do the implicit reference to Pindar at ll. 3–6, might make us think of Solon, also a relevant model for this poem (cf. Sol. 13, ll. 37–70, p. 71), whose Roman counterpart might be Cicero.

herdlings of Romulus: Horace is characteristically disdainful of the urban *plebs*.

triple rungs of office: i.e., the *cursus honorum*, the 'ladder of magistracies' aspirants to high office climbed, from quaestor to praetor to consul.

l. 15. *wild siroccos wrestling*: Horace commonly employs this agonistic metaphor for the unpredictable and violent crosswinds so salient to daily life on the Mediterranean, especially in winter; cf. Hor. *Odes* 1.3, ll. 12–16 (p. 463) and 1.9, l. 10 (p. 467). For sudden winds as a motif in poetry, see Ar. 212 (p. 15) and n.

l. 16. *the Sea of Icarus*: See n. on *Odes* 1.3, l. 34 (p. 464), below.

l. 19. *a swig of the old Massic*: An apparently well-regarded wine, though lacking the reverence attached to the best (such as Falernian and Caecuban; cf. Tib. 2.1, l. 28, p. 418, and n., and Hor. *Odes* 2.14, l. 26, p. 477, and n., respectively). Massic came from the Massic Hills (now Monte Massico) between Latium and Campania. Geographically, it is hard to distinguish from Falernian, farmed on the slopes of Mount Falernus in the same general area, but Massic is said to have been a bit harsher. Horace drinks Massic again with his friend Pompey at *Odes* 2.7, l. 22 (p. 473), while Martial (3.26, l. 4, p. 540) describes a rich man who drinks both Massic and Caecuban, the former perhaps as an everyday wine.

l. 28. *Marsian boar*: For Marsian, cf. Hor. *Epod.* 16, l. 3 (p. 460) and n. Sulpicia's boyfriend Cerinthus (see Sulp. 3.9, p. 448, and n. at l. 1) may have been on Horace's mind here, or someone like him. The genre of 'cynegetics' (hunting literature) had Xenophon as its chief exponent.

l. 31. *nymphs and dancing satyrs*: These traditional companions of Bacchus/Dionysus suggest Horace's lyrical interest in wine and associate him in particular with Archilochus (pp. 5–15) and Alcaeus (pp. 55–67).

463. l. 33. *Euterpe, and Polyhymnia*: Muses, eventually associated with lyric poetry, and sacred poetry and hymns, respectively.

l. 35. *slip this Roman songster among the lyric Greeks*: i.e., as Maecenas might slip a new volume into his library among the old Greek favorites already there. Horace is telling us that he wishes to be not a lyric *poet* ('poet', like 'lyric', is originally a Greek word) but a lyric *vates*, a specifically Italic poet-priest figure, counterpart of the Greek *aoidos*, which is what Homer was and somewhat closer to a 'bard' than a 'poet': see n. on Call. *Hy.* 2, p. 269; cf. also Tib. 2.1, ll. 18–25 (p. 418) and n., Hor. *Epod.* 16, l. 66 (p. 461) and n., Hor. *Odes* 2.20, l. 2 (p. 477) and n., and Hor. *Odes* 3.1, ll. 1–4 (p. 478) and n. Thus *lyricus vates* (or 'songster') suggests that Horace is positioning himself as a Greco-Italian hybrid: specifically, the Roman inheritor of Alcaeus (pp. 55–67). As a program poem, the ode bespeaks Horace's high ambition, tempered by the mild amusement and philosophical distance with which he regards all actors in the human comedy – himself included, as the goofy last line makes clear.

1.3. The first of two (or three) odes addressed by Horace to his friend – though perhaps not a close one – the poet Virgil (pp. 398–410); cf. Hor. *Odes* 1.24 (p. 469) and n. Virgil is undertaking a sea voyage to Greece; as a send-off, Horace offers him this *propempticon* ('bon voyage' poem; cf. nn. on Sap. 5, p. 41, and Theoc. *Id.* 7, l. 58, p. 291). After the first eight lines, however, he leaves Virgil behind to rail at the audacity of the first seafarer in particular and of mankind in general. The ode (which is written in an asclepiadean quatrain – see *Note on Meters*, p. xl) has an associative movement reminiscent of Tibullus, and indeed the motif was one of Tibullus' favorites; cf. Tib. 1.3, ll. 37–40 (p. 414). Yet the rather negative tone might remind us of Hor. *Epod.* 16 (p. 460), and from there of the vision in Vi. *Ecl.* 4 of a Golden Age when all sailing would end (ll. 45–6, p. 404): perhaps Virgil's prophecy is undermined by his own voyage. Then again, starting in the early 20s, Virgil was widely known to be embarking on another major journey, the composition of the *Aeneid* – the sort of epic task Horace rejects in more than one *recusatio* (refusal poem; see n. on Prop. 2.1, p. 427, and Hor. *Odes* 1.6, p. 466, and n.). Is the second half of this poem intended as a criticism, whether literary or personal, of Virgil? Or is Horace rather expressing admiration (as in ll. 9–20, which seem more impressed than critical), while sounding, by way of contrast with Virgil's Homeric undertaking, a landlocked Hesiodic note of his own ('as for me, / I've never sailed the broad sea on a ship, / Not yet, except to Euboea, my one trip': *W&D*, ll. 650–51, trans. Stallings)? Whatever the case, Prometheus' gift of fire (ll. 27–30) was the beginning of the end of the Golden Age, preceding the invention of ship, sword and plow; Horace may be associating that god's 'frauds' with the 'ancient crime' or 'fault' of Vi. *Ecl.* 4, ll. 16–36 (p. 404).

l. 1. *May Venus guide you*: Venus was associated with the sea both because of her ocean birth (as referred to in Mel. 6, p. 327) and because her temples were often situated on coasts, the better to service sailors. Cf. Nos. 4 (p. 311) and n., and this epigram from Mnasalces (*AP* 9.333):

> Stand on that coast the waves slap, that we might see
> the shrine of Oceanic Aphrodite,
> and the fresh spring those poplars shade, whence throngs
> of halcyons sip the spates and lift their songs.

Other examples of the goddess's saltwater association may be found at (perhaps) Sap. 26 (p. 43), Mel. 6 (p. 327), Phil. 15 (p. 336) and Hor. *Odes* 1.5, ll. 12–16 (p. 465).

l. 2. *Helen's starry brothers*: The Dioscuri (Sons of Zeus), Castor and Pollux, patrons of mariners; cf. Alc. 34 (p. 57) and Cat. 68b, l. 64 (p. 392). They are called 'starry' because of their association with St. Elmo's fire (see n. at Alc. 34, l. 12).

l. 3. *Aeolus*: God of the winds.

ll. 3–4. *one wind ... from Calabria*: The west-northwest wind, called Iapyx, which carried ships from Brundisium (modern Brindisi) to Greece.

l. 8. *half my soul*: Horace is quoting an epigram of Callimachus (*AP* 12.73), who claims that half his soul has been kidnapped by a handsome boy. Cf. also Milton, *Paradise Lost* 5, l. 95 ('Best image of myself and dearer half'), and Dizzie Gillespie on Charlie Parker ('He's the other half of my heartbeat').

ll. 9–10. *He had a heart encased in oak ...*: Lines imitated by Herrick in 'A Country Life' (ll. 75–6):

> A heart thrice wall'd with Oke, and Brasse, that man
> Had, first, durst plow the Ocean.

l. 10. *whoever first set sail*: The first ship is usually said to have been the *Argo* (cf. n. on Hor. *Epod.* 16, l. 57, p. 461). The malediction (*schetliasmos*, opposite of *makarismos* – for which, see n. on Alcm. 1, ll. 37–9, p. 32) of the inventor of seafaring owes something to the beginning of Euripides' *Medea* (cf. also Call. *Ep.* 45, p. 280), as well as the association of sailing with the end of the Golden Age (see Tib. 1.3, ll. 35–40, p. 414, and n.).

ll. 12–16. *the hurtling southern gale ...*: Cf. Hor. *Odes* 1.1, l. 15 (p. 462) and n., and 1.9, l. 10 (p. 467); and, more generally, see n. on Ar. 212 (p. 15).

l. 14. *rainy stars*: The Hyades, whose morning setting in November and evening rising in October brought rain; their name is perhaps derived from Greek *hyein*, 'to rain'. Cf. Alcm. 1 (p. 32) and nn.

l. 20. *Acroceraunia*: A mountain ridge in northern Epirus (southern Albania) near the sea, and an important landmark for sailors from Brundisium (modern Brindisi); so named for frequent thunderstorms (Greek *akros*, 'height', + *keraunos*, 'thunderbolt').

464. ll. 27–31. *Reckless Prometheus's frauds ...* : Besides stealing fire, Prometheus (see n. on Prop. 2.1, ll. 67–72, p. 429) taught mankind to deceive the gods in their sacrifices by covering the bones with fat and keeping the

good meat for themselves (Hes. *Th.*, ll. 535–616). Their punishment was Pandora, who opened her jar and let all the world's evils out (Hes. *W&D*, ll. 100–104).

l. 34. *Daedalus soared*: Escaping from the Cretan king Minos and the palace of Cnossus, where he had built the Labyrinth, Daedalus fashioned wings of wax for himself and his son Icarus – whose wings, however, melted when he flew too close to the sun, causing him to plummet from the sky and drown. The Icarian Sea (the part of the Aegean between the Cyclades and Asia Minor) was named after him. Cf. Vi. *Aen.* 6, l. 14, Ov. *Met.* 8, ll. 183–235, and W. H. Auden, 'Musée des Beaux Arts'.

l. 36. *toiling Hercules sacked Acheron*: Required to capture Cerberus for his Twelfth Labor. Cf. Bacch. 5, ll. 69–77 (p. 173) and n.

l. 38. *though our bravado would assail the sky*: The line recalls Daedalus' flight from the previous stanza, but also suggests the Giants' assault on Olympus, which in turn provokes the thunderous conclusion.

1.4. The first of three odes on spring, two of which (4.7, p. 489, and this one) are among Horace's most beloved. (The third, 4.12, isn't too bad either.) The literary backdrop for all three poems is the Hellenistic spring epigram (in this volume, see Leo. Tar. 85, p. 309, and Ant. Si. 41, p. 322), a genre also adapted in Cat. 46 (p. 386). Hellenistic epigrams follow a tripartite pattern: the first part offers a weather report (calm seas, mild breezes, birds returning); the second exhorts sailors to set sail; and in the third the speaker reveals himself as a statue of Priapus in the harbor. Catullus turns the genre to personal ends, but Horace enlarges and universalizes, transforming a simple slice-of-life poem into an illustration of its brevity and preciousness. As often with Horace, there may also have been a precedent from Alcaeus – a fragment (Alc. 286) which has barely survived seems a likely candidate – and/or Archilochus, from whom the meter is derived (cf. Ar. 188, 191, p. 12).

464–5. ll. 1–12. *Spring . . . seal our vows*: Varying and expanding on his Hellenistic models (see poem note), Horace makes his first stanza report on the weather, while the next two add Greek mythological and Italian religious dimensions.

l. 1. *west winds warm the earth*: The west wind – *Zephyr* in Greek, *Favonius* in Latin – is said by Latin authors (with great precision) to begin blowing between 5 and 8 February.

ll. 5–8. *Venus leads out her chorus line . . .*: With her husband Vulcan, the god of fire and the forge, occupied in manufacturing thunderbolts – in high demand in spring and autumn (cf. Lucretius, *De Rerum Natura* 6, ll. 357–78) – Venus and her cohort are at leisure to play. Compare Hor. *Odes* 4.7, ll. 6–7 (p. 489), as well as Theog. ll. 1275–8 (p. 85). Vulcan's forge, typically associated with volcanic activity, is variously placed on Mount Etna in Sicily, on Lemnos or in the Lipari islands; cf. Theoc. *Id.* 2, l. 137 (p. 290).

465. l. 11. *Faunus*: The archaic Italian deity, a particular favorite of Horace's (cf. *Odes* 3.18, p. 485, and n. on l. 1), credited at one point (*Odes* 2.17) with having saved him from a tree which nearly killed him (*Odes* 2.13, ll. 1–4, p. 474). Generally, however, his role in Italian cult had, by Horace's day, been usurped by Pan. Here Faunus takes the place occupied by Priapus in Hellenistic epigrams (see poem note, above). It is interesting that sacrifice to Faunus in his temple in Rome on Tiber Island (13 February) directly preceded the festival of the dead called the Parentalia: 'Therefore, when death knocks so unexpectedly at the door, the sequence of thought may be justified by the facts of the Roman calendar' (R. G. M. Nisbet and Margaret Hubbard, *A Commentary on Horace: Odes, Book I*, pp. 66–7).

l. 13. *Pale Death*: This turn, from the renewal of spring to the inevitability of death (complete with propulsive alliteration in the Latin – *pallida mors pulsat pede*), is made not by the usual logical steps (as in *Odes* 4.7, p. 489), but via a sudden leap, or jolt. This has bothered readers like Walter Savage Landor, who wrote in a marginal note that '*pallida mors* [Pale Death] has nothing to do with the above'. Today we are less likely to furrow our brows at the inexplicit logic. Still, no reader schooled in Hellenistic epigram could fail to be shocked when Pale Death comes knocking in this poem – almost as shocked, perhaps, as we would be if we heard the rap on our own door. (In Latin, he knocks with his foot, recalling perhaps the epiphany of Apollo at Call. *Hy.* 2, l. 3, p. 269.)

l. 14. *Sestius*: Lucius Sestius Quirinalis Albinianus was the son of the senator Publius Sestius defended by Cicero's speech *Pro Sestio*. Like Horace, he joined the tyrannicide Marcus Junius Brutus' army in 44 BCE and was later pardoned by Octavian; he served as consul in 23, the year Bks. 1–3 of the *Odes* were published, and thus receives an appropriately prominent place in the collection (behind only Maecenas, Augustus and Virgil, the addressees of the first three odes). He was a very rich man ('blessed' in Latin meaning both 'fortunate' and 'wealthy'); it is possible, as David West argues in his commentaries on Horace, that the references to merchant shipping (l. 2) and forges (ll. 7–8) may have evoked Sestius' large commercial operations at Cosa (modern Ansedonia) on the Etruscan coast.

l. 15. *but life's brief compass* . . . : This line in Latin (*vitae summa brevis spem nos vetat inchoare longam*) gave Ernest Dowson the title of one of his two famous Horace-inspired poems; for the other, see *Odes* 4.1, ll. 3–4 (p. 487).

l. 16. *the Ghosts*: The *Di Manes*, chthonic deities often believed to be the shades of deceased ancestors.

l. 18. *Lord of Wine*: The symposiarch, or *rex bibendi* – president of the symposium, appointed by a dice-throw. Cf. Hor. *Odes* 1.9, l. 6 (p. 467) and n., and 2.7, ll. 25–6 (p. 473) and n.

l. 19. *Lycidas*: Prior to Horace, the name is used in pastoral, by Bion, Theocritus (*Id.* 7, p. 291) and Virgil (*Ecl.* 9, (p. 405)). The pederastic element here is more appropriate to the Greek symposium Horace evokes, though the practice was common enough in Rome. In this volume, cf. Ligurinus in Hor. *Odes* 4.1 (p. 487), and perhaps Thaliarchus in *Odes* 1.9 (p. 466) and the anonymous boy in Hor. *Odes* 1.38 (p. 471); as well as Juventius in Cat. 48 (p. 386) and 99 (p. 396); Marathus in Tibullus (see *Intro* to Tibullus, pp. 411–12); and Mart. 2.62 (p. 539), 4.48 (p. 541), 9.21 (p. 548), 11.63 (p. 551) and 12.18 ll. 25–30 (p. 553).

1.5, The Pyrrha Ode. This ode integrates a number of Hellenistic subgenres and motifs with a seamlessness and metaphorical panache that make it much more than the sum of its parts; even its stanzaic form – which employs the third asclepiadean meter – is expressive of Hellenistic inspiration (see *Note on Meters*, p. xxxix). The imaginative starting point is the 'ocean of love' motif (cf. Theog. ll. 1375–6, p. 85, and n.) and the comparison, at least as old as Semonides of Amorgos, of women to the sea (cf. Semonides of Amorgos 7, ll. 27–42, p. 18). On this metaphorical base, Horace fashions a poem in the temple-dedication genre (cf. all of *Greek Anthology* Bk. 6, but especially, say, Philetas 1, p. 301, Ascl. 6, p. 305, and Nos. 5, p. 311; Ov. *Am.* 1.11, p. 496, offers another Roman example). Rescued from shipwreck in love's waters, Horace imagines himself making a thanks-offering to the god(s) who saved him. In doing so, he bids 'farewell to love', as at Phil. 18 and 21 (pp. 337, 338), though not, as in Philodemus, to all love, only to Pyrrha, and perhaps also to the kind of moody, tempestuous affair she represents. The gesture has both poetic and philosophical implications: Pyrrha may stand for the fickle mistresses of love elegy, and hence for that (highly unphilosophical) genre also, as well as for the kinds of passionate entanglements which, as Epicurus taught, put serenity of mind (*ataraxia*) out of reach. (Horace was himself an armchair Epicurean.) And yet, the poem betrays a certain ambivalence, in its jealous fascination with Pyrrha's new lover, its admiration of her in her good moods, and its elaborate performance of renunciation; one senses that, should Pyrrha experience a change of heart (like the one in *Odes* 3.9, p. 482), the poet might renounce his renunciation, too.

Beyond all that, the ode is a classic test case for the impossibility of translation. Milton's famous attempt ('What slender youth bedew'd with liquid odours . . .') has been lauded and deplored ad infinitum. It is true that Horace's word order, especially in the final stanza, is inimitable in English (or almost any language); nowhere is the effect praised by Nietzsche as 'Roman' and '*noble par excellence*', of a 'mosaic of words in which every word . . . pours forth its power to left and right and over the whole' (*Twilight of the Idols*, 'What I Owe to the Ancients', section 1, trans. Hollingdale), more in evidence, or more visually effective, than in the offering which Horace makes here – as I believe, to both Neptune and Venus (see n. on l. 15, below).

l. 1. *Pyrrha*: 'Fiery Ginger', a common name for a courtesan, as in Argent. 15 and 16 (p. 349). The name's masculine form, 'Pyrrhus', happens to be the Latin name given to Achilles' excessively violent son, Neoptolemus, and might import further negative connotations. Virgil gives the definitive portrait of Pyrrhus' evil for Latin readers in *Aen.* 2 (ll. 469–553).

l. 9. *golden through and through*: *Aurea* (golden) in Latin refers to Pyrrha's character, of course, but also to her 'fiery' or strawberry-blond locks (implied by the name), as well as to the brilliant glittering of the Mediterranean on a sunny day. There is a pun with *aura*, wind (l. 10), which shifts as rapidly and deceptively as her moods.

l. 15. *the great Power of Ocean*: Commentators debate whether Horace's dedication is to Neptune or to Venus; whether, that is, it pertains more to the vehicle (the shipwreck) or its tenor (the failed affair). The manuscript points to the former, but Venus is also a goddess of the ocean (see n. on Hor. *Odes* 1.3, l. 1, p. 463, above); my own suspicion is that Horace left things ambiguous because he wanted it both ways.

466. 1.6. l. 1. *Your bard will be Varius*: The 'you' (named in l. 5) is Augustus' right-hand man, Marcus Vipsanius Agrippa, the most distinguished general and statesman of the age apart from the *princeps* (Augustus) himself. The poem is a classic Augustan *recusatio* (refusal poem) in the Callimachean mold (see n. on Prop. 2.1, p. 427); its meter, too (the second asclepiadean – see *Note on Meters*, p. xxxix), is one which evokes a certain Hellenistic air. Horace, politely declining to write a grand, serious

poem in Agrippa's praise, instead suggests Lucius Varius Rufus, an important epic poet ('a swan, like Homer, grand') and a friend of his and Virgil's; indeed, he was one of the posthumous editors of Virgil's *Aeneid*. (Varius and Virgil introduced Horace to Maecenas.) Varius was the author of a famous tragedy, *Thyestes*, which Quintilian deemed as good as any written in Greek, and which Augustus paid Varius a million sesterces to put on at the Actian Games in 29 BCE. It is at any rate clear why the *recusatio* format appealed to Horace: it allowed him to compliment his friend Varius and also Agrippa while still maintaining a certain degree of artistic independence from his patrons.

ll. 5–8. *no more than rouse* . . . : In this stanza, Horace alludes, in turn, to the two major Homeric epics ('the acid of Achilles' refers to the *Iliad*; 'devious Ulysses', the *Odyssey*), and then to both Aeschylus' *Agamemnon* and Varius' own *Thyestes* ('the cruelties of Pelops' house'), since Thyestes and Atreus (the father of Agamemnon) were both sons of Pelops.

ll. 9–12. *I'm too small for grandeur* . . . : The claim is quintessentially Callimachean. Horace reverses this refusal to 'soar to Caesar's' praise (i.e., Augustus') in *Odes* 3.25 (p. 486), where Bacchus, the god of wine and tragedy, helps him overcome this sudden attack of modesty – or, in other words, Horace is only foolish enough to attempt to praise Augustus when drunk. See also n. on Hor. *Odes* 2.20, l. 1 (p. 477) and n., and *Odes* 3.30, ll. 13–14 (p. 487) and n.

ll. 13–16. Both *Mars decked out for rage* and *Diomedes, peer of gods* seem to refer to Hom. *Il.* 5, the star turn of the Greek hero Diomedes, where Pallas Athena gives him strength and even helps him attack and wound Ares/Mars (he also wounds Aphrodite/Venus; cf. n. on Call. *Hy.* 5, ll. 35–6, p. 273). The Cretan hero *Meriones* is a lesser character in the *Iliad*, who nonetheless plays a significant supporting role with his cousin Idomeneus in Hom. *Il.* 13; the apparent reference to his death, however, makes one suspect either some scene from a lost poem in the Epic Cycle (cf. Call. *Ep.* 2, l. 1, p. 276, and n.), or perhaps an unknown epic, starring Diomedes and featuring Meriones, which Varius may have been planning. We are also told (by an anonymous ancient commentator on Hom. *Il.* 2, l. 96) that Diomedes had a herald named Meriones; perhaps this, and not the Cretan hero, is the figure intended by Horace.

ll. 17–20. *I sing the drunken soirée* . . . : Horace's own preferred subject matter belongs squarely in the Greek symposium, in the realm of Anacreon (pp. 100–108) and the *Anacreontea* (pp. 357–64), and Hellenistic epigram – or, perhaps, of Latin love elegy, one of whose key tropes is the 'warfare of love' (*militia amoris*; see n. on Ov. *Am.* 1.9, p. 495, and cf. Hor. *Odes* 4.1, l. 1, p. 487, and n.). Compare also the similar list of subjects in Prop. 3.3, ll. 47–50 (p. 434).

1.9, The Soracte Ode. Since this is Horace's first ode in what would become his signature stanza, the alcaic (see *Note on Meters*, pp. xxxviii_ xxxix), we should not be surprised that a poem of Alcaeus – Alc. 338 (p. 65) – is lurking in the background. If we had all of Alc. 338, I suspect it would show the originality of Horace's poem – specifically, of its sequence of thought and movement of time and tone. Although cf. the close parallels in Hor. *Epod.* 13 (p. 458), similarly descended from Alc. 338.

l. 1. *Soracte*: Modern Monte Soratte, about twenty-five miles north of Rome and visible on a clear day from the Janiculum Hill, lends local color to what is otherwise a universal scene, as at home on Lesbos as in Latium.

467. l. 6. *Thaliarchus*: Greek for 'Master of the Revels'. The name evokes the 'king of drinking' (*rex bibendi*) or symposiarch, often chosen by a dice-throw, as in Hor. *Odes* 1.4, l. 18 (p. 465), and 2.7, ll. 25–6 (p. 473); yet the absence of others from the scene, combined with Thaliarchus' apparent role, suggests that he might be a servant, and the (rare, though real) Greek name applied in jest. David West suspects that Horace's interest in him is pederastic, a theory which would certainly fit the Alcaean context (see Hor. *Odes* 1.4, l. 19, p. 465, and n.); in that case, the advice of stanzas 4–6 would be inspired by the recognition that, like Lycidas in Hor. *Odes* 1.4 (ll. 19–20 and n.), Thaliarchus will soon be old enough to attract women.

l. 7. *house Sabine*: A rustic (and, no doubt, rather rough) wine produced on the country estate which Maecenas gave to Horace (see *Poet Intro*, p. 453, and n. on Hor. *Epod.* 2, l. 41, p. 457). Both here and throughout, Horace serves Italian wine in a Greek vessel – a metaphor for the Italian wine of his poems in the Greek bottles of his stanzas.

l. 10. *storm-blasts fighting the churning seas*: Cf. Hor. *Odes* 1.1, l. 15 (p. 462) and n., and 1.3, ll. 12–16 (p. 463); and, more generally, see n. on Ar. 212 (p. 15).

ll. 18–20. *Now make for the public squares* . . . : The great Italian philologist Giorgio Pasquali confirmed in 1920 the longevity of the tradition that Horace describes: 'At night indeed in the solitary piazzas of Rome, where the grass grows, even today one finds the young lovers in pairs, even today one hears their tender sibilance; but in the daytime no one makes love in piazzas, in Rome or anywhere else' (quoted, in the original, in Nisbet and Hubbard, *Commentary on Horace: Odes, Book I*, p. 124).

No doubt his description is as accurate in the twenty-first century as it was in the twentieth.

1.11, Carpe Diem. To the extent that 'lodging a phrase where it'll be hard to get rid of' (to vary a quip of Robert Frost's) should be the measure of a poem's success, it would be difficult to think of a more successful poem than this ode, in which Horace coined the phrase *carpe diem* ('seize' or, here, '*pluck* the day'). The poem stands at the head of the long tradition of *carpe diem* poetry, a vast body of Renaissance and modern verse, of which the best-known examples in English are by Robert Herrick and Andrew Marvell. Yet, within its own context, Horace's ode comes relatively late in a tradition of sympotic exhortation which looks back to Alcaeus. Indeed, the metrical line used by Horace is the same one as in Alc. 346 and 347 (pp. 65–6; see *Translator's Preface*, pp. xxi–xxii, and *Note on Meters*, pp. xxxv–xxxvi), and there may be a lost poem of Alcaeus even more directly behind this one.

l. 2. *Leuconoë*: The name has not been satisfactorily explained, but seems to mean something like 'white mind', whether in a positive sense, suggesting innocence and purity, or a negative one, implying gullibility.

ll. 2–3. *that astrology from Babylon*: This art or science was invented by the Babylonians, and disseminated throughout the Hellenistic world in the wake of Alexander. It had reached Rome by the second century BCE and was regarded by educated Romans as the most scientific form of divination, though there were naysayers: Cicero, the Elder Pliny, Augustus (sometimes) and, apparently, Horace.

l. 5. *the Etruscan sea*: i.e., the Tyrrhenian Sea, on Italy's western coast ('Tyrrhenian' is another name for 'Etruscan'). Some have placed the setting of this poem in southern Italy, near Herculaneum. David West (*Horace Odes I: Carpe Diem*, pp. 50–51), on the grounds that 'the only part of the mainland of Italy where volcanic rock lies along the shore is the Bay of Naples', speculates that Horace may be looking out on the sea from somewhere near Herculaneum, perhaps even from a dining room in Philodemus' villa (see *Intro* to Philodemus, pp. 333–4).

468. l. 6. *Be wise; have taste*: One verb, *sapere*, gives us both *sapientia* (wisdom) and *sapor* (flavor). The Latin language, speaking through Horace, wants to convince us that wisdom *is* taste.

l. 8. *until tomorrow*: The distrust of the future is related to the threat of heirs battening on pleasures from which the deceased abstained in life; cf. *Odes* 2.3, ll. 17–20 (p. 472), 2.14, ll. 25–8 (p. 477), and 4.7, ll. 24–5 (p. 489).

pluck today: Anyone who has conversed with a Latin teacher about the famous phrase *carpe diem*, which Horace coins here, has probably heard that *carpe*, conventionally translated 'seize', might better be rendered 'pluck'. The reason has to do with the focus on wines and viticulture in the second half of the ode: *carpe* balances *reseces*, 'prune back' (l. 6), an action which keeps the vines healthy and allows the grapes to ripen. The metaphor slips a little, since pruning is done in winter for the sake of the spring and summer crop (that is, for the future); still, we might say that good pruning lets a vine luxuriate in each day's sun.

1.22. Another of Horace's *Odes* beloved in later centuries, this one was even set to 'mournful music' by the German composer F. F. Flemming (1778–1813) 'and sung at German and Scandinavian funerals' (Nisbet and Hubbard, *Commentary on Horace: Odes, Book I*, p. 262); it was particularly dear to Petrarch, who imitated it at *Canzone* 145, 159 and 176. In English, Thomas Campion's version (*A Booke of Ayres* 18, ll. 1–4) reflects the solemnity with which it was typically read:

> The man of life upright,
> > Whose guiltlesse hart is free
> From all dishonest deedes,
> > Or thought of vanitie . . .

For these readers, the point made in the first stanza is the point of the poem: the good man is under God's protection. It is hard to believe that Horace took this idea so seriously, despite the grandiloquence of his opening: really he is echoing, or perhaps satirizing, a commonplace of elegiac poetry, that lovers are protected by Cupid; cf. Prop. 3.16, ll. 11–20 (p. 438), Sulp. 3.10, ll. 15–16 (p. 449), and Tib. 1.2, ll. 29–34:

> Sacred and safe we wander where we please,
> we lovers, and need fear no treacheries.
> For me, the torpid winter midnights pose
> no threat, nor yet the rains the tempest blows.
> I'll feel no pain, if Delia's door swings wide
> and her hushed finger ushers me inside.

l. 2. *Fuscus*: Marcus Aristius Fuscus, a noted Stoic, grammarian and author of comedies or tragedies (or both), is also the addressee of Hor. *Epist.* 1.10, and appears as a character in Hor. *Satires* 1.9, in which Horace has been roped into conversation in the Forum and Fuscus (with malicious wit) declines to rescue him. If there is humor in this poem, we can be sure Fuscus would have gotten the joke. The 'Moorish' spears would have been of particular use in Numidia (l. 15).

l. 5. *Libya's sweltering sands*: See n. on Hor. *Odes* 2.20, l. 14 (p. 477).

l. 10. *Lalage*: Greek for 'babbler', 'chatterbox'; cf. Prop. 4.7, l. 46 (p. 441). The name occasionally appears in later Latin and English poetry (it is used by Kipling and Hardy), usually as a nod to Horace.

l. 12. *took off like a shot*: We are reminded of Dios. 16 (p. 314), in which a eunuch priest of Cybele scares off a lion with a kettledrum – which, incidentally, Dioscorides calls a *lalagema* (see Dios. 16, l. 16, and n.). By contrast, Horace's portent is rather less impressive: wolves (like lions, associated with Cybele) are shy of human beings, and would be likely to flee the poet as he wandered through his estate in the Sabine Hills (see *Poet Intro*, p. 453, and n. on Hor. *Epod.* 2, l. 41, p. 457), with or without the divine protection due a lover.

l. 23. *lovely laughter*: With *dulce ridentem*, Horace is quoting Cat. 51, l. 5 (p. 387), itself a translation of Sap. 31, l. 5 (*gelaisas imeroen*, p. 45). This layered literary reference, combined with the allusive Greek name of Horace's beloved and his babbling tambourine of Cybele (see nn. on ll. 10 and 12, above), makes one wonder whether this beautiful and silly poem is really about the silliness and beauty of poetry: what Horace can't help loving is its idealistic, grandiose, mellifluous prattle, which, though spouting nonsense, does so with charm, grace and style.

469. 1.23. This delicate ode, perhaps one of Horace's earliest forays into lyric, is modeled on Anac. 408 (p. 107), though Anac. 346 fr. 1 (p. 101) and 417 (p. 108) also seem relevant, as does Ar. 196a, l. 46 (p. 15), which compares the young girl the poet seduces there to a fawn. We may note as well the traditional use of similes in *epithalamia* (cf. Sap. 104–16, pp. 51–3, and Cat. 62, p. 388, and 68b, p. 391); yet it is difficult to think of earlier poems that work the way this one does. Horace offers advice and exhortation in the usual way, but the poem consists essentially of an epic-style simile (Homer was often comparing heroes to lions and their victims to animals like fawns: cf., e.g., *Il.* 11, ll. 113–21) whose vehicle is expanded to take up almost the entire poem. We are not so far away from a modern poem completely given over to its conceit, with the tenor only implied.

l. 1. *Chloe*: 'Green Shoot' in Greek; a name used elsewhere by Horace (here, in *Odes* 3.9, p. 482). Its suggestion of freshness and naivety is particularly apt here.

ll. 9–10. *I'm not some vicious tiger or ... lion*: The amorous predator disclaiming his predatory intent is a pastoral motif; the key passage is Theoc. *Id.* 11, ll. 25, p. 297 (echoed at Vi. *Ecl.* 2, ll. 71–74, p. 402, and Ov. *Met.* 1, ll. 504–7).

1.24. The second of two (or three) odes addressed by Horace to the poet Virgil (pp. 398–410). The first is Hor. *Odes* 1.3 (p. 463); the possible third, *Odes* 4.12, invites one Vergilius, a 'client of noble youths', to a symposium that may or may not have taken place after the death of the poet Virgil, but scholars disagree about whether this Virgil is likely to be the author of the *Aeneid*.

The present poem offers consolation for the death of a mutual friend, Quintilius (see n. on l. 5, below). While the exhortations to Virgil within the poem are thoroughly plausible within the rhetorical and poetic sub-genre of the consolation (*consolatio*), of which Ar. 13 (p. 7) is an early example, many readers have detected a note of personal criticism – a feature this poem shares with *Odes* 1.3 (p. 463). Virgil is a deeply elegiac poet, not only in *Geo.* 4 (which this poem alludes to at ll. 13–18, and which David West has described as 'awash with tears': *Horace Odes I: Carpe Diem*, p. 113), but throughout the *Aeneid*, which is equally a celebration of Rome's triumph and a lament for those lost along the way; one might merely point to one of its most famous lines: *sunt lacrimae rerum et mentem mortalia tangunt*, 'Our story runs with tears, and so much death touches the mind' (*Aen.* 1, l. 462). Does the present ode suggest that Virgil the man was as piously weepy, or weepily pious, as his poetry? Is Horace criticizing that trait, on a personal level, a poetic level, or both? Or is he merely making Virgil an offering of friendship and solidarity, filled with truisms to which Aeneas' creator couldn't help but assent? It is worth noting that Horace's firm advice here is echoed in *Aen.* 5, l. 710, when old Nautes advises Aeneas (trans. Fagles):

> Whatever Fortune sends, we master it all
> by bearing it all, we must!

l. 3. *Melpomene*: One of the nine Muses, eventually the Muse of tragedy. See also *Odes* 3.30, l. 15 (p. 487).

l. 5. *Quintilius*: Quintilius Varus, literary critic, and friend of Horace, Virgil and, possibly, Catullus (see n. on Cat. 10, l. 2, p. 379). He is otherwise little known, apart from a passage in Horace's *Ars Poetica* (ll. 438–44, trans. Ferry):

> If Quintilius read a manuscript of yours,
> He'd say, 'Please, if you will, change this, and this,'
> And if, after you tried and failed to make
> The corrections he'd advised you to make, he'd tell you
> To tear it up and take it back to the forge
> To be remade. And if you got defensive
> And wouldn't even try, he wouldn't say
> Another word or waste another minute,
> To come between yourself and your self-love.

l. 10. *piety*: This word will have evoked the *Aeneid*, well known to be underway in 23 BCE when Bks. 1–3 of the *Odes* were published; Aeneas' main characteristic was, of course, *pietas*, a concept encompassing devotion to one's family, one's people and the gods. Horace is critical of it again in *Odes* 2.14 (p. 476) and 4.7 (p. 489).

470. l. 13. *Orpheus*: This reference will have conjured Virgil's breathtaking treatment of Orpheus' descent into the underworld in Bk. 4 of his *Georgics* (ll. 453–527), published in 29 BCE, as well, perhaps, as his self-comparison with Orpheus at *Ecl.* 4, ll. 63–6 (p. 404). Cf. also Hor. *Odes* 2.13, ll. 21–40 (p. 475) and n., and Ov. *Tri.* 4.1, ll. 17–18 (p. 516) and n.

1.37, The Cleopatra Ode. Yet another ode it would be trivial to call 'famous', Horace's polemic-turned-panegyric on Cleopatra has captured the imagination of the ages. The alcaic strophe (see *Note on Meters*, pp. xxxviii–xxxix) – here complete with precedent in Alcaeus (see n. on l. 1, below) – came to be Horace's preferred measure for political subjects, as Alcaeus was for him the prototypical political lyricist; cf. Horace's comparison of Alcaeus with Sappho at *Odes* 2.13, ll. 25–32 (p. 475). Though Horace was forever refusing to tackle epic subject matter (in, e.g., *Odes* 1.6, p. 466, and 4.2), this ode, as well as the first six of Bk. 3 (pp. 478–82), show how a lyric poet might rise to the task. The headlong syntax, enjambed within and between stanzas from the second strophe on, creates a feeling – not, it must be said, especially historical – of speed and inevitability. The queen's sudden transformation, in the last three strophes, from drunken to clearheaded, contemptible to magnificent, can be read, and might have been intended, as mere propaganda: to praise the conquered is, implicitly, to praise the conqueror. Yet it is the tragic dignity of Cleopatra, in Horace's portrayal, which has made the ode an all-time classic, along with the impeccable Horatian performance of such virtuosity in the service of such ambivalence.

l. 1. *High time to drink now*: This opening echoes Alcaeus' drunken joy at the death of the tyrant Myrsilus (Alc. 332, p. 64), implicitly dwarfing the small goings-on of Archaic Lesbos with the great ones of the Roman present.

ll. 3–4. *a seat for the gods at the feast of our Priests of War*: In these lines, Horace sounds a specifically Roman note after the Greek beginning. Horace describes a kind of public thanksgiving called the *lectisternium*, where feasts were laid out before couches on which images of the gods were placed. The 'Priests of War', the Salii, were a byword for luxurious banqueting. One of their dinners is catalogued by Macrobius (*Saturnalia* 3.13.12, trans. Kaster):

> as a prelude, sea-urchins, raw oysters (as many as they wanted), cockles and mussels, thrush over asparagus, fattened hen, a dish of baked oysters and cockles, white and black acorn-mollusks; mussels again, clams, jellyfish, fig-peckers, loin of roe-deer, loin of boar, fattened fowl wrapped in dough, fig-peckers, murex and purple-shell; for the main courses, sow's udders, boar's cheek, a dish of baked fish, a dish of baked sow's udder, ducks, boiled water-fowl, hares, fattened fowl roasted, gruel, and bread of Picenum.

Appropriately here, the Salii were also famous for their dancing (cf. ll. 1–2, and see Hor. *Odes* 4.1, l. 28, p. 488, and n. on *Odes* 3.18, l. 16, p. 485), as well as for their custodianship of sacred relics integral to Rome's survival (see n. on Hor. *Odes* 3.5, ll. 9–12, p. 481).

l. 7. *the queen*: Cleopatra VII Philopator (69–30 BCE) was the last of the Ptolemies to rule Egypt, the end of a line which began with Alexander's general Ptolemy, son of Lagus (r. 303–282 BCE; see *Intro* to Post-Classical Greek Lyric, p. 249). She was the lover of Julius Caesar – said by Plutarch to have first gained his presence by sneaking into the palace in a laundry bag (*Life of Julius Caesar* 49.1) – and the mother of his son, Caesarion; after Caesar's assassination, she took up with Mark Antony, in whom she reposed her hopes for the continuance of her dynasty, and to whom she bore three children (cf. Crin. 18, p. 341, and n.). Their relationship provoked the eventual rift between Antony, who controlled the eastern part of the Roman Empire, and Caesar's heir, Octavian, who controlled the west, including Rome. Octavian made good use of Antony's alliance with Cleopatra to paint the civil war between them as a foreign one, waged by the morally rigorous Romans against the barbaric licentiousness of

Egypt; the ode's omission of Antony, to focus on and demonize the foreign queen, follows the Caesarian party line.

l. 9. *a flock of 'men'*: Horace refers insultingly to the many eunuchs of Cleopatra's Alexandrian court.

l. 12. *luck's sweet liquor*: The ode's emphasis on Cleopatra's drunkenness, both metaphorical and literal – Antony was a notorious drunkard, a vice for which he had been thoroughly vilified by Cicero in the *Philippics* – fits neatly with the sympotic interests of the lyric genre in general and Alcaeus in particular. The lack of moderation attributed to Cleopatra, slanderous in itself, in Horace takes on a philosophical cast; she has failed to observe the golden mean: see *Odes* 2.10 (p. 473) and n.

l. 13. *scarcely a ship slipped burning*: A hyperbolic reference to the naval Battle of Actium, fought off a coastal promontory of northwestern Greece in September 31 BCE, when Octavian (the 'Caesar' of l. 17) secured his dominance over the Roman world, defeating his Alexandria-based rival, Mark Antony. Cleopatra is said to have panicked and retreated with all sixty of her ships while the outcome of the battle hung in the balance; Antony followed close behind, while most of the fleet – according to Plutarch (*Life of Antony*, 61.1 and 68.1), 300 out of 500 ships – surrendered intact. Horace's claim is thus a bald exaggeration.

l. 14. *the Mareotic grape*: Alexander laid out Alexandria between the sea and a large, brackish lake called Mareotis (modern Mariout), which dried up in the Middle Ages but was flooded again in the nineteenth century. The region's wine was light and sweet and apparently not strong enough for Cleopatra to serve to Caesar; Horace, having chosen the word for its sinister, foreign sound, is not concerned with such details. Cf. Shakespeare, *Antony and Cleopatra* 5.2, ll. 280–81: 'Now no more / The juice of Egypt's grape shall moist this lip.'

471. ll. 21–32. *steeled to meet a nobler end* ... : Cleopatra did not kill herself until August 30 BCE, almost a year after the battle; Horace therefore simplifies the timeline dramatically. The notion, dubious in itself, that she committed suicide by venomous asps reflects the official Augustan version.

1.38. After the grandest and most ambitious poem of his first book, Horace ends with the simplest and slightest. The analogy with other bookending poems in which Horace speaks explicitly about his own poetry (Hor. *Odes* 2.20, p. 477, and 3.30, p. 487) has led commentators to look for programmatic resonance in this one as well: Horace hints at his preference for simplicity of style, or reaffirms his commitment to the poetry of wine and love, eschewing the grander themes.

As usual, Horace has assimilated a large number of Greek precedents. The main model is Anacreon (cf. Anac. 356, p. 103, and 396, p. 107), while for the rejection of eastern luxury we might point to Ar. 19 (p. 8) and *Anacreontea* 8 (p. 359). Phil. 21 (p. 338) adumbrates, not without irony, the kind of fussily extravagant symposia the poet 'hates'. If there is a homoerotic subtext in Horace's address to his cupbearer, one might point to Ant. Thess. 3 (p. 345), as well as any number of epigrams on Ganymede in Bk. 12 of the *Greek Anthology*; cf. also Hor. *Odes* 1.4, l. 19 (p. 465) and n. Though we need not be versed in his models to enjoy Horace's poem, we may be curious about the process by which he has absorbed and fused them with his own sensibility to create two charming stanzas which, all would agree, are quintessentially 'Horatian'.

l. 1. *crowns of linden*: Linden bast (a fibrous part of the phloem) was used to bind complicated garlands woven of different kinds of flowers; Horace, however, wants myrtle and myrtle only (l. 5).

l. 2. *Persian frill*: The Persian Empire was a byword for extravagant luxury (cf., in Horace, *Epod.* 13, l. 13, p. 459, and *Odes* 3.1, l. 44, p. 479, and 3.9, l. 4, p. 482).

l. 5. *myrtle*: The association of the myrtle with Venus has often been thought relevant, whether because Horace asserts his preference for love poetry in a general way, or because he has his eyes on the boy pouring his wine.

2.3. l. 4. *you, Dellius*: Quintus Dellius, described by Marcus Valerius Messalla Corvinus, patron of Tibullus (see *Intro* to Tibullus, p. 411), as the 'stunt-rider of the civil wars' (i.e., *desultor*, one skilled at leaping between horses; David West's translation). He began his career with Julius Caesar and, after Caesar's death, joined up in turn with the conspirator Gaius Cassius Longinus, then with *his* conqueror, Mark Antony, and finally, just before the Battle of Actium (see n. on Hor. *Odes* 1.37, l. 13, p. 470), with Octavian. He wrote a history of Antony's unsuccessful war with Parthia (cf. n. on Hor. *Odes* 2.13, l. 17, p. 475) and addressed a series of 'salacious letters' to Cleopatra. He was also rumored to be Antony's *eromenos* (boy love); when he changed sides prior to Actium, he claimed that Cleopatra resented him and, if Antony won, would have had him killed. Octavian received him generously and left him to prosper and grow rich, seemingly without overburdening him with responsibilities. The Epicurean-themed ode which Horace here addresses to him presumably exhorts him to do what he was already doing, that is, enjoy however much of his life he had left. Horace's thinking in this ode is unexceptional, but his Latin is scintillating; the poem makes a brilliant introduction to the more philosophical odes of Bk. 2.

l. 8. *Falernian Grand Reserve*: Dellius loved his Falernian (see Tib. 2.1, ll. 28–9, p. 418, and n.), complaining bitterly when he could not get it in Alexandria (Plutarch, *Life of Antony* 59.4).

472. l. 13. *Come, bid the boy* . . . : Horace envisions himself at an al fresco symposium on one of Dellius' estates (ll. 17–20).

l. 14. *roses, all too briefly in flower now*: Modern roses, which flower throughout spring and summer, are descendants of Chinese cultivars imported to Europe in the nineteenth century; before this, European roses bloomed only once – though the roses of Paestum were apparently an exception; cf. Ov. *Ex Pont.* 2.4, l. 28 (p. 521) and n. It is odd to think that, had the rose been as assiduously cultivated in Europe as in China, we would not have poems like Ronsard's 'Mignonne, allons voir si la rose' or Waller's 'Go, lovely rose'.

ll. 17–20. *You'll leave . . . to your heir*: Cf. Hor. *Odes* 2.14, ll. 21–8 (p. 477), and 4.7, ll. 24–5 (p. 489), for recurrences of the trope.

ll. 19–20. *your beachfront home, piled on the whitecaps*: See n. on Hor. *Odes* 3.1, ll. 33–7 (p. 479).

l. 22. *Inachus*: The legendary first king of Argos (see n. on Call. *Hy.* 5, l. 49, p. 273), and father of Io (see Bacch. 19, ll. 15–45, pp. 183–4, and nn.).

ll. 26–8. *all lots are shaken in a single urn* . . . : Cf. Tib. 1.3, ll. 11–12 (p. 413) and n., and Hor. *Odes* 3.1, ll. 14–16 (p. 478).

2.7. There are plenty of precedents for this ode. Alc. 350, for example, addresses the poet's brother Antimenidas, returned from a campaign fighting with the Babylonians:

From the world's farthest verges   you've come back, bringing with you
a chryselephantine sword-hilt –   ivory, bound in gold . . .

Cat. 9 is an effusion of pure emotion:

> Veranius, of all my three
> hundred thousand friends, the best,
> have you come home to your family,
> your loving brothers and old mother?
> You have! You have! The best news ever! . . .

Horace, the more cerebral worker, has not produced a poem of Catullan immediacy; but by the comparison one can see how much more ground he has had to cover, and how deftly he has done it: in deflecting grand geopolitics to the personal realm while dishing out elliptical compliments to everyone but himself, this ode reveals the essence of Horatian tact (see also Hor. *Odes* 2.10, p. 473).

ll. 3–4. *who brought you back, a citizen . . .* : Octavian did; the compliment is tactfully oblique. Pompey (l. 5) must have lost his citizenship and had it recently restored, after the end of the civil war in 30 BCE, or sometime later.

l. 5. *Pompey*: Horace's friend, but not Pompey the Great (or his son Sextus Pompeius) – the man is unknown beyond this ode. Horace and Pompey first got to know each other when they fought under Marcus Junius Brutus at the Battle of Philippi in 42 BCE (see n. on l. 9, below), where Horace was actually a high-ranking officer. This stanza (along, perhaps, with *Epod.* 13, p. 458: see n. on l. 15 *ad loc.*) describes the exotic symposia enjoyed in those heady days of high principle and higher danger.

l. 8. *the Indian bay*: Malabathrum, or tamala leaf; an exotic Eastern luxury no doubt more easily accessible to Republican soldiers in Macedonia.

473. l. 9. *Philippi*: A Macedonian city in northeast Greece, where the anti-Caesarian faction, helmed by Brutus and Gaius Cassius Longinus, was defeated by the then-allied Mark Antony and Octavian. It was a savage battle – 24,000 dead on the first day (Appian, *Civil Wars* 4.112)! – which Horace paints in jocular and literary terms, with plenty of self-deprecation.

l. 10. *I dropped my shield*: This may or may not have actually happened, but as a poetic motif the 'shield-dropper' had been around at least since Archilochus (Ar. 5, p. 6) – Alcaeus (see *Poet Intro*, p. 55) and Anacreon (Anac. 381b, p. 105) also confessed to the same faux pas. Archilochus was in Thrace when he dropped his shield, in the same general area as Philippi.

l. 13. *I was saved by Mercury*: Men in Homer are often saved from battle by gods (e.g., *Il.* 3, ll. 380–82, 5, ll. 344–6, 11, ll. 749–51), though never by Mercury, perhaps because of his usual role as usher to the underworld (cf. Hor. *Odes* 1.24, ll. 16–18, p. 470). Elsewhere Horace claims that, as a poet, he is under Mercury's special protection (*Odes* 2.17). Horace's mock-epic account glorifies Octavian, the victor at Philippi; yet, by dwelling on his own personal cowardice, he praises Pompey's bravery by implication.

ll. 15–16. *sucked back into . . . the fight*: Pompey continued campaigning for losing causes, first with Sextus Pompeius in Sicily (cf. n. on Hor. *Epod.* 16, l. 1, p. 460), then with Mark Antony at the Battle of Actium (cf. Hor. *Odes* 1.37, l. 13, p. 470).

l. 21. *bright goblets*: These *ciboria* are drinking cups in the shape of the Egyptian bean-plant (cf. Vi. *Ecl.* 4, l. 24, p. 403), probably nostalgically associated with the old eastern campaign, like the 'Indian bay' of l. 8, above.

l. 22. *Massic wine*: See Hor. *Odes* 1.1, l. 19 (p. 462), and n.

ll. 25–6. *Venus, whom will the next dice-roll make king of drinking?*: See n. on Prop. 4.8, ll. 45–6 (p. 444). As in Propertius, erotic connotations may also apply to the 'Venus' roll, in the usual way that wine leads to love. For the 'king of drinking' (*rex bibendi*, symposiarch), cf. Hor. *Odes* 1.4, l. 18 (p. 465) and n., and 1.9, l. 6 (p. 467) and n.

2.10. The subject of this ode, the golden mean, is a well-known doctrine of the Peripatetic school of philosophy founded by Aristotle (see *Intro* to Aristotle, p. 223), though the phrase *aurea mediocritas* is Horace's inimitably felicitous coinage. It is also, of course, an oxymoron, gold being a substance of no middling preciousness. Although the ode's generality was much beloved in the aphoristic eighteenth century, it is somewhat uncharacteristic of Horace; it is, however, an example of his tact (like *Odes* 2.7, p. 472): to speak more concretely would have been impolitic, and perhaps dangerous, given the poem's addressee (see n. on l. 1, below). With particulars carefully excluded, the poetic drama Horace presents is one of stanza construction, of balance and antithesis, and of a syntax uniquely calibrated to the central theme.

l. 1. *Licinius*: This seems to have been Lucius Licinius Murena, brother-in-law of Horace's patron Maecenas, and a devotee of the Peripatetic (Aristotelian) school of philosophy. This Murena incurred Augustus' anger at a court trial shortly before the publication of Bks. 1–3 of the *Odes* and, shortly after, was convicted of treason and put to death. In the gap between those two events Horace may have had time to write this poem, warning Murena away from extremes of behavior in good Aristotelian terms.

474. ll. 9–12. *Often the tallest pines writhe in the wind's teeth . . .*: The illustration goes back at least to Herodotus (*Hist.* 7.10, trans. Grene):

Do you see how it is the living things that exceed others in size that the god strikes with lightning and will not let them show their grandeur, while the little ones do not itch the god to action? Do you see how it is always the greatest houses and the tallest trees that the god hurls his bolts upon?

Osip Mandelstam may have had l. 9 (or one of its descendants) in mind when he wrote in the classically infused 'He Who Finds a Horseshoe' (trans. Brown and Merwin):

> We look at the forest and say
> here are many ships already in the trees, masts . . .
> they should creak in the storm
> like solitary pines,
> in the raging treeless air . . .
>
> And breathing the smell of the tears
> of resin that seep from the ship's timbers . . .
> we say
> these too once stood on the earth,
> uncomfortable as a donkey's spine,
> their tops forgetting their roots . . .

ll. 16–17. *the same god clears // the clouds away*: This sole interstanzaic enjambment, in a poem of otherwise consistently closed strophes, has always reminded me of the enjambment between stanzas 6 and 7 in Thomas Hardy's great poem on the sinking of the *Titanic*, 'The Convergence of the Twain': 'The Immanent Will that stirs and urges everything // Prepared a sinister mate / For her . . .' The schematics of balanced construction in Hardy's poem bear some comparison to those in the present ode.

2.13. ll. 1–4. *On a black day that fellow planted you* . . . : Another parody of the *schetliasmos* (imprecation) against the *arche kakon*, 'inventor of evils'; cf. Hor. *Odes* 1.3 (p. 463) and Ov. *Am.* 1.12 (p. 497). Hor. *Epod.* 3 uses similar language when the poet's patron Maecenas mischievously slips him some garlic:

> If some inhuman thug's own fingers strangled
>   his father's neck, for his last meal
> I'd give him garlic – it's deadlier than hemlock!
>   Reapers who eat it have guts of steel.

l. 3. *Tree*: This tree, which almost killed Horace by falling on his head (ll. 11–12), is mentioned three other times in the *Odes*. In 2.17 (ll. 27–30), Horace claims to have been saved from the tree by Faunus, 'protector of Mercury's men' (i.e., poets). In 3.4 (ll. 25–8), he includes the tree among the three gravest threats to his life:

> A friend to your [i.e., the Muses'] dances and springs, I managed to flee
> death when our side turned tail at Philippi,
>> and when that tree took aim at me,
>> and the waves off Sicily's coast waxed high.

And in 3.8 (ll. 1–12), he says he celebrates the anniversary of his lucky dodge every 1 March. Of course, we can't know what really happened; but as with the wolf in *Odes* 1.22, ll. 9–12 (p. 468), there was presumably *something*, however inflated into personal mythology.

l. 8. *No Black Sea toxin*: Horace nods to Medea (see n. on. Prop. 2.1, ll. 53–4, p. 428), and perhaps Mithridates VI of Pontus (see n. on Mart. 6.19, l. 6, p. 545), two famous poisoners of the region.

475. ll. 13–20. *Of all our hours of danger . . .* : A sentiment entirely at home in Archaic Greek lyric; compare Sim. 521 (p. 122).

l. 14. *Punic sailor*: Horace is referring to the Phoenicians, famed for their seafaring exploits; cf. Hor. *Epod.* 16, l. 59 (p. 461) and n.

l. 15. *the stormy Bosporus*: Ancients believed the current of the Bosporus (the strait connecting the Sea of Marmara to the Black Sea and dividing Turkey from Thrace) flowed constantly west; cf. Shakespeare, *Othello* 3.3, ll. 516–19. See also Hor. *Odes* 2.20, l. 16 (p. 477) and n.

l. 17. *the shots of the Parthian*: Parthia was an empire founded in the mid-third century BCE whose territory stretched from central Turkey to eastern Iran. For Augustus' poets, the Parthians were the great foreign menace; in one of Rome's worst-ever military disasters, they destroyed seven legions led by Julius Caesar's rival and fellow triumvir, Marcus Licinius Crassus, at the Battle of Carrhae (Harran, in southeastern Turkey) in 53 BCE, taking 10,000 soldiers prisoner and capturing the legionary standards. Augustus negotiated the return of those standards, along with the surviving captives, in 20 BCE, in what he and his poets trumpeted as a great diplomatic victory (cf. Prop. 3.5, ll. 47–8, p. 435, and Hor. *Odes* 3.5, ll. 4–12, pp. 480–81), and which is commemorated on the breastplate of one of the most famous statues of the *princeps*, the

Augustus of Prima Porta. The 'Parthian shot' was the signature battle tactic by which they had defeated Crassus: on horseback the Parthians galloped away as if in flight, drawing the Romans into rash pursuit, then swiveled around and launched their arrows. Our expression 'parting shot' is corrupted from this term. For the Parthians, cf. also Cat. 11, l. 6 (p. 380), Vi. *Ecl.* 10, l. 69 (p. 410), Hor. *Odes* 3.2, l. 4 (p. 479), and Mart. 2.53, l. 10 (p. 539) and 5.58, l. 4 (p. 544).

l. 19. *the Tullianum*: The dungeon, located at the foot of the Capitol Hill in Rome, where the state's most important enemies – domestic and foreign – were executed.

ll. 21–40. *How close I came* ... : This scene, of the shades of the dead listening rapt to Sappho's and Alcaeus' poetry in the afterlife, owes much to Orpheus' descent into the underworld in Vi. *Geo.* 4, ll. 453–527; cf. also Hor. *Odes* 1.24, ll. 13–20 (p. 470) and n., and Ov. *Tri.* 4.1, ll. 17–18 (p. 516) and n. But here Horace adds some characteristic comedy, especially with the drooping ears of Cerberus (ll. 33–4).

l. 22. *Proserpine's realm*: Proserpina (the Greek Persephone), queen of the underworld.

Aeacus' judgments: Aeacus, the Aeginetan hero (cf. Pi. *Py.* 8, ll. 98–100, p. 155) and grandfather of Achilles, is made one of three judges of the souls of the dead, perhaps for the first time, by Plato in his *Gorgias* (523e–34a); the other two are Rhadamanthys and his brother, the Cretan king Minos (see n. on Theaetetus 3, l. 4, p. 318, and Hor. *Odes* 4.7, ll. 26–7, p. 490).

ll. 25–6. *Sappho ... and you, Alcaeus*: See pp. 38–54 and 55–67, respectively. Meeting one's favorite authors was a traditional perk of being dead: see especially Aristophanes' *Frogs*, but also Plato, *Apology* (41a), Cicero, *De Senectute* (83), and Aelian, *Various Histories* (13.20). Dante borrows the motif in *Inferno* 4, ll. 85–90, where, with Virgil as his guide, he meets Homer, Ovid, Lucan and *Orazio satiro*, 'Horace the satirist' – according to Paget Toynbee, Dante, 'like his contemporaries, shows no direct knowledge' of the odes (*A Dictionary of Proper Names and Notable Matters in the Works of Dante*, s.v. 'Orazio').

l. 27. *golden pick*: The plectrum, used by citharodes to pick the strings of the lyre (cf. *Intro* to the Classical Period, p. 189).

ll. 30–32. *the closely packed populace's ear prefers* ... : Horace's preference for Alcaeus over Sappho is both programmatic for his own work and no doubt polemical against the tastes of Catullus and the Neoterics (see *Intro* to Catullus, p. 374). Ovid (or an imitator) disagreed; he has her say, in *Sappho to Phaon* (*Heroides* 15, ll. 29–30):

> Nor is my countryman, Alcaeus, prouder;
> he's no more lauded, though his sound is louder.

ll. 33–4. *the barking black beast of a hundred heads*: Though likewise given a hundred heads by Hesiod (*Th.*, l. 312) and Pindar (fr. 249b), Cerberus usually, and elsewhere in Horace, only has three. Cf. Bacch. 5, ll. 75–7 (p. 173) and n.; Tib. 1.3, ll. 71–2 (p. 415); Prop. 3.5, l. 43 (p. 435), and 4.7, l. 53 (p. 441).

ll. 35–6. *the Furies' twisted, snaking curls*: Compare with Tib. 1.3, ll. 69–70, p. 415 and n.

l. 37. *Prometheus*: Cf. n. on Prop. 2.1, ll. 67–72 (p. 429), as well as Hor. *Odes* 1.3, ll. 27–31 (p. 464) and n.

Pelops' father: Tantalus; see Pi. *Ol.* 1, ll. 45–79 (pp. 137–8), and Tib. 1.3, ll. 77–8 (p. 415).

l. 38. *Orion*: A great hunter, sometimes portrayed as a son of Poseidon, depicted here as doing, in the underworld's fields of asphodel, what he did in life: pursuing beasts through meadows. Some versions suggest that, like Ixion (see n. on Tib. 1.3, ll. 73–4, p. 415) and Pirithöus (see n. on Hor. *Odes* 4.7, l. 34, p. 490), he ended up there because he became overly fond of a goddess – in Orion's case, his hunting partner, Artemis.

476. 2.14. The present ode, widely considered one of Horace's greatest and most memorable, is also an uncharacteristic one, due to its unrelieved melancholy, eschewing all but the most oblique exhortations to enjoyment. *Per contra*, David West argues that the tone is light and teasing, but I am not sure who agrees (though I grant the consciously absurd exaggerations of daily 'triple hecatombs', l. 5, and the 'hundred keys', l. 26). The ode does not state a creed, but a mood; even the jovial Horace, it seems, sometimes tapped into more abyssal currents. (*Odes* 4.7, p. 489, is similarly gloomy.) Why does the poem give such pleasure? Shelley was right that 'Our sweetest songs are those that tell of saddest thought' ('To a Skylark', l. 90).

l. 1. *Postumus*: Somewhere between nothing and almost nothing can be said of this person, who just might be one Gaius Propertius Postumus, a relative of the elegist (pp. 421–45) and the addressee of Prop. 3.12. Whoever he was, it seems relevant that the name 'Postumus' was bestowed on a boy born after his father's death (see also Mart. 5.58, p. 544).

l. 5. *not even triple hecatombs, daily done*: i.e., not even if you sacrificed 300 oxen a day. This is an absurdly large number; no one was doing such a thing. Postumus' evidently earnest but futile piety can be compared with Virgil's in Hor. *Odes* 1.24, ll. 10–12 (p. 469).

ll. 7–8. *three-bodied Geryon and Tityus*: Mighty Giants slain, respectively, by Heracles (see Stes. *Geryon*, p. 90, and nn.) and by Apollo and Artemis (see Tib. 1.3, ll. 75–6, p. 415, and n.).

l. 16. *stinging siroccos*: The sirocco is a southerly autumn wind that brings clouds, rains and malaria. Those rich enough to do so escaped to the country or the coast.

l. 17. *Cocytus*: The River of Lamentation, one of the five rivers of the underworld.

l. 18. *Danaus' daughters*: See Tib. 1.3, ll. 79–80 (p. 415) and n.

l. 20. *Sisyphus*: See Prop. 3.5, l. 42 (p. 435) and n.

ll. 23–4. *cypress trees will follow*: Romans associated cypress trees with death because they were planted in cemeteries and their branches strewn over pyres; so they do follow the dead, but not for long.

477. l. 25. *Some heir who deserves it more*: Cf. *Odes* 2.3 (p. 471) and 4.7 (p. 489); and see also n. on *Odes* 1.11, l. 8 (p. 468). Horace could be thinking of the famous orator and bon viveur Quintus Hortensius Hortalus (see Cat. 65, p. 390), who was said by the Elder Pliny to have left 10,000 casks of Chian wine to his heir (*Natural History* 14.17; cf. n. on Tib. 2.1, ll. 28–9, p. 418); Pliny also tells us that he was the first Roman to dish up peacock for dinner (*Natural History* 10.23). His house on the Palatine Hill was the modest one later occupied by Augustus (Suetonius, *Life of Augustus* 72.1).

l. 26. *Caecuban*: This wine, mentioned occasionally by Horace and several times by Martial (in this volume, cf. Mart. 3.26, p. 540, 12.17, p. 552, and 12.60, l. 9, p. 555), seems to have been the most prized wine of the late Republic – at least, the Elder Pliny (*Natural History* 14.8) dubs it the *grand cru*, followed closely (in his estimation) by the Falernian (see Tib. 2.1, ll. 28–9, p. 418 and n.). Caecuban was produced in the Pontine Marshes, a tract of swampy land on the western coast of Latium southeast of Rome.

hundred keys: An exaggeration, but cellars were locked to keep servants from drinking on the sly.

l. 27. *pavé floor*: i.e., one adorned with an elaborate mosaic.

l. 28. For sumptuous priestly banquets, cf. *Odes* 1.37, ll. 3–4 (p. 470) and n.

2.20. Horace speaks directly about his poetry in three major odes at key points in Bks. 1–3 (published together as single collection): in 1.1 (p. 462), he announces his ambitions with jokey self-parody, imagining the stars as a low roof he hits his head on (ll. 35–6); in 3.30 (p. 487), all jokes are cast to the winds as he confidently proclaims his achievement. This poem falls in between, both in its placement, at the end of Bk. 2, and in its tone of confident grandiloquence offset by bizarre literalism, as the poet depicts himself being physically transformed into a swan. Naturally, his metamorphosis makes us think of Ovid and Apuleius, but there was plenty of earlier Hellenistic precedent, in obscure (to us) works by such authors as Antigonus of Carystus (cf. n. on Alcm. 26, p. 36), Nicander, Parthenius of Nicaea (see Erucius 13, l. 2, p. 343, and n., and *Intro* to Latin Lyric, pp. 367–8) and Theodorus; according to R. G. M. Nisbet and Margaret Hubbard, this was 'a minor category of literature' (*A Commentary on Horace: Odes, Book II*, p. 334). Yet the fact that Horace is being funny doesn't mean that he isn't also being serious, as a modest barrage of allusions (to Theognis, Simonides, Callimachus and Ennius – see below) would seem to suggest. Horace returns to several of these sources in the even more triumphant *Odes* 3.30 (p. 487).

l. 1. *not weak*: The Latin word *tenui*, related to 'tenuous', suggests that Horace is here rejecting the 'slender' Callimachean poetics he embraces elsewhere (cf. Hor. *Odes* 1.6, ll. 9–12 and 17–20, p. 466, and 3.30, ll. 11–14, p. 487 and nn.).

l. 2. *part bard*: Horace once again announces himself as a *biformis vates* (poet-priest of double form). Usually the doubleness combines Greek and Latin, but here it also melds man and bird. For other discussions of the *vates* in Horace, see *Epod.* 16, l. 66 (p. 461), *Odes* 1.1, l. 35 (p. 463), 3.1, ll. 1–4 (p. 478).

I fly: This poem's flight echoes two illustrious precedents, one Greek, one Roman: Theog. ll. 237–55 (pp. 80–81), and the verse epitaph of the early epic poet Ennius:

> Let none adorn my grave or weep there. Why?
> I'm still alive on the lips of men. I fly.

ll. 4–5. *too high for Envy's grasp*: This echoes an epitaph of Callimachus (*Ep.* 29, p. 279). Thus the two implicit allusions to Callimachus in this poem (see n. on l. 1, above) seem to point in opposite directions, both toward and away from the waspish Alexandrian.

ll. 5–6. *a child of mere subsistence*: Horace also emphasizes his common birth at *Odes* 3.30, ll. 10–12 (p. 487).

ll. 10–11. *a snow-white swan*: The choice of bird evokes both Apollo (cf. Call. *Hy.* 2, l. 5, p. 269) and Pindar, whom Horace, praising his inimitability, calls the 'swan of Dirce' (*Odes* 4.2, l. 25); Pindar, however, would never let details such as shriveling legs (l. 9) interrupt the sublimity of his flight.

l. 13. *Daedal Icarus*: 'Daedal' is a word much used by, e.g., Shelley to evoke the intricate craftsmanship of Daedalus (see n. on Hor. *Odes* 1.3, l. 34, p. 464), often in reference to the 'daedal earth'. Horace, of course, is alluding to Daedalus as the father of Icarus, while also implying the construction of his own intricately made verse. One might further note that the poet's comparison of himself to Icarus, well-known high flyer and hard faller (see n. *ad. loc.*), suggests that his tongue is somewhere in his cheek.

l. 14. *Libya's sandbanks* refers to the Syrtis (the modern Gulf of Sidra, on the north coast of Libya), often used metonymically for the Sahara (cf. Hor. *Odes* 1.22, l. 5, p. 468).

l. 15. *Boreas*: The north wind; north of him dwelt the Hyperboreans, a magical people beloved of Apollo.

l. 16. *the bellowing Bosporus*: Horace plays on the etymology of Bos‑ porus as 'Cow-Ford', which Io was said to have crossed in bovine form (see Bacch. 19, ll. 15–45, pp. 183–4, and nn.). See also n. on Hor. *Odes* 2.13, l. 15 (p. 475), above.

ll. 17–20. Horace sketches the northern limits of the Empire, from *Colchis* (Medea's hometown, on the eastern coast of the Black Sea, annexed by the emperor Nero in 64 CE) to *Dacia* (modern Romania, conquered by the emperor Trajan in 106 CE), to the semi-legendary *Geloni*, Scythians in southern Russia, to the River *Ebro*, used as a metonym for Spain (the conquest of which Augustus was completing as Horace wrote his *Odes*), to the *Gauls*. Horace is being facetious, especially in calling Spain 'well-read'; in the envoi to his first book of *Epistles*, he makes fun of it for its provincial readership (*Epist.* 1.20, ll. 11–14). Horace's prophecy here, that he would be read and admired by all manner of hirsute barbarians at the fringes of the Empire, has proved more true than even he is likely to have imagined.

ll. 21–2. *My grave will be empty* . . . : Besides Ennius' epitaph (see n. on l. 2, above), Horace is echoing Sim. 531, ll. 3–5 (p. 123), the famous elegy on the dead at Thermopylae.

478. *3.1.* The first six poems of Bk. 3 have been known as the 'Roman Odes' ever since Theodor Plüss called them that (*Römeroden*) in 1882. All in

alcaic stanzas (see *Note on Meters*, pp. xxxviii–xxxix), they are elevated in tone, ambitious in scope and patriotic in subject matter; they are not generally modern readers' favorite Horace. Yet they are deeply significant, both for our understanding of Horace at his most public and serious, and as eloquent articulations of Augustan ideals. This first ode, however, has been thought an unusual introduction to the series, since it seems more a manifesto for Epicurus than for Augustus, more a brief for personal happiness than for public order. In a series of examples drawn from contemporary Roman life, Horace illustrates the following maxim of Epicurus (trans. Bailey):

> The disturbance of the soul cannot be ended nor true joy created either by the possession of the greatest wealth or by honour and respect in the eyes of the mob or by anything else that is associated with causes of unlimited desire.

This does not sound especially Roman. The point of overlap Horace seizes on, between his personal Epicureanism and Augustan propaganda, lies in the rejection of luxury. The Augustan narrative held that Rome had conquered the world thanks to the rustic austerity of her citizen-soldiers, the hard-nosed country toughness which encompassed simplicity and restraint; but afterwards, Rome was corrupted by the wealth and luxury success brought with it. In resurrecting this old-fashioned ideal, Augustus would discourage the sorts of extravagant senatorial competition which led to the civil breakdown from which he himself eventually emerged triumphant (cf. *Intro* to Latin Lyric, pp. 368–9). However, when Horace inveighs against tyrannical ambition and insatiable accumulation, he does so on the familiar Horatian (and Epicurean) grounds that such *pleonexia* (grasping for more, money-grubbing) cannot inoculate us against death or secure our happiness. Rather than merely repeat Augustan talking points like a press secretary, therefore, Horace seems to have found a way to accommodate them to his own poetry and principles – at least in this first ode. Interestingly, the way the ode, after the first two stanzas, breaks consistently into two-stanza sections, with enjambment after odd stanzas and a full stop after even ones, has led some scholars to posit that the poem was originally a personal one, and that Horace added the two grandiose opening stanzas later, to introduce the 'Roman Odes' as a whole.

ll. 1–4. *Out of the temple, profaners whom I hate . . .* : An imitation of Call. *Hy.* 2, l. 2 (p. 269). Horace adopts the Callimachean posture of the poet-priest (*vates*): see n. on Call. *Hy.* 2, and cf. Tib. 2.1, ll. 18–25 (p. 418) and n., Hor. *Epod.* 16, l. 66 (p. 461) and n., Hor. *Odes* 1.1, l. 35 (p. 463) and n., and Hor. *Odes* 2.20, l. 2 (p. 477) and n.

l. 1. *profaners*: From *pro fano*, i.e., those 'outside the fane', or temple – here, the uninitiated and/or unpurified who would contaminate the rites. Cf. Tib. 1.3, ll. 25–6 (p. 413), and 2.1, ll. 12–15 (p. 418).

l. 7. *the Giants' lucent vanquisher*: Elsewhere (in *Odes* 3.4), Horace uses Jupiter's defeat of the Giants as a metaphor for Octavian's victory over Mark Antony at Actium (see n. on Hor. *Odes* 1.37, l. 13, p. 470). For the war with the Giants (Gigantomachy), see note on Xen. 1, 1.9 Prop. 2.1, ll. 19–20 (p. 427) and n., and Ov. *Am.* 2.1, ll. 14–21 (p. 498) and nn.

l. 8. *who rattles the world when his eyebrow moves*: For the Homeric precedent, see n. on Call. *Hy.* 5, ll. 132–7 (pp. 275–6).

ll. 9–14. *Compare two vineyards . . .* : A mini priamel; cf. Hor. *Odes* 1.1, ll. 3–34 (pp. 462–3) and n.

ll. 10–14. *in the consular campaigns . . .* : Our word 'candidate' derives from the white robe (*toga candida*) worn by aspirants to the consulship; similarly, 'ambition' is from *ambitio*, 'going around', viz., to solicit votes (a process which often included bribing voters). Here the first candidate is a blue-blooded patrician, the second a 'new man' (like Cicero, striving to be the first in his family to attain the consulship), the third a man of great influence and probably wealth.

ll. 14–16. *. . . from one great urn shakes everyone's name*: Cf. Tib. 1.3, ll. 11–12 (p. 413) and n., and Hor. *Odes* 2.3, ll. 26–8 (p. 472).

ll. 17–18. *the tyrant's unholy neck*: Horace is thinking of Dionysius I or II, tyrant of Syracuse, and his courtier Damocles. The story goes that in response to Damocles' flattering exclamations about Dionysius' good fortune and happiness in being king, the tyrant offered to switch places with him. Damocles was given supreme power and seated on the throne, but with a sword hanging over his head, suspended by a single horsehair (Cicero, *Tusculan Disputations* 5.61–2). The *Feast* of Philoxenus (Phil. 836b+c, p. 216), perhaps written with reference to Dionysius I's court (see *Intro* to Philoxenus, p. 215), might suggest the kinds of 'flavors of Sicily' the Syracusan tyrants enjoyed.

ll. 24–23. *vale of Tempe*: The valley of the River Peneus in Thessaly, often used for any pleasantly wooded vale.

l. 28. *when Arcturus sets and the Kids return*: The evening setting of Arcturus and the evening rising of the Kids (the *Haedi*; see Theoc. *Id.* 7,

l. 60, p. 291, and n.) happened around the end of October, a season of inclement weather. A merchant reckless enough to sail under these constellations would be especially greedy.

479. ll. 29–30. *his farm's deceit . . . his trees complain*: Farms and crops often cheated a farmer's hopes. The trees making excuses for poor productivity is a particularly surreal touch.

ll. 33–7. *Fish feel the ocean shrinking . . .* : Villas artificially erected over water were a common target in diatribes against luxury. Cf. Hor. *Odes* 2.3, ll. 19–20 (p. 472).

l. 41. *purple robes*: For the costly murex dye, see n. on Sulp. 3.8, l. 16 (p. 447).

l. 42. *Phrygian marbles* were white with purple streaks.

l. 43. *Falernian*: See n. on Tib. 2.1, ll. 28–9 (p. 418).

l. 44. *Achaemenid crown*: The Persian royal house was founded by Achaemenes; for the proverbial opulence of Persians and especially Persian kings, cf. Hor. *Epod.* 13, l. 13 (p. 459), and *Odes* 1.38, l. 2 (p. 471), and 3.9, l. 4 (p. 482).

l. 47. *my Sabine valley*: See *Poet Intro* (p. 453) and n. on Hor. *Epod.* 2, l. 41 (p. 457).

3.2. If you could see the gassed soldiers writhing in the trenches, Wilfred Owen says to his old school chum, Horace:

> My friend, you would not tell with such high zest
> To children ardent for some desperate glory,
> The old Lie: Dulce et decorum est
> Pro patria mori.

Owen is, of course, quoting this ode: 'A fine thing and sweet, to die for the fatherland' (l. 13), as this translation has it. Today, this is one of Horace's least beloved poems: Owen is devastating and irrefutable. Does it matter that, for centuries, Horace's line consoled soldiers in the thick of battle, and, later, their grieving families? Does it matter if the poem, for all its propagandistic idealism and earnest naivety, can still get the blood pumping? I don't know. The translation tries to do justice to the poem's rhetorical and poetic virtues, but it is included for its importance, and because, if we are to see Horace, we must see him not only as we prefer him, but as he was.

In contrast to *Odes* 3.1 (see poem note), this one is predominantly Stoic in philosophy.

l. 4. *fierce Parthians*: See n. on Hor. *Odes* 2.13, l. 17 (p. 475), above. The scene that follows is Homeric and romantic rather than rooted in the actualities of Roman warfare as practiced in Horace's day.

480. l. 13. *A fine thing and sweet . . .* : The famous tag clearly owes something to Tyr. 10, ll. 1–2 (p. 22): 'It's beautiful for a brave man to fall . . .'

l. 14. *Death still catches deserters*: For the sentiment, cf. Callinus 1, ll. 12–16 (p. 21), and especially Sim. 524 (p. 122). That the poem carries several other references to Simonides (see nn. on ll. 21–5, below) seems significant – but the poems to which they point are so fragmentary it is hard to say what the significance is.

l. 17. *True Manhood*: The root of the Latin word here given as 'man-hood', *virtus*, is *vir*, 'man'. *Virtus* refers, in the first place, to the virtues befitting a man, especially to courage in battle; but, to the patriarchal Romans, the word's semantic range could be easily extended somewhere close to our 'virtue' or 'excellence.' At any rate, it is on the hymn to *virtus* in this and the next stanza that the present ode turns, from the military virtues of the soldier in the first half of the poem to the virtues of states-men and poets in the second half, a progression which might be felt loosely to track the career of Augustus himself.

l. 19. *the sovereign axe*: The fasces were a bundle of elm or birch rods tied together with a single-bladed axe and carried by lictors, subordinate offi-cials who accompanied elected magistrates and symbolized the majesty of the Roman state. The axe embodied the state's power to carry out execu-tions. Horace's stanza seems to be celebrating, with a deeply undemocratic enthusiasm, Augustus' transcendence of the old requirements of Roman electoral politics.

ll. 21–4. *True Manhood . . . flees on the wing*: Here Horace perhaps looks forward to Augustus' apotheosis, in the manner of Hellenistic monarchs (as well as his adoptive father, Julius Caesar); cf. also Hor. *Odes* 3.25, ll. 5–6 (p. 486). There may be an echo of Sim. *Ep.* 9 (p. 131), on the dead of Thermopylae.

l. 25. *The tact of the faithful*: Horace adapts a fragment of Simonides (Sim. 582): 'Tact, too, has its own reward: it comes risk-free.' The saying was evidently a favorite of Augustus.

ll. 26–7. *the mystical sacraments of Ceres*: A reference to the Eleusinian Mysteries, in which Augustus was initiated; initiates were forbidden from divulging details about the ceremony. Cf. Pi. fr. 137 (p. 164), Phil. Scar. *PaeDi.*, ll. 27–36 (p. 230) and nn., Call., *Acontius and Cydippe* (*Aet.* 3.75), ll. 29–30, and Crin. 35 (p. 343). Horace seems to be hinting that Augustus' own secrets will be safe with him. This ending, a classic example of Horatian diminuendo, points up Horace's own more modest virtues of loyalty and discretion, and hints at the ruin that may be faced by those without them (such as Lucius Licinius Murena; cf. Hor. *Odes* 2.10, p. 473, and nn.).

l. 29. *the Father of Day*: Jupiter, under his archaic name *Diespiter* (*pater diei*).

3.5, The Regulus Ode. Horace inveighs against ransoming back the lives of Roman soldiers taken captive by the Parthians after the disastrous Battle of Carrhae in 53 BCE (see n. on Hor. *Odes* 2.13, l. 17, p. 475). The ode itself is less remarkable for its ferocity and inhuman indifference to the fate of captive Romans than for its arrestingly beautiful and quiet conclusion.

ll. 2–3. *a god at hand, Augustus*: Cf. n. on Ov. *Tri.* 1.4, l. 23 (p. 512). The name 'Augustus', meaning 'majestic, august, venerable, worthy of honor' (Charlton T. Lewis and Charles Short, *A Latin Dictionary*, s.v.), was conferred on Octavian by the Senate in 27 BCE, the likely date of this ode; it signified, according to Cassius Dio (*Roman History* 53.16.8) 'that he was more than human; for all the most precious and sacred objects are termed *augusta*' (trans. Cary). Horace clearly expected an imminent campaign against Britain and Parthia which did not occur.

481. ll. 5–8. *Crassus' troops lie in barbarous beds . . .*: Crassus was the Roman general killed at Carrhae (see n. on Hor. *Odes* 2.13, l. 17, p. 475). According to Horace, the captive soldiers have been so far assimilated into the culture of their conquerors that they have married Parthian women and taken enemies of the Roman state as in-laws.

ll. 9–12. The *Twelve Shields* were kept by the Salii (priests of Mars; cf. Hor. *Odes* 1.37, ll. 3–4, p. 470, and n.); one shield supposedly fell from heaven during the reign of Rome's semi-mythical second king, Numa Pompilius, who, to prevent it from being stolen, had eleven replicas made (see Ov. *Fasti* 3, ll. 352–92). Both Numa's shield and the cult he introduced, which tended the *everliving flame* of *Vesta* (see n. on Hor. *Odes* 3.30, l. 9, p. 487), were associated with the continued survival of Rome. As for the *toga*, apparently it had fallen into some disuse, upsetting Augustus. Suetonius tells us (*Life of Augustus* 40.5) that he once happened on a crowd in brown cloaks and harangued them, sarcastically quoting Virgil, 'Look, Romans, masters of the world, the toga-clad race' (*Aen.* 1, l. 282)! Finally, *Jove* (l. 12) refers not to the god himself so much as to his great temple on the Capitoline Hill.

l. 13. *Regulus' foresight*: Marcus Atilius Regulus, a Roman general during the First Punic War, was captured by Carthage in 255 BCE but sent back to Rome by his captors in hopes that he would persuade the Romans to return some Carthaginian officers in exchange for himself. Clearly the Carthaginians expected him to speak in his own self-interest, but they were mistaken; according to Cicero, Regulus advised the Senate not to accept Carthage's offer, because he was old and would be useless in battle, while the Carthaginians whom the Romans held captive were still young and strong. He then knowingly returned to Carthage to be killed by torture. Accounts of his manner of death vary: either he was subjected to alternating light and dark with his eyelids sewn open, or he was put in a device like an iron maiden, or he was killed slowly by 'enforced wakefulness' (Cicero, *On Duties* 3.100). The truth of this anecdote – which Polybius, the earliest historian of the Punic Wars, does not mention – is less important than the fact that it was known to Horace's audience and accepted as a valorous example of what it meant to be a good Roman.

ll. 18–19. *I've seen many a Roman standard ...* : The standards are depicted as hanging from Carthaginian temples. After a victory, Romans hung up trophies in the manner described; characteristically, Horace (and, no doubt, the people at large) assumed that their enemies did the same.

ll. 23–4. *lands replanted we ravaged ...* : An allusion to Regulus' own military successes in Carthaginian territory, as described in Polybius, *Histories* 1.29–31.

l. 29. *true Manhood*: See n. on Hor. *Odes* 3.2, l. 17 (p. 480).

482. l. 41. *uncitizened*: As a prisoner of war, Regulus was no longer a citizen and thus legally no longer his wife's husband or his sons' father.

ll. 55–6. *Venafrum* (modern Venafro) was a pleasant town about 100 miles southeast of Rome, known for its olive groves. *Tarentum* (modern Taranto, formerly Greek Taras) was a popular resort town on the heel of the Italian boot; it is called 'Lacedaemonia's jewel' because it was founded by Sparta. A Roman like Regulus might head to one of these places either to enjoy his retirement or for a holiday.

3.9. This ode was admired extravagantly by the great sixteenth-century scholar Julius Caesar Scaliger, who said he would rather have written it, or something like it, than be the king of Spain (taking a clue, no doubt, from Horace's l. 4). The poem is *amoebaean*, that is, a kind of competitive dialogue, in which the second speaker tries to 'cap' or outdo the statements of the first. In this volume Cat. 62 (p. 388) takes this form (see n. *ad loc.*); Theoc. *Id.* 7 (p. 291) and Vi. *Ecl.* 9 (p. 405) work in a similar way. Even closer to the present poem in spirit is Cat. 45 (p. 385); both poems are concerned with using their formal symmetries as metaphors for the relationships they depict. Catullus' poem, however, is more visual and static (it could be depicted by a painting), while Horace's is a mini-drama of antagonism and reconciliation.

l. 3. *pale white neck*: A compliment, since, as R. G. M. Nisbet and Niall Rudd say, 'ladies of leisure in the Mediterranean world were not admired for their tan' (*A Commentary on Horace: Odes, Book III*, p. 135).

l. 4. *more richly than a Persian king*: Cf. Hor. *Epod.* 13, l. 13 (p. 459), *Odes* 1.38, l. 2 (p. 471), and *Odes* 3.1, l. 44 (p. 479).

483. l. 8. *Romulus's mother*: Rhea Silvia. Lydia's boast is closer to home. If Horace is her interlocutor, she is returning his compliment, since her fame will have been due to his poetry.

l. 9. *Thracian Chloe now rules my heart*: The epithet for Horace's new girlfriend, Chloe, suggests not only low birth or servile status, but perhaps also a stormy disposition (cf. references to Thracian barbarism in Alc. 72, p. 59, Anac. 356, p. 103, and Call. *Aet.* fr. 178+2.43, ll. 12–13, p. 259). 'Rules my heart' suggests that, though Horace was a king with Lydia (like Croesus), with Chloe he is now a subject.

l. 14. *Calaïs, son of Ornytus*: Lydia's new lover shares a name (supposedly derived from *kalos*, 'handsome') with a Thracian-born son of Boreas (the north wind; cf. n. on Ant. Si. 26, l. 2, p. 322) who sailed with the Argonauts; *Ornytus* probably means 'rushing' in Greek, like the wind. (One might contrast Calaïs' impressive pedigree with Horace's own freedman birth; see *Poet Intro*, p. 453.) Calaïs and Chloe would thus seem to make a well-matched, if tempestuous, pairing, while the associations of Lydia's name with easy-living eastern luxury would plainly appeal to the pleasure-loving Horace.

l. 23. *Adria*: The Adriatic.

3.12. This slight but charming poem is notable mostly as a metrical experiment – the only poem in Latin composed entirely in minor ionics (see *Note on Meters*, p. xl). In both meter and content it is an imitation of Alcaeus 10b (p. 56), though the speaker is named 'Neobule', after Archilochus' sometime love interest (cf. *Intro* to Archilochus, p. 5).

484. ll. 6–7. *Venus's fluttering boy*: Cupid.

l. 8. *Minerva's duty*: Weaving, which fell under Minerva's patronage, was the traditional occupation of Roman female virtue (cf. Tib. 2.1, ll. 64–7, p. 419).

l. 9. *Hebrus*: Named for a river in Thrace (cf. Alc. 45, l. 3, p. 58, and n.), Neobule's love interest, as Horace's Latin makes clear, hails from the island of Lipara (modern Lipari) near Sicily – *liparos* in Greek means 'glistening', as with oil. The geographical reference may point to Simaetha's infatuation with Delphis in Theoc. *Id.* 2 (cf. l. 137, p. 290).

l. 11. *in the Tiber's waves*: Presumably Hebrus' ablutions took place before 25 BCE, when the Baths of Agrippa supplanted the Tiber as the go-to swimming spot; cf. n. on Hor. *Odes* 4.1, l. 40 (p. 489), below, and Mart. 5.20, l. 10 (p. 543) and n.

l. 13. *Bellerophon*: The quintessential horseman, he slew the monstrous Chimera on the back of the winged steed, Pegasus. But, like other high flyers, he overreached, and he was bucked from his horse while trying to ascend to Olympus. See n. on Hor. *Odes* 4.11, ll. 25–31 (p. 491), below.

ll. 19–20. *the bristling boar he's ready for*: For more on boar-hunting, see Sulp. 3.9 (p. 448) and nn. The beautiful young boy hunting boar ominously evokes Adonis, for whom see Call. *Ia.* 3, ll. 36–7 (p. 263) and n.; combined with the reference to Bellerophon above, one rather doubts Neobule's infatuation will end well, perhaps like Simaetha's in Theoc. *Id.* 2 (see n. on l. 9, above).

3.13. Just as Horace seeks a place for himself in the canon of Greek lyric poets, he also seeks a place for his favorite local fountain among the Muses' great springs: to Hippocrene, Aganippe, Castalia and Arethusa, Horace adds . . . Bandusia. Where is Bandusia? It certainly could be the lovely, fresh fountain near the archaeological site at Licenza in the Sabine Hills, dubbed 'Horace's Villa' and visited by many a literary pilgrim (cf. *Poet Intro*, p. 453, and n. on Hor. *Epod.* 2, l. 41, p. 457). Yet the word *Bandusia* isn't at home in Latium; rather, it sounds like a southern Italian corruption of a Greek name (*Pandosia*, 'Place of All Gifts'). Because we can do no better, we will assume that Horace grew up near a spring called Bandusia in Apulia and gave that name to another spring near his beloved Sabine villa.

Much ink has also been spilled trying to determine this ode's occasion: the leading contender is the Fontanalia, a sacrifice to the Roman god of springs, Fons (Font), which took place every 13 October. Formally the ode is a hymn, but it clearly owes more to Greek epigram (cf. Anyte 16, p. 303, and Leo. Tar. 5, p. 307).

l. 4. *to stain your coldness*: Some commentators have been troubled by this aestheticizing contrast of blood and water. Horace plainly does not possess the sentimental feelings toward the baby goat we might expect of a nature poet.

l. 9. *while the fierce Dog Star burns*: This reference to the midsummer heat associated with Sirius (see n. on Prop. 2.28, l. 3, p. 431, and cf. Hor. *Epod.* 16, ll. 61–2, p. 461, and n.) might suggest July as a likely setting for the poem and thus would present difficulties to those who think the poem celebrates the October Fontanalia.

485. *3.18*. This charming little invocatory ('kletic') hymn is directed to the god Faunus (see n. on l. 1, below) and strikes as pure a note of Italian pastoral lyric as anything in Horace. Compare Hor. *Odes* 3.23 (p. 485), below.

l. 1. *Faunus* was an ancient Italic deity, perhaps originally Etruscan, and early associated with Pan. He was a god of fertility and prophecy – his name was variously derived from *favere*, 'to favor', and *fari*, 'to speak, prophesy' – and his prophecies were often chanted in saturnians, the obscure native Italian verse form into which Livius Andronicus translated the *Odyssey* at the beginning of Latin literature (see *Intro* to Latin Lyric, pp. 365–6). There were also plural *fauni*, Fauns, eventually assimilated to the Greek satyrs as Faunus was to the Greek Pan. Faunus had no iconography; his female counterpart, similarly aniconic, may have been Pales. Faunus appeared (or uttered) unpredictably, at no prescribed place or season. When a Roman smallholder stepped off his property and ventured forth, he left the protection of his Lares (see n. on Tib. 1.10, ll. 15–29, p. 416) and entered the capricious realm of Faunus. Horace's fondness for this deity – who, he says in *Odes* 2.17, saved him from a falling tree (see *Odes* 2.13, ll. 1–4, p. 474 and nn.) – was probably already a bit antiquarian, whether inspired by Augustus' preference for the old religion or his own Epicurean need for being versed in country things. Cf. Faunus' presence in *Odes* 1.4, ll. 11–12 (p. 465) and n.

l. 9. *December's Nones*: i.e., 5 December, during the festival of the Faunalia.

l. 16. *a three-step jig*: This old-fashioned style of dance was characteristic of the leaping priests of Mars, the Salii; see Hor. *Odes* 1.37, ll. 3–4 (p. 470), 3.5, ll. 9–12 (p. 481) and n., and 4.1, l. 28 (p. 488).

3.23. Like Hor. *Odes* 3.18 (p. 485), above, a quiet little ode on rustic Italian religion in the vein of Tibullus (here cf. also Tib. 1.10, ll. 15–29, p. 416). The Elder Cato (*On Agriculture* 143.2) gives his villa manager the task of tending to the hearth gods, the Lares (or, as he has it, the singular Lar): 'On the Kalends, the Ides and the Nones, and any other holiday, she should deck the hearth with a wreath, and make offering to the household Lar according to her means.' Horace's Phidyle (Greek for 'thrifty') has a similar task: to ward off the plagues of the second stanza by the observances of the first, performed at the start of every month (marked in the country by the new moon, l. 1). In the contrast between Phidyle's modest offerings (ll. 15–16) – to be given, as Cato has it, 'according to her means' – and the lavish pontifical flocks (ll. 11–12), it is easy enough to hear the poem talking about itself.

l. 3. *Lares*: See n. on Tib. 1.10, ll. 15–29 (p. 416), and cf. Hor. *Epod.* 2, l. 43 (p. 457).

l. 5. *the sirocco*: See Hor. *Odes* 2.14, l. 16 (p. 476) and n.

486.   l. 10. *Algidus*: A dormant volcano (modern Monte Algido) in the Alban Hills, about twelve miles southeast of Rome.

l. 12. *fattened by pontiffs*: The pontifical college – one of Rome's four chief priestly orders – owned pastureland in the Alban Hills, where animals for public sacrifice were raised.

3.25. The Apollinian Horace gives himself over to the Dionysiac dithyramb (see n. on Ar. 120+121, l. 2, p. 10). He imagines himself as a Bacchant or maenad, one of the ecstatic followers of Dionysus/Bacchus. This poem is the closest Horace ever came to the Romantic enthusiasm of a Schiller. Compare *Odes* 1.6 (p. 466), where Horace strikes his usual pose of refusal (*recusatio*) to hymn the truly great; this poem abandons that pose, under the influence of the god of wine.

l. 7. *My song is a new star*: The 'star of Julius' (*sidus Iulium*) was a comet observed every night during the seven days of funeral games for Julius Caesar which Octavian held four months after the assassination in 44 BCE; it was taken as a sign of Caesar's apotheosis, a prerogative Roman emperors came to enjoy after death. Cf. n. on Vi. *Ecl.* 4 (p. 403), and *Ecl.* 9, ll. 59–60 (p. 407). With this translation I follow the lead of David West, who hears in Horace's *insigne* a reference to *signa*, 'constellations'.

ll. 10–12. *Hebrus* is a great river (cf. Alc. 45, l. 3, p. 58, and n.), and *Rhodope* a mountain range, of Thrace, a region of perpetual snow associated with Bacchus in his sublime and uncanny aspect.

l. 14. *King of the Naiad bands*: Dionysus is often associated with Naiads. See Pi. *Dith.* 2, ll. 17–20 (p. 159).

ll. 15–16. *whose strength shivers and topples towering ash trees*: Bacchants had superhuman strength when the god possessed them; they even uprooted trees (Euripides, *Bacchae*, ll. 1104–10) and tore large animals, like bulls, limb from limb (*ibid.* ll. 737–47), and, driven mad, did the same to people.

487. *3.30.* In the final ode of his third book, Horace returns to the meter with which Bk. 1 began (stichic lesser asclepiads – see *Note on Meters*, p. xxxv), and proclaims authoritatively here the fulfillment of ambitions announced somewhat comically in *Odes* 1.1 (p. 462). (It's worth recalling that all three books were published together, in 23 BCE, when Horace may have had no intention of writing a fourth.) As pointed out elsewhere in the notes, this poem, *Odes* 1.1 and *Odes* 2.20 (p. 477) are the only three in which Horace speaks directly about his own achievement.

l. 2. *the kingly decay of pyramids*: Romans had pyramids on the brain after the annexation of Egypt in 30 BCE (see *Intro* to Latin Lyric, p. 369, and Hor. *Odes* 1.37, p. 470); the ode begins with a nod to Augustus' greatest achievement, and ends with Horace's. The present passage is imitated by Prop. 3.2 (ll. 19–26), as well as by Ovid at the end of the *Metamorphoses*; Shakespeare repurposed it several times, most obviously with 'Not marble, nor the gilded monuments' (Sonnet 55). The Romans' simple bronze plaque (l. 1) and the grandiose Egyptian pyramids are both funeral monuments.

ll. 3–5. *which not the needling raindrops ... :* As Horace began with Pindar at *Odes* 1.1, ll. 3–34 (pp. 462–3; see n. *ad loc.*), here he ends with him as well: these lines are based on *Py.* 6, ll. 8–14, where Pindar compares his own ode to 'a treasure house of melodies'

> which neither winter storms from the throaty thunder
>   of clouds like the arriving
> of far harsh armies marching, nor winds driving
>   the silt-churn sucking under
> can sweep into the chambers deep below
>   the seething ocean.

l. 7. *untouched by the death goddess*: Libitina, goddess of funerals, associated with the cemetery on the Esquiline Hill, where Horace would eventually be buried (see *Poet Intro*, p. 454).

l. 9. *Vestals keeping silence*: Vestal Virgins, priestesses dedicated to Vesta, who tended the everliving fire of Vesta (cf. Hor. *Odes* 3.5, l. 11, p. 481, and n.) in her round temple in the Forum, and swore a thirty-year vow of chastity. See also Ov. *Am.* 3.7, l. 22 (p. 508).

l. 10. *where vocal Aufidus pours his floods*: The Aufidus (modern Ofanto) was the main river of Apulia, where Horace was born.

ll. 11–12. *Daunus* ... : A legendary Apulian king – a Greek immigrant from Illyria – whose 'country' subjects remind Horace of his own humble beginnings ('mighty from slender means'), which of course he connects to the Callimachean 'slenderness' of his poetry. See the next note, and also the n. on *Odes* 2.20, l. 1 (p. 477) – another poem where Horace emphasizes his common birth ('a child of mere subsistence', ll. 5–6).

ll. 13–14. *the first to lead in triumph Aeolia's exquisite music to Roman rhythms*: The Latin, whose nuances neither literal nor poetic translation can exhaust, is worth quoting: *princeps Aeolium carmen ad Italos / deduxisse modos* – literally, 'the first to have led Aeolic song to Italian measures'. Horace is *princeps*, i.e., the 'first', the 'chief', the 'prince' (in the way that Augustus is *princeps inter pares*, the 'first among equals'), 'to have led', *deduxisse*, Greek song to Italian measures. But Horace has it backward, since what he really did was compose Italian songs in Greek measures. The key is *deduxisse*, which has three quite different senses: 'to lead on a colonizing expedition'; 'to lead in triumph'; and 'to lead or draw out, finely spin, as a yarn or thread'. All three senses are active. First, Horace has, as it were, led Greek song from Archaic Lesbos to contemporary Rome; in his poetry, Greek lyric has colonized Latin. That may sound as if Rome has been conquered, and, in a sense, it has: as Horace himself wrote in *Epist.* 2.1, l. 156, 'Greece, taken, took its feral captor captive'. Yet, in truth, Rome is the real conqueror, and the triumph Horace's. Horace here is like a belated Lucius Mummius, parading before the citizens' eyes myriads of bronze statues and paintings lifted from the sack of Corinth (see *Intro* to Latin Lyric, p. 367). For Horace there was no contradiction between homage and rivalry: he clearly implies that he has surpassed his forebears. Finally, there is also a trace of Horace's ambivalence toward Callimachus (pp. 255–81): *deducere* elsewhere in Latin poetry (e.g., Vi. *Ecl.* 6, l. 5) conveys that 'slenderness' (*leptotes*) and attention to detail associated with the influential Alexandrian. If Horace has 'finely spun' Aeolic song into Latin, the implication, almost off-hand, is that he has refined the rough old stuff to meet modern aesthetic standards. In short, Horace here confronts us with such a seamless and thoroughgoing fusion of Greek and Latin, colonizer and colonized, conquered and conqueror, that it is hard to tell where one ends and the other begins. His Greek rhythms have been naturalized in Italy; his Italian music is at least half Greek.

l. 15. *Melpomene*: The Muse. See Hor. *Odes* 1.24, l. 3 (p. 469) and n.

l. 16. *Apollo's laurel*: The prize for victory in the Pythian Games, including its poetic competitions (cf. Call. *Ia.* 4, l. 33, p. 264; and see n. on ll. 3–5, above, for this ode's quotation of Pi. *Py.* 6), and also the coronal of a Roman general in a triumph. Not, however, previously applied to the brows of poets simply for being poets: the *poet laureate* is invented here.

4.1. After retiring from love in *Odes* 3.26, the aged Horace, now in his fifties, reluctantly reenters the lists of Venus. Via an easy conceptual slide from love to love poetry, Horace is usually also thought to be returning to the genre of lyric, which he had put away in 23 BCE when the *Odes* came out and he turned his *Epistles*. But, according to Suetonius (*Life of Horace*) commissions straight from the top pulled him back in: first the *Centennial Hymn*, composed for the Centennial or 'Secular' Games in 17 BCE (see *Intro* to Latin Lyric, p. 372), then, in 15, two odes celebrating the victory of the emperor's stepsons, Drusus and Tiberius, over the Vindelici, a people living in what is now Switzerland and Bavaria. Suetonius further reports that Augustus had written to Horace kiddingly, but with a definite edge: 'You should know I'm mad at you, since, in all the many poems you've written, you never address me directly; or are you afraid that posterity will think worse of you if you admit to being my friend?' Horace took the hint, and addressed to Augustus the first poem of *Epist.* 2, as well as two odes in Bk. 4 (4.5 and 4.15); the book ends in direct praise of 'your epoch, Caesar'. Yet biographical skeptics might wonder if, having been asked by Augustus to write two odes, Horace now felt compelled to write thirteen more, just so he could have a book to publish them in.

Bk. 4 is more doggedly political than the first three books, and is full of a tension or opposition between poetry and politics; it is also concerned with new generations of Romans entering the stage while Horace himself is on the way out. Ode 4.1 engages both themes, contrasting the aged Horace, painted in the colors of Greek epigram, with the poem's suave young addressee, Paullus Fabius Maximus (see n. on l. 11, below). Today, Bk. 4's odes about the poet's own death and the consolations of poetry will be the ones we respond to most warmly, as indeed in this poem the praise of Maximus functions mostly as a foil for the poet's futile pursuit of the boy Ligurinus.

l. 1. *Venus, must I rejoin your fray*: The motif of lover as soldier of Venus is an elegiac one (cf. especially Ov. *Am.* 1.9, p. 495), though Horace uses it too, as in *Odes* 1.6 (p. 466), where he insists on writing love poetry instead of epic. Horace is influenced by Iby. 287 (p. 99) and Sap. 1 (p. 39), the first poem in the Alexandrian edition of her poems (as this is the first in Horace's Bk. 4); but while Sappho summons Aphrodite for her own sake, Horace dismisses Venus from himself and sends her to the younger Paullus Maximus instead (cf. ll. 9–12).

ll. 3–4. *That man I was ... Cinara ... no more*: The Latin (*non sum qualis eram bonae / sub regno Cinarae*) furnishes the title of Ernest Dowson's greatest poem, which in turn gave Margaret Mitchell the title for *Gone with the Wind* (cf. n. on Hor. *Odes* 1.4, l. 15, p. 465, for Dowson's other famous Horace-inspired poem). Cinara herself is mysterious, as Horace for some reason only mentions her after her death. An Augustan inscription from Horace's hometown of Venusia marks the grave of a slave girl called Cinara (or similar; the spelling is up for debate) whom he may have known in his youth; alternatively, the reference may be to the Hebrew word for 'lyre', which appears in Greek as *kinyra*.

488. l. 11. *Paullus Maximus*: Paullus Fabius Maximus (*c.*46 BCE–14 CE) was an important young aristocrat (or youngish – he would have been in his thirties when the ode was written sometime in the mid-teens BCE, clearly before his consulship in 11 BCE) and confidant of Augustus. He is the only person besides Augustus himself to be addressed by both Horace and Ovid (cf. *Ex Pont.* 3.3, p. 522).

l. 12. *whose liver will be perfect for your skewers*: The liver was believed to be the seat of passionate emotions, such as lust and anger.

ll. 17–20. *Whenever a richly second-rate ...* : Horace imagines Maximus in a stock elegiac situation, competing with a rival for a woman's attention (cf., e.g., Prop. 1.11, ll. 7–8, p. 426); except that Maximus, unlike Propertius, has so many advantages that there is no competition. Casually the great man vows an expensive shrine and statue of Venus in gratitude for his inevitable victory.

l. 19. *Alban Lake*: The modern Lago Albano, near Rome on the Appian Way. A swanky suburban retreat area in Republican Rome, it was increasingly co-opted by the emperors. Presumably Maximus had a villa there.

l. 23. *Phrygian oboe*: A reed instrument associated with Mount Berecynthus in Phrygia and the Cybele worship which traveled thence to Rome at the end of the third century BCE; see Anon. 935 (p. 237) and n.

ll. 27–8. *footing the triple dance . . . like the Salii*: The Salii were the leaping priests of Mars, famed for their triple-time dance; cf. Hor. *Odes* 1.37, ll. 3–4 (p. 470), and 3.18, l. 16 (p. 485), and see n. on *Odes* 3.5, ll. 9–12 (p. 481).

l. 32. *drinking competitions*: Probably competitive toasting (as in Call. *Ep.* 5, p. 277, and Mel. 42, p. 328) rather than the *cottabus* (or *kottabos*; cf. Alc. 72, p. 59, and n.).

l. 33. *why oh why*: Such puzzled questions are typical of Greek epigram; cf. Ascl. 16 (p. 305).

l. 34. *Ligurinus*: The name, which means 'the Ligurian' (that is, a native of maritime northwest Italy), is probably a nickname, but not much more can be said about this mysterious boy. Only here in the *Odes* (in a context redolent of Greek epigram) does Horace speak openly of pederasty, though there are possible hints in Bk. 1: see *Odes* 1.4, l. 19 (p. 465) and n.

ll. 35–6. *Why . . . does my articulate tongue fail*: Horace is surely thinking of Sappho's failure of speech at Sap. 31, l. 9 (p. 45).

489. l. 39. *Mars's Field*: The Campus Martius, outside the sacred boundary (*pomerium*) of Rome proper, a place where young men went to exercise and be seen.

l. 40. *through . . . tides*: Latin *per aquas*; the translation assumes Ligurinus is swimming in the Tiber, as was generally done up until 25 BCE, when Agrippa's heated baths were built nearby, in a bend of the river, whereupon they immediately became the go-to spot. Cf. Hor. *Odes* 3.12, l. 11 (p. 484) and n., and Mart. 5.20, l. 10 (p. 543) and n.

4.7. A few days after the death of the great English poet and philologist A. E. Housman, one of his former students, a Mrs. T. W. Pym, contributed the following recollection to a column of 'Appreciations' in *The Times* (5 May 1936):

> At five minutes past 11 he used to walk to the desk, open his manuscript, and begin to read. At the end of the hour he folded his papers and left the room. He never looked either at us or at the row of dons in the front. One morning in May, 1914, when the trees in Cambridge were covered with blossom, he reached in his lecture Ode 7 in Horace's Fourth Book . . . This ode he dissected with the usual display of brilliance, wit, and sarcasm. Then for the first time in two years he looked up at us, and in quite a different voice said: 'I should like to spend the last few minutes

considering this ode simply as poetry.' Our previous experience of Professor Housman would have made us sure that he would regard such a proceeding as beneath contempt. He read the ode aloud with deep emotion, first in Latin and then in an English translation of his own. 'That,' he said hurriedly, almost like a man betraying a secret, 'I regard as the most beautiful poem in ancient literature,' and walked quickly out of the room.

Of the same incident, another undergraduate recalled: 'I felt quite uncomfortable. I was afraid the old fellow was going to cry.'

Ode 4.7 shows the influence of Simonides (Sim. 521, p. 122, and *El.* 19+20, p. 129), and contains many reminiscences of other odes of Horace – most obviously 1.4 (p. 000), with its shared theme of spring; for other examples, see below.

ll. 6–7. *The nymphs ... dare to dance ...* : Compare Hor. *Odes* 1.4, ll. 5–7 (p. 464).

l. 19. *Tullus, Ancus and Aeneas*: Aeneas, of course, makes us think of Virgil, as does the *pietas* ('godliness', l. 29) whose effectiveness against death Horace denies farther on. Tullus Hostilius and Ancus Marcius were the third and fourth legendary kings of Rome, also grouped together in the underworld at *Aen.* 6, ll. 812–16.

l. 25. *grasping heir*: For such legacy hunting or captation in Rome, see n. on Mart. 1.10, l. 4 (p. 535); in Horace, cf. also *Odes* 2.3, ll. 17–20 (p. 472), and 2.14, ll. 25–8 (p. 477), and n. on Hor. *Odes* 1.11, l. 8 (p. 468).

490.   l. 26. *strict Minos*: See n. on Theaetetus 3, l. 4 (p. 318).

l. 28. *Torquatus*: Surely the same Manlius Torquatus addressed in Hor. *Epist.* 1.5; an orator otherwise little known to us, his name will have evoked the Titus Manlius Torquatus who sternly condemned his own son to death in 340 BCE (Livy, *History of Rome* 8.7.19), and who is mentioned in Vi. *Aen.* 6 (ll. 824–5), shortly after Tullus and Ancus (l. 19, above).

l. 29. *godliness*: *Pietas*, famously the chief virtue of Virgil's Aeneas, also comes in for criticism in Horace in *Odes* 1.24 (p. 469) and 2.14 (p. 476).

l. 32. *Hippolytus who fell*: Hippolytus was a chaste youth dedicated to Artemis/Diana – Ovid mentions him jokily at *Am.* 2.4, l. 32 (p. 500); he spurned the advances of his stepmother Phaedra, who accused him of attempted rape. Cursed by his father Theseus, his grandfather Poseidon spooked his horses, causing him to be thrown from his chariot and trampled to death. For the story, see Euripides' *Hippolytus* and Racine's

Phaedra. In Vi. *Aen.* 7, ll. 761–77, Diana rescues Hippolytus from the underworld and installs him, now called Virbius (Twice a Man), in a grove sacred to her. Horace pointedly contradicts Virgil's account.

l. 34. *Pirithöus*: The son of Ixion (see Tib. 1.3, ll. 73–4, p. 415, and n.) – or, rather, the son of Zeus by Ixion's wife – and king of the Lapiths, who attempted, with his best friend Theseus, to abduct Persephone from the underworld and marry her. The pair were tricked onto a bench (or Chair of Forgetfulness) and chained there; when Heracles came down to abduct Cerberus (cf. Bacch. 5, ll. 69–83, p. 173), he was allowed to free Theseus, but not Pirithöus.

l. 35. Hor. *Odes* 3.4 ends similarly, with Pirithöus in the underworld:

> the bird that gnaws unbridled Tityus' liver
> will never leave that grossness it guards over;
>   nor will three hundred fetters ever
> let go of Pirithöus, the lover.

(For Tityus, see n. on Tib. 1.3, ll. 75–6, p. 415.) Intriguingly, a poem of A. E. Housman's – little known because he wrote it in Latin and prefixed it to his edition of the first-century CE astronomical poet Manilius – also concludes in the same manner. In the wonderfully Housmanesque version of A. E. Stallings ('To my Comrade, Moses J. Jackson, Scoffer at this Scholarship', ll. 35–40):

> Take them: for that day will come
> To add us to the canceled sum
> And give our bones to earth to rot
> (For we have no immortal lot,
> And souls that will not last forever)
> And the chain of comrades sever.

Stallings is echoing Housman's own rendering of Ode 4.7 ('Diffugere Nives'), one of the great translations of classical poetry. It ends (ll. 27–8):

> And Theseus leaves Pirithous in the chain
> The love of comrades cannot take away.

Both Housman's translation and Horace's ode have the feel of a summation of their authors' careers and a crystallization of their undeceived and uncompromising classicism.

4.11. Horace is celebrating his patron Maecenas' birthday on the Ides of April and invites one Phyllis to join him. Such invitation poems comprise a minor subgenre, more Roman than Greek, perhaps invented by Philodemus (see Phil. 23, p. 338 and n.); cf. Cat. 13 (p. 381), Hor. *Odes* 1.20 and Mart. 10.48 (p. 549). This poem is both invitation and persuasion, most poignant for its finality: it is indeed the last of Horace's love poems.

l. 1. *Phyllis*: Her name means 'Leaf', not unlike *Chloe* (Green Shoot) in Hor. *Odes* 1.23 (p. 469) and 3.9 (p. 482) and is a conventional name in pastoral. It may be relevant that in Vi. *Ecl.* 3 (l. 76) a Phyllis is requested as a birthday present. Horace could also be thinking of the Phyllis of Prop. 4.8 (p. 442), a lady of easy virtue.

l. 2. *aged over nine years*: Interestingly specific; if the grape harvest had happened in 23 BCE, when Bks. 1–3 of the *Odes* were published, the party for Maecenas at which the resulting wine is now being opened might also celebrate the publication of Bk. 4 of the *Odes* in 13 BCE.

l. 14. *the Ides*: In April, as in all thirty-day months, the 13th.

l. 15. *the month of Venus Born from Foam*: Horace here takes sides in the ancient debate on the etymology of April – whether to regard it as the 'opening' of the year (from *aperire*, 'to open'), or as derived from *Aphrodite* – *aphros* meaning 'foam' – and relating to the sexual energy of the season. Horace is wrong about the etymology but clearly correct about his own intentions.

491.   l. 21. *Telephus*: 'Far-Shining', the name also given to a more successful amatory rival of Horace's in *Odes* 1.13 and 3.19. There might be a distant connection to the mythical hero Telephus (see Ar. *Achaeans at Mysia*, p. 7), since he, having been cured by the weapon used to wound him, bears some resemblance to a typical lover; cf. Prop. 2.1, ll. 65–6 (p. 429), and Ov. *Tri.* 4.1, l. 36 (p. 517).

ll. 25–31. *Phaethon* (l. 25) and *Bellerophon* (l. 27) both provide Horace with examples of overreaching. Phaethon flew Phoebus' chariot, but could not control it, and was blasted by Zeus/Jupiter as a result (Ov. *Met.* 1, l. 750–*Met.* 2, l. 400). Bellerophon was bucked off by Pegasus while trying to fly to Olympus (according to Pi. *Isthmian* 7, ll. 44–8) and fell to earth. There is something Pindaric in Horace's high-minded argument here – jokily inappropriate to his real, quite lowbrow goal of convincing Phyllis to settle for a shortish, fattish, oldish man like him (as he describes himself in *Epist.* 1.4, l. 15, and 1.20, l. 24). After such Pindaric excess, the poem's melancholy conclusion is the more touching and sincere.

Ovid

492. *Poet Introduction. carmen et error*: Ov. *Tri.* 2, l. 207.

494. *which thematize their 'two-ness'*: In the translations that follow, the alert reader will notice my own occasional resort to triplets where the content of Ovid's Latin couplets did not naturally compress into English ones, or need to be unpacked into four lines (an approach to the 'heroic' couplet that is perhaps a little more Dryden than Pope).

Amores. First published *c*.16 BCE (though later pruned and reissued, perhaps around 1 or 2 CE), the *Amores* (*Experiences of Love*, as the German classicist Niklas Holzberg asserts the title should be rendered) stand at the beginning of Ovid's prolific career, as the *Tristia* (pp. 512–20) and *Letters from Pontus* (pp. 521–6) stand at the end. These three works, bookending Ovid's more ambitious productions, approach most closely to our own Romantic-inflected conceptions of first-person lyric, and so are the works of Ovid excerpted here. It seems unlikely that Ovid himself would have viewed them as we do: he certainly denies (echoing Catullus – see Ov. *Tri.* 3.2, l. 6, p. 513, and n.) any overlap between the three books of the *Amores* and his own autobiography. Holzberg has seen the *Amores* influentially as an 'erotic novel' (*Ovid: The Poet and His Work*, trans. Goshgarian, pp. 46–70), an experiment in and extension of Callimachean discontinuous narration, as hinted at Call. *Aet.* 1.1, ll. 3–5 (p. 258); he points not only to the novelty of the situations limned (cf. especially Ov. *Am.* 2.13, p. 506), but also to their concreteness, finding them more reminiscent of scenes from a fiction than of the dreamy and passionate subjectivity of love elegy in the hands of Tibullus (pp. 411–20) and Propertius (pp. 421–45). Ovid is a poet far less of sentiment than wit. Plainly, part of his intent was to parody his two predecessors (and, no doubt, the father of Latin love elegy, Gaius Cornelius Gallus as well, whose work has not survived; see Vi. *Ecl.* 10, l. 2, p. 408, and n.), and, in the process, perhaps to mock the moral anxieties of the late Republic with an insouciance born in the boom years of the early Empire. Whether he also intended, in his relentlessly logical way, to push and extend the genre of Latin love elegy up to and past its breaking point cannot be determined; yet this is precisely what he did. The *Amores* broke the love elegy, and no one (up until, say, Goethe) ever tried to write it again.

1.5. There are really only two 'sex' poems in Latin: this one, and Prop. 2.15 (p. 429), to the first ten lines or so of which Ovid is clearly indebted. Propertius' poem, though, is a personal monologue, in which the ecstatic blurt yields to thoughtfulness and reflection; Ovid's, by contrast, is an impersonal narrative, cool, witty and controlled. And yet it represents the height of Ovid's amorous happiness with his mistress, Corinna ('Dollface', or 'Little Girlie', named for the Greek poetess of uncertain date, pp. 199–203); two other relatively explicit poems (*Am.* 2.10, p. 504, and 3.7, p. 507) chart his decline into promiscuity and decadence. Those poems are also connected to this one by a shared reliance on Greek epigram, specifically Philodemus: this poem opens with a nod to Phil. 9 (p. 336) – as well as, no doubt, to Prop. 1.3 (p. 425), which also uses it – and touches upon two others (see nn. on ll. 18–23 and 26, below).

l. 1. *Noon sizzled*: Noon in Hellenistic poetry is an hour of torpor and danger, in which epiphanies occur, as in Call. *Hy.* 5, ll. 72–4 (p. 274), and Theoc. *Id.* 1, ll. 15–19; the epiphanic resonances are foremost here. Ovid may also be thinking of Mel. 79 (p. 331).

ll. 3–4. *The shutters* ... : Cf. Phil. 9 (p. 336), Prop. 1.3, ll. 31–3 (pp. 425–6), and Ov. *Ex Pont.* 3.3, ll. 6–13 (p. 522).

ll. 12–13. *famed Semiramis ... or Lais*: Semiramis was a semi-mythical Assyrian queen said, in one story reported by Diodorus Siculus (*Library of History* 2.20.3), to have been a prostitute. Lais of Corinth certainly was; in this volume Antipater of Sidon (Ant. Si. 23, p. 321) has written her an epitaph. The passage bears some similarity to the rampant similitudinizing of Prop. 1.3, ll. 1–6 (p. 425), or Cat. 68b (p. 391).

ll. 14–17. *I tore the gown* ... : For fighting with one's lover as erotic, see Tib. 1.10, ll. 53–6 (p. 417) and n., and Prop. 2.15 (p. 429) and 3.8 (p. 435).

ll. 18–23. *She stood there naked ... how young*: Since the sixteenth century, such a 'catalogue of charms' has been known as a 'blazon' and is used, without undue seriousness, by authors such as Shakespeare (Sonnet 130: 'My mistress' eyes are nothing like the sun'), John Donne ('Love's Progress') and Andrew Marvell ('To His Coy Mistress'). Ovid's own example no doubt looks to Phil. 12 (p. 336); for another example, see Dios. 1 (p. 313).

495. l. 26. *Who doesn't know the rest*: Ovid's poem closes coyly with an allusion to Phil. 1 (p. 334); compare also Argent. 13 (p. 349).

1.9. The motif of lover as soldier (*militia amoris*, the 'warfare of love') may have had its origin in Hellenistic epigram (cf. Dios. 2, p. 314, and *Anacreontea* 26, p. 362), but it came into its own in Latin love elegy; cf. Tib. 1.10, ll. 53–66 (p. 417) and n., Prop. 2.15, ll. 41–8 (p. 430), Hor. *Odes* 1.6, ll. 17–18 (p. 466), and Ov. *Am.* 2.12 (p. 505) and *Ex Pont.* 3.3, l. 84 (p. 524). Ovid treats the theme with typical fulsomeness, via the rhetorical trope of *comparatio* (comparison), but gives it an Ovidian twist. Lovers are conventionally thought to be lazy and idle (cf. Cat. 51, p. 387), in contrast with the sheer energy of soldiers; Prop. 1.6 expresses the usual attitude:

> Let me, whom Lady Luck debarred from action,
> breathe my last breath in slothful stupefaction . . .
> I'm not cut out for glory or for war:
> my destiny's to march in Cupid's corps!

Ovid, however, emphasizes the enterprise and perseverance of the elegiac lover – more accurate, no doubt, in the case of the prolific poet than the indolent urban debauchee.

l. 2. *Cupid, too, has tents pitched on the plain*: The 'camp' of Cupid may be an intentional oxymoron, as the word 'camp' (*castra*) was often derived from *casta*, 'chaste', on the grounds that women were forbidden from the camps of soldiers. Cf. also Ov. *Ex Pont.* 3.3, l. 84 (p. 524).

l. 3. *Atticus*: Presumably a soldier, this Atticus cannot be identified, though he is also addressed by Ovid at *Ex Pont.* 2.4 (p. 521). In general, addressees play a minimal role in the *Amores*.

l. 25. *Thracian Rhesus' armies met disaster*: The story is in Hom. *Il.* 10, ll. 433–563, and alluded to at Vi. *Aen.* 1, ll. 469–73. The Thracian king Rhesus, an ally of the Trojans, just arrived in Troy, was killed as he slept in his camp by Diomedes and Odysseus; they also stole his horses. It had been prophesied that, should those horses ever drink from the River Xanthus, Troy would not fall.

496. ll. 36–43. *Briseis, taken, set Achilles burning . . .*: The point of these examples seems to be that the warriors named (Achilles, Hector, Agamemnon, Mars) were not rendered idle and impotent by their amours. Achilles is a sort of exception; in the *Iliad*, when his favorite slave girl, Briseis, is taken by Agamemnon, he petulantly refuses to fight, the tide turns and the Trojans attack with great success.

ll. 38–9. *Straight from Andromache's arms . . .*: In Hom. *Il.* 6, ll. 392–496, Hector's wife, Andromache, attempts to persuade her husband not to fight, but is not able to stop him.

ll. 40–41. *Agamemnon stopped to stare . . .*: Agamemnon falls for Priam's daughter Cassandra at first sight, like a stereotypical elegiac lover, and, according to Aeschylus (*Agamemnon*, ll. 1438–47), is eventually killed by his jealous wife.

ll. 42–3. *Mars once was fettered* . . . : The farcical story of Mars/Ares being caught *in flagrante* with Venus/Aphrodite by her husband Vulcan/Hephaestus ('the crafty smith'), who creates a magic net to ensnare them, is told by Homer at *Od.* 8, ll. 266–366, and by Ovid at *Art of Love* 2, ll. 561–92.

l. 44. *born to forget my belt*: Belts were essential gear for travelers and an important part of military dress.

1.11. This poem and the next (*Am.* 1.12), both addressed to Corinna's servant Napé, make a diptych, a device of which Ovid was quite fond (see *Poet Intro*, p. 494). Here it is especially apt as an analogue for the sort of double writing tablets mentioned in the poem, which W. A. Camps describes thus (*Propertius: Elegies, Book III*, p. 162):

> These tablets are oblong slabs of wood, hinged so as to open and shut like a book; the inside surfaces are overlaid with wax, in which messages can be scratched with a pointed metal stylus, and erased again at will to free the surfaces for re-use; the edges of the blocks on the side that is written on are raised in relation to the waxed surfaces, so that these do not touch one another when the tablets are 'shut'.

Ovid's diptych is further doubled by a contrasting one at *Am.* 2.7 and 2.8 (pp. 502–3). Both poem-pairs address a hairdresser of Corinna's, but, while this one merely uses her to carry messages (the slave go-between is a stock motif in Greek and Roman comedy), the latter shows the poet and servant intimately entangled.

The present poem elaborates Mel. 71 (p. 330): the poet, breathless with excitement, delays his courier, Napé, with an amusing litany of digressive, contradictory and pointless instructions.

l. 7. *wax tablets*: See poem note, above.

497. ll. 26–30. *These glorious tablets . . . would hang in Venus' shrine* . . . : Ovid anticipates the jubilant dedication of the tablets to Venus. Such dedications are, of course, rife in the *Greek Anthology*, whose entire sixth book is taken up with them; cf., for example, Philetas 1 (p. 301), Ascl. 6 (p. 305) and Nos. 5 (p. 311), as well as another Roman entry into the genre, Hor. *Odes* 1.5 (p. 465).

1.12. See n. on *Am.* 1.11, above.

ll. 7–31. *Out of my sight, death-notes* . . . : The blessing (*makarismos*: see n. on Alcm. 1, ll. 37–9, p. 32) of the tablets in the previous poem turns to a curse (*schetliasmos*: see Hor. *Odes* 2.13, ll. 1–4, p. 474, and n.) in this one.

ll. 9–10. *Corsican honey ... from hemlock*: The proverbial bitterness of Corsica's honey is not elsewhere attributed to hemlock, the flowers of which have little nectar and do not much interest bees. Hemlock, however, being both bitter and poisonous, is a conventional antonym to honey.

l. 11. *reddish lead*: The wax was commonly red or black.

497–8. ll. 19–20. *hoot-owls ... vulture ... scritch-owl*: Birds of ill-omen; cf. Folk Songs 859 (p. 244) and n., and Prop. 2.28, l. 38 (p. 432).

498. 2.1. Ovid opens his second book by signaling the essentially literary nature of the game he is playing. J. C. McKeown notes that the present poem is an elaborate riff on the 'fundamental elegiac concept', which boasts the mellifluous name of *Nützlichkeitstopik*: the 'utility motif' (*Ovid: Amores – Text, Prolegomena and Commentary*, Vol. 3, p. 2). Traditionally, epic poetry is ranked above other genres for the useful moral instruction it offers; but Ovid turns the valuation upside down, preferring elegy because only it helps him in his amours. Meanwhile, Ovid travesties two elegiac conventions, the *recusatio* (refusal poem; see n. on Prop. 2.1, p. 427) and the magic catalogue (see n. on ll. 26–31, below), giving each a typically Ovidian twist.

l. 1. *Sulmo*: Ovid's hometown (modern Sulmona) in Abruzzo, about eighty miles east of Rome. His people were the Paeligni, a Samnite tribe, and thus, similar to the Sabines (see n. at *Am.* 2.4, l. 15, p. 499), likely to be included among the 'genteel' prudes he warns away in l. 3.

ll. 14–21. *that supernal scuff ...*: Ovid's *recusatio* parodies Propertius' in Prop. 2.1; both poems reference the Gigantomachy (battle with the Giants; see n. on Xen. 1, l. 24, p. 110, and Prop. 2.1, ll. 19–20, p. 427, and n.). Yet Ovid does not say, as usual in such refusals, that his powers aren't up to the epic task (quite the opposite: per l. 15, his 'mouth was big enough'); rather, he claims that elegy is actually the superior genre – because it holds his mistress Corinna's attention.

l. 15. *Gyges* is a hundred-handed brother of Briareus and Cottus at Hes. *Th.*, l. 149. Hor. *Odes* 3.4 suggests the political dimensions of the subject. There Horace offers a lyric Gigantomachy as an analogy for Augustus' triumph at Actium (see n. on Hor. *Odes* 1.37, l. 13, p. 470) in which the Giants clearly stand for Antony and Cleopatra (*Odes* 3.4, ll. 49–52):

> What a fulsome fear Jove felt at that juvenile crowd
> brash and bristling with arms they presumed upon!

At brothers hot to top the cloud-
capped peaks of Olympus with Pelion!

l. 17. *Pelion piled on Ossa on Olympus*: See Prop. 2.1, ll. 19–20 (p. 427) and n. Propertius mentions 'Titans'; Ovid, more accurately, 'Giants'.

499. l. 25. *which often soften hard doors with their charms*: A wistful nod to the *paraclausithyron* (locked-door song) motif – see n. on Call. *Ep.* 8 (p. 277) – since the poets generally complain that their verse does *not* have this softening effect, and the only thing that opens doors is money.

ll. 26–31. *Song brings the blood-horned moon down from the sky* . . . : For the magic catalogue, see Prop. 1.1, ll. 19–24 (p. 423), and 2.28, ll. 35–40 (p. 432). Yet closest to Ovid's passage is this from Vi. *Ecl.* 8 (ll. 69–71):

Spells coax the high moon down to earth again.
Circe used spells to change Ulysses' men.
Spells make cold-blooded snakes burst in the den.

Ovid's twist is a glib conflation of the magical *carmen* (the meanings of which run from 'spell' or 'charm', to 'chant' or 'song', to 'poem') with his own poetry. Specifically, Ovid reverses Tib. 2.4 (ll. 15–20), whose art is worthless for seducing his venal inamorata:

Muses, if you can't serve my love, depart;
I need no help with wars or epic art,
or singing the Sun's path, or how the Moon
wheels round her horses when her circuit's done.
I need an easy way to her hard heart;
Muses, if you can't give me that, depart.

For a further Ovidian repurposing of the magic catalogue, cf. Ov. *Am.* 3.7, ll. 29–38 (p. 508).

ll. 32–5. *What good would songs* . . . : Ovid refers to the Homeric epics. The two sons of Atreus are Agamemnon and Menelaus, and 'he who roamed as many years as fought' is, of course, Odysseus.

l. 35. *Hector, sadly dragged by the chariot*: After killing Hector, Achilles ties him by the heels to his chariot and drags him around the walls of Troy; see Hom. *Il.* 22, ll. 395–405.

2.4. Like *Am.* 2.1, *Am.* 2.4 has precedents in Propertius (Prop. 2.22 and 2.25), but, while Propertius seems genuinely tormented by his promiscuity,

Ovid deploys his rhetorical gifts and artistic shamelessness in a cheerful taxonomic romp. The poem is a textbook example of the rhetorical technique of *amplificatio* (elaboration). John Donne, who plainly considered Ovid a kindred spirit, draws on this poem in 'The Indifferent'.

l. 8. *I'm like a ship huge currents toss*: Ovid wittily adapts the old 'ocean of love' motif to his torrid sensualism; cf. Theog. ll. 1375–6 (p. 85) and n.; compare also *Am.* 2.10, ll. 9–10 (p. 504).

l. 15. *One's like the Sabines*: An ancient Italic people based in the Apennines, absorbed into Rome, as legend has it, via mass abduction in the days of Romulus. (The 'no means yes' tenor of l. 16 makes it hard not to think of the Rape of the Sabine women orchestrated by Romulus; cf. n. on Ov. *Am.* 2.12, ll. 24–5, p. 506.) The Sabines exemplify the rustic austerity at the heart of traditional Roman identity – an identity which Ovid undermines, but Augustus was trying to restore. Cf. Hor. *Epod.* 2, l. 41 (p. 457) and n., and Prop. 2.32, ll. 47–8:

> If you still think Rome's home to the severe
> Sabines, and ancient Tatius, you're new here.

500. ll. 19–22. *One says Callimachus* . . . : Ovid plays on the overlap between the *docta puella* and the Callimachean *doctus poeta* (see n. on Prop. 1.2, ll. 27–30, p. 424): a girl who is 'learned', whether in the arts of the courtesan or the literary critic, can lecture him all she wants, provided she does it in bed. This passage is briefly touched on in the *Intro* to Ovid (p. 493).

l. 32. *she'd coax Priapus from Hippolytus*: In other words, she'd turn the conventional paradigm of male chastity (cf. n. on Hor. *Odes* 4.7, l. 32, p. 490) into the conventional paradigm of a raging hard-on (cf. n. on Hor. *Epod.* 2, ll. 21–2, p. 457).

l. 33. *tall as the couch is lengthy*: The ancients had a special fondness for tall women; part of the beauty of goddesses was their size.

l. 41. *dark complexions also reel me in*: See n. on Phil. 8, ll. 1–2 (p. 335).

l. 43. *black-haired Leda*: The mother of Castor, Pollux, Helen and Clytemnestra, Leda was raped by Zeus in the form of a swan. How Ovid decided her hair was black is unknown – perhaps she was so depicted in art for greater contrast with the swan.

501. 2.6. This dirge (*epicedion*) for Corinna's pet parrot owes its existence to Hellenistic pet epitaphs (see Anyte 9, p. 303, and n.) and, especially, to Cat. 3 (p. 376). Ovid, however, is the first to write a full, formal lament

for a pet; Statius imitates him at *Silv.* 2.4 (p. 528). Ovid's entry in the genre is as witty and fulsome as one would expect.

ll. 8–11. *Philomela* . . . : The nightingale. For her, Procne, Itys (or Itylus) and Tereus ('that Thracian tyrant'), see Cat. 65, ll. 13–14 (p. 391) and n. Here Philomela appears to be Itys' mother, though in Ovid's *Metamorphoses* (*Met.* 6, ll. 440–674) she is his aunt.

ll. 13–14. . . . *the parrot's lifelong, loyal friend*: Doves and parrots were great friends according to the Elder Pliny (*Natural History* 10.96).

l. 16. *Like Pylades and the Argive Orestes*: Ovid frequently refers to Pylades and Orestes as a paradigm for friendship: the two princely cousins were raised together at the court of Pylades' father while Clytemnestra was consorting with Aegisthus. Pylades is far the lesser figure – he gets only three lines in Aeschylus' *Libation Bearers*, and none in both Sophocles' *Electra* and Euripides' version.

ll. 28–9. *Look how quails always fight* . . . : This couplet seems out of place and many editors move it to follow l. 33.

502. l. 36. *the crow, loathed by Minerva*: Minerva's bird was the owl. According to Aristotle (*History of Animals*, 609a), there was mutual enmity 'between the crow and the owl; for, owing to the fact that the owl is dim-sighted by day, the crow at midday preys upon the owl's eggs, and the owl at night upon the crow's, each having the whip-hand of the other, turn and turn about, night and day' (trans. Thompson). Cf. also n. on Stat. *Silv.* 2.4, ll. 16–22 (p. 529), for Ovid's account of how the raven became black.

l. 42. *Thersites saw Protesilaus' death*: According to some authors (including Ovid, at *Met.* 12, ll. 67–8), Protesilaus was the first Greek soldier killed at Troy; Ovid's *Heroides* 13, a verse letter from Laodamia to Protesilaus, is entirely built on the dramatic irony of Laodamia not knowing Protesilaus is already dead. For more on those two, see Cat. 68b, ll. 72–5 (p. 392) and nn. For Thersites, see Theaetetus 3, l. 4 (p. 318) and n.

l. 51. *an Elysian hill*: For Elysium, see Tib. 1.3, ll. 58–66 (p. 414) and n., and Ov. *Am.* 3.9, ll. 60–68 (p. 511) and n.

l. 57. *Juno's peacock*: The peacock was sacred to Juno, who studded its vibrant tailfeathers with the many eyes of her Giant watchman Argus after he was killed by Hermes; see Bacch. 19, ll. 15–45 (pp. 183–4) and nn.

ll. 57–8. *doves in amorous couples*: Doves were thought to mate for life; cf. Cat. 68b, ll. 127–30 (p. 393), and Prop. 2.15, ll. 25–8 (p. 430).

2.7. This poem and the next (*Am.* 2.8) form a diptych in which Ovid's duplicity and invention are on full display, recapitulating and varying the theme of *Am.* 1.11 and 1.12 (pp. 496–7; see n. *ad loc.*, and *Poet Intro*, p. 494). Ovid the poet makes Ovid the character intentionally outrageous, showcasing the ingenious manipulations, the lies, specious arguments, flatteries and threats he uses to get his way with the objects of his attentions – here, his mistress, Corinna and her hairdresser, Cypassis. The poet, no doubt, wants us to laugh at his own expense, to find humor in the shocking reversals and incorrigible shamelessness of the character. The modern reader, though, may well be drawn to the plight of the slave girl Cypassis with an empathy and even horror that clashes with the jaunty tone; this, too, albeit hardly intended by Ovid, is part of the poem's effect, and the witness it bears to its place and time.

l. 3. *Pompey's theater*: This theater complex, inaugurated by Pompey the Great in 55 BCE and the site of Julius Caesar's murder, is a common topos (literal and rhetorical) in treatments of cruising for girls; cf. Prop. 4.8, ll. 76–7 (p. 444) and n. Both Ovid and Propertius must glance up because, by an edict of Augustus, equestrians like them sat in the first fourteen rows, while women were sequestered in the upper tiers.

503. l. 18. *Cypassis*: Her name in Greek means 'short frock'. She is literally a piece of skirt.

l. 21. *What freeborn man would so engage a maid*: Slaves were not legally permitted to contract a marriage (*conubium*). *Concubitus* ('sleeping together', rendered as 'activities' at *Am.* 2.8, l. 6, below) was another story.

l. 27. *I swear by Venus and by Cupid's bow*: Oaths sworn in love were proverbially worthless – cf. Call. *Ep.* 11 (p. 277) and n. Ovid asks forgiveness for this peccadillo at 2.8, ll. 19–21 (p. 504).

2.8. See n. on *Am.* 2.7, above.

504. ll. 11–12. *Briseis … Cassandra … :* Ovid's point is perhaps less the *a fortiori* argument (if slave girls were good enough for Achilles and Agamemnon, 'Mycenae's king', they should be good enough for me) than the flattery of the implicit comparison of Cypassis to the legendary heroines Briseis and Cassandra – who, however, both brought their lovers rather more than they bargained for; cf. nn. on *Am.* 1.9, ll. 36–41 (p. 496).

l. 19. *In Venus' name, no less*: See *Am.* 2.7, l. 27 and n., above.

l. 21. *Carpathian seas*: The Carpathian Sea, in the southern Aegean, southwest of Rhodes, was famously stormy.

l. 22. *sable Cypassis*: Cypassis may have been African or Asian, both in high demand as slaves in Rome.

ll. 26–7. *Keep saying no* ... : The threat, for all its wit, or perhaps even because of it, is chilling: Cypassis, if discovered, has far more to fear than Ovid; compare, for example, *Am.* 2.7, l. 22 (p. 503).

2.10. This poem is the second of what has been called a trilogy of sexy poems illustrating Ovid's slide into promiscuity and debauchery; see also *Am.* 1.5 (p. 494) and 3.7 (p. 507). Like the other two, this one riffs on an epigram of Philodemus (here Phil. 16, p. 337). Echoes of this poem are especially rife in *Am.* 3.7, where the context humorously undermines the laddish boasting here. The present poem also provides fine sport for Ovid's natural love of pairs, or doubles; see *Poet Intro* (p. 494).

l. 1. *you, Graecinus*: Gaius Pomponius Graecinus, to whom Ovid addresses three of the *Letters from Pontus* (*Ex Pont.* 1.6, 2.6 and 4.9). In 16 CE, Graecinus was voted suffect consul (i.e., he was elected to complete another consul's term).

ll. 9–10. *caught in the crosswinds' welter* ... : Compare the simile at Ov. *Am.* 2.4, ll. 7–8 (p. 499). Cf. also Theog. ll. 1375–6 (p. 85) and n.

505. ll. 21–2. *Let love exhaust me* ... : Up to, and including, this couplet, Ovid merely seems to elaborate the emotional tribulations of a double love affair; but starting with l. 23 he wittily shifts his focus to the physical challenges of so much sex.

l. 23. *I'm slender*: A conventional attribute of the elegiac love poet; cf. Prop. 3.16, ll. 19–20 (p. 438). There is a conceptual link to the Callimachean 'slenderness' of modern poetry; cf. Call. *Aet.* 1.1 (p. 258), and nn. on Hor. *Odes* 1.6, ll. 9–12 (p. 466), 2.20, l. 1 (p. 477), and 3.30, l. 13–14 (p. 487).

ll. 29–39. *Happy the man* ... : Rapt contemplation of one's own decease is common in the elegiac poets, especially Propertius (cf., e.g., Prop. 2.1, ll. 49–58 and 73–80, pp. 428, 429, and Prop. 3.16, ll. 21–30, p. 438), but Ovid indulges in it only here, in this parodic *makarismos* (see n. on Alcm. 1, ll. 37–9, p. 32).

2.12. This poem of sexual triumph extends the 'warfare of love' (*militia amoris*) motif verbosely set forth in 1.9 (p. 495). The ecstatic tone shares something with Prop. 2.15 (p. 429), as does Ovid's insistence that his triumph has been won 'with no bloodshed' (ll. 6 and 29) – compare Prop. 2.15, ll. 41–8. It also sets up a shocking contrast with the next poem (*Am.* 2.13, below): Ovid's was not, we will learn, a harmless victory.

l. 1. *Laurel of triumph*: Ovid is thinking of the laurel crown worn by the victorious general in a triumph, rather than the laurels of athletic and poetic victory (Horace, at *Odes* 3.30, l. 16, p. 487, combines them all).

ll. 9–10. *When Troy fell in ten years to many men* . . . : Hyperbolic comparisons to the Trojan War are a common trope of Greek and Latin oratory and comedy; see also ll. 18–19, below. Here, Ovid may have been inspired by a passage from Plautus' *Bacchides* (*The Bacchises*, ll. 925–30). 'Atreus' sons' are Agamemnon and Menelaus.

506. ll. 18–19. *Had Helen stayed home* . . . : The view of the Persians, too; see Sim. *El.* 11, ll. 10–11 (p. 128) and n.

ll. 20–21. *Centaurs and the woodsy Lapiths* . . . *fought*: At the marriage of the Lapiths' king Pirithöus (see n. on Hor. *Odes* 4.7, l. 34, p. 490) with Hippodamia (not the Hippodamia, daughter of Oenomaus, married by Pelops in Pi. *Ol.* 1, ll. 86–115, pp. 138–9), the drunken Centaurs attempted to carry the bride away, provoking the war known as the Centauromachy, described at length by Ovid at *Met.* 12, ll. 210–535 (see also n. on Xen. 1, l. 24, p. 110).

ll. 22–3. *A girl* . . . : Lavinia, daughter of King Latinus of Latium; the war Ovid alludes to, between the Trojan settlers and the native Rutulians, forms the subject of the second half of Virgil's *Aeneid*.

ll. 24–5. . . . *to battle their in-laws*: Romulus' abduction of the Sabine women, and the resulting war with the Sabines, are described in Livy's *History of Rome* at 1.9–13, and Ovid's *Fasti* 3, ll. 201–28.

2.13. Ovid's mistress, Corinna, has fallen desperately ill after an abortion. The subject matter is unusual, and shocking after the previous poem of sexual triumph. But Ovid is merely varying a traditional elegiac theme – the illness of the beloved, cf. Prop. 2.28 (p. 431) and Sulp. 3.10 (p. 448) and 3.17 (p. 452)– in a new way. Abortion was legal in the ancient world, and far from the charged political topic it is today; Ovid's goal is the shock of novelty, not *épater la bourgeoisie*. This personal-seeming poem appears to express genuine distress over Corinna's danger; the following one (*Am.* 2.14), however, makes a more general argument against abortion, in Ovid's wittily elaborate rhetorical style. For the modern reader the second poem makes for uncomfortable reading; Ovid's usual flippancy and wit there feel like a moral failure. He writes (ll. 15–18; the first couplet refers to Rhea Silvia, mother of Romulus and Remus):

> Had Ilia offed the twins that made her rounder,
> the world's chief city would have lost its founder.
> Had Venus snuffed Aeneas' life to ease hers,
> the world would have been cheated of the Caesars.

I find the present poem much more sympathetic.

ll. 8–12. *O Queen of Memphis* . . . : In prayers it was common practice to list places associated with the deity invoked; all the locations Ovid mentions are in Egypt, dotted around Alexandria, and may have been invoked due to their particular association with Isis, or merely for their exotic, Isiac flavor. (Ovid deploys an almost identical list when invoking Isis at *Met.* 9, ll. 774–5.) For Isis' worship by non-aristocratic women like Cynthia and Corinna, see n. on Tib. 1.3, l. 23 (p. 413).

l. 13. *by the rattles in your hands*: See n. on Tib. 1.3, l. 24 (p. 413), and cf. Ov. *Am.* 3.9, ll. 34–5 (pp. 510–11) and n.

l. 14. *Anubis' worshiped countenance*: Anubis was the nephew/grandson/ adopted son of Isis (Plutarch, *Isis and Osiris*) and an Egyptian god of the underworld.

507. ll. 15–17. *Osiris . . . Apis*: For these two Egyptian deities together, whose names combined to form that of the Alexandrian god Serapis, see *Intro* to Post-Classical Greek Lyric (p. 253). The bull god Apis, worshiped at Memphis, was, at least by some accounts, the son of Isis and Osiris. To the serpent (l. 16), compare the rite described by Propertius at Prop. 4.8, ll. 3–15 (pp. 442–3), and the snake which feeds at an altar at Vi. *Aen.* 5.84–96. Asps in particular were associated with Isis; one species, the thermuthis, was fed at temples in Egypt (Aelian, *On the Nature of Animals* 10.31).

l. 21. *where your priests splash the laurels*: That is, at the Temple of Isis and Serapis in the Campus Martius; see nn. on Cat. 10, l. 27 (p. 380) and Tib. 1.3, l. 23 (p. 413). The specific rite referred to is deeply obscure; the Latin may well be corrupt.

l. 24. *Ilithyia*: Goddess of childbirth; see Cat. 34, l. 13 (p. 384) and n.

3.7. Ovid narrates an embarrassing failure of virility at amusing length; taken with *Am.* 1.5 (p. 494) and 2.10 (p. 504) – which latter it echoes frequently – *Am.* 3.7 has been thought to limn the third and final stage of the poet-narrator's sexual and moral decline, perhaps as a result of the promiscuity he cheerfully admits. (The present girl is clearly not his mistress, Corinna.) Like those other two poems, this one has a precedent in

Philodemus (here Phil. 27, p. 339). Impotence is an occasional topic of Greek epigram (see also, e.g., Automedon 1 and 2, pp. 352–3), but this is the only Latin poem dedicated to it, unless we accept the bawdy allegorical reading of Cat. 2 and 3 (p. 376; see n. on Cat. 2). Tibullus (see n. on ll. 29–38, below) and Propertius (cf. Prop. 4.8, ll. 47–8, p. 444) admit in passing to similar episodes, but qualify their failures – thinking of Delia or Cynthia, neither can concentrate on the girl(s) of the moment. Ovid offers no such excuse. In 'The Imperfect Enjoyment', the Earl of Rochester imitates the present elegy with gleeful vulgarity.

508. l. 22. *a priestess tends that deathless flame of Vesta's*: The reference is to Vestal Virgins; see n. on Hor. *Odes* 3.30, l. 9 (p. 487).

ll. 25–8. All three girls are suggestively named: *Chlide* (Wantonness), *Libas* (Dripping Wet) and *Pitho* (Persuasion). The reference to 'nine tilts' with Corinna may recall Catullus inviting a certain Ipsitilla to 'nine uninterrupted fuckings' (Cat. 32).

ll. 29–38. *Did drugs from Thessaly . . .* : In using the present opportunity to expatiate on the favorite elegiac subject of magic (cf., e.g., Ov. *Am.* 2.1, ll. 26–31, p. 499, and n.), Ovid was clearly inspired by Tib. 1.5, ll. 39–42:

> I slept with others; Delia, as I neared
> completion, scowled and Venus disappeared.
> Going, the girls said I was in your spell;
> ashamed, they claimed you knew the dark arts well.

Compare also the girl's complaint to Ovid at ll. 82–4, below.

ll. 31–2. *transfix my . . . liver*: The liver was thought to be the seat of the passions (cf. Hor. *Odes* 4.1, l. 12, p. 488).

ll. 43–4. *Nestor . . . Tithonus*: Both archetypal oldsters. For the Iliadic hero Nestor, cf. Pi. *Py.* 3, ll. 162–4 (p. 151) and n., and Mart. 5.58, l. 5 (p. 544). For Tithonus, see Tyr. 12, l. 7 (p. 25) and n.

509. ll. 54–5. *Tantalus' thirst . . . apples he can't touch*: See Tib. 1.3, ll. 77–8 (p. 415) and n.

l. 64. *Phemius*: The Ithacan bard in the *Odyssey*, often thought of as an alter ego of the Homeric narrator.

510. 3.9. Tibullus (pp. 411–20) died in 18 BCE, perhaps two or so years before Ovid published the first (five-volume) edition of his *Amores*. Much later, writing in exile, Ovid described his relationship, such as it was, with other poets of the age (Ov. *Tri.* 4.10, ll. 49–54):

> When Horace, meter man, strummed his advanced
> songs on Italian strings, I was entranced;
> Virgil I just saw once. My all-too-jealous
> fate cheated me of friendship with Tibullus;
> Gallus, he followed you; Propertius, him.
> Then I came next in line, the fourth of them.

(For Gallus, see n. on Vi. *Ecl.* 10, l. 2, p. 408.)

The present elegy, then, is an act less of personal than literary homage. I do not, however, believe it to be chiefly parodic, as some modern commentators have claimed; if it offers a few, sad smiles, they are not mocking, but rueful. Ovid was not serious about much, but he was serious about poetry, and his indebtedness to those who make it. As might be expected, the poem is in frequent and detailed conversation with the poems of Tibullus – especially with 1.3 (p. 413), where the poet imagines his death while stranded on the island of Corfu, which he calls Phaeacia; but there are echoes of several others as well, along with pastoral elegy – cf. Theoc. *Id.* 1 (p. 283), and Vi. *Ecl.* 10 (p. 408). It is true that Tibullus was among the majority of elegiac poets fascinated by morbid visions of their own death, while Ovid was among the minority who avoided the subject. Ovid's was a colder, more disenchanted eye; he took death too seriously to romanticize it. The vision here of a Poets' Elysium (ll. 60–67, below) is wish-fulfillment, not conviction, and Ovid knows it.

ll. 1–2. *Memnon's mother . . . Achilles' mother*: Aurora/Eos and Thetis, respectively. Memnon was a Trojan ally slain by Achilles in the poem named for him, the *Aethiopis* (*Ethiopian*), which formed part of the lost Epic Cycle (see Call. *Ep.* 2, l. 1, p. 276, and n.). Both the fight and the maternal grief were staples of classical art and literature. In Aeschylus' lost *Psychostasia* (according to Plutarch, *How the Young Man Should Study Poetry* 17a–b), Eos and Thetis entreat for their sons' lives as Zeus weighs their souls in his scales of justice; the scene was also popular in both red- and black-figure pottery.

l. 5. *Alas, how true – too true! – your name will be*: Ovid alludes to an etymology of 'elegy' which derived it from Greek *e e legein* ('to say "eh! eh!"' in mourning).

l. 14. *Iulus*: Aeneas' son, Ascanius, receives this name in the *Aeneid* (see *Aen.* 1, ll. 267–8) to justify the line of descent claimed by the Julii. Cf. Vi. *Ecl.* 9, l. 60 (p. 407) and n., and Prop. 2.1, l. 44 (p. 428) and n.

l. 15. *Aeneas', his brother's*: Aeneas and Cupid were both sons of Venus; see Theoc. *Id.* 1, ll. 107–9 (pp. 284–5) and n., and cf. also Ov. *Ex Pont.* 3.3, l. 64 (p. 523).

l. 17. *when her young love was savaged by a boar*: Adonis; see n. on Call. *Ia.* 3, ll. 36–7 (p. 263).

l. 22. *Orpheus' mother, or Apollo*: The parents of Orpheus (see Ov. *Tri.* 4.1, ll. 17–18, p. 516, and n.) were the Muse Calliope and Apollo. For the question, compare Milton's 'Lycidas' (ll. 58–63):

> What could the Muse herself, that Orpheus bore,
> The Muse herself, for her enchanting son . . .

ll. 24–5. *That sire wept Linus too . . .*: Like Orpheus, Linus was considered to be a son of Apollo and a Muse (cf. Vi. *Ecl.* 4, ll. 64–6, p. 405); however, he also shared his name with an early genre of lyric dirge mentioned by both Homer (*Il.* 18.570) and Hesiod (fr. 255). The 'Linus song' involved the mournful refrain *Ailinon*, 'Alas for Linus!' The Linus of this lament is sometimes identified with the music teacher who was killed when he struck the boy Heracles for singing off-key.

l. 27. *the spring of the Pierian mountain*: For Pieria, see Sap. 55, l. 3 (p. 47) and n.

ll. 30–31. *Yes, poems endure . . .*: The reference is, of course, to the *Iliad* (l. 30) and the *Odyssey* (l. 31), in which Odysseus' wife Penelope, to put off the suitors for her hand, spent her days weaving a funeral shroud for her father-in-law Laertes and her nights unweaving it.

l. 32. For *Nemesis* and *Delia*, Tibullus' beloveds, see *Intro* to Tibullus (pp. 411–12).

510–11. ll. 34–5. *Egypt's rattles . . .*: A reference to the rites of Isis. See Tib. 1.3, ll. 23–6 (p. 413) and nn., and cf. Ov. *Am.* 2.13, ll. 8–21 (pp. 506–7).

511. ll. 42–3. *O holy bard . . . Did they not shrink . . .*: Surely this is a sardonic reference to the 'lovers are holy' motif commonplace in elegiac poetry, not least Tib. 1.2, ll. 29–30: 'Sacred and safe we wander where we please, / we lovers . . .' See further Hor. *Odes* 1.22 (p. 468) and n.

l. 46. *Maid of Eryx*: Venus; Eryx was a city and mountain (now Monte Erice) in western Sicily sacred to the goddess.

l. 48. *Phaeacia*: See poem note, above.

ll. 54–9. *Nemesis and Delia moan* ... : The competitive grieving between Tibullus' two literary girlfriends has often been read as humorous. Line 59 ('His failing grip held *my* hand as he died') quotes Tib. 1.1, ll. 59–60, where Tibullus is addressing Delia:

> May I see you as my demise draws nigh,
> my failing hand in your hand as I die.

Ovid, however, gives the line to Nemesis, as Tibullus' final amour.

ll. 60–67. *If more remains of us* ... : The vision of a Poets' Paradise in Elysium recalls the whimsical avian Elysium of Ov. *Am.* 2.6, ll. 51–60 (p. 502), and the Elysium of beautiful women in Propertius (Prop. 2.28, ll. 25–30, p. 431, and 4.7, ll. 61–70, p. 441), as well, of course, as Tibullus' own journey there at Tib. 1.3, ll. 57–66 (p. 414).

l. 63. *Calvus*: See Cat. 50 (p. 387) and n. on l. 1 *ad loc.*

ll. 64–5. *Gallus ... betrayed your friend*: Gaius Cornelius Gallus, whose 'friend' here is Augustus. See Vi. *Ecl.* 10 (p. 408), and n. on l. 2 *ad loc.*

512.   *Tristia.* In exile on the shore of the Black Sea, Ovid composed two major collections of verse epistles: the five books of the *Tristia* (*Lamentations*), written during the first four years of banishment from *c.*9 to 12 CE, and the *Epistulae ex Ponto* (*Letters from Pontus*), the first three books of which were published in 13 CE, the fourth a year or two after that (for the background to Ovid's exile, see *Poet Intro*, pp. 492–3). In both works, Ovid writes to friends and acquaintances back in Rome, describing the conditions of his exile, defending himself from the charges leveled against him and begging them to intercede with Augustus on his behalf. The chief difference between the two books lies in the way the *Tristia* cautiously suppresses the names of its addressees, while the *Letters from Pontus* speaks boldly and directly to specific individuals.

In the past, assessment of the poems' quality too often followed the lead of Ovid himself, who frequently, and somewhat disingenuously, disparages them. Recently, more objective assessments have noticed how many motifs from the elegies of the *Amores* (pp. 494–511) are repeated with variation in the poems of exile. The German classicist Niklas Holzberg calls the setting of the exile poetry 'an elegiac world out of joint'; he notes that Ovid plays the paradigmatic role of the excluded elegiac lover (*exclusus amator*), begging the beloved (in this case, Augustus) to open the door and let him in (*Ovid: The Poet and His Work*, 'Exile as an Elegiac World Out of Joint: The *Tristia* and the *Epistulae ex Ponto*', trans. G. M. Goshgarian, pp. 176–98). Like love in the elegies, poetry in the exile letters is both cause and cure of Ovid's sufferings. In the elegies, Ovid is a soldier of love, but, in exile, he is an actual soldier. Et cetera. Noting these, as well as other features of the exile poetry, like the fact that many of its descriptions seem derived from literature rather than firsthand reportage, some twentieth-century scholars went so far as to argue that Ovid never actually traveled to Tomis, that his banishment was all a literary fiction. But this is to misunderstand how poets work. A writer like Ovid is always on the lookout for the felicitous coincidence, the rhyme between literature and life. If sometimes he bends the one to fit the other, it is because the poetic work is more important than the prosaic fact.

(The title *Tristia* would later be borrowed by Osip Mandelstam for his second collection of poems, in 1922, parts of which he wrote while on Crimea's Black Sea coast seeking respite from revolutionary St. Petersburg. A little over a decade on, Stalin's regime would sentence him to three years' exile, this time for real, in punishment for his scathing 'Stalin Epigram'.)

1.4. Bk. 1 of the *Tristia* charts Ovid's long, sad journey from Rome to Tomis (modern Constanţa, in Romania). On the way, he encounters several storms, which suggest his inner turmoil and are derived at least as much from storms in epic poetry (cf. Hom. *Od.* 5, ll. 291–391, and Vi. *Aen.* 1, ll. 81–156) as from firsthand experience.

ll. 1–3. *The guardian . . . makes the waters stormy*: This learned Callimachean periphrasis (not at all untypical of Ovid's 'high' style in the *Metamorphoses* and the *Fasti*) marks the season as late November or early December, the stormiest time on the Mediterranean.

l. 1. *Erymanthus* was a mountain and river near Elis, in the northern Peloponnese; the name as used by Ovid here simply means 'Arcadian'.

Bear: The Big Dipper or Great Bear (Ursa Major). The hapless Arcadian princess Callisto and her son Arcas (see n. on Theoc. *Id.* 1, ll. 128–9, p. 285), persecuted by Juno, were transformed first into bears and then into constellations, as narrated by Ovid elsewhere (*Met.* 2, ll. 401–507; cf. Prop. 2.28, ll. 23–4, p. 431). Callisto appears frequently in the *Tristia* in order to persecute Ovid with the rigors of the frozen north. According to Suetonius (*Life of Augustus* 80), Augustus had a birthmark in the shape of Ursa Major.

l. 2. *Boötes*: The Plowman (or Herdsman), a constellation containing the brilliant Arcturus ('Bear Guardian' in Greek). Cf. Ant. Thess. 96 (p. 346) and Prop. 3.5, l. 35 (p. 435) and Hor. *Odes* 3.1, l. 28 (p. 478).

l. 19. *the land where I can't go*: Italy, from which Ovid has been permanently exiled.

ll. 20–21. *For on the left . . .* : Ovid is sailing south, with the boot of Italy to his right and Illyria (Macedonia, the Balkans) to his left.

l. 23. *a mighty god*: Augustus. Though Augustus wasn't formally deified until his death in 14 CE, he had technically been the son of a god (*divi filius*) since 42 BCE, and his Lares (household gods; see note on Tib. l. 10, ll. 15–29 (p. 416)) and *genius* (personal spirit) had been officially worshiped in Rome since 7 BCE. Augustus is referred to again in the same fashion at Ov. *Tri.* 3.2, l. 28 (p. 513). Horace also makes Augustus a 'god at hand' in, e.g., *Odes* 3.5, ll. 2–3 (p. 480); cf. n. *ad loc.*

513. 3.2. In his new home, Tomis, on the Black Sea, Ovid's instinct for narrative gives way, yielding to depression and stagnation. On the journey, at least, there is physical movement and progress toward a destination, albeit a bad one; but once Ovid arrives in Tomis, time loses its meaning and the exiled poet has nothing but a life he equates with death. In the *Amores* (e.g., 2.10, ll. 29–39, p. 505), Ovid had made fun of other elegists with their incessant death-wishes. Sadly, in Tomis he changes his tune.

l. 2. *Scythia*: Ovid is exaggerating. Scythia refers to southern Russia, the Eurasian landmass north of the Black Sea (see n. on Hor. *Odes* 2.20, ll. 17–20, p. 477), while the climate in Constanţa resembles that of northern Italian cities on roughly the same latitude, like Bologna and Rimini. For Scythia's boreal climes, see also Philip of Thessalonica 55, l. 2 (p. 356), and Prop. 3.16, l. 14 (p. 438).

l. 6. *more decorous in my life than in my rhyme*: Ovid picks up Catullus' self-defense in Cat. 16, ll. 7–8 (p. 382), claiming that he himself lived less decadently than his poems (especially the *Art of Love*) would suggest. See, further, n. on the *Tristia* (p. 512), above.

l. 7. *now, after many trials on land and sea*: Ovid alludes to the proem of the *Odyssey*, implicitly comparing himself to Odysseus/Ulysses.

l. 8. *the Pontus*: i.e., the Black Sea and its littoral, not the kingdom of Asia Minor formerly ruled by Mithridates VI (for whom, see n. on Mart. 6.19, l. 6, p. 545).

l. 28. *Rome's great deity*: Augustus, as at Ov. *Tri.* 1.4, l. 23 (p. 512), above.

514. 3.7. The 'Perilla' addressed here is clearly a pseudonym, often thought to represent Ovid's stepdaughter, or perhaps a Greek freedwoman of his. The unusual name was also applied to the mistress of one of Catullus' contemporaries, Lucius Ticida, a neoteric poet (see *Intro* to Catullus, p. 374) whose work has not survived; this Perilla is commonly identified as

being the daughter of Clodia Metelli (Catullus' 'Lesbia'). Besides Sulpicia (pp. 446–52), women poets were vanishingly rare in Rome (hence Ovid's comparison of his correspondent to the Greek Sappho in l. 20), and we know nothing of Perilla's own poetry, beyond what Ovid tells us. This verse epistle is remarkable for its defiant statement of independence from Augustus ('Caesar's sovereignty') at ll. 47–52.

l. 16. *Hippocrene*: See n. on Ant. Thess. 3, ll. 1–2 (p. 345), and Prop. 3.3, l. 2 (p. 432).

ll. 27–30. *Perhaps the harm ... the art of love*: See *Poet Intro* (pp. 492–3).

515. l. 42. *Irus ... Croesus*: These two figures, representing the penniless beggar and the pinnacle of wealth, are also paired at Prop. 3.5, l. 17 (p. 434).

3.13. This inverted *genethliacon* (birthday poem) laments the living death into which Ovid has been banished. For the genre, and for Roman birthdays more generally, see n. on Sulp. 3.11 (p. 449).

l. 1. *the barren day that marks my birth*: Ovid was born on 20 March 43 BCE.

l. 2. *that day's god*: As explained in the note on Sulp. 3.11 (p. 449), Ovid is referring to his *genius*, his personal guardian god.

l. 11. *Pontus*: See n. on Ov. Tri. 3.2, l. 8 (p. 513), above.

516. ll. 21–2. *a funeral altar, hung with cypress*: See n. on Hor. Odes 2.14, ll. 23–4 (p. 476).

l. 28. *the 'Welcoming' ... Euxine*: 'Euxine', another name for the Black Sea, derived from the Greek for 'welcoming' or 'hospitable' (*euxeinos*), under the same principle (i.e., that of giving a positive name to a maleficent entity) by which the Furies are known as the *Eumenides* (Kindly Ones). Its original name was apparently *Axeinos*, 'Inhospitable', as noted by Ovid (*Tri.* 4.4, ll. 55–6) and Strabo (*Geography* 7.3.6).

4.1. Ovid combines a vivid account of his unelegiac hardships in Tomis, on the Thracian frontier of the Roman Empire (where Cupid's old soldier now must fight for real: see n. on l. 36, below), with a description of poetry as both cause and cure of his troubles – not unlike love in the world of love elegy.

ll. 15–16. *Achilles ... turned to his lyre*: Ovid is thinking of Hom. *Il.* 9, ll. 185–91, in which the embassy from Agamemnon finds Achilles alone with Patroclus in front of his tent, singing of the great deeds of heroes.

ll. 17–18. *Orpheus ... sang his love, twice lost*: Orpheus, the archetypal poet-singer, son of Apollo and the Muse Calliope, fabled inventor of the lyre, lost his beloved Eurydice twice, the first time due to a snakebite, the second to his own sad lapse: the King and Queen of the Dead agreed to restore her to the upper world, on condition that Orpheus not look upon her until both were safely above – but Orpheus, on the threshold of felicity, fatefully, fatally, turned his head, only to see Eurydice's shade slip away forever. The story is told brilliantly by Vi. at *Geo.* 4, ll. 453–527, and also by Ovid himself in the *Metamorphoses* (*Met.* 10, ll. 1–63). For further references to Orpheus, see *Intros* to the Archaic Period (p. 2), the Classical Period (p. 187) and Post-Classical Greek Lyric (p. 251); n. to Alc. 45, l. 3 (p. 58) and n.; Sim. 567 (p. 126); Tim. 791, ll. 225–7 (p. 211); Vi. *Ecl.* 4, ll. 63–6 (p. 405); Prop. 1.3, l. 42 (p. 426); Hor. *Odes* 1.24, ll. 13–14 (p. 470), 2.13, ll. 21–40 (p. 475) and n.; Ov. *Am.* 3.9, ll. 22–36 (p. 510) and nn., *Ex Pont.* 3.3, l. 42 (p. 523).

517.   ll. 23–6. *She also knows ... the same crime*: See *Poet Intro* (pp. 492–3).

ll. 27–8. *I could wish ... I had never touched the Muses' hem*: Ovid is probably thinking of Prop. 3.5, ll. 19–22 (p. 434), pointedly reversing the older poet's gratitude toward his profession.

ll. 31–2. *It's like the lotus ... *: Odysseus describes the Land of the Lotus-Eaters in Hom. *Od.* 9 (ll. 82–104). The lotus is a tree whose fruits and flowers induce such forgetfulness and sloth that all memory of home disappears, along with any desire to return.

l. 36. *and love the javelin once used to wound me*: Ovid is clearly thinking of Telephus; cf. Prop. 2.1, ll. 65–6 (p. 429), and n. on Hor. *Odes* 4.11, l. 21 (p. 491). The implied comparison between love (for the elegiac poet) and poetry (for the exile) as both cause and cure of illness is intended.

ll. 41–6. *As a gored Bacchant ... so my heart ... soars above ... *: Ovid's language strongly recalls Horace's hymn to Bacchus (*Odes* 3.25, p. 486), as well as comments of Plato's about the divine, Bacchic madness of poetry (e.g., *Ion* 534a–b, *Phaedrus* 245a). At the end of the *Amores* (*Am.* 3.15, ll. 15–18), Ovid had said farewell to elegy, as if abandoning it for the Bacchic genre of tragedy:

> Venereal mother, boy I have extolled,
> from my field take your gonfalons of gold;
> Bacchus the Bull strikes with heavier thyrsus;
> a greater race awaits my greater horses!

Now, Ovid's life is shown to be the tragedy for which he abandoned his love poetry. (For the *thyrsus* in l. 43 see Ion, Elegy 26, l. 1, p. 197, and n.). There may also be a contrast with Orpheus, mentioned above (ll. 17–18), who, of course, met his death at the hands of a pack of raving Bacchants in Thrace, in the same general area as Tomis.

l. 42. *Ida's peak*: Probably not the Cretan, but the Phrygian Mount Ida (near Troy), associated with a form of ecstatic worship (of the Great Mother, Cybele: see Anon. 935, p. 237, and n.) which Ovid seems here to be conflating with maenadism (see n. on Prop. 1.3, ll. 5–6, p. 425). In particular, he may be thinking of Catullus' poem 63, in which a priest called Attis castrates himself in a religious frenzy on the slopes of Mount Ida, only to regret it afterwards. This could give point to the wound of l. 41.

l. 46. *the shores of Scythia*: See Ov. *Tri.* 3.2, l. 2 (p. 513) and n.

518. l. 61. *the Euxine's left*: Tomis is to the left (north) of ships entering the Euxine, or Black Sea (cf. n. on Ov. *Tri.* 3.13, l. 28, p. 516).

l. 68. *Gets and Bessi*: Both Thracian tribes, the Gets (or *Getae*) were also called Dacians; they lived to the west of Tomis, on the lower Danube below the Carpathian Mountains, and were praised by Herodotus (*Hist.* 4.93). Ovid eventually learned Getic and even claims in *Ex Pont.* 4.13 (ll. 17–38) to have composed a panegyric to Augustus in it. The Bessi lived to the south, on the upper Hebrus River (modern Maritsa), along the southern slopes of Mount Haemus. Ovid does not seem overly troubled by distinctions between tribes and names them (along with the Sarmatians: see n. on l. 95, below) more or less interchangeably. None of these peoples had yet been fully pacified by Rome.

ll. 72–5. *When I was young . . . old now . . .* : The reversal is generic as well as personal; Ovid, who was a soldier of love in youth (*Am.* 1.9, p. 495), now faces genuine combat. See, further, n. on the *Tristia* (p. 512), above.

519. l. 95. *Sarmatians*: A nomadic Scythian people, known for their horsemanship and horsebreeding. Ovid refers to the region north of the Black Sea and east of the Carpathians generally as Sarmatia.

4.6. Ovid is primarily a narrative poet; almost all of his poetry depicts change over time. However, when he goes to Tomis, time grinds to a halt (cf. *Tri.* 4.1, ll. 47–8, p. 517). Seasons alternate, birthdays come and go (*Tri.* 3.13, p. 515), but Ovid's condition remains essentially static. This poem therefore comments obliquely on the *Tristia* as a whole, suggesting that the collection's lack of narrative development (which contrasts so pointedly with, say, the 'erotic novel' of the *Amores* – see n. on the *Amores*, p. 494, above) reflects the poet's exilic lot.

520.   l. 47. *Scythians, Gets in pants*: i.e., Sarmatians and Thracians. See nn. on Ov. *Tri.* 4.1, ll. 95 and 68 (pp. 519, 518), respectively. In the classical world, trouser-wearing was a defining mark of the barbarian.

521.   *Letters from Pontus*. See n. on the *Tristia* (p. 512), above. The chief difference between the *Tristia* and the *Letters from Pontus* is that, in the latter, Ovid names his addressees directly. Formally, then, the collection more closely resembles his *Letters of Famous Heroines* (*Heroides*), while the *Tristia* aligns with the *Amores*.

2.4. The Atticus addressed here is also the addressee of Ov. *Am.* 1.9 (p. 495). Although he is otherwise unknown, the literary friendship he shared with Ovid (to adapt Sir Philip Sidney) 'to those who've felt the like, his state descries'.

l. 1. *Hister*: The lower Danube, which flows near Tomis (now Constanța in Romania).

l. 20. *adjacent theater seats*: This will mean that Atticus was an equestrian; for theater seating, see n. on Ov. *Am.* 2.7, l. 3 (p. 502).

l. 22. *Achilles and Antilochus*: According to Hom. *Od.* 24, ll. 78–9, Nestor's son Antilochus came second only to Patroclus in Achilles' affections, and was buried in the same tomb with them. Just as in the *Iliad*, Achilles kills Hector after the death of Patroclus, so Achilles is spurred to kill the Ethiopian Memnon after Memnon kills Antilochus in the *Aethiopis*, one of the poems of the lost Epic Cycle (see Call. *Ep.* 2, l. 1, p. 276, and n., and cf. n. on Ov. *Am.* 3.9, ll. 1–2, p. 410). Antilochus' death is also limned in Pi. *Py.* 6.

l. 24. *I'd not believe you could forget all this*: This line, rendered by translator Peter Green as 'I cannot believe these things could fade from your mind', appears in Bob Dylan's song 'Spirit on the Water' on his 2006 album *Modern Times*, in which a number of songs contain borrowings from Green's translation of Ovid's exile poetry. See further Richard F. Thomas, 'The Streets of Rome: The Classical Dylan', *Oral Tradition* 22:1 (2007), pp. 30–56.

ll. 25–8. *The long, slow winter days will grow . . .* : These lines use the trope of *adynaton* (catalogue of impossibilities); see n. on Prop. 2.1, ll. 67–72 (p. 429), and cf. Ov. *Ex Pont.* 3.3, ll. 99–101 (p. 524) and n.

l. 27. *Pontus*: See n. on Ov. *Tri.* 3.2, l. 8 (p. 513), above.

l. 28. *the Paestum rose*: Paestum (Poseidonia in Greek) was a wealthy Greek city in southern Italy annexed by the Romans after the war with Pyrrhus in 273 BCE. It was famous for its roses, which flowered twice a year.

522. 3.3. The Maximus addressed here – as well as in *Ex Pont.* 1.2 and 3.8 – is Paullus Fabius Maximus, scion of an ancient and distinguished aristocratic family ('star of the Fabians', l. 2) and confidant of Augustus. He is also the addressee of Hor. *Odes* 4.1 (p. 487); if he was in his thirties when Horace addressed his ode to him (in the mid-teens BCE), he would likely be in his sixties now, as the triumph of Tiberius over the Pannonians and Illyrians mentioned at l. 88 took place in October of 12 or 13 CE. The present poem bears a clear resemblance to a number of literary dreams, such as the appearance of Patroclus' ghost to Achilles (Hom. *Il.* 23, ll. 65–107), of Hector's ghost to Aeneas (Vi. *Aen.* 2, ll. 270–97) and (perhaps more to the point) of Cynthia's ghost to Propertius (Prop. 4.7, p. 440). This poem was imitated in the Middle Ages by the poet of *Carmina Burana* 105.

l. 2. *star of the Fabians*: A patrician family of ancient pedigree, whose most famous member, Quintus Fabius Maximus Verrucosus Cunctator, is mentioned by Propertius at 3.3, l. 9 (p. 433). Coincidentally, at l. 7, so is the illustrious ancestor (Lucius Aemilius Paullus) from whom Maximus took his unusual first name.

ll. 6–7. *sifting through shutters, soft moonlight . . .* : In alluding to Prop. 1.3 (p. 425) and its precedent in Phil. 9 (p. 336), Ovid may actually be recalling his own prior use of the same allusion in *Am.* 1.5 (p. 494), where love appears embodied in the form of a willing Corinna. The allusion enhances the pathos of this moment by contrast with the pleasure of that one.

l. 27. *the barbaric Hister*: See n. on *Ex Pont.* 2.4, l. 1 (p. 521).

523. l. 30. *You gave me marching orders first when young*: A reference to Ovid's *Amores* (see pp. 494–511); Ovid blames his frivolous and unmanly (slender – cf. l. 35, and Ov. *Am.* 2.10, l. 23, p. 505) output on Cupid.

l. 39. *my* Art of Love: Ovid's *Ars Amatoria*, in which he now claims to have taken leadership, and Cupid as his pupil – though in what follows (ll. 42–50) he shifts blame back to the god.

ll. 40–41. *And paid the price . . .* : See *Poet Intro* (pp. 492–3).

l. 42. *Eumolpus*: A mythical king of Eleusis mentioned in the *Homeric Hymn to Demeter* (ll. 154 and 475), sometimes credited with initiating the Eleusinian Mysteries (for which, see Pi. fr. 137, l. 2 (p.230) and n.). Ovid likewise makes Orpheus the teacher of Eumolpus (as well as of Midas) at *Met.* 11, ll. 92–3.

l. 44. *Olympus ... Marsyas*: Early proponents of the *aulos* (double-reed pipe). Marsyas was a satyr of whom two stories are told. The first (discussed in Ath. *Deip.* 616e) claims that the double pipe was invented by Athena, who, after she saw how silly she looked while playing it, threw it away, to be picked up by Marsyas, who then introduced the instrument to men. In the second, Marsyas (on the double pipe) challenges Apollo (playing the lyre) to a musical contest; Apollo wins and, as penalty, flays Marsyas alive (Ov. *Met.* 6, ll. 382–400). Olympus was generally said to have been a pupil of Marsyas (Ov. *Met.* 6, ll. 393–4); to him was attributed the composition of a number of old-fashioned musical *nomes* (see *Intro* to the Classical Period, p. 187).

l. 45. *Achilles ... Chiron*: See n. on Hor. *Epod.* 13, l. 16 (p. 459).

l. 46. *Numa ... Pythagoras*: Numa Pompilius was the semi-mythical second king of Rome, known for his peaceable nature and religious laws. Cicero and Livy reject the tradition that Numa was taught by Pythagoras as chronologically and geographically implausible; according to Dionysius of Halicarnassus's exhaustive investigations (*Roman Antiquities* 2.59), the sixth-century Pythagoras was four generations younger than Numa, whose reign was traditionally dated to 715–673 BCE. Ovid, however, is untroubled by such quibbles.

ll. 51–2. *lawful marriage ... disparage*: Arguably, one of the failings of Ovid's *Art of Love*, at least from Augustus' perspective, was that it ran afoul of his marriage legislation, intended to discourage adultery and encourage procreation in citizens.

l. 64. *whose ancestor, Aeneas, was your brother*: i.e., Love's/Cupid's. Ovid also makes this point at *Am.* 3.9, l. 15 (p. 510).

524. ll. 81–2. *The first time I ... pierced Medea's heart*: Aphrodite sends Eros to the Black Sea on this mission at the beginning of the third book of Apollonius of Rhodes' *Argonautica* (cf. n. on Theoc. *Id.* 2, ll. 19–20, p. 286).

l. 84. *stalwart of my camp*: Cf. Ov. *Am.* 1.9, l. 2 (p. 495) and n.; also, for the *militia amoris* trope more generally, poem note *ad loc.*

l. 88. *Tiberius triumphs*: In 12 or 13 CE; see poem note, above.

l. 89. *Your house and sons*: Ovid, in Cupid's voice, shifts into a direct address to Augustus.

l. 91. *our leader's ... father*: Augustus had become Tiberius' father by adoption in 4 CE; then, in 13, Tiberius had been awarded powers equal to those of Augustus.

l. 95. *now, we must hope these pleas of ours have force*: Cupid's last line is echoed and contradicted by Ov. *Ex Pont.* 3.7, l. 2 (p. 525), below.

l. 99. *I'd say swans are Memnon's birds*: That is, black: Memnon was an Ethiopian hero killed by Achilles at Troy (see n. on Ov. *Am.* 3.9, ll. 1–2, p. 510). (It is beside the point to note that black swans do, in fact, exist, but in Australia – Ovid traveled far, but not that far.) The swans introduce another example of an *adynaton* (catalogue of impossibilities): see n. on Prop. 2.1, ll. 67–72 (p. 429), and cf. Ov. *Ex Pont.* 2.4, ll. 25–8 (p. 521) and n.

l. 100. *terebinth*: According to the Elder Pliny, the wood of the terebinth tree is 'a shiny black colour' (*Natural History* 13.12, trans. Rackham).

l. 103. *Hercules's double*: Maximus's family, the Fabii, claimed descent from Hercules; cf. Ov. *Fasti* 2, ll. 237–42. It may be that, when Ovid notes in l. 110 that Paullus' 'house helps the weak who count on [them]', he is alluding to the Fabians taking on Hercules' mantle as champion.

525. 3.7. l. 2. *these useless, endless pleas*: A disillusioned echo and contradiction of *Ex Pont.* 3.3's more optimistic l. 95 (p. 524), above.

l. 19. *I'm in Get-country*: See n. on Ov. *Tri.* 4.1, l. 68 (p. 518).

Statius

527. *Poet Introduction. his elegy for his father*: Stat., *Silv.* 5.3.

not to have spent more than two days: Stat., *Silv.* 1, preface.

Dante . . . gives Statius a major role: See Dante, *Purgatorio* 21–33.

528. *'wanted the Poyze of Judgement'*: John Dryden, 'The Authors Apology for Heroique Poetry; and Poetique Licence', preface to *The State of Innocence, and Fall of Man: An Opera*.

culture of 'the impromptu': See Gianpiero Rosati, 'The *Silvae*: Poetics of Impromptu and Cultural Consumption', in *Brill's Companion to Statius*, ed. W. J. Dominik, C. E. Newlands and K. Gervais, pp. 54–72.

2.4. This playful consolation on the death of a pet parrot models itself after Ov. *Am.* 2.6 (p. 501) and Cat. 3 (p. 376), which in turn are indebted to the Hellenistic genre of pet epitaphs (see n. on Anyte 9, p. 303). Yet while Ovid condescends to the parrot, emphasizing the vacuity of its speech, Statius commends its eloquence in terms that might suggest a degree of poetic self-identification – after all, the present poem 'parrots', as it were, both Ovid and Catullus. There is a further hint of political allegory to the description of the bird's cage (ll. 11–15), which evokes the rich houses of the aristocracy; we might think of a court poet 'parroting' platitudes to his imperial patrons. One court poet of Neronian stamp, Petronius, implicitly compares himself to a parrot in an epigram attributed to him in the *Latin Anthology* (fr. 41 Bücheler = *AL* 691R):

> The purple shores of India bore me,
> where day's bright orb is reborn, burningly.
> Reared among banquet halls that gods get fat in,
> I traded barbarisms in for Latin.
> Now, Delphic Healer, let your swans fly south;
> more worthy of your temple is my mouth.

Here Petronius seems to assert the primacy of his own brand of satire, represented by the parrot, over more 'serious' or epic poetry, represented by Apollo's swans. It is therefore not implausible, as Leah Kronenberg argues, to identify Statius' parrot with Petronius – who, accused of treason by a powerful enemy in 66 CE, as Tacitus tells us (*Annals* 16.18–19), enjoyed a leisurely suicide at a banquet, conversing with friends as he had always done, and listening to 'light songs and frivolous verses' (see Leah Kronenberg, 'A Petronian Parrot in a Neronian Cage: A New Reading of Statius' *Silvae* 2.4', *Classical Quarterly* 67:2, 2017, pp. 558–72). Certainly this reading is not incompatible with Statius' description of the parrot's last night at ll. 4–8.

l. 1. *your owner's favorite*: Atedius Melior, the dedicatee of the second book of *Silvae* and of three poems within it (2.1, 2.3 and this one); he is also addressed in several epigrams of Martial (2.69, 4.54, 6.28, 6.29 and 8.38). Nothing is known about him beyond what can be gleaned from Statius and Martial. He seems to have been rich, elderly and reclusive, with a house on the Caelian Hill (cf. Mart. 12.18, l. 6, p. 553, and n.). The total lack of politics in the poems leads to the inference that either he was apolitical by temperament or he had been driven from politics by some mischance.

l. 9. *Cycnus' tale*: Ovid (*Met.* 2, ll. 367–80) tells how Cycnus, while mourning the death of his lover Phaethon, was transformed into a swan; Statius combines the story with the popular tradition of the 'swan-song'.

529.   ll. 16–22. *Call the bird-poets* ... : Statius' first catalogue of birds is rife with allusion to Ovid. The raven (l. 17) was turned from white to black for informing on Apollo's mistress Coronis (Ov. *Met.* 2, ll. 534–632; see

also Pi. *Py.* 3, ll. 42–3, p. 147 and n.); the daughters of Pierus (l. 19) lost a contest with the Muses and were changed into magpies (Ov. *Met.* 5, ll. 294–333 and 662–78); and the partridge (l. 21) had been an inventor called Perdix who was envied and murdered by Daedalus (Ov. *Met.* 8, ll. 236–59), while the story of Procne and Philomela (l. 22), changed into nightingales, is told in Ov. *Met.* 6, ll. 440–674 (see also Cat. 65, ll. 13–14, p. 391, and n.). There are no starlings (l. 18) in Ovid, but the Elder Pliny claims that Nero as a boy had a trained starling which could speak Greek and Latin (*Natural History* 10.59).

ll. 27–30. *Not peacocks* ... : The second catalogue groups three birds (the peacock, the pheasant and the guinea fowl) known less for poetic resonance than taste – along with parrots, they were considered fine dining by wealthy Romans (cf. Hor. *Epod.* 2, ll. 53–4, p. 458). The peacock, however, as both a delicacy (cf. n. on Hor. *Odes* 2.14, l. 25, p. 477) and a literary bird, was an exception: see Ov. *Am.* 2.6, l. 57 (p. 502) and n. There Ovid has Corinna's parrot welcomed to Elysium by the peacock and the phoenix, which also makes an appearance here (l. 39, below).

ll. 37–8. *Arabian spice ... his ashes*: See n. on Tib. 1.3, l. 7 (p. 413).

l. 39. *more fortunate than the phoenix*: According to legend, when the phoenix grew old, it built a nest which was both pyre and cradle and, immolating itself, was reborn from the ashes (see Ov. *Met.* 15, ll. 391–407; Hdt. *Hist.* 2.73; Elder Pliny, *Natural History* 10.3–5). Melior's parrot is 'more fortunate' because it will now never grow old or die. Statius, of course, is one-upping Ovid, whose parrot meets the phoenix in Elysium; see n. on ll. 27–30, above.

4.5. This poem is addressed to a friend of Statius: the equestrian Septimius Severus, a first- or second-generation immigrant to Rome from Leptis Magna in Libya (modern Khoms, east of Tripoli), and possibly grandfather or granduncle to the future emperor of the same name. In addition to his 'footloose prose' (l. 57), Septimius seems also to have composed lyric poetry, providing Statius, at least in part, with the rationale for the stanza form – this ode being Statius' only composition in alcaics (see *Note on Meters*, pp. xxxviii–xxxix), and indeed one of the few surviving Latin attempts at the meter for the three centuries between Horace and Prudentius (348–after 405 CE). The ode is full of Horatian reminiscences and motifs – the coming of spring, praise for the simple life, and a very Roman approach to lyric panegyric.

ll. 1–2. *old Alba*: i.e., Alba Longa, the town in Latium founded by Aeneas' son Ascanius. Statius had his country estate in the surrounding Alban

Hills – a gift from Domitian – and also won a poetry contest put on by the emperor at his own Alban estate, as described below (ll. 21–8).

l. 3. *silver-tongued and bold*: Severus is praised as both an effective orator and a literary talent.

530. l. 5. *the Arctic Bear*: Ursa Major. Cf. n. on Ov. *Tri.* 1.4, ll. 1–3 (p. 512).

l. 8. *the zephyrs have vanquished the North Wind*: The west wind's defeat of the north (Aquilo) is commonly associated with the coming of spring (cf. Cat. 46, l. 3, p. 386; Hor. *Odes* 1.4, l. 1, p. 464, and n., and 4.7, l. 11, p. 489). The image of winds locked in combat is a favorite of Horace's (see Hor. *Odes* 1.3, ll. 12–16, p. 463, and n.).

ll. 13–16. *A little land* ... : The stanza may generally be modeled on the second stanza of Horace's *Soracte Ode* (1.9, ll. 5–8, p. 467), but the emphasis on smokiness also resonates with Hor. *Odes* 4.11, ll. 9–12 (p. 490), and Mart. 2.90, ll. 8–9 (pp. 539–40).

ll. 17–20. *I have no thousands of wooly sheep that bleat* ... : Compare, e.g., Hor. *Odes* 3.23, ll. 9–14 (p. 486), or the end of Hor. *Odes* 2.16 (ll. 33–40):

> A hundred Sicilian cattle and sheep-flocks nose
> your fields and bellow; your whinnying thoroughbreds stride
> fit for the chariot race, and all your clothes
>   are wool twice dyed

> with African purple – while I have a tiny tract
> and the Italian Muses' slender song
> by dint of my honest Fate, and I can reject
>   the vicious throng.

ll. 23–4. *Minerva, crowned my verse with Caesar's wreath*: The emperor Domitian founded a festival in honor of Minerva (with whom he claimed a special relationship), held on the emperor's own Alban estate in the first quarter of the year, where Statius won first prize in 90/91 CE with a poem about Domitian's triumphal victories in Germany and Dacia (86–9 CE).

l. 26. *delicious risk*: Statius' phrase is influenced by Hor. *Odes* 3.25, l. 18 (p. 487): 'This danger is delight ...'

ll. 27–8. *as Castor quailed* ... : The boxing match between Polydeuces/Pollux and Amycus, the barbarous king of the Bebrycians, is described both by Apollonius of Rhodes (*Argonautica* 2, ll. 1–97) and by the 'Flavian Apollonius', Valerius Flaccus (in his own *Argonautica* 4, ll. 199–343).

ll. 31–2. *Indian harvests . . . scented Sabaea*: India was famed for producing two harvests a year. The land of the Sabaeans, located in the southern Arabian peninsula, roughly coincides with modern Yemen. Like Arabia generally, it was famed for the production of luxurious spices.

531. l. 34. *Romulus's every mountain*: i.e., all seven hills (mountains) of Rome. Septimius, whose name means 'Seventh', seems even more Roman than most native Romans.

l. 36. *Juturna's fountain*: Juturna, the sister of Aeneas' great enemy Turnus, given a prominent role in Bk. 12 of the *Aeneid*, had a sacred spring in the Roman Forum, near the temple of Vesta.

ll. 41–2. *content with the narrow equestrian stripe*: Men of equestrian rank were entitled to wear togas with a narrow purple stripe (or perhaps two), in contrast to the broad purple stripe (*latus clavus*) of senators. 'Content' may imply that Septimius could have received the broad stripe, and thus run for office, if he had wished to.

ll. 45–6. *Phoenician . . . you're pure Italian-bred*: 'Phoenician' here means 'Carthaginian', i.e., North African. 'Pure Italian-bred' is a more exclusive compliment than if Statius had called Septimius 'Roman', since to be *Italus* required Italian birth, whereas *Romanus* referred only to Roman citizenship, which could be – and increasingly was – awarded to anyone irrespective of nationality.

ll. 54–6. All of the places listed by Statius, via their proximity to Rome and the large role they played in Roman history, are steeped in associations of traditional *Romanitas*, with which they endow Septimius. *Veii* (modern Isola Farnese) was a powerful Etruscan city conquered by its near neighbor Rome in 396 BCE. The *Monti Ernici* (Hills of the Hernici) belong to the Apennines; Septimius' estate may have been located at Capitulum Hernicum, in modern Piglio, some thirty miles east of Rome. Finally, ancient *Cures*, located near the modern town of Arci, was supposedly the first town annexed to Rome by Romulus, and source of the other name for Roman citizens, who were also known as *Quirites*.

532. 5.4. This short, personal poem is among the most beloved of Statius' works. The poet, in the grip of prolonged insomnia, prays feelingly to the god Sleep (Somnus) for relief. In form, the poem is a 'kletic' or invocatory hymn like Sap. 1 (p. 39); it owes much to literary predecessors, especially Virgil (pp. 398–410) and Ovid (pp. 492–526), but also to the many epic appeals to Sleep, starting with Hera's in Hom. *Il*. 14 (ll. 231–41). Alcm. 89 (p. 37) may be in the background of ll. 5–7, though the more immediate precedent is Vi.

Aen. 4, ll. 522–32, contrasting the insomnia of Dido with the sleeping night-time world of Carthage. At any rate, both the poem's personal immediacy (Statius here seems almost Romantic) and its aura of mystery (we never learn the cause of his insomnia) no doubt help explain its enduring popularity.

l. 3. *sweet youthful Sleep*: Sleep is depicted as an infant in Hesiod's *The-ogony* (ll. 755–9) and an old man in Ovid's *Metamorphoses* (*Met.* 11, ll. 592–649); there is a similar range of variation among vase-paintings and sarcophagi from Classical Greece through to the Roman period. Statius here, and perhaps in Bk. 10 of the *Thebaid* (ll. 84–155), chooses to make him a youthful god.

l. 10. *Vesper and Lucifer*: i.e., the evening and morning stars. Cf. 'Plato' 1–2 (p. 221) and nn. Here both stars – which the Romans knew were, in fact, the same celestial body; cf. Cat. 62, l. 35 (p. 000) – together indicate that Statius' sleepless invigilations have spanned the daytime (from Luci-fer to Vesper) as well as the night (from Vesper to Lucifer).

l. 14. *Juno's Argus*: The many-eyed watchman; see Bacch. 19 (p. 183) and/or the account in Ov. *Met.* 1, ll. 622–723, and cf. n. on Tib. 1.3, l. 23 (p. 413).

l. 21. *just tap me with your wand's tip*: When Sleep seduces Aeneas' helmsman Palinurus in *Aen.* 5, ll. 854–6, Virgil writes: 'Look! – above his temples the god spritzes a bough, dripping with Lethe's liquor, drugged with the narcotics of the Styx, and, despite his resistance, closes his swim-ming eyes.' Palinurus then 'gives his life into the waves' embrace' (cf. Ar. 213, p. 15); Statius here prays to share his fate.

ll. 21–2. *just tap me . . . knees uplifted*: The paradox of Sleep being asked, if he will not pay the poet a proper visit, then at least to pass by quietly without disturbing him, brings the poem to a mysterious and disquieting conclusion.

Martial

533. *Poet Introduction. client*: This word is used (like 'patron' several lines later) in the specialized Roman sense, in which wealthier, more influential men served as 'patrons' (*patroni*) for less wealthy or influential 'clients' (*clientes*). Middling types like Martial could be at the same time both patrons of lower-status men and clients of wealthier ones. For more on patron–client customs and responsibilities, see poem 4.8 (p. 541) and n.

535. *1.10. l. 1. Gemellus*: For the most part, it should be assumed that the names Martial employs are not intended to refer to or pseudonymize

historical individuals so much as conjure a character and/or exemplify a type. Exceptions will be detailed in the notes below.

l. 4. *She's a cougher*: Legacy hunting or captation was a common, and commonly satirized, practice in Rome from the late Republic on. People like Gemellus would seek out the elderly or sickly rich (Maronilla), and pay them assiduous respect, take care of them, offer gifts and even sexual favors, in hopes of being written into the will. The wealthy 'prey' in turn would sometimes feign illness in hopes of encouraging such attentions (as in Mart. 2.26, p. 538); this is the plot of Ben Jonson's *Volpone*. Cf. also Mart. 10.8 (p. 548) and 12.10 (p. 552); and Horace's more oblique allusions to the phenomenon at *Odes* 2.3, ll. 17–20 (p. 472), 2.14, ll. 25–8 (p. 477), and 4.7, ll. 24–5 (p. 489).

536.   *1.32.* This little squib is included mainly as the source of one of our most famous English epigrams (Tom Brown, 1680):

> I do not like thee, Doctor Fell,
> The reason why – I cannot tell;
> But this I know, and know full well,
> I do not like thee, Doctor Fell.

The (apocryphal) story goes that Dr. John Fell, Dean of Christ Church, Oxford, was about to expel Tom Brown from the college, but decided to offer a last-second reprieve, if he could translate Martial's couplet extempore. The epigram Brown came up with is one of those rare translations that surpasses its original. The portrait of the unlikeable doctor glowers upon visitors to the Great Hall at Christ Church; it is not recorded whether Brown's performance was sufficient to earn his reinstatement.

1.34. l. 2. *Lesbia*: Martial borrows the pseudonym Catullus used for his mistress; see *Intro* to Catullus (p. 373). Catullus' is probably the single most salient influence on Martial's work.

l. 7. *Chione and Ias*: 'Snow-White' and 'Violet', Greek type-names for prostitutes, who (the poem says) at least have the decency to conceal their professional activities in the relative privacy of cemeteries, which tended to be outside the city walls, and would have offered plenty of places to hide.

1.61. In this priamel, far more modest than, e.g., Hor. *Odes* 1.1, ll. 3–34 (pp. 462–3, and see n. *ad loc.*), Martial aligns himself and his hometown of Bilbilis with other famous poets from the provinces. Martial's list begins with Cisalpine Gaul (i.e., 'Gaul on this side of the Alps'; ll. 1–4), then moves to Egypt (l. 5) and Abruzzo (l. 6), and finally to Spain (ll. 7–12).

l. 1. *Verona . . . her best bard*: Catullus (pp. 373–97).

l. 2. *Virgil*: See pp. 398–410.

l. 3. *Livy*: Titus Livius (59 BCE–17 CE), Roman historian and author of a monumental *History of Rome* (*Ab Urbe Condita*, 'From the Founding of the City') in 142 books, thirty-five of which survive.

l. 4. *Stella*: Lucius Arruntius Stella was an important political figure, an elegiac poet and a patron of both Statius (pp. 527–32) and Martial, who invites him to dinner in Mart. 10.48 (p. 549).

ll. 4–11. *Flaccus, Apollodorus, Canius, Decianus* and *Licinianus* are little known outside Martial but were friends of his. Flaccus and Canius Rufus are among the invitees to dinner in Mart. 10.48 (p. 549).

l. 6. *Ovid*: See pp. 492–526.

l. 7. *both Senecas*: The elder Lucius Annaeus Seneca (*c.*54 BCE–39 CE) was a Roman oratorical and historical writer, father of the Younger Seneca and grandfather of the poet Lucan (see n. on l. 8, below). Lucius Annaeus Seneca the younger (*c.*4 BCE–65 CE) was a Stoic philosopher and tragedian; tutor to the emperor Nero, he was implicated in a conspiracy to assassinate him and forced to take his own life.

l. 8. *Lucan*: Marcus Annaeus Lucanus (39–65 CE), author of the *Pharsalia*, an epic poem about the civil war between Caesar and Pompey. A fellow conspirator with his uncle, the Younger Seneca, against Nero, he quoted from the *Pharsalia* as he committed suicide.

537. 1.117. Lupercus wants to read Martial's poetry but doesn't care to pay for it, a predicament plenty of artists today will recognize; see also 5.16 (p. 542). Martial tells Lupercus not to send his slave boy schlepping all the way to Martial's place, but instead to, actually, you know, have him go buy the thing in a bookstore. Despite its self-deprecation, the poem likely served as an advertisement to listeners or readers letting them know where they could go to scratch their epigrammatic itch.

l. 6. *the Quirinal Pear Tree*: Martial lived on the Quirinal Hill – one of the canonical seven hills, in the northeast of the city – on a street with a pear tree, in an upper story or attic, probably a cramped little garret with a sloping roof easy to knock your head against.

l. 9. *the Argiletum*: A major road which connected the Forum to the Subura neighborhood (see Mart. 12.18, p. 553, and Prop. 4.7, l. 17, p. 440, and n.) and was eventually incorporated into the Forum Transitorium of Domitian and his successor, Nerva.

l. 10. *Caesar's Forum*: It is not easy, on archaeological grounds, to determine whether this refers to the Forum of Julius Caesar (typically referred to as the *forum Caesaris*) or the Forum Transitorium.

538. l. 16. *a Martial for five denarii*: A denarius was about one day's wage for a skilled laborer (like a Greek drachma; cf. Phil. 25, ll. 2–4, p. 339, and n.). Little is known about the price of books in the ancient world. Peter Howell (*A Commentary on Book One of the Epigrams of Martial*, p. 352) remarks that '5 denarii seems a rather high price, but then this is a smart copy'. For more on physical books, see Cat. 1 (p. 376) and Cat. 22 (p. 382).

2.26. l. 3. *Bithynicus*: Evidently a provincial, from Bithynia, and a legacy hunter; see n. on Mart. 1.10 l. 4 (p. 535), above.

2.38. l. 1. *Nomentum*: Now Mentana, about fifteen miles northeast of Romye, on the fringes of Sabine country, where Martial had an estate which was for him what the Sabine farm was for Horace (see *Intro* to Horace, p. 453, and n. on Hor. *Epod*. 2, l. 41, p. 457). Other notables, such as Cicero's friend Atticus and the Younger Seneca, had villas in the same area; there is a common scholarly assumption that the estate was gifted to Martial by Seneca (cf. *Poet Intro*, p. 533), but there is no evidence for this. In 10.48 (p. 549), Martial serves friends in Rome his own Nomentan wine; and in 10.92 (p. 551), he has sold his farm to one Marrius, whom he asks to look after it while he is back in Spain.

539. 2.53. l. 4. *Veii*: See Stat. *Silv*. 4.5, l. 54 (p. 531) and n.

l. 10. *Parthia's king*: See n. on Hor. *Odes* 2.13, l. 17 (p. 475). Martial could mean 'Parthian' specifically, or merely 'Persian'; both signifiers of proverbial opulence, the two are also used interchangeably at times by Horace. The striking final line owes much to Hor. *Odes* 3.9, l. 4 (p. 482).

2.62. l. 3. *Labienus*: This name may have been chosen by Martial for its similarity to *labia*, 'lips', with clear sexual implications.

2.90. l. 1. *Quintilian*: The famous orator and teacher of oratory, Marcus Fabius Quintilianus, who today is best known for his twelve-book rhetorical and pedagogical guide the *Institutes of Oratory* (*Institutio Oratoria*), written *c*.95 CE, at the end of Domitian's reign. He ran a school of rhetoric, with a salary granted, at public expense, by the emperor Vespasian, where he educated the Younger Pliny, Domitian's nephews and heirs, and perhaps Tacitus. Like Martial, he was also a native of Spain, born around the Rioja region in 35 CE. The fact that this is the only epigram addressed by Martial to Quintilian might imply that they were not much in sympathy with each other; here, Quintilian seems to have suggested that Martial use his gifts more seriously, but Martial, ever the earthy Epicurean, demurs.

539–40. ll. 8–12. *I'm happy with a roof . . . I call that life*: Compare Mart. 12.18, ll. 21–30, for a similarly simple, and rusticated, vision of the good life – not to mention Hor. *Epod.* 2, ll. 39–48 (pp. 457–8), for it in a Sabine setting again. For the 'smoky hearth' (l. 8), cf. Stat. *Silv.* 4.5, ll. 13–14 (p. 530) and n.

540. 3.26. l. 4. *Massic, and . . . Caecuban*: See Hor. *Odes* 1.1, l. 19 (p. 462) and n., and Hor. *Odes* 2.14, l. 26 (p. 477) and n., respectively.

3.53. ll. 1–4 . . . *why describe you bit by bit*: A sort of anti-blazon; compare Phil. 12, ll. 1–6 (p. 336), and Ov. *Am.* 1.5, ll. 20–23 (p. 494) and n.

3.65. Martial, through a series of comparisons reminiscent of that other nosiest of poets, Charles Baudelaire, exhorts a young slave to kiss him in a more grown-up manner. (The kisses of the young were proverbially sweet-scented.) The poem owes much to Catullus' amatory epigrams addressed to the boy Juventius (see Cat. 48, p. 386, and 99, p. 396).

l. 2. *Corycus*: A mountain in Cilicia famous for its saffron.

l. 6. For the Arabian *spice harvest*, cf. Stat. 4.5, ll. 31–2 (p. 530) and n.

well-thumbed amber: Carried by Roman ladies as a perfume, amber gives off a piny scent when 'thumbed'.

l. 7. *incense*: i.e., frankincense, which, when burned, gives the flame its pale amber color as well as its odor of balsam.

l. 8. *nard*: An unguent made from spikenard, a flowering herb in the honeysuckle family, and used, along with wreaths, to adorn hair at drinking parties.

l. 9. *Diadumenos*: 'With Hair Bound Back', a common slave moniker and the name of a much-admired statue by the fifth-century BCE Greek sculptor Polyclitus, which was frequently copied by Roman artists.

541. 3.89. l. 2. *that look as if you're working hard to shit*: The characteristic expression of Domitian's father, the emperor Vespasian, according to Suetonius (*Life of Vespasian*, 20).

4.8. Martial combines an account of a typical Roman day with a dedication of his book and a compliment to the emperor Domitian. Roman days and nights were divided into twelve hours each, with the first daylight hour starting at sunrise and the twelfth ending at dusk. The length of an hour would therefore change depending on the season, and reckoning was never very exact; cf. also Mart. 10.48, ll. 1–5 (pp. 549–50).

The first two hours of the day, from around 6 to 8 a.m., were occupied with the *salutatio* (l. 1's 'morning greeting', or 'levee'), in which clients would dress up in their togas (monkey suits, they might as well have called them; cf. Mart. 12.18, l. 5, p. 553, for the unpleasantness of this garment) and wait on their patrons. At the *salutatio*, clients might ask patrons for favors, and patrons might ask clients to accompany them somewhere, such as the forum – a patron's prestige was enhanced by a large train of followers. Martial particularly hated this custom and complains about it frequently. Cf. Mart. 5.20, ll. 5–7 (p. 543), 7.39 (p. 546), 12.18, ll. 1–6 (p. 553), and 12.68 (p. 555), and Horace's allusion, *Epod.* 2, ll. 7–8 (p. 456).

Martial was also not a fan of the law courts, which got going after the *salutatio*; cf. Mart. 6.19 (p. 544), 7.65 (p. 546) and 10.47, l. 5 (p. 549). The fifth hour (l. 3), around 11 a.m., was lunchtime, which was followed by a siesta (l. 4). After the siesta, the put-upon client seems to have been home free: mornings in Rome were for work, afternoons for exercise and leisure activities; not a bad set-up.

Martial's final couplet (ll. 11–12) is a kind of miniature *recusatio* (refusal poem; see n. on Prop. 2.1, p. 427), in which the poet excuses his Muse – as too unserious and salacious – from attending the emperor's *salutatio* ('Jove's *Good mornings*'), but sends her instead with a greeting more suited to cocktail o'clock.

542. *5.9.* Doctors are frequent objects of satire, for their high fees and often deadly results (cf. Mart. 8.74, p. 548). They are often given Greek names: the Elder Cato warned his son that Greeks had a plot to kill all barbarians with medicine, and that their fees were a confidence scheme (Elder Pliny, *Natural History* 29.7). *Symmachus* (Ally) at any rate is a fictional name, which Martial gives to a doctor in two other places.

543. *5.16.* l. 5. *Treasury lawyer*: The Treasury was housed under the stairs of the temple of Saturn in the Forum. The Younger Pliny (*Letters* 4.12) gives an example of the sort of case such a lawyer might argue: a provincial scribe died before he could be paid, and there was a trial about what to do with the money: one lawyer spoke on behalf of his heirs; the other, for the People – that is, the Treasury.

l. 10. *you enjoy them – only if they're free*: For the same complaint, cf. Mart. 1.117 (p. 537).

l. 12. *Alexis*: The love interest of the shepherd Corydon in Vi. *Ecl.* 2 (p. 400; and see n. *ad loc.*). In his *Life of Virgil* (28–31), no doubt extrapolating from the poem, Donatus claims that the character of Alexis represented a beloved slave boy given to the poet by his early patron, Gaius Asinius

Pollio, though Martial elsewhere attributes the gift to Virgil's later, greater patron, Gaius Maecenas (Mart. 8.55). At any rate, Martial is saying that patrons in the old days thought nothing of giving a poet such an extravagant gift ('a knickknack') in addition to their praise.

5.20. l. 1. *Sweet Julius*: Julius Martialis, Martial's best friend in Rome, and a frequent addressee in philosophically tinged epigrams about happiness and friendship. See also Mart. 10.47 (p. 549) and 12.34 (p. 554).

l. 5. *palatial homes of the powerful*: Martial, as client, would have to visit these during the morning *salutatio*; see n. on Mart. 4.8 (p. 541), above.

l. 10. *the Virgo's baths, the colonnade*: The Aqua Virgo was an aqueduct built by Augustus' right-hand man Marcus Vipsanius Agrippa in 19 BCE to supply his previously built baths in the Campus Martius (see also Hor. *Odes* 3.12, l. 11, p. 484, and n., and 4.1, ll. 39-40, p. 489, and nn.). 'The colonnade' might refer to any number of them, including the temple of Quirinus, near Martial's house, the Portico of Europa, the Portico of the Argonauts and the Portico of Pompey (for which, see Prop. 4.8, l. 76, p. 444 and n.).

5.34. This epitaph on Erotion, a slave girl who died young – six days short of her sixth birthday (ll. 5-6) – is Martial's most tender poem and a worthy addition to antiquity's great epitaphs (e.g., Call. *Ep.* 34, p. 280, Mel. 56, p. 329, Cat. 101, p. 397; compare also Crin. 17, p. 341, and Ben Jonson's 'On My First Son' and 'On My First Daughter'). Martial commends Erotion's spirit to the care of his deceased parents, and asks that they look after her in the underworld.

544. l. 4. *Cerberus' huge bark*: See Bacch. 5, l. 75 (p. 173) and n. Martial may have been thinking of Prop. 4.7, l. 53 (p. 441).

5.58. l. 1. For the name *Postumus*, see n. on Hor. *Odes* 2.14 l. 1 (p. 476). The name also appears at Mart. 2.12 (p. 538), above, and Mart. 6.19 (p. 544), below.

ll. 5-6. *as old as Nestor or Priam*: Archetypes of venerable old age, from Homer's *Iliad* onward. For Nestor, cf. also Pi. *Py.* 3, ll. 162-4 (p. 154) and n., and Ov. *Am.* 3.7, l. 43 (p. 508).

6.19. This epigram Latinizes a Greek epigram of the Neronian court poet Lucillius (*AP* 11.141; for Lucillius, see *Intro* to Martial, p. 534). In it, Martial's lawyer Postumus unleashes a rhetorical cannonade in an attempt to crush a forensic fly. Postumus inappropriately thunders through a number of crises of the Roman Republic, glossed below; cf. the lists in Prop. 3.3, ll. 7-12 (p. 433), and Hor. *Epod.* 16, ll. 3-14 (p. 460).

Martial's scorn for the workings of the legal system finds further outlet in Mart. 7.65 (p. 546), below.

545. l. 6. *Carrhae*: Site of the devastating defeat of the Romans, under Crassus, by the Parthians in 53 BCE; see n. on Hor. *Odes* 2.13, l. 17 (p. 475). The *Mithridatic War* was actually a series of wars waged against one of Rome's bitterest enemies, Mithridates VI of Pontus, from 89 BCE until his death by suicide in 63, when his kingdom became a province of the Roman Empire.

l. 7. *Hannibal*: Traditionally Rome's greatest antagonist, in the Second Punic War (218–201 BCE); cf. *Intro* to Latin Lyric (p. 365), Prop. 3.3, ll. 9–11 (p. 433) and nn., and Hor. *Epod.* 16, l. 8 (p. 460) and n.

l. 8. *the Sullas and the Mariuses*: The Roman general Lucius Cornelius Sulla (138–78 BCE) won one victory over Mithridates in 84, but it took twenty more years before Pompey the Great finished him off. The civil unrest between the aristocratic Sulla and the populist Gaius Marius (see also Prop. 2.1, l. 24, p. 427, and nn. on Prop. 3.3, ll. 43–4, p. 434, and 3.5, l. 16, p. 434), both prominent generals in the Social War (91–88 BCE), was the major theme of the 80s BCE (cf. *Intro* to Latin Lyric, p. 368).

l. 9. *Muciuses*. The most famous Mucius was Gaius Mucius Scaevola, a failed assassin who burned off his own hand in the war with the Etruscan king Lars Porsena in 508 BCE (cf. Livy, *History of Rome* 2.12, and Hor. *Epod.* 16, l. 4, p. 460, and n.). D. R. Shackleton Bailey, however, in his Loeb Classical Library edition of Martial, thinks the reference is to Quintus Mucius Scaevola, a famous jurist who was consul in 95 BCE, but who 'seems to have been thrown in merely for the sake of assonance' (Vol. 2, p. 15).

546. 7.39. Gout, which involves painful swelling of the joints in the sufferer's hands and feet, was frequently satirized for its associations with luxurious living. Martial, rather originally, combines this subject with one of his favorite pet peeves, the *salutatio* (see n. on Mart. 4.8, p. 541, above).

7.65. Disdain for the law courts was one of Martial's characteristic attitudes; cf. Mart. 6.19 (p. 544), above. Then, as now, the slowness of lawsuits was proverbial.

l. 1. *Three forums*: Probably the Roman Forum, the Forum of Julius Caesar and the Forum of Augustus, all of which were edged by porticoes and basilicas, where the law courts were located – though the Forum Transitorium, begun by Domitian and completed by his successor, Nerva, also finds its way into Martial's work.

547. 7.95. Kissing was originally an aristocratic form of greeting, which by Martial's day had spread to all levels of society. There may therefore be a

classist element to Martial's invective against Linus' wintry osculations; or he may only be inveighing against sycophants and spongers.

ll. 13–14. *mohair coats . . . Cilicia's and Libya's goats*: 'In modern times,' write the commentators Lindsay and Patricia Watson, 'mohair wool is obtained from the angora goat, named from its place of origin Ankara, the modern name for Cilicia' (Martial, *Select Epigrams*, ed. Watson and Watson, p. 313). North Africa, near the Syrtis (the modern Gulf of Sidra, on the north coast of Libya), was also known in antiquity for the hairiness of its goats.

ll. 16–17. *cunt-lickers . . . fellatio*: Martial's main objection to oral sex acts was sanitary: cunnilingus was thought bad for oral hygiene. Eunuch priests were supposed to be particularly zealous fellators.

8.69. l. 3. *Vacerra*: This name, which refers to 'a wooden post or stake', was apparently used as an insult by the emperor Augustus instead of *cerritus*, 'crackbrained' (Suetonius, *Life of Augustus* 87.2).

548. 8.74. Doctoring was a ticklish business in the ancient world; doctors were in high demand, but subjected to little of the extensive training and oversight of modern medicine (cf. Mart. 5.9, p. 542, and n.). Martial's comparison, therefore, between the eye doctor (*ophthalmicus*) and the Greek-style gladiator (*oplomachus*) is not implausible: both professions will have been much employed in lancing eyeballs.

10.8. On legacy hunting, see n. on Mart. 1.10 1.4 (p. 535), above.

549. *10.14.* Martial satirizes the *paraclausithyron* (locked-door song) genre prevalent in Greek epigram and Latin love elegy (cf. Call. *Ep.* 8, p. 277, and n.). Martial is mocking the conventional posture of slavery and poverty among courtiers or poets who, like Ovid (pp. 492–526), may have been rich indeed, but nonetheless hung around haunting the foyer of some courtesan very much their social and financial inferior.

l. 3. *Baiae*: See Prop. 1.11 (p. 426) and n. on l. 1.

l. 5. *Setine wine*: The favorite wine of Augustus (and, consequently, of many of his successors), produced in the hills above the Pontine Marshes at Setia (modern Sezze), southeast of Rome. Martial repeatedly refers to it in his poems as a luxury (cf., in this volume, Mart. 12.17, l. 5, p. 552).

10.47. One of Martial's most famous epigrams, this is another semi-philosophical piece of Epicureanism addressed to his great friend, Julius Martialis (see n. on 5.20, l. 1, p. 543). Julius is an appropriate choice of addressee, since friendship was of prime importance in Epicurean doctrine. Martial's vision of the good life in the country has much in common with, say, Tib. 2.1 (p. 417) and Hor. *Epod.* 2 (p. 456), though he is less intellectual than Horace and less religious than Tibullus; he is clearly more interested in creature comforts than philosophical conversation. Martial also benefits from the servants who do all the hard work for him, while himself being absolved from the burdensome urban obligations of a client to his patrons (see n. on Mart. 4.8, p. 541, above). To this poem compare also Martial's Epicurean portrayal of his native Bilbilis in Mart. 12.18 (p. 553).

10.48. Perhaps the most charming of Martial's contributions to the minor subgenre of the dinner invitation poem; cf. Phil. 23 (p. 338), Cat. 13 (p. 381) and Hor. *Odes* 4.11 (p. 490) and n. Dating from after Domitian's downfall in 96 CE, it takes a turn in its final lines when it comments on the kind of malicious informing which happened under the ill-fated emperor's regime.

l. 1. *the eighth hour*: Mid-to-late afternoon; see n. on Mart. 4.8 (p. 541), above, for more on Roman timekeeping.

Isis' doors: For the temple of Isis in the Campus Martius, see n. on Tib. 1.3, l. 23 (p. 413).

550. l. 5. *Nero's glut of gold*: i.e., the *Domus Aurea* (Golden House), Nero's extravagantly gilded 300-acre palace complex, built after the great fire of 64 CE and extending over parts of three of Rome's seven hills. After Nero's death in 68, portions of the palace remained for around forty years as an embarrassing symbol of imperial extravagance until they finally burned down in a fire of 104 CE and were not restored.

ll. 6–7. For *Stella, Flaccus* and *Canius*, see nn. on Mart. 1.61, ll. 4 and 9 (p. 536), above. *Nepos* was a neighbor of Martial, both on the Quirinal Hill in Rome, and in the country at Nomentum (cf. n. on Mart. 1.117, l. 6, p. 537, and n. on Mart. 2.38, l. 1, p. 538, respectively); he seems to have been an oenophile. The poet Julius *Cerialis* is the recipient of another of Martial's invitation poems (Mart. 11.52), where he appears as the author of *Georgics* in the manner of Virgil (pp. 398–410), and of a *Gigantomachy* (cf. Prop. 2.1, ll. 19–20, p. 427, and n., and Ov. *Am.* 2.1, ll. 14–21, p. 498, and nn.).

l. 9. *Lupus*: Not known outside Martial's epigrams; he may or may not be the debtor at Mart. 7.10, l. 7 (p. 546).

l. 17. *a kid a wild wolf killed*: See n. on Hor. *Epod.* 2, ll. 59–60 (p. 458).

l. 23. *when Frontinus ran things*: Sextus Julius Frontinus was consul in 72 or 73 CE, then again in 98 or 100; cf. n. on Hor. *Epod.* 13, l. 9 (p. 458), for the convention associating consulships with wine vintage.

ll. 24–7. *we'll have candid speech, and friendly laughter* ... : Edwin Post suggests in his 1908 commentary that Martial 'is thinking of the dangers that beset men under rulers like Tiberius and Domitian, when innocent remarks of a private conversation were purposely misconstrued and when traps were set to tempt men to utter words that turned out to be their death-warrants' (*Selected Epigrams of Martial*, ed. Post, pp. 255–6).

10.63. The sting of this satirical funerary epigram is very much in its tail. The 'one-man woman' (*femina univira*), of whom Martial's anonymous speaker is a parodically exaggerated archetype, would never use *that* word. Nor, frankly, was she even supposed to enjoy sex so much as endure it for the sake of the family/clan.

l. 3. *Mausolus's stony sepulcher*: The Mausoleum of Halicarnassus, named after Mausolus, the Persian satrap of Caria between 377 and 353 BCE, who initially commissioned it. Like the 'pyramids of Egypt' (l. 2), one of the seven wonders of the ancient world.

l. 4. *Caesar's jubilees*: The Centennial or 'Secular' Games were a religious celebration held roughly every 110 years. They occurred twice in the Roman Republic (in 249 and the 140s BCE), then were revived by Augustus in 17 BCE (see *Intro* to Latin Lyric, p. 372) and held again by Domitian in 88 CE. However, Claudius held his own Centennial Games in 47 CE to celebrate the 800th year of Rome's founding, so it was just possible that one woman could have participated in both Claudius' and Domitian's games.

551. *10.80.* l. 1. *Eros*: The Greek name for Cupid, commonly given to slaves (cf. Crin. 17, p. 341, and n.). Meaning 'desire', it is an appropriate moniker for this poem's protagonist.

10.92. Martial has sold his beloved farm in Nomentum (see n. on Mart. 2.38, l. 1, p. 538, above) and is moving back to Spain.

ll. 1–2. *Marrius ... Atina's pride and glory*: Martial's friend, to whom he entrusts care of his Italian farm, is not otherwise known, though there is an inscription with this name from Atina, a town in central Latium, southeast of Rome.

l. 4. *the Fauns' sacred grove*: See n. on Hor. *Odes* 3.18, l. 1 (p. 485).

l. 6. *rude Silvanus*: See Hor. *Epod.* 2, ll. 21–2 (p. 457) and n.

ll. 9–10. *Mars ... in whose holy month I had my birth*: For Martial's March birthday, see also Mart. 12.60 (p. 555).

ll. 11–12. *exquisite Flora escaped Priapus*: The story of Flora, a rustic goddess of springtime and blossoming whose festival was celebrated from late April to early May, and her escape from Priapus is nowhere fully narrated, but bears some resemblance to that of the nymph Chloris, who flees from Zephyrus at Ov. *Fasti* 5, ll. 183–212, and is transformed into Flora; she subsequently helps Juno conceive (via a magic flower) and give birth to Mars (*Fasti* 5, ll. 229–58). It is also possible Martial was thinking of Priapus' pursuit of the nymph Lotis at Ov. *Met.* 9, ll. 340–48. For more on Priapus, see n. on Hor. *Epod.* 2, ll. 21–2 (p. 457).

552. *11.71*. l. 1. *'Hysterical'*: Hysteria, the word derived from Greek *hystera*, 'uterus', was a condition of adult women attributed by Greeks and Egyptians to a 'wandering uterus', but by Romans to reproductive abnormalities.

11.76. ll. 1–2. *Paetus* means 'cross-eyed', and *Bucco*, 'fathead'.

12.10. Another epigram on legacy hunting / captation; see Mart. 1.10 l.4 (p. 535) and n.

12.17. ll. 5–6. *Falernian . . . Setine . . . Caecuban wine*: For Falernian wine, see Tib. 2.1, l. 28 (p. 418) and n. For Setine, see Mart. 10.14, l. 5 (p. 549) and n. And for Caecuban, see Hor. *Odes* 2.14, l. 26 (p. 477) and n.

l. 10. *why would your fever leave your life for Dama's*: 'Dama' is a typical slave name.

553. *12.18.* After thirty-four frenetic years in Rome, Martial has retired to his ancestral home of Bilbilis in northeastern Spain, which he presents as a rustic Epicurean paradise. Compare also Martial's vision of the good life in the Italian countryside in Mart. 10.47 (p. 549), above, and his praise of Spain in Mart. 12.31 (p. 554) and 12.60 (p. 555), below.

l. 1. *Juvenal*: Most likely the satirist, who must have been a pretty good friend of Martial's; two other epigrams (Mart. 7.24 and 7.91) are also addressed to him.

l. 3. *Diana's hill, or Subura's din*: The oldest temple to Diana in Rome stood on the Aventine Hill; cf. Prop. 4.8, l. 29 (p. 443). For the Subura neighborhood, cf. Prop. 4.7, l. 17 (p. 440) and n. Neither of these neighborhoods was what we would call tony.

l. 5. *your sticky toga*: The toga, composed of up to fourteen square yards of heavy wool, was complicated to put on and uncomfortable to wear, particularly in summer; by Martial's day, its use was restricted to holidays and ceremonial occasions, including the morning greeting (*salutatio*: see n. on Mart. 4.8, p. 541, above).

l. 6. *the Caelian Hills*: The Greater and Lesser Caelian, the latter being a (particularly posh) spur of the former.

l. 13. *Platea, Boterdus*: Towns near Bilbilis; Platea lay on the River Salo (modern Jalón); Boterdus perhaps overlaps with the village of Campiel. For *Celtic Spain*, or Celtiberia, see n. on Cat. 37, l. 18 (p. 385).

l. 16. *nine o'clock*: For Roman timekeeping, see n. on Mart. 4.8 (p. 541), above.

ll. 21–30. *I wake up to the welcome . . .* : Note the similarity between these lines and Martial's definition of happiness at 2.90, ll. 8–12 (pp. 539–40).

ll. 27–8. *The foreman, with his cheeks still bare . . .* : And thus at the perfect age for sexual enjoyment. The rustic setting might rather have led us to expect a paragon of country rectitude, but this seems not to have been high on Martial's list of interests.

554.   12.20. l. 1. *Themison*: A name derived from *themis*, 'right, good, correct' – in other words, everything Themison's relations with his sister are not.

12.31. Homer's description of the gardens of Alcinous, king of the magical land of Phaeacia (*Od.* 7, ll. 112–32), provides the *locus classicus* to which Roman writers, from Horace to the Younger Seneca, Statius and the Younger Pliny, hearken back in their descriptions of idyllic country villas. Martial, thanking his patroness Marcella (likely a rich widow of Spanish birth and Roman mores) for the gift of a villa at Bilbilis, claims extravagantly that his new residence is superior to that of Alcinous. He also praises his life in Spain in Mart. 12.18 (p. 553) and 12.60 (p. 555).

l. 3. *Paestum's roses*: See Ov. *Ex Pont.* 2.4, l. 28 (p. 521) and n.

l. 10. *Nausicaä*: Alcinous' daughter, princess of Phaeacia, whose hand in marriage her father offers to Odysseus (*Od.* 7, ll. 311–21); Odysseus, however, refuses, being eager to get home – in the same way that Martial refuses the imagined offer of Phaeacia's gardens.

12.34. l. 1. *Thirty-four years*: See *Poet Intro*, p. 533.

l. 2. *Julius*: For Julius Martialis, see n. on Mart. 5.20, l. 1 (p. 543).

ll. 5–7. *if all the pebbles . . . outweigh the black*: According to the Elder Pliny (*Natural History* 7.40), Thracians, for every day of their lives, would lay aside a white or a black stone, depending on whether the day had been good or bad.

555.   12.60. Another contrast of Martial's simpler life in Spain with the requirements of Rome (cf. Mart. 12.18, p. 553, and 12.31, p. 554, above), where he apparently was expected to play the punctilious host – a role which he found onerous and nerve-wracking, as this poem makes clear. For more

on birthday rituals, see n. on Sulp. 3.11 (p. 449). As Martial also tells us in Mart. 10.92 (p. 551), he was born in March.

l. 9. *the cloudy Caecuban*: See Hor. *Odes* 2.14, l. 26 (p. 477) and n.

12.68. Martial, ever the client in Rome (at least, according to him), finds that, back home in Bilbilis, his Spanish countrymen are looking to him for patronage – a role which he finds equally annoying (for the client– patron relationship, see n. on Mart. 4.8, p. 541, above). The poet will have been around sixty years old at the time of this epigram.

Index of Genres

Poems' page numbers are given in **bold**.

bucolic **276** (Call. *Ep.* 3), **283–96**
(Theoc. *Id.* 1, 2, 7, 10, 11), **308**
(Leo. Tar. 19), **400–8** (Vi. *Ecl.* 2,
4, 9, 10), **456** (Hor. *Epod.* 2),
485 (Hor. *Odes* 3.23), **549**
(Mart. 10.47), **551** (Mart.
10.92), **553** (Mart. 12.18)

didactic **112–13** (Xen. 11, 15–6,
23–26, *, 30, 34), **258–61** (Call.
Aet.), **346** (Ant. Thess. 96)
dirge
all **163–4** (Pi. frr. 129, 131, 137,
140d), **376** (Cat. 3), **501** (Ov.
Am. 2.6), **510** (Ov. *Am.* 3.9),
528 (Stat. 2.4)
for a pet **376** (Cat. 3), **501** (Ov.
Am. 2.6), **528** (Stat. 2.4)

elegy
all **6–7** (Ar. 1–5, 11, 13, *The
Achaeans at Mysia*), **21** (Callinus
1), **22–5** (Tyr. 10–12), **28–30**
(Mimn. 1–7, 11+11a, 12, 14),
77–85 (all Theognis), **69–73**
(Sol. 4–6, 9, 11, 13, 24, 27),
86–7 (Phocylides 1, 3, 5–6), **88**

(Demodocus 1), **110–12** (Xen.
1–2, 7a, 8), **128–9** (Sim. *El.* 11,
19+20), **195** (Tim. Rhod. Elegy
10), **197** (Ion of Chios Elegy 26),
212 (Tim. Epitaph for
Euripides), **221–2** ('Plato' 1–5),
225 (Aristotle 673), **258–61**
(Call. *Aet.*), **391** (Cat. 68b), **395**
(Cat. 76), **413–17** (all Tibullus),
423–42 (all Propertius), **447–50**
(Sulp. 3.8–12), **494–526** (all
Ovid)

didactic **258–61** (all Call. *Aet.*)
dirge **510** (Ov. *Am.* 3.9)
dream vision **432** (Prop. 3.3), **440**
(Prop. 4.7), **522** (Ov. *Ex Pont.* 3.3)
epistolary **512** (Ov. *Tri.* 1.4),
521–5 (all Ov. *Ex Pont.*)
exilic **512–19** (all Ov. *Tri.*), **521–5**
(all Ov. *Ex Pont.*)
love- **413–17** (all Tibullus),
423–42 (all Propertius), **447–50**
(Sulp. 3.8–12), **494–507** (Ov.
Am. 1.5, 1.9, 1.11–12, 2.1, 2.4,
2.6–8, 2.10, 2.12–13, 3.7)
love- (proto-) **391** (Cat. 68b), **395**
(Cat. 76)

elegy – *cont'd.*

  martial 21 (Callinus 1), 22–5 (Tyr.
10–12)

  political 69–73 (Sol. 4–6, 9, 11,
13, 24, 27), 128–9 (Sim. *El.* 11,
19+20)

  sympotic 28–30 (Mimn. 1–7,
11+11a, 12, 14), 77–85 (all
Theognis), 110–12 (Xen. 1–2,
7a, 8), 197 (Ion of Chios Elegy
26)

  votive 496 (Ov. *Am.* 1.11)

encomium 129 (Sim. *Ep.* 1), 185
(Bacch. fr. 20b), 342 (Crin. 27),
391 (Cat. 68b), 417 (Tib. 2.1),
466 (Hor. *Odes* 1.6), 480 (Hor.
Odes 3.5), 486 (Hor. *Odes* 3.25),
529 (Stat. 4.5), 541 (Mart. 4.8)

epigram

  all 129–33 (all Sim. *Ep.*), 195
(Tim. Rhod. Elegy 10), 212
(Tim. Epitaph for Euripides),
221–2 ('Plato' 1–5), 225
(Aristotle 673), 276–81 (Call.
Ep. 1–3, 5, 8, 10–11, 13–15,
29–32, 34, 37, 41–5, 56, 50–1,
53, 58, 63), 301–56 (all *Greek
Anthology*), 394 (Cat. 70, 72),
395–7 (Cat. 83, 84, 85, 92, 99,
101, 109), 535–6 (Mart 1.23,
1.32, 1.34), 537 (Mart. 1.68,
1.73, 1.79), 538 (Mart. 2.12,
2.26), 538–40 (Mart. 2.38, 2.53,
2.58, 2.62, 2.88, 2.90, 3.26),
340–42 (Mart. 3.65, 3.89, 4.8,
4.24, 4.48, 4.71), 542 (Mart.
4.87, 5.9, 5.16), 543–4 (Mart.
5.34, 5.58), 544 (Mart. 5.83),
545 (Mart. 6.60), 546 (Mart.
7.65), 548–9 (Mart. 8.74,

9.14–15, 9.21, 9.81, 10.8,
10.14), 549–51 (Mart. 10.48,
10.63, 10.80), 552 (Mart. 11.71,
11.76), 552 (Mart. 12.17),
554–5 (Mart. 12.31, 12.34,
12.42, 12.60, 12.68)

amatory 221–2 ('Plato' 1–5),
276–8 (Call. *Ep.* 1–3, 5, 8, 10–11,
13), 281 (Call. *Ep.* 63), 304–5
(Ascl. 1–2, 4–5), 305–6 (Ascl. 12,
15–17, 42), 311 (Nos. 1), 312
(Pos. 2), 313 (Rhianus 10),
313–14 (Dios. 1–3, 6), 317 (Alc.
Mess. 6–7), 323 (Ant. Si. 61),
323–4 (Anon. 4, 6, 8, 10), 327–9
(Mel. 6, 23, 25, 29, 31, 36, 41–2,
46, 49, 52, 56), 330–32 (Mel. 69,
71, 72, 79, 90, 94, 102–3), 334–7
(Phil. 1–3, 5–6, 8–9, 12, 14–18),
338 (Phil. 21), 339 (Phil. 25, 27),
345 (Ant. Thess. 3, 7), 348
(Argent. 1, 2, 6, 7, 10), 349
(Argent. 11, 12, 13, 15), 350
(Argent. 16), 352 (Automedon 1),
353 (Automedon 2, 11), 354
(Evenus 7), 354 (Maccius 1), 394
(Cat. 70, 72), 395–6 (Cat. 83, 85,
92, 99), 397 (Cat. 109), 451–2
(Sulp. 3.13–18), 536 (Mart. 1.34),
537 (Mart. 1.68, 1.73), 538
(Mart. 2.26), 540 (Mart. 3.65),
542 (Mart. 4.71, 4.81)

aubade 350 (Argent. 16), 354
(Antiph. Mac. 1)

bucolic 276 (Call. *Ep.* 3), 308
(Leo. Tar. 19)

carpe diem 344 (Zonas 9), 346
(Ant. Thess. 38), 347
(Apollonides 8), 349 (Argent.
11), 350 (Argent. 30), 355 (Ant.

Mac. 7), **538** (Mart. 2.53), **539**
(Mart. 2.90), **544** (Mart. 5.58)
comastic **277** (Call. *Ep.* 8), **324**
(Anon. 6), **350** (Argent. 26)
convivial **555** (Mart. 12.60); *see
also* epigram, sympotic
dedicatory **130** (Sim. *Ep.* 6), **131**
(Sim. *Ep.* 27–8), **132** (Sim. *Ep.*
40a+b+c), **278** (Call. *Ep.* 14–15),
301 (Phil. Sam. 1), **311** (Nos.
11), **332** (Mel. 129), **340** (Crin.
3, 4), **342** (Crin. 34), **351** (Ant.
Byz. 1, 2), **352** (Ant. Byz. 16),
542 (Mart. 5.16); *see also*
epigram, votive
didactic **346** (Ant. Thess. 96)
encomial **129** (Sim. *Ep.* 1), **342**
(Crin. 27), **541** (Mart. 4.8)
epideictic **132** (Sim. *Ep.* 45), **212**
(Tim. Epitaph for Euripides),
225 (Aristotle 673), **303** (Anyte
16), **308** (Leo. Tar. 33), **309–10**
(Leo. Tar. 77, 85, 91), **310**
(Phalaecus 5), **311** (Nos. 4), **320**
(Phanias 7), **322** (Ant. Si. 41),
323 (Ant. Si. 59), **326** (Anon.
53), **332** (Mel. 129), **342** (Crin.
27, 33), **343** (Crin. 37), **346**
(Ant. Thess. 80, 82), **352** (Ant.
Byz. 9, 33), **354** (Maccius 10),
545 (Mart. 6.60), **549** (Mart.
10.48), **554** (Mart. 12.31)
hortatory **303** (Anyte 16), **308**
(Leo. Tar. 33), **309** (Leo. Tar. 77),
310 (Phalaecus 5), **322** (Ant. Si.
41), **343** (Crin. 35), **343** (Crin.
48), **538** (Mart. 2.53), **555**
(Mart. 12.68)
kletic **336** (Phil. 15), **338** (Phil.
19), **342** (Crin. 34)

maledictory **195** (Tim. Rhod.
Elegy 10), **356** (Phil. Thess. 55)
invective **343** (Erucius 13), **355**
(Ant. Mac. 9), **356** (Phil. Thess.
55), **537** (Mart. 1.79)
invitatory **338** (Phil. 23), **549**
(Mart. 10.48)
philosophical **554** (Mart. 12.34)
polemical **345** (Ant. Thess. 20,
37), **355** (Ant. Mac. 6, 9)
satirical **320** (Phanias 7), **339**
(Phil. 25), **348** (Argent. 7, 10),
349 (Argent. 12, 15), **353**
(Automedon 2, 7, 11), **395** (Cat.
83), **396** (Cat. 84), **535–6** (Mart.
1.23, 1.32, 1.34), **537** (Mart.
1.68, 1.73, 1.79), **538** (Mart.
2.12, 2.26), **538** (Mart. 2.38),
539 (Mart. 2.58, 2.62, 2.88),
540 (Mart. 3.26), **541** (Mart.
3.89), **541–2** (Mart. 4.24, 4.48,
4.71), **542** (Mart. 4.87, 5.9), **544**
(Mart. 5.83), **546** (Mart. 7.65),
548–9 (Mart. 8.74, 9.14–15,
9.21, 9.81, 10.8, 10.14), **550**
(Mart. 10.63, 10.80), **552** (Mart.
11.71, 11.76), **552** (Mart.
12.17), **555** (Mart. 12.42)
sepulchral **130** (Sim. *Ep.* 2),
130–31 (Sim. *Ep.* 7–9, 22a,
22b), **132–3** (Sim. *Ep.* 46, 84–5),
279–81 (Call. *Ep.* 29–32, 34, 37,
41, 45–6, 50–51, 53), **302** (Phil.
Sam. 2), **302** (Erinna 1), **303**
(Anyte 5, 9), **307–8** (Leo. Tar.
17, 19, 21), **308–9** (Leo. Tar. 57,
71), **312** (Heraclitus of
Halicarnassus 1), **315** (Dios. 30,
32), **315–16** (Mnasalces 8, 11),
316–17 (Theodoridas 12, 15,

19), 318 (Alc. Mess. 14), 318 (Theaetetus 3), 319 (Diotimus 10), 319 (Tymnes 2, 5), 321–2 (Ant. Si. 22, 23, 26), 322 (Ant. Si. 58), 325 (Anon. 47, 49, 50, 52), 326 (Mel. 4), 329–30 (Mel. 56, 65), 338 (Phil. 20), 341–2 (Crin. 15, 17–20), 343 (Erucius 13), 344 (Zonas 5), 347 (Apollonides 8), 351 (Bianor 2), 397 (Cat. 101), 543 (Mart. 5.34), 530 (Mart. 10.63)

sepulchral (for a pet) 303 (Anyte 9), 308 (Leo. Tar. 21), 316 (Mnasalces 11), 319 (Tymnes 5), 330 (Mel. 65)

sympotic 277 (Call. *Ep.* 5), 278 (Call. *Ep.* 13), 305 (Ascl. 16), 312 (Pos. 1), 317 (Alc. Mess. 2), 324 (Anon. 6), 328 (Mel. 42), 337 (Phil. 17), 338 (Phil. 21), 344 (Zonas 9), 345 (Ant. Thess. 3), 345–6 (Ant. Thess. 20, 37, 38), 347 (Apollonides 8), 350 (Argent. 23, 26, 30), 352 (Automedon 1), 353 (Automedon 7), 355 (Ant. Mac. 6, 7); *see also* epigram, convivial

votive 130 (Sim. *Ep.* 3), 303 (Anyte 13), 305 (Ascl. 6), 307 (Leo. Tar. 5), 308 (Leo. Tar. 45), 311 (Nos. 3, 5), 313 (Hedylus 2), 314 (Dios. 16), 316 (Theodoridas 2), 318 (Diotimus 1), 319 (Pancrates 1), 320 (Phanias 2), 322 (Ant. Si. 51), 324 (Anon. 35), 340–41 (Crin. 9, 10), 350 (Argent. 23), 352 (Ant. Byz. 16); *see also* epigram, dedicatory

genethliacon 436 (Prop. 3.10), 451–2 (Sulp. 3.14–15), 515 (Ov. *Tri.* 3.13), 555 (Mart. 12.60)

hymn
 kletic 39 (Sap. 1), 57 (Alc. 34), 64 (Alc. 308b), 213 (Ariph. Sic. 813), 224 (Aristotle 842), 226 (Arist. Hymn to Hestia), 234 (Anon. Hymn to Zeus), 237–9 (Anon. 935–7, 939), 240–41 (Anon. 1018a+b, 1019), 269–72 (Call. *Hy.* 2, 5), 336 (Phil. 15), 338 (Phil. 19), 383 (Cat. 34), 485 (Hor. *Odes* 3.18), 486 (Hor. *Odes* 3.25), 487 (Hor. *Odes* 4.1), 532 (Stat. 5.4)
 mimetic 269–72 (Call. *Hy.* 2, 5), 417 (Tib. 2.1)

iambus
 all 8–12 (Ar. 19, 21+22, 30+31, 41–2, 48, 105, 108, 114–6, 118–9, 120+121, 122, 124, 125–6, 128, 130–31), 12–13 (Ar. 168, 184, 188, 191, 193, 196, 196a), 16–17 (all Semonides of Amorgos), 62 (Alc. 140), 74–5 (Sol. 33, 34, 36), 102 (Anac. 347a, 347b), 106 (Anac. 388–9), 108 (Anac. 417, 419), 115–19 (all Hipponax), 261–6 (all Call. *Ia.*), 378 (Cat. 6), 379 (Cat. 8, 10), 381–3 (Cat. 13, 16, 22, 31), 384 (Cat. 37), 385 (Cat. 41), 387 (Cat. 50), 388 (Cat. 58, 60), 456–60 (all Hor. *Epod.*), 464 (Hor. *Odes* 1.4), 489 (Hor. *Odes* 4.7), 535 (Mart. 1.10), 536 (Mart. 1.61), 537 (Mart. 1.117), 538 (Mart. 2.33),

540 (Mart. 3.53), 542 (Mart. 4.81), 544 (Mart. 5.73), 544 (Mart. 6.19), 545 (Mart. 6.82), 546 (Mart. 7.39), 547 (Mart. 7.95, 8.54, 8.69), 549 (Mart. 10.47), 551 (Mart. 10.92, 11.63), 552 (Mart. 12.10), 553–4 (Mart. 12.18, 12.20)

amatory 547 (Mart. 8.54)

bucolic 456 (Hor. *Epod.* 2), 549 (Mart. 10.47), 551 (Mart. 10.92), 553 (Mart. 12.18)

carpe diem 464 (Hor. *Odes* 1.4)

convivial 458 (Hor. *Epod.* 13)

epideictic 383 (Cat. 31), 464 (Hor. *Odes* 1.4), 489 (Hor. *Odes* 4.7)

epistolary 387 (Cat. 50), 551 (Mart. 10.92), 553 (Mart. 12.18)

epodic 12–13 (Ar. 168, 184, 188, 191, 193, 196, 196a), 62 (Alc. 140), 119 (Hipp. 115, 117), 456–60 (all Hor. *Epod.*), 464 (Hor. *Odes* 1.4), 489 (Hor. *Odes* 4.7), 536 (Mart. 1.61)

hortatory 379 (Cat. 8), 460 (Hor. *Epod.* 16), 537 (Mart. 1.117), 545 (Mart. 6.82)

invective 379 (Cat. 8), 382 (Cat. 16), 384–5 (Cat. 37, 41), 388 (Cat. 58, 60), 538 (Mart. 2.33), 547 (Mart. 7.95)

invitatory 381 (Cat. 13)

philosophical 549 (Mart. 10.47), 552 (Mart. 12.10)

polemical 460 (Hor. *Epod.* 16)

satirical 378 (Cat. 6), 379 (Cat. 10), 382 (Cat. 22), 456 (Hor. *Epod.* 2), 535 (Mart. 1.10), 540 (Mart. 3.53), 542 (Mart. 4.81), 544 (Mart. 5.73), 544 (Mart. 6.19),

545 (Mart. 6.82), 546 (Mart. 7.39), 547 (Mart. 8.69), 552 (Mart. 12.10), 554 (Mart. 12.20)

lyric

all 32-7 (all Alcman), 39–54 (all Sappho), 56–67 (all Alcaeus), 90–95 (all Stesichorus), 97–9 (all Ibycus), 101–8 (all Anacreon), 121–7 (all Sim. *Lyrics*), 135–64 (all Pindar), 167–85 (all Bacchylides), 194–95 (Tim. Rhod. 727, 729, 731), 197 (Ion of Chios 744–6), 198 (Praxilla 747), 200–3 (all Corinna), 205–12 (Tim. 791, 796), 213 (Ariph. Sic. 813), 216 (Philox. 836b+c), 224 (Aristotle 842), 226–7 (Arist. Hymn to Hestia, Paean to Apollo), 229 (Phil. Scar. Paean to Dionysus), 233 (Hermolochus 846), 234–41 (all Anonymous Classical Lyric), 242–4 (all Folk Songs), 245–8 (all Scolia), 358–63 (all Anacreontea), 380 (Cat. 11), 387 (Cat. 51), 462–3 (Hor. *Odes* 1.1, 1.3), 465–87 (Hor. *Odes* 1.5–6, 1.9, 1.11, 1.22–4, 1.37–8, 2.3, 2.7, 2.10, 2.13–14, 2.20, 3.1–2, 3.5, 3.9, 3.12–13, 3.18, 3.23, 3.25, 3.30, 4.1), 490 (Hor. *Odes* 4.11), 529 (Stat. 4.5)

amatory 359 (Anacreontea 7), 360 (Anacreontea 10), 361 (Anacreontea 22), 362 (Anacreontea 26, 35), 465 (Hor. *Odes* 1.5), 468–69 (Hor. *Odes* 1.22–23), 482 (Hor. *Odes* 3.9), 483 (Hor. *Odes* 3.12), 487 (Hor. *Odes* 4.1), 490 (Hor. *Odes* 4.11)

lyric – *cont'd.*
  anti-sepulchral 477 (Hor. *Odes*
    2.20); *see also* lyric, sepulchral
  bucolic 485 (Hor. *Odes* 3.23)
  carpe diem 466 (Hor. *Odes* 1.9),
    467 (Hor. *Odes* 1.11), 471 (Hor.
    Odes 2.3)
  choral 32–4 (Alcm. 1, 3), 36
    (Alcm. 56), 37 (Alcm. 89),
    135–61 (Pi. *Ol.* 1, 7, 12; *Py.* 3,
    8; frr. 29–30, 33c, 33d; *Pae.* 6, 9;
    Dith. 2, 4; frr. 108a+b, 109–10),
    167–84 (Bacch. 3, 5, 17, 19, fr.
    4), 200–1 (Cor. 654a, 654b),
    226–7 (Arist. Hymn to Hestia,
    Paean to Apollo), 234–7 (Anon.
    Hymn to Zeus, 934, 935), 238
    (Anon. 937)
  convivial 466 (Hor. *Odes* 1.9),
    467 (Hor. *Odes* 1.11), 470–72
    (Hor. *Odes* 1.37–38, 2.3, 2.7);
    see also lyric, sympotic
  consolatory 469 (Hor. *Odes* 1.24)
  dedicatory 462 (Hor. *Odes* 1.1)
  dirge 163–4 (Pi. frr. 129, 131, 137,
    140d)
  aubade 360 (Anacreontea 10)
  carpe diem 359 (Anacreontea
    7, 8)
  ekphrastic 358 (Anacreontea 4)
  encomial 185 (Bacch. fr. 20b), 466
    (Hor. *Odes* 1.6), 480 (Hor. *Odes*
    3.5), 486 (Hor. *Odes* 3.25), 529
    (Stat. 4.5)
  epideictic 362 (Anacreontea 46),
    484 (Hor. *Odes* 3.13)
  epinician 167–71 (Bacch. 3, 5)
  epithalamion 51–3 (Sap. 104,
    105a, 105c, 110a, 111–2,
    114–6), 54 (Sap. 141)

hortatory 473 (Hor. *Odes* 2.10),
    476 (Hor. *Odes* 2.14), 478–79
    (Hor. *Odes* 3.1–3.2), 480 (Hor.
    Odes 3.5), 485 (Hor. *Odes* 3.23)
invitatory 490 (Hor. *Odes* 4.11)
invective 380 (Cat. 11), 470 (Hor.
    Odes 1.37), 474 (Hor. *Odes*
    2.13)
monodic 36 (Alcm. 26), 39–54 (all
    Sappho), 56–67 (all Alcaeus),
    194–95 (Tim. Rhod. 727, 729,
    731), 213 (Ariph. Sic. 813), 224
    (Aristotle 842), 239 (Anon.
    939), 240–41 (Anon. 1018a+b,
    1019)
'Nine', the 32–7 (Alcman), 39–54
    (Sappho), 56–67 (Alcaeus),
    90–95 (Stesichorus), 97–9
    (Ibycus), 101–8 (Anacreon),
    121–7 (Sim. *Lyrics*), 135–64
    (Pindar), 167–85 (Bacchylides)
paean 156–7 (Pi. *Pae.* 6, 9), 178
    (Bacch. 17), 184 (Bacch. fr. 4),
    227 (Arist. Paean to Apollo),
    229 (Phil. Scar. Paean to
    Dionysus), 236 (Anon. 934)
philosophical 473 (Hor. *Odes*
    2.10), 479 (Hor. *Odes* 3.2)
scolion 64 (Alc. 332), 65–6 (Alc.
    346–7), 161–3 (Pi. frr. 122–3,
    124a+b), 185 (Bacch. fr. 20b),
    245–8 (all Scolia); *see also* lyric,
    sympotic
sympotic 56–67 (all Alcaeus),
    161–3 (Py. Frr. 122–3, 124a+b),
    185 (Bacch. fr. 20b), 213 (Ariph.
    Sic. 813), 224 (Aristotle 842),
    245–8 (all Scolia), 358
    (Anacreontea 1, 4), 359–60
    (Anacreontea 8–9), 361

(Anacreontea 21), 363
(Anacreontea 53, 60b); *see also*
lyric, convivial

mime 330 (Mel. 71, 72), 502–3 (Ov.
Am. 2.7–8)

nome, monodic 205 (Tim. 791)

verse, miscellaneous
  amatory 376 (Cat. 2), 377 (Cat.
    5), 378 (Cat. 7), 385 (Cat. 45),
    386–7 (Cat. 48, 50)

dedicatory 376 (Cat. 1), 390
  (Cat. 65)
dirge 376 (Cat. 3)
epideictic 385–6 (Cat. 45–6)
epistolary 390 (Cat. 65)
epithalamion 388 (Cat. 62)
hortatory 395 (Cat. 76)

Index of Poets

Alcaeus 55
Alcaeus of Messene 317
Alcman 31
Anacreon 100
Anacreontea 357
Antipater of Sidon 320
Antipater of Thessalonica 344
Antiphanes of Macedonia 354
Antiphilus of Byzantium 351
Anyte 302
Apollonides 347
Archilochus 5
Ariphron of Sicyon 213
Aristonous of Corinth 226
Aristotle 223
Asclepiades 303
Automedon 352

Bacchylides 165
Bianor 351

Callimachus 255
Callinus 21
Catullus 373
Corinna 199
Crinagoras 339

Demodocus 88
Dioscorides 313
Diotimus 318

Erinna 302
Erucius 343
Evenus 354

Hedylus 313
Heraclitus of Halicarnassus 312
Hermolochus 233
Hipponax 114
Horace 453

Ibycus 96
Ion of Chios 196

Leonidas of Taremtum 306

Maccius 354
Marcus Argentarius 347
Martial 533
Meleager 326
Mimnermus 27
Mnasalces 315

Nossis 310

Ovid 492

Pancrates 319
Phalaecus 310
Phanias 320
Philetas of Samos 301

Philip of Thessalonica 355

Philodamus of Scarphea 229

Philodemus 333

Philoxenus 215

Phocylides 86

Pindar 134

'Plato' 221

Posidippus of Pella 312

Praxilla 198

Propertius 421

Rhianus 313

Sappho 38

Scolia 245

Semonides of Amorgos 16

Simonides 120

Solon 68

Statius 527

Stesichorus 89

Sulpicia 446

Theaetetus 318

Theocritus 282

Theodoridas 316

Theognis and the *Theognidea* 76

Tibullus 411

Timocreon of Rhodes 193

Timotheus 204

Tymnes 319

Tyrtaeus 22

Virgil 398

Xenophanes 109

Zonas 344

Index of First Lines

A dream: I lay on Helicon, in shade
432

A female love is best for us, if we 348

a hyacinth, which shepherds in the
mountains 51

A kingfisher 8

A man whose life is whole, whose
heart is clean 468

A poet has the planet's briefest boast
281

A saying of Demodocus, this too 88

A shipwrecked man lies here.
Stranger, no slowing 317

Accept this note from Hister's icy
crust 521

Adonis, by your bier she wounded
me 314

Aethiopian gods are dark-skinned
with flat noses 112

After twelve years, here Philip had to
lay 280

Again the lyre, again the snowdrop
bloom 338

Again, Love, doing Aphrodite's
bidding 37

Against three million Persians in this
spot 131

Ageanax will smoothly sail the brine
291

Ah, Anticles! and ah me, who upon
309

Alas for me in my misery, forced to
share in all sorts of care! 56

All hail, Lord of Cyllene, you're the
one 64

All Hellas, Pylades, wails for you
gone 318

*All space is brimming with god, his
ears in all places* 113

All things – great excellences and
fortunes – are in one boat 122

All you who pass this tombstone,
know that I 279

All you who wait on Pallas' bath,
come forth 272

Already your time is past, and your
prime is spent 60

Although a glen of Dirphys cradles
us 130

Although he's underground, pour out
a splash 343

Although this stone is small, do not
prefer 550

Although your life is sedentary, and
343

Am I stuck, then, on the defendant's
dais? 502

Amalthea's horn obsesses 105

Ambracian Cleómbrotus said, 'Sun, farewell!' 281
Ameana, you've been fucked silly – 385
An apple a young beauty bites; fresh puffs 540
An apple on a bough hangs redly, sweetly 51
and all night let 44
And, Cypris, about Doricha: don't let 41
and I know the airs of every 36
'. . . And of your daughters, Zeus, the royal head 201
And others came for plunder, with high hopes to strike it rich 74
and out of heaven, Love came down and had a purple mantle on 47
and that hair of yours, which softly 102
and then, moreover, you're 101
and they dissolved in tears as the unweaned 125
and threw the shield down nigh where   the lovely stream 105
and toward you who are lovely my regard 45
And two boys, working double 216
and while night overshadows 163
[and you collapsed, as when 128
Antiodemus, nursed with Cypris' milk 323
Apollo, how I wish I lived in bygone days 263
Archinus, if my own free choice convinced me 277
Arsinoë gave Sosipater her oath 314
Artemis, [you haunt] the Cretan pastures 266
Artie sold his land for a boy toy 548

As I was giving Agathon a kiss 221
As if to stiff the Erythraeans, the literal 115
As languidly as Ariadne lay 425
As she was buffeted 124
as the waves rolled 90
As whose largesse with lavish hand should lift 140
Asclepiades, drink! Why all these tears? 305
Asclepias, with her oceanic eyes 327
Asclepius' high virtuosity 238
Asleep are all the mountain peaks and the crevasses 37
At noon I saw the boy Alexis where 331
At Pytho's sacrosanct foundation 227
At seven years, a boy's still infantile 73
Athenium sang the *Horse*, and did me wrong 314
Attalus, you push lawsuits, products, deals 537
Atthis, I loved you   long ago 46
Away, away with the dire 244
Awful to mourn the death of groom or bride 325

Bacchus, where to, now that I'm filled and flown 486
Back to the barn through snow, of their own will 319
Be my ally, Lord Hephaestus: hear your supplicant 9
Because Tyndareus once 92
Before now, dancers in the dithyramb 158
Before this plaque, you won, Simonides 131
Bent on deceit, she carried 12

Boar, spare that boy, whether a gentle glade 448

Bocotian Helicon, once from your course 345

Breastbone glued to breastbone, breast to breast 349

Bridegroom, how do you seem to me? 52

Bring wine and water; bring 107

Bucaeus, what's wrong, buddy? Why this moping? 294

But *I* 'm in love with the soft and sensuous. This [is my fire], and this 48

But if oxen had hands, or horses or lions had them 112

But you too, even you, at one time [were] 44

By god, don't make a stink 360

By Timo's curls that love to be caressed 327

By Zeus who rules Olympus, I implore 156

Call her; you're ready. But what will you do 353

Callistratus and Afer, Rough and Hairy 555

Carpenters, raise the roof up! There is – 52

Catullus, lovesick, heartsick, quit this stupid mooning 379

Cease from seafaring, if you would survive 310

Cerinthus, are you worried for me now 452

Chalk it all up to the gods; for they have often caught 11

Chaste Atys, chambermaid of Cybele 314

Civil war is wasting a second generation 460

Cleina has often wailed beside this tomb 303

Come here! The girl is sick; come bring the cure 448

Come join the dance, Oympians! 160

Come kindly, you who happen on these grounds 417

Come on, my boy, it's time for wine and truth 67

Come on, what's wrong with you? Don't stay 132

Come to my place, you'll dine in style 381

Come to this holy place from your Cretan home 40

Come, Attic jug, let Bacchus' raindrops spill 312

Come, bring the cup across this man-of-war 6

Come, goddess, tell me how, by the lovely purling 94

Come, Muse, whose hymns and high notes ring 35

Come, you sons of unconquered Heracles! 23

Conveyed through many nations, many seas 397

Cool waters rushing where the rock is cleft 307

Corinna's reckless bid to bid goodbye 506

Cruelest of girls that were or are 547

Cynthia – it was those eyes – captured me first 423

Cypris loosed from her breast her sensual 354

Cypris, sea-calmer, Cypris, who adore 336

Damn raucous birds, be silent! Leave
    me be 324
Daughters of Zeus and Memory, you
    fair 71
Day breaks, Chrysilla; the cock is
    urging on 345
Dead poets from a bygone era 547
Dead, you'll possess five feet, and not
    see one 350
Dear girls, [I'm still possessed] of the
    lovely gifts [of the Muses,] 47
Dear Hermes, Hermes, Maia's kid,
    Cyllene's kingpin 116
Dear Juno, birthday goddess, take
    this mass 450
Dear Thrasybulus, here: I'm sending
    you this little craft 163
December's bristling with cold
    547
Demaeneta sent eight to the war
    zone 315
Demo and Thermion are killing me!
    337
Descend from on high, divine 237
Didyme's eyes have ravished me; I
    stare 305
– Does Charidas lie here? 279
Don't ask – it's not for us to know –
    what end the heavens 467
'Don't fan our fears 93
Don't let the drifter's lifestyle grind
    you down 308
Don't touch the millstone, grinding
    girls; sleep on 346
Drink and get drunk   with me,
    Melanippus! 57
Drink! Is it lamps we're waiting for?
    A finger of day is left 65
Dust is enough for me. Let a too-
    great 307

Each friend Lycoris courted in her
    life 541
Each lover is a soldier on campaign
    495
Each time Cydilla holds me, if I call
    334
Each time I look into your eyes
    reveals 43
Each time we've met, here's what
    you've said 537
Earth holds them in their glory, these
    who died 130
Earthquake, most shuddersome of
    cataclysms 342
Erinna's themes are few, her poem
    not long 322
Eros bends over, Linus gives head –
    who cares 545
Eros weeps, gazing on the glitz of
    good 551
Eudemus, coming to famous Attica
    225
Euripides' memory all Hellas owns
    212
Euryalus, bloom of the ocean-eyed
    Graces 99
even to battle-deserters Death catches
    up 122

Fabulla read the epigram in which I
    crow 542
Fair Heraclitus' beauty has declined
    331
Faunus, who love nymphs on the
    run, to my 485
First of my friends, Aristocleides, for
    your bravery 108
Flavius, your new girlfriend – spill!
    378
Fleeing from Love again 107

For all the sun does every day is work 30

For Delos in the early days was tossed 156

For I know how to strike up Dionysus' lovely strain 10

For mortals it is Peace gives birth 184

For mortals, best is a healthy constitution 127

For my sake, Lady Nereids, please grant 41

for over every mortal frame 164

[For Pollis didn't skimp on or] ignore 259

For sixty years of seasons Grace has made it 334

for wise old Dionysus with his thyrsus 197

from Argos, by Zeus's will, they sailed 97

From ophthalmologist to gladiator 548

Fronto, my father, mother Flaccilla, here 543

Frustrated by recent setbacks, Father Zeus 59

Gemellus really wants to marry Maronilla 535

Ghosts do exist. Not all things end with dying 440

gingerly 107

Girlish glancer, whom I pursue 105

Glaucus, son of Leptines, our hearts are built this way 12

Glowing with pleasure, she held a myrtle sprig 8

'Go, hurry right 95

Go tell the men of Sparta, passerby 131

Go to Perilla, hastily scrawled letter 514

Gongyla 49

Greatness, the cause of humanity's sweat and striving 224

Grind, mill, grind the barley down 244

Hades, implacable, unswerving, why 325

Hail to you, heaven's seedling, love 156

Hail, Clio, hymn Demeter's name 167

Hail, Young Man, mightiest of all 234

Hang here above this door, garlands my pain 305

Happy the man who sees, before he goes 164

Happy the man who, far from the rat race 456

Harmodius and Aristogiton's 246

He called on Maia's son, grand poobah of Cyllene 115

He hates his beauty now, but give him time 317

he sacrificed 117

He seems like the gods' equal, that man, who 44

He used to wear this cap, striped like a wasp, so tight it hurt 106

He wasn't any backward yokel 35

heaping humiliation on the head 63

Hear me, o Fates, you who sit 240

Heart, you should pluck love's harvest in good time 162

'Hector and company are heading here now 45

Heliodora's nail is Love's own dart 329

Hera most high, who often stoop to
    view 311
[Heracles decided] the greatest
    advantage lay 91
Here is the man you read and want
    535
Here lies Mnasalces, writer of elegies
    316
Here lies the blood of Battus, who
    could write 279
Here Philocles has hung on Hermes'
    wall 308
Here Saon of Acanthus shuts each
    eye 280
Here, hold my cloak, I'm going to
    bash the eye of Bupalus 119
Here, Lady Cypris, by your temple
    door 305
Here, take this apple, and, if you love
    me 222
Hey, it's Sunshine, Sweetheart's
    son 12
Hey, where's that furry coat, my
    antidote to freezing? 116
High on the mountains, when the
    gods enjoy 36
High time for ships to surge their
    ocean path 322
High time to drink now, time with
    unfettered feet 470
High time to get drunk now and to
    drink with all 64
Hipparchus slain! New dawn makes
    Athens brighten 129
Hippe has put up her luxuriant 322
His body pummeled, pummeled in
    each eye 197
[His] judgment sifts the noble from
    the vile 123
his music and his lyrics 36

His pointing stick, his strap, its
    nearby mate 320
Hitting me again today 104
Holding his Acme in his lap 385
Holy heart of the great Earthshaker,
    be 342
Homer and Hesiod have larded the
    gods with all kinds 112
Honored guests, goodnight, and
    goodnight, bride 53
Horsing around, I stole a kiss from
    you 396
How I wish that I could touch the
    hand of Neobule! 10
How long will you shiver in the
    clouds, poor dope 343
How long, boys, will you lie there
    and hang back? 21
How many kisses must come before
    378
How nice, Cerinthus, that you feel so
    free 452
Hunt me, I'll flee you. Flee from me,
    I'll hunt 544
Hunters, dear Epicydes, stalk the
    hare 276
Hysteria and brouhaha – 107
'Hysterical' is Leda's diagnosis 552

I – glyph that signifies the finish line
    332
I am a quince from the last year, kept
    fresh 351
I am an apple, fruit of your lover's
    praying 222
I can't cure this by weeping, nor can I 7
I can't do this weaving,   sweet
    mother, since in truth 51
I dined last on goat's foot and a
    ten-day-old 353

I don't like tall generals who strut with a long stride 9

I don't need your face or lips 540

I don't want golden Gyges' anything – 8

I dreamt the Troubadour 358

I fell for young Alcippe hard, when she 349

[I] fell on that hard-working wineskin and began to thrust 10

I gave the mass such privilege as was due it 70

I had cake (honey- sesame) 105

I hate and I love. How can that be? you scoff 396

I hate Love. Why, why won't the god pursue 317

I hate the Epic Cycle, and refuse 276

I have a child as gorgeous as gold flowers, and I love her 53

I have heard that famous dear – she 102

I honestly wish that I were dead 48

I know how to do one major thing 11

I know. No – shh! No tricks. I've found you out 330

I lie here pierced with longing 13

I love that Asian dancing girl who drips 352

I loved Demo of Paphos. Fair enough 335

I need to tell you something, but shame stops me 53

I owe ten thousand. Paetus wants it now 552

I serve Lord Ares on the battlefield 6

I shall die young – so says astrology 346

I sing steep Rhegium in Italy 325

I was a joke at parties, feasts, events 439

I was a shellfish, Cypris by the Sea 278

I was a speedy, big-eared bunny, torn 330

I was just loafing in the Forum 379

I was lamenting my Theonoë 351

I wish I could be a grand clay bowl, well thrown by hand 247

I wish that Chiron – sovereign 146

I wish we could see the truth of appearances 245

I wish, I wish I could be a lyre of ivory 246

I wouldn't dare excuse my grievous faults 499

I, who once chased off starlings and the crane – 321

I'd fight off Zeus himself, if he should try 332

I'd never praise a man or pay him heed 25

I'll fuck you in the ass and throat 382

I'll give up and give in, all groans, to a bad fate 117

I'll hide my sword in a myrtle bouquet 246

I'll pile this cold shore-shingle in a heap 344

I'll weave snowdrops with dainty daffodillies 329

I'm in love with Cleobulus 104

I'm litigating, not a matter 544

I've loved; who hasn't? I've reveled in her name 337

I've raised a monument   more permanent than bronze 487

I've searched through the whole city, head to toe 542

If a man wins the footrace, or
    prevails 111
If hate is pain and love is pain, I
    would 354
If I could kiss-kiss-kiss, nonstop 386
If Memnon's mother, mistress of the
    Dawn 510
If my books are flawed (they are),
    please don't abuse them 516
If only sailing ships had never been!
    280
If to die well is of all high acts best
    130
If we had sense, we wouldn't think
    about 17
If you care for me, take a younger
    woman 53
If you have a little time for an exiled
    friend 522
If your mistakes have brought you
    grief and shame 71
If, country Phidyle, as soon as the
    moon is born 485
Impossible 196
In Adimantus' days, the tripod went
    131
In iron chains their enemies are
    pinched 130
In my desire for sex, blind lust 12
In plush sedans your rouged-up
    stooges travel 549
in Sardis 50
In spring, the Cretan quinces grow
    99
In the beginning, god created women
    17
Infinite, man, the days before your
    birth 309
Instead of writing Major Verse, I
    make 542

Ionis thrilled when Callignotus swore
    277
Islands before have yielded their
    unknown 341
It's a woman's lot that we may not 483
It's arduous truly to perfect 123
It's beautiful for a brave man to
    fall 22
It's sailing season! Swallows are on
    the wing 309
It's the eighth hour. Isis' doors are
    barred 549
It's Venus! On your feet, boys! Venus,
    long 388
It's your month, Mars. Sulpicia's
    dressed the part 447

Jason could not have done it on his
    own 29
John Doe gives Jane (who isn't that
    good-looking!) 339
Join me in drink and youth and
    daring, join me in love and 247
Joining   the party, a playful
    lyre 59
Just let me sleep in the stern on a
    strawy bed 352
Juvenal, while you no doubt 553

Kind Sun, ever the same yet other
    still 372

Lady of Cyprus, Adonis is dying
    – what should we do? 54
Lady, I don't have much, and yet I
    boast 351
Lake Camarina drained could not
    bring doom 260
Laurel of triumph, come, surround
    my brow! 505

Leave the island where Pelops once was master 57

Leaving the sea-stream, Dawn 203

Leophilus is leader now, Leophilus has sway 9

Lesbia bashes me when hubby's near 395

Lesbia never stops complaining of 396

Lesbia, Caelius, Lesbia 388

Let somebody come over and surround 66

Let's go to Cypris' temple and behold 311

Lettuce and mallow, Phoebus, *might* loosen it – 541

Lie here for Cypris, loaded flask of mine 350

Life has no maps, nor any grounds for confidence 233

Lifted on wings not weak or of common worth 477

[Light of the spangled sash,] the Graces' [star] 261

'Light-hearted love', my life, you offer me 397

Like a man parched for water, so I long to skirmish with you 11

Like a Phrygian or a Thracian sucking 9

Like Harmodius and Aristogiton's 246

Listen to Hipponax! And can the disbelief 261

Live for yourself, not reputation. Yes 29

Lofty oak-branches, helping men evade 352

Long winter night. The Pleiades have set 306

Look at me climbing, yet again 105

Look, Glaucus, as the breakers thrash the bottomless ocean there 9

Look, it's the barren day that marks my birth 515

Look, look how the crown of Apollo's laurel is shivering! 269

Lord Dithyramb, the Bacchants' Lord 229

Lord, come yourself, and join us at a bound 354

Love hit my heart 46

Love like a smith 108

Love once again out from under his eyelids of jet 99

Love once overlooked 362

Love's awful, awful! But what's the value of 327

Love's come at last – and such a love that I 451

Love's got me again, that impossible 53

Lovers of boys, rest from your fruitless toil 324

Lust, that makes limbs slack 13

Lyre, leap down from your peg! Don't linger 185

Made rich by the goods of my little farm, where old 529

Maecenas, lordly scion sprung from Etruscan kings 462

Mamercus, though you don't recite or write 539

Many were the quinces cast 93

Marcellus, spoil-rich from the western war 341

Marrius, the simple life's devoted friend 551

May my fate take me after sixty
      years 29
May Venus guide you as you go 463
May you too sleep through nights
      like those you force 281
Megistes, that 103
Melissa, you're the same as your
      namesake 348
'Menecrates, I'll catch you! Better fly!
      277
Menoetes, offspring of Diaphanes 347
Menophila's tasted everything. Her
      stars 348
Millionaire seeks billionaire to die
      and leave him stuff 552
Mimnes, who boast an asshole as big
      as your whole back 116
More fiercely, Bacchus, than the
      Cyclops when 317
Mother of vision, beam of the sun
      157
Muses, strike up, strike up the
      country song 283
My audience thinks my lines are
      first-rate stuff 548
My birthday's nearing – miserable
      day! 451
My boy, bring me the bowl 103
My bread's aboard a ship, aboard a
      ship is my wine 6
'My dear, I pay with love the love I
      find 335
My dear Philaenis, don't be too
      distressed 319
My friend, turn over any stone and
      you will find a scorpion 247
My friend, who at my side again and
      again 472
My girl tells me there's no one she'd
      prefer 394

My Lesbia, let's live and love! 377
my life is like some hick's – 61
My love stays here; don't let it go
      elsewhere 323
My mother was named Earth, and
      earth's dark mat 341
My riches are in my sword and my
      spear together 248
My soul says: 'Heliodora's trouble;
      go! 328
My sweetheart's sick: Jupiter, show
      some pity! 431
My temples have turned gray 106
Myiscus' eyes first pierced my
      haughty heart 332

Naevia is Rufus' idée fixe 537
Naevia's panting, and her cough
      won't quit 538
Napé, expert at primping disarrayed
      496
Necessity's behest 123
Neither the setting of the Pleiades
      345
Never again may I so feed your blaze
      452
Nicias, now past her fiftieth year 301
Night's Moon, horned Moon of the
      dance that lasts all night 336
No man has pierced through to the
      truth; none will unravel 113
No man or government will fault our
      grief 7
No man, no city, without god 122
No more surprises now, no stunning
      miracles, no thought 10
No more, you honey-voiced maidens
      whose songs have a 36
No tears, no wheedling; I won't
      swallow it 312

No windy bluster, filling the leaves
with noise 127

No, no, it isn't true, that tale 93

Nobody cared to take the liberty
537

Noon sizzled, and the sun stood
overhead 494

Not 'commodities', 'commoditae'
396

Not Cypris, that 37

Not diamonds or gold in its
lustrousness – most rare gleam
240

not even the beauty of wisdom is a
blessing 127

Not if the whole sea up the coast
comes pouring 342

[Not one st]ood by Zeus, [the gods'
uni]versal [king 91

Not only do I sing sweet melodies
310

Not since the day Europe from Asia
parted 132

Not twenty-two, and life is too much
for me 305

nothing in poems that never end 134

'Nothing is sweeter than love; no
goods compete 311

Now hear what shocked the
Esquiline last night 442

Now heaven's birds can rest their
wings and sit 315

Now I'll sing beautifully to my
companions 54

Now must the lad hard fighting has
rendered stout 479

Now my ideas for sixty-seven years
112

Now seven years have joined with
thirty, ripped 337

Now snowdrops are in bloom, as
daffodils 328

Now take your lyre and sing 43

Now that the thought of me rubs you
raw 53

'Now this here ac'rn may be mine,
but I want that 'un!' 247

Now Zeus is sleeting, and out of
heaven a mighty 65

Now, Cyrnus, let these verses bear
my seal 77

Now, Dica, with soft hands cull some
anise strands 48

O Artemis, torch-wielder, Savioress
318

O Calm, well-wisher, Justice's
daughter 151

O column, o Sirens, o urn with
anguished air 303

O deathless Aphrodite, enthroned in
glamor 39

O evening star, you bring home
everything 51

O feet, o calves, o thighs I'd die to
taste 336

O Fortune, start and finish line
241

O graced with grace and the bloom
of health 244

O great good luck! O gorgeous
night! O you 429

O Health, among the Blest 213

O heart, my heart, turned upside
down by cares that have no
cures 11

o herald of spring and its fragrance
sweet and clean 127

O husband, blessed now the request
made in your prayers 52

O lord whom gracious fortune
     blesses 171
O Lord, whom Love, that tames and
     dazes 104
O Melicertes, and you too, sea-green
     338
O my heart, why has the best 363
O need for Heliodora, nights awake
     329
O sacred, sacramental queen 226
O spring of Bandusia,   brighter
     than glass, which should 484
Of girls who gaze upon the sun, I
     can't imagine even one 47
Olympian singers, [now descend! 34
On a black day that fellow planted
     you 474
On one side, steel; and on the
     other 36
On seven husbands' tombs, Chloe
     composed 548
Once I was good for five or nine.
     Now – one 339
once, my mother said 50
Once, when he saw a puppy being
     whipped 111
One god, who is greatest among both
     gods and humans 112
One last time, Arethusa, bless my
     efforts 408
One of them lived it up on Easy
     Street, Hog Heaven 116
One time you came to visit in the
     true Myconian style 11
Only you two were privy to the oath
     330
Our fight was sweet beneath the
     lamps last night 435
Our guest was wounded, and we
     didn't see 278

Our parrot, parodist from lands of
     Dawn 501
Our state will never perish by decree
     69
Our time is brief, however much
     we've got 355
Out of stormclouds, snow falls and
     hailstones crash 70
Out of the temple, profaners whom I
     hate 478
Out of this city to Troy's great
     battlefield 132
over that city – 66
Over the head of Orpheus a throng
     125

Pan, I sing you, lord of nymphs
     238
Parasite – reason I left Rome – awake
     555
Parrot, o prince of birds, your
     owner's favorite 528
Pass me the cup, shaped of the
     selfsame clay 344
Paula wanted to marry me. I told her
     548
Philaenis, why, why won't I kiss you?
     538
Philainion is short, and somewhat
     brown 335
Phileas' brilliance seemed to have no
     peers 318
Philistion, always difficult, who never
     354
Philostratus, hapless in your
     happiness 342
Phyllis, I have a caskful of Alban
     wine 490
Pipe down, get out, dull tribe,
     thorn-gatherers 345

Piso, tomorrow your poet-friend will
    tow 338
Plastered on words – I drink my
    madness neat 324
Please, boy, no crowns of linden for
    my hair – 471
Polycrates gives hammer, tongs and
    pliers 319
Poor Corydon was yearning for
    Alexis 400
Postumus, Postumus, ah, how the
    fleeting 476
Postumus, you always wear cologne
    538
Pounded by thrashing waves,
    [storm- thumped and sodden,]
    60
Poverty's pain,   an impossible
    evil 67
Priestesses of Persuasion, dears 161
Proclus, this spearlike silver pen, with
    fine 340
Put silver to the hammer 358
Pyrrha, now who's the
    skinny   young thing on top
    of you 465

Queen Hera, on this ground [the
    chorus rings,] 42
Queen of the Wayside, Antiphilus
    offers you 352
Queen of the Wild, with golden hair
    103
Quintilian, our Roman exemplar
    539

Rain, rain, sweet Zeus, let it rain
    132
Reading the *Works and Days* of
    Hesiod 349

Rehearsing our sorrows won't get us
    anywhere 65
Remember in uphill climbing to keep
    a level 471
Rome praises, loves and quotes my
    little verses 545

Sabidius, I do not like you – who
    536
Samytha's gift, I'm sure, will satisfy
    311
Saving yourself?! What for? When
    you've crossed over 304
Say 'Seagull', for she's buried here,
    my friend 316
See how Soracte, buried in
    snowdrifts, gleams 466
See how the springtime uncloses 362
seeing him coming, his mother said 91
Seems to me, Nicias, that there's no
    cure 296
setting the heart in Argive Helen's
    chest 63
she came 117
She spewed some Lydian magic, in
    the dialect 118
She who was lapped in purple, love
    and gold 321
Shepherds who walk these hills in the
    wind's teeth 307
Shh, stranger, softly! With the dead
    devout 326
Sicilian Muses, let's make a grander
    poem 403
Simus, you're one of us then? You?
    That's what you think? 264
Sing Allius! I can't hush, goddesses
    391
Sing Paean, boys, the Famed for Art
    236

Siren Hermione and I once played 304

Sit in the shade where the laurel riots green 303

Small, home-born Hymnis the sweet-talker, shine 342

So long untaken, uninvaded, Sparta 326

So long, Paros, with those figs and that seafaring life! 10

So now the floor and cups are clean and all 110

So. Fate wanted me to visit even far 513

So: a lioness bore you on African bluffs 388

Sober Eubulus lies here. Let's recall 308

Some say that horsemen, some a host on foot 42

Some Thracian now enjoys the faultless shield 6

Someday I'll give you a tripod pot, where you 35

Someone, someday, I say, will remember us 54

Sparrow, my sweetheart's favorite baby 376

Spring is here, and the cold is melting 386

Spring, and the bitter winter thaws as west winds warm 464

Staffless, Cinesias, you walked the road 316

straight from the bucket 115

Sublimest of deities 239

[Suddenly speechless sweat rivers my face 29

Summer is over, Epicles, and bright 346

Swallow, you windbag, you 360

Sweet day, nursling of Mars's month, when I 555

Sweet in the summer heat to gulp down snow 304

Sweet Julius, if we were free 543

Sweet Julius, let me express 549

Sweet Sirmio, dearest of waterfronts – lake isles 383

Sweetly you pluck the lyre, Zenophila 327

Sweet-scented Isias, though your limbs breathe 349

Symmachus, I felt a little sick 542

Take her this message, Dorcas. Say it one 330

Take off those nets, coy, cruel Lysidice 348

Tantalus' daughter grew 361

Tears are my gift, tears terrible to shed 329

Terpsichore requires verses! 202

Thanks to this man, Simonides is living 133

That boxing left me black and blue 101

That bunk that blew in from Ceos? I thought it stunk 195

That none today could rival that man's might 30

That wine, those toasts, Nicagoras' love, all crept 313

The chickpea's rife, the rose is at its prime 338

The citizen who would increase 161

The crab spoke up 246

The crushing gravestone says, 'Hades took hold 302

'. . . the Curetes hid the goddess's 200

The daughters of all Samos still ask
    after 280
The day, Cerinthus, you were born, I
    rate 449
The dead of night. A letter comes to
    me 437
The doorman's feet stretch seven
    fathoms 52
The earth imbibes the rain 361
The earth is freshly dug, and the
    leaves wave 312
The endless scurrying about 546
The equal of a god that man appears
    387
The first two hours bring the
    morning greeting 541
the force of Seeming subjugates even
    Truth 127
The fox knows many tricks, the
    hedgehog one 15
The full moon showed 54
The girls are all appalled 359
The goals I summoned the assembly
    for 75
The god of peace is Love. Lovers are
    wed 434
The great house scintillates 62
[the Greek ships bashed the enemy
    boats] 205
The guardian of Erymanthus' Bear
    512
The guest who stands and drones by
    the brimming wine 108
The kids have muzzled you, poor
    billy goat 303
The Lesbians erected 60
The loveliest of rivers where you
    race 58
The loveliest thing I left is the light of
    the sun 198

The masses will obey their leaders
    best 70
The men who murdered me, may
    Zeus destroy 133
The mixing bowl 54
The moon drops down the sky 54
The Moon herself, climbing on
    evening's skirt 341
The Muses, dressed   in their
    saffron best 36
The ocean-colored prow was knifing
    toward 178
[the offspring of mighty Chrysaor
    and] undying 90
The other day for dinner I dropped
    by 353
The paths are numberless which
    wind 183
The prostitute's and bath attendant's
    chosen trades share this 247
The sea is the source of water, the
    source of wind 113
The ship sat on a knife-edge 15
The snows have fled; meadows put
    on their blooms 489
The Son of Sulmo also wrote these
    pieces – 498
The stars that in their glimmering
    orbits hover 45
The story goes that your bad
    behavior cruelly 58
The strength of man 121
The swallow, the swallow is here! 242
The tacit lamp, trustworthy
    bystander 334
The wealth of Gyges, Lord 359
The weather has brought the sky
    low; a scowl on its face 458
The will of Zeus the Thunder, my
    boy 16

The young ladies scattered, their jobs
    half done 37
their nurse brought them, with
    scented hair and breasts 9
Themis, who counsels only right 155
Then did Hyperion's powerful son
    embark 90
then she bent over lampward, Arete,
    for me 115
then you scoot close. Hipponax,
    more than most 119
There are four Graces – the three
    have just made room 278
There are two happy days in a
    woman's life: the day 117
There comes no pain, no crime 122
There is an old vignette 126
There *is* revenge the gods exact 32
Theron is dead to me, and the
    once-hot 331
These brave, who fought the
    bowmen Medes beside 132
These springs, this trellis-wovenvine,
    this shade 554
Thessalian Eugethes once rejected
    320
They drive me wild, those chatty lips
    flushed rose 313
They gave their lives into the waves'
    embrace 15
Thirty-four years, if I recall 554
This Damis built for his brave horse,
    who died 303
This feather from a hook-beaked
    eagle's wing 340
This is the best thing said by the
    Chian bard 129
This island, arching like an ass's
    backbone 8
This lyre that Arion used to play 251

This magic wheel of Nico's, on a
    string 324
This man in pursuit   of
    supreme power 62
This man your food and table have
    won over – 548
This roller, like the roller before it,
    slaps 56
'This Solon is no wise man – why, he
    doesn't have a clue! 74
This stone marks famed Megistias's
    slaughter 130
This tomb holds the white hound
    from Melite 319
This we believe: our king in the
    heavenly spheres 480
This, too, a saying of Phocylides 86
This, too, a saying of Phocylides 86
This, too, a saying of Phocylides 86
[*This, too, a saying of Phocylides:*]
    87
Those ancient songs I do not sing
    212
Those who died at Thermopylae 122
Though constant grief confounds me
    and its fetters 390
Three forums, twenty winters, and
    your one 546
Time breaks the farmer's bull and
    makes him bow 519
Timon, is Dark or Light worse? You
    can tell 281
To all the nymphs on Amarynthus'
    sheer 316
To Pitana Thrasybulus was borne
    315
To those who haven't been, war
    seems a dear 161
To you, daughter of Freeborn Zeus, I
    pray 145

To Zeus Accomplisher and Artemis
     340
Toast Diocles. Again! Let glasses
     clink 277
Tomorrow, tomorrow, Postumus, you
     swear 544
Top off the wine, and toast, and toast
     again 328
tossed in the slap of the waves 119
Traveler, though the stone at my
     grave-mound 308
True honor, mortal and divine, is due
     that man who would decline
     248
Two men have wealth: one owns
     estates replete 73
Two traps: one plucked a fat thrush
     from the air 346

Under a plane tree Dexionicus
     trapped 313
Under Diana's faithful wing 383

Varus, you said *Suffenus*. I know you
     know him well 382
vehemently 59
Venus, must I rejoin your fray 487
Verona loves the works of her best
     bard 536

Was she not beautiful? Was she not
     kempt? 507
Watching the stars pulse in their
     golden trances 350
Water is best, while of all riches, gold
     135
We are like leaves born in the
     teeming spring 28
We buried Melanippus in the
     morning 279

We waited for the star of dawn 197
Wealth's never found his way to *my*
     house – too damn blind – 117
Weep for the news these tablets bring
     to me! 497
Weep, you Venuses and Cupids 376
Well, well! Timocreon is not 194
Well: shall we hymn Ismenus River
     155
Wet your whistle – have some wine!
     Soon Sirius will rise 66
What a love-charm the Cyclops hit
     upon – 276
What are these birds, come from the
     sea – the world's 65
What can a woman do, if you don't
     love [her,] 43
What have I done? What was my
     fault or fraud 532
What hill – deserted, sunless –
     brought you forth 356
What immigrants, o abject, have
     replaced 343
What is god? 164
What is this limp lethargy of limb
     459
What life, what pleasure, without
     golden Love? 28
What shame is there in
     weeping?   What limit to
     desire 469
What sort of life could satisfy the
     heart 126
What's in Nomentum, Linus, that I
     go there?
Whatever life is left me, for god's
     sake 306
When a god goads us with necessity 7
When a man's past his prime, though
     handsome once 28

When Cleodemus, still a suckling, was 322

When god shows where to set forth from 160

When he said this, the distantly radiant 240

When I gaze at handsome young men 363

When I heard, Heraclitus, you were dead 280

when the nightingale goes warbling 127

Where are my bay leaves? Thestylis, bring them! 286

Where are my roses, where are my violets 243

Where are you headed, Moeris? The same way 405

Where is that charm the world flocked to behold 323

Where, o where, Virginity, where have you gone, deserting me? 52

Which way the winds are blowing, I can't tell 62

While I was worthy of your love 482

While you were still alive, your brightness shone 221

While you're in Baiae, Cynthia, at ease 426

Who are you, stranger? A corpse wrecked on the foam 281

Who gets this smart new chapbook, freshly 376

Who in the world whose mind is right 126

Who midwifed your cord-snipping, you accident 115

Who was the first swordsmith, parent of peril? 415

Whoever shuns the flute or the divine 355

'. . . wholly restraining yourself 13

Why doesn't Themison have a wife? 554

Why rip me, rooster, from sweet dreams? The charms 350

Why so cagey, Thracian filly 108

Why step out, love, with labyrinthine hair 424

Why were the Muses smiling by my bed 436

wine shines right through a man 65

With a good bird – a heron – on the right, I went 115

With fame imperishable these have endowed 131

Words fail me, always saying the same thing 525

Would that none had caught your scent 195

Xantho, my fragrant Muse-faced waxwork toy 336

Yesterday, Calvus, we were free 387

Yesterday, Rufus, a strange guy 545

You adore being buggered, yet you cry 541

You and you only have a large estate 540

You ask why love, love, love, is all I sing 427

You busybody grammar-mongers, brutes 355

You came, when I was wild with wanting 46

You doll to strangers, you're no tease 106

You gold-horned Moon, do you
see – and you, swarms 348
You Naiads, and you drafty stalls, in
spring 325
You once claimed – I remember! –
you, Graecinus! – 504
You only dine with your bath
buddies, Cotta 535
You pluck your arms, legs, chest, and
keep them slick 539
You pubic pub, and you, its pubey
regulars 384
You set no guards and do not close
the door 536
You stalwart sons of citizens 132
You there might want to praise
Pausanias 194
You used to say I was your only love
394
You want your freedom, Maximus? I
doubt it 538
You watch me bathing, Philomusus
551
You watch the stars, my star. Were I
the wide 221
You with the arms of roses, Zeus's
daughters, come here, holy
Graces 47
You won't see many bent bows, nor a
throng 6
You, who are man, do not
foretell what tomorrow
will be like 122
You, who teach all styles of hair
what class is 503
You'd stick beside Catullus, your old
friend 380
You'll lie low when you're dead, and
be forgotten by posterity 47

You'll live a better life, Licinius
473
You'll sail without me the Aegean
blue 413
You're [always] croaking at my
music's strains 258
You're begging me to send my books
544
You're off to Mytilene, land of
dances 311
you're on the lips 98
You're running from me,
Chloe, just like a baby
deer 469
You're sleeping, though your cup is
shouting, friend 347
You're too proud of your beauty, girl:
you're wrong 438
You've had this fever now for many
days 552
You've heard!? The trip and weight
are off! I'm free! 452
Your bard will be Varius, a
swan, like Homer, grand
466
Your Bassa's baby always is nearby
542
Your skin has lost the bloom of
spring 12
Your theme is Thebes' attack 362

Zenophila the rosebud is asleep
328
Zeus gave Tithonus an everlasting
curse 29
Zeus, Father Zeus, grand poobah up
on Mount Olympus 117
Zoilus, my cloak is fraying, yours is
fine 539

Thematic Index

Page numbers for introductory text and commentary are in Roman text. Page numbers in **bold** indicate poems, and in *italics* indicate notes.

Abas 153, *637*

Achaea 128

Achaean League *723*

Achaemenes *479*

Achelous (river) **277**

Acheron (river) 49, 57, **195**, 316, 432

Achilles 404, **428**, 499, 521, 523, 648, *798*
  addresses to 120, 128, *621*
  Aegina, patron of 152, 155, *636*
  birth 58
  and Briseis **496**, **504**, **516**
  death 128, 150–1, 224, 269, 510
  education 459, 523, *648*, *777*
  as soldier 98, *466*, *734*

Acis (Fiume di Jaci, river) **284**, *705*, *715*

Acis (youth) *715*

Acraephen 201–2, *659*

Acragas (Agrigento) **260**

Acroceraunia (mountain) **463**, *808*

acrostics 271–2, 388, *697*

Actaeon 275, *634*, *698*, *702*

Adastrus 153, *636*, *637*

Adimantus 131

Admetus 170, 270, *644*, *648*, *695*

Adonia (festival) 263, *589*, *687*

Adonis **285**
  Aphrodite/Venus and 311, 510, *706*
  death and mourning of 54, 263, 314, *589*, *687*
  in the underworld **198**, *198*

Adrastus 25, *577*

Aeacids 152, *636*

Aeacus 152, 155, 475, *828*

Aegeus 179, *651*, *776*

Aegina (daughter of Asopus) **202**, *659*, *784*

Aegina (island) 144, 152, **154**, 155, *636*, *637*

Aelian *675*

Aemilius Paullus, Lucius **433**, *781*

Aeneas **489**, 510, 523, *757*, *819*

Aenus (Enez, Turkey) 58, *591*

Aeolia 60, 211, 278, 475, 487
  see also Lesbos

Aeolus 57, **463**

Aeschylus 189, 579, *653*
  Persians *661*, *663*

Aethra 179, **180**, *651*

aetiology 141–2, 630

Aetna (Etna) 149, 284–5, 633, 705

Aetolia 175, 176, 646, 648

Agaleus 175

Agamemnon 7, 42–43, 97, 496, 504, 505, 585, 607

Aganippe spring 408

Agathon 204, 221, 666–7

Agave 150, 634

Agenor 184, 651

Agrigento (Acragas) 260

Agrippa, Marcus Vipsanius 372, 454, 466, 774, 812–3

Aiora (Swing festival) 259, 681–2

Aisa 240, 675

Ajax (son of Oileus, the 'Lesser Ajax') 63–64, 594

Ajax (son of Telamon, the 'Greater Ajax') 98, 152, 224, 360, 636, 735, 746

Alba Longa 432, 529, 780

Alcaeus 38, 304

  allusions to 483–4, 839–40

  influence of 455, 463–4, 466–8, 470–1, 483–4, 676, 809, 814–5, 819–20

  mentions 475, 828–9

Alcaeus of Messene, influence of 396, 419, 752, 770

Alcathous 83

Alcmaeon 153, 360, 435, 636–7, 735, 784

Alcman 252–3

Alcmene 174, 647

Aldigo (Aldigus, volcano) 486

Alexander, Prince of Macedon 185, 654

Alexander the Great 223, 224, 249, 593, 654

  Successors to 249, 252

Alexandria 249–54

  Library 165, 192, 223, 250–1, 252–4, 255

  Museum 250, 252

Alexandrianism 253–4, 255, 373–4, 454, 739, 747–8

allegory 60, 417, 528–9, 875–6

  food 323

  political 528–9

  religious 403, 754–5, 757

  sexual 376–7, 390, 737–8

  'ship of state' 9, 56, 62–63, 573, 590, 594

  sporting 317

alliteration 367, 810

Allobroges 460, 801

Alonissos (Icus) 259, 682

alphabets 4, 120, 192, 683, 688

Alpheus (river) 136, 139, 167, 172, 177, 627

Althaea 648, 649

Alyattes, King of Lydia 27, 591

Amalthea 105, 610

Ambarvalia (festival) 417–8, 767

Amnisus (river) 266, 691

amoebaean (capping/competitive dialogue) 194, 482–3, 839

Amorgos 16

Amphalces 262–3, 685–6

Amphiaraus 153, 605, 636

Amphion 401, 753–4

Amphitrite 182, 206, 239, 661

Amphitryon 647

Amphrysus (river) 270

amplificato (elaboration) 499–500, 856–7

Amycus 530, 878

Amyntor 141, 629

Anacreon 96, 357–8

  allusions to 609

influence of 363, 730, 735
mentions 358, 359, 364, 459
Anacreontea 357–8
Anapo (Anapus, river) 284, 293, 705
Anatolia
   Ionia 109, 114
   Magnesia 102, 577, 609
Ancaeus 175, 648
Ancus Marcius 489, 848
Androgeon 429, 777
Andromache 45–46, 431, 496
Andromeda 53, 336, 431, 441, 726, 773
Andronicus, Livius 365–6, 371–2
Aniene (Anio, river) 437, 442
animal imagery 17–20, 112, 308, 519–20, 817–8
   boars 175, 448, 462, 484, 646–8, 792
   deer 469
   dogs 81
   insects 258–9
   see also horse imagery
Ankara (Cilicia) 547
anthropomorphism 99, 608
Antilochus 521, 872
Antioch-on-the-Orontes 249
Antiochus 131
Antiope 432, 753–4, 780
Antipater of Thessalonica 198, 199
antistrophe 94–95, 124–5, 204
Antony *see* Mark Antony
Anubis 506
Anyte, influence of 310
Apelles 424, 772
Apennines (mountains) 460, 802
aphorisms 3, 77, 86, 86–87, 135, 259
Aphrodite/Venus 213, 392, 464
   addresses to 39–40, 41, 54, 327
   and Adonis 311, 510, 706

Amphitrite, gift to 182
anger and revenge 43, 92–93
appeals to 287, 323, 336–7, 449–50, 487–9, 504, 584
and Ares/Mars 496, 785
Arsinoë II, assimilated to 278, 683
birth of 490
and Daphnis 284–6, 706
doves of 433
epithets 321, 511, 722
and Eros/Cupid 362, 447
gifts of 451
grief of 321
hymns to 388
judgment of Paris 272–3, 431, 699
myrtle, association with 471
oaths to 503, 504
offerings to 161–2, 305, 324, 465, 497
parentage 63, 594
powers 52, 85, 101, 364
powers, over love 37, 51, 99, 102, 104, 177, 185, 201, 391
prayers to 156–7, 289–90, 443
as psychopomp 414
sash 354, 733
sea, association with 463, 807
as teacher 424
temples 311, 313, 488, 718
Apidanus (river) 425
Apis (god) 253, 507, 862
Apis (mythical king) 267, 691
apolelymenon ('free verse') 188–9, 204
Apollo/Phoebus 72, 211, 631–2, 756
   Achilles, death of 128
   addresses to 36, 153–4, 184–5, 263
   Admetus, rescue of 644, 695

Apollo/Phoebus – *cont'd.*
  appeals to 83–84, 168, 211, 403,
    448–9
  Asclepius, father of 146–8, 632–3
  and Asopus's daughters 201
  birth 156, 638, 693
  and Coronis 147–8
  Croesus, rescue of 168–70
  Daphnephoria 660
  descendants 146–8, 510, 632–3,
    757
  epithets 271, 696, 760; Loxias
    157, 170, 639; Lycian 258, 680;
    Paean 46, 72, 210, 227–8,
    229–32, 236–7, 269, 574
  and Gigantomachy 152, 635
  grief of 318
  Hebe, gifts for 267–8, 690
  hymns to 226, 227–8, 229–32,
    269–72
  laurel and 264, 265, 693, 845
  and Marpessa 424, 772
  music of 447, 474
  prayers to 83, 157, 639
  swans, associated with 832
  as teacher 424, 772
  temples 167, 231, 262, 269, 270,
    292, 671
  Tlapolemus, guidance to 141–2
  worship of 210, 669–70
Apollonius of Rhodes 252, 255, 691
apophasis 97, 606
apotrophaic verse 157–8
Appian Way 443, 790
Apuleius 412, 421
Apulia 453, 468, 487, 781, 844
Aquitania 411, 418, 769
Arcadia 144, 409–10, 572
  Cyllene 64, 393
  Tegea 302

Arcas 285, 707, 867
Archelaus of Macedon 204
Archemorus/Opheltes 125, 620
Archilochus
  attributions 119, 617
  influence of 101, 114, 193, 301,
    730, 799, 802
  mentions 345
Ares/Mars (War) 6, 24, 52, 132, 176,
  447, 466
  and Aphrodite/Venus 496, 785
  attributes 159
  prayers to 172, 551
  weapons, compared to 206
Arethusa (nymph) 408, 759
Arethusa (spring) 149, 285, 633,
  707
Arganthonius 105
Argo (ship) 404, 757
Argonauts 461, 803
Argos 97, 273, 652, 700
  Games of Hera 144
Argus 425, 532, 583, 652, 858
  killing of 37, 183–4, 653
Ariadne 287, 425, 709, 716, 773
Arion 31, 239, 251–2, 675
Aristaeus 275, 694, 702
Aristarchus of Samos 251
Aristarchus of Samothrace
  165, 651
Aristides 131, 194, 655–6
Aristogiton 129, 246, 622–3, 677
Aristomenes of Aegina 151–4, 637
Aristophanes 115, 617
Aristotle 250, 825
  on Alcman 31, 582
  on Archilochus 574
  on Sappho 589
  on Simonides 120
  on Timotheus 204

Aristoxenus 204
Armenia 544
Arrius, Quintus 396
Arsinoë II 251, 261, 278, 683, 704
Artaxerxes III of Persia 223
Artemis/Diana 448
  and Actaeon 275
  and Apollo 228, 270
  appeals to 287, 318, 322
  birth 156, 638
  childbirth, goddess of 266, 403
  epithets 175, 649, 762, 770
  and Hippolytus 490, 847–8
  as Phoebe/Moon 384, 778
  punishments/vengeance 147–8,
    174–6, 633, 647
  worship of 209, 664; hymns to
    383–4; offerings to 340, 432;
    prayers to 103; temples 288,
    443, 551, 553, 609, 720, 790
Ascanius (Iulus) 510
Asclepiades 703
  allusions to 370
  influence of 304, 310
Asclepius 146–9, 213, 213–4, 238,
    632–3, 634, 777
  hymns to 236–7, 673
  Serapis, influence on 253
Asia 132
Asia Minor 204, 577
  Atarneus 223
  Bithynia 373, 379, 740
  Clazomenae (Urla) 114
  Ephesus 21, 114
  Erythrae 115, 236–7, 615, 673
  Lampsacus 116, 615
  Miletus 86, 88, 211
  Mysia 7–8, 208, 663
  Pamphylia 625
  Rhoetum 391, 746

Smyrna (Izmir) 27, 579
  Thebe 45, 587
Asine 184–5, 653
Asopus (river and god) 201–2, 318,
    659, 720, 784
Astraea 403, 756
Astydameia 141
Atabyrium (mountain) 194, 630
Atalanta 175, 376, 423, 648, 738,
    771
Atarneus 223
Athena/Minerva (Pallas) 30,
    142–3, 402
  aegis 159, 640
  Athens, support for 179, 651
  birth 630
  crows, dislike of 502
  epithets 699
  eyes of 779
  festivals 530
  and Geryon 91
  Greek fleet, drowning of 594
  Hebe, gifts for 267, 268
  Heracles, protection of 647
  judgment of Paris 272–3, 431
  and Odysseus 615
  olive, creation of 265, 689
  Palladium (sculpture) 273, 698,
    700
  patronage 466
  pipe, inventor of 310
  powers of 275–6
  as teacher 424, 772
  and Trojan War 128
  weaving, goddess of 419, 483–4,
    769
  worship of 130, 597, 699, 701;
    hymns to 272–5; offerings to
    316; temples 64, 227–8, 669,
    698

Athenaeus 579, 615, 641
  on Alcaeus 595
  on Alcman 583
  on Archilochus 574, 575
  on Ariphon of Sicyon 213
  folk songs, quoted by 676, 677
  on Ion of Chios 657
  on Philoxenus 215
  on Praxilla 198
  scolia, quoted by 245
  on Simonides 656
  on Xenophanes 612
Athenis 114
Athens 74, 211, 725
  Acropolis 100
  Athena's support for 179, 651
  Ceramicus cemetery 625
  decline 249
  democratic 188
  Great Panathenaea 189
  heroism of 132
  Lyceum 223-4, 250
  Odeion of Pericles 189, 661
  Persian wars and 660-5
  Piraeus 338
  political organization 68, 69-70
  social organization 624
  verse dedicated to 160, 183-4
Atreus 97, 499, 607
Attic drama 89, 120, 188, 367
Attica (Pandion) 129, 225, 265, 342, 622, 668
Atys/Attis 314, 719
Augustus (Octavian) 369, 399, 421, 754-5, 757-8, 776, 800
  Centennial ('Secular')
    Games 372
  and Cleopatra 470-1, 820-821
  Crinagoras and 339
  cult of Isis and 764

deification 480, 512, 513, 824, 868
Gallus and 760
Horace and 453-4, 455
Ovid, banishment of 492-3, 515, 517, 523-4
Parthians, negotiations with 827-8
praise for 342, 428, 473, 729, 775, 836-7
Tibullus and 411
Virgil and 398
Aulis 98
Aurora see Dawn
Autonoë 150, 275, 634, 702
Averno (Avernus, lake) 426, 510, 774
Babylon 467, 521, 815
Bacchantes see maenads/Bacchates
Bacchus see Dionysus/Bacchus
Bacchylides 165
  attributions 123, 240, 618, 675
  influence of 365
  makarismos in 173
Baiae 426-7, 549, 773
Ballıhisar (Pessinus) 314, 719
Bandusian spring 484, 840
bathos 116
Bathycles 262, 685-6
Bathyllus 459, 799
battles see Persian wars (490-479 BCE); wars and battles
Battus 270-1, 279, 378, 695, 696
Bellerophon 484, 491, 840, 850
Berenice I 694, 704
Berenice II 278, 694, 704
Bessi (Thracian people) 518, 871
Bianor 407, 759
Bias of Priene 262-3, 685, 686

Bible 755
bird imagery 39, 171, 242, 244,
    251–2, 644
  doves 406, 430, 470, 502
  eagles 172, 406, 645
  halcyons (kingfishers) 36, 291,
    323, 582, 711
  sparrows 39, 584
  swans 34, 264, 466, 476–7, 502,
    528, 831
Bithynia 373, 379, 740
Black Sea 32, 474, 518, 526, 591,
    827, 874
  as Pontus 513, 515, 521
Blessed Isles 460–1, 799, 802–3
Boebias (Karla, lake) 148, 632–3
Boeotia 1, 130, 144, 202, 638,
    658–9
  Aulis 98
  Tanagra 199, 202, 659
book culture 192, 253–4, 299,
    332, 376
Boreas 25, 99, 322, 476, 483, 722
Bosporus (strait) 475, 476
Branchus 264, 688
break-off formulas 177, 650
Briseis 496, 504, 516
Britain 480
Brutus, Marcus Junius 399, 453,
    472, 754, 776, 797, 810
Bupalus 16, 114, 115, 118, 119,
    614, 615

Cabiri (deities) 117, 616
Cadmus 4, 275
  descendants 94, 638
  Harmonia, marriage to 150,
    155, 159
  parentage 184, 651, 660
Caelius Rufus, Marcus 388, 745

Caicus (river) 7, 573
Callimacheanism 367–8, 697–8, 772
  in Horace 454, 478–9
  opposition to 730
  in Ovid 512
  in Philip of Thessalonica 355
Callimachus 253–4
  allusions to 454, 463, 477, 478,
    794, 808, 831
  on Antimachus 697
  on Bacchylides 165, 651
  influence of 373–5, 412, 432–4,
    454, 487, 492–3, 534, 780,
    799, 844
  mentions 355, 391, 428, 500, 747
Callinus, influence of 479, 836
Calliope 177, 183, 433–4, 650, 782
  Orpheus, mother of 211, 405,
    510, 757
Callirhoë 90, 91, 603
Callisto 285, 431, 707, 779, 867
Calvus, Gaius Licinius 387, 511, 744
Calydonian Boar 646–8
Camarina (lake) 260, 682
Campania 336, 726
Cannae 433, 781
Cape Taenarum (Cape Matapan)
    239, 675
capping/competitive dialogue
    (amoebaean) 194, 482–3, 839
Capua 460, 801
Carneia (festival) 271, 664, 696
Carpathian Sea 504
Carthage 249, 365–6, 427, 481–2,
    531
Cassandra 63–64, 97, 496, 504, 594
Cassius Longinus, Gaius 399, 453,
    754, 822–3
Castalian spring 141, 157, 168, 228,
    293, 639

Castor *see* Dioscuri/Tyndarids
Catullus 121, 368, 371–2, 454
  allusions to 430, 528–9, 536, 540,
    778, 875, 881, 884
  influence of 412, 459, 482–3,
    501–2, 513, 534, 536, 779,
    839, 868
  mentions 511, 536
Caucasus 291, 544
Celer, Quintus Caecilius Metellus
    395, 752
Centauromachy 110, 506, 612–3
Centaurs 293, 713
  Hylaeus 423, 771
  Pholus 293
  Rhoecus 423, 771
  see also Chiron
Centennial ('Secular') Games 372,
    453–4, 550, 889
Ceos (Kea) 120, 165, 171, 195,
    278, 644
Cephalus, Constantine 299, 300
Cephisus (river and god) 202–3,
    659, 660
Cerberus 158, 415, 416, 435,
    441, 544
  Heracles's capture of 173–7, 464
  number of heads 475, 829
Cercylas of Andros 38
Ceres *see* Demeter/Ceres
Chalcis (city) 62, 130, 593
Chalcis (daughter of Asopus)
    202, 659
Chaldeans (Babylonians) 348
Chance *see* Tyche
Charaxus 38, 41, 584–5
Chariclo 273–5, 698, 701
Charis 98
Charites see Graces
Charon 416, 442, 767

Charybdis 122, 618
Chilon of Sparta 262–3, 685, 686
Chiron (Centaur) 58, 146–7, 293,
    591, 632, 798
  as Achilles's tutor 459, 523
  as healer 148, 149, 429, 777
Choerilus 204
Choes (Pitcher-Feast festival) 259,
    681
Chrysaor 90, 603
Cicero 320, 333, 347, 373, 374, 411,
    761, 838
Cilicia (Ankara) 547
Cimbri (German tribe) 427, 775, 801
Cimon 132, 196, 624, 625
Cinna, Gaius Helvius 367, 380, 406,
    741, 759
Cinyras, King of Cyprus 25, 577–8
Circe 286, 428, 708
Cirrha 152, 636
Cithaeron (mountain) 200, 658–9
Claudius 550
Clazomenae (Urla) 114
Cleanthes 312, 350, 718
Cleis (daughter of Sappho) 38, 51, 53
Cleobulus 126, 262–3, 620, 685, 686
Cleopatra Selene 341, 728
Cleopatra VII Philopator 366,
    470–1, 764, 819–21, 822
Clio 167, 642
Clitomachus 152, 636
Clodia Metelli 373, 752
Clodius Pulcher, Publius 373
Clotho 136, 240, 627, 675
Clytemnestra 92–93, 441, 604, 788
Cnidus 312
Cocytus (river) 343, 476, 830
Colchis 476, 529, 832
Colophon 109, 614
comedy 114–5, 215, 367, 477, 831

comets ('star of Julius') 407, 486, 842

competitive dialogue (capping, *amoebaean*) 194, 482–3, *839*

constellations *see* stars

Corcyra (Corfu) 202, 413, *659, 763*

Corinna (poet) 199, *638*

Corinth 226
  Isthmus of 129, 194, 267
  Pirene (spring) 321, *722*
  prostitution, associated with 161, 321, *641, 656*
  repopulation of 343, *729*
  sack of 323, 367, 434, *722, 783*

cornucopia (horn of plenty) 105, *610*

Coronis 146–8, 236, *632–3*

coronis (glyph indicating conclusion) 332, *725, 727*

Corycian cave 228, 232, *669, 672*

Corycus (mountain) 540

Cos (Kos) 282, 326, *772*

Crassus, Marcus Licinius 435, 481, *784, 827–8*

Crete 40, 266–7, 432, *584*, 672, *691*
  Amnisus (river) 266, *691*
  Cnossus 146
  Eleutherna 319, *721*
  Mount Dicte 234–5, 266, *672, 691*

Croesus 27, 168–9, 434, 515, *643*

Cronus 57, 200, *594, 658, 668*
  see also Saturn

Croton (Crotone) 311, *717–8*

Cupid *see* Eros/Cupid

Curetes (people of Aetolia) 175–6, *648, 649*

Curetes (protectors of Zeus) 200, 234–5, *658, 672–3*

Curiatii 433, *781*

Cyanippus 98, *607*

Cybele 149, 158–9, 208, *634, 663*
  cult of 263, *673–4, 687, 719, 846*
  hymns to 237
  priests/consorts of 314, *719*

Cyclades 16
  Ceos (Kea) 120, 165, 171, 195, 278, *644*
  Delos 156, 265, 269, 270, *638, 651, 656*
  Melos 83

Cyclopes 25, 215, 276, 296–8, 317, 464, *703, 714–5*

Cycnus 528

Cyllene 64, *393*

Cynthus (mountain) 270, *695*

Cypris *see* Aphrodite/Venus

Cyprus 132

Cyrene (city) 255, 270–1, 378

Cyrene (nymph) 271, *694, 696*

Cythera *see* Aphrodite/Venus

Dacia 476, *832*

Daedalus 464, 476, *809, 832*

Damocles 478, *834*

Danaë 124–5, *619*

Danaids 415, 429, 476, *700, 766*
  Amymone 273
  Physadeia 273

Danaus 273, *700, 766*

Danube (Hister, river) 521, 522

Daphnis 283–6, 291, 401, 407, *705–7*

Daunus 487, *843*

Dawn (Aurora, Eos) 51, 203, 290, 415, 510, 532
  epithets 30, 33, 48, 172, 306, 329, 345, 500
  hymns to 32, 33
  and Tithonus 48, 345, *588–9*

Deianira 177, 646, 650
Deiphobus 64, 594
Delian League 194, 656
Dellius, Quintus 471-2, 822-3
Delos 156, 265, 269, 270, 638,
　651, 656
Delphi 169, 173, 292
　Apollo/Phoebus and 270, 631-2
　epithets 153, 157, 226, 637
　omphalos (navel) stone 226, 668
　Pythia (priestess) 264
　rites at 167-8, 669-70
　Tlapolemus and 141-2
　verse for 156-7, 226, 226-8, 229,
　　229-32, 638-9, 668-9
　see also Theoxenia (festival)
Demeter/Ceres 167, 267, 346,
　627, 731
　altars of 294
　appeals to 295-6, 416
　Bees (priestesses) 272, 697
　see also Eleusinian Mysteries
Demetrius of Phalerum 250-1
Demosthenes 229
demotic language 190, 192,
　245, 253
Di Manes 465, 811
Diagoras of Rhodes 139-45, 629
Diana *see* Artemis/Diana
dice 233, 334, 465, 473, 790
　of love 107, 244, 305, 437
Dicte (mountain) 234-5, 672
Didyma 262
Dike (Justice) 155, 160, 203, 235,
　240-1, 638, 673
diminuitives 116
Diogenes of Sinope 306
Diomedes 285, 466, 700, 706-7,
　813
　Shield 273, 698, 700

Dione 63, 292, 713
Dionysius II of Syracuse 215, 478,
　834
Dionysius of Halicarnassus
　on Alcaeus 56
　on Pindar 134, 640
　on Sappho 583
　on Simonides 619
Dionysus/Bacchus 185, 220, 312,
　363
　addresses to 317, 416, 486-7
　and Apollo 228
　appeals to 197, 229-32
　and Ariadne 709, 716
　birth 634
　bull's horns of 196, 657
　dithyramb, dedicated to 10,
　　158-60, 183-4, 639, 640
　epithets 61, 229, 669-70
　festivals 259, 419, 681-2, 769
　hymns to 155
　parentage 43, 66, 585, 595, 652-3
　prayers to 60-61, 101-2, 104
　rites 36-37, 230-1, 669-70
　sculptures of 231, 671-2
　temples 592
　Thrace, association with 842
　thyrsus of 197, 657
Dioscorides, allusions to 468, 817
Dioscuri/Tyndarids (Castor and
　　Polydeuces/Pollux) 224, 530,
　　618, 699, 743, 749
　appeals to 57, 238, 392, 463, 590
　and death of Scopas 260-1
　Hippocoön and 578
　marriage 424
　parentage 604
　statue of 384, 743
　in Trojan War 128
Dipsas 321

diptychs 494, **496–8**, **502–4**, *854*
Dirce **401**, *753–4*
Dodecanese
    Kos (Cos) **282**, **326**, *772*
    Leros **86**, **88**, *602*
    see also Rhodes (island)
Dodona **406**, *758*
Domitian **533–4**, **541**, **550**
Doricha **41**, *584–5*
doublings/pairings 493–4,
    504–5, *854*

Ebro (river) **476**, *832*
Echidna **173**, *647*
Echinades (Spines, islets) **341**, *728*
Egypt **184**, **292**, **319**, **428**, **461**, **536**,
    653
    annexation of **487**
    Canopus **506**
    Oxyrhynchus **31**, **166**, *603*
    Pyramids **487**
Eilythyia/Ilithya **146**, **507**, *632*, *743*
Eirene *see* Peace
ekphrasis (description) **358–9**, *734*
elaboration (*amplificato*) **499–500**,
    856–7
Elea **109**
elegaiac couplets **7–8**, **272–5**, **375**,
    493–4, *572*, *698*
elegaiac mode **120**, **121**, **124–5**
Eleusinian Mysteries **164**, **230**, **343**,
    480, *616*, *643*, *670–1*
Eleusis **129**, **230**, *622*
Elis **1**, **138**
Elysium (underworld) **414**, **441**, *765*
Endymion **336**, **429–30**, *726*
Enez (Aenus, Turkey) **58**, *591*
enjambment **478–9**, *826*
Ennius, Quintus **367**, **368**, **372**, **374**,
    433, *600*, *775*, *781*

Eos *see* Dawn
Epaphus **184**
Epeius **94–95**, *606*
Ephesus **21**, **114**, **215**
Epic Cycle **276**, *702–3*, *735*
Epicureanism **549–50**, *888–9*
    Horace and **478–9**, *833*
    Martial and **534**
    Philodemus and **333–4**, *725*, *727*
    Virgil and **398–9**
Epicurus **320**, *721*, *727*, *811*
Epidaurus **213**, **239**, *673–4*
Epigones **153**
epithets **116**, **145**, **146**, **157**, **166**,
    174, **483**, *615*
    Aphrodite/Venus **321**, **511**, *722*
    Apollo/Phoebus **271**, *696*, *760*;
        Loxias **157**, **170**, *639*; Lycian
        258, *680*; Paean **46**, **72**, **210**,
        227–8, **229–32**, **236–7**, **269**, *574*
    Artemis/Diana **175**, *649*, *762*, *770*
    Athena/Minerva (Pallas) *699*
    compound **190**
    Dawn (Aurora, Eos) **30**, **33**, **48**,
        172, **306**, **329**, **345**, **500**
    Delphi **153**, **157**, **226**, *637*
    Dionysus/Bacchus **61**, **229**,
        669–70
    Helen **63**, **459**, *594*
    Hermes/Mercury **115**, *614*
    Pittacus **66**, *596*
    Zeus/Jupiter/Jove **145**, **234–6**,
        480, *631*, *672–3*
epode **124–5**, **170**, **456–61**, *619*,
    644, *799*
Ergoteles of Himera **145–6**, *630–1*
Erigone **259**, *681–2*
Erinna
    influence of *310*
    mentions **322–3**, **355**

Eros/Cupid (Love) 362, 385–6, 437, 483, 496
  appeals to 313, 503
  colors associated with 47, 394
  grief of 321, 510
  as hunter 37, 99, 305–6, 317, 419, 770
  love poetry, blamed for 522–4
  parentage 327
  as soldier 495
Erymanthus (mountain) 512
Erythrae 115, 236–7, 615, 673
Eryx (Monte Erice) 511
Eteocles 94, 605, 606
Ethopia (Aethiopia) 30, 112
Etna (Aetna) 149, 284–5, 633, 705
Etruria 267
Euboea 6, 84, 230
  Amarynthus (mountain) 316, 720
  Chalcis 62, 130, 593
  Dirphys 130
Euclid 251
Eudemus 225
Euhemerus of Messene 261, 266, 684, 691
Eumedes 273
Eumolpus 523
Eunomia (Good Order) 155, 160, 203, 235, 240–1, 596, 638, 673
Euonymus 202, 659
Euphorbus 262, 686
Euphorion of Chalcis 367, 409, 746, 760, 761
Euphrates (river) 272
Euripides 189, 204, 211, 665
  Bacchae 670
  Heracles 614
  Iphigenia in Tauris 668
  Medea 808
Euripus (strait) 130

Europa 179, 432, 651, 780
Eurotas (river) 84, 128, 326, 621, 723
Eurus (east wind) 435
Euryalus 99
Eurydice (love of Orpheus) 516, 870
Eurydice (wife of Lycurgus of Nemea) 125, 620
Euryganea 93–94, 605
Eurymedon (river) 132
Eurypylus 271, 696
Eurystheus 393
Eurytion 603
Euterpe 463
Euthydemus 263, 686–7
Euthymus 169, 644
Euxine see Black Sea
Evenus (mythical figure) 424, 772
Evenus (poet), influence of 396, 733
exaggeration 475–6

Fabius Maximus 'Cunctator,' Quintus 433, 781
Fates 21, 238, 392, 404, 441, 449, 644
  Aisa 240, 675
  Clotho 136, 240, 627, 675
  hymns to 240–1
  Lachesis 143, 240, 630, 675
  loom of 459
  on Meleager 649
Faunalia (festival) 485
Faunus 465, 485, 551, 810, 827, 841
festivals 2–3
  see also Adonia; Aiora; Ambarvalia; Carneia; Choes; Faunalia; Fontanalia; Pithoigia; Pythais; Termialia; Theoxeia
first person voice 151, 170–1, 293–4, 634, 644, 711

Fiume di Jaci (Acis, river) **284**, *705*, *715*

Flavian dynasty **527**, **528**, **533**

Flora **551**, *890–1*

Foça (Phocaea) **460**, *801–2*

Fontanalia (festival) *840*, *841*

form
'modern' **412–3**, **454–5**
Platonic **191**

Fortune *see* Tyche

'free verse' (*apolelymenon*) **188–9**, **204**

Frontinus, Sextus Julius **550**, *889*

full stops, use of **478–9**

Furies **61**, **343**, **415**, **435**, **475**, *765*

Furius Bibaculus, Marcus *741*

Fuscus, Marcus Aristius **468**, *816–7*

Gaea (Earth) **142**, **227**, *612–3*, *635*, *658*, *668*

Galatea **215**, **296–8**, **407**, *715*

Gallus, Gaius Cornelius **370**, **408–10**, **511**, *758*, *759–62*

Ganymede **137**, **332**, *724*, *725*

Garda (Benacus) **373**, **383**, *742*

Gaul **373**, **433**, **476**, *801*

Gediz (Hermus, river) **27**, **30**, *579*

Geloni (people) **476**, *832*

genius (personal spirit/god) **449**, **515–6**, *767*, *793*, *868*

Germanicus **339**, **493**, *729*

Germany **342**, **434**, **460**, *782*, *801*

Gets (Thracian people) **518**, **519**, **520**, *871*

Giants **110**, *612–3*
Enceladus **259**, *681*
Geryon **90–92**, **476**, *602–4*, *635*
Gyges **498**, *855*
Porphyrion **152**, *635*
Tityus **138**, **415**, **435**, **476**, *765*
see also Argus

Gigantomachy **110**, **272**, **498**, *612–3*, *635*, *699*, *775*

Glaucus (friend of Archilochus) **9**, **12**, **498**, *573*

Gonglya **43**, **49**, *585–6*

Graces (*Charites*) **214**, **261**, **278**, **362**, **464**, **489**
appeals to **47**, **156**, **313**, **318**
Euryalus **99**
poetry, role in **3**, **171**, **183**, *652*
preferences **48**

Graecinus, Gaius Pomponius **504**

Gyges, King of Lydia **8**, **27**, **359**, *573*

Hades (underworld) **49**, **80**, **163–4**, **279**, *627–8*
katabasis (descent to) **173–7**, **475**, *646–7*

Hades/Pluto (god) **253**, **267**, **316**, **325**, **432**, **465**, *784*

Haemus (mountain) **291**

Hannibal **365**, **433**, **460**, **545**, *801*

Harmodius **129**, **246**, *622–3*, *677*

Harmonia **150**, **155**, **159**, *637*, *638*

Harpargus *614*

Hasdrubal Barca **365**

Hebe **267**, **393**, **690**, *750*

Hecate **261**, **286**, **384**, *685*, *743*

Hector **45–46**, **436**, **496**, **499**, **502**, *594*

Helen **97**, **321**, **392**, **429**, **436**, *604–5*, *799*
approval of **42**, *585*
beauty of **431**, **459**
criticism of **20**, **58**, **63**, **92–93**, **102**, **393**, **428**, *590*, *594*
cult titles **31**, **32–34**
epithets **63**, **459**, *594*

Heliadae **142–3**, **144**, *629*

Helicon (mountain) 97, 200–201,
    607, 658–9
  Aganippe spring 408
  Hippocrene spring 261, 344, 432,
    433, 514, 683, 701
Helius 141–3, 630, 652
Hellenism 221–2, 238, 666, 674,
    712, 745–6, 764
  and the Blessed Isles 461, 802–3
  Cyclops in love theme 276–7,
    296–7, 703, 714–5
  foundations theme 270, 695
  influence of 464–6, 477, 528–9,
    809, 811
  magic theme 286–7, 431–2,
    708, 779
  style and form 292, 465, 811
Hellespont 207, 662–3
Hephaestus/Vulcan 319, 464, 496,
    734, 785, 809–10
  appeals to 358–9
  and birth of Athena 142
  cup for the Sun, maker of 30
  Hebe, gifts for 267–8
  prayers to 9
  worship of 72, 597
Hera/Juno 267, 365, 384, 394,
    550, 653
  appeals to 42–43, 450
  and Io 183, 652
  jealousy of 432, 779
  judgment of Paris 272–3, 431
  Kallisteia (festival) 61–62, 585,
    587, 592
  as mother of Typhus 635
  peacock, associated with 502
  punishments/vengeance 708, 765
  as Queen of Aeolia 60
  and sack of Troy 128
  temples 311, 442–3, 592, 718

Heracles/Hercules 89, 155, 158
  Cerberus, capture of 173–7, 464
  Chiron and 293, 713
  death 650
  descendants 23, 141, 224, 524,
    572, 577
  Dryopians, relocation of 653–4
  Geryon, fight with 90–92, 602–4
  and Iphitus 360, 735
  Meleager, meeting with 173–7,
    646–50
  olive, brought to Olympia by
    699–700
  parentage 629
  Stymphalian birds, slaying of 393
  Thebes and 638
  Tibur (Tivoli), founding of
    442, 789
  and Trojan War 8
  white poplar, brought to Greece
    by 710
Heraclitus of Ephesus 109
Heraclitus of Halicarnassus,
    mentions 280, 704
Herculaneum 333, 726
Hercules see Heracles/Hercules
Hermes/Mercury 183–4, 200,
    470, 583
  appeals to 49, 116, 615–6
  Argus, killing of 37, 183–4, 653
  and Daphnis 284, 706
  epithets 115, 614
  as god of good luck 349, 732
  as gods' cupbearer 54
  hymns to 64, 595
  lyre, invention of 797
  offerings to 308, 320
  as psychopomp 588
  soldiers, saved by 473, 824
  and Tanagra 201

Hermias 223, 224
Hermione 43
Hermus (Gediz, river) 27, 30, 579
Herodotus 825–6
    on Alexandria 252
    on Anacreon 100
    on Arion 675
    on Battle of Plataea 621, 623–4
    on Charaxus 584–5
    on Croesus 643, 644
    on Egypt 653
    on Isis 763
    The Persian Wars 4, 775
    on Phocaea 802, 803
    on Phoenician sailors 803
    on Solon 597
    on Xerxes 663, 664
Herophilus of Chalcedon 251
Hesiod 659, 668, 703, 730
    on Archilochus 573
    Catalogue of Women 633, 722
    on Hyperion 578
    influence of 399, 595–6, 596, 607
    mentions 112, 178, 261, 344,
        349, 683
    Theogony 255–6
Hesperides 30, 90, 603
Hesperus/Vesper (evening star) 221,
    410, 532, 746
Hestia 226–7
Hesychia 151–2, 635
Hibrias (Hybrias) 248, 677–8
Hieron I of Syracuse
    Bacchylides on 165, 167, 169–73,
        178, 642–3, 644, 645, 649
    Pindar on 135–6, 139–40, 146,
        149–50, 626, 628, 632, 650
Hilaïra 424
Himera 89, 145–6, 291, 631,
    645–6

Hipparchus 100, 129, 246,
    622–3, 677
Hippias 100, 622–3
Hippocrene spring 261, 344, 432,
    433, 514, 683, 701
Hippodamia (daughter of
    Oenomaus) 138, 139, 424
Hippodamia (wife of Pirithoüs) 861
Hippolytus 490, 500, 847–8
Hipponax
    influence of 115, 264–6, 683–4,
        687
    mentions 261–3
Hister (Danube, river) 521, 522
Homer 192, 251, 366
    influence of 367, 399, 583–4
    mentions 112, 128, 129, 151, 343,
        427, 466, 510
    quotations from 239, 682
Homeric allusions
    in Bacchylides 174–7, 647,
        648, 649
    in Callimachus 271–2, 697
    in Catullus 397, 747, 753
    in Hipponax 115, 615
    in Horace 466, 813
    in Ibycus 97–98, 607
    in Martial 554, 892
    in Mimnermus 28, 578
    in Ovid 513, 515, 516–7
    in Pindar 150, 634
    in Propertius 436, 444, 791
    in Solon 69–70, 596
    in Theocritus 294, 714
Honor 469
Horace 367, 370, 372, 398–9, 618,
    622, 697–8
    influence of 415–7, 517, 530,
        539–40, 766–7, 870–1, 878
    mentions 864

Horae *see* Seasons
Horatii 433, *781*
horn of plenty (*cornucopia*) 105, *610*
Hornblower, Simon 134
horse imagery 32, 345, 518, 520
    day/dawn and 33, 240, 415
    Moon and 290
    sexual 85, 99, 108
Hortalus, Quintus Hortensius
    390–1, *746*
Hyades 33
Hydra 92, *604, 629*
Hylaeus 423, *771*
Hylaeus (Centaur) 423, *771*
Hyllus 577, *650*
Hymen 52, 314, 388–90, *719*
Hyperboreans 169, *644*
Hyperion 30, 90, *579*
Hypermestra 441, *766*
Hypseus 271
Hyrieus 202, *659*
Hyrrhas 59–60, *592*

Iacchus 230, *670–1*
Ibycus 100
    mentions 325
Icarian Sea 462, *809*
Icarius *681–2*
Icarus 476, *809, 832*
Icus (Alonissos) 259, *682*
Ida (mountain) 173, 179, 517, 647,
    651, 658
Idas 424, *772*
Ilithya *see* Eilythyia/Ilithya
Ilium 46, 98
Illyria 512
Inachus 273, 276, 472, 652, *700*
India 336, *726*
Ino (Leucothea) 150, 322, 337, 431,
    634, 722, 779

invocation 171, 286, 288–91, 335–6,
    644, 709
Io 183–4, 425, 431, *652–3, 763–4,*
    779
Ion of Chios, influence of 215
Ionia 109, 114
Ionian League 211, *665*
Ionian Sea 335, 512
Iphitus 360, *735*
irony 114, 256, 456–8, 460–1,
    795, 804
Irus (beggar, *Odyssey*) 434, 515
Ischys 147, *632*
Isis 413–4, 432, 652, *763–4, 780*
    appeals to *506–7*
    temples 549
Ismenus (river) 155, *639*
Isthmian Games 134, 146, 152,
    634, 656
Italy 89, 512, *725*
    Alba Longa 432, 529, *780*
    Aldigo (Aldigus, volcano) 486
    Aniene (Anio, river) 437, 442
    Appian Way 443, *790*
    Apulia 453, 468, 487, *781, 844*
    Assisi (Asisium) 421
    Averno (Avernus, lake) 426,
        510, 774
    Baiae 426–7, 549, *773*
    Calabria 398
    Cannae 433, *781*
    Capua *801*
    Croton (Crotone) 311, *717–8*
    Garda (Benacus) 373, 383, *742*
    Lanuvium (Lanuvio) 442–3
    Locri 310, *717*
    Lucrino (Lucrine, lake) 426, *774*
    Mantua 398, 406, 407, 536, *758*
    Mentana (Nomentum) 533, 538,
        550, 551, *883*

Miseno (Misenum) 426, 774
Naples 398, 400
Ofanto (Aufidus, river) 487
Padua 536
Perugia (Perusia) 421, 428
Reggio Calabria (Rhegium)
    96, 325
Road of Hercules 426, 774
Sabine Hills 453, 468, 479,
    484, 796
San Benedetto dei Marsi
    (Marruvium) 800
Sirmio (Sirmione) 383, 742
Soratte (Soracte, mountain)
    466, 814
Sulmona (Sulmo) 492, 498, 536
Taranto (Tarentum) 482, 838
Teuthras (lake) 426
Tivoli (Tibur) 437, 442, 789
Venafro (Venafrum) 482, 838
Venosa (Venusia) 453
Verona 373, 375, 536
    see also Rome; Sicily
Itylus 391
Itys 501
Iulus (Ascanius) 510
Ixion 138, 415, 435, 765
Izmir (Smyrna) 27, 579

Jason 29
Jerome, Saint 367
Jocasta 93–94, 605
Jove see Zeus/Jupiter/Jove
Jove-Ammon shrine 378
Jugurtha 434
Julian the Apostate 166
Julius Caesar 369, 373, 381, 729,
    754–5, 800, 820
Julius Martialis 543, 549, 554
Juno see Hera/Juno

Jupiter see Zeus/Jupiter/Jove
Justice 69–70, 98, 154, 596
Juturna 531
Juvenal 553

Kallisteia (festival) 61–62, 585,
    587, 592
Karla (Boebias, lake) 148, 632–3
katabasis 173–7, 646–7
Kea (Ceos) 120, 165, 171, 195,
    278, 644
kennings 190, 205, 205, 207, 268,
    661, 692
Keres (Spirits of Death) 92, 604
Kore see Persephone/Proserpina
Kos (Cos) 282, 326, 772

Labdacus 275, 702
Lachesis 143, 240, 630, 675
Lais of Corinth 321, 494, 852
Lakereia 147, 633
Lampsacus 116, 615
Lanuvium (Lanuvio) 442–3
Laodamia 392, 393, 394, 748,
    749–50
Lapiths 506, 613
Lares (hearth gods) 414, 416, 419,
    485–6, 764, 767, 842
Lars Porsena 460, 801
Lavinia (daughter of Latinus) 506
lectisternium (thanksgiving
    ceremony) 470
Leda 57, 224, 500, 857
Leonidas, king of Sparta 22, 123,
    130, 624
Leonidas of Tarentum, influence of
    320
Leotychidas 194, 655, 656
Lepidus, Marcus Aemilius 421
Leptis Magna 530

Lerna 142, 629
Leros 86, 88, 602
Lesbos 55–56, 59–62, 104, 587,
    588, 592, 610, 676
  Antissa 187, 211, 591
  Ialysus 190
  Mytilene 1, 38, 55–56, 291, 311,
    339, 588
  Pyrrha 584
Lethe (river) 415, 440, 442,
    517, 521
Letheaus (river) 102
Leto 156, 194, 265, 383, 638, 689
Leucothea see Io
Libitina 487
Library of Alexandria 165, 192, 223,
    250–1, 252–4, 255
Libya 270–1, 476, 530, 547
Libye 203, 653, 660
Licinius Murena, Lucius 473–4, 825
Licymnius 141, 629
Linus 405, 510, 865
literacy 1, 3–4, 192
Lityerses 295, 714
Livius, Titus (Livy) 365, 372,
    536, 781
Locri 310, 717
Longinus see Pseudo-Loginus
Lucan (Marcus Annaeus Lucanus)
    536, 882
Lucian of Samosata 16, 213
Lucifer (morning star) 532
Lucilius, Gaius 454
Lucillius 534, 887
Lucretius 374, 741
Lucrino (Lucrine, lake) 426, 774
Lycaeon 285, 707
Lycaeus (mountain) 285, 408
Lycambes 5
Lycurgus 188, 356

Lydia 59, 100, 482–3, 588, 591
  Sardis 34, 50, 51, 208, 577, 588
  Sipylus 137
Lynceus 766
'Lyric I' (first-person narrative) 5

Macedon 212
  Pella 249
Machaon 236, 428, 777
Maecenas, Gaius Cilnius 369, 493,
    754, 769
  and Horace 453, 454, 455, 462,
    490–1, 799, 804–5, 850
  and Propertius 421, 427–9, 775
maenads/Bacchantes 230, 486–7,
    773, 842, 843
  imagery of 425, 436, 473, 517
  Muses and 231, 671
Maenalus (mountain) 285, 408,
    409, 707
Magnesia 102, 577, 609
Maia 64
makarismos 580
  in Bacchylides 167, 173, 643, 646
  in Hipponax 119
  in Horace 456
  in Ovid 497, 505
  in Philodamus of Scarphea 231
  in Pindar 140, 164, 629
  in Theognis 84, 85, 602
malediction (schetliasmos) 463, 474,
    497, 808, 826
Malta (Melite) 319, 721
Mantua 398, 406, 407, 536, 758
Marcellus, M. Claudius 340, 728
Marcus Aurelius 676
Marcus Furius Camillus 725
Mareotis (Mariout, lake) 471, 821
Marius, Gaius 368, 427, 434, 545,
    775, 782, 800, 801

Mark Antony 369, 411, 421, 754, 757, 776, 800, 820–821, 822

Marpessa 424, 772

Mars see Ares/Mars

Marsians 460, 800

Marsyas 523

Martial 528, 737

Matinus (mountain) 460, 802

Mausoleum of Halicarnassus 550

Maximus, Paullus Fabius 488, 522–5, 846, 873

Maximus of Tyre 213

Maximus Planudes 300

Medea 286, 428, 461, 474, 524, 708, 776–7

Medusa 159, 640

Megara 76, 77–78, 83, 129, 144, 601, 622

Megistias 130, 623

Melanchrus 55

Meleager (mythical figure) 89, 174–7, 646–50

Meleager of Gadara (poet) 221 influence of 347, 370

Melia 155, 638

Melicertes (Palaemon) 322, 337, 634, 722

Melior, Atedius 528

Melos 83

Melpomene 469, 487

Memmius, Gaius 373, 741

Memnon 510, 524, 864

Memory (Mnemósyne) 3, 157, 224

Menelaus 42–43, 63, 128, 505, 585, 604, 607

Menestheus 132

Menippus 326

Mentana (Nomentum) 533, 538, 550, 551, 883

Mercury see Hermes/Mercury

Meriones 466, 813

Messalla Corvinus, Marcus Valerius 411, 418, 446, 451, 453, 492, 769

Messenia 22

Messina, Straits of 408

metamorphosis 476, 831

metaphors 156, 217
of the body 157
formal 482–3
hunting 99, 608
of hybridity 476
meteorological 336, 462, 463, 504, 575–6, 805–6
'ocean of love' 43–44, 85, 327, 465, 586, 602, 811, 857
for poetry 477, 832
proverbial 65, 595
ships 60, 586, 590, 592
temporal 519
of touch 151–2
of victory 478

metempsychosis 111, 614, 686

meter 139, 204, 215, 339, 493–4, 558–9, 715
alcaic stanza 53, 466–7, 478–82, 589, 814, 833
alcaic strophe 470–1
anacreontic 100–101, 357–8
asclepiadean, second 466, 812
asclepiadean, third 465, 811
asclepiads, stichic lesser 462–3, 487
elegaiac 257
epic 283
hexameter, dactylic 256, 375
hexameter, Greek 367
hexameter, iambic 261–8
iambic 379
'limping iambic' 114, 117–8, 683–4, 687

meter – *cont'd.*
lyric 304, 375
minor ionics 483–4, 839–40
in translation 367
trochaic pentimeter 266–7
trochaic trimeter catalectic 690
varied 527
Methe 323, 722
metynomy 206, 346, 661, 731
Midas 25, 313, 577–8, 600, 620, 718
Midea 141, 629
Milanion 423, 771
Miletus 86, 88, 211, 262, 292
mimesis 256, 692–3
Mimnermus
attributions 76
influence of 620, 697
mentions 258
Minerva *see* Athena/Minerva
Minos 179–82, 318, 345, 490,
650–1, 652, 721, 730
Minotaur 651
Miseno (Misenum) 426, 774
Mithridates VI 740
Mithridates VI of Pontus 474, 887
Mnasalces, mentions 316, 720
Mnemósyne (Memory) 3, 157, 224
Monte Erice (Eryx) 511
moon (satellite) 45, 50, 54, 126,
198, 203, 239, 347, 384, 708
Moon (Selene/Phoebe) 341
Artemis/Diana, identified with
384, 778
and Endymion 429, 726
invocations 286, 288–91,
335–6, 709
motifs 136
of country living 417–20, 478,
485–6, 554
dead pets 376, 501–2

hunting 175–6, 448, 484
'lovers are holy' 511, 865
of lovers as soldiers 487, 489
of predation 297
shield-dropping 6, 55, 105, 473, 824
sight/blindness 272–6
of witchcraft 423
see also dice
Mucius Scaevola, Gaius 545
Mummius, Lucius 367, 729, 783
Murena, Licinius 455
Muses 36, 211, 433–4, 782
anger of 335
appeals to 71, 236, 238, 284–6,
295, 337, 391, 403, 410
Clio 167, 642
and Daphnis 292
and daughters of Pierus 529
and Dionysus 231, 671, 671–2
Euterpe 463
favour of 170
gifts of 424, 436–7
grief of 318
Hesiod and 255–6, 261
loyalty of 516–7
maenads, performance of 231, 671
Melpomene 469, 487
as patrons 376, 737
poetry as gift of 3, 6, 37, 47, 72,
183, 652
Polyhymnia 463
power of 97, 156–7, 171, 200, 711
as psychopomps 80, 184
Sicilian 403–5, 756
singing of 150
Terpsichore 202
Urania 171, 645
see also Calliope
musical accompaniments 187–92,
204–5, 234–5, 487, 559–60

Mutina 428
Mykonos 11, 574–5
Myrsilus 55, 59, 64, 588, 590, 592, 593, 594
Myrtis 199
Mysia 7–8, 208, 663

Naevius, Gnaeus 366–7, 371–2
Naiads 159, 238, 325, 486
narrative form 135, 166
Nausicaä 554
Nemean Games 134, 144, 620, 720
Nemesis 331, 387, 392, 724
neologisms 207, 208
Nepos, Cornelius 376, 737
Neptune see Poseidon/Neptune
Nereids 40, 181–2, 239, 323, 337, 404, 652
  see also Thetis
Nereus 58, 128, 150, 634
Nero 533, 550
Nestor 151, 508, 544, 635
New Poets (Neoterics) 368, 369–70, 374–5
Nicaea 386, 744
Nicias 296, 715
Night 32, 33, 419, 580
Nile (river) 184, 319, 342, 428, 506, 536
Niobe 269, 361, 437, 694, 735
Nisus 129, 622
Nomentum (Mentana) 533, 538, 550, 551, 883
Numa Pompilius 523, 837

Octavian see Augustus
Odysseus/Ulysses 461, 466, 513, 517, 615, 804
Oedipus 93, 605
Oeneus 175, 177, 647, 649

Oenomaus 138, 139, 628
Oenopion 659
Oeta (mountain) 389
Ofanto (Aufidus, river) 487
Olympia 111, 139, 141
Olympic Games 1, 134, 625–6, 628–31, 645–6
  champions, celebration of 135–6, 139–41, 145–6, 167
  fame and 111
  prizes 265
Olympus 230, 393, 498
omphalos (navel) stone 226, 668
Opheltes/Archimorus 125, 620
oracles 201–2
oratory 320, 396, 752
  pre-rhetorical 69–70, 596
  public 188
Orchomenus 230, 638, 670
Orestes 203, 360, 501, 660, 681, 735, 858
Orion 202, 203, 291, 475, 659, 672–3, 829
Oroetes 100, 609
Orpheus 211, 405, 470, 523, 664, 870
  death and afterlife 187, 510, 591
  music, impact of 126, 516
Osiris 253, 507, 763–4
Ovid 38, 371–2, 585, 600, 612
  allusions to 446, 528–9, 532, 875, 876–7, 879
  mentions 536
oxymoron 473–4, 495, 825, 853
Oxyrhynchus 31, 166, 603

Pactolus (Sart Çayı, river) 169, 266, 643, 690
Padua 536
Paean see Apollo/Phoebus

Paestum 521, 554, 873

Palaemon (Melicertes) 322, 337, 634, 722

palinode (recantation) 93, 590–1, 604, 605

Palladium (sculpture of Athena) 273, 698, 700

Pallas *see* Athena/Minerva

Pamphylia 625

Pan 149, 238, 285, 292, 408–9, 674, 701, 707, 754, 761
  pastoral song, patron of 405, 757
  pipes of 433, 782
  rites 713
  see also Faunus

Panacea 236

Pandion (Attica) 129, 225, 265, 342, 622, 668

Pandion I 361, 735

Panhellenism 199–200, 200, 230, 231, 252–3, 671

Panhellenization 68, 625

paraclausithyron (locked-door motif) 277, 280, 290, 305, 450, 499, 703, 705
  satires of 547

Paris 63, 97, 128, 272–3, 402, 429, 436, 605, 699, 754

Parmenides of Elea 109

Parnassus 141, 157, 228, 230, 408, 639

parody 115, 119, 474–5, 498, 615, 617, 851
  of *makarismos* 505
  self 831

Paros 5, 10, 572

Parthenius (mountain) 409, 771

Parthenius of Nicaea 343, 367–8, 370, 729, 759

Parthia 475, 479, 480–1, 539, 544, 827–8

Pasiphaë 432, 441, 652, 780

pastoral mode 282–3, 297–8, 302–3, 399–400, 412

Patroclus 128, 428

Pausanias 129, 593, 621, 656
  on Apollo's temple at Delphi 671
  on Battle of Plataea 623
  on Boeotia 659
  on Cyanippus 607
  on Cybele 634
  on Olympic Games 630–1
  on Pheneus 750
  on public burial 625
  reputation of 194, 655
  on Timotheus 664

Peace 161, 184–5, 404, 653–4, 767
  Eirene 155, 160, 235, 240–1, 673

Pegasus 432, 491, 730, 840

Peleus 155, 260, 648
  as Aeacid 152, 636
  cult of 682
  Thetis, marriage to 58, 150, 591

Pelias 29, 776–7

Pelion 146, 150, 427, 498

Pellana 144

Peloponnese 1, 57, 136, 165, 590, 627
  Cape Taenarum (Cape Matapan) 239, 675
  Sicyon 198

Pelops 25, 136–9, 424, 466, 626, 627–8

Penelope 431, 510

Pentekontaetia 196

Pentheus 634

Periander of Corinth 262–3, 685, 686

Pericles 100, 196

Perimede 286, 708

periphrasis 267, 512

Persephone/Proserpina (Kore) 167, 173, 267, 307, 325, 642–3, 828
appeals to 351, 432

Perseus 124–5, 336, 431, 619, 726

Persia (Media) 83–84, 193–4, 601–2
luxury, association with 479, 482
perfume/scent, association with 459

Persian wars (490–479 BCE) 120, 194–5, 601–2, 654, 655
Battle of Plataea (479 BCE) 128–9, 130–1, 621–2, 623
Battle of Salamis (480 BCE) 205–11, 660–5
Battle of Thermopylae (480 BCE) 130, 131, 623–4

personification 334, 457

Perugia (Perusia) 421, 428

Pessinus (Ballıhisar) 314, 719

Phaeacia (mythical land) 338, 413, 511, 554, 728, 763

Phaethon 491, 850

Pharos lighthouse 249–50, 428, 506

Phemius 509

Pheneus 393, 750

Pherenicus (horse) 136, 172–3, 178, 627, 632, 644, 646

Philinus 290

Philip II of Macedon 229, 249

Philip V of Macedon 317, 720, 723

Philitas of Cos 301, 434, 680, 697, 709, 783

Philoctetes 428

Philodemus
allusions to 494–5, 504–5, 507–8, 852, 860
influence of 370, 398–9, 504, 507–8, 862–3

Philomela 361, 501, 735, 746–7

Philostratus of Athens 342, 599, 729

Philoxenus of Cythera 215, 714–5
influence of 276, 703

Philoxenus of Leucas 215

Philyra 146, 632

Phíneus 435, 784

Phlegyas 146–7, 236, 673

Phocaea (Foça) 460, 801–2

Phocylides, attributions 88

Phoebe (daughter of Leucippus) 424

Phoebe (Moon) see Moon (Selene/Phoebe)

Phoebus see Apollo/Phoebus

Phoenicia 320
skilled sailors, association with 475, 803

Phoenix (Achilles' tutor) 429, 648, 777

Phoenix (king of Phoenicia) 260, 651

Pholus 293

Pholus (Centaur) 293, 713

Phosphorus (morning star) 221

Phrygia 209, 269, 488, 663, 846

Phrynis of Mytilene 188, 204

Phrynon 55

Phthia 150

Pieria 47, 71, 211, 230, 510, 587

Pindar 4, 121, 166, 199, 252, 577–8, 645, 646–7
allusions to 462–3, 477, 487, 805, 832, 843
influence of 266–8, 490–1, 690, 850

Pindus (mountain range) 283, 408, 435, 705

Pirene (spring) 321, 722

Pirithöus 428, 490, 613, 848, 861

Pisa (near Olympia) 111, 136, 177–8, 627

Pisistratus 68, 70–71, 250, 596–7

Piso Caesoninus, Lucius Calpurnius (101–c.43 BCE) 333, 338, 344, 727, 728
Piso Frugi, Lucius Calpurnius 344
Pithoigia (Cask-Opening festival) 259, 681
Pittacus 55–56, 124, 244, 262–3, 588, 676, 685, 686
    Alcaeus on 59–60, 61, 62, 592, 593, 596
    Sappho and 38
Plataea 202, 659
Plato 4, 110
    influence of 291–4, 711
    mentions 225, 281, 667, 704
    poetry, criticism of 120, 190–2, 204, 205, 253, 678–9
    Protagoras 619
Pleiades 33, 54
Pleisthenes 97
Pleuron 176
Plotius Tucca 334
Plutarch 802–3
    on Aemilius 781
    on Archilochus 572
    on Bacchylides 165
    on Corinna 199
    Life of Themistocles 656–7
    on Pindar 638, 639, 641
    on Simonides 620
    on Solon 68
    on Timocreon 193–4
    on Timotheus 204, 664
    on Tyrtaeus 577
Plutus (Wealth) 117, 616
Po (river) 460, 802
Podalirius 236
Pollio, Gaius Asinius 399, 403–5, 758, 759
Pollux see Dioscuri/Tyndarids

Polycrates 96, 100, 319, 608, 609
Polydeuces/Pollux see Dioscuri/Tyndarids
Polyhymnia 463
Polynices 94, 153, 606, 636
Polyphemus 215, 276, 296–8, 317, 703, 714–5
Polyzelus 626, 645, 646
Pompey (soldier, friend of Horace) 472–3, 824–5
Pompey the Great 369, 740, 791, 800
Pontus (Black Sea) 513, 515, 521
Porphyrion 152, 635
Poseidon/Neptune 91, 439, 652
    and Apollo 227
    appeals to 337, 342
    and Asopus's daughters 201
    descendants 179–80, 202, 591, 603, 651
    Hebe, gifts for 267
    hymns to 239
    offerings to 465
    and Pelops 136, 137, 138–9, 627
Posidippus of Pella, translations of 251
Postumus, Gaius Propertius 476–7, 829
praeteritio 97, 606
Priam 46, 58, 97, 544
priamels
    in Asclepiades 304
    in Horace 462, 478, 805
    in Martial 536
    in Nossis 311
    in Pindar 135–6, 626
    in Sappho 42, 585
Priapus 284, 310, 322, 457, 500, 551, 706, 717, 796, 890–1
Procne 361, 391, 437, 735, 746–7

programmatic verse 256, 261–3, 376, 423, 427–8, 474–5
Prometheus 429, 434, 464, 475, 777, 807, 808–9
Pronomus 188
Propertius 412–3
  allusions to 498, 522, 855
  influence of 448, 494–5, 499–500, 792, 851–2, 856–7
  mentions 864
prose 256, 261
Proserpina *see* Persephone/Proserpina
Protesilaus 392, 393, 502, 748, 749–50, 858
proverbs 70, 82, 596, 600
Pseudo-Longinus 166, 586
Ptolemy, son of Lagus (Ptolemy I Soter) 249, 250
Ptolemy II Philadelphus 251, 255, 282, 683, 694
Ptolemy III Euergetes 255, 694
punctuation 478–9
puns 238, 674
  in Callimachus 271, 697
  in Hipponax 116, 117, 616
  in Horace 465, 477, 812, 832
  in Ovid 508
  in Pindar 141, 629
  in Tibullus 415, 767
Pygmies 258, 680
Pylades 318, 501, 720, 858
Pythagoras 109, 111, 262, 523, 614, 686
Pythais (festival) 264, 688–9
Pythia (priestess) 264
Pythian Games 134, 146, 151–5, 625, 631–2, 646, 672
  and Dionysus 232
  prizes for 487
Python 271, 696

quatrains 302–3
Quintilian 89, 121, 412, 539, 883–4
Quintilius Varus 334, 469

realism 354, 733
recantation (*palinode*) 93, 590–1, 604, 605
Reggio Calabria (Rhegium) 96, 325
Regulus, Marcus Atilius 481–2, 838
Remus 427, 756, 801
Rhea 200, 234, 658
  Cybele, conflated with 237, 674
Rhea Silvia 482
Rhesus 495, 853
Rhodes (island) 139–45, 629, 675–6
  Ialysus 193
  Lindus 620
Rhodes (nymph) 141, 144
Rhodope (mountain) 291, 486
Rhoecus 423, 771
Rhoecus (Centaur) 423, 771
Rhoetum 391, 746
Road of Hercules 426, 774
Robbins, Emmet 634
Romanization, literary 367, 369, 371–2, 399, 434–5, 461, 804, 805
Rome 249, 365–9, 541, 751–2, 884–5
  Alban Lake (Lago Albano) 488, 846
  Aqua Virgo 543
  Argiletum 537
  Aventine Hill 553
  Caelian Hills 553
  Campus Martius (Mars's Field) 489, 507, 549, 847, 862
  Capitoline Hill 433, 487, 492
  Centennial ('Secular') Games 372, 453–4, 550, 889

Rome – *cont'd.*
  civil wars 368–9, 399, **428**, **460**,
    754, 820–821
  Colosseum 533
  Domus Aurea (Golden House)
    550, 889
  Empire 369
  Esquiline Hill 421, **442**, 454
  Forums 444, 537, 546, 791
  Greece, conquest of 366–7
  Isis, cult of 764
  Juturna's spring 531
  Pact of Brundisium 754, 755
  Pompey's theater 502
  Quirinal Hill 537
  Republic 368–9
  sack of 801
  Subura 440, **553**, 787–8
  Tarpeian Rock **443**, 790
  Tiber (river) 847
  Treasury 885
  Tullianum (dungeon) **475**
Romulus 384, 460, 506, 756, 801

Sabaea (Yemen) 530
Sabine Hills 453, 468, 479,
    484, 796
Sabine women, abduction of 506
Sakarya (Sangarias, river) 315, 719
Salamis 202, 659
Salii (Priests of War) **470**, **488**,
    820, 837
Samos 16, 96, 100, 304, 609
San Benedetto dei Marsi
    (Marruvium) 800
Sangarias (Sakarya, river) 315, 719
Sappho 4, 304
  influence of 188, 487, 846
  mentions 336, 475, 514, 828–9
Sardis 314, 719

Sarmatians (Scythian people) **519**,
    520, 871
Sarpedon 151, 635
Sart Çayı (Pactolus, river) 169, 266,
    643, 690
Saturn 403, 413, 414, 764
  see also Cronus
Saturnalia 534
Scamander (river) **459**
Scarphea 229
schetliasmos (malediction) **463**, **474**,
    497, 808, 826
Sciron **438**, 786
Scopas 122, 618
Scylla **388**, 745
Scythia 438, 513, 517, 868
Seasons (Horae) 155, 160, 203, 235,
    240–1, 271, 673
Secular Games *see* Centennial
    ('Secular') Games
Selene *see* Moon (Selee/Phoebe)
Semele (Thyone) 159–60, 184, 230,
    431, 585, 595, 634
Semiramis **494**
Semonides of Amorgos, influence of
    128–9, 620
Seneca the Elder 347, 411,
    536, 882
Seneca the Younger 533, **536**, 882
Septimius Severus 529–30
Serapis 250, 253, 261, 350, 380,
    740, 763, 764
  temples 507, 862
Sestius Quirinalis Albinianus, Lucius
    465, 810
Sibyl 403
Sicily 38, 84, 89, 136, 167, 705–6
  Agrigento (Acragas) 260
  Anapo (Anapus, river) 284, 293,
    705

Arethusa (spring) **149, 285,**
    633, 707
Etna/Aetna **149, 284–5,** *633, 705*
Fiume di Jaci (Acis, river) **284,**
    705, 715
Himera **89, 145–6, 291,** *631,*
    645–6
Lake Camarina **260,** *682*
Megara Hyblaea **76**
Monte Erice (Eryx) **511**
Persephone's assocation with
    642–3
Straits of Messina **408**
Syracuse **149, 171, 282,** *626, 633*
Silenus **433,** *600, 709, 782*
Silvanus **408, 457, 551,** *796*
similes **289, 499**
    astronomical **50,** *588*
    for beauty **323, 507**
    floral **92**
    Homeric **128, 173,** *621, 647*
    for love **108, 381, 393**
    sexual **391,** *747*
    for warfare **206**
Simois (river) **94, 272, 459,** *699*
Simonides **165, 191**
    allusions to **479–80, 480,** *618, 836*
    attributions **240–1,** *636, 657, 675*
    influence of **213–4, 224, 370,**
        489–90, *667, 847, 848*
    mentions **260–1, 316,** *656–7*
Sinope **202,** *659*
Sirens **34, 302,** *581*
Siris **8,** *573*
Sirius **33, 66**
Sirmio (Sirmione) **383,** *742*
Siro **398**
Sisyphus **57, 138, 435, 476,** *784*
Smyrna (Izmir) **27,** *579*
Solon **4, 68, 76,** *685*

influence of **462,** *805*
    mentions **262–3**
song **2–4**
    folk *676*
    pastoral **405,** *757*
    Spartan culture of **31–32**
Sophia (wisdom) **3**
Soratte (Soracte, mountain) **466,** *814*
Spain **385, 536, 553,** *832*
    Bilbilis **533, 536**
Sparta **22, 31–32, 57, 84, 122–3,**
        128–9, *572, 590, 621*
    Apollo, founded by **271**
    Carneia (festival) **271,** *664, 696*
    decline **249**
    invasion of **326,** *723*
    patriotism of **315,** *719*
    Persia, treaties with *660*
    Pitana **315,** *719*
    song culture **31–32, 243**
    Terpander, cult of **187–8**
    Timotheus on **211**
Spartacus **460,** *801*
Spartoi **156,** *638*
sphregis ('seal,' conclusion) **211,**
        271–2, 286, *597–8, 665, 697*
stanzas, form of **77, 473–4,** *559*
stars **50, 51, 347,** *734*
    Arcturus **346, 478, 512,** *732–3,*
        834–5
    Boötes **346, 359, 512,** *732–3*
    comets ('star of Julius') **407,**
        486, *842*
    Corona Borealis (Spring Wreath)
        304, 350, *716*
    Gemini **348,** *731–2*
    Haedi ('the Kids') **60, 478,** *711,*
        834–5
    Hyades **463,** *581, 808*
    Lyra **350**

stars – *cont'd.*
  Orion 60, 359
  Pleiades 54, 306, 345, 359, 435
  Quintus 435
  Sirius 348, 431, 484, 731–2,
    778–9
  Ursa Major 262, 359, 435, 512,
    530, 779, 867
  Ursa Minor 262
Stobaeus, Ioannes 233, 622, 675
strophe 95, 124–5, 204
Styx (river) 318, 415, 765
Suda (Byzantine encyclopedia) 199,
  204, 678
Suetonius 373, 837–8, 845
Sulla, Lucius Cornelius 368–9,
  545, 800
Sulmona (Sulmo) 492, 498, 536
Sulpicius Rufus, Servius 446, 452
Sun 32–33, 136, 198, 239, 361, 363,
    372, 430, 435
  cup for 12, 30, 579
  obscuring of 10
  in underworld 163
  see also Helius
symbols/symbolism
  phallic 117
  of prophecy 153
  quinces 93, 99, 351, 604, 608
Syracuse 149, 171, 282, 626, 633

Tacitus 411
Tanagra 199, 202, 659
Tanagra (city) 199, 202, 659
Tanagra (daughter of Asopus) 202, 659
Tantalus 137–8, 415, 429, 435, 475,
  509, 627–8, 765–6
Taranto (Tarentum) 306, 482, 838
Tartarus (underworld) 137–8, 195,
  415, 635, 765

Tartessus (Guadalquivir, Spain) 105
Tegea 302
Telamon 152, 155, 636
Telchines 143, 258, 630, 679, 680
Telephus 7–8, 429, 572, 850
Tenedos 162–3
Teos 100
Tereus 360, 501, 735, 746–7
Terminalia (festival) 458, 796–7
Terpander 187–8, 211, 664
Terpsichore 202
Tethys 265, 689
Teuthras (lake) 426
Teuthras (Teuthrantia) 7, 573
Thales of Miletus 262–3, 676,
  685–6
Thasos 5, 8, 572, 573
Theagenes 76
Theban Cycle 427, 605, 636, 735, 775
Thebe 45, 155, 202, 587, 638, 659
Thebes 1, 144, 203, 427, 432,
    577, 638
  Daphnephoria 660
  decline 249
  Dionysus and 230, 670
  Seven Against Thebes narrative
    153, 636
  temples Apollo Ismenius 639
  Theban Cycle 605
  Tiresias's prophecies for 93–94
  verse dedicated to 157–9
Themis 155, 227, 638, 668
Themistocles 193–4, 194–5, 655–7
Theocritus
  allusions to 399, 400–402, 408–9,
    753, 761
  mentions 715
Theocritus, influence of 283
  in *Anacreontea* 359, 734
  on Catullus 385–6, 744

on Horace 465, *811*
on Tibullus 412–3
on Virgil 398
Theognetus 152, *636*
Theognis
    allusions to 477, *831*
    influence of 299
Theophrastus 250, *615*
Theoxenia (festival) 156–7, 229–30,
    231, *638*, 668–70
Theoxenus of Tenedos 162–3, *641*
Thera 271
Thermopylae 130
Thersites 318, 502, *721*
Theseus 178–82, 425, 428, 490,
    613, 650–1, *709*
Thespia 202, *659*
Thessaly 35, 236, *613*, *673*
    Crannon *618*
    Erysiche 35, *582*
    Mount Pelion *591*
    Peneus 283, *705*
    Phthia *591*
    Tempe 227, 264, 265, 283, 478,
        668, *705*
    witchcraft, association with 324,
        423, 508, *771*
Thesus *776*
Thetis 128, 150, 510, *798*
    Achilles, mother of 269, 459,
        694, *864*
    Peleus, marriage to 58, *591*
Thoösa 297, 298, *715*
Thrace 102, 292, *572*
    Abdera 100
    barbarism, associated with 322,
        483
    Chalcidice 244
    drunkenness, associated with
        103, *610*

Eion 132, *624*
Hebrus (Maritsa, river) 58, 292,
    484, 486, *591*
    horses of 108, *611*
    Salmydessus 119, *617*
Thrasybulus of Acragas 163, *641*
Thyone *see* Semele
Tiberius 339, 493, 524, *729*
Tibullus 446
    allusions to *763*
    influence of 458, 463–4, 499, *797*,
        807, *842*, *856*
    mentions 510–511, *864*,
        865–6
Timon 280, *704*
Timotheus 188, 189–90, 204, *664*
    influence of 239, *675*
Tiphys 404, *757*
Tiresias 94, 273–5, *605*, *698*,
    701, *702*
Tisamenus 129, *622*
Tisiphone 415, 435, *765*
Titanomachy 110, 427, *612–3*,
    635, *775*
Titans 110, *612–3*
Tithonus 25, 29, 48, 265, 345, 508,
    578, *588*, *689*
Titus 533
Tivoli (Tibur) 437, 442, *789*
Tlapolemeia (games) *630*
Tlapolemus 141–2, 144, *629–30*
Tmolus (Bozdağ, mountain) 208,
    264, *663*
Tomis 492–3, 513, 515
Torquatus, Manlius 490, *847*
translation 365–7, 387–8,
    744–5
triadic form 89, 188, *559*
Troilus 98, *606*, *607*
Trojan horse 95

Trojan War 63–64, 97–98, 128–9,
    150–1, 392–3
  allusions to 404, 757
  commemoration 132, 510
  Helen blamed for 58, 63, 505–6
  Heracles/Hercules and 8
  love, motivation for 496
  Sack of Troy 94–95, 128
tropes
  adynaton (catalogue of
    impossibilities) 285, 430, 460,
    521, 524, 707, 777
  catalogue of charms 313
  comparitio (comparison) 495–6
  dice of love 107, 244, 305, 437
  militia amoris (warfare of love)
    314, 417, 430, 435–6, 440,
    495–6, 505–6, 777, 813–4, 846
  servitium amoris ('slavery of love')
    324
Troy 58, 128, 132, 392–3, 397, 744
  Sack of 94–95, 128
Tullus, Gaius Volcacius 421,
    423, 771
Tullus Hostilius 489
Tyche (Fortune, Chance) 145,
    241, 631
Tydeus 153, 636
Tyndareus 92–93, 604
Tyndarids see Dioscuri/Tyndarids
Typhus 152, 635
Tyro 432, 780
Tyrrhenian (Etruscan) Sea 467, 815
Tyrtaeus
  attributions 76, 243, 676
  influence of 479–80, 577, 579,
    620

Ulysses see Odysseus/Ulysses
underworld

Acheron (river) 49, 57, 195, 316,
    432
Cocytus (river) 343, 476, 830
Elysium 414, 441, 765
Hades 49, 80, 163–4, 279, 627–8
katabasis (descent to) 173–7, 475,
    646–7
Styx (river) 318, 415, 765
Tartarus 415, 765
Urania 171, 645
Uranus 118, 146, 158, 594, 658

Varius Rufus, Lucius 333, 398, 406,
    466, 759, 813
Varus, Publius Alfenus 406,
    740, 758
Varus, Quintilius 398, 740, 818–9
Venafro (Venafrum) 482, 838
Venosa (Venusia) 453
Venus see Aphrodite/Venus
Verona 373, 375, 536
Vertumnus 447
Vespasian 527, 533
Vesper see Hesperus/Vesper
Vesta 481, 487, 508, 837
Vesuvius 333
Virgil 333, 578, 647
  allusions to 418–9, 434–5, 460–1,
    489, 769, 783, 789, 802–3, 819,
    848
  influence of 372, 499, 532, 856,
    879
  mentions 463, 463–4, 469–70,
    536, 807, 818
Volumnia (Cytheris/Lycoris) 408–9,
    760
Vulcan see Hephaestus/Vulcan

wars and battles 130, 175, 189,
    572, 775

Battle of Actium (31 BCE) 411, 428, 430, 453, 470–1, 498, 798, 821, 855–6

Battle of Carrhae (53 BCE) 480–2, 545, 827

Battle of Chaeronea (338 BCE) 229, 249

Battle of Cumae (474 BCE) 626

Battle of Cyprus (449 BCE) 132, 624

Battle of Philippi (42 BCE) 399, 428, 453, 473, 754, 797, 800, 824

Battle of Sigeum (612/608 BCE) 55

Calydonians vs. Curetes 175–6, 646–8

Centauromachy 110, 506, 612–3, 613

Gigantomachy 110, 272, 498, 612–3, 612–3, 635, 699, 775

Lelantine War 572, 676

Mithridatic War 545

Peloponnesian War 132, 196, 249

Perusine War 428, 776

Punic Wars 365–6, 433, 481–2, 801

Roman civil wars 368–9, 399, 428, 460, 754, 820–821

Second Messenian War 22

'Social War' (91–88 BCE) 368, 800

Third Sacred War 231, 671

Titanomachy 110, 427, 612–3, 635, 775

western 340, 728

see also Persian wars (490–479 BCE)

'Wheel of Virgil' (rota Vergiliana) 399–400

White Rock of Leucas 105, 610–611

writing 3–4, 299, 692

Xanthippe 221, 667

Xanthippus 100, 194, 655–6

Xanthus (Eşen, river) 34, 581

Xenarces 154

Xenophanes 120
    influence of 215, 256

Xenophon of Corinth 162, 641

Xerxes 193, 207, 210, 427, 601, 661, 662–4

Zeno of Citium 312, 350, 718

Zeno of Sidon 333

Zenobius 198

Zenodotus of Ephesus 251

Zephyr/Favonius (wind) 809

Zephyrus 271

Zeus/Jupiter/Jove 23, 59, 158–60, 258, 394, 461, 498
    and Apollo/Phoebus 226
    appeals to 81, 117, 144–5, 243, 266, 431–2
    and Asopus's daughters 201
    and Croesus 168, 169
    and Cybele 236
    descendants 141, 753–4;
        Aphrodite/Venus 63, 594;
        Dionysus/Bacchus 66; Hermes/
        Mercury 64; Minos 179–81
    eagle, symbol of 172
    epithets 145, 234–6, 480, 631, 672–3
    fear of 332
    and Ganymede 137, 332, 724, 725
    and Geryon 91
    Giants, defeat of 478
    and Hebe 267
    as huntsman 457
    infant 200, 234–5, 610, 658
    and Io 652

Zeus/Jupiter/Jove – *cont'd.*
  and Iunx *708*
  judgments of *79, 80, 599*
  love as protection from *324*
  mortality of *266, 691*
  punishments/vengeance *10, 28,*
    29, 71–72, 73, 149, 464, 474,
    512
  reign of *414*
  as Sabazius *116, 615*
  Seasons and *203*
  and Semele *150, 634*
  Serapis, influence on *253*
  and Sisyphus *784*
  and Themis *155–6*
  women created by *16, 19, 20*
  worship of *43, 60, 110, 139, 177,*
    210, 585, 629; hymns to *155–6,*
    224, 234–5, 637–8; offerings to
    340, 473, 551; prayers to *83,*
    178, 261, 439; temples *481,*
    592, 672
Zeuxippus *98, 607*
Zeuxis *204*